Quattro® Pro 4.0 Handbook

FOURTH EDITION

OTHER TITLES IN THE BORLAND BANTAM SERIES

Borland C++ Programming for Windows
by Peter Norton and Paul Yao

ObjectVision 2.0 Developer's Guide
by Allen G. Taylor

Paradox 3.5 Handbook, 3rd Edition
by Douglas Cobb, Jane Richter, Jeff Yocom, and Brian Smith

Turbo Pascal for Windows 3.0 Programming
by Tom Swan

BORLAND BANTAM

Quattro® Pro 4.0 Handbook

FOURTH EDITION

Mary Campbell

BANTAM BOOKS
NEW YORK • TORONTO • LONDON • SYDNEY • AUCKLAND

Quattro Pro 4.0 Handbook, 4th Edition

A Bantam Book/April 1992

All rights reserved.
Copyright © 1992 by Mary Campbell.
Cover Design © 1992 by Bantam Books

Produced by Pageworks, Old Saybrook, Connecticut

Borland and Quattro are registered trademarks of Borland International.

Throughout this book, tradenames and trademarks of some
companies and products have been used, and no such uses
are intended to convey endorsement of or other affiliations with the book.

No part of this book may be reproduced or transmitted in any form or by any means,
electronic or mechanical, including photocopying, recording, or by any information storage
and retrieval system, without permission in writing from the publisher.
For information address: Bantam Books.

ISBN 0-553-37041-3

Bantam Books are published by Bantam Books, a division of Bantam Doubleday Dell
Publishing Group, Inc. Its trademark, consisting of the words "Bantam Books" and the
portrayal of a rooster, is Registered in the U.S. Patent and Trademark Office and in other
countries. Marca Registrada, Bantam Books, 666 Fifth Avenue, New York, NY 10103.
Printed in the United States of America

0 9 8 7 6 5 4 3 2

To my husband Dave

Foreword

At Borland we are justifiably proud of the Quattro Pro success story. With each new version, Quattro Pro has leaped forward in both functionality and market share. More than one million users have experienced first-hand why Quattro Pro has earned an unprecedented 38 international awards for excellence, and top ratings in all major spreadsheet reviews.

Quattro Pro has always been an innovative spreadsheet. It was the first to combine multipage consolidation technology and spreadsheet publishing. Its electronic slide show features and automatic font-building add graphic presentation capabilities that are yet to be found in any other PC spreadsheet.

Quattro Pro 4.0 continues that innovative tradition. With its versatile and powerful SpeedBar for quick access to frequently used commands, its custom styles, Intelligent Graph option, Netware support, and the ability to load libraries of custom @ functions, Quattro Pro 4 brings a whole new generation of power to spreadsheet users.

At a time when many spreadsheets require more powerful PCs with more memory to take advantage of advanced features, our incorporation of VROOMM (Virtual Runtime Object-Oriented Memory Manager) technology lets us continue adding functionality to Quattro Pro without requiring you to invest in expensive hardware. You can use your current hardware—whether it's an XT, a 486-based PC or somewhere in between—while enjoying state-of-the-art spreadsheet features and the productivity gains of a graphical user interface. Also, Quattro Pro 4 provides easy installation for Windows 3.x and is a smooth transition path for users who plan to migrate later to Windows.

Since the first version of this software application came out, author Mary Campbell has been widely recognized for her spreadsheet mastery and her keen ability to teach thousands of users to use Quattro Pro easily and productively. With each version of the product, she has led a new and larger group of users to higher levels of spreadsheet skills.

It is with great pleasure that we have worked with Mary on Quattro Pro 4.0 and now endorse her latest book, *Quattro Pro 4.0 Handbook*, as the official Borland guide to our powerful software package. This is a revision of the first title in the Borland-endorsed series of books from Bantam Electronic Publishing, and it continues the high standards of readability, comprehensiveness, and clarity.

We know that the many detailed examples of usage, as well as the novice-oriented "Getting Started" sections, will help the beginning Quattro Pro user get up to speed and become productive immediately. For the more advanced user, the many tips and shortcuts she provides, and the complete reference summaries of commands, will be of great value. The book is topped off with copious illustrations and a detailed index of topics.

We are extremely proud of Quattro Pro *and* Mary Campbell's *Quattro Pro 4.0 Handbook*. Together they will help you achieve maximum spreadsheet proficiency with productivity and pizazz.

Philippe Kahn
CEO, Borland International

Contents

Foreword vii
Preface xiii
Acknowledgments xvii

1   **Overview of the Quattro Pro 4 Environment 1**

   Quattro Pro's Basic Concepts 1
   Equipment Requirements 3
   The Display 5
   The Keyboard 11
   Package Defaults 20
   Menu Selections 20
   Using HELP 23
   Getting Started 24

2   **Basic Spreadsheet Entries 27**

   Making Entries on the Spreadsheet 27
   Entering Labels 32
   Entering Values 38
   Entering Formulas 41
   Entering Dates and Times 54
   Documenting Dates, Formulas, and Numbers 57
   Getting Started 57

3   **Working with Multiple Cells 61**

   Basic Block Commands 62
   Copying 70
   Advanced Block Commands 85
   Column and Row Commands 104

Titles 116
Window Options for a Single Spreadsheet 117
Adding Fonts, Bullets, Lines, Boxes, and Shading 122
Using Undo to Correct Mistakes 134
Getting Started 138

4 Printing 143

The Basic Print Procedure 143
Print Options 150
Advanced Print Options 161
Changing Printers 172
Getting Started 174

5 File Options 177

File Basics 177
Saving Quattro Pro Spreadsheets 181
Retrieving Data 189
Changing Directories 194
Using Multiple Files 195
Using Data from Other Spreadsheets 202
Accessing DOS 217
Quattro Pro's File Manager 218
Creating Workspaces 227
Getting Started 227

6 Functions 231

Function Basics 232
Statistical Functions 238
String Functions 249
Date and Time Functions 265
Logical Functions 276
Mathematical Functions: Introduction 306
Mathematical Functions: Basic 306
Mathematical Functions: Trigonometric 312
Mathematical Functions: Logarithmic 318
Cell and Table Functions 321
System Functions 333
Getting Started 335

Contents xi

7 Graphic Features 339

Creating Basic Graphs 340
Customizing a Graph 358
The Graph Annotator 377
Saving the Graph 392
Creating a Slide Show 394
Adding a Graph to a Spreadsheet 399
Printing Graphs 400
Getting Started 407

8 Data Management 409

Data Management Concepts in Quattro 410
Creating a Quattro Pro Database 411
Entering and Editing Data 412
Sorting a Database 412
Searching for Quick Answers 419
Building Exception Reports with Quattro Pro's Extract Features 431
Using an External Database 435
Creating an Input Form for Data Entry 440
Restricting the Data Types 441
Database Statistical Functions 442
Getting Started 449

9 Advanced Analytical and File Features 453

Sensitivity Tables 454
Frequency Distribution 462
Matrix Math 464
Regression Analysis 471
Solving for a Value 474
Optimizing a Spreadsheet 476
Auditing Spreadsheets 483
Saving Part of a File 486
The Combining Files Command 487
Importing Data 498
Exporting Data 501
Splitting the Long Labels 503
Getting Started 507

10 Customizing Quattro Pro 511

Selecting an Options Set 513
Updating Defaults 514
Changing Hardware Defaults 514
Changing Color Options 521
International Currency and Punctuation 529
Changing the Display Mode 533
Defaults at Startup 534
Setting the SpeedBar 538
Telling Quattro Pro When to Build Bitstream Fonts 538
Setting Other System Options 539
Quattro Pro Settings For Using Quattro Pro 4 on a Network 541
Format Defaults 542
Recalculation Defaults 546
Protection Defaults 551
Assigning Shortcut Keystrokes to Quattro Pro Commands 552
Quattro Pro's Menu Builder 553
Getting Started 566

11 Automating Quattro Pro Tasks 569

Macro Basics 569
Sample Keyboard Macros 582
Using Quattro Pro's Transcript Features 592
Getting Started 597

12 Advanced Macro Options 601

Advanced Macro Features 602
Command Language Options 610
Cells Commands 610
Getting Started 679

Appendix A: Installing Quattro Pro 683
Appendix B: Command Reference 689
Appendix C: Menu Equivalent Commands 813
Appendix D: Quattro Pro Menus 841

Index 853

Preface

Quattro Pro 4.0 is an exciting spreadsheet product offered by Borland. Although Borland is somewhat of a newcomer to the spreadsheet market, Quattro Pro's features indicate they did the right research to offer a product containing exactly what the spreadsheet user needs, whether he is a novice or an established expert.

Quattro Pro provides a state-of-the-art software solution for users with a wide variety of hardware types. You can run Quattro Pro on any system with a hard disk and 512K of memory. This means that you can use an IBM PC, XT, AT, or PS/2. If you have additional memory on a LIM 3.2 or 4.0 card Quattro will recognize and use this memory.

Quattro Pro provides an excellent online help system and full mouse support. Shortcuts to menu commands, choice lists for selection, up to 32 windows, spreadsheet publishing and a single-key Undo feature make it an exciting product. You can retrieve files from most releases of 1-2-3, Paradox, Reflex, or Symphony without the need for a special translation step. Search and replace features and a file manager make your information management tasks easier. Over 100 functions and a set of macro commands add significant power to the package.

WHO SHOULD BUY THIS BOOK

This book is designed as a one-stop source for all the information you need to use Quattro Pro effectively, whether you are a novice or an experienced spreadsheet user. If you are using an earlier release you can use this book, since many of Quattro Pro's features are the same in both releases. Unless a specific release is mentioned, *Quattro Pro* in the book refers to all releases.

We provide plenty of examples to guide the new user through an uneventful transition to this time-saving new product. The experienced user will find that this book continues where others leave off by providing full coverage of more advanced topics and tips. Although the new user may elect to skip these advanced topics initially, he or she will be able to continue learning from this book as his or her experience level grows.

CONVENTIONS

A set of conventions was used throughout this book to offer consistency and make learning easier.

Throughout the book, file names are shown in all capital letters to distinguish them from the surrounding text.

Special keys such as ENTER, ESC, and F1 are also shown in capital letters.

Examples in the Getting Started sections and elsewhere where an entry is expected are shown in boldface, as in: Type **ABC Company**.

Menu commands are indicated by the letter in boldface that you need to type to make a selection.

The spreadsheets in this book are enlarged (using /Options WYSIWYG Zoom %) to make it easier to see the spreadsheet information. Your spreadsheets will look different with the spreadsheets shown at 100% of their size and if you use the text display mode instead of Quattro Pro's WYSIWYG display mode.

ORGANIZATION OF THIS BOOK

This book consists of 12 chapters covering every aspect of Quattro Pro. The chapters proceed from the basics to more sophisticated topics, but you can skip to the advanced topics once you have mastered the preliminary material.

Chapter 1 provides an overview of the Quattro environment and features. These topics include equipment supported, the display, and the keyboard options. In this chapter you will learn how to use the help system, the new SpeedBar, and the package defaults.

Chapter 2 covers basic worksheet entries and the rules you must follow for these entries. You will learn how to make corrections to any type of entry and how to build formulas with both pointing and typing methods.

Chapter 3 teaches you how to work with more than one cell. You will learn how to block, and select row and columns commands. These commands allow you to complete your work quickly, since they affect many cells at once. You will learn how to customize how the spreadsheet appears by using Quattro's spreadsheet publishing commands and the WYSIWYG (what-you-see-is-what-you-get) display that shows the spreadsheet as it will appear when printed. Quattro Pro 4 includes styles that represent a collection of desktop publishing features including fonts, lines, shading, alignment, and data entry limitations.

Chapter 4 starts with the basic print features. You will first learn how to obtain a quick printed copy, but then you can master the advanced features such as adding headers and footers, previewing the printed spreadsheet, and background printing.

Chapter 5 covers basic save and retrieve procedures. It also covers some of the advanced file features like data, reading and writing other file formats, and importing and exporting data.

Chapter 6 covers each of the @ functions by type. The chapter includes a brief description of the function types. Each of the functions has a short description and an example showing its use. Where functions are similar, the same example may illustrate several functions.

Chapter 7 covers all the options for creating a graph with Quattro including customization options and printing, and new features such as bubble graphs, analytical graphs, and dialog boxes.

Chapter 8 covers data management concepts, including sorting, querying, form input, and database statistical functions.

Chapter 9 covers advanced features that can add power to data analysis. You will learn how to use Quattro Pro 4 to create tables for sensitivity analysis, frequency distributions, linear programming, matrix math, auditing, splitting long labels, and combining files.

Chapter 10 covers the full range of options for customizing Quattro. You will learn how to change the hardware defaults, color and mouse options, the defaults at startup, and any other default changes that Quattro supports.

Chapter 11 covers Quattro's shortcuts and keyboard alternative macros. Keyboard alternative macros let you capture Quattro Pro keystrokes and commands and then execute the macro to repeat the keystrokes and commands. A number of sample keyboard macros will help you master the required techniques.

Chapter 12 focuses on the automation possibilities offered by the macro command language. A short example showing how each macro command can be used is provided. The transcript feature and transaction back out are also covered in this chapter.

Four appendixes provide help on a variety of other features. Appendix A provides detailed instructions for installing Quattro. Appendix B is a command reference that includes a description of each command. Its organizational structure derives from the Quattro menu. Appendix C provides a description of the Quattro menu command and the menu equivalent command that a user will select to create macros. Appendix D displays Quattro Pro menus and the chapter in which the command is discussed.

GETTING THE MOST FROM THIS BOOK

You must assess your current knowledge of Quattro and other spreadsheet products to select the most productive path through this book. If you have little or no knowledge of Quattro or of another spreadsheet, start at the beginning of the book and complete the first six chapters before attempting to skip around.

If you have used the older release of Quattro or know another spreadsheet product well you will want to take a look at Chapters 1 and 2, and then begin to browse through the other chapters for the features you use most frequently as well as new Quattro Pro options with which you are unfamiliar.

Acknowledgments

I would like to thank the following people who contributed so much to the quality of this book:

Gabrielle Lawrence for her work on the entire project. Her many bright ideas and her knowledge of Quattro contributed so much.

Kenzi Sugihara, Steve Guty, Jeff Rian, and Maureen Drexel of Bantam Books for the in-house effort necessary to achieve a quality product.

Nan Borreson at Borland who helped in many ways throughout the many beta releases.

Art Chavez of Borland, who provided an excellent technical review. Not only were Art's comments helpful, his knowledge of both the product and its users' needs made his advice invaluable.

Rainé Young, who did the copy editing.

Margaretha Campbell for capturing and printing the book's figures.

1
Overview of the Quattro Pro 4 Environment

Quattro Pro 4 is a powerful spreadsheet product with features that meet the needs of almost every spreadsheet user. In fact, the many options are so diverse that the average user will not work with all of them unless he or she is designing applications for a large number of other users. To access any of these features you must understand the basics of the Quattro environment.

This chapter takes you on a quick tour of a few of Quattro's major features. It provides the basics you need to understand to start using Quattro. You will learn about the equipment supported, the display, and the keyboard options. You will learn how to begin and end a Quattro session as well as how to ask for help at any point.

QUATTRO PRO'S BASIC CONCEPTS

Quattro is a spreadsheet product. As in other spreadsheet products, its basic features are to provide an electronic grid for the entry of numbers, labels, and formulas. The row and column arrangement of the entries makes it easy to enter information.

Spreadsheet Features

Each entry in a Quattro spreadsheet is placed at the intersection of a row and a column called a cell. Your entries can consist of labels, numbers, and formulas. In most cases, labels describe the entries on the spreadsheet, and they consist of characters and numbers. Numbers represent a measure or a count of some type. Formulas are the real power of the product and allow you to calculate business, mathematical, and scientific computations.

A spreadsheet enables you to update formula results as conditions change. When you change a cell that has an impact on a formula, Quattro updates the result for the formula. Because Quattro is aware of the impact of every change, the package is an ideal tool for tasks that involve calculations that are updated frequently. Budget projections, profit analysis, receivables aging, and expense computations are tasks that are suited to a spreadsheet. Once you tell Quattro how to perform the necessary calculations for each of these tasks, Quattro can calculate them effortlessly each time a number changes.

In Chapter 2, you will begin to focus on the components of the spreadsheet environment. You will begin to build a set of model construction techniques that can apply to any business problem. Besides simply showing your entries in the spreadsheet, Quattro Pro 4 can display the spreadsheet with many enhancements. This lets you give your calculations a professional appearance. In Chapter 3 you will learn the commands that let you alter the appearance of your spreadsheet data.

Quattro Pro also allows you to link spreadsheets. This makes it easy to create consolidated reports for several divisions of a company or to transfer forward totals as the figures with which to start the next period. Although this linkage is an advanced feature that will not be covered until Chapter 5, its presence tells you that Quattro Pro is a package that you will not outgrow. You can continue to build more and more sophisticated applications, and Quattro Pro will meet your needs.

Graphics Features

Quattro has features by which you can graph spreadsheet entries. These visual representations of your data convey the essence of your entries without requiring knowledge of every detail. You will find that people can interpret your projections more easily from a graph than from a spreadsheet.

Without reentering any of your data, you can present it in a line, bar, bubble, stacked bar, pie, XY, area, rotated bar, column, high-low, text, or 3D graph. Quattro's graph features are presented in the same familiar menu structure as spreadsheet commands. After reading Chapter 7, you will be able to create basic graphs and customize them to present your data in a unique fashion. Once you create a basic graph, you can add annotations to the graph by using a WYSIWYG (what-you-see-is-what-you-get) display to draw additional information on the graph. You can also insert the graph into the spreadsheet so the graph will appear with the data it represents.

Data Management

The calculations performed in the spreadsheet environment are sufficient to make Quattro an invaluable product for many business users. Quattro's features extend beyond calculations and provide a vehicle for data management. In data management, the user normally is more interested in data storage and retrieval than in calculations. With Quattro, you can have both since the data management features use the spreadsheet.

As you build a database with Quattro, information is still stored in the rows and columns of a spreadsheet. In a data-management application, a column is used to store a field. A *field* is one piece of information about an item. For example, if you are storing employee information, fields might include name, salary, job code, and location. The information for any one employee consists of an entry in each of the fields. A record is stored across one row of the spreadsheet.

Quattro provides special menu commands to control activities in the data-management environment. In Chapter 8, you will begin to add these techniques to the spreadsheet skills acquired in earlier chapters. New Quattro Pro features let you use data from Paradox and dBASE databases as an external query. Data in other databases, such as Symphony, can be retrieved to a spreadsheet file in order to execute a query.

EQUIPMENT REQUIREMENTS

Borland has designed Quattro as a flexible package that runs on most popular brands of computer hardware. It will run on an IBM XT, AT, or PS/2 computer with a minimum of 512K. It also runs on any 100% IBM-compatible system (for example, a Compaq, Leading Edge, or AT&T system). You must run Quattro Pro on a system with a hard drive. In addition to the hardware requirements, you will need a copy of the DOS operating system 2.0 or higher to start Quattro Pro.

Quattro uses a simple installation process. The procedures needed to install Quattro are described in Appendix A. When you install Quattro, the installation program guides you through the steps to copy the files to your hard disk and make selections about the equipment you are using.

Print Output Devices

When you install Quattro, you will make a selection that tells Quattro which printer you plan to use and, therefore, which printer driver file Quattro will use. A *printer driver file* contains information Quattro uses to print your spreadsheets and files. Once Quattro knows the selected printer, it can invoke printer features like underlining and boldface and also print graphs. After you have installed Quattro, you can later change the printer settings with the /Options Hardware Printers command.

To make it easy to print spreadsheet entries, Quattro assumes that you are using a standard parallel printer for all your text output connected to the first parallel slot on your system. It also assumes that you are using continuous-form paper rather than feeding individual sheets of paper into your printer. It will generate line feeds at the end of every line since it assumes that your printer does not generate these line feeds. If Quattro's defaults are not correct for your printer, you can change them after the program is loaded with the /Options Hardware Printers command. On the other hand, when you print using Quattro Pro's graphics features, you will want to make sure you have selected the correct printer so your data prints correctly.

Quattro Pro also provides many Bitstream soft fonts that you can use with your spreadsheets and graphs. *Fonts* provide characters in different sizes and styles that can give your output a professional appearance. The Bitstream soft fonts are created with software (unlike font cartridges, which create fonts with printer hardware). You can use any of the Bitstream fonts that Quattro provides. You can also use other Bitstream fonts provided with other software packages or sold separately.

Another new feature of Quattro Pro is the ability to see how Quattro will print your spreadsheets and graphs. Now you can look at the spreadsheet and see how it will appear before you start printing. You can make any needed changes before taking the time to print the entire spreadsheet on your printer.

Memory Options and Storage Capacity

Quattro requires 512K of memory but can use the full 640K possible in the DOS environment. Quattro uses Virtual Real-Time Object-Oriented Memory Manager (VROOMM), which is a memory-management technology that stores only the portions of the Quattro program that you need. As your spreadsheet grows, Quattro will remove part of the program that is not being used so your spreadsheet has more memory. This feature does not limit the spreadsheet size as did earlier spreadsheet packages. Quattro's VROOMM feature is an adaptation of a popular memory-extension technique known as overlays, which has worked in both mainframe and microcomputer environments for years.

Because large models can require more memory, Quattro supports the Lotus/ Intel/Microsoft (LIM) expanded memory specification. Intel, AST, and other vendors market special memory expansion boards that conform to the LIM 4.0 standard. The expanded memory board can supply up to 32 megabytes (MB) of additional memory. Quattro Pro can use up to 8MB of this memory. Quattro Pro can put the entire spreadsheet, format settings, and graphs in its expanded memory, whereas other spreadsheets limit the use of this memory.

Using a Mouse with Quattro

A mouse is a hand-held pointing device, and Quattro automatically knows if a mouse is installed on your system. For a mouse to be installed on your system, it must be physically attached, and the software that tells your operating system to use a mouse must be run. It points by moving across either a special surface called a mouse pad or any other flat surface (such as a desk). As you move the mouse, Quattro moves the pointer on the screen accordingly. Although a mouse may contain as many as three buttons, Quattro uses only one of them. The default is set to the left button. Throughout this book, this button is referred to as the mouse button. When you press the mouse button, it selects whatever the pointer is on. This is called *clicking*. You can use the mouse to make menu selections, move to a position in the spreadsheet, or select a group of cells. Throughout this book, directions for using a mouse are included along with the directions for using the keyboard. A mouse can take advantage of the SpeeedBar, which appears above or to the right of the spreadsheet. The SpeedBar makes frequently used commands available by clicking a button.

THE DISPLAY

The main Quattro display is the screen that follows the introduction screen that appears when you load Quattro. In this second screen, you will make entries in spreadsheet cells and invoke menu commands for any Quattro task. When you are finished working with Quattro, you can remove this screen from the display and return to your operating system by typing /File Exit or by pressing CTRL-X.

The display screen is divided into several distinct areas: a spreadsheet area, an input line, the menu bar, a status line, and a SpeedBar (called a mouse palette in prior releases). The initial screen using the WYSIWYG display looks like Figure 1.1. If you are using Quattro Pro 3 and 4 and select the WYSIWYG display during installation, the display shows the spreadsheet as it will appear when you print it using a graphics printer. If you select the text mode display when you install Quattro Pro 3 or 4, or if you are using a prior release of Quattro Pro, the screen will look more like Figure 1.3. If you are using Quattro Pro 3, your mouse palette will always be on the side and include different buttons. In Quattro Pro 4, the SpeedBar always appears on the side in text mode and on the top in WYSIWYG mode. You can change the display between these two display modes by typing /ODB to display Quattro Pro 3 or 4 in WYSIWYG mode or /ODA to display Quattro in text mode. If you are using a mouse, you can switch between the two displays by clicking the WYS or CHR button on the SpeedBar.

If you are using a mouse, the rectangle or arrow in the middle of the screen indicates the position of the mouse. Throughout the book, the discussion of these areas will assume that the default Quattro options are still in effect. The spreadsheet data will use larger fonts than Quattro's defaults for legibility purposes, so the figures may look different from your Quattro Pro screens.

The Spreadsheet Area

The spreadsheet area is the major portion of the Quattro screen. It begins after the input area at the top of your screen and continues to the status line. This area

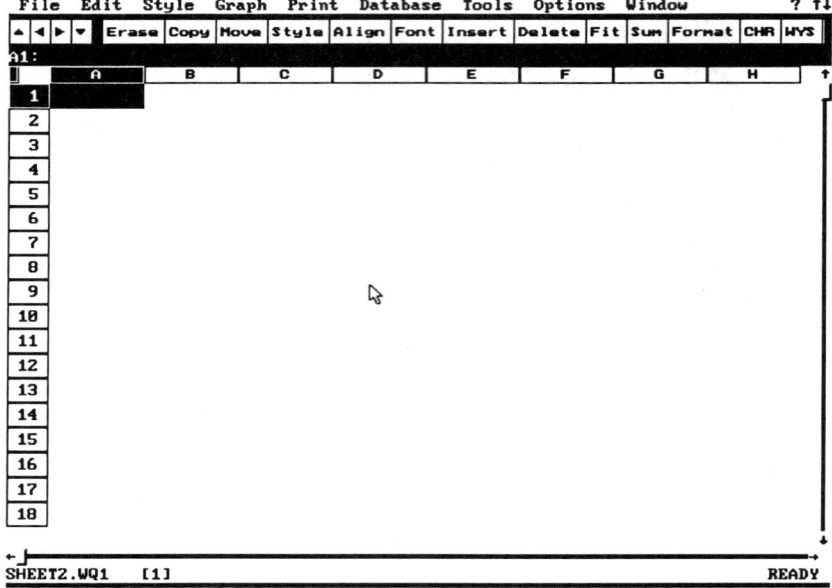

Figure 1.1 Initial Quattro Screen

initially contains one spreadsheet window. A spreadsheet window is framed by vertical and horizontal bars showing the names of the rows and the columns that are currently visible on the screen. At the bottom and right of the spreadsheet window are the horizontal and vertical scroll bars, with a block on each scroll bar indicating the cursor's position relative to the number of cells the spreadsheet contains.

Quattro's column names begin with A and continue to the right through Z, followed by AA to AZ and finally IA through IV as shown by the spreadsheet overview in Figure 1.2. Although there are 256 columns, you will see only a few columns at any one time. The number of columns visible at one time depends on the column width.

When you want to make an entry in a spreadsheet, move the selector to the desired cell and type the entry. The *selector* is the rectangle that tells you where Quattro will put an entry. You can tell the column and row of the selector, since the row and column labels are in a different color from the other row and column labels.

The bar at the left of the spreadsheet window displays row numbers. They are assigned sequentially, beginning with 1 and continuing to 8192. Initially, Quattro displays 20 or 23 rows; but the number of lines that appear in this area will change as you open multiple spreadsheet windows or as you change the display mode.

Quattro can have up to 32 windows open at a time. Each window contains either a spreadsheet or a File Manager. Quattro provides many options that let you choose how to view the windows you are using.

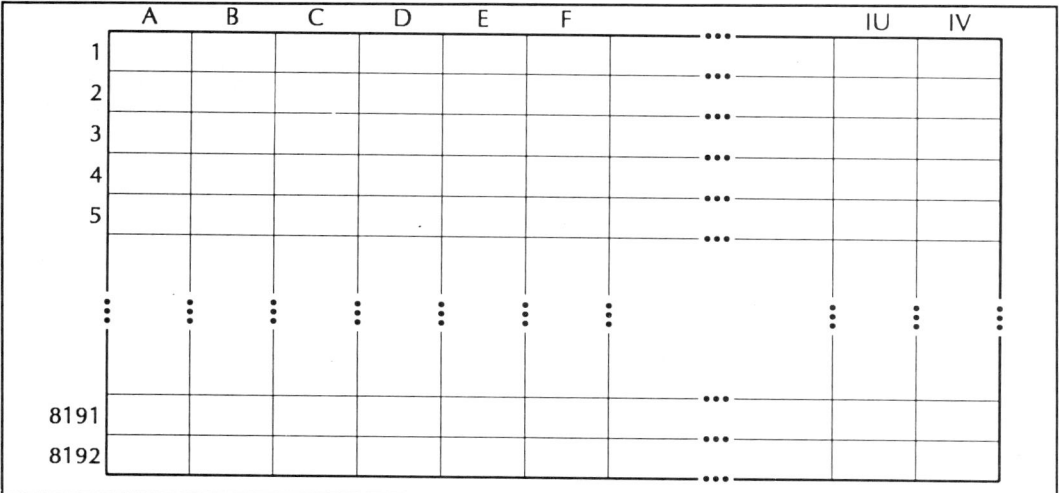

Figure 1.2 Spreadsheet Overview

At the top or right side of the spreadsheet area is the SpeedBar, which only appears when a mouse is connected to your system. A SpeedBar contains up to 15 buttons. You can use your mouse to select any one of these. Clicking the button performs the task the button is assigned. Initially, these buttons are assigned specific tasks. Later, when you are more comfortable using them, you can change the tasks assigned to these buttons.

The Menu Bar

The top line in the screen contains the menu bar. This line always appears even if you are in the middle of a task during which a menu selection is inappropriate. To activate the menu, type a slash (/): File becomes highlighted to indicate that your selections will activate menu commands. Once you select an item from the menu bar, the menu item's pull-down menu will appear. If you are using a mouse, you can point to a menu item in the menu bar, and when you press the first button on the mouse, the pull-down menu for that selection will appear.

The Input Line

Quattro's input lines are the top lines on the screen that do not contain spreadsheet windows. While this usually uses one line, it can use more. The information contained in the input line depends on your current activity. The input line can be used to show the contents of a cell, the menu, or a prompt message.

At a minimum, the input line displays the current cell address. If a cell contains an entry, its contents also display in this area as shown in Figure 1.3. If the cell has

```
     File Edit Style Graph Print Database Tools Options Window          ? ↑↓
F4: [W10] @NA
        A           B           C            D            E        F       End
                            Warehouse    Amount                Percentage Discount    ▲
              Item Code    Location    In Stock Supplier        Discount  Quantity   ◀ ▶
                                                                                      ▼
  4    04-97-UAF    Mentor         88 Office Supply      0.0%       NA
  5    N4-32-FMR    Lorain        313 Office Needs      2.0%       100    ERS
  6    P6-07-NBS    Ashtabula      23 Office Needs       0.0%       NA
  7    Q1-56-UVY    Ashtabula      42 Computer Supplier  5.0%        50    CPY
  8    P6-19-FWJ    Elyria         83 Meaden Corp.       0.0%       NA
  9    Z5-46-MRX    Akron          83 Office Supply      3.0%        10    MOU
 10    K5-69-UTI    Mentor         14 Office Supply      0.0%       NA
 11    K4-75-XJZ    Painesvill     80 Bulk Suppliers     3.0%         5    STY
 12    K7-49-WBK    Mentor         89 Office Needs       0.0%       NA
 13    M1-54-WRX    Lorain        702 Office Needs       3.0%       500    ALN
 14    L2-30-URT    Painesvill    474 Meaden Corp.       1.0%       100
 15    Q7-92-UWL    Elyria         89 Computer Supplier  4.0%         5    FNT
 16    U0-86-GXU    Elyria         55 Bulk Suppliers     4.0%         5
 17    U3-29-GWR    Ashtabula      51 Daley Brothers In  4.0%        25    INS
 18    W7-79-GTW    Lorain        464 Computer Supplier  4.0%       200
 19    Y4-97-IYO    Mentor         71 Office Supply      2.0%        50    BAR
 20    X5-27-WZJ    Mentor         59 Acme Inc.          2.0%       200
QFIG1_3.WQ1  [1]                                                           READY
```

Figure 1.3 Input Line Showing Cell Contents

settings applied to it, indicators will appear to the left of the cell entry. The word "Date" or "Label" may appear if the /Database Data Entry command has set the cell to accept only date or label entries. If the width of the cell's column has been changed from the default, a "W" and the new width appear in brackets [W12] indicates that the width has been changed to 12 characters. If the format of the cell has been altered with the /Style Numeric Format command, an abbreviation representing the selected format and the number of decimal places appears in parentheses (P2) indicates a selection of Percent with two decimal places. Table 1.1 displays other format abbreviations you may see in this area. If the cell has a style added to it, the style name will appear in brackets, as in [Headings].

The input line also displays the contents of a cell when you are editing the cell. Since a cell can contain up to 254 characters, Quattro will expand the input line to up to four lines to display the entire cell entry as shown in Figure 1.4. Once an entry is finalized, Quattro displays as much of the entry as it can fit in the input line.

When Quattro needs additional information to complete one of your requests, it prompts you to supply this information. The prompt message is often displayed in the input line. As you type a response, it is displayed in the input line with the prompt message. Figure 1.5 shows a prompt ("Source block of cells:") and the response to the prompt ("A1..A7") for the /Edit Copy command that duplicates spreadsheet entries.

The Status Line

The status line contains general information about the current Quattro session. The information that appears is determined by the mode Quattro is in.

Table 1.1 Format Abbreviations Used in the Cell Identifier

Symbol	Format
,	Financial
+	+/−
C	Currency
D	Date
F	Fixed
G	General
P	Percent
S	Scientific
T	Text
H	Hidden

Figure 1.4   Input Line Using Spreadsheet Area for a Long Entry

10 *Quattro Pro 4.0 Handbook*

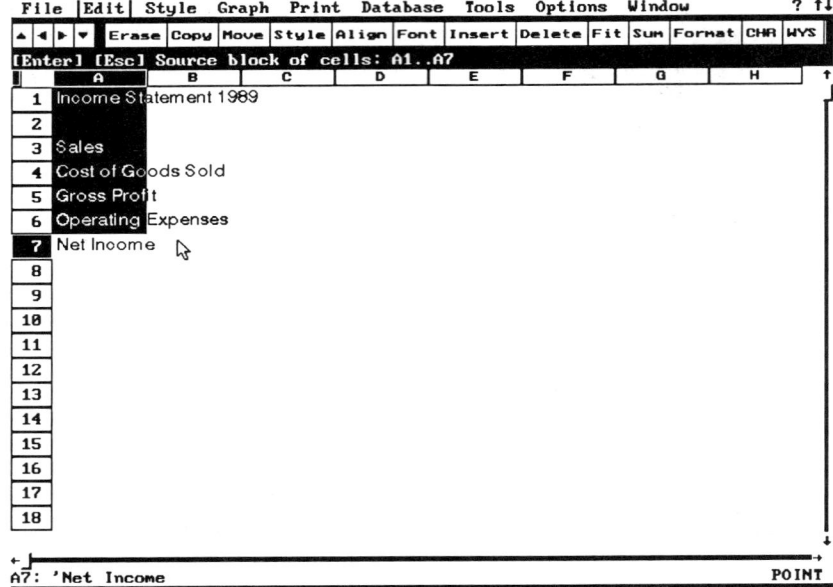

Figure 1.5 **Prompt for Additional Information**

When Quattro is in the EDIT mode because you pressed F2 (EDIT) to modify the current cell's contents, the status line displays the cell contents and cell settings that appeared previously in the input line. When the menu is activated, the status line contains descriptive information about the highlighted menu selection. Figure 1.6 provides an example of the description Quattro provides for the /Edit Copy command. As the highlighted menu item changes, the information in the status line changes to correspond to the highlighted choice. In the READY mode, when Quattro is ready for data entry or commands, the status line provides four different pieces of information. The file name, window number, status indicators, and the mode indicator display in this area.

FILE NAME The file name indicates which spreadsheet window contains the selector. If the current spreadsheet window has not been saved yet, it appears as SHEET# (# represents a number Quattro assigns automatically). If more than one spreadsheet window is open, the file name indicates which file contains the selector. When multiple spreadsheet windows appear on the screen simultaneously, Quattro displays the file name for each spreadsheet window at the top of each window.

WINDOW NUMBER The window number indicates which spreadsheet window is current (that is, which contains the selector). This is initially [1], but as spreadsheet windows are added, each added spreadsheet window is assigned the next highest number.

Overview of the Quattro Pro 4 Environment 11

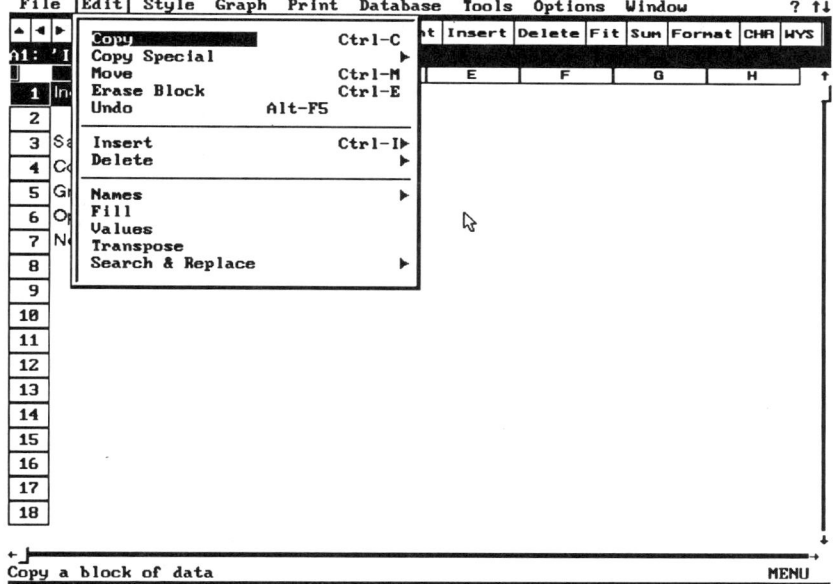

Figure 1.6 Status Line Displaying Information About a Command

STATUS INDICATORS The status indicator is designed to tell you about Quattro's current state. Some of the indicators tell you that a particular key has been pressed. Others inform you of potential problems or macro activities. Table 1.2 provides a list of Quattro's status indicators.

MODE INDICATORS The mode indicator is at the far right side of the status line. Like the status indicator, it tells you something about the package. The mode indicator is able to tell you exactly what task Quattro is working on and its state of completion.

The mode indicator is a more comprehensive indicator than the status indicator, since it affects everything you attempt to do. Table 1.3 provides a list of Quattro's mode indicators. When you want Quattro to start a new task, the mode indicator must read READY before it can begin.

THE KEYBOARD

Quattro makes effective use of the keyboard, using all the special keys to perform tasks quickly. The location of the special keys will depend on which computer model you are using. Figures 1.7 and 1.8 show two popular IBM keyboards. Many IBM-compatible machines have keyboards that are almost identical to these.

Table 1.2 Quattro's Status Indicators

Status Indicator	Meaning
BKGD	Quattro is performing calculations in the background.
CALC	Spreadsheet requires recalculation. One or more formulas have not been recalculated, since a change that affects these formulas. Do not print the spreadsheet with this indicator displayed.
CAP	The CAPS LOCK key is depressed. Pressing the alphabetic keys will result in uppercase letters.
CIRC	One or more spreadsheet formulas contain circular references.
DEBUG	The macro DEBUG feature is invoked. If you execute a macro, the debug window appears at the bottom of the screen.
END	Quattro is waiting for you to press an ARROW key since the END key has been pressed.
EXT	SHIFT-F7 has been pressed to select a block. The next command you enter will use this block.
MACRO	Quattro is executing a macro.
NUM	The NUM LOCK key has been pressed. Entries from a numeric keypad will generate numbers rather than cursor movement commands.
OVR	Quattro will type over characters in entries that you are editing. Overwrite mode is the opposite of insert mode.
SCR	The SCROLL LOCK key has been pressed. Pressing an arrow key scrolls the spreadsheet in the direction of the arrow.

Keys for Typing Letters and Numbers

On all keyboards, the keys in the center are almost identical to a typewriter keyboard. These keys are used for typing letters and numbers into cells. To type letters, press any of the alphabetic keys for a lowercase letter. For uppercase letters, you can press the CAPS LOCK key, and note the CAP indicator in the status line. Each letter key pressed will result in a capital letter until you turn the feature off by pressing the CAPS LOCK key again. Another option for capital letters is to press the SHIFT key while you press the letter that you want to see capitalized.

To type numbers, you can use the top row of keys or a numeric keypad, if one is provided on your machine. The numbers on the numeric keypad are arranged in the same fashion as a 10-key adding machine to speed up entry for those familiar with that device. Some numeric keypads are dedicated solely to the entry of

Table 1.3 Quattro's Mode Indicators

Mode Indicator	Meaning
DATE	Quattro is processing your current entry as a date or time.
EDIT	The current cell entry is being edited.
ERROR	Quattro encountered an error. Press ESC or ENTER to acknowledge the associated error message.
FILES	Quattro expects you to enter or select a file name.
FIND	Quattro is looking for matching records that you ask for using the /Database Query commands.
FRMT	The selected format line is being edited with the /Tools Parse Edit command.
HELP	A help screen is displayed, since you pressed F1 (HELP).
LABEL	Quattro is processing your current entry as a label entry.
MENU	Quattro is waiting for you to make a menu selection.
POINT	Quattro is expecting you to point to a cell or block.
READY	Quattro is waiting for you to make a new entry or request.
REC	Quattro is recording your keystrokes with the macro recorder.
VALUE	Quattro is processing your current entry as a value entry or a formula.
WAIT	Quattro is processing your last request. New requests or entries will not be processed until it has completed this task.

numbers. Others require that the NUM LOCK key be pressed to set these keys into their numeric mode. On these keypads, pressing the keys without NUM LOCK depressed causes movement from one cell to another on the screen.

To type the special symbols such as {, ^, %, :, and #, press the SHIFT key while you press the key that has that special symbol at the top. The CAPS LOCK key will not generate the special symbols shown at the tops of keys, since it is only designed to capitalize letters.

Function Keys

The function keys are labeled F1 through either F10 or F12 (that is, your keyboard may have 10 or 12 function keys). Quattro has assigned tasks to F1 through F10, so it will work consistently with either type of keyboard.

14   *Quattro Pro 4.0 Handbook*

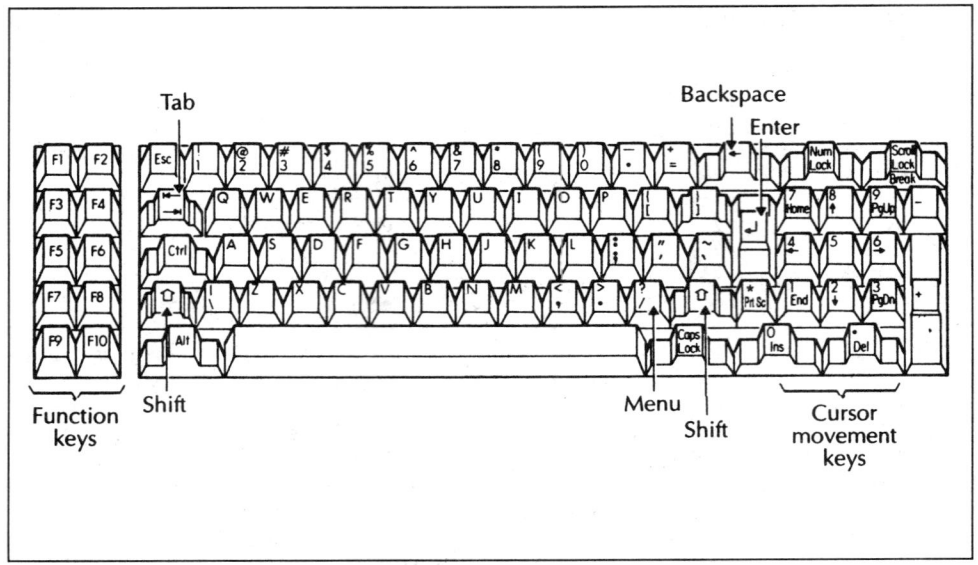

Figure 1.7   Regular IBM Keyboard

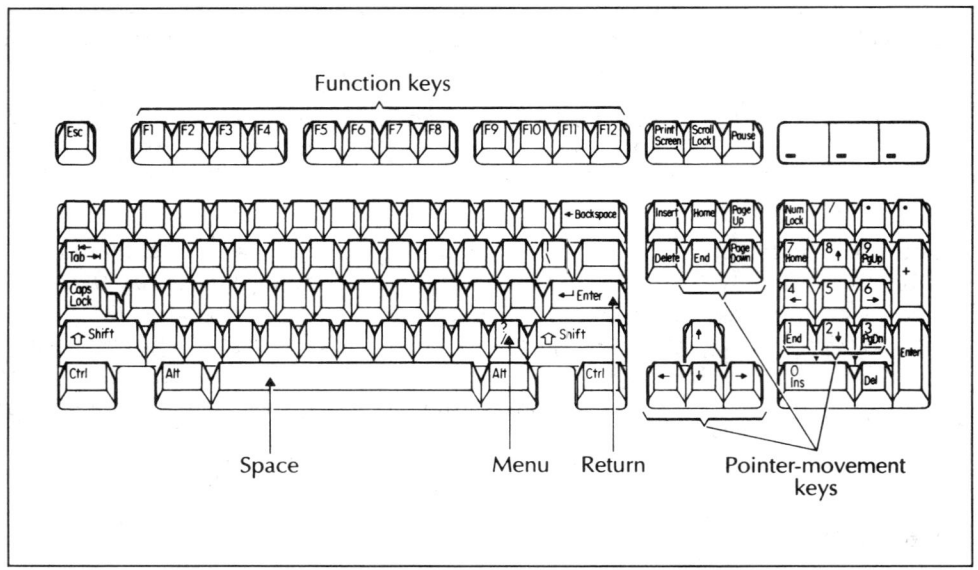

Figure 1.8   Enhanced IBM Keyboard

Table 1.4 provides a list of the tasks assigned to the function keys. Some of the keys have multiple tasks, which are activated by pressing the function key by itself or in combination with the ALT or SHIFT key. For example, pressing F3 displays a list of the names that have been assigned to blocks of spreadsheet cells. Pressing

Table 1.4 Function Key Assignments

Function Key	Action
F1	Help
F2	Edit
F3	Choices
F4	Abs
F5	GoTo
F6	Pane
F7	Query
F8	Table
F9	Calc
F10	Graph
ALT-F2	Macro Menu
ALT-F3	Functions
ALT-F5	Undo
ALT-F6	Zoom
ALT-F7	Select All
SHIFT-F2	Debug
SHIFT-F3	Macro List
SHIFT-F5	Pick Window
SHIFT-F6	Next Window
SHIFT-F7	Select
SHIFT-F8	Move
SHIFT-F9	Copy
SHIFT-F10	Paste
CTRL-F10	Switches between Quattro Pro and Paradox Access

F3 and the SHIFT key together displays a selection box of macro commands, and pressing F3 and the ALT key together displays the names of the @ functions Quattro provides. The tasks performed by the function keys will be discussed as each new feature is introduced.

Quattro provides a template, which will fit over your function keys, that serves as a quick reminder of what each key does. Templates are provided for both major keyboard types in the Quattro Pro package.

Special Keys

In addition to the function keys, there are other keys on the keyboard whose purpose may not be obvious. Some of these keys affect entries you have typed, others allow you to move around the keyboard, and still others are used in combination with other keys.

DIRECTION KEYS When you first load Quattro, a selector marks your position in cell A1. To make entries in other cells, you need to move the selector to other locations on the spreadsheet. You can use the ARROW keys to move one cell in the direction indicated by the arrow. Many other keys also reposition the selector much faster than repeatedly pressing the ARROW keys. Table 1.5 summarizes the effect of each of these keys.

Moving an entire screen at one time is easy. To move a screen to the right, use the CTRL and RIGHT ARROW keys in combination (or press the TAB key). Your view of the spreadsheet will scroll one screen to the right. The CTRL-LEFT ARROW (or SHIFT-TAB) combination scrolls one screen to the left. Moving an entire screen up or down requires only one key each: the PGUP and PGDN keys, respectively.

The END and HOME keys warrant special attention, since they can save considerable time in a large spreadsheet. Pressing the HOME key always returns the selector to A1, which is known as the HOME position. Pressing the END key and then the HOME key positions the selector in the lower rightmost cell in the area used on the spreadsheet. In a spreadsheet with entries in K1 and A40, pressing END then HOME places the selector in K40.

Unlike the HOME key, the END key is never used alone. If you press END, the END indicator is shown in the status line. Quattro waits for you to press an

Table 1.5 Direction Keys

Key Sequence	Action
LEFT ARROW	Selector moves one cell to the left.
RIGHT ARROW	Selector moves one cell to the right.
UP ARROW	Selector moves up one cell.

Table 1.5 Direction Keys *(continued)*

Key	Action
DOWN ARROW	Selector moves down one cell.
SHIFT-TAB or CTRL-LEFT ARROW	Selector moves one screen to the left.
TAB or CTRL-RIGHT ARROW	Selector moves one screen to the right.
PGUP	Selector moves up one screen.
PGDN	Selector moves down one screen.
HOME	Selector moves to A1.
END	Status indicator is set to END; Quattro awaits pressing of an arrow key.
END HOME	Selector moves to the lower right cell in the active spreadsheet area.
END LEFT ARROW	Action depends on whether current cell contains an entry. If the current cell contains an entry, this key sequence moves selector left to the first cell with an entry that is followed by a blank cell. If the current cell is blank, this sequence moves the selector left to the first nonblank cell.
END RIGHT ARROW	Action depends on whether current cell contains an entry. If the current cell contains an entry, this key sequence moves the selector right to the first cell with an entry that is followed by a blank cell. If the current cell is blank, this sequence moves the selector right to the first nonblank cell.
END UP ARROW	Action depends on whether current cell contains an entry. If the current cell contains an entry, this key sequence moves the selector up to the first cell with an entry that is followed by a blank cell. If the current cell is blank, this sequence moves the selector up to the first nonblank cell.
END DOWN ARROW	Action depends on whether current cell contains an entry. If the current cell contains an entry, this key sequence moves the selector down to the first cell with an entry that is followed by a blank cell. If the current cell is blank, this sequence moves the selector down to the first nonblank cell.

*A hyphen between two key names indicates that the keys should be pressed simultaneously; otherwise press the keys in the order indicated.

ARROW key, and then it moves the selector in the direction indicated. The distance traveled depends on the contents of the current cell and other entries in the direction indicated. If you press the END key and then the DOWN ARROW key when the current cell contains an entry, Quattro moves down to the next nonblank cell that is above an empty cell. If the current cell is blank, Quattro moves to the next cell containing an entry in the direction indicated. Four of the SpeedBar buttons with the arrows perform the same tasks as the END and the arrow keys. In text mode, these buttons are labeled END followed by four arrows. Clicking one of the arrows is equivalent to pressing END and then the ARROW key for the direction.

With a mouse, you have other options for moving in a spreadsheet. The arrows that appear at the beginning and end of the horizontal and vertical scroll bars move the selector one cell in the direction of the arrow. You can also use the mouse and the scroll bars to move within the spreadsheet cells that the spreadsheet uses. For example, if your spreadsheet uses rows 1 to 60, moving the pointer to the bottom of the vertical scroll bar without highlighting the down arrow and pressing the button on the mouse will move the selector to row 60. If you want to move to a cell visible in the spreadsheet area, you can quickly move there by pointing to the cell you want to be at and pressing the mouse button.

The direction keys assume different functions when used in EDIT or MENU mode. The actions of these keys in other modes will be explained later in the chapter.

EDITING KEYS There are some special keys that operate only for editing entries, and direction keys that take on new functions if used while you are editing. Editing entries means modifying cells in a spreadsheet or changing a setting (such as the information that you want printed at the beginning of a report). When you edit a cell, Quattro places the cell's contents in the input line and uses a cursor to indicate your position within the cell for editing purposes. A *cursor* is a small line the width of a character. Moving the cursor is different from moving the selector. Understanding the range of options for editing keys will make error correction easy. These editing keys are listed in Table 1.6.

The BACKSPACE key performs the same function when you are editing as it does when you are typing an entry: It deletes the previous character. In EDIT mode, you can use BACKSPACE to remove a character anywhere in your entry if you first position the flashing cursor to the right of the character you want to remove.

The DEL key removes the character that is just above the cursor. If you want to remove all characters in an entry, you can press CTRL-BACKSPACE. You can also remove part of an entry by moving the cursor to the first character you want to remove and pressing CTRL-\ (backslash). This removes all characters from the cursor's position to the end of the entry.

While you are in EDIT mode, the HOME key moves the cursor to the first character in the entry. The END key moves the cursor to a position immediately after the last character in the entry.

Table 1.6 Editing Keys

Key Sequence	Action
BACKSPACE	Deletes the character to the left of the cursor.
DEL	Deletes the character at the cursor's position.
HOME	Moves to the first character in the entry.
END	Moves to the last character in the entry.
INS	Switches between Insert (INS) and Overwrite (OVR) modes.
CTRL-BACKSPACE	Deletes the entire entry.
CTRL-\	Deletes all characters to the right from the cursor's position.

The INS key toggles between insert and overwrite. Initially when you enter EDIT mode, Quattro is set to insert any new characters you type to the left of the cursor. By moving the cursor with the ARROW keys, you can add characters at any location within the entry. Pressing the INS key toggles to Overwrite mode, so that each character typed replaces a character in the current entry. The status line will display OVR, and the cursor indicates where the character will be replaced. To begin inserting characters again, press the INS key to toggle to Insert mode. Whenever you complete an entry, Quattro toggles to the Insert mode.

OTHER SPECIAL KEYS The remaining special keys Quattro uses provide different features. Some change the meanings of keys, and others remove characters from an entry. These keys are listed in Table 1.7.

There are three special keys that lock other keyboard keys to perform a specific task. These keys are NUM LOCK, SCROLL LOCK, and CAPS LOCK. NUM LOCK is used to lock the numbers on dual-function keys in place. With NUM LOCK on, these keys enter only numbers; with NUM LOCK off, these keys act as directional keys. SCROLL LOCK changes the way information scrolls off the screen. With SCROLL LOCK off, pressing the DOWN ARROW key does not scroll information off the screen until you are in the last row on the screen. With SCROLL LOCK on, each row you move down scrolls a row at the bottom of the screen. CAPS LOCK produces an uppercase letter when you press any alphabet key. CAPS LOCK does not result in entry of the special symbols at the top of keys; you must use the SHIFT key to access these symbols.

The other special keys provide advanced features, which are introduced later in the book. For example, the GRAY PLUS and GRAY MINUS keys, respectively, expand and contract menu and selection boxes. The PRTSC key prints the contents of the screen (if it does not use graphics); however, it does not provide the printing enhancements of the /Print command (described in Chapter 4).

Table 1.7 Special Keys

Key Sequence	Action
+ (GRAY PLUS)	Expands the menu or selection box to include additional information.
– (GRAY MINUS)	Contracts the menu or selection box after it has been expanded.
ALT-#	Selects which window is active.
CAPS LOCK	Makes typed letters appear in uppercase.
CTRL-ENTER	Assigns a shortcut to a keystroke.
NUM LOCK	Toggles the numeric keypad between numbers and directional keys.
SCROLL LOCK	Determines whether the spreadsheet is scrolled when the cell selector moves.
PRTSC	Prints the (nongraphics) information shown on the screen.

PACKAGE DEFAULTS

Every time you load Quattro, it uses a set of standard defaults that affect the initial spreadsheet presented. These defaults affect the column width, the format of numeric entries, the location used for the storage of data files, and other settings. You can alter any of the default settings for the current session or spreadsheet, or you can change the defaults that are used for all new sessions. Permanent changes can be made by making changes through Quattro's menus and selecting the Update option to save the changes permanently. You can also create a spreadsheet file named QUATTRO.WQ1, which will be loaded automatically anytime you load Quattro. Any changes you have made for the current spreadsheet will take precedence over the defaults while you work in that spreadsheet. You will find more details on changing Quattro's defaults in Chapter 10.

MENU SELECTIONS

For most tasks other than entering data, you need to access the commands in Quattro's menus. The slash key (/) is used to activate the main menu. All other menu options are branches from Quattro's main menu. Quattro stores the initial menu selections along the top line of the screen. When you type a slash, the File menu item is highlighted. You can select this menu item or one of the other items.

To select a menu item, use the LEFT or RIGHT ARROW to move to the item, and press ENTER. Another method is to type the first letter of the menu item you want. For example, if you want to see the Tools pull-down menu, type a slash and a **T**. If you change your mind, press ESC until you are at the menu level you want or you have returned to the READY mode.

If you are using a mouse, you can activate any pull-down menu by pointing to the menu item on the menu bar and pressing the mouse button. For example, if you point to Tools in the menu bar and press the mouse button, Quattro activates the Tools pull-down menu. If you want to leave a menu, you can either press ESC on the keyboard or click on the spreadsheet. Using the slash to activate the menus will not finish your current activity, but using a mouse will. For example, if you are editing a cell, pointing to a menu and pressing the mouse button to activate it finalizes the cell editing and activates the selected pull-down menu.

Menu Options

After one main menu item is selected, Quattro displays a pull-down menu box for the menu item. Figure 1.9 shows the pull-down menu for File. As you highlight each menu item, a description of the highlighted choice appears in the status line.

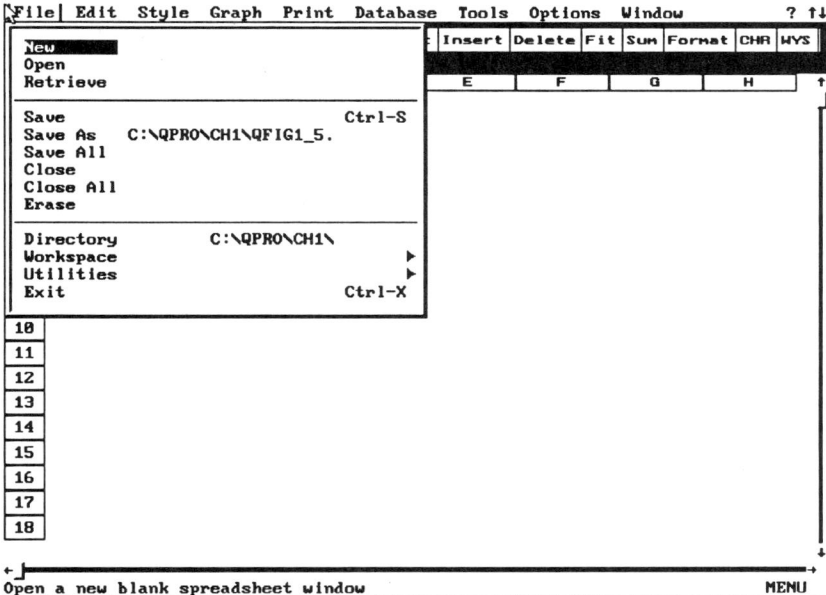

Figure 1.9 Pull-down Menu for File

Making Selections from the Menus

The same method is used for selecting options from any Quattro menu. To select a menu item by using the keyboard, use the UP or DOWN ARROW to move to the item you want, and press ENTER. To use a mouse, point to the menu item, and press the mouse button. As in selecting a menu item from the menu bar, another option is to type the highlighted letter of the menu item you want. For example, if you want to see the current directory, type a slash (/), an **F**, and a **D** for Directory. In this book, the letter you must type to select a command is boldfaced when the command is discussed. You can also press HOME or END to move to the first or last menu item in the pull-down menu box. If you decide that you want to see the pull-down menu for another menu item in the menu bar, you can use the LEFT or RIGHT ARROW key to switch pull-down menu boxes displayed, or use a mouse to point to the desired menu item and press the mouse button. If you change your mind, press ESC until you are at the menu level you want or until you have returned to the READY mode. If you want to leave the menu system altogether, press CTRL-BREAK.

As you select options from Quattro's menus, additional menus are sometimes presented. Figure 1.10 shows the menu that is presented after the Search & Replace option is selected from the Edit pull-down menu. As additional menu selections are made, lower level menus are sometimes superimposed on previous menus, as shown in the screen displayed when /Edit Search & Replace is selected. You can

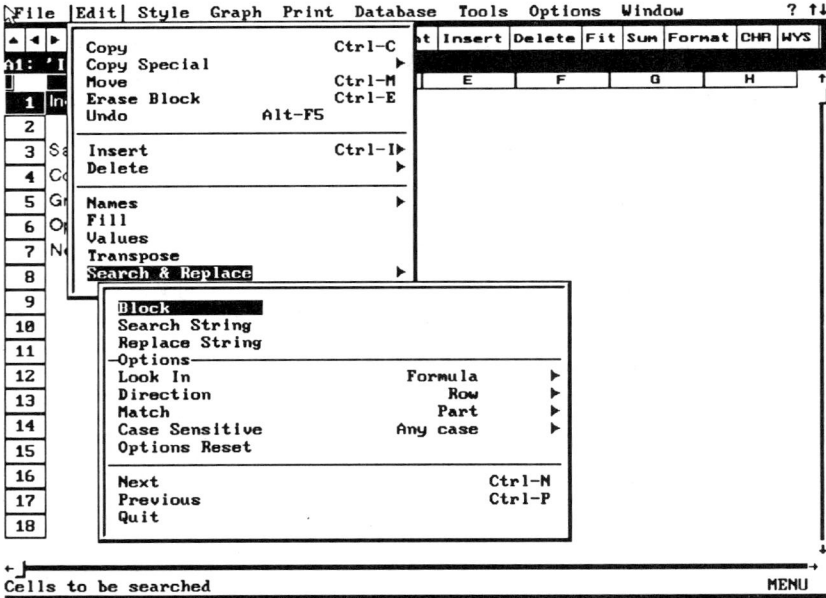

Figure 1.10 A Second Menu Presented When a Menu Selection Is Made

tell which menu items in a menu box will display another menu when they are selected, since they have a triangle next to them such as the triangles shown next to Row and Part in Figure 1.10.

Some tasks require multiple selections from lower level menus. These menus are displayed in expanded form to show the entries that already have been made. Figure 1.11 shows the menu box when Search & Replace is selected after making several menu selections. Pressing the GRAY MINUS key contracts this menu to show only the basic selections. Pressing the GRAY PLUS key expands it again to show the entries that already have been made.

When you use a mouse, you can switch between visible menu boxes by pointing to the menu box you want and pressing the mouse button. For the menu boxes in Figure 1.10, if you point to Insert in the partially hidden Edit pull-down menu and press the mouse button, you remove the menu box for Search & Replace and select Insert. If you are outside the menus, pressing a mouse button will remove all the menus from the screen.

USING HELP

Quattro's on-line help provides a quick source of information. At any time, you can press the F1 (HELP) key to see information pertaining to your current menu selection or other entry. If you are using a mouse, you can move the mouse so the

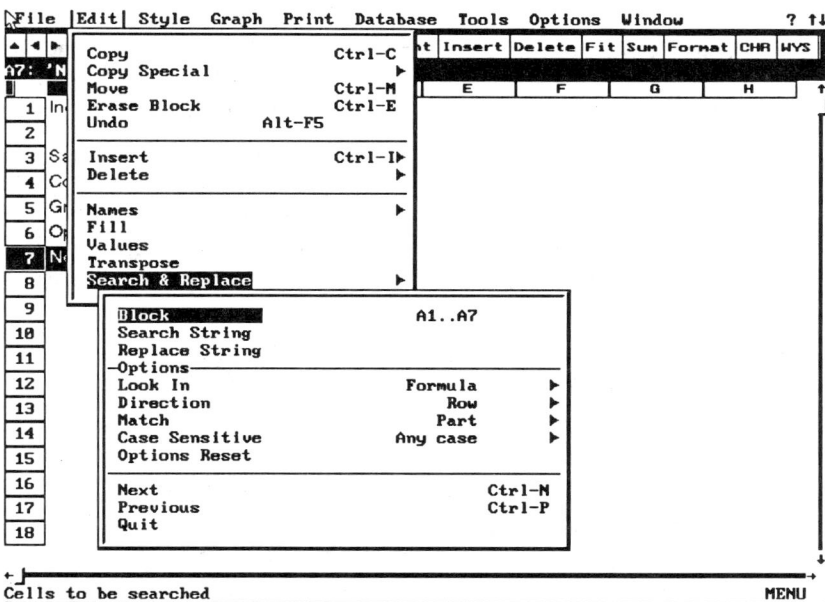

Figure 1.11 Menu Box, After Selections Have Been Made

pointer is on the question mark in the menu bar, and press the mouse button. The help information temporarily displaces the spreadsheet from the screen. Pressing ESC returns you to the spreadsheet without affecting what you were doing at the time you requested help.

The selectable options on the help screen are referred to as *keywords*. Selecting any one of them presents the help screen on the topic you selected. If you want to know more about using help, press F1 (HELP) to display the help screen for Using the Quattro Help System. You can return to a prior help screen by pressing BACKSPACE. You can also press F3 (CHOICES) to display a list of the available topics, and select one from the list by highlighting it and pressing ENTER or by clicking it with the mouse. You can also type the name of the topic you want to quickly move through the list.

While you are building models, Quattro will display an error message whenever it finds an error. You can learn more information about the topic of the error message by pressing F1 (HELP), while the error message is displayed. When you press F1 (HELP), Quattro displays a help screen for the topic that caused the error message. When you press ESC to leave help, you are returned to the original error message.

GETTING STARTED

All the chapters in this book end with a special hands-on section. These sections are designed to give you a set of short exercises for the material in the chapter. While these exercises do not cover all the Quattro features covered in the chapter, they do provide a starting point from which you can try the more advanced features.

To try some of the keystrokes introduced in the chapter, follow these steps:

1. At the DOS prompt, type a **Q** and press ENTER. If you do not have a PATH command in your AUTOEXEC.BAT file, you first need to change to the Quattro subdirectory. Notice how the file name, in this case SHEET1.WQ1, appears in the status line. You may also notice status indicators such as CAP, NUM, or SCR if the CAPS LOCK, NUM LOCK, or SCROLL LOCK keys have been pressed.

2. Type a / to invoke the menu. The file name disappears as Quattro uses this area for menu item descriptions.

3. Type an **F** for File. Selecting a menu item from the menu bar displays the pull-down menu for the menu item.

4. Press the RIGHT ARROW to display the menu for Edit. You can use the LEFT ARROW and RIGHT ARROW to change the menu. (This only applies to the pull-down menus belonging to the menu items in the menu bar.)

5. Press the UP ARROW, and ENTER. When you press UP ARROW on the first menu item, the highlight wraps around to the bottom menu item. When you press ENTER, you are selecting the highlighted menu item.

6. Press F1 (HELP) to display the Search & Replace Command Settings help screen. This help topic uses three screens to display the help information. Many other Quattro help topics use more than one screen.
7. Press END and LEFT ARROW to move to the Next (Command Settings 2/3) keyword, and select it by pressing ENTER. Selecting a keyword displays another help screen, in this case, Search & Replace Command Settings (2/3). Selecting Previous (Command Settings 1/3) displays the first help screen that you saw and Next (Command Settings 3/3) will display the third Search & Replace Command Settings help screen.
8. Press ESC to leave the help screen. When you leave the help screen, you return to your original location. This allows you to display help information while you are in the middle of a command or an entry.
9. Press CTRL-BREAK. This key combination quickly leaves the Quattro menus. You also could have pressed ESC several times, but the CTRL-BREAK option is better when you are several layers into Quattro's menus.
10. Press CTRL-X. This shortcut key, which is equivalent to /File Exit, leaves Quattro. If you have made entries in the spreadsheet, Quattro will prompt you to see if you want to save your changes.

2

Basic Spreadsheet Entries

Mastering spreadsheet entries is the most important first step you can take with Quattro. Every spreadsheet you create consists of the same types of entries. With these basic entries, you can create financial projections, supply the data needed for data-management features of the package, or complete the necessary entries on the spreadsheet for the creation of Quattro graphs. Your time investment in mastering the basics of each type of Quattro entry provides benefits in everything else you do with the package.

MAKING ENTRIES ON THE SPREADSHEET

In Chapter 1, you learned how Quattro's spreadsheet is organized into rows and columns. Each intersection of a row and a column forms a unique location referred to as a cell. The location of every cell is uniquely identified by its cell address, consisting of the cell's column letter immediately followed by its row number (for example, A1, Z10, and AX5000). If you tell anyone familiar with spreadsheets that an entry is stored in A10, they know to look at the intersection of column A and row 10 to find the data.

Although you can make an entry in any cell on the Quattro spreadsheet, you normally will want to organize your entries to make them easy to read and understand. Figure 2.1 displays product sales by month with the data neatly arranged to make it easy to find information quickly. Cell entries strewn about on the spreadsheet do not meet this objective, even though Quattro does not prevent you from making entries that way.

Each entry you make on the spreadsheet uses some of the memory available in your system. Since all spreadsheet entries must be stored in memory, the number of cells that you are able to use on any spreadsheet depends on the average length

```
               File  Edit  Style  Graph  Print  Database  Tools  Options  Window        ? ↑↓
               ▲ ◀ ▶ ▼  Erase Copy Move Style Align Font Insert Delete Fit Sum Format CHR WYS
               F14: 15000
                            A          B         C         D         E         F         G
                 1                          QUICK STOP GAS
                 2                        JAN       FEB       MAR       APR       MAY
                 3    Automotive Products
                 4      Tires              30        40        30        50        60
                 5      Oil             1,210     1,320     1,250     1,190     1,330
                 6      Gas(Gallons)   20,900    21,000    21,200    19,900    22,000
                 7      Sparkplugs        500       540       550       480       490
                 8    Food Items
                 9      Eggs(dozens)   1,200     1,300     1,410     1,220     1,150
                10      Milk           1,980     2,000     2,200     1,890     1,990
                11      Bread         10,500    10,800    11,000     9,900    11,200
                12      Rolls          1,100     1,200     1,050     1,320     1,250
                13      Donuts         1,300     1,320     1,370     1,400     1,450
                14      Soda(cans)    13,900    14,000    14,300    14,500    15,000
                15
                16
                17
                18

               QFIG2_1.WQ1  [1]                                                    READY
```

Figure 2.1 Spreadsheet Displaying Product Sales by Month

of the entries you are making and the amount of memory in your system. Whether you have added expanded memory to your system also affects the number of possible entries. Quattro uses efficient memory-management techniques so that the location of your entries on the spreadsheet does not affect the amount of memory used.

Before you can start a new spreadsheet entry, the mode indicator in the status line must read READY as shown in Figure 2.2, indicating that Quattro is ready to allow you to begin a new activity (for example, a cell entry). If the mode indicator displays MENU, POINT, or EDIT, you must take some action to return the indicator to READY mode before Quattro allows you to make an entry. This action may be as simple as pressing ESC to back out of a menu or completing your specifications for an activity. Once you have started your entry, you can continue if the indicator shows EDIT, LABEL, or VALUE, since these indicator values are also acceptable after an entry has been started. In these modes, the buttons on the SpeedBar change to buttons that are more appropriate when you are creating and editing entries. For example, the SpeedBar contains buttons such as +, -, *, /, (, and) to add these operators to a calculation.

Entry Types

Quattro supports two basic types of entries, label entries and value entries. John Smith, 34 North Ave., 216-89-6754, and AX-56-7890 are examples of label entries.

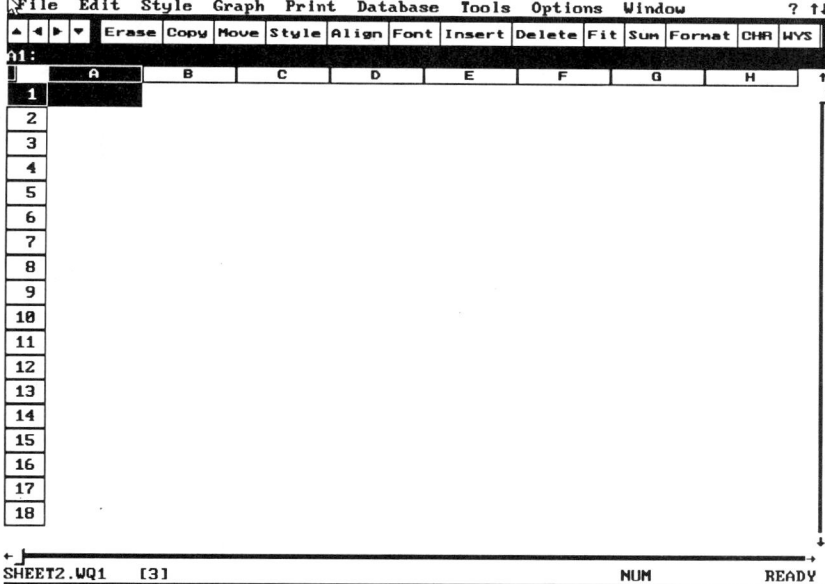

Figure 2.2 Spreadsheet Ready for Data Entry

In each case, the entry contains at least one text character, distinguishing it from a value entry. The entry 216-89-6754 consists of numbers and dashes, so Quattro will not treat it as a label unless you take some special action. If it is entered as shown, Quattro performs two subtraction operations and displays the result. To have Quattro display the number as you entered it, you need to tell Quattro to treat it as a label by entering **'216-89-6754**. The apostrophe at the beginning tells Quattro that your entry must be treated as a label.

Value entries are numbers that are designed to be used in calculations. You can enter either numeric constants like **57, 89765**, or **-.0987865** or formulas like **+B2/B3** or **+D11*(B2+B3)** as Quattro value entries.

Quattro assesses the type of data you intend to place in a cell by the first character you type. If the first character you type is a text character, Quattro treats the cell as a label, and the mode indicator in the bottom right corner of the screen immediately changes to LABEL as shown in Figure 2.3. When you press ENTER to finalize the entry, Quattro will add a label indicator at the beginning of the cell. If the first character you type is a numeric character, Quattro sets the mode indicator to VALUE. Once Quattro has decided that the cell contains a value or a label, you have only two choices for changing it: (1) You can press ESC to clear the cell and start your entry again, or (2) you can press F2 (EDIT) to edit the cell and add or remove the label indicator.

You control the location at which you make an entry by positioning the selector before you begin typing. As you make an entry into a cell, Quattro displays the characters you type in the input line at the top of the screen; the characters do not

```
File   Edit  Style  Graph  Print  Database  Tools  Options  Window          ? ↑↓
 ▲ ◀ ▶ ▼  Name  Abs  Calc  Macro  @   +   -   *   /   (   ,   )
[Enter] [Esc] Unit Sal
             A              B         C         D         E         F         G
                                  QUICKSTOP GAS
  1
  2                              JAN       FEB       MAR       APR       MAY
  3  Automotive Products
  4    Tires                      30        40        30        50        60
  5    Oil                     1,210     1,320     1,250     1,190     1,330
  6    Gas (Gallons)          20,900    21,000    21,200    19,900    22,000
  7    Sparkplugs                500       540       550       480       490
  8  Food Items
  9    Eggs (dozens)           1,200     1,300     1,410     1,220     1,150
 10    Milk                    1,980     2,000     2,200     1,890     1,990
 11    Bread                  10,500    10,800    11,000     9,900    11,200
 12    Rolls                   1,100     1,200     1,050     1,320     1,250
 13    Donuts                  1,300     1,320     1,370     1,400     1,450
 14    Soda (cans)            13,900    14,000    14,300    14,500    15,000
 15
 16
 17
 18

A2: [W20]                                                                LABEL
```

Figure 2.3 Quattro Ready for Label Entry in Cell (Entry Starts with a Text Character as Shown in Input Line)

appear in the designated cell until you have finalized your entry. Figure 2.3 shows an entry being made in cell A2. You can verify where the entry will be stored by checking the location of the selector on the screen, or the cell address displayed at the bottom of the screen in the status line.

You can finalize the entry of a number or a label by pressing ENTER or any of the direction keys such as the arrow keys or PGUP and PGDN. A formula can be finalized by pressing ENTER in all situations. Depending on the formula and the method used for building it, you can finalize some formulas by pressing the arrow keys. Once finalized, the entry is displayed in the cell designated by the selector during entry. The input line also displays the contents of the cell. If you build your formulas by pointing to cell addresses rather than typing them, you will not be able to finalize the formulas by moving with the arrow keys.

Making Corrections

Quattro provides many different options for correcting data entry mistakes. The tactic you use depends on the length of the entry, the extent of change, and whether the entry has been finalized. You can correct an entry that has not been finalized by pressing the BACKSPACE key to delete the previous character. If the mistake affects the entire entry, you can eliminate all the characters entered by pressing ESC, CTRL-BREAK, or CTRL-BACKSPACE.

To make a subtle change to an entry that has not been finalized, the BACKSPACE key is too destructive. A better approach is to press F2 (EDIT). If you are using a mouse, you can also enter the EDIT mode by pointing to the cell, pressing the mouse button, pointing to the cell entry in the input line, and pressing the mouse button. The EDIT mode allows you to use the LEFT and RIGHT ARROW keys to move within the entry. With a mouse, you can point to the characters you want to edit, and press the mouse button to move the cursor to that position. You can use the BACKSPACE more selectively by positioning the small cursor in the entry before pressing the BACKSPACE key. You can also use other keys, like the DEL key (which deletes the character at the cursor), CTRL-\ (which removes all characters from the cursor's position to the end of the line), the HOME key (which moves the cursor to the front of the entry), the END key (which moves the cursor to the end of the entry), and the INS key (which toggles between Insert and Overstrike).

Figure 2.4 provides an example of the entry in A3 being edited to correct a spelling mistake. After pressing F2 (EDIT), press the HOME key (the error occurred closest to the beginning of the entry). Next, press the RIGHT ARROW key three times to move to the letter d and the DEL key once to remove the d; the entry can be finalized by typing a **t** and pressing ENTER.

Once an entry is finalized, you cannot use the BACKSPACE key to make corrections, since BACKSPACE does not have an effect on a finalized entry. You can type a new entry for a cell, replacing its current entry. You can use the edit

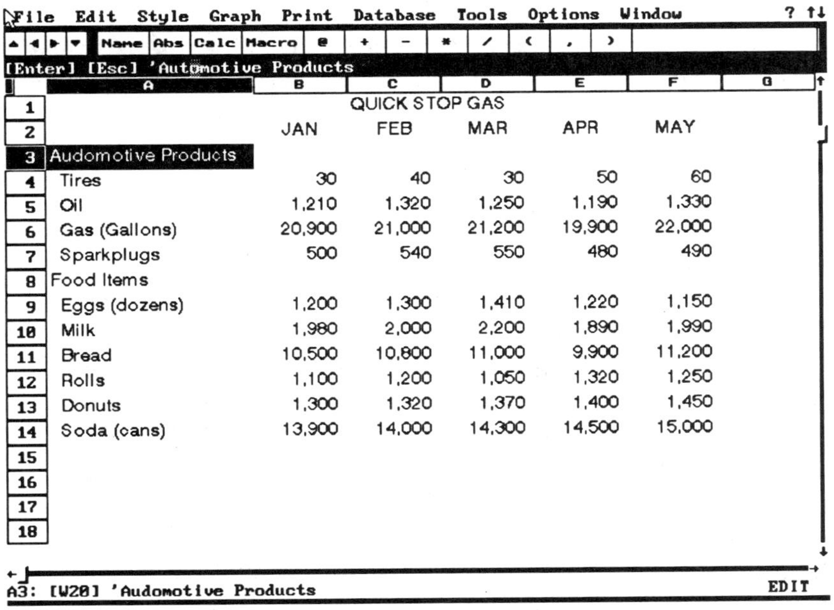

Figure 2.4 Cell Entry Edited to Correct Spelling Mistake

technique just described to make a less extensive change to the cell entry. Or, you can erase the current cell by pressing the DEL key.

ENTERING LABELS

Label entries serve several purposes in Quattro. You use them to add descriptive information to a spreadsheet. Without label entries, your numbers and formulas appear as a sea of value entries with no apparent meaning. By adding the account names, months of the year, or other descriptive information as labels, your colleagues can better understand your spreadsheet entries.

Label entries also supply character information when you use Quattro's data-management features. A column of employee names, addresses, or social security numbers contains label entries.

The macro features of Quattro allow you to record keystrokes and commands to automate Quattro tasks using label entries. In Chapters 11 and 12, you will learn that label entries are required in all cells that are part of a Quattro macro.

Following the Rules

Quattro has a certain discipline that must be followed when entries are made on the spreadsheet. The rules that Quattro follows for label entries are summarized in the box "Rules for Label Entries."

You can place your label entry anywhere on the spreadsheet. It is the first character, not the location, that causes Quattro to recognize your entry as a label. If your first character is anything other than the numeric digits 0 through 9 or one

---

Rules for Label Entries

1. Label entries must begin with a label indicator, a space, an alphabetic character, or a special symbol other than @, ., $, +, -, (,), #, or /.
2. Label entries cannot exceed 254 characters.
3. Labels wider than the current cell width borrow space from empty cells to the right for display purposes. If these labels are printed to a file and the cells that they borrow space from are not included in the spreadsheet area to print, the printed labels are truncated.
4. The ' label indicator left-aligns the label entry, "right aligns the entry, and ^ centers the entry.
5. An entry that starts with a label character or indicator is treated as a label even if it also contains numbers.

of several symbols, (., +, -, (,), $, #, @, /), Quattro recognizes the character as the beginning of a label entry.

The default width for a spreadsheet cell is nine characters, but this does not restrict the length of your label entries. A label entry can contain as many as 254 characters, even though they all cannot be displayed within the cell. If a cell contains more characters than can fit in the cell, the cell uses the space of the cells to the right to display the additional characters (provided that the adjacent cells are empty). With the WYSIWYG display, the column width is measured in the average character width of the default font, so the number of characters you can actually fit varies according to the width of the characters in the entry. In a character display, such as in earlier releases, each character is the same width so the character width is exactly the number of characters that fits in the column.

LONG LABELS An entry that exceeds the current cell width borrows space from the cells immediately to the right if they are empty. Figure 2.5 shows a long label entered in C1; the long entry borrows space from cells D1 and E1 to complete the display. If these cells contain entries, the display of C1's contents is truncated to the number of characters that fit within the current cell. You do not need to be concerned with data loss, since Quattro retains the entire entry in memory. If the current cell is widened or the cells to the right are erased, the entire entry may then be displayed.

As you enter a label that fills the input line, Quattro begins to use the second

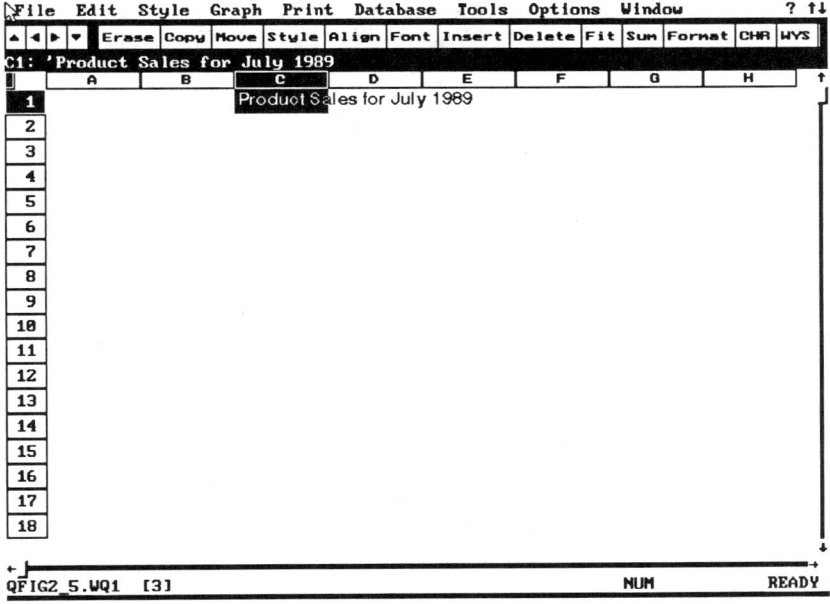

Figure 2.5 Cell Entry That Spills Over into Adjoining Cells

input line for the display. If your entry fills the second line, Quattro borrows space from the spreadsheet area to allow room for a third and fourth input line as shown at the top of Figure 2.6. This expansion allows you to review a complete entry up to the maximum 254 characters. While you are entering a long label, you cannot use the UP ARROW or DOWN ARROW to move to different lines of the entry.

Since a long label entry resides completely in the cell where you make the entry, changes can only be made through this cell. To replace the entry, you move to this cell and type a new entry. To edit the entry, this cell must be the current cell when you press F2 (EDIT). If you try to change the entry by moving to other cells where space is borrowed for the display, the input line shows an empty cell even though information is displayed in these cells within the spreadsheet.

ALIGNMENT When you enter a label, Quattro generates a label indicator and places it at the beginning of your entry. The default label indicator on a new spreadsheet is an apostrophe (') that causes Quattro to left-align your entry. Quattro has other label alignment characters that can change how the label is aligned within the cell.

A quotation mark (") entered at the start of a label entry makes the label right-align within the current cell. This feature is useful if the cell is used at the top of a column that contains value entries (since value entries are initially right-aligned). Figure 2.7 presents a spreadsheet with right-aligned labels at the top of the Salary, Medical Benefits, and Disability Benefits columns.

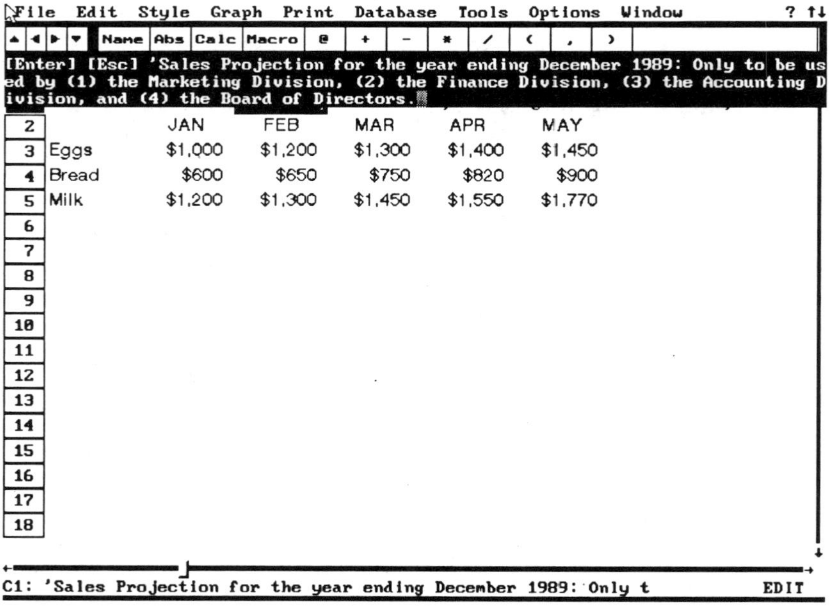

		JAN	FEB	MAR	APR	MAY
3	Eggs	$1,000	$1,200	$1,300	$1,400	$1,450
4	Bread	$600	$650	$750	$820	$900
5	Milk	$1,200	$1,300	$1,450	$1,550	$1,770

C1: 'Sales Projection for the year ending December 1989: Only t   EDIT

Figure 2.6   Cell Entry Using Three Lines in Input Line

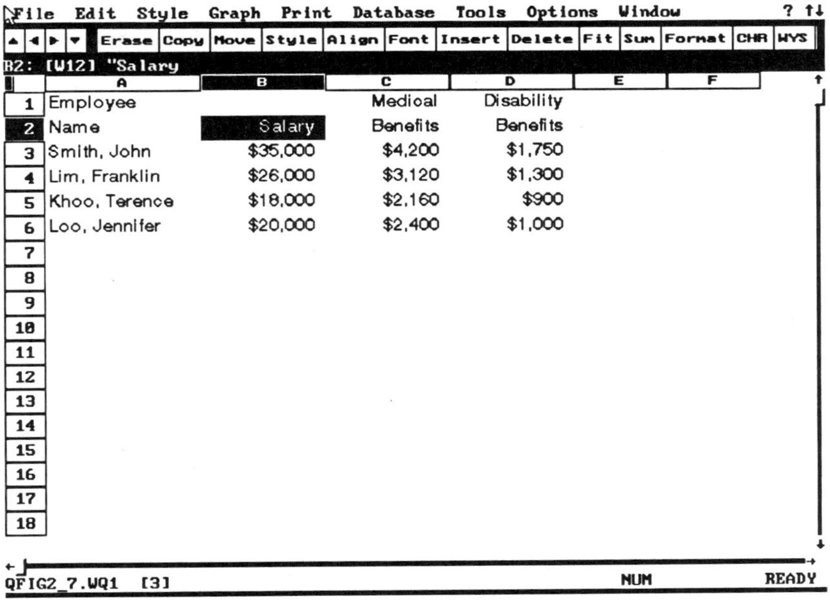

```
File  Edit  Style  Graph  Print  Database  Tools  Options  Window        ? ↑↓
 ▲ ◄ ► ▼  Erase Copy Move Style Align Font Insert Delete Fit Sum Format CHR WYS
B2: [W12] "Salary
         A              B            C           D          E          F
   1  Employee                     Medical    Disability
   2  Name             Salary      Benefits   Benefits
   3  Smith, John      $35,000     $4,200     $1,750
   4  Lim, Franklin    $26,000     $3,120     $1,300
   5  Khoo, Terence    $18,000     $2,160     $900
   6  Loo, Jennifer    $20,000     $2,400     $1,000
   7
   8
   9
  10
  11
  12
  13
  14
  15
  16
  17
  18
QFIG2_7.WQ1  [3]                                      NUM           READY
```

Figure 2.7 Spreadsheet with Right-Aligned Labels

You can center label entries by beginning your entry with a caret symbol (^). Frequently, the months of the year are centered at the tops of columns as they are entered across the spreadsheet. Figure 2.8 presents a spreadsheet with centered labels at the top of each column. If you look at the input line when the selector is on one of these labels, you will see the caret symbol at the front of the entry for the current cell.

For now, you must type the appropriate label indicator if you want your labels to be centered or right-aligned. In Chapter 3, you will learn how to change the default label prefix that is generated automatically for all label entries. You will also learn how you can change the label prefix for existing entries without editing the cell or retyping the entire entry.

REPEATING LABELS Quattro provides a special label indicator that causes Quattro to repeat the entry that follows until the current cell is filled with a repeated pattern of this entry. If the backslash (\) begins a label entry, the label repeats the designated character the required number of times to fill the cell regardless of its width. For example, entering * generates *'s to fill the cell, and entering \+- generates a series of +- entries to fill the cell. This feature is especially useful for creating dividing lines on the spreadsheet. The top and bottom lines for the box that contains the assumptions for the current spreadsheet is shown in Figure 2.9. It was generated with a series of \+- entries in rows 1 and 8.

```
 File  Edit  Style  Graph  Print  Database  Tools  Options  Window          ? ↑↓
 ▲ ◀ ▶ ▼  Erase Copy Move Style Align Font Insert Delete Fit Sum Format CHR WYS
 B2:  [W9] ^JAN
              A              B          C          D          E          F          G
   1                                  QUICK STOP GAS
   2                         JAN       FEB        MAR        APR        MAY
   3    Automotive Products
   4      Tires               30        40         30         50         60
   5      Oil              1,210     1,320      1,250      1,190      1,330
   6      Gas (Gallons)   20,900    21,000     21,200     19,900     22,000
   7      Sparkplugs         500       540        550        480        490
   8    Food Items
   9      Eggs (dozens)    1,200     1,300      1,410      1,220      1,150
  10      Milk             1,980     2,000      2,200      1,890      1,990
  11      Bread           10,500    10,800     11,000      9,900     11,200
  12      Rolls            1,100     1,200      1,050      1,320      1,250
  13      Donuts           1,300     1,320      1,370      1,400      1,450
  14      Soda (cans)     13,900    14,000     14,300     14,500     15,000
  15
  16
  17
  18

 QFIG2_8.WQ1  [3]                                              NUM           READY
```

Figure 2.8 Spreadsheet with Centered Labels

```
 File  Edit  Style  Graph  Print  Database  Tools  Options  Window          ? ↑↓
 ▲ ◀ ▶ ▼  Erase Copy Move Style Align Font Insert Delete Fit Sum Format CHR WYS
 A1:  \+-
              A         B            C          D          E          F          G
   1    +-+-+-+-  +-+-+-+-    +-+-+-+-   +-+-+-+-   +-+-+-+-   +-+-+-+-   +-+-+-+-
   2    +                        ASSUMPTIONS                                  +
   3    +           Salary Increase %                5%                       +
   4    +           Benefit Increase %               4%                       +
   5    +           Rent Increase %                 10%                       +
   6    +           Commission Increase %          10%                       +
   7    +           Advertising Increase %          8%                       +
   8    +-+-+-+-  +-+-+-+-    +-+-+-+-   +-+-+-+-   +-+-+-+-   +-+-+-+-   +-+-+-+-
   9
  10                          1992        1993
  11         Salaries      $240,000    $252,000
  12         Benefits       $48,000     $49,920
  13         Rent           $60,000     $66,000
  14         Commission     $25,000     $27,500
  15         Advertising    $30,000     $32,400
  16
  17
  18

 QFIG2_9.WQ1  [3]                                              NUM           READY
```

Figure 2.9 Backslash Used to Create a Repeating Label

Labels That Contain Numbers

At times you may want to create label entries that begin with a numeric character. Since Quattro automatically categorizes your entry as a label or a value based on the first character you type, you want to begin these entries with a label indicator. If you want to use the default (left-alignment), type **'34 North Avenue** to record the address 34 North Avenue.

Although it is not a common situation, you may sometimes want to create label entries that consist solely of numeric characters. This feature is useful if you are creating a spreadsheet in which a year appears at the top of each column. Since you do not want these year numbers to include any numeric formatting characters such as decimal points or dollar signs, you may wish to treat these entries as labels by entering a label prefix before you start your entry. Later, if you change how Quattro displays numbers, the format for the years will not change.

Entries like phone numbers and social security numbers that have special characters like dashes or slashes to separate components of an entry are likely to cause problems for a new spreadsheet user. If you enter **213-46-1245** with the intention of recording a social security number, you may be surprised to see that Quattro displays your entry as -1078, as shown in column C of Figure 2.10. The symbols you entered as dashes are interpreted as minus signs, and Quattro performs two subtraction operations to arrive at the resulting negative number. Using the label indicator at the front of each entry produces a correct display such as the one in Figure 2.11.

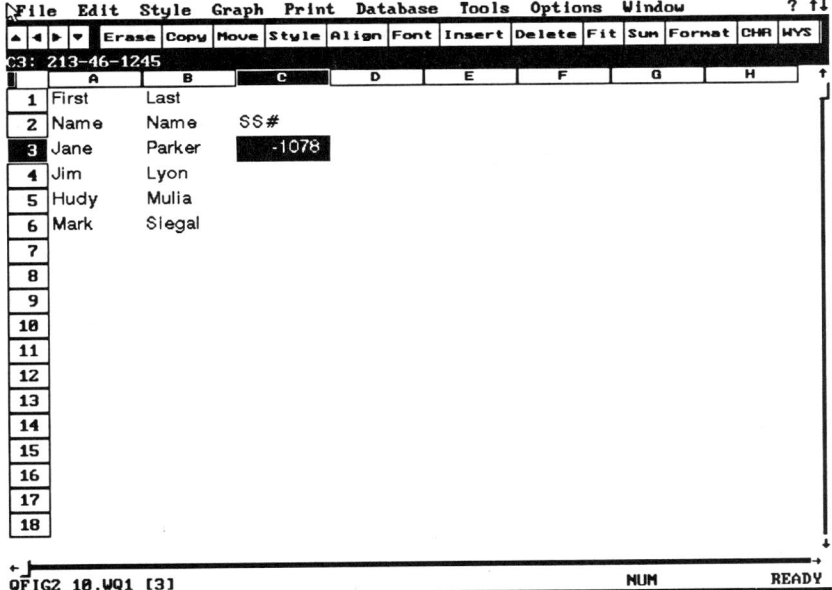

Figure 2.10 Quattro Subtracting a Social Security Number

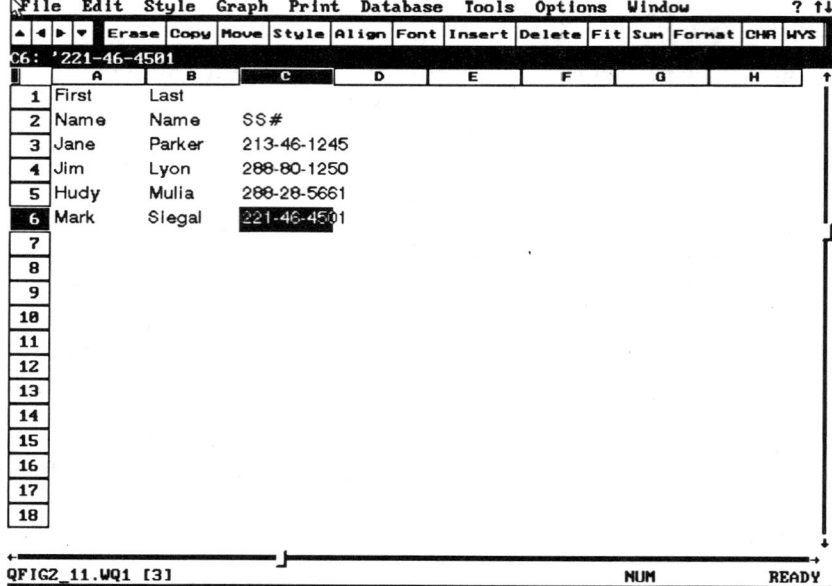

Figure 2.11 Storing Social Security Numbers as Labels

ENTERING VALUES

Although label entries provide descriptive information on your spreadsheets, value entries form the backbone of any spreadsheet. These entries are used to record the current and projected numbers for your business operation and any calculations that you might want Quattro to perform.

There are two basic types of value entries: numeric constants and formulas. Numeric constants are composed of the numeric digits from 0 through 9 with an optional + or - sign. Formulas offer a little more variety, since Quattro supports arithmetic formulas, logical formulas, and string formulas. Each type of formula offers new possibilities for model creation, and each type is examined in depth in the sections that follow.

Rules for Numeric Entries

1. Numbers cannot exceed 254 characters.
2. If the first key you press is a digit or one of a few symbols (., +, -, (,), $, #, @), the entire entry is considered a numeric entry. Numeric entries are restricted to the following symbols: 0, 1, 2, 3, 4, 5, 6, 7, 8, 9, ., +, -, (,), $, #, @, E, ^, %, *, and /. However, the last five symbols (E, ^, %, *, /) cannot begin a numeric entry.
3. Spaces and commas can never be part of a numeric entry unless they are part of a formula.

Entering Numeric Values

Entering a number in Quattro is easy; the basic rules are summarized in the box "Rules for Numeric Values Entries." If you want to enter a positive number, the + sign is optional and is normally not used. All you do is enter the numeric digits, and press ENTER or an arrow key to finalize your entry. To enter a negative number, you must type a minus sign in front of the number. Entering **99** records a positive 99, and entering **-99** records a negative 99. If you want to enter a percentage, you can enter the percent using the % sign like **15%** or you can type the decimal equivalent like **.15**.

LENGTH Like labels, numbers can be up to 254 characters in length. Quattro can handle numbers as large as 1.7976931E+308 and as small as 1.7967931E-308 if scientific notation is used to record the entries as a power of ten, as in these two examples. Quattro retains 15 decimal digits of accuracy.

Numbers do not borrow space from cells to the right to continue the display if a cell is not wide enough. If the cell uses a general numeric format (the default until you set a different format), Quattro displays any number that is too wide for the current cell width by using scientific notation. If the number is too wide for the cell, the number appears as * 's that fill the cell width. The asterisks are sometimes generated when a number is entered but may also appear when an entry is reformatted with another display format that shows additional decimal places, added commas, or other edit characters like $ or %. To eliminate the asterisks, you can reformat the affected cells with a display format that requires less space or widen the column to show more digits. Both techniques are covered in Chapter 3.

THE DEFAULT DISPLAY The initial display format for numeric entries uses Quattro's General format. The General format does not provide a consistent display for numeric entries since the magnitude of the number and the current cell width affect the display. Table 2.1 summarizes the types of entries you might see displayed with the default cell width of nine.

Using whole numbers that fit within the cell width causes the numbers to display exactly as you enter them. Extremely large or small numbers are displayed in scientific notation. Scientific notation displays a number times a power of 10. An E is used to precede the power that the number is being raised to (for example, 2.38E+05 tells Quattro to multiply 2.38 by 10 to the fifth power—or 2.38 × 100,000).

Quattro determines whether a number formatted with the General format is converted to scientific notation based on the magnitude of the number and the cell width (if a whole number entry is used). If you enter **-23456789**, Quattro displays the entry as -2.3E+07 meaning that -2.3 is multiplied by 10 raised to the seventh power. Even though you do not see the other digits of the number, Quattro remembers them and uses the full number in calculations.

The evaluation process is different for an entry consisting of a decimal fraction. If the first four digits after the decimal point are zeros, the number is converted to scientific notation regardless of the cell width. An entry of **.00008** is displayed as 8E-05 even if the current cell width is 40. If any of the first four digits is a number

Table 2.1 Potential Cell Displays*

Number Entered	Quattro's Display
15	15
1234567890	1.23E+09
6.022E27	6.02E+27
-.0000032	-3.2E-06
5.6E-200	5.6E-20
1.5%	0.015
.0000008	8E-07
.0001008	0.000101

*This table lists several possible ways Quattro displays your data when your cell uses the default column width and the default format.

other than zero, the display is rounded to fit within the cell width (for example, an entry of **.123456789** is displayed as 0.123457 when the cell width is nine).

Decimal fractions have a zero added to the left of the decimal point of the entry in the General default display format. For example, entering **.9** causes Quattro to display your entry as 0.9. Percentages in Quattro are recorded as the equivalent decimal fraction. You can enter 10 percent as **10%** or **.1**. Quattro displays your entry as 0.1 with either entry method. In Chapter 3, you will learn to use the format options to display the % symbol with your entry.

Negative numbers are displayed with a preceding minus sign when the General format is used. Typing **-99** in a cell causes Quattro to display your entry exactly as you typed it. Quattro has other options for displaying negative numbers, including enclosing them in parentheses and changing the color of the display. These options are covered in Chapters 3 and 10, respectively.

HANDLING ERRORS IN NUMERIC ENTRIES Once Quattro determines that you plan to enter a value in a spreadsheet cell, it checks your entry to ensure that every character entered is a value character. If you enter a character that is not a value character and attempt to finalize your entry, Quattro displays the error message shown in Figure 2.12. When you press ENTER to continue, Quattro places you in EDIT mode. This is Quattro's way of telling you that you need to correct your entry before it can be finalized.

Once you are in EDIT mode, everything functions as if you had pressed F2 (EDIT) to invoke EDIT mode yourself. You can use the arrow keys to move within the entry. Your options are (1) delete the characters that are not value characters, or (2) insert a label indicator at the front of the entry, and press ENTER to finalize the entry.

```
File  Edit  Style  Graph  Print  Database  Tools  Options  Window    ? ↑↓
◄ ► ▼  Name Abs Calc Macro  @  +  -  *  /  (  ,  )
[Enter] [Esc] 1992 December 31
        A              B         C         D         E         F         G
 1                               QUICK STOP GAS
 2                    JAN       FEB       MAR       APR       MAY
 3  Automotive Products
    ┌Error─────────────────────┐  40        30        50        60
    │Invalid cell or block address│ 1,320    1,250     1,190     1,330
 6  Gas(Gallons)     20,900   21,000    21,200    19,900    22,000
 7  Sparkplugs          500      540       550       480       490
 8  Food Items
 9  Eggs(dozens)      1,200    1,300     1,410     1,220     1,150
10  Milk              1,980    2,000     2,200     1,890     1,990
11  Bread            10,500   10,800    11,000     9,900    11,200
12  Rolls             1,100    1,200     1,050     1,320     1,250
13  Donuts            1,300    1,320     1,370     1,400     1,450
14  Soda(cans)       13,900   14,000    14,300    14,500    15,000
15
16
17
18

A1: [W20]                                                       ERROR
```

Figure 2.12 Error Caused by Invalid Character

ALIGNMENT OF NUMERIC ENTRIES Numeric entries are normally right-aligned within a spreadsheet cell. A label indicator cannot change this alignment. If you enter a label indicator at the front of a number in an attempt to change its alignment, Quattro uses the alignment you indicate with the label indicator, but the entry is a label (not a number). This prevents you from using the entry in any subsequent calculations. Figure 2.13 shows quantities that were entered as centered labels. When these entries are referenced in a formula, the labels are treated as 0, resulting in totals of 0. In Chapter 3, you will learn how you can change the alignment of numbers.

ENTERING FORMULAS

Quattro's formulas are invaluable because they produce results that depend on the current contents of the spreadsheet cells referenced. You can use formulas to total a column of sales figures, forecast sales growth, calculate the federal withholding tax for a given level of earnings, or compute the monthly payment amount for a loan. Formulas can perform logical comparisons and combine character-string entries into one longer entry. Creating updated results for any of these calculations is as easy as placing a new entry in a spreadsheet cell referred to in the formula.

Many new users are a little intimidated at the prospect of entering formulas, but the thought process is exactly the same as the one used to enter the correct series of calculations with a hand-held calculator. In both cases, your results reflect the attention to detail and planning involved in the effort.

```
┌[File  Edit  Style  Graph  Print  Database  Tools  Options  Window        ?  ↑↓┐
│▲◀▶▼ Erase│Copy│Move│Style│Align│Font│Insert│Delete│Fit│Sum│Format│CHR│WYS│
│D2: +B2*C2                                                                     │
│        A         B         C         D         E    F    G    H              │
│  1  Item      Price  Quantity   Total                                         │
│  2  Desk      $550       2         0                                          │
│  3  Chair     $220       4         0                                          │
│  4  Credenza  $375       8         0                                          │
│  5  Lamp       $65      10         0                                          │
│  6  File      $275       5         0                                          │
│  7                                                                            │
│  8                                                                            │
│  9                                                                            │
│ 10                                                                            │
│ 11                                                                            │
│ 12                                                                            │
│ 13                                                                            │
│ 14                                                                            │
│ 15                                                                            │
│ 16                                                                            │
│ 17                                                                            │
│ 18                                                                            │
│QFIG2_13.WQ1 [3]                                            NUM         READY  │
└───────────────────────────────────────────────────────────────────────────────┘
```

Figure 2.13 Formulas Computed Improperly Because Quantity is Stored as a Label

Formula Types

Quattro supports three types of formulas: arithmetic, logical, and string formulas. Arithmetic formulas are used to perform mathematical calculations involving addition, subtraction, multiplication, division, and exponentiation. Also, you can use Quattro's @ functions in your arithmetic formulas to access higher-level mathematical features like random numbers, absolute values, and trigonometric functions. Many other categories of @ functions exist and offer additional calculations, such as present value, internal rate of return, and depreciation calculations.

Logical formulas are used in Quattro to test a condition and ascertain if the condition is true or false. The result of a logical formula evaluated as true is displayed as a 1. The result of a logical formula evaluated as false is displayed as a 0. The ones and zeros resulting from these evaluations can influence other calculations on the spreadsheet.

A string formula can concatenate two or more strings. Once joined together with this process, the strings can be used as if they were one string. Concatenating two strings allows you to create a heading or other entry from two different pieces of spreadsheet information. String functions are especially useful when you transfer data to a Quattro spreadsheet from another source and need to manipulate the information before it can be used.

Regardless of the type of formula you select, all cells that contain formulas display the results of calculations. The formula itself is still visible in the input line when you point to the cell, but it is not displayed within the cell unless you change the display format for the cell to Text, an option described in Chapter 3.

Quattro uses different operators for each of the different types of formulas. Quattro scans formulas from left to right, assessing the priority of each operator and evaluating the operators with the highest priority first. Each operator that is included in one of your entries is evaluated according to the priority sequence shown in Table 2.2. Besides typing the operators, you can also click them in the SpeedBar to add them to your formulas.

Entering Arithmetic Formulas

Arithmetic formulas are constructed with numeric constants, cell references, and operators for addition (+), subtraction (-), multiplication (*), division (/), and exponentiation (^). Cell references are included in formulas by entering the cell address or the optional block names like Sales, Profit, or Benefits (Chapter 3 will explain how to assign these names to cells).

If you enter a formula that uses numeric constants, you can type these constants into the cell without any preparation (for example, 5*4), and Quattro will compute

Table 2.2 Order of Calculation

Operator	Action performed
( )	Parenthesis group operations to be performed
^	Exponentiation (raises the number on the left to the power on the right)
+ or -	Indicates a positive or negative number to the right of this operator
/ and *	Division and multiplication, respectively
+ and -	Addition and subtraction respectively
=, <>, <, >, <=, >=	Logical operators (equals, not equals, less than, greater than, less than or equal to, and greater than or equal to)
#NOT#	Logical NOT
#AND#, #OR, &	Logical AND, Logical OR, and string combinator

*Quattro evaluates mathematical calculations by using several rules. One rule is the order of calculation. This table lists each operator in the order it is evaluated within a formula. The higher on the list an operator is, the sooner it is evaluated within a formula. The other rule Quattro uses when it finds multiple operators that should be evaluated at the same time is to evaluate the operators left to right. The list above gives the available operators in the order that they are evaluated.

and display the result of 20. Cell references used as variables in a formula make it easy to update the results of the formula. To use cell references, you must begin your entry with a value character rather than the first letter in a cell address. If you forget to begin a formula with a value character, Quattro treats your entry as a label.

If you enter **B2*C2** in a spreadsheet cell, Quattro enters 'B2*C2 in the cell and displays the entry as a label as shown in Figure 2.14. If you enter **+B2*C2**, the + does not change the value of B2, but it causes Quattro to treat the entry as a value and to process B2 and C2 as cell addresses. Using the current contents of these cells, Quattro calculates the result of the formula and displays this result in cell D2 where the formula was entered. Parentheses are value characters and can be used, except they are needed at both ends of the entry, as in (A2*B3). The plus sign is a better choice, since one less keystroke is required for each formula entered. Figure 2.15 shows the edited formula in D2 that calculates the total cost for an order. The formula appears in the input line when the selector is on the cell, and the result appears in the cell.

You are not restricted to entering formulas with a single operator. With Quattro, you can enter formulas as long as 254 characters with as many operators as necessary. When you use more than one operator, Quattro follows the order in Table 2.2 to determine which operation to perform first. If more than one operation of the same level is in a single formula, the operation at the left is performed first, because Quattro always moves from left to right when evaluating an expression. For example, since multiplication has a higher priority than addition, the entry **6+2*4** yields 14, not 32. (Quattro calculates $2 \times 4 = 8$, then $6 + 8 = 14$.)

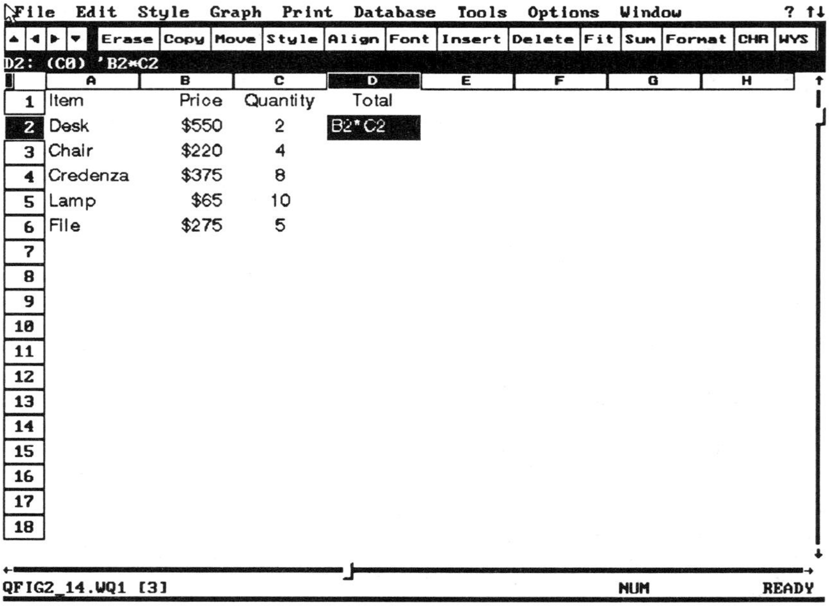

Figure 2.14 Formula Typed as a Label

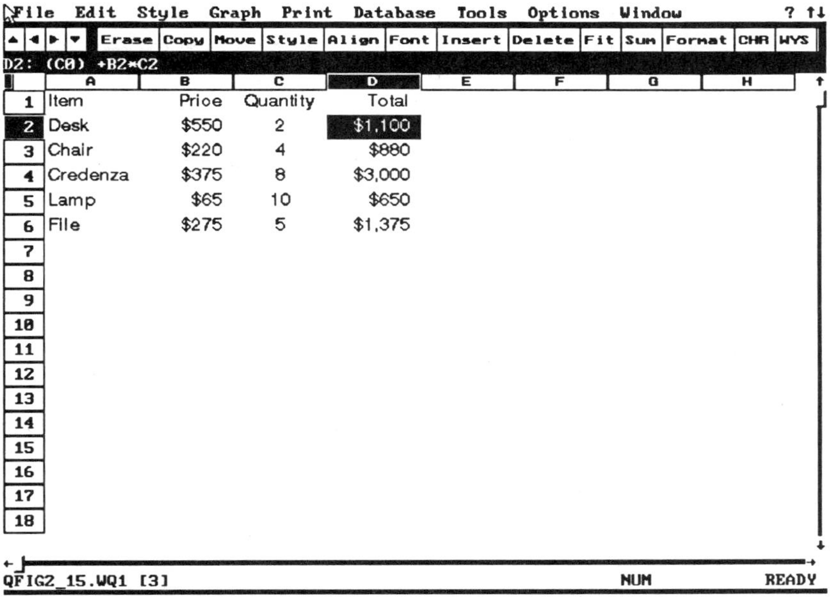

```
File  Edit  Style  Graph  Print  Database  Tools  Options  Window         ? ↑↓
     Erase Copy Move Style Align Font Insert Delete Fit Sum Format CHR WYS
D2: (C0) +B2*C2
         A          B        C          D        E      F       G      H
  1  Item        Price   Quantity    Total
  2  Desk         $550       2       $1,100
  3  Chair        $220       4        $880
  4  Credenza     $375       8       $3,000
  5  Lamp          $65      10        $650
  6  File         $275       5       $1,375
  7
  8
  9
 10
 11
 12
 13
 14
 15
 16
 17
 18

QFIG2_15.WQ1 [3]                                    NUM         READY
```

Figure 2.15 Formulas in Column D to Compute Totals

USING PARENTHESES To override the natural priority sequence of operations, use parentheses. Enclosing an expression within parentheses causes Quattro to evaluate the expression within parentheses before performing any other operations. Typing the previous expression as **(6+2)*4** produces a result of 32. Parentheses can also be nested, as in **((9+3)*(2+3))**, which causes Quattro to perform the two addition operations before the multiplication, and produces 60 as a result for the expression.

BUILDING FORMULAS WITH THE POINTING INSTEAD OF TYPING METHOD Most formulas you enter are built with cell references rather than numeric constants. This tactic allows you to change the results calculated by entering new numbers in spreadsheet cells rather than having to alter formulas to produce the new results. You can type any formula into the current cell by typing the arithmetic operators and the cell addresses, but the pointing method offers an alternative approach with an added advantage.

The advantage of the pointing method for formula construction is that pointing to each reference used in a formula causes you to visually verify that you are including the proper information in your calculation. This minimizes the possibility of including an incorrect cell reference in a calculation.

To build a formula with the pointing method, you type the arithmetic operators, parentheses, and numeric constants and point to the correct cell reference each time you want to include one in the formula. Before you decide that the steps involved seem to take more time than typing the formula, remember that the lower formula error rate actually saves time and improves the accuracy of your calculations. To enter +D4/F2 in the current cell the following steps are required:

1. Type a plus (+).
2. Move the selector to D4. As you move the selector, the mode indicator changes to POINT as shown in Figure 2.16, and Quattro displays the cell address in the input line as part of the formula just as if you had typed it.
3. Type a /. The selector returns to the cell where the formula is being recorded when the operator is typed and can be moved to the next cell reference required.
4. Move the selector to F2 as shown in Figure 2.17.
5. Press ENTER. Pressing ENTER is your only option for finalizing the formula, since moving the selector to a new location changes the last reference in the formula. The exception to this rule is a formula that ends with a parenthesis or a numeric constant, since the arrow keys finalize these formulas.

As you are entering a formula in POINT mode, you may decide to abandon POINT mode and type the remainder of your formula. The mode indicator switches back to VALUE. You can switch back to POINT mode after you type the next operator. If you try pointing to a cell after typing the formula and if the formula does not end with an operator, Quattro finalizes the formula.

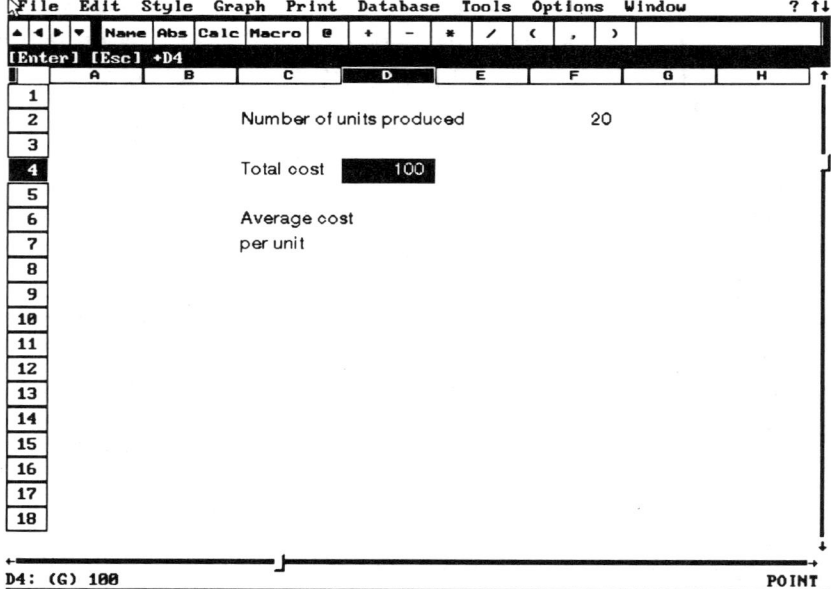

Figure 2.16 Pointing to Incorporate the Value for Cell D4 into a Formula

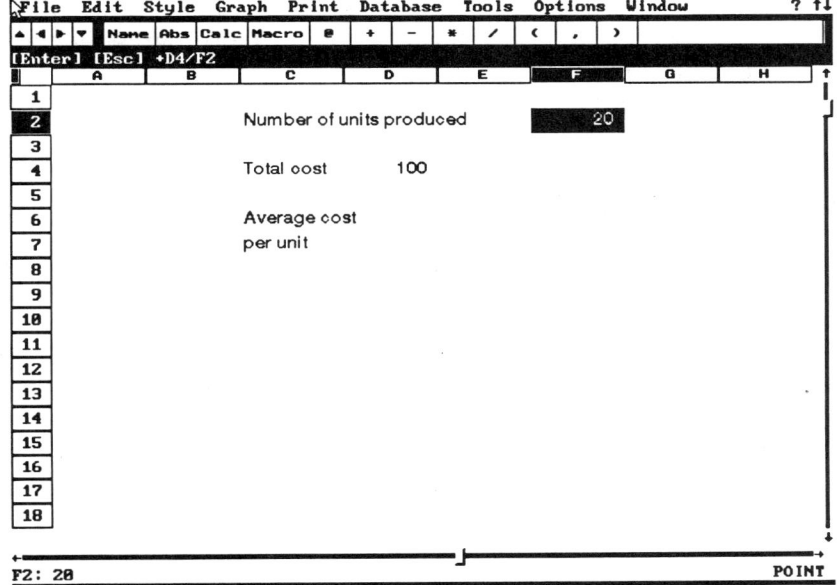

Figure 2.17 Pointing to Incorporate the Value for Cell F2 into a Formula

Pointing with a Mouse Pointing with a formula using a mouse is different from pointing using the keyboard directional keys. Quattro does not use what the mouse is pointing to until you select it by pressing the mouse button. To build a formula with the pointing method using a mouse, you type the arithmetic operators, parentheses, and numeric constants and select the correct cell reference each time you want to include one in the formula. As in pointing with the keyboard directional keys, it may take longer to point to a cell with a mouse, but the time lost is balanced by the increased accuracy. Also, pointing with a mouse is quicker when the cells are farther apart or in different files. To enter +D4/F2 in the current cell the following steps are required:

1. Type a plus (+).
2. Point to D4. The mode indicator does not change (as it does when you are using the keyboard directional keys).
3. Press the mouse button. Quattro adds D4 to the cell's contents. If you selected the wrong cell, you can select a different cell by pointing to it and pressing the mouse button. Quattro then replaces the previous cell with the more recently selected cell. For example, if you point to D3 and press the mouse button by mistake, you can point to D4 and press the mouse button to replace D3 with D4.
4. Type a /.
5. Point to F2 and press the mouse button.

6. Point to [Enter] in the input line, and press the mouse button. As when the keyboard directional keys are used, pressing ENTER is your only option for finalizing the formula. If you press an arrow key or point to another cell and press the mouse button, the last reference in the formula is changed.

@ Functions in Arithmetic Formulas

Quattro has additional computational capabilities beyond the simple arithmetic operators. These additional calculations are accessed through @ functions to round numbers, compute financial calculations, and perform conditional computations and many additional sophisticated options. Each @ function begins with the @ symbol and is followed by a keyword and your requirements for its specific use. Chapter 6 provides an in-depth look at the various categories of @ functions that Quattro offers. After you have mastered the basic formulas the package offers, Chapter 6 is a must-see chapter to add additional power to your spreadsheets.

Reference Types

Quattro supports three types of cell references: relative, absolute, and mixed. Each formula discussed so far has used the default option of relative references. This style reference might look like A2, Z33, ST100, R94. An absolute reference has a **$** in front of each portion of the address (A4), and in a mixed reference style, half of the address is relative and the other half is absolute ($A2 or A$2).

All three reference styles produce the same results in the cell where the formula is entered initially. The difference in the three reference styles is not apparent until you copy the cell containing the formula. Relative references are adjusted as the formula is placed in another cell. Absolute references are not adjusted when they are copied. The updating of a mixed reference depends on which portion of the cell address is absolute and whether the formula is being moved to a new row or a new column. This topic is covered in more detail in Chapter 3 in the section on copying formulas. For now it is only important to recognize the various types of cell addresses shown in the box "Cell Reference Types" and to realize that the type of reference you select can have far-reaching effects later in the model development process.

How Quattro Pro Recalculates Formulas

Early versions of spreadsheet packages recalculated the entire spreadsheet every time a single cell was changed. A more recent technique maintains a table of row and column dependencies so that only the rows and columns affected by a change are recalculated. However, even this slows you down; if you make a change that affects many cells, you must wait for Quattro to finish recalculating the cells.

> ## Cell Reference Types
>
> Quattro has three types of cell references. These types of cell references to not affect the formula, but they do modify how the cell references change when a formula is copied.
>
> | Type | Examples |
> |---|---|
> | Relative Reference | A1, G13, AV1520 |
> | Absolute Reference | A1, G13, AV1520 |
> | Mixed Reference | A$1, $G13, $AV1520 |

Quattro, therefore, provides background automatic recalculation. With background automatic recalculation, Quattro recalculates the necessary formulas only when you are not entering keystrokes. The BKGD indicator will appear in the status line while Quattro has formulas that it needs to recalculate, but you can continue to enter data. If you are going to print the spreadsheet, you must wait until the BKGD indicator disappears before printing.

Quattro can also recognize an 8087 or 80287 math coprocessor chip; iterative calculations, complex formula recalculations, and recalculations for large models are noticeably faster with one of these chips.

Formulas That Result in Special Values

Normally the formulas you enter produce either arithmetic results, string entries, or a logical 0 or 1 result. In error situations or other special circumstances, the result produced by a formula is not what you expect. If you enter a formula with a missing parenthesis, a missing operator, or an incorrectly spelled @ function keyword, Quattro displays an error message. When you press ENTER to continue, Quattro places you in EDIT mode to make the correction. If you cannot find the source of the problem, you might want to convert the formula into a label temporarily by adding a label indicator at the front of the entry. This allows you to look at the formula later from a fresh perspective (pressing ESC eliminates the formula, and you must retype the formula again).

In other situations, a special value may display in the cell where you enter the formula. If you attempt an operation like dividing by zero or a label entry, Quattro displays ERR in the cell. ERR also appears when you have provided an improper function argument for one of the @ functions. Also, ERR appears when you reference a cell that contains a value that is an error. When a formula references a cell containing @NA or ERR, the formula returns @NA or @ERR. In Chapter 9, you will learn how you can have Quattro Pro identify formulas that reference a cell equalling @NA or @ERR.

The last special value that can appear is a row of *'s that fill the cell. Although these entries are not really values, they occur anytime a cell is not wide enough to display the current result of the formula in the current format. Changing the width of the column containing the formula or reformatting the cell with a different format, as described in Chapter 3, can solve the problem.

Using Logical Formulas

Logical formulas allow you to compare two values. Logical formulas add power to spreadsheet applications, since you can check the result of the comparison and use it to influence other operations on the spreadsheet. The results produced by the logical formulas are not the result of arithmetic calculations. Logical formulas always return either a 0 (representing a false result for the condition test) or a 1 (indicating that the condition tested as true).

You use logical operators when you build a logical formula. These operators are listed in Table 2.3. They test for equality (=), inequality (<>), greater than (>), greater than or equal to (>=), less than (<), or less than or equal to (<=).

In Figure 2.18, a logical formula determines if a customer has met the minimum purchase amount for a discount. The logical formula +B8>B2 compares the amount of the purchase against the minimum purchase. If the condition tests true, the discount is multiplied by one; if it tests false, the discount is multiplied by zero, effectively negating the discount calculation.

Logical operators all have the same priority level and are evaluated from left to right if more than one occurs in an expression. When logical operators are combined with arithmetic operators, the arithmetic operations are computed first, since they have a higher priority. Figure 2.19 provides an example of a formula that combines both logical and arithmetic operations.

Table 2.3 Logical Operators

Operator	Result
=	Returns a 1 if the value on the left of the equal sign equals the value on the right; returns a 0 otherwise.
<>	Returns a 1 if the value on the left of this operator does not equal the value on the right; returns a 0 otherwise.
<	Returns a 1 if the value on the left of this operator is less than the value on the right; returns a 0 otherwise.
>	Returns a 1 if the value on the left of this operator is greater than the value on the right; returns a 0 otherwise.
<=	Returns a 1 if the value on the left of this operator is less than or equal to the value on the right; returns a 0 otherwise.
>=	Returns a 1 if the value on the left of this operator is greater than or equal to the value on the right; returns a 0 otherwise.

Basic Spreadsheet Entries 51

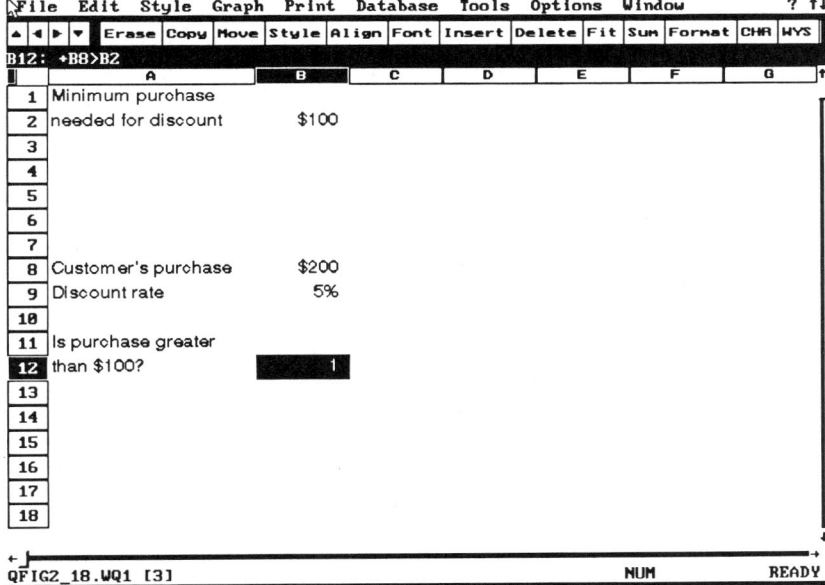

Figure 2.18 Logical Formula Used to Determine if Customer is Eligible for a Discount

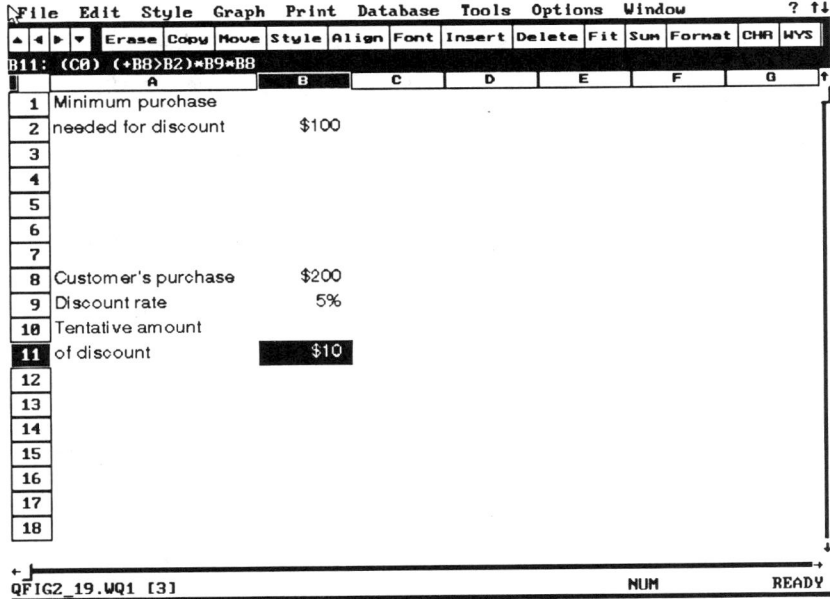

Figure 2.19 Logical Formula Used in Computing Discount

Logical formulas can use text as the two quantities it compares. For example, +"Smith">"Jones" returns a 1, since it is true that Smith is after Jones in the alphabet. When you use logical operators with strings, the comparisons are usually (1) whether one string is the same as the other or different or (2) which string comes before the other.

Using String Formulas

String formulas are used to join or concatenate two strings or groups of characters into one longer string. The ampersand (&) is the only operator used in string formulas and must be used between any two strings that you wish to join. Because a string formula is a type of value entry, it must begin with a value character like the plus sign, as in the formula **+A2&D3** that joins the string entries in A2 and D3.

String constants can be incorporated into string formulas and are often used either to provide spaces between two string variables or to add a constant entry. Anytime a string is included directly in a formula it must be enclosed in quotation marks. Figure 2.20 shows a formula in C1 that joins the department number in B5 with a constant to create a string that appears at the top of the report.

Another application of string entries joins many separate entries into a longer string. Figure 2.21 shows first names, middle initials, and last names in columns A through C. By using the formula **+C2&", "&A2&" "&B2&"."**, the separate entries in row 2 are joined into one name entry with the appropriate spacing and punctuation, which appears in column D.

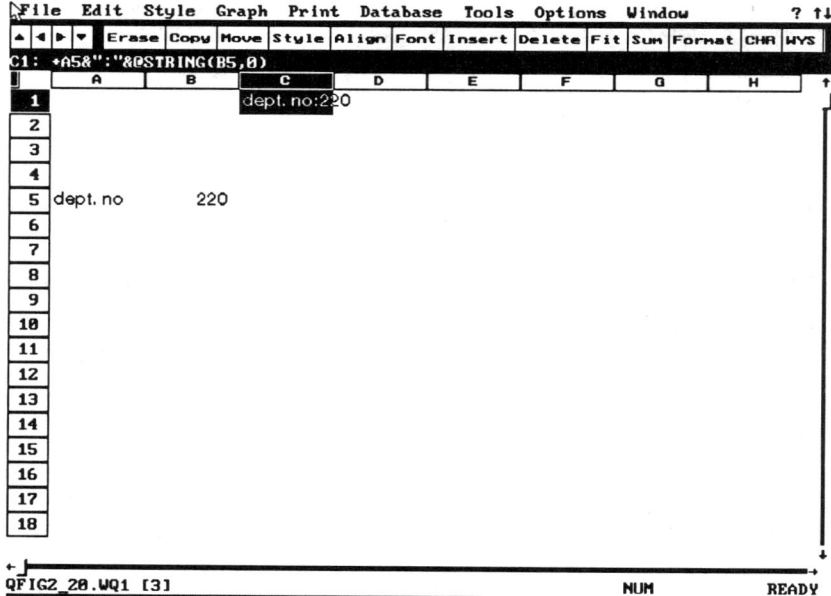

Figure 2.20 String Formula Used to Join Two Cells' Contents

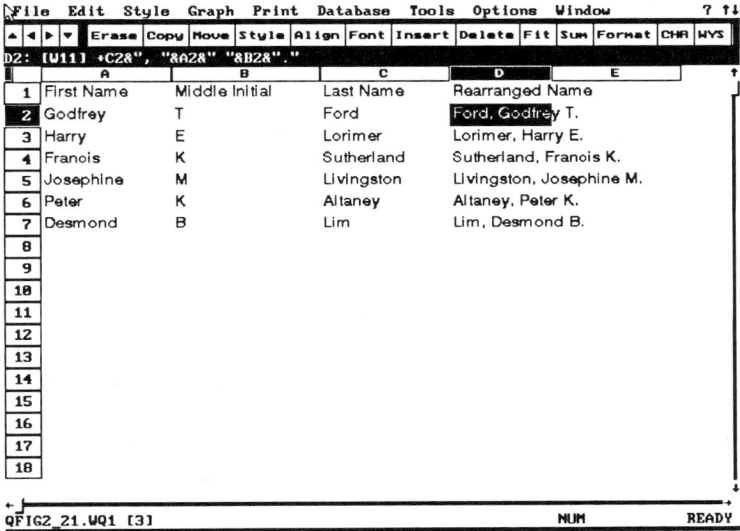

Figure 2.21 String Formula Used to Combine Several Strings into a Longer One

Testing Spreadsheet Formulas

Even though your formulas produce normal-looking results, you must test the results to ensure their accuracy. The potential problem with inaccurate results does not stem from any deficiencies in Quattro's ability to calculate, but from the possibility of inadvertent errors on your part. In Chapter 9 you will learn how you can audit a spreadsheet to test its formulas but for now you can test a spreadsheet by putting numbers in it.

The most efficient testing is conducted in phases. If you plan to use a set of calculations to process periods of data, enter the formulas for the first period, and test them before copying the formulas for the other periods. Although the other periods still need to be verified, you minimize your total time investment.

Another part of the step-by-step approach is to increase the vigorousness of the test gradually. Your first test should be a reasonableness test. If sales are $100,000 and are the sole source of revenue for the company, it is totally unreasonable for profits to be $1,000,000. A quick check can tell you if the results produced by a model are reasonable.

The next set of data entered while testing should be easy-to-manage round numbers like 10, 100, or 1,000. It is easy to check the results of simple calculations in your head with this type of entry (multiplying 10 units by a selling price of $100 obviously yields a total of $1,000).

Once your model has passed both a reasonableness test and the entry of simple numbers, check the model with some real data. The best data to use are data from a previous period; you already have the manually calculated results and can check the results produced by the model quickly.

Once the accuracy of your model is verified, you do not need to check your model every time you use it. If you later modify the formulas in your model, you ought to repeat the testing process.

ENTERING DATES AND TIMES

Spreadsheet packages handle dates as date serial numbers to allow calculations that can determine if a loan is past due, the aging of your receivables, or the rental charge on a home-improvement product with a daily rental rate. Quattro also stores times as time serial numbers, so you can use times in calculations such as calculating the time each person spent on a project. Most spreadsheet packages require you to use @ functions to enter a date serial number that determines how many days a given date occurs after a past date. Quattro makes the date-entry task easy, since a simple key sequence tells Quattro that you are about to enter a date.

Quattro's Date Features

To enter a date in Quattro, you need to press CTRL-D and type a date in any of the formats shown in Table 2.4. Quattro accepts date entries between January 1, 1900, and December 31, 2099. Quattro displays your entry with the date display format that is initially entered. Figure 2.22 displays a column of date entries entered with the CTRL-D option, and the cell widened so asterisks do not appear.

Table 2.4 Formats That CTRL-D Accepts as a Date

Format	Examples
DD-MMM-YY	25-Dec-91, 20-Aug-92
DD-MMM	25-Dec, 20-Aug (assumes current year)
MMM-YR	Dec-91, Aug-92 (assumes first day of the month)
Long International (initially set at MM/DD/YY)	12/25/91, 8/20/92, 08/20/92
Short International (initially set at MM/DD)	12/25, 8/20 (assumes current year)

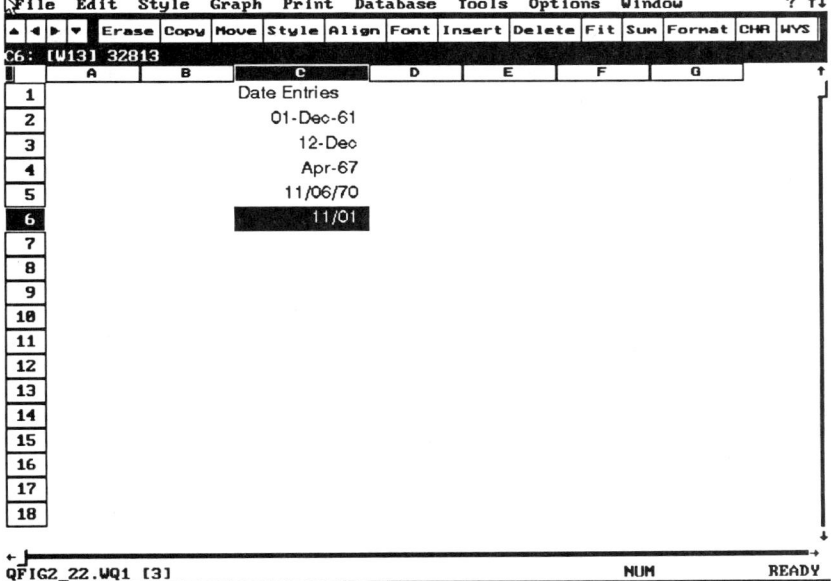

Figure 2.22 Dates Entered with CTRL-D

Although your date entry is displayed as a date, it is stored as a date serial number so you can perform date calculations. An entry of January 1, 1900 produces a date serial number entry of 2, since it is two days after December 30, 1899, which is the zero reference point for all Quattro dates. An entry of July 7, 1989 produces a date serial number entry of 32696, since it is 32696 days after December 31, 1899. Although 1900 was not a leap year, other spreadsheet packages count February 29, 1900 as an actual date. To maintain compatibility over the vast range of useful dates, Quattro uses December 30, 1899, rather than December 31, 1899, as a zero point. Negative numbers represent the number of days before December 30, 1899.

Performing Date Calculations

Once dates are recorded in a Quattro spreadsheet, date calculations can be performed with the same operators used in other arithmetic calculations. Figure 2.23 shows dates representing invoice dates in column B. According to the terms of the invoice, payment should be made within 10 days of the invoice date. The payment due date is calculated easily by adding 10 days to the invoice date. The formula to perform this calculation is stored in column C. These entries have not been formatted as dates and appear as serial date numbers. To change the display to a date

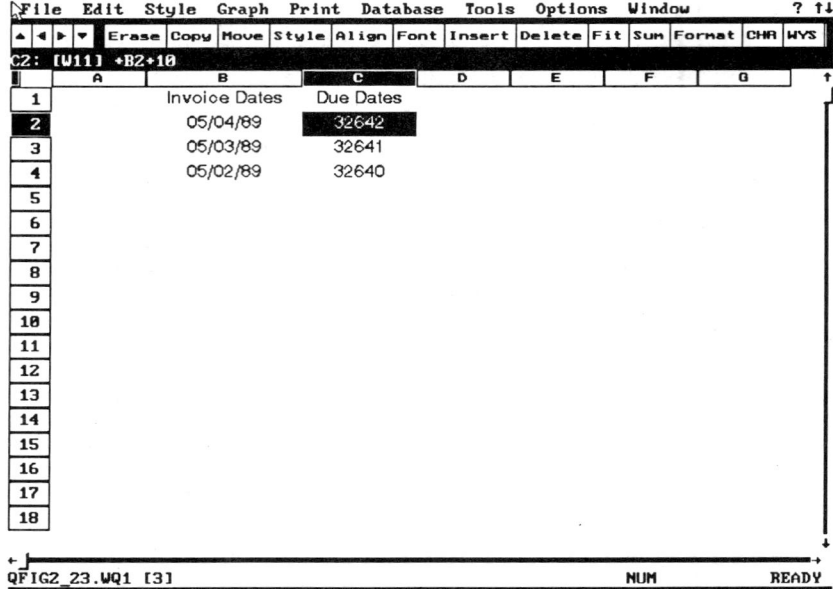

Figure 2.23 Date Serial Numbers Used to Compute Invoice Due Dates

format, you enter /Style Numeric Format Date, and select one of the four date options. This command is discussed in more detail in Chapter 3.

Quattro's Time Features

To enter a time in Quattro, you must press CTRL-D and type a time in one of the acceptable time formats. These time formats are HH:MM:SS AM/PM, HH:MM AM/PM, HH:MM:SS, and HH:MM. The last two formats are the international time formats; so if you later change how the international time formats are displayed, the last two formats for directly entering dates change. Also, the international time formats use a 24-hour clock, which means that hours after noon are 12 plus the hour as in 18 for 6 PM. When you press CTRL-D and enter a time, Quattro converts the time into a time serial number in the input line (which looks nothing like the time it represents) and displays the time using the time format you used. Times are represented as the portion of the day. For example, noon is .5, since it is half of the day. Once times are entered, you can use them in calculations. For example, if A1 and A2 contain times, you can calculate the difference between the times with the formula **+A1-A2**. When you format the result using one of the time formats described in the next chapter, Quattro will display the time difference in hours, minutes and seconds.

DOCUMENTING DATES, FORMULAS, AND NUMBERS

When you create models in your spreadsheet, the formulas and numbers you add will seem very clear to you. However, when you use the spreadsheet model later, you may forget why you entered certain dates, formulas, or numbers. You can add cell notation to dates, formulas, and numbers. Quattro uses a semicolon to separate the date, formula, or number part of a cell entry from the cell notation. After the semicolon, you can type the description of the cell's contents. The number of characters that you use in a comment is limited to 254 for each cell entry. Figure 2.24 shows a cell containing cell notation. The comments only appear in the input line when the selector points to a cell containing a cell notation. If you want to show the comments, you must change the format to Text, as Chapter 3 will describe. You can print comments by printing the cell formulas, as Chapter 4 will describe.

GETTING STARTED

In this chapter, you learned how to make entries in spreadsheet cells. The options available for you include entering data, changing label alignment, and creating formulas to perform computations. You can practice these types of entries by

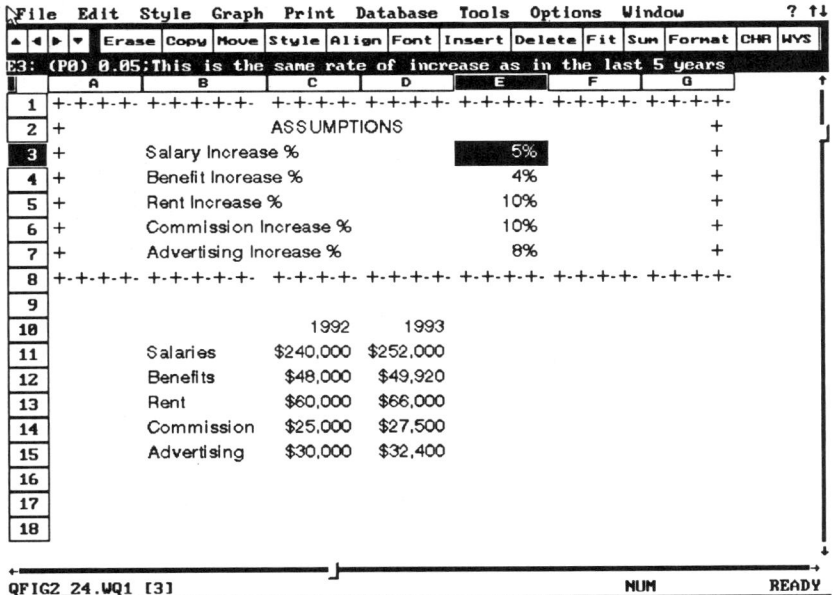

Figure 2.24 Cell Containing Cell Notation

58 *Quattro Pro 4.0 Handbook*

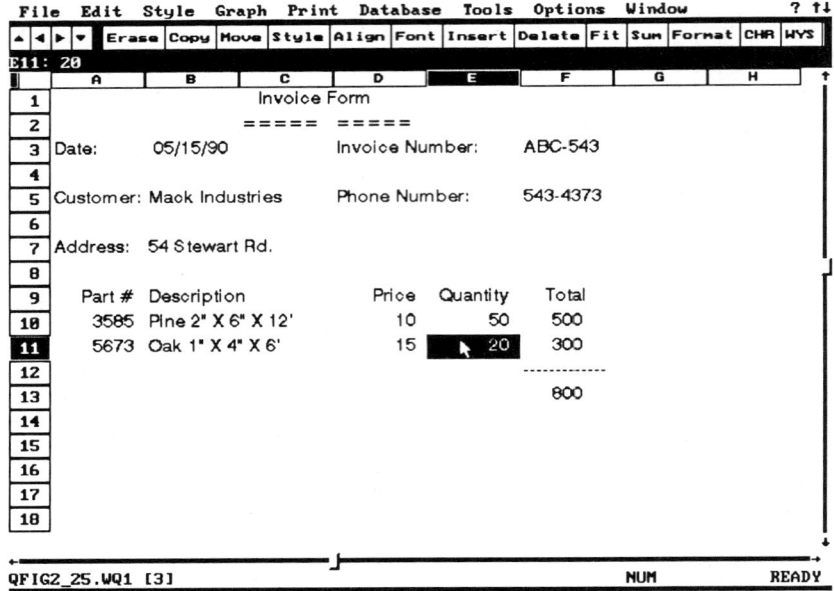

Figure 2.25 Invoice Form Created with Getting Started Section

creating an invoice order form and entering the data for an invoice. Figure 2.25 shows the final spreadsheet. To create an invoice in the spreadsheet, follow these steps:

1. Move to C1. Type three spaces and **Invoice Form**. The three spaces at the beginning center the label in columns C and D.

2. Press the DOWN ARROW or point to the cell C2, and press the mouse button. Type \=, and press the RIGHT ARROW to create a dashed line in C2. Type \=, and press the DOWN ARROW to create a dashed line in D2. You can use repeated labels to divide the spreadsheet and to create headings.

3. Make the following entries. For each cell, you must first position the selector to the cell address or point to it and press the mouse button. Once the cell is selected, type the entry. To finish the entry, you can either (1) press ENTER, (2) click the [Enter] button in the input line, or (3) press an arrow key. Notice how some of the entries listed below have a quotation mark at the beginning so the label will be right-justified in the cell. You can use this feature for column headings for columns that will contain numbers.

A3: **Date:**
D3: **Invoice Number:**
A5: **Customer:**
D5: **Phone Number:**
A7: **Address:**

A9: "**Part #**
B9: **Description**
D9: "**Price**
E9: "**Quantity**
F9: "**Total**

4. Move to F10 by using the arrow keys or by pointing to the cell and pressing the mouse button. This cell needs a formula that multiplies the value in the Price column with the value in the Quantity column. Type +. Press the LEFT ARROW twice or point to D10 and press the mouse button. Type *. Press the LEFT ARROW or point to E10 and press the mouse button. Press ENTER or press the mouse button on [Enter] in the input line.

5. Move to F11 by using the arrow keys or by pointing to the cell and pressing the mouse button. This cell needs the same formula as does F10. You will learn in the next chapter how to copy formulas, but now simply type the formula. Type **+D11*E11**. Since you did not enter this formula by pointing, you can use the DOWN ARROW or point to F12 and press the mouse button to finalize the entry and move to F12.

6. Type **\-**, and press the DOWN ARROW (or point to F13 and press the mouse button) to create a repeating label of dashes. You can use the repeating labels to indicate that the value above or below the line is a summary figure.

7. The cell in F13 needs a formula that adds the value in F10 to the value in F11. Type +. Press the UP ARROW three times or point to F10 and press the mouse button. Type +. Press the UP ARROW twice or point to F11 and press the mouse button. Press ENTER or click [Enter] in the input line.

You have now completed the form and are ready to enter invoice data. To fill in the form you have just created, follow these steps:

1. Press HOME to move to A1, then press the DOWN ARROW twice and the RIGHT ARROW once to move to B3.

2. Enter the date by pressing CTRL-D and typing **5/15/90**. Press ENTER. Quattro converts your entry in the input line to 33008, which is the integer value that represents May 15, 1990.

3. Move to F3 by pressing the RIGHT ARROW four times or by pointing to F3 and pressing the mouse button. Type **ABC-543**. You can use ENTER to finalize the entry or you can press the DOWN ARROW twice and the LEFT ARROW four times to move to B5. If you are using a mouse, point to B5 and press the mouse button. Type **Mack Industries**. Either press the RIGHT ARROW key four times to move to F5 or point to F5 and press the mouse button. This finalizes the entry in B5 and moves the selector to where you will be making your next entry.

4. Type **543-4373**, and press ENTER or press the mouse button. Since this entry starts with a number, Quattro treats this entry as a value and displays -3830. As you can see in the input line, Quattro stores this entry as you entered it.

To change this entry so it is treated as a label, press F2 (EDIT) or point to the cell's contents in the input line and press the mouse button. Move to the 5, and type an apostrophe ('). Finalize the modified entry by pressing ENTER or pressing the mouse button.

5. Move to B7 by pressing the DOWN ARROW twice and the LEFT ARROW four times. If you are using a mouse, point to B7 and press the mouse button. Type **54 Stewart Rd.**, and press ENTER. Since the first character is a number, Quattro tries to evaluate this entry as a value or formula. In a formula, an entry like Stewart looks like a block name. A block name is a name assigned to one or more cells that you can use in place of the cell or block address in formulas and commands. Since this spreadsheet does not have a block named Stewart, Quattro does not know how to evaluate this formula and displays an error message. Since you really want this entry treated as a label, you need to tell Quattro to treat this entry as a label. After pressing ENTER or pressing the mouse button, move to the beginning of the entry and type an apostrophe.

6. Move to A10 by pressing the DOWN ARROW three times and the LEFT ARROW once or by pointing to A10 and pressing the mouse button. Type **3585** for the part number. Press the RIGHT ARROW or point to B10 and press the mouse button to finalize the entry in A10 and move the selector to where you want to make the next entry. Type **Pine 2" @ 6" @ 12'**. When you use apostrophes, quotation marks, and carets in a label entry for other than the first character, these characters will appear in the label. Press the RIGHT ARROW twice or point to D10 and press the mouse button. Type **10**, and press the RIGHT ARROW or point to E10 and press the mouse button to finalize the first item's price. Type **50** to enter the first item's quantity. Press the DOWN ARROW to move to the row for the next item, and press END followed by LEFT ARROW to move the cell selector to A11. With a mouse, point to A11 and press the mouse button. Notice that as you entered the price and quantity, the formula in F10 automatically computed the total for the item and the formula in F13 computed the total for the invoice.

7. Type **5673** for the part number. Press the RIGHT ARROW or point to B11 and press the mouse button to finalize the entry in A11 and move the selector to where you want to make the next entry. Type **Oak 1" X 4" X 6'**. Press the RIGHT ARROW twice or point to D11 and press the mouse button. Type **15** and press the RIGHT ARROW or point to E11 and press the mouse button to enter the second item's price. Type **20** to enter the second item's price. Press ENTER or press the mouse button. Your screen now looks like Figure 2.25. The formulas in F10 and F11 automatically compute the totals for the items, and the formula in F13 computes the total for the invoice.

8. You can quickly save this spreadsheet by pressing CTRL-S and typing a file name such as **INVOICE**. The first time you save a spreadsheet with CTRL-S, Quattro prompts you for the file name. If you pressed CTRL-S a second time, Quattro would save the file using the same file name. When the file name is entered, press ENTER or press the mouse button.

3

Working with Multiple Cells

As you become more proficient in making cell entries, you will find that model building is slow when you work with one cell at a time. Fortunately, Quattro provides many commands that allow you to affect multiple cells. When you work with multiple cells at once, you are working with a *block* of your spreadsheet. By using a block of your spreadsheet, you can apply one command to the block and have it affect all cells in the block. Working with blocks is a time-saving feature that enables you to complete many tasks quickly. Many of the block commands have shortcut keys, so you can execute the command with fewer keystrokes than the menu selections require.

    This chapter addresses Quattro commands that operate on blocks of data. First, this chapter teaches you the rules for defining blocks of the spreadsheet to Quattro. Second, you will learn how you can change the format and alignment used to display your information. You will learn commands for changing a block of spreadsheet entries or all the entries on the spreadsheet. You will also learn to copy, move, or erase a block of your spreadsheet.

    Other block features you will be introduced to offer a little more sophistication. You can name blocks of your spreadsheet so that you can use the name instead of the block address. Names are much easier to remember than spreadsheet cell addresses. You can also add notes to the blocks just like the cell notation you learned about in Chapter 2. Another advanced feature is protecting your spreadsheet from inadvertent damage. You can also change how Quattro stores a section of your spreadsheet by transposing the rows and columns or by converting formulas into their string or numeric values. Quattro also has a Search & Replace feature that finds spreadsheet data and provides several options for modifying that data. When you have text extending for many cells, you can direct Quattro to reformat the text to fit different margins. You will also learn how to make Quattro input data into your spreadsheet by filling in numbers according to your specifications. By the time you finish this chapter, you will have mastered a set of block commands that will provide speed features for your model-building activities.

Quattro's commands that work with multiple cells are not limited to block activities. Quattro also has commands that let you work with columns and rows. You can direct Quattro where to insert and remove columns and rows. You can also change the width of columns and select which columns are displayed. Quattro lets you change how your spreadsheet appears as you move around in your spreadsheet by creating rows and columns that are frozen on the screen. Finally, Quattro lets you create windows to view two sections of your spreadsheet at the same time.

Quattro Pro also has many features that change the appearance of your entries. You can set the font and add bullets, lines, boxes, and shading to your spreadsheet entries. Quattro Pro 4 makes using these appearance enhancements easy by letting you create named styles to represent sets of appearance enhancements, and apply named styles to cells rather than to the separate commands that are represented by the named styles.

A feature of Quattro Pro is the Undo feature. While you can use this feature to simply undo a change to a cell entry, the Undo feature is also a more powerful feature by which you can undo changes made to blocks of data. Using the Undo feature provides a safety net in case you make a mistake.

BASIC BLOCK COMMANDS

Quattro's basic block commands provide simple features that are powerful because they can operate on blocks rather than on individual cells. With each of the basic block commands, you must specify the group of cells on which the command should operate. Specifying a block is easy, since Quattro provides several methods for indicating which block you want to use. Once you master the rules for specifying a block, you can format, copy, move, erase, or change the alignment of the block, as well as use the more advanced block commands.

In Quattro Pro, you can select the block and then select the command that will use the block. For example, if you want to format a block so the numbers in the block include currency signs, you have the choice of selecting the block and then selecting the /Style Numeric Format command or selecting the /Style Numeric Format command and then selecting the block. In most of this book, you will see the commands selected before selecting the block that the command uses. You have the choice of selecting the block or the command first—the results are the same. If you select the block before selecting the command, you will not see the prompt for the block the command uses. Also, if a command uses more than one block, a preselected block is used for the first block the command uses. For example, if you preselect a block and then use the /Edit Move command, Quattro only prompts for where you want the block moved. If you had not preselected a block, Quattro would separately prompt for the block to move and its new location. So you will see prompts for subsequent blocks the command uses. In Quattro

Pro 4, the block you select before selecting a command will remain selected, so you can use the block and select more than one command that will use the block. The block will remain selected until you move the selector to another cell.

Specifying a Block

A block is a rectangular section of your spreadsheet. It can be as small as one cell or include cells in many rows and columns. Figure 3.1 shows a block specified (using a mouse or SHIFT-F7). All the cells that are highlighted are included in the block. To describe a block to Quattro, indicate two diagonally opposite corners of the block. Blocks are frequently specified by their upper-left corner and lower-right corner, but Quattro also lets you describe a block using any combination you wish. In Figure 3.1, the block is specified by the two corners, B4 and D16 (the selector has a different color than the other cells in the block).

When Quattro asks you for a block, one method of describing it is by typing the cell address of one corner, typing a period, and typing the cell address of a diagonally opposite corner. Another method is to use the arrow keys to highlight one corner, type a period, and move the highlight to the diagonally opposite corner. If you have a mouse attached to your system, you can select a block by using the mouse. You can use the SHIFT-F7 (SELECT) key or mouse to specify a block before requesting the Quattro command that will operate on the contents of the block.

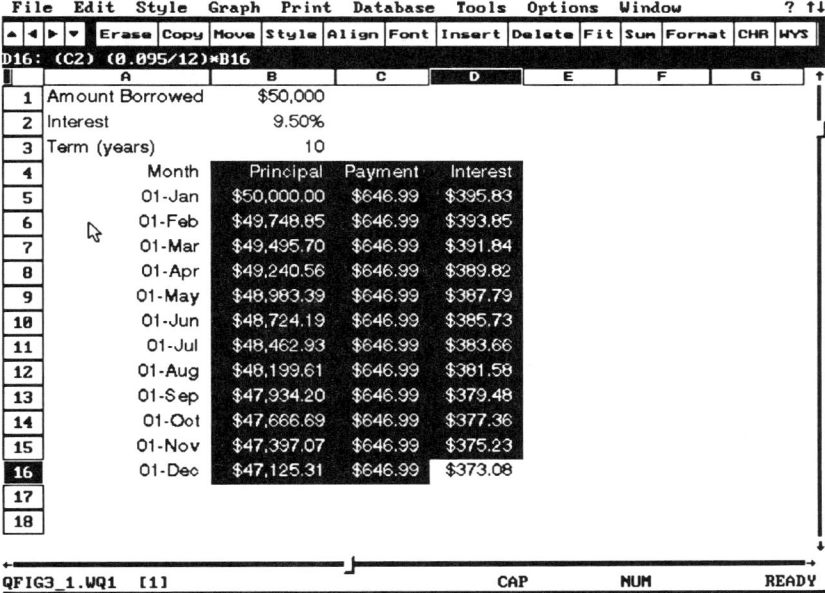

Figure 3.1 Spreadsheet with Block Highlighted

A little planning on your part makes it even easier to use the block commands. Before invoking a block command, position the selector on a cell that is on a corner of the block. Then, when Quattro prompts for the block you want to use in the command, direct Quattro to the other corner of the block. Quattro assumes that the selector is on one of the corners in the block shown by the block address at the top as in Figure 3.2. In this figure, Quattro assumes that B4 is one corner of the block. This is a block address, since the cell address is shown twice separated by two periods. When Quattro assumes that the selector is on one of the corners of a block, it *anchors* the block address to that point. By anchoring one corner of a block, you can stretch the other corner to include the information you want. You can change the other corner of the block with the arrow keys and the other keys that move the selector.

If the selector is not on the desired corner of the block, press ESC once and Quattro changes the block address to a single cell address. Since the address is no longer expressed as a block, the beginning is no longer anchored. You can move the selector to a corner of the block, and type a period. Typing a period changes the cell address to a block address and anchors one corner of the block to the current cell address. This allows you to stretch the sides of the block as you move the selector to the opposite corner.

Some Quattro commands (such as Print) remember the block reference used in the previous command. If you want to use the same block a second time, you do not have to reenter it. To change the block reference for the current command, you can use either the ESC key or the BACKSPACE key. The ESC key unlocks the

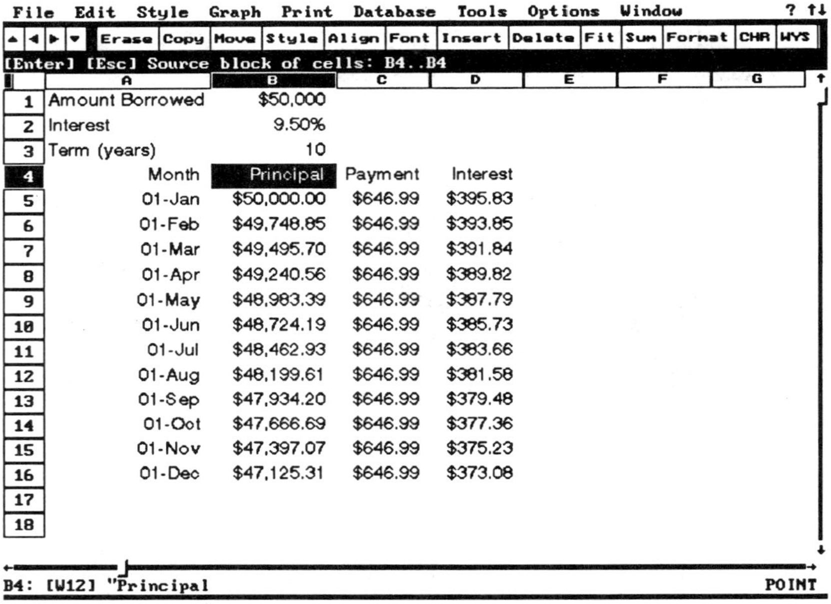

	A	B	C	D	E	F	G
1	Amount Borrowed	$50,000					
2	Interest	9.50%					
3	Term (years)	10					
4	Month	Principal	Payment	Interest			
5	01-Jan	$50,000.00	$646.99	$395.83			
6	01-Feb	$49,748.85	$646.99	$393.85			
7	01-Mar	$49,495.70	$646.99	$391.84			
8	01-Apr	$49,240.56	$646.99	$389.82			
9	01-May	$48,983.39	$646.99	$387.79			
10	01-Jun	$48,724.19	$646.99	$385.73			
11	01-Jul	$48,462.93	$646.99	$383.66			
12	01-Aug	$48,199.61	$646.99	$381.58			
13	01-Sep	$47,934.20	$646.99	$379.48			
14	01-Oct	$47,666.69	$646.99	$377.36			
15	01-Nov	$47,397.07	$646.99	$375.23			
16	01-Dec	$47,125.31	$646.99	$373.08			
17							
18							

B4: [W12] "Principal   POINT

Figure 3.2 Spreadsheet with Block Anchored at B4

beginning of the block reference and expresses it as a single cell address. You can move the selector to a new location and respecify the beginning of a block by typing a period. The BACKSPACE key changes the block address to a single cell address and moves the selector to the position it held before the command was invoked.

Another alternative for changing a block is to use the period to restate the block address when Quattro displays the block address. When you type a period, Quattro moves the selector in the highlighted block to the next corner in a clockwise direction.

When you specify a block by using the arrow keys and select the lower-right corner when Quattro has anchored the upper left-corner, the selector is at the lower-right corner of the block. If you press the period, Quattro moves this selector to the lower-left corner. When it switches the corner the selector is on, the corner opposite the one with the selector is anchored. For example, if the block address is originally stated as B1..D10 and the selector is at D10, typing a period moves the selector to B10, and the corner of the block at D1 is anchored. Typing a period again moves the selector to B1 with the block corner at D10 anchored. Typing another period causes the selector to move to D1. Typing one more period returns the selector to the original position (D10). The new orientation for the block address allows you to expand and contract the block from various sides with the directional keys.

SELECTING A BLOCK WITH A MOUSE When you are using a mouse, you have other options for selecting a block. To select a block with a mouse, move the pointer to the first cell of the block. Then press down on the mouse button. Without releasing the mouse button, move to the opposite corner of the block. As you move, Quattro highlights the cells in the block. When the opposite corner is selected, release the mouse button. This process is referred to as *dragging* the mouse. The block remains highlighted. If you use a mouse or the SHIFT-F7 (SELECT) key, you can select a block before you enter the command for the block. For example, you can use the mouse to select a block of cells, then enter the command to move a block. Since Quattro assumes the selected block is the block you want to move, it does not ask you for this information and immediately prompts you to provide the location to which the block should be moved. If you can select a block before entering the command, you can use that block for more than one command. As an example, you can use the same block (1) to center the labels and (2) to show the numbers in the block with currency symbols and commas to separate thousands.

SELECTING A BLOCK WITH THE SELECT KEY Just as if you were using a mouse, you can select a block before you enter a Quattro command by using SHIFT-F7 (SELECT). To select a block, move the selector to the first cell of the block. Then press SHIFT-F7 (SELECT). Quattro displays EXT in the status line. Move the selector to the opposite corner of the block. As you move, Quattro highlights the cells in the block. When you select a block using this method,

Quattro uses the block with the next command you enter that operates on a block of data.

Changing the Numeric Format

As discussed in Chapter 2, when you enter formulas and numbers in a cell, Quattro displays as much of the entry as possible that can fit in the current cell width. Using the default display format also results in scientific notation (1.04E+26) for extremely large and small numbers. Decimal entries also are displayed with varying numbers of decimal digits. The default format display shows numbers inconsistently, as shown by the numbers in Figure 3.3. Changing the display for values entries can make the data much easier to read and understand.

You can change how Quattro displays numbers by formatting them. *Formatting* numbers and formulas does not change their value. Formatting only changes the appearance of the entry. The contents of the cell to be used in all calculations that reference the cell remain the same. Therefore, if you enter 3.333 and format the cell as a whole number, only 3 is displayed, but 3.333 is used in all calculations that reference the cell.

To change how the numbers are displayed in the spreadsheet, select the **/Style Numeric Format** command. When you select this command, Quattro displays the Format menu shown in Figure 3.4. To choose one of these formats, highlight your

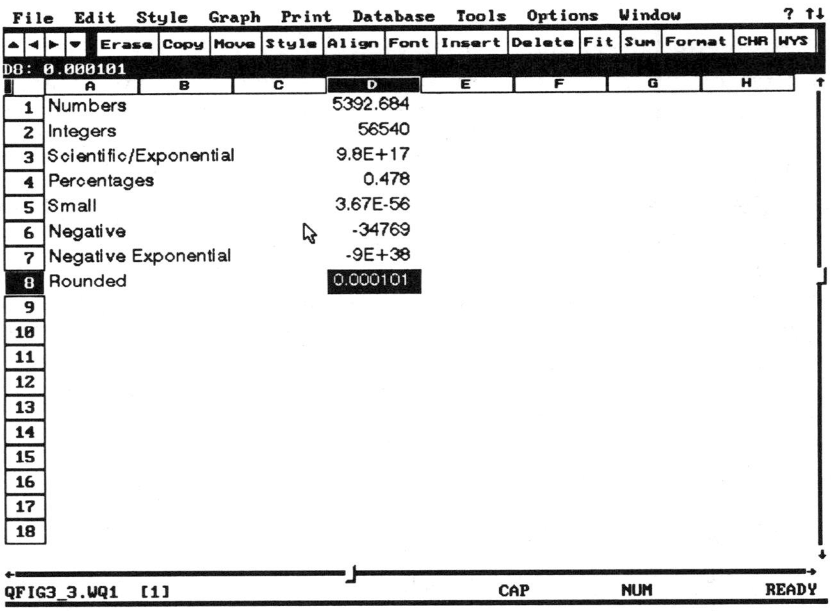

Figure 3.3 Different Displays for Unformatted Numbers

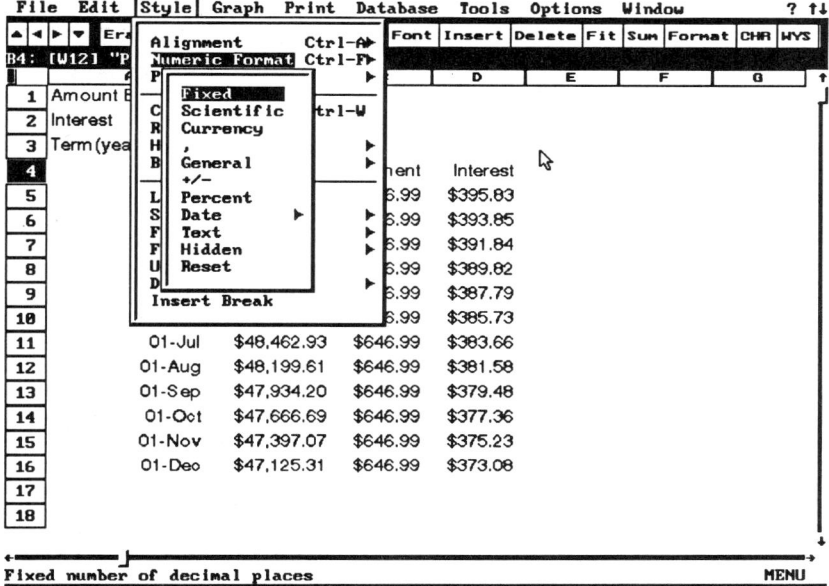

Figure 3.4 Formats Available for Formatting a Block

choice and press ENTER. If you choose Date, you need to refine your selection further by selecting from another menu. The second menu provides format selections for date and time serial numbers. If you select Time, a third menu appears with a set of specific options for time serial numbers. A list and examples of the available formats are given in Table 3.1. Later in the chapter, you will learn how to create your own defined numeric formats that offer additional options for how you format the numbers in your spreadsheet. The /Style Numeric Format command also has a shortcut key, CTRL-F, which you can press instead of entering /Style Numeric Format. A third alternative is to click the FORMAT or FMT button in the SpeedBar. (You may need to click BAR first if you are not in WYSIWYG mode.)

When you select a Fixed; Scientific; Currency; , (Financial); or Percent format, Quattro prompts you for the number of digits you want after the decimal point. Type a number between 0 and 15, and press ENTER. Next, if you have not already selected a block, Quattro prompts you for the block to format. Type in the block address, use the directional keys to select the block to format, or select a block with the mouse, and press ENTER; Quattro then formats the data in the selected block. The values stored in memory are not changed by formatting even though the value's appearance may change. Spreadsheet calculations are performed on the numbers as stored in memory, not on the numbers as displayed. If a cell is too narrow to fit the cell's contents in the selected format, Quattro displays asterisks in the cell. Changing the format or widening the column eliminates the asterisks and returns the cell's contents to the display.

Table 3.1 Choices for the /Style Numeric Format Command

Format	Effect on 9123.456	Effect on 195.4	Effect on .00987
Fixed (two decimals)	9123.46	–195.40	0.01
Scientific (two decimals)	9.12E+02	–1.95E+02	9.87E–03
Currency (two decimals)	$9,123.46	($195.40)	$0.01
, (Financial) (two decimals)	9,123.46	(195.40)	0.01
General	9123.456	–195.4	0.00987
+/–	9123 +'s	195 –'s	0.00987
Percent (two decimals)	912345.60%	–19540.00%	0.99%
Date/Time	22-DEC-24	N/A	12:14:13AM
Text	9123.456	–195.4	0.00987
Hidden			

Note: N/A = not applicable; blanks appear in Hidden format because no numbers or characters appear on the screen when you choose that format.

When you format a block of cells, the format you select applies to all the cells in the block. Cells in the block that contain values immediately change their appearance for the new format. Cells that are empty or contain labels retain the numeric format information in case the cells later contain values. When the selector is on a cell that has been formatted with the /Style Numeric Format command, Quattro displays a format indicator after the cell address in the input line. The input line entry shows a letter representing the format that you have chosen. If the format is one that requests the number of digits you want displayed after the decimal point, the number of decimal digits selected is displayed after the format letter. The format for date or time serial numbers is a D followed by a number 1 through 9 indicating which of the date/time formats are chosen.

When you format a block of cells, the /Style Numeric Format command overrides the default format. If you want to return part of your spreadsheet to the default format, use the /Style Numeric Format Reset command. To change the default format, use the /Options Formats Numeric Format command. When you execute this command, you must select the format you want and the number of digits after the decimal point, if Quattro prompts for it. You do not have to select a block since this format applies to all cells that are not explicitly formatted.

Quattro provides two formats with special features. The Text format displays formulas in the specified block instead of showing the formula results. This can be a good solution for documenting the contents of a worksheet. You will probably need to widen the cells to print all the formulas. Any cell notation also appears. The Hidden format, the only numeric format that affects label entries as well as numbers and formulas, hides the cell contents from the display. When the selector is on a cell with a Hidden format, the cell contents are visible in the input line but do not appear in the spreadsheet cell. When you print a block that includes the hidden cells, the contents of these cells are not printed. This feature allows you to print a spreadsheet containing salary data without printing the confidential salary information. While a cell is hidden, it can still be edited, changed, and referenced in calculations. To expose a hidden cell, use the /Style Numeric Format command again, and select another format or choose Reset to return to the default format selected for the spreadsheet.

Changing Alignment

Chapter 2 discussed how Quattro initially left-aligns text unless a special label prefix is typed as the first character for a cell entry and how it right-aligns numbers. However, if you have many labels to type or want to change the alignment of existing labels, typing the label prefix is not an efficient solution. Also, you cannot use label prefixes on value entries. You can change the alignment of existing entries with the /Style Alignment command. If you prefer, you can use the shortcurt key, CTRL-A, or click the ALIGN or ALN button in the SpeedBar to invoke the command. To change the alignment of cells, press / and select Style and Alignment. Quattro displays a menu from which you can choose General, Left, Right, or Center alignment. After you have made your selection, Quattro prompts for which block to align, unless you already have selected a block with the mouse or SHIFT-F7 (SELECT). Select the block, and press ENTER. Quattro replaces the existing label prefixes in the selected block with the appropriate label prefix for the alignment that you have chosen. Also, if you select Left or Center, Quattro changes the alignment of any numbers in the selected block. This is different from other spreadsheet packages in which the alignment of numbers cannot be changed.

Any labels that you subsequently enter in the selected block do not have the alignment that you have chosen with this command. These new entries use the setting of the /Options Formats Align Labels command. If you want to change the alignment of empty cells, the /Options Formats Align Labels command (discussed in Chapter 10) can change the default label alignment. However, you cannot change the default alignment of numbers. With numbers, the alignment setting remains with the block. This means that if you apply this command to a block, any number you enter into the block will continue to use the selected alignment. This includes numbers in the block when you enter the command and numbers you enter in the block after using this command.

COPYING

Often the formulas you need in a spreadsheet are similar to those you have already entered. Rather than typing the entries in many places, you can save time and effort by copying them. Quattro's /Edit Copy command helps you copy the entries from one cell to another. This command has a shortcut key, CTRL-C, which you can use instead of /Edit Copy. In addition, you can also use Copy in the SpeedBar, which may be lapeled CPY. When you copy a cell or block, you are copying both the cell contents and any formatting applied to the cells. This includes numeric format, alignment, protection status, lines, shading, and fonts, features described later in this chapter.

The /Edit Copy command is extremely flexible and powerful. You can use /Edit Copy to copy one cell to another cell, one cell to an entire block of the spreadsheet, or an entire block of cells to another section of your spreadsheet. When Quattro's copy options are combined with relative, absolute, and mixed addressing, the options of the copy command are extended even farther. Also, Quattro Pro 4 has a new command that lets you selectively copy a block's contents or its format.

COPYING ONE CELL TO ANOTHER You can copy the number, label, or formula entry in any spreadsheet cell to any other cell on the spreadsheet. Once you master this process, only a few modifications are required to expand the scope of the copy operation. To copy one cell to another follow these steps:

1. Move the selector to the cell that you want to copy.
2. Type / and select Edit Copy, click Copy in the SpeedBar, or simply press CTRL-C. Quattro prompts you for the source block as shown in Figure 3.5. As you can see in the top line of the figure, Quattro assumes that the current cell is one of the corners of the block. Since you only want to copy the one cell, this address is adequate for the source of the data to be copied.
3. Press ENTER. Quattro prompts you for the destination of the cells. Since Quattro only needs to know where the upper-left corner of the copied block should be, it prompts for a cell address rather than a block. G8 is the destination for copying E8 in Figure 3.5.
4. Move the selector to the cell where you want the copy to appear.
5. Press ENTER. Quattro copies the source entry to the address you chose in step 4.

Figure 3.6 shows the selector on G8 after the formula was copied from E8. When Quattro copies formulas, it adjusts cell references based on the new location for the formula, unless you take some special action to prevent this from occurring by using absolute references. This is because Quattro records the original formula as the relative distance and direction needed to access the correct cell entries rather than using the actual cell addresses. This approach uses Quattro's default reference style referred to as relative references. With relative references, Quattro changes the cell references based on the location of the copy. In Figure 3.5, the

Working with Multiple Cells 71

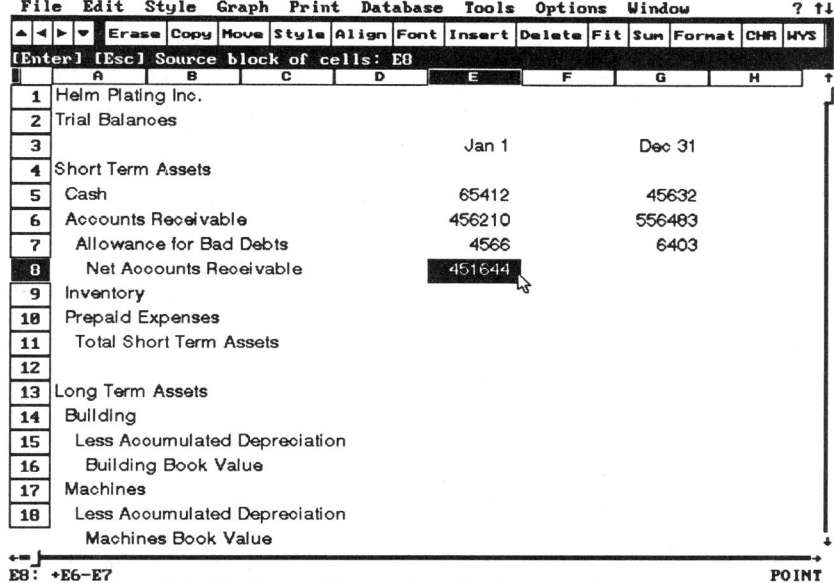

Figure 3.5 Quattro Prompting for Source Block to Copy

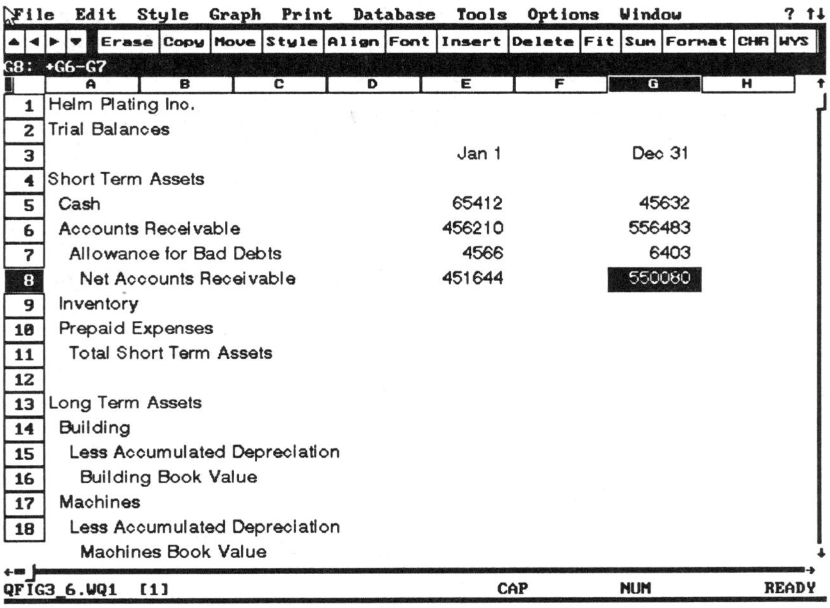

Figure 3.6 Cell Copied to Another Location

formula in E8 subtracted the value in the cell above it from the value two cells above it. When the formula is copied to G8, Quattro changes the cell addresses in the formula so that the new formula subtracts the value in the cell above it (G7) from the value two cells above it (G6). When Quattro adjusts the cell references, it only affects the cells in the destination of the /Edit Copy command.

REFERENCE STYLES IN COPIED FORMULAS When the formula in the previous section was copied, Quattro adjusted all the cell addresses in the formula based on their new location, because each cell reference was a relative reference. Quattro always changes the relative cell references in copied formulas. Quattro also supports absolute and mixed references to allow you to hold some or all references constant.

Changing the cell addresses that formulas use allows you to create formulas in one cell and copy them to other cells after you have tested the results produced by these formulas. By copying tested formulas rather than typing them, you reduce errors in spreadsheet models. The method that Quattro uses for changing the cell addresses in copied formulas applies whether one cell or multiple cells are copied.

Relative Addresses A relative address is the default reference style in Quattro. It consists of a column designation followed by a row designation, and is consistent with the cell references used in all the examples to this point. When you use a relative address, Quattro displays a cell address in the formula but does not specifically remember the cell addresses of all pertinent cells; rather, Quattro remembers the distance and directions of the cells to be used.

In Figure 3.7, cell A3 contains the formula +**A1**+**A2**. Since both of these are relative

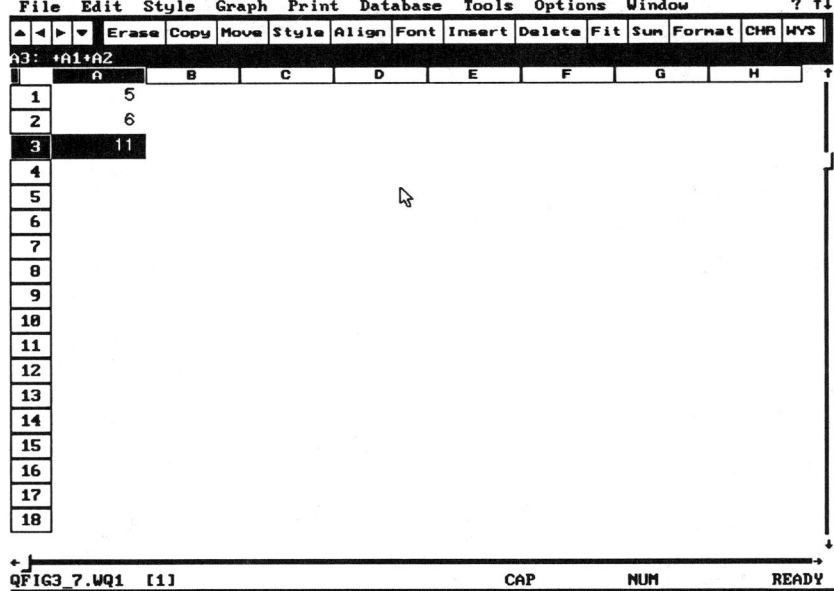

Figure 3.7 Cell Formula Containing Relative Cell References

addresses, Quattro stores its instructions for computing the formula in A3 as adding the value that is in the cell two rows above the formula to the value that is in the cell one row above the formula. This is referred to as a *relative address*, since the actual addresses used in the computation depends on the location of the cell where the formula is stored.

If the formula in A3 is copied to F5, Quattro's relative addresses for the formula in F5 will be altered. The formula in F5 will still add the value of the cell two rows above the formula (F3) to the value of the cell one row above the formula (F4), as shown in Figure 3.8.

Absolute Addresses Absolute cell addresses in copied formulas do not change. This feature allows you to make constant any cell references in a formula. To indicate to Quattro that you want a cell reference to be absolute, you must put a dollar sign ($) in front of both the row and the column position of the address as in A5 or Z1. You can type these $ symbols or, if you are at a cell or block address in VALUE, POINT, or EDIT mode, you can press F4 (ABS) or click Abs in the Edit SpeedBar while the cursor is positioned on the cell address. Quattro then inserts the $ symbols for you. When you copy a cell containing a formula with absolute references, the new copy refers to the same cells as the original. For example, when you copy D5 to E5 in the spreadsheet in Figure 3.9, the cell reference to D1 does not change even when the formula is copied to E5.

Mixed Cell Addresses Mixed addresses have a $ in front of one portion of the cell address. Mixed addresses combine the features of relative and absolute addresses.

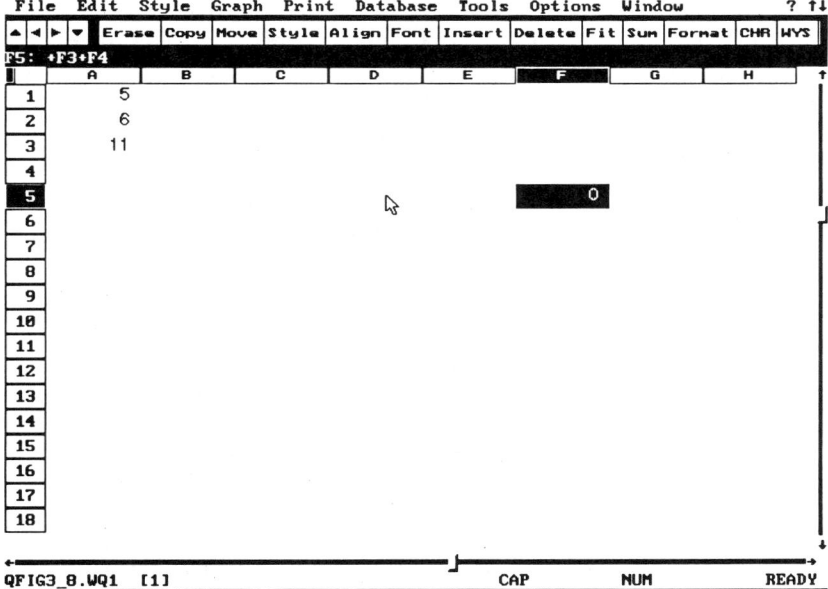

Figure 3.8 Formula Copied with Relative Addresses

74   Quattro Pro 4.0 Handbook

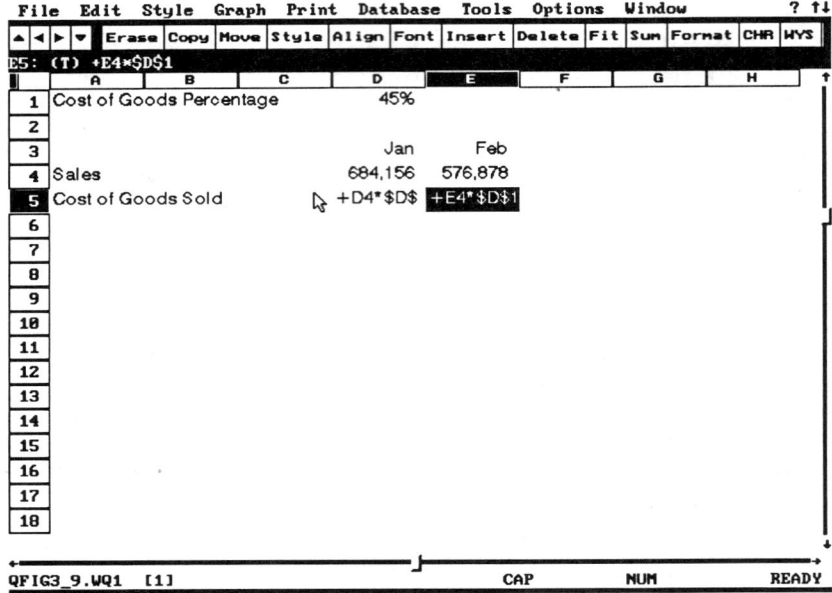

Figure 3.9   Cell Copied with Absolute Cell Address (D1)

With a mixed address, either the row or the column portion of the address is held constant, while the other portion is allowed to change. With mixed addresses, Quattro treats the part of the cell address that has the dollar sign in front of it as absolute and the part that does not have a dollar sign in front of it as relative. When a cell containing a formula using mixed addresses is copied, the addresses in the formula of the new copy are adjusted for the parts of the address that are relative and remain fixed for the parts of the address that are absolute. For example, Figure 3.10 shows a spreadsheet that has a default format of Text and has the formula from A3 copied to H3, H10, and A10. The original formula adds the value that is in the same column as the formula in row 1 to the value that is in column A one row above the cell with the formula. In H3, the formula still adds the value that is in the same column as the formula in row 1 to the value that is in column A one row above the cell with the formula; but the first cell reference has the column changed from A to H. In H10, the formula has changed the column from A to H for the first cell address and changed the row number in the second cell address from row 2 to row 9. In A10, the formula has changed the row of the second cell address from 2 to 9. In each case, Quattro treats the portion of the cell address without the dollar sign as relative and the portion with the dollar sign as absolute.

A practical application of the mixed address is creating pro forma spreadsheets. Figure 3.11 shows a spreadsheet that projects the cost of different expenses. For this type of spreadsheet, the absolute addresses may seem to be the best address type for referring to the expected percentage growth. If you use an absolute address, you will have to create a new formula for each of the different types of

Working with Multiple Cells 75

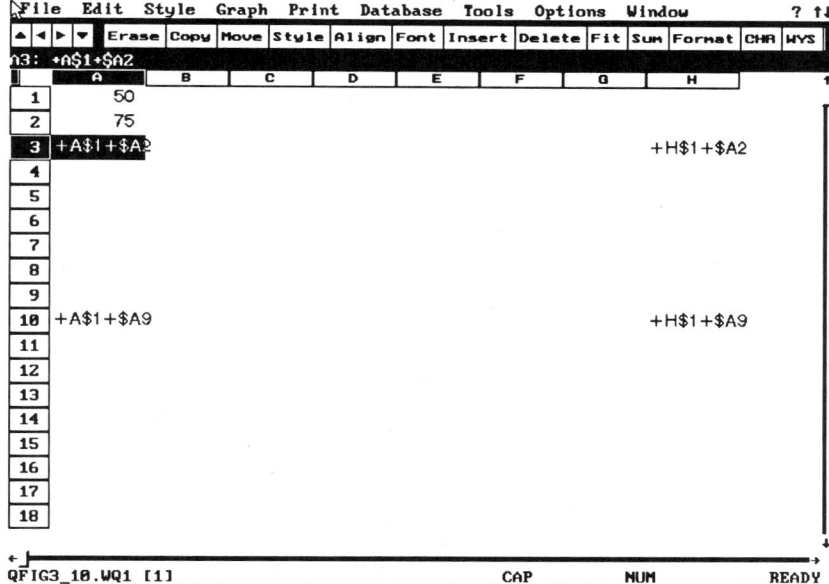

Figure 3.10 Cell Copied with Mixed Cell Addresses

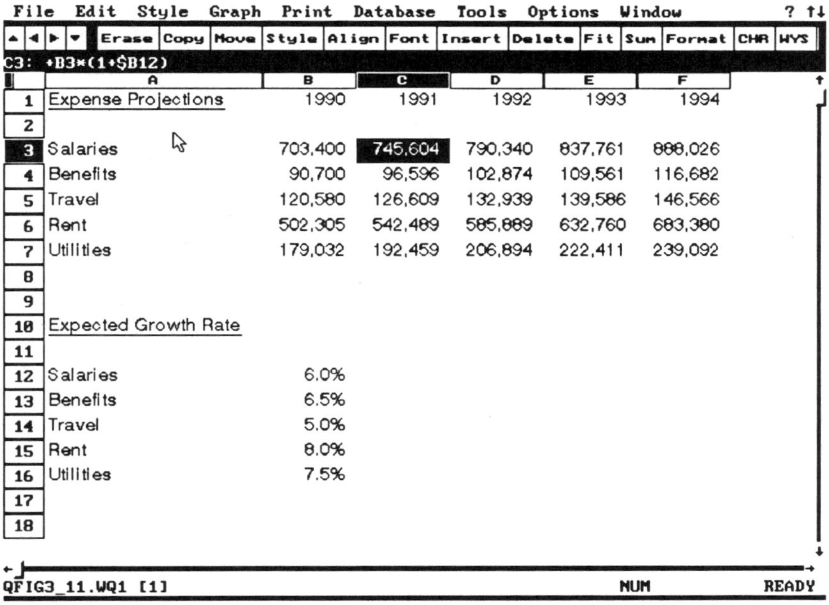

Figure 3.11 Using Mixed Addresses to Project Cost Growth

expenses before copying the formulas to columns C through F. Using a mixed cell address when referencing the expected growth percentage is the best method for generating the formulas, since Quattro will not adjust the column that the formula gets the percentage of growth from as it copies the formulas. By putting the formula +B3*(1+$B12) in C3 and copying it to the block C3..F7, you have only typed one formula for the entire spreadsheet. Since the row portion of the mixed address for the growth percentage is relative, Quattro adjusts the formula for each row so that each type of expense refers to the appropriate growth rate. Since the column portion of the mixed address is absolute, Quattro does not adjust the column in the growth rate cell reference as the formula is copied across the columns.

COPYING ONE CELL TO SEVERAL CELLS Often after you have entered the formulas to calculate the first month, year, or company totals, the difficult task of model construction is complete. Since all future periods and entities follow the same pattern for their calculations, the copy operation provides a quick solution for model completion.

Copying from one cell to several cells is used frequently to copy a formula for one month's sales projection, depreciation, or production estimates to other periods across a spreadsheet. For example, in the trial balance spreadsheet used for copying one cell to another, you may also want to know the change during the year for each account. In Figure 3.12, putting a formula that subtracts the January 1 balance from the December 31 balance in column H computes the difference for

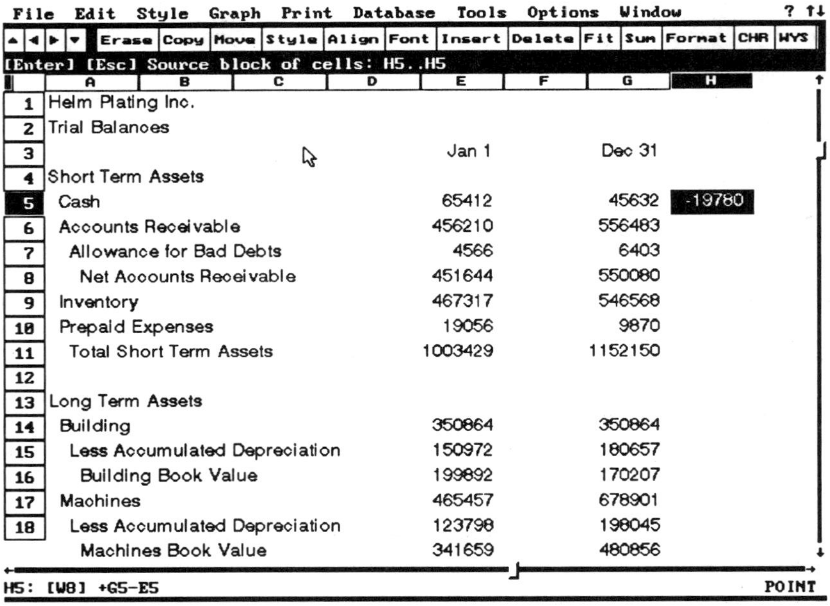

Figure 3.12 Quattro Prompting for Source Block to Copy

each of the accounts. Using the /Edit Copy command reduces the typing, since you only have to put the formula in H5 and copy the formula for the remainder of the column.

To copy one cell to several cells, follow these steps:

1. Move the selector to the cell that you want to copy.
2. Type / and select Edit Copy, press CTRL-C, or click Copy in the SpeedBar. Quattro prompts you for the source block of cells. Quattro assumes that the current cell is one of the corners of the block. Since you only want to copy one cell, the cell address is both corners of the block. In Figure 3.12, the source block is H5..H5.
3. Press ENTER. Quattro then prompts you for the destination of the cells. Although Quattro presents a cell address to describe where you want the original block copied to, you can change it to a block to indicate that you want multiple copies.
4. Move the selector to the first cell that you want the original cell copied to. In the spreadsheet in Figure 3.12, the first cell the formula should be copied to is H6. When you make multiple copies of a single cell, you can include the cell you are copying in the block of cells you are copying to. However, when you copy multiple cells, you do not want the cells you are copying to be included in the block you are copying to.
5. Type a period. This converts the cell address to a block address and anchors one of the block's corners to the current selector position.
6. Stretch the block to include all the cells that you want the original cell copied to. The destination block for this example is H6..H20.
7. Press ENTER. Quattro copies the cell to all the cells that were in the block you selected with steps 4 through 6.

The final result of copying H5 in Figure 3.12 to H6..H20 is shown in Figure 3.13. For each of the copied formulas, Quattro adjusts the cell references so that the new formulas refer to cells that are the same distance and direction as are the original formula's cell references. The formulas that are in H12 and H13 are meaningless and may be deleted. Including them in the copy block and then deleting them eliminates repeating the /Edit Copy command for the Long-Term Assets section.

Normally, the source and the destination block cannot overlap. If you use the same blocks for the source and destination, the original copy is often damaged. Copying one cell to a block is the one exception where including the source block as part of the destination block does not harm the original cell.

COPYING ONE BLOCK TO ANOTHER Copying one block to another spreadsheet location is a powerful tool, since it generates the same block in a different place. Like the previous copy examples, if you copy formulas, Quattro adjusts the relative and mixed cell references in the copied block.

To copy one block to another follow these steps:

1. Move the selector to the first cell of the block that you want to copy.

```
  File   Edit  Style  Graph  Print  Database  Tools  Options  Window            ? ↑↓
 ▲|◄|►|▼  Erase|Copy|Move|Style|Align|Font|Insert|Delete|Fit|Sum|Format|CHR|WYS
 15: +G5-E5
            A           B           C        D        E       F       G         H
   1  Helm Plating Inc.
   2  Trial Balances
   3                                                 Jan 1           Dec 31
   4  Short Term Assets
   5    Cash                                         65412           45632     -19780
   6    Accounts Receivable                         456210          556483    100273
   7      Allowance for Bad Debts                     4566            6403      1837
   8      Net Accounts Receivable                   451644          550080     98436
   9    Inventory                                   467317          546568     79251
  10    Prepaid Expenses                             19056            9870     -9186
  11    Total Short Term Assets                    1003429         1152150    148721
  12                                                                               0
  13  Long Term Assets                                                             0
  14    Building                                    350864          350864         0
  15      Less Accumulated Depreciation             150972          180657     29685
  16      Building Book Value                       199892          170207    -29685
  17    Machines                                    465457          678901    213444
  18      Less Accumulated Depreciation             123798          198045     74247
         Machines Book Value                        341659          480856    139197
 QFIG3_13.WQ1 [1]                                           CAP       NUM       READY
```

Figure 3.13 Spreadsheet After Single Cell Is Copied to a Block

2. Type /, and select Edit Copy, press CTRL-C, or click Copy in the SpeedBar. Quattro prompts you for the source block of cells. Quattro assumes that the current cell is one of the corners of the block.

3. Move the selector to cover the entire block that you want to copy. For example, in Figure 3.14, the block to copy is A3..A16.

4. Press ENTER. Quattro prompts you for the destination of the cells. Since Quattro only needs to know the location of where it should start copying the block, you only need to provide it with the location of the upper-left corner of the block.

5. Move the selector to the desired upper-left corner of the copied block. For the example in Figure 3.14, type **E3**.

6. Press ENTER. Quattro copies the block to the address selected in step 4. Even though you only specified one cell for the block's destination, Quattro copies the entire block as shown in Figure 3.15 after a new label is typed in E1. If there are any entries in the destination block before the copy, these entries will be replaced with information from the cells being copied.

COPYING A BLOCK MORE THAN ONCE When you are creating your own spreadsheets, you will want to copy a block to several other locations. Copying a block multiple times is used frequently when you have a block consisting of a

Working with Multiple Cells 79

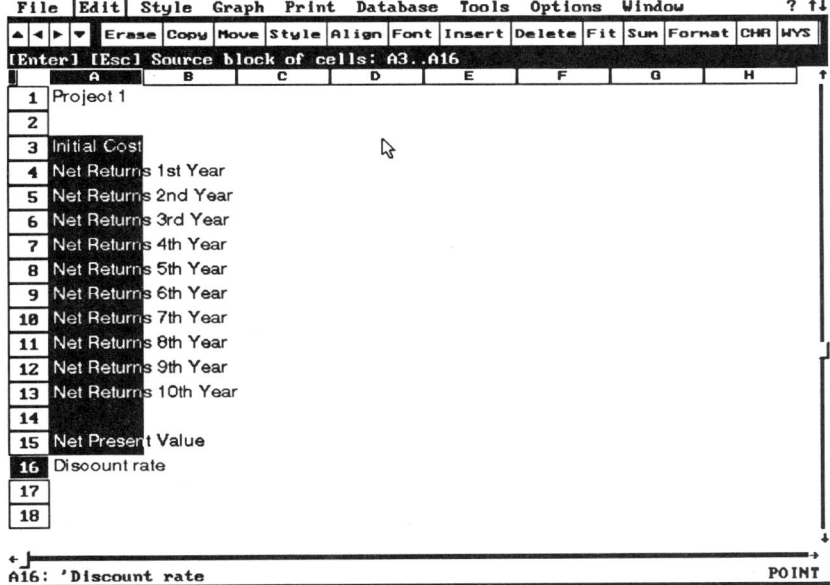

Figure 3.14 Spreadsheet with Block to Copy

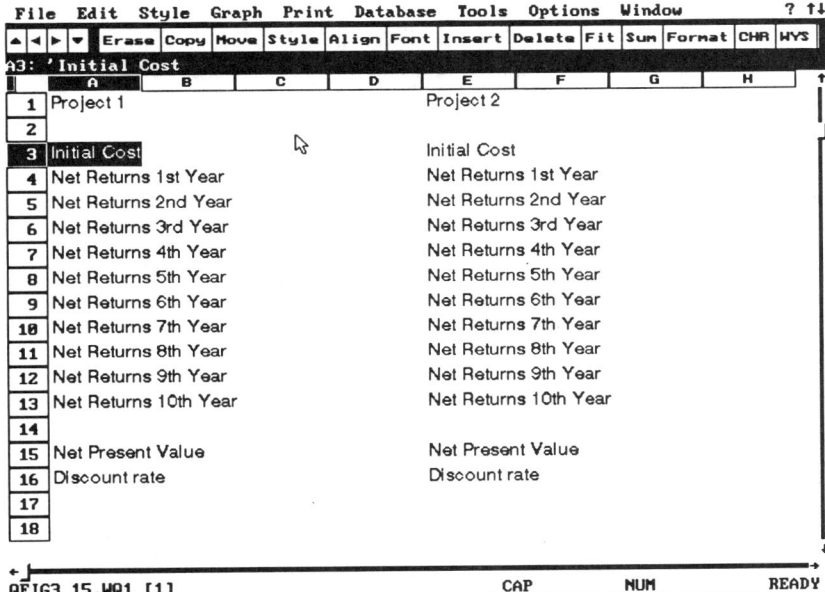

Figure 3.15 Spreadsheet After Block is Copied

column or row of formulas that you want to copy across to several other columns or rows. To copy a block multiple times, follow these steps:

1. Move the selector to the first cell of the block that you want to copy.
2. Type /, and select Edit Copy, press CTRL-C, or click Copy in the SpeedBar. Quattro prompts you for the source block of cells. Quattro assumes that the current cell is one of the corners of the block. Since you are copying a block multiple times, you are restricted to using a block that contains only one column or that contains only one row.
3. Move the selector to cover the entire block that you want to copy. (For example, in Figure 3.16, you can select D4..D20.)
4. Press ENTER. Quattro then prompts you for the destination of the cells. Since Quattro only needs to know the destination of the upper-left corners of each block, you only need to provide it with the locations across row 4 where you want the column of entries in D4..D20 to be placed. Since you want the block to be copied multiple times, you must select E4..H4 to have the entries copied to these columns.
5. Move the selector to the first cell that you want to become the upper-left corner of the first copied block. For this example it is E4.
6. Type a period. This converts the cell address to a block address and anchors one of the block's corners to the current cell address.

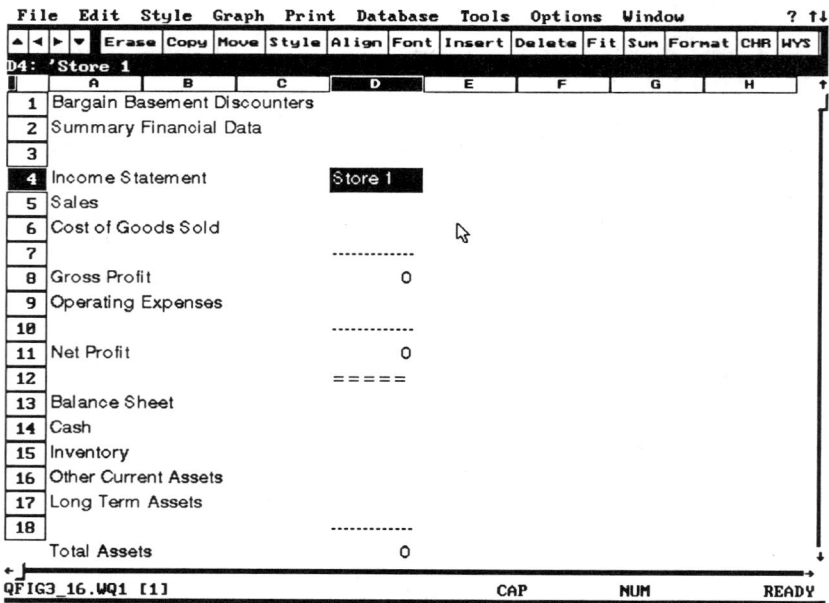

Figure 3.16 Spreadsheet with Block to be Copied

7. Stretch the block to include all the cells that you want to be the upper-left corners of the copied blocks. To create multiple copies of the block selected in Figure 3.16, enter E4..H4 as the destination block.

8. Press ENTER. Quattro copies the block to the address you selected in steps 5 through 7. Since you only specified several cells for the block's destination, Quattro copies the entire block using each of the selected destination cells as the upper-left corner of the copied block, as shown in Figure 3.17.

SELECTIVELY COPYING A BLOCK When you copy cell entries with the /Edit Copy command, you are copying both the cell entries and the formats you have assigned to the cells in the block. In Quattro Pro 4, you can also copy either the cell entries or the formats. For example, after you have changed the numeric format of one block, you can apply the format to another block so both sections of the spreadsheet have the same format. Copying only the cell entries or the cell formats is just like copying both. You can copy one cell to another, one cell to a block, a block to another location, or a block to several locations. First, you select /Edit Copy Special and then select Contents or Formats. Then, like using the /Edit Copy command, you select the cell or block to copy and the cell or block where copies are made. Besides copying the numeric formats, when you copy only the format, you will also copy any numerical alignment, protection status, lines, shading, and fonts that you will learn about adding to the spreadsheet later in the chapter. You can use this command to give a spreadsheet a consistent appearance by copying

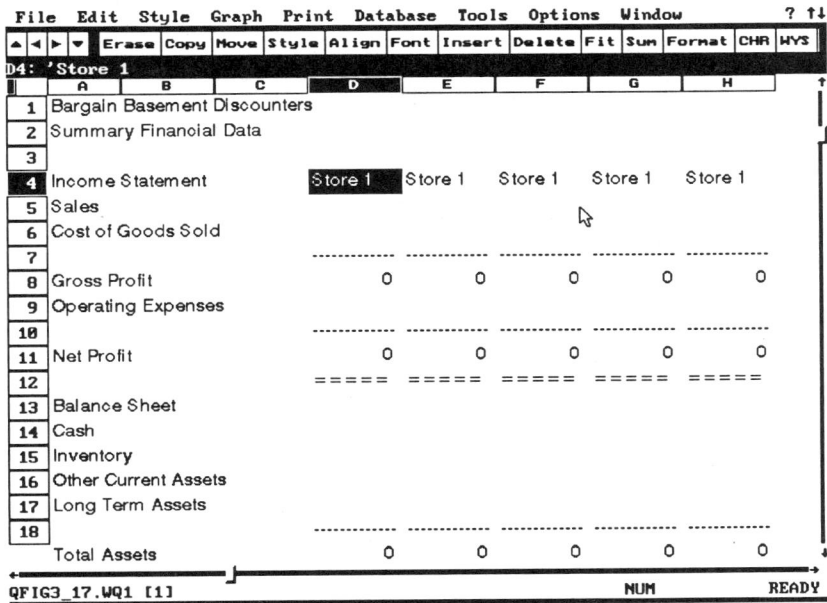

Figure 3.17 Spreadsheet with Block Copied Multiple Times

formats to other entries. You can also copy entries to a new location where you have already assigned the formats you want the entries to use.

Moving

Good spreadsheet design makes your spreadsheet easier to understand. When you are beginning to create your own spreadsheets, it takes time to achieve optimal designs. You may want to move existing entries to improve the appearance of your spreadsheets. You may find yourself moving information around until you achieve an appearance that works best for your application. Quattro's /Edit Move command moves spreadsheet entries without changing the values of cells containing formulas. This command has a shortcut key, CTRL-M, which you can use in place of /Edit Move. In Quattro Pro 4, you can also select the /Edit Move command by clicking Move in the SpeedBar, which may also appear as MOV. When you move cells, you move both the cells' contents and their numeric format, alignment, block names, protection status, lines, shading, and fonts.

MOVING A BLOCK Moving a block is similar to copying a block. You can move a single cell or a block—the process is the same. To move a block, follow these steps:

1. Move the selector to the first cell of the block that you want to move.
2. Type /, and select Edit Move, click Move in the SpeedBar, or press CTRL-M. Quattro prompts you for the source block of cells (as in Figure 3.18), if you have not selected a block yet. As you can see in the top line of

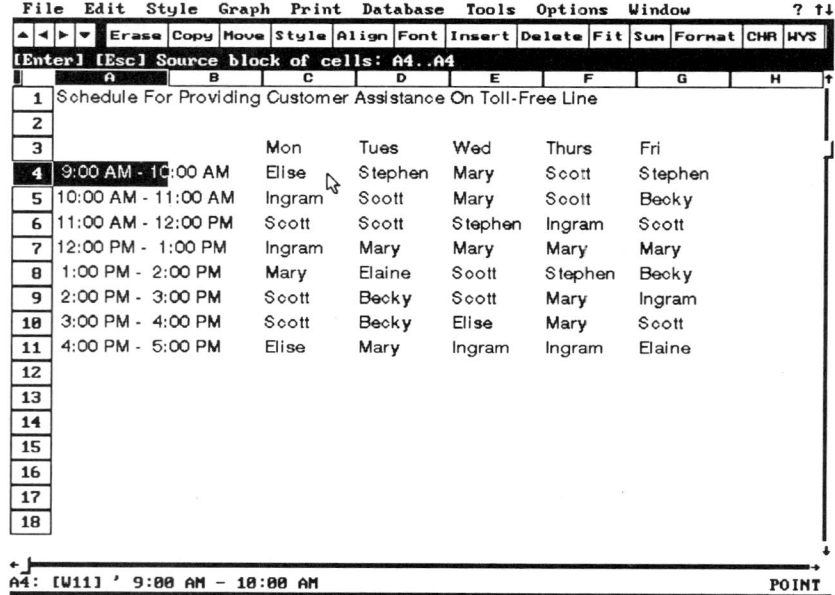

Figure 3.18 Quattro Prompting for Source Block to Move

the figure, Quattro assumes that the current cell is one of the corners of the block.

3. Move the selector to cover the entire block that you want to move. For Figure 3.18, you want to move the block A4..G11.
4. Press ENTER. Quattro prompts you for the destination of the cells. Since Quattro only needs to know the beginning location of where the cells will be moved, you only need to provide the desired location of the upper-left corner of the moved block.
5. Move the selector to the cell that you want to be the upper-left corner of the moved block. For the spreadsheet in Figure 3.18, the destination is A5.
6. Press ENTER. Quattro moves the block to the address you selected in step 5, as shown in Figure 3.19. Even though you only specified one cell for the block's destination, Quattro moves the entire block using the selected destination cell as the upper-left corner of the moved block. Any information that was in the section of the block's destination is replaced by the moved block.

RELATIVE VERSUS ABSOLUTE ADDRESSES IN MOVED FORMULAS When you move formulas containing cell addresses, Quattro modifies the cell addresses to maintain the formula values. Therefore, moving a block does not change the values in the block as the /Edit Copy command does. The /Edit Move command also differs, since it changes formula references of cells that are not in the moved block but refer to it. Examples of Quattro changing the cell references are Figure 3.20 and Figure 3.21, which show a block before and after it has been moved. When

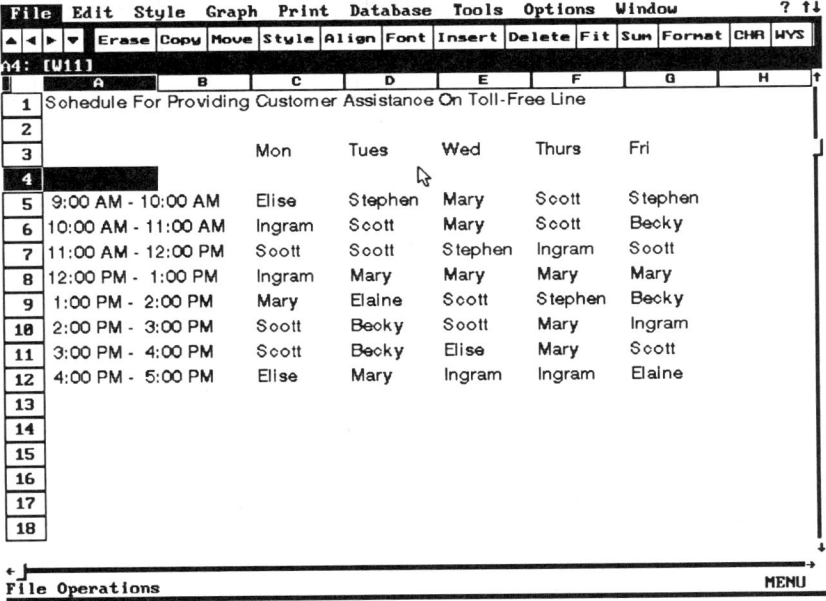

Figure 3.19 Spreadsheet After Block Is Moved

84 *Quattro Pro 4.0 Handbook*

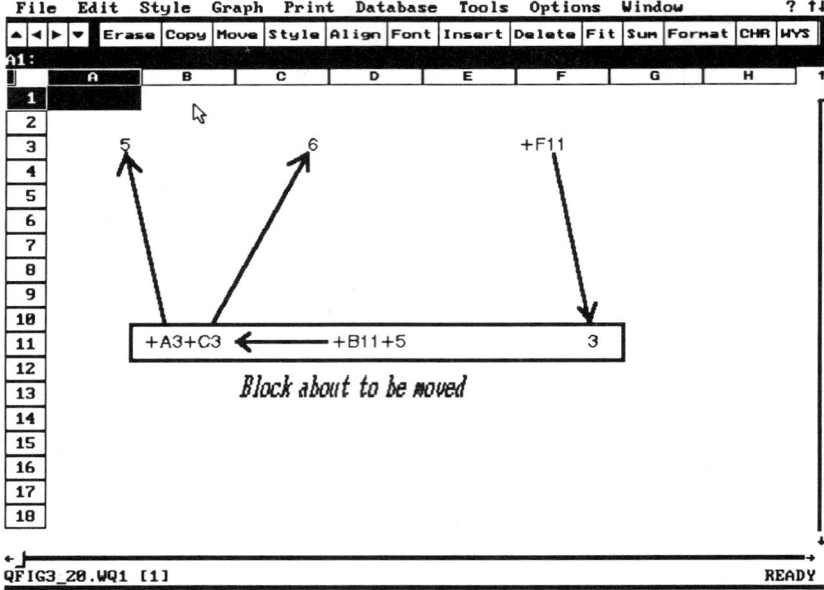

Figure 3.20 Block About to be Moved

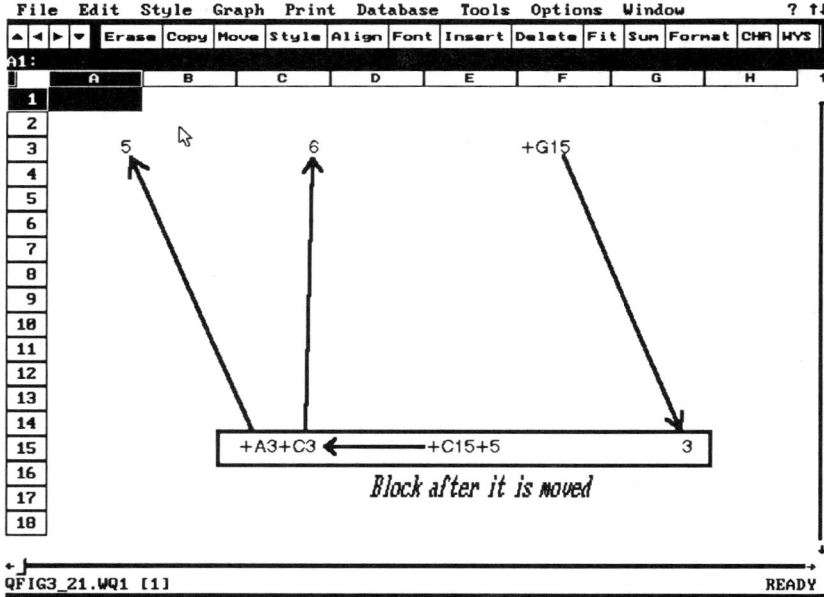

Figure 3.21 Block After It Is Moved

a cell in a moved block references cells outside of that block, Quattro does not change the formulas. For example, the formula that was moved from B11 to C15 (+A3+C3) has not changed. When a cell in the moved block references cells inside the moved block, Quattro changes the formulas to reflect the referenced cells' new positions. For example, a formula moved from D11 to E15 changed from +B11+5 to +C15+5. When a cell outside the moved block refers to cells inside the moved block, Quattro changes the formula to reflect the referenced cell's new position. For example, since F11 moved to G15, Quattro changes the formula in F3 from F11 to G15.

Erasing

As you add to a spreadsheet, you may want to remove existing data. For example, if you are changing an income statement from January's figures to February's figures, you want to remove January's data before you type in February's data. Chapter 2 discussed how you delete individual cells with the DEL key. This key is not efficient when you have many cells to erase. The /Edit Erase Block command erases any block you specify. In Quattro Pro 4, you can also erase a block by clicking Erase or ERS in the SpeedBar. To use this command, type /, and select Edit Erase Block, click Erase or ERS in the SpeedBar, or press CTRL-E. When Quattro prompts you for the block to modify, type the block address or use the directional keys to highlight the block or select the block with the mouse, and press ENTER. When you erase a block, any formulas that reference cells in the erased block remain intact, but the formula treats the empty cells as 0 in numeric formulas and empty labels in string formulas. If you want to protect some of your spreadsheet entries from being erased, you will want to use spreadsheet protection, since Quattro Pro will not erase protected cells when spreadsheet protection is enabled.

ADVANCED BLOCK COMMANDS

Quattro's block commands extend beyond the basic features that change the display formats and label prefixes. These advanced commands let you substitute names for block addresses, protect your spreadsheet, convert a formula to the current result of that formula, transpose entries, search and replace spreadsheet data, reformat a text block, and generate a series of values in a block.

Naming Blocks of Data

In all the previous examples, blocks have been referenced by their addresses. Quattro supports the assignment of names to block addresses. Using block names instead of block addresses has several advantages. Most users find that a block name is easier to remember than an address. Quattro updates a block name's address automatically when the block is moved. The use of a block name in a formula makes the formula easier to comprehend.

Block names can be used any place that a block address or cell address is used. Quattro provides commands to create block names, delete block names, and make a table listing the block names and their addresses. Block names are easier to use for formula references to another spreadsheet, a feature covered in Chapter 5. Block names are also useful in macros (see Chapters 11 and 12).

The use of block names is not any more difficult than the use of a cell address, as long as you are aware of potential problems. Misspelling a block name in a block command prevents the block command from executing. Misspelling a block name in a formula causes Quattro to not accept the entry until the spelling error is corrected. Misstating a block address makes the block command operate on the wrong cells.

CREATING A BLOCK NAME Assigning a block name to a block address is as simple as telling Quattro the name and the block address. Quattro provides two methods of creating block names. The first method offers complete flexibility in the size of the block. The second method has limited applicability, since (1) the block name must be stored on the spreadsheet already, and (2) it can only apply to a single cell.

Using The /Edit Names Create Command The simplest method of creating a block name is using the /Edit Names Create command. To use this command, press /, and select Edit Names Create. Enter the block name or select an existing name when Quattro prompts you for this entry. Existing block names are listed in a box to help you avoid duplication.

You can use up to 15 characters in a block name. Quattro will convert all letters to uppercase letters. Although you can use any character available on your keyboard, you should not use mathematical operators, since the operators make a formula difficult to understand if a block name with these symbols is included in a formula. Also, use an underscore (_) instead of a space to separate words, since spaces, especially at the end of a block name, can be misinterpreted in a formula. Quattro prompts you for the coordinates of the block. Type the address (or use the arrow keys to define the block that you want or use the mouse to select a block) before pressing ENTER to finalize the block.

Using The /Edit Names Labels Command If you have label entries already on the spreadsheet that you want to use to name individual cells that are adjacent to the names, the /Edit Names Labels command is a quicker approach to naming the cells. Figure 3.22 displays a spreadsheet that computes the cash flows from sales for six months. The formulas in rows 9 through 12 each refer to a different month's sales to compute the portion of sales receipts that is expected to be collected. These formulas are not difficult but would be easier to understand if they used the month names rather than the cell references. By attaching block names to these cells, you can use the month names in the formulas. To apply the block names to these cells, move the selector to B5, press /, and select Edit Names Labels. The Labels menu

```
File   Edit   Style   Graph   Print   Database   Tools   Options   Window           ? ↑↓
 ◄ ► ▼  Erase Copy Move Style Align Font Insert Delete Fit Sum Format CHR WYS
A2: [W22] 'Cash Flow For Last Half of 1990
            A              B         C         D         E         F         G
 1  Acme Incorporated
 2  Cash Flow For Last Half of 1990
 3
 4
 5                        July       Aug      Sept       Oct       Nov       Dec
 6  Forecasted Sales    450,000   500,000   475,000   525,000   600,000   550,000
 7
 8  Paid Invoices from:
 9    This Month's Sales  45,000    50,000    47,500    52,500    60,000    55,000
10    Last Month's Sales 219,450   247,500   275,000   261,250   288,750   330,000
11    Sales 2 Months Ago 150,000    99,750   112,500   125,000   118,750   131,250
12    Sales 3 Months Ago  47,500    60,000    39,900    45,000    50,000    47,500
13  Total                461,950   457,250   474,900   483,750   517,500   563,750
14
15  Assumptions:
16  Percentage Paid: Current Month          10%       April Sales        475,000
17  Percentage Paid: Next Month             55%       May Sales          600,000
18  Percentage Paid 2 Months Later          25%       June Sales         399,000
    Percentage Paid 3 Months Later          10%
QFIG3_22.WQ1 [1]                                        NUM            READY
```

Figure 3.22 Spreadsheet Computing Cash Flows from Sales

permits you to choose whether the cells that you want to name are to the right of, left of, above, or below the labels that Quattro will use to name the blocks. For example, in Figure 3.23, you should choose **Down**. Next, you specify the block containing the labels. You do not specify the blocks that you want to name—you specify the block containing the labels. In this example, it is B5 to G5. Once you press ENTER to finalize the block, Quattro creates block names for each month's sales entry. If you look at the formulas in the cells that refer to the sales of July through December, Quattro has changed the cell addresses to their block names. For example, the formula in B9 is **+JULY*C16**. This command is restricted in its application, but if you have the correct set of conditions, it can save a significant amount of time.

USING BLOCK NAMES Once you have created a block name, you can use it in formulas, functions, and block commands. For example, when you want to copy a named block, you can type the block name instead of describing the coordinates. You can also use the block name in formulas and, as discussed in Chapter 6, @ functions. Using block names instead of cell or block addresses creates formulas that are easier to understand.

When the selector is on a cell containing a formula that uses a block name, the block name appears in the input line instead of the actual cell reference. When you edit a cell with a block name in a formula, the formula appears in the input line using the cell references. Quattro continues to use the block names instead of the cell addresses when the cell formulas are displayed in the input line and when the cells use the Text format. When you enter block names in a formula, you achieve

```
File  Edit  Style  Graph  Print  Database  Tools  Options  Window            ? ↑↓
      Erase Copy Move Style Align Font Insert Delete Fit Sum Format CHR WYS
[Enter] [Esc] Enter label block: B5..G5
            A                    B         C         D         E         F         G
  1  Acme Incorporated
  2  Cash Flow For Last Half of 1990
  3
  4
  5                            July       Aug      Sept       Oct       Nov       Dec
  6  Forecasted Sales         450,000   500,000  475,000   525,000   600,000   550,000
  7
  8  Paid Invoices from:
  9    This Month's Sales           0    50,000   47,500    52,500    60,000    55,000
 10    Last Month's Sales     219,450         0  275,000   261,250   288,750   330,000
 11    Sales 2 Months Ago     150,000    99,750        0   125,000   118,750   131,250
 12    Sales 3 Months Ago      47,500    60,000   39,900         0    50,000    47,500
 13  Total                    416,950   209,750  362,400   438,750   517,500   563,750
 14
 15  Assumptions:
 16  Percentage Paid: Current Month       10%            April Sales          475,000
 17  Percentage Paid: Next Month          55%            May Sales            600,000
 18  Percentage Paid 2 Months Later       25%            June Sales           399,000
     Percentage Paid 3 Months Later       10%
G5: [W8] "Dec                                                                    POINT
```

Figure 3.23 Selecting the Cells That Contain the Block Names

the same results as entering the address. You can create block names that are handled as absolute references by adding a dollar sign ($) in front of the block name when you type the block name (as in $SALES). Another option for making the reference absolute is using F4 (ABS) or the Abs button in the SpeedBar to change the relative block name into an absolute block name.

When you type in a formula with cell addresses or use the point method to highlight it, Quattro automatically converts addresses with assigned block names to these names for displaying the formulas. When you initially name a block, Quattro searches your spreadsheet for any references to the named block and converts them so the block name (not address) will be displayed.

Quattro has a function key to provide quick access to block names. When you press F3 (CHOICES) or click the Block or BLK button in the SpeedBar, Quattro displays a list of the existing block names (as shown in Figure 3.24) as long as Quattro is waiting for you to specify a block. If you press the GRAY PLUS, Quattro widens the box and shows the cell addresses referenced by each of the block names. Pressing the GRAY MINUS reduces the box size to its original size that just lists the block names. If you press F3 (CHOICES) while Quattro is listing the block names, the box expands. To include a block name in the input line using F3 (CHOICES), move the selector to the desired block name, and press ENTER. You can also use this key whenever you want to use a block name for a Quattro command such as pressing F3 (CHOICES) when Quattro prompts for a block to format. You do not have the Block or BLK button in the SpeedBar for selecting

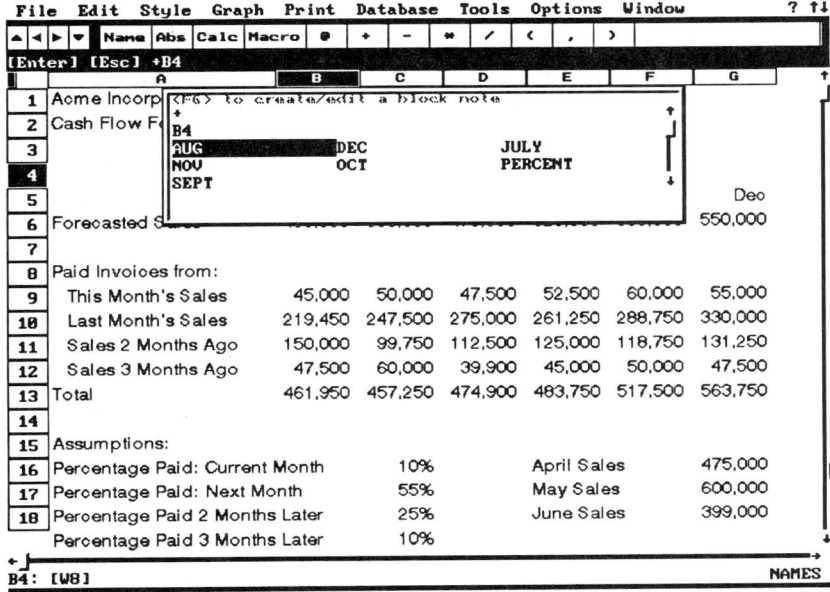

Figure 3.24 Using F3 (CHOICES) to List Spreadsheet's Block Names

block names in response to Quattro Pro command prompts. If you press F3 (CHOICES) when Quattro is not expecting a block name Quattro displays the menu just as if you had pressed /.

REMOVING A BLOCK NAME As you create names for blocks, you may want to remove some of them. For example, if you enter a name of a block incorrectly when you type it, you must delete the block name, and create it again. To remove a block name, press /, and select Edit Names Delete. Quattro prompts for the block name that you want to delete. Type the block name (or move the selector to the one that you want to remove), and press ENTER. Once you have deleted a block name, you must recreate it if you want to use it again. Formulas that reference the deleted block name will convert the block names to the cell addresses. Removing a block name does not change the information that is stored inside the block.

If you want to remove all block names, use the /Edit Names Reset command. When you use this command, Quattro displays a confirmation menu prompting you to confirm your request. If you delete one or all the block names and then change your mind, you can restore the block names if the Undo feature is enabled.

ADDING A NOTE TO A BLOCK In the last chapter you learned how to document a formula or number by typing a semicolon and then typing the text that describes the value. You can also do this for a block. For example, with the percentages that you have named PERCENT for the cash flow forecast, you may want to describe the source of the percentages so future users will know where the values come from so they can determine if they need to be updated. To add a note to a block name, use the /Edit Names Notes Create Command. When Quattro Pro lists the spreadsheet's block names, highlight the block name you want to add the note to, then press F6 or double click the block name. Type the note, and press ENTER. Unlike cell entries, you will only see one line of the note at a time even when it is longer than fits on the line. Once you have created a note, you can change it at a later point by displaying the spreadsheet's block names, highlight the block name with the note to edit, and then press F6. Edit the note, and press ENTER. When a block has a note added to it, it will appear at the top of the list of the spreadsheet's block names.

CHANGING A BLOCK NAME'S ADDRESS After you create a block name, Quattro keeps track of the current location of your named block. If you move the block, Quattro changes the block address referenced by the block name. In some instances, you may need to change the address Quattro uses for a block name (if, for example, an original specification was incorrect or you wish to use that name elsewhere).

To change the address that Quattro uses for a block name, use the /Edit Names Create command, and select the block name from the box displaying the existing block names. When Quattro prompts for the address of the block, enter the new address that you want Quattro to use.

CREATING A BLOCK NAME TABLE When you have many block names, it may be difficult to keep track of all the locations that the blocks represent. You can list the block addresses of block names by pressing the GRAY PLUS key after you have pressed F3 (CHOICES) as shown in Figure 3.25. To create a list of the existing block names and their addresses, use the /Edit Names Make Table command after moving the selector to a blank section of your spreadsheet. By moving to a blank section of the spreadsheet, you prevent the table of names from affecting the existing spreadsheet entries. If the spreadsheet has any entries in the section where the block name table is created, the table data replace the existing entries. A sample table created with this command is shown in Figure 3.26. The table you create, as shown in Figure 3.26, contains the spreadsheet's block names, the cell or block address the block name represents, and any note attached to a block name.

Using Protection

Protecting a spreadsheet ensures that formulas and other entries you want to keep are not damaged inadvertently. In Quattro, protection is a two-step process that includes determining a protection status for a block of cells and enabling the protection features. You can tailor the protection features to your needs, since Quattro lets you choose which portions of your spreadsheet to protect. Once you have instructed Quattro to protect your spreadsheet, you cannot modify any of the protected locations without disabling protection for the cells first. In Quattro Pro

Working with Multiple Cells 91

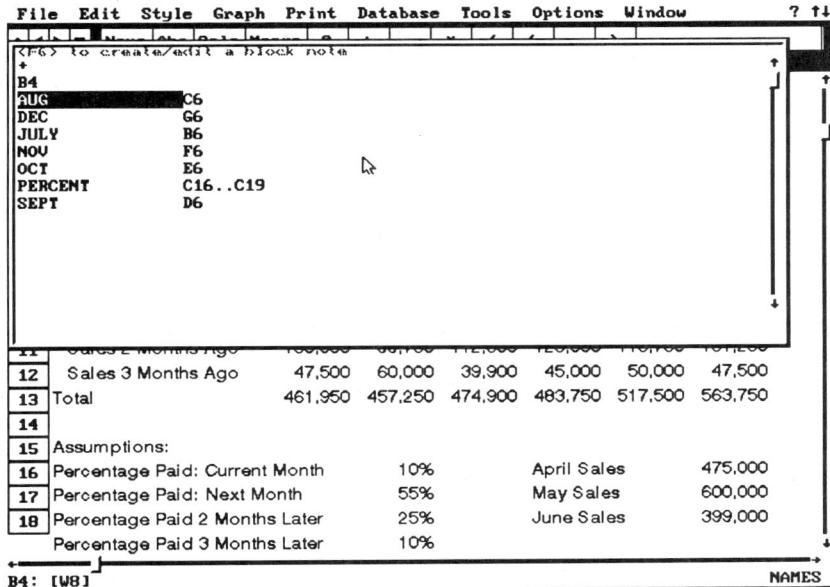

Figure 3.25 Pressing F3 to Show Block Names and Addresses

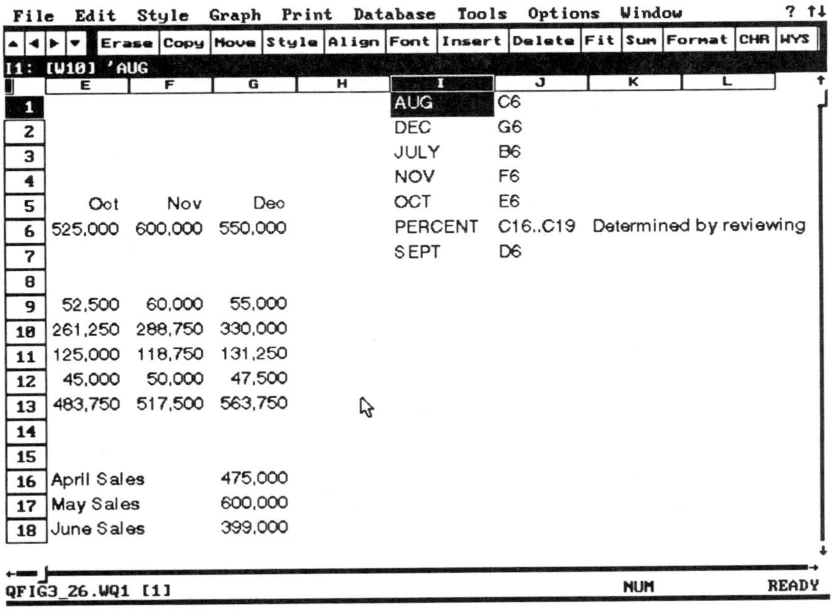

Figure 3.26 Table of Block Names and Addresses Made with the /Edit Names Make Table Command

4, you can also protect formulas in the spreadsheet without protecting the label and value entries. This type of protection works differently from the other protection features.

ENABLING PROTECTION To have Quattro use the protection status of the spreadsheet cells, use the /Options Protection Enable command. Once protection is enabled, any cells that are protected display PR between the cell width and format descriptors. Whenever you attempt to make an entry in a cell that is protected, Quattro displays the message shown in Figure 3.27. A protected cell cannot be edited, replaced, or deleted. Also, a column or row containing one or more protected cells cannot be deleted. The only method of erasing a protected cell is by erasing the entire spreadsheet. When you want to disable the protection of an entire worksheet, use the /Options Protection Disable command.

CHANGING THE PROTECTION STATUS Quattro assumes that you want the entire spreadsheet protected unless you tell it otherwise. Since you will normally only want to change specific spreadsheet cells, you must tell Quattro which sections of the spreadsheet may be changed by unprotecting these blocks. To unprotect a cell or block, use the /Style Protection Unprotect command. When you use this command, Quattro prompts you for the block that you want to modify.

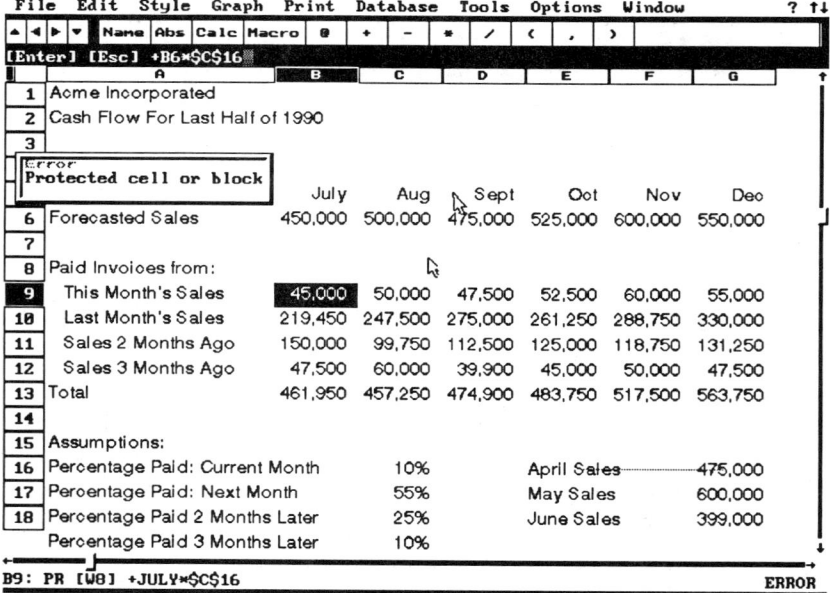

Figure 3.27 Error Message Related to a Protected Cell

Select the block that you want to unprotect. In a typical spreadsheet, this command may have to be repeated to remove the protection from different sections of the spreadsheet where data entry is required. You can also unprotect cells while spreadsheet protection is enabled.

Any unprotected cell displays a U between the cell width and format descriptors. Once a cell is unprotected, its color or attribute changes. For example, using Quattro's default colors and a color monitor, the unprotected cells become a bright light cyan (text mode) or have a cyan background (WYSIWYG mode).

To reinstate a protected status for a block of cells, use the /Style Protection Protect command. This command performs the opposite action from /Style Protection Unprotect, since it returns every cell in the block to a protected status. However, the cells that you instruct Quattro to protect are not actually protected until you enable protection for the entire spreadsheet.

PROTECTING SPREADSHEET FORMULAS Besides using the overall spreadsheet protection provided by the /Style Protect and /Options Protection commands, you can also protect the formulas without protecting the value and label entries. This type of protection applies to all the formulas in the spreadsheet. This feature allows you to create a spreadsheet for someone else knowing that they cannot change the spreadsheet's formulas. To add formula protection, select /Options Protection Formulas Protect. Quattro Pro prompts for a password. Type the password, and press ENTER. As confirmation, you must type the password again, and press ENTER again. The password is case sensitive so the password "MINE" is different from the password "Mine." When formula protection is added, you cannot change any formula in the spreadsheet regardless of whether the /Style Protection command has protected or unprotected the cell, and whether spreadsheet protection is enabled with /Options Protection Enable. When you want to remove the formula protection, select /Options Protection Formula Unprotect. You must enter the password in the same case as the original, and press ENTER for the protection to be removed. Like other changes you make to a spreadsheet, you must make sure to save the spreadsheet after adding formula protection, so later when you work with the spreadsheet the formula protection is enabled.

Converting Formulas

Quattro provides a command for conversion of formula entries to the current result of the formula, effectively freezing the current value of the entry. You can use this command to freeze formulas that are no longer subject to variations. You can convert formulas to allow you to replace other cells with the results of the formulas. Also, you may want to compare the values produced by the formulas with the same formulas used with different assumptions. For example, Figure 3.28 displays a spreadsheet that contains the formulas needed to construct a vendor

```
File   Edit   Style   Graph   Print   Database   Tools   Options   Window           ?  ↑↓
Erase Copy Move Style Align Font Insert Delete Fit Sum Format CHR WYS
F2:  [W11]  @UPPER(@LEFT(A2,3))&C2&"-"&@STRING(E2,0)&"-"&C2&@STRING(D2,0)
```

	A	B	C	D	E	F	G	H
1	Vendor Name	Type		Region	Year	Vendor-Id		
2	Anderson, Ino.	B		6	60	ANDB-60-B6		
3	Walkers	Q		5	82	WALQ-82-Q5		
4	Teachman's	B		5	42	TEAB-42-B5		
5	Naoe Eleotrio	A		2	59	NACA-59-A2		
6	Boyd's Repair	F		5	38	BOYF-38-F5		
7	Harris Plumbing	F		3	43	HARF-43-F3		
8	Severenoe, Ino.	C		4	56	SEVC-56-C4		
9	HELPMATE	H		4	66	HELH-66-H4		
10	Partles Plus	A		4	79	PARA-79-A4		
11	Fordman Toys	T		5	41	FORT-41-T5		
12	Vanoe Food	Y		6	43	VANY-43-Y6		
13	Food Lion	J		4	82	FOOJ-82-J4		
14	Warehouse, Inc.	N		2	60	WARN-60-N2		
15	Brownstone	V		3	69	BROV-69-V3		
16	Lawlers	R		2	61	LAWR-61-R2		
17	Soup And Stuff	F		1	71	SOUF-71-F1		
18	Stuff& More	L		4	46	STUL-46-L4		
	York Tailor	W		3	47	YORW-47-W3		

```
QFIG3_28.WQ1 [1]                              CAP         NUM           READY
```

Figure 3.28 Using the Edit Values Command

identification (ID) number. Once the vendor numbers have been constructed from the detail entries, you can freeze the column of entries at its current value and eliminate the component entries if they are not required for other tasks. The /Edit Values command takes the current results from the formula entries with the block selected and copies the values over the old entries or to a new location. All formulas are converted to their resulting numeric or string values.

To use this command, type /, and select Edit Values. When you use this command, Quattro prompts for the source block, which contains the formulas that you want to convert. If vendor names in this example are entered through A500, the source block is F2..F500. After you have selected the source block, Quattro prompts for the destination address, the location to which you want the upper-left corner of the block to be copied. To convert entries without relocating them, specify a source and target block that are the same. Copying the values to their original location replaces all the formulas in the source block with their values (in this example, F2). When you press ENTER, Quattro copies the values of the block to the new location. Any numeric formulas are converted to values. This command is useful when you are correcting data-entry errors.

Transposing Entries

Restructuring a spreadsheet to meet new requirements can require changing the orientation of rows to columns or vice versa. Quattro can handle this change automatically with a menu command.

Figure 3.29 shows a table in a spreadsheet that is extended so far to the right that you can no longer see all the table's columns on the screen. Since the table is only a few lines in length, changing the orientation so that the sales personnel are in the top row and the months are in the left column provides a better table.

The /Edit Transpose command copies the values of a block, switching the row and column entries. To execute this command, type /, and select Edit Transpose. Next, specify the block of your spreadsheet that you want to transpose. In Figure 3.29, it is A2 to M6. After you press ENTER, Quattro prompts for the block where you want the transposed data copied. The location that you choose should be separate from existing spreadsheet data to prevent the transposed information from writing over your existing information. Unlike the /Edit Values command, you cannot copy over the block from which you are copying. In this example, we choose A8 as the location to receive the transposed table. Since Quattro only needs to know the upper-left corner of the receiving block, you only need to specify a single cell and press ENTER. The table shown in Figure 3.29 looks like the one in Figure 3.30 after it is transposed. When the source block contains formulas with relative cell references, the formulas do not convert properly. If the original formula contains relative references, the new relative references are incorrect. If the formulas contain absolute references, the new formulas refer to the data in the old table. If you are planning to remove the original block after you have successfully transposed it, you must change the formulas.

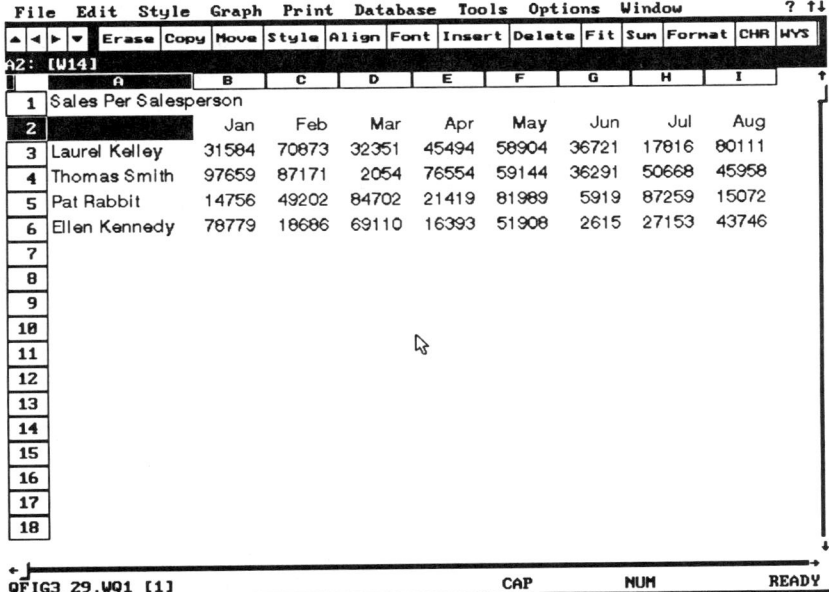

Figure 3.29 Spreadsheet Before Transposition

```
     File   Edit   Style   Graph   Print   Database   Tools   Options   Window              ?  ↑↓
   ┌─┬─┬─┬──────┬────┬────┬─────┬─────┬────┬──────┬──────┬───┬───┬──────┬───┬───┐
   │▲│◄│►│▼ Erase│Copy│Move│Style│Align│Font│Insert│Delete│Fit│Sum│Format│CHR│WYS│
   A2: [W14]
              A              B       C       D       E       F       G       H       I
      1  Sales Per Salesperson
      2                     Jan     Feb     Mar     Apr     May     Jun     Jul     Aug
      3  Laurel Kelley    31584   70873   32351   45494   58904   36721   17816   80111
      4  Thomas Smith     97659   87171    2054   76554   59144   36291   50668   45958
      5  Pat Rabbit       14756   49202   84702   21419   81989    5919   87259   15072
      6  Ellen Kennedy    78779   18686   69110   16393   51908    2615   27153   43746
      7
      8                   Laurel  Thoma   Pat Rab Ellen Kennedy
      9             Jan    31584   97659   14756   78779
     10             Feb    70873   87171   49202   18686
     11             Mar    32351    2054   84702   69110
     12             Apr    45494   76554   21419   16393
     13             May    58904   59144   81989   51908
     14             Jun    36721   36291    5919    2615
     15             Jul    17816   50668   87259   27153
     16             Aug    80111   45958   15072   43746
     17             Sep    20689    5645   92272   19070
     18             Oct    34917    6923   63115   96111
                    Nov    96762   25918   67663   49723

   QFIG3_30.WQ1 [1]                                               NUM              READY
```

Figure 3.30   Spreadsheet After Transposition

Search and Replace

Quattro has a special command that lets you find characters in a block and replace them with other characters. This command can be used to locate all occurrences of a particular cell reference. This command can correct a misspelling that occurs repeatedly in a spreadsheet.

To use Quattro's search and replace feature, follow these steps:

1. Type /, and select Edit and Search & Replace. Quattro displays the Search & Replace menu shown in Figure 3.31.

2. Select Block. With this command, you specify the section of the spreadsheet to be checked. If you do not provide a block address or name, Quattro searches through the entire spreadsheet.

3. Type in the coordinates, move the selector to one corner of the block that you want to use, type a period, and use the direction keys to highlight the block that you want Quattro to use (or select a block with the mouse).

4. Press ENTER.

5. Select Search String. Quattro prompts you with a box for entering the search string. This string can be one or more numbers, letters, or both. When Quattro searches for this string, it looks at all the cells, whether they contain labels, numbers, or formulas. If you are searching for a cell reference, such as A1, Quattro finds it even if it is buried in a formula. If you are looking

Working with Multiple Cells 97

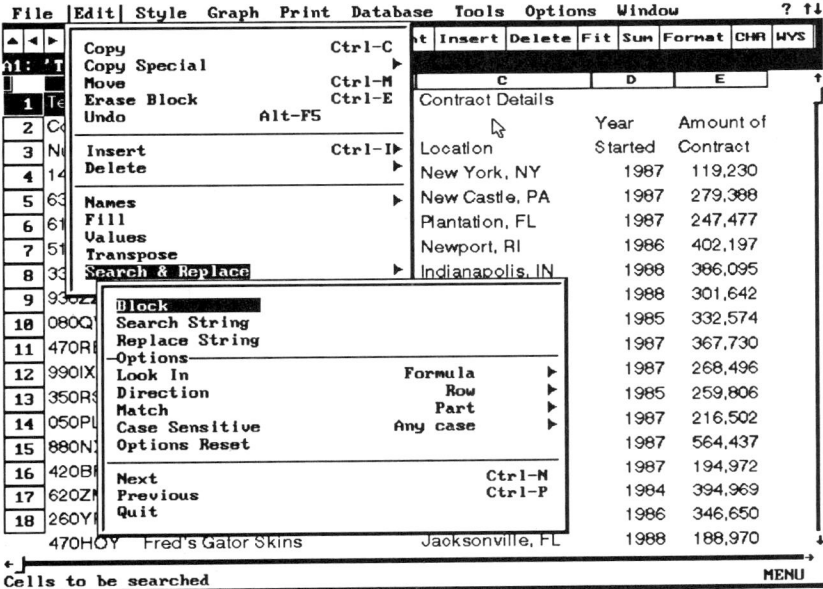

Figure 3.31 Search / Replace Menu

for an absolute or mixed cell address, the search string must include the dollar signs in that address.

6. Press ENTER.

7. Select **Replace String**. Quattro prompts you with a box asking which string it should replace the search string with. This string can be one or more numbers, letters, or both. If you only want to find occurrences of the search string but do not want to replace them, leave this setting empty.

8. Press ENTER.

9. Select **Next**. Quattro searches for the specified search string. If Quattro does not find a match, it beeps and displays the error message "Not Found." When Quattro finds a match, a box like the one in Figure 3.32 is presented. From this box, you have five choices. If you choose **Yes**, Quattro replaces the search string with the replace string, and then searches for the next occurrence of the search string. If you choose **No**, Quattro does not make the replacement, and looks for the next occurrence of the search string. **All** replaces all occurrences of the search string in the specified block with the replace string. **Edit** enters the EDIT mode so you can edit the cell containing the search string; when you press ENTER to finalize editing, Quattro searches for the next occurrence of the search string. If you choose **Quit**, you abort Quattro's search and replace operation. When you choose **Yes**, **No** or **Edit**, Quattro continues to look for all occurrences of the search string until it cannot find any more matches or **Quit** is selected. When the operation is

```
File  Edit  Style  Graph  Print  Database  Tools  Options  Window           ? ↑↓
 ▲ ◄ ► ▼  Erase Copy Move Style Align Font Insert Delete Fit Sum Format CHR WYS
[Enter] [Esc]   'Termite Construction Company
         A              B                     C              D         E
  1  Termite Cons    Replace this string:  Contract Details
  2  Contract        Yes                                   Year      Amount of
  3  Number       C  No                    Location        Started   Contract
  4  140UPY       Fo All                   New York, NY    1987      119,230
  5  630SEF       M  Edit                  New Castle, PA  1987      279,388
  6  610QZZ       B  Quit                  Plantation, FL  1987      247,477
  7  510FDO          Boaters, Inc          Newport, RI     1986      402,197
  8  330ZEJ          Speeders, Ltd.        Indianapolis, IN 1988     386,095
  9  930ZZD          Crooked Towers        Chicago, IL     1988      301,642
 10  080QVM          Mappers Galore        Elm Creek, TX   1985      332,574
 11  470RBP          Rusty's Automotive Parts  Tuscon, AZ  1987      367,730
 12  990IXZ          Alonzo's Fish & Tackle    Mobile, AL  1987      268,496
 13  350RSH          New Worlds Horizons   Fort Knox, TN   1985      259,806
 14  050PLK          Portuguese Foods, Inc.  Fall River, MA 1987    216,502
 15  880NXF          Crystal Ball Glass Makers  Salem, CT  1987      564,437
 16  420BFY          Stanton Leather Company    Stanton, MO 1987     194,972
 17  620ZMB          Birdfeeders Inc.      Buffalo, NY     1984      394,969
 18  260YPS          Stitch In Time Crafts  Atlanta, GA    1986      346,650
     470HOY          Fred's Gator Skins    Jacksonville, FL 1988     188,970
A1:  'Termite Construction Company                                      EDIT
```

Figure 3.32 Replacement Selection Box

finished, Quattro returns to the READY mode. Quattro remembers the settings that you used with this command, making it easier to use this command again.

SEARCH AND REPLACE OPTIONS Quattro provides other options for finding cells containing the search string. If you select **Previous**, Quattro searches from the current cell to the beginning of the search block. **Next** searches from the current cell to the end of the search block. You can also perform the /Edit Search & Replace Next and /Edit Search & Replace Previous commands using the accelerator keys CTRL-N and CTRL-P. The /Edit Search & Replace command makes several assumptions that you can change. These options are listed in the middle of the menu in Figure 3.31. You can also change the search direction to either rows or columns with the **Direction** option of the command.

Look In determines how Quattro searches formulas. The default setting (Formula) searches the formulas themselves. Value searches the results that the formulas display. Condition searches the formulas' results and other cell entries to find cells whose values meet the condition provided by the search string. When this option is selected, the search string must be entered first. The search string is a logical condition. As an example, if you want to find cells with values greater than 400,000 for the spreadsheet shown in Figure 3.31, you enter **A1>400000**. The current cell address is used so that every cell in the search block is checked to see if it matches the condition. You can see the current cell address below the File menu item on the menu bar. When the search string is a condition, the cell address in the search string is always updated for the current cell position, so that, when you look at the search string at another time, the cell reference in the search string will be different.

Direction determines whether Quattro searches by rows or by columns. Match determines whether Quattro will match the search string to a cell entry if it matches the entire cell entry or part of a cell entry. If Smith is the search string, it matches with Smithfield if **Match** is set to **Part** but does not match if **Match** is set to **Whole**. Case Sensitive determines if the search string must have the same capitalization pattern as a cell entry. If this is set to **Any Case**, Quattro matches with any capitalization pattern as long as the entry meets the other match criteria. If this is set to **Same Case**, Quattro matches only if the capitalization pattern and other characteristics of the entry are exactly the same as the search string. **Options Reset** returns the options to the default settings of checking formulas, searching by rows, finding cells that contain at least the search string, and including matches that have a different capitalization pattern as well as removing the search string and the replace string.

Reformatting Text Blocks

When you create a spreadsheet, you usually include text to describe it. It may be a quick heading at the top and one- or two-word descriptions for row and column headers. Other spreadsheets demand more extensive documentation. For example, Figure 3.33 shows a spreadsheet that contains notes at the bottom of the screen.

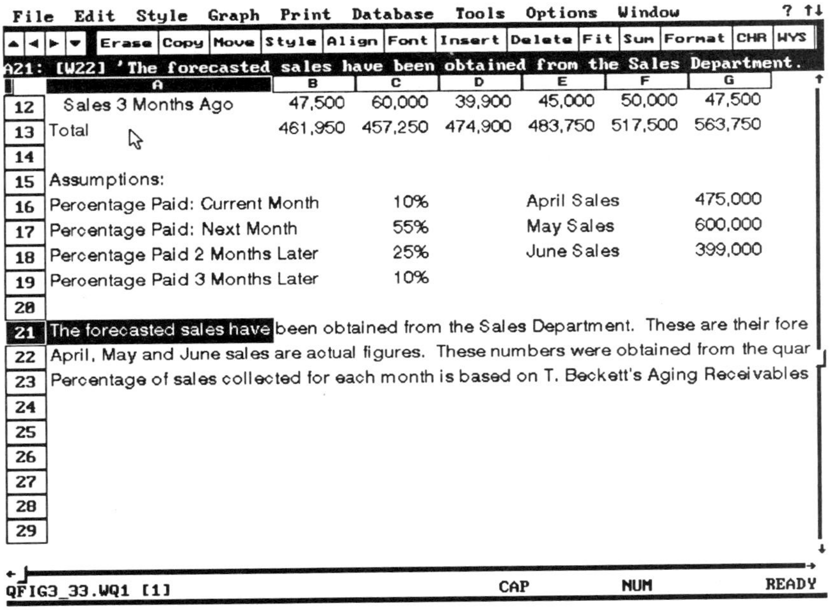

Figure 3.33 Spreadsheet Containing Labels That Extend Beyond the Display

> ▼ **TIP: Unprotect cells that might be used.**
>
> Remove protection of cells below the zones you are reformatting, if protection is enabled so Quattro can use these cells if necessary.

Since the descriptive information is lengthy, only the portion that fits on the screen is displayed. The /Tools Reformat command can restructure text in a block to fit within the width of selected columns. To use this command, press /, and select Tools Reformat. Next, select the columns over which you want the cell's contents to be redistributed, and press ENTER. Quattro word-wraps the long-label entries, splitting the long labels between words to fit within the allotted space. The reformatted text is shown in Figure 3.34. When Quattro performs the reformatting command, it uses as many rows as necessary to store the restructured data. Another option for reformatting text is including the rows to be used as well as the columns. When you include more than one row in the block to reformat, Quattro only uses the number of rows in the block to reformat. If you have not included enough rows in the block, the last cell contains the remaining data that did not fit in the block. Like the original labels that were only stored in one cell but displayed across several columns, the reformatted labels are stored in the first column of the display area. With the WYSIWYG display, you may notice that the text does not exactly fill up the width that you have selected. The /Tools Reformat command bases the number

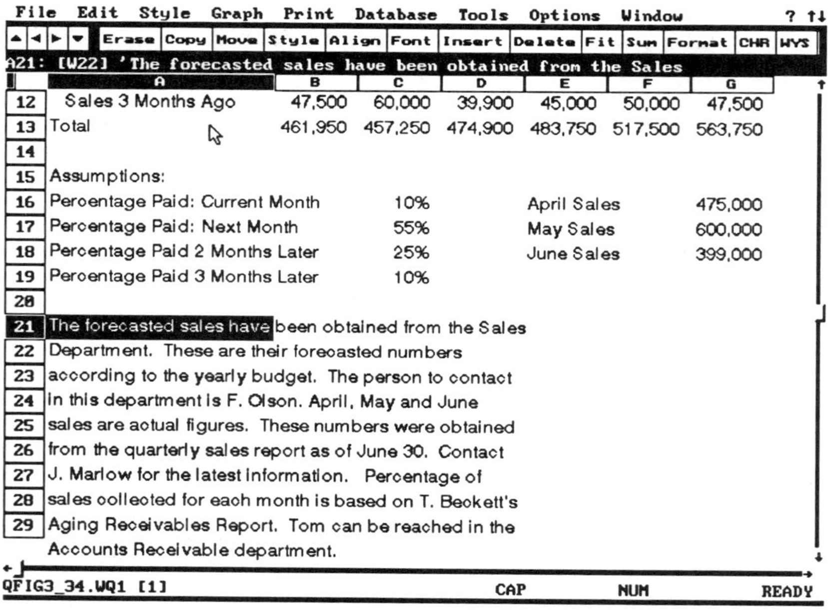

Figure 3.34 Labels Reformatted to Fit into the Display

of characters that fits on each line using the average character width of the default font. Since your text may have different widths or different fonts, the block you reformat may be wider or narrower than the block you selected. You may want to select a wider or narrower block to reformat if you plan to print your spreadsheet using a graphics printer and the fonts Quattro Pro provides.

When there are numeric entries below the area that you are reformatting, Quattro inserts rows to provide sufficient space to reformat the labels. For example, in Figure 3.35, the formula in A25 totals the sales for the last quarter. When the long labels above it are reformatted, Quattro inserts seven new rows between the original labels and the numbers so that it has enough room to reformat the labels, as in Figure 3.36.

Generating Values in a Block

Most data you enter into your spreadsheet models are provided by external sources. When you enter data, you may find that some data are monotonous, such as consecutive dates or numbers. Quattro eliminates this monotonous data entry by generating a series of values that are an equal distance apart. The following three lines contain samples of series you can create:

1 2 3 4 5 6 7 8 9 10

01/07/90 01/14/90 01/21/90 01/28/90

100 60 20 -20 -60 -100

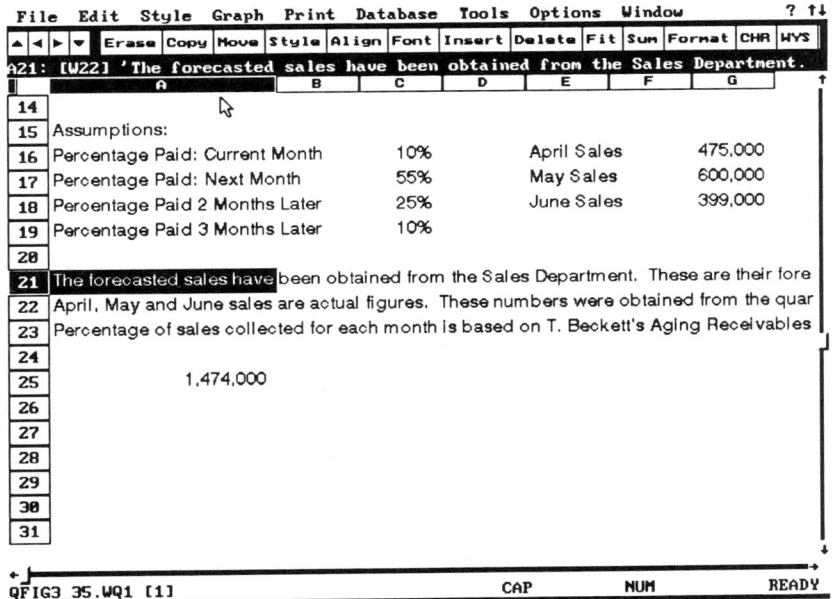

Figure 3.35 Long Labels with Additional Information Below

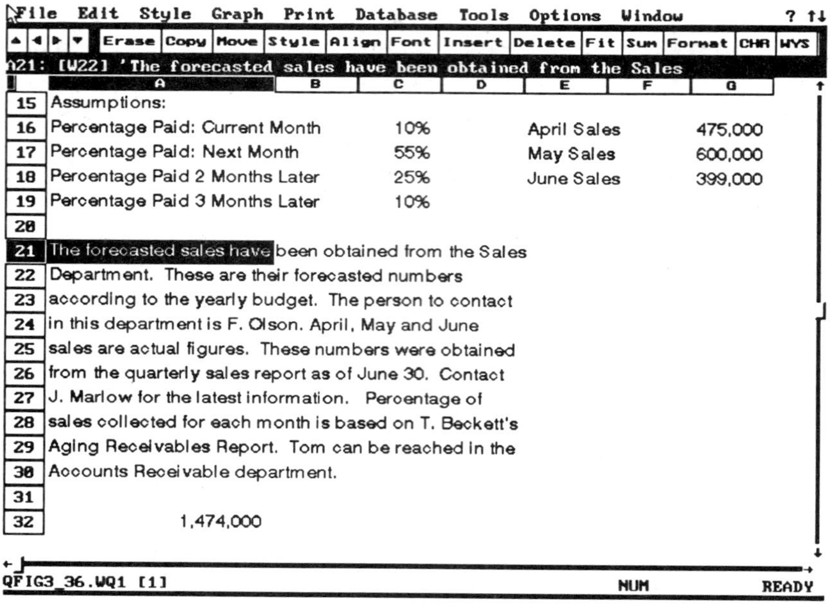

Figure 3.36 Reformatted Labels with Rows Inserted

The /Edit Fill command generates a series of numbers in a spreadsheet block when you tell Quattro the appropriate block name or address, the number you want to start with, the increment between numbers, and the highest possible number. To generate a series of values, follow these steps:

1. Type /, and select Edit and Fill. Quattro prompts you for the block to fill first unless you have already selected a block with the mouse or SHIFT-F7 (SELECT). When you select the block and press ENTER, Quattro prompts for the first value in a box (see prompt shown in Figure 3.37).

2. Press ENTER to accept the default value of 0. Quattro prompts for the step value, the amount each value generated by Quattro increases or decreases. If the step value is positive, the numbers generated by Quattro increase. If the step value is negative, the numbers generated by Quattro decrease.

3. Type 10, and press ENTER. Quattro prompts for the stop value and displays 8192. Quattro uses this number and the block size to determine when to stop generating numbers. Quattro continues to generate numbers until it reaches the stop value or it has filled all the cells in the block.

4. Press ENTER to accept the default of 8192. Quattro fills the block and creates the block of numbers shown in Figure 3.38. Notice how Quattro fills each column in the block before filling the next row.

Quattro is very flexible with the values that you provide for the start, step, and

Working with Multiple Cells 103

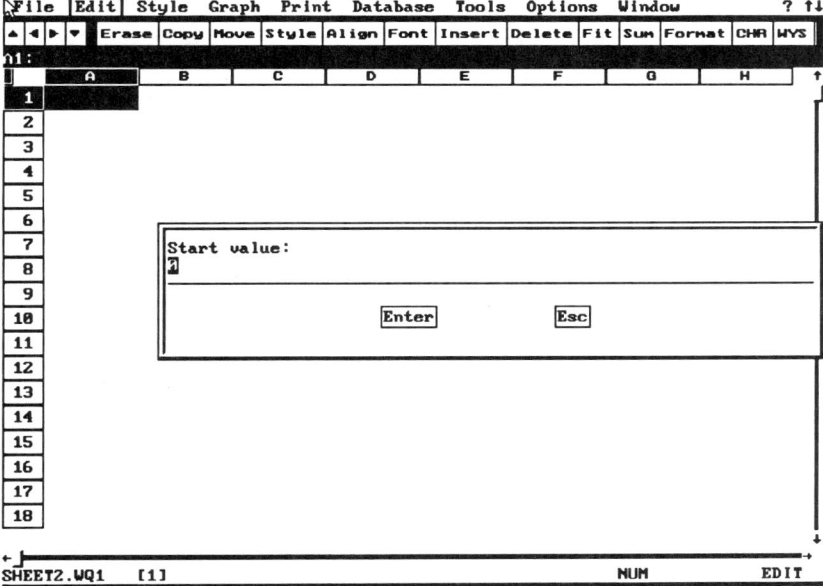

Figure 3.37 Prompt for Start Value to Generate Number Sequence

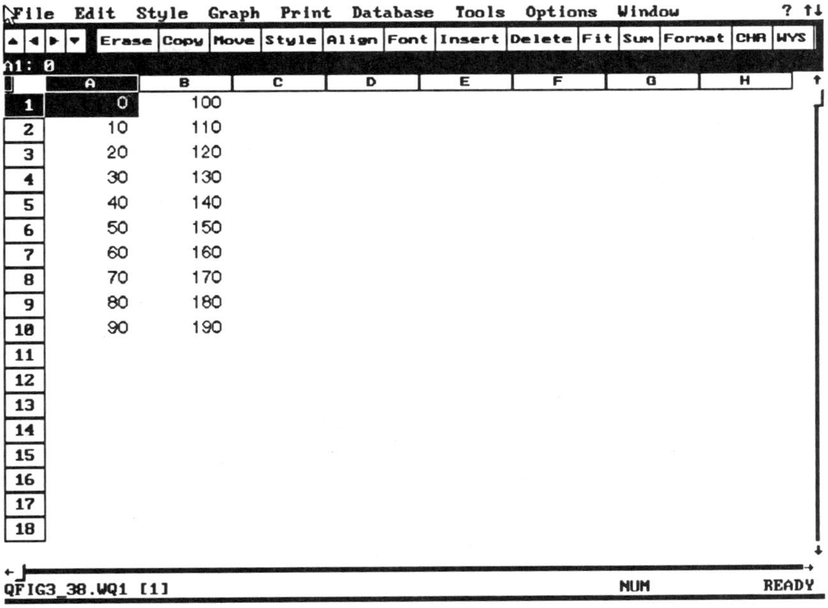

Figure 3.38 Result of Numbers Generated by Quattro

> ▼ **TIP: Use large stop values for dates.**
>
> If you are using /Edit Fill with dates, remember to increment the stop value to about 90000, since most date numbers are greater than the 8192 default stop value.

stop values. You can use functions such as @DATE and @TIME to create date and time serial numbers. You can also use CTRL-D to enter a date or time directly.

COLUMN AND ROW COMMANDS

The block commands covered so far in the chapter have operated on blocks of data consisting of a rectangle of entries. Quattro has several commands that let you operate on columns and rows. The column and row commands let you add and delete columns and rows. Additional options for columns let you hide and expose columns and also change the column widths.

Inserting Columns

As you create a spreadsheet, you may realize that you have forgotten to include a column of entries. You may also decide that the addition of bland columns would make the existing data easier to read. Quattro makes it easy for you to enter blank columns. You can leave them blank or make entries in these inserted columns.

Quattro allows you to insert columns anywhere on the spreadsheet. To insert one or more columns into your spreadsheet, move the selector to the right of the column where you want the new columns inserted. Type /, and select **Edit Insert** and **Columns**. You can also use the shortcut key: Press CTRL-I, and select **Columns**. In Quattro Pro 4, you can also insert columns by clicking the Insert or INS button in the SpeedBar and then selecting **Columns**. Quattro prompts for the columns that you want inserted. Since one column is already highlighted, press the RIGHT ARROW key for each additional column that you wish to insert, and then press ENTER. Quattro inserts the number of columns that you highlighted and adjusts all the formulas accordingly. Like the /Edit Move command, inserting columns adjusts absolute, mixed, and relative cell references so all formulas refer to the same cells after the new columns are inserted. For example, Figure 3.39 shows a spreadsheet before a column is inserted, and Figure 3.40 presents the same spreadsheet after a blank column is inserted. The formulas in Figure 3.40 are adjusted after the blank column is inserted. Each reference to the right of the insertion is adjusted by one column for each column inserted. When Quattro adjusts the

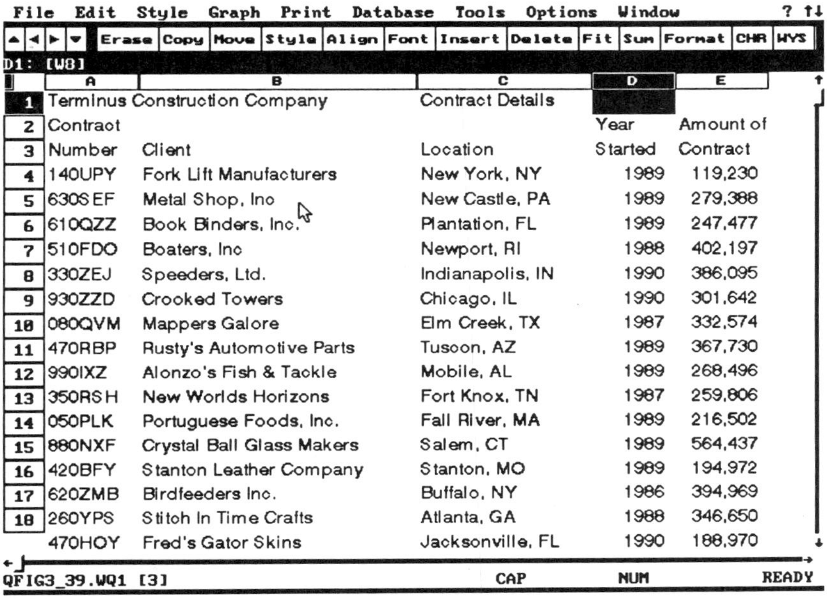

	A	B	C	D	E
1	Terminus Construction Company		Contract Details		
2	Contract			Year	Amount of
3	Number	Client	Location	Started	Contract
4	140UPY	Fork Lift Manufacturers	New York, NY	1989	119,230
5	630SEF	Metal Shop, Inc	New Castle, PA	1989	279,388
6	610QZZ	Book Binders, Inc.	Plantation, FL	1989	247,477
7	510FDO	Boaters, Inc	Newport, RI	1988	402,197
8	330ZEJ	Speeders, Ltd.	Indianapolis, IN	1990	386,095
9	930ZZD	Crooked Towers	Chicago, IL	1990	301,642
10	080QVM	Mappers Galore	Elm Creek, TX	1987	332,574
11	470RBP	Rusty's Automotive Parts	Tuscon, AZ	1989	367,730
12	990IXZ	Alonzo's Fish & Tackle	Mobile, AL	1989	268,496
13	350RSH	New Worlds Horizons	Fort Knox, TN	1987	259,806
14	050PLK	Portuguese Foods, Inc.	Fall River, MA	1989	216,502
15	880NXF	Crystal Ball Glass Makers	Salem, CT	1989	564,437
16	420BFY	Stanton Leather Company	Stanton, MO	1989	194,972
17	620ZMB	Birdfeeders Inc.	Buffalo, NY	1986	394,969
18	260YPS	Stitch In Time Crafts	Atlanta, GA	1988	346,650
	470HOY	Fred's Gator Skins	Jacksonville, FL	1990	188,970

Figure 3.39 Spreadsheet Before Column Is Inserted

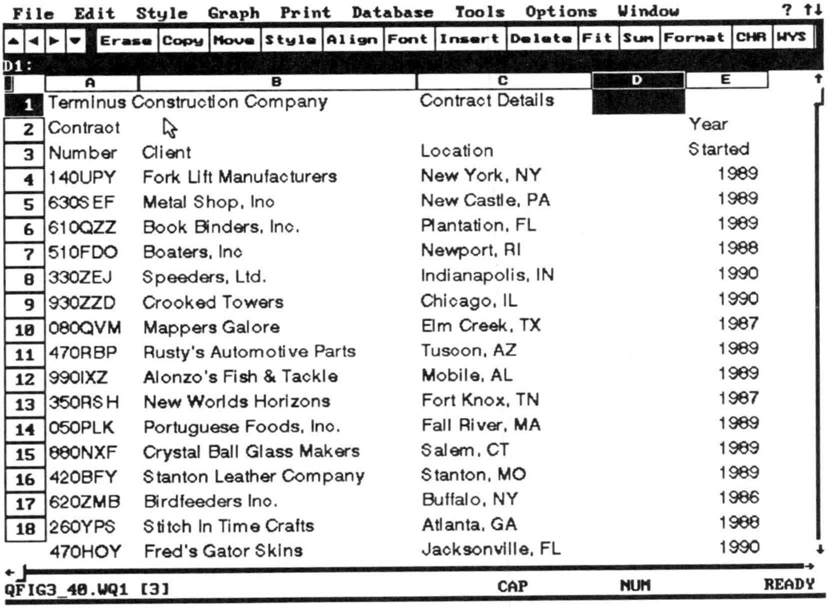

	A	B	C	D	E
1	Terminus Construction Company		Contract Details		
2	Contract				Year
3	Number	Client	Location		Started
4	140UPY	Fork Lift Manufacturers	New York, NY		1989
5	630SEF	Metal Shop, Inc	New Castle, PA		1989
6	610QZZ	Book Binders, Inc.	Plantation, FL		1989
7	510FDO	Boaters, Inc	Newport, RI		1988
8	330ZEJ	Speeders, Ltd.	Indianapolis, IN		1990
9	930ZZD	Crooked Towers	Chicago, IL		1990
10	080QVM	Mappers Galore	Elm Creek, TX		1987
11	470RBP	Rusty's Automotive Parts	Tuscon, AZ		1989
12	990IXZ	Alonzo's Fish & Tackle	Mobile, AL		1989
13	350RSH	New Worlds Horizons	Fort Knox, TN		1987
14	050PLK	Portuguese Foods, Inc.	Fall River, MA		1989
15	880NXF	Crystal Ball Glass Makers	Salem, CT		1989
16	420BFY	Stanton Leather Company	Stanton, MO		1989
17	620ZMB	Birdfeeders Inc.	Buffalo, NY		1986
18	260YPS	Stitch In Time Crafts	Atlanta, GA		1988
	470HOY	Fred's Gator Skins	Jacksonville, FL		1990

Figure 3.40 Spreadsheet After Column Is Inserted

formulas with cell references, it does not matter if the cell addresses are relative or absolute. The only situation in which Quattro does not allow you to insert another column is when you have data stored in the last possible column (column IV). The new columns use the spreadsheet defaults for alignment, display format, and column width.

Inserting Rows

While creating a spreadsheet, you may decide to put additional information at the top of your spreadsheet, such as titles, dates, or time-stamp entries. You may want to put information between existing rows to accommodate missing entries. Quattro allows you to insert rows wherever you choose.

To insert one or more rows into your spreadsheet, move the selector to the row below where you want the new rows inserted. Type /, and select Edit Insert Rows. In Quattro Pro 4, you can also insert rows by clicking the Insert or INS button in the SpeedBar and then selecting Rows. You can also use the accelerator key: Press CTRL-I, and select Rows. Quattro prompts for the rows that you want inserted. Since one row is already highlighted, press the DOWN ARROW key for each additional row that you want inserted, and then press ENTER. Quattro inserts the number of rows that you highlighted and adjusts all the formulas accordingly. The only situation in which Quattro does not let you insert another row is when you have data stored in the last possible row (row 8192). The new rows use the spreadsheet defaults for alignment, display format, and column width.

Deleting Columns

Columns that are no longer needed can be removed from the spreadsheet. As Quattro makes this adjustment, it automatically moves information to the left of the deleted columns and adjusts the formulas.

You may want to delete columns between a column of numbers and the text that explains these entries after widening the text column to contain the entire entries. Quattro lets you delete columns at any location in the spreadsheet. To delete one or more columns from your spreadsheet, move the selector to the leftmost column that you want to delete, type /, and select Edit Delete and Columns. You can also delete columns by clicking the Delete or DEL button in the SpeedBar and selecting Columns. Quattro prompts for the columns that you want to delete. Highlight the contiguous columns that you want deleted, and press ENTER.

If you want to delete several columns that are not adjoining, you must use the /Edit Delete Columns command for each group of adjoining columns that you want to delete. Quattro deletes the columns that you highlighted and adjusts all the formulas accordingly. Any formulas that referenced cells in the deleted columns have that cell reference changed to ERR. Quattro does not allow you to delete a column that contains protected cells when the spreadsheet protection is enabled or when formula protection is enabled.

Deleting Rows

After building a spreadsheet model, you might have extra blank rows or rows containing entries that are no longer needed. These rows can be deleted with Quattro's /Edit Delete Rows command or by clicking the Delete or DEL button in the SpeedBar and selecting Rows.

You can delete rows at any location in the spreadsheet. To delete one or more rows, move the selector to the first row that you want to delete, type /, and select Edit Delete Rows. Quattro then prompts for the rows that you want deleted. Highlight all the rows that you want deleted, and press ENTER. If you want to delete several rows that are not adjoining, you must use the /Edit Delete Rows command for each adjoining group of rows that you want to delete.

When Quattro deletes the highlighted rows, it adjusts all the formulas accordingly. Any formulas that referenced cells in the deleted rows display as ERR. The one situation in which Quattro rejects a request to delete a row is when the row contains protected cells and the spreadsheet protection is enabled or when formula protection is enabled.

Inserting Blocks of Columns and Rows

Another option for inserting columns and rows is to insert portions of columns or rows. This is similar to cutting a section of the spreadsheet and shifting it right or down. You may want to think of it as an earthquake on your spreadsheet, since only the columns or rows you select are affected while the remaining data stays in place. As an example of inserting a block of a column or row, look at Figure 3.41. In this spreadsheet with the B2..C3 block selected, Quattro Pro uses the selected block to indicate how many rows or columns to insert as well as the columns and rows that are affected. With the data in Figure 3.41, if you select the /Edit Insert Row Block command, Quattro adds two rows in columns B and C; columns A and D through the end of the spreadsheet do not have any rows inserted. If you select the /Edit Insert Columns Block command with the data in Figure 3.41, Quattro adds two columns in rows 2 and 3; rows 1 and 4 through the end of the spreadsheet do not have any rows inserted. Figure 3.42 shows the spreadsheet after inserting two partial rows. When you insert a partial column or row to a spreadsheet, you must select a block that includes the number of columns to insert and the rows that are affected, or the number of rows to insert and the columns that are affected. Use inserting partial columns and rows as an alternative to the /Edit Move command when you want to make sure that you do not accidentally move data on top of other data. Like moving data, when you insert a partial column or row, Quattro Pro will adjust the cell addresses so the formulas in your spreadsheet continue to refer to the same data.

Deleting Blocks of Columns and Rows

Besides inserting partial columns and rows, you can also delete partial columns and rows. This lets you shift a section of a spreadsheet up and to the left. For

108 *Quattro Pro 4.0 Handbook*

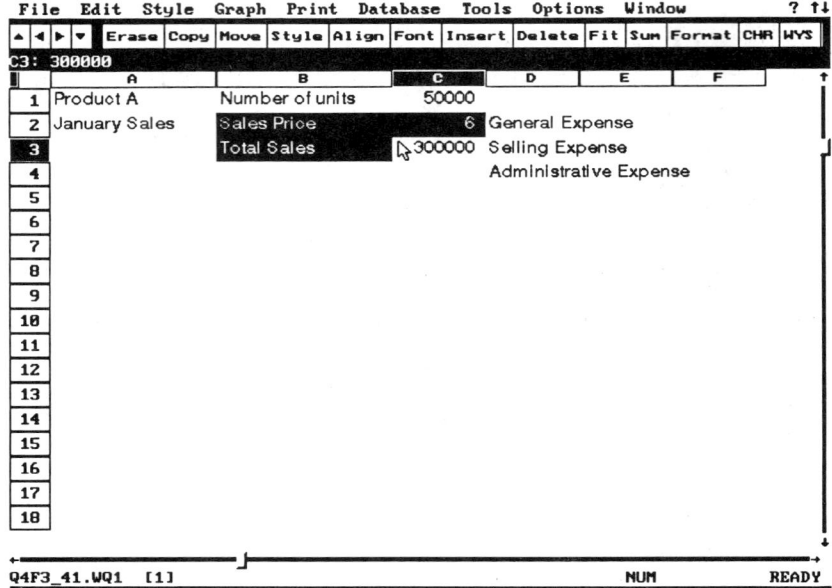

Figure 3.41 Spreadsheet before Inserting Partial Rows

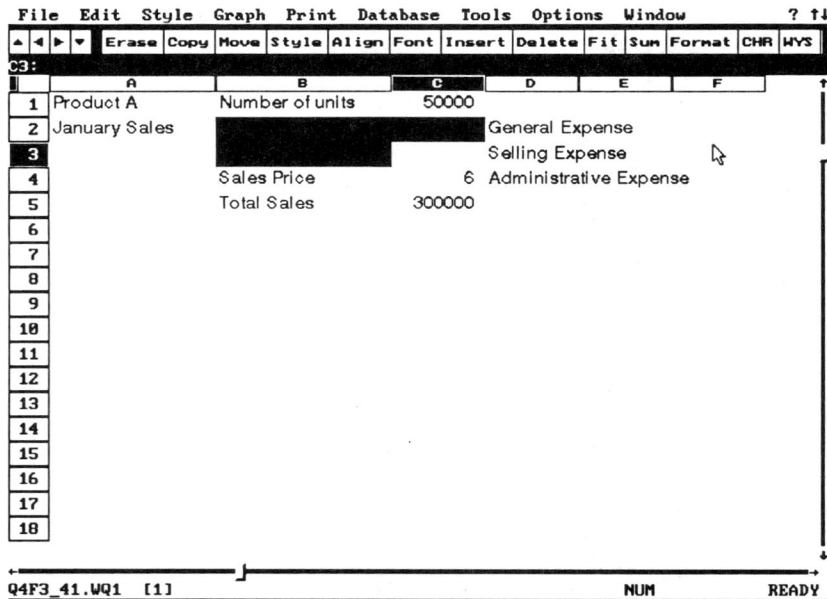

Figure 3.42 Spreadsheet after Inserting Partial Rows

example, you have many reports on a spreadsheet and then if you delete one, you can shift the remaining reports using the same columns up or the other reports using the same rows to the left. This is similar to cutting a section out of the spreadsheet and shifting the data to the right or below it into its place. For example, if you deleted the partial columns selected in Figure 3.41, the general and selling expenses would move from columns D and E to columns B and C. The block you select to delete partial columns or rows selects the columns or rows to delete and the rows or columns that are affected by the deletion. To delete partial rows, select the /Edit Delete Row Block command, the block containing the rows to delete, and the columns in which the rows are deleted. To delete partial columns, select the /Edit Delete Columns Block command, the range containing the columns to delete, and the rows in which the columns are deleted.

Hiding Columns

You can elect to hide columns from the display when you do not need to work with data in every column. Columns that are hidden from the display are also not printed, even if they are in the block that you select to print. This feature is useful for hiding salary and other confidential information. It is also useful to make it easier to work with a very wide spreadsheet.

If you have a spreadsheet that tracks payroll costs for all the employees and this spreadsheet contains prior data that is not relevant to the current period, you may elect to hide some of these columns. To hide a column, move the selector to one of the columns that you want to hide, press /, and select Style, Hide Column, and Hide. If you want to hide more than one contiguous column, type a period, and select the columns Quattro should hide by moving the selector to cover the adjoining columns that you want to hide. Then press ENTER.

When Quattro hides columns, it adjusts the display of the rest of the spreadsheet columns to the right of the hidden columns to display in the place of the hidden columns. However, Quattro does not reletter the columns as you can see in Figure 3.43, which has several hidden columns.

The contents in the hidden columns are still retained in memory. Any formulas that rely on hidden data are still accurate. Quattro will display these hidden columns whenever it is in POINT mode. This includes when you point to cells or blocks in formulas and commands that prompt for a block of cells. When the hidden columns are displayed, an asterisk appears next to the column letter.

To make hidden columns visible again, type /, and select Style, Hide Column, and Expose. When Quattro prompts for which columns to expose, move the selector to the column that you want to expose; or, if you want to expose more than one column, type a period, and stretch the selector to cover the remaining columns that you want to expose. If the columns that you want to expose are not adjoining, you can still expose them with one use of the command, since you can have the highlight extend over columns currently exposed. When the columns that you want exposed are highlighted, press ENTER.

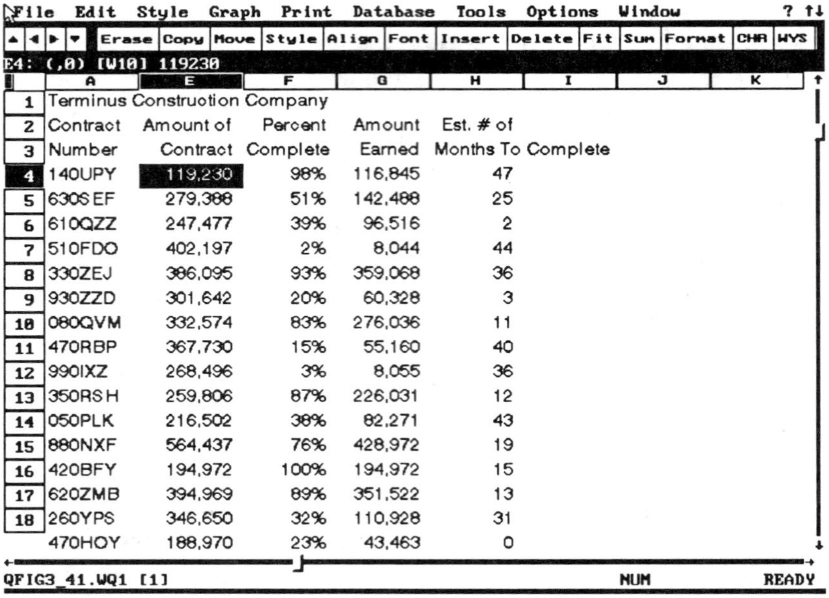

	A	E	F	G	H
1	Terminus Construction Company				
2	Contract	Amount of	Percent	Amount	Est. # of
3	Number	Contract	Complete	Earned	Months To Complete
4	140UPY	119,230	98%	116,845	47
5	630SEF	279,388	51%	142,488	25
6	610QZZ	247,477	39%	96,516	2
7	510FDO	402,197	2%	8,044	44
8	330ZEJ	386,095	93%	359,068	36
9	930ZZD	301,642	20%	60,328	3
10	080QVM	332,574	83%	276,036	11
11	470RBP	367,730	15%	55,160	40
12	990IXZ	268,496	3%	8,055	36
13	350RSH	259,806	87%	226,031	12
14	050PLK	216,502	38%	82,271	43
15	880NXF	564,437	76%	428,972	19
16	420BFY	194,972	100%	194,972	15
17	620ZMB	394,969	89%	351,522	13
18	260YPS	346,650	32%	110,928	31
	470HOY	188,970	23%	43,463	0

Figure 3.43 Spreadsheet with Hidden Columns

Changing Column Widths and Row Heights

When you start a new spreadsheet, the width of every column is set at the default width. This width is nine characters unless you change Quattro's default column width. This width lets you see eight or ten columns on the screen at once depending on the screen mode. You may want to change the width of a column to be either wider or narrower, depending on your data. Options in Quattro Pro let you set the column width for several columns and allow an automatic width setting that sets one or more columns to fit the widest data in a block. Quattro can change the width for all columns or a single column and can also reset a column width to the current default values. You can also change the height of a row or use the font size as the basis of the row's height.

CHANGING A COLUMN'S WIDTH To change the column width for a single column, use the **/Style Column Width** command. Move to the column whose width you want to change, press **/**, select **Style Column Width**, and respond to the prompt for another column width. This command has a shortcut key, CTRL-W, which you can press instead of entering **/Style Column Width**. Although you can type in a new number for a column width, Quattro provides another method: You can change the setting of the column width by pressing the right and left arrow keys. When you press the RIGHT ARROW key, the width of the column increases by one. As the column widens, Quattro displays formatted numbers that appear as asterisks as soon as the column is wide enough. On the other hand, when you press the LEFT ARROW key, the width decreases by one. If the new column width becomes too narrow to display any formatted numbers within the column, Quattro displays them as asterisks instead of numbers. When you have the column width that you want, press ENTER. Quattro shows the column whose width is being changed by displaying two arrows next to the column letter.

Using the arrow keys is the best method for changing the column width when you need to change it by a small amount. If you need to make a dramatic change in the width, typing the new column width or using Quattro's automatic column width is easier. This command can only change the width of one column at a time.

You can also change the column width with the mouse. To make the change, point to the column letter, press and hold the mouse button, and move the mouse left or right until the column is the desired width.

If you want to change the width of several adjacent columns you can use the **/Style Block Size** command (covered later in this section) or select a block containing several columns with the mouse or SHIFT-F7 (SELECT) before you select the **/Style Column Width** command. If you have a mouse, you can also change a column or a block of column's width using the mouse. First select the block containing the columns to change, and then click one of the column letters of the selected block and drag the mouse left or right to set the column width.

RESETTING THE WIDTH FOR A SINGLE COLUMN A column width set for an individual column remains fixed regardless of the changes you make to the default width. If you change the default width, you may want to reset columns that you previously had set individually. To reset a column width, move to the column that you want to reset, press **/**, and select **Style Reset Width**. Once you have chosen Reset Width, Quattro returns the column width to nine (or the current default column width).

CHANGING THE WIDTH OF SEVERAL COLUMNS If you have three adjacent columns that you want to change to the same width, altering the width for each of them separately is a waste of time. You can use the **/Style Block Size** command (called **/Style Block Widths** in previous releases). This command is an improvement over the **/Style Column Width** command, since it can change multiple columns at once. This command also can set the column widths based on the data in a block.

To reset the widths of multiple columns, move the selector to the first column whose width you wish to reset. Press **/**, and select **Style Block Size** to see the menu shown in Figure 3.44. Select Reset Width. When Quattro prompts for a block, select one cell from each column whose width you want to reset. You can type the block address, point to it with the directional keys, or use the mouse to select the block. When you press ENTER, Quattro resets the widths of all columns included in the block.

To set the widths of multiple columns, move the selector to the first column whose width you want to set. Press **/**, and select **Style Block Size Set Width**. When

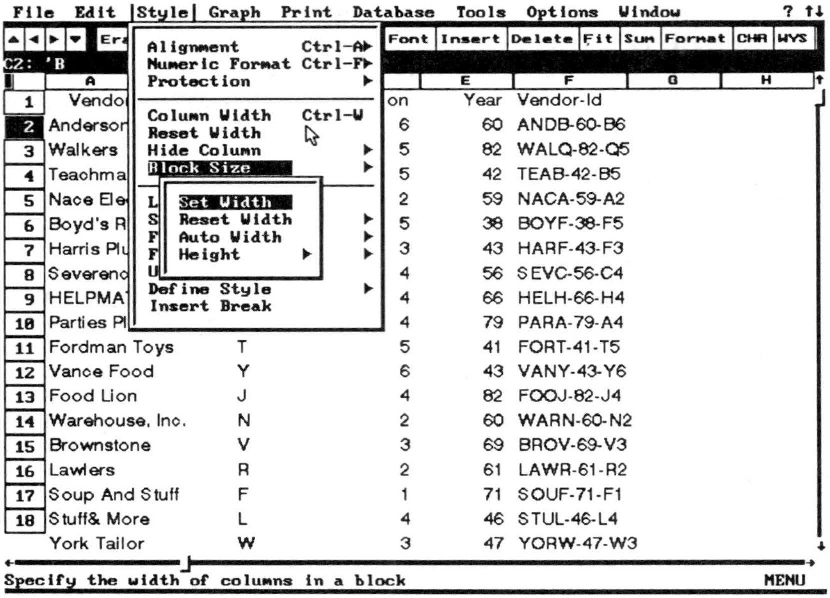

Figure 3.44 Menu Box for /Style Block Widths

Quattro prompts for a block, select one cell from each column whose width you want to set. You can type the block address, point to it with the directional keys, or use the mouse to select the block. When you press ENTER, Quattro prompts for the width for the columns. Like setting the width for a single column, you can type the column width or you can use the LEFT and RIGHT ARROW keys to set the width. When you have the column width that you want, press ENTER. Quattro shows the columns that are affected by displaying two arrows next to the column letter (as shown in Figure 3.45).

You can also use this command to tell Quattro to set the width of one or more columns so that it fits the columns' entries. To use this command to automatically set the widths of multiple columns, move the selector to the first column whose width you want set. Press /, and select Style Block Size Auto Width. Quattro will prompt you for the number of spaces you want between columns. This is the additional number of spaces above the minimum the column needs to display the widest entries in the block you will select. You can enter a new number, and press ENTER; or just press ENTER to accept Quattro's default of 1. Next Quattro prompts for a block, which should include all the cells that you want Quattro to use to determine how wide the column should be. This usually means that the block should include the widest entry in each column. You can also use this command with the default of one character between columns by clicking the FIT button in the SpeedBar to apply this command to the column containing the selector or to all columns in the selected block before you click the button. Figure 3.46 shows a spreadsheet that contains several columns that need to be widened

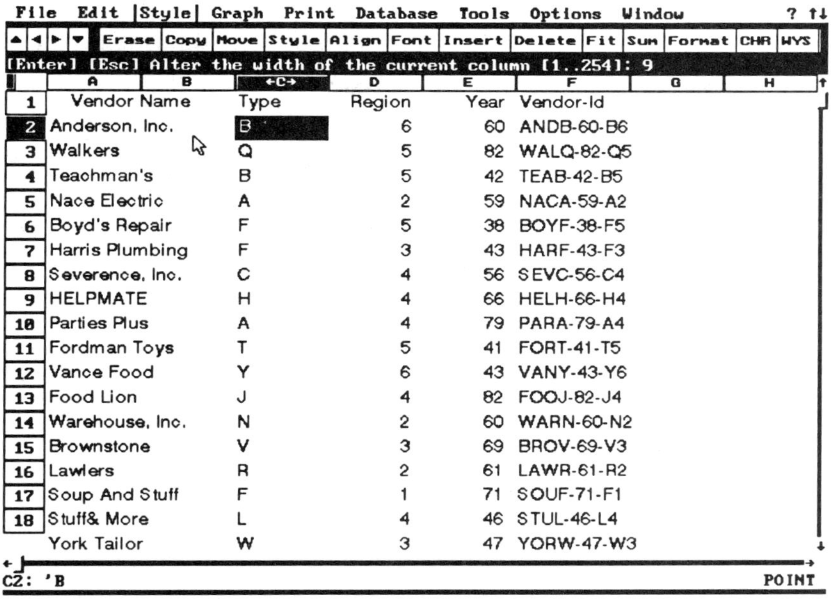

Working with Multiple Cells 113

	A	B	C	D	E	F	G	H
1	Vendor Name		Type	Region	Year	Vendor-Id		
2	Anderson, Inc.		B	6	60	ANDB-60-B6		
3	Walkers		Q	5	82	WALQ-82-Q5		
4	Teachman's		B	5	42	TEAB-42-B5		
5	Nace Electric		A	2	59	NACA-59-A2		
6	Boyd's Repair		F	5	38	BOYF-38-F5		
7	Harris Plumbing		F	3	43	HARF-43-F3		
8	Severence, Inc.		C	4	56	SEVC-56-C4		
9	HELPMATE		H	4	66	HELH-66-H4		
10	Parties Plus		A	4	79	PARA-79-A4		
11	Fordman Toys		T	5	41	FORT-41-T5		
12	Vance Food		Y	6	43	VANY-43-Y6		
13	Food Lion		J	4	82	FOOJ-82-J4		
14	Warehouse, Inc.		N	2	60	WARN-60-N2		
15	Brownstone		V	3	69	BROV-69-V3		
16	Lawlers		R	2	61	LAWR-61-R2		
17	Soup And Stuff		F	1	71	SOUF-71-F1		
18	Stuff& More		L	4	46	STUL-46-L4		
	York Tailor		W	3	47	YORW-47-W3		

Figure 3.45 Quattro Marks the Columns Whose Widths are Being Set

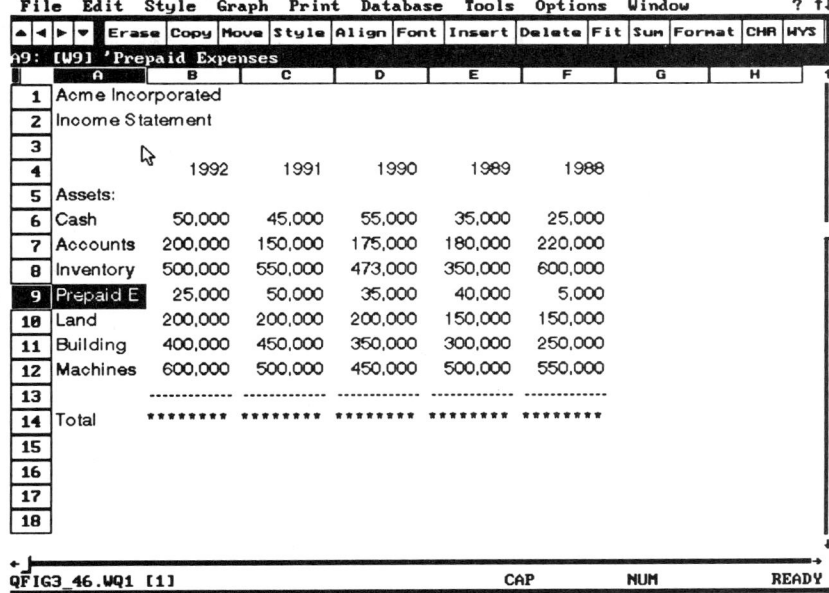

Figure 3.46 Spreadsheet with Columns Needing to be Widened

because of lengthy entries. In this spreadsheet, A1..F14 is selected as the block to automatically format. You can type the block address, point to it with the directional keys, or use the mouse to select the block. When you press ENTER, Quattro makes each column as wide as necessary to fit the widest entry in each column of the selected block plus the additional number of spaces you requested. Figure 3.47 shows Figure 3.46 after the columns have been widened automatically. This command will calculate the width of the column of characters either, in WYSIWYG display mode, taking into account the different widths of the characters in the font they use, or, if you are using Text mode, using the number of characters in the entries.

SETTING THE WIDTH FOR ALL COLUMNS You can change the widths of every column in the spreadsheet with the **/Options Formats Global Width** command. To use this command, press **/**, and select **Options Formats Global Width**. When you use this command, Quattro prompts you for a new column width. You can type a new width number or you can use the arrow keys to adjust the width one position at a time. Quattro adjusts all widths that have not been set with **/Style Column Width** or **/Style Block Size**. The number of columns that currently appear on the screen changes to fit the maximum number of columns. Some numbers in the spreadsheet may change to asterisks if the column width is insufficient or change from asterisks to numbers if the column width is expanded sufficiently. When you have the column set at the number of spaces that you want, press ENTER.

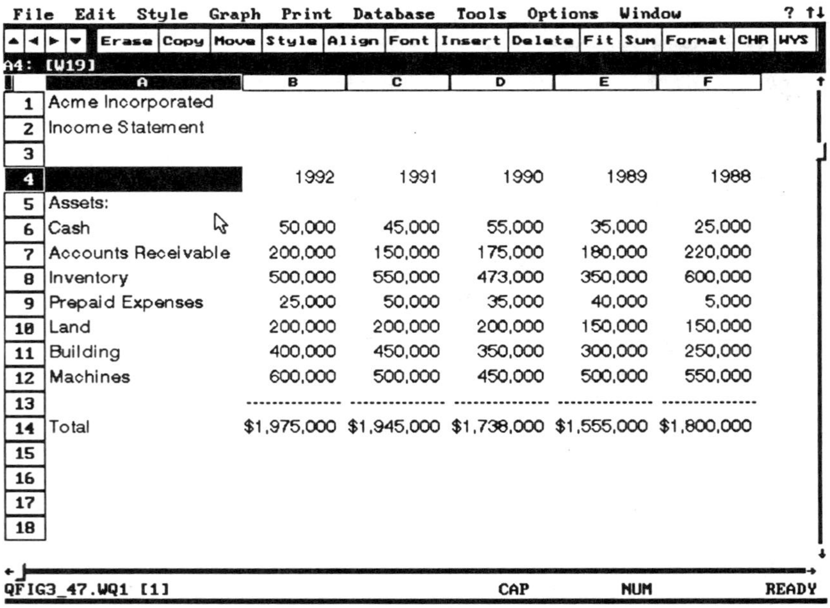
File Edit Style Graph Print Database Tools Options Window ?
Erase Copy Move Style Align Font Insert Delete Fit Sum Format CHR WYS
A4: [W19]
A B C D E F
1 Acme Incorporated
2 Income Statement
3
4 1992 1991 1990 1989 1988
5 Assets:
6 Cash 50,000 45,000 55,000 35,000 25,000
7 Accounts Receivable 200,000 150,000 175,000 180,000 220,000
8 Inventory 500,000 550,000 473,000 350,000 600,000
9 Prepaid Expenses 25,000 50,000 35,000 40,000 5,000
10 Land 200,000 200,000 200,000 150,000 150,000
11 Building 400,000 450,000 350,000 300,000 250,000
12 Machines 600,000 500,000 450,000 500,000 550,000
13
14 Total $1,975,000 $1,945,000 $1,738,000 $1,555,000 $1,800,000
15
16
17
18
QFIG3_47.WQ1 [1] CAP NUM READY

Figure 3.47 Spreadsheet with Columns Automatically Widened

> ▼ **TIP: Use space setting between columns for narrower columns.**
>
> If you need your columns narrower so more columns appear on the screen, set the column widths automatically using 1 space between columns containing labels and 0 spaces between columns containing numbers.

Just as when you are setting the width of an individual column, changing all columns by a few positions is best accomplished with the arrow keys. If you need to change the column width dramatically, typing the new column width is easier.

Since you are changing the widths of all columns, it does not matter which column you are in when you perform this command. Changing the global width of columns only affects the current spreadsheet. Also, this command does not affect any columns that have had their widths changed with the /Style Column Width or /Style Block Widths commands. To use the default column width for columns that have been changed with the /Style Column Width command, you must first reset the column width to the default setting.

SETTING THE ROW HEIGHT In Quattro Pro 3 and above, you can also set the height of the rows. Initially, Quattro Pro sets the row heights to the appropriate height of the tallest font in the row. You may want to use a different row height than the default or return a modified row to the default. For example, you may have a block to print and you want it printed double spaced, which you can do by doubling the row height of the block of text. To change the row height, select a block containing cells from the rows you want to change, and select the /Style Block Size Height command. This presents an additional menu containing Set Row Height and Reset Row Height. After selecting an option, you must select the block containing the rows you want to change, unless you selected a block before selecting the command. If you select Reset Row Height, the row height is returned to the default of the row height most appropriate for the tallest text on the row. If you select Set Row Height, you must also enter a number between 1 and 240 representing the number of points high you want the row or rows. A point is 1/72 of an inch. You will want a row height larger than the height of the text. If the row height is shorter than the text, the larger text will be cut off at the top of the row. If you are in WYSIWYG display mode, you will see the changed row height. If you are in text display mode, you will not see a difference; but when you print using a graphics printer as described in the next chapter, you will see the printed copy uses the row height you select.

You can also change a row or a block of rows height using the mouse. First select the block containing the rows to change, and then click one of the row numbers of the selected block and drag the mouse up or down to set the selected rows to the new height.

TITLES

When your spreadsheets stretch beyond one screen, it is difficult to remember what every row and column represents. Quattro lets you freeze rows and/or columns in the spreadsheet to keep labels at the top and left of the spreadsheet. With rows and/or columns frozen, Quattro uses the remaining portion of the display window for other spreadsheet information.

To create a title, move the selector so the columns and/or rows you always want displayed on the screen are to the left and/or at the top of the spreadsheet area. Then move the selector to the row just below the title row and/or to the column to the right of the title column. Next, type /, and select **Window Options Locked Titles**. Then choose Horizontal, Vertical, or Both. If you select Horizontal, every row above the selector is frozen in place. If you select Vertical, every column to the left of the selector is frozen in place. If you select Both, every row above the selector and every column to the left of the selector are frozen in place.

After you have chosen an option to control the extent of the title freezing, Quattro freezes the rows and/or columns and displays them in a different color. In Figure 3.48 rows 1 through 3 and columns A and B are frozen. Chapter 10 will describe how you can make the titles appear in a different color. When you have frozen rows and/or columns, Quattro does not allow you to move the selector into the title row and/or columns. However, if you press F5 (GOTO) and type in the

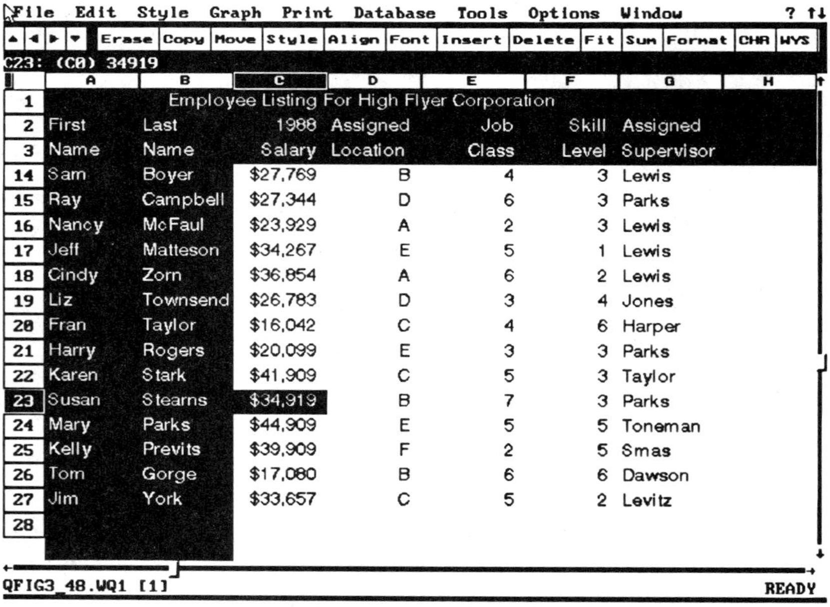

Figure 3.48 Spreadsheet with Titles

address of a cell in one of the title rows and/or columns, Quattro moves the selector to the cell in the remaining spreadsheet window and displays two copies of the titles, as shown in Figure 3.49. Any change that you make to one copy of a title cell is reflected in the other. Moving out of the title area in any direction that causes the screen to scroll removes the second copy from the display.

To clear your titles, use the **/Window Options Locked Titles Clear** command. After this command, Quattro no longer freezes any rows or columns.

WINDOW OPTIONS FOR A SINGLE SPREADSHEET

Quattro uses the spreadsheet area to display spreadsheet windows. Quattro has many features that change how it displays your spreadsheet windows. Some of these options that apply to multiple spreadsheets are discussed in Chapter 5. However, several features accessed through Quattro's **/Window** pull-down menu also apply to a single spreadsheet. You can split a single spreadsheet window into two panes (either vertically or horizontally) and look at two different portions of your spreadsheet at once. You can also choose whether the panes move independently or together. Additional options for a spreadsheet window or a single pane can hide the row and column labels and can show the entries in a map view, which shows the types of entries made in each cell.

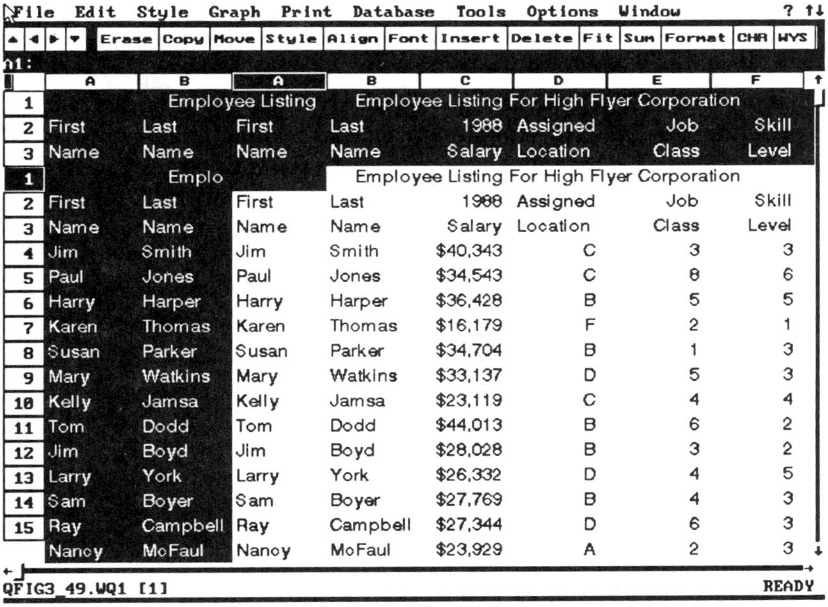

File Edit Style Graph Print Database Tools Options Window ? ↑↓

▲ ◄ ► ▼ Erase Copy Move Style Align Font Insert Delete Fit Sum Format CHR WYS

A1:

	A	B	A	B	C	D	E	F
1		Employee Listing		Employee Listing For High Flyer Corporation				
2	First	Last	First	Last	1988	Assigned	Job	Skill
3	Name	Name	Name	Name	Salary	Location	Class	Level
1		Emplo		Employee Listing For High Flyer Corporation				
2	First	Last	First	Last	1988	Assigned	Job	Skill
3	Name	Name	Name	Name	Salary	Location	Class	Level
4	Jim	Smith	Jim	Smith	$40,343	C	3	3
5	Paul	Jones	Paul	Jones	$34,543	C	8	6
6	Harry	Harper	Harry	Harper	$36,428	B	5	5
7	Karen	Thomas	Karen	Thomas	$16,179	F	2	1
8	Susan	Parker	Susan	Parker	$34,704	B	1	3
9	Mary	Watkins	Mary	Watkins	$33,137	D	5	3
10	Kelly	Jamsa	Kelly	Jamsa	$23,119	C	4	4
11	Tom	Dodd	Tom	Dodd	$44,013	B	6	2
12	Jim	Boyd	Jim	Boyd	$28,028	B	3	2
13	Larry	York	Larry	York	$26,332	D	4	5
14	Sam	Boyer	Sam	Boyer	$27,769	B	4	3
15	Ray	Campbell	Ray	Campbell	$27,344	D	6	3
	Nancy	McFaul	Nancy	McFaul	$23,929	A	2	3

QFIG3_49.WQ1 [1] READY

Figure 3.49 Spreadsheet with Two Copies of Titles

Creating Window Panes

To split the spreadsheet window into two window panes, move the selector to the location where you want the split to occur. Type /, and select Window Options. Select Horizontal if you want to split your spreadsheet horizontally as shown in Figure 3.50. Select Vertical if you want to split your spreadsheet vertically as shown in Figure 3.51.

When you select Horizontal, Quattro puts all the rows above the selector into the first pane and all the remaining rows into the second pane. When you select Vertical, Quattro puts all columns to the left of the selector into the first pane and the rest of the columns in the second pane.

While you are using panes, some Quattro commands affect both panes, and some affect only one. For example, you can hide columns, expose columns, make titles, clear titles, change column widths, and change the default display format in one pane without affecting the other pane. The remaining commands operate on both panes.

Even though the display looks as if it is splitting the spreadsheet into two, it is not. The panes do not split the spreadsheet but provide two different views of the same spreadsheet.

To switch from one pane to another, press F6 (PANE) or click a cell in the other pane with the mouse. The selector is in the current pane at all times.

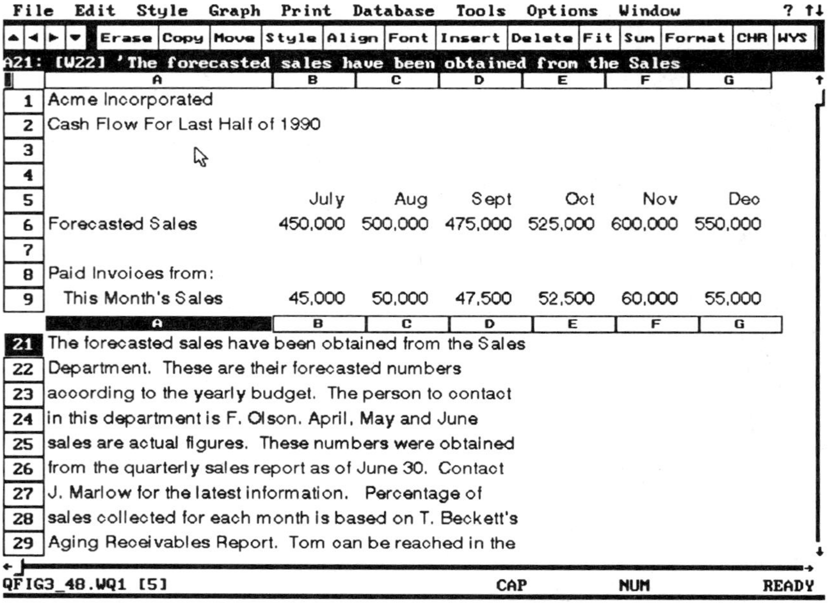

Figure 3.50 Spreadsheet with Horizontal Panes

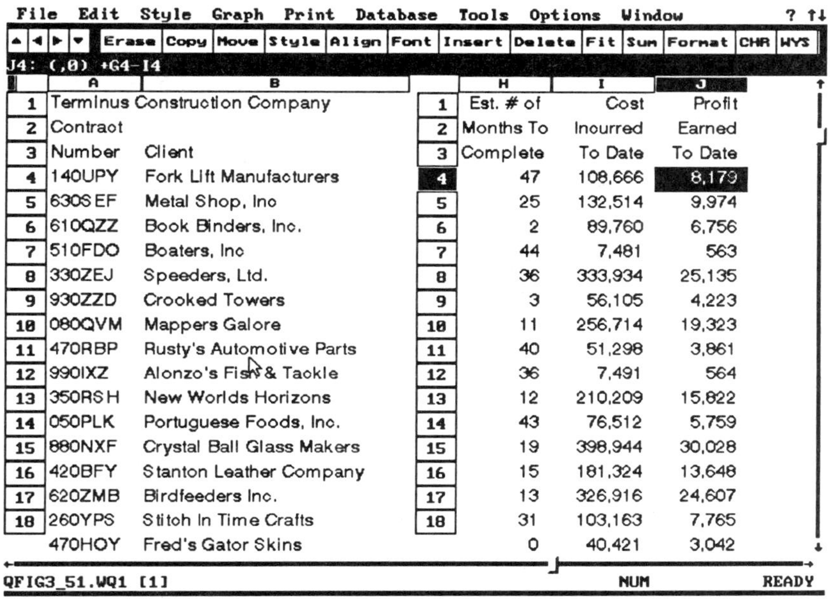

Working with Multiple Cells

[spreadsheet screenshot]

Figure 3.51 Spreadsheet with Vertical Panes

Synchronizing Windows

Each pane can display information from different areas of the spreadsheet. As you move in one pane, it can affect the current pane, and it also can be synchronized with the other one. For example, if your spreadsheet with horizontal panes is synchronized, both panes display the same columns. Quattro moves the inactive pane when you move the current pane to the left or right. If your spreadsheet with vertical panes is synchronized, both panes display the same rows. Quattro moves the inactive pane when you move the current pane up or down. If a spreadsheet with either type of pane is not synchronized, moving one pane around in the spreadsheet has no effect on the other pane's position.

Quattro normally has the panes move in synchronization. However, to make them unsynchronized, use the /Window Options Unsync command. To make unsynchronized panes synchronous again, use the /Window Options Sync command.

Removing a Window

To return the two panes to a single spreadsheet window, use the /Window Options Clear command. When you execute this command, Quattro removes the right or bottom pane. Any changes that were made in an upper or left pane are retained when the spreadsheet is returned to one view.

Showing a Map of a Spreadsheet

The types of entries you make in each cell may seem obvious by its appearance. However, an entry can be a formula, label, or number but seem like a different type of entry. Quattro can show a spreadsheet in a map view that identifies the type of entry made in each cell. The map view tells if each cell contains a circular reference, formula, label, link formula (discussed in Chapter 5), or number. To show a map view of the current spreadsheet, enter /Window Options Map View Yes. If the spreadsheet window is split into panes, this command only affects the current pane. Figure 3.52 shows a spreadsheet window divided into two panes with the

---

▼ **TIP: Use map view to search for types of entries**

You can use the /Edit Search & Replace Command with a map view to find types of entries by entering the character for the type of entries (such as c) as the search string and set Look In to Value.

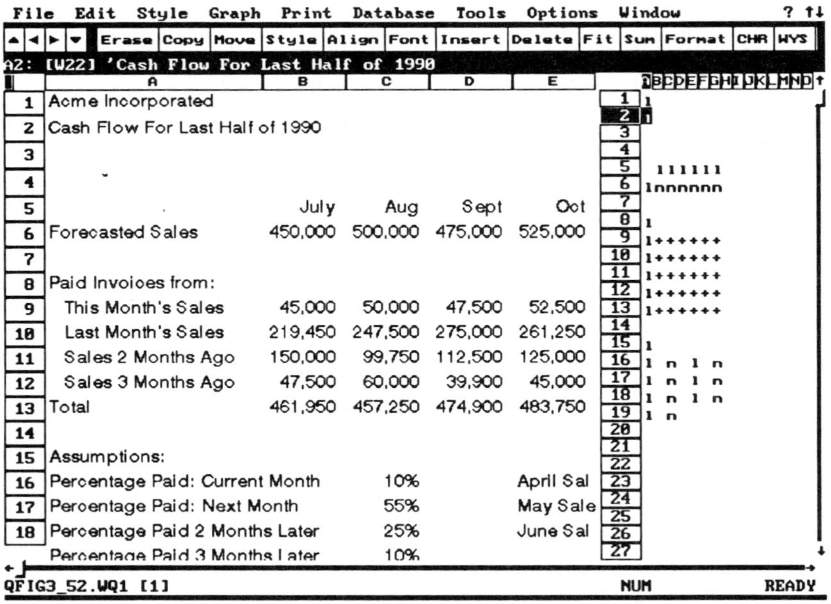

Figure 3.52 One Pane Showing Map View of Spreadsheet in Other Pane

right window showing the map view. In a map view, a "c" represents a circular reference, a "g" represents an inserted graph (covered in Chapter 7), an "l" represents a label, a "+" represents a formula, a "-" represents a link formula, and an "n" represents a number. To return to the regular display enter /Window Options Map View No.

Hiding and Displaying Cell Grid Lines

With the WYSIWYG display, Quattro Pro can display grid lines indicating the boundaries of each cell. You can display or hide these lines. To hide these lines, select /Windows Options Grid Lines Hide. This hides the grid lines just like the grid lines in Figure 3.53 (which also has the row and column borders in the left pane hidden as described below). When you want to display the grid lines, select /Windows Options Grid Lines Display.

Hiding Column and Row Borders

Quattro has several methods of letting you know your current location in the spreadsheet. It shows the selector's address in the input line, and it has the

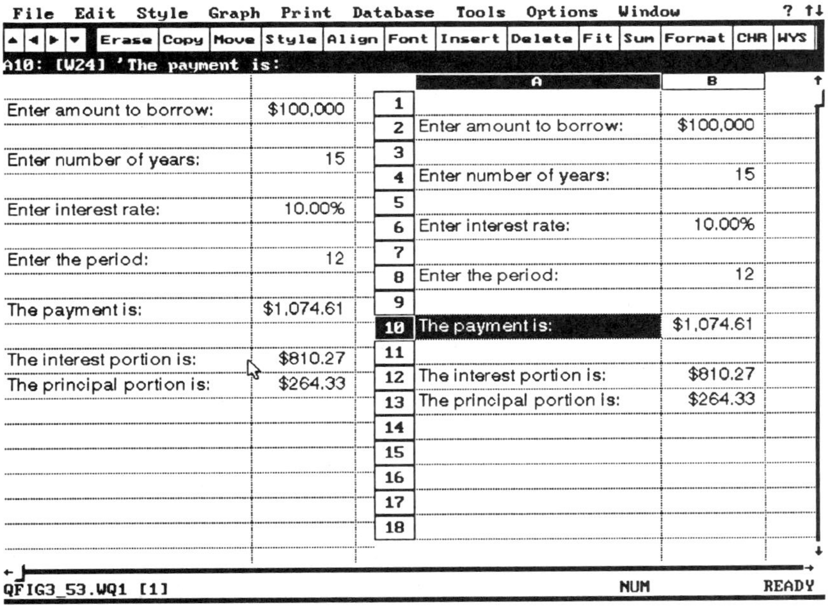

Figure 3.53 Pane Showing Spreadsheet Without Column and Row Borders

selector's position and the column letters and row numbers along the left and top side of the spreadsheet area marked with a different color. You can hide the column letters and row numbers. If you do so, Quattro will use this area for spreadsheet data. You may want to hide the column letters and row numbers when you are creating a model that someone else will use. For example, you can limit which cells a user can access to enter data and hide the column and row borders so the data entry screen looks customized. To hide the column letters and row numbers, enter /Window Options Row & Col Borders Hide. If the spreadsheet window is split into panes, this command only affects the current pane. Figure 3.53 shows a spreadsheet window with one pane displaying the column letters and row numbers and the other pane hiding them. To restore the column letters and row numbers, enter /Window Options Row & Col Borders Display.

ADDING FONTS, BULLETS, LINES, BOXES, AND SHADING

So far you have learned a few ways to enhance a spreadsheet's appearance. Quattro Pro offers additional spreadsheet enhancements by letting you add lines, boxes, and shading to your spreadsheets. You can also change the fonts the spreadsheet uses and add bullet characters. Quattro Pro 4 has added new features through named styles. Named styles let you create a group of spreadsheet formats that you can assign to spreadsheet blocks rather than applying separate commands to add the formats that the named styles represent. Named styles also provide additional features such as letting you create numerical formats that are not part of the default numerical formats available with the /Style Numeric Format command. You can use these features to customize the spreadsheet's appearance.

Using Different Fonts

Up to this point, your printouts have used one font. A font is typeface, size, style, and color in which the characters appear. You can use multiple fonts to create a professional looking spreadsheet. The many fonts that Quattro provides can be classified into three types. Quattro supplies Hershey fonts, which can be used with most printers. Quattro also provides Swiss, Dutch, and Courier Bitstream fonts (fonts that are created with software). These fonts take more disk space but look the best. Finally, Quattro can use the PostScript or Hewlett-Packard printer fonts that your printer can provide. If you have a Hewlett-Packard LaserJet with printer cartridges, you must tell Quattro which cartridges you are using as described later in this chapter. With Quattro, you can use menu commands to select which cells use which font. This is an advantage over other spreadsheet packages that require you to supply special printer codes if the entire spreadsheet or a line of the spreadsheet uses a different font. When you change the fonts in Quattro's WYSIWYG display mode, Quattro displays the fonts properly. In text display mode and in earlier Quattro Pro releases, Quattro does not change the appearance of the spreadsheet. When you preview the spreadsheet or print it to the graphics printer, you will see the new font. To use different fonts in your spreadsheet, you must select the fonts you want, and then select the cells in which you want to use the font. Changing fonts in Quattro Pro 4 is different from changing the fonts in earlier releases, since Quattro Pro 4 has two commands for setting spreadsheet fonts.

When you use a Bitstream font for the first time, Quattro Pro will build a font file for the font size you are using and display a message on the screen. These font files are kept on disk, so the next time you use the font combination, the font file is readily available to be used. Quattro Pro 4 includes both regular Bitstream fonts and faster Bitstream fonts which have a -SC suffix.

You can use the Bitstream fonts to print international characters (characters that are not used in the English language). Unless you selected Standard European for the character set during the installation program, you will need to make two changes. First, you will need to rename all files in your Quattro Pro directory with .SFO extensions so that they have .SFR extensions. Next, you will need to delete all the files in the \QPRO\FONTS subdirectory. After making these two changes, the Bitstream fonts Quattro builds will contain an additional 42 characters. Since building font files with international characters takes longer and the files are bigger, only make these changes if you are printing international characters with graphics quality. If your spreadsheet includes a character that is not part of the Bitstream font character set, it is displayed as a question mark.

SELECTING FONTS FOR A SPREADSHEET IN QUATTRO PRO 4 To select the font a block uses, use the **/S**tyle Font command, or click Font or FNT in the SpeedBar. Next, select the block that you want to change the font and press ENTER. This presents the menu in Figure 3.54. With **T**ypeface, you can select any of the installed Bitstream, Hershey, and printer typefaces shown in Figure 3.55 for the default printer. With some printer fonts, you will select the size and style as well as the typeface. With **P**oint Size, you can select from any of the available sizes listed. With **B**old, **I**talic, and **U**nderlined, you can select them to turn the style on or select it again to turn the style off. You can also remove the styles you have added by selecting **R**eset. With **C**olor, you can select the color a font uses. Once the font you want is selected, choose **Q**uit. Figure 3.56 shows a spreadsheet that is enhanced using additional fonts as well as bullets and lines. Different fonts are used to italicize and boldface text as well as different typeface styles.

If you want to apply the same font changes to multiple blocks, you may want to use the **/S**tyle Font**T**able command described next to assign up to eight fonts, and use the font numbers instead of changing the font for each block you want to change. Another option for fonts that you can combine with other style changes is to create a named style that represents the font you want and any other changes you want to apply to blocks.

124 *Quattro Pro 4.0 Handbook*

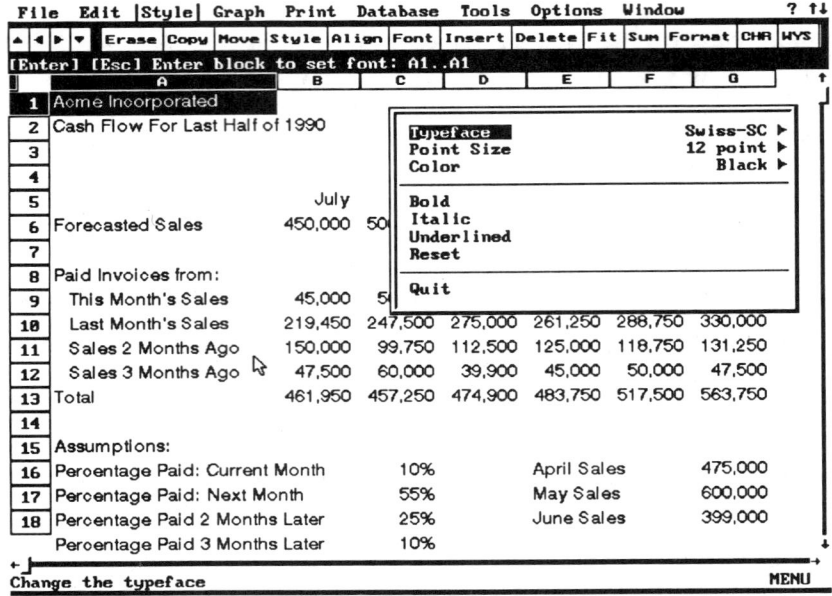

Figure 3.54 Menu for Editing Fonts

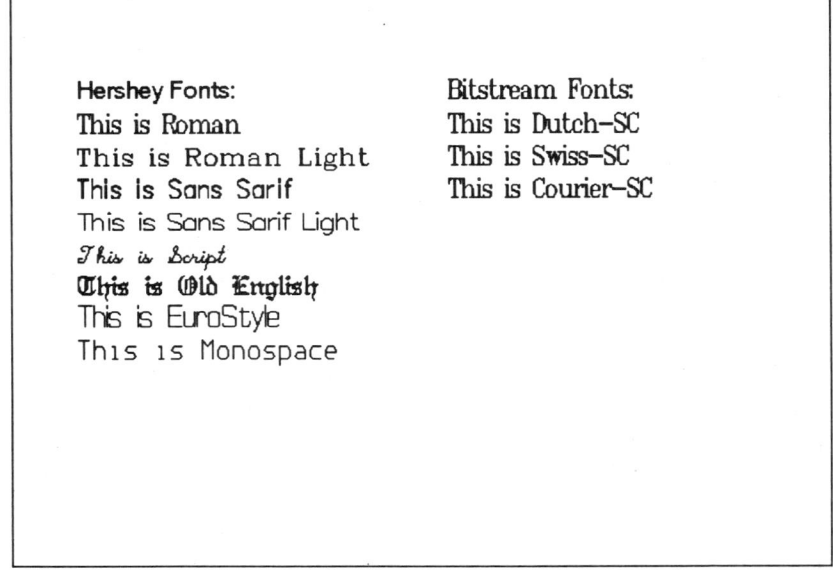

Figure 3.55 Sample Fonts

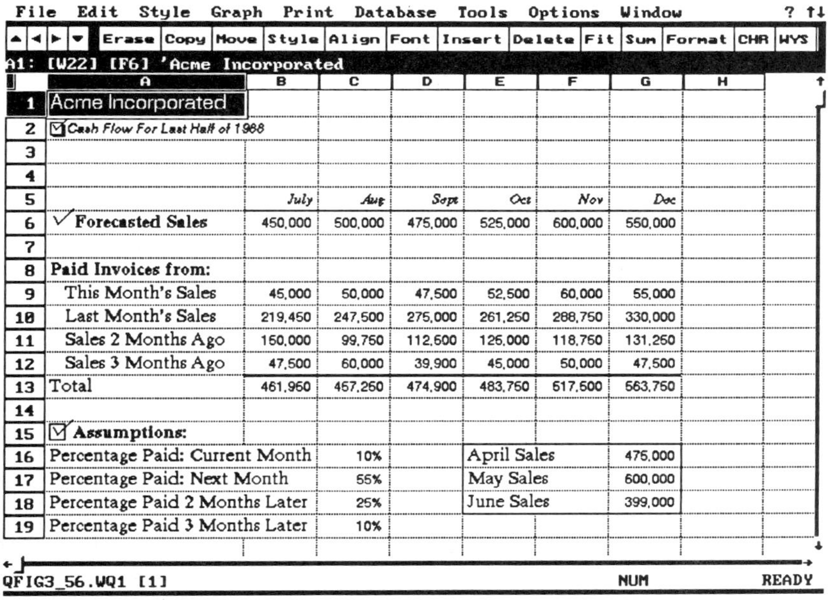

Working with Multiple Cells 125

```
  File   Edit   Style   Graph   Print   Database   Tools   Options   Window            ? ↑↓
```

	A	B	C	D	E	F	G	H
1	Acme Incorporated							
2	☑ Cash Flow For Last Half of 1988							
3								
4								
5		July	Aug	Sept	Oct	Nov	Dec	
6	✓ Forecasted Sales	450,000	500,000	475,000	525,000	600,000	550,000	
7								
8	Paid Invoices from:							
9	This Month's Sales	45,000	50,000	47,500	52,500	60,000	55,000	
10	Last Month's Sales	219,450	247,500	275,000	261,250	288,750	330,000	
11	Sales 2 Months Ago	150,000	99,750	112,500	125,000	118,750	131,250	
12	Sales 3 Months Ago	47,500	60,000	39,900	45,000	50,000	47,500	
13	Total	461,950	457,250	474,900	483,750	517,500	563,750	
14								
15	☑ Assumptions:							
16	Percentage Paid: Current Month		10%		April Sales		476,000	
17	Percentage Paid: Next Month		55%		May Sales		600,000	
18	Percentage Paid 2 Months Later		25%		June Sales		399,000	
19	Percentage Paid 3 Months Later		10%					

QFIG3_56.WQ1 [1]   NUM   READY

Figure 3.56   Spreadsheet Enhanced by Using Additional Fonts

SELECTING FONTS WITH THE FONT TABLE The other method of changing the fonts in a spreadsheet is to change the table of eight fonts. This is the only method for changing the fonts in Quattro Pro 3 or earlier, although you can also use it in Quattro Pro 4 in place of the /Style Font command.

The first step to using fonts with Quattro is selecting the eight fonts in the font table. To select fonts, use the /Style FontTable Edit Fonts command (/Style Font Edit Fonts in Quattro Pro 3 and earlier). After you enter /Style Font, Quattro displays a box with numbers (1-8) for the font table. Next to each number is a font description. After you enter Edit Fonts, Quattro lists fonts 1 through 8 with descriptions, Reset, Update, and the Quit option, which returns you to the READY mode. You can select Reset when you want to return the fonts listed to the default fonts, or Update when you want to make the fonts listed to be the default fonts. Next, you select a number between 1 and 8 to change a font in the current font table. Since Quattro uses font 1 as the default font, this is always the font used when no other font is selected. Once you select a number, Quattro displays the menu containing Typeface, Point Size, Style, Color, and Quit. The Typeface, Point Size, Color, and Quit are identical to the same named options for the /Style Font command described previously. When you select Style, you can have the Bold, Italics, Underlined, and Reset options that you previously saw with the /Style Font command. You can make font selections for each of the eight slots in the font table. These eight fonts can be assigned to your spreadsheet entries.

USING FONTS IN A SPREADSHEET Once you select fonts for the font table, you select the fonts for particular spreadsheet cells with the /Style FontTable command (/Style Font in Quattro Pro 3 and earlier), and select a number, 1 through 8, to represent the font in the font table that you want a block to use. Then you select the block to use this font, unless you have selected a block before selecting the command. Quattro Pro 3 and 4 will show the font on the screen as it will appear when printed. Earlier releases will only show the selected font when you print the spreadsheet.

The entire spreadsheet uses font 1 unless another font is selected. If you want the fonts you have selected to become the default fonts to be used by all new worksheets, select /Style FontTable Update. Later, if you want to return to the default font selections, select /Style FontTable Reset.

SETTING WHEN QUATTRO BUILDS FONTS Quattro initially builds Bitstream fonts whenever it needs a font that is not already created. The /Options Graphics Quality command lets you decide when Quattro builds a Bitstream font. The Draft option does not build Bitstream fonts. If you try using a Bitstream font that is not built yet, Quattro substitutes a similar Hershey font in its place. The Final option builds fonts whenever Quattro needs a Bitstream font that you have not built yet. Quattro uses different Bitstream fonts for previewing and printing. Changing when Quattro Pro builds fonts also affects the WYSIWYG display and when Quattro Pro builds fonts that appear on the screen.

The font files, which have .FON and .FN2 extensions, can use much space on your hard disk. If your hard disk needs space, you can delete the files with .FON and .FN2 extensions in the fonts subdirectory. After you delete the font files, Quattro must rebuild them as it needs them, but you will end up with less font files on your disk. If you selectively delete font files, you also must delete INDEX.FON. This file contains a list of the Bitstream fonts, which have been built. If you do not delete this file, Quattro might try using a font that needs to be rebuilt.

USING BSINST TO LOAD NEW FONTS While Quattro includes some Bitstream fonts, the Bitstream company creates other fonts that you can also use with Quattro. To use a Bitstream font other than the ones supplied with Quattro, you will need to use the SPDINST or BSINST program to load the Bitstream fonts to your hard disk. Use SPDINST for Bitstream-SC fonts and BSINST for old Bitstream fonts. To load a Bitstream font, you must be in DOS (either exit Quattro or temporarily exit Quattro with the /File Utilities DOS Shell command). At the DOS prompt, enter **SPDINST** or **BSINST** followed by the drive and directory containing the .BCO font files. The program creates the .SFO or .SFR font files in the QPRO directory that Quattro uses to build the .FON and .FN2 files. If you only want to load one Bitstream font, include the name of the .BCO file you want to load after the drive and directory information. You must load the font files for Quattro even if you have already loaded the same font files for another program. Loading the files is not the same as building fonts to preview and print the spreadsheets. As you use the Bitstream files you have loaded, Quattro builds the individual font file for that particular point size and style of font.

USING PRINTER CARTRIDGE FONTS Two of the most popular printers, the Hewlett-Packard LaserJet and the Canon LBP, offer additional character sets through cartridges that are inserted in the machine. Quattro can also use these fonts. To use one of these fonts, you must tell Quattro which cartridge you have in either the left or right cartridge holder. You can give Quattro this information by using the /Options Hardware Printers Fonts Cartridge Fonts command. After you select Left Cartridge or Right Cartridge, Quattro lists the available font cartridge names. Once you select a font cartridge, you can select Quit, Update, and Quit to save the changes and return to the spreadsheet. The next time you edit the typeface of one of the fonts, the font cartridges are listed with the printer-specific fonts.

Using Bullet Characters

You can add bullet characters to your printouts for emphasis. A bullet character is primarily used for text. To add a bullet character to a spreadsheet cell, enter **\bullet #** (instead of the # symbol, enter a number between 0 and 6). Each number represents a different bullet character as shown in Figure 3.57. If the bullet character is the first character in the cell, you must type a label prefix character first so Quattro does not misrepresent the cell's contents as a repeating label. You can put a bullet character anywhere in a cell's entry. When you preview or print a spreadsheet with a bullet character, or if you are using Quattro Pro's WYSIWYG display mode, Quattro displays the **\bullet #** entry as the actual bullet character. In text display mode, you will see **\bullet #** in place of the bullet.

Adding Lines and Boxes

Adding lines and boxes can separate data and provide dividing lines between sections of the spreadsheet. To create a line or box, use the /Style Line Drawing command. When Quattro prompts you for a block, select the cells that you want to draw a line in or around. Once you press ENTER, Quattro displays the menu in Figure 3.58. This option describes all the choices for line placement in the block you select, including a line box around the entire block. If you want a box around the entire group of cells, select Outside. If you want lines drawn in other places, select the appropriate option. Once you select the location of the line, Quattro prompts for the type of line. Your selections are None, Single, Double, or Thick. Once the line type is selected, you are returned to the box in Figure 3.58 to select more lines or to select Quit to return to the spreadsheet. Figure 3.59 shows several

128 Quattro Pro 4.0 Handbook

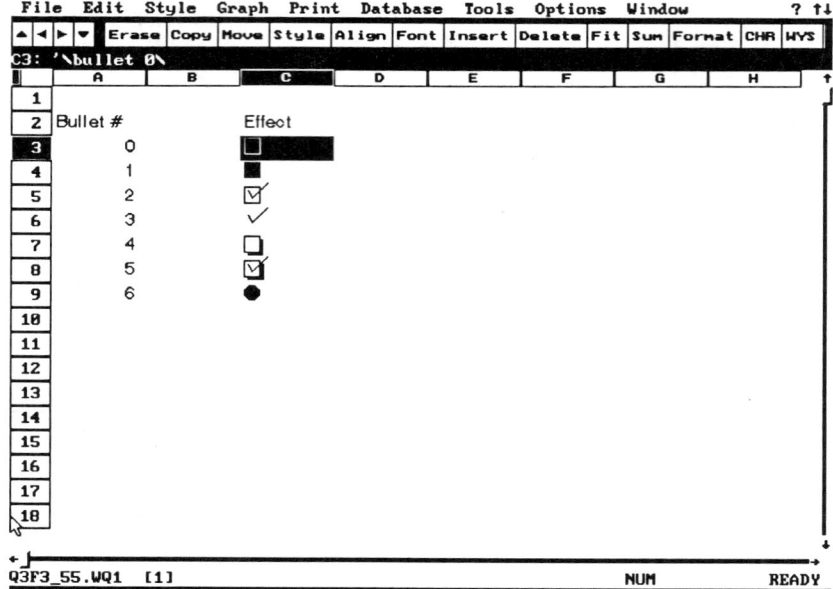

Figure 3.57 Sample Bullet Characters

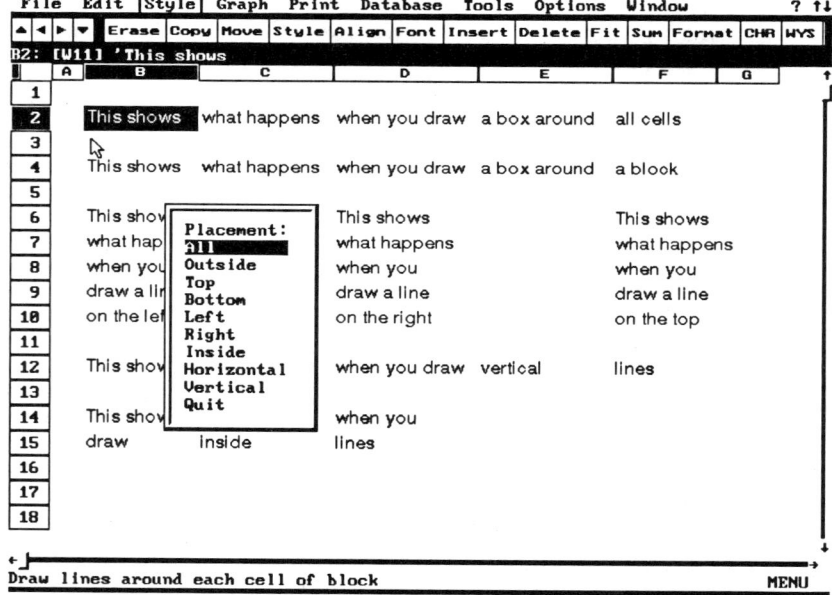

Figure 3.58 Selection Box for Line Types

Working with Multiple Cells

examples of lines drawn in a spreadsheet. In WYSIWYG display mode, these lines appear as shown in Figure 3.59. In text display mode, when you draw lines, Quattro adjusts the heights and widths of the cells. When you draw boxes in cells (the **All** option), the width of each column must be sufficient to show all of the text; otherwise, the box will truncate the display. Also, if you are drawing a box around a block of cells (the **Outside** option), the block you select must include the cells that the labels borrow space from. For example if you are drawing a box around the text in A1 and A2 and the text in these two cells uses the display space of columns B and C, you must use the block A1..C2 as the block you want to draw a line around (or you must widen column A).

If you want to remove some lines, use the **/Style Line Drawing** command, select the block from which you want to remove lines, select the type of lines you want to remove, and choose **None** for the line type. The line types stay with the cells. If you copy the cells, the lines are also copied. If you erase the cell's contents, the lines will remain. When adjoining cells also have lines, Quattro will join the line types if possible.

Adding Shading

Just as you can use lines and boxes to emphasize and customize the spreadsheet data, you can use shading for the same purposes. To shade cells, you use the **/Style**

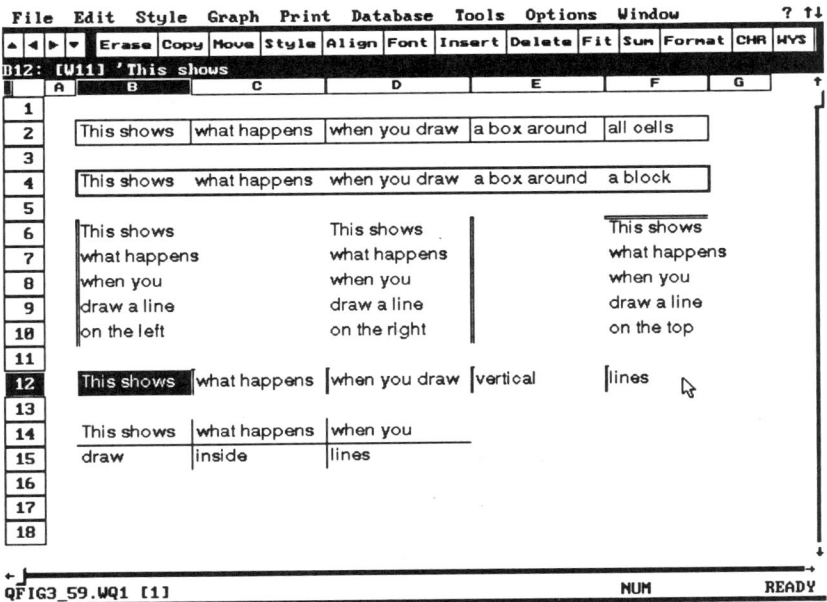

Figure 3.59 Spreadsheet with Different Types of Lines

Shading command. After entering this command, Quattro prompts you for the type of shading with the selections of **None**, **G**rey, and **B**lack. When Quattro prompts you for a block, select the cells that you want shaded. Once you press ENTER, all the cells in the block are shaded. In text display mode, Quattro displays characters in a grey-shaded area as white characters with a black background. Figure 3.60 shows a spreadsheet using shading to emphasize the sections of the spreadsheet that will be filled in by the people taking inventory. If you are using a Hewlett-Packard LaserJet Series III printer, you can select the shading level the printer uses for the shade block as described in the next chapter.

If you want to remove shading, use the **/**Style **S**hading **N**one command, and select the block in which you want to remove the shading. Shading stays with the cells. If you copy or move the cells, the shading appears in the copied cells or with the cells in their new location.

Named Styles

Quattro Pro 4 has named styles that let you assign a name to a group of styles just as you learned earlier that you could assign a name to a block and use the block name to refer to the block's contents. Once a named style is created, you can assign the styles that the named style represents by assigning the named style to blocks in your spreadsheet. Named styles can include fonts, line drawings, shading, alignment, data entry limitations made with the **/D**atabase **D**ata **E**ntry command, and numerical formats. With the numerical format you can create more numerical formats in addition to those available with the **/S**tyle **N**umeric **F**ormat command.

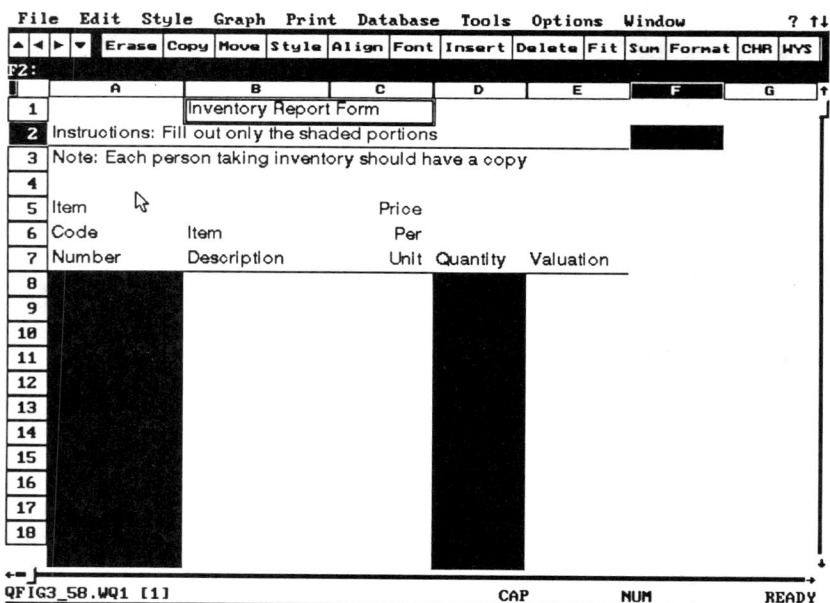

Figure 3.60 Spreadsheet Using Shading to Emphasize Columns

Named styles makes enhancing your spreadsheet's appearance easier. You can assign blocks in your spreadsheet to a style, and then edit the style to change the block's appearance rather than separately apply the commands. For example, when you are developing a report, you can assign blocks that you want to be treated identically, and then edit the styles until the report has the appearance you want.

CREATING A NAMED STYLE Creating a named style is as simple as telling Quattro Pro the name you want to use for the named style and the Quattro Pro styles the named style represents. You have two choices. You can assign the styles to a block that you want the named style to represent and then use the block to tell Quattro Pro the styles the named style represents. You can also tell Quattro Pro the named style you are creating and use a menu to select the styles that are represented by the named style. For example, suppose you want a named style called HEADING that centers its entries, boldfaces them with a Swiss 16 point font, and has a line at the bottom of the cell. You can use the /Style commands to change a cell's font, alignment, and lines, and then use this cell to tell Quattro Pro what styles HEADING represents; or you can tell Quattro Pro that you want to create a named style called HEADING, and then use its own menu to tell Quattro Pro that HEADING centers its entries using a Swiss 16 point bold font and a line at the bottom of the cell. To create a named style, select **/Style Define Style Create**. Next, type the name for the named style, and press ENTER. This displays a menu like the one in Figure 3.61. The initial settings of each of the menu options matches the first cell in any block currently selected when you select this command or the styles assigned to the

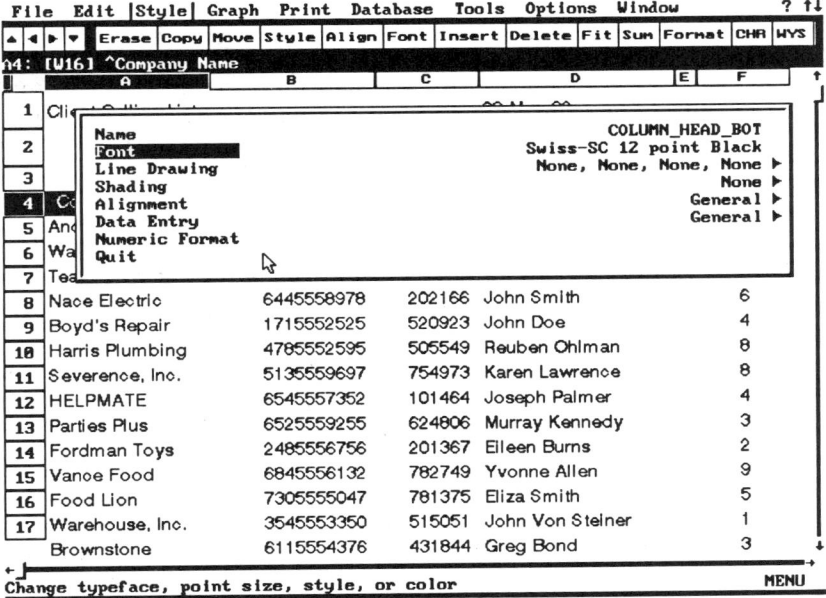

Figure 3.61 Menu for Selecting Styles a Named Style Represents

current selector's cell. In Figure 3.61, the menu is blank except for the font, since the current cell has no styles assigned to it. Like using the commands in the Style menu, you can select these menu options and make selections similar to the ones you would make with the individual /Style commands. The only difference is Line Drawing and Numeric Format. When you select Line Drawing, you select the side of the cell that you will draw a line and then select the type of line you are drawing. When you select Numeric Format, you have the additional option of User Defined, which you can select to create additional numerical formats that Quattro Pro does not automatically provide. When you have finished defining the styles represented by the style name, select Quit to return to the menu that you selected when you chose /Style Define Style. Next, select Quit. You are returned to the spreadsheet, so at this point you can use the /Style Use Named Style command to apply the named style. You can continue adding named styles for the different styles your spreadsheet uses up to 120 styls names.

If you later want to change a named style, use the /Style Define Style Create command again, and select the style name you want to alter. Then from the same menu you used to create the named style, change the styles of the style name. When you select Quit, the changes you make to the named styles are retained. Any spreadsheet blocks that use the changed named style, changes to use the style changes you have made. If you want to change the default style of a spreadsheet, change the named style NORMAL, which is the style all spreadsheet cells automatically use unless they are assigned to another style name.

USING NAMED STYLES When you have named styles that you want to apply to your spreadsheet cells, you can apply the named style either using a command or using the SpeedBar. You can use the menu by using the /Style Use Style and selecting the named style to use. You can also click Style or STY in the SpeedBar, and then select the named style to use. Like other Quattro Pro commands, you can select the block to assign the named style to either before you select the command or after you select the style name. When a style name is assigned to a cell, the style name appears in the input line as in Figure 3.62. Since NORMAL is the default named style, you will not see it in the input line.

REMOVING NAMED STYLES You will have two reasons to delete a named style. In one case, you may want to remove the style name assignment between one of the named styles and a block in the spreadsheet. In another case, you may want to entirely remove a named style from a spreadsheet so it is no longer available. To only remove a named style from a block, select the /Style Define Style Erase command and the style to remove, and either select the block to remove the named style from before or after you select the command. To remove a named style from a spreadsheet, select the /Style Define Style Remove command and the style name you want removed from the spreadsheet. If the named style is currently assigned to any blocks, you must also select Yes as a confirmation. When you use either command to remove a named style from a block or an entire spreadsheet, the blocks that used the named style retain all the style settings except for the ones that

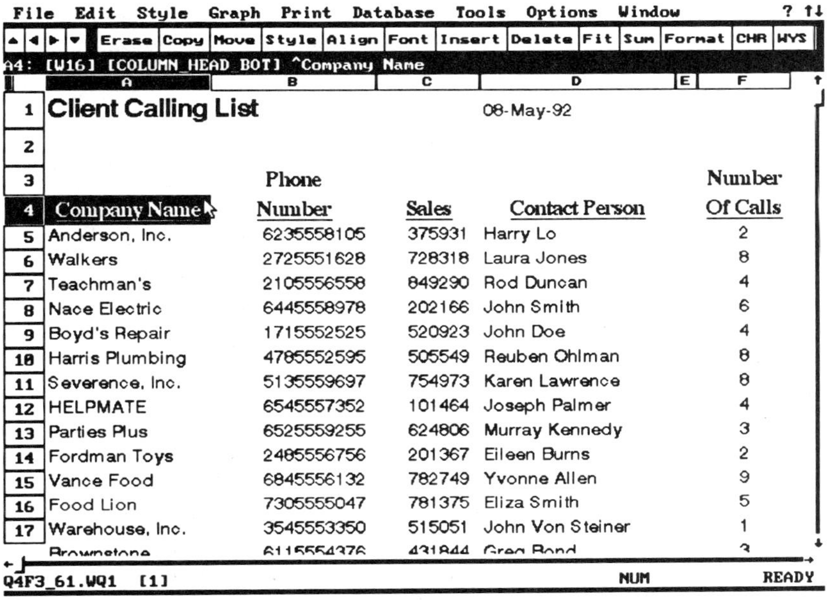

Working with Multiple Cells 133

Figure 3.62 Adding a Named Style to a Spreadsheet

would be set with /Style Font and /Database Data Entry. The style name will also no longer appear in the input line.

CREATING STYLE FILES One use of named styles is to give your reports and spreadsheet data a consistent appearance. You may develop a group of styles in a spreadsheet that you want to use with other spreadsheets so you have a consistent appearance among your spreadsheets. To share the named styles from one spreadsheet with others, you need to put the styles you want to share into a file, and then bring that file into the spreadsheets where you want to use those style names. To put the style names and the styles they represent in a file, select /Style **Define Style File Save**, type a name for the style file, and press ENTER. Quattro Pro will add an .STY extension. Then, when you are in a spreadsheet that you want to use the named styles, select /Style **Define Style File Retrieve**, select the style file from the list or type its name, and press ENTER. Retrieving a style file adds the named styles in the style file to the named styles in the current spreadsheet instead of replacing them.

NUMERICAL FORMATS Quattro Pro lets you create custom numerical formats that expand on the formatting options that are provided with the /Style **Numeric Format** command. You can create custom formats that provide additional ways of displaying values, dates, and times. For example, you can create your own numeric formats to set Quattro Pro to add the day of the week to a date and time format.

To create a user-defined format, select /Style Define Style Create, enter the name for the named style that will include the customized numeric format, and press ENTER. From the menu box that lets you select the styles that are represented by the named style, select Numeric Format and User Defined. Quattro Pro prompts for a format code for the customer numeric format. Type the format code for the numeric format you want to create, and press ENTER.

The first character of a format code is an N or a T to indicate whether the format applies to values or dates or times. After the N in each section are the numeric format symbols that define the format. Table 3.2 lists characters you might use in a format code for values. You can also use other characters such as using ( ) for negative numbers. These characters are not listed, because they are typed in directly.

For date or time formats, the first character is T. After that are the codes for the parts of the date or time you want to display. The case of the dates and times for text controls the case the text appears in. For example, WEEKDAY may return SUNDAY, but Weekday may return Sunday. Table 3.3 shows the format code characters for date entries, and Table 3.4 shows the format code characters for time entries.

Once you create the user-defined numeric format, it is available to be used by assigning that named style to any block using the /Style Use Style command as described above.

An example of user-defined formats is shown in Figure 3.63. In this spreadsheet, the date is formatted with a format definition of T Weekday, Month D, YYYY. This format lets you include the weekday with the date, an option not possible with the other date and time formats. For phone numbers, the range B5..B17 is formatted with a format definition of N(999)999-9999. Also, the range C5..C17 is formatted with a format definition of N$9999. In column F, the number of previous phone calls are formatted with the format description of N99 times. The format definitions let you create new formats that specifically meet your needs.

USING UNDO TO CORRECT MISTAKES

When you make a mistake in an entry, you can correct the mistake by editing the data or entering the entry again. However, you cannot correct a mistake this way if you accidentally use the wrong cells for an /Edit Erase Block command. Fortunately, Quattro has an Undo feature that removes the effect of your most recent action. In the Undo feature, Quattro remembers the differences in a spreadsheet from the time before you made a change, and so can undo the latest spreadsheet change. The types of changes Quattro can undo are changes to cell entries, removing block or graph names, erasing spreadsheets (including erasing a spreadsheet by retrieving another file in its place), and erasing blocks. However, the Undo

Table 3.2 Format Code Symbols for Value Entries

Character	Effect	Sample Format Code	Results on 5474.983	Results on -3891.4852
N or n	Indicates that the following format code is for values	N999990.99	5474.98	-3891.49
0	Displays a digit in place of 0, substituting 0 where a digit is needed	N00000.00	05474.98	-03891.49
9	Displays digit in place of character, only if number has a digit in that place	N999999.99	5474.98	-3891.49
%	Displays a number as percentage	N999990.9%	547498.3%	-389148.5%
,	Inserts a comma separator	N999,999	5,475	-3,891
.	Inserts a decimal separator	N999,999.9	5,475.	-3,891.5
E- or e-	Displays a number using scientific notation with - or nothing after the E as appropriate	N9.99E-99	5.47E3	-3.89E3
E+ or e+	Displays a number using scientific notation using + or - after the E as appropriate	N9.99E+00	5.47E+03	-3.89E+07
\	Displays next character as it literally appears	N9999.99	5474.98*	-3891.49*
*	Fills column not occupied with other characters with the character after the asterisk	N*9999.0	- - - - - 5474.0	- - - - 3891.4
""	Adds characters between quote to the entry	N"Price-"99.99	Price-5474.98	Price - -3891.49

Table 3.3 Format Code Symbols for Dates

Character	Effect	Sample Format Code	Results on May 5, 1992	Results on December 12, 2010
T or t	Indicates that the format code is for a date or time	TMMO/DD/YY	05/05/92	12/12/2010
M or Mo	Displays the month as a number between 1 and 12	TMo-D-YYYY	5-5-1992	12-12-2010
MM or MMO	Displays the month as a number between 01 and 12	TMMO/DD/YY	05/05/92	12/12/2010
MON	Displays the month as a three-letter abbreviation	tMon d	May 5	Dec 12
MONTH	Displays the month spelled out	tMonth d	May 5	December 12
D	Displays the day as a number between 1 and 31	TMo-D-YYYY	5-5-1992	12-12-2010
dd	Displays the day as a number between 01 and 31	TMMO/DD/YY	05/05/92	12/12/2010
WDAY	Displays the day as a three-letter abbreviation	tWday Mon d	Tue May 5	Sun Dec 12
WEEKDAY	Displays the weekday spelled out	tWeekday	Tuesday	Sunday
YY	Displays the last two digits of the year (00-99)	TMMO/DD/YY	05/05/92	12/12/2010
YYYY	Displays four digits of the year (1900-2099)	TMo-D-YYYY	5-5-1992	12-12-2010

Table 3.4 Format Code Symbols for Time

Character	Effect	Sample Format Code	Results on 9:48:02 AM	Results on 3:09:12 PM
h	Displays the hour as a number between 1 and 12 if ampm or AMPM is used, or between 1 and 24 if ampm or AMPM is not used	Th:m:s AMPM	9:48:2 AM	3:9:12 PM
hh	Displays the hour as two digits between 01 and 12 if ampm or AMPM is used, or between 01 and 24 if ampm or AMPM is not used	Thh:mm:ssAMPM	09:48:02AM	03:09:12 PM
M or MI	Displays the minute as a number between 1 and 60	Th:m:s AMPM	9:48:2 AM	3:9:12 PM
MM or MMI	Displays the minute as a number between 01 and 60	Thh:mm:ssAMPM	09:48:02AM	03:09:12PM
S	Displays the second as a number between 1 and 60	Th:m:s AMPM	9:48:2 AM	3:9:12 PM
SS	Displays the second as a number between 01 and 60	Thh:mm:ssAMPM	09:48:02AM	03:09:12PM
AMPM	Displays am or AM after times before noon, and pm or PM after times after noon	Thh:mm:ssAMPM	09:48:02AM	03:09:12PM

feature does not remove the effect of the following actions: file actions performed in the File Manager (see Chapter 5); command settings (such as the settings for the /Edit Search & Replace command); format settings (such as label alignment); and style changes such as fonts, line drawing, and shading. To use the Undo feature, you must tell Quattro you want to use it by entering /Options Other Undo Enable. When Undo is enabled, Quattro runs slower, since it must keep track of the

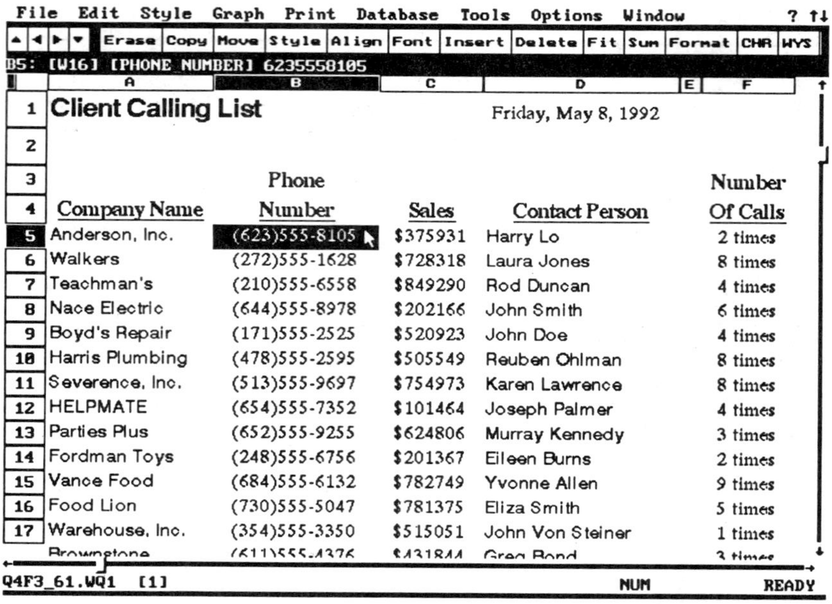

	A	B	C	D	F
1	Client Calling List			Friday, May 8, 1992	
2					
3		Phone			Number
4	Company Name	Number	Sales	Contact Person	Of Calls
5	Anderson, Inc.	(623)555-8105	$375931	Harry Lo	2 times
6	Walkers	(272)555-1628	$728318	Laura Jones	8 times
7	Teachman's	(210)555-6558	$849290	Rod Duncan	4 times
8	Nace Electric	(644)555-8978	$202166	John Smith	6 times
9	Boyd's Repair	(171)555-2525	$520923	John Doe	4 times
10	Harris Plumbing	(478)555-2595	$505549	Reuben Ohlman	8 times
11	Severence, Inc.	(513)555-9697	$754973	Karen Lawrence	8 times
12	HELPMATE	(654)555-7352	$101464	Joseph Palmer	4 times
13	Parties Plus	(652)555-9255	$624806	Murray Kennedy	3 times
14	Fordman Toys	(248)555-6756	$201367	Eileen Burns	2 times
15	Vance Food	(684)555-6132	$782749	Yvonne Allen	9 times
16	Food Lion	(730)555-5047	$781375	Eliza Smith	5 times
17	Warehouse, Inc.	(354)555-3350	$515051	John Von Steiner	1 times

Figure 3.63 Spreadsheet Using Custom Numeric Formats

changes you make. Once Undo is enabled, you can undo the effect of the last action (of the actions that Undo can remove) by entering **/Edit Undo** or pressing ALT-F5. To disable the Undo feature, enter **/Options Other Undo Disable**. Another method for removing the effects of commands you have performed is to use the Transcript utility discussed in Chapter 11.

GETTING STARTED

In this chapter, you learned how to use Quattro commands that operate on more than one cell. With these commands, you learned how to align, copy, erase, format, move, and name cells. Other commands let you insert and delete rows or columns, protect the spreadsheet entries, search and replace entries, change column widths, and change how Quattro displays the spreadsheet by using titles, panes, and map views. You can try some of these commands by creating the sales projection spreadsheet shown in Figure 3.64. To create this spreadsheet, follow these steps:

1. Make the following entries. If you are not using a mouse, press ENTER or an arrow key to finalize the entry. If you are using a mouse, click [Enter] in the input line or another cell.

   A1: **Units**
   A2: **Price**
   A3: **Sales**

Working with Multiple Cells   139

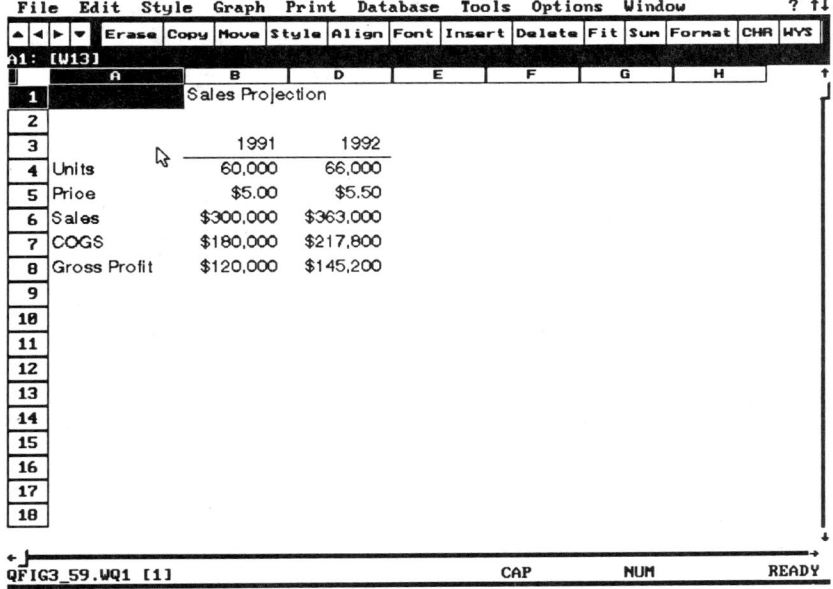

Figure 3.64   Spreadsheet Used with Getting Started Section

    A4: **COGS**
    A5: **Gross Profit**
    B1: **60000**
    B2: **5**

2. Enter the following formulas by pressing ENTER or by clicking [Enter] in the input line. For each of the formulas, you can either type the cell address or point to the cell address (as described in Chapter 2).

    B3: **+B1*B2**
    B4: **+B3*.6**
    B5: **+B3-B4**

3. You can use /Edit Copy to copy one value to another. Move to C1. Type **10%** and press ENTER or click [Enter] in the input line. Press CTRL-C or click Copy in the SpeedBar to enter the /Edit Copy command. Quattro prompts the current cell as the block you want to copy, although you can expand this block address. Press ENTER or click [Enter] in the input line. When Quattro prompts for the destination for the cells, move to C2, and either press ENTER or click [Enter] in the input line.

4. You can also use /Edit Copy to copy formulas. Move to D1. Enter the formula **+B1*(1+C1)**. You can either point to the cells or type the cell addresses. Finalize the formula by pressing ENTER or clicking [Enter] in the input line. Press CTRL-C or click Copy in the SpeedBar to enter /Edit Copy. Since

Quattro prompts the current cell as the source block, either press ENTER or click [Enter] in the input line to accept this block address. When Quattro prompts for the destination, move to D2, and press ENTER or click [Enter] in the input line.

5. You can also use /Edit Copy to copy multiple formulas. Move to B3. Press CTRL-C or click Copy in the SpeedBar to enter the /Edit Copy command. When Quattro prompts for the source block, stretch the block address to B3..B5; then, either press ENTER or click [Enter] in the input line. When Quattro prompts for the destination, move to D3, and either press ENTER or click [Enter] in the input line.

6. Since this spreadsheet needs column headings for the values in columns B, C, and D, you need to move the entries. Move the selector to A1 by pressing HOME or by clicking A1. Press CTRL-M or click Move in the SpeedBar to enter the /Edit Move command. When Quattro prompts the source block, press END, HOME, and ENTER to select the block A1..D5. If you are using a mouse, point to A1, hold the mouse button down, and point to D5 before releasing the mouse button. Once the block is selected, click [Enter] in the input line. When Quattro prompts for the destination, move to A3 and either press ENTER or click [Enter] in the input line.

7. Expand column A so the text in A7 is not clipped. Press CTRL-W to enter /Style Column Width. Expand the column's width to 13 by typing **13** or by pressing the RIGHT ARROW four times. If you are using a mouse, point to the A in the column heading, and press the mouse button. Then move the mouse to the right until the column width is 13, and release the mouse button.

8. Make the following entries, finalizing each entry either by pressing ENTER or by moving to the next cell.

    B1: **Sales Projection**
    B2: **1991**
    C2: **% Increase**
    D2: **1992**

9. Draw a line under the column headings by selecting the block B2..D2. If you are using a mouse, point to one of these cells, hold down the mouse button, and point to the opposite cell in the block before releasing the mouse button. If you are not using a mouse, move the selector to one corner of the block, press SHIFT-F7 (SELECT), and move to the other corner of the block. Then enter /Style Line Drawing Bottom Single and Quit to return to READY mode. Quattro draws a line below the cells and adjusts the height of the row to fit the line. You did not have to enter a block to modify, since you selected it before entering the command.

10. Expand columns B, C, and D to fit the entries. With B2..D2 still selected, enter /Style Block Widths Set Width. Expand the width of the columns to 10 by pressing the RIGHT ARROW once and by either pressing ENTER or clicking [Enter] in the input line.

Working with Multiple Cells 141

11. You may want to add space between the report title and the report body. You can increase the spacing by inserting a row between the title in B1 and the column headings in row 2. To insert a row, press CTRL-I or click Insert in the SpeedBar to enter /Edit Insert. When Quattro prompts you to select between columns and rows, select Rows. Next, Quattro prompts you for a block containing the number of rows you want to insert. Since you only want to insert one row and the block address at the prompt contains one row, press ENTER or click [Enter] in the input line.

12. The formulas that you have created do not provide much information about why these calculations are being performed. A quick method of documenting this spreadsheet is to name some of the cells. For each of the cells listed below, enter /Edit Names Create followed by the name of the cell. When Quattro prompts for the block address of the cell, enter the cell address of the cell that you are naming. After you have named the cells, move to the cells that use the named cells in the formulas, and notice how Quattro substitutes the cell names in place of the cell address. If you press F2 (EDIT) to edit the cell's contents, Quattro changes the block names to the cell or block addresses they represent.

    B4 named **Units_1991**
    B5 named **Price_1991**
    B6 named **Sales_1991**
    D4 named **Units_1992**
    D5 named **Price_1992**
    D6 named **Sales_1992**

13. The next step is to format the values so the numbers of units appear with commas separating the thousands, prices appear with two digits after the decimal point, the percentages appear as percents, and the remaining numbers appear using the currency format. First, move to B4, and select the block B4..D4. If you are using a mouse, hold down the mouse button, and drag the block selection to D4 before releasing the mouse button. If you are not using a mouse, press SHIFT-F7 (SELECT) and move the selector to D4. Press CTRL-F or click Format in the SpeedBar to enter /Style Numeric Format. Select **,**, type **0**, and either press ENTER or click [Enter] in the box. You do not need to select a block to format, since you selected a block before entering this command.

    For the prices, move the selector to B5. Press CTRL-F or click FORMAT in the SpeedBar to enter /Style Numeric Format. Select **Currency**, then either press ENTER or click Enter in the box to select a currency format with two digits after the decimal point. Select B5..D5 as the block to format before finalizing the block selection with ENTER. Without these block commands, you would have to format B4, D4, B5, and D5 individually.

    For the percentages, move the selector to C4. Press CTRL-F or click Format in the SpeedBar to enter /Style Numeric Format. Select **Percent**, then type **0**, and either press ENTER or click Enter in the box to select a percent format with no digits after the decimal point. Select C4..C5 as the block to format before finalizing the block selection with ENTER.

For the remaining numbers, format them as currency by entering **/Options Formats Numeric Format Currency**. Type **0**, and either press ENTER or click Enter in the box. Select **Quit** twice to return to the READY mode.

14. In this spreadsheet you may want to hide column C. To hide column C, enter **/Style Hide Column Hide**. When Quattro prompts for a cell that contains the columns you want to hide, select a cell from column C, and press ENTER. Your spreadsheet now looks like Figure 3.64.

4
Printing

Once you have created a spreadsheet, you will want to share the information it contains with others. Since a screen is not as portable as a piece of paper, printing the spreadsheet affords you this opportunity. Quattro provides many options to control the appearance of your printed output. Its default settings provide a quick method for printing your spreadsheet data without being bogged down in the specifics of the various print operations. Quattro can also provide you complete control of the printed output and let you choose how much or how little detail you want to use in printing your spreadsheet.

This chapter covers the basic print procedure as well as the more advanced print options. You will be introduced to the terms to use for Quattro's more advanced print features. Once you have covered the basics, you will be prepared to use as many of the special options as you need. As a final step, this chapter describes how you can change Quattro's printer defaults.

THE BASIC PRINT PROCEDURE

Printing a Quattro spreadsheet is as simple as telling Quattro which part of the spreadsheet you want to print and starting the print process. Once you select the block to print, Quattro uses all its default settings to determine the appearance of the printed page. In addition to understanding how to invoke printing, you need to understand the default settings completely so that you will know when and how to change them.

Printing a Spreadsheet with the Default Settings

The first step of printing your spreadsheet is defining a print block. This action informs Quattro which part of the spreadsheet you want to print. The process requires these steps:

1. Press /, and select **Print** to display the Print menu shown in Figure 4.1.
2. Select **Block**.
3. Move the selector to the upper-left corner of the block that you want to print. If you want to start printing from A1, press HOME. If you do not want to start printing from A1, use the arrow keys to move to the upper-left corner of the block that you want to print. If a block is already highlighted, you must press ESC if you want to change the beginning of the print block. Another option is to press BACKSPACE which returns the selector to the selector's original position before you typed /.
4. Press the period, which anchors the beginning point of the block that you want to print.
5. Move the selector so that the entire block that you want to print is highlighted.
6. Press ENTER. The Print menu reappears on your screen.
7. Select **Spreadsheet Print**. Quattro will start printing your spreadsheet.

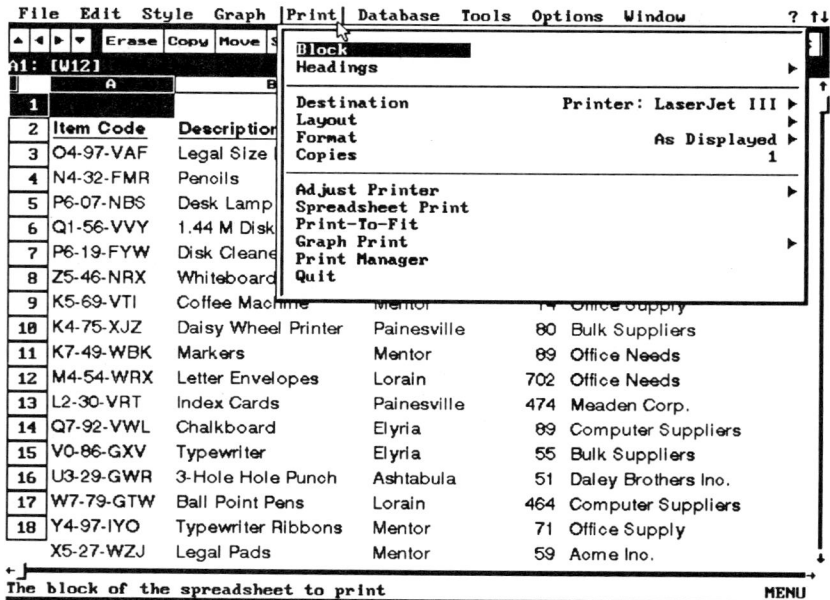

Figure 4.1 Print Menu

THE DEFAULT PAGE LAYOUT When you print a spreadsheet with the default settings in effect, Quattro makes a number of decisions that affect the appearance of your spreadsheet. You need to know the different options available before you can make changes to the default settings. The special terms that Quattro uses to describe print options are illustrated in Figure 4.2. The definition and default settings for the terms are as follows:

- Top Heading—The top heading is one or more rows of a spreadsheet that prints above spreadsheet data at the top of every page. Quattro does not have a default top heading, but you can specify one to create column headings for every page of your spreadsheet.

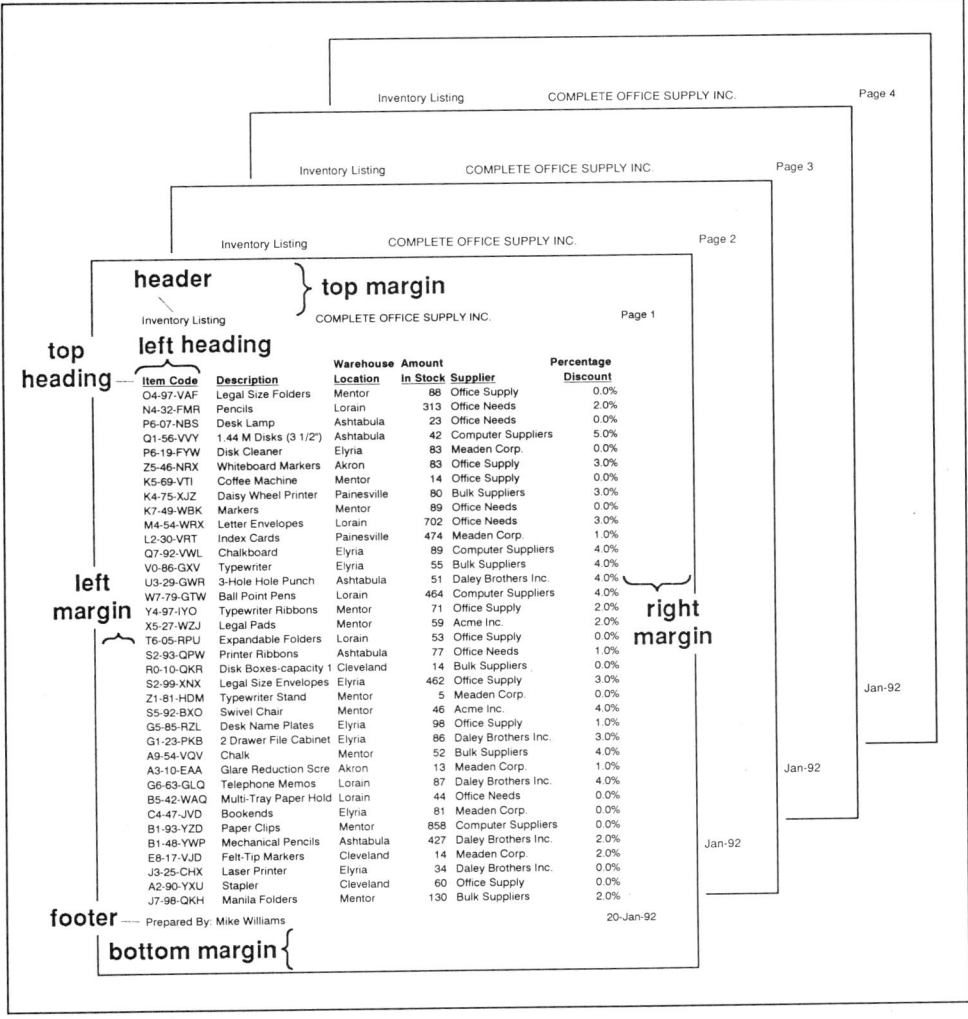

Figure 4.2   Printout Illustrating Different Printer Terms

- Left Heading—The left heading is one or more columns of a spreadsheet that prints to the left of spreadsheet data on every page. Quattro's defaults do not have a left heading, but you can specify one to create row headings for every page of your spreadsheet.
- Format—Quattro defaults to print the spreadsheet data as it appears on the screen. You can change Quattro's default to print the cell contents instead.
- Header—The header is the first three lines at the top of every page. Quattro's default settings leave these lines blank, but you can specify text to be placed in the first line.
- Footer—The footer is the last three lines at the bottom of every page. Quattro's default settings leave these lines blank, but you can specify text to be placed in the third line.
- Page Breaks—Quattro breaks the printed text into pages according to the page length setting. You can instruct Quattro to put page breaks at any location on the spreadsheet.
- Setup String—A setup string is a sequence of characters that is set to your printer to use printer-dependent features. Quattro's default settings do not use setup strings.
- Page Length—The page length is the number of lines on a page. Quattro's default for this setting is 66 lines per page.
- Top Margin—The top margin is the number of blank lines between the top of the paper and the first line of the header. Quattro's default setting is two lines.
- Bottom Margin—The bottom margin is the number of blank lines between the last line of the footer and the bottom of the paper. Quattro's default setting for the bottom margin is two lines.
- Left Margin—The left margin is the number of spaces on the left side of the page before printing spreadsheet data. Quattro initially leaves four blank spaces.
- Right Margin—The right margin is the number of spaces from the left side of the page that Quattro uses for the left margin and the spreadsheet. The difference between the number of characters that fit on a page and the right margin setting is the space Quattro leaves blank on the right side of the page. The right margin is initially set to 76, leaving four blank spaces for a right-hand margin.

A CLOSER LOOK AT SELECTING A PRINT BLOCK You have already looked at the basic steps for selecting a print block on a new spreadsheet, but there are a few specifics that you will want to know. If the contents of a cell within the print block borrows display space from cells that are not part of your print block, the portion of these entries that uses the display space of other cells will not print. To print these entries, you can change the column width so the entire cell contents display in their own column, or expand the print block to include the cells where the long cell entries borrow display space.

If the block that you are printing exceeds the page in width or length, Quattro prints the data on multiple pages, automatically breaking the pages at the appropriate location. A print block must consist of a contiguous block of cells. For example, you cannot print the information in columns A, B, G, and L unless you first hide the columns that you do not want to print. For example, you can hide columns C through F and columns H through K and specify the print block using columns A through L to achieve the desired result.

Your print block will appear in the Print menu on the right side next to **Block**. You can also indicate the print block in Quattro Pro 4 by adding a dotted line around the block area. To display the dotted line around the print block, select **/Windows Options Print Block Display**. After selecting this command, the dotted line will surround the area to print when you print to a graphics printer, binary file, or the screen preview. When you later want to remove the dotted lines, select **/Windows Options Print Block Hide**.

RESETTING THE PRINT BLOCK Once you have selected a print block, Quattro remembers your selection. The next time you use the print features, the block setting is the same unless you change it. Quattro provides four ways of changing the print block. The best method for changing the print block depends on the type of change that you want to make.

Changing a Print Block by Pressing ESC If you need to completely reset a print block, the quickest method is pressing the ESC key and selecting a new print block. If a block is already set, this key eliminates the block specification and places the selector in the upper-left corner of the specified block. You can specify the new print block by moving the selector to the upper-left cell in the block, typing a period, moving to the lower-right cell in the block, and pressing ENTER.

Pressing the BACKSPACE key is similar to pressing the ESC key with one exception. When you press the BACKSPACE key, Quattro removes the current print block and moves the selector to its previous position before you invoked the **/Print Block** command. Using the BACKSPACE key instead of the ESC key works best when the selector is located in a section of the spreadsheet that you want to print.

Changing the Print Block with the /Print Layout Reset Print Block Command Another method for completely resetting a print block is the **/Print Layout Reset Print Block** command. When you execute this command, Quattro removes the print block specification. After using this command, you can set a new print block by entering **Block**, moving the selector to the upper-left cell that you want to be in the block, typing a period, moving to the lower-right cell in the print block, and pressing ENTER. This reset option is useful when you want to print a block that is completely different from the one currently selected.

Using the Arrow Keys to Expand and Contract the Print Block If you need to expand or contract the width of the print block, use the arrow keys to make the change quickly. When you execute the **/Print Block** command and the current print block is highlighted, you can expand or contract the print block at the bottom or at the right with the arrow keys. The upper and left settings for the block are unaffected. Quattro marks the selector's position in the block with a different color. This lets you know which corner of the block will change when you press the arrow keys.

Using the Period to Change the Print Block If you need to expand or contract the upper or left side of the print block, changing the block specification makes this task easy. When you invoke the /Print Block command and Quattro highlights the current print block, the selector is at the lower-right corner. The selector at the lower-right corner indicates that you can change this corner of the block with the arrow keys. If you type a period, Quattro moves the selector to the next corner in a clockwise direction. Therefore, if you press the period once, the selector moves to the lower-left corner. From this position, you can alter the left edge of the print block with an expansion or contraction. You can also change the bottom edge of the print block up or down.

Each use of the period continues to rotate the corner of the print block, which you can then adjust. For example, suppose your current print block is D10..G17 and you want to expand it to B7..J20. First, you perform the /Print Block command. This highlights the block anchored at D10 and provides a selector at G17. By moving the selector to J20, you have expanded the right and bottom limit of the current print block. To change the upper and left limit of the block, press the period twice. The selector is now at D10. The block is currently anchored at J20. Next, move the selector to B7, and press ENTER. As these steps illustrate, you can modify all four sides of a print block without retyping the block specification.

Adjusting the Printer

The key to correct print output is setting the printer correctly at the beginning of each print session and following a specific procedure after printing each block. If you ignore these steps you will be frustrated by half pages of printed output and other errors that render the output unusable.

To maintain the printer setting, the first step in each Quattro session that uses the printer is to position the paper at the top of a form and then turn the printer on. Quattro provides several commands to advance to the next line or page and to zero the line count when you have advanced to a new page.

ADVANCING PAPER When a print block is printed, the printer head often stops at the middle of a page. Rather than manually advancing the paper or pressing buttons on the printer to do so, you should have Quattro instruct the printer to advance to the next page. The /Print Adjust Printer Form Feed command instructs your printer to advance to the next page. To maintain proper print alignment, you also need to reset the internal line counter with the instructions covered in the next section.

To advance the paper in the printer to the next line, use the /Print Adjust Printer Skip Line command. This command advances the paper in the printer to the next line. Use this command to create space between blocks printed on the same page.

RESETTING THE TOP-OF-PAGE INDICATOR Since Quattro cannot look at the printer to see if it is at the beginning of the page, Quattro must keep track of the number of lines it prints to decide when a page break should occur. Several things can cause page breaks to occur in the wrong locations. For example, if you have manually readjusted the paper, Quattro does not add to its counter the number of lines you advanced the paper. If you adjust the printer, you can tell Quattro when the printer is at the top of the page with the /Print Adjust Printer Align command. This command resets Quattro's line counter at zero, which is appropriate for the top of the page. The command also zeros the page and line counter. You want to use this command whenever you advance the paper to the top of the page or you have included the page number in the header or footer and you want the next printing task to start numbering pages with 1.

Handling Print Problems

Once you define the block to print and tell Quattro to begin by selecting Spreadsheet Print from the Print menu, you expect the print output to be directed to your printer immediately. Most of the time your expectations are met, but you also want to be prepared to handle problem situations.

RESPONDING TO AN ERROR MESSAGE If Quattro is unable to print your file, it displays a message box, which lets you choose whether you want to abort or continue the printing process. An error message can be caused by a printer that is turned off, off-line, or out of paper, or by a loose cable, a missing disk, or an open disk drive door. If you correct the problem and want to continue printing, choose Continue. If you want to abort the print operation, choose Abort, and you will be in READY mode. To retry the print operation, the /Print Spreadsheet Print command must be invoked again. If you select Continue, Quattro will try to print the spreadsheet.

INTERRUPTING PRINT There are times when you want to interrupt printing before the entire block is printed. For example, you may want to quickly abort printing if you are using continuous feed paper and the printer becomes jammed. Other reasons include incorrect page breaks and print settings. Press the CTRL-BREAK keys simultaneously to interrupt the flow of information to the printer. Although this stops Quattro from transmitting information to the printer, your printer may continue printing for a while if it has a buffer to store information about to be printed. Be patient, and wait for the contents of the buffer to print. Once

---

▼ **TIP: Reset the first page number to 1.**

Use the /Print Adjust Printer Align command before printing each spreadsheet, so Quattro starts printing at the top of the page using 1 as the first page number.

150   *Quattro Pro 4.0 Handbook*

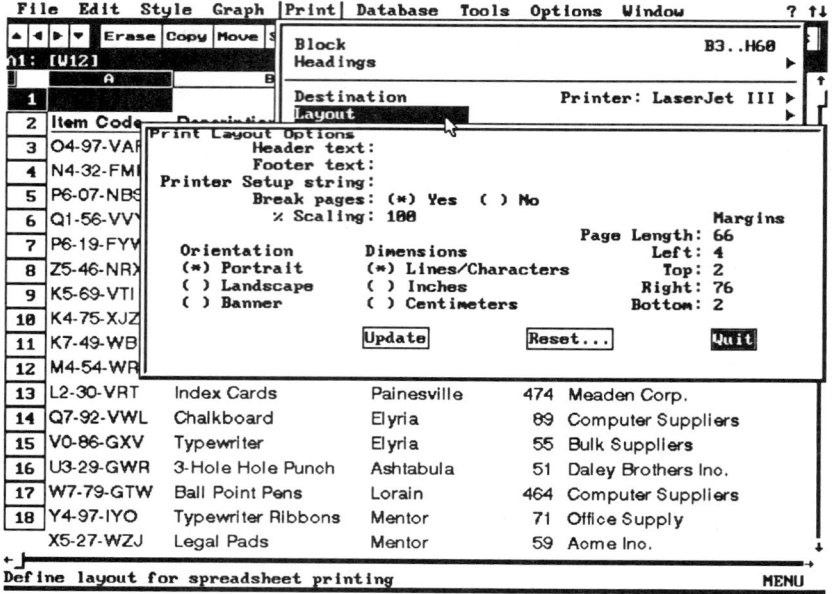

Figure 4.3   Dialog Box for Setting Print Options

printing has stopped, press ESC, correct the problem, and use /Print Spreadsheet Print to start printing again.

PRINT OPTIONS

While printing your spreadsheet can be as simple as defining a block to print, creating customized, professional-looking reports normally requires the use of Quattro's special print features. These special options include selecting where Quattro Pro prints your data, setting the margins, adding headings, controlling page breaks, printing cell contents, and hiding columns to select which columns are printed. Most print options and commands are set by selecting /Print Layout. In Quattro Pro 4, this displays the Print Layout Options dialog box shown in Figure 4.3. If Quattro Pro 4 is set to not use dialog boxes or you are using an earlier release, the printing commands can have their current settings displayed when you select /Print Layout Values. This displays the menu box shown in Figure 4.4, which disappears when you press any key. The printing settings that you select are saved with the spreadsheet so they are available the next time you print.

With the Print Layout Options dialog box, you can make all of your selections at once. A dialog box removes nested menus by bringing up only the options you may possibly change. The dialog box in Figure 4.3 shows several print layout options grouped together, such as the choices for orientation and dimensions. With the choices marked with parentheses, you can select one from the group. To move to an item on the dialog box, you can press TAB and SHIFT-TAB. Another option is to type the highlighted letter. When you want to select an item within a group, you will select the group, such as **Orientation** or **Dimensions**, and then the

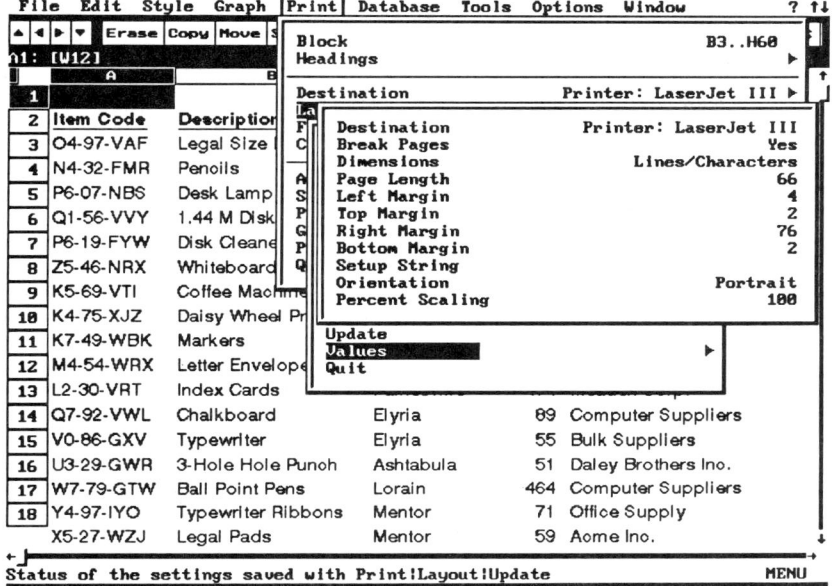

Figure 4.4 /Print Layout Values Displays Current Print Settings

specific choice you want. With a mouse, you can just click the setting you want to change, such as clicking Inches to change the dimensions Quattro Pro uses to measure distances. With the dialog box choices that do not have parentheses next to them, you must type your entry. Some of the choices are in boxes like **Update**, **Reset**, and **Quit** in Figure 4.3. These perform some action. **Reset** will show another dialog box which you can tell by the three periods after **Reset**. Dialog boxes have the **Quit** button for when you are finished with a dialog box and you want to leave it.

Specifying the Destination

Quattro provides other output options for your spreadsheet data. Quattro can print your spreadsheet to a draft quality printer, a final quality printer, a file, or to Quattro's screen previewer. Changing where Quattro prints the spreadsheet is simple and allows you to change from one destination to another without having to change the other settings. When you select **Destination** from the Print pull-down menu, you have five choices. The first choice, **Printer**, is the default. This sends the block to the printer in draft quality using the printer's default font, which prints your spreadsheets quickly but does not print graphics features such as fonts, lines, shading, and inserted graphs (discussed in Chapter 7). If you want the spreadsheet to include these features, select **Graphics Printer**. When you select **Graphics Printer**, the printed output will use a different font. **Screen Preview** will activate Quattro's screen previewer, which shows how the printer will print your spreadsheet if you select Graphics Printer. The two remaining selections, **File** and **Binary File**, send the information to a file instead of to the printer in a draft or graphics format, respectively.

Directing the print output to a file instead of the printer offers new possibilities. You can print the file at a later time, or transfer the information the file contains into another program. Deferring the print operation until later is useful if you do not want to tie up your printer with a long print job. By writing the print output to a file, you can print the file with the DOS COPY command when you no longer need to use the printer for other jobs. When you print to a file, Quattro sends all the headers and footers, headings, and other print settings to the file so the file contains the same information that is sent to the printer. **File** is equivalent to selecting **Printer**. **Binary File** is equivalent to selecting **Graphics Printer**. When you select **File** or **Binary File**, Quattro prompts for the name of the file that you want to store the information. Quattro provides a box listing all the .PRN files that currently exist. Either type the name of the file or highlight the filename, and press ENTER. You do not need to add an extension, since Quattro adds a .PRN extension. If the file you select exists, you have the option of canceling the command, replacing the old file with the new one, backing up the old file before replacing the file with the new one, or appending the file to the old one (with the **File** option only). Quattro sends information to the file when you select **S**preadsheet Print and closes the file when you select **Q**uit. To print the file later, return to DOS, and type COPY followed by the filename. If you plan to use the printed file in another software package, you need to change other print settings as described in the section on special considerations for printing to a text file.

Selecting the Number of Copies to Print

Quattro usually assumes you want only one copy of your printed spreadsheet. Besides selecting /Print Spreadsheet Print for each copy you want, you can also print multiple copies of your spreadsheet by selecting /Print Copies and entering a number between 1 and 1000. To prevent you from printing out more copies of subsequent spreadsheets, this setting always reverts to the default of 1 after you print.

Changing Margins and Page Length

Quattro allows you to change all the margins and the page length for printing your spreadsheet. When you select Layout and Margins from the Print menu or display the Print Layout Options dialog box, Quattro displays the measurements it will use for margins and the page length. Initially, Quattro displays this information as the number of characters or lines.

When you print in draft mode (printing to the File or Printer), the characters and lines are measured using the font you use to print. In graphics printing mode, the characters and lines are converted into the distance they represent using your printer's default font. This means that changing the number of lines or characters in a margin may affect the actual margin in graphics printing mode by a different number of characters. If you are printing mostly in graphics printing mode, you may want to change the measurement of margins and page length from characters and lines in text mode to inches or centimeters.

> ▼ **TIP: Only 60 lines per page are printed on some printers.**
>
> Page printers such as the Hewlett-Packard LaserJet print only 60 lines per page.

If you want these numbers to appear as the number of inches or centimeters, select **Dimensions** from the Layout menu, and select **Inches** or **Centimeters** for the measurement it uses. When you enter a new margin or page length, you will enter the number of characters and lines, inches, or centimeters to match the dimensions chosen. Quattro displays the range of acceptable values for the margins or page length using the selected dimensions when you are not using dialog boxes.

ADJUSTING THE RIGHT AND LEFT MARGINS Quattro's initial default setting of a left margin of 4 and a right margin of 76 provides approximately a 1/2-inch margin at each side. Both margins may range from 0 to 511 (254 in Quattro Pro 1 and 2) characters or an equivalent number of inches or centimeters. You should increase the right margin setting if you are using a wide carriage printer, using a smaller font in the text printing mode, or printing to a file rather than a printer when you use the file in another software package.

To change the left or right margin, select **Layout** from the Print menu. With the Print Layout Options dialog box, select **Right** or **Left** and type the new margin setting. If you do not see the dialog box, select **Margins**, then **Right** or **Left** before you type the margin and press ENTER.

TOP AND BOTTOM MARGIN SETTINGS Quattro's initial default settings leave two blank lines at the top and bottom of each page, which provides 1/3-inch margins. The top or bottom margin may range from 0 to 32 lines, which equals 5 1/3 inches or 13 1/2 centimeters. The top and bottom margins may be changed if you need to increase the amount of information that appears on each page or if you change the line spacing. From the Print Layout Options dialog box, you can change the top or bottom margins by selecting **Top** or **Bottom** and typing the new margin. If you do not see the dialog box, select **Top** or **Bottom**, type the new margin, and press ENTER.

PAGE LENGTH OPTIONS Quattro uses a setting of 66 lines per page. Sixty-six will fit on an 11-inch sheet of paper if the printer uses a standard setting of six lines to the inch. The page length setting can range from 0 to 100 lines, 0 to 24 inches, or 0 to 60 centimeters. When you print in a graphics printing mode, Quattro Pro converts the number of lines into the distance Quattro Pro can fill with as many lines as will fit using the selected fonts.

The actual number of lines of spreadsheet data per page is the page length, less the top margin, the bottom margin, three lines for a header, three lines for a footer, and the number of lines used for a top heading. This setting may need to be changed for some printers, when you are printing a different number of lines per inch or using paper of a different size. To change page length, select Layout from the Print menu and **Page Length**. If you are not using dialog boxes, you must select **Margins** before you select **Page Length**. Type the number of lines per page, and press ENTER.

Adding Headings to a Page

When you are printing a spreadsheet that spans many pages, you may want to include identifying information for each row or column. For example, if your spreadsheet is very long, you will want column headings on each page to explain what the entries in each column represent. On the other hand, if your spreadsheet is very wide, adding row headings identifies the information in each row on every page of the report.

USING HEADINGS AT THE TOP Creating a top heading allows you to include entries from multiple rows at the top of every page that you print. When you choose a top heading, you do not have to specify the entire block that you want to use as a top heading; you only have to include one cell in a row for the entire row to be used. Which columns from that row are used is dictated by which columns are in the print block.

If you have a top heading, do not include the rows of the top heading as part of the print block. If you accidentally include the data in both places, the top heading is printed once as a top heading and a second time as part of the spreadsheet data on the first page of the report.

To create a top heading, follow these steps:

1. Press / to activate the menu.
2. Select **Print Headings** and **Top Heading**.
3. Move the selector to the first row that you want as your top heading. You do not have to be in any specific column.
4. Type a period to anchor the first row as the beginning of the block or rows in the top heading.
5. Move the selector to include one cell from each row that you want as part of your top heading.
6. Press ENTER.

When you print your spreadsheet, Quattro uses the rows that you specify at the top of each page. The columns match the columns selected in the print block. A top heading should not include any setup strings (discussed later in the chapter), since Quattro prints them just as they are entered. To remove the top heading, use the **/Print Layout Reset Headings** command.

USING INFORMATION AT THE SIDE The addition of a left heading allows you to print a wide spreadsheet spanning several pages without losing track of what the data in each row represents. When you choose a left heading, you do not have to specify the entire block that you want to use as a left heading; you only have to include one cell in a column for the entire column to be used.

If you have a left heading, do not include the columns of the left heading in the print block. If you include the left heading columns in the print block, the information is printed once as a left heading and then again as part of the spreadsheet data.

To create a left heading, follow these steps:

1. Press **/** to activate the menu.
2. Select **Print Headings** and **Left Heading**.
3. Move the selector to the first column that you want as the left heading. You do not have to be in any specific row.
4. Type a period to anchor the column as the beginning of the block.
5. Move the selector to include one cell of each column that you want as part of your left heading.
6. Press ENTER.

When you print your spreadsheet, Quattro prints the entries in the columns that you specify at the left side of each page. The rows that Quattro uses match the rows in the print block. A heading should not include any setup strings (discussed later in the chapter), since Quattro prints them as they are entered in the spreadsheet. To remove the left heading, use the **/Print Layout Reset Headings** command.

Adding Headers and Footers

Quattro lets you add headers and footers to the top and bottom of each page. Header and footer information is not stored on the spreadsheet and must be entered. The header and footer are the same on each page with the exception of the page number. The header and footer are excellent locations for the name of your spreadsheet, your name, a reference to the current date, and the page number.

To create a header press **/**, and select **Print, Layout,** and **Header**. To create a footer press **/**, and select **Print, Layout,** and **Footer**. In either case, type the text that you want to appear for the header or footer (within the limit of 241 characters on one line). The header is printed before the top heading is printed. The footer is printed below the spreadsheet. Quattro separates the header and the footer from the spreadsheet data with two blank lines.

SPECIAL HEADER AND FOOTER CHARACTERS Quattro provides several special characters that you can use in a header or footer. These special characters let you print the current date and the appropriate page number, and they allow you to divide the header into several sections that are left-aligned, centered, or right-aligned. The special characters for headers and footers include the following:

- #—A pound sign prints the current page number on every page in place of this character.

- @—Sign (@) is converted to the current system date when the spreadsheet is printed.
- |—A vertical line divides the header or footer text into three parts. Quattro normally left-aligns headers and footers. To center text, start the header with a vertical bar, and enter the text to be centered immediately after the vertical bar. To right-align text, start the header with two vertical bars, and place the text to be right-aligned after these bars. You can combine the three types of alignment in a header or footer by entering the text to be left-aligned before the first vertical bar, entering the text to be centered between the first and second vertical bar, and entering the text to be right-aligned after the second vertical bar. A sample header or footer may look like this:

Smith & Co. | Income Statement | Date: @, Page #

When this header is printed, Smith & Co. is left-aligned, Income Statement is centered in the middle of the line, and the date and the page number are right-aligned. When the header is printed, it looks like this:

Smith & Co.   Income Statement   Date: 9/27/92, Page 1

This printed header assumes that the current date is 9/27/92 and that the first page is printed.

Controlling Page Breaks

For long spreadsheets, Quattro breaks the text into pages according to the Page Length setting. Quattro automatically adjusts the page breaks every time you print. However, Quattro provides you with several options to insert page breaks at different locations. For example, if you have one spreadsheet that contains several reports, creating your own page breaks can force each report to start on a new page. Also, you can instruct Quattro not to use page breaks except for the ones that you have created.

ELIMINATING PAGE BREAKS You can suppress Quattro's page breaks by selecting Break Pages and No in the Print Layout Options dialog box or by selecting /Print Layout Break Pages and No. When you print your file, Quattro will not print headers or footers and will not insert automatic page breaks. Quattro prints the top and left headings once at the beginning and again at each of the page breaks that you insert. While this setting is normally set to Yes, you will want to set it to No when you are planning to print the spreadsheet data to a file for later incorporation into another software package.

ADDING PAGE BREAKS Quattro provides two methods of manually inserting page breaks. You can either enter a page break directly into the spreadsheet or use a menu command.

Adding a page break directly into your spreadsheet is as simple as moving to a blank row and typing |:: (a vertical line and two colons) in the first column of the print block. If you do not have a blank row, you must create one with the **/E**dit **I**nsert **R**ows command. Entries in the same row as the page break are ignored. This method is quicker when you already have a blank row available. If you do not have a blank row, you will want to use the menu option.

Quattro's menu command for adding a page break is **/S**tyle **I**nsert Break. When you execute this command, Quattro inserts a blank line above the selector and puts |:: (a vertical line and two colons) in the first column. Any entries later inserted in the same row as the page break are not printed.

Hiding Columns to Change the Print Output

Since print blocks must be a contiguous rectangle, you cannot selectively choose scattered information to print. However, you can hide columns from the view, which automatically eliminates them from printing. For example, if your spreadsheet is set up as an inventory database that you want to print with the item code, description, amount in stock, percentage discount, and discount quantity (columns A, B, D, F, and G), you want to hide the warehouse and supplier in columns C and E. To hide these two columns, move the selector to column C, press /, and select **S**tyle **H**ide Column **H**ide. At the prompt, you only have to press ENTER, since the proper column is already chosen. Repeat this command for column E. After this command, the columns disappear from the display as in Figure 4.5 and are not

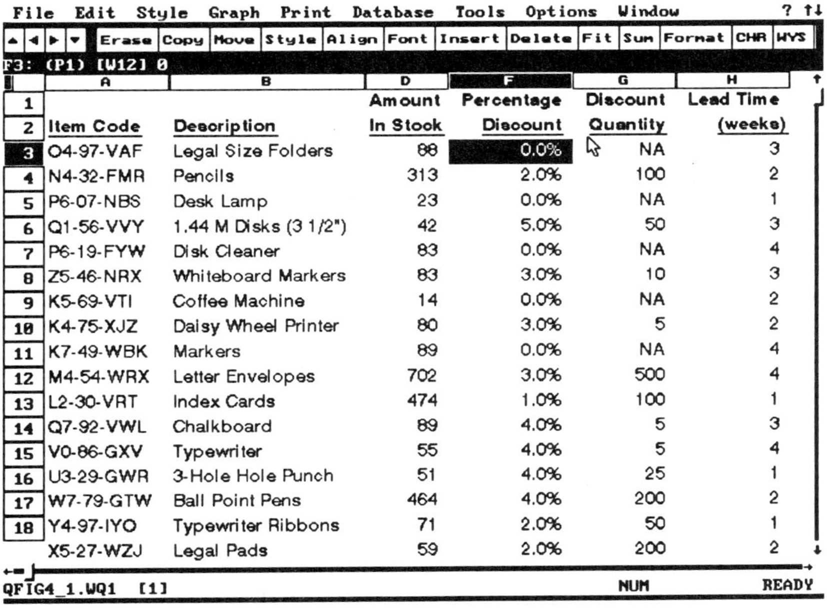

	A	B	D	F	G	H
1			Amount	Percentage	Discount	Lead Time
2	Item Code	Description	In Stock	Discount	Quantity	(weeks)
3	O4-97-VAF	Legal Size Folders	88	0.0%	NA	3
4	N4-32-FMR	Pencils	313	2.0%	100	2
5	P6-07-NBS	Desk Lamp	23	0.0%	NA	1
6	Q1-56-VVY	1.44 M Disks (3 1/2")	42	5.0%	50	3
7	P6-19-FYW	Disk Cleaner	83	0.0%	NA	4
8	Z5-46-NRX	Whiteboard Markers	83	3.0%	10	3
9	K5-69-VTI	Coffee Machine	14	0.0%	NA	2
10	K4-75-XJZ	Daisy Wheel Printer	80	3.0%	5	2
11	K7-49-WBK	Markers	89	0.0%	NA	4
12	M4-54-WRX	Letter Envelopes	702	3.0%	500	4
13	L2-30-VRT	Index Cards	474	1.0%	100	1
14	Q7-92-VWL	Chalkboard	89	4.0%	5	3
15	V0-86-GXV	Typewriter	55	4.0%	5	4
16	U3-29-GWR	3-Hole Hole Punch	51	4.0%	25	1
17	W7-79-GTW	Ball Point Pens	464	4.0%	200	2
18	Y4-97-IYO	Typewriter Ribbons	71	2.0%	50	1
	X5-27-WZJ	Legal Pads	59	2.0%	200	2

Figure 4.5 Spreadsheet with Hidden Columns

printed, even when the columns are included in the print block. Quattro still keeps track of the hidden columns and therefore, does not relabel the displayed columns. To display a hidden column, use the /Style Hide Column Expose command. Data in a hidden column is still maintained and is also available for access by formulas in columns that are still displayed.

Resetting Print Settings

When you need to change your print settings, it may be easier to undo the existing settings. With Quattro, you can reset a portion of your print settings or all of them. You can reset the print block, the top and left headings, and the page layout settings.

When you reset the print block or the heading, the current setting is removed. When you request Print Block, the current cell is highlighted, and you can enter a new block specification. When you reset the page layout settings, the current settings are replaced with the default settings. The default settings are Quattro's default settings or the entries you made for these options with the /Print Layout Update command. To reset any or all settings, select Reset in the Print Layout Options dialog box or press / to activate the menu, and select Print Layout and Reset. Make your selection from the Reset menu to control the impact of the reset print settings. When you choose Layout or Headings, Quattro clears the settings made in the Layout menu or the top and left headings.

Printing Cell Contents to Document the Worksheet

Quattro provides three types of documentation for your spreadsheets. One of them, Audit, provides information about the formulas in your spreadsheet as described in Chapter 9. Another one is the Transcript Add-in, which creates an audit trail of the changes that you have made to a spreadsheet. This feature is covered in Chapter 11. A third type of documentation for your spreadsheet is printing your entries. Quattro provides two methods for printing the information in spreadsheet formulas. One method is to change the default format to Text so that Quattro displays the formulas and then prints the resulting spreadsheet. The other method changes the format of your printed spreadsheet so that Quattro prints a list of the cells and their contents. Although the second method may be used more often, the first method usually provides better results.

PRINTING THE SPREADSHEET WITH FORMULAS DISPLAYED You can use Quattro's display formats to show your entire spreadsheet as text, numbers, and formulas. Once the spreadsheet displays the formulas instead of the results, printing the spreadsheet provides you with a printed version of each cell's contents with the same row and column orientation that you are familiar with. Although this method has more steps, the resulting printout is easier to understand. To print out your spreadsheet's formulas, numbers, and labels, follow these steps:

Printing   159

1. Retrieve the file containing formulas you want to print.
2. Enter /File Save As to save the file under a different name. Saving the file under a different name provides you with something to return to if you want to reprint this copy of your spreadsheet. Using this command also prevents you from accidentally saving this copy over the copy that has all the formats you want.
3. Change the default format to text by typing / to activate the menu and selecting Options, Formats, Numeric Format, and Text. Cells containing formulas and the default format are displayed as formulas. Cells containing formulas that have been formatted with the /Style Numeric Format command, text, and unformatted numbers remain unchanged. Any cells that have cell notation show the notation. Select Quit twice to return to READY mode.
4. Reset cells formatted with the /Style Numeric command by pressing / to activate the menu, and selecting Style, Numeric Format, and Reset. When prompted for the block to modify, press ESC to remove the block's anchor from the current position, press HOME to move the selector to A1, type a period to anchor the block, press END HOME to stretch the block to cover the portion of the spreadsheet that you have used, and press ENTER.
5. Enter /Style Block Widths Auto Width, and type 1 for the number of characters between columns, or click Fit in the SpeedBar. You may need to further widen columns with cells containing cell notation, since /Style Block Widths Auto Width does not widen the columns to show cell notation. An example is shown in Figure 4.6.

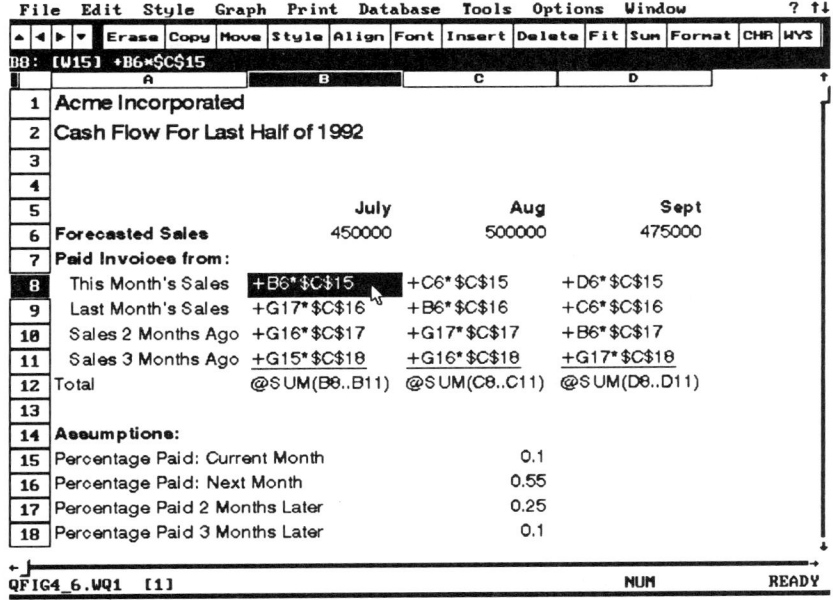

Figure 4.6   Spreadsheet with Default Format Set to Text

6. Activate the menu by pressing /, and choose **Print**.
7. Select **Block**, and highlight the area of the spreadsheet that you want to print.
8. Choose **Spreadsheet Print**. Quattro then starts printing your file in the format that appears on the screen, as the example shown in Figure 4.7.

CHANGING THE PRINT FORMAT TO PRINT CELL CONTENTS The Format setting from the Print menu provides another method for printing formulas. This method is quicker, but the printout is more difficult to work with. Quattro initially sets the Format setting to As Displayed, but if you change this to Cell-Formulas, Quattro prints out the cell address, its cell width (if different from the default setting), its format setting (if different from the default setting) and the contents (including any cell comments in a cell within the print block). Quattro omits headings, headers, footers, and explicit page breaks. A sample line from the printed output with this setting at Cell-Formulas looks like this: C8: (C2) [W11] (C1+C3+C5)/C7. This sample is the output for cell C8. In this cell, the format has been set to Currency with two decimal places, and the width has been set to 11. Finally, this cell contains the formula (C1+C3+C5)/C7. Figure 4.8 provides a look at some output produced with the Format set to Cell-Formulas.

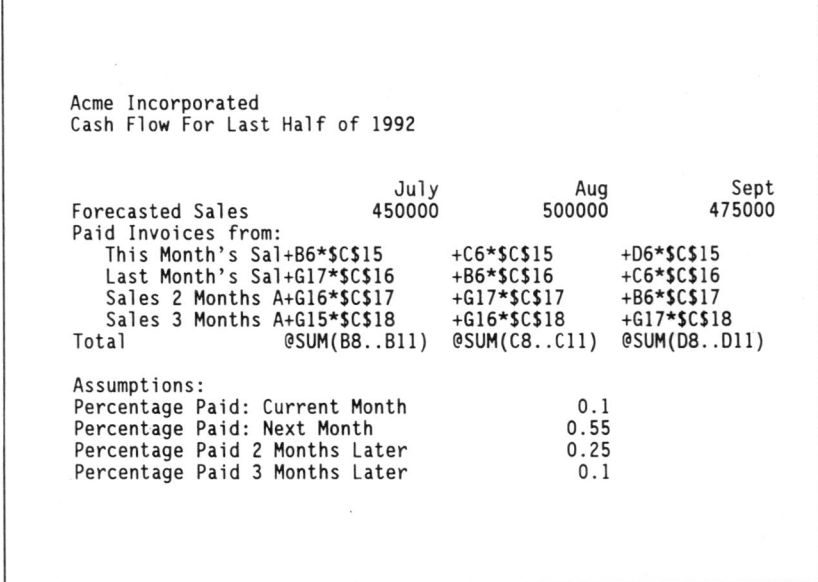

Figure 4.7 Printed Output with Default Format Set to Text

```
B5: [W15] "July
C5: [W15] "Aug
D5: [W15] "Sept
A6: [W19] 'Forecasted Sales
B6: [W15] 450000
C6: [W15] 500000
D6: [W15] 475000
A7: [W19] 'Paid Invoices from:
A8: [W19] '   This Month's Sales
B8: [W15] +B6*$C$15
C8: [W15] +C6*$C$15
D8: [W15] +D6*$C$15
A9: [W19] '   Last Month's Sales
B9: [W15] +G17*$C$16
C9: [W15] +B6*$C$16
D9: [W15] +C6*$C$16
```

Figure 4.8 Format Set to Cell-Formulas

ADVANCED PRINT OPTIONS

To print most of your spreadsheets, you will use the basic Quattro print commands. However, Quattro provides other features that help you customize the printed spreadsheet's appearance. Quattro's screen preview feature shows you the spreadsheet before you print it, so you can quickly see if the document's appearance meets your expectations. You can take advantage of other printer features, such as rotating the output or changing the line spacing using menu commands or setup strings, codes that tell your printer to perform a specific printer feature. Finally, you can use Quattro Pro 4's background printing to let you continue using Quattro Pro 4, as information is sent to the printer to be printed.

Previewing the Printed Spreadsheet

The first time you print a spreadsheet, you may find that you need to reprint it, because the output is missing information or includes lines and boxes that are inappropriately placed. Rather than halting the printing process or waiting until Quattro finishes printing, you can save time by viewing the spreadsheet on the screen before Quattro prints it. This is Quattro's screen previewer. When you preview a spreadsheet, Quattro displays the spreadsheet as if you were sending the printed output to a graphics printer. This feature expects that the printer is selected correctly before printing or previewing a document, because different printers vary in regard to appearance of output.

To tell Quattro that you want to preview a spreadsheet, enter /Print Destination

Screen Preview. Once Quattro knows you want to preview the output instead of printing it, enter Spreadsheet Print to preview the spreadsheet. Quattro may occasionally show a box telling you it is building a font. Figure 4.9 shows the screen Quattro displays for previewing a spreadsheet.

The white rectangle that represents the page Quattro will print does not show the actual text well. If you want to look closer at the text, press the PLUS or GRAY PLUS key to look at a section of the page closer. If you want to return the display to show the entire page, press the MINUS or GRAY MINUS key. You can press these keys more than once to expand or contract the text farther. The superimposed rectangle in the upper-right corner in Figure 4.10 represents the page. This is called the *guide*, and a rectangle on the guide indicates which portion of the page currently is enlarged (zoom box). You can change the portion of the screen that Quattro enlarges by moving the UP and DOWN ARROWS to move the zoom box. When the zoom box is positioned at the portion of the sheet you want to see, press ENTER. If the spreadsheet will use more than one page when it is printed, press the PGDN and PGUP keys to switch between pages.

The screen preview feature also has a menu bar, which is activated with the slash (/). Entering /Zoom is the same as pressing the + key. Entering /Unzoom is the same as pressing the - key. If you want to remove the guide that selects the portion of the page Quattro displays, enter /Guide. Entering the same command again returns the guide to the display. When the guide is hidden, you can continue to use the UP and DOWN ARROWS to change the portion of the page that is enlarged. You do not have to press ENTER, since pressing an arrow key automati-

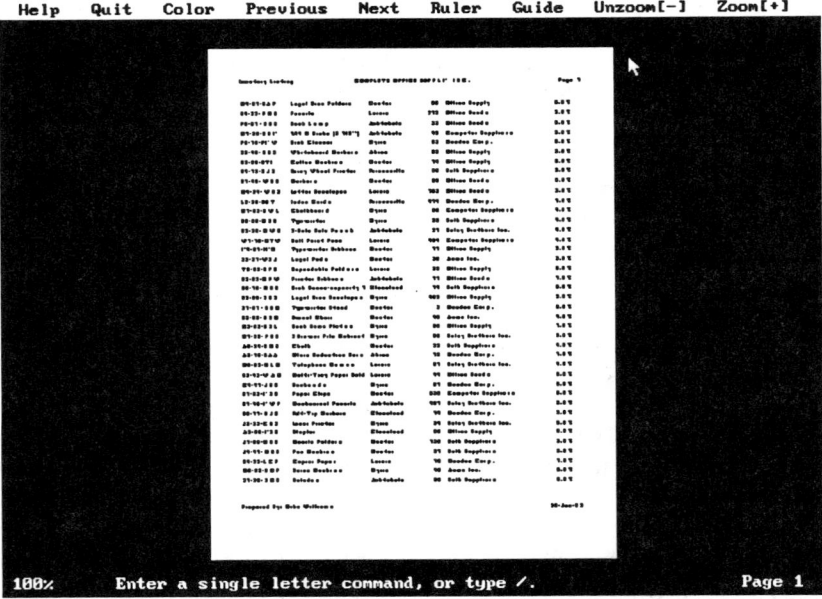

Figure 4.9 Preview of a Spreadsheet

Printing 163

Figure 4.10 Closer Look at Previewed Spreadsheet

cally changes the portion of the page that is enlarged. /Next and /Previous perform the same functions as the PGUP and PGDN keys. Selecting /Ruler adds lines to indicate inches down and across the page. Selecting /Ruler again removes these lines. The /Color command changes the screen preview display to various screen color settings that may work better with certain equipment. Each time you enter /Color, Quattro uses the next color setting for the screen preview. Entering /Quit or pressing ESC will return you to the Print pull-down menu. If you need help, you can enter /Help, or press F1 (HELP).

If you are using a mouse, you can select a menu command by pointing to the command you want and pressing the mouse button. To change the portion of the page Quattro displays when the display is enlarged, point to the section of the page you want to view on the guide, and press the mouse button.

Rotating the Spreadsheet

Quattro is initially set to print the spreadsheet from the top to the bottom of the page. If you are printing a wide block, it may be more convenient for you to print the spreadsheet sideways. To print a spreadsheet sideways, use the /Print Layout Orientation Landscape command. When you select Spreadsheet Print, the text will be rotated. To return the orientation of the printing to the default, use the /Print Layout Orientation Portrait command. The Landscape option can only be used when you select a graphics printer as the destination. A third option for Quattro

> ▼ **TIP: Previews save paper.**
>
> Preview any spreadsheet before you print it so you can check that the printed spreadsheet will appear as intended.

Pro 3 and 4 is selecting /Print Layout Orientation Banner. This option prints the selected block rotated like landscape printing, except that it does not break between pages. This option lets you print out wide blocks in landscape mode without the page breaks the Landscape option creates. Banner printing ignores the right margin and prints the spreadsheet as wide as necessary. Banner printing cannot be done with laser printers, since these automatically include page breaks. If the block includes top and left headings, these headings are printed for every page in Portrait or Landscape printing; but Banner printing only prints these headings on the first page.

Expanding or Compressing the Printed Spreadsheet

If you want to make the printed copy of your spreadsheet smaller or larger, Quattro Pro 3 and 4 include two options that make it easier. In prior releases, you had to alter the font, margins, and page size until you got the results you wanted. With Quattro Pro 3 and 4, you can use two menu commands to enlarge or compress the printed spreadsheet. Both commands require that you print to a graphics printer by selecting Graphics Printer or Binary File as the destination. One of the two commands you can use is /Print Print-To-Fit. When you use this command in place of /Print Spreadsheet Print, Quattro Pro contracts your printed spreadsheet to fit on one page or as few pages as possible. Quattro Pro makes the determination as to how much to compress the spreadsheet so the text is still readable based on the selected printer and the printer resolution. This command uses the page breaks you have added with the /Style Insert Break command. This command is most frequently useful when you have a spreadsheet to print that you want to fit on one page.

The other option, using the % Scaling in the Print Layout Options dialog box or the /Print Layout Percent scaling command when you are not using dialog boxes, lets you select how much Quattro Pro expands or compresses the printed spreadsheet. When you select this command, you must enter a number between 1 and 1000 for the percentage of the original size you want to expand or compress the printed copy. Entering a number less than 100 prints the spreadsheet smaller, and entering a number greater than 100 prints the spreadsheet larger. When you use this command, Quattro Pro divides the output into pages based on the amount of information that fits on each page. When you use this command, Quattro Pro will not reduce the point size of any font below 1 point or expand the point size of any text beyond 72 points. When you change the percent scaling, use **S**preadsheet **P**rint to print the data, since using **P**rint-**T**o-**F**it ignores the percent scaling setting.

Using Setup Strings

Setup strings can tap into the array of special print features available on your printer. Although you might think setup strings have a strange appearance, a setup string is a sequence of characters that has a specific meaning to your printer. Setup strings allow you to use nonstandard features of your printer such as boldface, compressed print, and a variety of line-spacing options. You can also use setup strings to reset the printer to remove settings made earlier. Since setup strings are printer dependent, a setup string created for one printer may not work on another. In some spreadsheet packages, setup strings are the method for using different fonts. Quattro Pro provides the setup strings automatically when you use a menu command, so you do not have to learn the printer codes for the printer feature you want to use. Setup strings are used primarily for accessing printer features for which Quattro Pro does not have a menu command.

ENTERING SETUP STRINGS THROUGH THE MENU Setup strings can be used for the entire output of a print operation. Setup strings are entered after Printer Setup String in the Print Layout Options dialog box or by selecting the **/P**rint **L**ayout **S**etup String command when you are not using dialog boxes. Next, type the setup string that you want to use, and pressing ENTER. When you print your spreadsheet, Quattro sends the setup string to the printer before it sends the data to be printed.

The feature invoked by a setup string continues until another setup string undoes the first setup string or until the printer is reset (by being turned off and then on again). Therefore, the printer feature activated by the setup string applies to the entire spreadsheet. Unfortunately, the exact setup string used varies from printer to printer. Therefore, if you change printers you may need to change the setup string.

To find a setup string for your printer, you must look in your printer manual. A printer manual contains a section that describes the printer codes that invoke each of the printer's features. A section with a name like Control Codes or Printer Command Table is a good place to begin your search. For example, to boldface characters on a Hewlett-Packard LaserJet printer, the entries in the printer manual might look like this:

Function	Parameter	Printer Command	Decimal Value	Hexadecimal Value
Primary Stroke Weight	Bold(3)	ESC (s3B	027 040 115 051 066	1B 28 73 33 42

In this example, the printer command to boldface text is the ESC key, a left parenthesis, an **s**, a **3**, and a **B**. When you enter a setup string, Quattro does not recognize characters with ASCII codes 32 or below. You must enter these characters using their ASCII code preceded by a backslash. For example, enter ESC as \027. Therefore, the setup string for boldfaced text is \027(s3B. You can enter the entire setup string using the ASCII codes. For example, you can enter the setup string of \027(s3B as \027\040\115\051\066. Using the combination of letters and numbers is shorter, but some printer manuals only provide the ASCII values. Since setup strings may be up to 39 characters, using the letter and number combination is more efficient. To combine setup strings, like boldfaced and compressed print, join the setup strings together, as in \027(s3B\027&k2S (the setup string for boldface and compressed print).

If you want to use the same setup string in later Quattro sessions, select **Update** from the Print Layout Options dialog box or the Layout menu. When you select **Update**, Quattro saves the page length, margins, dimensions, orientation, and setup string settings. Any spreadsheets that you create after saving the layout settings use the settings that you saved. You can use this feature to include a setup string that resets the printer before printing so that the spreadsheet will not inadvertently include printer features from a previous printing.

INCORPORATING SETUP STRINGS IN A SPREADSHEET A setup string entered in the Print Layout Options dialog box or with the /Print Layout Setup String applies to the entire document. Quattro also lets you use setup strings within a spreadsheet to use printer features for a smaller portion of a spreadsheet. For example, you can change the line spacing of different portions of the spreadsheet. To incorporate a setup string in your spreadsheet, create a blank row just above the row in which you want the special printer feature. At the beginning of this new blank row type two vertical bars (| |), and type the setup string that you want to use. Entries in the same row as the setup string are not printed. Therefore, you can use the cells to the right of the setup string to document your setup string. When you use a printer feature, the printer continues to use that feature until the feature is disabled by another setup string or the printer is reset. You must create another setup string to turn off the printer feature, or reset the printer before printing another spreadsheet. You cannot use setup strings in the top and left headings, since in headings Quattro prints setup strings as they appear in the spreadsheet instead of activating printer features.

USING SETUP STRINGS TO TAP THE HEWLETT-PACKARD LASERJET'S FEATURES Figure 4.11 provides an example of setup strings in a spreadsheet. When this report is printed, the setup string in A4 tells the printer to start underlining. The setup string in A6 tells the printer to stop underlining. The setup string in A15 instructs the printer to start printing with compressed print for the assumptions. This spreadsheet has another setup string in A21, which instructs the printer to return to the regular printing size. If this last setup string is missing, the printer will continue to print using compressed characters until the printer receives a setup string to deactivate the special feature or you turn your printer off and then on again. Figure 4.12 shows the finished product when the block of data shown in Figure 4.11 is printed.

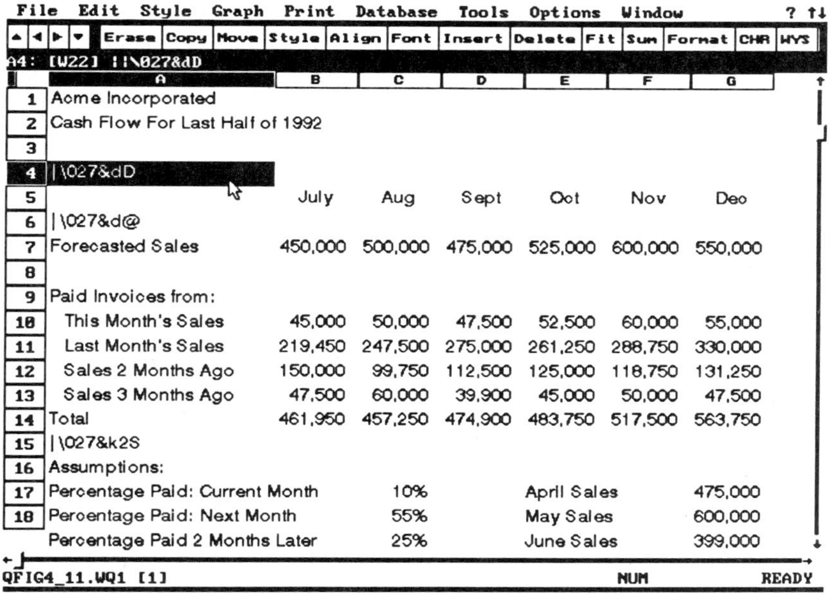

Figure 4.11 Spreadsheet with Setup Strings

Acme Incorporated
Cash Flow For Last Half of 1992

	July	Aug	Sept	Oct	Nov	Dec
Forecasted Sales	450,000	500,000	475,000	525,000	600,000	550,000
Paid Invoices from:						
This Month's Sales	45,000	50,000	47,500	52,500	60,000	55,000
Last Month's Sales	219,450	247,500	275,000	261,250	288,750	330,000
Sales 2 Months Ago	150,000	99,750	112,500	125,000	118,750	131,250
Sales 3 Months Ago	47,500	60,000	39,900	45,000	50,000	47,500
Total	461,950	457,250	474,900	483,750	517,500	563,750

Assumptions:			
Percentage Paid: Current Month	10%	April Sales	475,000
Percentage Paid: Next Month	55%	May Sales	600,000
Percentage Paid 2 Months Later	25%	June Sales	399,000
Percentage Paid 3 Months Later	10%		

Figure 4.12 Printed Spreadsheet with Setup Strings

Special Considerations When Printing to a Text File

When you print your output to a text file that you are planning to import to another program, you need to make a few adjustments. These changes help eliminate changes usually required after importing the data to another program. If you are planning to import your Quattro spreadsheet to another package, you should also look at the Exporting Data section in Chapter 5. Quattro provides several quick methods of converting spreadsheets to dBASE and Lotus files that you can use in place of printing spreadsheet data to a file and importing the file to another software package. When you are printing to a file that will later be imported into another software package, you first want to select **File** as the destination. When you print to a text file you do not want to use the WYSIWYG display mode, since you will not see if the column widths are appropriate for the file you will create.

ELIMINATING PAGE BREAKS When Quattro prints to a file, page breaks cause blank lines to be included in the file. If you are importing this information into another program, you often do not need these extra lines. To remove the page breaks that Quattro automatically inserts, use the **Break Pages** command after selecting **/Print Layout**. To remove page breaks, choose **Break Pages**. Choose **No** from the box superimposed on the screen. When you print your spreadsheet, Quattro no longer inserts automatic page breaks. Quattro also does not print the header and/or footer. Quattro uses the left and right margins set in the Margins menu. Although the top heading and left heading continue to be used, the top heading only appears at the beginning of the printed file. Suppressing the page breaks only affects the page breaks that Quattro automatically adds. The file still contains any page breaks that you create with the **/Style Insert Break** command or with a **|::** entry in the beginning of the row. To remove these page breaks, you must remove them from the spreadsheet. If you later want to restore the page breaks, enter **/Print Layout** and then select **Break Pages** and **Yes**.

WIDENING COLUMN WIDTHS In a printed file, you cannot always see all the information seen in a spreadsheet on the screen. For example, if a cell has a long string of text that is partially hidden by the contents of other cells, only the portion that appears is included in the print file. Frequently, you need to change the widths of columns. To change the width of a column, use one of three commands: **/Style Column Width, /Style Block Widths Set Width**, or **/Style Block Widths Auto Width** (all covered in Chapter 3). These enable you to widen the columns so that all the cell's contents appear.

Just as with direct printer output, any columns that are hidden in the spreadsheet do not appear in the printed file. Therefore, before you print your information to a file, check that all the information that you want is visible and included in the print block.

MARGIN SETTINGS When you print to a file, you do not need blank margin space on all four sides of the data. For some applications, blank spaces surrounding your data is best eliminated. If you are planning to include the printed file in another program, you should reset all margins to make the margins as small as possible. Also, by instructing Quattro to print more characters on each line, you can prevent a wide spreadsheet from being broken into sections.

To reset the margins, press **/** to activate the menu, and select **Print, Layout**, and **Margins**. Next, set the Left, the Top, and the Bottom margins to 0. Finally, set the

Right margin to 511 (254 in prior releases). Even if you do not use all 511 characters, setting the right margin to 511 characters prevents a row within a print block from being divided into sections.

SETUP STRINGS Although the setup strings are useful for direct print output, they may acquire a different meaning if you access them in another program. You should remove all setup strings before creating a print file for use by another program. You must remove both the setup strings located within your spreadsheet and the setup strings contained in the Printer Setup String setting of the Print Layout Options dialog box.

Printing with a Hewlett-Packard LaserJet Printer

A Hewlett-Packard LaserJet printer has several features that can enhance your spreadsheets printed with Quattro Pro 3 and 4. These features include using cartridge fonts, changing the shading level, and downloading Bitstream fonts.

As described in Chapter 3, Hewlett-Packard LaserJet and Canon LBP printers can use cartridges to provide more fonts. To use these fonts in Quattro Pro, you must tell Quattro Pro which cartridges are attached to the printer. To do so, select /Options Hardware Printer Fonts Cartridge Fonts, Right Cartridge or Left Cartridge, and the cartridge installed in the printer's cartridge font slot.

Another feature of a Hewlett-Packard LaserJet series III printer is the seven different shading levels to select the shading level Quattro Pro uses when you print cells shaded with the /Style Shading Grey command, select /Options Hardware Printer Fonts Cartridge Fonts Shading Level, and enter the percentage Quattro Pro should use. One to 2 percent uses the first shading level, 3 to 10 percent uses the second shading level, 11 to 20 percent uses the third shading level, 21 to 35 percent uses the fourth shading level, 36 to 55 uses the fifth shading level, 56 to 80 percent uses the sixth shading level, 81 to 99 percent uses the seventh shading level, and 100 percent uses solid black.

When you print in Quattro Pro 2.0 and above and your spreadsheet uses Bitstream fonts that are smaller than 20 points, Quattro Pro downloads the fonts to the printer before it prints the spreadsheet. The Bitstream fonts are bitmapped, which means that each character is defined by where the printer places the dots that compose each character. With Bitstream fonts smaller than 20 points, Quattro Pro sends the definition of each character to the printer for the fonts the spreadsheet uses, so the printer has this stored in its memory. This is called *downloading*. Once the font is downloaded, Quattro Pro only needs to tell the printer which characters to print. This is faster than Quattro Pro 1 or printing fonts larger than 20 points, which require Quattro Pro to tell the printer individually how each character is printed. This is also how Quattro Pro prints graphs so in Chapter 7, when you learn how to print the graphs you create, you know why printing them takes longer than printing a spreadsheet.

Updating Print Defaults

If you use the same print settings for many of your spreadsheets, you can make your specifications the default settings that Quattro uses. To make your current page layout settings the default settings, press / to activate the menu, and choose Print, Layout, and Update. When you update the default settings, Quattro takes the current settings in the Page Layout menu, except for the header and footer, and uses them as the default settings for the page layout for all new spreadsheets in both current and subsequent sessions. Quattro always stores changes made to the Page Layout menu with the spreadsheet to which you make the changes. The changes saved with the Update command are used with all subsequent spreadsheets; for other spreadsheets, use the /Print Layout Reset All or /Print Layout Reset Layout command.

Background Printing in Quattro Pro 4

Just as you can print to a file, you do not have to wait until a file is printed to continue to use Quattro Pro, you can also use background printing. Background printing means that when you print a spreadsheet, Quattro Pro stores the information it will send to the printer in a file and as you continue using Quattro Pro, Quattro Pro sends the information from the file to the printer. Background printing is used because your computer can send information to the printer faster than your printer can print it. Without background printing, the computer sends some information to the printer and waits until the printer has printed that information before sending more. This means that the computer must do nothing while the printer is printing, and you cannot use the printer. Background printing makes your work easier by letting you continue working with Quattro Pro as you are printing spreadsheet data.

To print in the background with Quattro Pro, you must start the program that handles the background printing. To do this, from DOS, without Quattro Pro loaded, type **BPS** and press ENTER. This loads the Borland print spooler. The spooler program handles receiving the information to print and sending the information to the printer as the printer is ready for it. Once the spooler is started you can start Quattro Pro. To tell Quattro Pro to use the spooler instead of printing directly to the printer, select /Options Hardware Printers Background Yes. Now when you print, the spooler will continue sending information to the printer as you continue working with Quattro Pro. You can change the printing by using Quattro Pro's Print Manager as described below.

When you finish using Quattro Pro and you want to remove the spooler from the computer's memory, return to the DOS prompt and type **BPS/U**, and press ENTER. You will not want to use the Borland print spooler for background printing if you are using a network printer, since the network will have its own print spooler.

USING THE PRINT MANAGER The Print Manager lets you view the printing tasks you will print with either the Borland print spooler or Novell's Netware

Printing   171

versions 2.0 and higher. To see and use the Print Manager (assuming you have loaded the Borland print spooler), select /Print Print Manager. Quattro displays the Print Manager as shown in Figure 4.13. Quattro lists every printing task that is being printed with the Borland or NetWare printer spooler. Each print task is called a *print job*. For each print job, the Print Manager lists the number assigned to it (Seq), the user name for the server (Banner Name) and the name of the print job on a network or the name of the temporary print file (File Name) when you are not using a network, the status of the print job (Status), the port that the printer is attached to (Port) or the job number assign by the server (Job), the size of the temporary file that stores the information to print (File Size), and the number of copies you are printing (Copies).The status of different jobs can be Adding if Quattro Pro is adding more information to print to the file on the network printer, Active if the spooler is printing the print job, Held if the print job has been suspended, Ready if the print job is waiting to be printed, or Waiting if the network print job will start printing after a specified time has elapsed. You can pause any print job by using the UP ARROW and DOWN ARROW to highlight the job in the list you want to pause and then select /Job Suspend. When a job is paused, it will not print until you select /Job Resume. You can also remove print jobs from the queue by selecting /Job Delete. If you are using a Novell Netware network, you can select the print queue displayed by selecting /Queue Network and the print queue to display. You can also return to displaying the Borland print spooler's queue by selecting /Queue Background. You can open multiple Print Manager windows so each one can display a different print queue. The commands in the File and

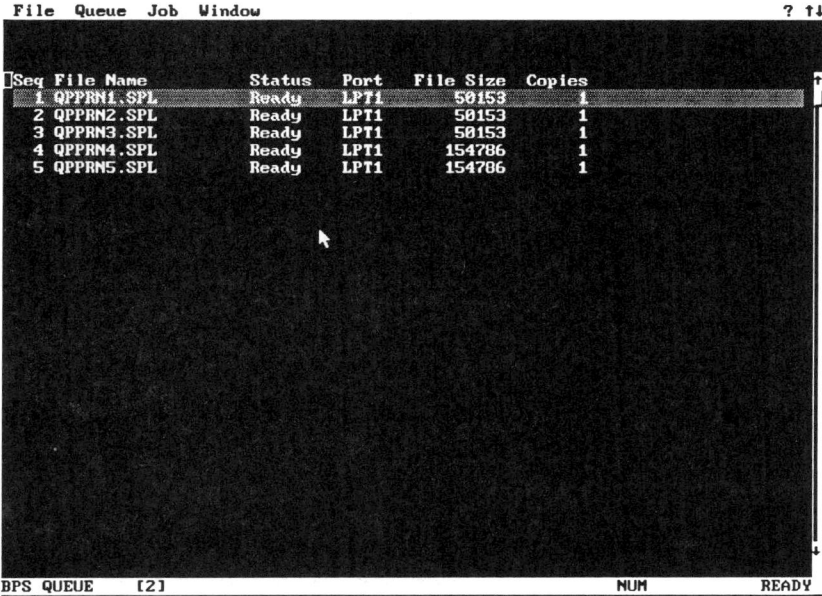

Figure 4.13   Print Manager Window

172 *Quattro Pro 4.0 Handbook*

Window menus are identical to the same commands when you are working with a spreadsheet. The print queue is updated according to the setting of the /Options Network Refresh command.

CHANGING PRINTERS

When you install Quattro, you have the opportunity to select the printer you will use with Quattro. Quattro needs to know the printer you use to enable printing with the graphics features like fonts, lines, and graphs. Quattro needs to provide the setup strings and other printer-specific information so the printer can print the spreadsheet and graphs as you want them to appear. If the printer that you have selected is not the one you are using, Quattro may not print your spreadsheet and graphs correctly. Quattro also assumes that you are using a parallel interface connected to your computer's first parallel slot, that the printer does not have automatic line-feed, and that the printer uses continuous paper. The last assumption also applies for many laser printers that do not use continuous feed paper but behave as if they do because of their automatic tray-feed mechanisms. If the printer selection is incorrect or Quattro's assumptions are incorrect, you must change Quattro's settings with these steps:

1. Press / to activate the menu.
2. Select Options, Hardware, and Printers. The menu in Figure 4.14 appears. Quattro remembers the settings for two printers at a time, although you can change which two printers Quattro remembers.

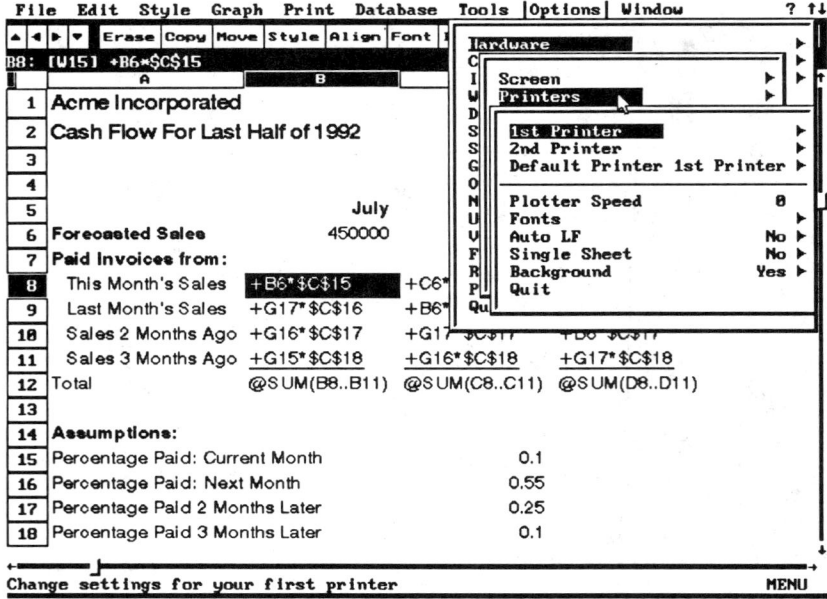

Figure 4.14 Hardware Printers Menu

3. If the printer you are using is not listed as the first or second printer, select **1st Printer** or **2nd Printer**. Then Quattro prompts you for information about the manufacturer, the model, and the mode (the quality level—many printers have more than one). For each selection box, choose the selection for your printer or a compatible printer.
4. If the printer is not connected to the first parallel port, press **D** for Device. Your choices are Parallel 1, Serial 1, Parallel 2, Serial 2, Parallel 2, LPT 1, LPT 2, LPT3, LPT4, EPT, and Network Queue. Highlight the one that you want, or type the number to the left of your choice and press ENTER. EPT is a logical device that works only with the IBM Postscript PagePrinter.
5. If you are using a serial port, press **B** for Baud rate, and choose the baud rate of your serial port. The correct baud rate should be listed in your serial printer's manual.
6. Press **P** for Parity if you are using a serial port. Your choices are Leave as is, **No**, **Odd**, and **Even**. Choose one by typing the first letter of your choice or moving the highlight to your choice and pressing ENTER. If you choose Leave as is, Quattro uses the parity set by DOS.
7. Press **S** for Stop bits if you are using a serial port. Your choices are Leave as is, **1** bit, or **2** bits. If it is set to Leave as is, Quattro uses the number of stop bits set by DOS. Choose one by typing the first letter of your choice or by moving the highlight to your choice and pressing ENTER.
8. Press **Q** for Quit to return to the previous menu.
9. Press **D** for Default Printer, and select **1st Printer** or **2nd Printer**. Quattro uses this selection when you print the spreadsheet to a graphics printer.
10. If you are printing to a plotter, you may need to adjust the speed. You may change the speed so the plotter draws thicker lines or so the plotter draws correctly on transparencies. Type **P** for Plotter Speed, and type a number representing the plotter speed (1 is the slowest speed; each higher number represents a faster speed, and 0 represents the quickest speed the plotter can use).
11. Type **A** for Auto LF if your printer is printing everything double-spaced or if the printer is not advancing to the next line. If the printer prints everything double-spaced, check that this setting is at **No**. If your printer is not advancing to the next line, check that this setting is at **Yes**. Choose one by typing **Y** or **N** or by moving the highlight to your choice and pressing ENTER.
12. Press **S** for Single Sheet if you are not using continuous-feed paper, and then press a **Y** for Yes. Although many laser printers use single sheets of paper, their automatic-feed capabilities conform with the continuous-feed specifications.
13. Press **Q** for Quit. Quattro remembers the printer settings that you have just created.

174 *Quattro Pro 4.0 Handbook*

14. Print a spreadsheet to check that your settings are correct. If your settings are not correct, you can make changes. Your changes are not stored permanently until you choose Update.

15. Make the changes permanent by pressing / to activate the menu, and select Options Update. Quattro now uses the new settings for printing out all subsequent spreadsheets.

GETTING STARTED

In this chapter you learned how to print your spreadsheets. With the options covered in this chapter, you learned how you can control your output's appearance. You can try some of these printing features by following these steps:

1. Make the following entries. You can use the inventory report in Figure 4.15 as a guide or use the cell addresses shown below. This spreadsheet is designed for you to try Quattro's printing features.

    A2: **Inventory Report**
    A4: **Nails**
    A5: **Rivets**
    A6: **Screws**
    A7: **Tacks**
    A8: **Total**

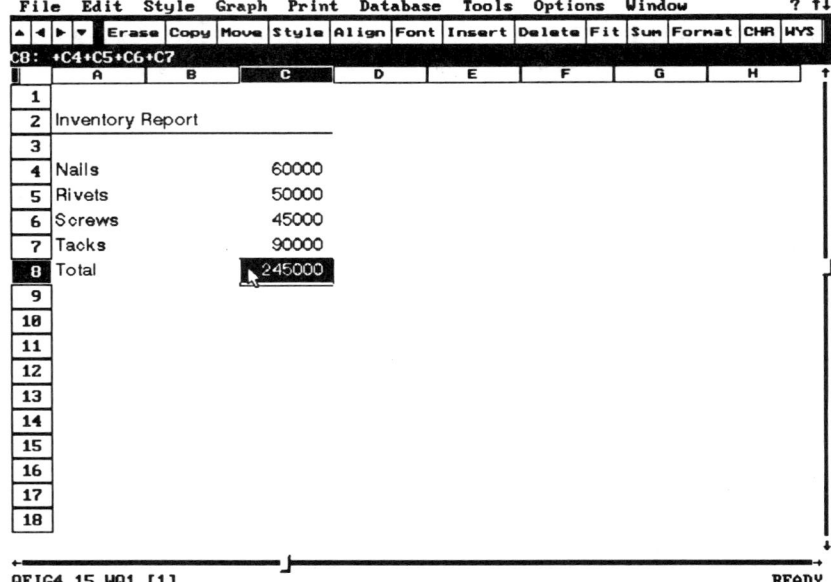

Figure 4.15 Inventory Report Used for Getting Started Section

C4: **60000**
C5: **50000**
C6: **45000**
C7: **90000**
C8: **+C4+C5+C6+C7**

2. To draw a single line under Inventory Report, move to A2, and enter **/Style Line Drawing**. Select the block **A2..C2**. Select **Bottom**, **Single**, then **Quit**. Move to C8. Add a line by selecting **/Style Line Drawing**, the block **C8..C8**, **Top**, **Single**, **Bottom**, **Double**, and **Quit**.

3. Enter **/Print Block**. When Quattro prompts for a block address, type **A2..C9** or point to the block using the selector or mouse. Press ENTER or click [Enter] in the input line.

4. Enter **Adjust Printer Align**, **Spreadsheet Print**, and **Adjust Printer Form Feed**. This prints the spreadsheet using the default print settings. As the line below Inventory Report indicates, printing to the Printer destination may not print the drawn lines as intended. Also, the output is in the upper-left corner. You can make this output more attractive by using the Bitstream fonts and centering the data on the page.

5. Enter **Quit** to return to the READY mode.

6. Select **/Style Font** and the block **A4..C8**. Next, select **Point Size** and **16** points. Since this is the only change you want to make, select **Quit** to return to the spreadsheet. This is the same as selecting **/Style Font Edit Fonts 1 Font 1** in Quattro Pro 3 or earlier, selecting **Point Size**, **16** points, and **Quit** since changing the first font in the font table sets the font of all spreadsheet entries that you do not otherwise assign.

7. Press ESC to return to the spreadsheet, and Move the selector to a cell in column C and press CTRL-W once, the RIGHT ARROW twice, and ENTER once to expand the column width to 11. You can also click the Fit button in the SpeedBar, and [Enter] in the input line.

8. Move to cell A2. Select **/Style Font**, or click FONT in the SpeedBar, and press ENTER or [Enter] in the input line. Next, select **Typeface** and **Dutch-SC**. Next, select **Point Size** and **20** points. Select **Bold** to boldface this font. Select **Quit** to apply the font and return to the spreadsheet. This is the same as selecting **/Style Font Edit Fonts 2 Font 2** in Quattro Pro 3 or earlier, selecting **Typeface**, **Bitstream Dutch**, **Point Size**, **20** points, **Style**, **Bold**, and **Quit**. Once this font in the font table was changed, you would use the **/Style Font 2** command, and press ENTER to assign this font in the font table to the cell A2. You do not need to include B2 even though A2 uses B2's display space since the font assignment is maintained with the cell contents.

9. Enter **/Print Destination Screen Preview**. This displays the spreadsheet on the screen as Quattro will print it.

10. Enter **Layout** so you can center the output on the page. If you do not see the Print Layout Options menu, select **Margins**. If Dimensions unit is Lines/Characters, select **Top**, type **15**, and press ENTER for the top margin; then

Inventory Report	
Nails	60000
Rivets	50000
Screws	45000
Tacks	90000
Total	245000

Figure 4.16 Spreadsheet Printed Using Graphics Printer

    select **Left**, type **25**, and press ENTER for the left margin. If it is inches, use **2.5** for the top margin and **2.5** for the bottom margin. If it is centimeters, use **6.35** for the top margin and **6.35** for the bottom margin. Select **Quit** until you return to the Print menu.

11. Select **Spreadsheet Print**. The inventory report appears in the screen previewer. Press **+** to zoom the report. Press the DOWN ARROW, and press ENTER to focus on the actual report. By checking this spreadsheet before printing it, you can focus on how the final document looks and decide whether to change any print settings before you print the document. Press ESC to return to the Print menu.

12. Select **Destination Graphics Printer**. Then select **Adjust Printer Align**, **Spreadsheet Print**, and **Adjust Printer Form Feed**. This prints your spreadsheet using the best quality your printer can produce. Figure 4.16 shows this report printed on a Hewlett-Packard LaserJet printer in high density (mode is set to 300 × 300 dpi). As you will notice, printing to a graphics printer takes longer, but the resulting printout looks better. Select **Quit** to return to the READY mode.

5

File Options

Spreadsheets created in the memory of your machine are lost if power to the machine goes off for even a brief instant. This loss occurs because random access memory (RAM) where the spreadsheet is stored is a transient storage medium. Files, however, offer permanent storage for your spreadsheets.

Quattro provides all the basic file handling commands and adds certain options for creating backups and protecting your files with passwords. Quattro's file-handling features surpass those of other packages by translating data directly from other popular packages into Quattro's format and from Quattro's format to the format required by other popular packages. An additional feature lets you use more than one spreadsheet at once. You can share data between spreadsheets by using Quattro's commands and by using data from other spreadsheets in formulas.

This chapter covers the basic concepts of DOS as they relate to the storage of Quattro files. You will learn how to save, retrieve, and erase files, and change the current directory. You will learn to use DOS commands from within Quattro. With the File Manager, many of the DOS commands are provided for you to use from menu selections.

FILE BASICS

Disks are like a file cabinet that provide an area for you to keep your information. Just as you can store printed information in a folder within a file cabinet, you can store your computer information in a file on a disk. However, unlike a file cabinet's contents, you do not see a file. Your operating system acts as an intermediary between you and your files. For DOS to store and retrieve your information, you must provide unique names for your files. To make it easier to find information on large-capacity disks, DOS supports the use of directories and subdirectories to organize your files.

Directories and Subdirectories

Directories and subdirectories contain information about the files that you store on your disk. The main directory on a disk is called the root directory. On a floppy disk, this may be the only directory, but a larger disk normally contains logical divisions called subdirectories. Subdirectories provide a method of logically organizing the information that you keep on your disks.

The file cabinet analogy also illustrates the concept of subdirectories. Most file cabinets contain several drawers, and typically each drawer is used for a different type of information. One drawer may contain financial information, and another may contain production information. Although subdirectories do not physically divide a disk the way drawers do a file cabinet, they also provide a logical structure for recording information on a specific type of data. One subdirectory can be used for production information, and another subdirectory can be used for financial information. The disk contains both types of files but has separated the information about them to help you locate the information more quickly.

Within each drawer of a file cabinet, the information can be further organized. For example, in the financial drawer, the information can be separated into inventory valuation, financial statements, and forecasting information. Likewise, the financial subdirectory on your disk can be divided into inventory valuation, financial statements, and forecasting information subdirectories. Any subdirectory can be broken into further levels of subdirectories. For example, the subdirectories can be established for the different years of financial statements.

Suppose you need to find last year's income statement. To find it in the file cabinet, you must first go to the financial drawer, locate the financial statements section, and then find the section for the financial statements for last year. Finally, you look for the specific folder you want. While it may seem to require a significant effort to choose a specific location before searching for the exact information that you need, it is much quicker than going through a pile of papers in random order. Accessing computer file information works the same way. Positioning yourself in a specific subdirectory locates the required file quickly.

Directories and subdirectories store information on your file and subdirectory entries. They are similiar to a piece of paper on top of a file cabinet that describes what each drawer contains; you can look at the piece of paper and know which drawer you want to use. On a disk, the initial or root directory lists all its subdirectories. If all your files are stored in either the production or financial subdirectory, the root directory contains only the entries for the production and financial subdirectories and not the file entries for the subdirectories. If you examine the financial's subdirectory entries, you may find that it has no direct file entries, only the entries for the subdirectories for inventory valuation, financial statements, and forecasting information. As you look down through each level, you will see entries for the files and subdirectories at each level. Figure 5.1 shows how the information stored in one file cabinet might be converted into computer directories.

Although subdirectories present the information on the disk in an orderly fashion, your disk does not store information in the order that it appears in the

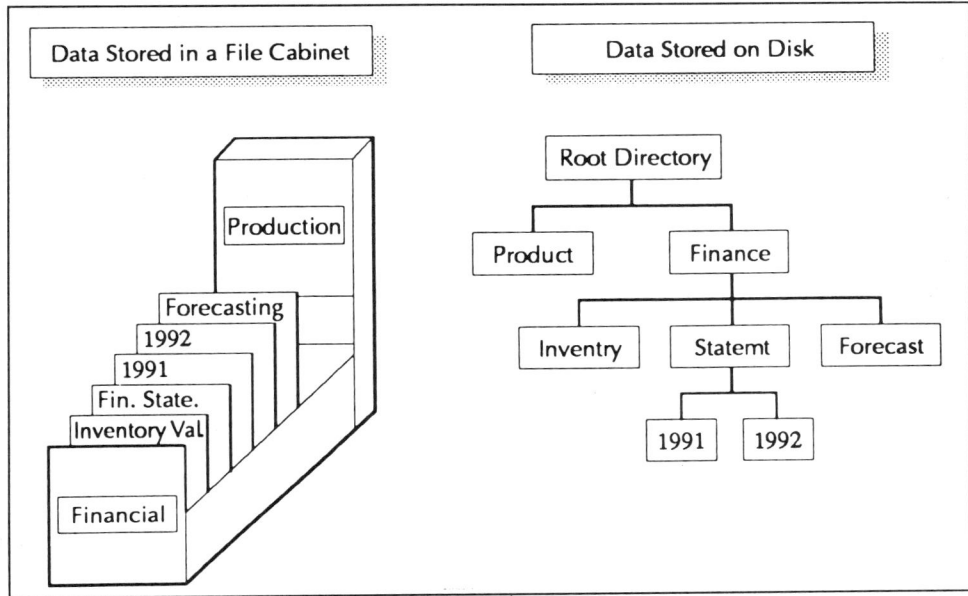

Figure 5.1 Directory Structures of File-Cabinet and Computer Disk Information

subdirectories. In other words, the operating system does not mark off an area of your disk to use for each subdirectory. If it assigned storage areas to each subdirectory, you would have to preset each directory's size and would not be able to expand beyond the preset limit. When you create a new file and add it at the level of the production subdirectory, the operating system stores the new file in the next free area. It puts the name and location of the new file in the production subdirectory, although you only see the name entry. When you ask for the file again, the operating system uses the location and finds the file. Your file's physical location on the disk is only important to the operating system. The subdirectory that contains the location information for a file is important in order to tell the operating system where to look for the information. The specification of the correct directory for a file is known as the *path*. The path begins with the drive destination and includes each directory level off the root directory that is required to reach the correct subdirectory. For example, a file inventory valuation subdirectory that is under the financial subdirectory on drive C may have the path of C:\FINANCE\INVNTRY.

File-Naming Conventions

The operating system in your computer uses several conventions to describe files. To tell it which file you want to use, you must present your information in a manner that the operating system understands. Once you understand these file name conventions, you will want to develop a set of standards to name your files consistently. A standard naming convention helps you locate files readily and allows you to use the DOS * and ? wildcards to copy your files quickly.

RULES FOR FILE NAMES DOS uses several rules for file names. You must follow the DOS rules for file names when you create files with Quattro or any other program. If you want to store a file in a subdirectory, you must include the path. C:\QPRO\FILENAME.EXT is an example of a usable file name.

The C: represents the disk drive that your operating system should refer to when looking for the file. Traditionally, drives A and B are floppy disk drives, and C is a hard disk. If you do not specify the disk, your operating system assumes it should use the one it is currently using. The \QPRO\ represents the path that lists the subdirectories in which the operating system can find the file. Since the subdirectory list starts with a backslash (\), your operating system starts in the root directory. A backslash also separates the different subdirectories from one another and the last subdirectory from the file name. Each subdirectory consists of one to eight characters. If you need to use a lower-level subdirectory, you can create a path that leads the operating system to the subdirectory that contains your file. For example, if your file is in the subdirectory FINANCE located under the subdirectory PRO, which is a subdirectory of the root directory, your description of the path is \QPRO\FINANCE\. If you do not specify a path, your operating system will use the current subdirectory.

If you indicate the drive to use and do not specify a path, your operating system will use the root directory of the specified drive. The FILENAME is the name of the file that you provide. It is from one to eight characters long and may include letters, numbers, and certain punctuation symbols, although no spaces. The EXT represents the file name's extension. While a file name extension is not necessary, it is frequently used to describe the format of the data in the file. A file's extension is normally provided by the program that you use to create a file. Unless you provide another, Quattro provides a .WQ1 extension. Later you will learn about other file extensions that you can use with the files you create in Quattro Pro.

The combination of the file name and extension must be unique within a directory. For example, you cannot have two files named SALES.WQ1 on your QPRO subdirectory, since your operating system cannot distinguish the two files. Your operating system will let you have multiple files with the same name in different subdirectories; for example, you can have a SALES.WQ1 file in the QUATTRO directory and a SALES.WQ1 file in the QPRO directory.

ESTABLISHING A WORKABLE NAMING STANDARD A set of file-naming standards can help you remember what is in a file and can make it easier to copy a group of files. First, although DOS permits the use of several punctuation symbols, you should restrict yourself to the underscore (_). Use the underscore when you prefer to use a space, since spaces are not allowed in some operating systems and create problems with operating system commands in other operating systems. Second, use a name for your file that describes the information stored in it to help you remember what is in the different files. Also, use similar names for related files. For example, if you have two files that contain production information, give them similar names, like PROD_1 and PROD_2. Similar names help organize the information and make it easier to execute DOS commands on the files as a group. Also, when you have many files containing related information, create a subdirectory and move the files to the new subdirectory.

SAVING QUATTRO PRO SPREADSHEETS

Quattro provides several options for saving your spreadsheet. You can password protect your spreadsheet or change the directory where Quattro saves your file. You can change the format that Quattro uses to save your file, save only a portion of your file, or make a backup copy.

The Basic Save Operation

Until you save a copy of your spreadsheet on disk, you are at risk of losing your time invested in building the model. A sudden loss of power erases the memory of your machine. When you reload Quattro, you will have to start from the beginning and rebuild the model. But, if the model is available on your disk, you can retrieve it and continue. Even if you do not think that you need a model later you should save it, because you may find a mistake in spelling or in one of the numbers or formulas and need to reprint the model and because a copy of the model on disk may serve as the basis for another model.

To save your file, follow these steps:

1. Enter /File to activate the File menu shown in Figure 5.2.
2. Select Save As.
3. Type the name you want to use for the file. If you are saving a new file, you can provide up to eight characters for a file name consisting of letters, numbers, and the special symbols that DOS accepts. If the spreadsheet has been saved previously, Quattro prompts at the top of the screen with the current spreadsheet name. If you want to save the spreadsheet under a different file name, type the new name. You can also modify the current file name that you want to save by pressing F2 (EDIT) and using the arrow keys to edit the file name. You do not need to add an extension, since Quattro automatically adds .WQ1.
4. Press ENTER. If you have previously saved the file, Quattro asks you if you want to cancel your /File Save As command, replace the existing file with the current spreadsheet, or backup the file before saving it. If you choose to create a backup, Quattro renames the existing file with a .BAK extension and saves the current spreadsheet under the file name with a .WQ1 extension.

Another option for saving the file is the /File Save command. Using this command to save a spreadsheet the first time is identical to using the /File Save As

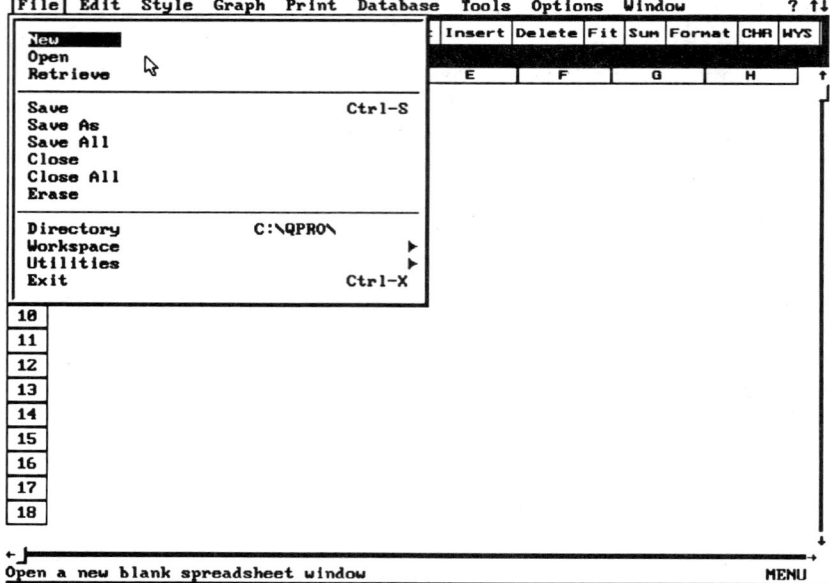

Figure 5.2 File Pull-down Menu

command. When you use the /File Save command to save a spreadsheet a subsequent time, Quattro asks you whether you want to cancel your /File Save command, replace the existing file with the current spreadsheet, or backup the file before saving. This command does not let you change the file name of the spreadsheet. You can also execute this command by pressing CTRL-S.

If Quattro is unable to save your file, it displays an error message. Normally, this error is caused by a situation that is easily remedied like an open disk drive, a missing disk, an unformatted disk, or a full disk. If Quattro is unable to save your spreadsheet because the diskette is unformatted, use the /File Utilities DOS Shell command, and format your disk before saving the spreadsheet again. If Quattro is unable to save your spreadsheet because the disk is full, replace the disk with another disk that has more room. You can also redirect Quattro to save the file to another drive by pressing CTRL-BACKSPACE and typing the desired drive, subdirectory, file name, and extension (if you are not saving it in Quattro's format). A third alternative is to remove files from the current diskette using the File Manager or the /File Utilities DOS Shell command. Once the problem is remedied, save your spreadsheet again.

Using Passwords

When you store information in a file cabinet, you can lock it to prevent unauthorized access. When you lock the cabinet, you then need the key the next time you need to look at those data. Quattro provides passwords to offer the same type of protection for your spreadsheet files. Just as you need a key to unlock the file cabinet, you need to use the password key to access password-protected Quattro files. To save a spreadsheet with a password, type a space and a **P** after the file name. Quattro asks you for the password. You can type a password up to 15 characters. For each character you type, Quattro displays a square bullet (■) as shown in Figure 5.3. After you finalize the password by pressing ENTER, Quattro asks you to verify the password by typing it and pressing ENTER again. If the two passwords are not identical, Quattro displays an error message and returns to the prompt for the file name.

When you try to retrieve a password-protected file, Quattro asks for the password. If you do not enter the correct password, Quattro does not retrieve the file. Since Quattro encrypts password-protected files, you cannot use the file in either Quattro or any other program if you forget your password. Quattro can retrieve 1-2-3 encrypted files when supplied with the correct password, although 1-2-3 cannot do the same with an encrypted Quattro file. To save and encrypt a file to be used in 1-2-3, make sure to use the .WK1 extension when you encrypt it.

To remove the password protection from your spreadsheet, when you save your file press F2 (EDIT), and then press the BACKSPACE key until the [P] is removed. After you press ENTER, the spreadsheet is saved without password protection if you elect to replace the file on the disk. To change the password, press F2 (EDIT), and use the arrow keys and the DEL key to remove the brackets ([]). Quattro prompts you for a new password and its verification before saving the file.

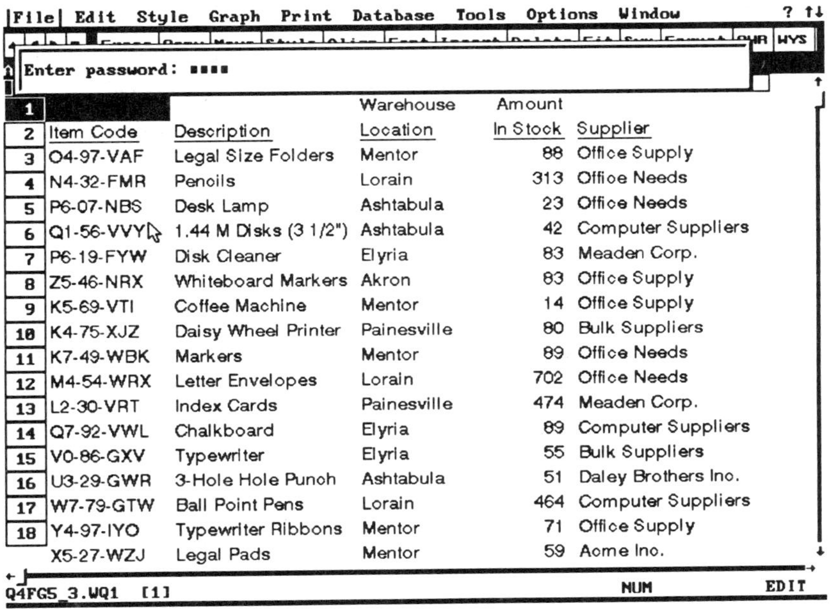

Figure 5.3   Entering a Password

Saving to a Different Directory

Quattro suggests saving a spreadsheet under its existing file name if it has been saved before. If you have not saved your spreadsheet previously, Quattro assumes that you want to save your file in the current directory. The current directory is either the subdirectory that Quattro is in or the one specified by the /File Directory command. To save a spreadsheet to a different directory, when you save a file press CTRL-BACKSPACE and type the entire file name, including the path. For example, to save the current spreadsheet as the file LOANS in the subdirectory FINANCE on drive C, after you press CTRL-BACKSPACE, type **C:\FINANCE\LOANS**, and press ENTER. If you type the path without a file name, Quattro lists the spreadsheet files in that directory. You can also save files to other locations using the buttons in the box when you see the list of files in a directory. These buttons are more frequently used to retrieve a file, and so you will learn more about them later.

Saving Files in SQZ! Format

Quattro can save your spreadsheet files in a compressed format called SQZ!. The SQZ! format significantly reduces the disk space requirements for your files. This storage method is effective for spreadsheet transmissions with a modem as well as for storage. To save a Quattro Pro file in an SQZ! format, change the file extension to .WQ!. Quattro 1.x files can be saved in an SQZ! format by using the extension .WKZ. To save a 1-2-3 file in an SQZ! format, change the file extension to .WK$ for 1-2-3 Release 1A or .WK! for 1-2-3 Release 2.0 and higher. When you press ENTER, Quattro automatically compresses the file as it saves it. To retrieve a SQZ! file, simply select the file that you saved; Quattro automatically expands the file as it is retrieved. Files saved with the SQZ! option are approximately half the size of the original file, although the space reduction depends on the contents of your spreadsheet.

The SQZ! format provides several settings that you can change to make the file more compact. To adjust these settings, use the /File Utilities SQZ! command. After making the selections you want, select **Quit** to return to the READY mode. The following settings are available:

- Remove Blanks—This setting determines whether the compressed file maintains blank cell features such as formatting and character font. While this setting is normally at No to maintain these blank cells, changing it to Yes provides a more compact storage.

- Storage of Values—This setting determines how formulas and their values are stored. The default setting, Exact, stores all formulas and their results up to 15 significant digits. The **Approximate** setting stores all formulas and their results up to seven significant digits, and the **Remove** setting stores only the formulas. Quattro recalculates the values of formulas when you

retrieve the file. If you want the maximum compression, change this setting to Approximate or Remove.
- Version—This setting determines whether Quattro uses SQZ! or SQZ! Plus. SQZ! Plus is more efficient. However, you must use SQZ! if you are using the SQZ! files with Symphony or Lotus 1-2-3, Release 1A. SQZ! Plus is compatible with other versions of SQZ! Plus and with SQZ! Version 1.5 for 1-2-3.

Saving Data in Another Format

Quattro changes the format it uses to save your spreadsheet to conform with the file name extension that you enter in the /File Save or /File Save As command. Using an extension other than .WQ1 changes the format in which the data are saved. To change the format for saving your data, use the /File Save As command. When Quattro prompts you for a name or provides you with an existing one, change the file name extension to match the desired format. For example, to translate your Quattro spreadsheet TEMPLATE to a 1-2-3 spreadsheet, change the file extension to .WK1 (for 1-2-3 Release 2.0, 2.2, and 2.3) by pressing F2 (EDIT), pressing the BACKSPACE key three times, typing **WK1**, and pressing ENTER. The file name extensions supported are summarized in Table 5.1. If you want to save the new spreadsheets you create to a different format, you may want to select /Options Startup File Extension. This sets the file extension and the format that all new files you create with Quattro Pro will have unless you select a different one. While the current setting is .WQ1 for Quattro Pro's format, you can type another extension that is in Table 5.1, and press ENTER to save your new files in a different format.

When you save data in a different format, Quattro only saves the data that are appropriate for the new format. For example, some graph information is not saved with 1-2-3 files. In dBASE files, Quattro's format settings are not saved. Also, in 1-2-3 absolute addresses in link formulas are converted into relative addresses.

EXPORTING QUATTRO DATA TO dBASE OR PARADOX Although exporting your Quattro spreadsheet to dBASE is as simple as using a .DB2, or a .DBF file extension, Quattro provides you with several options that are particular to a database. When Quattro translates a spreadsheet to a database file, Quattro normally uses the first row of the spreadsheet as the field names for the database. For example, in the spreadsheet shown in Figure 5.4, Quattro uses Warehouse and Item_Code as field names (Quattro converts spaces in the field name to underscores). When the first row contains a blank column, a date, numbers, or a label that starts with a number, Quattro uses the letter representing the row. Every row below the first row is a record in the database with each column representing a different field. Quattro lets you change the field name and its characteristics before it translates it into a file with the View Structure command. The database-type information in Figure 5.4 illustrates the process of converting your spreadsheet to a dBASE

Table 5.1 File Name Extensions for Saving and Retrieving Files

.WQ1	Saves and retrieves Quattro Pro's spreadsheets. This is normally the default setting. To save files in this format, you do not have to specify an extension.
.WKQ	Saves and retrieves Quattro 1.x spreadsheets.
.WK1	Saves and retrieves 1-2-3 Release 2.0, 2.2, and 2.3 spreadsheets.
.ALL	Saves and retrieves Allways format file for 1-2-3 Release 2.x spreadsheets.
.FMT	Saves and retrieves Impress or WYSIWYG format file for 1-2-3 Release 2.x spreadsheets.
.WKS	Saves and retrieves 1-2-3 Release 1A spreadsheets.
.WK3	Saves and retrieves 1-2-3 Release 3 spreadsheets.
.FM3	Saves and retrieves Impress or WYSIWYG format file for 1-2-3 Release 3.
.WKE	Saves and retrieves 1-2-3 Educational spreadsheets.
.WRK	Saves and retrieves Symphony data files.
.WR1	Saves and retrieves Symphony version 2.0 spreadsheets.
.WKP	Saves and retrieves Surpass data files.
.DB	Saves and retrieves Paradox data files.
.DBF	Saves dBASE III data files and retrieves dBASE II, dBASE III, or dBASE IV data files.
.DB2	Saves and retrieves dBASE II files.
.WQ!	Saves and retrieves a compressed Quattro Pro spreadsheet.
.WKZ	Saves and retrieves a compressed Quattro 1.x spreadsheet.
.WK$	Saves and retrieves a compressed 1-2-3 Release 1A spreadsheet.
.WK!	Saves and retrieves a compressed 1-2-3 Release 2.0, 2.2, or 2.3 spreadsheet.
.DIF	Saves and retrieves Multiplan data files.
.RXD	Saves and retrieves Reflex data files.
.R2D	Saves and retrieves Reflex 2 data files.
.CHT	Saves and retrieves Harvard Graphics charts.
.SLK	Saves and retrieves Multiplan files.

```
File   Edit   Style   Graph   Print   Database   Tools   Options   Window        ? ↑↓
 ▲ ◀ ▶ ▼  Erase Copy Move Style Align Font Insert Delete Fit Sum Format CHR WYS
A1: [W12] 'Item Code
```

	A	B	C	D	E
1	Item Code	Description	Warehouse	In Stock	Supplier
2	O4-97-VAF	Legal Size Folders	Mentor	88	Office Supply
3	N4-32-FMR	Pencils	Lorain	313	Office Needs
4	P6-07-NBS	Desk Lamp	Ashtabula	23	Office Needs
5	Q1-56-VVY	1.44 M Disks (3 1/2")	Ashtabula	42	Computer Suppliers
6	P6-19-FYW	Disk Cleaner	Elyria	83	Meaden Corp.
7	Z5-46-NRX	Whiteboard Markers	Akron	83	Office Supply
8	K5-69-VTI	Coffee Machine	Mentor	14	Office Supply
9	K4-75-XJZ	Daisy Wheel Printer	Painesville	80	Bulk Suppliers
10	K7-49-WBK	Marker	Mentor	89	Office Needs
11	M4-54-WRX	Letter-size Envelopes	Lorain	702	Office Needs
12	L2-30-VRT	Index Cards	Painesville	474	Meaden Corp.
13	Q7-92-VWL	Chalkboard	Elyria	89	Computer Suppliers
14	V0-86-GXV	Typewriter	Elyria	55	Bulk Suppliers
15	U3-29-GWR	3-Hole Hole Punch	Ashtabula	51	Daley Brothers Inc.
16	W7-79-GTW	Ball Point Pens	Lorain	464	Computer Suppliers
17	Y4-97-IYO	Typewriter Ribbons	Mentor	71	Office Supply
18	X5-27-WZJ	Legal Pads	Mentor	59	Acme Inc.
19	T6-05-RPU	Expandable Folders	Lorain	53	Office Supply
	S2-93-QPW	Printer Ribbons	Ashtabula	77	Office Needs

```
QFIG5_4.WQ1  [1]                                    NUM              READY
```

Figure 5.4   Spreadsheet Set Up as a Database

database and the different options available. For other database packages such as Paradox and Reflex, the steps are similar but the rules for field definitions follow the conventions of the particular database package. To convert this file to dBASE III or IV, follow these steps:

1. Press **/**, and select File Save As.
2. Type or select the file name. In this example, the file was originally saved as ITEMS.WQ1. This is changed to ITEMS.DBF by pressing F2 (EDIT), pressing the BACKSPACE key three times, and typing **DBF**.
3. Press ENTER to accept your file name. Quattro then displays a dBASEL File Save menu like the one shown in Figure 5.5.
4. Select View Structure. This choice lets you change the database structure before it is saved to a file. Choosing **Write** immediately saves the database. Choosing **Quit** aborts the **/File Save As** command. Choosing **View Structure** presents a box like the one shown in Figure 5.6. This box shows the database structure as Quattro plans to save it.

As you can see in the figure, Quattro uses the text from the first line of the spreadsheet for the field names. For each column, Quattro uses the first 10 characters of the first row and replaces any blanks with underscores (_). If

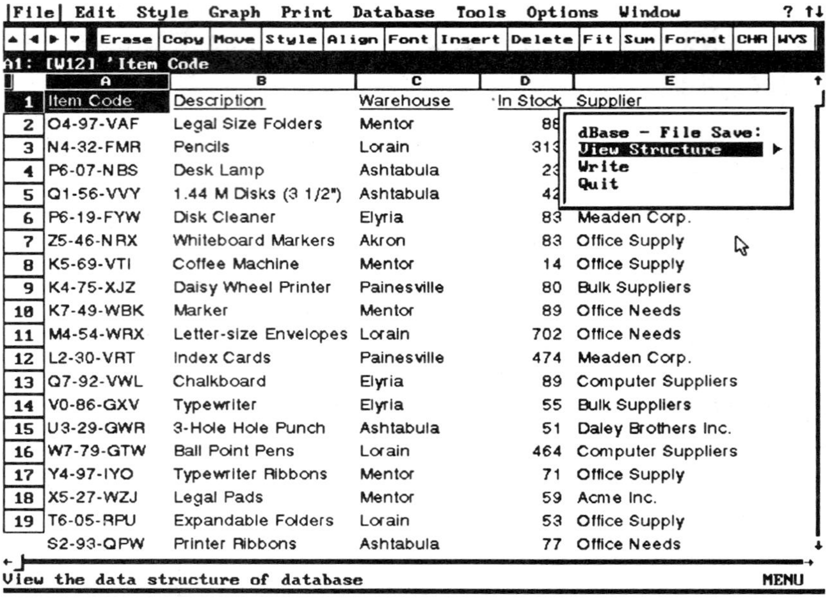

188 *Quattro Pro 4.0 Handbook*

Figure 5.5   dBASE IV File Save Menu

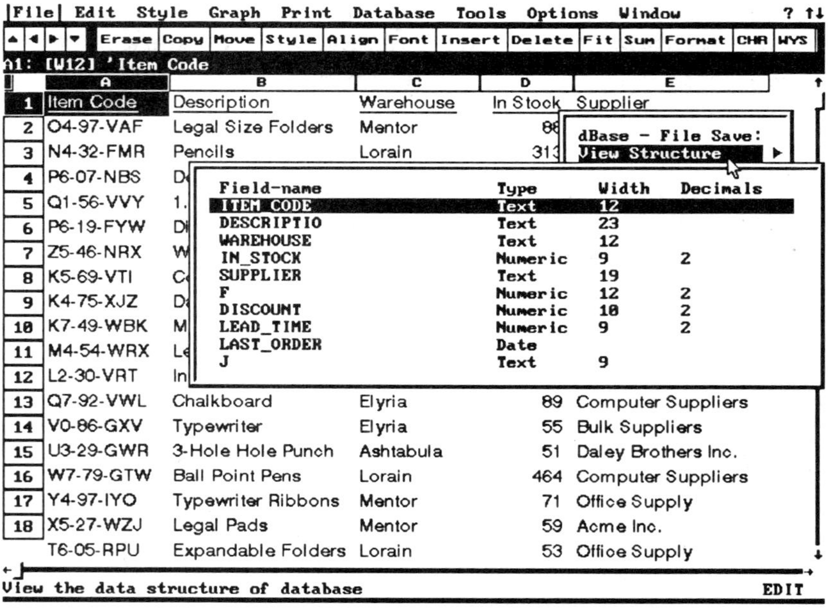

Figure 5.6   Viewing the Database Structure Before Quattro Saves It

the text in the first line of the spreadsheet is not a valid field name, Quattro uses the column letter. Quattro determines the data type by looking at the information in the second row of the data. Quattro uses the column width for each column as the field width.

5. Modify the structure to meet your needs. To change a field's characteristics, move the highlight to the field, and press ENTER. This presents you with a box to change the name or the type of the highlighted field. From this box, choose whether you want to change the **Name** or **Type**. When you change a field's characteristics, the rules of that database package apply. For example, dBASE field names can have up to 10 characters, may not start with a number, and must be unique. For a field's type, you can choose from **Text, Numeric, Date,** and **Logical**. (Quattro Pro does not use dBASE memo fields, which is also why .DBF is the extension for the dBASE III and dBASE IV databases, since only the format of their memo fields is different.) For columns that are to become date fields, Quattro converts the dates into the database's date format, regardless of how the dates appear in the spreadsheet. When you make a column a logical field, Quattro converts cells containing a 1 to T and cells containing a 0 to F. If you select a type of Text or Numeric, Quattro prompts for the field width. Type the number, and press ENTER. If you select Numeric, Quattro prompts for the number of decimal places. Type the number, and press ENTER.

In this example, F was renamed to DSCNT_PCNT, since the entry in F was unacceptable as a dBASE field name. IN_STOCK, DSCNT_PCNT, DISCOUNT, and LEAD_TIME have their widths modified. Also, the last field, J, was included because the column had a few miscellaneous entries. This column is removed from the database by moving to this field and pressing the DEL key. To restore a field, press the DEL key again, which removes the asterisk that indicates which columns are omitted. Figure 5.7 shows the database structure after all modifications have been made.

6. Press ESC to return to the prior menu, and select **Write**. Quattro translates and stores your spreadsheet as a dBASE III or IV file.

This example shows how to convert a spreadsheet to a dBASE III or IV file; however, the process of converting the file to another database format is the same, except the extension in step 2 is different. When you convert a file to the dBASE II format, you have to rename it later to a .DBF extension. dBASE II, dBASE III, and dBASE IV use the same file extension.

RETRIEVING DATA

Retrieving a file is as simple as telling Quattro what file you want to work with. Quattro's support for multiple file formats makes it easy to work with data in many file formats. To retrieve a file, type / to activate the menu, and select **File** and **Retrieve**. Quattro displays a box like the one in Figure 5.8, which lists all spread-

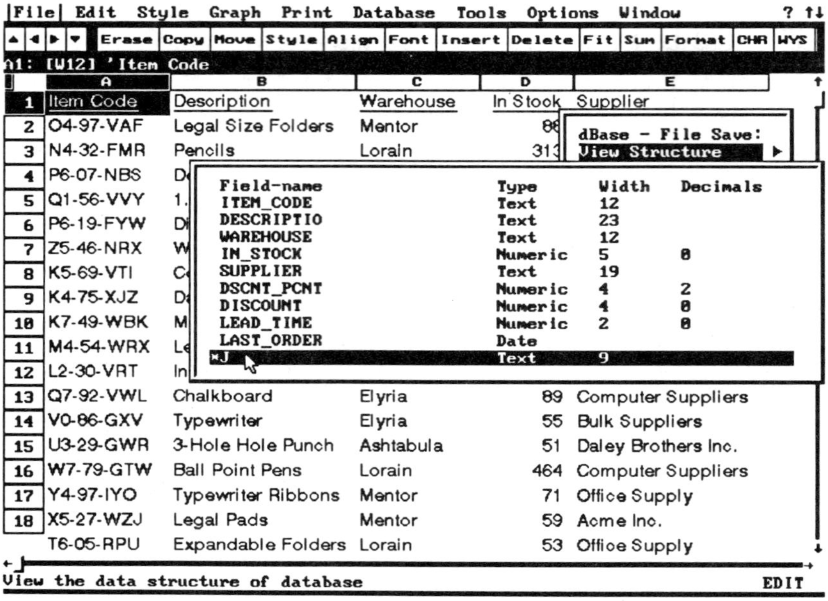

```
[File]  Edit  Style  Graph  Print  Database  Tools  Options  Window        ? ↑↓
```

	A	B	C	D	E
1	Item Code	Description	Warehouse	In Stock	Supplier
2	O4-97-VAF	Legal Size Folders	Mentor	88	
3	N4-32-FMR	Pencils	Lorain	313	
4	P6-07-NBS				
5	Q1-56-VVY				
6	P6-19-FYW				
7	Z5-46-NRX				
8	K5-69-VTI				
9	K4-75-XJZ				
10	K7-49-WBK				
11	M4-54-WRX				
12	L2-30-VRT				
13	Q7-92-VWL	Chalkboard	Elyria	89	Computer Suppliers
14	V0-86-GXV	Typewriter	Elyria	55	Bulk Suppliers
15	U3-29-GWR	3-Hole Hole Punch	Ashtabula	51	Daley Brothers Inc.
16	W7-79-GTW	Ball Point Pens	Lorain	464	Computer Suppliers
17	Y4-97-IYO	Typewriter Ribbons	Mentor	71	Office Supply
18	X5-27-WZJ	Legal Pads	Mentor	59	Acme Inc.
	T6-05-RPU	Expandable Folders	Lorain	53	Office Supply

Overlay dialog: **dBase - File Save: View Structure**

Field-name	Type	Width	Decimals
ITEM_CODE	Text	12	
DESCRIPTIO	Text	23	
WAREHOUSE	Text	12	
IN_STOCK	Numeric	5	0
SUPPLIER	Text	19	
DSCNT_PCNT	Numeric	4	2
DISCOUNT	Numeric	4	0
LEAD_TIME	Numeric	2	0
LAST_ORDER	Date		
*J	Text	9	

View the data structure of database   EDIT

Figure 5.7 Database Structure After It Is Modified

sheet files in the current subdirectory in alphabetical order as well as the new Quattro Pro 4 buttons. This list displays the file name extensions so you can distinguish Quattro files from files stored in other formats. Quattro also lists non-Quattro spreadsheets such as 1-2-3 worksheets. To select a file to retrieve, highlight your selection, and press ENTER. If the list of files is long, typing the name of file and pressing ENTER may take less time. You also can select a file to retrieve with your mouse by clicking it twice or double clicking it. You can also change how the list appears in the file selection box using the buttons. If you are using Quattro Pro 3 or a prior release, Quattro Pro has several keys to change the list of files in the file selection box. These are described in the next section, since they provide many of the same features that are provided by Quattro Pro 4 buttons.

If the file that you want is in a subdirectory under the Quattro directory, press END to go to the bottom of the file list, and select the subdirectory. If the file that you want is in another subdirectory, press ESC twice, and type the path and file name. If you type a new path without a file name, Quattro lists all the spreadsheet files in the path. If your file is in a format that Quattro can automatically retrieve but does not display as a spreadsheet file, such as dBASE or Reflex files, press ESC once, and type an asterisk, a period, and the extension that Quattro should look for.

If Quattro cannot retrieve the file, it displays an error message. A disk drive that is not ready, an unformatted disk, or a file not on the specified drive can cause the error. An error also occurs when a file is renamed using an extension that is inappropriate for the data format the file contains.

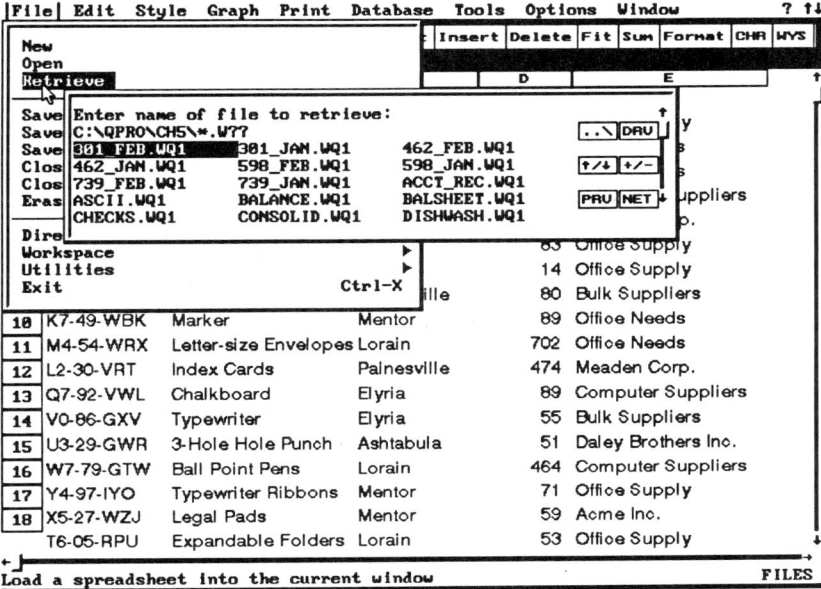

Figure 5.8 File Selection Box Showing Files in Current Directory

---

▼ **TIP: Spelling counts!**

If you enter a file name and Quattro cannot find it, check the spelling of the file name and entries that you have specified.

Once Quattro has found the file, it starts loading the file into memory. If the file is password protected, you will have to supply the correct password when Quattro prompts for it. If the file is in a format that Quattro can translate to a Quattro spreadsheet, Quattro will automatically translate the data when you retrieve the file.

Using the Buttons To Select A File

When you initially have to select a file, the file selection box includes six buttons instead of the two you usually see for ENTER and ESC. These buttons provide features that make selecting a file easier. While you saw these buttons earlier when you save a spreadsheet the first time, these buttons are more useful for retrieving a file. You will also see these buttons when you use other commands where you must select a file.

The first button (..\) displays the files in the parent directory. This is the same as pressing BACKSPACE. The DRV button lists the other drives available to your system that you can click to select, type the letter of the drive, or highlight and press ENTER. Besides just telling you the available drives, the list of drives also indicates whether the drive is fixed, removable, or part of a network drive. The ↑/↓ button expands or contracts the file selection box so you can see more of the file list on the screen. This is the same as pressing F3 (CHOICES). The +/- button adds or removes file information to the files in the list. The file information includes the file's size and the date and time the file was last saved. This button is the same as pressing + or -. Figure 5.9 shows the file selection box expanded and showing the file information of the files in the current directory. The PRV button lists the last nine files you have used in Quattro Pro so you can easily save a file to a frequently used name or, more commonly, you can use the PRV button to retrieve the files you use most frequently. The NET button shows network drive mappings so you can see to select the files on the network that you want to use. To select any of these buttons, click them or type /, and then press the arrow keys until the one you want is highlighted; then press ENTER.

Automatically Retrieving a File

Quattro provides two features that can automatically retrieve a file at the beginning of a Quattro session. You can have Quattro retrieve the same file for each session or you can specify a different file for each session. Normally, you start Quattro by typing **Q**. If you add a space after the Q and type a file name, Quattro retrieves the file after loading Quattro. For example, if the first spreadsheet that

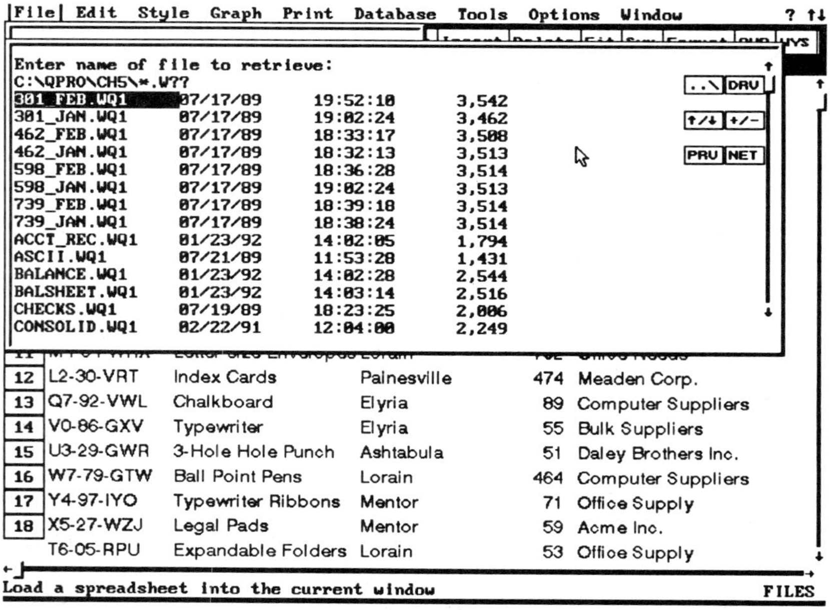

Figure 5.9 Expanded File Selection Box Showing Information About Files in Current Directory

you want to use is MYFILE.WQ1, you type **Q MYFILE** to tell Quattro to immediately retrieve this file. If the file is not in Quattro's .WQ1 format, you need to type the proper file extension. For example, type **Q MYFILE.WK1** if MYFILE is a 1-2-3 spreadsheet with a .WK1 extension.

The second alternative lets you set up a default file for retrieval at startup with the /Options Startup Autoload File command. When you use this command, Quattro asks you for the name of the file to automatically retrieve every time you load Quattro. Quattro initially is set to automatically load a file named QUATTRO.WQ1 if it is available in the directory when you load Quattro. Changing the name of the automatic load file with /Options Startup Autoload File also requires the /Options Update command to make this change permanent. If Quattro cannot find the autoload file when the program is loaded, an empty spreadsheet is presented.

Retrieving Data in a Different Format

Quattro makes it easy to work with data in a variety of formats since it does not require a separate translation process. To retrieve a file in a supported format, add an extension after the file name; Quattro automatically translates the file as it retrieves it. For example, to use a 1-2-3 Release 2 file called SALES.WK1, enter or select the file name from the file list box. Quattro automatically translates the file to Quattro as it loads the spreadsheet. The list of file name extensions in Table 5.1 provides a summary of the various file types supported.

When you retrieve a file, the file selection box lists only files with extensions that start with W. To list other types of files, press ESC once, and type an asterisk (*), a period, the desired file extension, and ENTER. For example, to list all the dBASE files on your current disk, press ESC, type ***.DBF**, and press ENTER.

If you are retrieving a 1-2-3 Release 2.2 or 2.3 file, Quattro converts file links (described later) into its own format. Addresses in link formulas are absolute in Quattro Pro even if they are missed or relative in 1-2-3. While previous versions of Quattro Pro ignored spreadsheet formatting stored in an Allways, Impress, or WYSIWYG format file, Quattro Pro 4 will prompt you if you want to load the formats with the spreadsheet. Most formatting is included although some features that do not have an equivalent in Quattro Pro 4 are not. This includes graphs inserted into a spreadsheet that are actually stored in another file. Graphs inserted in the spreadsheet that are part of the spreadsheet file, as you will learn about in Chapter 7, are brought into the spreadsheet in Quattro Pro 4.

If you are retrieving a 1-2-3 file that uses the Lotus International Character Set (LICS) or the Lotus Multibyte Character Set (LMBCS) to create foreign and graphics characters, you may want to change the /Options International LICS/LMBCS Conversion command to Yes so Quattro translates these characters into their closest ASCII character approximation when the file is retrieved just as this setting tells Quattro to use the LICS or LMBCS for 1-2-3 files when one is saved. If the setting for the /Options International LICS/LMBCS Conversion command is No, the foreign and graphics characters will not appear correctly in Quattro. This command is not needed if the 1-2-3 files are created with the ASCII No-LICS driver. If you want the change in this command to become permanent, you must use the /Options Update command.

If you are retrieving a 1-2-3 Release 3 file, Quattro Pro will split the individual pages in the notebook or sheets into separate Quattro Pro 4 files as long as the original file has 32 or less pages or sheets. The file created by each sheet will use the first six letters of the original file name followed by the letters A through Z and AA through AF to distinguish the different pages or sheets. If the original file has more than 32 pages or sheets, you must split it into smaller files in Quattro Pro for Windows or 1-2-3 Release 3. The references in formulas to separate pages or sheets in the original file change to link formulas like the ones described later in the chapter. Formulas with @functions not in Quattro Pro 4 become labels. Graph features that are not part of Quattro Pro 4 are lost.

CHANGING DIRECTORIES

When Quattro saves and retrieves files, it uses the current disk drive and subdirectory and directory specified by the /Options Startup Directory command unless you override it. You are not restricted to that directory and can use several methods to change the directory, depending on whether you want the change to affect an individual file, the current session, or all future sessions.

Changing the Directory for a Single File

To change the directory for a single file, you will not want to make a permanent change to Quattro's directory settings. You can change the directory for Quattro's file commands (like Save and Retrieve) by pressing the ESC key several times when Quattro prompts you for a file name. Once the current file and path disappears, you can type the new path and the file name that you want. You can also press the BACKSPACE key or select the ..\ button to change the display of files to the parent directory of the current directory.

Changing the Directory for the Current Quattro Session

When you are planning to use files in another directory for your current Quattro session, you can change the directory for the entire session. For example, if you are planning to work with a group of Lotus 1-2-3 Release 2 files in your 123 subdirectory, changing the directory to C:\123 eliminates the extra typing required for each file operation. To change the directory, type /, and select File Directory. Quattro displays the current directory and allows you to type the new one in. After you press ENTER, Quattro uses the new directory for all subsequent file operations in the current session.

Making a Permanent Change to the Directory

Quattro also allows you to make a permanent change to the directory used for data files. If you have a partitioned hard disk with a drive C and a drive D, you may want to use drive C for your programs and drive D for your data. You may want to change the directory if you prefer to store your data on a floppy disk, reserving the hard disk space for additional programs.

To change the directory for your data permanently, type **/**, and select **Options Startup** and **Directory**. Type the directory that Quattro should use for data files. Once you have chosen the new directory, press ENTER and select **Quit** to return to the Options menu and select **Update** command to change the data directory for subsequent sessions.

USING MULTIPLE FILES

So far the spreadsheets you have created have used a single spreadsheet window. Quattro can have up to 32 windows open at once. In each window you can have a spreadsheet, Print Managers, or a File Manager window. When you have multiple windows open, Quattro provides many options for moving between the windows and displaying them. You can also use the data from the different spreadsheets in Quattro commands to move and copy data. When you have a group of spreadsheets that you want to treat as a group, you can assign these spreadsheets to a workspace so you can retrieve and save with a single command.

Opening a Second Spreadsheet

Using more than one spreadsheet at a time is as simple as telling Quattro that you want to open another spreadsheet window and designating which file you want in the window. To open another spreadsheet window, type **/** to activate the menu, and select **File** and **Open**. Just as when you retrieve a file, Quattro displays a box listing all spreadsheet files in the current subdirectory in alphabetical order. To select a file to open, highlight your selection (or type a file name), and press ENTER. Once you have selected the file, Quattro may prompt for the password (if the file uses one); then, Quattro loads the file into another spreadsheet window. Once the second spreadsheet window is open, the screen looks like Figure 5.10. This looks just as if you had used the **/File Retrieve** command to load the spreadsheet in memory with one exception—the file name in the status line has a [2] next to it indicating that this file is in the second spreadsheet window. Each window that you open has a unique number in square brackets. Later you will learn different options for displaying multiple windows on the screen. You can

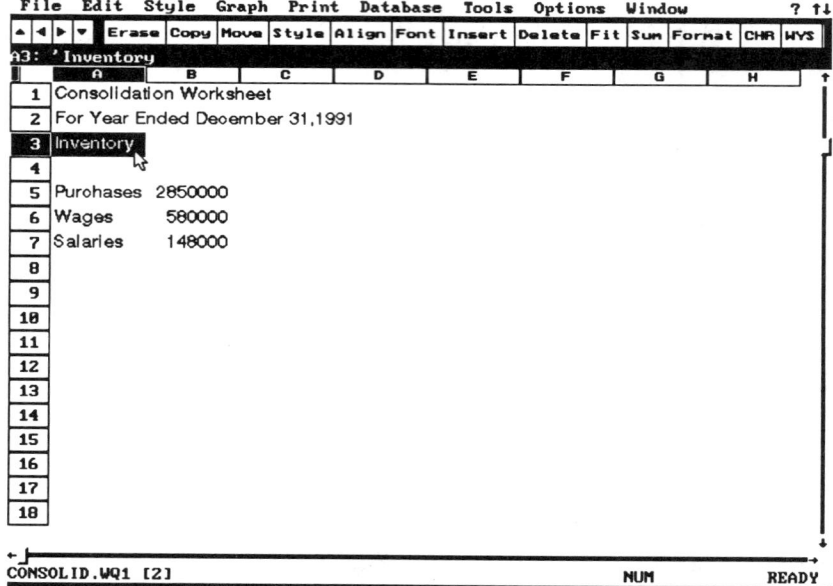

Figure 5.10 Second Spreadsheet Window Opened

always tell which window is the current window (the one that will be affected by your keystrokes) by the file name in the status line.

Once this window is open, it will remain open until you explicitly close it. If you perform a /File Retrieve command later, the command changes which spreadsheet is in the current window but does not close the window.

Saving a spreadsheet when multiple windows are open is the same as saving a spreadsheet with a single window open. The /File Save and /File Save As commands save the current window whose file name is shown in the status line. You can save all the open files at once by using the /File Save All command. This command saves all open spreadsheets. For each spreadsheet, you will need to select among Cancel, Replace, and Backup. When you exit Quattro with multiple windows open, Quattro will prompt you for each window with unsaved changes to check if you want to save the spreadsheet before exiting Quattro.

Opening a Window with a New Spreadsheet

The windows that you create with the /File Open command use files that have already been created. To open a new window with a blank spreadsheet, use the /File New command. This command opens a window and puts an empty spreadsheet in the window. This spreadsheet initially has the name SHEET# where # represents the next unused number. You can provide a name for this spreadsheet when you save the file.

Closing a Window

When you are finished with a window, you may want to remove it from memory so Quattro can use the memory for other features or spreadsheet data. To close a window, use the /File Close command. With a mouse you can close a window by clicking the upper-left corner of the window. This removes the spreadsheet window from Quattro's memory. If the spreadsheet has unsaved changes, Quattro will first prompt you if you want to abandon the changes, save the file before closing the window, or cancel the command. Once Quattro closes the window, the window number of the closed window is unassigned, and Quattro assigns that number to the next window that is opened.

You can also close all the open windows with the /File Close All command. This command acts as the /File Close command for each window. Once all the windows are closed, only the File menu item remains, which lists only the menu selections that can be used.

Moving Between Windows

Although having multiple spreadsheets open in different windows is convenient, the real advantage of using multiple spreadsheets is using data from one spreadsheet in another. Before you can use the data from another spreadsheet in the current spreadsheet, you must know how to move to the other spreadsheet. Quattro provides several options for moving between spreadsheets. As you change which window is current, Quattro may change the display, depending on how the windows are displayed.

The /Window Pick command selects the current window using Quattro's menu structure. When you execute this command, Quattro displays a selection box like the one shown in Figure 5.11, which lists the window numbers and the files contained in each window. When you pick a window from the list, Quattro makes that one current. You can also access a box like the one in Figure 5.11 by pressing SHIFT-F5 (PICK WINDOW) or ALT-0. If you press the ALT key and a number between 1 and 9, the window with that number becomes the current window. For example, pressing ALT-3 makes window 3 current. The SHIFT-F6 (NEXT WINDOW) key makes the next window current. The order of the windows that SHIFT-F6 (NEXT WINDOW) will move you to depends on the order that the windows were created. If you are using a mouse and the window you want appears (using one of the display options discussed in the next section), you can always point to the window that you want to make current, and press the mouse button.

Display Options for Multiple Spreadsheets

So far you have looked at one window at a time. Quattro has other options for showing multiple windows. You can use these options to change how many windows appear and which ones appear. All of the options for displaying multiple

198   *Quattro Pro 4.0 Handbook*

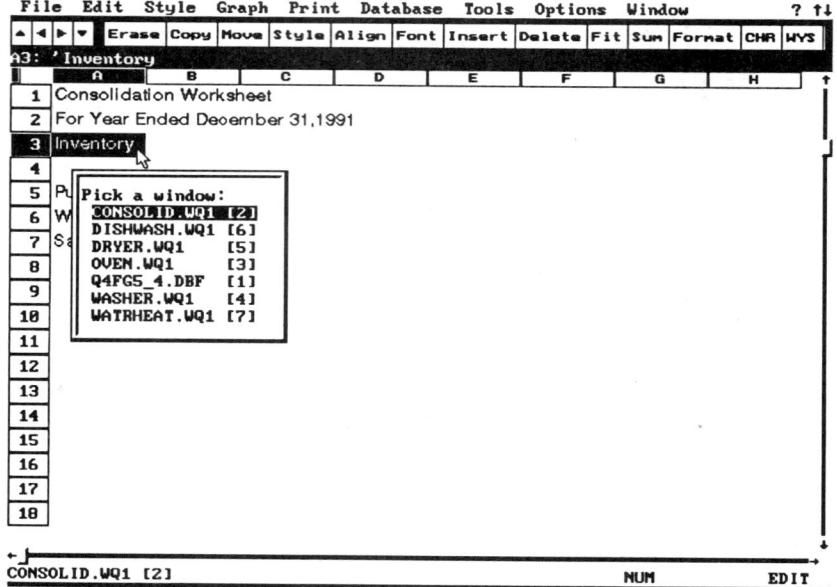

Figure 5.11 Pick List to Select Window

windows are available in a text display mode but only some of them are available from the WYSIWYG display mode. Each of these windows is separate from the other, which means you can move each one or change its size. You can make changes in one window without affecting the other. For example, you can split any window into two panes (discussed in Chapter 3), while the other windows do not use panes. Most of the display options for multiple windows reduce the display area of a window so you can see other windows. If you want to temporarily use the entire screen for the current window, use the /Window Zoom command or press ALT-F6 (ZOOM). This expands the current window to use the entire screen. Repeating the /Window Zoom command or pressing ALT-F6 (ZOOM) returns the current window to its previous size. In WYSIWYG display mode, you must use the /Window Tile command again to return the window to its previous size. With a mouse, you can click the ↑ arrow in the upper-right corner to expand the current spreadsheet to fill the desktop area. If you click the ↓ arrow, also in the upper-right corner, the current spreadsheet returns to its original size, except in the WYSIWYG display mode.

One simple method of showing the windows and their contents is to stack the spreadsheets. This is like taking a pile of papers and staggering their placement so you can see the top line from each page. To stack spreadsheets, use the /Window Stack command. When you use this command, Quattro creates a three-dimensional effect, and the first line of each window in the stack shows the name and window number of the spreadsheet. Figure 5.12 shows several windows stacked. Stacking cannot be done in a WYSIWYG display mode. If you are using a mouse, you can make any window the current window by pointing to the top line of a window and pressing the mouse button.

File Options 199

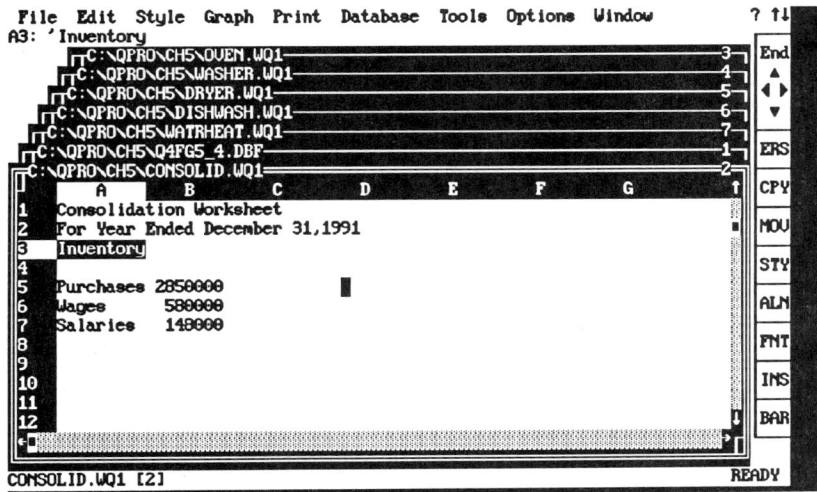

Figure 5.12 Multiple Windows Stacked

Another option for showing all the windows and some window contents is to display a small section of each window. This is done by dividing up the screen into tiles. To divide the screen into tiles, use the /Window Tile command or press its accelerator key, CTRL-T. When you execute this command, Quattro divides the spreadsheet area into small, equal-sized windows and displays as much as possible in each window. Figure 5.13 shows four windows displayed with the /Window Tile command. As the number of windows increases, the amount of space allocated to each window decreases. In Quattro Pro 4, unlike prior releases, you can tile windows in WYSIWYG display mode.

The windows options described so far allow Quattro to decide the position and size of each window. However, you can set the size and position of any window (assuming you are not in a WYSIWYG display mode). First, the window that you want to change must be the current window. Then, use the /Window Move/Size command or use its shortcut key, CTRL-R. When you enter /Window Move/Size, Quattro displays Move in the corner of the screen, as shown in Figure 5.14. While Move appears in the upper-left corner, the

---

▼ **TIP: Getting the most from your display.**

If you are displaying multiple windows and you have a EGA or VGA monitor, you can display more lines on the screen (and therefore more rows in each window) with display options available with the /Options Display Mode command covered in Chapter 10.

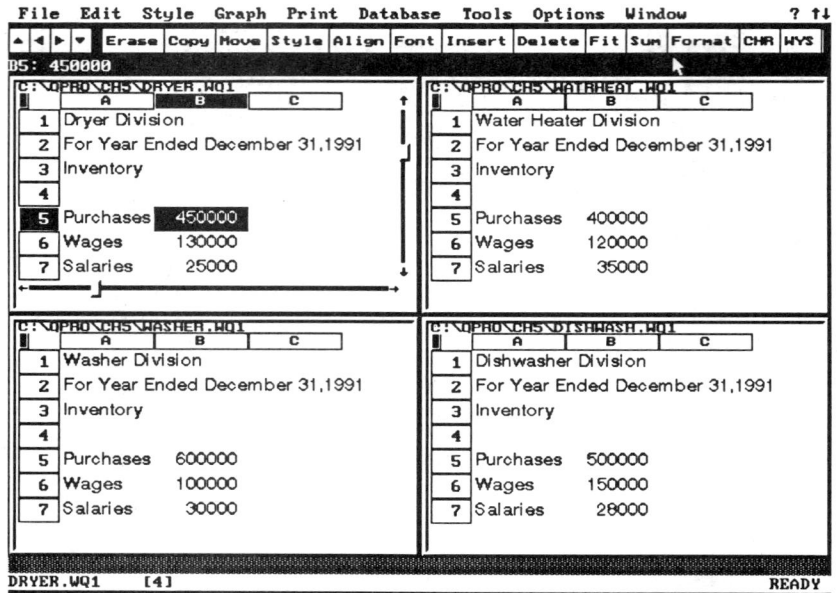

Figure 5.13   Spreadsheet Area Split into Tiles

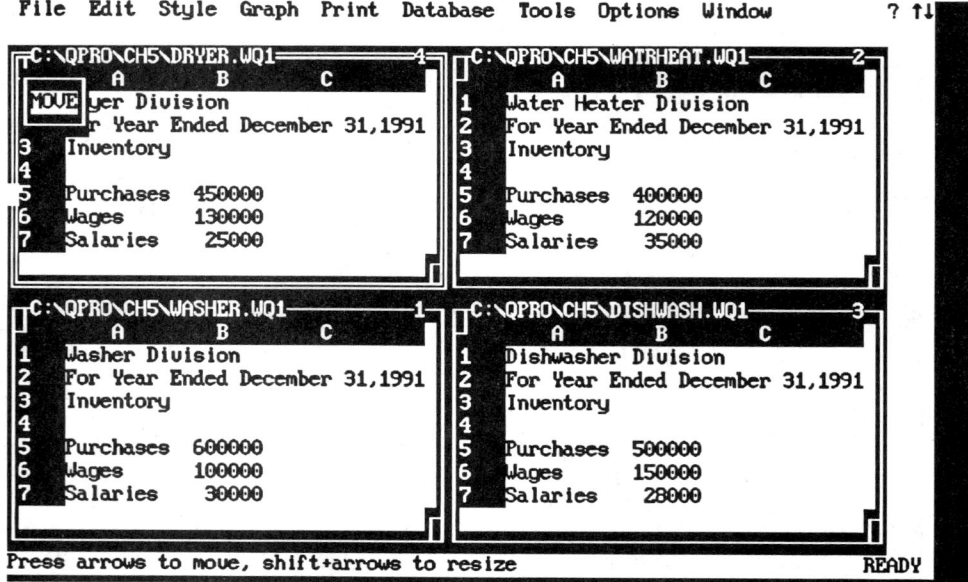

Figure 5.14   Moving Current Window

keys you press affect the position of the window. You can use the arrow keys to move the box in any direction. You can use the mouse to move the window by pointing to one window corner (holding down the mouse button and pointing to where you want the selected corner of the window to be moved). To change the size of the window, press SCROLL LOCK. This changes Move to Size. Each time you press SCROLL LOCK, Quattro switches between Move and Size. Pressing LEFT ARROW or RIGHT ARROW decreases or increases the window's width one character at a time. Pressing UP ARROW or DOWN ARROW decreases or increases the window's height one row at a time. When you are finished changing the size and position of the window, press ENTER to return to READY mode. You can also size and position a window with a mouse. To size a window with a mouse, click the lower-right corner, and drag it to a new position. To move a window with a mouse, click an edge of the window, and drag it to a new position.

When you are positioning or sizing a window, you can type letters to change the window quickly. If you type **SHIFT-T** while moving the window, Quattro will move the window to the top of the spreadsheet area. If you type **SHIFT-B** while moving the window, Quattro will move the window to the bottom of the spreadsheet area. If you type **SHIFT-L** while moving the window, Quattro will move the window to the left side of the spreadsheet area. If you type **SHIFT-R** while moving the window, Quattro will move the window to the right side of the spreadsheet area. If you type **SHIFT-Z** while sizing the window, Quattro will expand the window to fill the entire spreadsheet area.

You can position the window over another window. In this case, Quattro displays the current window over the other window using the same spreadsheet area.

Using Multiple Windows

Once the windows are open and displayed in the desired manner you are ready to use the windows in your applications. You can use windows for commands and formulas. Using them in formulas reduces data entry time and eliminates errors. Since this is a major feature of Quattro, it is covered in its own section, the next section in this chapter.

USING OTHER SPREADSHEETS IN QUATTRO'S COMMANDS You can use cells from other spreadsheets in Quattro's commands. You will frequently use cells from other spreadsheets with the /Edit Copy and /Edit Move commands to duplicate and transfer data between spreadsheets. You can also use this feature in other commands as well.

As an example, suppose you want to copy the block A2..A7 in the WASHER spreadsheet shown in Figure 5.15 to the new, unnamed spreadsheet. First, you move to A2 in the WASHER spreadsheet. Then you enter /Edit Copy, click Copy in the SpeedBar, or press CTRL-C. When Quattro prompts for the source block to copy from, either type or point to block **A2..A7** before pressing ENTER. When Quattro prompts for a destination for the copied cells, press ALT-2 to switch to the new spreadsheet, and move to A2 before pressing ENTER. Once you press EN-

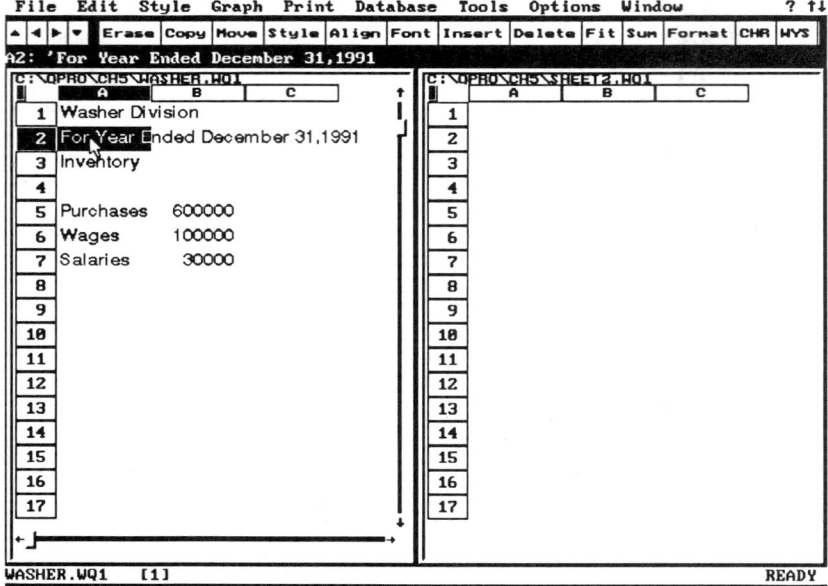

Figure 5.15 Spreadsheet Data to Copy to New, Unnamed Spreadsheet

TER, Quattro copies the cells from the WASHER spreadsheet to the new spreadsheet. If you are using a mouse, the steps are slightly different: You can point to a cell in another spreadsheet and Quattro will include the information it needs to know to use a cell from the other spreadsheet.

USING OTHER SPREADSHEETS IN FORMULAS Once you know how to pick the window you want, you can use data from other spreadsheets in formulas. This lets you build formulas using values from other spreadsheets by moving to the appropriate window and pointing to the appropriate cells. The exact steps are described in the next section.

USING DATA FROM OTHER SPREADSHEETS

If you limit the data that your file can use to a single spreadsheet, you end up with spreadsheets that contain data duplicated in other spreadsheets. When spreadsheets contain duplicate data, you increase the chances that one or more of the spreadsheets will not have the most current data. If the data that appear in many spreadsheets are changed in one spreadsheet, there is no guarantee that the numbers are also changed in the other appropriate spreadsheets. A better solution is to enter the data in one spreadsheet, and other spreadsheets, as needed, can reference the data in the original spreadsheet. You can reference a single cell or a block of any size from another spreadsheet. A block can only include cells from one

> ▼ TIP: Save before linking.
>
> If you are planning to use a new spreadsheet in formulas in other spreadsheets, save the spreadsheet before creating the formulas so Quattro uses the correct file names in the formulas.

spreadsheet, so if you want to use blocks from multiple spreadsheets, you must select the block from each spreadsheet individually. Creating formulas that reference data in other spreadsheets is creating a link between spreadsheets. The spreadsheet that contains the formula(s) with references to other spreadsheets is the *primary spreadsheet*. The spreadsheets that the formula references are the *supporting spreadsheets*. The supporting spreadsheets can be in any data format that Quattro can read, but the primary spreadsheet must be a .WQ1, .WK1 or .WK3 file.

If the primary spreadsheet has a .WK1 file extension, when you save it, Quattro displays an extra prompt telling you that the spreadsheet contains Hotlinks (links to other spreadsheets) and wants to know if it should save the link formulas as their values. From this box, select **Yes** to save the file using the values of the links as the cell entries; select **No** to abort the command, which displays the warning that the file on disk is erased (you must save the file to have a permanent copy); or select **Use 2.2 syntax** to save single-cell link formulas using the 1-2-3 Release 2.2 format and save more complex link formulas as their values. 1-2-3 Release 2.2 and 2.3 have the requirement that a cell containing a link formula cannot perform other calculations, so using the Quattro Pro file format provides more flexibility.

Linking spreadsheets provides several advantages. First, it lets one spreadsheet share the information it contains with other spreadsheets. Second, a complex spreadsheet can be broken into smaller and more manageable spreadsheets so that each spreadsheet is easy to understand. Third, when an application is divided between many people, linking each person's spreadsheet in a consolidating spreadsheet allows each person to use his or her spreadsheet without interfering with the other people's work. In this case, the overall spreadsheet contains the most up-to-date information. Fourth, with large applications, a single spreadsheet may be too small for all the data. Using multiple spreadsheets surpasses the memory limitations of your machine. Fifth, if the supporting data are in a nonspreadsheet format, such as a Paradox format, file links allow you to access the portions of the data you want without loading the file into a spreadsheet.

Linking to Another Spreadsheet

Quattro provides several methods for linking to other spreadsheets. Although the steps used to select the cells are different, the end result is the same. In all cases, a sequence like **+[filename]address_to_use** is needed for the link.

The file name in the link provides Quattro the information it needs to find the file. Quattro assumes that the supporting spreadsheet has a .WQ1 extension and is in the current drive and directory. If these assumptions are not correct, you must provide the information Quattro needs to find the spreadsheet. [SALES]TOTAL, [BUDGET.WK1]B3, [D:\QPRO\FOCUS.WKQ]B3.D10 are examples of links to cells in other spreadsheets. The *address_to_use* is a cell address, block address, or block name that you want to use from the supporting spreadsheet. You can have links to as many as 62 spreadsheets

The formula in a Quattro Pro format file can use other formula features besides the link to a supporting spreadsheet. The link to another spreadsheet can be by itself, or it can be part of a larger formula as in the examples listed below.

+[SALES]TOTAL
@PMT([LOANS]B3,[INT_RATE]SHORT_TERM,30)
@AVG([AREASALE]B2.B25)*.025

You can create links to supporting spreadsheets by pointing to the cells, by typing the cells that you want, or by using two special characters that will reference all open spreadsheets. Once the link references are established, you can change and delete them using Quattro commands.

CREATING FORMULA LINKS BY POINTING You can point to a cell or block in another spreadsheet that you want to include in the current spreadsheet. This is just like pointing to a cell or block in the current spreadsheet. You can use this method when the supporting spreadsheet that you want to use is open. This method ensures the greatest accuracy, since you can visually select the cell that you want.

To create a formula link by pointing, enter the formula up to the point where you want to add the link. If the formula is only referencing a single cell from the supporting spreadsheet, type a plus sign. Then switch to the spreadsheet that you want by either (1) pressing ALT and the number between 1 and 9 that applies to that spreadsheet, (2) pressing ALT-0 or SHIFT-F5 to display the Pick a window list and select one from the list, or (3) pressing SHIFT-F6 (NEXT WINDOW) until you are in the window. As you change to different windows, Quattro adds the [filename] and cell address of the selector in the current window. When the cell or block you want is selected, press ENTER to finalize the formula or enter the rest of the formula.

If you are using a mouse and you can activate the spreadsheet to which you want to link, the steps are slightly different. First, enter the formula up to the point where you want to add the link. Second, activate the spreadsheet you want by pointing to the spreadsheet and pressing the mouse button. Third, point to the cell or block you want to use in the other spreadsheet. Fourth, either press ENTER to finalize the formula or enter the rest of the formula and then press ENTER.

For example, look at Figure 5.16. Suppose you want B8 in the TRIALBAL spreadsheet to add the contents of cell B6 in the TRANSFER spreadsheet and the block B3..B8 in the CHECKS spreadsheet. First, you move the cell pointer to B8 in the TRIALBAL spreadsheet. Then you would type **@SUM(** to begin the formula. To select the B6 cell from the TRANSFER spreadsheet, you press ALT-2 to move to the TRANSFER spreadsheet. Notice how Quattro automatically adds the file name reference for you. Then point to B6 and type ,. Typing the comma locks the cell reference to B6 in the TRANSFER spreadsheet. To select the block to add, press

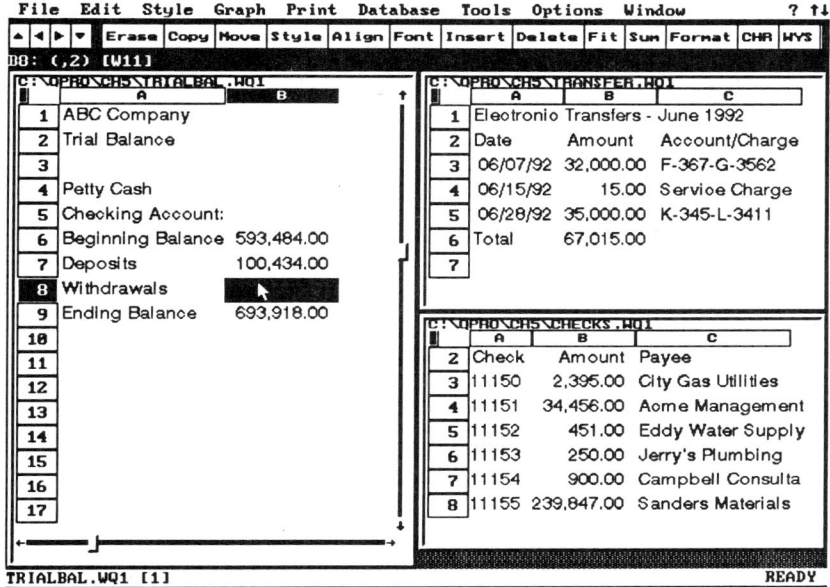

Figure 5.16 Spreadsheet Used to Add Numbers for TRIALBAL, Cell B8

ALT-3 to move to the CHECKS spreadsheet, move to B3, type a period, and move to B8. Then type) to finish the formula, and press ENTER to finalize the formula. The results appear in Figure 5.17.

If you are using a mouse, the steps are slightly different. First, you would point to B8 in the TRIALBAL spreadsheet, and press the mouse button. Then you would type **@SUM(** to begin the formula. To select the B6 cell from the TRANSFER spreadsheet, you would point to B6 in the TRANSFER spreadsheet and press the mouse button. Quattro automatically adds the file name reference. Then click **,** in the Edit mode SpeedBar to lock the cell reference to B6 in the TRANSFER spreadsheet and select the next function argument. To select the block to add, point to B3 in the CHECKS spreadsheet, hold down the mouse button, and move to B8. Then click **)** in the SpeedBar to finish the formula, and press ENTER to finalize the formula. The results are the same ones shown in Figure 5.17.

CREATING FORMULA LINKS BY TYPING You can type a link to a supporting spreadsheet just as you can type an entire formula without pointing to the cells that you want to use. You can use this method when the supporting spreadsheet that you want to use is not open (such as when the supporting spreadsheet is too big to fit into memory with the primary spreadsheet).

To create a formula link by typing, enter the formula up to the point where you want to add the link. If the link to the supporting spreadsheet is at the beginning of the formula, you type a plus sign so Quattro does not treat the entry as a label. Then, type an opening square bracket ([) followed by the drive, directory, file name, and extension. The drive and directory only need to be included if it is different

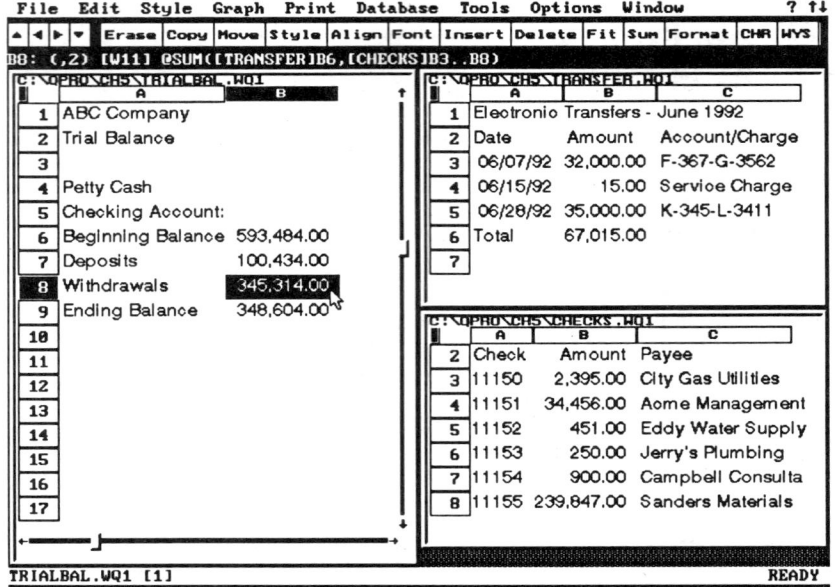

Figure 5.17 Spreadsheet After Adding Numbers for B8 Entry from Spreadsheets CHECKS and TRANSFER

from the current drive and directory. The extension only needs to be included if it is not .WQ1. Then type a closing square bracket (]) and the rest of the formula before pressing ENTER to finalize the formula.

As an example, suppose you want B8 in the TRIALBAL spreadsheet to add the contents of cell B6 in the TRANSFER spreadsheet and the block B3..B8 in the CHECKS spreadsheet using the data in Figure 5.16. First, you move the cell pointer to B8 in the TRIALBAL spreadsheet. Then you type **@SUM(** to begin the formula. Next, you type **[TRANSFER]** to select the spreadsheet and **B6** to select the cell from the spreadsheet. After typing a **,** to start the next part, you enter **[CHECKS] B3..B6** to add the block from the CHECKS spreadsheet. Finally, you type **)**, and press ENTER to finalize the formula. The results appear in Figure 5.17.

CREATING LINKS TO ALL OPEN FILES Quattro provides two special characters that can reference any open spreadsheets. When an asterisk or question mark is used in the file name in a link reference, it represents one or more characters. You can use these special characters to quickly consolidate all open files. The asterisk represents zero or more characters in a file name. The question mark represents one character in a file name. Some examples of these characters in file names are

[*]   Represents all open spreadsheets, such as SALES_89, BUDGET

[SALES_*]   Represents all open spreadsheets with file names beginning with SALES_, such as SALES_89, SALES_90, SALES_IV

[SALES_9?]   Represents all open spreadsheets with file names that have the first seven characters of SALES_9 followed by a single character such as SALES_90, SALES_91

[??????90]   Represents all open spreadsheets with file names of eight characters that end with 90 such as BUDGET90, SALES_90, SALE1990

When you use these characters in the file name, they only apply to open spreadsheets. Since they apply to all open spreadsheets, you will want to check that only those files that you want to include are open. Once you enter the formula in a cell, Quattro converts the formula to list all the files included in the formula. For example, if you enter @SUM([*]B3) to add B3 from the GAS, ELECTRIC, and COAL spreadsheets, Quattro will convert the formula to @SUM([GAS]B3,[ELECTRIC]B3,[COAL]B3).

An example of link references that use these special characters is a consolidation spreadsheet like the one shown in Figure 5.18. In this spreadsheet formula @SUM([*]PURCHASES) has been entered in B3. Each of the supporting spreadsheets contains data that the primary spreadsheet combines. Since all the supporting spreadsheets are in the same format, you can use a formula like +@SUM([*]B4) to add the purchases for all the divisions. However, a better alternative is to use block names. In each of the supporting spreadsheets, the cells containing the values to combine have been labeled using the adjacent labels. As a result, the formula to combine purchases is +@SUM([*]PURCHASES). If the PURCHASES

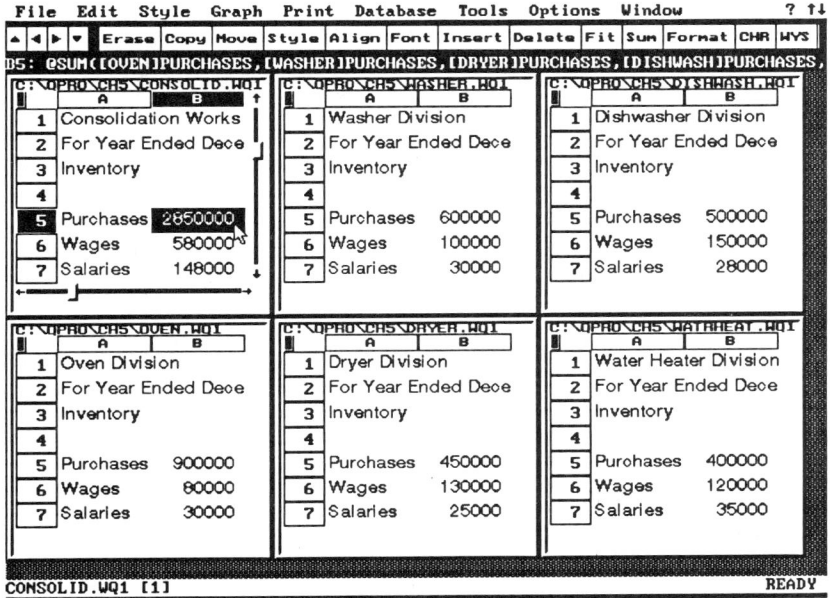

Figure 5.18 Consolidation Spreadsheet That Links to Open Spreadsheets

cell in one of the spreadsheets is later moved, the formula will adjust for the cell's new location in one of the supporting spreadsheets.

CHANGING AND DELETING LINK REFERENCES As you create link references, you may need to edit them. One method of changing link references is to enter the EDIT mode and type the corrections to the cell formula. Another possibility is to use the /Edit Search & Replace command. Quattro provides two different options for changing and deleting link references; these options prevent errors, since Quattro will find all instances of linked references for you. If you need to find which cells have link references, you can set the window or pane display to show a map view of the spreadsheet. A map view of the spreadsheet displays link references as hyphens.

Changing a file name in link references may be needed in several situations. For example, if your BUDGET spreadsheet has link references to your PLANNING spreadsheet and you rename PLANNING.WQ1 to PLAN_90.WQ1, you need to change all the link references from PLANNING to PLAN_90. Rather than find each cell with a link reference to the PLANNING spreadsheet, you can tell Quattro to make the change for you. To change the name of the file in a spreadsheet's link references, enter /Tools Update Links Change. When Quattro displays a list of the supporting spreadsheets, select the one you want to replace and press ENTER. Next Quattro prompts for the name of the spreadsheet for the replacement. You can either (1) type a file name, (2) press F2 (EDIT) and edit the existing file name, or (3) press ESC and pick a file name from the list Quattro displays. Quattro automatically finds all instances of the first file name in link references and replaces them with the second file name.

Just as you add link references, you also can delete them. For example, if you have a consolidation spreadsheet that consolidates the results from six divisions and one of them is liquidated, you need to remove the link references to that spreadsheet. To remove link references, use the /Tools Update Links Delete command. When you execute this command, Quattro lists the supporting spreadsheets. From this list, you can select the spreadsheets you want to delete by highlighting the file name and pressing SHIFT-F7 (SELECT). You can select all the spreadsheets by pressing ALT-F7 (ALL SELECT). If you press ALT-F7 (ALL SELECT) again, it unselects all the files. Quattro marks the selected spreadsheets with a check next to the file name. Once you press ENTER, Quattro deletes all the link references from the selected spreadsheets and replaces them with ERR. Once the link references are deleted, you can edit the cells containing the ERR and replace them with valid references or remove them from the formula.

Linked References in Quattro Commands

When you create a link reference, it performs the same way that a formula referencing a cell in the same spreadsheet does. Some of Quattro's commands behave differently with linked references.

RETRIEVING A FILE WITH LINK REFERENCES When you load a spreadsheet that contains formulas with link references, Quattro checks if the supporting spreadsheets are loaded. If the supporting spreadsheets are not loaded, Quattro provides three options to treat the link references. When you load a file with link references and the supporting spreadsheets are not loaded, Quattro displays the selection box in Figure 5.19. The first option, Load Supporting, opens any supporting spreadsheets that are not already open. If the supporting spreadsheets also have link references, Quattro will display another selection box to select whether to load the supporting spreadsheets of the original supporting spreadsheet. This will continue until a selection is made from the selection box shown in Figure 5.19 for all loaded spreadsheets that contain link references to unloaded spreadsheets.

The second option, Update Refs, checks the current value of the cells in the supporting spreadsheets and uses these values in the link references. These values can be rechecked with the /Tools Update Links Refresh command. The actual spreadsheets can be loaded later with the /Tools Update Links Open command. This option works best when you do not have the memory to load the supporting spreadsheets and you know that the supporting spreadsheets contain the most current values.

The last option, None, temporarily substitutes the values of the link references with NA. This lets you know that the values of the link formulas have not been computed. Any formulas that reference formulas containing link references will also have the value @NA. This option is best when you want to change the text or formulas that do not use link references. If you want to change the formulas to use the values in the link references, you can use the /Tools Update Links Refresh

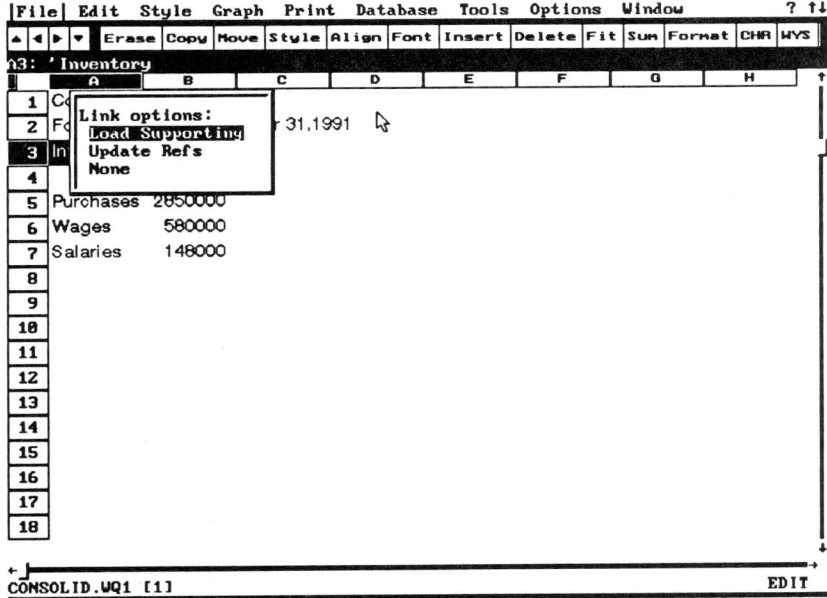

Figure 5.19 Menu Box to Select Action for Supporting Spreadsheets

command to use the values from the supporting spreadsheets or the /Tools Update Links Open command to load the supporting spreadsheets and update the formulas in the primary spreadsheet.

If you later want to open an unloaded supporting spreadsheet, use the /Tools Update Links Open command. When you execute this command, Quattro lists the supporting spreadsheets as shown in Figure 5.20. From this list, you can select the spreadsheets you want to open by highlighting the file name and pressing SHIFT-F7 (SELECT). You can select all the spreadsheets by pressing ALT-F7 (ALL SELECT). If you press ALT-F7 (ALL SELECT) again, it unselects all the files. Quattro marks the selected spreadsheets with a check next to the file name. Once you press ENTER, Quattro opens all the selected spreadsheets. If you try executing this command when all the supporting spreadsheets are open or when the current spreadsheet does not contain any link references, Quattro displays an error message.

RECALCULATION WITH LINK REFERENCES Quattro is designed to recalculate the spreadsheet in the background and minimize the amount of recalculation. This does not affect linked spreadsheets, since it only applies to formulas that use the current and loaded spreadsheets. When a spreadsheet contains link references to an unloaded spreadsheet, the values from the supporting spreadsheets are only checked and updated when the primary formula is loaded and the Update Refs option is chosen or when the /Tools Update Links Refresh command is executed. When you use Quattro on a network and other people may be using the supporting spreadsheets, you will want to update this command before printing the spreadsheet to ensure that your spreadsheet is using the most current values from the supporting spreadsheets.

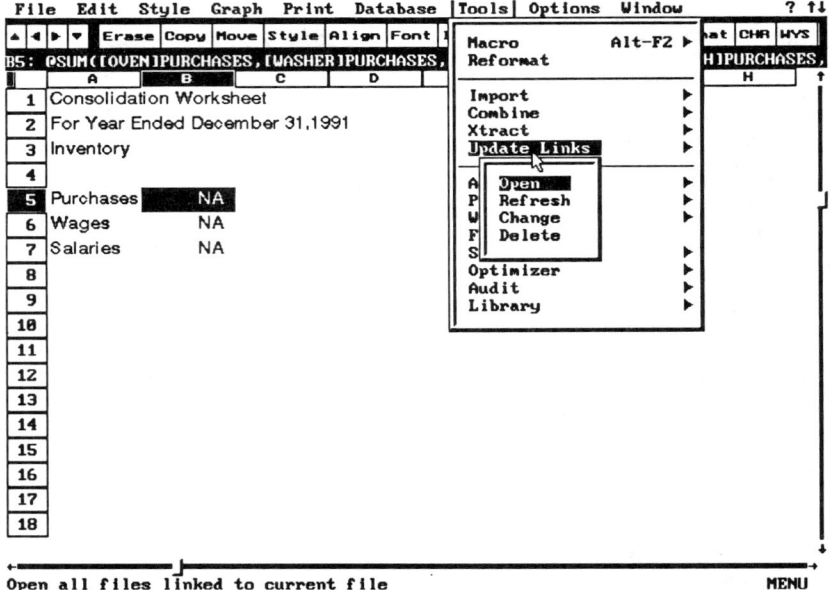

Figure 5.20 Selecting Supporting Spreadsheets to Open

COPYING AND MOVING LINK REFERENCES Quattro will let you copy and move cells that contain link references. The results produced depend on whether the Copy or Move command moves formulas with link references in the same spreadsheet or between different spreadsheets.

When you copy a formula containing a link reference to another area in the same spreadsheet, Quattro treats the formulas just as if you were copying cells in one spreadsheet without link references. When you copy formulas containing link references, Quattro adjusts the formulas and the cells that the link reference refers to, depending on whether the original block copied contains absolute, mixed, or relative addresses. For example, suppose you want to copy the block B3..B5 to A8 in the RECEIVE spreadsheet in Figure 5.21 to produce the results shown in Figure 5.22 (the formulas are formatted Text). Quattro has adjusted the relative references in the formulas to refer to the same relative address as the original formula. The cells used by the link references are also adjusted by the same number of rows and columns as the other data.

When you copy a block to another spreadsheet, the file names in link references cells remain unchanged, although the cell or block address may change depending on the address types. As an example, Figure 5.23 shows the results of copying B3..B5 in the RECEIVE spreadsheet shown in Figure 5.21 to A13 in the BALSHEET spreadsheet. The cell addresses have been changed to reflect the new relative position the copy has in the BALSHEET spreadsheet to the previous relative position the original has in the RECEIVE spreadsheet. The file names in the link references are unchanged. The link references even remain when a link reference refers to itself.

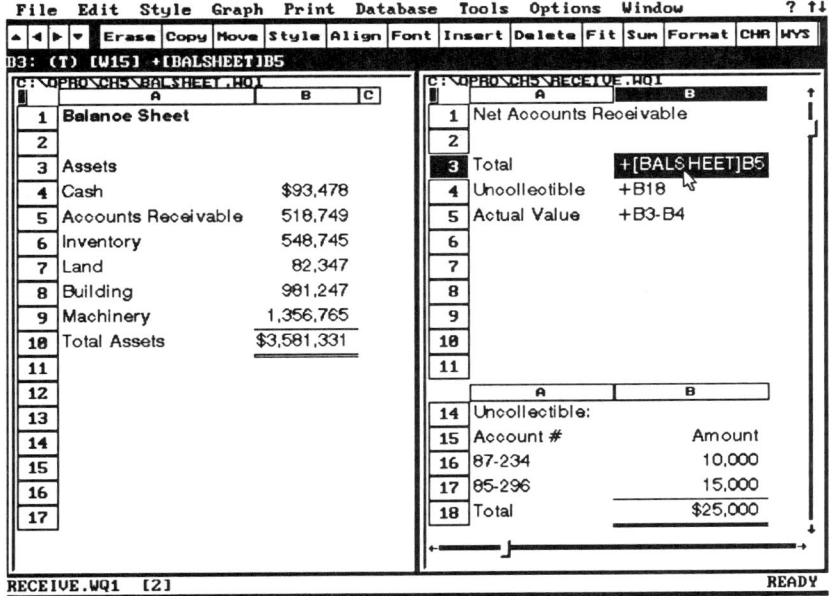

Figure 5.21 Spreadsheet for Manipulating Data

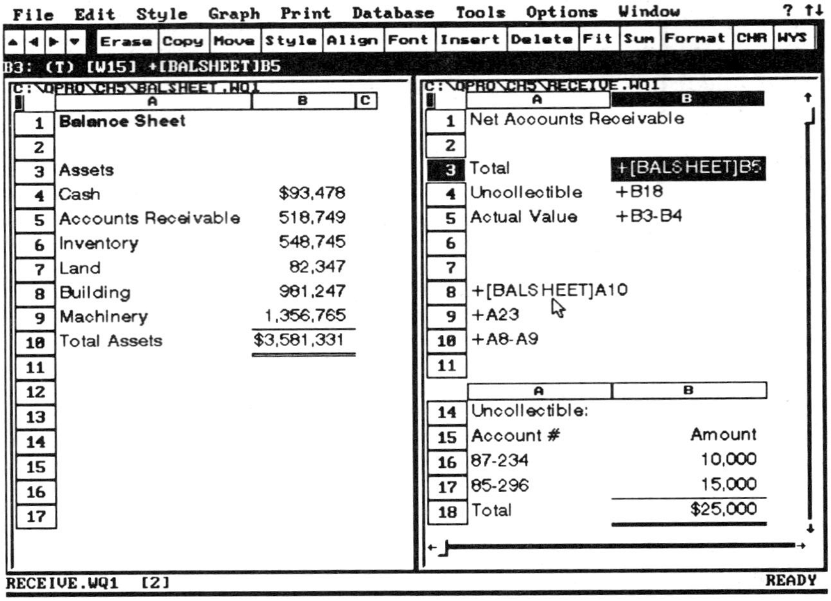

212 *Quattro Pro 4.0 Handbook*

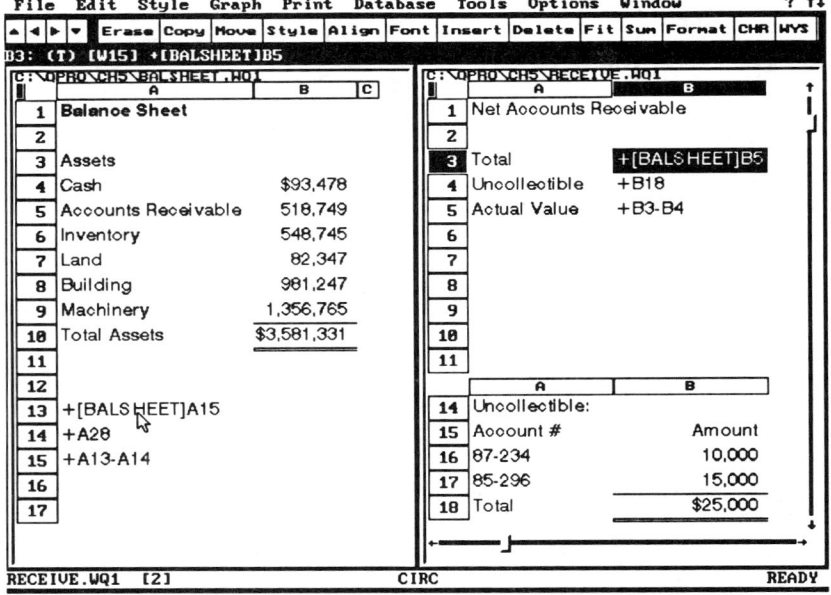

Figure 5.22 Copying Link References Within the Same Spreadsheet (shown in Figure 5.21)

Figure 5.23 Copying Link References to Another Spreadsheet (See Two Spreadsheets Shown in Figure 5.21)

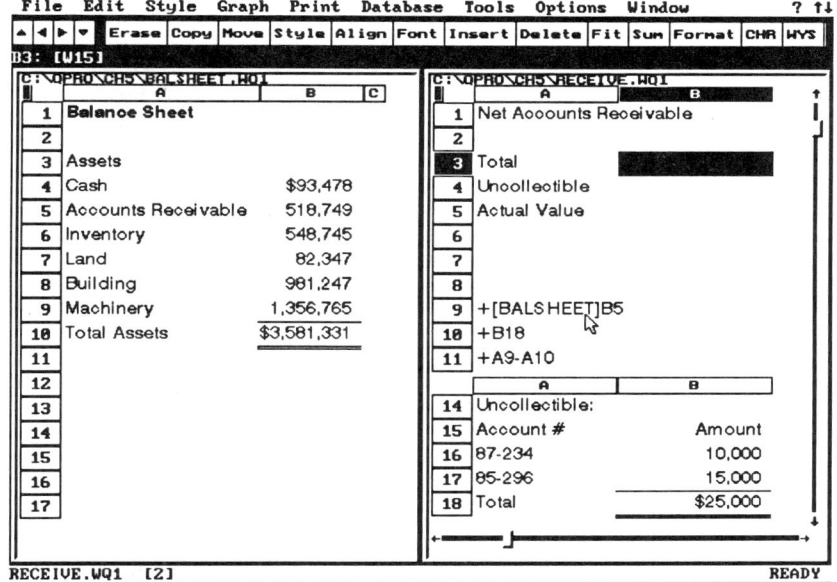

Figure 5.24 Moving Link References in the Same Spreadsheet (See Original Placement of Link References in RECEIVE in Figure 5.21)

When you move a block containing link references to another position in the same spreadsheet, the link references do not change. When you move the block B3..B5 in Figure 5.21 to A8..A10, you obtain the results shown in Figure 5.24; Quattro does not change the link references.

When you move cells between spreadsheets, link references can be changed, created, or deleted as Quattro Pro adjusts formulas so they refer to the same data as they did before you moved the entries. Quattro determines which cell and block addresses need to be changed. Quattro also must determine which cell or block addresses become link references, which link references are no longer link references but simple cell or block addresses, and which file names in link references need to be changed. An example of moving a block with link references is moving B3..B5 in the RECEIVE spreadsheet shown in Figure 5.21 to A13 in the BALSHEET spreadsheet. The result shown in Figure 5.25 shows how Quattro adjusts link references. In A13, Quattro removes a link reference, since the reference is moved to its own spreadsheet. A link reference is created in A14, since the cell it references is in the RECEIVE spreadsheet. The formula in A15 specifies the same relation to cells A13 and A14 as it did when it was in B5 referring to B3 and B4.

Using Block Names with Link References

When you create link references, it is preferable to use a block name rather than a cell or block address. Since the correct block name is easier to remember than the correct block address, using block names reduces initial entry mistakes. Also,

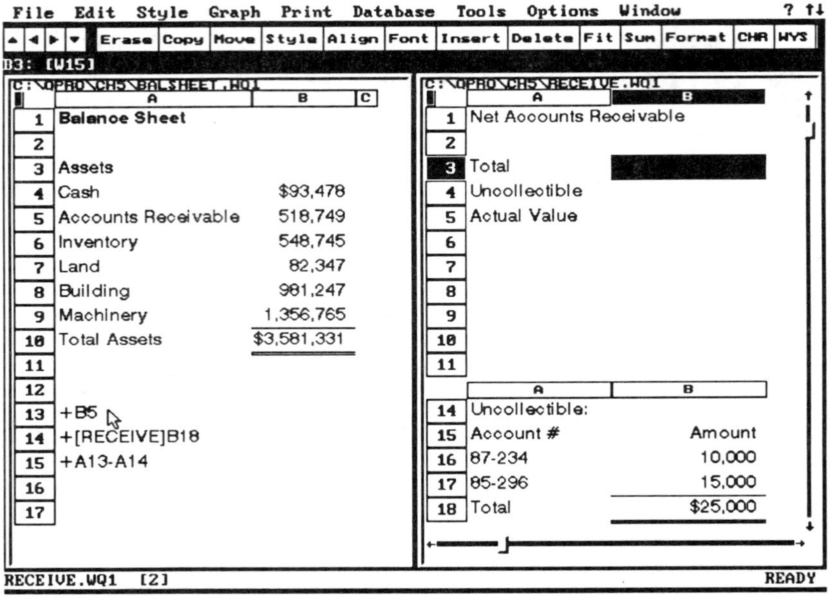

Figure 5.25 Moving Link References to Another Spreadsheet (See Original Placement of Link References in Figure 5.21)

using block names prevents mistakes when the application is used later if the cells containing the data have been moved. Since a block name is adjusted when the cell is moved, any link references that use the block name automatically use the relocated cell. Quattro also provides other features by using block names for link addresses. You can create a block name that is actually a link reference to another spreadsheet. You can create a block name whose contents are a link reference and use the block name in place of the link reference without reentering the link reference. Finally, you can create a link reference library that is a spreadsheet containing references to other spreadsheets.

USING A BLOCK NAME AS A LINK REFERENCE Chapter 3 introduced using block names to refer to one or more cells in a spreadsheet. With link references, you can have a block name that refers to another spreadsheet. You might use this feature instead of typing a link reference into a cell directly. For example, in a consolidating balance sheet, you may get the number for accounts receivable from the block TOTAL in the ACCT_REC spreadsheet. Rather than entering +[ACCT_REC]TOTAL in the balance sheet spreadsheet, you can enter /Edit Names Create and enter **ACCOUNT_RECEIVE** as the block name. When Quattro prompts for the block location, you can select the TOTAL block in the ACCT_REC spreadsheet by typing the location or pointing to it. Then when you are ready to use the value stored in ACCOUNT_RECEIVE, you can type + and press F3 (CHOICES) or click Name in the SpeedBar. Quattro will include ACCOUNT_RECEIVE in the list of block names even though the block is in another spreadsheet. Using this method is more convenient when you are entering formulas since you do not have to enter a lengthy link reference and you can use the F3 (CHOICES) key or the Name button in the SpeedBar to select the block.

ASSIGNING A BLOCK NAME TO A LINK REFERENCE When your spreadsheet contains multiple link references to the same block, one way to simplify your work is (1) create one link reference to the block, (2) name the cell containing the block reference, and (3) use the named block in other locations where you would use the link reference. For example, you may have a spreadsheet that uses the monthly production stored in a cell called MONTH_PROD from the MONTHLY spreadsheet several times. Rather than typing in a link reference every time you need the monthly production, you can enter a link reference once, name the cell containing the link reference, and use the named cell in place of the link reference in the other places in the spreadsheet where you need the monthly production. In this example, you would enter +[MONTHLY]MONTH_PROD in a cell and use the /Edit Names Create command to name the cell. Then each time you needed the monthly production, you would press F3 (CHOICES) or click Name in the SpeedBar and select the name of the cell containing the link reference. As in the previous section, using this method is convenient for entering formulas, since you do not have to enter a lengthy link reference and you can use the F3 (CHOICES) key or the Name button in the SpeedBar to select the block.

CREATING A LINK LIBRARY Another problem with link references is remembering which spreadsheet contains the data you want. One solution to remembering the file names is to create a link library. A link library contains formulas that are link references to other spreadsheets. Instead of browsing through many spreadsheets to find the value you want, you can look at the link library and use the cell containing the link reference. The link library also has the advantage of letting you change the file reference in the link library; then, any spreadsheet that uses the link library will automatically use the value from the replaced spreadsheet.

As an example, suppose you want to combine the monthly totals of the production costs for each department. Each department has a spreadsheet that looks something like Figure 5.26. Rather than make the consolidation spreadsheet so that it adds the total from each department, you can create a link library like the one in the bottom half of Figure 5.27. Such a library has in memory all the file names and block names for each department. As each month changes, the file name in the link library changes, and the consolidation as shown at the top of Figure 5.27 is updated for the new figures. The formulas in the consolidation use the block names assigned to the link reference formulas in the LIBRARY spreadsheet. For example, if you need to change the consolidation data shown in Figure 5.27, to February's data, you can use the /Edit Search & Replace command to change the JAN in the file names to FEB. A link library has a greater advantage when multiple spreadsheets use the same link references, since changing the link reference in the link library spreadsheet automatically changes the spreadsheet that the other spreadsheets get their data from.

216 Quattro Pro 4.0 Handbook

```
File   Edit  Style  Graph  Print  Database  Tools  Options  Window        ? ↑↓
▲ ◀ ▶ ▼ | Erase | Copy | Move | Style | Align | Font | Insert | Delete | Fit | Sum | Format | CHR | WYS
B3: (,2) 89.82
        A              B          C          D         E       F      G
  1              Department 301              Month:  January
  2     Job Number    Labor    Materials   Overhead
  3        1001       89.82      36.58       50.96
  4        1002       85.58      10.26       69.31
  5        1003       54.65      23.82      136.43
  6        1004       88.78      16.72       62.35
  7        1005       90.17      18.06       65.41
  8        1006       98.94      29.41       94.18
  9        1007       59.92      33.90       85.00
 10        1008       98.78      25.65       53.27
 11        1009       72.30      33.70      131.61
 12        1010       72.06      11.37      132.78
 13        1011       77.12      13.37      103.29
 14        1012       51.83      30.29       86.12
 15        1013       68.35      25.13      134.83
 16        1014       58.87      12.72      133.39
 17        1015       72.89      29.30       70.96
 18        Total  $1,140.06    $350.28   $1,409.89

301_JAN.WQ1  [1]                                                         READY
```

Figure 5.26 Spreadsheet Showing Departmental Data (Department 301)

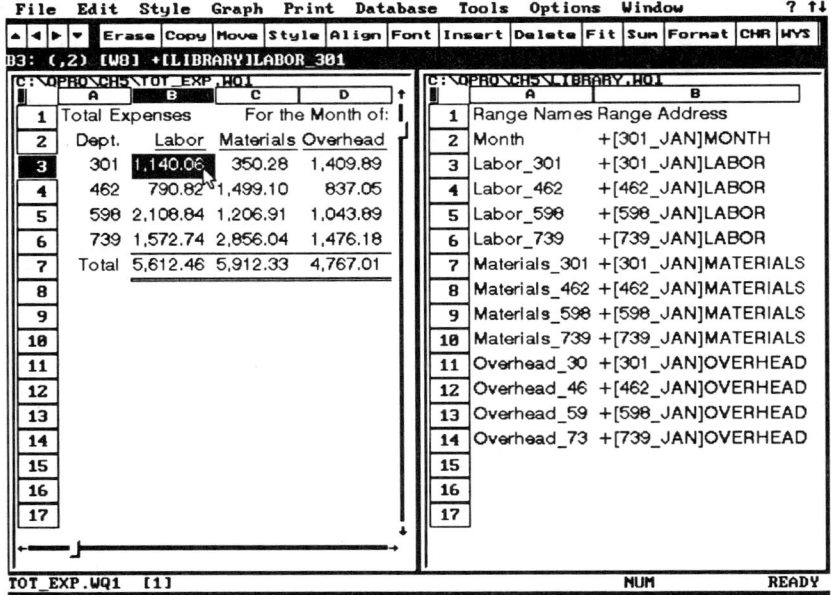

Figure 5.27 Spreadsheet Using Link Library and Link Library Spreadsheet

ACCESSING DOS

Quattro's file commands provide the basic file features that you need to use your spreadsheet. Additional options are available if you are willing to enter DOS instructions directly. Naturally, the DOS commands can be executed if you quit Quattro and type the DOS commands at the DOS prompt. However, you may occasionally want to use a DOS command but not want to exit Quattro and have to reload it. Quattro permits you to temporarily access the operating system without leaving Quattro. This procedure leaves your spreadsheets in memory. To access the operating system, type /, and select File Utilities DOS Shell. In Quattro Pro 3 and 4, you will need to press ENTER for the prompt for the DOS command. Quattro clears the screen and replaces it with the information shown in Figure 5.28. After you have finished using DOS and want to return to Quattro, type **EXIT**. After you press ENTER, you are returned to the same location in the current spreadsheet as before your request for the temporary exit. Another option available in Quattro Pro 3 and 4 is to enter the command you want to perform in the box Quattro Pro 3 and 4 display and press ENTER. If you do this, DOS performs the command you enter and then returns to Quattro without having to type **EXIT** and pressing ENTER.

You can use most DOS commands with this procedure. You can run another program; however, some programs require more memory than you may have available. Many commands for which you use DOS in other spreadsheets and earlier releases of Quattro can be performed by using the File Manager discussed later in this chapter.

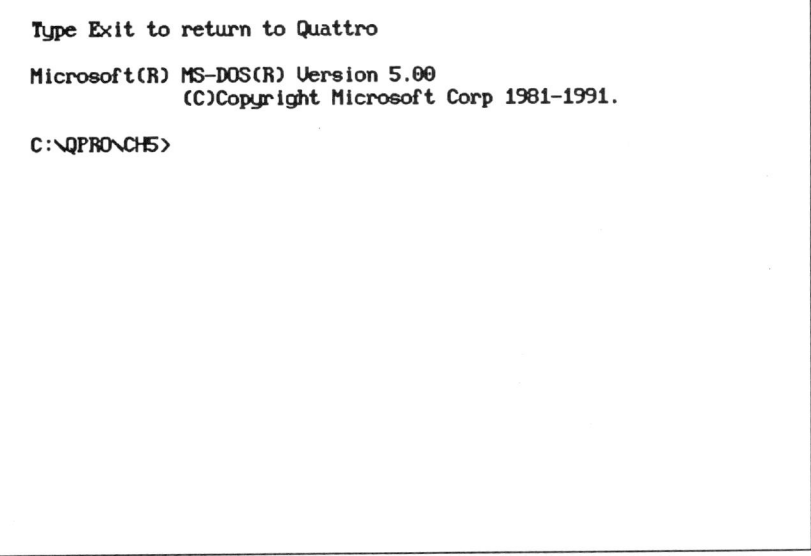

Figure 5.28 Screen Display When You Invoke DOS Within Quattro

Practical Applications

Using DOS commands from within Quattro provides several features that are not supported as Quattro menu commands in the File Manager. You can use the FORMAT command to format a disk to save your current spreadsheet. You can execute other programs while keeping Quattro and the open spreadsheets in memory.

FORMATTING A DISK If you are using diskettes to save your work it is important that your disk has enough room to save a file. If you try saving your file and your diskette does not have enough room, Quattro displays an error message. Any new disk you try to use must be formatted before you can store information on it. Although there is no Quattro option to support formatting, you can accomplish it easily after a temporary DOS exit. First, type **FORMAT A:** to format your disk. Second, press ENTER, and the operating system tells you to put in a new diskette and press ENTER. Any information that was on a disk before it is formatted is removed by the formatting process. Next, for some DOS versions, you will type the label for the disk or the name of the disk that appears at the top of the directory listing. Type the disk label up to 11 characters, and press ENTER. Next, type **N** to tell DOS that you do not want to format the disk, and press ENTER.

RUNNING OTHER PROGRAMS When you access the operating system from within Quattro, you can run other programs. For example, if you printed your spreadsheet to a file and want to print it sideways, you can run the program SIDEWAYS from DOS. If you run another program, you must make sure that it does not interfere with Quattro. If you are going to try to run another program with Quattro in memory you should save the current spreadsheet before attempting the task: Use the **/File Utilities DOS Shell** command, run the program, and return to Quattro to check that your spreadsheet is intact. The larger your spreadsheets are, the less memory is available with the temporary exit.

Commands and Programs to Avoid

Although you can use many DOS commands, there are a few you should avoid. DOS commands that overlay memory cause problems when you execute the DOS command or when you return to Quattro. For example, you should avoid DOS commands like GRAPHICS and PRINT that remain in memory after you use them.

Another problem you will encounter is limited memory. When you use DOS from within Quattro, the operating system reserves part of the memory for the Quattro program and for your spreadsheets. As your spreadsheets grow, there is less memory to run DOS commands and other programs. With large spreadsheets, you can only execute DOS commands that require a small amount of memory.

QUATTRO PRO'S FILE MANAGER

When you access DOS, you can perform a variety of operations, but this assumes that you know the DOS commands needed to perform those operations. Quattro provides a simpler approach by providing a File Manager that you can open as a window in the spreadsheet area. From a File Manager window, you can perform many DOS commands, and you do not have to remember the syntax of the commands, because you perform them using menu commands and a menu structure just like those in the other Quattro menus.

Opening and Closing a File Manager Window

Even though the File Manager window is treated as a window in the spreadsheet area, the command that opens a File Manager window is different from the command to open a spreadsheet window. To open a File Manager window, enter /File Utilities File Manager. A sample File Manager window is shown in Figure 5.29. As you can see in the figure, a File Manager window uses its own menu structure. Most options for the Print, Options, and Window pull-down menus are identical to those options for a spreadsheet window. The major change is that some of the menu options are missing, since they are inappropriate for a File Manager window. The other menus provide more specific features than you need in a File Manager window. Quattro lets you have multiple File Manager windows open. You can have different File Manager windows look at files in different directories. You can use ALT-0, SHIFT-F5 (PICK WINDOW), ALT and a number between 1 and 9, SHIFT-F6 (NEXT WINDOW), and the /Window Pick command to switch between spreadsheet and File Manager windows. A File Manager window is assigned a window number just as the spreadsheets are.

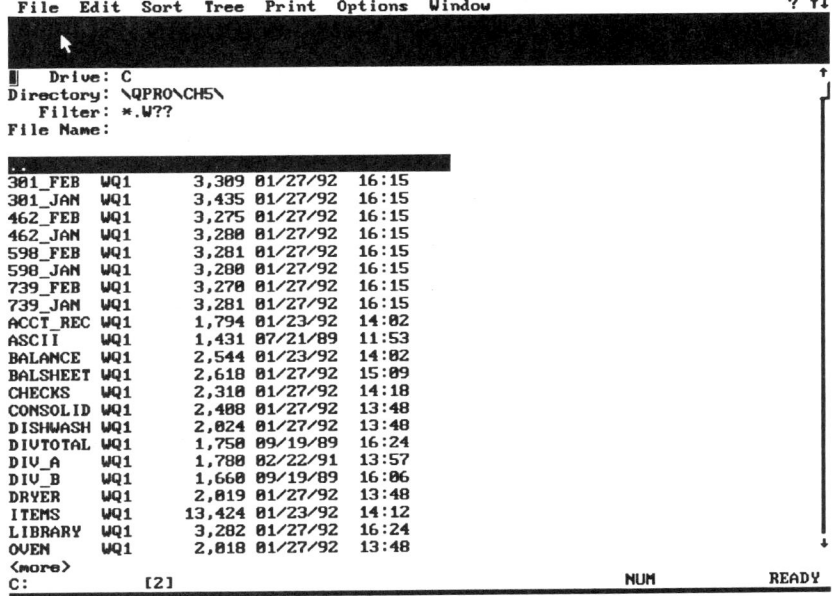

Figure 5.29 File Manager Window

The File Manager window can be divided into panes just as any spreadsheet can. The initial File Manager window contains two panes. At the top is the control pane. This contains the current drive, directory, and filter. The lower pane contains the file list. This lists all the files that are in the drive and directory and that meet the filter conditions imposed in the control pane. You can use the control pane to select which files appear in the file list pane. To move between panes, you can press F6 (PANE). You can also use the UP and DOWN ARROWS to move between these two panes. Later, you will learn how you can add a tree pane to quickly change the drive and directory of the files in the file list pane.

Once you have finished using a File Manager window, you can remove it using the same commands that you use to close a spreadsheet window. To close the current spreadsheet or File Manager window, use the /File Close command. To close all spreadsheet and File Manager windows, use the /File Close All command. Of course, all windows are closed when you exit Quattro Pro.

Selecting the Files for the File List Pane

Quattro provides four lines in the control pane that determine which files appear in the file list pane. By changing the drive, directory, filter, and file name settings, you change which files are displayed in the file list pane.

Quattro initially sets the control pane to display the files that you looked at the last time you used the File Manager. You can change the setting so Quattro displays the files in the current directory. Enter /Options Startup Directory Current. If you want to change the setting back to always displaying the last directory that you looked at with the File Manager, enter /Options Startup Directory Previous. Selecting Update from the Options pull-down menu makes the selection permanent for all later Quattro sessions.

For the Drive setting, you can change the current letter to any letter that is valid for your system. For the Directory setting, you can change the current directory to any directory that is valid for the selected drive. The Directory setting must separate each directory in the path with a backslash (\). You can also change the directory from the file list pane by highlighting the directory you want and pressing ENTER. For the Filter and Filename options, the next two sections describe your choices.

SETTING THE FILTER The filter setting selects which files you want to include or omit in the file list pane. The filter contains a file name description of the files you want to see. Filters normally use the question mark and asterisk wild card characters to represent one or any number of characters. For example, to see all the Quattro files, the filter is *.WQ1. You can also limit which files Quattro lists by entering part of the file name such as **SALES*.WQ1**. This lists any Quattro file in which SALES comprises the first five characters of the file name.

You can also select which files you do not want in the file list by including the file name description in square brackets. For example, a filter of [*.WQ1] lists all files except Quattro Pro files. You can combine file descriptions into a filter by putting a comma between each file description. A filter such as *.W*,[*.WQ1] lists all spreadsheet files except for Quattro Pro spreadsheets. This filter remains in effect even as you change the drive and directory. If you need to remove the filter, either replace it with *.* or highlight the Filter prompt, press ESC, and press ENTER.

SETTING THE FILE NAME The File Name prompt lets you select a spreadsheet that you want to open in another window or finds a file anywhere in a drive. If you type a file name at the prompt and press ENTER, Quattro opens that spreadsheet if it finds a file in that directory with that file name or it creates an empty spreadsheet with that name and opens the spreadsheet. When you type an existing file name at the File Name prompt, Quattro can find the spreadsheet even if it is excluded from the file list pane by a filter. You can also open a spreadsheet from the file list pane by highlighting the spreadsheet file you want and pressing ENTER.

The other option you have for the File Name prompt is to have Quattro find the file for you. When Quattro finds a file for you, it looks through every directory in the selected drive. To find a file, enter the file name, and press F5 (GOTO)—do not press ENTER. Quattro changes the directory and filter to match the directory and filter containing the selected file, and the file name is highlighted in the file list pane. If Quattro cannot find the file, Quattro displays an error message. If you press F5 (GOTO) again, Quattro looks for the next occurrence of that file name. When Quattro cannot find another file with the same name, the File Manager window remains in the same drive and directory. Quattro only searches the files that match the filter setting.

The file name you enter for the File Name prompt can include the question mark and asterisk wild card characters. This allows you to find files when you are unsure of the file name. For example, use **SALES.W*** when you want to find a spreadsheet called SALES and you are unsure of its extension, or **BUDGET*.WQ1** when you want to find all Quattro Pro spreadsheets with BUDGET as the first six characters in their file names.

Using the File List Pane

The file list pane contains all the files that meet the filter conditions and are in the selected drive and directory. The information the file list pane displays is identical to the file information DOS shows when you ask for a directory listing. The information includes the file name, the extension, the size (in bytes), and the date and time the file was last altered. If the files listed are not in the root directory, the file list pane contains two periods (..) at the top of the list, which represent the parent directory. If the files listed are in a directory that contains other directories, the file list pane contains the subdirectory names at the bottom of the list. The file list pane displays **<more>** if the file list is longer than the pane. You can move through the file list a screen at a time by pressing PGUP and PGDN. Pressing HOME or END moves you to the first or last entry in the file list pane. At the bottom of the list of files is the number of files listed in the file list, the number of files in the directory, the number of bytes used by the files in the directory, and the number of bytes available for additional files.

If you want to open a highlighted spreadsheet, press ENTER and Quattro opens a spreadsheet window containing the selected spreadsheet. If you press ENTER while highlighting a file that Quattro cannot understand, Quattro displays the invalid spreadsheet error message.

Several of the commands in the File Manager operate using one or more files from the file list. To select a file to use with a File Manager command, press SHIFT-F7 (SELECT) or the GRAY +. When you press SHIFT-F7 (SELECT) or the GRAY + on an unselected file, it selects it. When you press SHIFT-F7 (SELECT) or the GRAY + on a selected file, it unselects it. With a mouse, you can select a file in the list by clicking it. Either method is equivalent to the /Edit Select command. Quattro Pro also has a / Edit All Select command to select all of the files in the file list. Another alternative for selecting all the files is pressing ALT-F7 (ALL SELECT). Selecting /Edit All Select or pressing ALT-F7 (ALL SELECT) a second time unselects all files. Quattro marks the selected files with a check next to the file name. Quattro only updates the files in the files list when a setting in the control panel changes or when you tell Quattro to recheck the files in the file list pane. To explicitly tell Quattro to recheck the files in the file list pane, press F9 (CALC) or select /File Read Dir.

Adding and Using a Directory Tree Pane

The third type of pane a File Manager window can have is a directory tree pane. A directory tree pane lists the directories of the current drive and highlights the path to the current directory. A directory tree pane shows how the drive is organized into directories. To add a directory tree pane, enter /Tree Open. Figure 5.30 shows a File Manager window with a directory pane added. If you want to change the portion of the window Quattro uses to display the directory tree pane, enter /Tree Resize and the percentage of the File Manager window the directory tree pane should use. You can move to this pane and move from it to another pane using F6 (PANE). Once the pane is the current pane, you can change the current directory of the file list by moving the highlight to the directory you want to use. As you move the highlight, Quattro changes the directory that the files in the file list pane use to display files.

Using Menu Commands in the File Manager

The File Manager commands can be divided into three categories. Some of the File Manager commands perform DOS commands. A second group of File Manager commands performs tasks that change the display of the panes and print information that the panes contain. Other File Manager commands perform commands

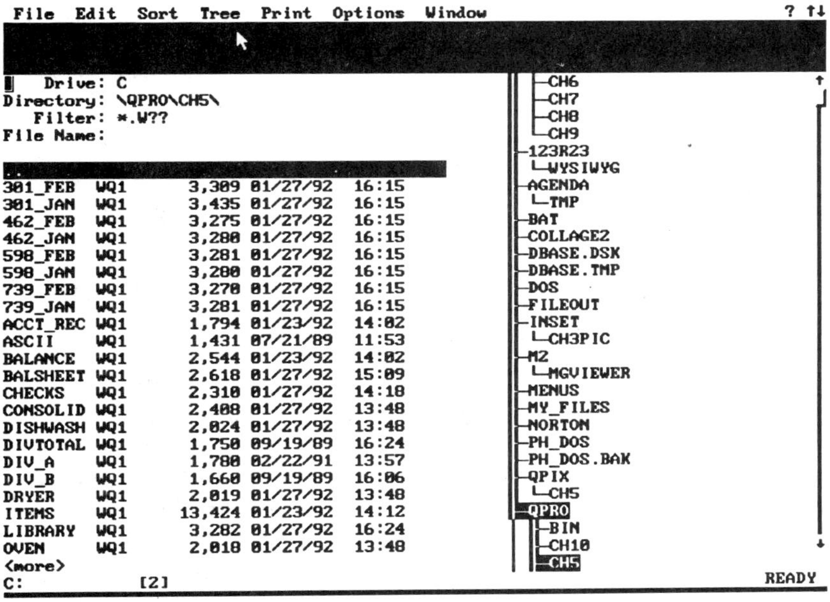

File Options 223

```
File  Edit  Sort  Tree  Print  Options  Window                    ? ↑↓

     Drive: C                                    ├─CH6              ↑
 Directory: \QPRO\CH5\                           ├─CH7
    Filter: *.W??                                ├─CH8
 File Name:                                      └─CH9
                                                ─123R23
                                                  └─WYSIWYG
 301_FEB  WQ1   3,309 01/27/92  16:15           ─AGENDA
 301_JAN  WQ1   3,435 01/27/92  16:15             └─TMP
 462_FEB  WQ1   3,275 01/27/92  16:15           ─BAT
 462_JAN  WQ1   3,280 01/27/92  16:15           ─COLLAGE2
 598_FEB  WQ1   3,281 01/27/92  16:15           ─DBASE.DSK
 598_JAN  WQ1   3,280 01/27/92  16:15           ─DBASE.TMP
 739_FEB  WQ1   3,270 01/27/92  16:15           ─DOS
 739_JAN  WQ1   3,281 01/27/92  16:15           ─FILEOUT
 ACCT_REC WQ1   1,794 01/23/92  14:02           ─INSET
 ASCII    WQ1   1,431 07/21/89  11:53             └─CH3PIC
 BALANCE  WQ1   2,544 01/23/92  14:02           ─M2
 BALSHEET WQ1   2,618 01/27/92  15:09             └─MGVIEWER
 CHECKS   WQ1   2,310 01/27/92  14:18           ─MENUS
 CONSOLID WQ1   2,408 01/27/92  13:48           ─MY_FILES
 DISHWASH WQ1   2,024 01/27/92  13:48           ─NORTON
 DIVTOTAL WQ1   1,750 09/19/89  16:24           ─PH_DOS
 DIV_A    WQ1   1,780 02/22/91  13:57           ─PH_DOS.BAK
 DIV_B    WQ1   1,660 09/19/89  16:06           ─QPIX
 DRYER    WQ1   2,019 01/27/92  13:48             └─CH5
 ITEMS    WQ1  13,424 01/23/92  14:12           ▓QPRO
 LIBRARY  WQ1   3,282 01/27/92  16:24            ├─BIN
 OVEN     WQ1   2,018 01/27/92  13:48            ├─CH10
 <more>                                          └─CH5           ↓
 C:           [2]                                           READY
```

Figure 5.30 Directory Tree in File Manager Window

that are similar to Quattro commands for spreadsheets. The menu selections available through the File Manager eliminate most of the times you need to exit to DOS. These commands are easier to use, since you can browse through the menus to select the command you want and let the menu command prompt you for the information the command needs. Since only the first two categories of File Manager commands are specific to the File Manager, the third group of commands are ignored, because they perform the same tasks they perform in a spreadsheet.

CHANGING THE FILE LIST PANE DISPLAY The file list pane initially shows the file name, extension, size, and date and time of the files with each file taking a separate line. You can change the display of file names so it is more like the file name display that you see when you press the GRAY PLUS or select the +/− button when Quattro lists the files (such as for the /File Retrieve command). If you want to change how the File Manager window displays the files, enter /Options File List Wide View. The resulting file list shows only the file names and the extensions but uses as many columns as can fit in the File Manager window. To return to the display that provides the size and date and time information for the files, enter /Options File List Full View. When you choose Update from the Options pull-down menu, the selection you make is retained and used in the next File Manager window you open.

SORTING THE FILES IN THE FILE LIST PANE Initially, the File Manager window lists all the files that the control pane selects in alphabetical order. The

/Sort command can change the order of the files in the file list pane to sort according to the file name, the extension, the size, or the date and time the file was last saved. This command can also list the files according to the order that DOS lists them when you ask for a directory of the files from the DOS prompt. To change the order of the files, enter /Sort, and select the order that you want to sort the files by. This command will sort by size or time and date even if that information is hidden by displaying the files in the file list pane with the wide view.

PRINTING THE FILE LIST AND DIRECTORY INFORMATION The /Print commands in the File Manager are very similar to the /Print commands for spreadsheets. The main difference is the type of information printed. In a File Manager window, you can print the files list, the directory tree, or both. To select the information to print, enter /Print Block. Then select Files to print the information in the file list pane, Tree to print the information in the directory pane, or Both to print the information in the file list pane and the directory pane. Printing this information also varies from printing spreadsheets by the destination. For printing in a File Manager window, you can either print to a printer or a file. Since the information that you can print from a File Manager window does not use special printer features, the Graphics Printer and Binary File options are unnecessary. The remaining options in the Print pull-down menu are identical to the options in the Print pull-down menu for spreadsheets. When you are ready to print the file or directory information, select Go. Before you print, you may need to check the settings of the default printer with the /Options Hardware Printers command.

COPYING FILES Copying files is quick to do in a File Manager window whether you have one file to copy or many. You may also want a copy of a file as a backup copy in case your original is accidentally damaged. Copying files is a three-step process. First, you must indicate which files you want to copy. Second, you must copy the files to the paste buffer, a temporary storage that Quattro uses to store files as it copies and moves them. Third, you must tell Quattro where you want the copies of the files.

To tell Quattro which files you want to work with, you must either select the files or highlight the single file you want to work with. To select a file, use the /Edit Select File command or press SHIFT-F7 (SELECT) or the GRAY +. To select all files, use the /Edit All Select or press ALT-F7 (ALL SELECT). Using the /Edit All Select command or pressing ALT-F7 (ALL SELECT) a second time unselects all the files. If you only want to copy one file, highlight the file in the file list. You do not have to select it, since the command to copy the file to the paste buffer uses the highlighted file if the file list pane does not have any files selected.

Once the files are selected, you can tell Quattro to copy the files to the paste buffer. Enter /Edit Copy or press SHIFT-F9 (COPY). Then change the drive and/or directory to the drive and directory that you want to copy the files to. It cannot be the same directory containing any of the files in the paste buffer. Once you have selected the drive and directory, copy the files from the paste buffer to the current drive and directory by entering /Edit Paste or pressing SHIFT-F10 (PASTE). The file will still be in the original location as well as the new location. When you copy a file with the File Manager, the original and the duplicates have the same name.

MOVING FILES Moving a file from one drive and directory to another is similar to copying a file from one drive and directory to another. Moving a file is different since it involves copying the original file to the paste buffer, erasing the original file and copying the file from the paste buffer to its new location. You may want to move a file when you are rearranging your data files so all data for a particular application are in the same directory. Moving files is a three-step process. First, you must indicate which files you want to move. Second, you must move the files to the paste buffer. Third, you must tell Quattro where you want the files moved.

To tell Quattro which files you want to work with, you must either select the files using the keys or commands described for copying files or highlight the single file that you want to move. After the files are selected, you can tell Quattro to move the files to the paste buffer. Enter /Edit Move or press SHIFT-F8 (MOVE). This copies the original file to the paste buffer and deletes the original file from the drive and directory. Then change the drive and/or directory to the drive and directory to which you want to move the files. Once you have selected the drive and directory, copy the files from the paste buffer to the current drive and directory by entering /Edit Paste or pressing SHIFT-F10 (PASTE). When you move a file with the File Manager, the resulting files have the same name as the original files.

DELETING FILES As your collection of files grows, you will have files that are no longer useful. Save and retrieve operations are much more efficient if you eliminate unnecessary files from your disk. This feature is also used when you have a file stored in multiple directories on a disk. Removing files is necessary when you are working with diskettes and are running out of space. Although erasing files is permanent, some file utilities provide methods of recovering files immediately after they are erased.

To remove a single file, highlight the file you want to remove, and enter /Edit Erase or press DEL. Quattro displays a box asking for your confirmation to erase the file. To remove more than one file, select the files you want to delete with the same commands or keys described for copying files. Once all the files are selected, enter /Edit Erase or press DEL. Quattro displays a box asking for your confirmation to erase the files.

When you erase a file, the operating system does not actually remove the file from your diskette. When you erase a file, the operating system changes the directory entry for the file and establishes the area that your file used as free space on the disk. The next time you save information on the disk, this free space is available for storage. If you immediately realize that you have erased an important file accidentally, you can use a utility program to help you recover the file. There are a number of these utility programs that you can purchase. Some examples of these utility programs are Norton Utilities, XTREE, and PCDISKID as well as the UNDELETE command available in DOS 5. The directions for using these utility programs accompany the software and vary from package to package. You can use the **/File Utilities DOS Shell** command to temporarily exit Quattro and use one of these programs.

RENAMING FILES When you name a file, you should provide a meaningful name. However, if you decide that you want a file to have a different name, you can rename it. Using the File Manager, you can also change the location of the file, thus combining changing the file name with moving the file. To rename a file and possibly relocate the file, enter **/Edit Rename** or press F2 (EDIT). Quattro will prompt for a new file name. If you want to move the file as you rename it, enter the drive and directory that you want to move the file to followed by a backslash (\). Next, enter the file name that you want the file to have, and press ENTER. Unlike some of the other options in the Edit pull-down menu, this command only operates on one file at a time.

When you use this command, you must make sure not to change the extensions of the files—especially if the extension indicates the type of data stored in the file. For example, renaming TEMPLATE.WK1 to TEMPLATE.WQ1 does not change the file's format from 1-2-3 Release 2 to Quattro Pro's format. In this case, changing the file extension causes problems. When you retrieve the file, Quattro tries to read the file as if it is in Quattro's format. Since the file contains the data in a different format, Quattro displays an error message.

DUPLICATING FILES When you use the **/Edit Copy** and **/Edit Paste** commands to make a second copy of a file, you are limited to using the same file name in the new location as the old location. You also are required to copy the file to a different drive or directory so DOS can distinguish the original from the new copy of the file. However, you may want to make a copy of a file using a different name or with a different name in a different drive and directory. For example, you may want to copy a spreadsheet so you can use the spreadsheet as the basis of a model you are creating. You can duplicate a file to create a copy of a file that has a name different from that of the original.

To duplicate a file and possibly relocate the file, enter **/Edit Duplicate** or press F2 (EDIT). Quattro will prompt for a new file name. If you want the copy in a different drive or directory, enter the drive and directory that you want the copy in followed by a backslash (\). Next, enter the desired file name, and press ENTER. Unlike some of the other options in the Edit pull-down menu, this command only operates on one file at a time. Like renaming a file, the new copy of the file must have the same extension as the original, especially if the file is a spreadsheet file.

CREATING AND USING SUBDIRECTORIES The only options in the File Manager's File pull-down menu that are different from those in the File pull-down menu for spreadsheets are the Read Dir and Make Dir options. The **/File Read Dir** command updates the files in the file list pane. Since this recalculates the files based on the most current settings of the control pane, you can also use F9 (CALC) to perform the same command. You can use this command when the drive in the control panel is a floppy disk drive or network drive. For a floppy disk drive, you should use this command every time you change the disk. The other unique command in the File pull-down menu is the command that creates a directory. When you enter /File Make Dir, Quattro prompts for the name of the subdirectory that you want to create. The subdirectory name should follow the naming conventions for file names but should omit an extension. If you want to add the new directory as a directory below the current one, only enter the directory name. If you want the new directory to branch from the root directory, precede the directory name with a backslash. If you want the new directory to branch from a directory other than the current one, you must precede the directory name with a backslash followed by all of the directories that lead to the new directory, each separated with a backslash. When you press ENTER, Quattro creates the subdirectory but the current directory does not change. If you want to make the newly created directory the current directory, you must change the directory specification in the control pane. If you later want to remove a directory, start by removing all the files and subdirectories in the directory, and then select the directory and press DEL or select /Edit Erase to remove a directory just as you would remove a file.

CREATING WORKSPACES

When you are designing an application, you can carefully size and position the windows so each one is where you want it. You may want to save the arrangement and files currently active so you can quickly retrieve the entire group at once. The group of windows, their contents, and their position is called a *workspace*. To save this workspace, enter /File Workspace Save. Quattro prompts for a workspace name. Quattro automatically adds an extension of .WSP. When you press ENTER, Quattro saves the spreadsheets and remembers the position and size of each window. Quattro also remembers the settings for each File Manager window. The workspace does not store the data in the spreadsheet windows. It only remembers which file is in each window and the size and position of the window. So, you can change data in a spreadsheet saved with a workspace without using a workspace, and the workspace still uses the updated contents when it's restored.

When you want to work with the same windows again, enter /File Workspace Restore, and select the workspace name from the list. This opens the windows in the spreadsheet area that you saved when you saved the workspace. Using workspaces is more convenient than retrieving each file in the group and then changing their sizes and positions.

GETTING STARTED

In this chapter, you learned how you can store and use data in files. You also learned how you can open multiple windows and put spreadsheets or File Man-

228   *Quattro Pro 4.0 Handbook*

ager windows in each window. You learned how you can use File Manager windows to perform file manipulations. You can try some of the commands you learned in this chapter by following these steps:

1. Make the following entries. You can use the report in Figure 5.31 as a guide or use the cell addresses shown below. This spreadsheet will be used as the model of a consolidation spreadsheet.

   A1: **Division A**
   A3: **Units Sold**
   A4: **Product A**
   A5: **Product B**
   A6: **Product C**
   A8: **Total**
   B4: **49523**
   B5: **12340**
   B6: **23480**
   B8: **@SUM(B4..B6)**

2. Expand column A so the text in the column does not run into the numbers in column B. Press CTRL-W to enter **/S**tyle **C**olumn Width. Expand the column's width to 15 by typing **15** or pressing the RIGHT ARROW until the column's width is 15. Then press ENTER. If you are using a mouse, point to the A in the column heading, and press the mouse button. Next, move the

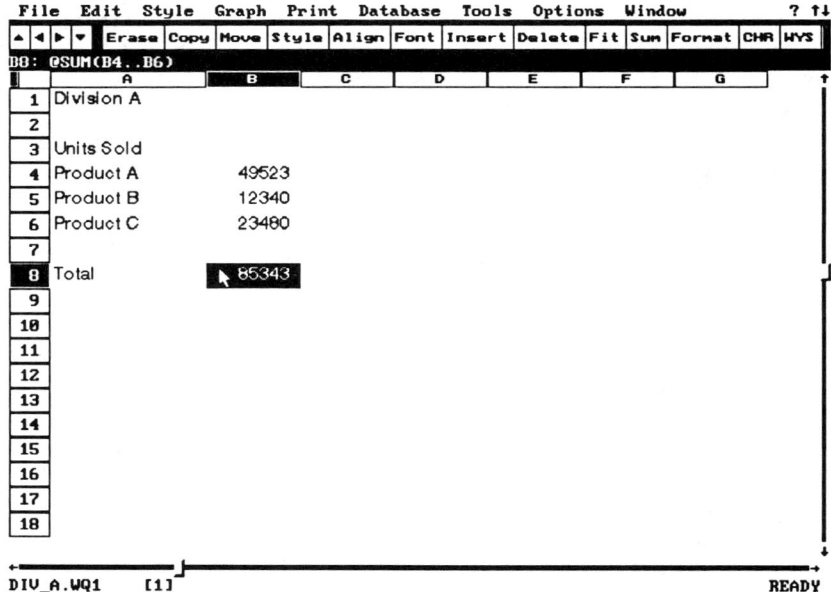

Figure 5.31   Spreadsheet Created in Getting Started Section

mouse to the right until the column width is 15 and release the mouse button.

3. Save this file as DIV_A by pressing CTRL-S and typing **DIV_A**. Then press ENTER or click Enter in the box.

4. Make the following entries replacing the entries you made in step 1.

   A1: **Division B**
   B4: **35702**
   B5: **93024**
   B6: **32408**

5. Save this file as DIV_B. Type **/**, and select File Save As. (With a mouse, point to File, press the mouse button, point to Save As, and press the mouse button.) You cannot use CTRL-S, since you want to save this file with a different name. Type **DIV_B**, and press Enter or click ENTER in the box.

6. Move to A1, and type **All Divisions** to replace Division B.

7. Save this file as DIVTOTAL. Type **/**, and select File Save As. (With a mouse, point to File, press the mouse button, point to Save As, and press the mouse button.) Type **DIVTOTAL**, and press Enter or click Enter in the box.

8. Load the files for Division A and Division B by entering /File Open followed by selecting **DIV_A**. With a mouse, point to File, press the mouse button, point to Open, press the mouse button, point to DIV_A, and point the mouse button. Repeat this command for DIV_B.

9. Press ALT-1 to move to the first window, the window containing the DIVTOTAL spreadsheet. Then press CTRL-T to execute the /Window Tile command.

10. Make the following entries replacing the entries you made in step 4.

    B4: **@SUM([*]B4)**
    B5: **@SUM([*]B5)**
    B6: **@SUM([*]B6)**

    Notice how Quattro converts these formulas into @SUM([DIV_A]B4, [DIV_B]B4); @SUM([DIV_A]B5,[DIV_B]B5); and @SUM([DIV_A]B6, [DIV_B]B6).

11. Open a File Manager window. Type **/**, and select File Utilities File Manager. (With a mouse, click File, Utilities, and File Manager.) If the File Manager window is not listing your files, change the drive, directory, and filter information so your newly created files are listed. Using the defaults, this means changing the drive to **C**, the directory to **\QPRO**, and the filter to ***.W??**.

12. Change the filter so only Quattro Pro spreadsheets starting with DIV are listed. Limiting the files in the file list pane lets you see your files without having to search for them. Move to the Filter setting, and type or edit the setting so it reads **DIV*.WQ1**. Then press ENTER.

13. Copy these files to drive A. If DIV_A.WQ1, DIV_B.WQ1, and DIVTOTAL.WQ1 are the only files in the file list pane, select these files by pressing ALT-F7 (ALL SELECT). Otherwise, move to each of the files, and press SHIFT-F7 (SELECT) while the highlight is on it. When these three files are selected, press SHIFT-F9 for the /Edit Copy command. Then place a formatted diskette in drive A, closing the disk drive (if any). Move to the drive setting. Type A, and press ENTER (or click the Directory settings). When Quattro reads the directory in drive A and lists the files in the drive and directory meeting the filter conditions, press SHIFT-F10 (PASTE). This copies the files to drive A. When Quattro finishes copying the files, Quattro displays the updated list in drive A that meets the conditions set by the filter.
14. Press CTRL-X to enter the /File Exit command and leave Quattro. Since you have changes you have not saved in the DIVTOTAL spreadsheet, select **Save & Exit** then **Replace** when Quattro prompts you about losing any changes.

6

Functions

Quattro Pro provides functions to make calculations easier for you. Quattro Pro's functions are prerecorded formulas that you can access with a special keyword. Some of Quattro Pro's functions provide computations that are impossible to achieve without a function (like the generation of a random number). Other functions calculate results that could be entered with a formula (like the payment for a loan). Quattro Pro still offers an advantage in the latter example, because you do not have to remember the correct formula. Also, since Quattro Pro's functions have already been tested, you can rely on them for more accurate results.

Quattro Pro provides 115 different functions. These functions are organized into categories based on the type of calculations they perform. Quattro Pro's function categories are statistical, string, date and time, logical, financial, mathematical, database aggregation, and system. The database aggregation functions are covered with Quattro Pro's other database features in Chapter 8. Once you have identified functions that are useful to you, take a look at other functions in the same category, since they probably will also apply to the Quattro tasks you perform.

The functions in this chapter are organized into the same categories that Quattro Pro uses in the Help menu. Each category includes functions that relate to the same types of feature. For example, this organization allows users working with financial calculations to review all financial functions quickly, without the need for sifting through functions that perform trigonometric calculations or other unrelated calculations. In this chapter, the material on each function includes a general description, the format of the function, and (in most cases) one or more examples that provide instant ideas for ways that you can use each function. Before looking at a specific group of functions, you need to master the basic syntax rules that apply to all Quattro Pro functions.

FUNCTION BASICS

Quattro Pro has a set of syntax rules that apply to all functions. Every Quattro Pro function starts with the commercial at sign (@). This character triggers Quattro Pro to treat the entry as a value, since all functions are considered formulas, even if the results they return are labels. Following the @ sign is a keyword that describes what the function does. Since function keywords are not case sensitive, you may type them lowercase or uppercase. Although you have an option with regard to the case used for entry, you cannot modify the spelling of the function name in any way. Quattro Pro recognizes only one keyword for each of its functions.

With a few exceptions, each function word is followed by a set of parenthesis enclosing specific arguments for the function. When functions are nested, each function must have its own set of parenthesis in order for Quattro Pro to determine where each function begins and ends.

The arguments for each function are enclosed within the parentheses. These arguments contain your specifications for the information the function uses when completing the computation. Each function requires a different number of arguments. Some functions like @INT require only one argument, while others like @PAYMT use up to six. Quattro Pro has a few functions like @NOW that do not require an argument. Multiple arguments are separated by commas (the comma can be changed to a semicolon or period with the /Options International Punctuation command). You must specify each argument listed for a function and cannot enter the comma by itself as a placeholder except to indicate that you are not using an optional argument. Entering @PMT(65000,,360) results in ERR, since Quattro Pro does not know what interest rate to use in calculating a payment amount. Table 6.1 summarizes each function and the arguments required to use the function.

Function Arguments

Quattro Pro accepts several types of information for function arguments. Every function description in this chapter indicates the acceptable types of data for each function argument. Using a different type of argument results in ERR or results other than what you expect. Quattro Pro's function arguments are numbers, integers, strings, cell references, blocks, block names, or lists of cell references and blocks.

A *number* is any group of digits that you can type with the number keys on your keyboard. Unless the default punctuation settings are altered, the period separates the whole number from the decimal portion of the number. An *integer* is in a subset of number entries since integers only include whole numbers. If you give Quattro Pro a number like 4.5 when it expects an integer, Quattro Pro truncates the number and uses the whole portion. In this example, Quattro Pro uses **4**.

A *string* is any combination of characters and special symbols. Quattro Pro cannot perform mathematical calculations on strings, but Quattro Pro does have a whole category of functions that operates exclusively on strings. When you use

Table 6.1 Quattro Functions and Their Arguments*

Function	Function with Arguments	Function Type
@ABS	@ABS(x)	Mathematical
@ACOS	@ACOS(x)	Mathematical
@ASIN	@ASIN(x)	Mathematical
@ATAN	@ATAN(x)	Mathematical
@ATAN2	@ATAN2(x,y)	Mathematical
@AVG	@AVG(list)	Statistical
@CELL	@CELL(attribute,block)	Cell & Table
@CELLINDEX	@CELLINDEX(attribute,block,column,row)	Cell & Table
@CELLPOINTER	@CELLPOINTER(attribute)	Cell & Table
@CHAR	@CHAR(code)	String
@CHOOSE	@CHOOSE(number,list)	Cell & Table
@CLEAN	@CLEAN(string)	String
@CODE	@CODE(string)	String
@COLS	@COLS(block)	Cell & Table
@COS	@COS(x)	Mathematical
@COUNT	@COUNT(list)	Statistical
@CTERM	@CTERM(rate,fv,pv)	Financial
@CURVALUE	@CURVALUE(category, action)	System
@DATE	@DATE(yr,mo,day)	Date & Time
@DATEVALUE	@DATEVALUE(date_string)	Date & Time
@DAY	@DAY(date_time_number)	Date & Time
@DDB	@DDB(cost,salvage,life,period)	Financial
@DEGREES	@DEGREES(x)	Mathematical
@ERR	@ERR	Logical
@EXACT	@EXACT(string1,string2)	Statistical
@EXP	@EXP(x)	Mathematical

*Optional arguments are shown in square brackets ([]).

(continued)

Table 6.1 Quattro Functions and Their Arguments *(continued)*

Function	Function with Arguments	Function Type
@FALSE	@FALSE	Logical
@FILEEXISTS	@FILEEXISTS(filename)	Logical
@FIND	@FIND(sub_string,string,start_number)	String
@FV	@FV(pmt,rate,nper)	Financial
@FVAL	@FVAL(rate,nper,pmt,[pv],[type])	Financial
@HEXTONUM	@HEXTONUM(string)	String
@HLOOKUP	@HLOOKUP(x,block,row)	Cell & Table
@HOUR	@HOUR(date_time_number)	Date & Time
@IF	@IF(cond,true_expr,false_expr)	Logical
@INDEX	@INDEX(block,column,row)	Cell & Table
@INT	@INT(x)	Mathematical
@IPAYMT	@IPAYMT(rate,per,nper,pv,[fv],[type])	Financial
@IRATE	@IRATE(nper,pmt,pv,[fv],[type])	Financial
@IRR	@IRR(guess,block)	Financial
@ISAAF	@ISAAF (addin.funct)	Logical
@ISAPP	@ISAPP (addin)	Logical
@ISERR	@ISERR(x)	Logical
@ISNA	@ISNA(x)	Logical
@ISNUMBER	@ISNUMBER(x)	Logical
@ISSTRING	@ISSTRING(x)	Logical
@LEFT	@LEFT(string,num)	String
@LENGTH	@LENGTH(string)	String
@LN	@LN(x)	Mathematical
@LOG	@LOG(x)	Mathematical
@LOWER	@LOWER(string)	String
@MAX	@MAX(list)	Statistical

Functions 235

Table 6.1 Quattro Functions and Their Arguments *(continued)*

Function	Function with Arguments	Function Type
@MEMAVAIL	@MEMAVAIL	System
@MEMEMSAVAIL	@MEMEMSAVAIL	System
@MID	@MID(string,start_number,num)	String
@MIN	@MIN(list)	Statistical
@MINUTE	@MINUTE(date_time_number)	Date & Time
@MOD	@MOD(x,y)	Mathematical
@MONTH	@MONTH(date_time_number)	Date & Time
@N	@N(block)	String
@NA	@NA	Logical
@NOW	@NOW	Date & Time
@NPER	@NPER(rate,pmt,pv,[fv],[type])	Financial
@NPV	@NPV(rate,block,[type])	Financial
@NUMTOHEX	@NUMTOHEX(x)	String
@PAYMT	@PAYMT(rate,nper,pv,[fv],[type])	Financial
@PI	@PI	Mathematical
@PMT	@PMT(pv,rate,nper)	Financial
@PPAYMT	@PPAYMT(rate,per,nper,pv,[fv],[type])	Financial
@PROPER	@PROPER(string)	String
@PV	@PV(pmt,rate,nper)	Financial
@PVAL	@PVAL(rate,nper,pmt,[fv],[type])	Financial
@RADIANS	@RADIANS(x)	Mathematical
@RAND	@RAND	Mathematical
@RATE	@RATE(fv,pv,nper)	Financial
@REPEAT	@REPEAT(string,num)	String
@REPLACE	@REPLACE(string,start_num,num, new_string)	String
@RIGHT	@RIGHT(string,num)	String

Table 6.1 Quattro Functions and Their Arguments *(continued)*

Function	Function with Arguments	Function Type
@ROUND	@ROUND(x,num)	Mathematical
@ROWS	@ROWS(block)	Cell & Table
@S	@S(block)	String
@SECOND	@SECOND(date_time_number)	Date & Time
@SIN	@SIN(x)	Mathematical
@SLN	@SLN(cost,salvage,life)	Financial
@SQRT	@SQRT(x)	Mathematical
@STD	@STD(list)	Statistical
@STDS	@STDS(list)	Statistical
@STRING	@STRING(x,num)	String
@SUM	@SUM(list)	Statistical
@SUMPRODUCT	@SUMPRODUCT(block1,block2)	Statistical
@SYD	@SYD(cost,salvage,life,period)	Financial
@TAN	@TAN(x)	Mathematical
@TERM	@TERM(pmt,rate,fv)	Financial
@TIME	@TIME(hr,min,sec)	Date & Time
@TIMEVALUE	@TIMEVALUE(time_string)	Date & Time
@TODAY	@TODAY	Date & Time
@TRIM	@TRIM(string)	String
@TRUE	@TRUE	Logical
@UPPER	@UPPER(string)	String
@VALUE	@VALUE(string)	String
@VAR	@VAR(list)	Statistical
@VARS	@VARS(list)	Statistical
@VERSION	@VERSION	System
@VLOOKUP	@VLOOKUP(x,block,column)	Cell & Table
@YEAR	@YEAR(date_time_number)	Date & Time
@@	@@(cell)	Cell & Table

a string in place of a number in a function, Quattro Pro treats the string as a zero and uses the zero value in the function. In other categories of functions, the use of a string entry can cause an error condition. Examples of strings are shown below:

"Tom Jones"

"The total of the numbers is:"

"December 14, 1989"

A *cell reference* is a single cell address. Rather than typing in a number or string as a function argument, you may want to reference the cell that contains these entries. When a function has a cell reference as one of its arguments, the function uses the value from the cell reference in place of the cell reference. Cell references provide flexibility, since they let you change a value of a function's argument without changing the function. A cell reference can reference a cell in another spreadsheet by including the file name in braces before the cell address.

A *block reference* is a rectangular group of cells on a spreadsheet. Rather than referring to one cell in your spreadsheet, a block refers to multiple cells in your spreadsheet. A block is defined by referring to two diagonally opposite corners of the group of cells you wish to reference. Typically, the reference is to the upper-left corner and the lower-right corner of the area of cells. When you type the block reference, one period separates the two corners; Quattro Pro, however, displays it as two periods. To include all cells from row 1 to 10 in columns A through D, the block is A1..D10, A10..D1, D10..A1, or D1..A10. A block reference can reference a block in another spreadsheet by including the file name in braces before the block address (see linking in Chapter 5).

You can also refer to a block or cell reference with a *block name*. A block name is a name that you assign to one or more cells. When you need to refer to the cells, you can use the block name instead of the cell references. Block names are discussed in Chapter 3. Block names provide an ideal solution when you need to reference blocks from other spreadsheets. When you move a named block, Quattro Pro adjusts the formulas that reference the block for the new address.

A *list* consists of either (1) a single block of cells on the spreadsheet, (2) a block of cells and several individual cells, or (3) several blocks of cells separated by commas. The cells in the list can refer to numbers or strings, although the statistical functions that support list entries expect values for most of the functions. A list allows you to combine several groups of information into one function. For example, @SUM, which uses a list as a function argument, allows you to total multiple areas of your spreadsheet, numbers, multiple cell references, and cells from multiple spreadsheets—all within the same function.

Using the Functions Key

Quattro Pro provides a quick method of choosing a function. If you press ALT-F3 (FUNCTIONS), Quattro Pro displays a box containing a list of all available functions. This is the same box that Quattro displays when you click the @ button on the SpeedBar in EDIT, POINT, VALUE, or LABEL mode. To choose one of these functions, highlight that function, and press ENTER or click it. Using the function key or SpeedBar prevents spelling mistakes and saves typing time.

Nesting Functions

In most examples in this chapter, the functions are covered individually. Quattro Pro also supports *nested* functions, which means that one function can be used as the argument for another function as long as the result of the nested function supplies the proper type of argument. This additional level of sophistication allows you to combine the different features of Quattro Pro's functions to create formulas to fit your spreadsheet's needs.

Using Added Functions

Besides the 115 functions available automatically with Quattro Pro 4, you can also add other functions to Quattro Pro. These functions are stored in add-in files. The add-in files let you add functions that expand Quattro Pro's features. To use one of these functions, select /Tools Library Load and the add-in file with a .QLL extension. When you press ENTER, you can use the functions just like you use other Quattro Pro functions. The only difference is that you put the name of the add-in file and a period before the function name. After the function name is the parentheses and any arguments the function uses. This means if you have a function called @TIMETOSTRING in the TIME.QLL add-in file that uses a time number as an argument, you would enter **@TIME.TIMETOSTRING(@now)**. The add-in remains loaded until you unload it by selecting /Tools Library Unload and the name of the loaded add-in file. If you want an add-in file constantly available, rename the add-in file AUTOLOAD.QLL. You can also use the two new functions, @ISAAF and @ISAPP, to test whether the add-in functions are loaded. The SAMPLE.QLL library that comes with Quattro Pro includes the @SINH, @COSH, @TANH, @HYPOT, @ADD_MONTHS, and @LAST_DAY functions.

STATISTICAL FUNCTIONS

Quattro Pro provides several functions that perform basic quantitative or statistical measures. All these functions except @SUMPRODUCT perform their computations on a list of arguments. Just as with any function, when multiple arguments are provided as part of the list, they are separated by commas. These functions perform simple arithmetic calculations like adding, counting, and averaging.

In this category, Quattro Pro also provides four functions to measure dispersion. Dispersion is a measure of the degree to which data is distributed within a range. The higher the dispersion, the more the data are spread out within the range. Dispersion is measured as a deviation from the mean (that is, from the average). Another function in Quattro Pro, @SUMPRODUCT, computes the dot product of two blocks. All statistical functions except @SUMPRODUCT have been used in the spreadsheet shown in Figure 6.1, which lists the expenses for a factory for the first six months of the year.

@MAX

The @MAX function returns the maximum value from the values provided in a list. The format of this function is @MAX(list). A list of arguments consists of a single block of cells on the spreadsheet, a block of cells and several individual cells, or several blocks of cells; arguments are separated by commas. Although numeric values are normally referenced in the lists, the inclusion of labels and character strings do not have an effect since they are treated as 0.

An example of the @MAX function is shown in Figure 6.2. For each type of expense, the last column shows the highest expense. This information tells you the largest amount expended in each category for any one month. You can use this information to locate costs that should be reviewed for possible cost reductions.

The @MAX function can also be used for determining the best performance figure for sales personnel, the highest grade on an examination for creating a curve, or the largest budget deviation. The ease with which the entire column or rows of data can be selected with the combinations of the END key and various arrow keys makes it easy to specify a contiguous block as the list.

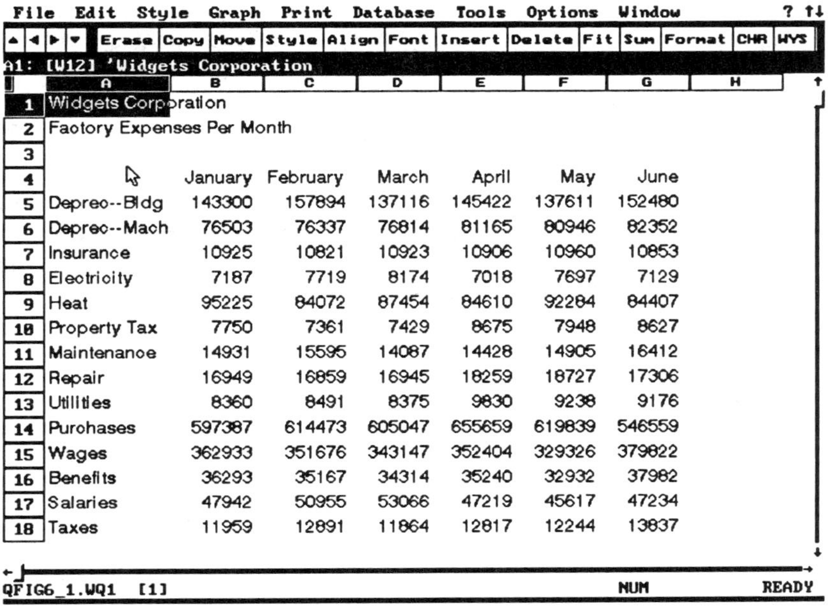

	January	February	March	April	May	June
Deprec--Bldg	143300	157894	137116	145422	137611	152480
Deprec--Mach	76503	76337	76814	81165	80946	82352
Insurance	10925	10821	10923	10906	10960	10853
Electricity	7187	7719	8174	7018	7697	7129
Heat	95225	84072	87454	84610	92284	84407
Property Tax	7750	7361	7429	8675	7948	8627
Maintenance	14931	15595	14087	14428	14905	16412
Repair	16949	16859	16945	18259	18727	17306
Utilities	8360	8491	8375	9830	9238	9176
Purchases	597387	614473	605047	655659	619839	546559
Wages	362933	351676	343147	352404	329326	379822
Benefits	36293	35167	34314	35240	32932	37982
Salaries	47942	50955	53066	47219	45617	47234
Taxes	11959	12891	11864	12817	12244	13837

Figure 6.1 Spreadsheet Used to Illustrate Statistical Functions

```
  File  Edit  Style  Graph  Print  Database  Tools  Options  Window           ? ↑↓
  ▲ ◄ ► ▼ Erase│Copy│Move│Style│Align│Font│Insert│Delete│Fit│Sum│Format│CHR│WYS
  I5: [W9] @MAX(B5..G5)
           A              B        C        D        E        F        G        H
     1  Widgets Corporation
     2  Factory Expenses Per Month
     3
     4                  January February  March    April     May     June   Maximum
     5  Deprec--Bldg    143300  157894   137116   145422   137611   152480   157894
     6  Deprec--Mach     76503   76337    76814    81165    80946    82352    82352
     7  Insurance        10925   10821    10923    10906    10960    10853    10960
     8  Electricity       7187    7719     8174     7018     7697     7129     8174
     9  Heat             95225   84072    87454    84610    92284    84407    95225
    10  Property Tax      7750    7361     7429     8675     7948     8627     8675
    11  Maintenance      14931   15595    14087    14428    14905    16412    16412
    12  Repair           16949   16859    16945    18259    18727    17306    18727
    13  Utilities         8360    8491     8375     9830     9238     9176     9830
    14  Purchases       597387  614473   605047   655659   619839   546559   655659
    15  Wages           362933  351676   343147   352404   329326   379822   379822
    16  Benefits         36293   35167    34314    35240    32932    37982    37982
    17  Salaries         47942   50955    53066    47219    45617    47234    53066
    18  Taxes            11959   12891    11864    12817    12244    13837    13837

  QFIG6_2.WQ1  [1]                                          NUM              READY
```

Figure 6.2 @MAX Used to Determine the Highest Cost Per Expense Type

@MIN

The @MIN function returns the minimum value from the values provided in a list. The format of this function is @MIN(list). A list of arguments consists of a single block of cells on the spreadsheet, a block of cells and several individual cells, or several blocks of cells. Arguments are separated by commas. Since character strings and labels are given a numeric value of 0, including them in the list with other positive numbers causes the @MIN function to return 0.

An example of the @MIN function is shown in Figure 6.3. For each type of expense, the last column shows the lowest expense. This information is used for variance analysis to determine why the minimum number varies from the average. @MIN quickly selects the lowest bid price for a contract, the lowest score on a test, or the lowest temperature reading.

@COUNT

The @COUNT function counts the number of nonzero cells in a list. This function counts both numbers and strings. The format of this function is @COUNT(list). A list of arguments consists of a single block of cells on the spreadsheet, a block of cells and several individual cells, or several blocks of cells. Arguments are separated by commas. If one or more arguments in the list are single-cell references, each single-cell reference is counted as a nonblank cell even if it is blank.

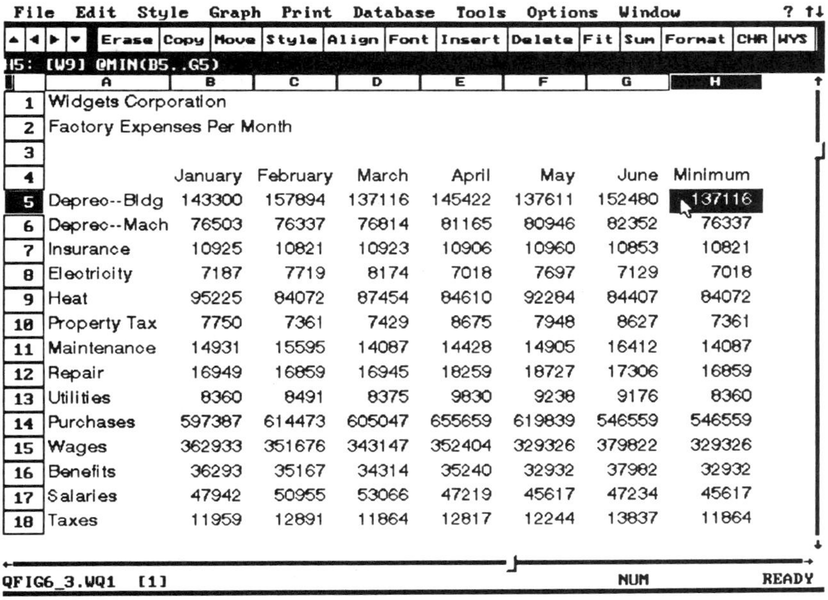

Figure 6.3 @MIN Used to Determine the Lowest Cost Per Expense Type

The @COUNT function is used in Figure 6.4 to count the number of expenses. A quick check of the counts tells you whether an entry was missing in any column in a long spreadsheet. As described above, a single-cell reference changes the count even if the cell referenced is blank. For example, if the formula in B20 is @COUNT(B5..B18,D2), the function returns 15, since it counts the number of nonblank entries in B5..B18 and then adds one for D2, even though D2 is blank.

@SUM

The @SUM function adds the values referenced in the list. The format of this function is @SUM(list). A list of arguments consists of a single block of cells on the spreadsheet, a block of cells and several individual cells, or several blocks of cells. Arguments are separated by commas. Since strings have a numeric value of zero, strings do not affect the result of this function.

Using the @SUM function in the bottom row of Figure 6.5 computes a total of the expenses. Using @SUM in column H totals the expenses for the first six months. This information is used for budget planning and variance analysis.

You can also easily add @SUM functions with the Sum button in the SpeedBar. You can select a block with SHIFT-F7 (SELECT) or a mouse that includes the values you want to total and the adjacent empty cells you want to contain the formulas. For example, you can select the block B5..H18 and click Sum in the

242 Quattro Pro 4.0 Handbook

```
File   Edit   Style   Graph   Print   Database   Tools   Options   Window       ? ↑↓
▲ ◄ ► ▼  Erase Copy Move Style Align Font Insert Delete Fit Sum Format CHR WYS
B20: [W8] @COUNT(B5..B18)
```

	A	B	C	D	E	F	G	H	I
1	Widgets Corporation								
2	Factory Expenses Per Month								
3									
4		January	February	March	April	May	June		
5	Deprec--Bldg	143300	157894	137116	145422	137611	152480		
6	Deprec--Mach	76503	76337	76814	81165	80946	82352		
7	Insurance	10925	10821	10923	10906	10960	10853		
8	Electricity	7187	7719	8174	7018	7697	7129		
9	Heat	95225	84072	87454	84610	92284	84407		
10	Property Tax	7750	7361	7429	8675	7948	8627		
11	Maintenance	14931	15595	14087	14428	14905	16412		
12	Repair	16949	16859	16945	18259	18727	17306		
13	Utilities	8360	8491	8375	9830	9238	9176		
14	Purchases	597387	614473	605047	655659	619839	546559		
15	Wages	362933	351676	343147	352404	329326	379822		
16	Benefits	36293	35167	34314	35240	32932	37982		
17	Salaries	47942	50955	53066	47219	45617	47234		
18	Taxes	11959	12891	11864	12817	12244	13837		
19									
20		14	14	14	14	14	14		
21									

```
QFIG6_4.WQ1  [1]                                              NUM          READY
```

Figure 6.4 @COUNT Used to Count the Number of Entries in Each Different Type of Cost Per Month

```
File   Edit   Style   Graph   Print   Database   Tools   Options   Window       ? ↑↓
▲ ◄ ► ▼  Erase Copy Move Style Align Font Insert Delete Fit Sum Format CHR WYS
B20: [W8] @SUM(B5..B18)
```

	A	B	C	D	E	F	G	H	I
1	Widgets Corporation								
2	Factory Expenses Per Month								
3									
4		January	February	March	April	May	June	Total	
5	Deprec--Bldg	143300	157894	137116	145422	137611	152480	873823	
6	Deprec--Mach	76503	76337	76814	81165	80946	82352	474117	
7	Insurance	10925	10821	10923	10906	10960	10853	65388	
8	Electricity	7187	7719	8174	7018	7697	7129	44924	
9	Heat	95225	84072	87454	84610	92284	84407	528052	
10	Property Tax	7750	7361	7429	8675	7948	8627	47790	
11	Maintenance	14931	15595	14087	14428	14905	16412	90358	
12	Repair	16949	16859	16945	18259	18727	17306	105045	
13	Utilities	8360	8491	8375	9830	9238	9176	53470	
14	Purchases	597387	614473	605047	655659	619839	546559	3638964	
15	Wages	362933	351676	343147	352404	329326	379822	2119308	
16	Benefits	36293	35167	34314	35240	32932	37982	211928	
17	Salaries	47942	50955	53066	47219	45617	47234	292033	
18	Taxes	11959	12891	11864	12817	12244	13837	75612	
19									
20	Total	1437644	1450311	1414755	1483652	1420274	1414176	8620812	
21									

```
QFIG6_5.WQ1  [1]                                              NUM          READY
```

Figure 6.5 @SUM Used to Total Expenses by Type and by Month

SpeedBar to get the same results that you see in Column H of Figure 6.5. Quattro Pro adds each of the rows in columns B through G and puts the @SUM formula that calculates the total in column H. Since the cells in column H are blank, Quattro Pro knows to put the formulas in these cells. You can also select B5..H19 if you want to total the expenses in Figure 6.1 by month as well as by expense category.

The @SUM function is also used for combining data from other spreadsheets. Figure 6.6 shows a consolidation spreadsheet and the five spreadsheets it totals. The formula in B6 of CONSOLID.WQ1 is **@SUM([*]WAGES)**. Quattro Pro converts this formula to use all spreadsheets that are open. A consolidation spreadsheet like this is often saved as a workspace so you can combine the spreadsheets.

@AVG

The @AVG function averages the values in the list. The @AVG function is equal to the @SUM function divided by the @COUNT function for the same list. The format of this function is @AVG(list). A list of arguments consists of a single block of cells on the spreadsheet, a block of cells and several individual cells, or several blocks of cells. Arguments are separated by commas. As with the @COUNT function, if one or more arguments in the list are single-cell references, each single-cell reference is counted as 0 even if it is blank. Also, since strings have a value of 0, their inclusion affects the result returned by the function.

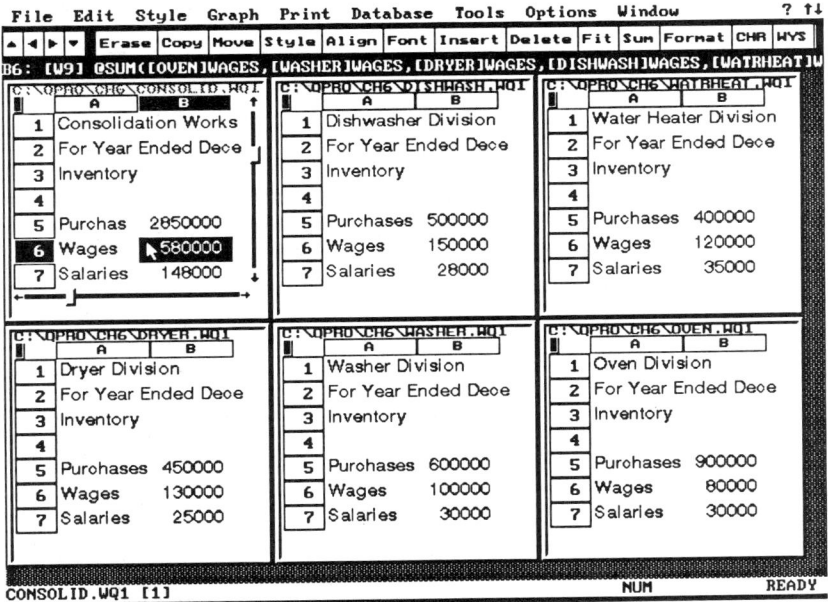

Figure 6.6 @SUM Used to Total Expenses from Several Spreadsheets

An example of the @AVG function is shown in Figure 6.7. For each expense category, the column H averages the expenses for the first six months of the year. In this example, the result indicates the approximate amount that is spent on each of the expense categories per month. Management can use this information for budget planning and variance analysis.

As described above, a single-cell reference that is blank or is a string changes the result. For example, entering the formula **@AVG(A5..G5)** in H5 returns 124,832, since it adds the values (873,823) and divides that number by 7, which is the number of nonblank cells in the block.

@VAR

@VAR measures the degree to which the individual values in a group of data vary from the average of that group. The lower the variance, the less individual values vary from the average. The lower the variance, the more reliable the average is as a representation of the data. The format for the variance function is @VAR(list). A list of arguments consists of a single block of cells on the spreadsheet, a block of cells and several individual cells, or several blocks of cells. Arguments are separated by commas. Cells containing labels and single-cell references cause this function to return an erroneous result.

Figure 6.8 shows the variance computed for each of the expense categories. The variance for Purchases is larger than the variance for Insurance, indicating that the monthly expense fluctuates more.

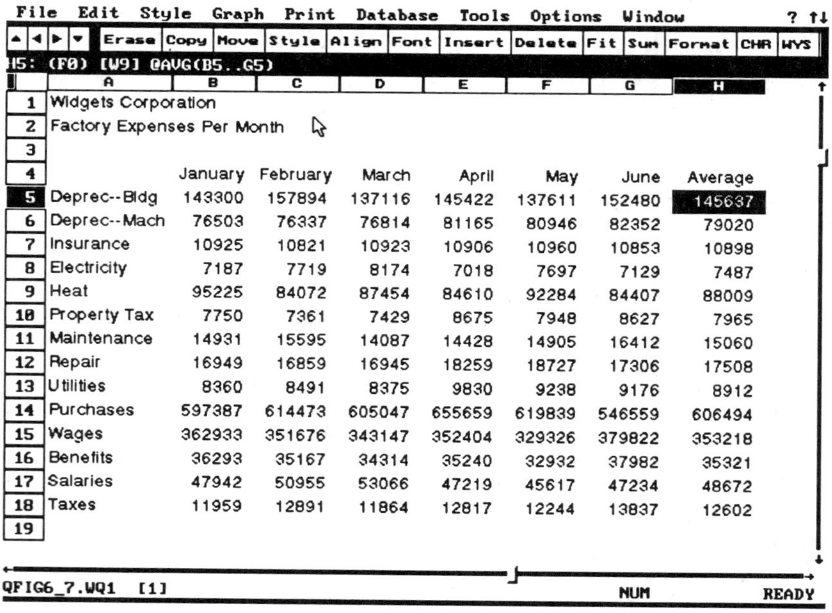

File Edit Style Graph Print Database Tools Options Window ? ↑↓

Erase Copy Move Style Align Font Insert Delete Fit Sum Format CHR WYS

H5: (F0) [W9] @AVG(B5..G5)

	A	B	C	D	E	F	G	H
1	Widgets Corporation							
2	Factory Expenses Per Month							
3								
4		January	February	March	April	May	June	Average
5	Deprec--Bldg	143300	157894	137116	145422	137611	152480	145637
6	Deprec--Mach	76503	76337	76814	81165	80946	82352	79020
7	Insurance	10925	10821	10923	10906	10960	10853	10898
8	Electricity	7187	7719	8174	7018	7697	7129	7487
9	Heat	95225	84072	87454	84610	92284	84407	88009
10	Property Tax	7750	7361	7429	8675	7948	8627	7965
11	Maintenance	14931	15595	14087	14428	14905	16412	15060
12	Repair	16949	16859	16945	18259	18727	17306	17508
13	Utilities	8360	8491	8375	9830	9238	9176	8912
14	Purchases	597387	614473	605047	655659	619839	546559	606494
15	Wages	362933	351676	343147	352404	329326	379822	353218
16	Benefits	36293	35167	34314	35240	32932	37982	35321
17	Salaries	47942	50955	53066	47219	45617	47234	48672
18	Taxes	11959	12891	11864	12817	12244	13837	12602
19								

QFIG6_7.WQ1 [1] NUM READY

Figure 6.7 @AVG Used to Average Expenses by Type

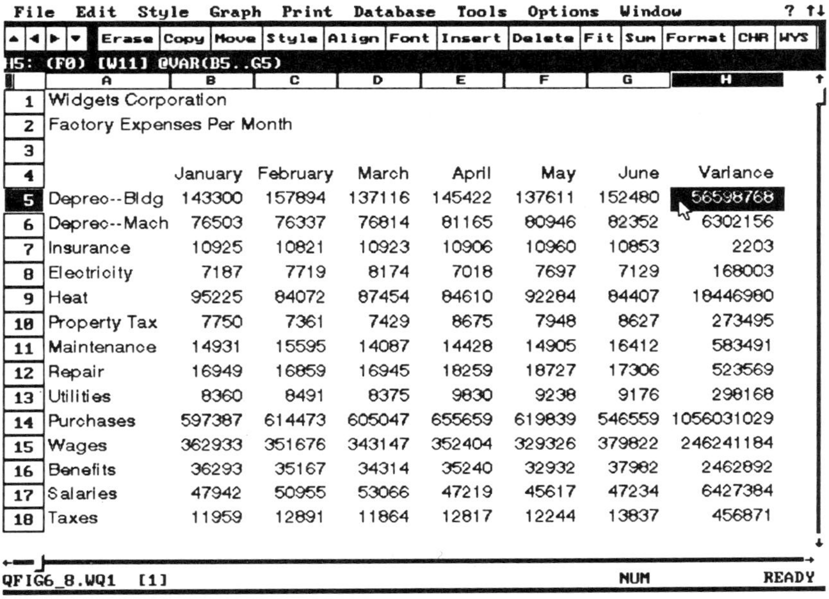

Functions 245

	A	B	C	D	E	F	G	H
1	Widgets Corporation							
2	Factory Expenses Per Month							
3								
4		January	February	March	April	May	June	Variance
5	Deprec--Bldg	143300	157894	137116	145422	137611	152480	56598768
6	Deprec--Mach	76503	76337	76814	81165	80946	82352	6302156
7	Insurance	10925	10821	10923	10906	10960	10853	2203
8	Electricity	7187	7719	8174	7018	7697	7129	168003
9	Heat	95225	84072	87454	84610	92284	84407	18446980
10	Property Tax	7750	7361	7429	8675	7948	8627	273495
11	Maintenance	14931	15595	14087	14428	14905	16412	583491
12	Repair	16949	16859	16945	18259	18727	17306	523569
13	Utilities	8360	8491	8375	9830	9238	9176	298168
14	Purchases	597387	614473	605047	655659	619839	546559	1056031029
15	Wages	362933	351676	343147	352404	329326	379822	246241184
16	Benefits	36293	35167	34314	35240	32932	37982	2462892
17	Salaries	47942	50955	53066	47219	45617	47234	6427384
18	Taxes	11959	12891	11864	12817	12244	13837	456871

Figure 6.8 @VAR Used to Determine the Variance in Expense Entries

@VAR uses the n method (biased) for computing the variances, which is designed to compute the variance for an entire population. When you are computing for a sample of a population, such as when you are evaluating questionnaires, you should either use the @VARS function or modify the @VAR formula slightly. To modify the @VAR formula to compute the variance for a sample, use this formula: **@COUNT(list)/(@COUNT(list)-1*@VAR(list)**. In this formula, **list** represents the data for which you are computing the variance. If you compute the sample variance of the expense categories, the variances become slightly higher. For example, the sample variance for Insurance becomes 2643, and the variance for Purchases is 1,267,237,235.

The variance is frequently used to measure deviations in production runs for different machines or shifts. In this type of application, the differences are normally much smaller, making the variance a much smaller number.

@VARS

@VARS is a function added to Quattro Pro that measures the degree to which the individual values in a group of data vary from the average of the sample of a population. The lower the variance is, the less individual values vary from the average and the more reliable the average is as a representation of the data. The format for the variance function is @VARS(list). A list of arguments consists of a

246   *Quattro Pro 4.0 Handbook*

single block of cells on the spreadsheet, a block of cells and several individual cells, or several blocks of cells. Arguments are separated by commas. Cells containing labels and single-cell references cause this function to return an erroneous result.

Figure 6.9 shows the variance computed for each of the expense categories. Since the expenses only include some of the months that the expenses are measured, the sample variance is more appropriate than the whole-population method. The variance for Purchases (1,267,237,235) is larger than the variance for Insurance (2,643).

@VARS uses the n-1 method (nonbiased) for computing the variances, which compensates for measuring the variance for a sample instead of the entire population.

The variance is frequently used to measure deviations in production runs for different machines or shifts. In this type of application, the differences are normally much smaller, making the variance a much smaller number.

@STD

@STD calculates the standard deviation of a group of data. The standard deviation measures the degree to which the individual values in the group vary from the average of that group. The standard deviation is the square root of the variance. The lower the standard deviation, the less individual values vary from the average and the more representative the average is. The format for the standard deviation function is @STD(list). A list of arguments consists of a single block of cells on the

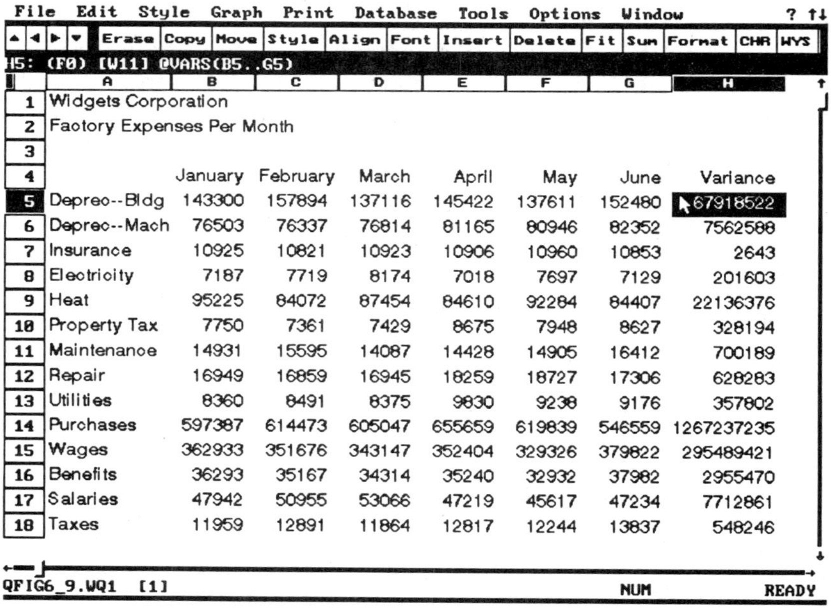

	January	February	March	April	May	June	Variance
Depreo--Bldg	143300	157894	137116	145422	137611	152480	67918522
Depreo--Mach	76503	76337	76814	81165	80946	82352	7562588
Insurance	10925	10821	10923	10906	10960	10853	2643
Electricity	7187	7719	8174	7018	7697	7129	201603
Heat	95225	84072	87454	84610	92284	84407	22136376
Property Tax	7750	7361	7429	8675	7948	8627	328194
Maintenance	14931	15595	14087	14428	14905	16412	700189
Repair	16949	16859	16945	18259	18727	17306	628283
Utilities	8360	8491	8375	9830	9238	9176	357802
Purchases	597387	614473	605047	655659	619839	546559	1267237235
Wages	362933	351676	343147	352404	329326	379822	295489421
Benefits	36293	35167	34314	35240	32932	37982	2955470
Salaries	47942	50955	53066	47219	45617	47234	7712861
Taxes	11959	12891	11864	12817	12244	13837	548246

Figure 6.9 @VARS Used to Compute the Variance for a Sample

spreadsheet, a block of cells and several individual cells, or several blocks of cells. Arguments are separated by commas. Cells containing labels and single-cell references are counted as 0 and cause this function to return an incorrect result.

Figure 6.10 shows the standard deviation computed for each of the expense categories. Like the variance computation, the standard deviation (32,497) for Purchases is larger than the standard deviation for Insurance (47).

The @STD function uses the n method (biased) for computing the standard deviation, which computes the standard deviation for an entire population. When you are computing the standard deviation for a population sample, such as evaluating questionnaires, you should use the @STDS function or modify the formula slightly. To modify the formula to compute the standard deviation for a sample, use **@SQRT(@COUNT(list)/(@COUNT(list)-1))*@STD(list)**. In this formula, **list** is all data for which you are computing the standard deviation. When you compute the standard deviation for a sample instead of the standard deviation for an entire group, the standard deviations become slightly higher. For example, the sample standard deviation for Insurance becomes 51, and the sample standard deviation for Purchases is 35,598.

@STDS

@STDS calculates the standard deviation of a group of data. Unlike the @STD function, the @STDS is designed for measuring the standard deviation of a sample

File Edit Style Graph Print Database Tools Options Window ? ↑↓

Erase Copy Move Style Align Font Insert Delete Fit Sum Format CHR WYS

H5: (F0) [W10] @STD(B5..G5)

	A	B	C	D	E	F	G	H
1	Widgets Corporation							
2	Factory Expenses Per Month							
3								Standard
4		January	February	March	April	May	June	Deviation
5	Deprec--Bldg	143300	157894	137116	145422	137611	152480	7523
6	Deprec--Mach	76503	76337	76814	81165	80946	82352	2510
7	Insurance	10925	10821	10923	10906	10960	10853	47
8	Electricity	7187	7719	8174	7018	7697	7129	410
9	Heat	95225	84072	87454	84610	92284	84407	4295
10	Property Tax	7750	7361	7429	8675	7948	8627	523
11	Maintenance	14931	15595	14087	14428	14905	16412	764
12	Repair	16949	16859	16945	18259	18727	17306	724
13	Utilities	8360	8491	8375	9830	9238	9176	546
14	Purchases	597387	614473	605047	655659	619839	546559	32497
15	Wages	362933	351676	343147	352404	329326	379822	15692
16	Benefits	36293	35167	34314	35240	32932	37982	1569
17	Salaries	47942	50955	53066	47219	45617	47234	2535
18	Taxes	11959	12891	11864	12817	12244	13837	676
19								

QFIG6_10.WQ1 [1] NUM READY

Figure 6.10 @STD Used to Compute the Standard Deviation to Determine the Variation in Expenses' Values

of the population. The standard deviation measures the degree to which the individual values in the group vary from the average of that group. The standard deviation is the square root of the variance. The lower the standard deviation, the less individual values vary from the average and the more representative the average is. The format for the standard deviation function is @STDS(list). A list of arguments consists of a single block of cells on the spreadsheet, a block of cells and several individual cells, or several blocks of cells. Arguments are separated by commas. Cells containing labels and single-cell references count as 0 and cause this function to return an incorrect result. The @STDS function uses the n-1 method (nonbiased) for computing the standard deviation, which computes the standard deviation for a sample. It compensates for not including the entire population in the standard deviation computation.

Figure 6.11 shows the standard deviation computed for each of the expense categories. Like the variance computation, the standard deviation (35,598) for Purchases is larger than the standard deviation for Insurance (51). It is also larger than the results for the @STD function, since the standard deviation for a sample compensates for not including the entire population. Use @STDS when you are using only a portion of the items you are measuring, such as when you measure the standard deviation of the rejection rate for 20 production runs instead of all production runs.

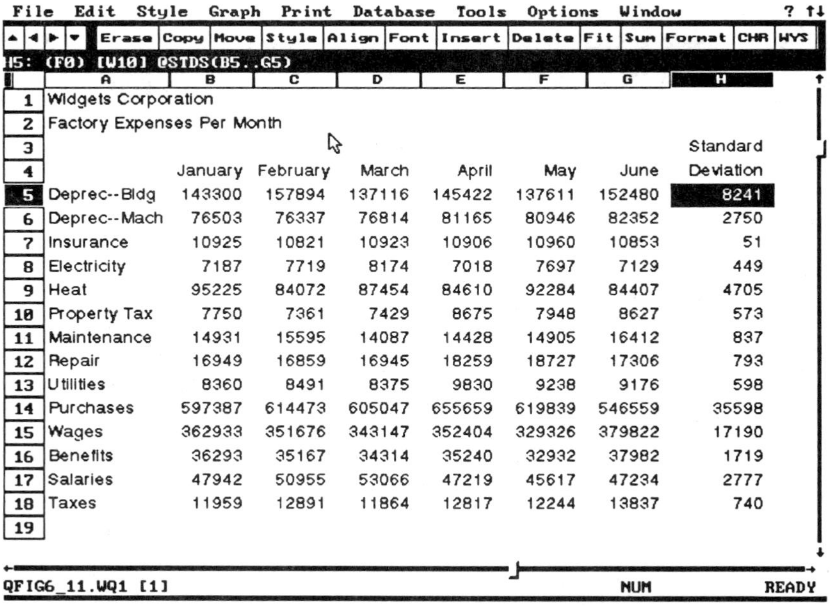

	A	B	C	D	E	F	G	H
1	Widgets Corporation							
2	Factory Expenses Per Month							
3								Standard
4		January	February	March	April	May	June	Deviation
5	Deprec--Bldg	143300	157894	137116	145422	137611	152480	8241
6	Deprec--Mach	76503	76337	76814	81165	80946	82352	2750
7	Insurance	10925	10821	10923	10906	10960	10853	51
8	Electricity	7187	7719	8174	7018	7697	7129	449
9	Heat	95225	84072	87454	84610	92284	84407	4705
10	Property Tax	7750	7361	7429	8675	7948	8627	573
11	Maintenance	14931	15595	14087	14428	14905	16412	837
12	Repair	16949	16859	16945	18259	18727	17306	793
13	Utilities	8360	8491	8375	9830	9238	9176	598
14	Purchases	597387	614473	605047	655659	619839	546559	35598
15	Wages	362933	351676	343147	352404	329326	379822	17190
16	Benefits	36293	35167	34314	35240	32932	37982	1719
17	Salaries	47942	50955	53066	47219	45617	47234	2777
18	Taxes	11959	12891	11864	12817	12244	13837	740

Figure 6.11 @STDS Used to Compute the Standard Deviation for a Sample

@SUMPRODUCT

The @SUMPRODUCT function computes the dot product of two vectors. Quattro Pro uses blocks of data for each vector. The format for this function is @SUMPRODUCT(block1,block2). The terms *block1* and *block2* represent block addresses or names that contain the same number of rows and columns. If the sizes of the blocks differ, Quattro Pro returns ERR.

While computing dot products of vectors may seem like a lot of math theory, the idea behind this function is simple. This function multiplies the first cell of the first block with the first cell of the second block. The function does this for the second cells of each block and so forth until the function has multiplied all the cells in both blocks. Then this function returns the total of the values from the multiplying operation. To illustrate how this function works, assume that you have to compute an invoice's subtotal before computing sales tax. The invoice might look like this:

Item Number	Quantity	Item Price	Item Total
AAGKF	5	6.49	$ 32.45
YOIWR	12	24.99	$299.88
JHKJH	30	5.39	$161.70
Total			$494.03

This invoice computes the dot product of two vectors—one containing the quantity and the other containing the item price. In the last column, the invoice multiplies the quantity and the item price for each item. In the bottom row, the invoice totals the results of the multiplication. If you use the @SUMPRODUCT function to compute the invoice total, the cells containing the quantity are the first block and the cells containing the item prices are the second block. When you enter the formula, Quattro Pro returns 494.03 as the result. This function can also be used to check other formulas in the spreadsheet.

STRING FUNCTIONS

Quattro Pro provides string functions to manipulate numbers and strings. Some of these functions change the capitalization of string entries and transform strings into uppercase, lowercase, or proper case. Other functions return part of a string. Most string functions operate on strings, although a few expect numbers as arguments.

@LENGTH

The @LENGTH function returns the length of the string reference by the argument. The format of this function is @LENGTH(string). *String* may either be a string enclosed in quotes, another function that results in a string, or a cell reference to either.

250   *Quattro Pro 4.0 Handbook*

Figure 6.12 shows an example of the @LENGTH function used to determine how many characters are in each string. The formula in F3 determines that the string in B3 is 14 characters long. This information can determine how narrow or wide a column must be to display the column's contents. The @LENGTH function is also used in combination with other string functions like @FIND and @MID to reverse name entries or perform other string manipulations.

@LOWER

The @LOWER function converts a string into lowercase letters. This function is often used to correct data entry inconsistencies by putting all entries into a consistent format. The syntax of the function is @LOWER(string). *String* is either a string enclosed in quotes, another function resulting in a string, or a cell reference to either.

Figure 6.13 shows an example of item descriptions that have not been entered consistently in column B. In column F, the @LOWER function converts the item description into lowercase letters. Once the item descriptions are in lowercase, you can use the /Edit Values command to freeze the string functions at their current values. You can then use the /Edit Move command to transfer the lowercase descriptions to the Description column without worrying about the effect of the formula.

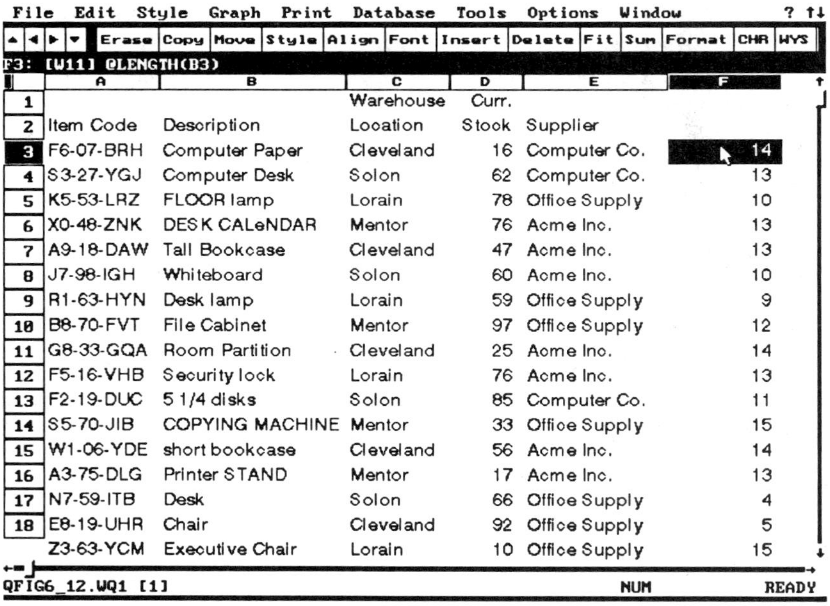

	A	B	C	D	E	F
1			Warehouse	Curr.		
2	Item Code	Description	Location	Stock	Supplier	
3	F6-07-BRH	Computer Paper	Cleveland	16	Computer Co.	14
4	S3-27-YGJ	Computer Desk	Solon	62	Computer Co.	13
5	K5-53-LRZ	FLOOR lamp	Lorain	78	Office Supply	10
6	X0-48-ZNK	DESK CALeNDAR	Mentor	76	Acme Inc.	13
7	A9-18-DAW	Tall Bookcase	Cleveland	47	Acme Inc.	13
8	J7-98-IGH	Whiteboard	Solon	60	Acme Inc.	10
9	R1-63-HYN	Desk lamp	Lorain	59	Office Supply	9
10	B8-70-FVT	File Cabinet	Mentor	97	Office Supply	12
11	G8-33-GQA	Room Partition	Cleveland	25	Acme Inc.	14
12	F5-16-VHB	Security lock	Lorain	76	Acme Inc.	13
13	F2-19-DUC	5 1/4 disks	Solon	85	Computer Co.	11
14	S5-70-JIB	COPYING MACHINE	Mentor	33	Office Supply	15
15	W1-06-YDE	short bookcase	Cleveland	56	Acme Inc.	14
16	A3-75-DLG	Printer STAND	Mentor	17	Acme Inc.	13
17	N7-59-ITB	Desk	Solon	66	Office Supply	4
18	E8-19-UHR	Chair	Cleveland	92	Office Supply	5
	Z3-63-YCM	Executive Chair	Lorain	10	Office Supply	15

Figure 6.12   @LENGTH Used to Compute the Length of the Item Descriptions

Functions 251

```
File  Edit  Style  Graph  Print  Database  Tools  Options  Window         ? ↑↓
     ▲◀▶▼  Erase Copy Move Style Align Font Insert Delete Fit Sum Format CHR WYS
F3:  [W14] @LOWER(B3)
           A              B              C         D         E              F
  1                                   Warehouse   Curr.
  2   Item Code    Description        Location    Stock     Supplier
  3   F6-07-BRH    Computer Paper     Cleveland     16      Computer Co.   computer paper
  4   S3-27-YGJ    Computer Desk      Solon         62      Computer Co.   computer desk
  5   K5-53-LRZ    FLOOR lamp         Lorain        78      Office Supply  floor lamp
  6   X0-48-ZNK    DESK CALeNDAR      Mentor        76      Acme Inc.      desk calendar
  7   A9-18-DAW    Tall Bookcase      Cleveland     47      Acme Inc.      tall bookcase
  8   J7-98-IGH    Whiteboard         Solon         60      Acme Inc.      whiteboard
  9   R1-63-HYN    Desk lamp          Lorain        59      Office Supply  desk lamp
 10   B8-70-FVT    File Cabinet       Mentor        97      Office Supply  file cabinet
 11   G8-33-GQA    Room Partition     Cleveland     25      Acme Inc.      room partition
 12   F5-16-VHB    Security look      Lorain        76      Acme Inc.      security look
 13   F2-19-DUC    5 1/4 disks        Solon         85      Computer Co.   5 1/4 disks
 14   S5-70-JIB    COPYING MACHINE    Mentor        33      Office Supply  copying machine
 15   W1-06-YDE    short bookcase     Cleveland     56      Acme Inc.      short bookcase
 16   A3-75-DLG    Printer STAND      Mentor        17      Acme Inc.      printer stand
 17   N7-59-ITB    Desk               Solon         66      Office Supply  desk
 18   E8-19-UHR    Chair              Cleveland     92      Office Supply  chair
      Z3-63-YCM    Executive Chair    Lorain        10      Office Supply  executive chair
QFIG6_13.WQ1 [1]                                                    NUM          READY
```

Figure 6.13 @LOWER Used to Convert the Item Descriptions into Lowercase Letters

@UPPER

The @UPPER function converts a string into uppercase letters. This function also is often used to put a group of data into a consistent format. The format of the function is @UPPER(string). *String* is either a string enclosed in quotes, another function or formula resulting in a string, or a cell reference to either.

Figure 6.14 provides an example of item descriptions that have not been entered consistently in column B. In column F, the @UPPER function converts the item description into all uppercase letters. Once the item descriptions are uppercase, you can use the /Edit Values command to transfer the uppercase descriptions to the Description column.

@PROPER

The @PROPER function converts a string into proper case (capitalization as used for proper nouns). This function also is often used to provide a consistent format to data entered with different capitalization styles. The syntax of the function is @PROPER(string). *String* is either a string enclosed in quotes, another function or formula that results in a string, or a cell reference to either.

Figure 6.15 shows an example of item descriptions that are entered inconsistently in column B. In column F, the @PROPER function converts the letters in the item

252 *Quattro Pro 4.0 Handbook*

```
File   Edit   Style   Graph   Print   Database   Tools   Options   Window        ? ↑↓
▲ ◄ ► ▼  Erase Copy Move Style Align Font Insert Delete Fit Sum Format CHR WYS
F3: [W16] @UPPER(B3)
```

	A	B	C	D	E	F
1			Warehouse	Curr.		
2	Item Code	Description	Location	Stock	Supplier	
3	F6-07-BRH	Computer Paper	Cleveland	16	Computer Co.	COMPUTER PAPER
4	S3-27-YGJ	Computer Desk	Solon	62	Computer Co.	COMPUTER DESK
5	K5-53-LRZ	FLOOR lamp	Lorain	78	Office Supply	FLOOR LAMP
6	X0-48-ZNK	DESK CALeNDAR	Mentor	76	Acme Inc.	DESK CALENDAR
7	A9-18-DAW	Tall Bookcase	Cleveland	47	Acme Inc.	TALL BOOKCASE
8	J7-98-IGH	Whiteboard	Solon	60	Acme Inc.	WHITEBOARD
9	R1-63-HYN	Desk lamp	Lorain	59	Office Supply	DESK LAMP
10	B8-70-FVT	File Cabinet	Mentor	97	Office Supply	FILE CABINET
11	G8-33-GQA	Room Partition	Cleveland	25	Acme Inc.	ROOM PARTITION
12	F5-16-VHB	Security lock	Lorain	76	Acme Inc.	SECURITY LOCK
13	F2-19-DUC	5 1/4 disks	Solon	85	Computer Co.	5 1/4 DISKS
14	S5-70-JIB	COPYING MACHINE	Mentor	33	Office Supply	COPYING MACHIN
15	W1-06-YDE	short bookcase	Cleveland	56	Acme Inc.	SHORT BOOKCASE
16	A3-75-DLG	Printer STAND	Mentor	17	Acme Inc.	PRINTER STAND
17	N7-59-ITB	Desk	Solon	66	Office Supply	DESK
18	E8-19-UHR	Chair	Cleveland	92	Office Supply	CHAIR
	Z3-63-YCM	Executive Chair	Lorain	10	Office Supply	EXECUTIVE CHAIR

```
QFIG6_14.WQ1 [1]                                           NUM         READY
```

Figure 6.14 @UPPER Used to Convert the Item Descriptions into Uppercase Letters

```
File   Edit   Style   Graph   Print   Database   Tools   Options   Window        ? ↑↓
▲ ◄ ► ▼  Erase Copy Move Style Align Font Insert Delete Fit Sum Format CHR WYS
F3: [W15] @PROPER(B3)
```

	A	B	C	D	E	F
1			Warehous	Curr.		
2	Item Code	Description	Location	Stock	Supplier	
3	F6-07-BRH	Computer Paper	Cleveland	16	Computer Co.	Computer Paper
4	S3-27-YGJ	Computer Desk	Solon	62	Computer Co.	Computer Desk
5	K5-53-LRZ	FLOOR lamp	Lorain	78	Office Supply	Floor Lamp
6	X0-48-ZNK	DESK CALeNDAR	Mentor	76	Acme Inc.	Desk Calendar
7	A9-18-DAW	Tall Bookcase	Cleveland	47	Acme Inc.	Tall Bookcase
8	J7-98-IGH	Whiteboard	Solon	60	Acme Inc.	Whiteboard
9	R1-63-HYN	Desk lamp	Lorain	59	Office Supply	Desk Lamp
10	B8-70-FVT	File Cabinet	Mentor	97	Office Supply	File Cabinet
11	G8-33-GQA	Room Partition	Cleveland	25	Acme Inc.	Room Partition
12	F5-16-VHB	Security lock	Lorain	76	Acme Inc.	Security Lock
13	F2-19-DUC	5 1/4 disks	Solon	85	Computer Co.	5 1/4 Disks
14	S5-70-JIB	COPYING MACHINE	Mentor	33	Office Supply	Copying Machine
15	W1-06-YDE	short bookcase	Cleveland	56	Acme Inc.	Short Bookcase
16	A3-75-DLG	Printer STAND	Mentor	17	Acme Inc.	Printer Stand
17	N7-59-ITB	Desk	Solon	66	Office Supply	Desk
18	E8-19-UHR	Chair	Cleveland	92	Office Supply	Chair
	Z3-63-YCM	Executive Chair	Lorain	10	Office Supply	Executive Chair

```
QFIG6_15.WQ1 [1]                                           NUM         READY
```

Figure 6.15 @PROPER Used to Convert the Item Descriptions into Proper Case (Capitalization as Used for Proper Nouns)

description to proper case. Once the item descriptions are in proper case, you can use the /Edit Values command to freeze the current results as the cell entries, and then use /Edit Move to transfer the proper case descriptions to the Description column.

@CLEAN

The @CLEAN function removes special characters from a string entry. These special characters can result from data that are imported from another spreadsheet or an ASCII file used to transmit information in the spreadsheet. The syntax of the function is @CLEAN(string), where *string* is a string enclosed in quotes, another function or formula resulting in a string, or a cell reference to either.

@TRIM

The @TRIM function strips a string of its extra spaces. It eliminates spaces at the beginning of a string up to the first nonspace character, the extra spaces between characters in the string, and the spaces after the last nonspace character. The format of the @TRIM function is @TRIM(string). *String* is a string enclosed in quotes, a formula or function that produces a string, or a cell reference to either.

The @TRIM function is often used for importing data. In Figure 6.16, the data illustrating most of the string functions were imported from a database file. Some columns (like Description) contain extra spaces from the original database file. The Description column is isolated from the rest of the spreadsheet. Column A contains the original item descriptions. Column B shows that the length of the original strings are all 18. Column C contains the @TRIM function, which trims the appropriate description from column A. Once the original descriptions are trimmed, column D lists the lengths of the shortened description entries. If you look at row 12, you will notice that the @TRIM function took out the extra spaces between the 5 and the 1 and between the 4 and the D. Once the extra spaces are removed, you can use the /Edit Values command to freeze the results of the function, and use the /Edit Move command to return the new copies of the descriptions to their original locations.

@LEFT

The @LEFT function returns a specified number of characters from the left side of the string. The format for the function is @LEFT(string,num). *String* is either a string enclosed in quotes, a formula or function resulting in a string, or a cell reference to a cell that contains a string. The term *num* is the number of characters that the function takes from the string.

Figure 6.17 shows an example of the @LEFT function used to obtain the first three characters from the warehouse location. This type of extraction is useful if the

254 *Quattro Pro 4.0 Handbook*

```
File  Edit  Style  Graph  Print  Database  Tools  Options  Window        ? ↑↓
▲ ◄ ► ▼  Erase Copy Move Style Align Font Insert Delete Fit Sum Format CHR WYS
C1:  [W17]  @TRIM(A1)
         A              B         C            D       E     F     G
    1  Description      18  Description        11
    2  Computer Paper   18  Computer Paper     14
    3  Computer Desk    18  Computer Desk      13
    4   Floor Lamp      18  Floor Lamp         10
    5  Desk Calendar    18  Desk Calendar      13
    6  Tall Bookcase    18  Tall Bookcase      13
    7  Whiteboard       18  Whiteboard         10
    8  Desk Lamp        18  Desk Lamp           9
    9  File Cabinet     18  File Cabinet       12
   10  Room Partition   18  Room Partition     14
   11  Security Lock    18  Security Lock      13
   12  5 1/4  Disk      18  5 1/4 Disk         10
   13  Copying Machine  18  Copying Machine    15
   14  Short Bookcase   18  Short Bookcase     14
   15  Printer  Stand   18  Printer Stand      13
   16  Desk             18  Desk                4
   17  Chair            18  Chair               5
   18  Executive Chair  18  Executive Chair    15
   19
   20
   21
QFIG6_16.WQ1 [1]                                                READY
```

Figure 6.16 @TRIM Used to Remove Extraneous Spaces

```
File  Edit  Style  Graph  Print  Database  Tools  Options  Window        ? ↑↓
▲ ◄ ► ▼  Erase Copy Move Style Align Font Insert Delete Fit Sum Format CHR WYS
F3:  [W13]  @LEFT(C3,3)
        A            B              C          D         E             F
    1                            Warehouse   Curr.                  Location
    2  Item Code  Description    Location    Stock  Supplier        Abbreviation
    3  F6-07-BRH  Computer Paper Cleveland     16   Computer Co.    Cle
    4  S3-27-YGJ  Computer Desk  Solon         62   Computer Co.    Sol
    5  K5-53-LRZ  Floor Lamp     Lorain        78   Office Supply   Lor
    6  X0-48-ZNK  Desk Calendar  Mentor        76   Acme Inc.       Men
    7  A9-18-DAW  Tall Bookcase  Cleveland     47   Acme Inc.       Cle
    8  J7-98-IGH  Whiteboard     Solon         60   Acme Inc.       Sol
    9  R1-63-HYN  Desk Lamp      Lorain        59   Office Supply   Lor
   10  B8-70-FVT  File Cabinet   Mentor        97   Office Supply   Men
   11  G8-33-GQA  Room Partition Cleveland     25   Acme Inc.       Cle
   12  F5-16-VHB  Security Lock  Lorain        76   Acme Inc.       Lor
   13  F2-19-DUC  5 1/4 Disks    Solon         85   Computer Co.    Sol
   14  S5-70-JIB  Copying Machine Mentor       33   Office Supply   Men
   15  W1-06-YDE  Short Bookcase Cleveland     56   Acme Inc.       Cle
   16  A3-75-DLG  Printer Stand  Mentor        17   Acme Inc.       Men
   17  N7-59-ITB  Desk           Solon         66   Office Supply   Sol
   18  E8-19-UHR  Chair          Cleveland     92   Office Supply   Cle
   19  Z3-63-YCM  Executive Chair Lorain       10   Office Supply   Lor

QFIG6_17.WQ1 [1]                                         NUM        READY
```

Figure 6.17 @LEFT Used to Create Location Abbreviations

first three characters indicate storage requirements, the vendor, or a product abbreviation.

A shortened version of the location allows you to hide the warehouse location column and use the extra space to display additional information. The @LEFT function in column F takes the first three characters from the warehouse location in column C. After the unique portion of the warehouse location is extracted, you can hide the unabbreviated warehouse location column and use the new column for other Quattro Pro features. Truncating the locations narrows the width required, since each of the locations are unique even when abbreviated to three letters.

@RIGHT

The @RIGHT function returns a specified number of characters from the right side of the string. The format for the function is @RIGHT(string,num). *String* is either a string enclosed in quotes, a formula or function resulting in a string, or a cell reference to a cell that contains a string. The term *num* is the number of characters that the function takes from the string.

Figure 6.18 provides an example of the @RIGHT function used to obtain the last three characters in the Item Code. In the Item Code, the last three characters are unique to each item. Having three alphabetical characters uniquely identifying each product allows up to 17,576 different items. The @RIGHT function in column

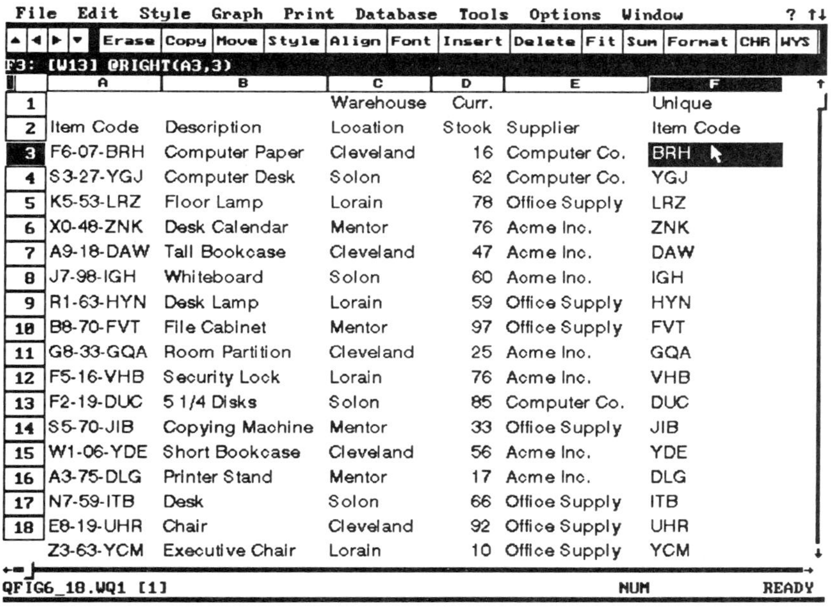

	A	B	C	D	E	F
1			Warehouse	Curr.		Unique
2	Item Code	Description	Location	Stock	Supplier	Item Code
3	F6-07-BRH	Computer Paper	Cleveland	16	Computer Co.	BRH
4	S3-27-YGJ	Computer Desk	Solon	62	Computer Co.	YGJ
5	K5-53-LRZ	Floor Lamp	Lorain	78	Office Supply	LRZ
6	X0-48-ZNK	Desk Calendar	Mentor	76	Acme Inc.	ZNK
7	A9-18-DAW	Tall Bookcase	Cleveland	47	Acme Inc.	DAW
8	J7-98-IGH	Whiteboard	Solon	60	Acme Inc.	IGH
9	R1-63-HYN	Desk Lamp	Lorain	59	Office Supply	HYN
10	B8-70-FVT	File Cabinet	Mentor	97	Office Supply	FVT
11	G8-33-GQA	Room Partition	Cleveland	25	Acme Inc.	GQA
12	F5-16-VHB	Security Lock	Lorain	76	Acme Inc.	VHB
13	F2-19-DUC	5 1/4 Disks	Solon	85	Computer Co.	DUC
14	S5-70-JIB	Copying Machine	Mentor	33	Office Supply	JIB
15	W1-06-YDE	Short Bookcase	Cleveland	56	Acme Inc.	YDE
16	A3-75-DLG	Printer Stand	Mentor	17	Acme Inc.	DLG
17	N7-59-ITB	Desk	Solon	66	Office Supply	ITB
18	E8-19-UHR	Chair	Cleveland	92	Office Supply	UHR
	Z3-63-YCM	Executive Chair	Lorain	10	Office Supply	YCM

Figure 6.18 @RIGHT Used to Extract Unique Item Codes

@MID

The @MID function returns a specified number of characters from a given starting point in a string. The format for the function is @MID(string,start_number,num). *String* is either a string enclosed in quotes, a formula or a function resulting in a string, or a cell reference to a cell that contains a string. The term *Start_number* is the position in the string where the extraction begins. Quattro Pro considers the first character in the string to be in position 0, so you must make this mental adjustment when you specify the location to begin the extraction. Subtracting 1 from the character location you obtain when counting the characters provides the correct number to Quattro Pro. *Num* is the number of characters that the function extracts from the string. Start_number or num may be numbers, formulas, or cell references to either.

Figure 6.19 shows an example of the @MID function used to obtain the reorder point for each of the items. The middle two characters in the Item Code contain the reorder point for each item. The @MID function in column F takes two characters from the Item Code, starting in position 3 (that is, the fourth character in the string). For example, the entry 07 in cell F3 and 06 in cell F15 are returned as strings. To transform the cells into values, you must use the @VALUE function.

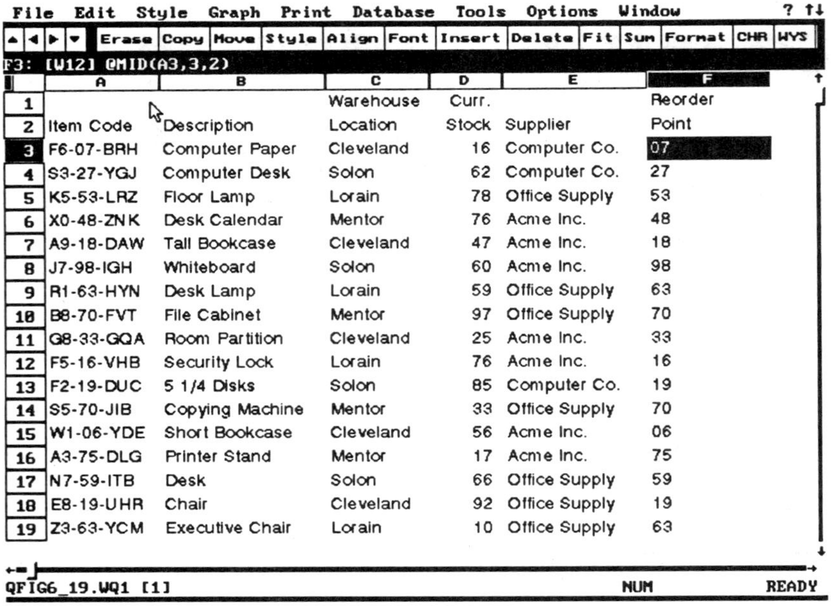

	A	B	C	D	E	F
1			Warehouse	Curr.		Reorder
2	Item Code	Description	Location	Stock	Supplier	Point
3	F6-07-BRH	Computer Paper	Cleveland	16	Computer Co.	07
4	S3-27-YGJ	Computer Desk	Solon	62	Computer Co.	27
5	K5-53-LRZ	Floor Lamp	Lorain	78	Office Supply	53
6	X0-48-ZNK	Desk Calendar	Mentor	76	Acme Inc.	48
7	A9-18-DAW	Tall Bookcase	Cleveland	47	Acme Inc.	18
8	J7-98-IGH	Whiteboard	Solon	60	Acme Inc.	98
9	R1-63-HYN	Desk Lamp	Lorain	59	Office Supply	63
10	B8-70-FVT	File Cabinet	Mentor	97	Office Supply	70
11	G8-33-GQA	Room Partition	Cleveland	25	Acme Inc.	33
12	F5-16-VHB	Security Lock	Lorain	76	Acme Inc.	16
13	F2-19-DUC	5 1/4 Disks	Solon	85	Computer Co.	19
14	S5-70-JIB	Copying Machine	Mentor	33	Office Supply	70
15	W1-06-YDE	Short Bookcase	Cleveland	56	Acme Inc.	06
16	A3-75-DLG	Printer Stand	Mentor	17	Acme Inc.	75
17	N7-59-ITB	Desk	Solon	66	Office Supply	59
18	E8-19-UHR	Chair	Cleveland	92	Office Supply	19
19	Z3-63-YCM	Executive Chair	Lorain	10	Office Supply	63

Figure 6.19 @MID Used to Extract Reorder Point from Item Code

If you are extracting characters from a string and wish to vary the position from which you take characters, you may need to start extracting characters based on the location of a specific character. For example, if you wanted the reorder quantity for the item code G-68-NHA, you could use the @FIND function to determine the location of the first hyphen. Since the reorder quantity is between two hyphens, you can use the @FIND function. For example, to find the reorder point for G-68-NHA, which is in A22, type **@MID(A22,@FIND("-",A22,0)+1,2)**. This formula accommodates an item code in which the location of the first hyphen varies.

@VALUE

The @VALUE function returns the numeric value of the string provided in the function argument. The format is @VALUE(string). The *string* may be a string enclosed in quotes, another function resulting in a string, or a cell reference to either. The string must look like a number. The string can contain dollar signs ($32); commas (32,967,586); extra spaces (" 45.34"); or percent signs (16%). This function is often combined with the @LEFT, @RIGHT, or @MID function to extract a portion of text from a string before converting it to a value. If you try converting a string that does not convert to a number, the function returns ERR.

Figure 6.20 provides an example of the @VALUE function used to convert the labels in column F to numbers in column G. The entries in column F were extracted from the Item Code using the @MID function, which extracted the number between

	A	B	C	D	E	F	G	H
1			Warehouse	Curr.		Reorder	Reorder	
2	Item Code	Description	Location	Stock	Supplier	Point	Point	
3	F6-07-BRH	Computer Paper	Cleveland	16	Computer Co.	07	7	
4	S3-27-YGJ	Computer Desk	Solon	62	Computer Co.	27	27	
5	K5-53-LRZ	Floor Lamp	Lorain	78	Office Supply	53	53	
6	X0-48-ZNK	Desk Calendar	Mentor	76	Acme Inc.	48	48	
7	A9-18-DAW	Tall Bookcase	Cleveland	47	Acme Inc.	18	18	
8	J7-98-IGH	Whiteboard	Solon	60	Acme Inc.	98	98	
9	R1-63-HYN	Desk Lamp	Lorain	59	Office Supply	63	63	
10	B8-70-FVT	File Cabinet	Mentor	97	Office Supply	70	70	
11	G8-33-GQA	Room Partition	Cleveland	25	Acme Inc.	33	33	
12	F5-16-VHB	Security Lock	Lorain	76	Acme Inc.	16	16	
13	F2-19-DUC	5 1/4 Disks	Solon	85	Computer Co.	19	19	
14	S5-70-JIB	Copying Machine	Mentor	33	Office Supply	70	70	
15	W1-06-YDE	Short Bookcase	Cleveland	56	Acme Inc.	06	6	
16	A3-75-DLG	Printer Stand	Mentor	17	Acme Inc.	75	75	
17	N7-59-ITB	Desk	Solon	66	Office Supply	59	59	
18	E8-19-UHR	Chair	Cleveland	92	Office Supply	19	19	
19	Z3-63-YCM	Executive Chair	Lorain	10	Office Supply	63	63	
20								
21								

Figure 6.20 @VALUE Used to Convert the Reorder Point Stored in Item Code into a Number

the two hyphens in the Item Code. For example, in F3, the @MID function extracted 07 from the Item Code. In G3, the @VALUE function converted the label 07 in F3 to the number 7. Once the reorder points are determined for each item, you can compare these numbers to the current stock using a logical formula to determine which items need to be reordered.

@STRING

The @STRING function transforms a number into a string. This function is frequently used to combine text and numbers. The format of this function is @STRING(x,num). The character *x* represents a number, a formula, or a cell reference to a number or formula. The term *num* is the number of digits after the decimal point that the function includes in the string. If the original value has fewer digits after the decimal point than num, zeros are added. If the original value has more digits after the decimal point than num, the extra digits are truncated.

The @STRING function is used to combine strings and numbers. For example, in Figure 6.21, if you want to compute the total number of items currently in stock, you add the numbers in column D. If you want an explanatory label, you must guess how far to the left you must be for the entire label to display and type your entry. By using the @STRING function you can combine the label and the total as shown in cell B20 in Figure 6.21. With the combination approach, you do not have to worry about the total obscuring the label. Also, as the number in stock changes, the total in B20 also changes.

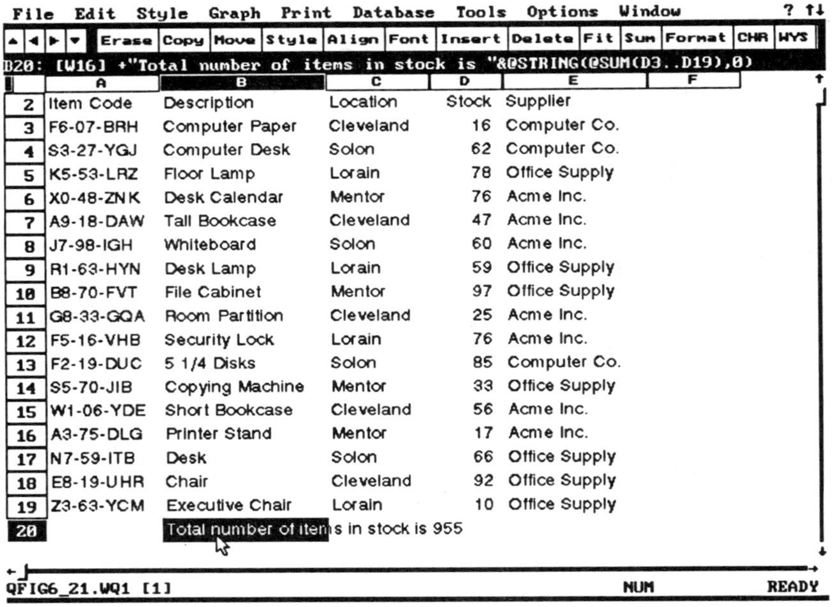

	A	B	C	D	E
2	Item Code	Description	Location	Stock	Supplier
3	F6-07-BRH	Computer Paper	Cleveland	16	Computer Co.
4	S3-27-YGJ	Computer Desk	Solon	62	Computer Co.
5	K5-53-LRZ	Floor Lamp	Lorain	78	Office Supply
6	X0-48-ZNK	Desk Calendar	Mentor	76	Acme Inc.
7	A9-18-DAW	Tall Bookcase	Cleveland	47	Acme Inc.
8	J7-98-IGH	Whiteboard	Solon	60	Acme Inc.
9	R1-63-HYN	Desk Lamp	Lorain	59	Office Supply
10	B8-70-FVT	File Cabinet	Mentor	97	Office Supply
11	G8-33-GQA	Room Partition	Cleveland	25	Acme Inc.
12	F5-16-VHB	Security Lock	Lorain	76	Acme Inc.
13	F2-19-DUC	5 1/4 Disks	Solon	85	Computer Co.
14	S5-70-JIB	Copying Machine	Mentor	33	Office Supply
15	W1-06-YDE	Short Bookcase	Cleveland	56	Acme Inc.
16	A3-75-DLG	Printer Stand	Mentor	17	Acme Inc.
17	N7-59-ITB	Desk	Solon	66	Office Supply
18	E8-19-UHR	Chair	Cleveland	92	Office Supply
19	Z3-63-YCM	Executive Chair	Lorain	10	Office Supply
20		Total number of items in stock is 955			

B20: [W16] +"Total number of items in stock is "&@STRING(@SUM(D3..D19),0)

Figure 6.21 @STRING Used to Combine a String and a Number in the Same Cell

@REPEAT

The @REPEAT function returns a specified string repeated the number of times specified. The format of the @REPEAT function is @REPEAT(string,num). *String* is a string, a formula or function that creates a string, or a cell reference to either. The term *num* is the number of times the string is repeated by the function.

This function is often used instead of the backslash for emphasizing labels or separating sections of a spreadsheet. For example, you can insert a row and put \- in A3 to E3 to create a line of hyphens between sections of a spreadsheet. The \- creates a solid line of hyphens. Combining the @REPEAT function with the @LENGTH function can create lines of hyphens the same length as the titles above them when you are not in WYSIWYG display mode. For example, Figure 6.22 shows a spreadsheet with a row inserted after the label entries and the results of the @REPEAT function used with the @LENGTH function to create lines that match the length of the text. The @LENGTH function determines the number of characters needed by the @REPEAT function as in @REPEAT("-",@LENGTH(A2)).

@EXACT

The @EXACT function takes two strings and compares them. If they are identical, the function returns a 1. If they are not identical, it returns a 0. These values are identical to the values that Quattro Pro uses for @TRUE and @FALSE. The syntax

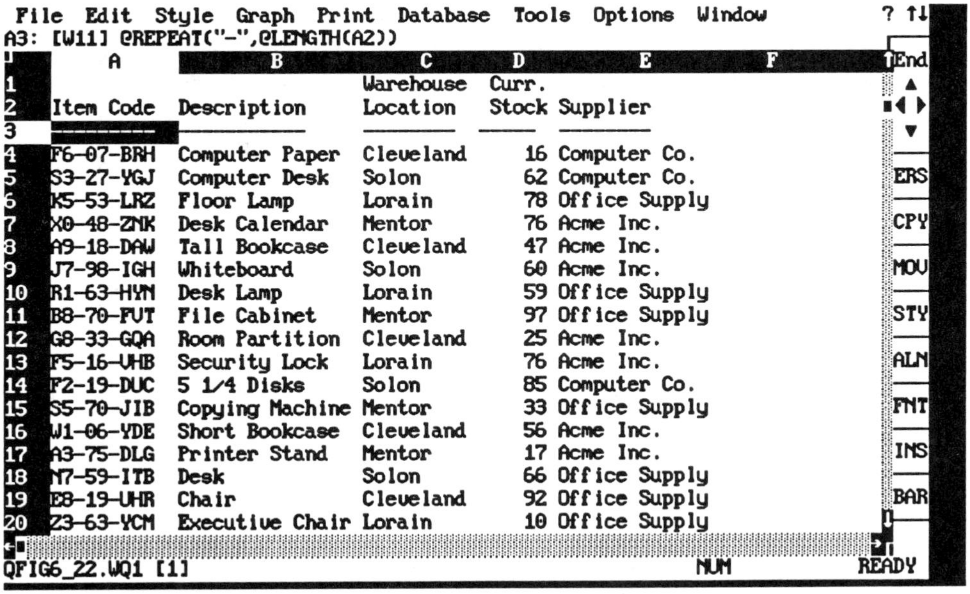

Figure 6.22 @REPEAT Used to Create Lines

of the function is @EXACT(string1,string2). Both *string1* and *string2* are strings, formulas or functions that create strings, or cell references to either. Since this function is case sensitive, the characters in the two strings must have identical capitalization.

The @EXACT function is frequently used in combination with the @IF function to check for errors. For example, by using the @MID function to return the third and fifth character, you can use the @EXACT function to check that these characters are hyphens. In Figure 6.23, any item code that does not have the hyphens in the proper position has Item Code Error in column F, and column F is blank for item codes with the hyphens in the proper positions. Once the formulas are entered in column F, you can fix the incorrect item codes. This function is unable to detect the error in the item code in row 4 since the item code does have two hyphens in their proper locations. Although this function screens for some errors, others are undetected.

@FIND

The @FIND function returns the position in a string where a specified string begins. This function is often used in combination with other functions. Quattro Pro begins counting position numbers for a string at 0, which is the first character of the string, and increments the count for each character to the right. If @FIND finds the string you are searching for in the second character in the string, it returns a 1. The format of this function is @FIND(sub_string,string,start_number). *Sub_string*

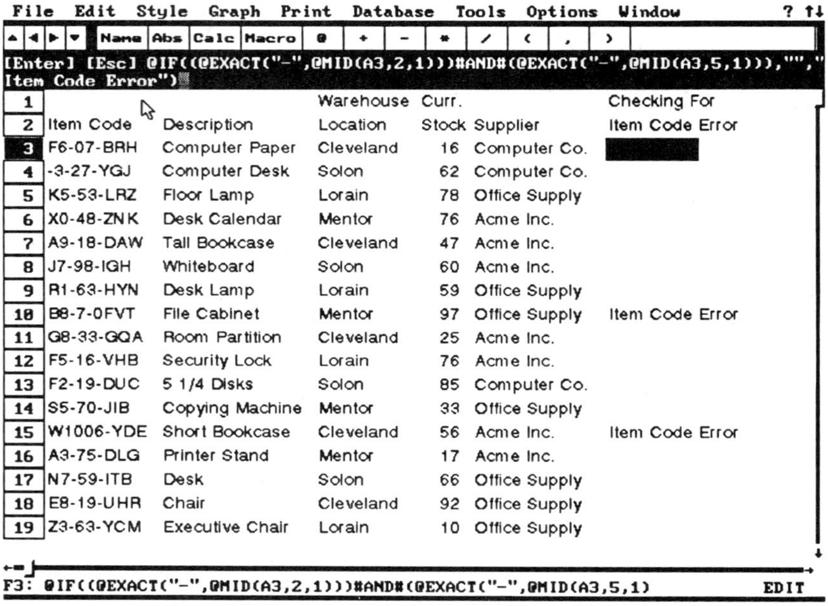

File Edit Style Graph Print Database Tools Options Window ? ↑↓

Name Abs Calc Macro @ + - * / (,)

[Enter] [Esc] @IF((@EXACT("-",@MID(A3,2,1))#AND#(@EXACT("-",@MID(A3,5,1))),"","Item Code Error")

1			Warehouse	Curr.		Checking For
2	Item Code	Description	Location	Stock	Supplier	Item Code Error
3	F6-07-BRH	Computer Paper	Cleveland	16	Computer Co.	
4	-3-27-YGJ	Computer Desk	Solon	62	Computer Co.	
5	K5-53-LRZ	Floor Lamp	Lorain	78	Office Supply	
6	X0-48-ZNK	Desk Calendar	Mentor	76	Acme Inc.	
7	A9-18-DAW	Tall Bookcase	Cleveland	47	Acme Inc.	
8	J7-98-IGH	Whiteboard	Solon	60	Acme Inc.	
9	R1-63-HYN	Desk Lamp	Lorain	59	Office Supply	
10	B8-7-0FVT	File Cabinet	Mentor	97	Office Supply	Item Code Error
11	G8-33-GQA	Room Partition	Cleveland	25	Acme Inc.	
12	F5-16-VHB	Security Lock	Lorain	76	Acme Inc.	
13	F2-19-DUC	5 1/4 Disks	Solon	85	Computer Co.	
14	S5-70-JIB	Copying Machine	Mentor	33	Office Supply	
15	W1006-YDE	Short Bookcase	Cleveland	56	Acme Inc.	Item Code Error
16	A3-75-DLG	Printer Stand	Mentor	17	Acme Inc.	
17	N7-59-ITB	Desk	Solon	66	Office Supply	
18	E8-19-UHR	Chair	Cleveland	92	Office Supply	
19	Z3-63-YCM	Executive Chair	Lorain	10	Office Supply	

F3: @IF((@EXACT("-",@MID(A3,2,1))#AND#(@EXACT("-",@MID(A3,5,1)) EDIT

Figure 6.23 @EXACT Used to Check for Item Code Errors

represents the string that you are trying to find. *String* represents the string that you are searching. These two strings must be strings enclosed in quotes, a function or formula that produces a string, or a cell reference to either. *Start_number* represents the position number in the string where the search should begin. Although this last parameter is usually set to 0 to start at the beginning of the string, it can be any integer or formula less than the length of the string.

An example of the @FIND function used with another function is shown in Figure 6.24. The @FIND function is used with the @IF function to check that each item code's hyphens are in the correct position. In this example, #AND# joins two @FIND functions. The first finds the position of the first hyphen in the Item Code. The second @FIND function recalculates the position of the first hyphen, adds one to the position and starts at that position to look for the second hyphen. If the result of the first @FIND function is 2, which is the third character, and the result of the second @FIND is 5, which is the sixth character, the @IF function puts a space into column F. If the item code does not match this pattern, the @IF function puts an error message in column F, as shown in F2, F4 and F10. In F15, the formula returns @ERR, since the @FIND function cannot find a second hyphen. These error codes inform you which Item Codes need correction.

@REPLACE

The @REPLACE function returns a string, replacing part of an original string with a new string at a specified position and removing a specified number of characters.

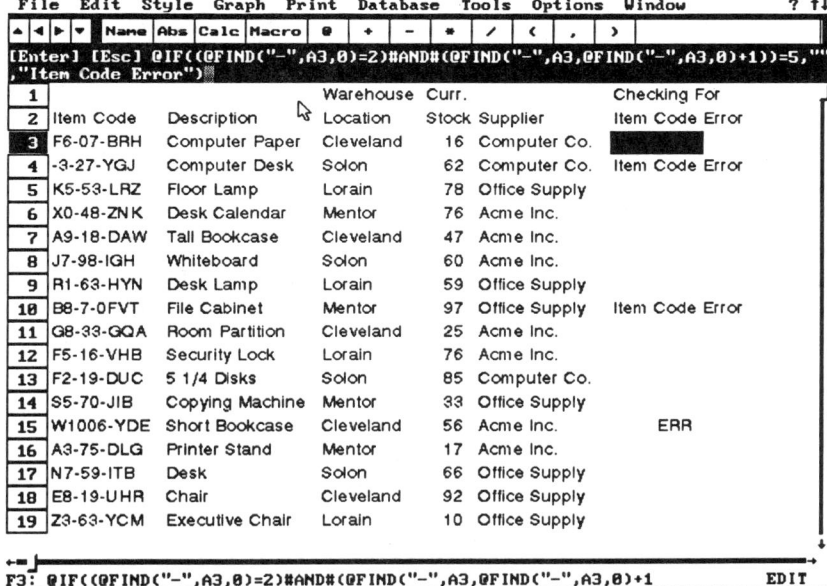

Figure 6.24 @FIND Used to Check for Item Code Errors

This function also lets you insert text in the middle of a string without removing any characters. You can also remove characters from the middle of the string without making a replacement. The format of the function is @REPLACE(string,start_num,num,new_string). *String* is a string in quotes, a formula or function resulting in a string, or a cell reference to either that the @REPLACE function operates on. *Start_num* is the position number where @REPLACE starts inserting and removing characters. The term *num* is the number of characters to be removed. The term *new_string* is a string in quotes, a formula or function resulting in a string, or a cell reference to either that @REPLACE inserts into string. The number of characters removed does not have to be the same as the number of characters inserted. If any of the arguments are omitted, a syntax error results. Therefore, if you are not deleting any characters or you are not inserting any characters, the appropriate values for num and new_string are **0** or "" respectively.

The @REPLACE function is used frequently to change characters in an entry to characters stored in another cell. If you want to change the item code so that the first two characters are the first letters of the warehouse that contains the item, the @REPLACE function can perform this task. In Figure 6.25, the function @REPLACE changes the item codes. The arguments indicate that the function starts at the beginning in position 0 (the function's second argument), deletes two characters (the function's third argument), and inserts the first two capitalized characters from the location in column C.

The @REPLACE function is also used to insert or remove characters from the middle of an entry without removing or replacing the inserted or deleted charac-

File Edit Style Graph Print Database Tools Options Window ? ↑↓

Erase Copy Move Style Align Font Insert Delete Fit Sum Format CHR WYS

F3: @REPLACE(A3,0,2,@UPPER(@LEFT(C3,2)))

	A	B	C	D	E	F
1			Warehouse	Curr.		New
2	Item Code	Description	Location	Stock	Supplier	Item Code
3	F6-07-BRH	Computer Paper	Cleveland	16	Computer Co.	CL-07-BRH
4	S3-27-YGJ	Computer Desk	Solon	62	Computer Co.	SO-27-YGJ
5	K5-53-LRZ	Floor Lamp	Lorain	78	Office Supply	LO-53-LRZ
6	X0-48-ZNK	Desk Calendar	Mentor	76	Acme Inc.	ME-48-ZNK
7	A9-18-DAW	Tall Bookcase	Cleveland	47	Acme Inc.	CL-18-DAW
8	J7-98-IGH	Whiteboard	Solon	60	Acme Inc.	SO-98-IGH
9	R1-63-HYN	Desk Lamp	Lorain	59	Office Supply	LO-63-HYN
10	B8-70-FVT	File Cabinet	Mentor	97	Office Supply	ME-70-FVT
11	G8-33-GQA	Room Partition	Cleveland	25	Acme Inc.	CL-33-GQA
12	F5-16-VHB	Security Lock	Lorain	76	Acme Inc.	LO-16-VHB
13	F2-19-DUC	5 1/4 Disks	Solon	85	Computer Co.	SO-19-DUC
14	S5-70-JIB	Copying Machine	Mentor	33	Office Supply	ME-70-JIB
15	W1-06-YDE	Short Bookcase	Cleveland	56	Acme Inc.	CL-06-YDE
16	A3-75-DLG	Printer Stand	Mentor	17	Acme Inc.	ME-75-DLG
17	N7-59-ITB	Desk	Solon	66	Office Supply	SO-59-ITB
18	E8-19-UHR	Chair	Cleveland	92	Office Supply	CL-19-UHR
19	Z3-63-YCM	Executive Chair	Lorain	10	Office Supply	LO-63-YCM

QFIG6_25.WQ1 [1] READY

Figure 6.25 @REPLACE Used to Change Item Code into Another Format

ters. If you want to include the location as part of the Item Code after the reorder point, the @REPLACE function in F3 looks like this: **@REPLACE(A3,5,0,@UPPER (@LEFT(C3,2)))**. This @REPLACE function inserts the first two capitalized characters from column C after the reorder point for the item currently shown in position 5. The first item code becomes F6-07CL-BRH after this @REPLACE function. The same function can also delete the reorder point from the Item Code. For example, if cell F3 contains **@REPLACE(A3,3,3,"")**, this @REPLACE function removes three characters starting at position 3 and does not insert anything in their place. For example, the first item code becomes F6-BRH. Use of the double quotes (with nothing between them) prevents a syntax error.

@S

The @S function retrieves the string from the upper-left cell of a block. This function prevents errors in string functions occurring due to a number, @NA, and @ERR occurring in one of the string function's arguments. The format is @S(block), where *block* represents a block's cell addresses or a block name. If you reference a single cell, Quattro converts it to a block address. If the upper-left cell of the block contains a number, @ERR, or @NA, the function returns a blank string.

The @S function is often combined with other functions. For example, suppose you are combining two cells that you expect to contain labels. If either of the cells contains a value, the formula combining the string will return ERR. You can use @S in the formula that combines the strings in case one of the cells contains a value. A formula might look like this: **+@S(A9)&@S(A10)**. In this example, if A9 or A10 contains a value, the @S function converts the value to a blank string for that portion of the formula.

@N

The @N function retrieves the numeric value from the upper-left cell of a block. This function prevents errors in formulas occurring in calculations due to a string entry for one of the formula's arguments. The format is @N(block), where *block* represents a block's cell addresses or a block name. If you reference a single cell, Quattro will change it to a block address.

The @N function is often used when one of the cells in a formula reference might contain a string. For example, if you need to add A1 and A2 and know that one of the two cells may contain a label, using the @N function around the two cell addresses prevents your formula from returning @ERR. Therefore, your formula looks like this: **+@N(A1)+@N(A2)**.

@CODE

The @CODE function returns the first ASCII code in a string. The format is @CODE(string). *String* is a string in quotes, a function that returns a string, a cell reference, or a block reference. If the argument is a block, this function returns the ASCII code of the first character in the upper-left-hand corner of the block.

@CHAR

The @CHAR function returns the character specified by an ASCII code. The format of this function is @CHAR(code). The term *code* represents any number or formula that has a value from 1 to 255. If the function's argument is not a whole number, it is rounded.

The @CHAR function can generate random characters when combined with the @RAND function. For example, if you want to add another item to the spreadsheet used for the string function examples, you need a unique item number. One method of generating a unique number is by combining the @CHAR and the @RAND functions. The @RAND function generates a number between 0 and 1. Since you need a number between 1 and 26, you must multiply the number by 27, one higher than you need and take the integer value of the result. Once you have the random number between 1 and 26, you must add 64 if you want an uppercase letter and 96 if you want a lowercase letter. (Adding 64 or 96 converts the random number between 1 and 26 to a number that is in the ASCII code range for uppercase or lowercase letters, respectively.) The @CHAR function converts this random number into a random letter. The formula can be written as **@CHAR((@RAND*27)+64)**. In its current form, this formula generates a random uppercase letter. To generate a random item code, use this formula three times, and join the result with an ampersand. The formula for the item code can be written as **@CHAR((@RAND*27)+64)&@CHAR((@RAND*27)+64)&@CHAR((@RAND*27)+64)**. Sorting your spreadsheet by the unique item code lets you scan the entries to ensure that your newly created item code is unique.

@HEXTONUM

The @HEXTONUM function takes a hexadecimal value stored as a string and converts it into a decimal number. The format of this function is @HEXTONUM(string). Here, *string* is a string in quotes or a cell reference to a string that contains a hexadecimal value.

One purpose of this function is to convert imported numbers that are in a hexadecimal format into decimal values. Since Quattro Pro causes values with the letters A through F to generate errors, hexadecimal values must be stored as a string. If data you have imported contain hexadecimal values, convert them to strings with the /Tools Parse command, then use this function to convert them into decimal values. Another purpose of this function is to determine the decimal values for a setup string to use when you are provided the hexadecimal equivalents. The setup string can change printer features, such as the line spacing or the font used to print the characters.

@NUMTOHEX

The @NUMTOHEX function takes a decimal value and converts it into a hexadecimal number stored as a string. The format of this function is @NUMTOHEX(x). The *x* represents a number, formula, or a cell reference to either.

DATE AND TIME FUNCTIONS

Quattro Pro provides a full complement of date and time functions. You can use these functions to create date and time serial numbers to work with the data in existing date and time entries. With these functions, you can perform all types of date and time calculations from computing an hourly payroll to aging your accounts receivable.

Quattro Pro assigns a unique serial number for every date it supports. The first date supported is assigned the date serial number 0 and represents December 30, 1899. The last date supported is December 31, 2099, and it is assigned the date serial number 73050. Although your date entries look a little strange when you enter them with one of Quattro Pro's functions, you can use the /Style Numeric Format Date command to change the display of the date serial number to an understandable format. You also have the option of making your entry in acceptable date format if you precede the entry with CTRL-D.

The inconvenience of the initial unformatted date serial number display is a small price to pay for the functionality which Quattro Pro's date serial numbers provide. Because all dates have a reference point of December 31, 1899, Quattro Pro supports all types of date calculations, like adding 10 days to an invoice date to determine the last date in the discount period or subtracting two dates to see how many days separate them.

Time serial numbers are decimal fractions. The decimal fraction .00 represents midnight. Noon is .5, 6 A.M. is .25, and 6 P.M. is .75. Every unique time of the day is represented by a unique time serial number.

Although it is the serial date and time numbers that support date and time calculations, you can change the display to any acceptable format for either. If a cell contains both a date and time serial number as in 32605.4873, you can elect to format the cell as either date or time, but it is not possible to select both formats simultaneously without using named style that includes a custom numeric format as described in Chapter 3.

Although most of the date and time functions generate date or time serial numbers, there are some that expect these numbers as arguments. These functions extract a portion of a date or time like the hour or day.

To format a date or time number, use the /Style Numeric Format Date command. For dates, you can choose from the DD-MMM-YY, DD-MMM (the year is not shown with this format but the full date serial number is maintained in memory), the Long International date format (initially set to MM/DD/YY), and the Short International date format (initially set to MM/DD).

To format time entries, you must first choose Time from the selection box showing the date formats, and then select from HH:MM:SS AM/PM, HH:MM AM/PM, Long International (initially set at HH:MM:SS), and Short International (initially set at HH:MM) formats. The last two time formats do not show A.M. or P.M., since they use a 24-hour clock. With these international time formats, all times after noon have 12 added to the hour; for example, 5:00 P.M. is displayed as 17:00.

For numbers that represent both date and time, such as 3716.44147185 for 10:35:43 on 22-APR-92, the appearance of the value as a date or time depends on the format of the cell. If a cell that contains only the time is formatted as a date, it displays the date for December 30, 1899. If a cell that contains only a date is formatted as a time, the display indicates a time of midnight.

Quattro Pro provides several specialized features. For dates and times that are typed in as labels, Quattro Pro has two special features that transform the strings into date values. Quattro Pro also has two functions that produce the current date and time. Two other functions create date or time values from the numbers that you provide. Finally, several functions extract the number of years, months, days, hours, minutes, and seconds from a time and/or date serial number.

@NOW

The @NOW function returns a date and time serial number. This function is entered as @NOW with no function arguments. This number is recalculated whenever another part of the spreadsheet is recalculated.

This function is often placed near the top of a spreadsheet to date reports printed from the spreadsheet. This feature enables you to identify the most recent copy of a spreadsheet when you have several printed copies. If you put the @NOW function in cell D1 and E1 as shown in Figure 6.26 (D1 formated as DD-MMM-YY and E1 formatted as HH:MM AM/PM), the date and time are printed whenever this spreadsheet is printed. The same formula and value are in both cells but the use of different formats causes the cells to display different results.

@TODAY

The @TODAY function returns a date serial number. This function is typed in as @TODAY with no function arguments. The @TODAY function is the integer value of @NOW. Therefore, @INT(@NOW) equals @TODAY.

This function is often used at the top of a spreadsheet to date a report printed from the spreadsheet. It is also used to show the day that a spreadsheet is printed to help keep track of the latest printout. For example, if you put the @TODAY function in cell D1, format D1 with the DD-MMM-YY format, and include this entry in the print block, the print output displays the date on which the report was printed.

```
File   Edit   Style   Graph   Print   Database   Tools   Options   Window      ?  ↑↓
  ▲ ◄ ► ▼   Erase Copy Move Style Align Font Insert Delete Fit Sum Format CHR WYS
D1:  (D1) @NOW
                A                    B            C            D            E
   1                                                       20-Jan-92    10:44 AM
   2
   3
   4                                        Product 1    Budget      Variance
   5   Gross Sales                          948073     1,000,000      -51927
   6     Less Sales                          50963        50,000         963
   7   Net Sales                            897110       950000       -52890
   8   Cost Of Goods Sold:
   9     Beginning Inventory                208595       200000         8595
  10     Purchases                          733681       700000        33681
  11       Total Goods For Sale             942276       900000        42276
  12     Ending Inventory                   235163       250000       -14837
  13     Inventory Sold                     707113       650000        57113
  14   Gross Profit                         189997       300000      -110003
  15
  16   Selling Expenses                      82854        80000         2854
  17   Administrative Expenses               90419        90000          419
  18     Total                              173273       170000         3273
  19   Income From Operations                16724       130000      -113276

QFIG6_26.WQ1  [1]                                                        READY
```

Figure 6.26 @NOW Used for Date and Time

@DATE

The @DATE function accepts values for a year, month, and day and converts them into a date serial number. The format of the @DATE function is @DATE(yr,mo,day). The *yr* represents the year, with a range from 0 to 199 for the number of years, since 1899 (for example, 1989 is 89 and 2001 is 101); *mo* represents the number of the month and has an acceptable range from 1 for January to 12 for December; and *day* represents the number of the day in the month (1 to 31).

The number of days used as the function's argument must be consistent with the month and year. For example, if month is 2, day can be 29 when year is 88, since in 1988, February has 29 days. Day cannot be 29 when year is 89, since February 1989 has only 28 days. Each of these arguments must be a number, a formula or function that returns a number, or a cell reference to either. Since you can also enter dates with the CTRL-D key, this function is often used when one or more of the function's arguments are formulas or cell references.

An example of @DATE function is shown in Figure 6.27, which uses the @DATE function in column B and column C. For each of these dates, the @DATE function includes the year, month, and day. By using the date values, you can compute the number of days between dental visits. In this example, it is easier to use CTRL-D to enter the dates in columns B and C.

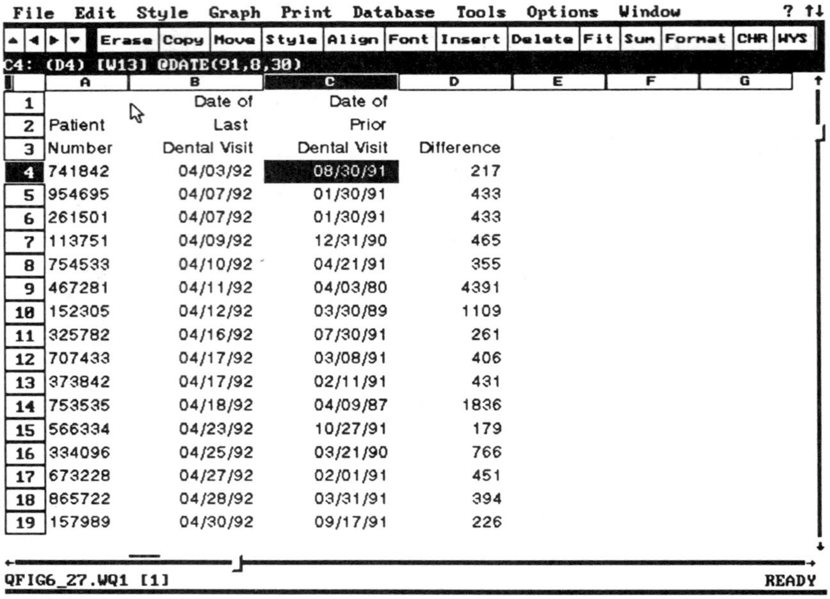

	A	B	C	D
1		Date of	Date of	
2	Patient	Last	Prior	
3	Number	Dental Visit	Dental Visit	Difference
4	741842	04/03/92	08/30/91	217
5	954695	04/07/92	01/30/91	433
6	261501	04/07/92	01/30/91	433
7	113751	04/09/92	12/31/90	465
8	754533	04/10/92	04/21/91	355
9	467281	04/11/92	04/03/80	4391
10	152305	04/12/92	03/30/89	1109
11	325782	04/16/92	07/30/91	261
12	707433	04/17/92	03/08/91	406
13	373842	04/17/92	02/11/91	431
14	753535	04/18/92	04/09/87	1836
15	566334	04/23/92	10/27/91	179
16	334096	04/25/92	03/21/90	766
17	673228	04/27/92	02/01/91	451
18	865722	04/28/92	03/31/91	394
19	157989	04/30/92	09/17/91	226

Figure 6.27 @DATE Used to Enter Dates

@YEAR

The @YEAR function returns the number of years in a date serial number. The format of the function is @YEAR(date_time_number).The *date_time_number* is a serial date number provided as a number, formula, or cell reference.

One purpose of the @YEAR function is to determine the number of years between two dates. Figure 6.28 shows one of the ways you can use the @YEAR function to compute the number of years between two dates. Column D contains a formula that subtracts column C from column B and displays the difference in number of days. The formula in column E determines the number of years based on the total number of days and does take leap years into consideration. From this information, a dentist knows which patients should be scheduled for a checkup.

@MONTH

The @MONTH function returns the month's portion of a serial date number. It does not return the total number of months, rather it returns the number of months of a date serial number in the current year. The formula of the function is @MONTH(date_time_number). The *date_time_number* is a serial date number given by a number, formula, or function or cell reference.

One use of the @MONTH function is to extract a month number to use in building another date. Another application is to determine the number of months

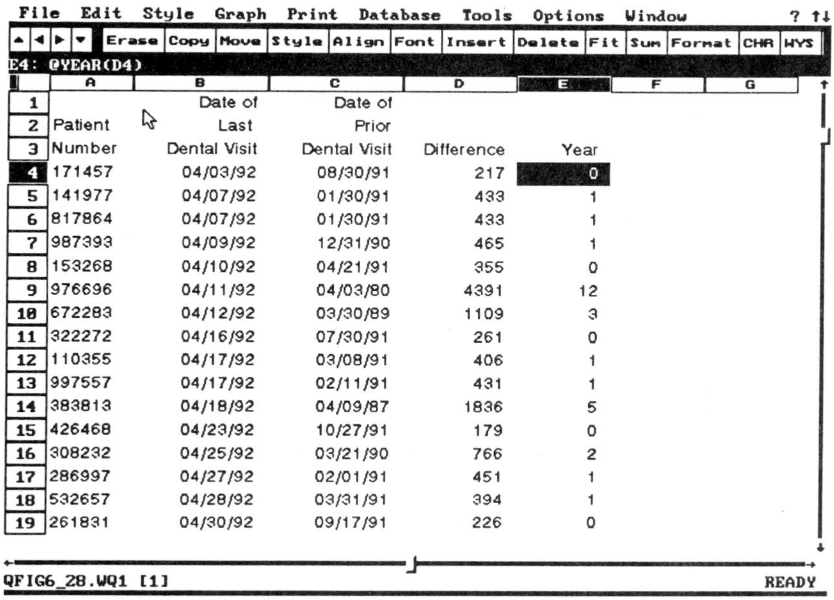

File Edit Style Graph Print Database Tools Options Window ? ↑↓

Erase Copy Move Style Align Font Insert Delete Fit Sum Format CHR WYS

E4: @YEAR(D4)

	A	B	C	D	E	F	G
1		Date of	Date of				
2	Patient	Last	Prior				
3	Number	Dental Visit	Dental Visit	Difference	Year		
4	171457	04/03/92	08/30/91	217	0		
5	141977	04/07/92	01/30/91	433	1		
6	817864	04/07/92	01/30/91	433	1		
7	987393	04/09/92	12/31/90	465	1		
8	153268	04/10/92	04/21/91	355	0		
9	976696	04/11/92	04/03/80	4391	12		
10	672283	04/12/92	03/30/89	1109	3		
11	322272	04/16/92	07/30/91	261	0		
12	110355	04/17/92	03/08/91	406	1		
13	997557	04/17/92	02/11/91	431	1		
14	383813	04/18/92	04/09/87	1836	5		
15	426468	04/23/92	10/27/91	179	0		
16	308232	04/25/92	03/21/90	766	2		
17	286997	04/27/92	02/01/91	451	1		
18	532657	04/28/92	03/31/91	394	1		
19	261831	04/30/92	09/17/91	226	0		

QFIG6_28.WQ1 [1] READY

Figure 6.28 @YEAR Used to Compute Number of Years Between Dental Visits

between two dates. The example for @YEAR presented the number of years in column E, but column F can be used to compute the number of months beyond the nearest whole year number. Figure 6.29 shows one way you can use the @MONTH function to compute the months portion of the difference between the two dates. Column D contains the number of days between dental visits. The formula in column F determines the months portion of the difference between dental visits.

@DAY

The @DAY function returns the day's portion of a date serial number. The formula of the function is @DAY(date_time_number). The *date_time_number* is a serial date number given by a number, formula, or cell reference.

The @DAY function can be used in the analysis of date entries. With dates representing machine breakdowns, employee absences, or delivery dates, you may be interested in the distribution of these dates by day of the month. Figure 6.30 provides a sample of entries representing machine breakdowns. The @DAY function is used to extract the day from the date of the problem occurrence. The records can be sorted by this field or these entries can be used with the /Tools Frequency command for a more rigorous analysis.

The @DAY function can also construct a set of dates for loan repayments that

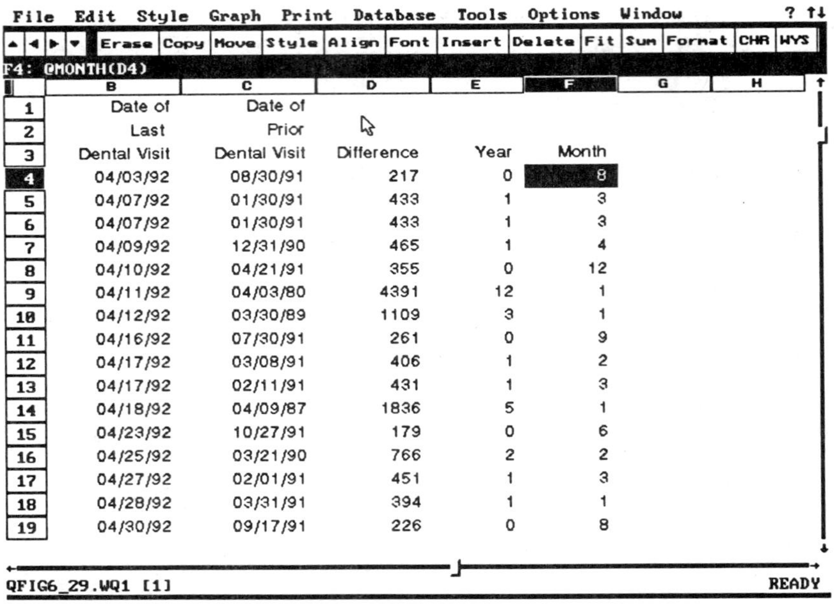

270 *Quattro Pro 4.0 Handbook*

	B	C	D	E	F
	Date of	Date of			
1	Last	Prior			
2	Dental Visit	Dental Visit	Difference	Year	Month
3	04/03/92	08/30/91	217	0	8
4	04/07/92	01/30/91	433	1	3
5	04/07/92	01/30/91	433	1	3
6	04/09/92	12/31/90	465	1	4
7	04/10/92	04/21/91	355	0	12
8	04/11/92	04/03/80	4391	12	1
9	04/12/92	03/30/89	1109	3	1
10	04/16/92	07/30/91	261	0	9
11	04/17/92	03/08/91	406	1	2
12	04/17/92	02/11/91	431	1	3
13	04/18/92	04/09/87	1836	5	1
14	04/23/92	10/27/91	179	0	6
15	04/25/92	03/21/90	766	2	2
16	04/27/92	02/01/91	451	1	3
17	04/28/92	03/31/91	394	1	1
18	04/30/92	09/17/91	226	0	8

Figure 6.29 @MONTH Used to Compute a Month's Portion of the Difference Between Two Dates

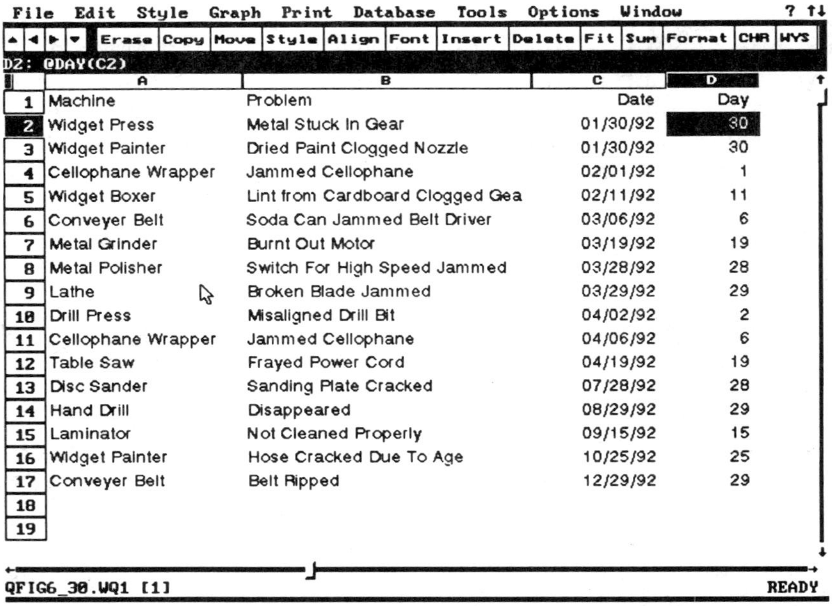

	A	B	C	D
1	Machine	Problem	Date	Day
2	Widget Press	Metal Stuck In Gear	01/30/92	30
3	Widget Painter	Dried Paint Clogged Nozzle	01/30/92	30
4	Cellophane Wrapper	Jammed Cellophane	02/01/92	1
5	Widget Boxer	Lint from Cardboard Clogged Gea	02/11/92	11
6	Conveyer Belt	Soda Can Jammed Belt Driver	03/06/92	6
7	Metal Grinder	Burnt Out Motor	03/19/92	19
8	Metal Polisher	Switch For High Speed Jammed	03/28/92	28
9	Lathe	Broken Blade Jammed	03/29/92	29
10	Drill Press	Misaligned Drill Bit	04/02/92	2
11	Cellophane Wrapper	Jammed Cellophane	04/06/92	6
12	Table Saw	Frayed Power Cord	04/19/92	19
13	Disc Sander	Sanding Plate Cracked	07/28/92	28
14	Hand Drill	Disappeared	08/29/92	29
15	Laminator	Not Cleaned Properly	09/15/92	15
16	Widget Painter	Hose Cracked Due To Age	10/25/92	25
17	Conveyer Belt	Belt Ripped	12/29/92	29

Figure 6.30 @DAY Used to Extract the Day Number from a Date

are exactly one month apart. If the original date is in A2, this formula calculates the date of the next payment:

@DATE(@IF(@MONTH(A2)=12,@YEAR(A2)+1,@YEAR(A2)), @IF(@MONTH(A2)=12,1,@MONTH(A2)+1),@DAY(A2))

By copying this formula farther down the column, you can list every loan repayment date. This formula changes the year every time the month equals 12.

@TIME

The @TIME function takes three values for the year, month, and date and converts them into a time serial number. The format of the @TIME function is @TIME(hr,min,sec). The *hr* represents the hour that ranges from 0 to 23 for the hours midnight to 11 P.M. (numbers greater than 12 represent the evening hours); *min* represents the number of minutes within the hour (this number ranges from 0 to 59); *sec* represents the number of the seconds within the minute (this number ranges from 0 to 59). Each of these arguments must be a number, a formula that returns a number, or a cell reference to either.

An example of @TIME function is in Figure 6.31, which uses the @TIME function in columns B and C. For each of these times, the @TIME function includes the hour, minute, and second. By using the time values, you can compute the time passed between when an employee clocks in and clocks out.

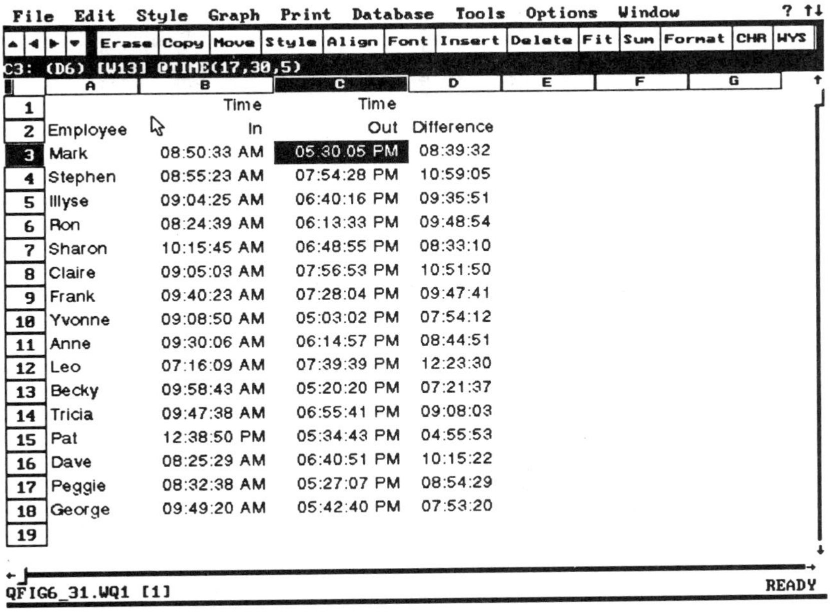

File Edit Style Graph Print Database Tools Options Window

Erase Copy Move Style Align Font Insert Delete Fit Sum Format CHR WYS

C3: (D6) [W13] @TIME(17,30,5)

	A	B	C	D
1		Time	Time	
2	Employee	In	Out	Difference
3	Mark	08:50:33 AM	05:30:05 PM	08:39:32
4	Stephen	08:55:23 AM	07:54:28 PM	10:59:05
5	Illyse	09:04:25 AM	06:40:16 PM	09:35:51
6	Ron	08:24:39 AM	06:13:33 PM	09:48:54
7	Sharon	10:15:45 AM	06:48:55 PM	08:33:10
8	Claire	09:05:03 AM	07:56:53 PM	10:51:50
9	Frank	09:40:23 AM	07:28:04 PM	09:47:41
10	Yvonne	09:08:50 AM	05:03:02 PM	07:54:12
11	Anne	09:30:06 AM	06:14:57 PM	08:44:51
12	Leo	07:16:09 AM	07:39:39 PM	12:23:30
13	Becky	09:58:43 AM	05:20:20 PM	07:21:37
14	Tricia	09:47:38 AM	06:55:41 PM	09:08:03
15	Pat	12:38:50 PM	05:34:43 PM	04:55:53
16	Dave	08:25:29 AM	06:40:51 PM	10:15:22
17	Peggie	08:32:38 AM	05:27:07 PM	08:54:29
18	George	09:49:20 AM	05:42:40 PM	07:53:20
19				

QFIG6_31.WQ1 [1] READY

Figure 6.31 @TIME Used to Enter Times

@HOUR

The @HOUR function returns the number of hours in the serial time number. The syntax of the function is @HOUR(date_time_number). The *date_time_number* is a serial time number provided as a number, a formula, or a numeric function, or as a cell reference.

One purpose of the @HOUR function is to determine the number of hours between two times. Figure 6.32 shows one way you can use the @HOUR function to compute the number of hours between two times. Column D subtracts column C from column B. The formula in column E determines the number of hours based on the total amount of time. From this information, an employer can determine the length of time an employee works.

@MINUTE

The @MINUTE function returns the minute's portion of a serial time number. It does not return the total number of minutes; rather it returns the number of minutes of a time serial number in the current hour. The syntax of the function is @MINUTE(date_time_number). The *date_time_number* is a serial time number given by a number, formula, function, or cell reference to any other.

One purpose of the @MINUTE function is to determine the number of minutes

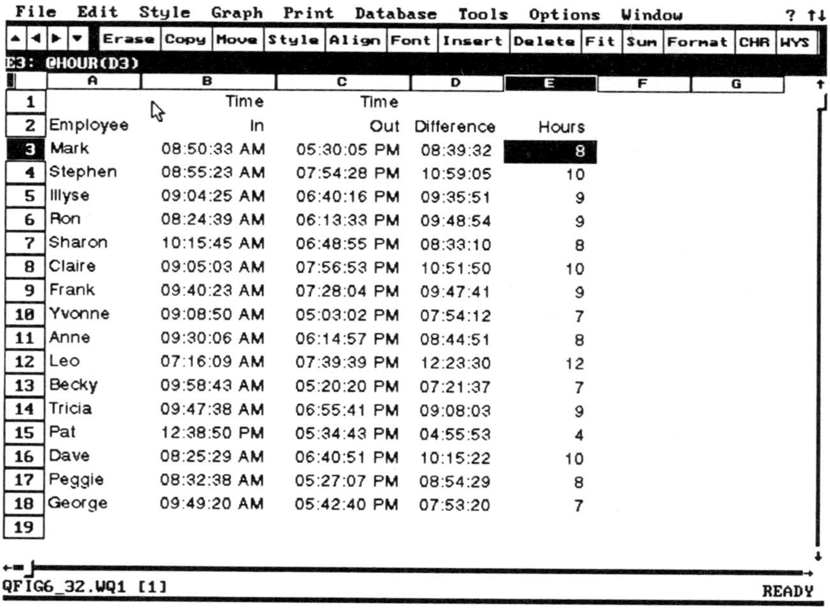

	A	B	C	D	E
1		Time	Time		
2	Employee	In	Out	Difference	Hours
3	Mark	08:50:33 AM	05:30:05 PM	08:39:32	8
4	Stephen	08:55:23 AM	07:54:28 PM	10:59:05	10
5	Illyse	09:04:25 AM	06:40:16 PM	09:35:51	9
6	Ron	08:24:39 AM	06:13:33 PM	09:48:54	9
7	Sharon	10:15:45 AM	06:48:55 PM	08:33:10	8
8	Claire	09:05:03 AM	07:56:53 PM	10:51:50	10
9	Frank	09:40:23 AM	07:28:04 PM	09:47:41	9
10	Yvonne	09:08:50 AM	05:03:02 PM	07:54:12	7
11	Anne	09:30:06 AM	06:14:57 PM	08:44:51	8
12	Leo	07:16:09 AM	07:39:39 PM	12:23:30	12
13	Becky	09:58:43 AM	05:20:20 PM	07:21:37	7
14	Tricia	09:47:38 AM	06:55:41 PM	09:08:03	9
15	Pat	12:38:50 PM	05:34:43 PM	04:55:53	4
16	Dave	08:25:29 AM	06:40:51 PM	10:15:22	10
17	Peggie	08:32:38 AM	05:27:07 PM	08:54:29	8
18	George	09:49:20 AM	05:42:40 PM	07:53:20	7

Figure 6.32 @HOUR Used to Compute Number of Hours Worked

between two times. While the example for @HOUR showed the number of hours in column E, an employer cannot ignore the minutes beyond the nearest whole hour that an employee works. In Figure 6.33, Column F computes these minutes to allow payroll calculations to include whole hours and fractional hours represented by the minutes. This shows one way you can use the @MINUTE function to compute the minutes portion of the difference between the two times. A more elaborate formula that included @IF would allow you to change the entry to zero if the employee works less than 5 minutes over the whole hour and to increase the hours worked by 1 if the minutes exceed 55.

@SECOND

The @SECOND function returns the second's portion of a time serial number. The formula of the function is @SECOND(date_time_number). The *date_time_number* is a serial time number given by a number, formula, or cell reference.

The @SECOND function is appropriately used where preciseness is important, as in monitoring the times for two production runs. For example, if you are deciding between several machines to perform a certain task, the time that each machine takes for each task is very important. You can use @SECOND to compute the amount of time for the different machines. In Figure 6.34, the start and stop times that each machine takes to produce 10 widgets is shown in columns B and

	A	B	C	D	E	F
1		Time	Time			
2	Employee	In	Out	Difference	Hours	Minutes
3	Mark	08:50:33 AM	05:30:05 PM	08:39:32	8	39
4	Stephen	08:55:23 AM	07:54:28 PM	10:59:05	10	59
5	Illyse	09:04:25 AM	06:40:16 PM	09:35:51	9	35
6	Ron	08:24:39 AM	06:13:33 PM	09:48:54	9	48
7	Sharon	10:15:45 AM	06:48:55 PM	08:33:10	8	33
8	Claire	09:05:03 AM	07:56:53 PM	10:51:50	10	51
9	Frank	09:40:23 AM	07:28:04 PM	09:47:41	9	47
10	Yvonne	09:08:50 AM	05:03:02 PM	07:54:12	7	54
11	Anne	09:30:06 AM	06:14:57 PM	08:44:51	8	44
12	Leo	07:16:09 AM	07:39:39 PM	12:23:30	12	23
13	Becky	09:58:43 AM	05:20:20 PM	07:21:37	7	21
14	Tricia	09:47:38 AM	06:55:41 PM	09:08:03	9	8
15	Pat	12:38:50 PM	05:34:43 PM	04:55:53	4	55
16	Dave	08:25:29 AM	06:40:51 PM	10:15:22	10	15
17	Peggie	08:32:38 AM	05:27:07 PM	08:54:29	8	54
18	George	09:49:20 AM	05:42:40 PM	07:53:20	7	53

Figure 6.33 @MINUTE Used to Compute Minute's Portion of the Difference Between Two Times

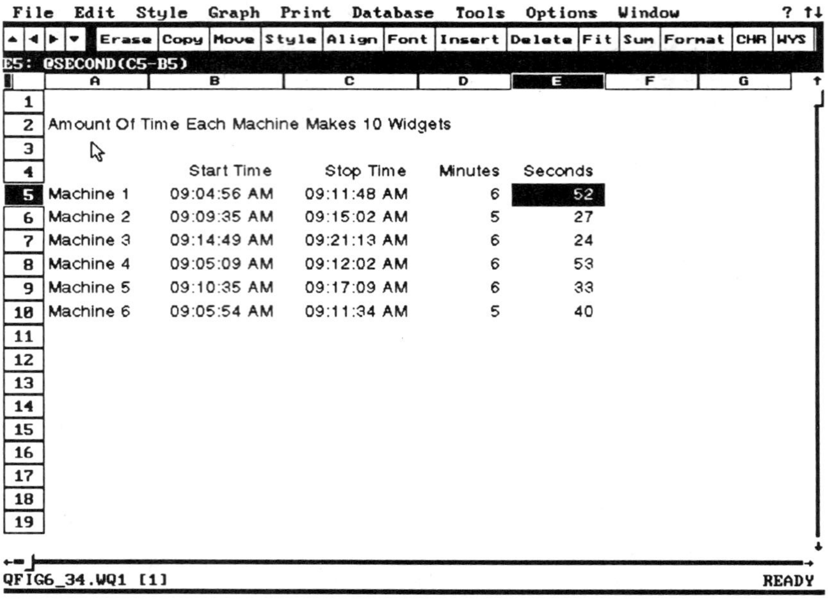

```
File   Edit   Style   Graph   Print   Database   Tools   Options   Window              ? ↑↓
▲ ◄ ► ▼  Erase  Copy  Move  Style  Align  Font  Insert  Delete  Fit  Sum  Format  CHR  WYS
E5: @SECOND(C5-B5)
         A              B            C          D         E          F         G
  1
  2  Amount Of Time Each Machine Makes 10 Widgets
  3        ▷
  4                  Start Time   Stop Time   Minutes   Seconds
  5  Machine 1     09:04:56 AM  09:11:48 AM      6        52
  6  Machine 2     09:09:35 AM  09:15:02 AM      5        27
  7  Machine 3     09:14:49 AM  09:21:13 AM      6        24
  8  Machine 4     09:05:09 AM  09:12:02 AM      6        53
  9  Machine 5     09:10:35 AM  09:17:09 AM      6        33
 10  Machine 6     09:05:54 AM  09:11:34 AM      5        40
 11
 12
 13
 14
 15
 16
 17
 18
 19
QFIG6_34.WQ1 [1]                                                              READY
```

Figure 6.34 @SECOND Used to Compute Second's Portion of the Difference Between Two Times

C. The @MINUTE function in column D computes the minute's portion of the difference between the two times. In column E, @SECOND computes the second's portion of the difference between the two times. This information can be used to determine which machines can produce the required production levels in minimal time.

@DATEVALUE

@DATEVALUE accepts a string that is in the form of a date and converts it into a date serial number. Since you can directly enter dates by pressing the accelerator sequence, CTRL-D, it is more efficient to use the accelerator key than to type date information in as labels. Still, you will want to be prepared to work with date labels entered by someone unaware of the importance of date serial numbers. The syntax of the function is @DATEVALUE(date_string). Here, *date_string* is a string, function or formula that produces a string, or a cell reference to either that is in the format of a date. This function permits transfer of date entries from another package that are stored as labels and conversion of them into date serial numbers.

An example of the @DATEVALUE function is shown in Figure 6.35. In this example, all dates are entered in as labels in the format 'MM/DD/YY. The @DATEVALUE function in columns D and E transform the two columns of strings into date serial numbers so they can be used in computations. Subtracting the two

Functions 275

```
File   Edit   Style   Graph   Print   Database   Tools   Options   Window           ?  ↑↓
▲ ◄ ► ▼  Erase Copy Move Style Align Font Insert Delete Fit Sum Format CHR WYS
D4: (D4) [W13] @DATEVALUE(B4)
```

	A	B	C	D	E	F
1		Date of	Date of	Date of	Date of	
2	Patient	Last	Prior	Last	Prior	
3	Number	Dental Visit	Dental Visit	Dental Visit	Dental Visit	
4	810963	4/3/92	8/30/91	04/03/92	08/30/91	
5	678162	4/7/92	1/30/91	04/07/92	01/30/91	
6	633689	4/7/92	1/30/91	04/07/92	01/30/91	
7	555259	4/9/92	12/31/90	04/09/92	12/31/90	
8	667628	4/10/92	4/21/91	04/10/92	04/21/91	
9	676589	4/11/92	4/3/80	04/11/92	04/03/80	
10	267367	4/12/92	3/30/89	04/12/92	03/30/89	
11	614856	4/16/92	7/30/91	04/16/92	07/30/91	
12	310203	4/17/92	3/8/91	04/17/92	03/08/91	
13	355445	4/17/92	2/11/91	04/17/92	02/11/91	
14	332825	4/18/92	4/9/87	04/18/92	04/09/87	
15	422526	4/23/92	10/27/91	04/23/92	10/27/91	
16	170636	4/25/92	3/21/90	04/25/92	03/21/90	
17	427823	4/27/92	2/1/91	04/27/92	02/01/91	
18	455346	4/28/92	3/31/91	04/28/92	03/31/91	
19	981489	4/30/92	9/17/91	04/30/92	09/17/91	

```
QFIG6_35.WQ1 [1]                                                        READY
```

Figure 6.35 @DATEVALUE Used to Convert Labels Containing Dates into Date Serial Numbers

date serial numbers determines the number of days between the two dental visits. Also, once you have the most recent dental appointment converted to a date serial number, you can easily compute when the next appointment should be by adding six months (180 days) to the number in column D. Even though columns D and E are serial numbers, they appear as dates because of the /Style Numeric Format Date command, which formats a date serial number to look like a date.

@TIMEVALUE

@TIMEVALUE accepts a string that is in the form of a time and converts it into a time serial number. This function converts times that were originally entered as labels when there was no plan to use mathematical capabilities on time values. The format of the function is @TIMEVALUE(time_string). Here, *time_string* is a string, function or formula that produces a string, or a cell reference to either which must be in the format of a time. This function is used frequently when you are updating a spreadsheet where the time entries are stored as labels.

An example of the @TIMEVALUE function is shown in Figure 6.36. In this example, all times are entered in as labels in the format 'HH:MM:SS with a PM following the times that are in the afternoon. The @TIMEVALUE function in columns D and E transform the two columns of strings into time serial numbers. The /Style Numeric Format Date Time command formatted columns D and E in

```
File   Edit   Style   Graph   Print   Database   Tools   Options   Window            ? ↑↓
Erase Copy Move Style Align Font Insert Delete Fit Sum Format CHR WYS
D3: (D7) [W12] @TIMEVALUE(B3)
```

	A	B	C	D	E	F
1		Time	Time	Time	Time	
2	Employee	In	Out	In	Out	
3	Mark	8:50:33 AM	5:30:05 PM	08:50 AM	05:30 PM	
4	Stephen	8:55:23 AM	7:54:28 PM	08:55 AM	07:54 PM	
5	Illyse	9:04:25 AM	6:40:16 PM	09:04 AM	06:40 PM	
6	Ron	8:24:39 AM	6:13:33 PM	08:24 AM	06:13 PM	
7	Sharon	10:15:45 AM	6:48:55 PM	10:15 AM	06:48 PM	
8	Claire	9:05:03 AM	7:56:53 PM	09:05 AM	07:56 PM	
9	Frank	9:40:23 AM	7:28:04 PM	09:40 AM	07:28 PM	
10	Yvonne	9:08:50 AM	5:03:02 PM	09:08 AM	05:03 PM	
11	Anne	9:30:06 AM	6:14:57 PM	09:30 AM	06:14 PM	
12	Leo	7:16:09 AM	7:39:39 PM	07:16 AM	07:39 PM	
13	Becky	9:58:43 AM	5:20:20 PM	09:58 AM	05:20 PM	
14	Tricia	9:47:38 AM	6:55:41 PM	09:47 AM	06:55 PM	
15	Pat	0:38:50 PM	5:34:43 PM	12:38 PM	05:34 PM	
16	Dave	8:25:29 AM	6:40:51 PM	08:25 AM	06:40 PM	
17	Peggie	8:32:38 AM	5:27:07 PM	08:32 AM	05:27 PM	
18	George	9:49:20 AM	5:42:40 PM	09:49 AM	05:42 PM	
19						

```
QFIG6_36.WQ1 [1]                                                                    READY
```

Figure 6.36 @TIMEVALUE Used to Convert Labels Containing Times into Time Serial Numbers

the HH:MM format. The time serial numbers can be subtracted to determine the amount of time each employee works.

LOGICAL FUNCTIONS

Quattro Pro's logical functions evaluate conditions to determine if the condition is true or false. Quattro Pro also provides several special logical functions that place special values in cells. Quattro Pro's logical functions that produce true and false values operate with Boolean logic. That is, the functions evaluate an expression and determine whether it is true or false. The logical functions that represent special values include the values Quattro Pro uses to store true and false and the values that Quattro Pro uses for data that is missing or contains an error.

@IF

The @IF function evaluates a condition as true or false and returns one value if the condition is true and another value if the condition is false. This function allows you to select an entry for a spreadsheet cell depending on other entries in the spreadsheet. The syntax of this function is @IF(cond,true_expr,false_expr). The term *cond* represents the condition that the function evaluates. The condition must be a logical condition that Quattro Pro can evaluate as true or false. Examples are B6>5 and @SUM(A1..A15)<100. The first formula is evaluated as true when B6 is greater than 5. The second one produces true as a result when the total of the values in the cells A1..A15 is less than 100. This function argument can contain strings, numbers, cell references, block references, and other formulas, as long as they are part of a logical formula.

@IF can have multiple conditions, since Quattro Pro allows the AND, OR, and NOT operators to be used within the condition expression. To use any of these conditions, you must precede and follow the operator with a number sign (#). For example, if you use **#AND#** in a condition, the condition to the left and to the right of the #AND# must be true for the @IF function to use the function argument for a true value. If either part of the condition is false, the @IF function uses the function argument for a false value. If a condition uses an **#OR#** connector, the condition to the left and/or the condition to the right of the #OR# connector must be true for the function to use the function argument for a true value. If a condition uses the **#NOT#** operator, the condition to the right of the #NOT# operator must be false to yield a true value or must be true to yield a false value. None of these operators can override parentheses.

The term *true_expr* represents the value that the function returns when the condition is true (this can be a formula, a value, or a string enclosed in quotes); *false_expr* represents the value the function returns when the condition is false (this can be a formula, a value, or a string enclosed in quotes).

The @IF function often is used to check for errors. For example, in Figure 6.37, the Zone column may contain numbers that are too large. For each row, the @IF

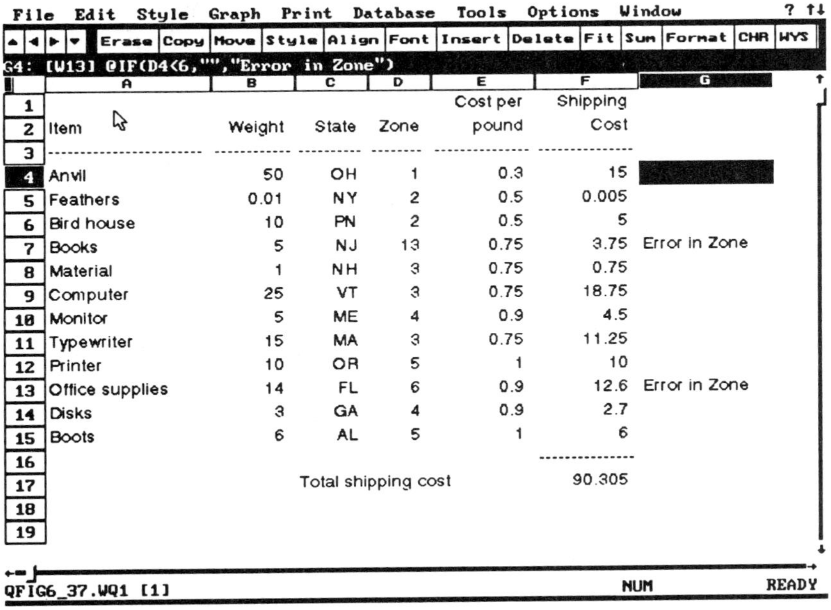

	A	B	C	D	E	F	G
1					Cost per	Shipping	
2	Item	Weight	State	Zone	pound	Cost	
3	----------------------	----------	--------	-------	-------------	-------------	
4	Anvil	50	OH	1	0.3	15	
5	Feathers	0.01	NY	2	0.5	0.005	
6	Bird house	10	PN	2	0.5	5	
7	Books	5	NJ	13	0.75	3.75	Error in Zone
8	Material	1	NH	3	0.75	0.75	
9	Computer	25	VT	3	0.75	18.75	
10	Monitor	5	ME	4	0.9	4.5	
11	Typewriter	15	MA	3	0.75	11.25	
12	Printer	10	OR	5	1	10	
13	Office supplies	14	FL	6	0.9	12.6	Error in Zone
14	Disks	3	GA	4	0.9	2.7	
15	Boots	6	AL	5	1	6	
16						-------------	
17			Total shipping cost			90.305	
18							
19							

Figure 6.37 @IF Used to Check the Validity of Zone Number

function in Column G takes the value in column D and compares it to six. If it is less than six, meaning that the zone number is within the acceptable range, it displays a blank label generated by the two double quotes after the first comma. If the value in column D is not less than six (any number that is six or higher), the function displays Error in Zone in column G. This technique provides a quick check for errors in zone entries since you only need to scan the column quickly for an error message display.

The @IF function can contain other @IF functions. This creates nested @IF functions that expand your choices from the two options provided in a single @IF function. When the true or false argument is expressed as another @IF function, the process proceeds normally with the first condition being evaluated and a true or false value selected for evaluation based on the outcome of the condition test. If the argument selected contains another @IF, Quattro Pro evaluates the second condition and determines whether to use the true or false argument of the second @IF function. An example of a nested @IF function is @IF(A1<100,@IF(B1>50,"A","B"), @IF(C1<=1,"C","D")). In this function, Quattro Pro first checks if A1 is less than 100. If A1 is less than 100, it then tests to see if the value in B1 is greater than 50. If B1 is greater than 50, the function returns A. If A1 is less than 100 but B1 is less than or equal to 50, this function returns B. If A1 is greater than or equal to 100, Quattro Pro checks if C1 is less than or equal to one. If C1 is less than or equal to one, this function returns C. If A1 is greater than or equal to 100 and C1 is greater than one, the function returns D.

A more complicated example using several levels of nested @IF functions can determine the proper cost per pound for shipping based upon the zone. In Figure 6.38, a series of nested @IF functions checks the zone and determines the correct cost per pound. The function first determines if the zone is equal to 1. If the zone is equal to 1, the function returns 0.3. If the zone is not equal to 1, the second @IF function checks if the zone is 2 and returns 0.5 if a true condition test results. If the function does not equal 1 or 2, and third @IF function determines if the zone equals 3 and returns 0.75 if the condition test is true. If the function does not equal 1, 2, or 3, the fourth function checks if the zone equals 4 and returns 0.9 for a true condition test. If the function does not equal 1, 2, 3, or 4, the fifth and final @IF function determines if the zone equals 5 and returns 1 if the test is true. If the zone does not equal 1, 2, 3, 4, or 5, the function returns the label Error. Since labels have a value of zero, this label causes an item with an incorrect zone to have a shipping cost per pound of zero. To avoid this problem, you can either add an @IF to the shipping cost calculation or use @ERR for the false value in the fifth @IF statement.

You need to be careful with the number of levels of nesting you use. A good rule of thumb for most users is not to exceed three levels. Other functions like @VLOOKUP and @INDEX offer alternatives for multiple levels of @IF statements.

@ISNUMBER

The @ISNUMBER checks the function's argument to determine if it is a number. This function returns a 1 if the argument is a number and a 0 if it is not. Quattro

```
File  Edit  Style  Graph  Print  Database  Tools  Options  Window        ? ↑↓
```
```
[Enter] [Esc] @IF(D4=1,0.3,@IF(D4=2,0.5,@IF(D4=3,0.75,@IF(D4=4,0.9,@IF(D4=5,1,"E
rror"))))))
```

	Item	Weight	State	Zone	Cost per pound	Shipping Cost
1						
2	Item	Weight	State	Zone	Cost per pound	Shipping Cost
3	--------	--------	--------	--------	--------	--------
4	Anvil	50	OH	1	0.3	15
5	Feathers	0.01	NY	2	0.5	0.005
6	Bird house	10	PN	2	0.5	5
7	Books	5	NJ	13	Error	0
8	Material	1	NH	3	0.75	0.75
9	Computer	25	VT	3	0.75	18.75
10	Monitor	5	ME	4	0.9	4.5
11	Typewriter	15	MA	3	0.75	11.25
12	Printer	10	OR	5	1	10
13	Office supplies	14	FL	6	Error	0
14	Disks	3	GA	4	0.9	2.7
15	Boots	6	AL	5	1	6
16					--------	
17			Total shipping cost			73.955

```
E4:  @IF(D4=1,0.3,@IF(D4=2,0.5,@IF(D4=3,0.75,@IF(D4=4,0.9,@IF(D4                EDIT
```

Figure 6.38 Nested @IF to Determine Cost per Pound

evaluates numbers and numeric functions as numbers. The format of this function is @ISNUMBER(x). Here, x is a number, formula, or cell reference.

The @ISNUMBER function is often used in combination with other functions to verify that an entry made in a spreadsheet cell is a number. For example, one type of data error that may occur in the calculations to determine the total shipping cost is that label entries are placed in the Zone column. Figure 6.39 shows the spreadsheet in which the state abbreviation was mistakenly entered in two rows instead of a numeric zone. In column G, the @ISNUMBER determines whether the value in column D is a number. This function returns the true or false value that the @IF function uses to determine which argument to place in column G. For those rows that have a numeric value in column D, the function returns a blank string. For those rows that have a label in column D, the @ISNUMBER and @IF functions return the error message displayed in rows 5 and 9.

@ISSTRING

The @ISSTRING checks the function's argument to determine if it is a string or label. This function returns a 1 if the argument is a string and a 0 if it is not. A string includes labels and strings in quotes. The format of this function is @ISSTRING(x). Here, x is a string, formula or function, or cell reference.

The @ISSTRING function is often used in combination with other functions to verify that entries made in a portion of the spreadsheet are labels. For example, one

```
File  Edit  Style  Graph  Print  Database  Tools  Options  Window        ? ↑↓
▲ ◄ ► ▼  Erase Copy Move Style Align Font Insert Delete Fit Sum Format CHR WYS
G4: [W14] @IF(@ISNUMBER(D4),"","Error in Zone")
```

	A	B	C	D	E	F	G
1					Cost per	Shipping	
2	Item		Weight	State	Zone	pound	Cost
3	-----	-----	-----	-----	-----	-----	-----
4	Anvil		50	OH	1	0.3	15
5	Feathers		0.01	2	NY	0	0	Error in Zone
6	Bird house		10	PN	2	0.5	5
7	Books		5	NJ	3	0.75	3.75
8	Material		1	NH	3	0.75	0.75
9	Computer		25	VT	VT	0	0	Error in Zone
10	Monitor		5	ME	4	0.9	4.5
11	Typewriter		15	MA	3	0.75	11.25
12	Printer		10	OR	5	1	10
13	Office supplies		14	FL	4	0.9	12.6
14	Disks		3		4	0.9	2.7
15	Boots		6	AL	5	1	6
16						-----	
17				Total shipping cost		71.55	

```
QFIG6_39.WQ1 [1]                                                          READY
```

Figure 6.39 @IF and @ISNUMBER Used to Check the Validity of Zone Entries

type of data error that may occur in the shipping cost spreadsheet is that the state is entered improperly. Figure 6.40 shows the spreadsheet in which a few of the states and zones have incorrect information. In column G, the @ISSTRING determines whether the value in column C is a string. This function returns the true or false value that the @IF function uses to determine which of its next two arguments it places in column G. For those rows that have a string value in column C, the function returns a blank string. For those rows that have a number in column C, the @ISSTRING and @IF combination returns the error message displayed in rows 5 and 14. This function cannot detect, however, the state entered as the zone in row 9.

@ISERR

The @ISERR checks the function's argument for @ERR. This function returns a 1 if the argument equals @ERR and a 0 if it does not. The format of this function is @ISERR(x). Here, x is a formula or cell reference.

The @ISERR function can be combined with @IF to remove @ERR from computations. Figure 6.41 shows an example of the @ERR value in B5, has preventing a computation for the cumulative shipping cost. While one method of computing the total cost is to substitute a 0 for the @ERR in B5, it is not the correct approach since the correct value may not be substituted at a later time. Another possibility

Functions 281

```
File   Edit  Style  Graph  Print  Database  Tools  Options  Window         ? ↑↓
 ▲ ◀ ▶ ▼  Erase Copy Move Style Align Font Insert Delete Fit Sum Format CHR WYS
G4:   [W14] @IF(@ISSTRING(C4),"","Error in State")
```

	A	B	C	D	E	F	G
1					Cost per	Shipping	
2	Item	Weight	State	Zone	pound	Cost	
3	---	---	---	---	---	---	
4	Anvil	50	OH	1	0.3	15	
5	Feathers	0.01	2	NY	0	0	Error in State
6	Bird house	10	PN	2	0.5	5	
7	Books	5	NJ	3	0.75	3.75	
8	Material	1	NH	3	0.75	0.75	
9	Computer	25	VT	VT	0	0	
10	Monitor	5	ME	4	0.9	4.5	
11	Typewriter	15	MA	3	0.75	11.25	
12	Printer	10	OR	5	1	10	
13	Office supplies	14	FL	4	0.9	12.6	
14	Disks	3		4	0.9	2.7	Error in State
15	Boots	6	AL	5	1	6	
16						---	
17				Total shipping cost		71.55	
18							
19							

```
QFIG6_40.WQ1 [1]                                                      READY
```

Figure 6.40 @IF and @ISSTRING Used to Check the Validity of State Entries

```
File   Edit  Style  Graph  Print  Database  Tools  Options  Window         ? ↑↓
 ▲ ◀ ▶ ▼  Erase Copy Move Style Align Font Insert Delete Fit Sum Format CHR WYS
G4:   [W13] @IF(@ISERR(B4),0,F4)
```

	A	B	C	D	E	F	G
1					Cost per	Shipping	
2	Item	Weight	State	Zone	pound	Cost	
3	---	---	---	---	---	---	
4	Anvil	50	OH	1	0.3	15	15
5	Feathers	ERR	NY	2	0.5	ERR	0
6	Bird house	10	PN	2	0.5	5	5
7	Books	5	NJ	3	0.75	3.75	3.75
8	Material	1	NH	3	0.75	0.75	0.75
9	Computer	25	VT	3	0.75	18.75	18.75
10	Monitor	5	ME	4	0.9	4.5	4.5
11	Typewriter	15	MA	3	0.75	11.25	11.25
12	Printer	10	OR	5	1	10	10
13	Office supplies	14	FL	4	0.9	12.6	12.6
14	Disks	3	GA	4	0.9	2.7	2.7
15	Boots	6	AL	5	1	6	6
16						---	---
17				Total shipping cost		ERR	90.3
18							
19							

```
QFIG6_41.WQ1 [1]                                                      READY
```

Figure 6.41 @IF and @ISERR Used to Substitute 0 for @ERR in Formula

is to use column G to add the shipping costs that do not have a value of @ERR. In column G, @ISERR is the condition for the @IF function. The @ISERR checks the value in column B to determine if it is @ERR. If the value in column B is zero, the @IF function returns zero. If the value in column B does not equal @ERR, the @IF function returns the shipping cost for that item. Therefore, you have the cumulative total shipping cost in column G, and a reminder in column F that information must be entered to make the spreadsheet complete.

@ISNA

The @ISNA checks to determine if its argument contains @NA. This function returns a 1 if the argument equals @NA and a 0 if it does not. The format of this function is @ISNA(x), and *x* is either a formula or a cell reference.

The @ISNA function is often used in spreadsheets in which you expect data to be missing for some time. The @ISNA function can help make preliminary computations before all the data is in, without forcing some @NA values to be removed. Figure 6.42 shows an example where the @NA value in E4 has prevented the computation of the cumulative shipping cost. While replacing all @NA entries with 0 produces these computations, it eliminates the reminder to complete the spreadsheet entries. In Figure 6.42, column G uses the @ISNA function and @IF function to create a temporary column that accepts the shipping cost if it does not equal @NA and returns 0 if the shipping cost per pound is @NA. The @ISNA

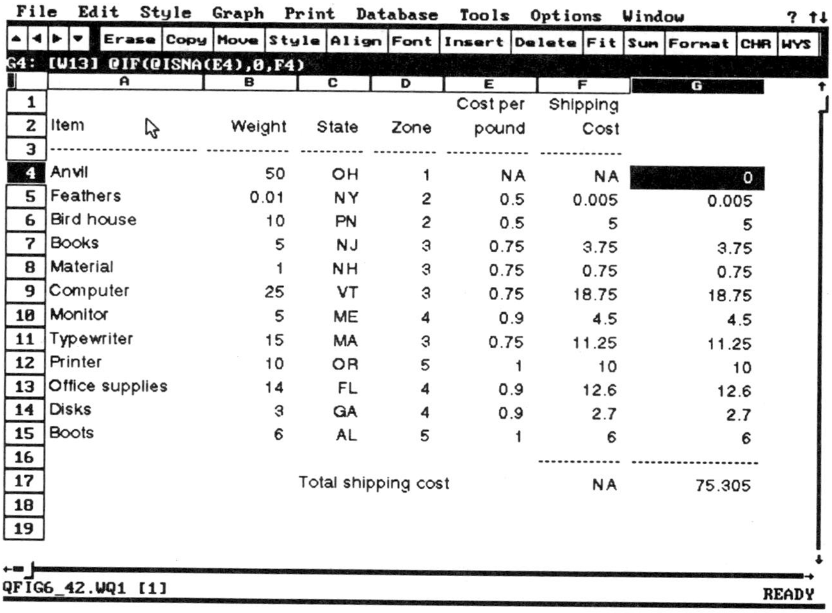

	A	B	C	D	E	F	G
1					Cost per	Shipping	
2	Item	Weight	State	Zone	pound	Cost	
3	---	---	---	---	---	---	---
4	Anvil	50	OH	1	NA	NA	0
5	Feathers	0.01	NY	2	0.5	0.005	0.005
6	Bird house	10	PN	2	0.5	5	5
7	Books	5	NJ	3	0.75	3.75	3.75
8	Material	1	NH	3	0.75	0.75	0.75
9	Computer	25	VT	3	0.75	18.75	18.75
10	Monitor	5	ME	4	0.9	4.5	4.5
11	Typewriter	15	MA	3	0.75	11.25	11.25
12	Printer	10	OR	5	1	10	10
13	Office supplies	14	FL	4	0.9	12.6	12.6
14	Disks	3	GA	4	0.9	2.7	2.7
15	Boots	6	AL	5	1	6	6
16						---	---
17			Total shipping cost			NA	75.305
18							
19							

G4: [W13] @IF(@ISNA(E4),0,F4)

Figure 6.42 @IF and @ISNA Used to Substitute 0 for @NA in Formula

compares the value in column E to @NA, the @IF function returns zero if the entry matches NA. If the value in column E does not equal @NA, the @IF function returns the shipping cost from column F for that item in column G. Therefore, you have the cumulative total shipping cost in column G and a reminder in column F that more entries must be made to complete the spreadsheet.

@ISAAF

@ISAAF checks whether an add-in function is loaded and available for use. This function returns a 1 if the add-in function is available and a 0 otherwise. The format of this function is @ISAAF(addin.function). *Addin* is the name of the add-in file containing the function you are testing. *Function* is the name of the function you want to test. An example of this is @ISAAF("TIME.TIMETOSTRING") to test whether the add-in function called TIMETOSTRING in the TIME add-in file is loaded and available for use. This function lets you know that cells that contain this add-in function will return the results of the function rather than @ERR.

@ISAPP

@ISAPP checks whether an add-in library file is loaded and available for use. This function returns a 1 if the add-in library file is loaded and a 0 otherwise. The format of this function is @ISAPP(addin). *Addin* is the name of the add-in file you want to test. An example of this is @ISAPP("TIME") to determine whether the TIME add-in file is loaded and available for use. This function is different from @ISAAF, since it does not check if a specific function in an add-in library file is loaded but only checks if the add-in file itself is loaded.

@FILEEXISTS

@FILEEXISTS returns a 1 for a true value if the specified file exists and a 0 for a false value if the specified file does not exist. The format of the function is @FILEEXISTS(filename). The *file name* is the name of the file that you want to check and is surrounded by quotes. The file name must include the file name extension and the path if the file is not in the default data directory.

The following are some examples of the @FILEEXISTS function used to check if the file MODEL.WKQ in Quattro Pro's PICTURE subdirectory exists.

@FILEEXISTS("MODEL") = 0 No file extension specified
@FILEEXISTS("MODEL.WQ1") = 0 Path not specified
@FILEEXISTS("C:\QPRO\PICTURE\MODEL.WQ1") = 1 Quattro Pro found the file

This function is used primarily with the {IF} macro command in macros to check that a file exists before performing other macro commands.

@TRUE

One of Quattro Pro's special logical functions is @TRUE. The @TRUE function has the same value that Quattro Pro uses when it evaluates a statement as true. Quattro Pro stores true and false values as 1 and 0, respectively. The @TRUE function is often used in place of a 1 since the @TRUE function provides documentation by its presence. The @TRUE function does not have parentheses or a function argument and is normally used with other functions. Often the @TRUE function is an argument in an @IF function. For example, you can use the @IF function to check if the weight is valid. If it is valid (that is, if it is a weight other than @ERR), the @IF function can return the value @TRUE. If the cost per pound is less than 0 or greater than 1, the @IF function can return the value @FALSE. Figure 6.43 shows the @TRUE and @FALSE functions used with an @IF function to determine which weight entries are valid and which are not. For each item, if the cost per pound for shipping is valid, the @IF function returns the @TRUE function. This function is displayed as a 1. If the cost per pound is not valid, the @IF function returns the @FALSE function, which is displayed as a 0. By sorting the rows according to this column, you can group the ones that do not have a valid cost per pound.

@FALSE

Another Quattro Pro special logical function is @FALSE. The @FALSE has the same value that Quattro Pro stores when it evaluates a true or false statement.

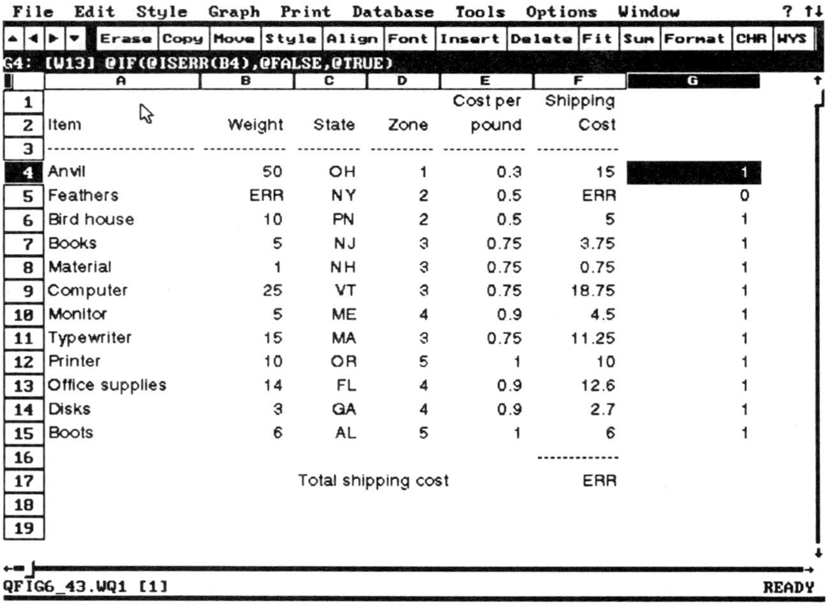

	A	B	C	D	E	F	G
1					Cost per	Shipping	
2	Item	Weight	State	Zone	pound	Cost	
3	---	---	---	---	---	---	
4	Anvil	50	OH	1	0.3	15	1
5	Feathers	ERR	NY	2	0.5	ERR	0
6	Bird house	10	PN	2	0.5	5	1
7	Books	5	NJ	3	0.75	3.75	1
8	Material	1	NH	3	0.75	0.75	1
9	Computer	25	VT	3	0.75	18.75	1
10	Monitor	5	ME	4	0.9	4.5	1
11	Typewriter	15	MA	3	0.75	11.25	1
12	Printer	10	OR	5	1	10	1
13	Office supplies	14	FL	4	0.9	12.6	1
14	Disks	3	GA	4	0.9	2.7	1
15	Boots	6	AL	5	1	6	1
16						---	
17			Total shipping cost			ERR	

Figure 6.43 @TRUE and @FALSE Used to Indicate the Results of Checking for @ERR

Quattro Pro stores true and false values as 1 and 0, respectively. The @FALSE function is often used in place of a 0 since the @FALSE function provides more information by virtue of its presence than the 0 does. The @FALSE function does not have parentheses or a function argument. These true and false values are usually used with other functions. An example of this special function is shown with the @TRUE example (in Figure 6.43).

@ERR

Quattro Pro provides two special logical functions for data that contain an error or are unavailable. The @ERR function is used when the data contain an error. The @ERR has the same value produced by the formulas or functions that contain an error. The @ERR function has a ripple effect. That is, every function that references a cell containing the @ERR value returns the @ERR value. This prevents you from using the information from your spreadsheet without being aware that some cells contain @ERR. The format of this function is @ERR. This function does not require parentheses or an argument. Often this function represents a piece of data that is incorrect.

An example of the @ERR function is in Figure 6.44. In this example, the weight for the feathers to be mailed was incorrect and @ERR was entered in the item's weight column instead of a weight. Since the @ERR value is part of the formula that determines the shipping cost, the @ERR value ripples through that computation and is displayed as the item's shipping cost. Likewise, the ripple effect also

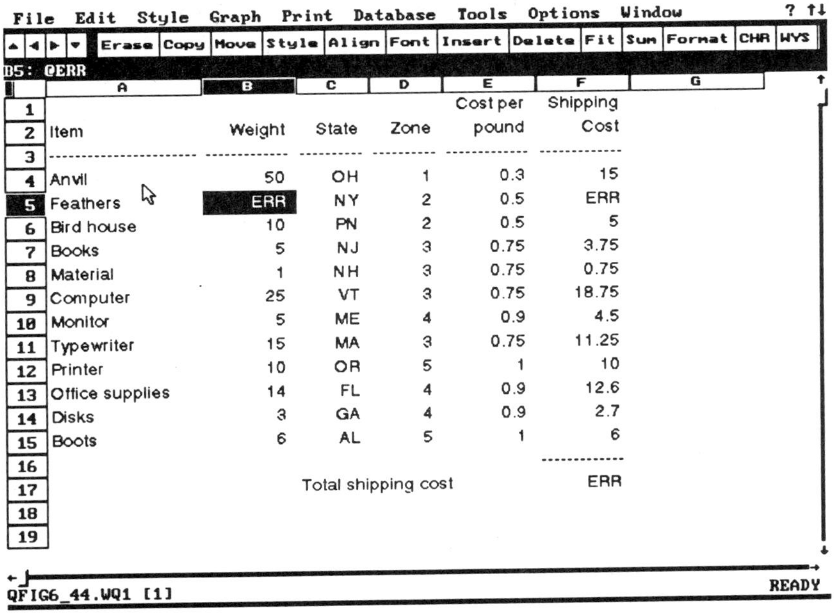

Figure 6.44 The Ripple Effect of @ERR

makes the total shipping cost in F17 equal @ERR. Therefore, you know that the error in the weight of the feathers must be corrected before you can know the correct total shipping cost.

@NA

The other special logical function for a data value is @NA. This function usually represents missing data or entries that are not applicable. Like the @ERR function, @NA has a ripple effect. That is, every function that references a cell containing the @NA value returns either @NA or @ERR. This prevents you from using the information from your spreadsheet without being aware that some cells contain @NA. The @NA function does not require parentheses or a function argument.

An example of the @NA function is in Figure 6.45. In this example, the cost per pound for shipping to Ohio is unknown, so @NA has been entered in cell E4. Since the @NA value is part of the formula that determines the shipping cost, the @NA value ripples through that computation and causes the item's shipping cost to equal @NA. Likewise, the ripple effect also makes the total shipping cost in F17 equal @NA. You must enter the cost per pound for the item before you know the total shipping cost.

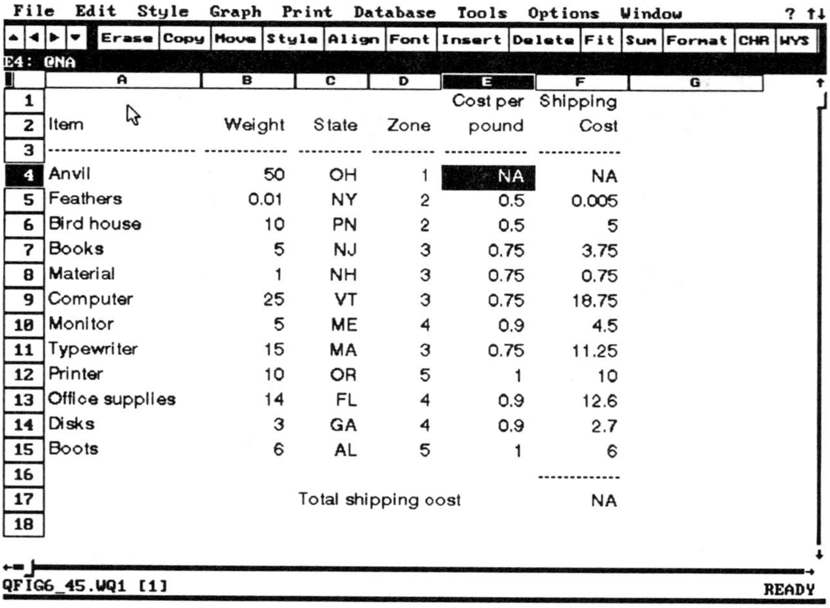

	A	B	C	D	E	F
1					Cost per	Shipping
2	Item	Weight	State	Zone	pound	Cost
3						
4	Anvil	50	OH	1	NA	NA
5	Feathers	0.01	NY	2	0.5	0.005
6	Bird house	10	PN	2	0.5	5
7	Books	5	NJ	3	0.75	3.75
8	Material	1	NH	3	0.75	0.75
9	Computer	25	VT	3	0.75	18.75
10	Monitor	5	ME	4	0.9	4.5
11	Typewriter	15	MA	3	0.75	11.25
12	Printer	10	OR	5	1	10
13	Office supplies	14	FL	4	0.9	12.6
14	Disks	3	GA	4	0.9	2.7
15	Boots	6	AL	5	1	6
16						
17			Total shipping cost			NA
18						

Figure 6.45 The Ripple Effect of @NA

Financial Functions

Quattro Pro provides several built-in functions for financial calculations. Several financial functions compute depreciation, a dollar value for how much of an asset's capacity you are using. Other financial functions focus on the time value of money, the concept that a dollar today is worth more than a dollar tomorrow. Several financial functions that are new to Quattro Pro are enhancements of earlier financial functions that expand the applications for which you will use the functions.

The financial functions that use the time value of money concept use time periods and interest rates in the calculations. The interest rate must match the time period. If the time period is a year, you use an annual interest rate. When you use a different time period, you must use the applicable rate of interest. For example, if you are computing an annuity that is paid monthly, you must use the monthly interest rate. Converting from a year to months for an interest rate or time period is easy: You divide an annual interest rate by 12 to get the monthly interest rate, and multiply the number of years by 12 to get the total number of months in the time period. You can express interest rates in percentage terms, such as 10% or 15.5% or in decimal notation such as .1 or .155.

@SLN

@SLN computes the straight-line depreciation for an asset. Straight-line depreciation depreciates the same amount each year for the life of the asset. The formula for straight-line depreciation is:

$$\frac{Cost - salvage\ value}{life\ of\ asset}$$

The format of the @SLN function is @SLN(cost,salvage,life). Here, *cost* is the amount paid for the asset; *salvage* is the amount that you expect to receive when you dispose of the asset at the end of the asset's useful life; and *life* is the length of time that the asset is useful to you. Since you do not know the exact period for which the asset will continue to be useful, you must make an intelligent approximation. Each of these arguments can be a number, formula, or cell reference to either.

Figure 6.46 shows the depreciation calculations for different assets. In this example, the function uses the information in the Cost, Salvage Value, and Life columns to determine the depreciation and ignores the period computation. For example, the metal grinder, the last item on the list, originally cost $70,000; the company expects to recover $5,000 when they dispose of it; and it is expected to last 7 years. Therefore, straight-line depreciation is one-seventh of the difference between the cost and the salvage value ($65,000/7 = 9,286).

288 *Quattro Pro 4.0 Handbook*

```
File  Edit  Style  Graph  Print  Database  Tools  Options  Window        ? ↑↓
▲ ◄ ► ▼  Erase Copy Move Style Align Font Insert Delete Fit Sum Format CHR WYS
G6:  (C0) [W12] @SLN(C6,D6,E6)
          A              B         C         D       E      F        G
 1  Widget Corporation                             Today's Date   01/20/92
 2  Depreciation Schedule
 3
 4                       Date               Salvage
 5  Asset                Acquired  Cost     Value   Life  Period  Depreciation
 6  Factory Building     09/29/73  $400,000 $40,000  35    18      $10,286
 7  Widget Press         03/06/84  $400,000 $40,000  35     7      $10,286
 8  Widget Painter       08/29/87  $45,000  $3,500   10     4       $4,150
 9  Cellophane Wrapper   05/31/86  $90,000  $200      8     5      $11,225
10  Widget Boxer         11/04/89  $150,000 $6,000   13     2      $11,077
11  Tools for Assembly   12/31/88  $200,000 $6,000    5     3      $38,800
12  Metal Polisher       04/09/79  $67,000  $3,000   15    12       $4,267
13  Metal Grinder        09/02/86  $70,000  $5,000    7     5       $9,286
14
15
16
17
18

QFIG6_46.WQ1 [1]                                      NUM            READY
```

Figure 6.46 Computing Straight-Line Depreciation

@SYD

@SYD returns the depreciation computed by the sum-of-the-years' digits method. Sum-of-the-years' digits method depreciates a greater portion of the asset's value at the beginning of the asset's life. This depreciates the asset more quickly than the straight-line method, although not as quickly as the double-declining balance method (discussed in a later section). The formula for sum-of-the-years' depreciation is:

$$\frac{(Cost - salvage\ value\ ) \times (life - period + 1\ )}{(asset\ life \times (asset\ life + 1))/2}$$

The format of this function is @SYD(cost,salvage,life,period). Here, *cost* is the initial price of the asset; *salvage* is the expected value when you sell the asset at the end of its useful life; *life* is the length of time that asset is expected to be used; and *period* is the year of the asset's life for which you are calculating the depreciation. The period must be supplied for the accelerated methods of depreciation, since more is depreciated at the beginning of the asset's life. Each of these arguments is a number, formula, or cell reference to either.

Figure 6.47 shows the sum-of-the-years' digits depreciation calculations for the same assets used in straight-line depreciation. This example uses the information in the Cost, Salvage Value, Life, and Period columns to determine the depreciation.

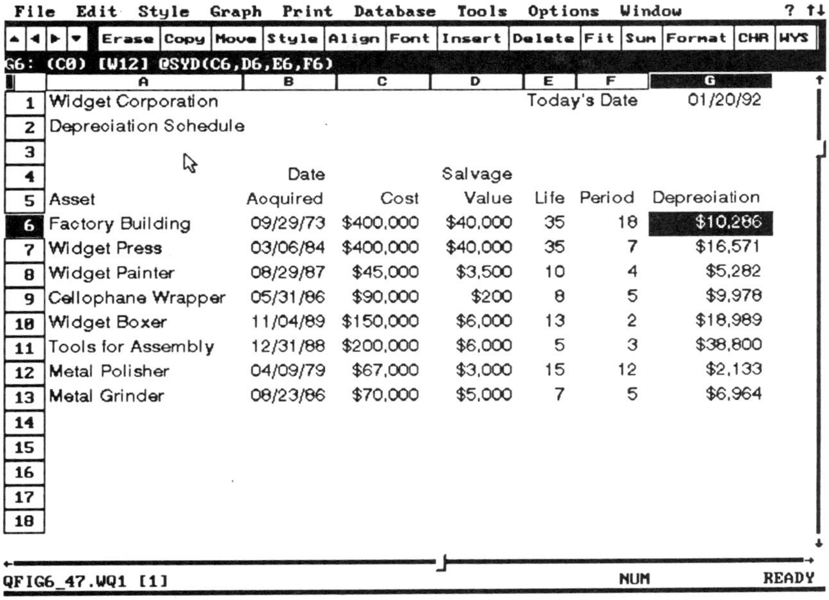

```
       File  Edit  Style  Graph  Print  Database  Tools  Options  Window        ? ↑↓
       ▲ ◄ ▼  Erase|Copy|Move|Style|Align|Font|Insert|Delete|Fit|Sum|Format|CHR|WYS
      G6:   (C0)  [W12]  @SYD(C6,D6,E6,F6)
              A           B         C          D       E     F         G
        1  Widget Corporation                       Today's Date    01/20/92
        2  Depreciation Schedule
        3
        4                         Date              Salvage
        5  Asset                Acquired    Cost    Value   Life  Period  Depreciation
        6  Factory Building     09/29/73  $400,000 $40,000   35    18      $10,286
        7  Widget Press         03/06/84  $400,000 $40,000   35     7      $16,571
        8  Widget Painter       08/29/87   $45,000  $3,500   10     4       $5,282
        9  Cellophane Wrapper   05/31/86   $90,000    $200    8     5       $9,978
       10  Widget Boxer         11/04/89  $150,000  $6,000   13     2      $18,989
       11  Tools for Assembly   12/31/88  $200,000  $6,000    5     3      $38,800
       12  Metal Polisher       04/09/79   $67,000  $3,000   15    12       $2,133
       13  Metal Grinder        08/23/86   $70,000  $5,000    7     5       $6,964
       14
       15
       16
       17
       18

      QFIG6_47.WQ1 [1]                                    NUM          READY
```

Figure 6.47 Computing Sum-of-the Years' Digits Depreciation

The period is computed as the difference between the current date and the date the asset was acquired. The first and second assets illustrate accelerated depreciation. Both assets have the same cost, salvage value, and life. Since the factory building is 10 years older than the widget press, the factory building has a lower depreciation. A larger percentage of the cost of the widget press is depreciated, since the period considered is closer to the beginning of the useful life of the widget press.

@DDB

@DDB computes an asset's double declining balance depreciation. The double declining balance method depreciates the asset most quickly by depreciating more in the beginning years of an asset's life than do the other two depreciation methods that Quattro supports. The double declining balance formula is

$$\frac{book\ value \times 2}{life\ of\ asset}$$

The book value of an asset is the cost of the asset less all depreciation taken.

The format is @DDB(cost,salvage,life,period). In this format, *cost* is the initial cost of the asset; *salvage* is the amount that you expect to receive when you dispose of the asset at the end of its life; *life* is the length of time that the asset is expected to be used; and *period* is the year of the asset's life that you are calculating the depreciation for. Each of these arguments is a number, formula, or cell reference to either.

Figure 6.48 shows the same assets used for the other depreciation functions using the double declining balance method depreciation. In this example, the function uses the information in the Cost, Salvage Value, Life, and Period columns to determine the depreciation. The first and second assets illustrate the effect of accelerated depreciation, since they have identical cost, salvage value, and life but were purchased almost 10 years apart. The widget press has a higher depreciation than the factory building, since it is newer. Of the three depreciation methods described, double declining balance produces the highest depreciation at the beginning of an asset's life and the lowest at the end of an asset's life.

@PMT

The @PMT function computes a payment based on the principal, an interest rate, and a number of periods. This function can compute loan and annuity payments. The format is @PMT(pv,rate,nper), where *pv* is the present value of the annuity or the loan principal; *rate* is the interest rate of the annuity or the loan per term; and *nper* is the number of periods that you are paying of the annuity or loan. Each of these arguments is a number, formula, or cell reference to either.

One application for the @PMT function is to determine the monthly payment

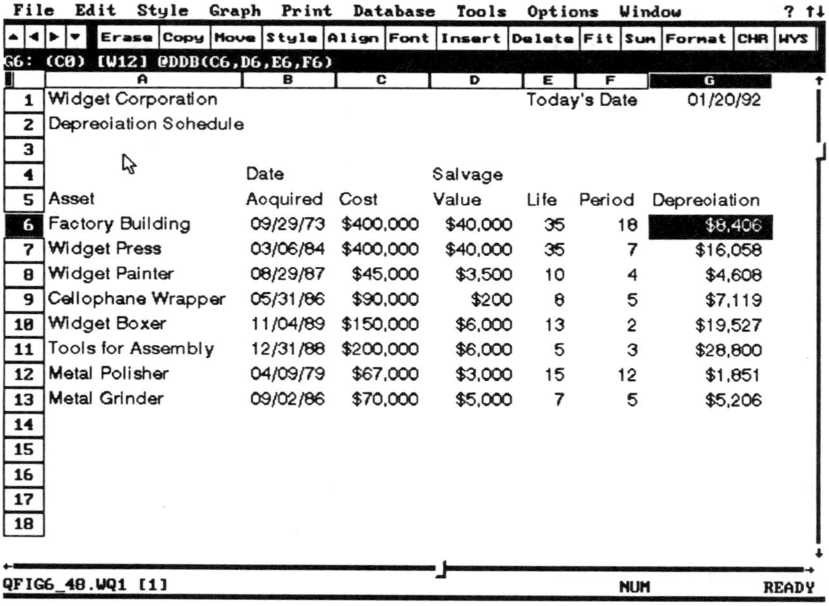

Figure 6.48 Computing Double Declining Balance Depreciation

for the house of your dreams. Figure 6.49 has the relevant information for six homes. For each home, make the assumption that the current home will be sold and the equity from it will be applied to the new home. Therefore, the amount borrowed is the difference between the cost of the new home and the equity of the old home. The mortgage rate and term are shown in annual terms. The basic formula in B7 is @PMT(B4-D1,B5,B6), which is then copied across the row. To compute the monthly payment, you must convert the rate and term to months. To convert the rate and term into the monthly interest rate and number of months for the loan, divide the annual rate by 12 and multiply the number of years by 12, respectively. By using the monthly rate and term, the @PMT function in row 8 computes the monthly payment. The monthly payment is not $\frac{1}{12}$ of the yearly rate. For example, $\frac{1}{12}$ of the yearly payment is 222.33. The difference is caused by the compounding interest rate effect. At the end of each period, the interest is computed based upon the balance at the end of the period. Since the balance declines more quickly when you pay monthly, the monthly payment is less.

@PAYMT

The @PAYMT function computes a payment based on the principal, its future value, an interest rate, a number of periods, and whether the payment is made at the beginning or end of the period. It can also compute annuity amounts. This

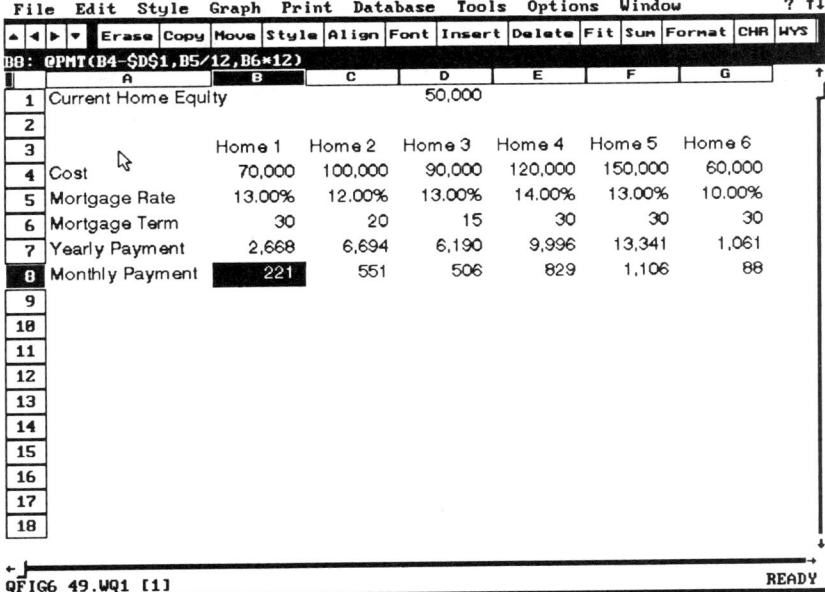

Figure 6.49 @PMT Used to Compute Monthly and Annual Payments on Different Houses

function is an enhancement of the @PMT function. The format is @PAYMT(rate,nper,pv[fv],[type],]), where *rate* is the interest rate you are paying on the loan per term; *nper* is the number of periods that you are paying on the loan; *pv* is the principal of the loan; *fv* is the future value that is still due at the end of the loan; and *type* indicates whether the payment is made at the beginning of the period (1) or end of the period (0). If the fv or type arguments are omitted, Quattro assumes they are 0—just as in the @PMT function. Each of these arguments is a number, formula, or cell reference to either.

This function is used instead of @PMT when the function uses one of the two optional arguments. As an example, if a fledgling business is borrowing $100,000 to buy a building, the lender may not want to offer a long-term loan. One option is to offer the loan for a shorter time period, such as five years. At the end of the loan period, some of the loan principal remains, so the borrower must take out another loan or sell the building to pay the remaining principal. The lender may also require that the loan payment is made at the beginning of the month. Figure 6.50 shows this example in a Quattro spreadsheet. This example assumes that the loan principal at the end of five years is $50,000. Since you are receiving $100,000 for the loan, this number, the present value, is positive. Since you will owe $50,000 at the end of the loan, the future value is negative. The function result of ($1,466.80) is the monthly payment the borrower will make for the next five years. It is negative since the borrower is paying this money instead of receiving it. At the end

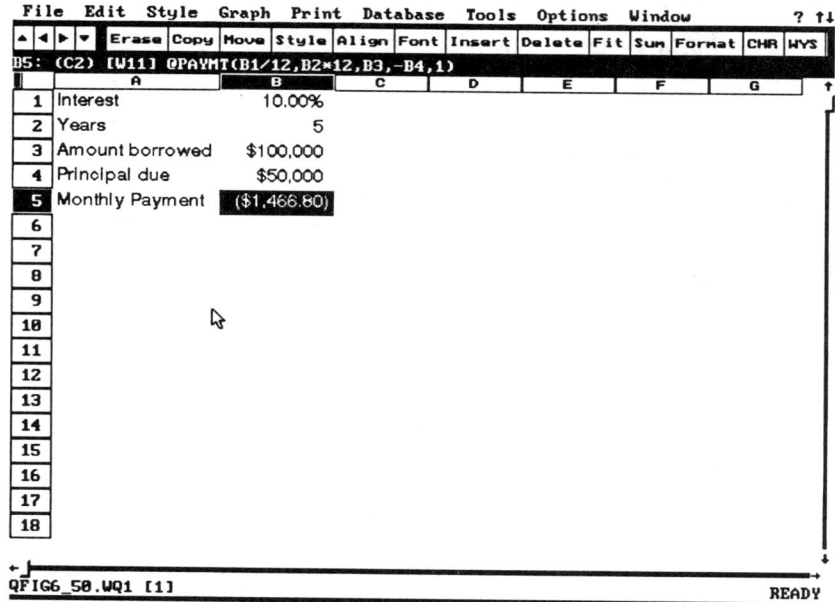

Figure 6.50 @PAYMT Used to Compute Short-Term Loan Payments

of five years, the borrower may seek another loan, the lender may offer to extend the loan, or the borrower may sell the building and pay the remaining principal.

Changing when the loan payment is made also changes the function's result. If the payment is made at the end of the month, the 1 in the formula in B5 is changed to a 0. The result of ($1,479.02) indicates how this payment amount is affected by when payment is made.

@IPAYMT

The @IPAYMT function computes the interest portion of a loan payment. The format is @IPAYMT(rate,per,nper,pv,[fv],[type]), where *rate* is the interest rate you are paying on the loan per term; *per* is the loan payment period for which you want to know the interest portion; *nper* is the number of periods that you are paying on the loan; *pv* is the principal of the loan; *fv* is the future value that is still due at the end of the loan; and *type* indicates whether the payment is made at the beginning of the period (1) or end of the period (0). If the fv or type arguments are omitted, Quattro assumes they are 0. These arguments are a number, formula, or cell reference to either.

Using the example described above for the @PAYMT function, suppose you want to know how much interest you will pay in the first year. Figure 6.51 shows the spreadsheet modified to compute the interest for the first year of the loan. As the results show, the interest portion of the loan payment decreases in each period.

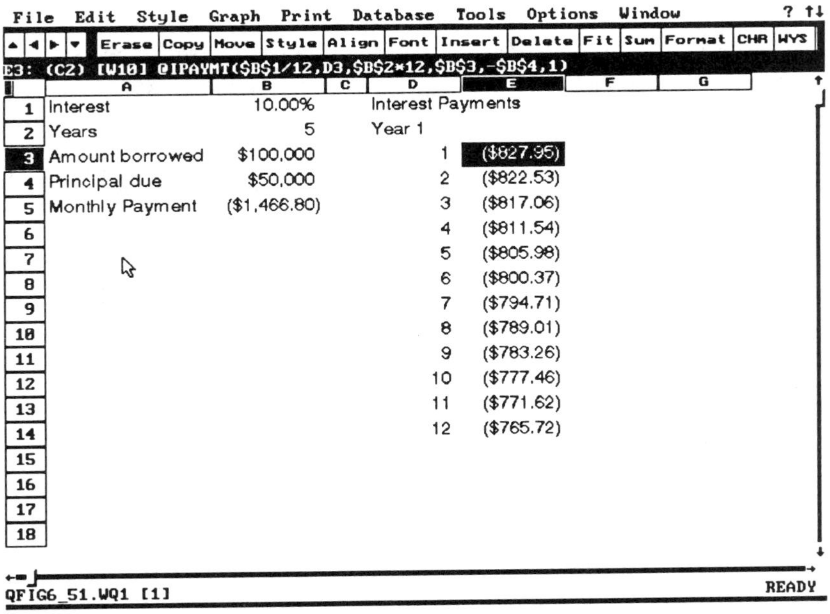

Figure 6.51 @IPAYMT Used to Compute Interest Portion of Loan Payments

@PPAYMT

The @PPAYMT function computes the principal portion of a loan payment. The format is @PPAYMT(rate,per,nper,pv,[fv],[type]), where *rate* is the interest rate you are paying on the loan per period; *per* is the loan payment period for which you want to know the principal portion; *nper* is the number of periods that you are paying on the loan; *pv* is the principal of the loan; *fv* is the future value that is still due at the end of the loan; and *type* indicates whether the payment is made at the beginning of the period (1) or end of the period (0). If the fv or type arguments are omitted, Quattro assumes they are 0. These arguments are a number, formula, or cell reference to either.

Using the example described above for the @PAYMT function, suppose you want to know how much principal you will pay in the first year. Figure 6.52 shows the spreadsheet modified to compute the principal for the first year of the loan. As the results show, the principal portion of the loan payment increases in each period. By adding the values in columns E and H, you will notice that the results of the @PPAYMT for each month is the result of @PAYMT less @IPAYMT.

@TERM

The @TERM function determines the number of periodic payments made each period at a specified rate of interest to accumulate a future value. The format is

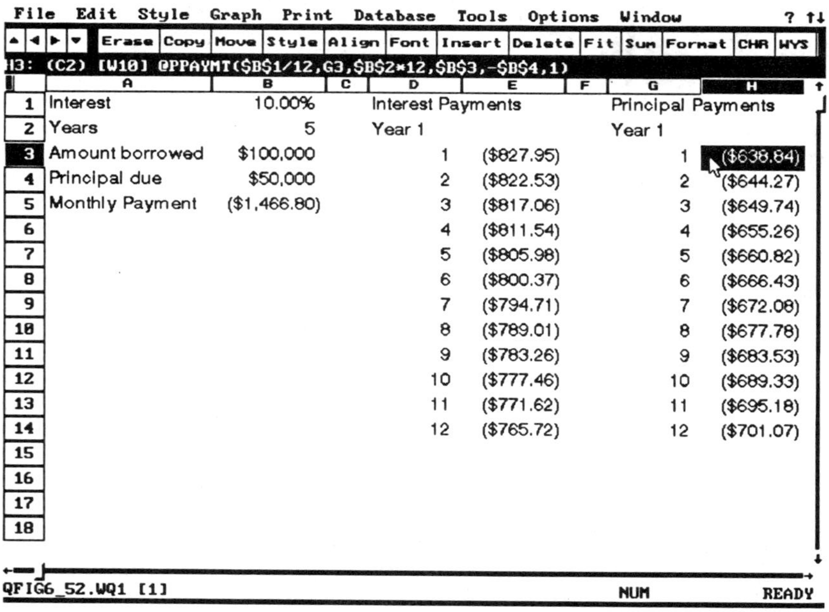

```
File  Edit  Style  Graph  Print  Database  Tools  Options  Window        ? ↑↓
     Erase Copy Move Style Align Font Insert Delete Fit Sum Format CHR WYS
H3: (C2) [W10] @PPAYMT($B$1/12,G3,$B$2*12,$B$3,-$B$4,1)
```

	A	B	C	D	E	F	G	H
1	Interest	10.00%		Interest Payments			Principal Payments	
2	Years	5		Year 1			Year 1	
3	Amount borrowed	$100,000		1	($827.95)		1	($638.84)
4	Principal due	$50,000		2	($822.53)		2	($644.27)
5	Monthly Payment	($1,466.80)		3	($817.06)		3	($649.74)
6				4	($811.54)		4	($655.26)
7				5	($805.98)		5	($660.82)
8				6	($800.37)		6	($666.43)
9				7	($794.71)		7	($672.08)
10				8	($789.01)		8	($677.78)
11				9	($783.26)		9	($683.53)
12				10	($777.46)		10	($689.33)
13				11	($771.62)		11	($695.18)
14				12	($765.72)		12	($701.07)

```
QFIG6_52.WQ1 [1]                                  NUM         READY
```

Figure 6.52 @PPAYMT Used to Compute Principal Portion of Loan Payments

@TERM(pmt,rate,fv), where *pmt* represents the present value that you have; *rate* represents the interest rate of the investment opportunity; and *fv* represents the future value you want to have. These arguments are a number, formula, or cell reference to either.

When a company sells a bond issue, it must make provisions to repay the bonds when they become due either by redeeming them or by reissuing another series of bonds. When bonds are redeemed, the company creates a bond-sinking fund that accumulates until the bonds are due, by which point the contributions to the bond-sinking fund and the earnings equal the bond's face value. One way to accumulate earnings in the bond-sinking fund is to invest a fixed amount every month. For example, suppose you invest $5,000 every month for the next 10 years, earning 10% annual interest. At the end of 10 years, you will sell the investments and use the proceeds to redeem the bonds, then totaling $1,000,000. However, before you start this investment program and deposit the first $5,000, you need to check if your assumptions are correct. Figure 6.53 shows a spreadsheet with the assumptions. The first assumption to be tested is if 10 years of investing $5,000 monthly is enough to reach your goal of $1,000,000. Cell B11 uses the @TERM function to determine the minimum number of years that you need to save. Because you are investing monthly, the function needs a monthly interest rate. Since you want the number of years and the function returns the number of months, the result of the function needs to be divided by twelve to convert the number of months to number of years. In B11, the @TERM function refers to the monthly saving of

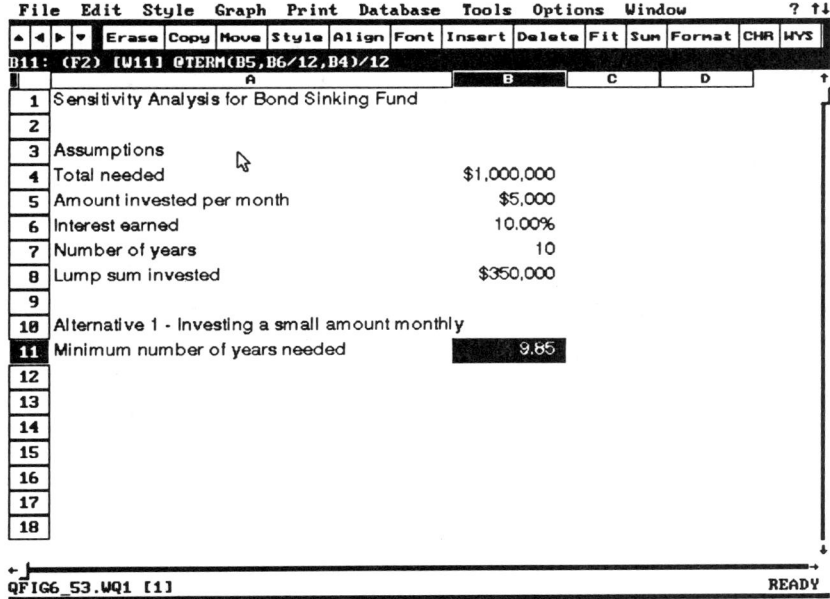

Figure 6.53 @TERM Used to Compute Minimum Years Needed of Weekly Savings

$5,000 entered in B5; the annual interest rate in B6 (which is divided by twelve to convert it to a monthly rate); and the targeted value of $1,000,000 entered in B4. By referring to the cell values instead of typing them directly into the formula, you can change your assumptions quickly without changing any formulas. The result of 9.85 years indicates that investing $5,000 a month for 10 years will earn enough to redeem the bonds in 10 years.

Another option for this example is to use annual figures by entering the invested amount as **B5*12** and not dividing the interest rate and the function's result by 12. The resulting answer of 10.29 is larger due to the compounding effects of investing annually instead of monthly; your investments accumulate more quickly if your interest is compounded monthly rather than annually.

@FV

The @FV function computes the future value of a series of equal cash flows, each earning interest. This function treats cash flows as it would treat an ordinary annuity. An ordinary annuity is an investment where you put in a fixed amount every period and at the end of a fixed number of periods, you receive the amount that you have saved plus the interest earned on all money invested.

The format is @FV(pmt,rate,nper); where *pmt* represents the periodic fixed payment; *rate* represents the interest rate each payment earns per period; and *nper* represents the number of periods the annuity covers. Each of these arguments is a number, formula or cell reference to either type of entry. The function assumes that interest is compounded at the end of each period within the term.

In the example for @TERM, the minimum number of years it takes to invest enough for the bond-sinking fund is computed. Since you found that it takes less than the 10 years that you planned to invest, the investment proceeds will exceed your needs at the end of the 10 years. The @FV function can determine the final amount that is actually saved and earned if you continue to save for the full 10 years.

Although both the @FV and @TERM work with the same basic problem, their approach and solutions are different, since both functions work with different unknowns. @TERM computes the minimum number of years and @FV computes the future value of your investments as shown in Figure 6.54. As you can see in the formula in cell B12 shown at the top of the screen, the annual rate is divided by 12 to generate the monthly interest rate, and the term of 10 years in cell B7 is multiplied by 12 to compute the number of months of the annuity. The result of $1,024,225 indicates that you will have $24,225 more than needed by saving $5,000 per month for 10 years at 10% interest.

@CTERM

The @CTERM function computes the number of time periods required for a present value to reach a future value by earning a fixed interest rate. The format is @CTERM(rate,fv,pv), where *rate* is the interest rate per period; *fv* is the future value that you are trying to reach; and *pv* is the present value that you currently

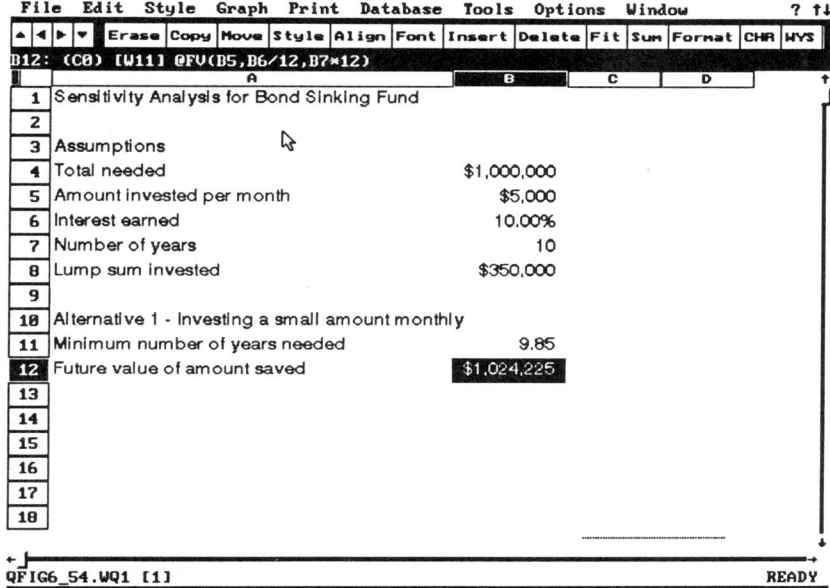

Figure 6.54 @FV Used to Compute the Future Value of Savings

have. Each of these arguments is a number, formula, or cell reference to either type of entry.

Using the example of the bond-sinking fund, an alternative to investing a fixed sum monthly is investing a larger sum now. For example, if you invest $350,000 for 10 years earning 10% interest, the original amount will grow to a larger amount due to compounding interest. To determine if the future value is enough for your goal, use the @CTERM function in B15 to compute the number of years for which you need to earn interest on the lump sum to reach your goal. Like the examples for @TERM and @FV, this example also uses monthly compounding. The @CTERM function uses the interest rate in B6 divided by 12, the future value in B4, and the present value in B8. To modify this function to return the number of years instead of the number of months, the interest and the function's result must be divided by 12. From the result shown in Figure 6.55, investing $350,000 and earning 10% annual interest yields your goal in 10.54 years, or approximately $10^1/2$ years. Since this is longer than desired, if you want to invest a lump sum now for redeeming bonds in 10 years, you would have to invest more than $350,000 or earn more than 10% interest.

@RATE

The @RATE function returns the minimum interest rate required for a present value invested over a period of time to equal a future amount compounded each time period. The format is @RATE(fv,pv,nper), where *fv* is the future value you

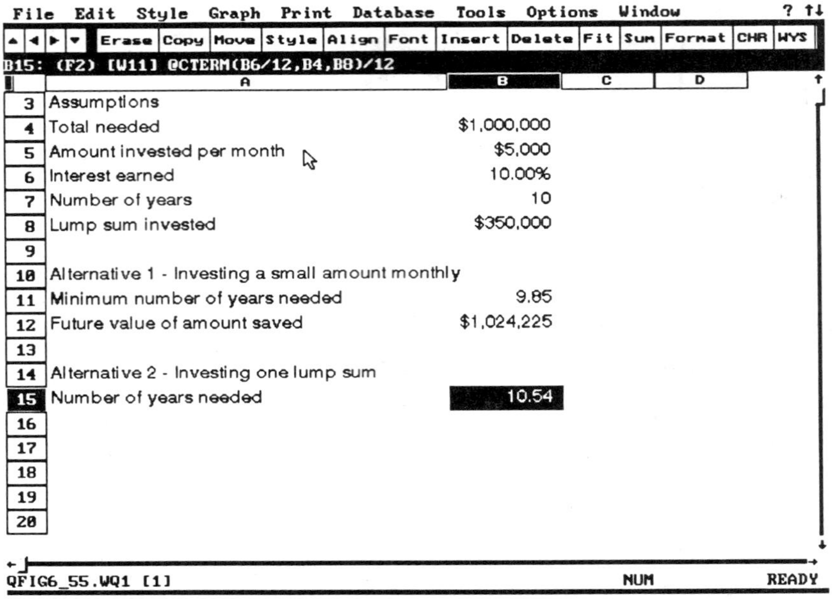

Figure 6.55 @CTERM Used to Compute the Number of Years to Reach the Financial Goal

want to earn; *pv* is the present value that you have; and *nper* represents the number of periods for the investment. Each of these arguments is a number, formula, or cell reference to either.

Using a current lump-sum investment approach for the bond-sinking fund, you can use the @RATE function to determine the minimum interest rate that your lump-sum investment must earn to accumulate the $1,000,000 goal at the end of the 10 years. Figure 6.56 uses the @RATE function to determine the interest rate required to accumulate $1,000,000 from your initial $350,000 investment in 10 years. In B16, the @RATE function computes the minimum annual interest rate that must be earned. This function produces a monthly rate, since the number of years in B7 is multiplied by 12. The function's result then is converted to an annual figure by multiplying the result by 12. Therefore, 10.54% is the minimum annual interest rate you can earn on a lump sum of $350,000 to accumulate $1,000,000 in 10 years when the interest is compounded monthly. If the interest is compounded annually, you need at least 11.07% interest. The difference illustrates the benefit of having interest compounded more frequently.

@NPER

The @NPER function returns the number of periods required for a lump sum and/or a number of periodic payments invested over a period of time and compounded

```
File  Edit  Style  Graph  Print  Database  Tools  Options  Window      ? ↑↓
  Erase Copy Move Style Align Font Insert Delete Fit Sum Format CHR HYS
B16:  (P2) [W11] @RATE(B4,B8,B7*12)*12
                A                              B           C       D
  4  Total needed                         $1,000,000
  5  Amount invested per month                $5,000
  6  Interest earned                          10.00%
  7  Number of years                              10
  8  Lump sum invested                       $350,000
  9
 10  Alternative 1 - Investing a small amount monthly
 11  Minimum number of years needed             9.85
 12  Future value of amount saved         $1,024,225
 13
 14  Alternative 2 - Investing one lump sum
 15  Number of years needed                    10.54
 16  Minimum interest rate needed             10.54%
 17
 18
 19
 20
 21

QFIG6_56.WQ1 [1]                                       NUM          READY
```

Figure 6.56 @RATE Used to Compute the Minimum Rate Needed to Reach the Financial Goal

each time period to equal a future amount. The @NPER function combines the @TERM and @CTERM, since it can handle a single amount at the beginning of the period, a fixed amount every period, or both. The format is @NPER (rate,pmt,pv,[fv],[type]), where *rate* represents the interest rate of the investment opportunity; *pmt* represents the payment made at the beginning or end of each period; *pv* is the present value the investment starts with; *fv* is the future value that will be earned at the end of the last period (pv and fv have opposite signs—if you think of the money that you earn or receive as positive numbers and money you have to pay as negative numbers, you will remember to put the correct sign in front of the pmt, pv, and fv function arguments); and *type* is 1 if the payment is made at the beginning of the period, or 0 or omitted if the payment is made at the end of the period. Each of these arguments is a number, formula, or cell reference to either.

A third approach to the bond-sinking fund example is investing $200,000 now and also $2,000 monthly. You can use the @NPER function to determine the minimum number of periods you must invest to accumulate the $1,000,000 goal. Figure 6.57 uses the @NPER function to determine the number of periods required to accumulate $1,000,000 from your initial $200,000 investment and the additional $2,000 monthly earning 10% interest (the $200,000 and $2,000 are in the input line). The function arguments are in a different order than for the @TERM or @CTERM function. Also, the fv argument has a minus sign, since you are paying it to the bondholders. In B19, the @NPER function computes the number of periods this

```
File   Edit   Style   Graph   Print   Database   Tools   Options   Window           ? ↑↓
▲◀▶▼ Erase Copy Move Style Align Font Insert Delete Fit Sum Format CHR WYS
B19: (F2) [W11] @NPER(0.11/12,2000,200000,-B4)/12
                        A                              B           C         D
  1   Sensitivity Analysis for Bond Sinking Fund
  2
  3   Assumptions
  4   Total needed                            $1,000,000
  5   Amount invested per month                  $5,000
  6   Interest earned                             10.00%
  7   Number of years                                 10
  8   Lump sum invested                         $350,000
  9
 10   Alternative 1 - Investing a small amount monthly
 11   Minimum number of years needed               9.85
 12   Future value of amount saved            $1,024,225
 13
 14   Alternative 2 - Investing one lump sum
 15   Number of years needed                      10.54
 16   Minimum interest rate needed                10.54%
 17
 18   Alternative 3 - Lump sum & monthly payment
 19   Number of years needed                       9.76

QFIG6_57.WQ1 [1]                                               NUM          READY
```

Figure 6.57   @NPER Used to Compute the Number of Years to Reach the Financial Goal

investment must be maintained. The function's result is divided by 12 to convert the resulting number of months to the number of years. Therefore, you must pursue this investment for 9.76 years.

@IRATE

The @IRATE function returns the minimum interest rate required for a present value invested over a period of time to equal a future amount compounded each time period. Unlike the @RATE function, the @IRATE function has two additional arguments that let you enter a final investment value and whether the periodic amount is deposited or withdrawn at the beginning or end of the period. The format of this function is @IRATE(nper,pmt,pv,[fv],[type]). Here, *nper* represents the number of periods for the investment and *pmt* represents the payment made at the beginning or end of the period. The *pv* is the present value the investment starts with, and *fv* is the future value that will be earned at the end of the last period. (The pv and the fv have opposite signs. If you think of the money that you earn or receive as positive numbers and money you have to pay as negative numbers, you will remember to put the correct sign in front of the pmt, pv, and fv function arguments.) The *type* is 1 if the payment is made at the beginning of the period, or 0 or omitted if the payment is made at the end of the period. These arguments are a number, formula, or cell reference to either.

Using the combined lump sum and monthly payment approach for the bond-sinking fund, you can use the @IRATE function to determine the minimum interest rate that your lump sum investment must earn to accumulate the $1,000,000 goal at the end of the 10 years. Figure 6.58 uses the @IRATE function to determine the interest rate required to accumulate $1,000,000 from your initial $200,000 investment and the additional $2,000 monthly in 10 years (see input line for entries **2000** and **2000000**). The function arguments are in a different order than in Figure 6.56 for the @RATE function. Also, the fv argument has a minus sign, since you are paying it to the bondholders at the end of 10 years. In B20, the @IRATE function computes the minimum annual interest rate that must be earned. This function produces a monthly rate, since the function uses the number of months for the nper argument. The function's result is converted to an annual figure by multiplying the result by 12. Therefore, 10.62% is the minimum annual interest rate you can earn on a lump sum of $200,000 and a monthly addition of $2,000 to accumulate $1,000,000 in 10 years when the interest is compounded monthly.

@PV

The @PV function computes the present value of an annuity, or series of equal cash flows, invested at a certain interest rate for a number of periods. The format is @PV(pmt,rate,nper), where *pmt* represents the amount of a fixed payment that is

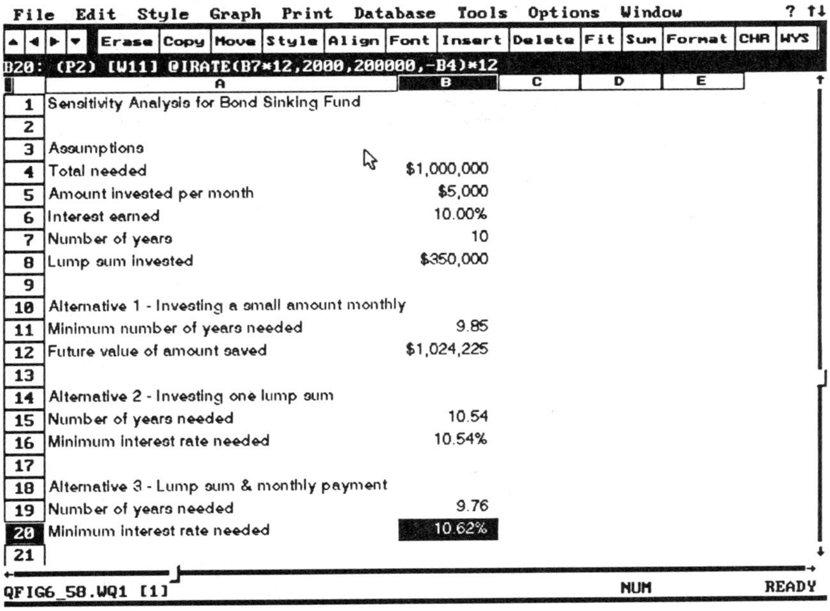

Figure 6.58 @IRATE Used to Compute Minimum Rate to Reach Financial Goal

made every period; *rate* represents the interest rate per period; and *nper* represents the number of periods that the investment covers. These arguments are a number, formula, or cell reference to either. The function assumes that interest is compounded at the end of each period within the term.

Most state lotteries award their prizes as annuities. For example, if you win a lottery of $1,000,000, you often do not receive a check for $1,000,000. Usually you get a payment once a year for a percentage of your winnings. For example, assume that you have just won a $1,000,000 lottery that is to be paid out at $50,000 for the next 20 years. As an option, the group operating the lottery allows you to choose a lump sum payment of $500,000 immediately. To decide which has the greater present value, you use the @PV function to compute the present value of the 20-payment option. In Figure 6.59, the three assumptions are listed in rows 1 through 3. This example assumes that the interest is computed annually. The function in B5 computes the present value of your annuity (lottery prize winnings). As you can see from this example, the present value of the $500,000 immediately is more than that of taking $50,000 for the next 20 years since you can earn more by putting the money in an investment that earns at least 8% and withdrawing $50,000 per year from your investment. (These results do not include the effects of taxes, which may change your decision.)

@PVAL

The @PVAL function computes the present value of an annuity, or series of equal cash flows, and an end of the term payment invested at a certain interest rate for

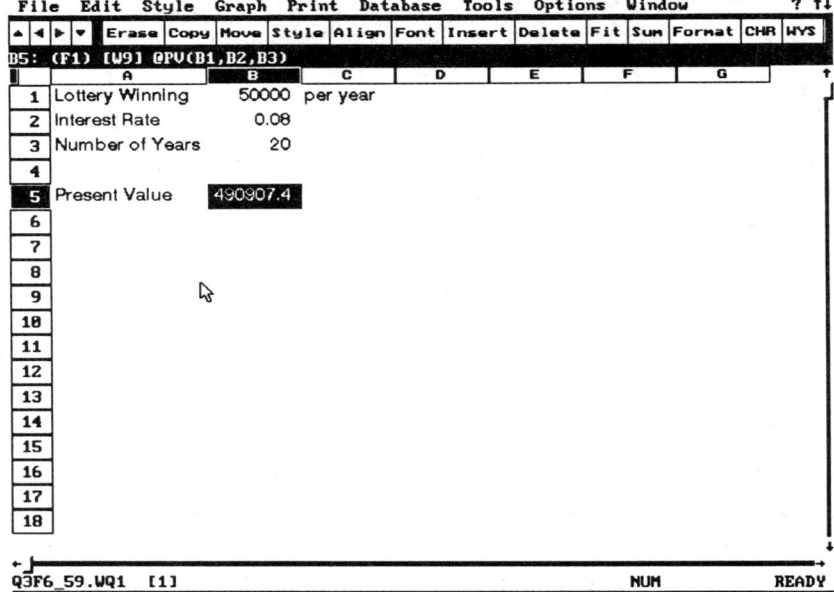

Figure 6.59 @PV Used to Compute the Present Value of Lottery Winnings

a number of periods. The format is @PVAL(rate,nper,pmt,[fv],[type]), where *rate* represents the interest rate per period; *nper* represents the number of periods that the investment covers; *pmt* represents the amount of a fixed payment that is made every period; and *fv* is the future value of the investment at the end of the last period. If you think of the money that you earn or receive as positive numbers and money you have to pay as negative numbers, you will remember to put the correct sign in front of the pmt and fv function arguments. The *type* is 1 if the payment is made at the beginning of the period, or 0 or omitted if the payment is made at the end of the period. Each of these arguments is a number, formula, or cell reference to either.

One application of this function is deciding if a sales offer is a good price. For example, suppose you own a restaurant and someone offers $300,000 to buy it. You can use the @PVAL function to determine if the sales offer is high enough to make selling the restaurant worthwhile. Assume that if you did not sell it now, you could expect to earn $40,000 per year for the next 10 years and that after 10 years it would be worth $100,000. To evaluate whether to sell now, you can check whether the selling price is greater than the present value of your expected cash flows. To find the present value of the restaurant, you would enter this formula in a cell: **@PVAL(.1,10,40000,100000)**. The **.1** (10%) represents the interest you would earn on a similar investment. This is an annual rate. The **10** represents the number of years you would receive the yearly income. The **100000** represents the restaurant value at the end of the 10 years. The function returns -284337. Since this is less than the sales offer, it is worthwhile to sell the restaurant now.

@FVAL

The @FVAL function computes the future value of a present value and the value of an annuity, or series of equal cash flows invested at a certain interest rate for a number of periods. The format is @FVAL(rate,nper,pmt,[pv],[type]), where *rate* represents the interest rate per period; *nper* represents the number of periods that the investment covers; *pmt* represents the amount of a fixed payment that is made every period; and *pv* is the present value of the investment. If you think of the money that you earn or receive as positive numbers and money you have to pay as negative numbers, you will remember to put the correct sign in front of the pmt and pv function arguments. The *type* is 1 if the payment is made at the beginning of the period, or 0 or omitted if the payment is made at the end of the period. Each of these arguments is a number, formula, or cell reference to either.

As an example, imagine that you are saving for a luxury vacation. So far, you have saved $500 and plan to put aside $50 per week in your bank account, which earns 5.25% interest. You can use the @FVAL function to learn how large your vacation budget is. To use the @FVAL function with this data, enter the following formula into a cell: **@FVAL(.0525/52,52,50,500)**. The number of periods is 52 for 52 weeks in one year, and the annual interest rate is divided by 52 to convert the annual rate to a weekly rate. The result of -3195.02 tells you how much you can spend on your vacation.

@NPV

The @NPV function computes the present value of a stream of future cash flows. The format is @NPV(rate,block,[type]). The *rate* is the interest rate for the period (which is a percentage, decimal value, formula, or cell reference). This function assumes that the same interest rate applies for each period. The *block* represents the area on your spreadsheet that contains the cash flows, which must be defined as either a block or a block name. This function assumes that cash flows occur on a regular basis in the order they appear in the block with blank cells representing periods with no cash flows. Positive numbers represent cash inflows, and negative numbers represent cash outflows. This function assumes the cash flows occur at the end of the period unless you enter 1 for the optional *type* argument. If the project's cash flows include an initial cost, use a 1 for the type argument. An alternative is to omit this cash outflow from the block for the @NPV function and subtract the initial cost from the result of the @NPV function. A cash flow at the beginning of a period is the same as a cash flow at the end of the previous period.

One use of the @NPV function is computing the net present value of investment opportunities. If you have several investment opportunities, the one with the highest net present value is the most valuable. Figure 6.60 shows four investment opportunities with different cash flows. The initial cost is in row 5, and the yearly cash flows are in rows 6 through 15. The formula in row 17 computes the net

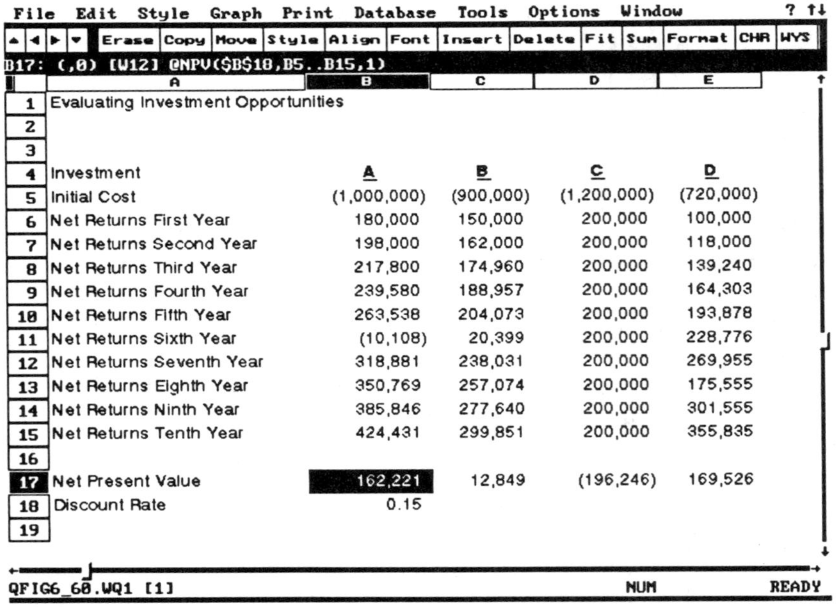

	A	B	C	D	E
1	Evaluating Investment Opportunities				
2					
3					
4	Investment	A	B	C	D
5	Initial Cost	(1,000,000)	(900,000)	(1,200,000)	(720,000)
6	Net Returns First Year	180,000	150,000	200,000	100,000
7	Net Returns Second Year	198,000	162,000	200,000	118,000
8	Net Returns Third Year	217,800	174,960	200,000	139,240
9	Net Returns Fourth Year	239,580	188,957	200,000	164,303
10	Net Returns Fifth Year	263,538	204,073	200,000	193,878
11	Net Returns Sixth Year	(10,108)	20,399	200,000	228,776
12	Net Returns Seventh Year	318,881	238,031	200,000	269,955
13	Net Returns Eighth Year	350,769	257,074	200,000	175,555
14	Net Returns Ninth Year	385,846	277,640	200,000	301,555
15	Net Returns Tenth Year	424,431	299,851	200,000	355,835
16					
17	Net Present Value	162,221	12,849	(196,246)	169,526
18	Discount Rate	0.15			
19					

B17: (,0) [W12] @NPV(B18,B5..B15,1)

Figure 6.60 @NPV Used to Evaluate Investment Opportunities

present value of each of the cash flows in rows 5 through 15 with a type argument indicating that the cash flows are made at the beginning of the period. In this example, B18 provides the discount or interest rate the @NPV function uses. Therefore, the investment opportunity D is the most valuable of the investment opportunities.

@IRR

The @IRR function computes the internal rate of return for a series of cash flows. The internal rate of return is the rate of interest the cash flows must earn to have a net present value of 0. This internal rate of return is the minimum interest rate a project or asset should earn to be considered a viable option.

The format of the function is @IRR(guess,block). Here, *guess* is your approximation of the internal rate of return. While your guess is probably different from the result of the function, it should be reasonably close. By using a reasonable guess, you shorten the time the @IRR function takes to compute the internal rate of return and ensure a correct internal rate of return. Every time the cash flows alternate between positive and negative numbers, there is another possible internal rate of return. Since some of the internal rate of returns are impractical, your guess indicates which one Quattro Pro should use. Your guess can be entered as a percent, decimal value, formula, or cell reference. The *block* is the area of cells that contain the cash flows. This function argument must be a block or block name. The @IRR function assumes that the first cell in the block is the initial cash outflow for the investment opportunity and is a negative number. Quattro Pro also assumes that cash flows occur on a regular basis in the order they appear in the block with blank cells representing periods with no cash flows. Positive numbers represent cash inflows and negative numbers represent cash outflows.

The internal rate of return is frequently used to help decide which projects should be considered for your investment dollars. For example, companies have a minimum internal rate of return for projects; a project must have an internal rate of return higher than the company's minimum before the company invests in the project. For example, when you have several possible investment opportunities, you must decide among them. Figure 6.61 displays four investment opportunities to be evaluated. The @IRR can determine which is providing the best return on investment. Since @IRR assumes that the first cell is the initial cash outflow, rows 5 through 15 are included in the formula. In this example, if you expect a minimum of 15% from your investments (entered in cell B18 as 0.15), you are willing to acquire the investment opportunities A, B, and D. Investment opportunity D is again the best of the three, since it has the highest internal rate of return. @IRR and @NPV usually agree on which is the best of several investment opportunities. When they do not agree, it is often due to an inappropriate guess in the @IRR function.

```
   File  Edit  Style  Graph  Print  Database  Tools  Options  Window         ? ↑↓
  ▲ ◀ ▶ ▼  Erase Copy Move Style Align Font Insert Delete Fit Sum Format CHR WYS
  B17: (P2) [W12] @IRR($B$18,B5..B15)
            A                    B            C            D            E          ↑
   1  Evaluating Investment Opportunities
   2
   3                             ▷
   4  Investment                 A            B            C            D
   5  Initial Cost          (1,000,000)   (900,000)   (1,200,000)   (720,000)
   6  Net Returns First Year   180,000     150,000      200,000      100,000
   7  Net Returns Second Year  198,000     162,000      200,000      118,000
   8  Net Returns Third Year   217,800     174,960      200,000      139,240
   9  Net Returns Fourth Year  239,580     188,957      200,000      164,303
  10  Net Returns Fifth Year   263,538     204,073      200,000      193,878
  11  Net Returns Sixth Year   (10,108)     20,399      200,000      228,776
  12  Net Returns Seventh Year 318,881     238,031      200,000      269,955
  13  Net Returns Eighth Year  350,769     257,074      200,000      175,555
  14  Net Returns Ninth Year   385,846     277,640      200,000      301,555
  15  Net Returns Tenth Year   424,431     299,851      200,000      355,835
  16
  17  Internal Rate of Return   18.58%      15.33%       10.56%       19.73%
  18  Minimum IRR                0.15
  19
  ────────────────────────────────────────────────────────────────────────────────
  QFIG6_61.WQ1 [1]                                          NUM           READY
```

Figure 6.61 @IRR Used to Evaluate Investment Opportunities

MATHEMATICAL FUNCTIONS: INTRODUCTION

Quattro Pro has a separate category of mathematical functions that perform one of three types of tasks. One type includes functions that focus on basic mathematical capabilities (like deriving absolute values) and rounding and other functions that provide basic mathematical values (like random numbers). The second type are used in logarithmic computations. The third type focuses on the trigonometric functions that relate to the properties of angles and allow you to perform computations on geometric shapes.

MATHEMATICAL FUNCTIONS: BASIC

@ROUND

The @ROUND function rounds a number to a specified place to the left or right of the decimal point. The format is @ROUND(x,num). Here, x is the value to be rounded (expressed as a number, formula, or cell reference to either); *num* is the number of places before or after the decimal at which the rounding should take place (expressed as a number, formula, or cell reference to either whose value ranges from -15 to 15). A positive value causes rounding to the right of the decimal. For example, if this argument equals 2, an entry of **2.5672** would be rounded to

2.57. A negative value causes rounding to the left of the decimal point. For example, if this argument equals -3, then **34,285.2** would be rounded to 34,000. A value of 0 causes the function to round the number to an integer. Rounding a value differs from truncating the value, since truncating a value ignores the numbers to the right of the point you are truncating from, and rounding a number uses the value to the right of the point that you are rounding to determine whether the number should be rounded up or rounded down. For example, **25.68** would be truncated to 25.6 but rounded to 25.7. Quattro follows the convention of rounding to the next higher digit if the number to the right of num is 5 or greater. Rounding changes the internal storage of the value to match the displayed value, unlike the /Style Numeric Format command, which changes the number's appearance but does not change how the number is stored. For example, if 1.00797 is stored in a cell, changing the format to Fixed with 2 decimal places does not affect the value of the cell. On the other hand, if the cell contains @ROUND(1.00797,2), the value is stored as 1.01 and used as that value in all subsequent computations.

One practical application of the @ROUND function is combining several measurements that have a different number of places of decimal accuracy. For example, if you are combining the weights of steel scrap from a process and each scrap was measured on one of three scales, the three different scales may provide different accuracy measurements, as in the example shown in Figure 6.62. Each piece of scrap is listed in column A. One of the scales measured to the nearest

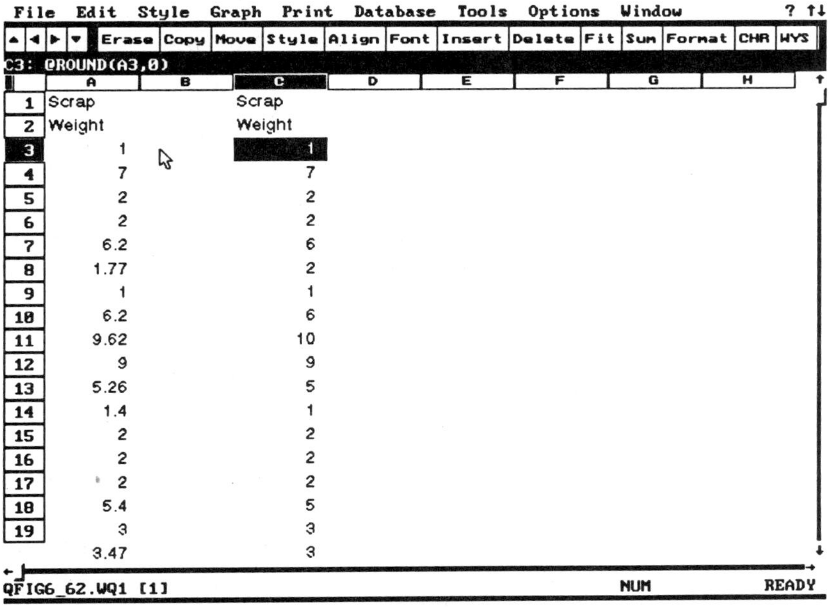

Figure 6.62 @ROUND Used to Convert Numbers to a Consistent Format

pound, another measured to the nearest tenth of a pound, and the third measured to the nearest hundredth of a pound. Since the accounting for scrap only requires accuracy to the nearest pound, it is not important to maintain the weight of the scraps to the nearest tenth and hundredth of a pound. In column C, each of the columns is rounded to the nearest whole number by using @ROUND with a 0 for the second function argument. By rounding the pieces of scrap to the nearest pound, you create a cleaner display without excessive detail. The @ROUND function is often used to control the accuracy of the results produced by other functions and formulas, as the example for the @RAND function later in the chapter illustrates.

@INT

@INT returns the integer portion of a number. Any digits after the decimal point are truncated. The format is @INT(x), where *x* is the number, formula, or cell reference to a value or number to be truncated. @INT differs from @ROUND with the second function's argument equaling 0 in that @INT ignores the numbers to the right of the decimal point while @ROUND uses the numbers to the right of the decimal point to round the value to the next higher or lower value. Like the @ROUND function, the @INT function changes the way the value is stored. Both @ROUND and @INT differ from the /Style Numeric Format command, which changes the number's appearance but does not change the way the number is stored. For example, if 6.022 is stored in a cell, changing the cell's format to Fixed with 0 decimal places does not affect the value of the cell. On the other hand, if the cell contains @INT(6.022), the value is stored as 6 and used as that value in all subsequent computations.

Figure 6.63 shows a schedule listing each piece of silver used for pressing charms. In this process, a press uses 0.75 ounces for each charm and presses as many as may fit on each piece of the silver sheet. Column B computes the number of 0.75-ounce pieces that are in each sheet. Since you cannot press only a portion of a charm from the piece of silver, the number of charms pressed from each piece is the integer portion of the calculation. You cannot use the @ROUND function since you do not want any of the calculations rounded to the next highest number.

@MOD

@MOD returns the modulo of two numbers. A modulo is the remainder when a number is divided by a divisor. For example, the modulo of seven divided by three is one since three goes into seven twice with a remainder of 1. The format is @MOD(x,y), where *x* is the number to be divided and *y* is the value being divided into x. Both function arguments are numbers, formulas, or cell references to either. The second argument must not equal 0.

Using the data from the @INT example, you can use the @MOD function to determine the remainder of each sheet of silver. As shown in Figure 6.64, once you

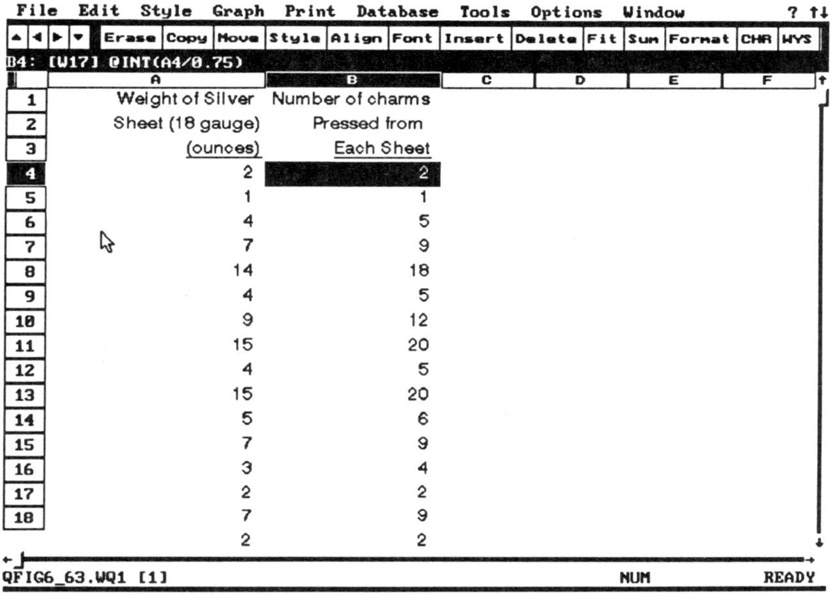

Functions 309

B4: [W17] @INT(A4/0.75)

	A	B
1	Weight of Silver	Number of charms
2	Sheet (18 gauge)	Pressed from
3	(ounces)	Each Sheet
4	2	2
5	1	1
6	4	5
7	7	9
8	14	18
9	4	5
10	9	12
11	15	20
12	4	5
13	15	20
14	5	6
15	7	9
16	3	4
17	2	2
18	7	9
	2	2

QFIG6_63.WQ1 [1]

Figure 6.63   @INT Used to Truncate Results of Division

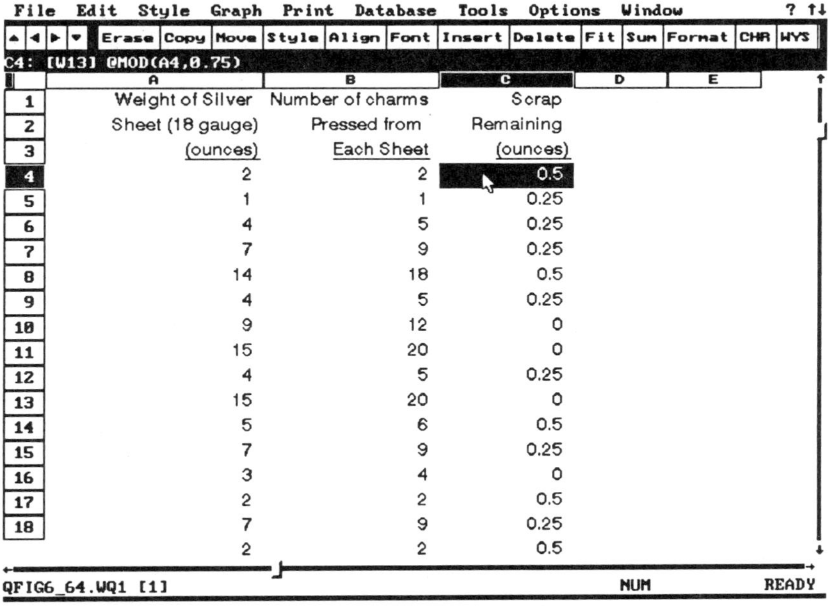

C4: [W13] @MOD(A4,0.75)

	A	B	C
1	Weight of Silver	Number of charms	Scrap
2	Sheet (18 gauge)	Pressed from	Remaining
3	(ounces)	Each Sheet	(ounces)
4	2	2	0.5
5	1	1	0.25
6	4	5	0.25
7	7	9	0.25
8	14	18	0.5
9	4	5	0.25
10	9	12	0
11	15	20	0
12	4	5	0.25
13	15	20	0
14	5	6	0.5
15	7	9	0.25
16	3	4	0
17	2	2	0.5
18	7	9	0.25
	2	2	0.5

QFIG6_64.WQ1 [1]

Figure 6.64   @MOD Used to Compute the Scrap Left

know the leftover silver from each sheet, you can determine the weight of the silver sheet you can create by melting the scraps into one sheet. In column C, the remaining silver from each sheet is computed. If you add the scraps from each sheet by using the @SUM function, you find that you can create a 4.25-ounce sheet by melting the scraps into one sheet.

@ABS

@ABS returns the absolute value of a number. The absolute value is a number's absolute distance from zero whether the number is positive or negative. This function returns a positive number equal to the function's argument if the argument is positive or a positive number equal to -1 times the function's argument if the argument is a negative value. The format is @ABS(x), where x is the value for which you want the absolute value. This argument is either a value, a formula or function resulting in a value, or a cell reference to either. This function is often used to process another function's argument before the other function uses the value, such as the @SQRT and the logarithmic functions described later in the chapter.

In some spreadsheet applications, you need to know the absolute value of a result. For example, when you compare a budget versus an actual spending plan, several differences appear. Since it is not worthwhile to check every variance, you can set a criterion, such as checking out all variances that exceed 10% of the budgeted expense. In Figure 6.65, the @IF function in column E determines which expense variances exceed 10% (0.1) of its budget. Since you want to know all variances that are over or under by 10%, you must use the absolute value of the variance (as the function in Figure 6.65 shows). If you do not use the @ABS function, you miss checking the variances for utilities and wages since their negative variances are much more than 10% of their budget.

The @ABS function is also used within other functions to ensure that a value used in or produced by a function is positive. For example, if you want the square root of a formula's result, you may take the absolute value of a formula's result to ensure that a positive value is used by the @SQRT function (described next).

@SQRT

The @SQRT function returns the square root of a number. The square root of a number is another number that, if multiplied by itself, produces the original number (for example, the square root of 9 is 3, because 3 × 3 = 9). The syntax of the function is @SQRT(x), where x is the value of which you want the square root, and x can be a value, a formula, or a cell reference to either. Quattro can only determine the square roots of positive numbers. You can also compute the square root by raising the number to the 0.5 power.

Various applications use the square root function, such as the Pythagorean theorem and the economic order quantity. The Pythagorean theorem states that, in a right angle triangle (one in which one of the angles is 90°), the square of the

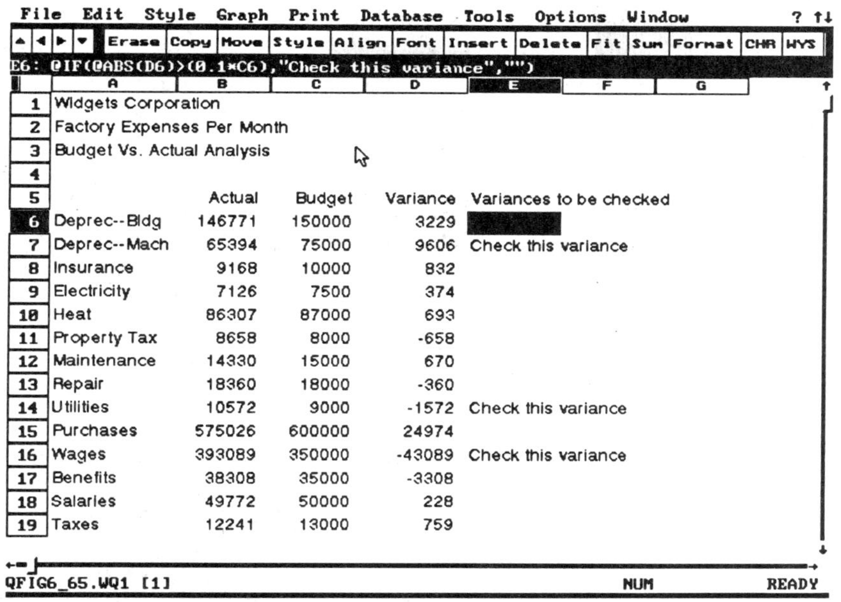

File Edit Style Graph Print Database Tools Options Window ? ↑↓

Erase Copy Move Style Align Font Insert Delete Fit Sum Format CHR WYS

E6: @IF(@ABS(D6)>(0.1*C6),"Check this variance","")

	A	B	C	D	E	F	G
1	Widgets Corporation						
2	Factory Expenses Per Month						
3	Budget Vs. Actual Analysis						
4							
5		Actual	Budget	Variance	Variances to be checked		
6	Deprec--Bldg	146771	150000	3229			
7	Deprec--Mach	65394	75000	9606	Check this variance		
8	Insurance	9168	10000	832			
9	Electricity	7126	7500	374			
10	Heat	86307	87000	693			
11	Property Tax	8658	8000	-658			
12	Maintenance	14330	15000	670			
13	Repair	18360	18000	-360			
14	Utilities	10572	9000	-1572	Check this variance		
15	Purchases	575026	600000	24974			
16	Wages	393089	350000	-43089	Check this variance		
17	Benefits	38308	35000	-3308			
18	Salaries	49772	50000	228			
19	Taxes	12241	13000	759			

QFIG6_65.WQ1 [1] NUM READY

Figure 6.65 @ABS Used to Measure the Absolute Amount of the Variances

longest side is equal to the sum of the squares of the other two sides. For example, if you have a triangle that has a height of 4 units and a base of 3 units with a 90° angle between the base and the height, you can use the Pythagorean theorem to compute the third side with this formula: **@SQRT(3^2+4^2)**. This formula squares 3 and 4, resulting in 9 and 16, respectively; then it adds them together for a result of 25, and computes the square root of 25, which is 5. While you can compute a square root of a value by raising it to its one-half root, the @SQRT function is quicker and easier to understand for someone who does not know that the two formulas are equivalent.

Generating a value's square root by raising a number to the inverse of the root that you want is usually not done for square roots; however, this formula can generate third and fourth roots for numbers. For example, to compute the cube (3rd) root of the value in A1, use this formula: **+A1^(1/3)**. For example, if +A1 is 125, this formula returns 5(5×5×5=125). This same formula works for the fourth root if you replace the **3** with a **4**.

@PI

The @PI function returns the value of pi (π), which equals approximately 3.14159. This function is primarily used in other formulas and functions. This function has no argument or parentheses.

The @PI function is often used for calculations involving circles. For example, suppose you had to purchase chairs for a large round table. You know that each chair requires approximately 3 feet, including some extra space for the comfort of the individual sitting in the chair. If you know that the diameter of the table is 10 feet, determining the perimeter is easy (perimeter = π × 10). Therefore to compute the perimeter of the table using Quattro, enter the formula **10*@PI**. To compute how many chairs you can comfortably fit at the table, use this formula: **@PI*10/3**. This formula calculates that you can put 10.47 chairs around the table. Since you can only order chairs in whole numbers, you can order 10 and be assured that each person has at least 3 feet of space.

@RAND

The @RAND function generates a random number between 0 and 1. By combining this function with other arithmetic operators, you can use this function to generate random numbers for any range. The function does not use parentheses or arguments.

To generate a group of numbers within a range, determine the range for the numbers you plan to generate and subtract the start of the range from the end of the range. Multiply this number by @RAND. For example, entering **@RAND*40** generates a random number between 0 and 40. If you want the random numbers to start at a different point than 0, add the starting point of the range to the number generated by @RAND. For example, if you want to generate integers between -20 and 20, the formula is: **@ROUND(@RAND*40,0)-20**. In this formula, the @RAND function generates a number that is multiplied by 40 to have the range spread over 40 integers. After this, the number is rounded to 0 decimal places to convert the number into an integer. Finally, this number has 20 subtracted from it to make the numbers start at -20 and extend to 20. An example of using @RAND to generate random alphabetic letters is demonstrated with the @CHAR function in an earlier section.

MATHEMATICAL FUNCTIONS: TRIGONOMETRIC

Trigonometric functions involve the relationships of the sides and angles of triangles. They provide information about a part of a triangle if you provide information about another part of the triangle.

Quattro Pro has nine trigonometric functions. The first two convert degrees to radians and radians to degrees. The next three are the basic functions for sine, cosine, and tangent. The last four are inverse functions. This means that these functions accept an appropriate ratio as an argument and return an angle rather than accepting an angle and returning a ratio. Each of these trigonometric functions is based on ratios that measure angles and are useful in applications that involve calculations with angles. The secant, cosecant, and cotangent are computed by using the basic trigonometric functions. Although you can use tables to determine the values for the trigonometric functions for various angles, Quattro Pro automatically calculates these ratios for you.

The trigonometric angle ratios can be understood by inscribing an angle in one of the four quadrants of a circle as shown in Figure 6.66. The angle in this circle that is the focus of trigonometric function examples is angle YXZ (an angle is described by listing the letters representing the points on the two lines that create the angle; the center letter is the pivot point for the two lines that form the angle). Angle YXZ is created by the rotation of the line XY to point Z on the circle's circumference.

By dropping a perpendicular line from the horizontal axis to Z, you create a right triangle, since the angle created by the line to the horizontal axis is 90°. This triangle has several key measurements used in trigonometric calculations. The hypotenuse is the distance from Z to X and is labeled r. This is the longest side of the triangle. The distance from Z to the vertical axis is b and is the same whether it is measured from Z to the vertical line or from X to the point where the dropped line meets the horizontal axis. The distance from the horizontal axis to Z is a. By comparing these three sides to one another, you create ratios that depend on the size of the triangle's angles. These ratios remain the same as the triangle is enlarged or contracted as long as the triangle's angles remain the same.

In any right triangle, if you know the length of any two sides, you can determine the length of the third side using the Pythagorean theorem. The Pythagorean theorem is $a^2 + b^2 = r^2$ (letters as in the triangle in Figure 6.66).

Angles are normally measured in one of two ways. An angle measured in degrees uses a circle divided up into 360°. In advanced mathematical calculations,

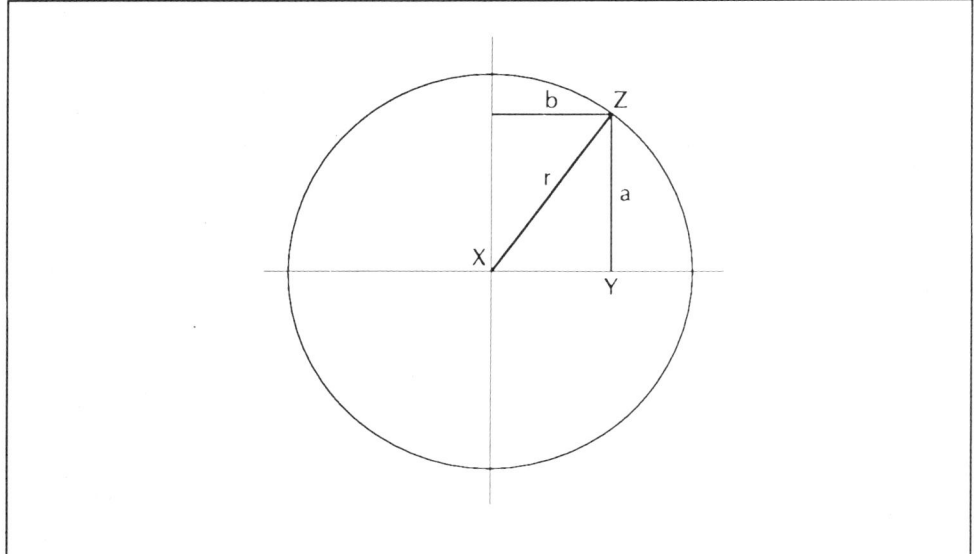

Figure 6.66 Triangle Illustrating Trigonometric Functions

the radian is used frequently as the unit of measure. One revolution around the circle is approximately two radians. A revolution through one quadrant of the circle is approximately 0.5 radians. One radian equals approximately 57.296°. For both methods of measuring angles, a positive angle is one that is measured counterclockwise starting from the positive X axis. A negative angle is measured clockwise from the positive X axis.

@DEGREES

The @DEGREES function converts radians to degrees. The format of the @DEGREES function is @DEGREES(x), where *x* is a number, formula, or cell reference to a value that equals an angle's radians. Since Quattro Pro uses radians in its trigonometric functions, this function converts the output of other trigonometric functions into degrees. Quattro Pro converts radians to degrees by multiplying the radians by 180/@PI.

The following are some examples using the @DEGREES function:

@DEGREES(0.5) = 28.64789
@DEGREES(1.0471975) = 60
@DEGREES(1) = 57.29578
@DEGREES(2) = 114.5916
@DEGREES(0.456456) = 26.153

@RADIANS

The @RADIANS function converts degrees to radians. The format of this function is @RADIANS(x), where *x* is a number, formula, or cell reference to a value that equals an angle's degrees. Since Quattro Pro uses radians in its trigonometric functions, this function converts angles measured in degrees to radians that are directly usable in the trigonometric functions. Quattro Pro computes radians by multiplying the degrees by @PI/180.

The following are some examples using the @RADIANS function:

@RADIANS(30) = 0.523599
@RADIANS(45) = 0.785398
@RADIANS(60) = 1.047198
@RADIANS(90) = 1.570796
@RADIANS(135) = 2.356194
@RADIANS(180) = 3.141593
@RADIANS(270) = 4.712389
@RADIANS(-30) = -0.523599

@SIN

The @SIN function returns the sine of an angle. The sine is the ratio of the side opposite the angle of which you are trying to compute the hypotenuse. For example, in Figure 6.66 the sine of YXZ is a/r. The format of this function is @SIN(x), where x is an angle, measured in radians. The radians can be entered directly, as a formula, or referenced by a spreadsheet cell.

The @SIN function can be illustrated by using Figure 6.66 and a few assumptions. The first assumption is that the triangle XYZ is a property on which you are constructing a building for lease. A potential lessee wants to know how much storefront is available if he leases the side r. Another assumption is that angle YXZ is 60°. The last assumption is that side a is 2,000 feet. To compute the length of r, you must first convert the degree measurement into radians by using the @RADIANS function. From earlier examples, 60° is 1.047198 radians. Then you must compute the sine of the angle (0.866025). Since the sine of the angle must equal a/r, r must equal a/(sine(YXZ)). Therefore, you divide 2,000 by 0.866025, which equals 2,309.4022. Combining all of these steps into one formula looks like this: **2000/@SIN(@RADIANS(60))**, which returns 2309.4022. Putting this formula into a Quattro cell quickly computes the result.

@COS

@COS returns the cosine of a given angle. The cosine is the ratio of the adjacent side of the angle of which you are trying to compute the hypotenuse. For example, in the triangle in Figure 6.66, the cosine of the angle XZY is a/r. The format is @COS(x), where x is the angle, measured in radians. The value for x can be entered directly in the function, as a formula, or as a reference to a spreadsheet cell.

Using the same assumptions described in the @SIN function, suppose you have another potential lessee who is interested in the smallest store-front area (side b). To compute the length of b, you must first convert the degree measurement into radians using the @RADIANS function. As in the earlier example, 60° is 1.047198 radians. Then you must compute the cosine of the angle, which is 0.5 in this example. Since the cosine of the angle must equal b/r, b must equal r*cosine(YXZ). Therefore, you multiply 2309.4022 by 0.5, which returns 1154.7011. Combining all these steps into one formula looks like this: **2309.4022*@COS(@RADIANS(60))**.

@TAN

@TAN determines the tangent of an angle. The tangent is the ratio of the side opposite the angle you are measuring to the side adjacent to the angle you are measuring. The tangent is equal to the sine divided by the cosine. The format is @TAN(x), where x is measured in radians. The value for x can be entered directly, as a formula, or referenced by a spreadsheet cell.

Using the same assumptions described in the @SIN function, the @TAN function can calculate the length of b in the Figure 6.66 triangle, also used in the @SIN and @COS examples. First, you must convert angle YXZ's 60° into radians with the @RADIANS function which returns 1.047198. Second, you must compute the tangent of this angle, which is 1.732051 in this example. Since the tangent of the angle must equal a/b, b must equal tangent(YXZ)/a. Therefore, you divide 2,000 by 1.732051, which equals 1154.701. Combining all these steps into one formula produces this entry: **2000/@TAN(@RADIANS(60))**. Putting this formula into a Quattro cell computes the same value that this illustration has provided in a step-by-step approach.

@ASIN

@ASIN returns the angle that has a sine of the specified ratio. This function returns the arc sine for a ratio. The format is @ASIN(x), where *x* is the sine of an angle and is either a number, a formula, or a cell reference that must be between -1 and 1. The sine of an angle is always in this range since the absolute value of the ratio of the side opposite the angle to the hypotenuse is always less than or equal to one. The result is the angle measured in radians.

All examples for the inverse trigonometric functions use different assumptions than used for @SIN, @COS, and @TAN. However, the examples of inverse trigonometric functions can use the same triangle (Figure 6.66). The inverse functions use the following assumptions. Side a represents a 40-foot telephone pole. Side b represents 26 feet on the ground. Side r represents a 47.7-foot guy wire holding the pole upright. The angle between the pole and the ground is 90, but the sizes of the other two angles are not known. You can calculate the angles by knowing the distances of each side of the triangle and by using the inverse trigonometric functions.

To use the @ASIN function to determine the angle YXZ, you must compute the ratio of the side opposite to the hypotenuse. In this example, it is 40/47.7 or 0.851064. Using this number as the input for the @ASIN function, the function returns 1.018008 radians. To convert this number to degrees, use the @DEGREES function on the output from the @ASIN function. Combining all the steps produces a formula like this: **@DEGREES(@ASIN(40/47.7))**. This function returns approximately 57 as the angle YXZ.

@ACOS

@ACOS returns the angle that has a cosine of the specified ratio. This function returns the arc cosine for a ratio. The format is @ACOS(x), where *x* is the cosine of an angle and is either a number, a formula, or a cell reference that must be between -1 and 1. The cosine of an angle is always in this range since the absolute value of the ratio of the side opposite the angle to the hypotenuse is always less than or equal to one. The result is the angle measured in radians.

Using the assumptions described in the @ASIN function, you can confirm the result. To use the @ACOS function to determine the angle YXZ, you must compute the ratio of the opposite side to the hypotenuse. In this example, it is 40/47.7 or 0.851064. Using this number as the input for the @ACOS function, the function returns 0.552788 radians. To convert this number to degrees, use the @DEGREES function on the output from the @ACOS function. Combining all the steps produces a formula like this: **@DEGREES(@ACOS(40/47.7))**. This function returns approximately 33° as the angle YXZ. Since the angle opposite the hypotenuse is 90°, 90 plus 33 is 123, and 180 minus 123 equals 57 as the third angle, which confirms the results of the @ASIN function.

@ATAN

@ATAN returns the arc tangent of a ratio. The arc tangent of a ratio is the angle that has a tangent of the specified ratio. The format is @ATAN(x), where x is the tangent of an angle and is either a number, a formula, or a cell reference. The result is an angle between 90° and -90°. All angles between 90° and 180° produce an @ATAN result between 0 and -90. All angles between 180 and 270 produce a result between 90° and 0°.

To illustrate @ATAN, use the assumptions described in the @ASIN function, with one exception. Since most wires stretch and sag to accommodate external pressures on the pole, assume that you do not know the distance between points Z and Y and cannot use the @ACOS or @ASIN function to determine the angle YXZ. To use the @ATAN function to determine the angle YXZ, you must compute the ratio of the opposite side to the adjacent side. In this example, it is 40/26 or 1.538462. Using this number as the input for the @ATAN function, the function returns 1.538462 radians. To convert this number to degrees, use the @DEGREES function on the output from the @ATAN function. Combining all these steps produces a formula like this: **@DEGREES(@ATAN(40/26))**. This function returns approximately 57° as the angle YXZ. Since you are certain that the two sides are correct, using the @ATAN function removes any problems caused by a loose wire.

@ATAN2

@ATAN2 is similar to @ATAN since it calculates an arc tangent, but @ATAN2 differentiates between angles larger than 90°. All angles start from the positive x axis (see Figure 6.67); negative angles are measured clockwise, and positive angles are measured counterclockwise.

The format for @ATAN2 is @ATAN2(x,y) where x is the x coordinate of the angle and y is the y coordinate of the angle. If x and/or y is negative, the negative sign must be entered, since a missing sign changes the result by 90° or 180°. Both x and y can be entered either directly in the function, as a formula, or indirectly by reference to a cell in the spreadsheet.

Figure 6.67 shows an x,y coordinate system that has several points marked in

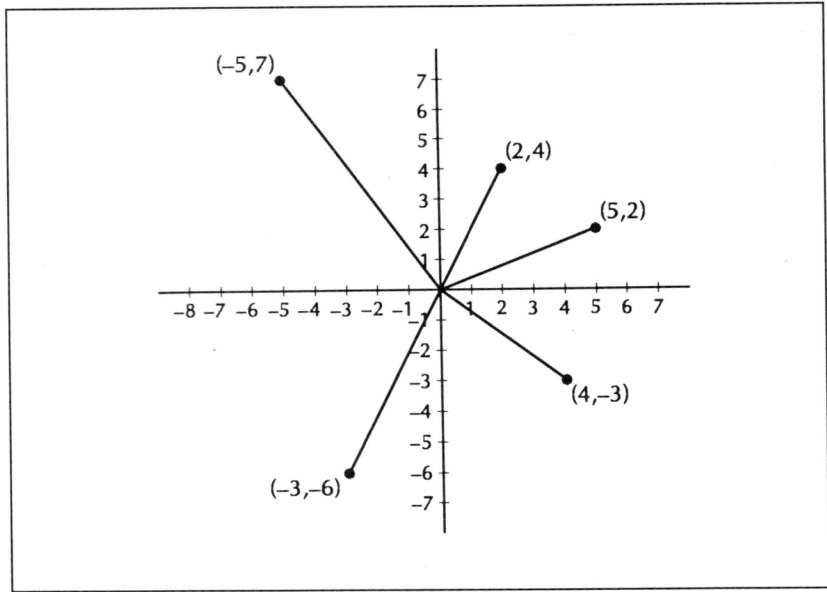

Figure 6.67 Inscribed Points

the different quadrants. For each point, a line is drawn to the origin of the x,y coordinate system. To determine the angle of each line, the @ATAN2 uses the x and y coordinates of each point. The following functions compute the angle for each point:

@ATAN2(5,2) = 0.380506 = approximately 38°
@ATAN2(2,4) = 1.107149 = approximately 63.4°
@ATAN2(-5,7) = 2.191046 = approximately 125.5°
@ATAN2(-3,-6) = -2.03444 = approximately -153.4°
@ATAN2(4,-3) = -0.643501 = approximately -36.9°

MATHEMATICAL FUNCTIONS: LOGARITHMIC

The logarithmic functions are useful in problems involving compound growth, such as populations studies, and computations in which very large numbers are multiplied and divided by very small numbers, as in scientific or engineering applications and in chemistry problems. A logarithm is defined as the power to which a number, called the base, must be raised to result in a specified number. The mathematical expression for a logarithm is $\log_b y = x$, which is read "the logarithm of y to the base b is x." This formula is expressed as $b^x = y$, which is read "b raised to the power of x is y." This formula expresses the same relationship as an exponential relationship.

The base b is any number greater than zero with the exception of the number one. The most widely used bases are base 10 and base e. The number represented by e is a real number approximated by 2.7182818285. When a base 10 is used, the logarithm is called a common logarithm or base 10 logarithm. When a base is not specified (for example, log 100 = 2), then the base is assumed to be 10. If a base of e is used, the logarithm is called a natural logarithm.

@LOG

The @LOG function determines the base 10 log of a number. The format for this function is @LOG(x), where *x* is a positive number that is a number, formula, or cell reference to either. An invalid function argument returns @ERR. To change a logarithm value to a decimal value, raise 10 to the power of the logarithm.

Logarithms can perform calculations on very large numbers and very small numbers without exceeding the computer's storage capacity for large numbers. Use of the @LOG function in Einstein's $E = mc^2$ equation illustrates this advantage. Figure 6.68 shows the computations necessary to compute the value of the energy in one atom of hydrogen. Column C shows the calculation using actual values, column D shows the calculation using logarithms, and column E shows the formulas in column D. In cell D4, the logarithm of the speed of light squared is

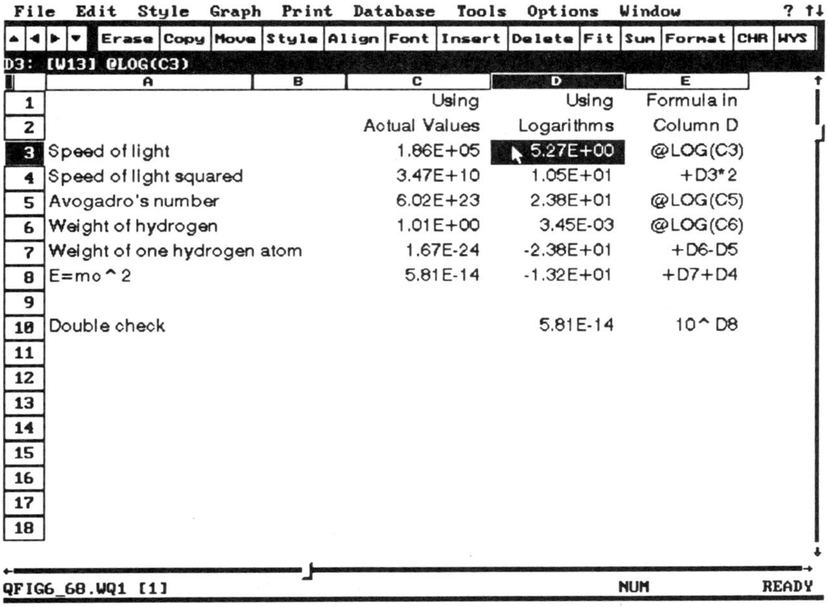
File Edit Style Graph Print Database Tools Options Window ?
Erase Copy Move Style Align Font Insert Delete Fit Sum Format CHR WYS
D3: [W13] @LOG(C3)
A B C D E
1 Using Using Formula in
2 Actual Values Logarithms Column D
3 Speed of light 1.86E+05 5.27E+00 @LOG(C3)
4 Speed of light squared 3.47E+10 1.05E+01 +D3*2
5 Avogadro's number 6.02E+23 2.38E+01 @LOG(C5)
6 Weight of hydrogen 1.01E+00 3.45E-03 @LOG(C6)
7 Weight of one hydrogen atom 1.67E-24 -2.38E+01 +D6-D5
8 E=mc^2 5.81E-14 -1.32E+01 +D7+D4
9
10 Double check 5.81E-14 10^D8
11
12
13
14
15
16
17
18
QFIG6_68.WQ1 [1] NUM READY

Figure 6.68 @LOG Used to Compute the Energy in a Hydrogen Atom

calculated by multiplying the logarithm of the speed of light by two. Multiplying a logarithm by a number is equivalent to raising the actual number of the logarithm to the power of the number. The weight of a single hydrogen atom is determined by dividing the weight of a mole in row 6 by the number of atoms in a mole (Avogadro's number) in row 5. To divide values using their logarithms, you subtract their logarithms as done in D7. D8 multiplies the values of the weight of one hydrogen atom by the speed of light squared by adding their logarithms together. The final result in D8 is the value of the energy in one hydrogen atom. In D10, D8 is raised to the power of 10 to confirm that the value obtained by using logarithms is the same as if actual numbers had been used. Since most of these numbers are too wide to fit into the columns with the regular default setting, the default display format setting is changed to Scientific.

@EXP

The result of the @EXP function is the value e, approximated by 2.718281828, raised to a specified power. The format is @EXP(x), where x is the power to which e is raised. The value can be a number, a formula, or a cell reference to either. To generate the value of e, use the formula, @EXP(1). To convert a natural logarithm to its actual value, use the natural logarithm as this function's argument.

The @EXP function can be used to compute continuous compounding. Continuous compounding is often used for savings accounts and other investment opportunities. For example, if you are putting $50,000 into savings at an 11% continuous compounding rate for the next 10 years, use the @EXP function in a formula to compute the value of your investment at the end of the investment's term. To compute the value of your investment at the end of 10 years, use this formula: +50000*@EXP(.11*10). Putting this formula into a Quattro cell computes the value of this investment at the end of 10 years as 150208.3.

@LN

The natural logarithm is written as either $\log_e y = x$ or $\ln y = x$. The format for the natural log function is @LN(x), where x is the number for which you want to determine the natural log (x must be a value greater than zero). If x is an invalid value, the function returns @ERR. The x can be a number, a formula, or a cell reference.

Natural logarithms can be used to perform calculations on very large and very small numbers without exceeding the computer's storage capacity for large numbers, just as can base 10 logarithms. This example uses the same information provided in the @LOG example. Figure 6.69 shows the computations necessary to compute the amount of energy in one atom of hydrogen by using the natural logarithm. The calculations are identical to the calculations used in the @LOG example. The only difference is the method used for double checking the computation by comparing it with the actual values. In the @LOG example, 10 was

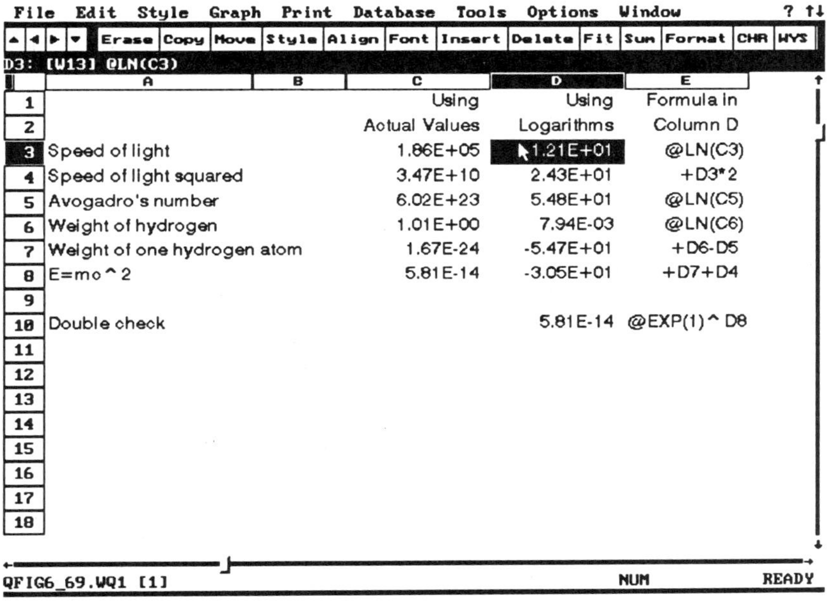

```
File  Edit  Style  Graph  Print  Database  Tools  Options  Window        ? ↑↓
   Erase Copy Move Style Align Font Insert Delete Fit Sum Format CHR WYS
D3: [W13] @LN(C3)
         A              B         C          D          E
  1                               Using     Using     Formula in
  2                           Actual Values Logarithms Column D
  3  Speed of light                1.86E+05  1.21E+01  @LN(C3)
  4  Speed of light squared        3.47E+10  2.43E+01  +D3*2
  5  Avogadro's number             6.02E+23  5.48E+01  @LN(C5)
  6  Weight of hydrogen            1.01E+00  7.94E-03  @LN(C6)
  7  Weight of one hydrogen atom   1.67E-24 -5.47E+01  +D6-D5
  8  E=mc^2                        5.81E-14 -3.05E+01  +D7+D4
  9
 10  Double check                            5.81E-14  @EXP(1)^D8
 11
 ...
QFIG6_69.WQ1 [1]                             NUM        READY
```

Figure 6.69 @LN Used to Compute the Energy in a Hydrogen Atom

raised to the logarithm result. In this example, e, computed as @EXP(1), is raised to the power of the result in D8. The two logarithms are different due to the different base used.

CELL AND TABLE FUNCTIONS

Quattro Pro's cell and table functions provide advanced features, such as looking up values in tables and returning information about the attributes of a block in your spreadsheet. Quattro Pro has three functions that provide you with specific attributes for the current or a specified cell. Two functions tell you the number of rows and columns in a block to describe the block's size. These cell and table functions are used in macros to add decision-making features. These functions also increase the logic features of your models by letting current values determine the next calculation or value used.

@@

The @@ function returns the value of a cell referenced by the function's argument. The @@ function uses indirect addressing, since the @@ function assumes that the argument is a cell address containing another cell address whose value the @@ function returns. If the function's argument is enclosed in quotes, this function returns the value of the cell referenced in the quotes. The format of the @@ function is @@(cell). The *cell* is either a cell name, a cell name enclosed in quotes, a block name, or a formula that produces a cell address. Examples of the four types of entries are: cell name, A1; cell name in quotes, "A1"; block name, "START" (where start is a predefined block beginning at cell A1); and a formula that produces a cell address is "A"&"1".

This function is normally used as an argument for other functions. Figure 6.70 shows an example of the @@ function that helps in determining the budget for labor cost. Since the labor cost varies for each type of job and each shift, a table is created to list the hourly cost for each job and shift. By using the @@ function in column C, this spreadsheet is created so that you only have to type in the number of hours for each department that you expect to use and the shift that you are making this budget for. The @@ function in column C takes the shift number and converts it to A, B, or C to correspond to the three different shifts by adding 64 to the shift number so that it generates an ASCII code number equal to A, B, or C. The ASCII code is transformed into a letter and appended after an A. Next, the row number is added to the cell reference. Since this cell reference is a string rather than directly entered, the @@ function takes the value of the cell for which you have created a cell reference. Once you have the value, you can multiply it by the number of hours in column B. Using the table and the formulas reduces the number of characters to type and so helps prevent mistakes.

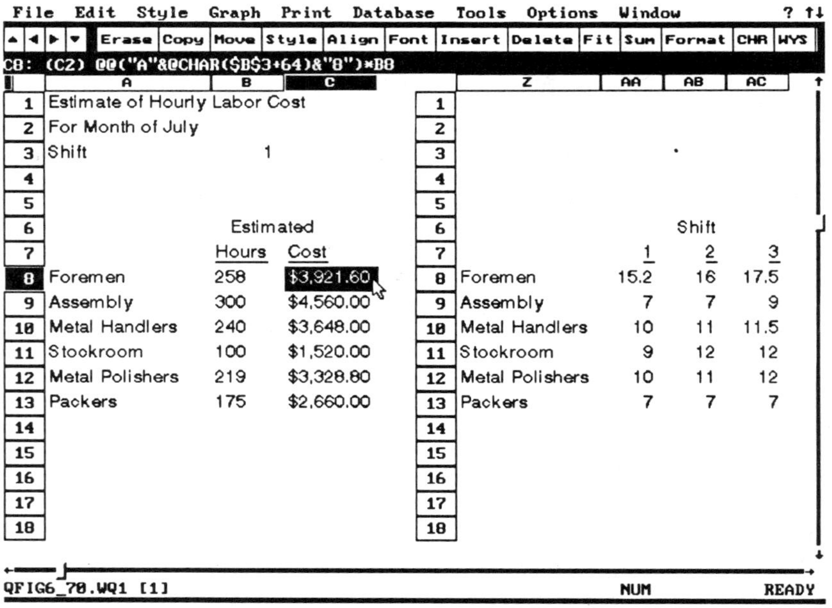

Figure 6.70 @@ Used to Reference a Table

@CELL

The @CELL function returns the requested attribute of the upper-left cell of a block. The format of the @CELL function is @CELL(attribute,block). The *attribute* can be any of a number of words discussed in the next section. The attribute must be enclosed in quotes or be a cell reference to a cell that contains a label with one of the attribute words. The *block* is a specified block of the spreadsheet. For all attributes except rwidth, @CELL uses only the upper-left cell in the block. If you enter a single address, Quattro converts it to a block address. The @CELL function is often used in macros to check a cell's attributes or to store an attribute to be used later in the macro. The possible attributes that may be checked are as follows:

- address—returns the absolute cell address with dollar signs preceding the row and column
- row—returns the row number
- col—returns the column number, which may range from 1 to 256 for the columns A through IV
- contents—returns the cell's contents
- type—returns a b for a blank cell, a v for a cell that contains a value, or a l for a cell that contains a label
- prefix—returns the label prefix: returns an apostrophe (') for a left-aligned label, a double quote (") for a right-aligned label, a caret (^) for a centered label, a backslash (\) for a repeating label, an empty string for a number or formula, or blank cell
- protect—returns 1 if protected and 0 if not
- width—returns the column width
- rwidth—returns the width of the sum of all the columns in the block
- format—returns letters or numbers to represent the numeric format; the following symbols returned indicating the different formats:

    Fn—Fixed with n representing the number of decimal places

    Sn—Scientific with n representing the number of decimal places

    Cn—Currency with n representing the number of decimal places

    ,n—Financial (,) with n representing the number of decimal places

    +—+/- for bar graph format

    G—General such as for unformatted cells, cells that have had their format reset, and labels

    Pn—Percent with n representing the number of decimal places

    Dn—Date or time; the number representing the format of the date or time:

    1   DD-MMM-YY
    2   DD-MMM
    3   MMM-YY
    4   MM/DD/YY,DD/MM/YY, DD.MM.YY or YY-MM-DD (long international)

324   *Quattro Pro 4.0 Handbook*

5   MM/DD, DD/MM, DD.MM or MM-DD (short international)
6   HH:MM:SS AM/PM
7   HH:MM AM/PM
8   HH:MM:SS 24hr, HH.MM.SS 24hr, HH,MM,SS 24hr, or HHhMMmSSs (long international)
9   HH:MM 24hr, HH.MM 24hr, HH,MM 24hr, or HHhMMm (short international)

T—Text which displays a cell's formula rather than the formula's result

H—Hidden, which prevents cell values from appearing on the spreadsheet

Figure 6.71 provides an example of the @CELL function used to check the format of the cells in column E. The attribute checked is in cell H2; therefore, the cell reference in the formula is absolute. In each function, the cell reference to the single cell is described as if it were a block. To change the attribute you are determining, type the new attribute in cell H2. If you want to change the cells that the function uses, you must modify the formula.

@CELLPOINTER

The @CELLPOINTER function returns a specified attribute of the current cell. The current cell is the cell that the selector is on. Quattro only updates this function when you press F9 (CALC) or edit a cell.

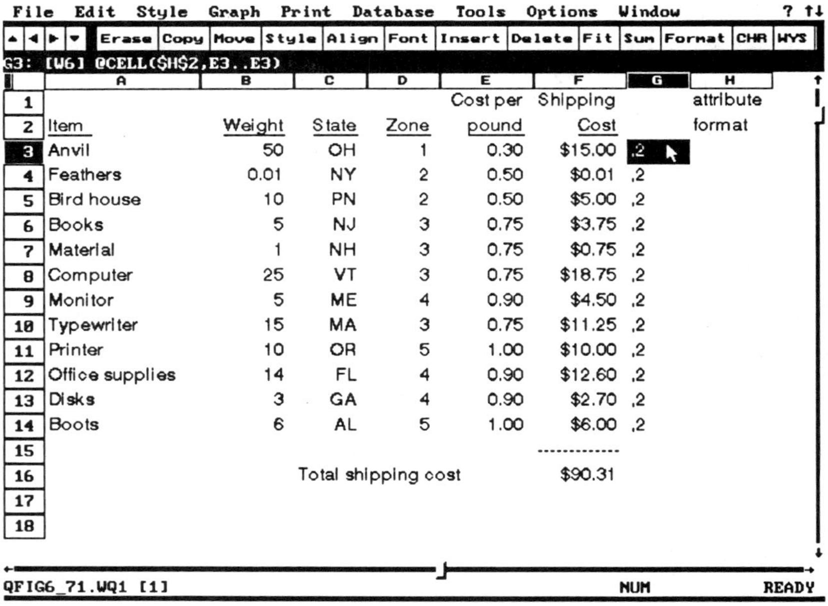

	A	B	C	D	E	F	G	H
1					Cost per	Shipping		attribute
2	Item	Weight	State	Zone	pound	Cost		format
3	Anvil	50	OH	1	0.30	$15.00	,2	
4	Feathers	0.01	NY	2	0.50	$0.01	,2	
5	Bird house	10	PN	2	0.50	$5.00	,2	
6	Books	5	NJ	3	0.75	$3.75	,2	
7	Material	1	NH	3	0.75	$0.75	,2	
8	Computer	25	VT	3	0.75	$18.75	,2	
9	Monitor	5	ME	4	0.90	$4.50	,2	
10	Typewriter	15	MA	3	0.75	$11.25	,2	
11	Printer	10	OR	5	1.00	$10.00	,2	
12	Office supplies	14	FL	4	0.90	$12.60	,2	
13	Disks	3	GA	4	0.90	$2.70	,2	
14	Boots	6	AL	5	1.00	$6.00	,2	
15						-------		
16			Total shipping cost			$90.31		

G3: [W6] @CELL(H2,E3..E3)

Figure 6.71 @CELL Used to Check That the Cost per Pound is Formatted Consistently

The format is @CELLPOINTER(attribute), where *attribute* is one of the words described for the @CELL function. The attribute must be enclosed in quotes unless it is placed in a cell.

Figure 6.72 shows an example of the @CELLPOINTER function in column H. For each cell in column H, the function uses the attribute in column G to determine the value of the function. In the previous section, the codes used for the attributes were explained. Every time you edit any cell or press F9 (CALC), Quattro recalculates the value of @CELLPOINTER functions.

@CELLINDEX

The @CELLINDEX function returns a specified attribute of a cell in a block as specified by the row and column number provided. This function differs from @CELL since @CELLINDEX lets you choose the cell in the block that you wish to examine.

The format is @CELLINDEX(attribute,block,column,row). The *attribute* is one of the words described for the @CELL function. The attribute must be enclosed in quotes unless it is a cell reference to a cell containing the attribute as a label. The *block* is a specified block of the spreadsheet. The *column* is the column number of the block that you want the value from (Quattro starts counting columns with 0 so that column 1 is the second column), and the *row* is the row number that you want

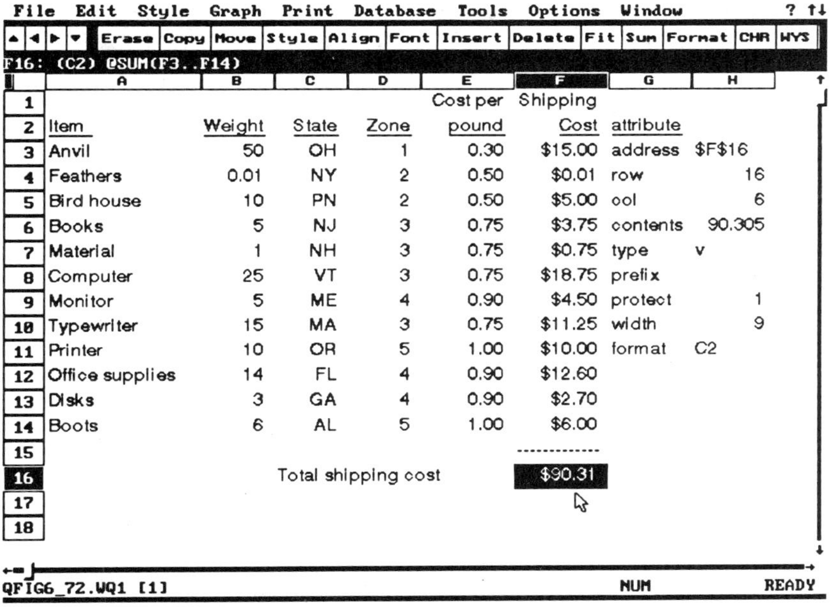

	A	B	C	D	E	F	G	H
1					Cost per	Shipping		
2	Item	Weight	State	Zone	pound	Cost	attribute	
3	Anvil	50	OH	1	0.30	$15.00	address	F16
4	Feathers	0.01	NY	2	0.50	$0.01	row	16
5	Bird house	10	PN	2	0.50	$5.00	col	6
6	Books	5	NJ	3	0.75	$3.75	contents	90.305
7	Material	1	NH	3	0.75	$0.75	type	v
8	Computer	25	VT	3	0.75	$18.75	prefix	
9	Monitor	5	ME	4	0.90	$4.50	protect	1
10	Typewriter	15	MA	3	0.75	$11.25	width	9
11	Printer	10	OR	5	1.00	$10.00	format	C2
12	Office supplies	14	FL	4	0.90	$12.60		
13	Disks	3	GA	4	0.90	$2.70		
14	Boots	6	AL	5	1.00	$6.00		
15						-------------		
16			Total shipping cost			$90.31		
17								
18								

Figure 6.72 @CELLPOINTER Used to Describe the Current Cell's Attributes

to use to determine the cell's attribute. Like the columns, the rows are numbered beginning with 0. The @CELLINDEX function uses the cell at the intersection of the row and column of the table. The column and row argument is a number, formula, or cell reference to either. If the row or column number is not a whole number, the decimal value is truncated. If the row or column number exceed the block's limits, the function returns ERR. If the row or column is a string or blank, the row or column number is treated as 0.

In Figure 6.73, the @CELLINDEX function checks the various sections of the spreadsheet to make sure that they are in proper format. This check might be appropriate before you print the spreadsheet. The function in column G determines the attributes of the table a column at a time. The attribute checked is the one displayed in H1. The column to be checked is determined in H2. The row to be checked is the same one as the @CELLINDEX function. The @CELL function determines the row of the block to use. To change the row number of the item in the spreadsheet to the row number of the block, subtract four. Subtracting four subtracts three for the first three lines of the spreadsheet that are not included in the block and one more since the @CELLINDEX function starts counting rows of the block with 0.

Several of the function arguments are expressed with their absolute address so that they maintain the correct references when copied in column G. These absolute references include the location of the block, the cell reference for the column

```
File  Edit  Style  Graph  Print  Database  Tools  Options  Window         ? ↑↓
|▲|◄|►|▼| Erase Copy Move Style Align Font Insert Delete Fit Sum Format CHR WYS |
G4:  [W9]  @CELLINDEX($H$2,$A$4..$F$15,$H$3,@CELL("row",H4..H4)-4)
```

	A	B	C	D	E	F	G	H
1								
2					Cost per	Shipping		format
3	Item	Weight	State	Zone	pound	Cost		4
4	Anvil	50	OH	1	0.30	$15.00	,2	
5	Feathers	0.01	NY	2	0.50	$0.01	,2	
6	Bird house	10	PN	2	0.50	$5.00	,2	
7	Books	5	NJ	3	0.75	$3.75	,2	
8	Material	1	NH	3	0.75	$0.75	,2	
9	Computer	25	VT	3	0.75	$18.75	,2	
10	Monitor	5	ME	4	0.90	$4.50	,2	
11	Typewriter	15	MA	3	0.75	$11.25	,2	
12	Printer	10	OR	5	1.00	$10.00	,2	
13	Office supplies	14	FL	4	0.90	$12.60	,2	
14	Disks	3	GA	4	0.90	$2.70	,2	
15	Boots	6	AL	5	1.00	$6.00	,2	
16						------------		
17				Total shipping cost		$90.31		
18								

```
QFIG6_73.WQ1 [1]                                           NUM        READY
```

Figure 6.73 @CELLINDEX Used to Check That the Cost per Pound Column is Formatted Correctly

number, and the cell reference containing the attribute that the function determines.

You can combine the @CELLINDEX function with the @IF function to confirm that the @CELLINDEX has returned the proper results. For example, in this example you can compare the results with a string containing a comma and a 2 to detect if any of the cells in column E are not in the Currency format with two decimal places. When you use @CELLINDEX to test a table for attributes, you should check the attribute contents first, which allows you to confirm that the function is checking the proper cell for the specified attribute. This function is also used with the map view created with the /Window Options Map View command to find data entry errors.

Using Quattro Pro's Table Features

Quattro Pro provides several useful functions for working with tables. A table is a block of information that contains information that you can access with Quattro Pro's table functions. You can retrieve information from a table based on one or more criteria. To use one of the table retrieval functions, you must have a table on a spreadsheet. A table is a block created by using columns and rows in the same way that you create a table on paper. You can create a vertical or horizontal table. The appearance of the table does not necessarily determine if the table is a horizontal or vertical table. The difference in the two types of tables is the function used to access the table entries. When the table is constructed vertically, the @VLOOKUP function searches the first column of entries in the table. With the @HLOOKUP function, the table is expected to have horizontal entries with the search conducted against the entries in the top row of the table. With Quattro Pro, you can use tables in other spreadsheets by including the file name in square braces.

@VLOOKUP

The @VLOOKUP function returns a value in a table within your spreadsheet based on the function arguments. @VLOOKUP can look up both strings and numbers.

The format of the function is @VLOOKUP(x,block,column). The x is the value that the command looks for in the first column of the block. With numbers, the @VLOOKUP command stops when it reaches an equal or higher value than the value of the function argument. Because the search is for the highest value that is not greater than the value you are searching for, the numbers in the @VLOOKUP table must be in ascending sequence. In a table with label entries, the sequence of the entries is not important since this function searches for an exact match. This x is a number, a string in quotes, a formula, or a cell reference to a number or string. The *block* is the area of a spreadsheet that contains the table. This area must include the index column (the column that contains the values the function will look for), the columns that contain the values to be returned, and all columns in between. The block is specified as a block address or a block name. The *column* is the number of columns to the right of the index column that the @VLOOKUP function uses to obtain the return values. The column number must be greater than or equal to 0. If the column number is zero, the function returns the value from the index column.

When the entry you are searching for is a value, Quattro returns the value determined by searching the index column for the largest value not greater than the search value. If the column number is negative or refers to a column that is beyond the block's limits, the function returns ERR. If the function is looking for a string and does not find it, the function returns ERR.

The @VLOOKUP function can determine shipping costs when the shipping rates are determined by a zone code assigned by state. Figure 6.74 shows the @VLOOKUP function in column D. The @VLOOKUP function determines the proper zone for each state by looking for the state in column AA. Since the last function argument is 1, the function takes the value in the cell one column to the right of the index column in the row where the state code is located. If the function does not find a match for the state, it returns ERR. This error message alerts you that your list of states and their appropriate zones is incomplete.

@HLOOKUP

The @HLOOKUP function returns a value in a table within your spreadsheet based on two function arguments. @HLOOKUP can look up both strings and

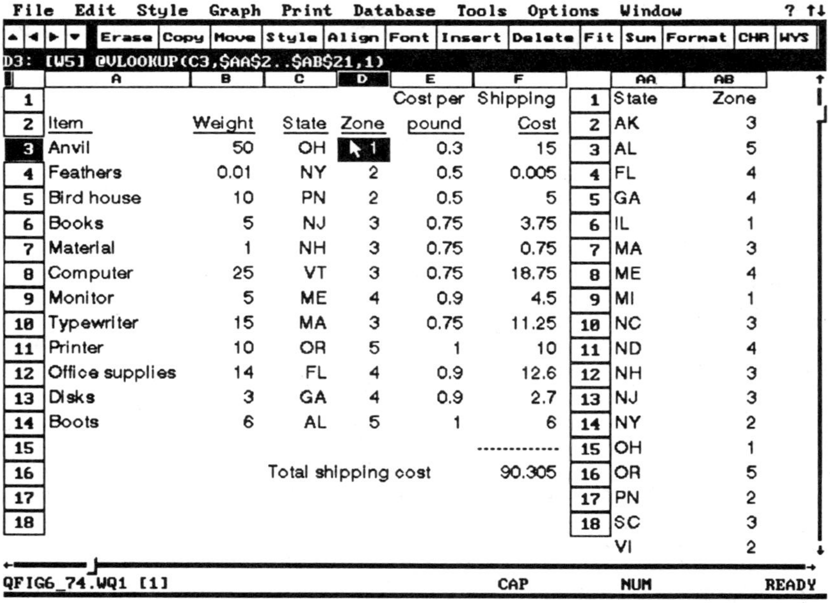

	A	B	C	D	E	F		AA	AB
1					Cost per	Shipping	1	State	Zone
2	Item	Weight	State	Zone	pound	Cost	2	AK	3
3	Anvil	50	OH	1	0.3	15	3	AL	5
4	Feathers	0.01	NY	2	0.5	0.005	4	FL	4
5	Bird house	10	PN	2	0.5	5	5	GA	4
6	Books	5	NJ	3	0.75	3.75	6	IL	1
7	Material	1	NH	3	0.75	0.75	7	MA	3
8	Computer	25	VT	3	0.75	18.75	8	ME	4
9	Monitor	5	ME	4	0.9	4.5	9	MI	1
10	Typewriter	15	MA	3	0.75	11.25	10	NC	3
11	Printer	10	OR	5	1	10	11	ND	4
12	Office supplies	14	FL	4	0.9	12.6	12	NH	3
13	Disks	3	GA	4	0.9	2.7	13	NJ	3
14	Boots	6	AL	5	1	6	14	NY	2
15						----------	15	OH	1
16			Total shipping cost			90.305	16	OR	5
17							17	PN	2
18							18	SC	3
								VI	2

Figure 6.74 @VLOOKUP Used to Determine the Zone for Each State

numbers. The difference between the @HLOOKUP and the @VLOOKUP functions is the entries that @HLOOKUP searches for are in the top row rather than in the left column in the table.

The format of the function is @HLOOKUP(x,block,row). The *x* is the value that @HLOOKUP searches for. It is a number, a string in quotes, or a cell reference to a number or string. When you use the @HLOOKUP function, the formula looks for the value of x in the table. It starts from the left corner of the table and looks for the value of x along the top row of the table, the index row. If x is a number, the search is conducted looking for the highest value that does not exceed x. If x is a string or a cell reference to a string, Quattro looks for an exact match between the value of x and the strings in the index row. The *block* is the area of your spreadsheet that contains the table. It must include the index row, the row that contains the values that the function will retrieve and all rows in between. The block is specified as either a block address or a block name. The *row* is the number of rows below the index row that @HLOOKUP gets the return value from. The column number must be greater than or equal to 0. If the column number is zero, the function returns the value from the index row.

If @HLOOKUP cannot find the value and it is a number, it returns the value associated with the largest entry that does not exceed the value you are searching for. When @HLOOKUP is searching for a number, the numbers must be in ascending sequence. If the value the function is looking for is a string and the function cannot find it, the function returns ERR. The function also returns ERR when column number is negative or refers to a row beyond the specified block of the function.

Figure 6.75 shows the @HLOOKUP function used to retrieve the proper cost per pound for each zone from the table shown at the bottom of the figure. The @HLOOKUP function looks for the Zone in the table's first row and then takes the number right below it, since the row number is 1. Using the @HLOOKUP table instead of typing the numbers in yourself reduces mistakes. Also, having the table with a different cost per pound for each zone makes it easier to change the cost per pound. Making a change in the table immediately reflects these new values in all the calculations.

@CHOOSE

The @CHOOSE function returns one argument from a list of choices, based on a specification of a choice number. The @CHOOSE function is different from the table lookup functions since the entries are all contained within the function rather than in an external table. Another difference between @CHOOSE and the table lookup functions is that the @CHOOSE function uses consecutive integers to determine the data that are used. The format of the function is @CHOOSE(number,list). The *number* is the number of the list entry that the function returns. It is a number, a formula, or a cell reference to a number or formula. If it is not a whole number, the value is truncated. If it exceeds the number of choices available or is a negative value, the function returns ERR. If the number is blank or a string, the @CHOOSE function assumes the value of 0 for number. The

330 Quattro Pro 4.0 Handbook

```
File  Edit  Style  Graph  Print  Database  Tools  Options  Window         ?  ↑↓
  ◄ ► ▼   Erase Copy Move Style Align Font Insert Delete Fit Sum Format CHR WYS
E3: [W9] @HLOOKUP(D3,$L$1..$P$2,1)
```

	A	B	C	D	E	F	G	H
1					Cost per	Shipping		
2	Item	Weight	State	Zone	pound	Cost		
3	Anvil	50	OH	1	0.3	15		
4	Feathers	0.01	NY	2	0.5	0.005		
5	Bird house	10	PN	2	0.5	5		
6	Books	5	NJ	3	0.75	3.75		
7	Material	1	NH	3	0.75	0.75		
8	Computer	25	VT	3	0.75	18.75		
9	Monitor	5	ME	4	0.9	4.5		
10	Typewriter	15	MA	3	0.75	11.25		
11	Printer	10	OR	5	1	10		
	Office supplies	14	FL	4	0.9	12.6		

	K	L	M	N	O	P	Q
1	Zone		1	2	3	4	5
2	Cost per pound		0.3	0.5	0.75	0.9	1
3							
4							
5							
6							

```
QFIG6_75.WQ1 [1]                              CAP        NUM        READY
```

Figure 6.75 @HLOOKUP Used to Determine the Cost per Pound for Each Zone

list represents the different choices that the @CHOOSE function has available. The first entry is choice 0. Thus, to select the second entry in the list, the number must be 1. While the number of choices are unlimited, the entire formula is limited to 240 characters. Each choice may be a number, string, formula, or cell reference. The different entries do not have to be the same type of entry. One entry can be a label, another a formula, and a third a number. To omit one of the choices, enter two double quotes in place of the entry you want to omit. For example, suppose A1 contains this function: **@CHOOSE(A3-1,B3*4,"","Marketing Strategy",16)**. Quattro first takes the value from A3 and subtracts one so that it is reduced by 1 to match the way @CHOOSE numbers its choices. If A3 equals one, A1 equals the value of B3 times four. If A3 equals two, A1 equals a blank cell. If A3 equals three, A1 equals "Marketing Strategy." If A3 equals four, A1 equals 16. If A3 equals five, A1 equals @ERR.

The @CHOOSE function can sometimes replace an @VLOOKUP or @HLOOKUP function. @CHOOSE is suitable for determining the cost per pound since there are a limited number of consecutive zone numbers. Figure 6.76 has the @CHOOSE function in column E for all of the items. Since all choices are integers ranging from one to five, the @CHOOSE function is a good alternative. For each item, the function takes the zone, subtracts one and uses the result to pick the correct cost per pound for shipping. This function is not optimal if there are many choices. A table is a clearer presentation of the different options and is easier to update than

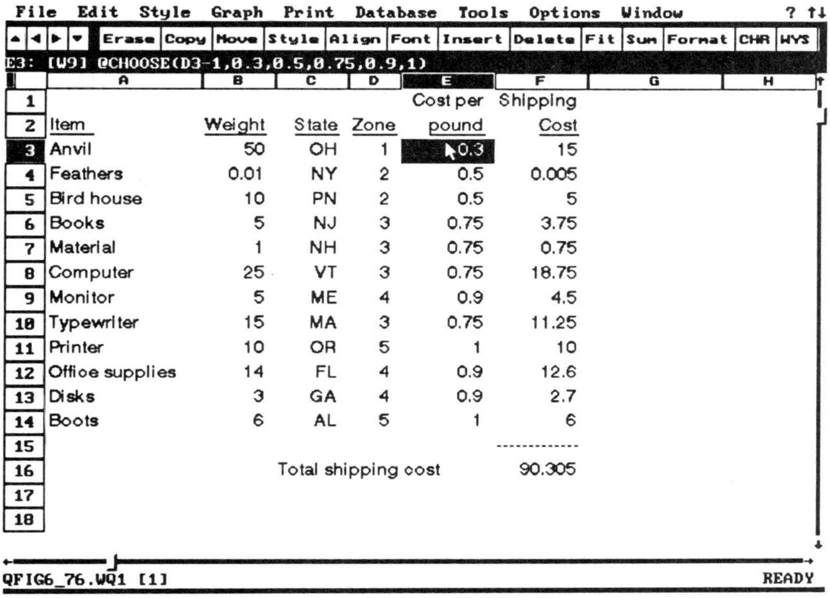

```
File  Edit  Style  Graph  Print  Database  Tools  Options  Window    ? ↑↓
   Erase Copy Move Style Align Font Insert Delete Fit Sum Format CHR WYS
E3:  [W9] @CHOOSE(D3-1,0.3,0.5,0.75,0.9,1)
        A           B        C      D        E         F          G        H
  1                                      Cost per  Shipping
  2  Item         Weight   State   Zone   pound     Cost
  3  Anvil          50      OH      1      0.3       15
  4  Feathers      0.01     NY      2      0.5      0.005
  5  Bird house     10      PN      2      0.5        5
  6  Books           5      NJ      3     0.75      3.75
  7  Material        1      NH      3     0.75      0.75
  8  Computer       25      VT      3     0.75     18.75
  9  Monitor         5      ME      4     0.9       4.5
 10  Typewriter     15      MA      3     0.75     11.25
 11  Printer        10      OR      5      1        10
 12  Office supplies 14     FL      4     0.9      12.6
 13  Disks           3      GA      4     0.9       2.7
 14  Boots           6      AL      5      1         6
 15                                              ----------
 16              Total shipping cost             90.305
 17
 18
QFIG6_76.WQ1 [1]                                          READY
```

Figure 6.76 @CHOOSE Used to Determine the Cost per Pound for Each Zone

the list in the @CHOOSE function. Also, @CHOOSE is limited to choices indicated by numeric entries and cannot work with strings as @VLOOKUP and @HLOOKUP can.

@INDEX

The @INDEX returns a value from a specified row and column in a table of information. @INDEX differs from @HLOOKUP and @VLOOKUP, since it does not search for a matching entry but selects information with a row and column designation.

The format is @INDEX(block,column,row). The *block* is the block address or block name for the location of the table. The *column* is the number of the column from the left column of the block that should be used for the return value, and the *row* is the number of rows away from the top row of the table from which you want the function to retrieve the value. Quattro starts counting the column and row numbers of a table from 0. For example, the top row is row 0 and the fourth row of the table is row 3.

The @INDEX function returns the value at the intersection of the row and column of the table. Each column and row argument is a number, a formula, or a cell reference to either. If the value is not a whole number, the value is truncated.

If the value refers to a column or row that is not included in the block or is a negative number, the function returns ERR. Strings or blank cells are treated as 0.

Many shipping companies provide different types of services for transporting packages. For each package, the cost per pound is determined by the distance the package has to travel and the type of service that you are paying for. The bottom of Figure 6.77 contains a table for the different zones and service types. At the top of the figure, the shipping costs for various packages are computed. The block of the function's argument includes the zone row and the service types columns. By including this row and column, you do not have to subtract one from the zone and service type to determine the proper row and column for the @INDEX function.

@ROWS

The @ROWS function determines the number of rows in a block. The format of the @ROWS function is @ROWS(block), where *block* is a block or block name that the function uses to count the number of rows.

The @ROWS command can number the items in a block better than the /Edit Fill command since one formula can handle the entire task. In Figure 6.78, the function @ROWS counts the number of rows between the absolute reference to B1 and the current row. Column A is not used for the computation since it creates a circular reference in the spreadsheet, which means the formula is referring to its own cell.

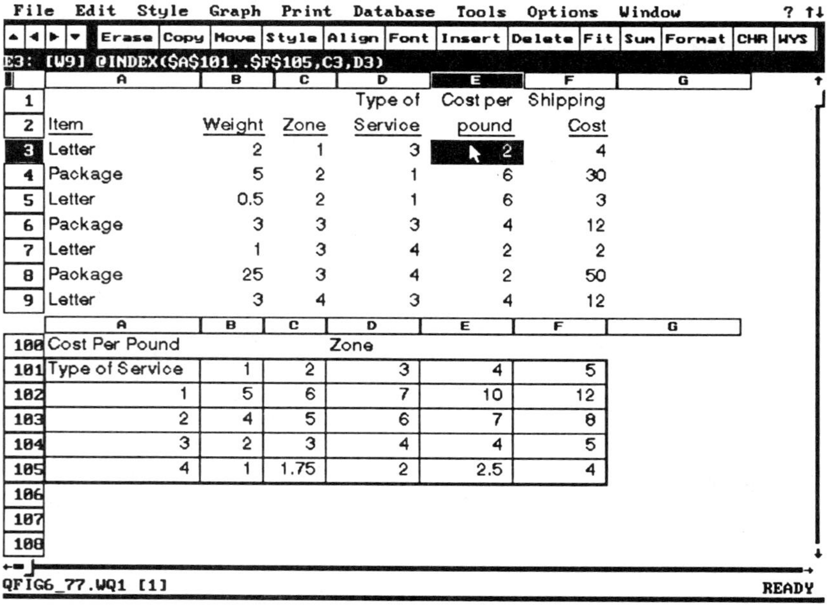

Figure 6.77 @INDEX Used to Find the Cost per Pound for Different Types of Service

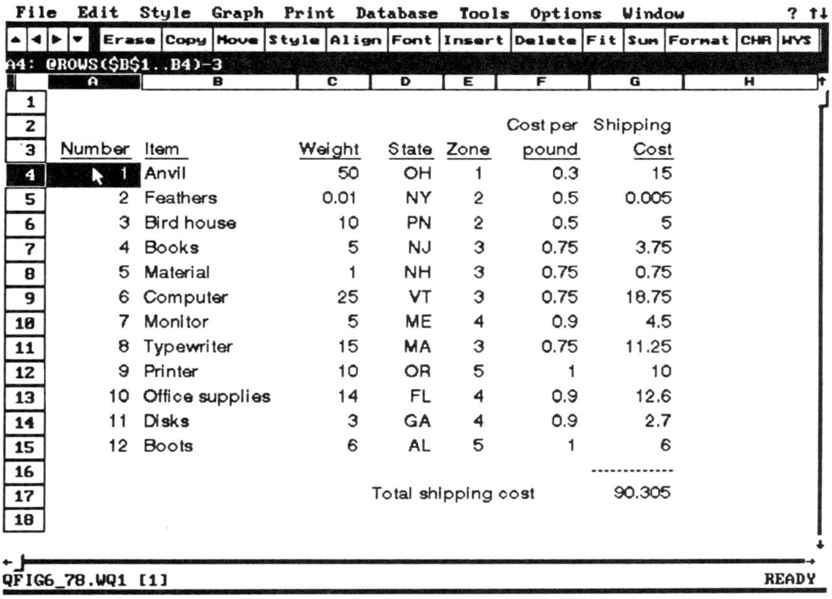

	A	B	C	D	E	F	G
1							
2						Cost per	Shipping
3	Number	Item	Weight	State	Zone	pound	Cost
4	1	Anvil	50	OH	1	0.3	15
5	2	Feathers	0.01	NY	2	0.5	0.005
6	3	Bird house	10	PN	2	0.5	5
7	4	Books	5	NJ	3	0.75	3.75
8	5	Material	1	NH	3	0.75	0.75
9	6	Computer	25	VT	3	0.75	18.75
10	7	Monitor	5	ME	4	0.9	4.5
11	8	Typewriter	15	MA	3	0.75	11.25
12	9	Printer	10	OR	5	1	10
13	10	Office supplies	14	FL	4	0.9	12.6
14	11	Disks	3	GA	4	0.9	2.7
15	12	Boots	6	AL	5	1	6
16							-------------
17				Total shipping cost			90.305
18							

Figure 6.78 @ROWS Used to Number Items

Three is subtracted from this result to compensate for the three lines of titles at the beginning. This function is better than using the /Edit Fill command since the function recalculates the numbers when a row is deleted. Also, as new items are added, the function takes them into account although you will need to copy the formula for the new items to have an item number assigned.

@COLS

The @COLS function returns the number of columns in a block. The format is @COLS(block), where *block* is a block or block name that the function uses to count the number of columns.

The @COLS command can number columns by using the @COLS function to count the number of columns between the current column and another column with an absolute address. In Figure 6.79, each zone is in a different column. The @COLS function counts the number of columns between the absolute reference to L2 and the current column. Therefore, if zones are added or removed, the @COLS function renumbers the columns for you.

SYSTEM FUNCTIONS

Quattro Pro provides several system functions that are not available in other spreadsheet packages. These functions are primarily used in macros.

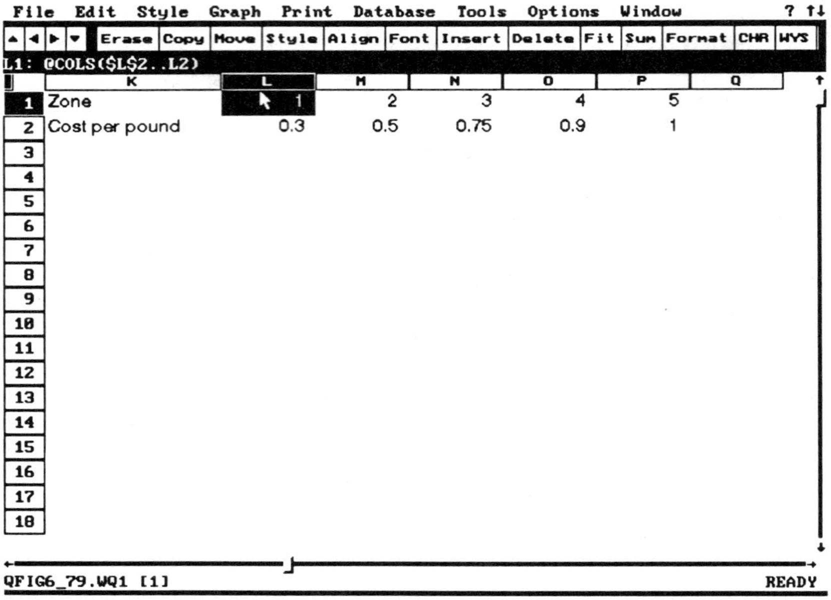

```
File    Edit   Style  Graph  Print  Database  Tools  Options  Window              ? ↑↓
▲ ◄ ▼  Erase Copy Move Style Align Font Insert Delete Fit Sum Format CHR WYS
L1: @COLS($L$2..L2)
```

	K	L	M	N	O	P	Q
1	Zone	1	2	3	4	5	
2	Cost per pound	0.3	0.5	0.75	0.9	1	
3							

QFIG6_79.WQ1 [1]   READY

Figure 6.79 @COLS Used to Number Columns

@CURVALUE

The @CURVALUE function returns the current value of a menu command setting. The format of the command is @CURVALUE(category,action), where *category* is the general menu category, and *action* is the specific menu action for which you want to know the setting. Both of these function arguments must be enclosed in quotes unless they are cell references to cells containing labels. Also, the function arguments must use the menu-equivalent commands. While some of the menu-equivalent commands are the same as Quattro Pro's menu commands, most of them are different. The function returns @ERR when Quattro Pro cannot determine what you want. The function returns an empty string when the menu command that you specify does not have a setting. The menu-equivalent commands are listed in Appendix C.

Here are a few examples of the function: **@CURVALUE("file","directory")** returns "C:\QPRO" if Quattro Pro is in the subdirectory QPRO on disk C. **@CURVALUE("print","format")** returns "As Displayed" if you have not changed this setting to Cell-Formulas. **@CURVALUE("intnl","currency")** returns "$ (Prefix)" if the currency symbol is the U.S. dollar sign, and $ appears as a prefix.

@MEMAVAIL

This function returns the amount of conventional memory available in your computer. This information can determine when you need to split a spreadsheet into two files. The format of this function is @MEMAVAIL. It uses no arguments and no parentheses. If you are planning a major expansion for your spreadsheet, use this function first to determine if you have sufficient memory for the expansion. If the available memory is limited, split the spreadsheet into smaller parts.

@MEMEMSAVAIL

This function returns the amount of expanded memory available in your computer. The format of this function is @MEMEMSAVAIL. It uses no arguments and no parentheses. If you are planning a major expansion of your spreadsheet, use this function first to determine if you have sufficient memory. If the computer does not have expanded memory, this function returns @NA.

@VERSION

This function returns the version of Quattro Pro you are using. This function has the format @VERSION. For Quattro Pro 4, this function returns 4. This function is for use in macros so that, as different versions are used, you can test the version of Quattro Pro in use as a macro runs and change the macro commands performed accordingly. For example, you might have two macro instructions like this: {IF @VERSION=4}{BRANCH Q_Pro_Instruct} and {BRANCH Other_Instruct}. In these macro instructions, Quattro Pro performs the macro instructions starting at the cell named Q_Pro_Instruct if you are executing this macro with Quattro Pro 4. If you are executing this macro using a different version of Quattro Pro, the macro would perform the macro instructions starting at the cell named Other_Instruct. Chapter 12 has more information on how you might use these macro commands.

GETTING STARTED

In this chapter you learned the functions available in Quattro Pro. As you use Quattro Pro you will develop your skills learning the different functions as you need them. Use the following steps to create the spreadsheet in Figure 6.80 and try a few of these functions:

1. Make the following entries into an empty spreadsheet. Do not worry about not seeing all of the entries since you will widen the columns later.

    E1: **Date:**
    E2: **Time:**
    A5: **Assets**
    B5: **Cost**
    C5: **Yr**
    D5: **Straight-Line**
    E3: **Double**

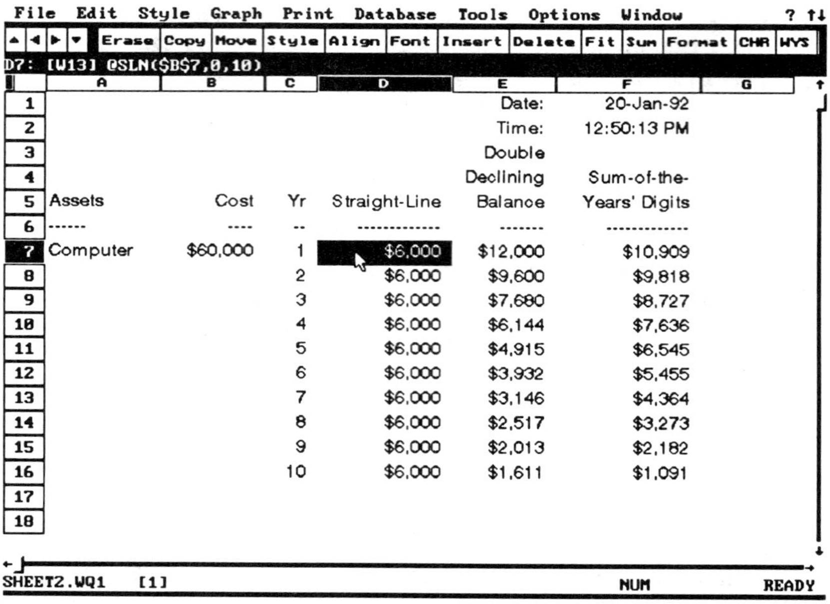

336 *Quattro Pro 4.0 Handbook*

```
 File   Edit  Style  Graph  Print  Database  Tools  Options  Window         ? ↑↓
       Erase Copy Move Style Align Font Insert Delete Fit Sum Format CHR WYS
D7:  [W13] @SLN($B$7,0,10)
           A          B        C         D             E            F           G
  1                                                 Date:      20-Jan-92
  2                                                 Time:     12:50:13 PM
  3                                                 Double
  4                                                 Declining  Sum-of-the-
  5    Assets       Cost       Yr    Straight-Line  Balance    Years' Digits
  6    ------       ----       --    -------------  -------    -------------
  7    Computer   $60,000      1        $6,000      $12,000    $10,909
  8                            2        $6,000       $9,600     $9,818
  9                            3        $6,000       $7,680     $8,727
 10                            4        $6,000       $6,144     $7,636
 11                            5        $6,000       $4,915     $6,545
 12                            6        $6,000       $3,932     $5,455
 13                            7        $6,000       $3,146     $4,364
 14                            8        $6,000       $2,517     $3,273
 15                            9        $6,000       $2,013     $2,182
 16                           10        $6,000       $1,611     $1,091
 17
 18

SHEET2.WQ1   [1]                                          NUM         READY
```

Figure 6.80 Spreadsheet Created in Getting Started Section

> E4: **Declining**
> E5: **Balance**
> F5: **Sum-of-the**
> F5: **Years' Digits**
> A7: **Computer**
> B7: **60000**

2. Add the date and time to the spreadsheet so you can tell at a quick glance when the spreadsheet was created or printed. Move to F1, and type **@TODAY**. Either press the DOWN ARROW or point to F2 and press the mouse button. Type **@NOW**, and either press ENTER or click [Enter] in the input line. While these values do not look like dates and times, you will format them later so they will look like dates and times.

3. Add dashed lines below the column headings. Move to A6, and type **@REPEAT("-",@LENGTH(A5))**. This formula creates a dashed line that is the length of the label. Either press ENTER or click [Enter] in the input line. Press CTRL-C or click Copy in the SpeedBar to enter /Edit Copy. When Quattro Pro prompts for the source block of cells, either press ENTER or click [Enter] in the input line. When Quattro Pro prompts for the destination cells, move to B6, type a period, press the RIGHT ARROW four times, and press ENTER. If you are using a mouse, click B6, hold down the mouse button and drag the mouse to point to F6; then click [Enter] in the input line.

4. Add the years in column C. First, move to C7. Enter /Edit Fill. When Quattro Pro prompts for a block to fill, type a period and press PGDN to select C7..C27. This selects a larger block that you will fill, but you can stop generating the numbers by entering a lower stop value. Either press ENTER or click [Enter] in the input line. When Quattro Pro prompts for a start value, type **1** and either press ENTER or click Enter in the box. When Quattro Pro prompts for a step value, either press ENTER or click Enter in the box to select the default of 1. When Quattro Pro prompts for a stop value, type **10**, and either press ENTER or click Enter in the box. Quattro Pro fills the first 10 cells in the block with the numbers 1 through 10.

5. Enter the following formulas either by pressing ENTER or by clicking [Enter] on the input line to finalize the entry. For each of the formulas, you can type the cell address or point to the cell as described in Chapter 2. These formulas compute the year's depreciation for the computer (assuming no salvage value) using the straight-line, double declining balance, and sum-of-the-years' digits methods.

D7: **@SLN(B7,0,10)**
E7: **@DDB(B7,0,10,C7)**
F7: **@SYD(B7,0,10,C7)**

6. Copy the formulas entered in step 5 for the other years of the asset's life. Move to D7. Press CTRL-C to enter /Edit Copy, and press the RIGHT ARROW twice and press ENTER. With a mouse select the block D7..F7 before clicking Copy in the SpeedBar. When Quattro Pro prompts for the destination, move to D8, type a period, press the DOWN ARROW eight times, and press ENTER. If you are using a mouse, point to D8, hold down the mouse button and drag the mouse to point to D16. Then click [Enter] in the input line. At this point you have the actual values entered in, but you need to improve the spreadsheet's appearance.

7. Most of these cells need formatting. Since most of the values represent dollars, enter /**O**ptions Formats **N**umeric Format **C**urrency. Type **0**, and either press ENTER or click Enter in the box. Select **Q**uit twice to return to the READY mode. Move to C7. Press CTRL-F or click Format in the SpeedBar to enter /**S**tyle **N**umeric Format. Select **F**ixed, type **0**, and either press ENTER or click Enter in the box. When Quattro Pro prompts for a block to format, press END and the DOWN ARROW followed by ENTER. If you are using a mouse, point to C7, hold down the mouse button, drag the mouse as you point to C16, release the mouse button and click [Enter] in the input line.

8. Move to F1. Press CTRL-F or click Format in the SpeedBar to enter /**S**tyle **N**umeric Format. Select **D**ate and **1**-(DD-MMM-YY). If Quattro Pro prompts for a block, press ENTER or click [Enter] in input line. Press the DOWN ARROW or click F2. Press CTRL-F or click Format in the SpeedBar to enter /**S**tyle **N**umeric Format. Select **D**ate **T**ime and **1**-(HH:MM:SS AM/PM). If

Quattro Pro prompts for a block, either press ENTER or click [Enter] in the input line.

9. Also, column widths on the spreadsheet need to be changed. Although you currently cannot see all of the labels and some numbers appear as asterisks, these values and labels are still in the spreadsheet. If you are not using a mouse move to A1 by pressing HOME. Enter **/Style Block Size Auto Width**. When Quattro Pro prompts for the number of spaces you want between columns, press ENTER. When Quattro Pro prompts for the block to use to determine the column widths, press END, HOME and ENTER to select all the spreadsheet entries. If you are using a mouse, point to A1, hold down the mouse button, drag the mouse as you point to F16, and release the mouse button. When the block is selected, click Fit in the SpeedBar.

10. The last change to the spreadsheet is the alignment of some of the labels. Move to B1. Press SHIFT-F7 (SELECT) END, DOWN ARROW, the DOWN ARROW a second time (to include the line of hyphens in B6), END, and RIGHT ARROW. This selects the block B1. F6. If you are using a mouse, point to B1, hold down the mouse button, drag the mouse as you point to F6 and release the mouse button. When the block is selected, either click Align in the SpeedBar to enter **/Style Alignment**. Select **Right** so your entries will align with the numbers. Your spreadsheet now looks like the one in Figure 6.80.

7
Graphic Features

Graphs provide a visual picture of the information in your spreadsheet. Graphs can show trends, patterns, and relationships between elements of data. Rather than emphasizing the actual values, graphs emphasize the essence of the data. A graph enhances the information in your spreadsheet by displaying a visual representation of your spreadsheet entries.

Graphing with Quattro is easy, since Quattro uses the data that are already in a spreadsheet. This reduces the number of steps that you must perform to create a graph. Since Quattro's graphics capabilities are an integral part of the program, you do not have to transfer data between programs or use another program to print your graph. Also, Quattro provides a what-if graphic feature by using the most up-to-date information for a graph and referring to the current values in a spreadsheet. Quattro's graphics commands use the same Quattro interface mastered for other commands. Quattro's graphs provide many customization features that allow you to tailor a graph to convey your message. Since Quattro keeps the current graph settings in memory, you can change any of the settings and Quattro immediately incorporates the change into the current graph. You can add other objects to the graph and link them. When the points in the graph move, the link objects move with them.

If you have a monitor that supports graphics, Quattro lets you view the graph as you create it. You can even include a graph in a spreadsheet. If your monitor cannot display graphs, you can still create graphs, but you cannot see the graph until it is printed.

This chapter covers all the options for creating a graph. First, you will look at the basics of graphics, including terminology, graph types, and ways to create a simple graph. Once the basics are covered, you will learn to customize your graph with all the features that Quattro provides. You will learn how to use the graph annotator to add free-form text and drawings to your graph. You will learn how to add and use graph buttons to change the order in which the graphs are displayed. Once the graph is complete, you will learn how to save and print a graph.

CREATING BASIC GRAPHS

Creating a graph with Quattro is easy, since you only have to tell Quattro what data to use and what kind of a graph you want. Quattro provides several graph types to choose from. The best type to use depends on the data and your specific presentation requirements.

Terminology

Because graphs are different from spreadsheets, you need to learn some new terms that describe features of the graph. The terms discussed below are also illustrated in Figure 7.1.

- Axis—The axis is the vertical or horizontal line to the left, right, or bottom. The x-axis is the horizontal line at the bottom of the graph, and the y-axis is the vertical line at the left or right of the graph. A graph can have two y-

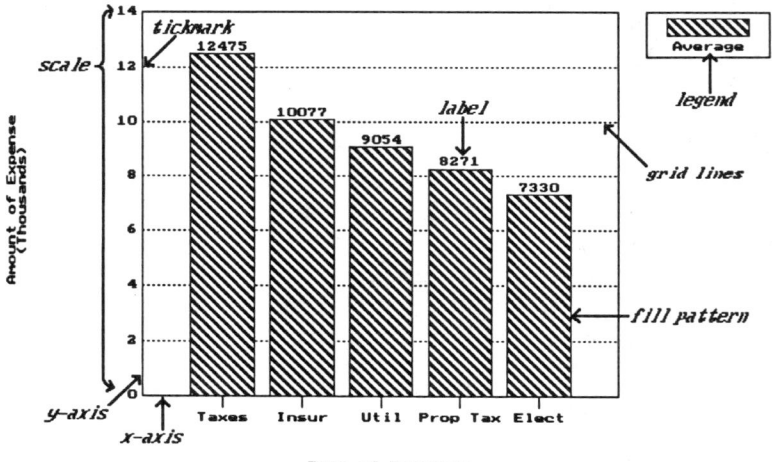

Figure 7.1 Sample Graph Illustrating Graph Terms

axes, so you can graph data measured in more than one way. Most graph types have both an x-axis and a y-axis. In Figure 7.1, the x-axis is divided into the different types of expenses, and the y-axis is divided into thousands of dollars to measure quantity. Axes are not used in pie charts or column and text graphs.

- Data Point—A data point is a spreadsheet value displayed in a graph. Data points are grouped into series. Quattro has a variety of options for displaying data points: They can be pie wedges, or bars in a column (as in Figure 7.1), or they can be marked with a symbol, a line, or both.

- Fill Pattern—The fill pattern is the special marking that Quattro uses to fill in areas like the diagonal stripes in the bars in Figure 7.1. Quattro has 16 different fill patterns.

- Font—The font is the style used for the graph lettering. In Figure 7.1, the title (Indirect Expenses) is in a different font from the rest of the graph text. In a graph, you can use any font available for your spreadsheet (see Chapter 3).

- Grid lines—The grid lines are the lines that connect to the tick marks stretching across the graph; they make the values easier to estimate by providing comparison points to the y-axis and/or x-axis. In Figure 7.1, the grid lines are the dotted lines from the numbers on the y-axis. For most graph types, the grid lines extend from the y-axis. Grid lines are not used in pie charts or column and text graphs.

- Label—In a graph, labels are text or numbers from the spreadsheet that describe the different points in the graph. In Figure 7.1, 12475, 10077, and 9054 are three labels. In pie charts and column graphs, these labels can be formatted.

- Legend—The legend is the box in line, bar, XY, stacked bar, and area and rotated bar graphs that describes the color, fill pattern, and marker indicating each series of values. For example, the legend in Figure 7.1 labels the data points as averages having a diagonally striped fill pattern.

- Scale—The scale is a numeric range divided into regular intervals along an axis. Quattro uses the scale to determine the position of points and lengths of bars in the graphs. For example, Figure 7.1 has a scale on the y-axis that determines the height of each of the bars.

- Series—A series is a group of related data points. Figure 7.1 has a series with five data points. Quattro permits up to six series of data in a graph. For the data on indirect expenses shown in Figure 7.1, direct expenses could be a second series.

- Tick Marks—Tick marks are the small lines that divide the scale into regular intervals. In Figure 7.1, the x-axis has tick marks that connect the bars to the x values they represent. Quattro has several options for tick marks.

Graph Types

Quattro provides 12 different graph types. The selection of a graph type depends on the data and the objective that you are attempting to achieve with your presentation. Unless you specify otherwise, Quattro uses a stacked bar graph. You can quickly change from one type of graph to another. A variety of graph types are shown in Figures 7.2A through 7.2K and described below:

- Line—A line graph (Figure 7.2A) consists of a line that connects the points for each series of data on the graph. Each series value is plotted against the y-axis. This graph effectively shows trends in sales, expenses, or profit projections.
- Bar—A bar graph has horizontal bars whose heights are determined by the value of the data points in the series measured against the y-axis scale. Figure 7.1 shows a bar graph. Bar graphs effectively compare and contrast values like profit contributions from several product lines or expense categories over time.
- Column—A column graph (Figure 7.2B) stacks bars representing each data point in a series to create a column. Each column section size is determined by the data point's percentage of the total. This is like a pie chart except the data points are represented by column sections instead of pie wedges. A column graph leaves more room for data labels and other text. You can use a column graph when you want to show the contributions several numbers have to the total, such as division sales relative to company sales.
- XY—An XY graph (Figure 7.2C) plots the values in one series against the values in a second series. You can use an XY graph to plot years of education against salary, age against sick days, or snow drift depth against wind velocity. This graph effectively shows series of data that are not divided into the same unit of measure.
- Stacked Bar—The stacked bar graph (Figure 7.2D) places each value of a series on top of the values from other series for each point on the x-axis. This graph effectively shows the total for different points on the x-axis as well as showing the individual series components. The profit contribution of various company units or the composition of expenses by quarter can be effectively shown with a stacked bar graph.
- Pie—A pie graph (Figure 7.2E) shows one series of values. Each value in the series is represented as a wedge in the pie. The size of each wedge is proportionate to the percentage that each value represents of the total (100%) of all values in the series. This type of graph is used to illustrate the proportions between numbers in the first series. If this graph type is chosen, Quattro ignores the other series of data that you might assign. The composition of company expenses can be shown effectively with a pie chart.
- Area—The area graph (Figure 7.2F) places a line graph for each series on top of another series matching each point in the x-axis. Instead of using bars as

Graphic Features 343

Growth In Sales
Line Graph

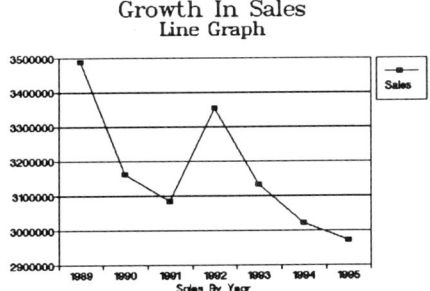

7.2A

Income From Operations Distribution
Column Graph

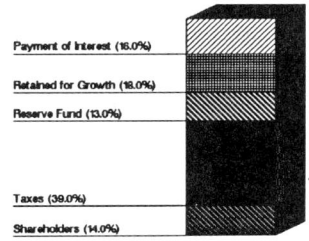

7.2B

Comparison Between Smoking & Sick Days
XY Graph

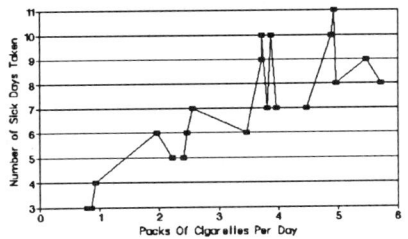

7.2C

Total Sales By Divisions
Stacked Bar Graph

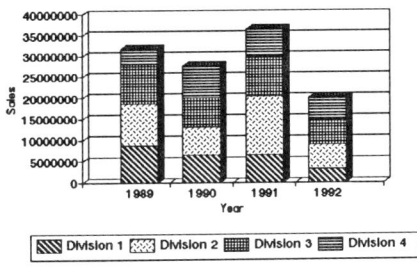

7.2D

Income From Operations Distribution
Pie Chart

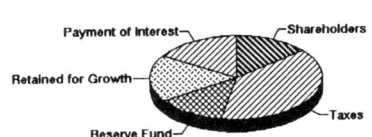

7.2E

Distribution of Sales Dollars
Area Graph

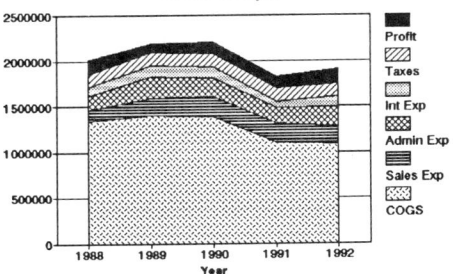

7.2F

Figure 7.2 Different Graph Types

does the stacked bar graph, the area graph fills the entire area between the line graphs with the fill pattern. This graph effectively shows the total for different points on the x-axis as well as showing the individual components.

- Rotated Bar—The rotated bar graph (Figure 7.2G) is a bar graph that has the x-axis as the vertical axis and the y-axis as the horizontal. This graph effectively compares and contrasts values just as the regular bar graph does. Rotated graphs are used as a variance of other bar graph types.

- High-Low—A high-low graph (or high-low-open-close graph, Figure 7.2H) plots statistical data showing the high, low, open, and close values for each point on the x-axis. The first series contains the high values, the second series contains the low values, the third series contains the values at the opening of the day or period, and the fourth series contains the values at the close of the day or period. Quattro draws a line from the high value to the low value then draws a horizontal line on the left side for the opening value and a horizontal line on the right side for the closing value. This graph type is used primarily for plotting financial commodities and statistical data.

- Text—A text graph (Figure 7.2I) provides a screen that you can fill using the graph annotator. This graph does not use data from the spreadsheet. It is used for creating drawings and text.

- Bubble—A bubble graph (Figure 7.2J) creates bubbles of different sizes in different places of the x-axis and y-axis to represent the combination of each of the values in the x-axis, first and second series. This graph type does not use the third through sixth series. For each bubble, the x-axis value determines its horizontal position, the first series value determines the bubble's center's position, and the second series value determines the bubble's size. You can use the bubble graph when you want to show three types of information at once, such as the median income for cities of different sizes.

- 3-D Graphs—A 3-D graph (Figure 7.2K) adds a different three-dimensional look to a bar, line, or area graph than the /Graph Overall Three-D command provides. After selecting 3-D Graphs, you must select **Bar**, **Step**, **Ribbon**, or **Area**. Select **B**ar or **A**rea to create a bar or area graph. Select **S**tep to create a bar graph with the bars for each series adjoining. Select **R**ibbon to create a line graph with the lines having depth. With these options, each new series is placed in front of the last instead of adjoining as in bar graphs, overlapping as in line graphs, or stacked as in area graphs, so the order of the series is important. You will want the largest values in the first series and the remaining series in descending order. You can use 3-D graphs to add variety to your other bar, line, or area graphs.

Quattro can also combine two graph types into one graph to emphasize one series of data. The combination options can be selected from line, bar, and XY graphs.

Graphic Features 345

7.2G

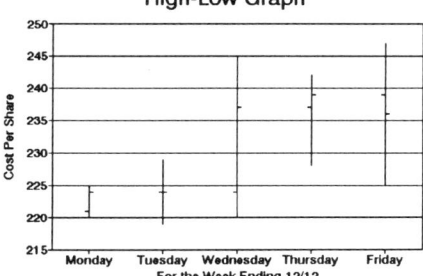

7.2H

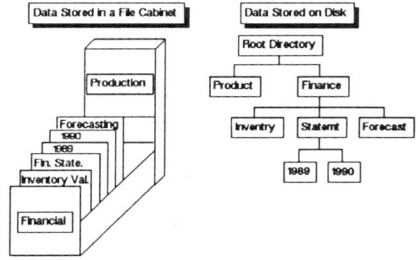

7.2I

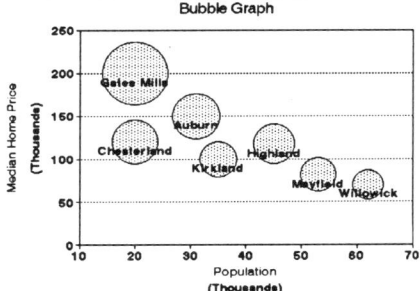

7.2J

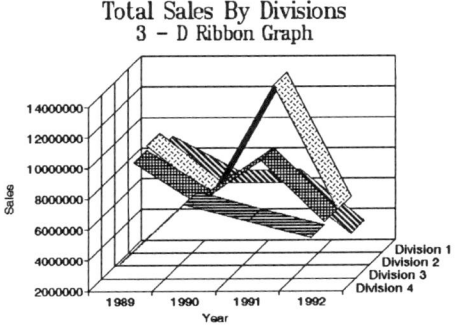

7.2K

Figure 7.2 Different Graph Types (continued)

Choosing a Graph Type and Assigning Data Values

Creating a graph with Quattro is easy. All you need to do is tell Quattro which data to use and which type of a graph to create. The steps for creating the graph in Figure 7.5 use the spreadsheet shown in Figure 7.3. To create a graph, follow these steps:

1. Type **/**, and select **G**raph. Quattro displays the Graph menu shown in Figure 7.4.
2. Select **G**raph Type, and select the type of graph that you want to create. Quattro lists the graph types it has available. Choose **L**ine for this example. When you display the spreadsheet in the WYSIWYG display mode (or graphics mode in earlier releases), many of the **/G**raph commands display how the menu selections will make your menu look rather than text to select. For example, the **/G**raph **G**raph Type in the WYSIWYG display mode shows samples of each of the selected graph types for you to select rather than the names of the different graph types. Other commands will display a palette that lets you select the color, fill pattern, or marker rather than a description.
3. Select **S**eries. This presents the Series menu to select the series values in the spreadsheet to be graphed. When Quattro graphs data, it uses the data

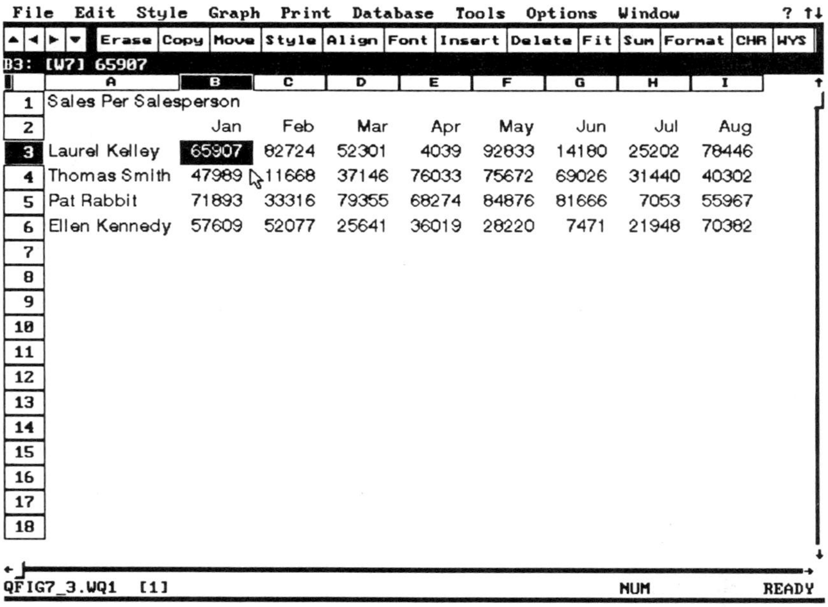

	A	B	C	D	E	F	G	H	I
1	Sales Per Salesperson								
2		Jan	Feb	Mar	Apr	May	Jun	Jul	Aug
3	Laurel Kelley	65907	82724	52301	4039	92833	14180	25202	78446
4	Thomas Smith	47989	11668	37146	76033	75672	69026	31440	40302
5	Pat Rabbit	71893	33316	79355	68274	84876	81666	7053	55967
6	Ellen Kennedy	57609	52077	25641	36019	28220	7471	21948	70382

Figure 7.3 Sample Spreadsheet

Graphic Features 347

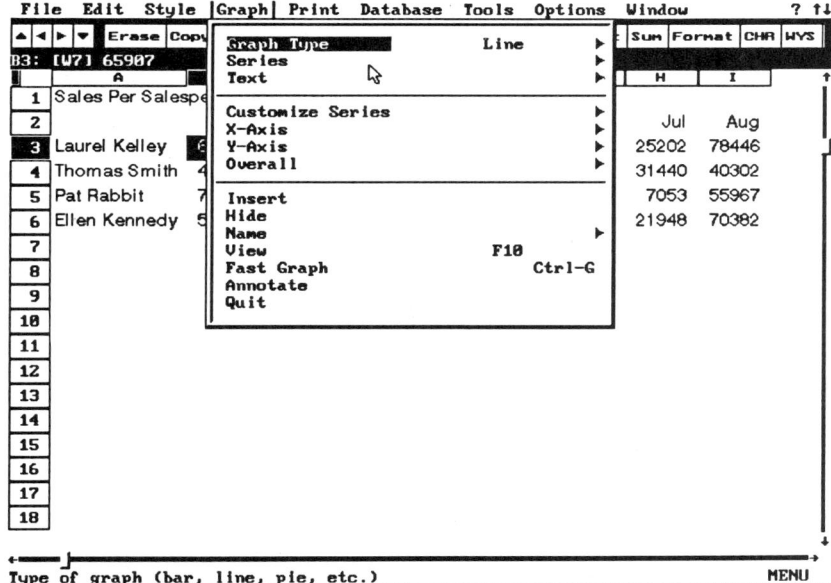

Figure 7.4 Graph Menu Box

values currently in a spreadsheet. As the data change, Quattro changes the graph.

4. Select **X-Axis Series**, and select the block to be used for the bottom axis of the graph. The block can come from any spreadsheet, including another one. You can use this feature to create a graph that graphs data from multiple spreadsheets. For this example, the block is B2..G2.

5. Select **1st Series**. Select the values that Quattro will graph as a single series. In this example, the block B3..G3 is chosen.

6. Repeat step 5 for each of the series to be graphed.

   In this example, block B4..G4 is chosen for the second series, block B5..G5 is chosen for the third series, and block B6..G6 is chosen for the fourth series.

7. Select **Quit** to return to the Graph menu.

8. View the graph by selecting **View**. The graph looks like Figure 7.5. Pressing any key except / returns you to the menu from which you selected **View**.

9. Select **Quit** to return to the READY mode.

Quattro has other commands for selecting the blocks used for the graph data. When the data for the first through sixth series are in contiguous blocks, you can select all the series with the /Graph Series Group command instead of using separate commands for each series of data. To create the same graph using the /Graph Series Group command, follow these steps:

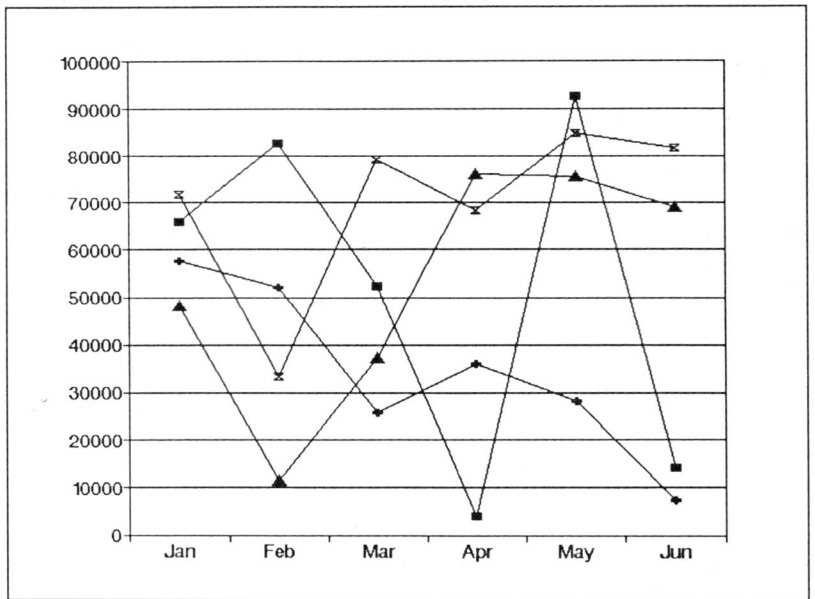

Figure 7.5 Graph of Information from Spreadsheet in Figure 7.4

1. Type **/**, and select **Graph**.
2. Select **Graph Type** and **Line** to create a line graph.
3. Select **Series X-Axis Series**, and select the block to be used for the bottom axis of the graph.
4. Select **B2..G2** as the block.
5. Select **Group**. Quattro prompts for dividing the block into series according to columns or rows. If you select **Columns**, each column is a separate series with the first column assigned to the first series, the second column assigned to the second series, and so on until Quattro runs out of series or columns in the block. If you select **Rows**, each row is a separate series with the first row assigned to the first series, the second row assigned to the second series, and so on until Quattro runs out of series or rows in the block.
6. Select **Rows** to divide the block into series according to rows. Quattro prompts for a block containing the data values you want to graph.
7. Select **B3..G6** as the block.
8. Select **Quit** to return to the Graph menu.
9. View the graph by selecting **View**. The graph again looks like Figure 7.5. Pressing any key except / returns you to the menu from which you selected **View**.
10. Select **Quit** to return to the READY mode.

Graphing Analytical Data

Quattro Pro 4 has several new features that make it easier to calculate and generate analytical data that is used in a graph. This means that if you want to graph the moving average of a series of numbers, rather than enter the calculations to generate the numbers that you will use in the graph, you can have Quattro Pro make the calculations as it graphs the calculation results. This type of analysis lets you focus on trends that may be hidden by an abundance of data. You can use these analytical features to consolidate the information presented in graphs when you have many data points.

The data to graph is analyzed by selecting /Graph Series Analyze. Next, you select the series you want to perform analysis to, or select All to analyze all the graph's series in the same method. You will only select X-Axis Series if you are using an XY graph. After the series is selected, select how you want to analyze the data. You can select Aggregation to perform simple statistical @functions on the data, Moving Average to calculate moving averages, Linear Fit to calculate a straight line that best fits the data points, or Exponential Fit to calculate a curved line that best fits the data points. When you no longer want to graph the analytical data and want to return to graphing the individual points in the series, select Reset. You can always return to the previous menu level by selecting Quit.

GRAPHING THE STATISTICS OF A SERIES In Chapter 6, you were introduced to statistical functions such as @SUM, @AVG, @STD, @STDS, @MIN, and @MAX. You can also use these statistical functions with groups of values in a data series. For example, if you have daily sales and you want to look at the average sales for each week, you can have Quattro Pro perform the calculations for you rather than you having to create the formulas to average each week's formulas. This type of graphical analysis will graph less data points than in the data series, since Quattro Pro will divide the values in the data series into groups, and each group will appear on the graph as a single data point.

Once you select Aggregation, you can select the statistical function Quattro Pro will perform on each group of values by selecting Function and selecting from SUM, AVG, STD, STDS, MIN, and MAX. Next, Quattro Pro needs to know how you want to divide the values in the series into groups. You do this by selecting the period each value represents and how you want these values grouped. To select the period each value represents, select Series Period and select from Days, Weeks, Months, Quarters, and Years. Next, select Aggregation Period and select how you want to divide the periods up into groups by selecting from Weeks, Months, Quarters, Years, or Arbitrary. If you select Arbitrary, type a number between 2 and 1000 for the number of values that are in each group, and press ENTER or click Enter in the box. If you use Arbitrary, you will want to set the Series Period to Days. Each value may not represent a different time period, but using the time periods lets you easily select ways of grouping the values in a series. You can use the Series Period and Aggregation Period to quickly divide the values into groups of 3 (months into quarters), 4 (weeks into months or quarters into years), 7 (days into weeks), 12 (weeks into quarters or months into years), 30 (days into months), 52 (weeks into years), 90 (days into quarters), 360 (days into years), or some other arbitrary period. For example, if the series contains financial data for stock and you want to use weekly data, you would use an arbitrary aggregation period of 5, since this type of information is only provided five days a week.

Figure 7.6 shows a graph that uses the @SUM function and groups the data from days into weeks. The first data point, 791,317, is the total of 108975+117474+ 109213+110921+113700+116598+114456. The graph uses other features that you will learn about later in the chapter such as changing the Y-axis so there is more room to display each data point's label and adding the data point labels.

GRAPHING A MOVING AVERAGE Another type of statistical analysis you may want to use when you want to graph data is showing a moving average. This shows the average for each value in the series using that value and a set number of previous values in the series. For example, if you are using four values to calculate your moving average, your values, the moving average and the formula that calculates the moving average might look like this:

```
         Moving
Value    Average    Formula
791317   791317     791317/1
877220   834269     (791317+877220)/2
989147   885895     (791317+877220+989147)/3
1042428  925028     (791317+877220+989147+1042428)/4
1132984  1010445    (877220+989147+1042428+1132984)/4
1185349  1087477    (989147+1042428+1132984+1185349)/4
1140721  1125371    (1042428+1132984+1185349+1140721)/4
```

You can see from this example that for the first few values, Quattro Pro calculates the moving average using the current value and the previous values until it has four values to average. When the formula includes the next value in the average calculation, it removes the oldest value in the formula. To graph a moving average without having to enter the formulas that calculate these values, select Moving Average. Next, select Period, type the number of values Quattro Pro will use to calculate the average, and press ENTER or click Enter in the box. Another option you have with moving averages is to weigh the different values in the calculation differently so the newest value has the most weight. For example, to calculate the weighted moving average for the fourth data point, the formula is **(791317*1+877220*2+989147*3+1042428*4)/(1+2+3+4)**. To use the moving average with weighted values, select Weighted and Yes. To return to not using weighted values in the moving average, select Weighted and No.

GRAPHING A TREND When you have many points in the graph, it may be hard to see a graph. But you can have Quattro Pro calculate the line that best describes the trend of the data points and graph that line instead of graphing the individual points. Quattro Pro can graph two types of trend lines: a straight line or a curved

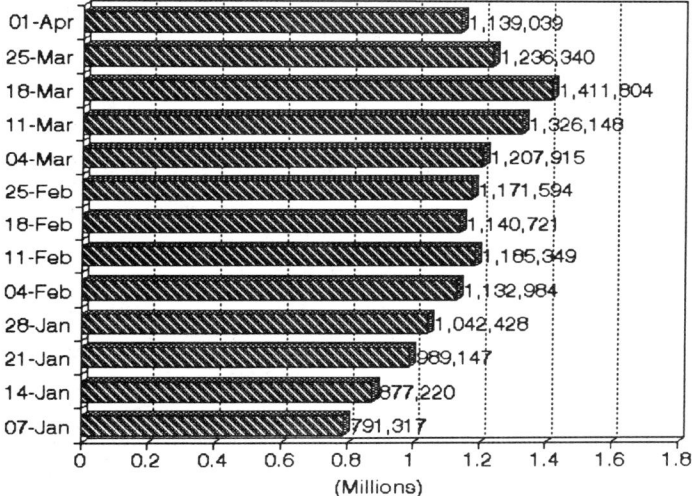

Figure 7.6 Graph of Aggregated Data Totaled by Week

line. To graph a straight line for the trend, select Linear Fit. To graph a curved line for the trend, select Exponential Fit. Once you have the trend line in place, you can see where the trend will continue in the future. The straight line you generate will be done with simple regression, which you will learn more about when you learn about the /Tools Advanced Math Regression command described in Chapter 9.

PUTTING THE DATA POINTS IN THE SPREADSHEET Graphing the analytical data means that Quattro Pro must calculate separate values for each of the data points. You can put a copy of the values the graph is using in the spreadsheet. For example, you may want a copy in the spreadsheet so you can print it out later. Also, if you want to label the data points in the analyzed series, you will need to put the values in the spreadsheet before you use the /Graph Customize Series Interior Label Block command. To put the calculated data points in the spreadsheet, select the series (you cannot select All for this) and select Table. Next, select a cell where you want the column of values for the series' data points placed, and press ENTER or click [Enter] in the input line. These values are not formulas, so as the data that Quattro uses in the graphical analysis changes, the values put in these cells will not (you will need to repeat the command to update the values). Figure 7.7 shows a spreadsheet that has two sets of analyzed data for the two graphs contained in the spreadsheet (you will learn how to have more than one graph in a spreadsheet later). The first set of numbers in E2..E14 sums the daily sales into weekly sales. Using these values for the second graph, the second set of numbers

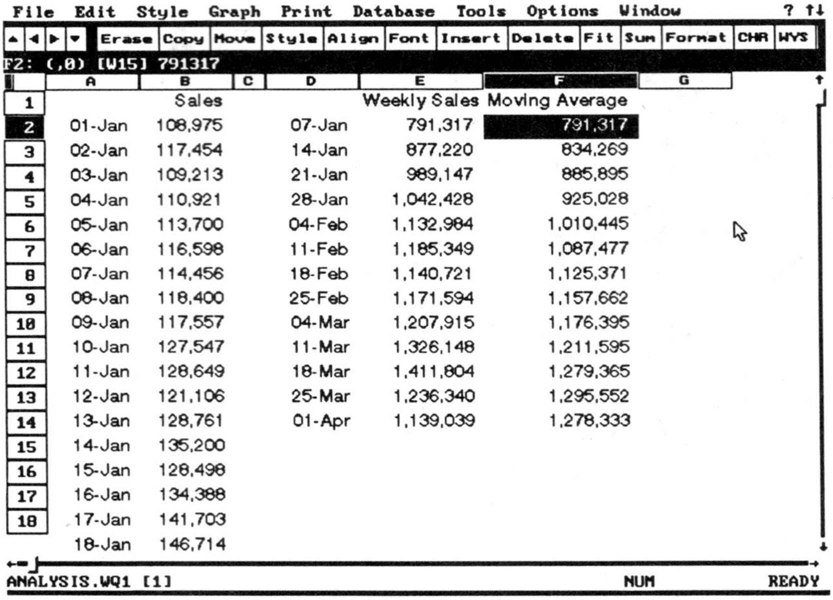

```
File   Edit   Style   Graph   Print   Database   Tools   Options   Window            ?  ↑↓
▲ ◄ ► ▼  Erase Copy Move Style Align Font Insert Delete Fit Sum Format CHR WYS
F2:  (,0)  [W15]  791317
      A         B       C      D           E              F              G
  1           Sales                  Weekly Sales  Moving Average
  2   01-Jan  108,975        07-Jan       791,317        791,317
  3   02-Jan  117,454        14-Jan       877,220        834,269
  4   03-Jan  109,213        21-Jan       989,147        885,895
  5   04-Jan  110,921        28-Jan     1,042,428        925,028
  6   05-Jan  113,700        04-Feb     1,132,984      1,010,445
  7   06-Jan  116,598        11-Feb     1,185,349      1,087,477
  8   07-Jan  114,456        18-Feb     1,140,721      1,125,371
  9   08-Jan  118,400        25-Feb     1,171,594      1,157,662
 10   09-Jan  117,557        04-Mar     1,207,915      1,176,395
 11   10-Jan  127,547        11-Mar     1,326,148      1,211,595
 12   11-Jan  128,649        18-Mar     1,411,804      1,279,365
 13   12-Jan  121,106        25-Mar     1,236,340      1,295,552
 14   13-Jan  128,761        01-Apr     1,139,039      1,278,333
 15   14-Jan  135,200
 16   15-Jan  128,498
 17   16-Jan  134,388
 18   17-Jan  141,703
      18-Jan  146,714
ANALYSIS.WQ1  [1]                                         NUM            READY
```

Figure 7.7 Calculated Graph Data Points Added to the Spreadsheet

in F2..F14 calculates a moving average for the weekly sales. Since the moving average calculates as many data points as are in the series, you would use D26 to D14 as the X-axis series for the graph.

Adding Text to a Graph

In the previous examples, the graph showed four series. However, it is not possible to determine which data the graph represents, since the graph is missing information that describes its contents. Adding titles to a graph provides two lines at the top of a graph and an x-axis and y-axis title. These are essential first steps in adding descriptive information to a graph. You can also add legends which will identify how each series is represented in the graph.

ADDING TITLES To add titles, activate the Graph menu. If you are in READY mode, type /, and select Graph. If you are in another graph menu, select Quit to return to the Graph menu. From the Graph menu, select Text. To put a title on the graph (like Indirect Expenses in Figure 7.1), select 1st Line, type the graph's title, and press ENTER. To create a secondary title below the first one (like Line Graph in Figure 7.2A), select 2nd Line, type the graph's secondary title, and press ENTER. The secondary title normally continues or explains the first title. To title the x-axis, select X-Title, type the title for the x-axis, and press ENTER. To title the y-axis, select Y-Title, type the title for the y-axis, and press ENTER. To title the second y-axis, select **Secondary Y-Axis**, type the title for the second y-axis, and press ENTER. To view the graph with the titles, select **Quit** and **View**. Using the graph created in Figure 7.5, the same graph with titles might look like Figure 7.8. To return to the Titles menu, press any key except /.

To use a cell's contents as a title, type a backslash followed by the cell address in place of the text for the title such as \A2 (which uses the contents of A2 as a title). To remove a title, select the title to be removed from the Text menu, press ESC, and then press ENTER.

ADDING A LEGEND The graph in Figure 7.8 displays several series of data in one graph. Each series has a different line and marker, but the series do not have any descriptions of what the lines and markers represent. Although you can look at the spreadsheet to match the different values with the different series, adding a legend to identify the salespeople makes the graph more meaningful. To define a legend, select **Legends** from the Text menu. A menu is presented to permit you to choose the series for which you want to define a legend. When you have chosen the series, Quattro prompts you for the legend for that series. Type the legend for the series, and press ENTER to return to the Legends menu. Selecting **Quit** returns you to the Text menu. When you view the graph, Quattro displays a box that contains the legend text and the line or symbol for each series. Figure 7.9 shows the graph, with a legend to label each series. If the graph is a bar graph, stacked bar, area, or rotated bar graph, the legend contains a small box filled with the fill pattern that identifies each series.

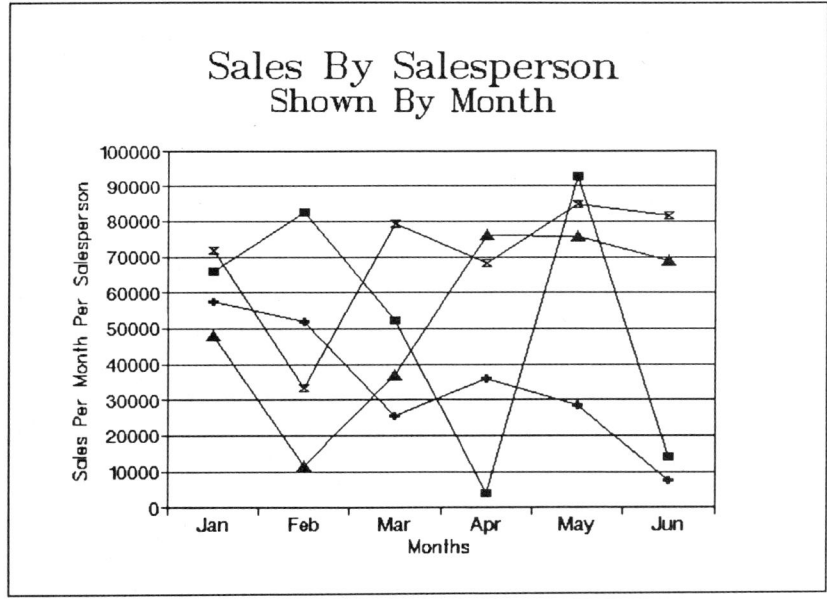

Figure 7.8 Graph in Figure 7.5 with Titles

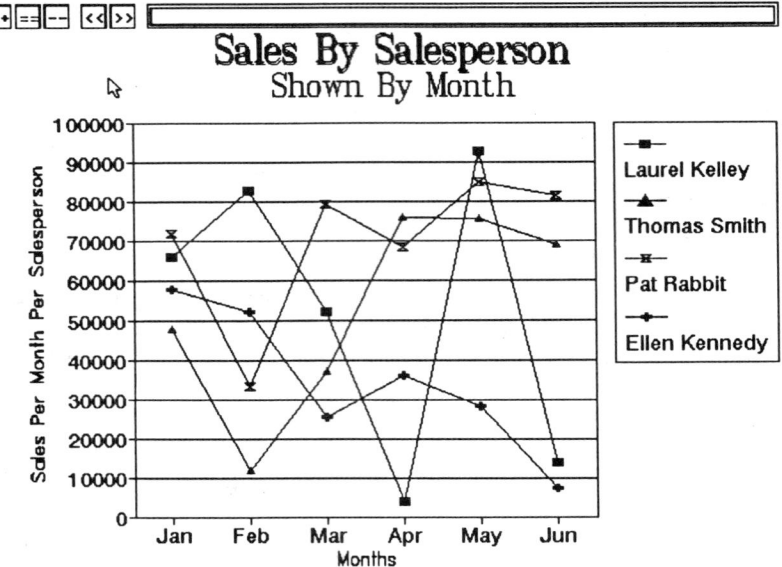

Figure 7.9 Graph Showing Legends and the Zoom and Pan Palette

Another option for adding a legend is to reference a legend entry in a spreadsheet cell rather than typing the legend. When prompted for the legend, type a backslash (\) and the address of the cell containing the legend. For example, using the data that created Figure 7.9, you can enter the legend for the first series by typing \A3.

Although Quattro puts the legends to the right of the graph, you can change the graph so the legends appear at the bottom of the graph or so they do not appear at all. To change the position of the legends, select **Legends** from the Text menu and **Position** from the Legends menu. If you select **Right**, the legend appears on the right side of the graph. If you select **Bottom**, the legend appears on the bottom of the graph. If you select **None**, the legend does not appear. This last option is a quick method to remove a legend. The **Right** and **Bottom** legend position options have no effect on 3-D graphs.

SETTING THE TEXT FONT In Chapter 3 you learned how you can set the fonts Quattro uses for text in spreadsheet. Setting the fonts for a graph requires fewer steps. Quattro can print graphs using the same fonts Quattro uses to print spreadsheets. When you change the fonts, Quattro shows the new fonts when you display the graph. To set the font for the text in a graph, select **Font** from the Text menu. Quattro will display a selection box to select the text for which you want to choose a font. Once you select the text, Quattro displays the menu to change the typeface, point size, style, or color—the same menu that Quattro displays when you select a font for a spreadsheet with **/Style FontTable Edit Fonts** and a font number. This is just like the **/Style Font** command except that the options **Bold, Underlined,** and **Italic** are under Style with the addition of **Drop Shadow** in Quattro Pro 3 and above to add a drop shadow as shown in Figure 7.9. After you make your selections, you can select **Quit** to return to the Text menu. If you are using a plotter, you must use one of the Hershey fonts. When you view the graph, Quattro may display a message that it is building a font if the Bitstream font that the graph uses has not already been built.

You can change the color of the shadow with the **/Graph Overall Drop Shadow Colors** command. After selecting the command, select the color of the text font that you want to change for the drop shadow color, and then select the color that is to be used for the shadow.

Quattro initially uses the Swiss-SC font for the graph text. On a screen that can display colors, the text initially displays in blue. The default sizes are the main title, 36 points; the second title, 24 points; and the remaining text, 18 points. If your computer cannot display some of the text attributes, Quattro makes the best substitution it can.

Viewing a Graph

As mentioned in previous sections on creating and labeling a graph, the current view can be displayed by selecting **View** from the Graph menu. Quattro also has a function key that presents an immediate view of the current graph—even from READY mode. Pressing F10 (GRAPH) displays the current graph. The difference between selecting **View** from the Graph menu and pressing F10 is that F10 can be pressed at any time. For example, if you are modifying the data in a graph and you want to see how the changes affect the graph, pressing F10 incorporates the latest data changes into the graph. Pressing F10 (GRAPH) to view a graph also works while a menu is active. When you have finished viewing the graph, you can press any key except / to remove the graph from the screen. Pressing / activates the graph annotator. If you accidentally press / or select **Annotate** from the Graph menu, type **/Q** to leave the graph annotator.

If you cannot see the graph when you press F10 or select **View** from one of the graph menu boxes, you may have a monitor that cannot display graphs. Nevertheless, you can still create graphs, save them, and print them (although you cannot monitor their creation on the screen).

Another special key to keep in mind as you work on graphs is F6. When you press F6 as you are working with the Graph menus (or any other Quattro Pro 4 menu), the menus disappear so you can see the data in the spreadsheet. The status line will remind you that once you press F6 again, the menus will reappear.

In Quattro Pro 4, you can look more closely at the graph using a mouse. This is just like looking at your screen preview of data that you will print more closely. When the graph is on the screen, press both mouse buttons simultaneously. Quattro Pro adds a Zoom and Pan palette to the top of the screen. This Zoom and Pan palette is shown in Figure 7.9. Clicking the ++ button enlarges the graph so you see less data points on the screen by expanding the X-axis, although the Y-axis will not change. You can continue zooming in on your graph to see fewer and fewer data points on screen at once. You are only changing the part of the graph that appears on the screen, so zooming the graph does not change it. When you want to shift the part of the graph that appears on the screen, you can either click the << and >> buttons or you can click the position bar for where you want to see the graph. This shifts the graph right or left (or on a rotated bar graph up or down). When you want to shrink the graph, click the - - button. You can always return the graph to its original size by clicking the ▬▬ button. When you are finished using the Zoom and Pan palette, you can remove it from the screen by pressing the right mouse button once.

Making a Fast Graph

Quattro has another version of the /Graph Series Group command that can quickly graph spreadsheet data. Quattro's /Graph Fast Graph command can assign data to the x-axis, up to six data series and the legends. When you create a fast graph, Quattro creates a graph using the data in the block you select and displays the graph. It uses any graph settings that are in effect when you create a fast graph, such as titles and graph type. To make a fast graph, enter /Graph Fast Graph or press CTRL-G. Quattro prompts for a block to graph. Select a block of data to be graphed. Quattro divides the block into the graph information it will use and displays the graph. Once you perform this command, Quattro has assigned portions of the block to the different series, the x-axis labels, and the legends so you can make additional enhancements to this graph without specifying the information again. Quattro analyzes the block's dimensions to determine how to divide the data in the block into the information the graph will use.

If the block uses more columns than rows, Quattro divides the data according to rows. If the first row contains labels, the row of labels becomes the x-axis data. If the first column contains labels, the first column of labels becomes the legend text. When the block contains data that Quattro uses as legends or x-axis labels, Quattro divides the remainder of the block into the first through sixth series according to rows. If the block does not contain text that Quattro uses as legends or x-axis labels, Quattro uses the entire block for the data series and divides it according to rows.

If the block uses more rows than columns, Quattro divides the data according to columns. If the first column contains labels, the first column of labels becomes the x-axis data. If the first row contains labels, the first row of labels becomes the legend text. When the block contains data that Quattro uses as legends or x-axis labels, Quattro divides the remainder of the block into the first through sixth series according to columns. If the block does not contain text that Quattro uses as legends or x-axis labels, Quattro uses the entire block for the data series and divides it according to columns.

As an example, suppose you want to quickly graph the data in Figure 7.10. To create this graph, follow these steps:

1. Enter **/Graph**.
2. Select **Text 1st Line**.
3. Type **Yearly Sales**, and press ENTER.
4. Select **Quit** and **Fast Graph**. Quattro prompts for a block to use for the graph.
5. Select **A1..H7**, and press ENTER. Your graph will look like Figure 7.11. Since this block has more columns than rows, Quattro divides these data into series by rows. Quattro uses **A2..A7** as the legend text for the six series. The years are right-aligned labels so they are the x-axis data. B2..H2 is the first data series; B3..H3, the second data series; B4..H4, the third data series; B5..H5, the fourth data series; B6..H6, the fifth data series; and B7..H7, the sixth data series. Because you already selected a graph type and entered a graph title, Quattro uses this information for the graph.
6. Press any key except / to remove the graph from the screen.
7. Select **Series**. As you can see from the settings on the right side of the menu, Quattro has set the addresses from the block as the current graph data.
8. Select **Quit** twice to return to the READY mode.

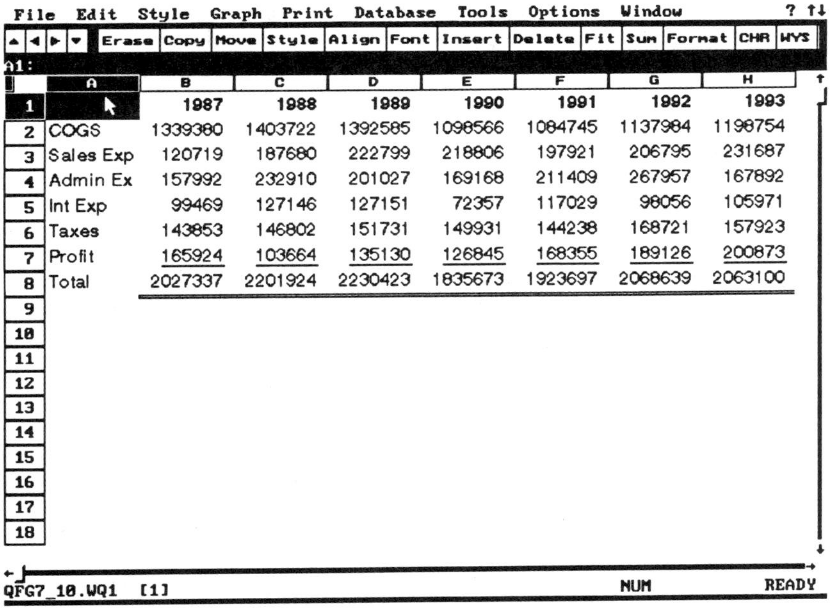

	A	B	C	D	E	F	G	H
1		1987	1988	1989	1990	1991	1992	1993
2	COGS	1339380	1403722	1392585	1098566	1084745	1137984	1198754
3	Sales Exp	120719	187680	222799	218806	197921	206795	231687
4	Admin Ex	157992	232910	201027	169168	211409	267957	167892
5	Int Exp	99469	127146	127151	72357	117029	98056	105971
6	Taxes	143853	146802	151731	149931	144238	168721	157923
7	Profit	165924	103664	135130	126845	168355	189126	200873
8	Total	2027337	2201924	2230423	1835673	1923697	2068639	2063100

Figure 7.10 Spreadsheet with Data to Graph

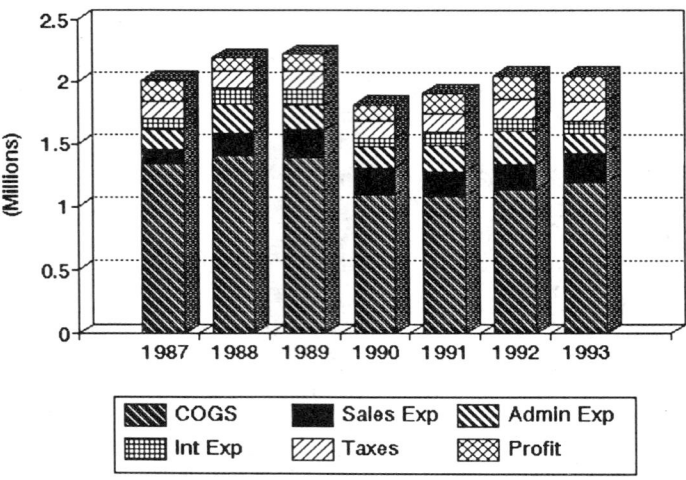

Figure 7.11 Graph Created from Spreadsheet in Figure 7.10 with /Graph Fast Graph

CUSTOMIZING A GRAPH

When you create a new graph, it is created with Quattro's default settings. To make the most out of the visual illustration which a graph can provide, you will want to customize the graph. When you customize a graph, you are giving Quattro specific presentation instructions that override default settings. With the customization options available through the Graph menus, you can add information, such as adding labels to the data points, setting the scaling of the axes, and adding boxes around the titles or legend. Customizing a graph can make the data easier to understand. All the customization options are available through the Customize Series, X-Axis, Y-Axis, and Overall menu boxes accessed from the Graph menu. In Quattro Pro 4, selecting **Customize Series, X-Axis, Y-Axis** or **Overall** displays a dialog box. While the X-Axis, Y-Axis, and Overall dialog boxes *do* not change, the Customize Series dialog box changes to fit the graph type selected with /**Graph Graph Type** as shown in Figure 7.12. The Graph Customize dialog box does not show any graph customization options that do not apply to the chosen graph type. If you are using Quattro Pro 3 or you have selected /**Options Startup Use Dialogs No**, selecting **Customize Series, X-Axis, Y-Axis,** or **Overall** displays menus that you can select to make the same customization options. You learned how to use dialog boxes in Chapter 4 with the Print Layout Options dialog box.

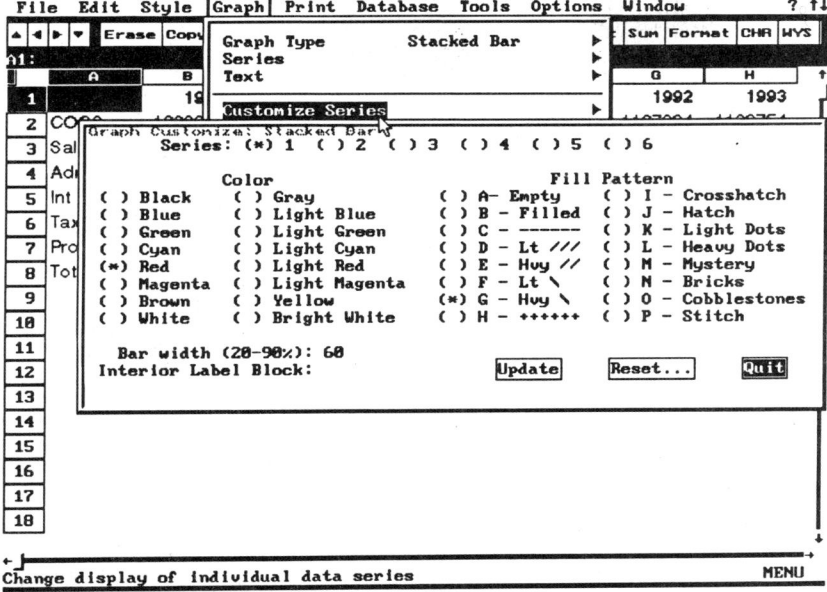

Figure 7.12 Graph Customize Dialog Box for a Stacked Bar Graph

Changing the Appearance of a Data Series

Quattro lets you change how each series of data is displayed. You can change the markers, fill patterns, labels, and override types. Each of these commands is available from the Graph Customize dialog box. In the Graph Customize dialog box, you must select the series you are customizing before you select any customizing options below.

CHANGING THE SERIES COLORS Each of the series is assigned a different color. Since Quattro can create graphs with many colors, you may want to change the color assigned to a series. To change the color, select the color from list below Color. If you do not see the Graph Customize dialog box, select Colors, the series to change, the color you want, and Quit. The appearance of the colors depends on the monitor, the graphics adapter card, and the setting for the /Options Hardware Screen command. When you view the graph, Quattro displays the graph using the colors you have selected (if your monitor can do so).

CHANGING THE FILL PATTERN When you create a bar, rotated bar, stacked bar, area, or 3-D graph, Quattro assigns each series a different fill pattern. Changing the fill pattern allows you to change the pattern that represents each series. You can change the fill pattern to emphasize or deemphasize different series. To change the fill pattern, select the pattern from the list below Fill Pattern. If you do not see the Graph Customize dialog box, select Fill Patterns, the series to change, the new fill pattern for the series, and Quit. When you view the graph, Quattro uses the fill pattern that you selected for the specified series.

CHANGING THE MARKERS, LINE STYLES, AND FORMATS For line graphs, Quattro assigns each series a different marker and connects the markers with a solid line. Changing the marker and lines allows you to select the symbol and line that represent the data points for each series. To change the markers and lines, use Line Style, Marker, and Format in the Graph Customize dialog box shown in Figure 7.13. If you do not see the Graph Customize dialog box, select Markers & Lines. To change the appearance of the lines, choose one of the options under Line Style or select Line Styles, the series, and the new line style if you do not have a dialog box.

To change the marker for a series, select an option below Marker in the Graph Customize dialog box or select Markers, the series, the new marker, and Quit.

To change whether Quattro marks the data points and connects the series with a line, select Format or, if you do not see a Graph Customize dialog box, select Formats and the series to change. Next, select how data points in that series is marked. If you select Lines, Quattro draws a line to each point in the series but does not display a marker at each data point. Selecting Symbols marks the data points with markers but does not connect the data points in each series with a line. Selecting Both marks the data points with markers and connects the data points in

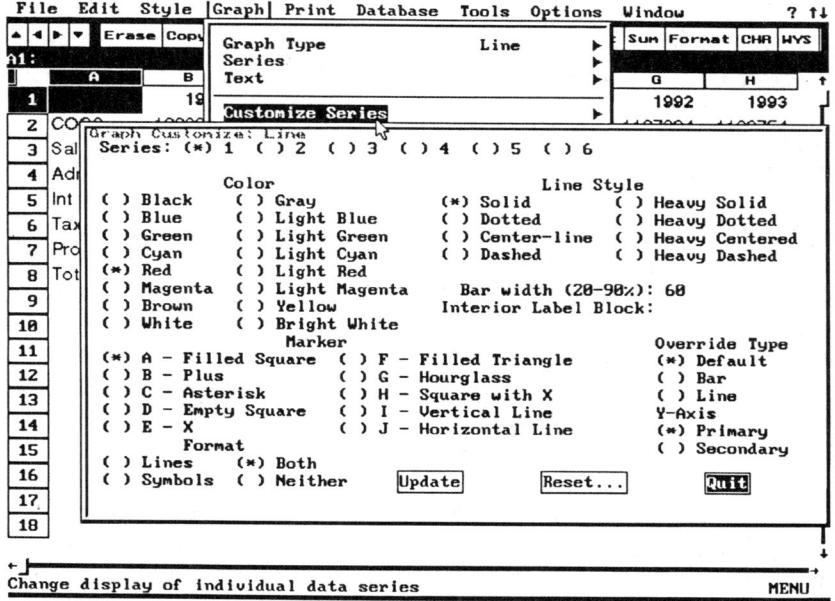

Figure 7.13 Graph Customize Dialog Box for a Line Graph

a series with a line. Selecting **Neither** does not mark the data points with lines or markers. This option is used when you want to mark the data points with their values instead of a marker by adding Interior Labels as described later.

SETTING THE BAR WIDTH In bar, rotated bar, 3-D bar, and stacked bar graphs, Quattro uses part of the x-axis for the bars and the remaining part of the x-axis for blank areas between bars. Each bar is the same width as the others. Quattro initially uses 40% of the x-axis for space between bars and 60% of the x-axis for the bars. You can change the percentage that Quattro uses for the bars. When you increase the percentage, the bars become wider. When you decrease the percentage, the bars become narrower. To change the percentage, select **Bar Width**. Quattro prompts for a percentage between 20% and 90%. When you enter a percentage, Quattro uses the new percentage if the graph type is bar, rotated bar, 3-D bar, or stacked bar.

CHANGING THE INTERIOR LABELS The graph in Figure 7.9 shows multiple series of data plotted in one graph, but the graph does not show the exact values for each point. You can approximate each point's value by its relation to the y-axis. If you need more exact information, you can instruct Quattro to display the values of each point in a graph. Displaying the interior labels, unlike setting series fill patterns and colors, can be done for bubble graphs as well as all other graph types except pie, column, and text.

To label the data points, select Interior Label Block from the Graph Customize dialog box, or select Interior Labels from the Customize Series menu and then the series to change. Quattro prompts for the block containing the labels for the series. While in many cases the labels are the same values as the data points, they do not have to be. Use the arrow keys and the period (or the mouse) to specify the block containing the labels, and press ENTER. After you press ENTER, Quattro displays a menu for the position of the labels like the one shown in Figure 7.14. Select the word representing your selected location for the labels in relation to the data points. If you select **None**, existing labels are removed. If you are planning to display the data values in place of the data points or displaying the labels in a bubble graph, select **Center**. When you view the graph, Quattro places the data labels in the selected position. Figure 7.15 shows two line graphs. Notice that the graph on the right does not display lines or markers but displays the data point values instead; for this graph, the interior label position is Center and the format for all the series is Neither (lines or markers).

Certain graph types change the way labels are displayed, regardless of the choices that you make. Labels are not shown in area graphs. In bar and 3-D graphs, the labels are always above the bars. In rotated bar graphs, the labels are always to the right of the bars. In stacked bars, only the labels of the last series are shown at the top of the bars; the other series' labels are not shown.

USING TWO GRAPH TYPES For bar, line, and XY graphs, Quattro can combine two types of graphs into a single graph. You can use two graph types in a single

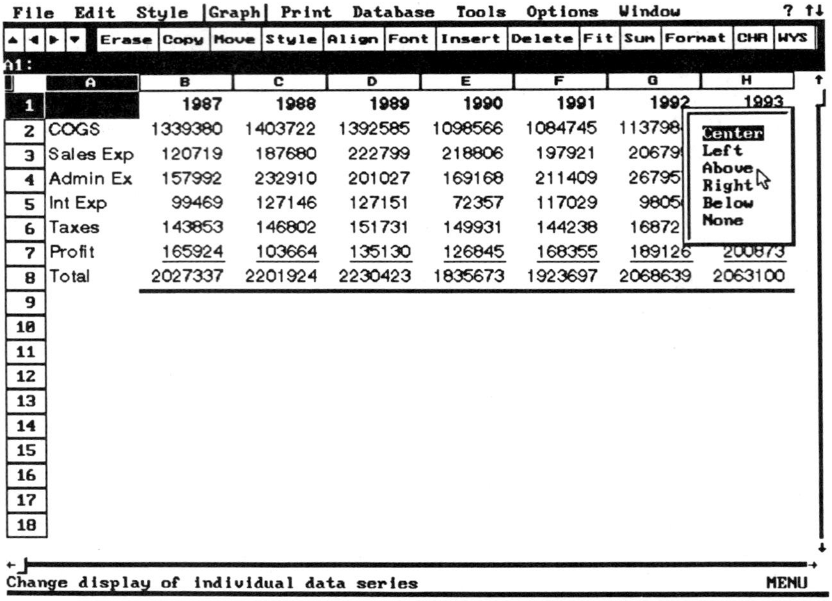

362   Quattro Pro 4.0 Handbook

```
 File   Edit   Style  |Graph|  Print   Database   Tools   Options   Window           ? ↑↓
 ▲ ◄ ► ▼  Erase Copy Move Style Align Font Insert Delete Fit Sum Format CHR WYS
A1:
        A         B        C        D        E        F        G        H
 1                1987     1988     1989     1990     1991     1992     1993
 2   COGS       1339380  1403722  1392585  1098566  1084745  113798 │Center
 3   Sales Exp   120719   187680   222799   218806   197921   20679 │Left
 4   Admin Ex    157992   232910   201027   169168   211409   26795 │Above
                                                                    │Right
 5   Int Exp      99469   127146   127151    72357   117029    9805 │Below
 6   Taxes       143853   146802   151731   149931   144238   16872 │None
 7   Profit      165924   103664   135130   126845   168355   189126   200873
 8   Total      2027337  2201924  2230423  1835673  1923697  2068639  2063100
 9
10
11
12
13
14
15
16
17
18
Change display of individual data series                              MENU
```

Figure 7.14   Menu for Positioning Labels

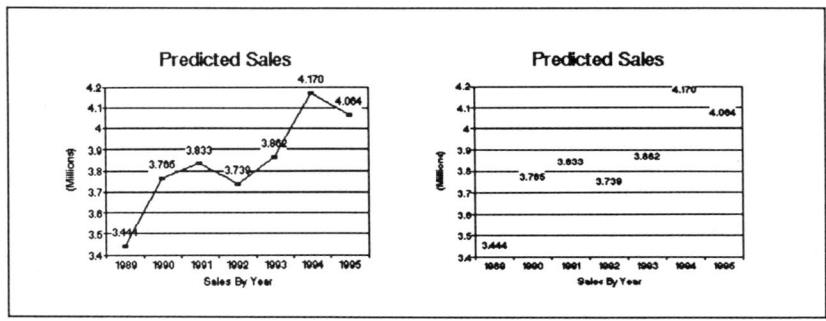

Figure 7.15   Graphs with Data Points Labeled and Label Position at Center; Format Set to Neither Only in the Graph on the Right

▼ TIP: Base the default graph type on the majority of series.

The graph type you select with /Graph Type should be the type that the majority of the series will use.

graph to display types of information that need to be graphed differently but have a relationship to each other. For example, you may graph defective products with product sales to illustrate how sales increase as defective products decrease. In this case, you may show the defective products in a bar graph and the sales in a line graph. To create a graph with two graph types, first select the basic graph type as bar, line, or XY. If you want one of the graph types to be an XY graph, you must make the default graph type an XY graph. To select the second graph type, select Override Type. If you are not in the Graph Customize dialog box, select the series that you want to use a different graph type. Select the graph type that you want the series to use. Your choices are Default (which makes the graph of the series the type selected with the /Graph Graph Type command), Bar, and Line. If you change your mind about overriding the graph type, select Default. Figure 7.16 shows a graph that combines two graph types. In this graph, the profits are shown as a bar graph and the sales are shown as a line graph. Since the number of sales dollars is so much larger than the number of profit dollars, the two data series are pushed to the opposite sides of the bar graph. By creating two y-axes, as discussed in the next section, you can display the data better. To change the graph's customization settings of the second graph type, temporarily change the default graph type to the overriding graph type, use the Graph Customize dialog box to customize the graph type, and return the graph type to the original default.

USING TWO Y-AXES When you combine graphs, the data you are displaying often are not measured by the same number of units. For example, in the data graphed in Figure 7.16, the sales are in millions while the profits are in the

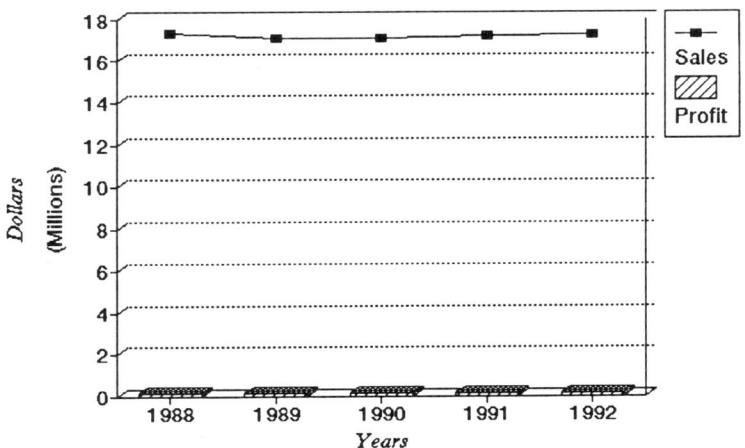

Figure 7.16 Combined Line and Bar Graph Using One Y-Axis

thousands. Since the data values are so different, the graphed data appears skewed with the sales squeezed at the top of the graph and the profits squeezed at the bottom of the graph. Another alternative is to have two axes. Using the graph in Figure 7.16, the sales data can be assigned to the first y-axis, and the profit data can be assigned to the second y-axis. When you assign data to a second y-axis, Quattro automatically creates it for you making the same assumptions Quattro uses to create the first y-axis. The second y-axis appears to the right of the graph. Only bar, line, and XY graphs can have a second y-axis. To assign series to the second y-axis, select **Y-Axis** from the Graph Customize dialog box, or Y-Axis and the series from the Customize Series menu. Then select Secondary or Secondary Y-Axis. If you change your mind, you can assign a series to the first y-axis by selecting **Primary** or **Primary Y-Axis**. Figure 7.17 shows a graph with two axes. In this graph, the profit uses the second y-axis, which is measured in thousands of dollars. By adjusting the axis using customization options for the axes (covered later in the chapter), you can control how Quattro places the data values on the graph.

RESETTING DEFAULT GRAPH SETTINGS Quattro uses many default settings when it creates a graph with your spreadsheet data. As you customize the graph's appearance, you are changing Quattro's defaults. You may want to use the settings that you have customized in place of the defaults. If you want the current settings in the Graph Customize dialog box or the Customize Series menu to be the defaults

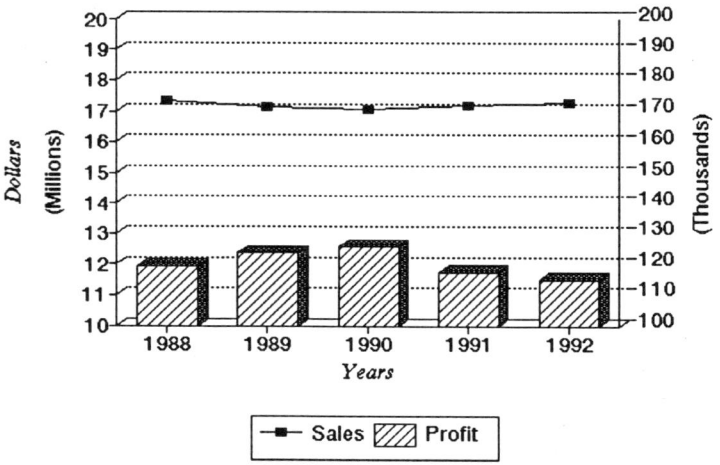

Figure 7.17 Combined Line and Bar Graph Using Two Y-Axes for the Same Information Displayed in Figure 7.16

for subsequent graphs, select **Update** from the Graph Customize dialog box or the Customize Series menu. The next graph you create uses the settings saved with this command. You can always override these defaults or create new ones. This command saves all settings made with /Graph Graph Type, /Graph Customize Series, /Graph X-Axis, /Graph Y-Axis, and /Graph Overall commands. /Graph Customize Series Update does not set defaults for either the series' blocks or the text the graph uses.

RESETTING THE GRAPH SERIES You can selectively reset any of Quattro's graph settings. To reset the values and settings for any of the series, enter /Graph Customize Series Reset, and select the series to be reset. To reset an entire graph, enter /Graph Customize Series Reset Graph. After Quattro resets a series or the entire graph, Quattro returns to the Graph Customize dialog box or the Customize Series menu. To reset other settings such as graph text, use the command for changing the setting, and press ESC and ENTER. Each setting is reset to Quattro's defaults. For some settings, the default settings may have been set previously by the **Update** command and may not be the default values used by Quattro when it was installed.

SPECIAL PIE, COLUMN, AND BUBBLE GRAPH OPTIONS Most of the customization options covered in the chapter so far are not used for pie charts or column graphs. Pie, column, and bubble graphs are very different from line and bar graphs: Only the first series of data is graphed by using a circle or column instead of axes. A second series of data is only used to select the colors and fill patterns of pie slices or column sections and to choose which pie slices are exploded. Bubble graphs use the second series to select the sizes of the bubbles that are placed in the location selected by the first series. Another difference in pie charts and column graphs is that the x-axis values are used as labels for the pieces of the pie created from the first series of data. In bubble graphs, the x-axis values can be either numbers or labels, since the bubble graph has an x-axis as part of its graph, although it shares many customization options with pie and column graphs.

Pie, column, and bubble graphs have their own set of customization options and have their own format commands to show the numeric labels for the series. Pie, column, and bubble graphs are the only types of graphs that allow each value within a series to have a different color and fill pattern. Quattro also lets you explode slices of the pie to focus attention on a particular data point. Therefore, when you select **Customize Series**, you must select which slice or bubble you want to customize before you make selections in the lower half of the dialog box. If you do not see the Graph Customize dialog box, select **Pies** for pie and column graphs or **Bubbles** for bubble graphs. From the menus you see when you select **Pies** or **Bubbles**, when you make a selection, you will then need to select which slice or bubble to change.

FORMATTING LABELS When you first create a pie graph or column graph, Quattro divides the pie into slices or the column into sections. Each slice of the pie or each section of the column represents a value in the series in proportion to the

> ▼ **TIP:** Customization options can prevent overlapping series.
>
> Use the axes' customization options to prevent one series from overlapping another series.

total. Quattro displays the proportion next to the pie slice or column section as a percentage. You can change the format of the proportion by selecting Label Format from the Graph Customize dialog box or the Pies menu.. You can then select Value, which shows the values as they appear on the spreadsheet; %, which shows the values as a percentage of the total; $, which shows the values with a preceding dollar sign and commas inserted; or None, which does not display the proportion. To add labels for bubble graphs, use the /Graph Customize Series Interior Labels command described earlier.

CHANGING THE COLOR OF PIE SLICES, COLUMN SEGMENTS, AND BUBBLES In pie charts and column graphs, Quattro automatically uses different colors for the different slices. In bubble graphs, Quattro Pro automatically uses different colors for each bubble. You can change Quattro's assignment of colors by selecting a color from the list under Color. From the Pies or Bubbles menu, select Colors, the slice or bubble to change the color, and Quit. Quattro only lets you select the colors for the first nine slices, sections, or bubbles, and then it repeats the colors selected for the first nine slices, sections, or bubbles as color selections for slices or sections 10 through 18. Changing the color assigned to a pie slice or column section also changes the color assigned to a bubble and vice versa.

CHANGING THE FILL PATTERNS OF PIE SLICES, COLUMN SECTIONS, AND BUBBLES Quattro automatically uses different fill patterns for the different slices in a pie chart, sections in a column graph, or bubbles in a bubble graph, but also allows you to customize them. To make the change, select a pattern under Fill Pattern in the Graph Customize dialog box. From the Pies or Bubbles menu, select Patterns, the slice or bubble to change, the new fill pattern, and Quit. Just as with color, Quattro only lets you change the first nine slices, sections, or bubbles, and it repeats the same fill patterns for the remaining slices, sections, and bubbles. Changing the pattern assigned to a pie slice or column section also changes the color assigned to a bubble and vice versa.

EXPLODING PIE SLICES Quattro allows you to explode pieces from a pie, effectively pulling slices out from the rest of the pie graph (see Figure 7.18). This option is not available for column or bubble graphs. Exploding a pie slice emphasizes the particular piece. You can explode a pie slice by entering Explode (and selecting

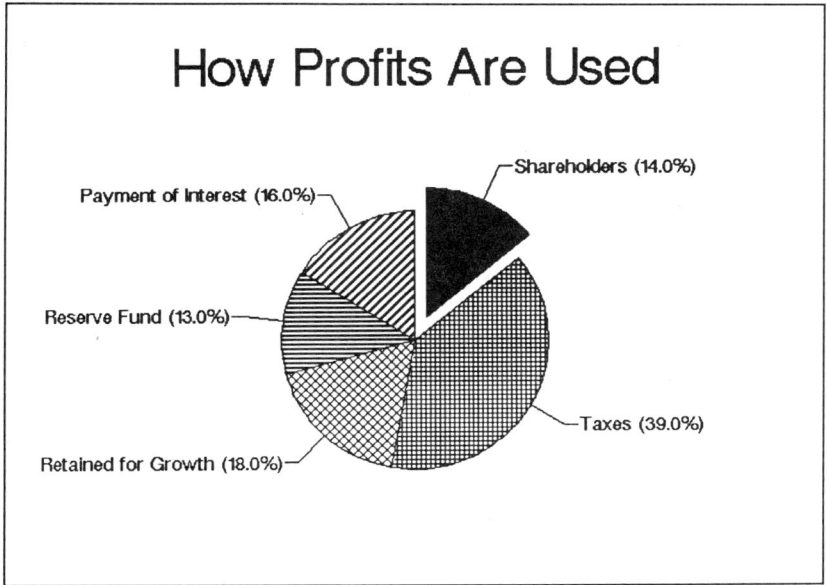

Figure 7.18 Pie Graph with Shareholders Slice Exploded

the slice that you want to explode if you are choosing Explode from the Pies menu). The menu that Quattro subsequently displays lets you choose from Explode or Don't Explode. When you explode a pie slice, the slice you selected is separated from the rest as shown in Figure 7.16.

DISPLAYING AND HIDING TICK MARKS The pie slices and column sections initially have tick marks that connect the labels to the slices or sections. You can remove them. To remove the tick marks, select Tick Marks, then select No. If you decide you want to add them at a later time, enter Tick Marks, and select Yes.

USING A SECOND SERIES FOR PIE CHARTS AND COLUMN GRAPHS You can also make many of the menu selections for pie charts and column graphs by selecting a second series that contains values Quattro understands as color, fill pattern, and exploding codes. The codes for the color and fill pattern are numbers ranging between 1 and 9. With numbers greater than 9 and less than 99, Quattro wraps the colors and the values. For example, a color and pattern code of 10 is the same as a color and pattern code of 1. Quattro uses values of 100 and greater to select which pie slices are exploded. When 100 is added to the color code, Quattro uses the code to select the color and fill pattern as well as exploding the pie slice. Figure 7.19 shows a spreadsheet that uses C3..C7 as a second data series. The

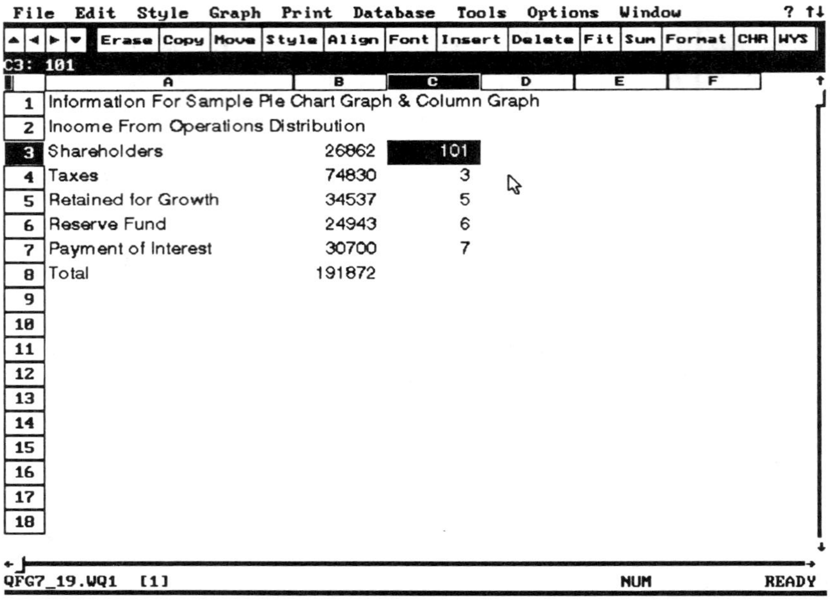

```
File   Edit   Style   Graph   Print   Database   Tools   Options   Window          ? ↑↓
 ▲ ◄ ► ▼  Erase Copy Move Style Align Font Insert Delete Fit Sum Format CHR WYS
C3: 101
          A                          B            C          D          E          F
  1  Information For Sample Pie Chart Graph & Column Graph
  2  Income From Operations Distribution
  3  Shareholders                26862         101
  4  Taxes                       74830           3
  5  Retained for Growth         34537           5
  6  Reserve Fund                24943           6
  7  Payment of Interest         30700           7
  8  Total                      191872
  9
 10
 11
 12
 13
 14
 15
 16
 17
 18

QFG7_19.WQ1  [1]                                              NUM             READY
```

Figure 7.19 Spreadsheet with Second Series for Setting First Series Appearance

values in the second series determine the fill pattern for the pie slices and which pie slices are exploded. The resulting graph is shown in Figure 7.18.

SETTING THE MAXIMUM SIZE OF BUBBLES In Quattro Pro 4 bubble graphs, you can set the maximum size of the bubbles so larger bubbles do not hide smaller ones. To set the maximum size of the bubbles, select **Max Bubble Size** from the Graph Customize dialog box or Bubbles menu. Next, type a number between 1 and 25 for the maximum percentage of the x-axis the bubble may occupy, and press ENTER. The maximum bubble size determines how large the bubbles are relative to each other, so entering a smaller number reduces the size of all bubbles.

▼ **TIP: Use formulas to choose which pie slice to explode.**

You can use formulas to select which pie slices explode so slices explode when other conditions are met (such as when sales exceed quotas).

Changing the Format and Scaling of the Graph Axes

When you create your first graphs, you will probably let Quattro use the default settings for the graph's axes. These assumptions include how the scale should be divided and where the tick marks should be placed on the axes. As you start to customize your graph, Quattro lets you change these assumptions so that you can design a graph to effectively present your specific data. You can also make your settings the defaults for all new graphs. All these commands are available through the /Graph X-Axis and /Graph Y-Axis, depending on the axis that you want to modify. These commands do not affect pie charts, column graphs, and text graphs (none of which have axes). When you have finished changing the axis, select Quit to return to the previous menu. If you want to make the new settings the defaults, use the /Graph Customize Series Update command.

CHANGING THE SCALING In most graphs, the y-axis is automatically scaled to fit the data points. In XY graphs, the x-axis is automatically scaled. Quattro creates the scale so that the graph has extra space on the top not used by the data points. You can reset the scale to any consistent format that you want. For example, if you are graphing the change in your company's gross margin profit percentage, you want to readjust the scale to show the small changes in the gross profit margin, since a small change can drastically change the company's profit. In this example, you may want to show only the range from 40% to 60%. Changing the scale requires these steps:

1. Type /, and select Graph.
2. Select X-Axis or Y-Axis, depending on which axis you want to change. If you want to alter the secondary y-axis select 2nd Y-Axis from the Y-Axis Options dialog box or Y-Axis menu.
3. Select Scale to choose whether the axis is set automatically by Quattro or manually by you.
4. Select Manual. When the scaling is set to automatic, the High, Increment, and Low choices for how the axis should be scaled are ignored.
5. Select Low, type the lowest number you want on the scale, and press ENTER. The number you provide should be as small or smaller than the lowest number in the series. If you are graphing negative numbers, make sure that this number has a minus sign before it. In the gross profit margin example, you would enter .4 or 40%.
6. Select High, type the highest number that you want on the scale, and press ENTER. The number you type should be as large or larger than the largest number in the series. In the gross profit margin example, you would enter .6 or 60%.

7. Select Increment, type the number representing the interval between each tick mark, and press ENTER. If this number is too small, the grid lines and tick marks become indistinguishable. In the gross profit margin example, the entry is .02 or 2%.

Once you have described the new scaling, Quattro changes the scaling of the current graph to the settings you have selected. When the scale numbers are very large or very small, Quattro divides the numbers for the scaling by a power of 10, such as thousands or millions. Quattro defaults to showing the scaling used next to the y-axis title. For the gross profit margin example, the rescaled graph looks like Figure 7.20.

DISPLAYING THE SCALING When Quattro changes the scaling numbers by multiplying the numbers by a power of ten, it displays a scale measurement next to the axis. You can hide this information from display by selecting Display Scaling No. To redisplay the information, select Display Scaling Yes.

CHANGING THE TICK MARKS When you create a graph, Quattro uses default settings for the tick marks but these can be changed. You can format the numbers next to the tick marks, change their frequency, or make other changes to the tick mark settings. Quattro initially creates tick marks that evenly divide the axis. You can instruct Quattro to place them at different intervals. Also, you can replace

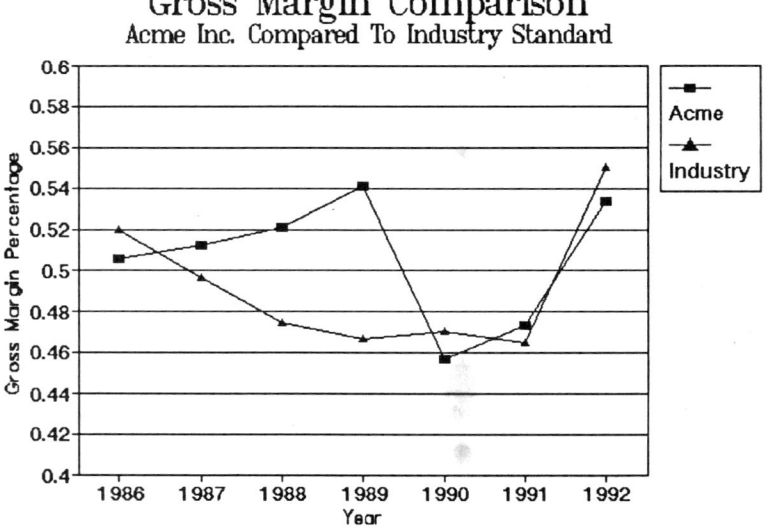

Figure 7.20 Graph Showing Fluctuations in Gross Margin Percentage

some of the tick marks with minor tick marks to keep the axis from appearing too crowded. Minor tick marks do not have numeric labels next to them and do not connect with grid lines. For the x-axis you can alternate the placement of labels on two lines next to the tick marks to prevent overlapping labels (for all graph types except XY graphs).

Setting the Format of Tick Mark Labels In Figure 7.20, the gross margin percentage is graphed over a period of time. The numbers on the y-axis are displayed with decimals. Here, it is more helpful to label the numbers as percentages. Quattro lets you format the numeric labels for the tick marks on either axis by selecting /Graph X-Axis or Y-Axis Format of Ticks. After you select Format of Ticks, Quattro displays a box listing all formats available with the /Options Formats Numeric Format command. After you have chosen the format for the scale numbers and specified the number of digits after the decimal point, Quattro returns you to the axis dialog box or menu. Figure 7.21 shows the same graph with the gross margin percentages formatted as percentages instead of decimals.

Creating Minor Ticks When a scale has small intervals, the numeric labels become jammed together, making it difficult to read the graph. Since the tick marks appear at regular intervals, removing some tick mark labels makes the remaining values

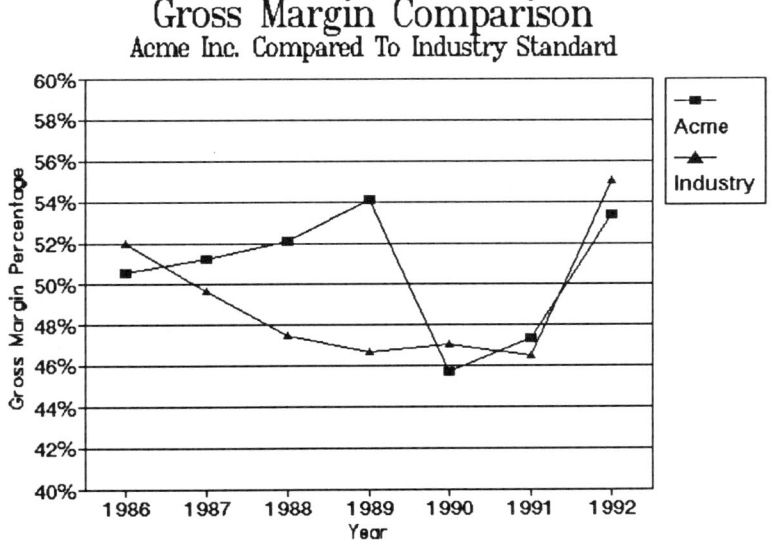

Figure 7.21 Graph in Figure 7.20 with Y-Axis Labels Formatted as Percentages

legible and makes it easier to determine the values on the graph. Minor ticks do not connect with grid lines.

You can convert some of the tick marks to minor tick marks to make their labels disappear. To convert tick marks to minor tick marks, select **No.** of Minor Ticks, type the number of minor ticks that you want between the major ones, and press ENTER. When you view the graph, the first tick is a major tick. After that, the tick marks alternate between major and minor, with the number of minor ticks dictated by your entry. Figure 7.22 contains a graph that combines minor and major ticks on the y-axis.

Making Labels Alternate When an x-axis has labels jammed together, you can make them more legible by placing them on two lines. Quattro alternates the label placement between the two lines. When you choose Alternate Ticks from the X-Axis dialog box or menu, you must select whether labels are alternated. If you choose Yes, the labels are alternated between two lines as in Figure 7.22. If you choose No, all labels are on the same line as in Figure 7.21. Even when you alternate tick marks, you can still have overlapping labels if the x-axis has more label entries than can fit.

SETTING SCALING FOR AN AXIS When you are graphing data, Quattro initially uses a standard scale. A standard scale means the increments are the same between each tick mark. Quattro also has a logarithmic scale. In a logarithmic

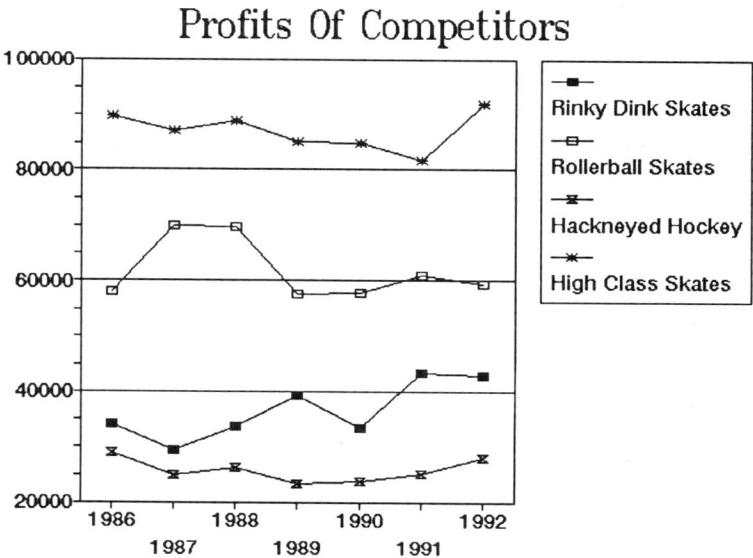

Figure 7.22 Graph Combining Major and Minor Ticks on the Y-Axis and Using Two Lines for Labels on the X-Axis

> ▼ **TIP: Change point size to make labels fit.**
>
> If labels still do not fit after alternating them, change the point size with the /Graph Text Font Data & Tick Labels command.

scale, the difference between each tick mark is a power of 10. For example, if the first tick mark is 1, the second tick mark is 10, and the third tick mark is 100. To change the tick mark scaling to logarithmic, select Mode and Log from the axis dialog box or menu. To return the axis to the standard scaling, select Mode and Normal. Figure 7.23 shows two versions of a graph, one scaled with a standard scale and one with a logarithmic scale.

Making Overall Changes to a Graph

Quattro lets you change several characteristics that affect the entire graph. You can change the grid Quattro displays, add outlines around the titles, legend, or entire graph, select the background color, add a three-dimensional effect, and select whether Quattro displays the graph in color or in monochrome. Each of these commands is available from the Graph Overall dialog box shown in Figure 7.24 that Quattro displays with the /Graph Overall command. If you want the new settings to become the defaults, use the /Graph Customize Series Update command, which saves the overall graph changes as the new defaults.

ADDING GRID LINES TO A GRAPH The grid marks that Quattro initially puts on a graph are designed to make it easier to estimate the exact values for data in a series. Quattro provides different settings that let you change the appearance of

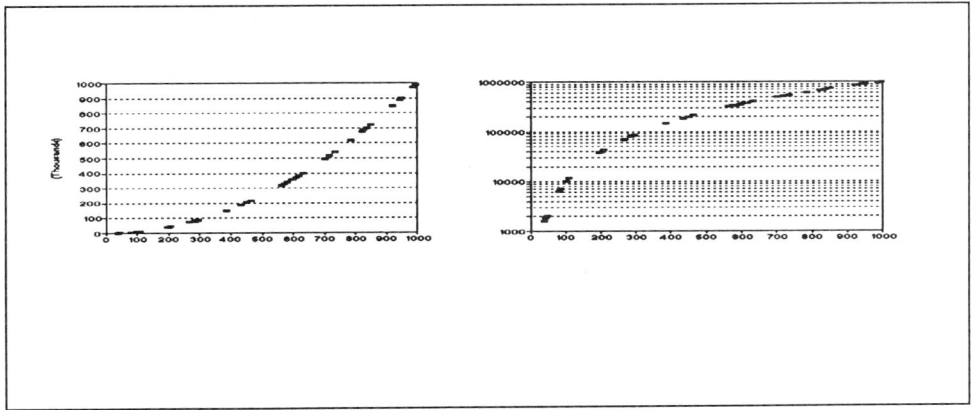

Figure 7.23 Standard and Logarithmic Scaling

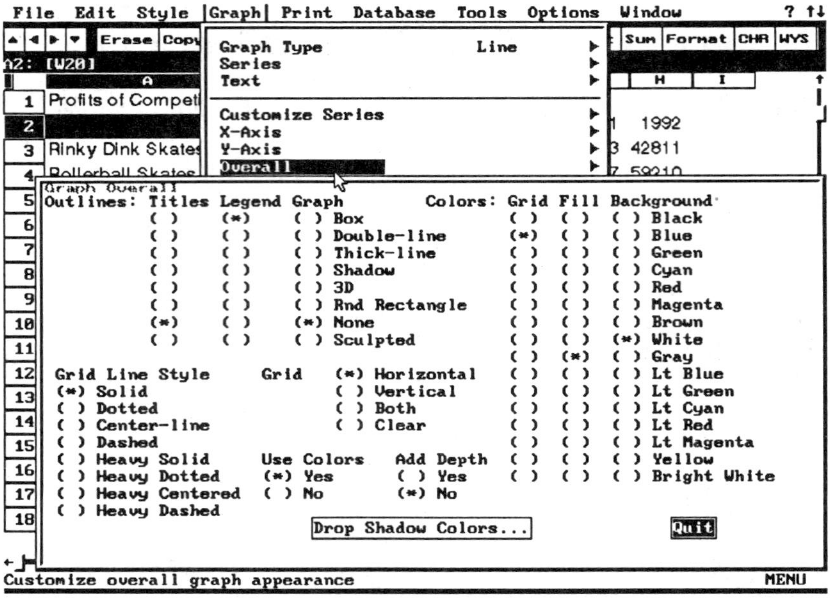

Figure 7.24 Graph Overall Dialog Box

the grid. With the options Quattro provides, you can change the grid lines to display the different series without cluttering the design. Quattro initially displays dotted grid lines starting from the tick marks on the y-axis.

The choices to the right of Grid selects the direction of the grid lines. If you do not see the Graph Overall dialog box, select Grid to change the graph's grid lines. Selecting Horizontal draws grid lines from the first y-axis. Selecting Vertical draws grid lines originating from the x-axis. Selecting Both draws grid lines originating from the x-axis and from the first y-axis. Selecting Clear removes grid lines created with the other selections. If you create a rotated bar graph, which has a vertical x-axis and a horizontal y-axis, the grid lines rotate so they start from the same axis from which the grid lines would start in a bar graph. For example, selecting Horizontal in a bar graph creates horizontal lines starting from the y-axis, and selecting Horizontal in a rotated bar graph creates vertical lines starting from the y-axis.

Selecting a color below Grid chooses the color of the grid lines. Selecting an option below Grid Line Style chooses the line style of the grid lines. Selecting a color below Fill chooses the color of the area behind the graphed data. Without the Graph Overall dialog box, select Grid Color and a color to set the color of the grid lines, select Line Style and a line style to change the lines of the grid lines, and select Fill Color and a color to set the color of the area behind the graphed data.

DRAWING BOXES IN A GRAPH Quattro initially only creates a box around the graphed data and legend. You can add boxes that surround the first and second title at the top of the graph, the legends, or the entire graph. To add a box in one of these locations, choose an option below Titles (the two lines at the top of the graph), Legend, or Graph. You can select from Box, Double-line, Thick-line, Shadow, 3D, or Rnd Rectangle. Quattro Pro 3 and above includes a Sculpted option that adds a sculpted outline such as the sculpted outlines around the row numbers and column letters in the WYSIWYG display mode. If you later want to remove a box, select None from the outline selections. Figure 7.25 shows a graph that uses three styles of boxes. You can also add boxes with the graph annotator (discussed later in the chapter). If you are not using dialog boxes, you can add outlines to the graph by selecting Outlines, where you want the outline added, and the type of line for the outline.

SETTING THE GRAPH'S BACKGROUND COLOR To change the color Quattro uses to draw the graph, select a color below Background from the Graph Overall dialog box. If you are not using dialog boxes, select Background Color and a color from the list. The appearance of the colors depends on the monitor, the graphics adapter card, and the setting for the /Options Hardware Screen command.

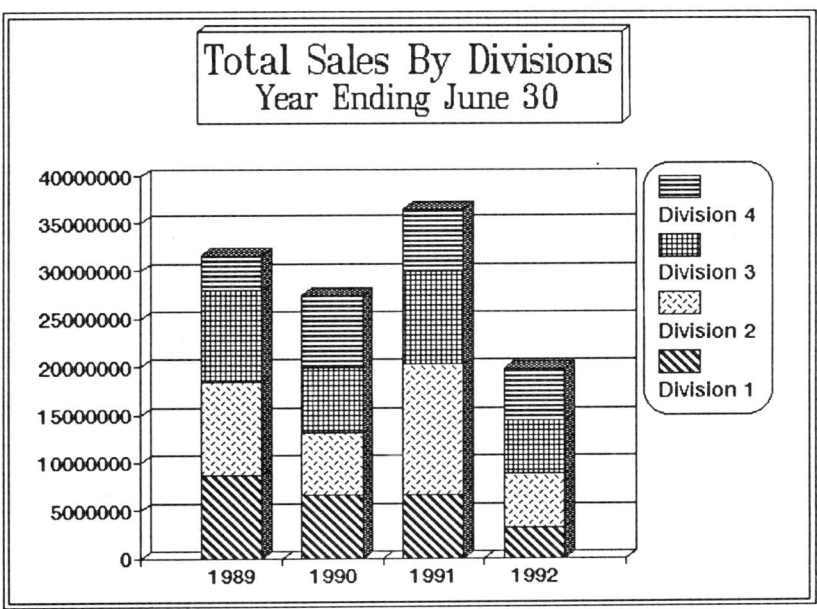

Figure 7.25   Graph with Three Different Outlines Around Boxes

ADDING A THREE-DIMENSIONAL EFFECT Another enhancement Quattro can make is adding a three-dimensional effect that makes the data series or points look like they are created with three-dimensional bars, column sections, or pie slices. This three-dimensional effect is different from the three-dimensional effect created with the 3-D graph types. A three-dimensional effect can be used in bar, rotated bar, stacked bar, 3-D graphs, column graphs, and in pie charts. Figure 7.26 shows both bar and pie graphs with a three-dimensional effect and their flat counterparts. If you want to remove the three-dimensional effect, select Add Depth and select No. If you change this setting to No for the bar, step, or area 3-D graph types, the graph will lose its three-dimensional appearance, but the graph will still look different from the bar or area charts, since the series are placed in front of each other. The ribbon graph will look like a line graph. If you later want to add the three-dimensional effect, select Add Depth and select Yes. You may want to remove the three-dimensional effect when you have so many data points that the three-dimensional effect creates a congested graph. If you are not using dialog boxes, select Three-D and then Yes or No to add or remove the three-dimensional effect.

With a pie chart, the three-dimensional effect slants the circle to show the depth of the pie slices. Without a three-dimensional effect, the circle is shown with its full perspective. In a pie chart with more than 50 data points, the pie chart is displayed without the three-dimensional effect regardless of the three-dimensional effect setting.

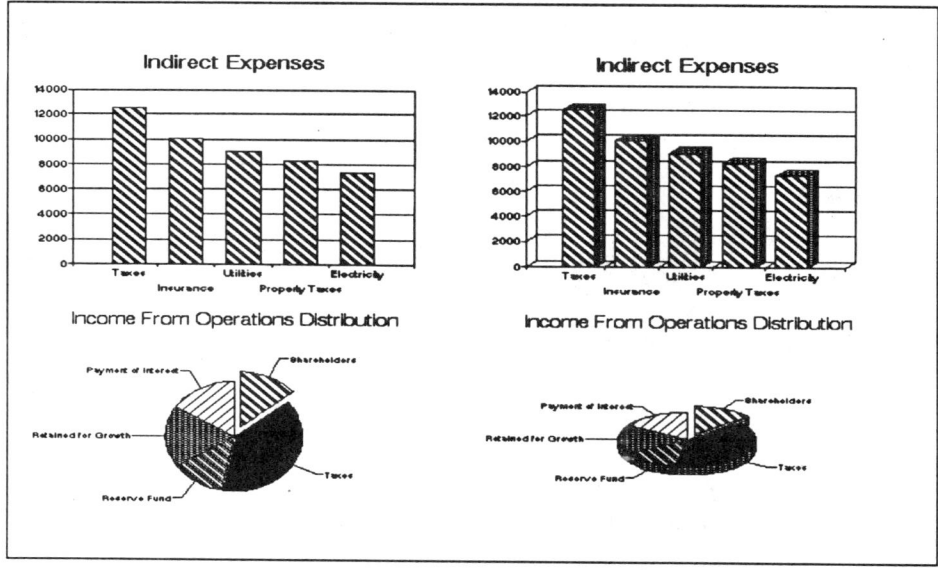

Figure 7.26 Three-Dimensional Effect on Bar and Pie Graphs

SETTING IF THE GRAPH USES COLOR Quattro provides many menu commands so you can take advantage of the color display capabilities of your screen. If you are planning to print the graph to a printer that cannot print colors or your screen cannot display colors, you do not want the graph to use colors to distinguish the different parts of the graph. To set Quattro to display the graph using one color, select No underneath Use Colors in the Graph Overall dialog box. If you later want to display the graph in color, select Yes underneath Use Colors. When you display a graph in black and white (or monochrome), Quattro distinguishes the series with different fill patterns. If you are not using dialog boxes, select Color/B&W and then either B&W or Color to select whether the graph is monochrome or uses colors.

THE GRAPH ANNOTATOR

Most of the graph features are available through Quattro's menus. These graphics features provide most graph enhancements although there are limitations on their placement. The graph annotator provides additional graph enhancements. Unlike the other graph features, the graph annotator is a free-form graph manipulator that allows you to draw and reposition any element in a graph. An element can be text, a box, a line, or an image stored in a clipboard file. The graph annotator provides the ultimate in graph manipulation since it has few restrictions on what you add or remove from the graph or where you put it. Text graphs often use the graph annotator since the text graph provides an empty screen that you can fill with the graph annotator. The graph annotator also can change the characteristics of the graph features that you set with Quattro's Graph menus.

Activating the Graph Annotator

Starting the graph annotator is simple—so simple that you might accidentally start using it without realizing it. To start the graph annotator, use the /Graph Annotate command. Another option is to view the graph and type /. This lets you use the graph annotator at any time. Once Quattro loads the graph annotator, the Quattro displays the current graph in the graph annotator screen like the one shown in Figure 7.27. If you want to use a named graph with the graph annotator, you must make the named graph the current graph before invoking the graph annotator. If a graph is not defined when you start the graph annotator, Quattro creates a text graph as the current graph so you have an empty graph screen to use.

The screen in the graph annotator is divided into four parts. The squares at the top of the screen make up the *toolbox*. This is just like the menu bar that Quattro displays above a spreadsheet. You use the toolbox to tell the graph annotator what you want to do. Each of the boxes in the toolbox contains a symbol (or *icon*) that represents the task that the box will perform if selected.

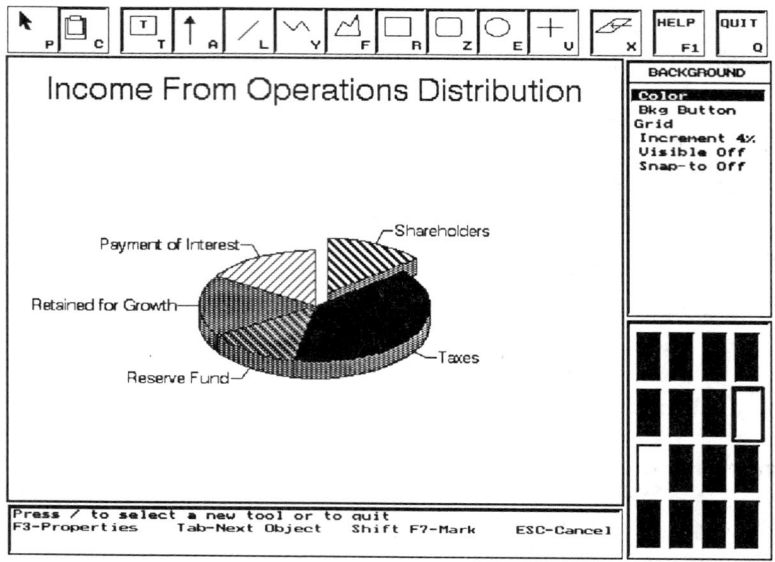

Figure 7.27 Initial Graph Annotator Screen

The rectangle containing the graph is the *drawing area*. This shows how the graph looks at any time. When you add to and change the graph, you use the drawing area to indicate the elements you want to change. The drawing area is filled with *elements*. An element can be a graph title, graph legend, the actual graph (without the titles or legend), or an item you add with the graph annotator. When you modify a graph with the graph annotator, you must select the element you want to change.

The text to the right of the drawing area and just below the toolbox is the *property sheet*. This is similar to the pull-down menus that Quattro displays when you select a menu item on the menu bar, since the selections in the property sheet are determined by which toolbox icon is selected. The property sheet contains the properties for the element that you can change. For example, if a text element is selected, you can change the color and font, and you can create a box around it.

The rectangle in the lower-right that contains smaller rectangles is the *gallery*. From the gallery you can select properties for an element such as colors, fill patterns, and line styles. Quattro automatically adjusts the selections in the gallery to match the highlighted attribute in the property sheet.

Many of the keys you use for spreadsheets work the same way for the graph annotator. Typing / activates the toolbox just as typing / in a spreadsheet activates the menu bar. If you ever need help, press F1 (HELP), which presents context-sensitive help. Pressing HOME or END moves you to the first or last icon in the toolbox or attribute in the property sheet. The PGUP, PGDN, END, and HOME keys perform differently in the drawing area, since they move diagonally. Another combination that is different in the drawing area is combining SHIFT and one of the arrow keys. Pressing an arrow key moves in the direction of the arrow. Pressing SHIFT and an arrow key also moves in the direction of the arrow. The difference is the amount the pointer moves. Combining SHIFT and an arrow key moves the pointer ten times more than does the arrow key alone.

You can tell which area of the screen your keystrokes will affect: The box around the current annotator area is a double line. If you want to return to the drawing area from the toolbox or property sheet, press ESC. A toolbox icon is selected by typing / and the letter at the lower-right of the icon. Like Quattro's other menus, you can also use the arrow keys to highlight the icon you want and press ENTER. To move to the property sheet, press F3. When you are ready to leave the graph annotator and return to the screen you had before you invoked the graph annotator, enter /Q. All changes you make with the graph annotator remain with the current graph. The next time you view the current graph, the graph appears as it did before you left the graph annotator. If you are using a mouse, you can select a toolbox icon, an attribute from the property sheet, a selection from the gallery, or an element from the drawing area simply by pointing to it and pressing the mouse button.

The elements that are in a graph are layered on top of one another. For example, if you add text in the middle of a graph, the text that is treated as an element is layered on top of the other element, the graph. Quattro also layers windows this way. When you select an element, Quattro displays the element on the top, just as selecting a window places that window on top of other windows.

Adding Elements to a Graph

Most of the icons in the toolbox are element icons. These are icons that you can use to draw elements. Quattro has the following element icons.

- Text (/T)—This icon adds an element that contains text surrounded with an optional box. This is used for adding text to describe and explain the graph. In a text graph, it can be used to create opening slides, flow charts, or organization charts. Options for the text include the font, justification, and color. Options for the box include the line style of the box, the color, and the fill pattern. To omit the box, select the None box from the gallery for box types. You can also use this icon to use a text element as a button, which will display another graph or perform a macro when selected.

- Arrow (/A)—This icon adds a line with an arrow at one side. This is used to connect an element to the data it represents or to emphasize part of the text. You can change the color of the arrowhead and the color and style of the line.

- Line (/L)—This icon adds a line. Lines are added to connect elements in a graph as well as to separate portions of the graph. You can change the color and style of the line.
- Polyline (/Y)—This icon adds connected lines. A polyline is used for drawing connecting lines without breaks. You can use this for drawing elements such as logos. You can change the color or style of the line.
- Polygon (/F)—This icon adds a multishaped element. To draw a polygon, you select each endpoint of the shape you are creating. When the element is completed, Quattro fills the polygon with the selected fill pattern and color. You can use this for drawing elements such as logos. You can change the color and fill pattern of the shape, as well as the color and style of the line.
- Rectangle (/R)—This icon creates a rectangle or square by the selection of two opposite corners. The difference between a square and a rectangle is that the height and width of a square are the same, but the height and width of a rectangle are different. This is used to put boxes around other elements or to create a box in which you can put other elements. You can select the color and fill pattern of the box, as well as the color and style of the line.
- Rounded Rectangle (/Z)—This icon creates a rectangle or square with curved corners by the selection of two opposite corners. The difference between a square and a rectangle is that the height and width of a square are the same, but the height and width of a rectangle are different. This is used to put boxes around other elements or to create a box in which you can put other elements. You can select the color and fill pattern of the box, as well as the color and style of the line.
- Ellipse (/E)—This icon creates a circle or ellipse by the selection of two opposite corners that create a box for the ellipse or circle to fill. The difference between an ellipse and a circle is that the height and width of a circle are the same, but the height and width of an ellipse are different. This is used to draw a circle or ellipse that is part of another drawing (such as a logo) or an area in which you can add text. You can select the color and fill pattern, as well as the color and style of the line that defines the ellipse.
- Vertical/Horizontal Line (/V)—This icon creates a perfectly straight vertical or horizontal line. This is used in place of the Line icon, so you do not have to worry whether the line is straight.

ADDING AN ELEMENT To add an element, first select the element you want to add, set the attributes, then tell Quattro where you want to put the element in the drawing area. When adding some elements, like text, you also must describe other information that is specific to the icon, such as the text you want to add. To add an icon without using a mouse, follow these steps:

1. Type / to activate the toolbox, and type the letter of the icon you want to add.

2. Press F3 to make the property sheet active.
3. Set the attributes for the element you want to create. Either type the first letter of the attribute or highlight the attribute, and press ENTER. For most of the attributes, you will either make a selection from the gallery or select from a superimposed menu. If you are selecting the font for text, the selections are the same for selecting the font for the graph text from the Graph menus. For text you may change the justification of the text within the box and how much a drop shadow is shifted from the original letters.
4. Press ESC to return to the drawing area.
5. Move the pointer to where you want the element to begin. If you are drawing an arrow, a line, a polyline, or a polygon, you will need to select the position where the element begins. If you are drawing a rectangle, rounded rectangle, or ellipse, you will need to select one corner of the rectangle that the element will fill.
6. Type the text you want to add as an element or type a period to lock the beginning of the element. For a text element, if you want the text to continue on a new line but in the same box, press CTRL-ENTER.
7. Finish the selections for the element. For a text element, press ENTER. For an arrow or line, point to where you want the line or arrow to end and press ENTER. For a polyline, move to the point where you want the first line to end, and press ENTER. Then move to where you want the second line to end, and press ENTER. Continue moving to the end of the next line and pressing ENTER until you have completed the line. When the polyline is finished, press ENTER a second time. For a polygon, move to the point where you want the first line or the shape to end and press ENTER. Then continue moving to the end of the next line and pressing ENTER until you have completed the lines that define the shape. You do not have to draw the line from the first point of the polygon to the last point since Quattro draws it for you. When the polygon is finished, press ENTER a second time. For a rectangle, rounded rectangle, and ellipse, move to the opposite corner and press ENTER.

Adding more of the same type of elements is easy. If you want to change the attributes for the new element, repeat steps 2 through 7. If you want to use the same attributes for the new element, repeat only steps 5 through 7.

If you are using a mouse, the steps are slightly different. To add elements with a mouse, follow these steps:

1. Point to the icon for the element type you want to add, and press the mouse button.
2. Set the attributes for the element you want to create by pointing to the attribute you want to change and pressing the mouse button. For most of the attributes, you will either make a selection from the gallery or select from a superimposed menu by pointing to your choice and pressing the mouse button. Selecting the font for text uses the same menus for selecting the font of the graph text from the Graph menus.

3. Move the pointer to where you want the element to begin in the drawing area. If you are drawing an arrow, a line, a polyline, or a polygon, you need to select the position where the element begins. If you are drawing a rectangle, rounded rectangle, or ellipse, you need to select one corner of the rectangle that the element will fill.
4. Type the text you want to add as an element or press the mouse button, and hold the mouse button while you move the pointer to the end of the element's position. For a text element, if you want the text to continue on a new line but in the same box, press CTRL-ENTER.
5. Finish the selections for the element. For a text element, press ENTER. For an arrow or line, release the mouse button. For a polyline, release the mouse button, then press it and hold it while you move to where you want the second line to end and press ENTER. Continue drawing the lines until you have drawn the last line. When the polyline is finished, press the mouse button a second time. For a polygon, release the mouse button when the pointer is where the first line should end. Then move to the next point where you want the shape to end, and press the mouse button. Continue moving to the next point of the shape and pressing the mouse button until you have completed the lines that define the shape. You do not have to draw the line from the first point of the polygon to the last point since Quattro draws it for you. When the polygon is finished, press the mouse button a second time. For a rectangle, rounded rectangle, or ellipse, move to the opposite corner and release the mouse button.

Adding another element of the same type is easy. To add another element with new attributes, repeat steps 2 through 5. To add a new element with the same attributes, repeat only steps 3 through 5.

Changing Elements in a Graph

Although adding elements lets you create graphs with unlimited possibilities, you probably do not always draw the elements the way you want the first time. You may want to change them to a different color, position, size, or remove them altogether. You can change the existing elements using the Edit icon (/P) and Clipboard icon (/C).

When you are adding objects or modifying them, you may want to display a grid. A grid looks like the dots in Figure 7.28. You can use these dots to gauge where you want to add or move objects, force objects to begin and end at grid points, and change how the grid appears. To add a grid, select Visible from the Background properties box to change the Off to On. The grid dots appear at four percent intervals (based on the graph size being 100 percent). You can change the frequency of the grid dots by selecting Increment and entering a number between

Graphic Features 383

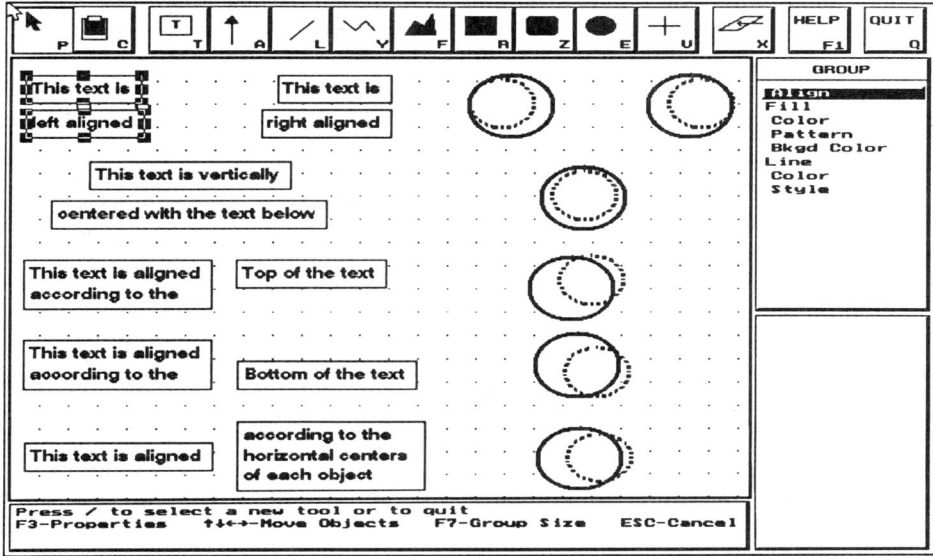

Figure 7.28 Graph Annotator Screen Showing Different Alignment Options and a Grid

1 and 25. When you want to use the dots as the starting and ending points of graph objects, select Snap-to in the Background properties box to change the Off to On. This means that when you add or move an object, Quattro moves the object to the nearest grid dot. Once you add an object it remains there even if you change the grid dot intervals.

When you select a group of objects, the properties sheet displays the settings that are common to a group of objects as shown in Figure 7.28. This property sheet changes all of the objects in the group. When you select a single object, the property sheet changes to apply to the specific type of object. Quattro Pro 3 and 4 includes the Align option in the properties sheet to change the alignment of objects. Figure 7.28 shows the different alignment options applied to groups of text objects and to groups of two circles.

CHANGING AN ELEMENT'S ATTRIBUTES When you add an element, you may not remember to set the attributes for the element before you create it. Also, you may change your mind and want different attributes. To change the attributes, you must tell Quattro you want to edit the graph by using the Edit icon. You can enter /P, or point to the first icon with the mouse and press the mouse button. When the Edit icon is active, you can tell Quattro which element or elements you

384 *Quattro Pro 4.0 Handbook*

want to change. Each time you press TAB or SHIFT-TAB, Quattro cycles forward or backward through the elements in the order they are added. If you are using a mouse, you can point to the element and press the mouse button to make the element current. The current element has *handles* (little boxes in its corners) to mark the element. Figure 7.29 shows an element with handles. As each element is made current, the property sheet automatically changes to match the current element. Press F3 when the element you want to change is current. Changing the attributes after adding the element is just like changing the attributes before creating the element.

If you want to change the attributes for more than one element, you must select the elements you want to use. To select an element, use TAB and SHIFT-TAB to make it the current element then press SHIFT-F7 (SELECT). When you press TAB or SHIFT-TAB to move to the next element, the handles remain on the marked element.

MOVING AN ELEMENT Moving an element is also done with the Edit menu. To move an element, activate the Edit icon and select the elements you want to move. Once the elements are selected, press the directional arrows to move the elements. When the elements are in the position you want them, press ENTER. If you are using a mouse, select the elements then point to one of the elements in the group, press and hold down the mouse button and move the pointer to where you want the group moved. Once the elements are where you want them, release the mouse button.

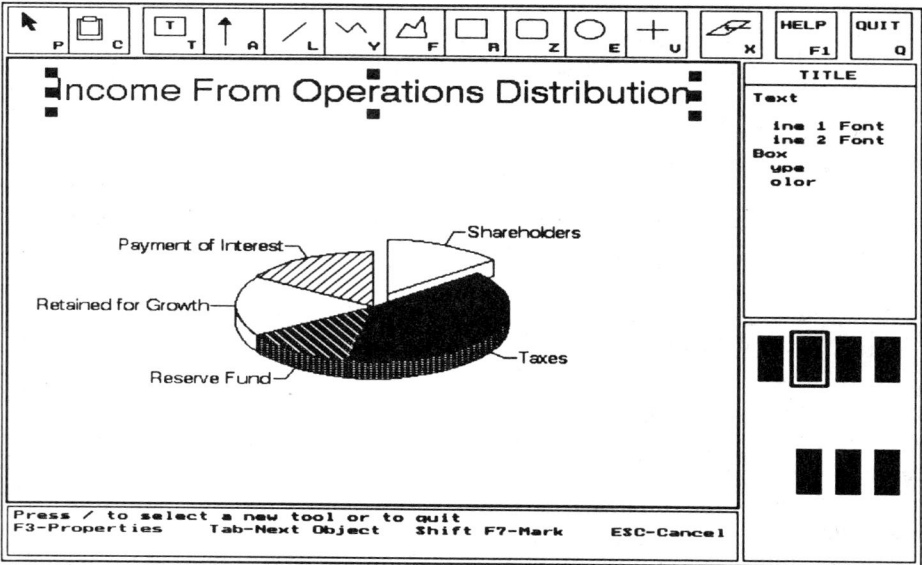

Figure 7.29 Element (Graph Title) with Handles

> ▼ **TIP: Use F2 to edit graph text.**
>
> If you want to change the text in a text element, make the text element current, and press F2 (EDIT) to edit the entry the same way you would edit a spreadsheet entry.

If you are moving a group of elements, make sure you have selected all elements that you want to move. One way to check is to move the selected elements so far away from the original that you can clearly see which elements remain. If some of the remaining elements are ones you intended to include, press ESC to return the elements to their original position so you can select all desired elements you want to move before final placement.

REMOVING AN ELEMENT If the element you added is not what you want, you can remove it. To remove an element, point to it and press the DEL key. The Edit icon does not have to be active for the DEL key to work. As long as the active icon is either the Edit or the type of element you are deleting, the DEL key will work. If multiple items are selected, pressing DEL removes all the selected elements.

RESIZING AN ELEMENT When you rearrange a graph, you may want to change the size of elements. To change the size of an element, use the Edit to make the element to be changed the current element or (select all elements you want to resize). When the elements you want to resize are marked, type a period. Quattro changes the outlines of the marked elements and only displays a handle in the lower-right corner of the outlines. When you press a directional key, Quattro changes the outlines to show the new size of the elements. If you want to change the corner that Quattro uses to change the size, type a period until the desired corner is marked with a handle. Once the element outlines are the size you want, press ENTER. Quattro redraws the elements using the smaller size. Since one corner of the element remains in the same position, resizing multiple elements may change their relative distance from each other.

CHANGING A GRAPH THAT YOU CREATED WITH QUATTRO'S GRAPH MENUS The graphs you create with the Graph menus also can be altered with the graph annotator. Changing the graph may produce different results than you expect, since Quattro treats many portions of the graph as a single element. The first and second titles are treated as one element. All parts of the legend are also

> ▼ **TIP: Resize from opposite corners.**
>
> When you resize a group of elements, resize equally from two opposite corners to minimize later repositioning.

treated as one element. The remaining parts of the graph are a single element. If you want to change a portion of the graph and the graph annotator does not let you make the change, exit the annotator and make the changes through Quattro's Graph menus.

When the main graph is the current element, you have the options shown in Figure 7.30. Selecting Reset Scale redraws the graph to fit the entire screen; use this option when you have changed the position or size of the graph and then change your mind and want to reinstate the old attributes. Selecting Grid Color and a color is the same as selecting the grid line color from the Graph Overall dialog box, which sets the color of the grid lines, the box around the legend, or the box around the titles. Selecting Chart Color and a color is the same as selecting the fill color from the Graph Overall dialog box, which sets the color of the chart area of the graph. Selecting Background and a color is the same as selecting the background color from the Graph Overall dialog boxes, which sets the color of the graph outside the chart area. The last three menu selections display the menu to select the typeface, point size, and style, which are just like those commands' counterparts in the Graph menus. The Label Font attribute is the same command as /Graph Text Font Data & Tick Labels command; the X Title Font attribute is the same as /Graph Text Font X-Title command; and the Y Title Font attribute is the same as /Graph Text Font Y-Title command.

When the legend is the current element, the menu selections are similar to those for elements that you create using the toolbox icons. Selecting Color under Box selects the color of the legend box. Changing the color for this attribute also

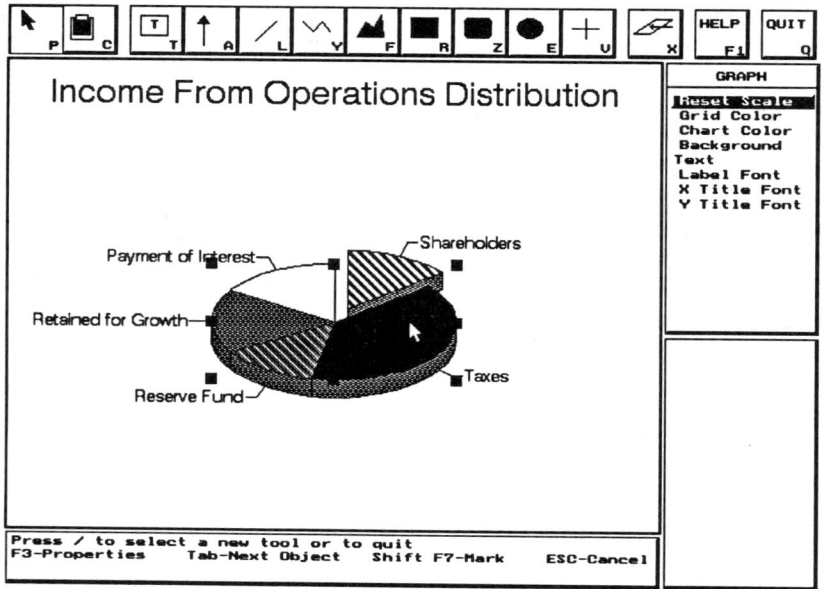

Figure 7.30 Property Sheet for Main Graph

> ▼ **TIP:** Use the rectangle icon to draw a different color title box.
>
> If you want the box around the titles or the legend to be a different color than the grid lines, draw a box for the titles or legend with the graph annotator Rectangle icon, and set the color of the box drawn with the icon active.

changes the color of the grid lines and the box around the graph titles (if any). Selecting **Type** selects the type of outline for the legend box (just like selecting an Option below Legend in the Graph Overall dialog box). Selecting **Color** under Text sets the color of the legend text (just like the /Graph Text Font Legends Color command). Selecting **Font** displays the same typeface, point size, and style options that the /Graph Text Font Legends command uses. You can delete the legend when it is the current element. If you delete the legend, Quattro performs the command /Graph Text Legends Position None command and resizes the main graph element.

When the element containing the two titles is the current element, the menu selections let you change the font and color of the text or the type and color of the box surrounding the text. Selecting **Color** under Text sets the color of the first and second titles; this combines the /Graph Text Font 1st Line Color and /Graph Text Font 2nd Line commands. Selecting **Line 1 Font** or **Line 2 Font** displays the same typeface, point size, and style options that the /Graph Text Font 1st Line (or 2nd line) command uses. Selecting **Type** selects the type of box outline surrounding the titles (just like selecting an option below Titles in the Graph Overall dialog box). Selecting **Color** under Box selects the color of the box containing the titles, as well as the legend box and the grid lines. If you want the box around the titles in a different color, draw a box using an icon from the toolbox. When the titles are the current element, you can delete them by pressing DEL. When you delete the titles from within the graph annotator, Quattro clears the title entered with the /Graph Text 1st Line and the /Graph Text 2nd Line commands and resizes the main graph element.

CHANGING THE LAYER OF AN ELEMENT When you add elements to a graph, they are layered in the order they are added. You can change the order of elements by moving elements to the top or bottom layer. When you move elements to the top or bottom, the other elements are adjusted to reflect the moved elements' positions. To move elements to the top, select the elements you want to move. Next, make the Clipboard icon active, and select To Top. You may want to do this when one element is blocking the display of another element. Figure 7.31 shows an example of one element blocking another. By selecting the text element, making the Clipboard icon active, and selecting To Top, the display now looks like Figure 7.32.

You can also move elements to the bottom. To move elements to the bottom,

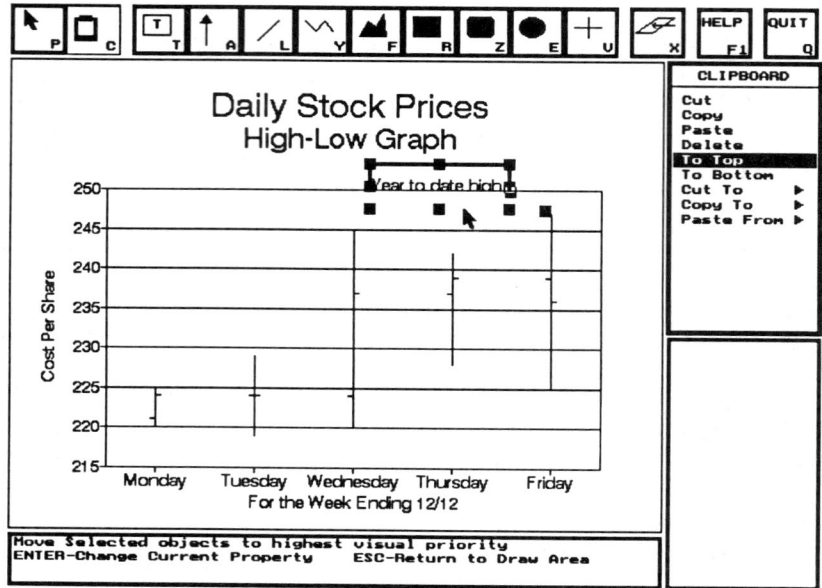

Figure 7.31 Graph with One Element Behind Another

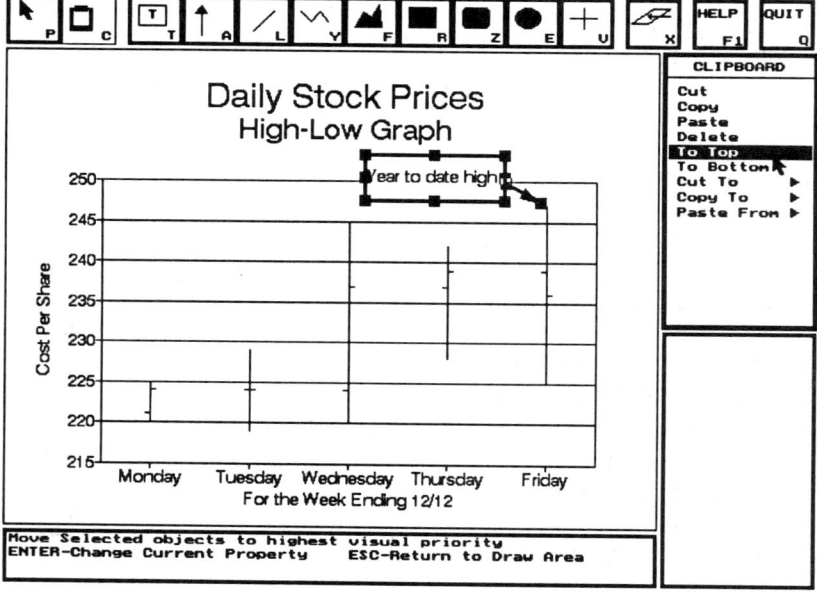

Figure 7.32 Graph After Moving Element to the Top

select the elements you want to move. Then make the Clipboard icon active, and select **To Bottom**. The elements become the bottom layers of the graph, and the remaining elements are placed above them.

Linking an Element to a Data Point

Some of the elements that you add with the graph annotator are pointing out features of the graph. You can point out the salesperson with the highest sales or the product with the lowest number of returns. When you are emphasizing a data-point value, you want the elements that highlight the data point to be near it. If the data change, the elements that emphasize the data point only move with the data if you link the elements to the data point. As the value of the data point changes and the position of the data point on the graph changes, Quattro adjusts the position of the linked elements, so the linked elements always have the same relative position to the linked data point.

To link elements to a data point, first position the elements to link in the desired positions relative to the data point. Second, select the elements you want to link. Third, make the Link icon active by typing /X or by pointing to the icon with the mouse and pressing the mouse button. When Quattro prompts you, select the desired series. Fourth, Quattro prompts you for the link index of the point that you want to link to the elements. This is the number that selects which data point in the series is used, a numeral from 1 to n, where n is the number of data points. For example, using the graph in Figure 7.33, if you want to select the third column section (the reserve fund), enter 3 for the link index. As the values change, Quattro automatically moves the linked elements so the linked elements always have the same relative location to the third data point. If you remove the series containing the data point to which the elements are linked, the linked elements also disappear. They reappear when the series is reassigned and has at least as many data points as the link index.

Using the Graph Annotator Clipboard

In Chapter 5 you learned how Quattro can store information in a temporary area as you copied files to a buffer and used the files in the buffer to make a copy of the file in another directory. The graph annotator also has a buffer area, which Quattro

---

▼ **TIP:** Position and size elements as they will be used.

Before creating a clipboard file, position the size the elements where you expect they will be used in the other graphs so you can minimize repositioning and resizing after you copy the elements into a graph.

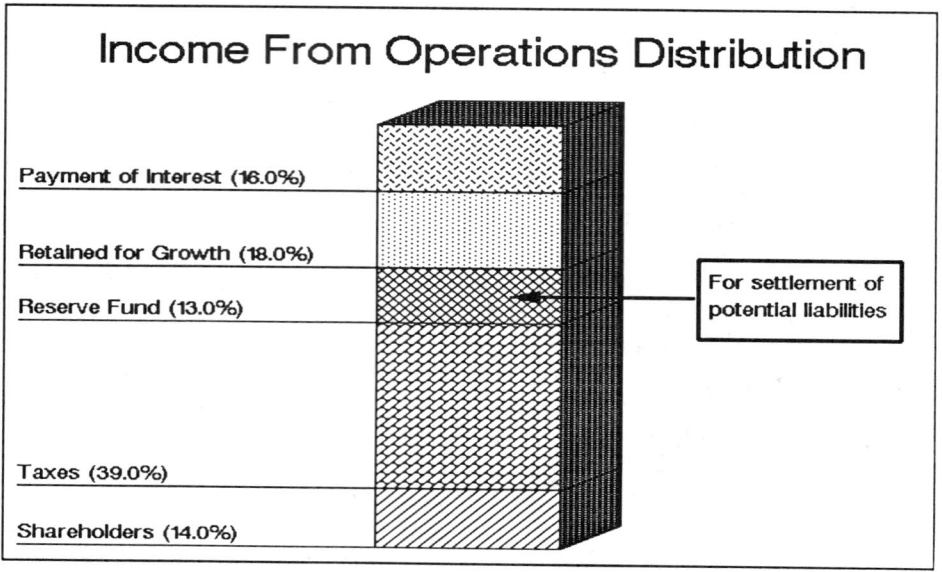

Figure 7.33 Linking an Element (Text Box and Arrow) to a Data Point

calls the Clipboard. You can use the Clipboard to store elements temporarily. Quattro remembers the elements that you store in the clipboard until you replace them with other elements. You can store elements in the clipboard and use them multiple times: in the same graph, in a different graph, in a different file, or in another Quattro session. This Clipboard is separate from other Clipboards such as Windows' Clipboard.

You can also store an image to a clipboard file so you can use the image in a different graph. For example, you may have a company logo that you want to appear at the top of many graphs. If you store the logo, you only have to draw it once and it is then available for use in any graph. In addition, Quattro provides 56 images created by Marketing Graphics, Inc. in clipboard files that you can incorporate into your graphs. These images include arrows, clocks, buildings, and maps. They are a sample of Marketing Graphics' products called Picture Pak libraries, which offer additional symbols. In addition to the clipboard art, you can also bring in .CGM files, which are a Metafile format that many graphics programs create. All clipboard and clipboard file options are accessed once the Clipboard icon is activated by either typing /C or by pointing to the icon with a mouse and pressing the mouse button. Unlike other icons, the Clipboard icon has the property sheet active (instead of the drawing area); but you can use ESC to make the drawing area active, and then F3 to return to the property sheet.

STORING ELEMENTS IN THE CLIPBOARD You have two options for storing elements in a clipboard, depending on whether you want to remove the original elements from the graph. If you want to remove the original elements from the graph as well as copy them to the clipboard, use Cut from the Clipboard property sheet. If you want to keep the original elements in the graph and copy them to the clipboard, use Copy from the Clipboard property sheet. To store elements in the clipboard, press ESC to make the drawing area active. Then select the elements that you want in the clipboard. Once the elements are selected, press F3 to make the property sheet active, and select Cut or Copy from the list. If you select Cut, the elements will disappear from the graph. If you decide you want to remove the elements without copying them to the clipboard, select Delete from the Clipboard property sheet. This performs the same action as pressing the DEL key.

COPYING ELEMENTS FROM THE CLIPBOARD Once elements are in the clipboard, you can add them back to a graph. To add the elements in the buffer to a graph, select Paste from the Clipboard property sheet. When Quattro copies the elements from the clipboard to the graph, the elements have the same location as they did when you copied the elements to the clipboard. You can paste elements that you have copied from the same graph, from a different graph, from a different graph in another spreadsheet, or from a graph created in another Quattro session. You can also paste the elements in a clipboard more than once. For example, you can paste a group of elements, move it to a new location, then copy the group of elements again to make a second copy. Once you paste elements from the clipboard, the elements are selected so you can use other Graph annotator menu selections (such as moving and resizing).

COPYING ELEMENTS TO A FILE Storing elements in a clipboard file is just like storing elements in the clipboard. However, the file is always available, but the clipboard only contains the last group of elements that you copied to it. Also, you can have an unlimited number of clipboard files, but only a single group of elements can be stored in the clipboard at any one time. A clipboard file is ideal for logos and other designs that you use in graphs from many different spreadsheets.

The graph annotator has two options for storing elements in a clipboard file. The one you choose is determined by whether you want to remove the original elements from the graph. To store elements in a clipboard file, press ESC to make the drawing area active and select the elements that you want in the clipboard file. Next, press F3 to make the property sheet active, and select either Cut To or Copy To from the list. If you selected Cut To, the elements disappear from the graph since this selection deletes the elements as it copies them to the clipboard file. Type the clipboard file name. If you want the clipboard file stored in a different drive or directory, you must include that information. Do not include an extension, since Quattro automatically adds a .CLP extension. When you press ENTER, Quattro stores the elements in the file.

COPYING ELEMENTS FROM A CLIPBOARD FILE Once you have a clipboard file, you can move it to any graph you want. To add a clipboard file to the current graph, make the Clipboard icon active, and select **Paste From**. Quattro prompts for the name of the clipboard file and lists the files with .CLP (Clipboard) and .CGM (Metafile) extensions. Select a file from the list, or type the file name and press ENTER. The elements from the clipboard file are copied to the graph in the same position they were in when you copied the elements to the clipboard file. Once you paste elements from a clipboard file, the elements are selected so you can use other graph annotator menu selections on them (such as moving and resizing).

Leaving the Graph Annotator

When you exit the graph annotator, Quattro continues to remember all changes made with the annotator. You can continue to make changes to the basic graph using the Graph commands without affecting the other changes you made with the graph annotator. If you use the **/Graph Customize Series Reset Graph** command, you will erase all the graph settings, whether they were made with the Graph menus or the graph annotator.

SAVING THE GRAPH

Once you have customized a graph, you want to save it. Since there are several ways of saving information relating to graphs, you should consider the options carefully. You can save the settings for the current graph within the spreadsheet in order to create a second graph on the spreadsheet. You can save the spreadsheet file in order to save the current graph and any other named graph on the spreadsheet. You can save the graph as a graphic image if you want to include the graphic image with other data, as you might do with a desktop publishing package.

Naming the Current Graph Specs

You can save the specification for the current graph within the current spreadsheet by naming the graph. A named graph can be restored as the current graph or deleted. Once a graph is named, you can use it for slide presentations with a special **/Graph Name** command.

NAMING A GRAPH WITHIN A SPREADSHEET To name a graph, enter **/Graph Name Create**. Quattro displays a list of the current named graphs. Select one of these names, or type a new name and press ENTER to be returned to the Graph menu. A graph name follows the same rules as block names. If you select an existing graph name, Quattro replaces the graph specifications referenced by this name with the current graph specifications.

A named graph is only available in the current spreadsheet and cannot be used by other spreadsheets although you can copy a graph to another spreadsheet. When you name a graph, you save the settings, not the exact data values in the graph series. Therefore, if you use the named graph later and the values for the series have changed, Quattro creates the graphs with the new numbers.

USING A NAMED GRAPH Once you have named a set of graph specifications, you can use these as the current graph by entering /Graph Name Display. Quattro lists the named graphs in the spreadsheet and lets you select the named graph that will become the current graph. After activating a named graph, any changes made to the graph settings are not stored under the graph name until you use the /Graph Name Create command again. In Quattro Pro 3 and 4, you can set Quattro Pro to save changes you make to a named graph as you make them. To do so, select /Graph Name Autosave Edits Yes before you start making changes to the current graph. Subsequently, all the changes that are made in the Graph menu are saved under the graph name assigned to the current graph. Quattro Pro will save the graph when you use the /Graph Name Display, /Graph Name Autosave Edits, /Graph Name Erase, /Graph Name Slide, /Graph Name Graph Copy, /Graph View, or /Print Graph Print Name commands. When you no longer want Quattro Pro to save the changes in the Graph menu, such as when you are using a named graph as the basis for a new graph, select /Graph Name Autosave Edits No.

REMOVING NAMED GRAPHS Quattro has two commands for removing named graphs. If you only want to remove one, enter /Graph Name Erase, move the highlight to the graph name that you want to remove, and press ENTER. If you want to remove all named graphs, enter /Graph Name Reset, and select Yes to confirm that you want to reset all named graphs. After you execute either command, Quattro returns you to the Graph menu.

COPYING A GRAPH TO ANOTHER SPREADSHEET Quattro provides the /Graph Name Graph Copy command to copy all of a graph's settings to another spreadsheet. To copy a graph, you must name the graph and open the spreadsheet containing the graph to copy and the spreadsheet where you want the graph copied. Next, select /Graph Name Graph Copy. Quattro prompts for the graph name and displays the named graphs. After selecting one, Quattro prompts for the target spreadsheet, or the spreadsheet where you want the graph copied. Use the mouse, ALT and a number, ALT-0, ALT-F5 or SHIFT-F6 to move the selector to a cell in the worksheet where you want the graph copied, and press ENTER. Quattro copies all the settings to the selected spreadsheet. Graph settings and objects added with the annotator are in the target spreadsheet just as if you originally entered them in there. The spreadsheet ranges the graph uses will continue referring to the data in its original location, usually in the spreadsheet that contained the original graph.

Saving the Spreadsheet

When you save a spreadsheet, Quattro also saves all the named graphs and the current graph. If you save the spreadsheet with an extension other than .WQ1 or

.WQ!, Quattro only saves the graph settings that the file format is designed to remember. For example, if you save a spreadsheet as a .WKS or .WK1 file, you lose graph color and font specifications, since th1is information is not stored in a 1-2-3 file. For 1-2-3 files, this information is determined every time you use PrintGraph or Allways.

Saving the Graphic Image

In most cases you have no need to save an image of the Quattro graph to a disk file, since you can print the graph directly with Quattro. If you need to save a graphic image in a file for use with 1-2-3's PrintGraph program or a desktop publishing package, you must create the graph in final form and print it to a file. This procedure is discussed later in the chapter in the section on printing a graph to a file.

CREATING A SLIDE SHOW

Once you name your graphs, you may want to review them. One method of quickly looking at your graphs is to create a slide show. You may also want to create a slide show as part of a presentation. Quattro Pro includes many slide show enhancements that you would normally expect to find in a separate graphics package. You can create a slide show by either creating a table that lists the named graphs you want to see in the slide show or by adding graph buttons to a graph that will display another graph or perform a macro command when selected.

Creating a Slide Show with a Spreadsheet Table

The easiest way to create a table is to fill a spreadsheet block with the graph names you want to appear and the number of seconds each named graph should appear. If these numbers are missing or are 0, the graph appears until the viewer presses any key. Unlike time serial numbers, the times in the second column of the block used for the slide show are the actual number of seconds. In Quattro Pro 3 and 4,

> ▼ TIP: Save the current graph before using Slide Show.
>
> Save the current graph if you want to keep it before using the /Graph Name Slide command, since this command makes each graph in the block the current graph, which removes the graph settings for the current graph.

you can add additional columns for other enhancements. Figure 7.34 shows a table created for this purpose (the last three columns are described below). To display this slide show, select /Graph Name Slide. When Quattro prompts for a block, enter the block containing the slide show information. For Figure 7.34, the block is I6..M11. When you press ENTER to finalize the block, Quattro starts at the top of the block and displays each named graph for the number of seconds specified. While a slide show is performing, you can return to a previous slide by pressing the BACKSPACE key.

QUATTRO PRO SLIDE SHOW ENHANCEMENTS In Quattro Pro 3 and 4, you can include three additional columns to the slide show block for transitional effect between slides, the speed of the transition, and audio effects. The third column of the slide show block contains integers from 1 to 24. Each of these numbers represents a different transition effect and is listed in Table 7.1. If you use a negative number, the next named graph is added on top of the currently displayed one and added using the transition effect you select. For example, if a slide show currently is displaying a graph named FIRST and the next graph called SECOND uses a transition effect of -20, the SECOND named graph will appear on top of the FIRST named graph by dissolving on top of it. Using negative numbers for transition effects is usually used to add parts of a graph one at a time or, when a text graph includes a list, to add one line of text at a time. Some video adapters cannot use all of Quattro Pro's transition effects. Most of the transition effects can operate at different speeds as shown in the last column of Table 7.1. The lower the number,

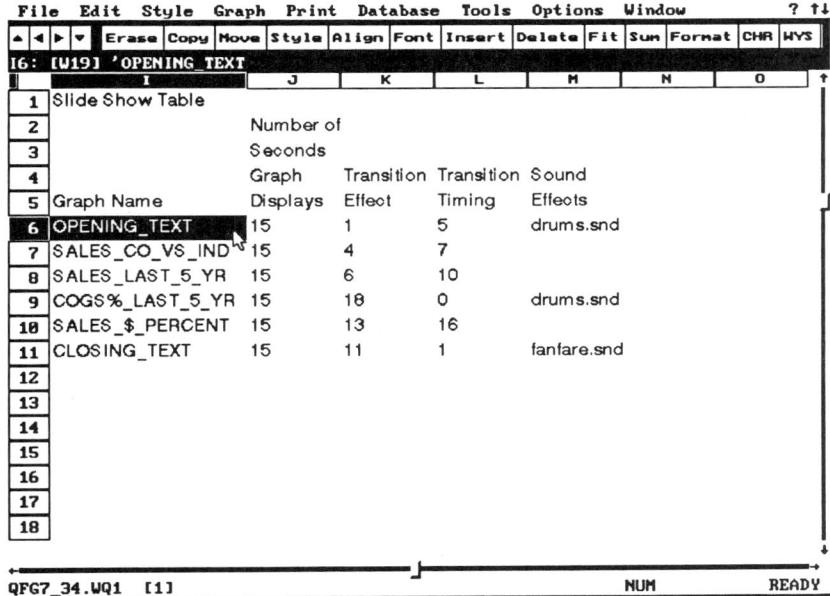

Figure 7.34 Spreadsheet Data for Slide Show

Table 7.1. Quattro Pro 4 Transition Effects

Transition Effect	Effect Number	Effect Speed
Switch instantaneously to the next graph	1	0
Switch to black then switch to next graph	2	0- (number of 1/70 seconds for black screen to display)
Wipe new graph on and old one on left to right	3	1-16
Wipe new graph on and old one on right to left	4	1-16
Wipe new graph on and old one on top to bottom	5	1-16
Wipe new graph on and old one bottom to top	6	1-16
Replace old graph with new one starting from the left and right sides and working to the vertical center	7	1-16
Replace old graph with new one starting from the vertical center and working to the left and right sides	8	1-16
Replace old graph with new one starting from the top and bottom and working to the horizontal center	9	1-16
Replace old graph with new one starting from the top and bottom and working to the horizontal center	10	1-16
Replace old graph with new one starting from the outside and working to the center	11	1-16
Replace old graph with new one starting from the center and working to the outside	12	1-16
Slide old graph up and replace with new one sliding up from the bottom	13	1-16
Slide old graph down and replace with new one sliding down from the top	14	1-16
Replace old graph with new one in small vertical strips working from left to right	15	1-16
Replace old graph with new one in two sets of horizontal strips working from left to right	16	1-16
Replace old graph with new one starting from the center and working a block at a time from the center in a counterclockwise circle	17	1-16

Table 7.1. Quattro Pro 4 Transition Effects *(continued)*

Transition Effect	Effect Number	Effect Speed
Replace old graph with new one by 2X1 rectangles	18	0
Replace old graph with new one by 2X2 squares	19	0
Replace old graph with new one by 4X4 squares	20	0-2
Replace old graph with new one by 8X8 squares	21	0-4
Replace old graph with new one by 16X16 squares	22	0-8
Replace old graph with new one by 32X32 squares	23	0-16
Replace old graph with new one by 64X64 squares	24	0-32

the faster the effect. The slide show block can also include a fifth column that contains audio effect files. These files have a .SND extension in the Quattro Pro directory and have file names that describe their effects such as DRUMS or THANKS. You can also combine sound effects by combining the names of sound files in the fifth column with semicolons. The sounds created this way may conflict with other software such as some TSRs and Windows running in 386 Enhanced mode, so you will not want them running when you run the slide show. When you use the transition effects with a slide show created with a table, Quattro Pro changes a VGA screen display to an EGA, screen display. Quattro Pro automatically changes the screen display of a slide shown when it contains a third column from VGA to EGA and then returns it to the default when the slide show is over.

Creating a Slide Show with Graph Buttons

In Quattro Pro 2 and above, you can create a slide show using graph buttons, which are text objects that you have selected to be graph buttons. In Quattro Pro 3 and 4, you can make the underlying graphic a graph button for when the person using the slide show selects something on the graph that is not a text graph button. When a graph button is selected, Quattro displays another graph or performs a macro. You can use graph buttons to create a slide show and by making selections you can change the order that the graphs are presented. You can also use graph buttons as part of a macro (which are discussed further in Chapter 12) to display a fancy opening screen from which the user can make selections. The text objects or graph background is selected to be graph buttons after you create the graph.

Once you select a text object that you want to be a graph button, press F3 and select **Graph Button** or select **Graph Button** with the mouse. In Quattro Pro 3 and

4, to make the graph background a button, select the graph background and select **Bkg Button** from the properties box. Quattro displays another box prompting you to enter the graph name. This is the graph name that Quattro will display, the macro instructions Quattro will perform, or the macro name Quattro will perform (enclosed in curly braces) when the button is selected. You can press F3 to display a list of the named graphs in the current spreadsheet. Figure 7.35 shows a graph with several graph buttons added. In this graph, you can select any one of the text in boxes to display another graph or to perform a macro. When the graph is displayed except in annotator or inserted into the spreadsheet, you can select the graph button by clicking any part of the text object with the mouse or by typing the first letter of the graph button. With this last method of selecting a graph button, it is important that the text of all graph buttons in a graph start with a different letter. If you click another part of the graph or type a letter that does not start with one of the graph buttons, you select the graph background button. If the graph is not a background button or you are using an earlier release of Quattro Pro, Quattro removes the graph.

When you add graph buttons, it is important that you name the graph when you finish using the annotator, since when a graph displays another graph, the original is no longer saved in the worksheet. Using graph buttons also requires that you create any graph or macro used by a graph button before you add the graph button. You will also want to include boxes around the text element so the graph users can see the boundaries of the graph buttons they can select. If the graph

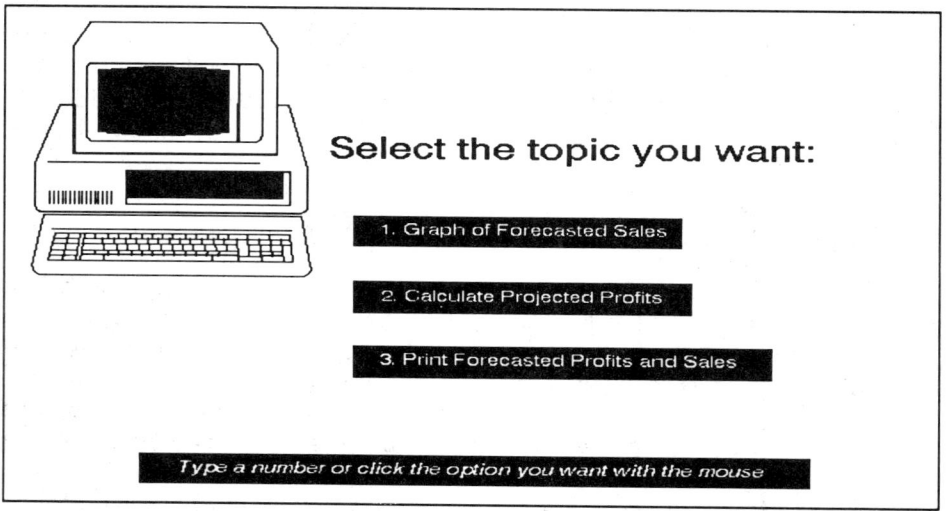

Figure 7.35   Graph with Graph Buttons to Display Other Graphs or Perform Macros

buttons include transition effects and you are using a VGA display, you must change the display to EGA by selecting /Options Hardware Screen Resolution and select one of the EGA options (you cannot do this from the WYSIWYG display mode).

USING QUATTRO PRO SLIDE SHOW ENHANCEMENTS WITH GRAPH BUTTONS In Quattro Pro 3 and 4, you can also use the transition effects and audio effects with graph buttons. To do so, do not name the graphs using semicolons. Then when you add the graph button and Quattro Pro prompts for the graph name, enter the graph name, the transition effect number, its speed, and any audio effect separating each part with a semicolon. For example, you can enter for a graph button prompt SECOND;-20;0;DRUMS so when the graph button is selected, Quattro Pro dissolves the SECOND named graph on top of the currently displayed graph and uses the sound effect stored in the DRUMS.SND file.

ADDING A GRAPH TO A SPREADSHEET

Quattro shows you the current graph every time you press F10 (GRAPH). Another option for displaying a graph is to add it to the spreadsheet. When you add it to the spreadsheet, you select the graph and its desired location within the current spreadsheet. Quattro displays the graph as it appears when you press F10 (GRAPH) if the display mode is graphics. If another mode is used, the graph's location appears highlighted or in a different color. To change the display mode Quattro uses, use the /Options Display Mode **B**: WYSIWYG command. This option appears in the selection box if you are using an EGA or VGA display card.

To add a graph to the spreadsheet, enter /Graph Insert. Quattro prompts you for the graph name. Either select a named graph or select <Current Graph> to add the current graph to the spreadsheet. Once a graph is selected, Quattro prompts for the spreadsheet block that you want the graph to fill. Select a block for the graph. When the block is selected, Quattro creates as large a graph as can fit into the selected block. Quattro may build fonts for the text in the graph. Since this graph has the same height-to-width ratio as the graph that appears when you press F10 (GRAPH), selecting an extremely narrow or wide block creates a small graph on the spreadsheet. As you change the data the graph uses, Quattro updates the graph in the spreadsheet. When the selector is at a cell in the block displaying the graph, the input line shows the graph name, as shown in Figure 7.36. Although you can have as many different graphs inserted in the spreadsheet as you want, you can insert any particular graph in the spreadsheet only once.

The size of the fonts in the inserted graph is determined by the /Options Hardware Printers Fonts Autoscale Fonts command. If this command is set to Yes, the fonts in the inserted graph maintain the same ratio to the graph's overall size. If it is set to No, the fonts in the inserted graph have the size set by the /Graph Text Font command. In small inserted graphs, this can cause text to overlap and be truncated.

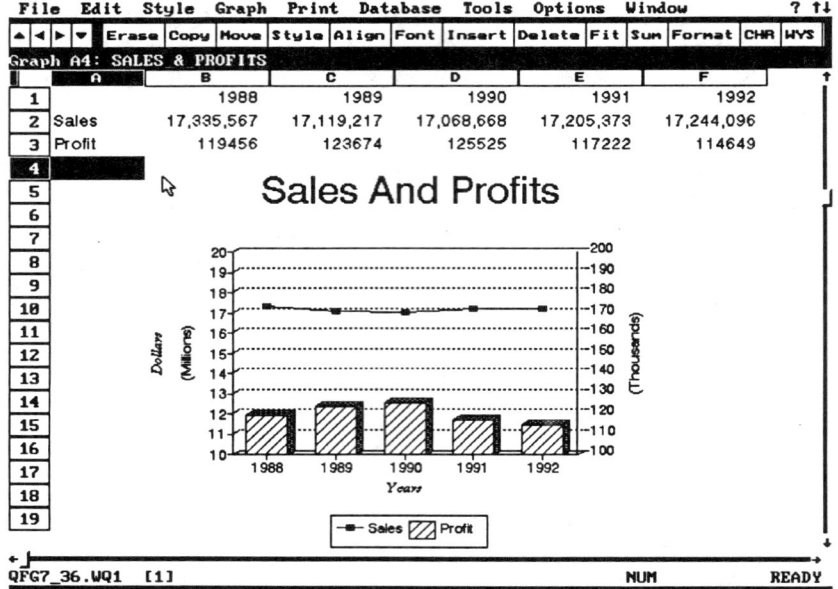

Figure 7.36 Graph Inserted into Spreadsheet

Once you add the graph, you may want to change its position or size. Quattro makes the current graph settings match the graph that is displayed at the selector's position. Then use the /Graph Insert command again, and select the same graph name that you want to move or resize. When Quattro prompts for the position, you can change the size of the block or select a new block in a different location.

Once a graph appears in a spreadsheet, you can print the graph by including the spreadsheet block containing the graph in the print block. The menu settings made through the normal Print menus affect the printing of the graph. You can print the graph with the spreadsheet if the destination is the **Graphics Printer** or **Binary File**. If you select **Printer**, the output does not include the graph. Before printing the spreadsheet and graph, preview them so the output meets your expectations.

If you want to remove an inserted graph, use the /Graph Hide command. When you use this command, Quattro prompts you for the name of the graph you want to remove. After you select a name from the list, Quattro removes the graph; you then can use that spreadsheet area for other data.

PRINTING GRAPHS

Once you have created a graph and saved the spreadsheet file to retain the graph settings, you may want to print the graph. Quattro allows you to print the graph directly and provides many options that allow you to select the printer, select the

▼ TIP: Save Changes before selecting another graph to print.

If you plan to use the /Print Graph Print Name command, save any changes to the current graph (if you want to keep them); selecting another graph to print makes the named graph the current graph.

format, and select the size of the printed graph. All the print options are available from the Graph Print menu (see Figure 7.37). If you have not selected a printer, you need to review Chapter 4 or Appendix A, which provides detailed instructions for selecting printers.

To print a Quattro graph, you must have a printer that can print graphs. This may be a dot matrix printer, a laser printer, or a plotter. You can tell Quattro which printer to use either during installation or during the current Quattro session (see Chapter 4 or Appendix A). Quattro lets you select two printers, and it remembers their settings. Also, you can change your selection of these two printers. Once Quattro knows which printers you selected, all the printer features can be used since Quattro knows the codes that activate them.

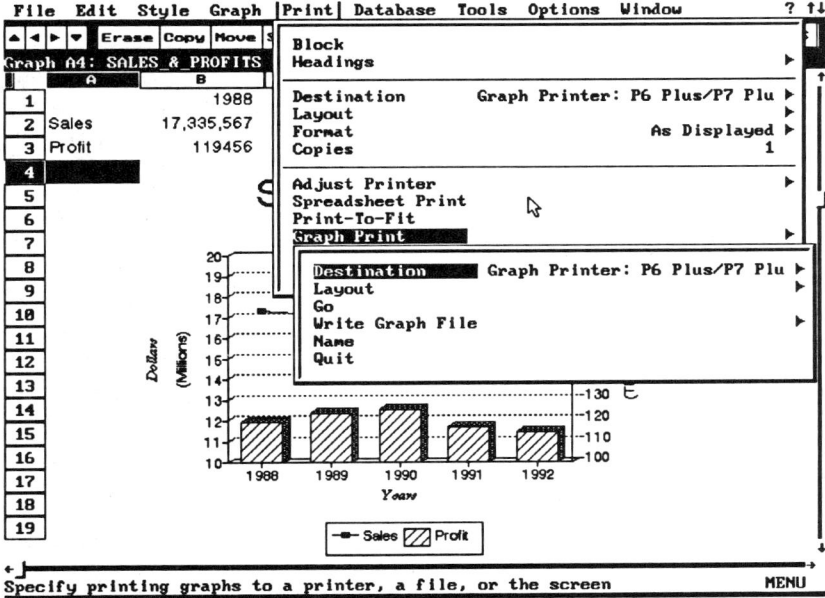

Figure 7.37 /Print Graph Print Menu Box

Printing a Graph

Once you select a printer, the graph is easily printed. To print a graph, select **Graph Print** and **Go** from the Print menu. Quattro uses the default graph print settings unless you change them. If you want to print a graph different from the one that appears when you press F10 (GRAPH), or if you want to redirect the graph to the second printer or to a file, a few more steps are involved. If the selector is on an inserted graph, selecting **/Print Graph Go** prints the inserted graph. If you want to print the current graph or another named graph, move the selector to a cell that is not used by an inserted graph.

PRINTING A DIFFERENT GRAPH Quattro initially prints the current graph when you select **Go** from the Graph Print menu. You can change the graph Quattro that prints to any named graph in current spreadsheet. To change the graph Quattro prints, select **Name** from the Graph Print menu. Quattro lists all the graphs in the current spreadsheet. Highlight one, and press ENTER or the mouse button. When you return to the Graph Print menu, Quattro prints the named graph as soon as you select **Go**. If you press F10 (GRAPH), you can see that the selected graph has become the current graph. The **/Print Graph Print Name** command performs the **/Graph Name Display** command, since it makes the named graph the current graph. All other settings in the Graph Print menu and in the menus accessed through Graph Print use the graph selected with the **/Print Graph Print Name** command.

SENDING A GRAPH TO THE SECOND PRINTER Quattro remembers the settings for up to two printers at a time. Initially, Quattro uses the printer defined as the first printer unless the second printer is selected with the **/Options Hardware Printers Default Printer** command. To print a graph using the printer defined as the second printer in the Printers menu, enter **/Options Hardware Printers Default Printer 2nd Printer**. Once you return to the READY mode, use the **/Print Graph Go** command. Quattro prints the graph to the printer described as the 2nd printer in the Printer menu. To change the default printer to the first printer, enter **/Options Hardware Printers Default Printer 1st Printer**.

SENDING A GRAPH TO A FILE Quattro also supports printing a graph to a file. When you print a graph to a file, Quattro writes the same information to the file that Quattro would otherwise send to the graphics printer. You may want to print a graph to a file if you are planning to print the file at a later time. To print a graph to a file, follow these steps:

1. Type **/**, and select **Print Graph Print** from the READY mode.
2. Select **Destination** and **File** to send the information to a file instead of a printer. Quattro prompts for a file name and lists the files on the current directory that have a .PRN extension.
3. Select a print file from the list or type the name of the file, and press ENTER. The printed graph file has a .PRN extension (unless you provide another

one). The file is saved in the same directory as spreadsheet files (unless you specify another drive and directory).

4. Select **Go**. Quattro prints the graph to the file. As the message displayed on the screen indicates, if you need to halt the process, press CTRL-BREAK. When Quattro is finished, it removes the message from the screen.

To print the graph file you just created, use the DOS command COPY instead of PRINT. For example, if the file containing the printed image of the graph is MYFILE.PRN, type: **COPY MYFILE.PRN /B PRN**. The **/B** indicates that the file is a binary file. LPT1 is DOS's reserved name for the first parallel printer, and the default value for PRN. If the printer that you are printing to is not the first parallel printer, substitute the appropriate DOS name for PRN. This command must be executed from the DOS prompt. You can access it without leaving Quattro by using the **/File Utilities DOS Shell** command.

SAVING THE GRAPH IN A FORMAT FOR OTHER PROGRAMS When you save the graph to a file, you are saving the graphic image that Quattro would display if you pressed F10 (GRAPH) before saving the file. Quattro cannot use the graphic image to display the graph or print the graph. However, other programs (such as 1-2-3's PrintGraph or a desktop publishing package that supports the Postscript format) can use an image file that Quattro can create. You can use these features to incorporate Quattro graphs into word-processing packages. To save a graph in one of these formats, select **Write Graph File** from the Print Graph menu. The menu displayed by Quattro lets you choose whether you want the graph stored in Postscript's format (EPS), 1-2-3's PrintGraph's format (PIC), Postscript's format for slides (Slide EPS), or PC Paintbrush and other graphic editing program's format (PCX). Select one. Once you have selected the format, Quattro prompts you for the name of the file. Select a file from the box that Quattro displays or type a file name. Quattro adds an appropriate file extension (EPS, PIC, or PCX) unless you provide a different one. When you press ENTER, Quattro immediately saves the graph to a file. If you are saving to a PIC file, the graph loses some information (like color and font settings) that are not supported in 1-2-3's .PIC files. You must redefine the colors and fonts in 1-2-3's PrintGraph.

Customization Selections

Quattro provides other customization settings that affect how a graph is printed. These customization settings handle the layout of the graph on the paper. While

---

▼ **TIP: Pies are not always round.**

If the pie in a pie graph is not round, use the **/Options Screen Aspect Ratio** command, not the **/Print Graph Print Layout 4:3 Aspect** command.

the customization settings are not necessary to print a graph, they allow you to tailor the graph's appearance to present a more effective graph.

SPECIFYING THE GRAPH LAYOUT When you press F10 (GRAPH), use the /Graph View command, or insert a graph into a spreadsheet, Quattro displays the graph as large as possible within the available area. When you print a graph, Quattro makes the graph as large as possible to fit in the area specified by the /Print Graph Print Layout command. If you do not select a layout, Quattro uses a 10-inch by 8-inch area for the graph, with half-inch margins on all sides. This uses the largest area available you can specify for printing the graph. The Layout commands describe to Quattro how you want your graph printed on the page. To change one of these settings, enter /Print Graph Print Layout and the setting that you want to change. The following options are available for your selection:

Dimensions—This setting determines whether the measurements for Left Edge, Top Edge, Height, and Width are in centimeters or inches.

Left Edge—This setting determines the distance between the left edge of the paper and the left edge of the graph.

Top Edge—This setting determines the distance between the top edge of the paper and the top of the graph.

Height—This setting determines the distance between the top and the bottom of the graph (the height of the graph).

Width—This setting determines the distance between the left and the right sides of the graph (the width of the graph).

4:3 Aspect—This setting determines if Quattro maintains the 4:3 width-to-height ratio when Quattro resizes the graph to use all available area. If set to Yes, the 4:3 ratio is maintained, and the graph may not use all available area set with the other layout settings. If set to No, Quattro expands the graph to use the largest available area. The chart may be stretched in either direction to fit the new size.

Orientation—This setting determines the rotation of the graph. The graph can be printed vertically with this setting at Portrait, which creates a printed image like the one in Figure 7.38, or horizontally with this setting at Landscape, producing a printed image like the one in Figure 7.39. When you change the rotation of the graph, the other layout settings apply to the new orientation. Rotating the orientation changes the corner that Quattro considers to be the upper-left corner of the page.

▼ **TIP: Some printers require half-inch margins.**

Hewlett-Packard LaserJet and other page printers must have a minimum margin of 0.5 inches.

> ▼ **TIP: Sometimes charts need to look taller.**
>
> To make a chart look taller, such as the column in a column chart, set the **/Print Graph Print Layout 4:3 Aspect** command to **No**, and make the graph width narrower.

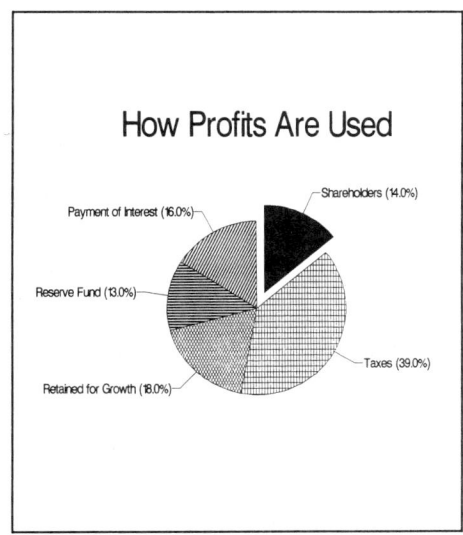

Figure 7.38 Graph Printed in Portrait Mode

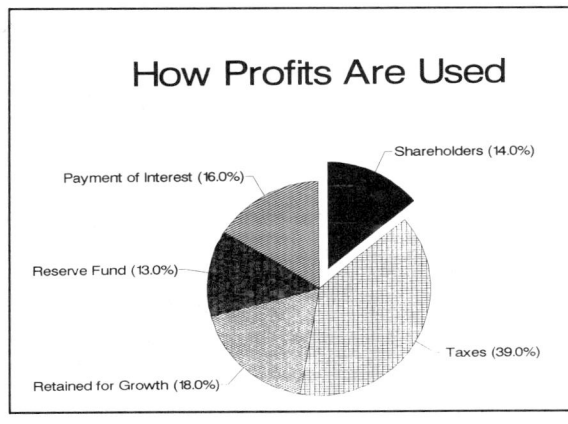

Figure 7.39 Graph in Figure 7.38 Printed in Landscape Mode

Plotters and printers work slightly different, since the origin (the upper-left corner) on a printer is determined with the long edge of the paper placed vertically. On a plotter, the origin is determined with the long edge of the paper placed horizontally. Therefore, a graph printed in the Landscape mode on a printer is the same as a graph printed in the Portrait mode on a plotter.

To limit a graph to a section of a page, such as the bottom-right corner, change the margins to move the beginning of the graph to the location where you want the graph to start printing and change the height and width to the desired size for the graph. Regardless of the dimensions that you choose, Quattro automatically sizes the graph to fit the space provided.

Previewing the Printed Graph

Chapter 4 introduced you to the Screen Preview, which you can use to see how Quattro will print the spreadsheet if it uses the most current settings. You can use the commands for the Screen Preview to print a spreadsheet containing a graph; use the same steps you used to preview a spreadsheet without a graph. When you are printing just the graph, you can preview how Quattro will print it by selecting **Destination** from the Graph Print menu and selecting **Screen Preview**. When you want to see how the graph will look, select **Go**. The menu for previewing a graph is the same as for previewing a spreadsheet. When you are ready to print the graph, select **Destination** and **Graph Printer** before selecting **Go**. The **/Print Destination Graphics Printer** and **/Print Graph Print Destination Graph Printer** commands send the output to the same printer.

Updating or Resetting Selection Options

Most changes that you make in the Graph Print menu affect only the graphs in the current spreadsheet that you are printing. The layout information is not maintained when you use another spreadsheet. As you change the settings for printing a graph, you can undo them by using the **Reset** command from the Layout menu from the Graph Print menu. The **Reset** command returns all print settings to the current default settings. The current default settings are the original Quattro settings or settings you specified as the default setting with the **/Print Layout Update** or **/Print Graph Print Layout Update** command.

To keep the changes that you have made with the **/Print Graph Print Layout** and **/Print Layout** commands, select **Update** from the Layout menu. When you use the **/Print Graph Print Layout Update** command, Quattro saves all printing layout changes you have made. These settings become the defaults that Quattro uses when you use the **/Print Graph Print Layout Reset** command. The **/Print Layout Reset** and **/Print Graph Print Layout Reset** commands are the same. Also the **/Print Layout Update** command is the same as **/Print Graph Print Layout Update** command.

GETTING STARTED

In this chapter, you learned how you can create graphs. With the customization options, you learned how you can tailor the graph's appearance. You can try some of your graphic skills by following these steps to create the graph in Figure 7.40:

1. Enter the following data in the spreadsheet. Notice that years are entered as right justified labels.

   A1: **VaporWrite Is Becoming the Market Leader**
   A3: **Units Sold**
   B3: **"1990**
   C3: **"1991**
   D3: **"1992**
   A4: **VaporWrite Products**
   B4: **60000**
   C4: **175000**
   D4: **450000**
   A5: **Leading Competitor**
   B5: **300000**
   C5: **350000**
   D5: **400000**

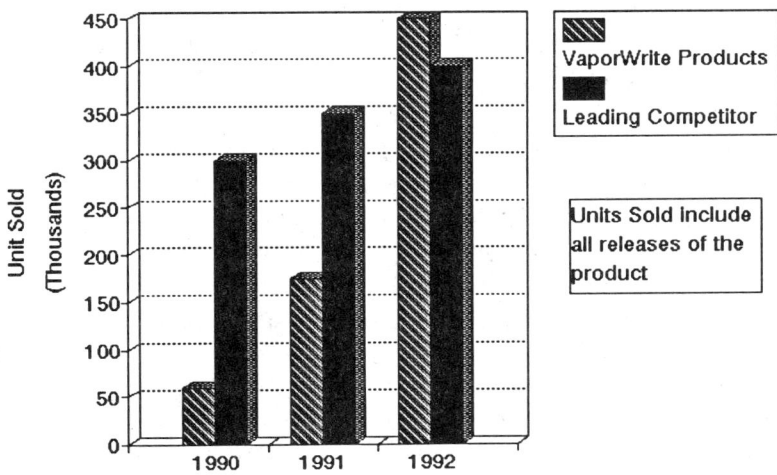

Figure 7.40   Graph Created with Getting Started

2. Expand column A so the text in column A is not clipped. Move to A3. Press CTRL-W to enter /Style Column Width. Expand the column's width to 20 by typing **20** or pressing the RIGHT ARROW 11 times. If you are using a mouse, point to the A in the column heading, and press the mouse button. Then move the mouse to the right until the column width is 20. When the column width is the width you want, release the mouse button.

3. Make a fast graph. Press CTRL-G to enter **/Graph Fast Graph**. When Quattro prompts for a block, press END, HOME, and ENTER. If you are using a mouse, point to A3, hold the mouse button down, and point to D5 before releasing the mouse button. Once the block is selected, point to [Enter] in the input line and press the mouse button. Since the block uses more columns (four) than rows (three), Quattro divides the data according to rows. Since row 3 contains the years entered as labels, the years entered as labels becomes the x-axis data. Since column A contains labels, the A4 and A5 become the legend text. Quattro divides the remainder of the block into the first and second series according to rows. The graph uses the remaining default graph settings. Press any key except / to remove the graph from the screen.

4. Add a title to the graph. Enter **/Graph Text 1st Line**. When Quattro prompts for the graph title, type **\A1**, and press ENTER or point to the Enter button in the box and press the mouse button.

5. Add a title to the y-axis. Select **Y-Title**. When Quattro prompts for the axis title, type **\A3**, and either press ENTER or point to the Enter button in the box and then press the mouse button.

6. Place the legend at the side of the graph. Select **Legends Position Right**. Then select **Quit** twice to return to the Graph menu.

7. Make the graph type a bar. Select **Graph Type** and **Bar**. Select **View** to display your graph. You can see how Quattro has adjusted the graph as you added titles and changed the legend position.

8. To activate the graph annotator, type **/**.

9. Add text below the legend box. Type **/T** (or point to the Text icon, and press the mouse button). Move the pointer or arrow to below the legend box. Type **Units Sold include**. Press CTRL-ENTER. Type **all releases of the**, and press CTRL-ENTER. Type **products**, and press ENTER.

10. Leave the graph annotator. Type **/Q** (or point to the Quit icon, and press the mouse button). Press any key except / to remove the graph from the screen. Select **Quit** to return to the READY mode.

11. Print the graph. Enter **/Print Graph Print Go**. The final graph looks like Figure 7.40. Yours may vary, depending on the location in which you placed the text you added in step 9 and on the printer you are using.

12. Select **Quit** twice to return to the READY mode.

8

Data Management

Quattro's data-management features can be used to supplement the spreadsheet techniques covered in earlier chapters. Data-management features can also be used alone to create a database of information on the spreadsheet that does not require any of the calculations of the spreadsheet environment. As a supplement to the spreadsheet features, the database commands can be used to resequence detail entries in a spreadsheet (as long as sorting these entries does not jeopardize the integrity of the formulas). The database features can also be used to produce an exception report from the calculations produced by spreadsheet formulas. An exception report can help you focus your attention on important issues rather than on the details.

In the more traditional sense, Quattro's data-management features can be used to maintain data for employees within your department, vendors that you contact on a regular basis, or the inventory codes and prices for merchandise items that you stock. This data may be stored as label and/or number entries without any formulas. The emphasis in these applications may be strictly on the storage and retrieval features of the package.

Quattro has features that parallel those found in traditional database-management systems: its abilities to present data in any sequence desired and to selectively present information from the database. Quattro differs from other systems in that the capacity of the database is limited to the storage capacity provided by the memory available on your machine. With Quattro's VROOMM technology, database size is only an issue with very large databases.

In addition Quattro can work with other database formats. In Chapter 5, you saw how you could save and retrieve database files. You can also work directly with these database files as part of Quattro's data management features. If you are using Paradox databases, you can switch between Quattro and Paradox by pressing a key. This allows you to use Paradox features in Quattro and Quattro features in

Paradox. Some of the features you may want to use include Quattro's graph features, Quattro macros, Paradox's sorting, and Paradox's query by example.

DATA MANAGEMENT CONCEPTS IN QUATTRO

Before you begin to learn the database functions and commands that Quattro provides, it is essential to first learn a few essential data-management terms. This section will introduce the basic concepts of database, record, and field.

A *database* is simply a collection of related information. The list of people and their telephone numbers found in a phone directory is an example of a database. Figure 8.1 is another example of a database. From its database, you can easily determine the vendor's name, as well as the invoice number, date, amount, and terms. Also, you can quickly check whether an invoice has been paid.

A *record* consists of all the information about one thing in the database. In Figure 8.1, a record consists of all the information about one vendor. The data contained in each row compose a record pertaining to a particular vendor.

Each individual piece of information is a *field*. Referring again to Figure 8.1, the fields are the vendor name, the invoice number, the invoice date, the invoice amount, the invoice terms, and the date of payment. The collection of one entry for each of these fields makes a record, and the collection of all the records makes a database.

```
File   Edit   Style   Graph   Print   Database   Tools   Options   Window           ? ↑↓
▲ ▶ ▼  Erase Copy Move Style Align Font Insert Delete Fit Sum Format CHR WYS
A1: [W17] 'Vendor
         A              B        C         D         E          F
  1  Vendor          Inv_#    Inv_Date   Amount    Term      Paid_Date
  2  ABC Company     A1105    15-Dec-91  $5,560.75 2/10 net 30  22-Dec-91
  3  Parker Inc.     A2301    01-Dec-91  $2,310.50 net          10-Dec-91
  4  ABC Company     A1111    23-Dec-91  $6,556.80 2/10 net 30
  5  Lim & Associates L2525   01-Dec-91  $9,899.00 2/10 net 30  14-Dec-91
  6  XYZ Company     X2364    17-Dec-91  $1,220.90 2/10 net 30
  7  Doolittle Corp  S6349    02-Dec-91  $2,398.70 net          14-Dec-91
  8  Lim & Associates L2601   20-Dec-91  $8,550.50 net
  9  The Ong Company K1877    18-Dec-91  $7,550.50 2/10 net 30
 10  Kelvin & Company K2312   17-Dec-91  $2,112.00 2/10 net 30
 11
 12
 13
 14
 15
 16
 17
 18
QFIG8_1.WQ1  [1]                                        NUM          READY
```

Figure 8.1 Quattro Spreadsheet Containing Invoice Database

CREATING A QUATTRO PRO DATABASE

A Quattro database is a block of cells on the spreadsheet that follow the row and column organization needed to effectively use the database commands. The top row in the database consists of as many as 256 fields. Beneath these fields the record entries are stored. As many as 8,191 records can be entered, although memory constraints preclude a database with both the maximum number of records and the maximum number of fields.

You can choose any location on your spreadsheet to start the database, but the actual location may be dictated to a certain extent by the other entries on your spreadsheet. If a database is sharing the same spreadsheet with calculations, the area immediately below and to the right of the calculations is best so that you can insert both rows and columns in the database without jeopardizing the integrity of your formulas. A better solution is to have the spreadsheet by itself, which allows you to insert and delete columns and rows without affecting other data. Since you can have separate spreadsheets open simultaneously, you can store the database in one spreadsheet and the formulas that use the database in another spreadsheet.

Once you have selected an area for your database, you can place the field names across the top row of the database. Observing the tips in the "Rules for Field Names" box helps insure success for your first Quattro database effort. The field names are in the first row of the database, like the ones shown in Figure 8.1. Quattro does not impose limitations on the field names as some database packages do. If the field names follow Quattro's rules for block names, you can take advantage of the /Database Query Assign Names command, which lets you refer to the fields in the database by the field name instead of by cell address. For this reason, you may want to replace spaces in the field names with underscores (_) so using the field names in formulas does not create confusion.

Rules for Field Names

1. A field name entry should be restricted to one cell immediately above the first field entry,
2. Do not place a dividing line between the field names and the first field entry. If you want a line, add it with the /Style Line Drawing command.
3. Select meaningful names, since they will be used in both the criteria table and output area.
4. Be especially careful not to include trailing spaces at the end of field names, since it will not be apparent that they are there, yet Quattro will require these spaces in other entries for the same field name.
5. Enter the field names in the same order in which they appear on the source document.
6. Use the underscore (_) instead of a space to separate words in the field name.

> ▼ TIP: Use **/S**tyle **L**ine command for a line under the field names.
>
> If you want a line between the field names and the field values, use the **/**Style **L**ine **D**rawing command instead of entering \- in the cells below the field names.

ENTERING AND EDITING DATA

Making entries in a Quattro database is the same as entering data into any other spreadsheet cell. You should place your first field entry in the cell directly beneath the first field name and move to the right to make the other entries for the first record. After completing the first record, move the selector to the next spreadsheet row to enter record 2.

Error corrections can be made by using the same methods used in a normal spreadsheet entry. If you realize a mistake immediately after typing a character, the BACKSPACE key can be used to eliminate the problem. If you have already finalized an entry, you need to retype the cell entry or edit the cell to make your corrections. Records can be inserted anywhere in the database with the **/**Edit **I**nsert **R**ows command and can be deleted with the **/**Edit **D**elete **R**ows command. Database fields can be added or removed with **/**Edit **I**nsert **C**olumns or **/**Edit **D**elete **C**olumns.

SORTING A DATABASE

As your database grows larger, finding entries may be difficult if the records are stored in their random entry sequence. Sorting the data may enable you to present the information in a more manageable sequence. For example, you may need a list of customer names in alphabetical order or a list of customer account balances in descending order (highest to lowest). Quattro provides an easy method to perform these sort features. In Quattro Pro 4, you can use the same command to sort columns of data into a different order.

Specifying the Records to Sort

Quattro provides you with the capability to sort all the records or just a portion of them. Whether you sort all the records or just a few, you should always make certain that you sort all the fields.

To sort database records in Quattro, you must follow a sequence of steps as summarized in the "Sort Steps" box. First, you need to specify the block to be sorted. To specify the block to be sorted, enter /Database Sort Block. Then specify the block to be sorted as shown in Figure 8.2. It is important to ensure that the field names are not included in the specified block. Otherwise Quattro treats your field names as a record and sorts them. If you are sorting spreadsheet data that is not part of a database, make sure the block to sort includes all the data in the rows or columns you want to sort. If you are sorting columns, make sure to include any column headings so the column headings are moved with the data they describe.

Selecting from One to Five Sort Keys

You are able to specify up to five sort keys. A *sort key* selects a column or row of entries that you will use to determine the order of the rows or columns. The first, or primary, sort key always controls the sequence of the records. Even when you specify a second sort key, Quattro ignores it unless there are duplicate entries of the first sort key. If this is the case, the second sort key determines the sequence of the records. If more than one record has the same values for the first and second sort keys, Quattro uses the value of the third sort key to order those records. Quattro continues to use the next sort key when multiple records have the same values for the preceding sort keys.

CHOOSING A PRIMARY KEY The command you need to choose a primary key is /Database Sort 1st Key. You need not enter /Database Sort if you have just

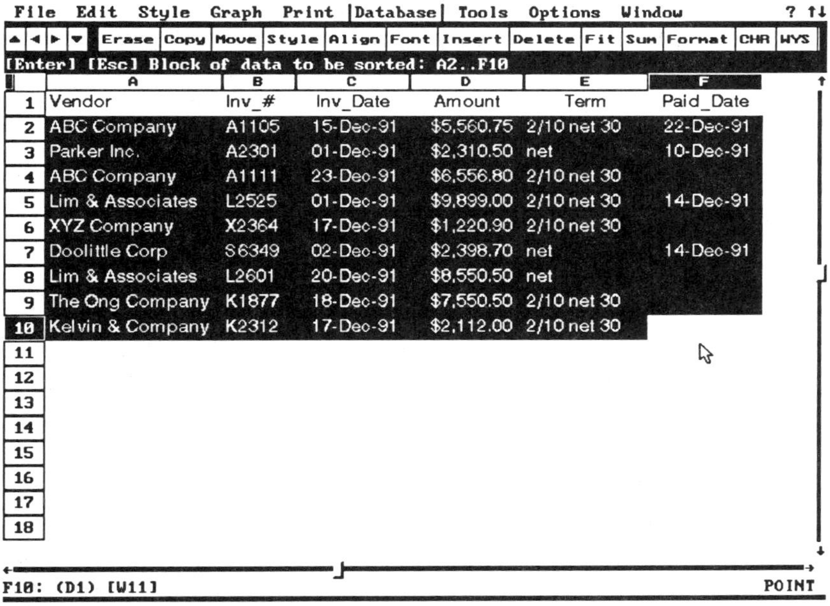

Figure 8.2 Selecting a Sort Block

> ### Sort Steps
>
> 1. Enter **/Database Sort Block**, and select a sort block. Do not include field names in this block.
> 2. Select the **1st Key**, and highlight a value within the database or a block name for a cell in the column you want to sort by.
> 3. Select the second through fifth sort keys if you want to establish multiple criteria.
> 4. Select **Go** from the menu.

specified the sort block. Quattro automatically returns you to the Database Sort menu. You can simply select **1st Key** and the field to be used as the first sort key. Next, move to a cell containing data for the field that is to be the first sort key. You need to select any entry in the column of values you want to use as the sort key when you are sorting by rows, and select any entry in the row of values you want to use as the sort key when you are sorting by columns. The cell you select must be in the block you selected with **/Database Sort Block**. If you use the **/Database Query Assign Names** command described later, you can also select a sort key by pressing F3 (NAME) and selecting the field name that you want to use to sort the records. For example, with the data in Figure 8.2, you might move the selector to A2 to indicate that the records should be sorted by vendor. When you press ENTER to confirm the first sort key, you are then prompted for either the **Descending** or **Ascending** order. If you choose the Descending order, Quattro sorts your data from highest to lowest (10,9,8 or Z,Y,X). Ascending order is just the reverse (8,9,10 or X,Y,Z).

CHOOSING ADDITIONAL SORT KEYS You can add four more sort keys that Quattro may use to sort the database. If you want to use a second sort key, simply select **2nd Key** and follow the same procedures used in specifying the first sort key. As mentioned previously, the second sort key is used as a tie-breaker to determine which data should be sorted first when the first sort key contains duplicates. The same procedure is followed for selecting sort keys three through five. With the sort block and keys selected, select Go to sort the database. If you want to sort by columns rather than by rows, you must select Sort Rules Sort Rows/Columns Columns Quit before selecting Go.

As an example of sorting, you might try sorting data by columns. First you would select the sort block, select the sort keys, tell Quattro Pro to sort by columns rather than by rows, and then tell it to sort the data. Figure 8.3 shows spreadsheet data that is sorted by columns. The values in row 10 are used as the first sort key. Since the values in this row are unique, it does not matter whether you have selected additional sort keys.

Figure 8.4 provides an example in which a primary and a secondary key are used to sort the data. The primary key is the Inv_Date field shown in column C, and the secondary key is the Vendor field shown in column A. Ascending order was specified for both of these keys. Note that the invoice dates are sorted from the earliest to the latest date. Also note that the secondary key comes into play only when sorting by the primary key results in a tie. Referring back to the example in Figure 8.4, notice that Lim & Associates is listed before Parker Inc. even though both records have an invoice date of December 1, 1989; the secondary sort key resulted in alphabetizing those two names. For the same reason, Kelvin & Company is listed before XYZ Company even though their invoice dates are the same.

Changing the Sort Order

Quattro provides three different sort order options. You can choose to sort numbers before labels, sort by columns, or by rows and can change the order of labels from a strict dictionary sequence to an ASCII code sequence that distinguishes between uppercase and lowercase entries.

The default sort order uses the following sequence when you choose Ascending:

Blank cells

Labels beginning with spaces

Labels beginning with numbers

Labels in alphabetical sequence

Labels beginning with special characters in their ASCII sequence

Value entries in numeric order.

Formulas are sorted with the labels or values according to the formulas' results. To change the sort order, you need to enter /Database Sort Sort Rules. If you select Numbers Before Labels, you can select Yes to sort the numbers before labels or No to sort the labels before the numbers. If you select Label Order you need to select either Dictionary (uppercase and lowercase are sorted together) or ASCII (uppercase and lowercase are sorted separately). If you select Sort Rows/Columns, you can select Rows to sort the sort block by rows (the default) or Columns to sort the sort block by columns. To use this new sort order on an ongoing basis, enter /Options Update.

If you are using international characters (ones not used in the English language), you will need to change how Quattro sorts characters, so Quattro incorporates the international characters in the proper alphabetical order. Select /Options International Use Sort Table. Select INTL.SOR to sort characters according to the alphabetic order of both English and International characters, NORDAN.SOR to sort characters according to their order in the Nordic and Danish Alphabets, or SWEDFIN.SOR to sort characters according to their order in the Swedish and Finnish alphabets.

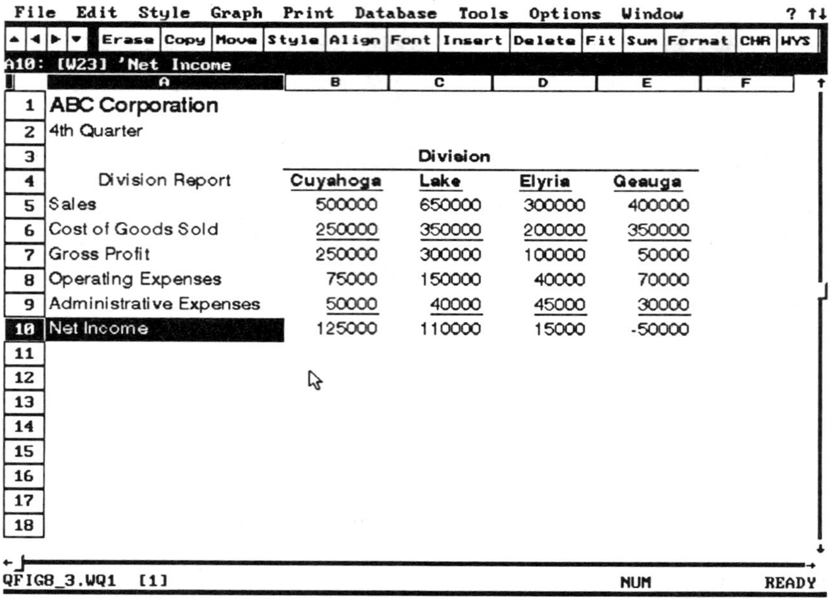

```
File  Edit  Style  Graph  Print  Database  Tools  Options  Window        ?  ↑↓
▲ ◄ ► ▼  Erase Copy Move Style Align Font Insert Delete Fit Sum Format CHR WYS
A10: [W23] 'Net Income
```

	A	B	C	D	E	F
1	ABC Corporation					
2	4th Quarter					
3				Division		
4	Division Report	Cuyahoga	Lake	Elyria	Geauga	
5	Sales	500000	650000	300000	400000	
6	Cost of Goods Sold	250000	350000	200000	350000	
7	Gross Profit	250000	300000	100000	50000	
8	Operating Expenses	75000	150000	40000	70000	
9	Administrative Expenses	50000	40000	45000	30000	
10	Net Income	125000	110000	15000	-50000	
11						
12						
13						
14						
15						
16						
17						
18						

```
QFIG8_3.WQ1  [1]                                           NUM         READY
```

Figure 8.3   Column Data Sorted By Net Income

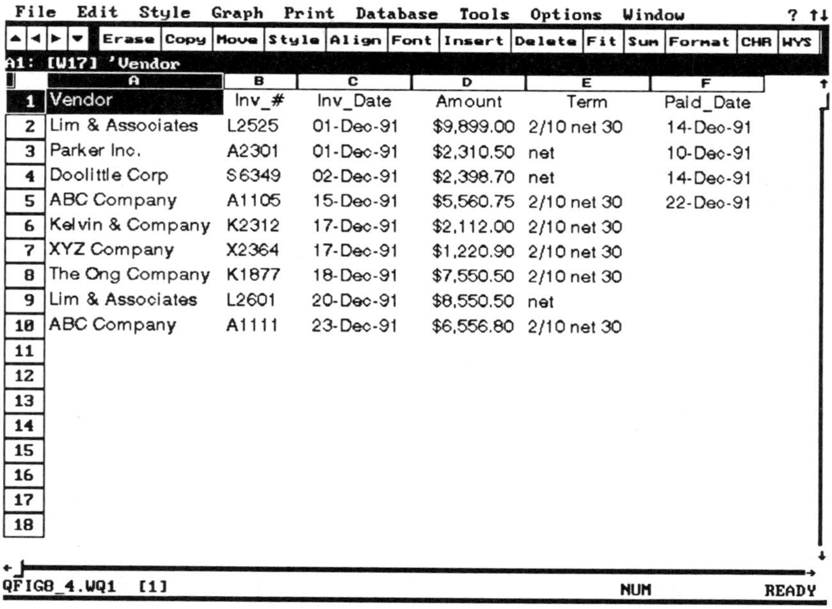

```
File  Edit  Style  Graph  Print  Database  Tools  Options  Window        ?  ↑↓
▲ ◄ ► ▼  Erase Copy Move Style Align Font Insert Delete Fit Sum Format CHR WYS
A1: [W17] 'Vendor
```

	A	B	C	D	E	F
1	Vendor	Inv_#	Inv_Date	Amount	Term	Paid_Date
2	Lim & Associates	L2525	01-Dec-91	$9,899.00	2/10 net 30	14-Dec-91
3	Parker Inc.	A2301	01-Dec-91	$2,310.50	net	10-Dec-91
4	Doolittle Corp	S6349	02-Dec-91	$2,398.70	net	14-Dec-91
5	ABC Company	A1105	15-Dec-91	$5,560.75	2/10 net 30	22-Dec-91
6	Kelvin & Company	K2312	17-Dec-91	$2,112.00	2/10 net 30	
7	XYZ Company	X2364	17-Dec-91	$1,220.90	2/10 net 30	
8	The Ong Company	K1877	18-Dec-91	$7,550.50	2/10 net 30	
9	Lim & Associates	L2601	20-Dec-91	$8,550.50	net	
10	ABC Company	A1111	23-Dec-91	$6,556.80	2/10 net 30	
11						
12						
13						
14						
15						
16						
17						
18						

```
QFIG8_4.WQ1  [1]                                           NUM         READY
```

Figure 8.4   Records Sorted by Vendor Within Invoice Date

Ensuring Data Integrity During Sorting

While using the database sort commands you must maintain data integrity. If your data contains relative cell references to cells outside the row in your database, the sort commands scramble your data. One example can show you how destructive a sort can be when you have relative cell references. Figure 8.5 is a loan amortization schedule with cell references to B1 (as seen in the input line), B2, and B3. These cell references are outside the database block. Figure 8.6 captures the spreadsheet after Quattro sorts the database in descending order with a primary sort key of the Month field. The entries in the Principal and Interest columns are now totally different from the entries shown in Figure 8.5. Integrity of the database is not maintained if the sort command is used when the database contains relative references to cells outside the database. Saving the file before performing a sort is one good way to prevent this problem, since you can always retrieve the file if a problem is found after sorting.

ACCEPTABLE FORMULA REFERENCES Although the sort command is easy to use, you must still be very cautious when you perform the sort process involving formula references. Failure to use caution can cause the sort command to change the entries in your database and make your database useless.

You must remember that if you use relative formula references within the same row of data in your database and if the fields that contain the formulas are sorted

	A	B	C	D
1	Amount Borrowed	$50,000		
2	Interest	9.50%		
3	Term (years)	10		
4	Month	Principal	Payment	Interest
5	01-Jan	$50,000.00	$646.99	$395.83
6	01-Feb	$49,748.85	$646.99	$393.85
7	01-Mar	$49,495.70	$646.99	$391.84
8	01-Apr	$49,240.56	$646.99	$389.82
9	01-May	$48,983.39	$646.99	$387.79
10	01-Jun	$48,724.19	$646.99	$385.73
11	01-Jul	$48,462.93	$646.99	$383.66
12	01-Aug	$48,199.61	$646.99	$381.58
13	01-Sep	$47,934.20	$646.99	$379.48
14	01-Oct	$47,666.69	$646.99	$377.36
15	01-Nov	$47,397.07	$646.99	$375.23
16	01-Dec	$47,125.31	$646.99	$373.08

Figure 8.5 An Amortization Table

418   *Quattro Pro 4.0 Handbook*

```
File  Edit  Style  Graph  Print  Database  Tools  Options  Window        ? ↑↓
▲ ◄ ► ▼  Erase Copy Move Style Align Font Insert Delete Fit Sum Format CHR WYS
B5: (C2) [W12] +B4-C4+D4
          A              B          C        D         E       F       G
  1  Amount Borrowed   $50,000
  2  Interest            9.50%
  3  Term (years)          10
  4              Month      Principal  Payment   Interest
  5              01-Dec       $0.00    $646.99    $0.00
  6              01-Nov     ($646.99)  $646.99   ($5.12)
  7              01-Oct   ($1,299.10)  $646.99  ($10.28)
  8              01-Sep   ($1,956.37)  $646.99  ($15.49)
  9              01-Aug   ($2,618.85)  $646.99  ($20.73)
 10              01-Jul   ($3,286.57)  $646.99  ($26.02)
 11              01-Jun   ($3,959.57)  $646.99  ($31.35)
 12              01-May   ($4,637.91)  $646.99  ($36.72)
 13              01-Apr   ($5,321.61)  $646.99  ($42.13)
 14              01-Mar   ($6,010.73)  $646.99  ($47.58)
 15              01-Feb   ($6,705.30)  $646.99  ($53.08)
 16              01-Jan   ($4,637.91)  $646.99  ($36.72)
 17
 18
QFIG8_6.WQ1  [1]                              NUM             READY
```

Figure 8.6 **The Effect of a Sort on the Amortization Table Shown in Figure 8.5**

simultaneously with the fields that these formulas reference, then the sort command does not change the data entries in your database.

If your data entries contain formula references to cells outside your database, you should make sure that these cell references are absolute before you use the sort command. This includes formulas that refer to data in another spreadsheet. This ensures that the sorting process does not affect the data entries in the cells. You can make cell references absolute by inserting $ signs in the cell addresses. For example, if you have a reference to cell A1, you can enter **A1** instead of just **A1**; Quattro knows the dollar signs indicate absolute cell references.

Furthermore, you cannot have absolute cell references between data entries within your database. If you do, the sort process changes your data entries and makes your database useless.

FORGETTING TO SORT ALL THE FIELDS Quattro only sorts the fields that you specify using the /Database Sort Block command. If you forget to specify a field, Quattro ignores this field when sorting, and some fields are lost in each record. For example, if you forget to include the salary field when sorting by employee name in an employee database, only the employee names are sorted. Therefore, the salary amounts are not properly matched with employee names after the sort. The database can no longer supply valid salary data. You should always check the fields included in the sort block before proceeding.

Data Management

It is especially important to recheck the sort block if you have added fields to the database. Otherwise, Quattro assumes that it should use its previous sort block, and the excluded fields remain stationary while the other fields are sorted.

SEARCHING FOR QUICK ANSWERS

When your database is large, searching for a specific record can be a time-consuming and tedious problem. Fortunately, Quattro provides query features that can eliminate this problem. For example, you may want to search for records pertaining to the vendor Lim & Associates in the vendor database shown in Figure 8.1. These database features also provide you with an exception-reporting capability. Information that does not conform to expectations can easily be brought to your attention using the query features. You also can use these features to remove unwanted records from your database or to prepare reports in response to requests.

Just as several steps are required for sorting your data, a special sequence of steps is required before you can use the query features. These steps are summarized in the "Query Steps" box.

Completing the Necessary Spreadsheet Entries

Quattro's query features are located on the Database Query menu, but there are a few steps that you may need to take before invoking them. The query features are

---

Query Steps

1. Enter the table criteria in the spreadsheet from READY mode.
2. Enter **/Database Query Block**, and select the database records (including the field names).
3. Select **Assign Names** to apply the names in the first row of the database to the fiels in the first database record.
4. Select **Criteria Table** and the spreadsheet block containing the criteria table.
5. To highlight matching records, select **Locate**.
6. To extract matching records, you must first enter the field names you wish to extract in a row of the database. Select **Output Block**, and highlight the block.
7. Select **Extract** or **Unique** to copy data from matching records to the output block.

used to tell Quattro the specific location of database records and a table of your specifications for matching records. These commands require that the entries be on the spreadsheet already when the command is invoked. Some of the query options also require an output area to which Quattro copies the records that match the criteria. The entries for the output area must also be completed before a command that uses them is invoked.

At a minimum, you should complete the entry of all database records and criteria before invoking the Database Query menu. You already know the rules to follow in creating database entries, but entering criteria offers a few more variations. Criteria are stored in a criteria table and contain exact match criteria or formula criteria. Exact-match criteria can match specific entries, like all invoices from ABC Company or all invoice dates of December 22, 1989. Formula criteria allow you to establish logical formulas for comparisons against the database field values, such as formulas for invoices that exceed $5,000.

If you want Quattro to find matching entries, you are ready to proceed to the menu. If you plan for Quattro to extract records that match your specifications, you must lay out at the top of the output area the fields for which data is to be extracted. You can select as many fields as you want and can place the fields in any order across a row in an empty area of the spreadsheet. You should be certain that you select an area for the output fields that allows adequate blank rows beneath it for Quattro to use when it copies the matching records to the extract area. You can also use a separate spreadsheet for the output area. For example, the spreadsheet file OUTPUT can be your output area, and you can use the resulting records for a report by adding the remaining information the report needs.

Defining the Block to Search

After preparing the spreadsheet entries, you are ready to begin making selections from the Database Query menu. The first step is defining the block of records to be searched. To do this, simply type /Database Query. A menu appears on the screen. Select Block, and then specify the block. Quattro will highlight the data that you have specified (such as A1..F10 for the database shown in Figure 8.7). Note that the field names must be included in your specification. Also you need not include the entire database to be searched, but the block must include all the fields in the criteria table and the output area if used. If the database is in a different spreadsheet, you must enter the file name in brackets ([ ]) before entering the block address. You can also use the PICK key (ALT-0) to point to another spreadsheet, then select the block from the other spreadsheet. If the drive or directory are different from Quattro's defaults, you must supply this information in the brackets. If the extension is not .WQ1, you must also supply this information in the brackets. The spreadsheet does not have to be open to use the Extract and Unique query features discussed later in the chapter. The spreadsheet must be open to use the Locate and Delete query menu options discussed later in the chapter.

When you use separate spreadsheets for the different blocks to be used by the

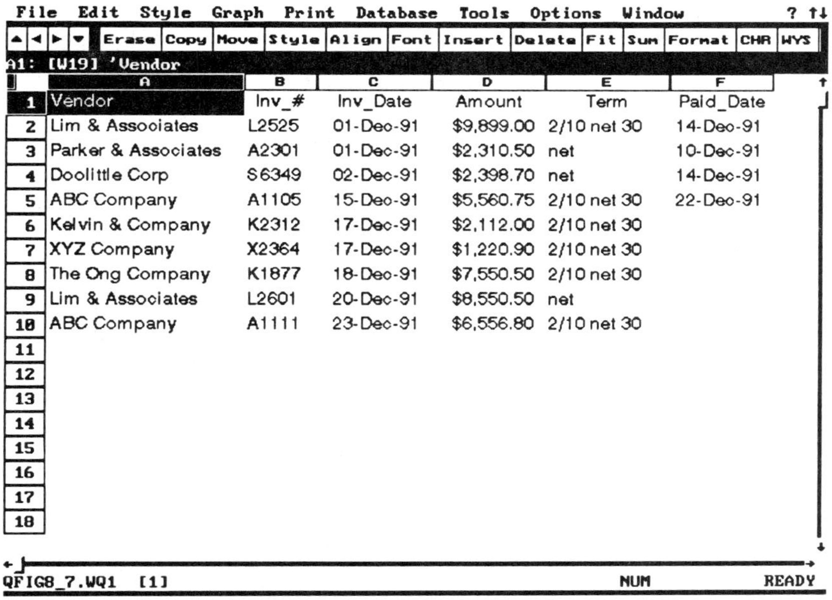

```
  File   Edit   Style   Graph   Print   Database   Tools   Options   Window          ?  ↑↓
  ▲ ◄ ▼  Erase Copy Move Style Align Font Insert Delete Fit Sum Format CHR WYS
  A1:  [W19] 'Vendor
```

	A	B	C	D	E	F
1	Vendor	Inv_#	Inv_Date	Amount	Term	Paid_Date
2	Lim & Associates	L2525	01-Dec-91	$9,899.00	2/10 net 30	14-Dec-91
3	Parker & Associates	A2301	01-Dec-91	$2,310.50	net	10-Dec-91
4	Doolittle Corp	S6349	02-Dec-91	$2,398.70	net	14-Dec-91
5	ABC Company	A1105	15-Dec-91	$5,560.75	2/10 net 30	22-Dec-91
6	Kelvin & Company	K2312	17-Dec-91	$2,112.00	2/10 net 30	
7	XYZ Company	X2364	17-Dec-91	$1,220.90	2/10 net 30	
8	The Ong Company	K1877	18-Dec-91	$7,550.50	2/10 net 30	
9	Lim & Associates	L2601	20-Dec-91	$8,550.50	net	
10	ABC Company	A1111	23-Dec-91	$6,556.80	2/10 net 30	

```
  QFIG8_7.WQ1   [1]                                          NUM           READY
```

Figure 8.7 Database to Select with /Database Query Block

/Database Query commands, the settings for the different blocks in the separate spreadsheets are only saved with the spreadsheet that is current at the time you define the blocks to use. Quattro uses the database, criteria, and output blocks defined in the Database Query menu of the spreadsheet in which the selector is located at the time that a /Database Query command is performed. For example, with the data in Figure 8.8 and the selector in the OUTPUT spreadsheet, the /Database Query Block command selects the database as [INVOICES]A1..F10. This setting is saved in the OUTPUT spreadsheet. The INVOICES spreadsheet may have its own settings in the Database Query menu.

Assigning Names to Fields

The Assign Names option of the Query menu allows you to assign block names to the first entry of each field. This is not a required step. However, this option makes entering search criteria much easier. You can reference fields by name instead of having to specify a cell address. When you create criteria that compare the values in a database, you must select which fields you want to compare. For example, if you want to find invoice amounts greater than $5,000, you must tell Quattro to use the fields in the column labeled Amount. One method is telling Quattro the first cell containing an amount value; Quattro then automatically compares all values in the Amount column using a formula like **+D2>5000**. Unfortunately, you cannot tell from looking at the formula which field it uses. Quattro offers a better solution

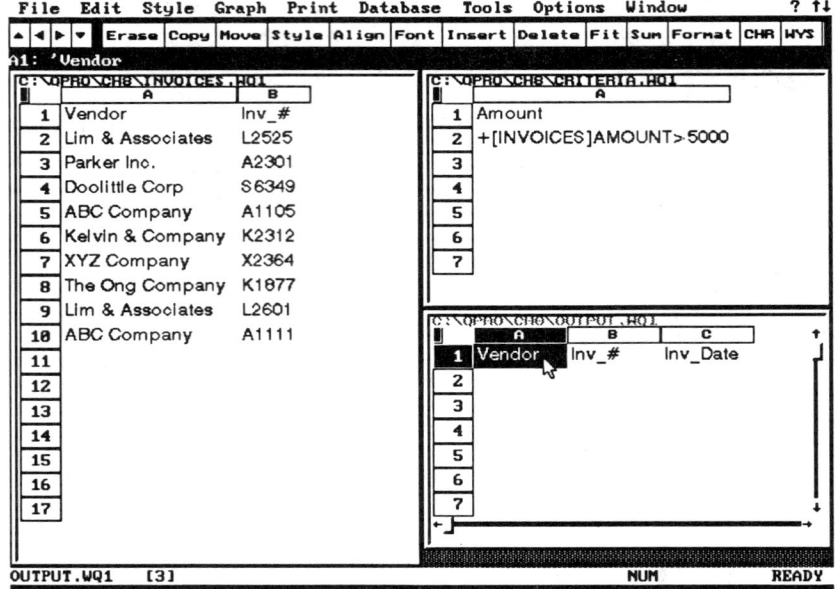

Figure 8.8 Using Separate Spreadsheets for Database, Criteria, and Output Blocks

with the /Database Query Assign Names command. When you enter /Database Query Assign Names, Quattro names the cells below the field names for each column in the block selected with /Database Query Block. After this command, you can enter formulas like **+AMOUNT>5000** and know exactly which fields this formula uses.

The /Database Query Assign Names command is different from the /Edit Names Labels Down command. Once you assign names with the /Database Query Assign Names command, the field names always apply to the cells below the field names. With the /Edit Names Labels Down command, the block names initially apply to the cells below the field names. As rows are inserted and deleted or the data is sorted, the position of the cells named with /Edit Names Labels Down changes. This does not happen with cells named with /Database Query Assign Names. Since Quattro treats cells named with /Database Query Assign Names as block names, you can use other Quattro features that apply to block names, such as pressing F3 (NAME) when Quattro prompts for a block address, cell address, or sort key.

Specifying the Criteria Table

After defining and assigning names to your database, you need to specify the criteria table. This allows Quattro to match the specified criteria with the records from your database. The other commands in the Database Query menu box use the criteria table to determine which records the command will use. The criteria use a table-type orientation with the field names in the top row and the values or formulas that the database records must match in the subsequent rows. The middle spreadsheet in Figure 8.8 shows a tabular format in which Vendor is the field name and Lim & Associates is the value criteria for this field for which you want to search; thus, Quattro searches for the records in which Lim & Associates is the vendor name field.

CHOOSING A LOCATION FOR CRITERIA Although the actual positioning of the criteria is not significant, you should position the table in an area that will not hinder the addition of records to your database. If the criteria is in the same spreadsheet as the database, you should position your criteria table to the right of your database so that you can add additional records without having to move the criteria entries. You may even want to leave a few columns between your database and criteria table so that you can add additional fields to your database in the future. However, you should try not to place your criteria table too far from your database, since that may make it inconvenient to access.

You can also put the criteria table in a separate spreadsheet; this prevents the database from interfering with the criteria. As an example, the data in Figure 8.8 can be in the spreadsheet file INVOICES, and the criteria could consist of Vendor in A1 and Lim & Associates in A2 of the CRITERIA spreadsheet file. The spreadsheet containing the criteria table must be open when the /Database Query command is performed.

To create a criteria table, simply enter the field names of the desired data followed by the desired data below the field names, as shown in the middle spreadsheet in Figure 8.8. Another option is to use the /Edit Copy command to copy the field names from the database to the criteria table. Copying the field names ensures that the field names in the database and the criteria table are identical. The field names indicate to Quattro the fields that the criteria should use. Below the field names, you put the exact match and/or formula criteria.

You can define the criteria table simply by selecting the Criteria Table option from the Query menu. Then highlight the block of cells in your criteria table, and press ENTER. Do not include any blank lines when you are highlighting. If you do, Quattro will locate every record in the database as matching, since a blank line serves as an ultimate wild card and matches everything in the database. You can include extra columns in the criteria table, since Quattro will ignore them. For the same reason, if the criteria table includes fields with no formulas or exact matches below them, Quattro will ignore those columns. A spreadsheet can contain more than one criteria table, which lets you change which records you are using by changing the block defining the criteria table. Before you proceed with selecting criteria, be sure to look at the criteria you can provide and the options you have for exact match criteria and/or formula criteria.

EXACT MATCH CRITERIA Criteria can be specified to exactly match the entries in your database. Quattro searches for the data in specific database fields that exactly match the specified criteria. Exact match criteria consist of a field name and a specific value or label that you want to search for in the field beneath the field names. For example, if you are searching the database shown in the top spreadsheet in Figure 8.8, you would specify your criteria so that Quattro would search for records with a vendor name of Lim & Associates. The criteria would have Vendor in the first row and Lim & Associates in the second row. You can also do exact matches with values, such as finding invoices with an invoice amount equal to $5,000. The criteria would have Amount in the first row and 5000 in the second row. Quattro does not care that the format of the number is different from the format of the numbers in the database. When entries in the database table are the results of formulas, Quattro uses the formula results to determine if the records match the criteria. For example, using the criteria to find invoices with amounts equaling $5,000, the criteria would match a record with an invoice amount of +4700+300.

With label exact match entries, Quattro does not distinguish between uppercase and lowercase labels. For example, Lim & Associates shown in the middle spreadsheet in Figure 8.8 can also be entered as LIM & ASSOCIATES or lim & associates with equivalent results. Exact match criteria for labels can also include the question mark and asterisk wild card characters, which increase the number of labels that match the criteria.

Wild Card Criteria for Label Fields Quattro provides wild card characters that can be useful in specifying criteria for fields that contain label entries. Special wild card characters can save typing time and provide flexible matching options. These wild card characters are *, ?, and ~.

The asterisk (*) tells Quattro to accept any database record that matches the specified part of the criteria. For example, if you specify a search criteria as **Sm***, Quattro searches for all records that begin with **Sm**. Entries such as Smith, Smyth, Smithsonian, and Smith & Company would match. Figure 8.9 shows criteria that uses the asterisk wild card. The specified criterion Lim* is matched by Lim & Associates in the first and eighth records (rows 2 and 9) shown in Figure 8.8. You can also include the asterisk at the beginning of the criteria; for example, the entry ***Company** matches with ABC Company, XYZ Company, and Kelvin & Company.

The question mark (?) is used to replace any one character in an entry. When you use the question mark as a wild card entry, you are telling Quattro to accept any character in place of the ? and to search for any entry that matches exactly the other characters in your specified criteria. Use the ? when you do not care what character is located in a specific position in an entry. Therefore, the criteria **L?m** would be matched by Lim, Lam, Lem, Lom, but not by Liming or Lin.

The ? wild card can be used several times in your specification. For example, if your specified criteria is **?????field**, Quattro matches it with Smithfield, Mellefield, and Bellefield. If your specified criteria is **?lf?rd**, Quattro finds such matches as Alford, Elford, and Alferd.

The tilde (~) is used whenever you want to negate an entry. For example, you might want to locate entries with last names other than Jones. You would then enter **~Jones** under the Last Name field in your criteria table. In this case, Quattro matches the criteria with all entries whose last name is not Jones.

FORMULA CRITERIA Formula criteria provide additional options for specifying your requirements to Quattro. This option also allows you to search for records that contain numeric and label characters. Formula criteria use the logical operators shown in Table 8.1, since all formula criteria are expressed as logical formulas. When you use formula criteria, Quattro analyzes the record to see if the values in the record make the formula in the formula criteria true (1) or false (0). If the formula evaluates to true for the record, the record matches that part of the criteria table. However, the criteria table may have other criteria the record must also match.

When the formula for formula criteria references a value from the database table, the formula references the first record in the database. After using /Database Query Assign Names, you can use the field names instead. For example, you can enter either **+D2>9000** or **+Amount>9000**. Quattro interprets both these logical conditions in a similar manner. The formula criteria will display in the criteria table as 0 or 1 unless you set the format of the cells containing the formula criteria to text. In the examples below, the formula criteria are formatted as text. This is a good habit to develop, since it provides documentation.

If the database is in a spreadsheet separate from the criteria, the formula criteria must reference the spreadsheet containing the database. For example, if the database

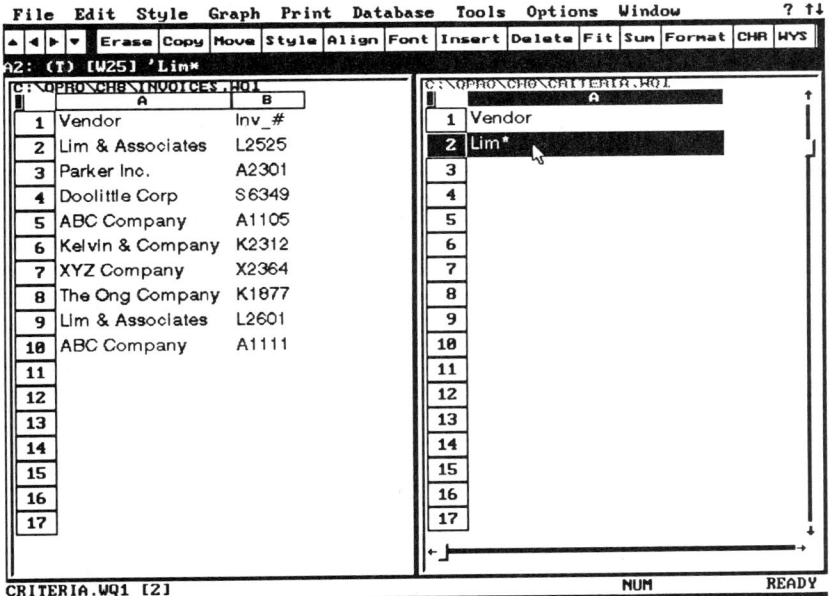

Figure 8.9 Using a Wild Card Character with Label Criteria

Table 8.1 The Logical Operators

Operator	Meaning
=	Equal to
>	Greater than
<	Less than
>=	Greater than or equal to
<=	Less than or equal to
<>	Not equal to

is in the INVOICES spreadsheet, criteria in a different spreadsheet to find the invoice amounts greater than $9,000 is +[INVOICES]AMOUNT>9000.

Creating Criteria as Logical Formulas for Values and Labels When you use formula criteria, you include the formula below the first row of the criteria table. The field name above the formula provides documentation about the formula. You can use cell references or blocks to build formula criteria by using the same entries as those in tables. The top line of Figure 8.10 shows the formula entered as **+AMOUNT>5000**. In this example, Quattro locates all the records with invoice amounts greater than $5,000. The **+AMOUNT** entered as part of the formula represents the invoice amount field. If you do not use the /Database Query Assign Names command, you must use the cell address of the first entry in the field for example, +D2>5000.

You can use formula criteria for fields that contain label entries. Any label included within the formula must be enclosed in quotation marks, as in **+VENDOR>>"L"** (which finds all database records with vendors that start between L and Z). Text in formulas that are used for comparison (like the L in the example) must be in quotes.

Formula Criteria Versus Quattro Formulas The formulas used for formula criteria follow the same rules as other Quattro formulas. You can use @ functions just as if you are building a logical function for another type of database entry. For example, you can use the @TODAY function to create a formula to find out which invoices are 30 days overdue: +INV_DATE+30>@TODAY. You may want to use the @EXACT function if you want to compare labels and you want the match to be sensitive to the uppercase or lowercase of the entries. For example, to find ABC Company and not Abc Company, enter the formula criteria of @EXACT(VENDOR,"ABC Company").

The only two differences are that in formula criteria cell references to the database fields use the cell address of the first entry below the field name or the field name itself, and cell addresses that reference outside the database must be

```
File  Edit  Style  Graph  Print  Database  Tools  Options  Window      ? ↑↓
 ▲ ◀ ▶ ▼  Erase Copy Move Style Align Font Insert Delete Fit Sum Format CHR WYS
A13:  (T)  [W17]  +AMOUNT>5000
         A              B        C          D         E         F
  1  Vendor          Inv_#    Inv_Date    Amount    Term      Paid_Date
  2  Lim & Associates L2525   01-Dec-91   $9,899.00  2/10 net 30  14-Dec-91
  3  Parker Inc.     A2301   01-Dec-91   $2,310.50  net         10-Dec-91
  4  Doolittle Corp  S6349   02-Dec-91   $2,398.70  net         14-Dec-91
  5  ABC Company     A1105   15-Dec-91   $5,560.75  2/10 net 30  22-Dec-91
  6  Kelvin & Company K2312  17-Dec-91   $2,112.00  2/10 net 30
  7  XYZ Company     X2364   17-Dec-91   $1,220.90  2/10 net 30
  8  The Ong Company K1877   18-Dec-91   $7,550.50  2/10 net 30
  9  Lim & Associates L2601   20-Dec-91   $8,550.50  net
 10  ABC Company     A1111   23-Dec-91   $6,556.80  2/10 net 30
 11
 12  Amount
 13  +AMOUNT>5000
 14
 15
 16
 17
 18

QFIG8_10.WQ1 [1]                                       NUM         READY
```

Figure 8.10 Entering Simple Formula Criteria

absolute addresses. When Quattro checks each record to see if it matches the criteria, Quattro makes imaginary copies down the column of the formula criteria. These are imaginary copies because the actual entries below the formula criteria do not change. Quattro uses each of these imaginary copies to determine which records match the criteria. This is also why you must reference the first entry below the field name in formula criteria, since the imaginary copies have the formula references adjusted. These imaginary copies are also why cell addresses outside the database must be absolute addresses. For example, with the database and criteria shown in Figure 8.11, Quattro makes imaginary copies of the formula criteria in B8 to B9..B11. The formulas in these imaginary copies are +D3>D9, +D4>D10, and +D5>D11. Since the cell address to D8 is not absolute, the formula criteria is only correct for the first record. The correct formula criteria in this case is +D2<D8.

COMPOUND CRITERIA Quattro has two ways of building compound criteria. You can use compound criteria to find records that meet one of several criteria or records that meet multiple criteria. You can create compound criteria in a single formula criteria by using the #AND#, #OR#, and #NOT# logical operators. You also have the option of creating compound criteria by putting the criteria on one or more rows in the criteria table. Compound criteria can combine exact match and formula criteria.

The #AND#, #OR#, and #NOT# operators can all be used in formula criteria. These operators are the same ones you use to build logical functions for applica-

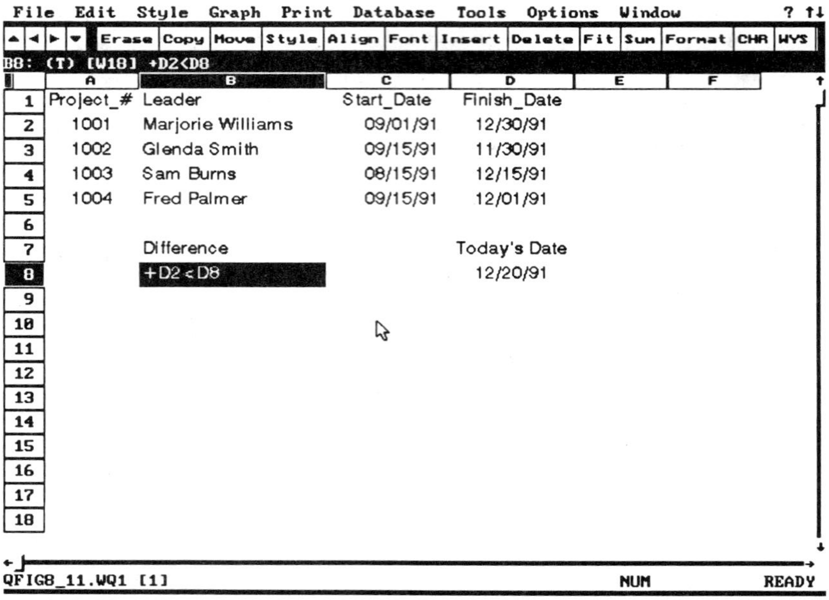

Figure 8.11 Formula Criteria that References Other Cells

tions not related to a database, as well as to create the conditions that an @IF function tests. When you use the #AND# logical operator, Quattro selects database records only if these records satisfy all the conditions specified by your search criteria. For example, if you specify your search criteria as **+Age=25#AND#Sex="Male"** in an employee database, Quattro finds those employees who are both 25 years old AND male. If you want to search for employees who are 25 through 40 years old, the criteria formula can be entered as **+Age>=25#AND#Age<=40**. In this instance, an age entry must match both criteria.

If you specify your search criteria using the #OR# logical operator, Quattro searches for any record that contains either of the specified criteria. Referring back to the employee example, any employee who is 25 years old or male will be matched if the criteria is entered as **+Age=25#OR#Sex="Male"**. Figure 8.12 contains another example of specified criteria using the #OR# logical operator. If you want to look at records for employees under 25 as well as those employees over 40, you can use this formula criteria entry: **Age<25#OR#Age>40**. The #OR# operator is perfect since it is not possible for one record to meet both conditions.

The #NOT# logical operator is used to match records that do not meet a set of criteria. For example, if your criteria is entered as **#NOT#Age= 25**, Quattro finds employees whose ages are not equal to 25. (The same criteria can be specified by using the <> operator.) You can also use the #NOT# logical operator to negate multiple formula criteria, and it is more practical in this situation. For example, if you enter **Age=25#OR##NOT#Sex="Female"**, Quattro finds employees whose

```
  File  Edit  Style  Graph  Print  Database  Tools  Options  Window      ? ↑↓
  ▲ ◄ ▼  Erase Copy Move Style Align Font Insert Delete Fit Sum Format CHR WYS
A13:  (T) [W17]  +AMOUNT<4000#OR#+AMOUNT>9000
          A              B         C          D          E          F
   1  Vendor           Inv_#    Inv_Date    Amount     Term      Paid_Date
   2  Lim & Associates L2525   01-Dec-91   $9,899.00  2/10 net 30  14-Dec-91
   3  Parker Inc.      A2301   01-Dec-91   $2,310.50  net          10-Dec-91
   4  Doolittle Corp   S6349   02-Dec-91   $2,398.70  net          14-Dec-91
   5  ABC Company      A1105   15-Dec-91   $5,560.75  2/10 net 30  22-Dec-91
   6  Kelvin & Company K2312   17-Dec-91   $2,112.00  2/10 net 30
   7  XYZ Company      X2364   17-Dec-91   $1,220.90  2/10 net 30
   8  The Ong Company  K1877   18-Dec-91   $7,550.50  2/10 net 30
   9  Lim & Associates L2601   20-Dec-91   $8,550.50  net
  10  ABC Company      A1111   23-Dec-91   $6,556.80  2/10 net 30
  11
  12  Amount
  13  +AMOUNT<4000#OR#+AMOUNT>9000
  14
  15
  16
  17
  18

QFIG8_12.WQ1 [1]                                         NUM          READY
```

Figure 8.12 Formula Criteria Using Complex Logical Operators

ages are equal to 25 OR whose sex is not female. The #NOT# logical operator can be used in another multiple criteria situation. For example you, can specify this search criteria: **#NOT#(Vendor="ABC Company"#AND#Amount =5560.75)**. Using the #NOT# logical operator in this manner alters the #AND# logical operator to an #OR# logical operator. In this particular example, Quattro matches any record in which the vendor is not ABC Company OR the invoice amount is not equal to $5,560.75.

You can also create compound criteria by selecting the row in the criteria table in which you want to place the exact match entries or formula criteria. Quattro interprets the relationship between data entered on the same horizontal line as having an "AND" relationship. This means that a record must satisfy both criteria before it can be located. For example, to create criteria that find unpaid invoices with payment terms of 2/10 net 30 (2% reduction if paid within 10 days or the full sum paid within 30 days), you can have **Term** and **Paid_Date** in the first row of the criteria table and **'2/10 net 30** and **@CELL("type",PAID_DATE)="b"** as the entries below these field names on the second row (the @CELL function returns a "b" when the cell it references is blank, which indicates an unpaid invoice).

When entries are on separate lines, Quattro interprets these entries as having an "OR" relationship. This means that a record is matched if it meets either of the specified criteria. For example, to create criteria that finds unpaid invoices or invoices greater than $8,000, you can enter **Amount** and **Paid_Date** in the first row of the criteria table, **+AMOUNT>8000** one row below the field names, and **@CELL("type",PAID_DATE)="b"** in two rows below the field names.

Locating Matching Records

Once you specify your criteria, you can locate all the records that match your specifications. To have Quattro highlight the first matching record, choose the **Locate** option from the Query menu. Quattro searches only the block specified by the **Block** option. When a matching record is located, Quattro highlights only the fields within the block. Figure 8.13 provides an example of a record highlighted with **Locate**. Notice the FIND mode indicator in the status line.

To view the next record, press the DOWN ARROW key. When you get to the last record, Quattro does not allow you to go down any farther. It beeps whenever you try to do so. Similarly, Quattro does not allow you to move above the first matching record. You can move to previous matching records with the UP ARROW key. Two other keys that can be used are the END and the HOME keys. The END key is used if you want to go to the last record matching your criteria, and the HOME key takes you back to the first record meeting your specifications.

You can edit the entry for any field when Quattro locates the desired database record. You can use the LEFT and RIGHT ARROW keys to move the selector to the cell within the record that you wish to edit. Next, press F2 (EDIT) to invoke the edit mode and make your changes, and then press ENTER to finalize the changes. You can move to other cells of the matching records to edit their entries. Instead of using the EDIT mode to change the cell entries, you can make the changes by typing in the entries. To exit from FIND mode, press ESC or ENTER, and Quattro will return you to the Query menu.

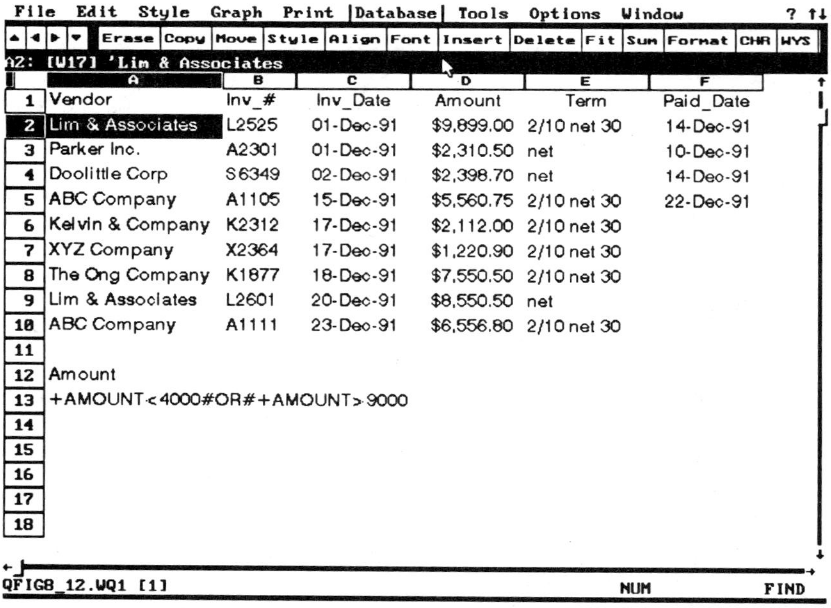

Figure 8.13 Matching Record Highlighted

If you want to quickly perform the same command from the Database Query menu box while you are in the READY mode, press F7 (QUERY). You can use this key when you return to the READY mode, change the criteria in the criteria table, and want to see the effect of the new criteria. You can use this for the Locate option in the Database Query menu box as well as the Delete, Extract, and Unique options covered later in the chapter.

BUILDING EXCEPTION REPORTS WITH QUATTRO PRO'S EXTRACT FEATURES

The Locate feature provides a quick answer for questions you might have about the data in your database. You can think of Locate as an ideal solution for handling telephone inquiries concerning data in your records. Sometimes you might want printed reports of records that meet your specifications. For example, you may need a report of all vendor invoice amounts over $7,000 to focus attention on the suppliers of large orders, or you may need to prepare a report of all invoices from a particular vendor. In these instances, the Locate feature in Quattro cannot serve your objectives efficiently, since you only can look at one matching record at a time. Quattro can handle this new task through Extract from the Database Query menu. This menu also has Unique, which finds unique records for you, and Delete, which removes records from the database that meet the criteria.

Before invoking Extract, you need to create an output area and define its location to Quattro. In other respects, Extract follows the same procedures as Locate and accepts either table or formula criteria for your specifications.

Creating an Output Area

You must create an output area on the spreadsheet from READY mode before you can define its location to Quattro with menu selections. Selecting an appropriate location will make it easier to work with your data-management application. If you want the output area in the same spreadsheet, the area beneath the database is frequently selected for the output area. If you choose this location, you should leave a number of blank rows after your database to allow for expansion. Alternatively, you can use an area to the right of your database.

Another possibility is to use a separate spreadsheet for the output area so your database and output do not interfere with each other as the database and output areas expand. When you use a separate spreadsheet for the output block, you must enter the file name in brackets ([ ]) before entering the block address. You can also use the PICK key (ALT-0) to change the spreadsheet to which the selector is pointing. When the selector is in a different spreadsheet, you can select the block from the other spreadsheet and let Quattro supply the file name for you. If the drive or directory are different from Quattro's defaults, you must supply this information in the brackets. If the extension is not .WQ1, the file name in the brackets must include the extension. The spreadsheet with the output block must be open to use the Extract and Unique query features. As an example, the database in Figure 8.14 is in the INVOICES spreadsheet file, the criterion is in the CRITERIA spreadsheet file, and the output block is in the REPORT spreadsheet.

After you choose a location for your output area, type in the field names you wish to extract from the records or copy the field names you used above your database records. The fields need not be in the same sequence as the fields in your database, and you do not need to include every field. However, correct spelling is essential, since Quattro matches these field names with the ones in your database. If you are including heading information above the field names in the output area for the report you are creating with the results of extracting records, you can hide the field names with the Hidden format. When you print the report, the hidden field names appear in the report as a blank line.

After typing or copying the field names to the top of the output area, you must define the output area to Quattro. This can be done by entering the Output Block command from the Database Query menu and specifying a block of cells to serve as the output block. When you specify the block, Quattro highlights the cells within the block, as shown in Figure 8.14. Since the output block is in a different spreadsheet, you can select the block by pressing ALT-3 to make the REPORT spreadsheet current. Then select A1..F1 as the output block before pressing ENTER. Quattro will add the [REPORT] for you.

The size of the output block you select affects the results of the extract operation. If you specify a block that consists of only the field names, Quattro interprets the

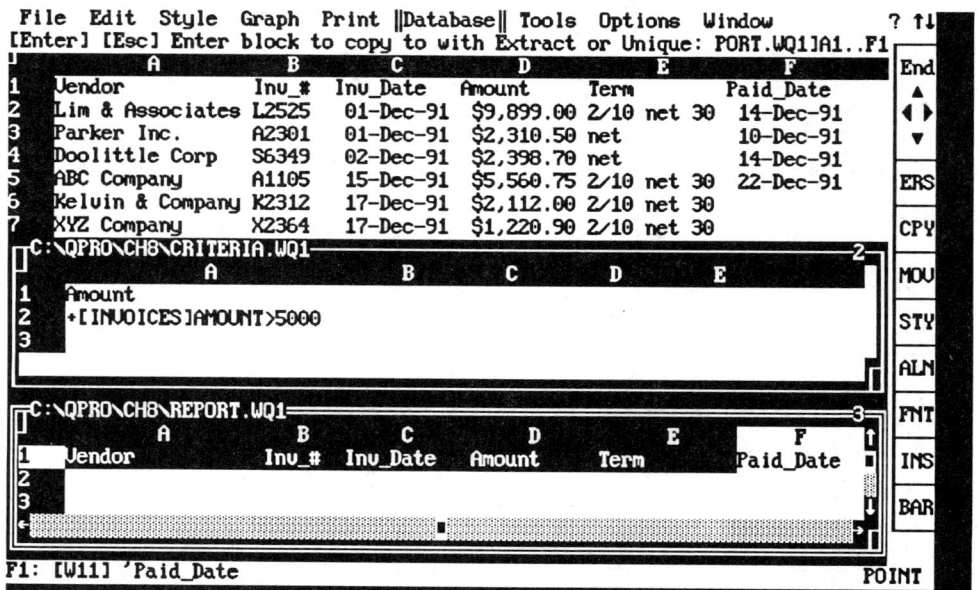

Figure 8.14 Locating an Output Area in a Separate Spreadsheet

output block to extend from the field names you selected as the output area to the bottom of the spreadsheet. Any previous data located in this area are lost, since Quattro erases the entire output area before copying new records to it. If you have data stored below the output block, you must select the output area carefully to ensure that any previous data is not lost.

Another option for the output block is including as many rows as you want the output block to fill. When Quattro copies records to the output block, it copies only as many records as it can fit in the block. If you specify an output block that is too small for the extracted data, Quattro stops copying records when the output block is full and displays an error message informing you that the output block is too small to contain all the desired data. To correct this situation, you need to expand the size of the output area and execute Extract or Unique again.

Extracting Matching Information

After you have set up the criteria table and defined the output block, select the Extract option from the Query menu. Quattro extracts the data from your database that meet your criteria and places them in your specified output block. At this point, you may want to press F6 (PANE) to temporarily hide the menus and see the results (press F6 (PANE) again when you want to see the menu). The Query menu remains on the screen until you select Quit. Figure 8.15 shows the extracted

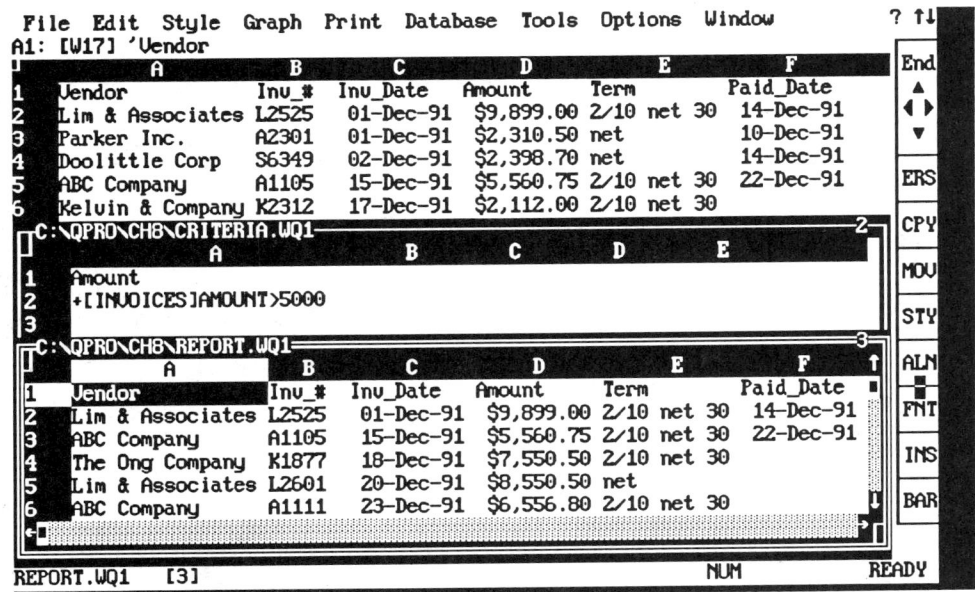

Figure 8.15 Extracted Records

data for invoice amounts above $5,000. Any formulas in the database are converted into numbers in the output area.

Extracting Unique Records

Your database may contain information in some fields in one record that exactly matches the contents of the same fields in another record within the database. This duplicate data may indicate duplicate records or specific fields with repeating entries. If you use the Extract feature, Quattro extracts all records that meet your specification and may produce a list that includes the duplicate data. These duplicate entries may be what you are looking for; however, in some cases, you may prefer to have a listing of each unique entry that meets your specifications. One such situation occurs when the output block does not include all the fields from the database. For example, if you are compiling a list of your customers to create a mailing list, you will want a list of all the unique names in the Vendor field. Using the /Database Query Extract command creates a list of all the vendors, but many of them will be listed more than once.

Quattro's Unique option lists only those records that are different from records already in the extract area. If two records have a different entry in any field that is copied to the output block, the records are considered unique. Quattro extracts the data from these records as separate and unique records. In this case, the two records are not unique. The bottom spreadsheet in Figure 8.16 shows a list of

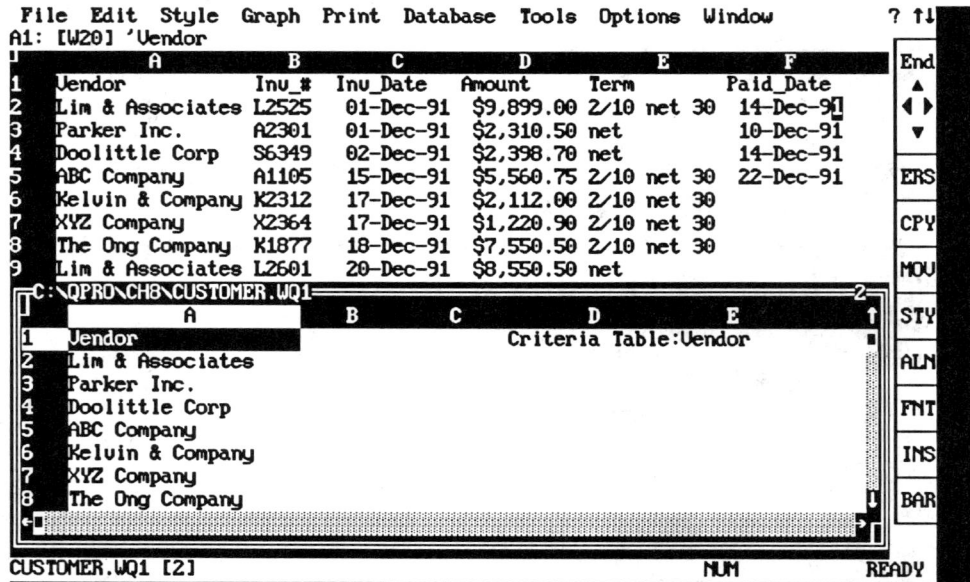

Figure 8.16 A List of Unique Vendor Names

company names, with each listed one time by use of the Unique option. The criteria table consists of Vendor with a blank cell below it to purposefully match with every record in the database. Note that Lim & Associates appears twice in the database shown in the top spreadsheet in Figure 8.15 but is only listed once in the output area.

Deleting Matching Records

Quattro's Query features allow you to delete database records that match your criteria. This feature is useful, for example, if your database includes obsolete inventory items. Instead of searching through the database to delete one item at a time, you can use the Delete option from the Query menu to delete them all at once based on the criteria set up in a criteria table.

To delete the matching records you must select a database block and criteria when you select the Delete option from the Query menu; Quattro prompts you to confirm your decision. A word of caution is necessary at this stage. You can purge outdated records in one easy step; however, if your criteria are not correct, you may lose some records that you want to retain. You should test your criteria with the Extract or Find option before electing to delete them. You can also delete database records by deleting the row containing the record, but you should only use this method if the spreadsheet does not contain information that might be erased by deleting the row and if you are not deleting the last record, which destroys the block address entered with /Database Query Block.

USING AN EXTERNAL DATABASE

While Quattro provides excellent database features, you also may need to use databases that are stored in different formats. For example, if you have your employee database applications developed for dBASE or Paradox, you may not want to switch the data files to Quattro's spreadsheet format to edit the data in Quattro. One option is to retrieve the file and let Quattro automatically translate the database into a spreadsheet. When you are finished editing, you can let Quattro automatically translate the spreadsheet containing your database to a file in the format you want. When you are performing queries on existing databases, you may not feel like translating all the files you want to translate. Instead, Quattro can perform queries on the file without translating the database file. There are so few differences between querying an external database and querying a database stored in another spreadsheet that you will find Quattro's advanced feature easy to use. When you query an external database, you can use the Extract and Unique menu options. Since the database already has field names assigned, you do not need to use the /Database Query Assign Names command.

The most distinctive feature of using an external database is how you tell Quattro which file to use. When you enter /Database Query Block and Quattro prompts for a block, you must enter the database file name and extension enclosed in square brackets followed by a block address. For example, if you want to use the EMPLOY dBASE IV database, type **[EMPLOY.DBF]A1..A2** as the block. The block address that follows the file name has no meaning but prevents Quattro from rejecting the external file name because of a syntax error. You can select any block address that contains at least two rows. If the file is in a drive or directory other than the default, you must supply the appropriate drive and path name. The file extension is required, since it is not Quattro's default of .WQ1.

The other distinctive feature of using an external database is that you must include the file name and extension just as if you were using a database in a separate spreadsheet. For example, if you are querying the EMPLOY database partially shown in Figure 8.17 to list the employees hired after January 1, 1989, you would enter +[EMPLOY.DBF]HIRE_DATE>@DATE(89,1,1) in a line in the table criteria.

The file that contains the information for the external database, the criteria, and the output area to use must be saved as a Quattro .WQ1 file. The other file formats are not designed to store the information to link to the external database. When you later retrieve this spreadsheet, Quattro prompts you to indicate whether you want to load the supporting files, update the references, or neither. Since the criteria are evaluated when a query is performed, you can select None (= neither). Even though the criteria are displayed as N/A, the criteria still work when you perform a /Database Query command.

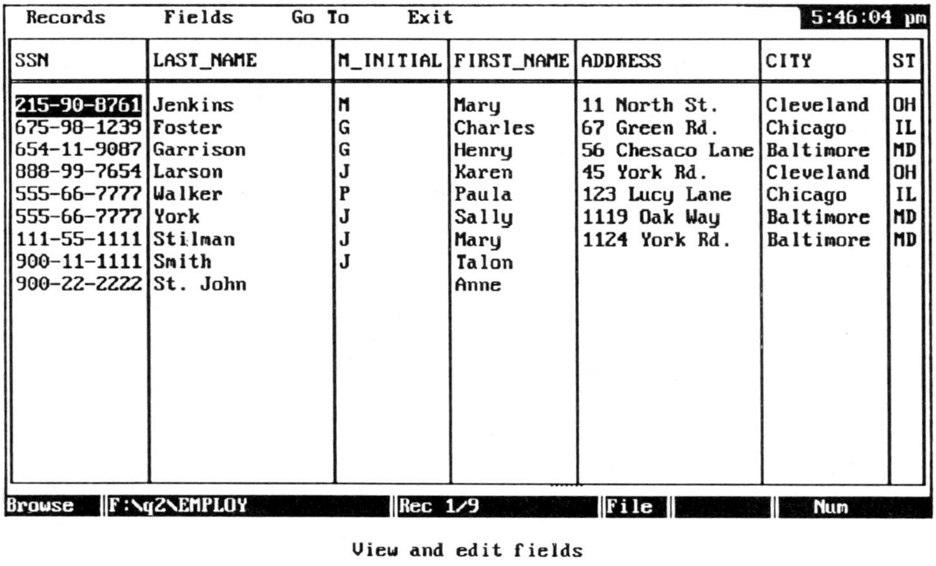

SSN	LAST_NAME	M_INITIAL	FIRST_NAME	ADDRESS	CITY	ST
215-90-8761	Jenkins	M	Mary	11 North St.	Cleveland	OH
675-98-1239	Foster	G	Charles	67 Green Rd.	Chicago	IL
654-11-9087	Garrison	G	Henry	56 Chesaco Lane	Baltimore	MD
888-99-7654	Larson	J	Karen	45 York Rd.	Cleveland	OH
555-66-7777	Walker	P	Paula	123 Lucy Lane	Chicago	IL
555-66-7777	York	J	Sally	1119 Oak Way	Baltimore	MD
111-55-1111	Stilman	J	Mary	1124 York Rd.	Baltimore	MD
900-11-1111	Smith	J	Talon			
900-22-2222	St. John		Anne			

View and edit fields

Figure 8.17 dBASE IV Database Containing Employee Records

Using a Paradox Database on a Network

Using Paradox database files follows the same rules described for dBASE databases. One difference between dBASE and Paradox is when you are using Paradox database files are stored on a network. When your Paradox database files are stored on a network, you need to tell Quattro the information it needs to use the network files. The /Options Other Paradox command tells Quattro how you want to use Paradox files. When you enter this command you have four selections. When you select Network Type, Quattro lists the types of networks that Quattro supports. Select yours from the list. When you select Directory, Quattro prompts for the directory containing the PARADOX.NET file. Enter the drive and directory that contains this file before finalizing it with ENTER. (You may need to use the /File Utilities DOS Shell command first so that you know the drive and directory containing the PARADOX.NET file.) When you select Retries, Quattro prompts for a number, which represents the number of milliseconds between retries. When you reserve a file on which someone else has the file reservation (a privilege given by the network to a user to control the file), Quattro tries to get the file reservation after the specified number of milliseconds following the previous attempt. When you are finished, select Quit to return to the Other menu. Selecting Quit again returns you to READY mode.

Combining Quattro Pro and Paradox

While you can use Quattro Pro to access your Paradox databases, you may want to use other features of Paradox. As an example, you may want to use Paradox to access SQL databases or to use Paradox's query by example to select a group of records to use. If your database is large, you may want to use Paradox to sort your records. You can quickly do these tasks as well as switch information between Quattro Pro and Paradox by using Paradox Access. Paradox Access lets you execute Quattro Pro 2 and above from within Paradox. When both Quattro Pro and Paradox are running, you can switch between the two programs by pressing a key.

To use Paradox Access, you must be using Paradox version 3.5 or later with 2 MB of RAM and a processor that is at least an 80286. For the first requirement DOS normally can only access 640K but Paradox can access the additional RAM that your machine has. The last requirement is met by most AT's and later computers. You may also want to have additional expanded memory so you have more room for your Quattro Pro spreadsheets. You will also want Paradox SQL Link if you will use Paradox to access SQL databases or file servers that run SQL.

Before you try executing Paradox and Quattro Pro, you will need to check that the CONFIG.SYS file has a statement such as FILES=40 (or a higher number). You will also need to execute the DOS SHARE program which Paradox and Quattro Pro need in order to be able to share files. You may want to include SHARE in a line in your AUTOEXEC.BAT file. You will also want to check that the Quattro Pro directory is included in the PATH command in your AUTOEXEC.BAT file. Both

Quattro Pro and Paradox must be installed in different directories. Since Paradox must be run in protected mode, you will need to use the Paradox Custom Configuration Program to make this the default. You must also use different directories for your Paradox working and private directories. If you are using Paradox on a network, this is already set up for you. You must also run the Paradox NUPDATE.EXE program. When you run this program by typing NUPDATE from the DOS prompt, you will select OTHER as the network type and provide the path containing the PARADOX.NET file. Next, load Quattro Pro and use the /Options Other Paradox command. Select Directory, and enter the path for the PARADOX.NET file. Also, select Network Type and Other. Finally, select Quit to return to the Options menu, and select Update to save the changes and Quit to return to READY mode. You can leave Quattro Pro by pressing CTRL-X.

Once Quattro Pro and Paradox are set up, you can use both by first starting Paradox and then starting Quattro Pro. Quattro Pro makes this easy for you by including a file, PXACCESS.BAT, that you can use to start both programs for you. Besides starting both programs, PXACCESS.BAT also starts Paradox with several parameters which help make the two programs behave more efficiently. Once both programs are loaded, you can switch between the two by pressing CTRL-F10. This is equivalent to the TOQPRO Paradox Application Language 3.5 command. You can set Paradox to immediately switch to Quattro Pro when you load Paradox by including a startup script named INIT.SC that contains the TOQPRO command. If you do not use PXACCESS.BAT to start Paradox and Quattro Pro, you will need to enter a command such as PARADOX -qpro to start Paradox and reserve memory for Quattro Pro. If you want Quattro Pro started and loaded with a specific spreadsheet, workspace, or Paradox database, follow -qpro with the file name in brackets as in PARADOX -qpro [MY_FILE MY_MACRO]. The MY_MACRO is the macro name Quattro Pro will execute once the MY_FILE spreadsheet is loaded. If you use any options to start Quattro Pro, they would follow the macro name before the closing bracket. Since Quattro Pro and Paradox have selections made for them as for how they will share the available memory, the /X option is ignored. Since Quattro Pro uses expanded memory, you will also improve Quattro Pro's performance by using the /Options Other Expanded Memory command and selecting Both.

If you are using Quattro Pro and Paradox to access a SQL database, you will need to use the SLQINST program to install Paradox for your SQL server. When you switch from Paradox to Quattro Pro, you will roll back any unfinished transactions, which means that if the SQL server has uncommitted transactions (changes that have not been saved), switching to Quattro Pro will return these modified transactions to their original value unless the Paradox command Tools SQL Preferences AutoCommit is set to Off. You cannot use Quattro Pro to load an SQL replica table, since it has no data. You can use Quattro Pro to store the answer tables (results of a Paradox database query operation). With SQL databases, the answer table may be very large. If it is too large for Quattro Pro, Quattro Pro will load as much of the table as it can fit into the spreadsheet and display a warning.

Quattro Pro has several commands you will want to use if you are using Quattro Pro with Paradox. These commands are in the /Database Paradox Access menu. You can select /Database Paradox Access Go instead of pressing CTRL-F10 to switch to Paradox. Using this command requires that you have first loaded Paradox with the PXACCESS.BAT file or with the -qpro option. You can use the /Database Paradox Access Load File command to select the name of the file that Quattro Pro loads every time you switch into Quattro Pro from Paradox. If you have included a file name in brackets when you started Paradox, Quattro Pro will load that file the first time you switch to Paradox and use the file name set by this command for the subsequent times. Quattro Pro assumes that this file is stored in the private directory used by Paradox. The default is ANSWER.DB, so Quattro Pro immediately pulls in the result of your last query by example in Paradox. Quattro Pro pulls these files in when the /Database Paradox Access Autoload command is set to Yes. When this command is set to No, Quattro Pro does not automatically load any file when you switch from Paradox to Quattro Pro. When this command is set to Yes, it overrides the setting of the /Options Startup Autoload File command. You can select Quit to return to READY mode.

Paradox has 12 temporary tables that you can access such as by using the /Database Paradox Access Autoload command. These tables provide different information about the databases you are using. The tables are:

ANSWER	Result of last query
CHANGED	Copy of changed records before they were changed
CROSSTAB	Results of a cross tab calculation
DELETED	Deleted records
ENTRY	New records for a table
FAMILY	Reports and forms used by a database table
INSERTED	Inserted records of a table
KEYVIOL	Records with duplicate key values
LIST	Lists of tables, scripts, files, network users, or locks
PASSWORD	Auxiliary passwords
PROBLEMS	Uconverted records
STRUCT	Table definition

Since these tables are temporary, Paradox removes them when you exit Paradox. Also, since Paradox uses the same names for each type of table, Paradox overwrites temporary tables. If you want to make a table permanent, you may want to switch to Quattro Pro to save the table to another file. You must use the /File Save As command, because Paradox reserves the right to write the file, even when you switch to Quattro Pro. These files are in the Paradox private directory so you will not see them until you change the directory of the files listed to the private directory. Normally, Quattro Pro finds these files without a problem, since Paradox tells Quattro Pro where the private directory is located. Storing these tables in the temporary directory makes them only available to you if you are on a network, whereas storing the tables in the working directory may allow others to access the data. When you are finished working with Quattro Pro, you can switch back to Paradox. If you switch back to Quattro Pro, you are returned to the workspace you had when you switched to Paradox. You may want to save your changes in Quattro Pro if you want to keep them so Quattro Pro will not overwrite the file with loading the file name selected with **/Database Paradox Access Autoload**. When you are finished using both Quattro Pro and Paradox, quit Paradox without worrying about exiting Quattro Pro, since Paradox will take care of it for you. If you have unsaved changes, Paradox will prompt you if you want to save the changes.

CREATING AN INPUT FORM FOR DATA ENTRY

You can enter the database records by moving the selector to the end of the database and entering the data in the appropriate columns. However, Quattro offers another solution that can reduce errors and create a more pleasing input screen for data entry. You can restrict input to unprotected cells in the spreadsheet with the **/Database Restrict Input**. As the name suggests, the Restrict Input command found in the Database menu allows you to enter data as if you were entering data in an entry form. This command restricts movement of the selector to cells in an unprotected block. All the other spreadsheet cells are visible but inaccessible to you. When you are in Restrict Input mode, you cannot use Quattro's menus. You can only move around the cells that are unprotected and are specified by the **/Database Restrict Input** command. You can enter or edit data in any of these cells.

To activate the Restrict Input command, you first need to unprotect all the cells to which you would like to allow access. When you activate the Restrict Input mode by entering **/Database Restrict Input**, Quattro prompts you to specify the block you want to use for data entry. Enter the block by pointing to it, typing the address, or using the mouse. You want the upper-left corner of the block to be the upper-left cell that Quattro will put on the screen. After you specify the block, the selector can only be moved to unprotected cells in the area referenced by the **/Database Restrict Input** command. You can press ESC to exit from the Restrict Input mode, or you can press ENTER without making an entry. Either action returns you to READY mode in which you can access all cells.

As an example, suppose you want to add five records to the database in Figure 8.18 and you want to ensure that data are added only to columns A, B, and D. First, enter **/Style Protection Unprotect**, and select the block A9..B13. Next enter **/Style Protection Unprotect**, and select the block D9..D13. Once the blocks are unprotected, activate the restricted input by entering **/Database Restrict Input**. When Quattro prompts for the block of unprotected cells, enter **A1..D13**. Since A1 is the upper-left corner of the block, it is the upper-left cell Quattro displays in the spreadsheet window. While data entry is restricted, you can only move in the blocks A9..B13 and D9..D13. When you press the RIGHT ARROW in column B, Quattro moves you to column D, which prevents you from accidentally typing an entry in column C. When you are finished entering the new records, press ESC or ENTER to return to the READY mode.

The **/Database Restrict Input** command is often used in macros in which you can design custom entry screens that mimic the appearance of the source of the data. With a macro, the macro prompts for the entries; when the user is finished, the macro can add the record to the end of the database. You can further prevent data-entry errors by restricting the types of data stored in a cell (you use the /Database Data Entry command, which is covered in the next section).

RESTRICTING THE DATA TYPES

When you enter a lot of data, it is easy to make a mistake. For example, if you press ENTER and you intended to press the LEFT ARROW, your remaining entries will be in the wrong column until you notice the mistake. One method of reducing errors is the /Database Restrict Input command discussed above. Another solution is to restrict blocks to accepting only labels or dates for entries. You can also use the same command to format blocks as dates or labels when you are entering a block of dates or labels beginning with numbers; Quattro then translates the dates into date serial numbers or automatically adds a label indicator at the beginning of the entry.

To control the type of entries made in a block of cells, enter /Database Data Entry, and select from General, Labels Only, and Dates Only. (The General option is for resetting a cell's data type after selecting one of the other options.) Then Quattro prompts for a block. Enter a block address, and press ENTER. After you press ENTER, Quattro adds Date or Label before the cell address in the input line when the selector is on a cell that is set for dates or labels only.

As an example of this command, suppose you had to enter the database records

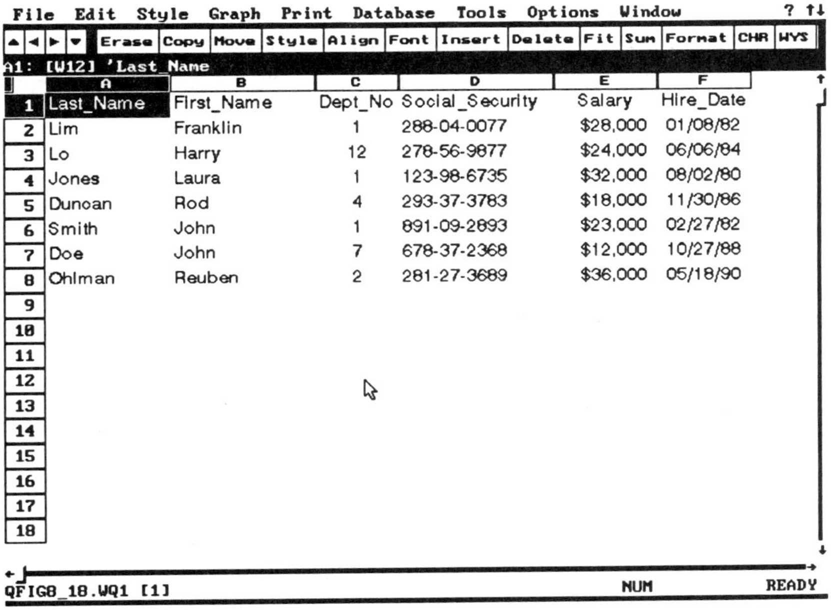

Figure 8.18 Employee Database

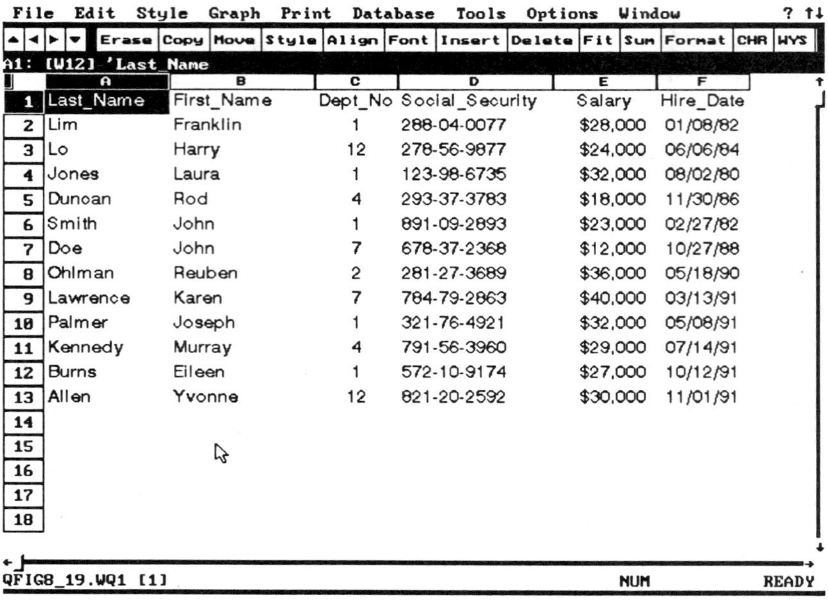

```
File  Edit  Style  Graph  Print  Database  Tools  Options  Window            ?  ↑↓
 ▲ ◀ ▶ ▼   Erase Copy Move Style Align Font Insert Delete Fit Sum Format CHR WYS
A1: [W12] 'Last_Name
         A            B          C         D            E         F
    1  Last_Name   First_Name  Dept_No  Social_Security  Salary   Hire_Date
    2  Lim         Franklin       1     288-04-0077    $28,000   01/08/82
    3  Lo          Harry         12     278-56-9877    $24,000   06/06/84
    4  Jones       Laura          1     123-98-6735    $32,000   08/02/80
    5  Duncan      Rod            4     293-37-3783    $18,000   11/30/86
    6  Smith       John           1     891-09-2893    $23,000   02/27/82
    7  Doe         John           7     678-37-2368    $12,000   10/27/88
    8  Ohlman      Reuben         2     281-27-3689    $36,000   05/18/90
    9  Lawrence    Karen          7     784-79-2863    $40,000   03/13/91
   10  Palmer      Joseph         1     321-76-4921    $32,000   05/08/91
   11  Kennedy     Murray         4     791-56-3960    $29,000   07/14/91
   12  Burns       Eileen         1     572-10-9174    $27,000   10/12/91
   13  Allen       Yvonne        12     821-20-2592    $30,000   11/01/91
   14
   15
   16
   17
   18

QFIG8_19.WQ1 [1]                                           NUM         READY
```

Figure 8.19 Employee Database from Figure 8.18 with More Records Added

shown in Figure 8.19. You can quickly enter the social security numbers as labels by entering /Database Data Entry Labels Only and selecting D2..D13 as the block. For the dates in column F, enter /Database Data Entry Dates Only, and select F2..F13 as the block. When you enter the first social security number, you enter only **288-04-0077**; you do not have to include a label prefix, since Quattro already knows that the entry is a label. For Franklin Lim's date of hire, you enter only **01/09/80**; you do not have to press CTRL-D, because Quattro knows that the entry must be a date.

DATABASE STATISTICAL FUNCTIONS

The database statistical functions combine the power of the statistical functions with the flexibility of the database features. You can selectively include the values in database records within these calculations by using criteria specifications like the ones used for the Query operations.

The database statistical functions can be used to perform a quick computation. They can also be used with the sensitivity analysis features covered in Chapter 9 to exhaustively perform computations for each unique field entry. A complete report composed of nothing but database statistical functions provides a quick solution for a management summary report.

You can use these functions to calculate the average salary paid to employees in a specific location or job code using the employee data in Figure 8.19. With a quick change in a function you can calculate the total amount of salaries paid employees whose records meet an established set of criteria.

Syntax of the Database Functions

The arguments for the statistical functions follow the same basic format as other arguments previously described. They begin with an @ followed by the keyword for the function and an open parenthesis. The three arguments for any of these functions are the input records, the offset column in the database, and the criteria location.

The *block* argument is the location of your database. The input records include the field names and all the database records. You can specify a block by highlighting it or you can assign a name to the block and specify the input records using the assigned name. You can also refer to a particular section of your database; however, the block must include all fields that are included in the criteria block and the column of the database that you want to use in the database statistical function. If the database is in a different spreadsheet, the block address or name must be preceded by the file name in brackets ([ ]).

The *column* refers to the position number of the field used for the computations. To specify the column of the field, remember that the first column in your database is column 0, and the second column is column 1 according to Quattro's numbering scheme. The field that you select should contain numeric entries, except for @DCOUNT, which counts label entries as well as numeric entries. If the column the function uses contains label entries other than the field name, the labels are treated as zeros for the computations (which distorts the results of functions like @DAVG, @DSTD, @DSTDS, @DVAR, and @DVARS).

The *criteria* is the location of your criteria table on the spreadsheet. You can specify the location of your criteria by referring to a block of cells or by referring to an assigned name. Remember to include the field names that appear at the top of your criteria when selecting the location.

@DAVG The @DAVG command allows you to compute the average of a set of values in a field within a selected group of records. @DAVG(block,column,criteria) is the syntax for this command. The function arguments are the ones defined in the previous section.

You can use @DAVG to obtain the average salary for all employees who work in department 1. The input line in Figure 8.20 shows the syntax and results of the @DAVG formula. The result of this computation is shown in cell D15. The block is located in **A1..F13**. This is the location of your database. Notice that the field names are included as part of your block. The column number is **4** since salary is the fifth column. Quattro averages the values for the salary field of the records that meet the criteria. The criteria is **A19..A20**. In this example, you have instructed

```
File  Edit  Style  Graph  Print  Database  Tools  Options  Window       ? ↑↓
  Erase Copy Move Style Align Font Insert Delete Fit Sum Format CHR WYS
D15: (C0) [W15] @DAVG(A1..F13,4,A19..A20)
      A              B          C         D              E         F
 1  Last_Name     First_Name  Dept_No  Social_Security  Salary  Hire_Date
 2  Lim           Franklin       1     288-04-0077      $28,000  01/08/82
 3  Lo            Harry         12     278-56-9877      $24,000  06/06/84
 4  Jones         Laura          1     123-98-6735      $32,000  08/02/80
 5  Duncan        Rod            4     293-37-3783      $18,000  11/30/86
 6  Smith         John           1     891-09-2893      $23,000  02/27/82
 7  Doe           John           7     678-37-2368      $12,000  10/27/88
 8  Ohlman        Reuben         2     281-27-3689      $36,000  05/18/90
 9  Lawrence      Karen          7     784-79-2863      $40,000  03/13/91
10  Palmer        Joseph         1     321-76-4921      $32,000  05/08/91
11  Kennedy       Murray         4     791-56-3960      $29,000  07/14/91
12  Burns         Eileen         1     572-10-9174      $27,000  10/12/91
13  Allen         Yvonne        12     821-20-2592      $30,000  11/01/91
14
15  Average salaries for Dept. #1           $28,400
16
17
18
19  Dept_No
            1
QFIG8_20.WQ1 [1]                                       NUM         READY
```

Figure 8.20 @DAVG Used to Find the Average Employee Salary for Department 1

Quattro to compute the average salary of all employees who are employed in department 1; that average salary is $28,400.

@DCOUNT The @DCOUNT command allows you to count the number of nonblank entries in a field within database records, which match your criteria. @DCOUNT(block,column,criteria) is the syntax for this command. The column argument for @DCOUNT differs from the other database statistical function arguments in that the offset can reference a field that contains label entries. Since the nonblank entities are counted and not involved in arithmetic computations, it is not necessary for them to contain values.

You can use the @DCOUNT function with the data in Figure 8.20 to obtain the total number of employees in department 1 by using the formula **@DCOUNT(A1..F13,0,A19..A20)**. The offset number is 0 for this example to reference the Last Name field. In this case, Quattro has been instructed to count the number of records in department 1 with a nonblank entry in the Last Name field, and it returns a 5.

@DMAX The @DMAX command allows you to locate the maximum value in a field within a selected group of database records. @DMAX(block,column,criteria) is the syntax for this command. @DMAX uses the same function arguments defined earlier. You can use the @DMAX function in place of @DAVG in Figure

8.20 to find the highest salary paid to an employee in Department 1 with the formula **@DMAX(A1..F13,4,A19..A20)**. The block is **A1..F13** and includes the field names. The offset number is **4** to work with the Salary field. The criteria is **A19..A20**, which directs Quattro to select records in department 1. Using the employee database, Quattro computes the maximum salary of the employees in department 1 as $32,000.

@DMIN The @DMIN command allows you to locate the minimum value in a field within a selected group of database records. @DMIN(block,column,criteria) is the syntax for this command. @DMIN uses the same function arguments defined earlier. You can use the @DMIN function in place of @DAVG to find the lowest salary paid to an employee in Department 1. This @DMIN formula is **@DMIN(A1..F13,4,A19..20)**. The block is **A1..F13** and includes the field names. The offset number is **4** to work with the Salary field. The criteria is **A19..A20**, which directs Quattro to select records in department 1. For the employee database, Quattro computes the minimum salary of the employees in department 1 to be $23,000.

@DSUM The @DSUM command allows you to selectively sum the values in a field within a group of records. @DSUM(block,column,criteria) is the syntax for this command.

For example, you can obtain the total salary for all the employees in department 1 as shown in Figure 8.21. The syntax for using the @DSUM function is shown in

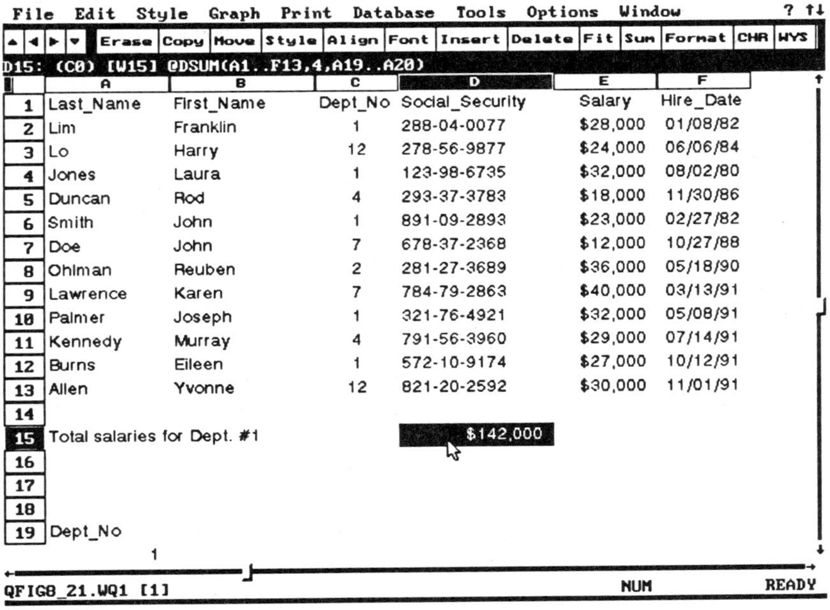

	A	B	C	D	E	F
1	Last_Name	First_Name	Dept_No	Social_Security	Salary	Hire_Date
2	Lim	Franklin	1	288-04-0077	$28,000	01/08/82
3	Lo	Harry	12	278-56-9877	$24,000	06/06/84
4	Jones	Laura	1	123-98-6735	$32,000	08/02/80
5	Duncan	Rod	4	293-37-3783	$18,000	11/30/86
6	Smith	John	1	891-09-2893	$23,000	02/27/82
7	Doe	John	7	678-37-2368	$12,000	10/27/88
8	Ohlman	Reuben	2	281-27-3689	$36,000	05/18/90
9	Lawrence	Karen	7	784-79-2863	$40,000	03/13/91
10	Palmer	Joseph	1	321-76-4921	$32,000	05/08/91
11	Kennedy	Murray	4	791-56-3960	$29,000	07/14/91
12	Burns	Eileen	1	572-10-9174	$27,000	10/12/91
13	Allen	Yvonne	12	821-20-2592	$30,000	11/01/91
14						
15	Total salaries for Dept. #1			$142,000		
16						
17						
18						
19	Dept_No					
	1					

D15: (C0) [W15] @DSUM(A1..F13,4,A19..A20)

Figure 8.21 @DSUM Used to Total Salaries for Department 1

the input line. The block is **A1..F13**, and the field names are included as part of the block. The column number (**4**) tells Quattro that the field you want to use for your calculations is the Salary field. The criteria is described in **A19..A20**. In this case, the $142,000 shown in cell D15 is the result of the @SUM computation.

@DSTD The @DSTD command allows you to compute the standard deviation of values in a field within a selected group of database records. This function uses the assumption that the database contains the records for all possible cases. If the database does not contain all records, use the @DSTDS function instead. The standard deviation measurement is very useful because it allows you to determine the amount of variation between a set of individual values and their mean. For example, the average time to complete a production run in department 1 is 3 hours. The range of completion times may be 1–5 hours, or it may be 2.5–3.5 hours. The standard deviation of the latter case is probably smaller than that of the former because of the smaller variance from the mean. This measurement is useful in this case because, if the standard deviation is large, it implies that there are many production runs that vary significantly from the average, indicating that potential problems exist in these runs. The standard deviation is the square root of the variance. The units for the standard measurement are the same as those of the field used to calculate this measurement. @DSTD(block, column, criteria) is the syntax for this command. The arguments for @DSTD are identical to those of the other database statistical function arguments.

You can use @DSTD to calculate the standard deviation of the completion time of product 1 as shown in Figure 8.22. The syntax for using the @DSTD function is shown in the input line and references block in **A1..B13**. An offset of **1** is used to reference the Completion Time field. Quattro calculates the standard deviation of the completion time for product 1 as 1.019804.

@DSTDS The @DSTDS command allows you to compute the standard deviation of values in a field within a selected group of database records. This function assumes that the database does not include all records that apply. @DSTDS(block, column, criteria) is the syntax for this command. The arguments for @DSTDS are identical to the other database statistical function arguments.

You can use @DSTDS to calculate the standard deviation of the completion time of product 1, if you are assuming the database does not contain all records for product 1. The formula is **@DSTDS(A1..B13,1,A15..A16)**. Quattro calculates the standard deviation of the completion time for product 1 as 1.140175. The difference between the standard deviation with @STD and @STDS is due to changing the assumption about whether the database includes all possible records for product 1.

@DVAR The @DVAR command allows you to compute the variance of a set of values in a field within a selected group of database records. The variance is the square of the standard deviation. It also measures the amount of variation between a set of individual items about its mean. This function uses the assumption that the

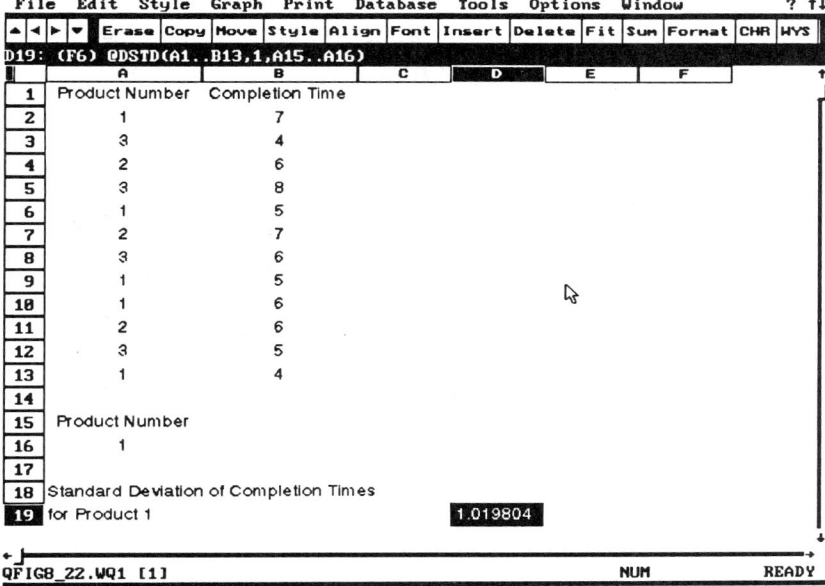

Figure 8.22 @DSTD Used to Calculate a Selective Standard Deviation

database contains the records for all possible cases. If the database does not contain all of the records, use the @DVARS function instead. @DVAR(block,column,criteria) is the syntax for this command. The arguments for @DVAR are identical to the arguments for the other database statistical functions.

You can use @DVAR to calculate the variance of the completion time of product 1 as shown in Figure 8.23. The syntax for using the @DVAR function is shown in the input line. The database is in **A1..B13**; an offset of **1** references the Completion Time field. Quattro calculates the variance to be 1.04.

@DVARS The @DVARS command allows you to compute the variance of values in a field within a selected group of database records. This function assumes that the database does not include all records that apply. The syntax for this command is @DVARS(block, column, criteria). The arguments for @DVARS are identical to the arguments for other database statistical functions.

You can use @DVARS to calculate the variance of the completion time of product 1, if you are assuming the database does not contain all records for product 1. The @DVARS formula for this example is **@DVARS(A1..B13,1,A15..A16)**. Quattro calculates the variance of the completion time for product 1 as 1.3. The difference between the variance with @VAR and @VARS is due to changing the assumption about whether the database includes all possible records.

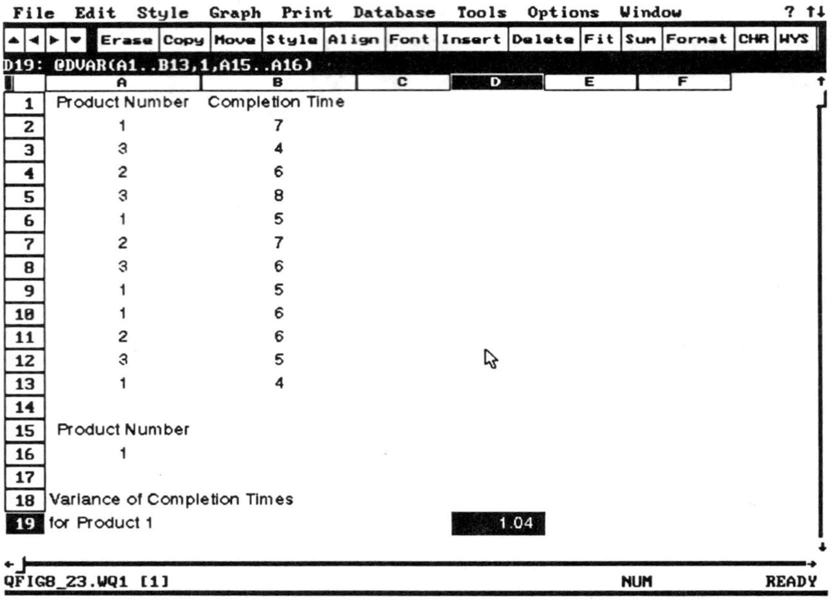

Figure 8.23 @DVAR Used to Calculate a Selective Variance

Building a Management Summary Report with Database Statistical Functions

The database statistical functions can be used to provide a simple total or average at the bottom of the database, but they also can be used to create an entire summary report. For databases that consist of large numbers of detailed transactions, the database statistical functions can help clarify the meaning of the data. You can use these functions to prepare a summary report consisting of totals and averages by product, sales region, or any other feature of the database. Use the database statistical commands described earlier to perform these computations.

Figure 8.24 provides an example from a management summary report that assimilates the detail in 2,500 database records into a few succinct totals. This report was prepared using only those database statistical functions already described. The entries in column D are the @DSUM functions that reference a database stored in **AA1..AG2500**. This database contains detailed sales transactions for the current quarter by region and product. A series of criteria entries on the spreadsheet reference the appropriate records. The criteria used in the formula displayed in D5 select records for June 1991 for the sales of computers in region 1. The offset of 1 references the sales column, totaling only the records that match the criteria.

Although it takes a little effort to create all the criteria areas required for this type of report, your efforts will be rewarded month after month. If you name the

Data Management 449

```
 File   Edit   Style   Graph   Print   Database   Tools   Options   Window        ? ↑↓
 ▲ ◄ ► ▼  Erase Copy Move Style Align Font Insert Delete Fit Sum Format CHR WYS
D5: (,0) [W11] @DSUM(AA1..AG2500,1,J1..L2)
         A         B         C         D        E        F        G        H
    1
    2                   Sales Summary for June 1991
    3
    4            Region 1
    5            Computers       987,000
    6            Disk Drives      98,700
    7            Printers        325,675
    8            Modems           25,000
    9                           1,436,375
   10            Region 2
   11            Computers       575,900
   12            Disk Drives      45,600
   13            Printers        279,000
   14            Modems           67,500
   15
   16            Region 3
   17            Computers       325,689
   18            Disk Drives      42,500
   19            Printers        875,000
                 Modems           29,500
QFIG8_24.WQ1 [1]                                   NUM           READY
```

Figure 8.24 A Portion of a Summary Report Created with Database Statistical Functions

database area with a block name, the formulas produce the correct results as the database size expands and contracts from month to month.

GETTING STARTED

In this chapter, you learned how to create databases and how to use the information stored in the databases to answer queries and create reports. You can try some of these skills by following these steps:

1. Set column A to accept only dates since the first field in this database contains date information. Enter **/Database Data Entry Dates Only**. When Quattro prompts for a block that will only accept dates, select A4..A20. Although you will not use all the cells in this column, you select a block with more rows than necessary so that your database can expand without your entering this command again. A1 through A3 is omitted so you can enter a title for your spreadsheet and a column heading for the date field.

2. Make the following entries to create a database. Since you have set A4..A20 to accept only dates, you can type them as they appear.

   A1: **Petty Cash Register**
   A3: **Date**

B3: **Amount**
C3: **Explanation**
A4: **9/20/92**
B4: **14.87**
C4: **Sugar for coffee**
A5: **9/18/92**
B5: **3.99**
C5: **Coffee filters**
A6: **9/15/92**
B6: **30**
C6: **Stamps**
A7: **9/21/92**
B7: **25.36**
C7: **Computer screen cleaner**

3. Set the global format to currency with two digits. Enter /Options Formats Numeric Format Currency. Press ENTER (or point to the Enter button in the box and press the mouse button) to accept the default of two decimal digits. Select Quit twice to return to READY mode. The global format does not affect the dates since Quattro automatically formats these numbers as dates when you enter them.

4. Find the records that are used for coffee supplies. Move to C3. Press CTRL-C or click Copy in the SpeedBar to enter /Edit Copy, since you will make fewer mistakes if you copy the field names to the criteria table instead of retyping them. Press ENTER or click [Enter] in the input line. When Quattro prompts for the destination, point to G1 and press ENTER or click [Enter] in the input line. Move to G2. Type ***Coffee*** and press ENTER or click [Enter] in the input line. Enter /Database Query Block. When Quattro prompts for a block, select A3..C7 and press ENTER or click [Enter] in the input line. Select Assign Names so you can use the field names instead of the addresses. Select Criteria Table. When Quattro prompts for a block containing the criteria table, select G1..G2 and press ENTER or click [Enter] in the input line. Select Locate. Quattro highlights the record in row 4. Since the search is not case sensitive, Quattro finds coffee whether the letters are uppercase or lowercase. Press ESC, and select Quit to return to the READY mode.

5. Sort the records you entered in step 1. Enter /Database Sort Block. When Quattro prompts for a block to sort, select A4..C7, and press ENTER or click [Enter] in the input line. Select 1st Key. When Quattro prompts for the primary sort field, press F3 (CHOICES), and select DATE. Type **A** to sort in ascending order. Press ENTER or click [Enter] in the input line. Select **Go** to sort the records according to their dates. Your entries should now be in the same sequence as those in Figure 8.25.

6. Change the criteria to a formula criteria that can find all amounts greater than or equal to $25.00. Move to G1. Type **Amount**, and press the DOWN ARROW (or point to G2 and press the mouse button). Since the field name

Data Management 451

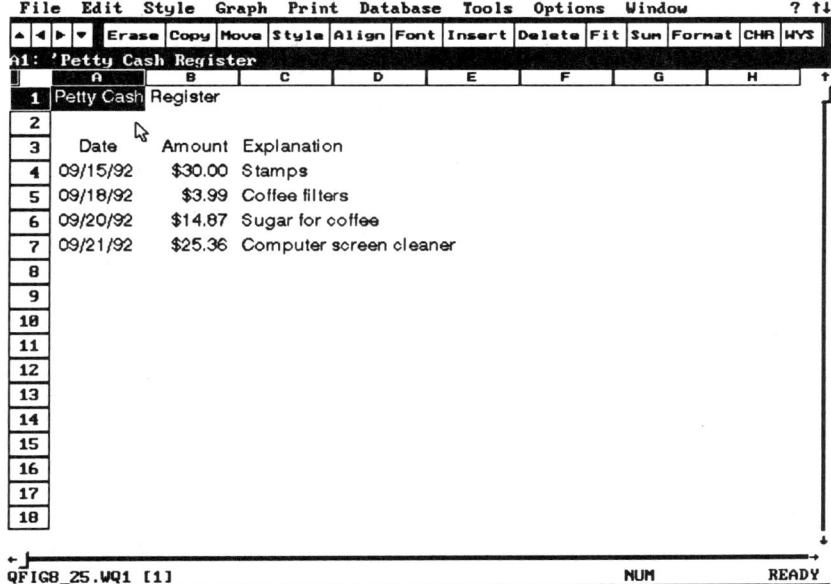

Figure 8.25 Database Created in Getting Started Section

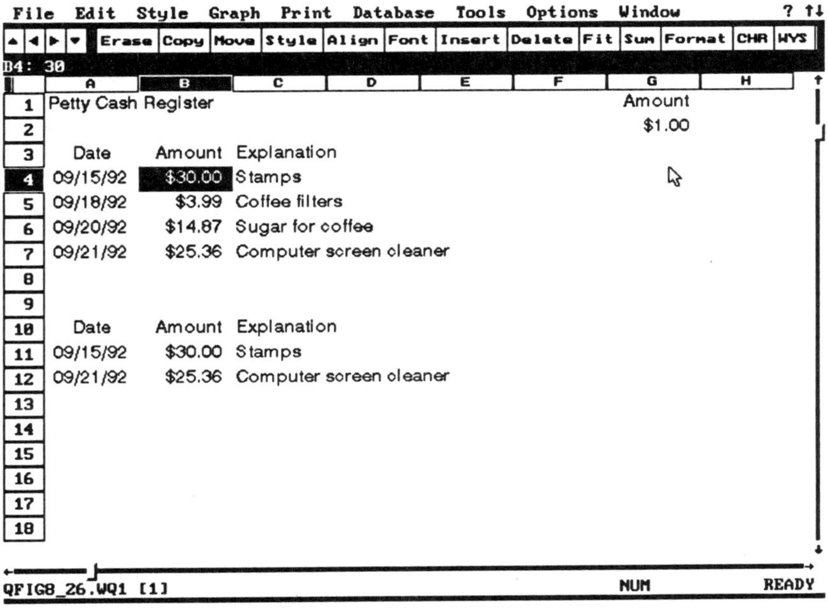

Figure 8.26 Extracted Records from Getting Started Section

is short, typing may be a shorter method, even if you have to correct typing mistakes. Type **+**. Press F3 (CHOICES), and select AMOUNT. Type **>=25** and press ENTER or click [Enter] in the input line

7. Create an output block that you can use as the basis for a report. Move to A3. Press CTRL-C or click Copy in the SpeedBar to enter **/Edit Copy**, since you want to copy all the fields to the output block. Select the block A3..C3 then press ENTER or click [Enter] in the input line. When Quattro prompts for the destination, point to A10 and press ENTER or click [Enter] in the input line. Enter **/Database Query Output Block**. When Quattro prompts for a block, select A10..C10 and press ENTER or click [Enter] in the input line.

8. Select **Extract** and **Quit**. This copies two of the records to the output block as shown in Figure 8.26. You may use this output block as the basis for determining which petty cash payments you want to check to confirm that the petty cash fund is being used correctly.

9

Advanced Analytical and File Features

In the previous chapter, you were introduced to the analytical features offered by Quattro's data-management commands. Quattro also provides advanced analytical features that are more mathematical in nature than the database options are. Also, each of these advanced analytical functions is more specialized in purpose than the general-purpose features found in data management.

In Chapter 5, you were introduced to the basic file commands offered through the File pull-down menu. Quattro also provides advanced file features that let you use data in other files without reentering that data (importing and exporting data). Once character data are imported, you may need to divide the data into smaller entries. Other advanced file commands include combining files into one and saving part of a spreadsheet as a separate file.

Both the analytical and file advanced features reduce the work needed to create spreadsheet models since you can take advantage of these tools to perform the work for you. Since these features are advanced, you may not feel ready to put them all to immediate use. You still should read through this chapter to obtain an understanding of the tasks that these features can handle so you can refer back to these techniques the next time you have a suitable application.

Each of the advanced analytical and file features consists of commands rather than functions or formulas. Because the analytical and file results are produced by commands rather than formulas, the results are values and are not updated automatically when spreadsheet entries are changed. For example, if you change a value referenced by one of these analytical commands, the values generated by the command are not recalculated until you execute the commands again.

The advanced analytical and file commands cover a variety of techniques that can solve a widely dispersed set of spreadsheet problems. Some commands allow you to automate a what-if analysis by storing the results of spreadsheet calculations in a table on the spreadsheet. The matrix features included in these commands allow you to simplify complicated mathematical operations. Other commands in this group can compute a frequency distribution or a regression analysis. The most advanced analytical features let you perform linear programming and have Quattro find the value of one cell that produces the desired result in another. In Quattro Pro 4, you can also trace how the different cell formulas affect one another as well as the formulas that use other spreadsheet entries. The one thing that all advanced commands have in common is the ability to save you a significant amount of time.

SENSITIVITY TABLES

Spreadsheets are designed for what-if analysis since changing a value in a cell causes the formulas relying on that cell to be updated immediately. Although these what-if features supply a quick answer when you want to look at the impact of one change, exploring a whole range of possibilities can still be quite time-consuming with this approach. Also, unless you print the results from each possibility, it is difficult to remember the impact of each change as you proceed through the range of options.

Quattro's What-If command can provide a solution that is much more sophisticated, yet it is still easy to use. With the What-If command, you can create a table of the results from your analysis that permits you to view the impact of each option at a glance. The what-if analyses that can be accommodated with this feature can be as simple as monitoring the effect of change on a single formula or as complex as analyzing the effects of changing many formulas and calculations. To analyze your model, Quattro's What-If command generates a table of results by varying the values for either one or two variables on the spreadsheet.

Creating a What-If Table for One Variable

When you use Quattro's What-If command for one variable, you need to store the values that you wish to substitute for the selected variable in a column on the spreadsheet. This type of what-if table is referred to as a 1 Variable table. In a 1 Variable table, the values on the left side of the table contain the input values of the variable. The values on the right side of the table contain the results when the variable replaces another spreadsheet entry.

The procedure required for using the What-If command is similar to the data-management commands, since some setup work is needed before the command can be executed. To set up the required spreadsheet entries for a 1 Variable table, follow these steps:

1. Select a blank area of the spreadsheet as the table location.
2. Enter the values you wish to substitute for the spreadsheet variable in the leftmost column of this table area.

3. Move one row above and one column to the right of the first variable value. Across the top row of the table, enter the formulas you wish to evaluate for each new value of the variable.

The formulas can be an integral part of the model, requiring many preliminary results to be calculated before the effect is evaluated. Rather than reentering a formula that is already stored elsewhere on the spreadsheet, you can reference it as in +B11, which references the formula currently stored in B11. With a 1 Variable table you can enter multiple formulas across the top row in the table, and the appropriate results are stored below each formula when the command is evaluated.

When the /Tools What-If 1 Variable command is executed, Quattro fills the cells in the right columns with the results of the formulas at the top of each column. Quattro evaluates each formula, one input value at a time, and places the evaluated results in the column beneath the formula and on the same row as the input value.

The what-if analysis has unlimited potential. For example, this command can compute a company's performance assuming different sales growth percentages. Figure 9.1 displays a spreadsheet that calculates different measurements of a company's performance, assuming a sales growth rate of 5%. To create the table area shown in Figure 9.2, the sales growth percentages are generated with the /Edit Fill command. The fill block is A10..A15. The /Edit Fill command uses a Start Value

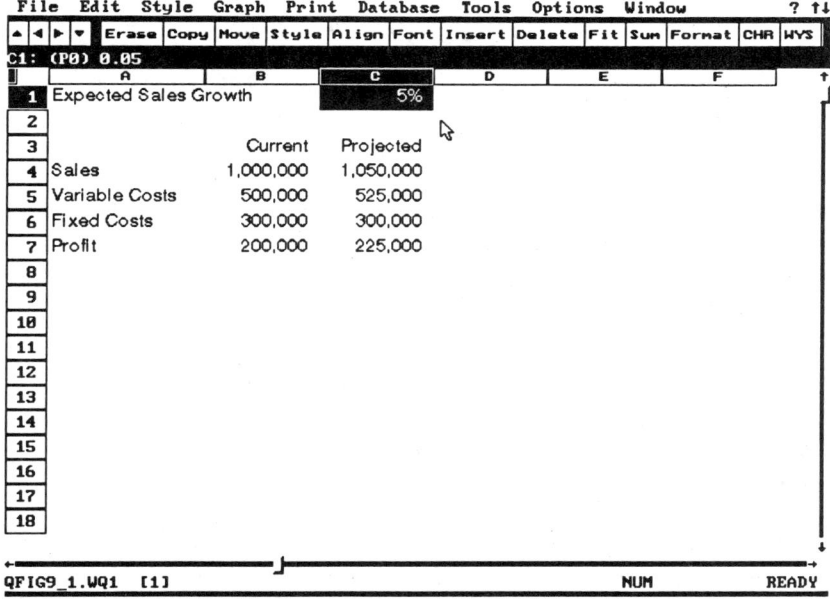

Figure 9.1 Spreadsheet Computing Company Performance for a Projected Growth Rate (5%)

456 Quattro Pro 4.0 Handbook

```
File  Edit  Style  Graph  Print  Database  Tools  Options  Window            ?  ↑↓
  ◄ ► ▼  Erase Copy Move Style Align Font Insert Delete Fit Sum Format CHR WYS
C9: (T) +C7
         A              B            C           D          E         F
  1  Expected Sales Growth          5%
  2
  3                       Current   Projected
  4  Sales              1,000,000   1,050,000
  5  Variable Costs       500,000     525,000
  6  Fixed Costs          300,000     300,000
  7  Profit               200,000     225,000
  8
  9                         +C4       +C7
 10                  5%
 11                  6%
 12                  7%
 13                  8%
 14                  9%
 15                 10%
 16
 17
 18
QFIG9_2.WQ1  [1]                                   NUM           READY
```

Figure 9.2 Table Set Up for /Tools What-If 1 Variable Command

of 5%, a Step Value of 1%, and a Stop Value of 10%. The generated numbers are formatted as percentages with the /Style Numeric Format command.

The first formula for this table is entered in B9 as +C4 to place the new sales figure next to the growth percentage. In C9, the formula +C7 is entered to place the new profit figure next to the sales figure for each sales growth percentage. As shown in this example, Quattro can fill in multiple values in a table for each of the growth rates. Figure 9.2 shows the completed setup work for the table with the two formulas at the top of the table formatted as text. Once the What-If command is invoked, this what-if analysis creates a table that shows performance measurements for different growth rates.

To create a single-variable what-if table after performing the initial setup, follow these steps:

1. Type **/** and select **Tools What-If 1 Variable**. Quattro prompts you for the location of the data table. The table's upper-left corner is the cell above the first input value. The lower-right corner is in the same row as the last input value and the same column as the last formula entered.

2. Select the block containing the table, and press ENTER. In Figure 9.2, the table location is A9..C15. Once the block is selected, Quattro prompts for the input cell of the column. This is the cell into which Quattro systematically places each input value from the data table before determining the result value to be placed on the right side of the table. Initially, the input cell can

Advanced Analytical and File Features 457

be blank or filled with other information. If the input cell already contains data, its contents are left unchanged after this command executes.

3. Enter the input cell for the column of entries, and press ENTER. In Figure 9.2, this is C1. Quattro fills in the data table with the results for the formula as each input value is used as a replacement value in the input cell. The calculated entries are values. As such, modifications to the input values or to any cells used in the calculations are not reflected in the table's results. For example, if you change the fixed costs from 300,000 to 250,000, the table values do not change until the /Tools What-If 1 Variable command is executed again. Quattro remembers the settings of the last /Tools What-If command, which makes executing the command again quicker. You can also execute the command again by pressing F8 (TABLE), which performs the /Tools What-If command again using the same addresses for the data table and the input cell. The values also have the same format as the formulas in the top of the column. Figure 9.3 shows the spreadsheet after Quattro fills in the table and the table's results have been formatted in the comma format.

The next time you execute the 1 Variable What-If command for the current spreadsheet, Quattro remembers the settings from your last use of the command on the spreadsheet. To reuse these settings, all you need to do is press ENTER after each prompt. To execute the command with new settings, you first eliminate the existing settings. Entering the /Tools What-If Reset command eliminates any settings used for creating a what-if table and makes it easier to specify a new table

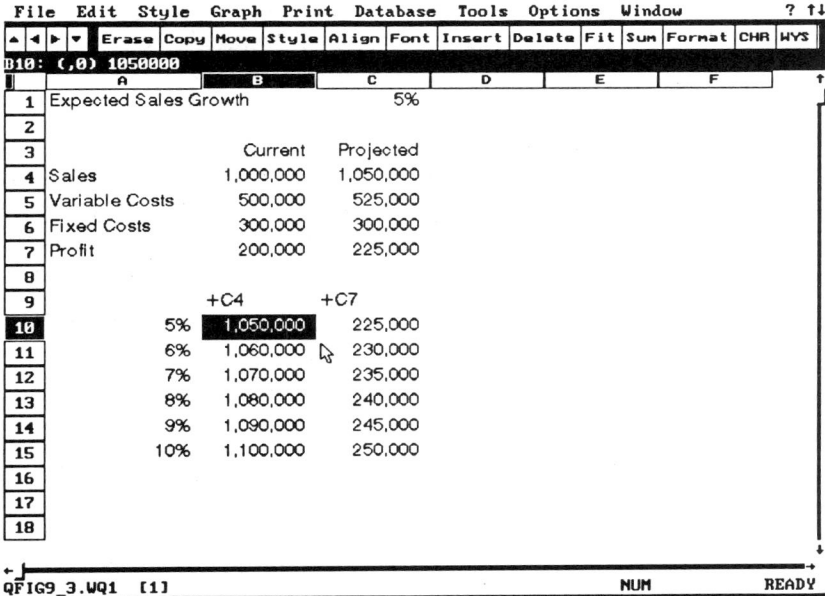

Figure 9.3 Table Filled in by /Tools What-If 1 Variable Command

location. Since the What-If menu remains on the screen after execution, you need to use the Quit option to exit from the menu.

Creating a What-If Table for Two Variables

Quattro's What-If command for two variables allows you to perform a what-if analysis while varying the values of two different variables. Since two variables are being evaluated, the command is only able to evaluate the effect on one formula. Just like the 1 Variable What-if, the 2 Variables What-if stores the results in a data table on the spreadsheet. The 2-variables table can be referred to as a two-way table.

With a 2 Variables What-if table, values on the left side of the table are used for one variable, and values in the top row of the table are used to provide values for a second variable. When the What-If command is executed, Quattro systematically substitutes one of the input values for the first variable and one of the input values for the second variable in place of their substitution cells and puts the formula's result at the row and column intersection of the two input values. You can determine the values of the variables used to produce any result value by looking to the left to obtain the variable value for variable 1 and looking across the top of the table to determine the value for variable 2.

Like the 1 Variable What-If command, the 2 Variables What-If command requires some setup work before it can be executed. What-if analysis saves time by mechanically performing many steps for you regardless of your spreadsheet application. One example of two-variable analysis is showing how different debt/equity ratios affect earnings per share at various income levels. As debt replaces stock in a company's capital structure, the interest expenses increase but the remaining profit is shared among fewer stockholders; therefore, the stock's value is increased. Figure 9.4 shows the shell for a table that computes the earnings per share (EPS) for different types of capital structure and different income levels. Variable costs are 50% of sales. Interest is 10% of the debt. Taxes are 40% of profit. The actual amount of debt is the debt-to-equity ratio multiplied by the 10 million dollars of total equity. The remaining equity is stock. The actual number of shares is the amount of stock divided by 1,000. A separate calculation is needed to compute the earnings per share for each income level. Quattro's /Tools What-If 2 Variables command can execute these computations automatically.

To create a two-variable what-if table, follow these steps:

1. Move to a blank area of your spreadsheet with sufficient space for the what-if table.
2. Enter the values to be substituted for the first variable in the leftmost column of the table. In this example, the values are generated with the /Edit Fill command with a fill block of **A2..A9**, a Start Value of 0, a Step Value of **.1**, and a Stop Value of **.70**.
3. Move to the cell that is one cell above and one column to the right of the first input value generated in step 2. In Figure 9.4, this is B1.

Advanced Analytical and File Features   459

```
File   Edit   Style   Graph   Print   Database   Tools   Options   Window        ? ↑↓
 ▲ ◄ ► ▼  Erase Copy Move Style Align Font Insert Delete Fit Sum Format CHR WYS
A1: (T) [W15] +B18
        A              B           C            D            E            F       ↑
  1  +B18           500,000    1,000,000    1,500,000    2,000,000    2,500,000
  2            0%
  3           10%
  4           20%
  5           30%
  6           40%
  7           50%
  8           60%
  9           70%
 10
 11  Sales                              Total Equity            10,000,000
 12  Variable Costs        0            Debt ratio
 13  Fixed Costs      200,000           Actual Debt                      0
 14  Interest              0            Actual Stock            10,000,000
 15  Profit          (200,000)          Number of Shares            10,000
 16  Taxes            (80,000)
 17  Net Profit     (120,000)           Assumptions:
 18  EPS             ($12.00)           Stock is $1,000/share
 19                                     Enough shares are sold
                                        for intended debt/equity ratio.
QFIG9_4.WQ1  [1]                                            NUM         READY
```

Figure 9.4 Table Set Up for 2 Variable What-If Analysis for Computation of Earnings per Share (EPS)

4. Enter the values for the second input variable across this row to form the top edge of the table. In this example, the values are generated with the /Edit Fill command with a fill block of **B1..F1**, a Start Value of **500,000**, a Step Value of **500,000**, and a Stop Value of **2,500,000**.

5. Move to the intersection of this row and column of values. In Figure 9.4, the intersection is A1.

6. Enter the formula to be computed for each combination of variable values. In A1, the cell reference **+B18** is typed to place the new EPS for each combination of debt/equity ratio and income level at the intersection of the two variables entries and this formula is formatted as text.

7. Type / and select Tools What-If 2 Variables. Quattro prompts you for the location of the data table. The table's upper-left corner is the cell with the formula. The lower-right corner is in the same row as the last value of the first variable and the same column as the last value of the second variable.

8. Select the block containing the table, and press ENTER. In Figure 9.4, the table is in A1..F9. Once the block is selected, Quattro prompts for the input cell for the column values. The input cell for the column values is the cell into which Quattro substitutes each value in the column of the table as it evaluates the result of the formula entered in the upper-left corner of the block. The input cell can be blank or filled with other information. If the input cell already contains data, its contents remain intact after the execution of this command.

9. Enter the input cell for the column, and press ENTER. In this example, it is **F12**. Then Quattro prompts for the input cell for the row values. Quattro will systematically substitute each value from this row into the specified cell while recording the impact on the formula in the table.

10. Enter the input cell for the row, and press ENTER. In this example, it is **B11**. Quattro fills the remainder of the data table with the results from the formula, as in Figure 9.5. The calculated table entries contain values. Therefore, modifications to the input values or to any other cells used in the calculations are not reflected in the table's results. For example, if you changed the last income level from 2,500,000 to 3,000,000, the table values do not change until the /Tools What-If 2 Variables command is executed again or until you press F8 (TABLE), which performs the /Tools What-If 2 Variables command using the same cell addresses for the table and the input cells. If you need to change a value, note that Quattro remembers the settings of the last /Tools What-If command.

Combining the What-If Analysis with the Database Statistical Functions

The what-if analysis can be combined with the database statistical functions to provide statistics on the entries in a Quattro database quickly. The values stored

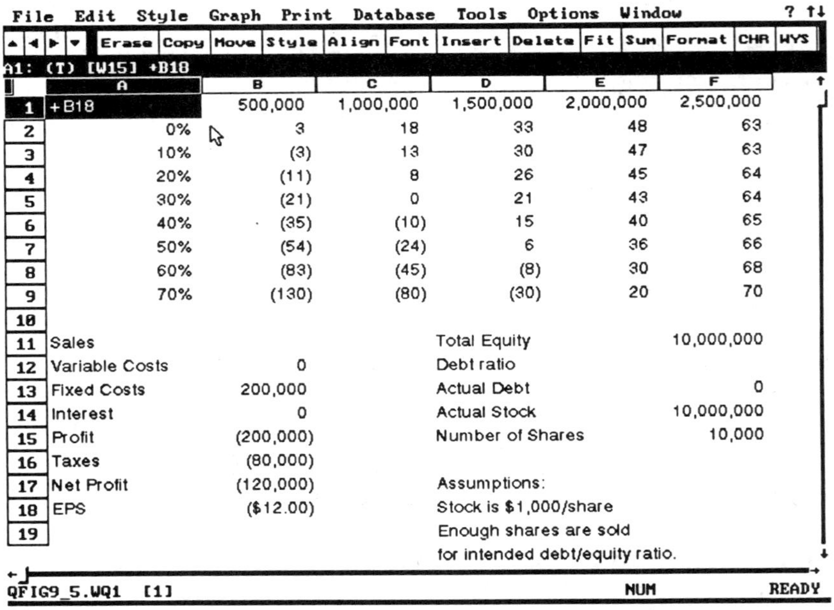

Figure 9.5 Table Filled in by /Tools What-If 2 Variable Command

in the columns and rows of the table can be used to replace criteria values, and the table's formula can be one of the database statistical functions that references these criteria entries.

Figure 9.6 shows a 2 Variables What-if table that uses a database statistical function. The table's formula adds the selling cost of the automobiles, depending on the salesperson and the type of automobile. The what-if analysis computes the total number of each type of automobile sold by each sales person.

After placing the input values in the rows and columns of the table, the database statistical function @DSUM is entered in E7. The /Tools What-If 2 Variables command is invoked, and the first input cell is specified as F2. The second input cell is specified as G2. Both of the input cells are criteria entries for the database function. The information in this table can be used for commission computations and sales reports.

Unlike using the database statistical functions directly, combining these functions with the /Tools What-If command does not recalculate the values in the table automatically if the values in the database change. However, combining the database statistical functions with the /Tools What-If command provides a quick approach for performing the same calculation with multiple criteria values.

When you are creating the table to be combined with a database statistical function, the input values that you are going to use as the criteria must all be acceptable criteria values. For example, if one of the criteria that the input value

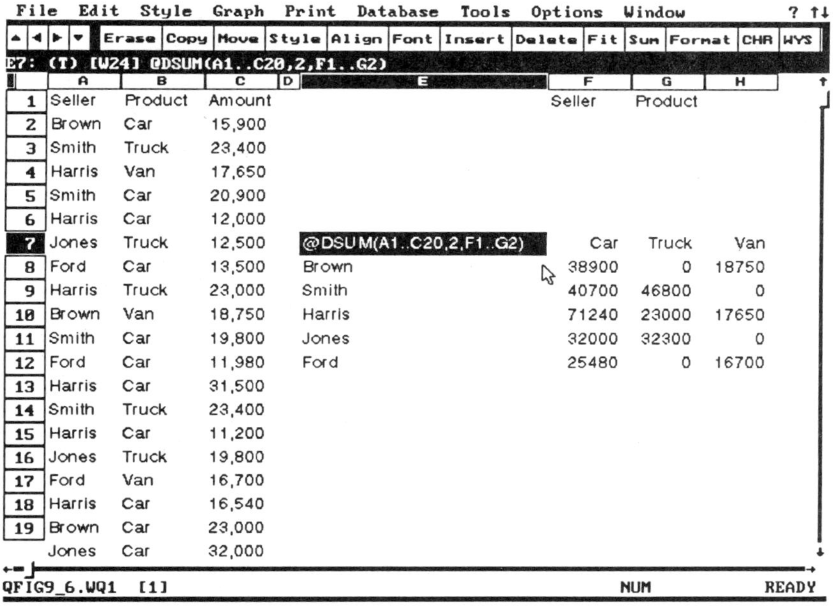

Figure 9.6 Two-Way Table Combined with a Database Statistical Function

replaces uses dates, all values for the input row or column must be valid date serial numbers. You can always generate a list of the unique entries in a database field by using the **/Database Query Unique** command, which you can also subsequently use for row or column input values.

Using Multiple Spreadsheets in a What-If Table

Just as you can use multiple spreadsheets for databases and spreadsheet calculations, you can also use multiple spreadsheets in a what-if table. For example, using the data in Figure 9.6, you may want the table in a spreadsheet separate from the spreadsheet containing the database. To use multiple spreadsheets with the What-If commands, enter the file name in square brackets before the cell or block address for the table address and the input cells. For example, if the VEHICLES spreadsheet contains the database in Figure 9.6 and you want to build the table in a spreadsheet containing only the data in columns E through H, the database formula in the other spreadsheet would be **@DSUM([VEHICLES]A1..C20,2,F1..G2)** with **F1..G2** containing the criteria in the same spreadsheet as the database statistical function. Even input cells can be in spreadsheets other than that containing the what-if table. All spreadsheets that have pertinent formulas should be open when you enter **/Tools What-If**, since Quattro does not update the formulas in the spreadsheets that are not open as the input cells are evaluated. In cases where the data values in the spreadsheet do not change as Quattro changes the values of the input cells, the spreadsheet may remain closed. For example, if the what-if table is evaluating a database statistical function and the spreadsheet containing the database is in a separate file than the what-if table, input cells, and criteria for the database statistical function, the spreadsheet containing the database does not have to be open to create the what-if table.

FREQUENCY DISTRIBUTION

Obtaining the average for a set of data values provides one meaningful piece of information about the entries. The functions @MIN and @MAX provide the highest and lowest values within the block of values, respectively. Knowing the average, minimum, and maximum values provides a partial picture of the entries but does not provide any indication about the distribution of these values. With a large number of entries, you may be interested in categorizing these values to get a better feeling for their distribution within the range represented by the minimum and maximum values.

Knowing the distribution of the data entries tells you how many entries are in each category. Categories can be established to group numeric entries. A distribution may be useful for dividing the records in an employee database into two groups of approximately equal size in order to assign two individuals an equal number of records for verification.

For numeric information, a distribution is of interest, for example, when you have a series of products that are assigned product numbers 1 through 5 and you want to know how many records are in the database for each product type. A distribution quickly tells you the number of records for each product type.

The /Tools Frequency command operates by using *bin* entries that you create. Each bin represents an entry within your data or a range of possible entries. Quattro analyzes the block that you specify and increments the frequency count for the appropriate bin as it processes each entry in the block.

To use this command, you first have to set up an area in your spreadsheet to record the bin values. Since your data is analyzed against these bins with a count supplied for these bins, the column immediately to the right of the bin values should be blank. To account for entries that are larger than any of the bin values that you supply, the row beneath your last bin value should also be empty, since Quattro supplies a count of entries exceeding the largest bin value at this location.

When you select bin values, the value you enter for each bin is the largest value to be included in the count for the bin. For example, if you are creating bin intervals of 1,000 and if the first bin value is 1,000, it includes the count of all entries equal to or less than 1,000. A second bin of 2,000 includes the count of all entries greater than 1,000 but less than or equal to 2,000. Cells equaling @NA are counted in the first bin and cells equaling @ERR are counted in the last bin.

A practical example of using frequency distribution is analyzing market survey data. For example, if you have computed that the average salary of the people who purchase your product is $35,000, you might want to know the distribution so that you can target your advertising. By knowing the distribution, you can learn whether your product appeals to people from many income groups or only from a few income groups close to the $35,000 average.

The steps to create a frequency distribution are shown below.

1. Select an empty area of a spreadsheet or a separate spreadsheet for the frequency distribution table. The area required for the frequency distribution table is determined by the number of categories you want to create. This area must have two columns with the number of rows for this area equal to the number of bins plus one.

2. Enter the highest value for each bin in each cell within the leftmost column of the table. Figure 9.7 shows the income values from respondents to a market survey. Bins can be created to categorize this data, with each bin having the highest income for each group. If the last bin value is 70,000, anything that is above 70,000 is counted in the cell to the right and below the last bin. The bin values must be in ascending sequence from the top to the bottom of the column.

3. Type / and select Tools Frequency. Quattro prompts you for the column where the values are entered. This is the block of entries for which Quattro

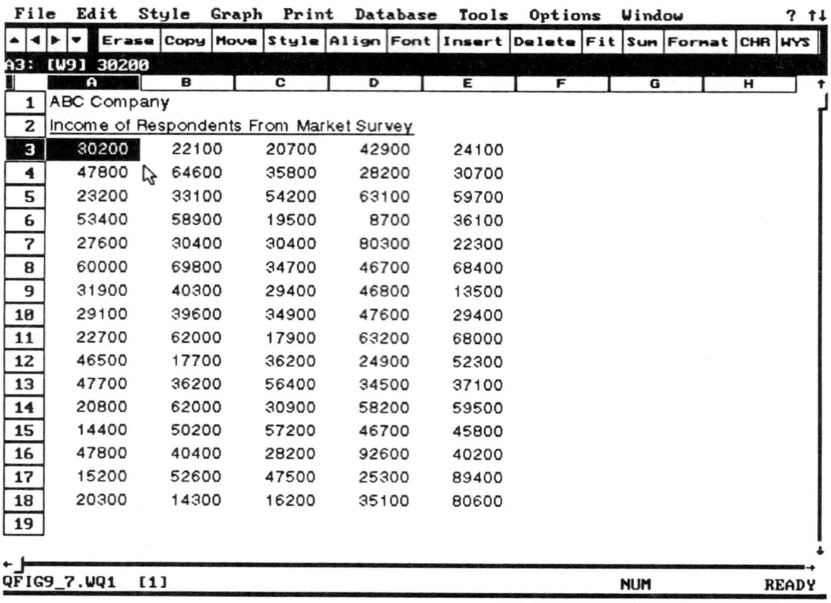

```
    File  Edit  Style  Graph  Print  Database  Tools  Options  Window           ? ↑↓
    ▲ ◄ ► ▼  Erase Copy Move Style Align Font Insert Delete Fit Sum Format CHR WYS
    A3: [W9] 30200
           A         B         C         D         E       F       G       H
    1  ABC Company
    2  Income of Respondents From Market Survey
    3    30200     22100     20700     42900     24100
    4    47800     64600     35800     28200     30700
    5    23200     33100     54200     63100     59700
    6    53400     58900     19500      8700     36100
    7    27600     30400     30400     80300     22300
    8    60000     69800     34700     46700     68400
    9    31900     40300     29400     46800     13500
   10    29100     39600     34900     47600     29400
   11    22700     62000     17900     63200     68000
   12    46500     17700     36200     24900     52300
   13    47700     36200     56400     34500     37100
   14    20800     62000     30900     58200     59500
   15    14400     50200     57200     46700     45800
   16    47800     40400     28200     92600     40200
   17    15200     52600     47500     25300     89400
   18    20300     14300     16200     35100     80600
   19

  QFIG9_7.WQ1  [1]                                    NUM              READY
```

Figure 9.7 Data from Market Research

determines the frequency distribution. It can be in the same spreadsheet as the frequency table or in a different one.

4. Move the selector to the first value in the values block, type a period, and highlight the entire value block or type in the block address. Press ENTER. In the spreadsheet shown in Figure 9.7, the values block is A3..E18. After specifying the values block, Quattro prompts you for the bin column.

5. Move the selector to the first bin value, type a period, and highlight all bins (or type in the block address of the bins). Press ENTER. If bin entries were placed in G3..G18, the bin column would be specified as **G3..G18**. After specifying the bin location, Quattro enters the frequency numbers in the column to the right of the bin numbers. The row immediately below the last bin is used to record the frequency number of the values that exceed the last bin value. For example, any salary above $70,000 is included in last row of the table, as in Figure 9.8. The numbers in the table are values and are not updated as the values in the values block change unless you execute the /Tools Frequency command again. Once this table is generated, it can be used for other Quattro features (such as bar graphs).

MATRIX MATH

Matrices are tabular arrangements of data used in many higher-level math applications. Matrix operations are popular because they can be used to simplify

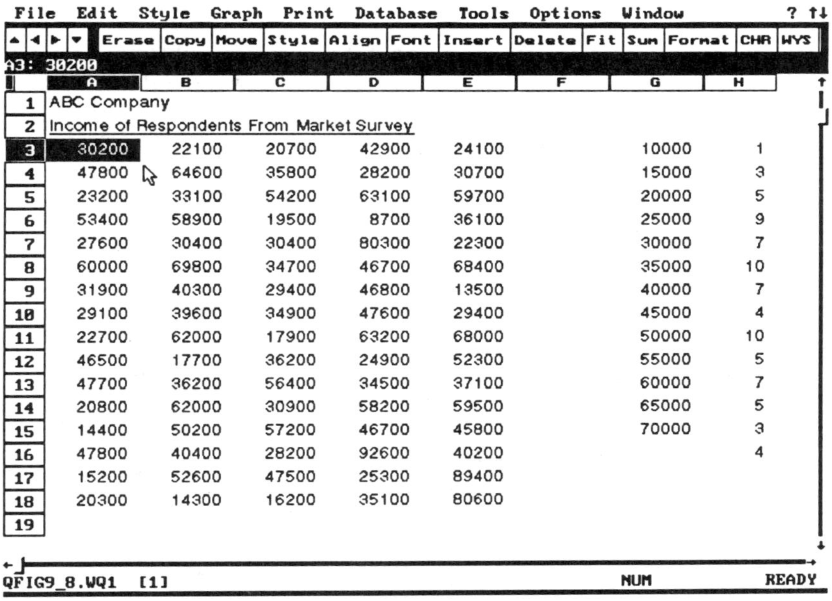

	A	B	C	D	E	F	G	H
1	ABC Company							
2	Income of Respondents From Market Survey							
3	30200	22100	20700	42900	24100		10000	1
4	47800	64600	35800	28200	30700		15000	3
5	23200	33100	54200	63100	59700		20000	5
6	53400	58900	19500	8700	36100		25000	9
7	27600	30400	30400	80300	22300		30000	7
8	60000	69800	34700	46700	68400		35000	10
9	31900	40300	29400	46800	13500		40000	7
10	29100	39600	34900	47600	29400		45000	4
11	22700	62000	17900	63200	68000		50000	10
12	46500	17700	36200	24900	52300		55000	5
13	47700	36200	56400	34500	37100		60000	7
14	20800	62000	30900	58200	59500		65000	5
15	14400	50200	57200	46700	45800		70000	3
16	47800	40400	28200	92600	40200			4
17	15200	52600	47500	25300	89400			
18	20300	14300	16200	35100	80600			
19								

Figure 9.8 Frequency Distribution of Incomes (Column H)

calculations and avoid complicated formulas. Quattro provides two commands that operate on matrices: matrix multiplication and matrix inversion. Although the rules for matrix operations may make them seem complex initially, they actually serve to simplify problem solutions and provide practical approaches to job-order costing, linear programming, and econometric modeling problems.

Since Quattro's matrix commands perform the matrix computations, you do not need to know the theory behind the required mathematics. Once you see how these operations can be used in problem solving you can focus on how to set up the matrix operation to have Quattro solve the problem.

Multiplying Matrices

Multiplying matrices can streamline formulas that require multiplying each of the values in one matrix by the values in a second matrix and adding the products of these operations together. One application for matrix multiplication is job costing. If you need to compute the labor cost for a multiphase project that requires several categories of labor, matrix multiplication can handle the tasks much easier than a formula can. A formula to determine costs for each project phase requires that you multiply each labor rate by the number of hours required at that rate and then total each of the products to obtain total labor costs. To solve the same problem with matrix multiplication, labor rates are stored in one matrix and the number of hours at each rate are stored in another matrix. The Matrix Multiply command provides the total charges for each project phase without the need for a formula.

When Quattro multiplies a matrix, Quattro multiplies the first element of the first row in the first matrix with the first element of the first column of the second matrix. It does this also with the second and third elements and so on until the elements in the first row of the first matrix are multiplied with the first column of the second matrix. For example, if your matrices look like this:

First Matrix:	6	5	8	Second Matrix:	3	5
	9	18	4		12	4
					5	2

Quattro multiplies 6 by 3, 5 by 12, and 8 by 5. Then Quattro totals all the products for the first row and column. In this example, it is 118. Quattro performs these computations for each row of the first matrix and column of the second matrix. Then Quattro multiplies the elements in the first row of the first matrix by the second column of the second matrix and totals the products. Quattro performs this for all columns in the second matrix. The resulting matrix has the same number of rows as the first matrix and the same number of columns as the second matrix. When Quattro multiplies the matrices, it creates this resulting matrix:

(6*3)+(5*12)+(8*5)	(6*5)+(5*4)+(8*2)	or	118	66
(9*3)+(18*12)+(4*5)	(9*5)+(18*4)+(4*2)		263	125

RULES FOR MATRIX MULTIPLICATION Although matrix multiplication offers the potential for streamlining your calculations, you must be willing to follow a set of specific rules to obtain these benefits. If your matrix multiplication operations deviate from these rules, Quattro cannot calculate usable results for you. The following rules are the ones you must adhere to:

- Each cell within either of the matrices used in the multiply operation must contain a value entry. Blanks are not equivalent to an entry of zero and must be replaced with zeros before attempting the operation.
- To multiply two matrices, you must look at the order of the matrices. Matrix order describes the size of a matrix as an x by y matrix, where x is the number of rows in the matrix and y is the number of columns. For example, a matrix with three rows and four columns is a 3 x 4 matrix. If the information in the 3 x 4 matrix is transposed, it becomes a 4 x 3 matrix. The two matrices are not interchangeable in a matrix multiply operation. To multiply matrices, the number of columns in the first matrix must be exactly equal to the number of rows in the second matrix. Without this relationship, it is not possible to multiply the contents of two matrices. Since the order of matrices are critical to successful multiplication, the sequence in which you specify the two matrices to be multiplied is important. You can multiply a 5 x 7 matrix by a 7 x 1 matrix, but you cannot multiply a 7 x 1 matrix by a 5 x 7 matrix. To determine whether two matrices are eligible for the matrix multiply operation, write the two matrix orders side by side, as in 2 x 3 and 3 x 2. When the two inside numbers are the same, the pair of matrices are compatible. The resulting matrix has the order of the two outside numbers, as in 2 x 2.

A MATRIX MULTIPLY EXAMPLE A closer look at a matrix multiply operation may clarify the process for its use. This procedure is useful for project-costing solutions like defense contract costs, which are sometimes awarded on a cost-plus basis. This requires the contractor to properly attribute all costs to specific products. For each project, the product manufactured must be processed by different departments. Each department has its own direct labor and overhead costs.

Figure 9.9 shows a list of the hours required for each project by department and a list of the hourly cost for direct labor and overhead. To compute the hourly cost for each project for the labor and the overhead cost, you must multiply the number of hours by the cost per hour. Rather than using a formula, you can use the /Tools Advanced Math Multiply command to compute the values.

First, the data must be stored in the proper form within matrices that are compatible for multiplication purposes. After storing the data and entering /Tools Advanced Math Multiply, Quattro prompts you for the first matrix. In Figure 9.9, the first matrix is B2..D3. After the first matrix is specified, you must specify the second matrix, B6..C8 in Figure 9.9. Next, Quattro prompts you for the destination of the resulting matrix, which can be indicated by supplying the upper-left corner of the matrix. In Figure 9.9, B12 is specified as the location for the results. Quattro multiplies the matrix and puts the result starting at B12 as Figure 9.10 shows. Like other analytical commands, the matrices may be stored in separate spreadsheets, as long as you include the file name before the block address.

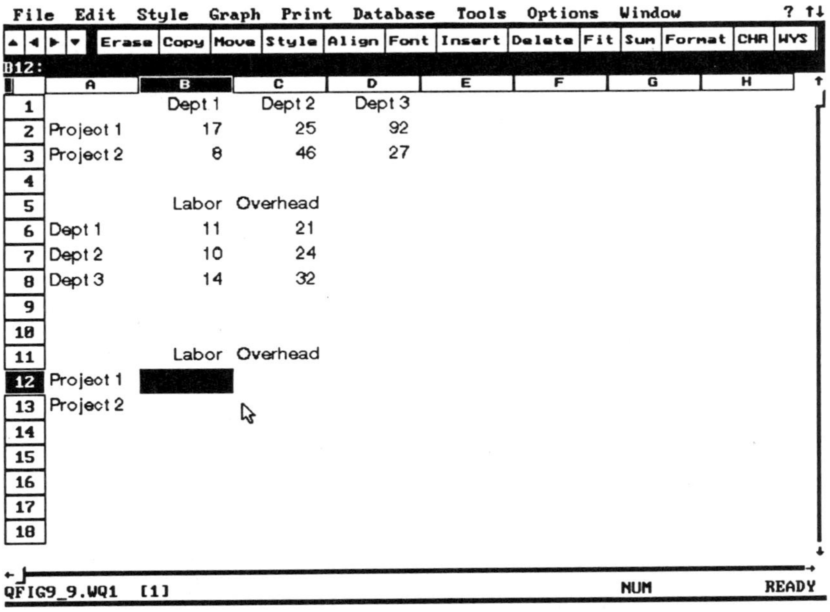

Figure 9.9 Matrices Containing Hourly Information for Two Projects

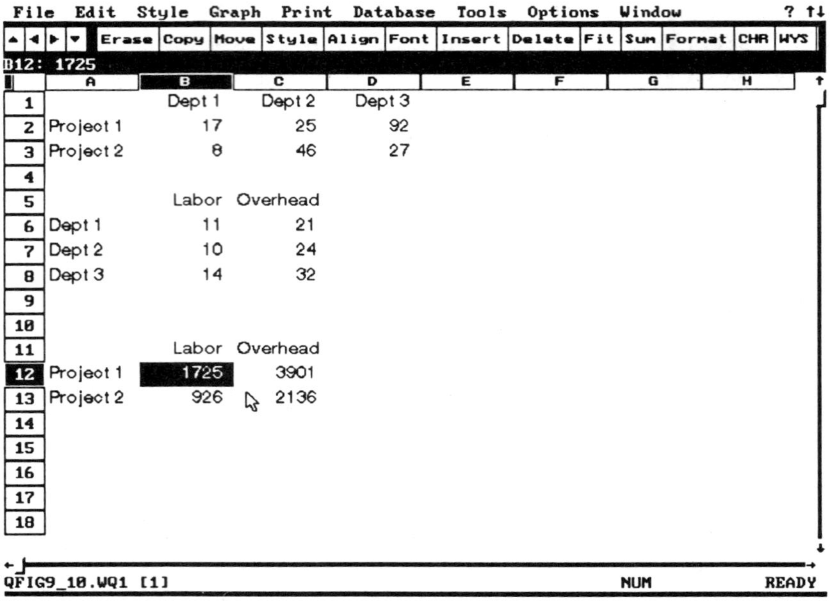

```
File  Edit  Style  Graph  Print  Database  Tools  Options  Window      ? ↑↓
  Erase Copy Move Style Align Font Insert Delete Fit Sum Format CHR WYS
B12: 1725
        A        B        C        D      E      F      G      H
   1           Dept 1   Dept 2   Dept 3
   2  Project 1   17       25       92
   3  Project 2    8       46       27
   4
   5           Labor   Overhead
   6  Dept 1     11       21
   7  Dept 2     10       24
   8  Dept 3     14       32
   9
  10
  11           Labor   Overhead
  12  Project 1  1725     3901
  13  Project 2   926     2136
  14
  15
  16
  17
  18
QFIG9_10.WQ1 [1]                                    NUM         READY
```

Figure 9.10 Multiplied Matrix Computing Total Labor and Overhead for Two Projects

Inverting Matrices

Inverting matrices is the first step in solving linear equations. A practical application of linear equations is production planning, which assumes several projects are competing for limited resources and computes the best distribution among the projects. Special rules apply to matrices used in an inversion operation since they must be square matrices with the same number of rows as columns and cannot be larger than 90 x 90.

An example of using an inverted matrix to solve for the best distribution between projects is shown in Figure 9.11. In the figure, the different requirements for three processes are shown for three products. Just below this information is the number or hours available in each department. To compute the best distribution among these resources, follow these steps:

1. Set up a matrix with the different resource requirements for each product. In Figure 9.11, the matrix is the block B2..D4. Each row contains the resource requirements of each department for a product, and each column contains the resource requirements for each product for a department.

2. Set up a matrix with the resource limitations. In Figure 9.11, the matrix is the block B8..B10. Each row in the matrix represents the resource limitation of each column in the first matrix.

3. Type /, and select **Tools Advanced Math Invert**.

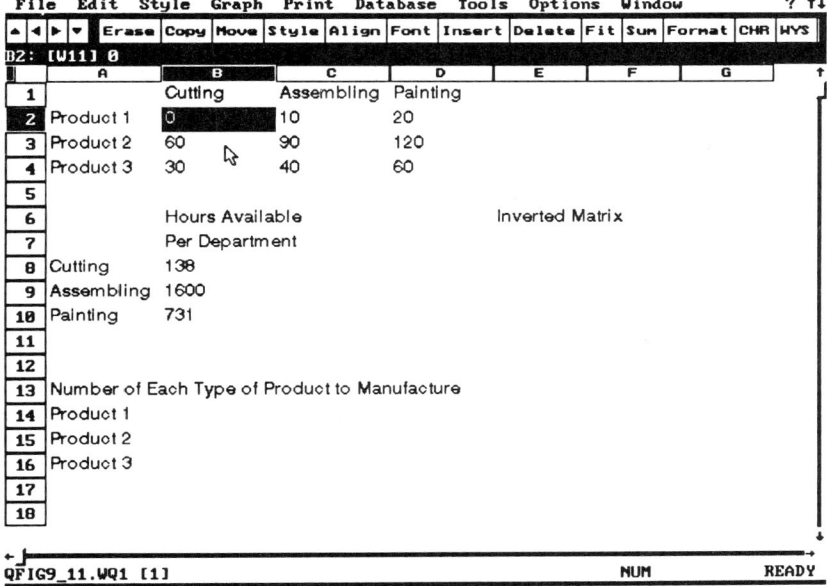

Figure 9.11 Matrices Containing Production Requirements

4. Select the matrix to be inverted, and press ENTER. For the example in Figure 9.11, the matrix block B2..D4 is selected.

5. Select the destination for the inverted matrix, and press ENTER. The inverted matrix is the same size as the original matrix. E7 is selected for the destination of the matrix in B2..D4. When you press ENTER, the matrix is inverted, as in Figure 9.12. The inverted matrix is used in determining the optimal production of the three products.

6. Type /, and select **Tools Advanced Math Multiply**.

7. Select the first matrix to be multiplied, and press ENTER. This is the matrix that is created in step 5. In the example in Figure 9.12, it is the matrix E7..G9.

8. Select the second matrix to be multiplied, and press ENTER. This is the matrix created in step 2. In the example in Figure 9.12, it is the matrix B8..B10.

9. Select the destination block, and press ENTER. The destination block is specified by the upper-left corner in which the multiplied matrix will be placed. In this example, it is B14. Figure 9.13 shows the spreadsheet after the matrices have been multiplied. As the figure shows, producing approximately 6 units of product 1 and 14 units of product 2 uses up all available hours in the departments. When you use matrix inversion and multiplication, the equation is forced to use all resources. In many cases, you can find a better solution using the linear programming available with **/Tools Optimizer**.

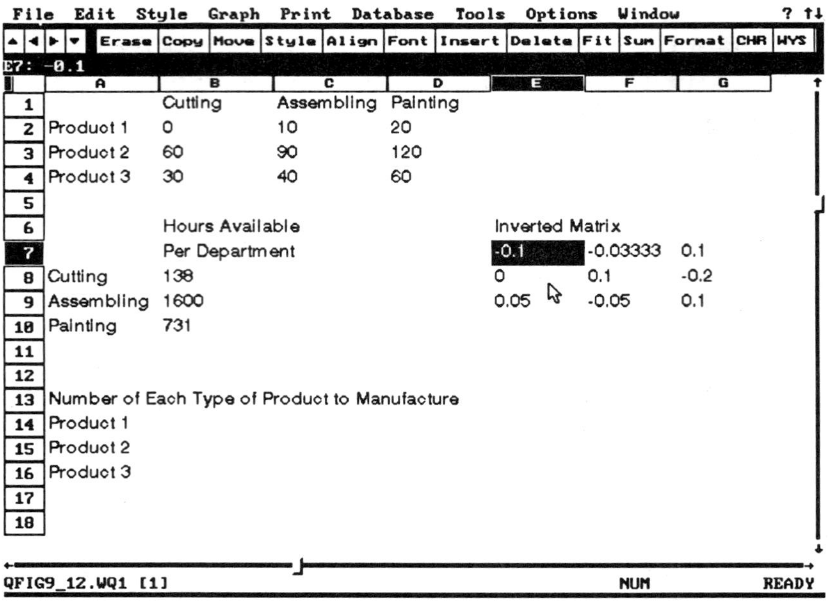

470 *Quattro Pro 4.0 Handbook*

```
File  Edit  Style  Graph  Print  Database  Tools  Options  Window          ? ↑↓
    Erase Copy Move Style Align Font Insert Delete Fit Sum Format CHR WYS
E7: -0.1
        A           B           C           D         E         F         G
 1                  Cutting     Assembling  Painting
 2  Product 1       0           10          20
 3  Product 2       60          90          120
 4  Product 3       30          40          60
 5
 6                  Hours Available                   Inverted Matrix
 7                  Per Department                    -0.1      -0.03333   0.1
 8  Cutting         138                               0          0.1      -0.2
 9  Assembling      1600                              0.05       -0.05     0.1
10  Painting        731
11
12
13  Number of Each Type of Product to Manufacture
14  Product 1
15  Product 2
16  Product 3
17
18

QFIG9_12.WQ1 [1]                                          NUM       READY
```

Figure 9.12 Result of Inverted Matrix

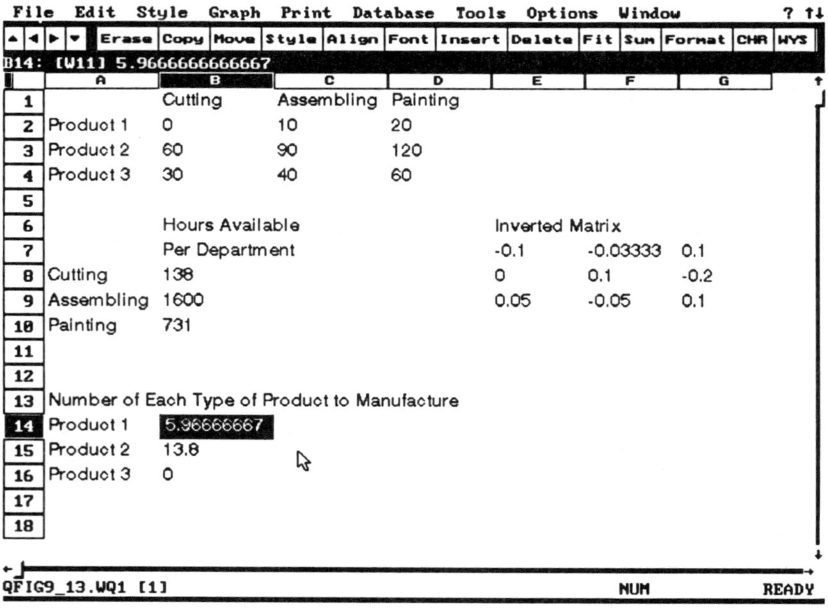

```
File  Edit  Style  Graph  Print  Database  Tools  Options  Window          ? ↑↓
    Erase Copy Move Style Align Font Insert Delete Fit Sum Format CHR WYS
B14: [W11] 5.9666666666667
        A           B           C           D         E         F         G
 1                  Cutting     Assembling  Painting
 2  Product 1       0           10          20
 3  Product 2       60          90          120
 4  Product 3       30          40          60
 5
 6                  Hours Available                   Inverted Matrix
 7                  Per Department                    -0.1      -0.03333   0.1
 8  Cutting         138                               0          0.1      -0.2
 9  Assembling      1600                              0.05       -0.05     0.1
10  Painting        731
11
12
13  Number of Each Type of Product to Manufacture
14  Product 1       5.96666667
15  Product 2       13.8
16  Product 3       0
17
18

QFIG9_13.WQ1 [1]                                          NUM       READY
```

Figure 9.13 Matrix Operations Computing Optimal Production

REGRESSION ANALYSIS

Regression analysis determines how an independent variable affects a dependent one and can be used to identify data that may have predictive ability. For example, advertising affects sales. Advertising is an independent variable and sales is a dependent variable. Regression analysis can help you determine how closely sales correlate with advertising to allow you to predict the likely sales growth from a given advertising expenditure. Quattro's regression analysis determines several statistics that measure how much the independent variable affects the dependent one. Quattro computes a regression line that predicts how much one value affects the other and how well one value predicts the other.

Like Quattro's other advanced analytical commands, the regression command requires a few preliminary steps. First, the dependent and independent data must be stored in spreadsheet columns. This data must only contain numeric values. Also, these columns must have the same number of entries. If the data has more than one potential independent variable, the potential independent variable columns must be adjacent if you intend to perform multiple regression. A sample data area is shown in Figure 9.14. This spreadsheet shows the direct labor hours, the material costs, and the total costs for each project that uses the Assembly Department. Each set of data for a different product is a different observation. Generating a regression equation helps predict future project costs.

To create a regression analysis, follow these steps:

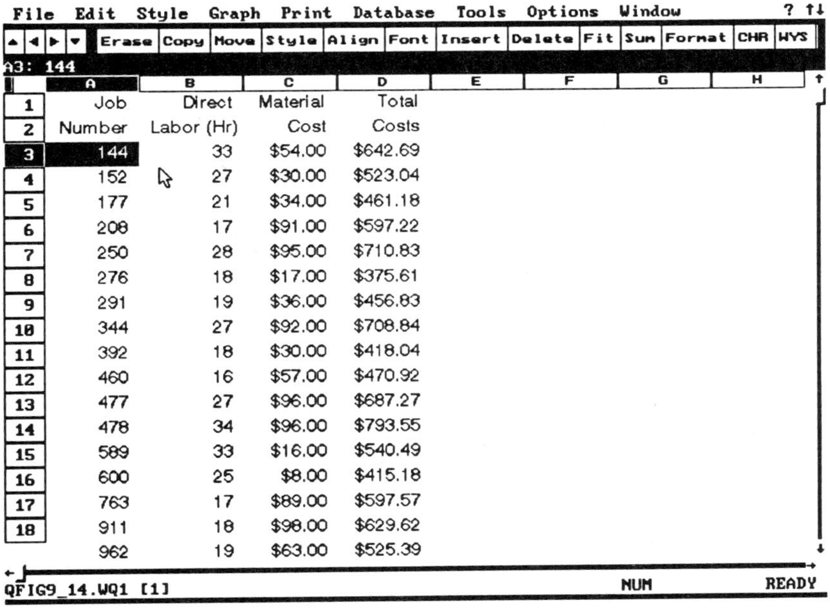

	A	B	C	D
1	Job	Direct	Material	Total
2	Number	Labor (Hr)	Cost	Costs
3	144	33	$54.00	$642.69
4	152	27	$30.00	$523.04
5	177	21	$34.00	$461.18
6	208	17	$91.00	$597.22
7	250	28	$95.00	$710.83
8	276	18	$17.00	$375.61
9	291	19	$36.00	$456.83
10	344	27	$92.00	$708.84
11	392	18	$30.00	$418.04
12	460	16	$57.00	$470.92
13	477	27	$96.00	$687.27
14	478	34	$96.00	$793.55
15	589	33	$16.00	$540.49
16	600	25	$8.00	$415.18
17	763	17	$89.00	$597.57
18	911	18	$98.00	$629.62
	962	19	$63.00	$525.39

Figure 9.14 Job-Costing Information

1. Create a data table that has the dependent and independent values for each observation. Figure 9.14 shows data entered for this example.

2. Type /, and select **Tools Advanced Math Regression** to display the menu shown in Figure 9.15.

3. Select **Independent**, and select the block that contains the independent variable values, then press ENTER. If you select multiple columns, Quattro computes the multiple regression for all variables selected. Otherwise, Quattro computes the simple regression for the one variable chosen. In the example in Figure 9.14, the independent variable block is B3..C20.

4. Select **Dependent**, and select the dependent variable block containing the data that are influenced by the other variables, then press ENTER. In the project-costing example, the dependent block is D3..D20.

5. Select **Output**, specify the upper-left cell in the regression output block, and press ENTER. In the example in Figure 9.14, the output block starts at B5. The regression table that Quattro creates is nine rows deep and two columns wider than the number of independent variables. If you have any existing information in the output area, it is overwritten when you execute the command.

6. Select **Intercept**, and choose whether the Y Intercept should be set to zero or computed. If the y intercept is set to zero, the regression equation does not have a y intercept. For some types of data, a y intercept is meaningless and is more appropriately set to zero instead of having Quattro compute the intercept. For example, suppose you are attempting to determine a correlation between age and trips to the doctor. At age zero, anything other than

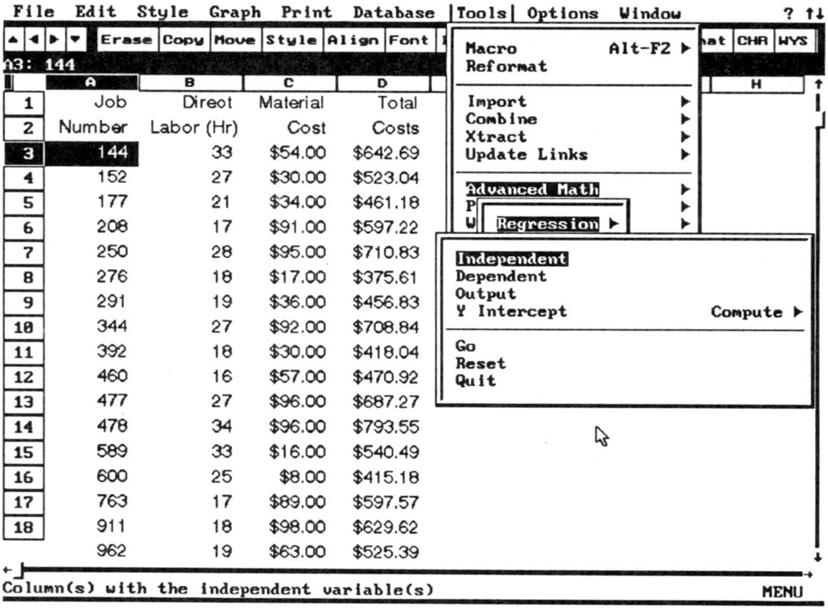

Figure 9.15 Regression Menu

zero trips is illogical; therefore, setting the intercept to zero is the best decision. In other situations, having Quattro compute the y intercept provides a more useful equation. With many regression equations, the equation has a relevant range. For example, in a regression equation for predicting the total production costs based on the number of units, the equation may only be useful for predicting costs for production between 100,000 and 500,000. A practical reason for this relevant range is that the fixed costs may change for production below 100,000 and above 500,000. In this case, you want to compute an intercept, since the resulting equation produces better results for values between 100,000 and 500,000. For values outside this range, you need to generate another equation.

7. Select **Go**. Quattro performs the regression analysis as shown in Figure 9.16. Selecting **Reset** eliminates all the specifications of the other options. Selecting **Quit** returns you to the spreadsheet in READY mode.

Applying the Results of Regression Analysis

Once you have the results of the regression analysis, you can use the information for different purposes. The X Coefficient(s) and Constant are the values for the regression equation. For example, the regression equation from Figure 9.16 is as follows:

$$(DIRECT\ HOURS \times 10.30261) + (MATERIAL\ COST \times 3.032367) + 143.2715 = TOTAL\ COST$$

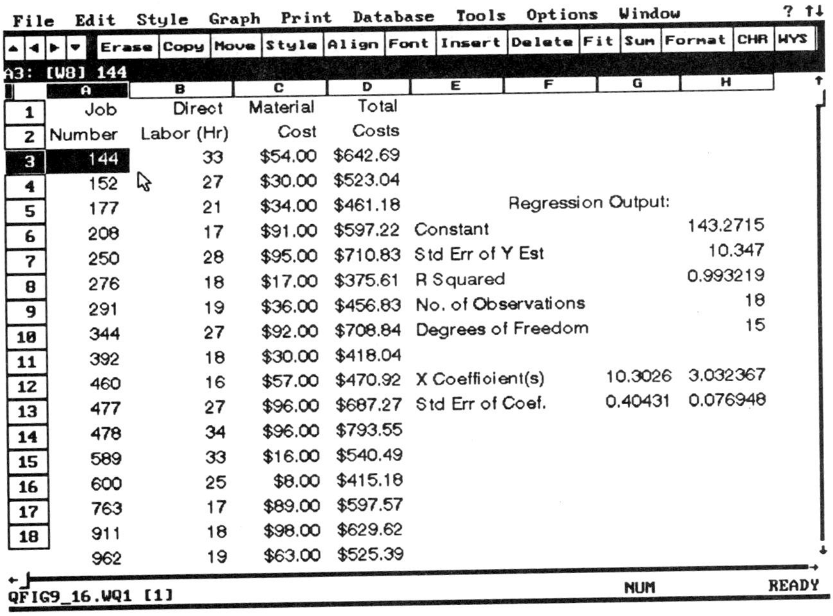

Job Number	Direct Labor (Hr)	Material Cost	Total Costs	Regression Output:		
144	33	$54.00	$642.69			
152	27	$30.00	$523.04			
177	21	$34.00	$461.18	Regression Output:		
208	17	$91.00	$597.22	Constant		143.2715
250	28	$95.00	$710.83	Std Err of Y Est		10.347
276	18	$17.00	$375.61	R Squared		0.993219
291	19	$36.00	$456.83	No. of Observations		18
344	27	$92.00	$708.84	Degrees of Freedom		15
392	18	$30.00	$418.04			
460	16	$57.00	$470.92	X Coefficient(s)	10.3026	3.032367
477	27	$96.00	$687.27	Std Err of Coef.	0.40431	0.076948
478	34	$96.00	$793.55			
589	33	$16.00	$540.49			
600	25	$8.00	$415.18			
763	17	$89.00	$597.57			
911	18	$98.00	$629.62			
962	19	$63.00	$525.39			

Figure 9.16 Output from Regression Analysis

This equation can predict the costs of future jobs in that department. For example, if the department is about to perform a job that is expected to require 30 hours of labor and $90 of materials, this equation predicts that the job will cost 725.26283. The Std Err of Coef. and the Std Err or Y Est describe how well the coefficients fit the data. The smaller the number, the better the coefficient describes the relationship between the independent variable and the dependent variable. The number of observations is the number of dependent variables that Quattro counted and used in the equation. The Degrees of Freedom result is the number of observations minus the number of independent variables and 1 for the y intercept (if it is computed). R Squared represents the validity of the model. The closer to 1 this value is, the better the independent variables predict the dependent variable. You can examine the variables as a group and then examine each one individually to see which analysis produces the highest R-squared result. A value close to 0 means that the regression equation is not a useful predictor of the dependent variable.

SOLVING FOR A VALUE

Quattro Pro 2 and above lets Quattro Pro work through calculations backward to find the value of a cell that makes another cell return the result you desire. For example, if you are reviewing production costs, you may want to determine the break-even points for production. Figure 9.17 shows a worksheet that calculates

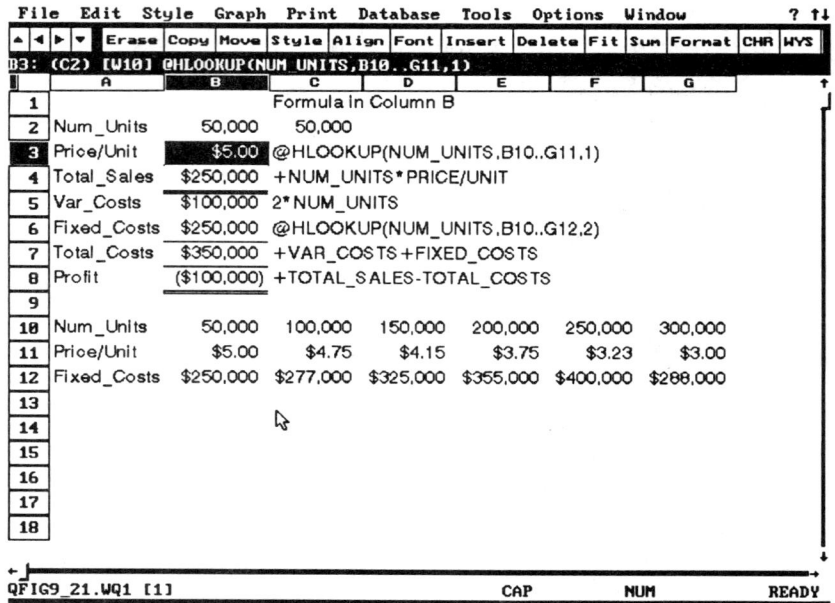

Figure 9.17 Problem to use with /Tools Solve For

the sales, total costs, and profits based on the number of units produced and sold. This model makes the assumption that the price and fixed costs vary at different quantities. When deciding how much to produce, you may want to find any breakeven points, that is, where the profit equals zero.

Before you can use the /Tools Solve For command, you must enter the formulas that the command will affect. For example, in Figure 9.17, you must enter the formulas in column B and the horizontal lookup table in B10..G12. The labels in column A and C are there for documentation, the lines are added for clarity, and the block names are added with /Edit Name Labels Right to make the formulas easier to understand. In this example, Quattro will find the value of B1 that makes B8 equal zero.

To find any values that make another cell equal a desired value, use the /Tools Solve For command. This displays a menu that includes Formula Cell, Target Value, Variable Cell, Parameters, Go, Reset, and Quit. The Formula Cell is the cell address or block name that contains a formula that you want to equal another value. For the example in Figure 9.17, it is B8. The Target Value selects the value that you want the Formula Cell to equal. In Figure 9.17, it is 0, but you can enter any value at the prompt. The Variable Cell is the cell or block name that contains a value that Quattro can alter in order to make the Formula Cell equal the Target Value. In the example in Figure 9.17, it is B2, which is the number of units. As this number changes, the @HLOOKUP functions return different numbers based on the number of units and the formulas in B4, B6, B7, and B8 use the new values. The value in the Variable Cell must affect the value of the Formula Cell. Before you try to solve for the value, you may want to change the parameters Quattro uses by selecting Parameters and Max Iterations or Accuracy. The Max Iterations is a number between 1 and 99 that selects the number of attempts Quattro performs to find an answer. The higher the number, the more attempts Quattro makes and the longer it may take. Accuracy selects how close the values the result of the Formula Cell can be from the Target Value for Quattro to assume that it has found an answer. For example, the default of .005 means that Quattro assumes that it has found an answer when the value of the Formula Cell is .005 more or less than the Target Value.

When you are ready to find the answer, select Go from the /Tools Solve For menu. You can also select Reset to remove the current settings for the other options in the /Tools Solve For menu. When you want to return to READY mode, you can select Quit. Figure 9.18 shows the result from Figure 9.17. Quattro uses the initial value of the Variable Cell as a starting point for generating the solution. Since this example abruptly changes the fixed costs and price per unit, it can have more than one potential solution. While the example shows the results of 83333, by starting with other different initial guesses you can also have results of 100727, 151163, and 202857. If Quattro cannot find an answer in the number of iterations set by /Tools Solve For Parameters Max Iterations, Quattro displays an error message. You will want to enter a new guess or increase the maximum number of iterations. This will also occur when the problem does not have a feasible solution. Using the example of Figure 9.17, if you tried finding a solution where the profit would be a negative $50,000, Quattro would not be able to find a solution because one does not exist.

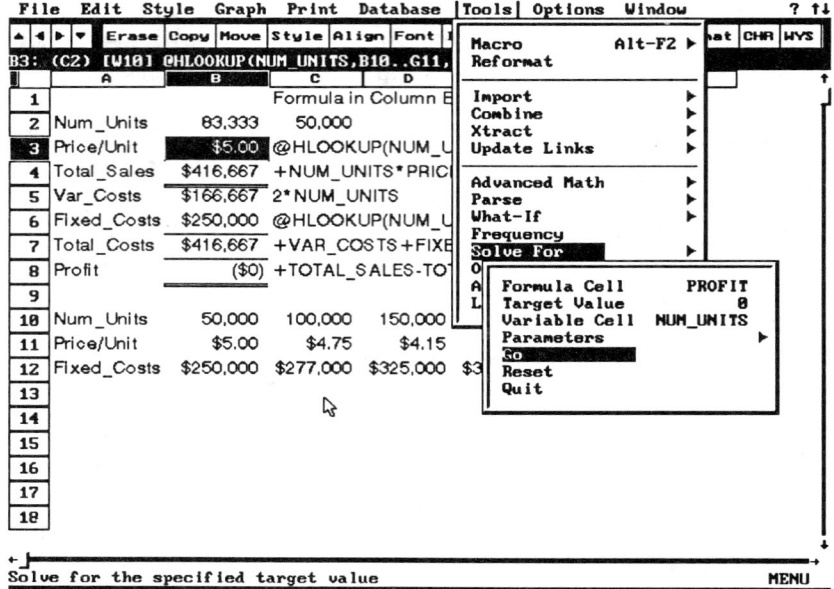

Figure 9.18 Answer Generated by /Tools Solve For

OPTIMIZING A SPREADSHEET

In the previous section, you learned about how you can have Quattro Pro work backward through a problem to find the value in one cell that makes another cell equal a stated value. This Quattro Pro feature works if you are calculating the number of products to reach a predetermined profit. If you need to consider how changing several variables at once will change the final result, you cannot use the /Tools Solve For command, because it only varies one cell's value at a time. When you have a model that you want to try varying several values at once, you will want to use Quattro Pro 4's Optimizer instead. The types of problems you will want to use the Optimizer with are the ones that you are thinking to yourself "What if I changed this, and this, and ..." or "What combination of these several values gets me the best results?"

The Optimizer takes at its input the values in the spreadsheet it can change, the constraints it must meet, and the results you want and then finds combinations of values that provide the desired results. The constraints the Optimizer uses are the limitations that you place on values in the spreadsheet. You can have many intermittent calculations between the values you tell Quattro Pro to change and the formula that calculates the final desired result. The Optimizer can solve many different types of equations. Some of the examples include linear and nonlinear programming problem solving. An example of linear problem solving is taking the problem that you used when you inverted and multiplied matrixes to find production quantities that would consume all the available resources and finding instead the product mix that maximizes profit. The company may be better off to not use all its resources and to concentrate production on the most valuable products instead. An example of a nonlinear problem is when you are calculating the change to overall sales volume with different prices when the change of price does not proportionally cause a change in volume.

Quattro Pro 4 can solve problems like this through its /Tools Optimizer command. Just as in the other analytical commands, you must set up data in a format for the /Tools Optimizer. This includes selecting the values that Quattro Pro may change, the formulas you want calculated as Quattro Pro tries a different set of values for the problem, and the limitations placed on the values in the spreadsheet.

Setting Up A Problem for the Optimizer

Before you can use the Optimizer, you must set up the model so Quattro Pro knows the values it will change and the formulas it will recalculate to find the solution to your problem. The values that Quattro Pro will change must be in an unprotected block. These values cannot be dates, formulas, or text. The cells that contain these values must be used by other formulas in the cell. They must be used to calculate the final formula that you want to optimize if you select a cell to optimize. The initial values in these cells can be important. Problems that you use with the Optimizer that are nonlinear (cannot be described in linear equations) may have more than one answer. The way to find the best answer for what you want is to put your best guess into these formulas. As an example, if you are using the model to plan future product mixes or sales, a good set of initial values would be the last period's production or sales.

The next type of information Quattro Pro needs to optimize a spreadsheet model is the constraints. These constraints limit other values in the spreadsheet that are affected by the values you tell Quattro Pro to change. For example, if you are working with a model to decide how much of several products you will produce, the model will have as constraints the amount produced of each product not exceeding the capacity or being less than zero. To decide on the constraints, decide which cells have limits on their values, then put that the value of this cell must be less than or equal to, equal to, or greater than or equal to in a cell (or written down) so you will have it ready to tell Quattro Pro.

The last step before you use Quattro Pro's Optimizer is to set up the formulas that you want Quattro Pro to calculate and any formula that you will use as a solution cell. The solution cell is the cell that you want to be the largest value possible, the smallest value possible, or equal to a specific value. For example, if you are working with different product mixes, you will use the cell that calculates sales or profit as the solution cell. If you are working with different expenses, you will minimize the cell that totals the expenses. You can omit using a solution cell as well. You would do this when you are only interested in finding a combination of values that will meet a set of constraints.

An example of a spreadsheet model set up for Quattro Pro's Optimizer is shown

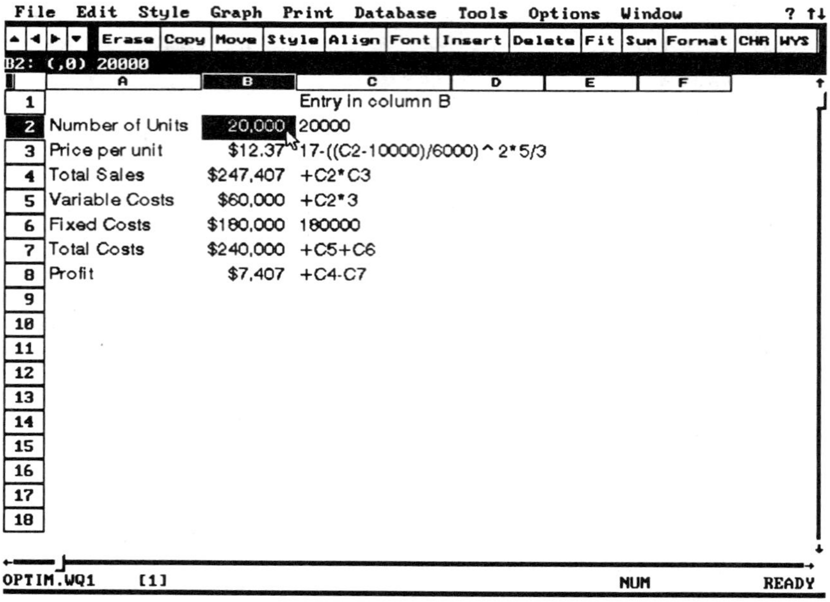

```
    File   Edit   Style   Graph   Print   Database   Tools   Options   Window        ? ↑↓
    ▲ ◀ ▶ ▼  Erase Copy Move Style Align Font Insert Delete Fit Sum Format CHR WYS
   B2: (,0) 20000
            A              B              C              D        E        F
    1                            Entry in column B
    2  Number of Units    20,000     20000
    3  Price per unit     $12.37     17-((C2-10000)/6000)^2*5/3
    4  Total Sales       $247,407    +C2*C3
    5  Variable Costs     $60,000    +C2*3
    6  Fixed Costs       $180,000    180000
    7  Total Costs       $240,000    +C5+C6
    8  Profit              $7,407    +C4-C7
    9
   10
   11
   ...
   18

   OPTIM.WQ1    [1]                                          NUM           READY
```

Figure 9.19 Problem Setup for /Tools Optimizer

in Figure 9.19. The value in B2, 20000, is the value you will tell Quattro Pro it can change. Many of the other spreadsheet formulas use B2's value in their own calculations. Your model may have different constraints depending on your production facilities. For example, one constraint is that the units sold cannot be less than zero. Other sample types of constraints might be that the units sold be more than sales commitments already made or less than the production capacity. You can also have constraints on other cells such as having a constraint that limits the total variable cost to a set amount.

Using Quattro Pro's Optimizer

When you have set up the spreadsheet to use with the Optimizer, you are ready to tell Quattro Pro to use the Optimizer with the spreadsheet. As an example of using the Optimizer, suppose you are thinking of changing a product's price to increase volume and you want to find the product price that will produce the maximum of profits. With all the data entered in the spreadsheet, follow these steps to tell Quattro to find the optimal solution:

1. Enter /Tools Optimizer to display the menu in Figure 9.20.
2. Select Variable Cell(s), and select the cells that contain the values Quattro Pro can change as it works through the problem you have given it in the spreadsheet. For the problem in Figure 9.20, the variable cell is B2, the number of units sold.

Advanced Analytical and File Features 479

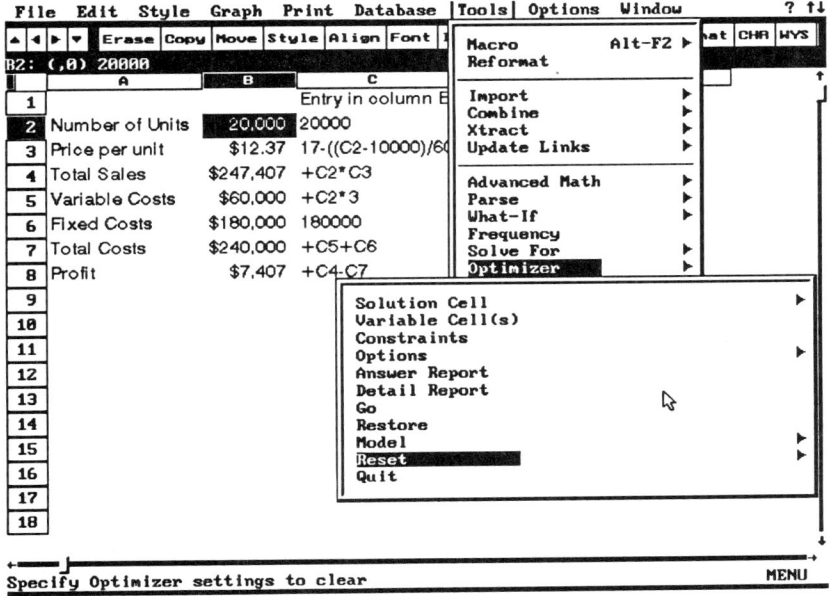

Figure 9.20 /Tools Optimizer Menu

3. Select **Solution Cell** if you will be using one, and select the cell that contains the formula that you want to minimize, maximize or make equal to a specific value. For the problem in Figure 9.20, the solution cell is B8, the profit.

4. Select **Max, Min, Equal**. Select from **Max** to maximize the result of the solution cell; **Min** to minimize the result of the solution cell; **Equal**, type the number you want the solution cell to equal and press ENTER; or select **None** if you do not want to use a solution cell in the problem.

5. Select **Constraints** and <Add New Constraint> to add the constraints for the problem. Then add a constraint in one of three ways:

   a. If you want one cell to have a relative value to another cell, select the cell and press ENTER. Next, select <=, =, or >= if you want the cell's value to be less than or equal to, equal to, or greater than or equal to the next cell you select. Select the cell containing the value you want the first cell less than or equal to, equal to, or greater than or equal to, and press ENTER.

   b. If you want one cell to be less than, greater than, or equal to another value, select the cell and press ENTER. Next, select <=, =, or >= to select whether you want the cell's value to be less than or equal to, equal to, or greater than or equal to another value. Type the value you want the cell less than or equal to, equal to, or greater than or equal to, and press ENTER.

   c. If you want multiple cells to be less than, greater than, or equal to another value that may be stored in a cell, select the block containing the cells you want to limit, and press ENTER. Next, select <=, =, or >= to select whether you want the cell's value to be less than or equal to, equal to, or greater than or equal to another value. Then, select the cell containing the value or type the value you want each cell in the block to be less than or equal to, equal to, or greater than or equal to, and press ENTER.

This step must be repeated for each constraint you want to add. For the problem in Figure 9.20, after you select Constraints and <Add New Constraint>, you will select B2, press ENTER, select >=, type 0, and press ENTER. If you later change you mind about a constraint, you can select Constraints, and then select the constraint that you want to modify in the list. You can repeat the selection of choosing a cell or block, then <=, =, or >=, and then the value or a cell with the value you want the first cell or the cells in the block to equal. You can also remove a constraint by highlighting it in the list of constraints and pressing DEL.

6. Select **Options**, and then select any of the options that you want to change as described later. You only need to perform this step if you want to change how Quattro Pro solves the problem you have created. You may only want to perform this step after you have tried solving the optimization problem once with the default settings. Do not forget to select **Quit** in the Options menu to return to the Optimizer menu.

7. Select **Answer Report**, and choose a cell where you want the answer report to start if you want one. For the sample problem, select J1, and press ENTER.

8. Select **Detail Report**, and choose a cell where you want the answer report to start if you want one. For the sample problem, select A30 and press ENTER.

9. Select **Go** and let Quattro Pro find the variables that will satisfy the constraints and optimize any solution cell you have selected.

At this point, you can select Quit to return to READY mode so you can see the new values (you can also press F6 (PANE)) to temporarily remove the menu and then press F6 (PANE) again. Another option is to select Restore to return the values in the variable cells to their original values. If you use Restore and you are using manual recalculation, you must press F9 (CALC) to update the formulas. If you want to start over, you can select Reset. Then you can select whether you want to reset some or all of the Optimizer's settings.

After you select Go, Quattro Pro puts the best values for the variable cells in those cells. When you return to the spreadsheet, you can look at the answer and detail report. Figure 9.21 shows the detail report created for the sample optimization problem. In this report Quattro Pro places the values of the variable cells and solution cell for each iteration Quattro Pro performs as it finds the solution. The number of columns this report uses is the number of variable cells and solution cell plus two, and the number of rows this report uses is the number of iterations plus 3. You would use this report when you want to see some of the intermediate values made in the Optimizer's calculations.

```
File   Edit   Style   Graph   Print   Database   Tools   Options   Window        ?  ↑↓
  ▲ ◀ ▶ ▼  Erase Copy Move Style Align Font Insert Delete Fit Sum Format CHR WYS
  A30:  [W15]  'Detail Report
            A              B            C          D         E         F
  30  Detail Report
  31                    Variable   Solution Cell:
  32                       B2
  33  Starting          20,000      $7,407
  34  Iteration 1       20,000      $7,407
  35  Iteration 2       17,218     $19,522
  36  Iteration 3       17,245     $19,523
  37  Final             17,245     $19,523
  38
  39
  40
  41  Solution Cell:
  42  +PROFIT           Maximize
  43  Variable Cells:
  44  @COUNT(NUMBER_OF_UNITS)
  45  Constraints:
  46  @COUNT(NUMB   >=               0
  47

  OPTIM.WQ1    [1]                               NUM          READY
```

Figure 9.21   Detail Report and Optimizer Model Settings

The answer report returns the values of the solution cell, variable cells, and constraint cells. An example of an answer report is shown at the top of Figure 9.22. Besides including information like cell addresses, starting and final values, and constraints, the answer report provides additional information. The Binding column tells you which of the constraints prevents the solution from equaling a higher or lower number. The Slack column indicates how are much the constraint cell's value must change before the constraint causes the solution to change. The Dual Value for the constraints indicates how much additional resources are worth. For example, if you are trying different product mixes and one of your departments is a binding constraint, the dual value indicates the value of increasing the department's capacity since increasing the department's capacity by one unit will increase the solution cell's value by the amount of the dual value. This means that if the cost of increasing the department's capacity is less than the dual value (the amount the solution will increase by adding the one unit), you would be better off increasing capacity.

If you have more than one optimization problem in a spreadsheet, you need to store the solution cells, variable cells, constraints, option settings, and report locations separately. You can put the settings for an optimization problem on the spreadsheet and then later when you want to use the same information for an optimization problem, you can tell Quattro Pro to use the information you have stored in the spreadsheet. To put the existing optimization problem information on the spreadsheet, use the /Tools Optimizer Model Save command and select a

482   *Quattro Pro 4.0 Handbook*

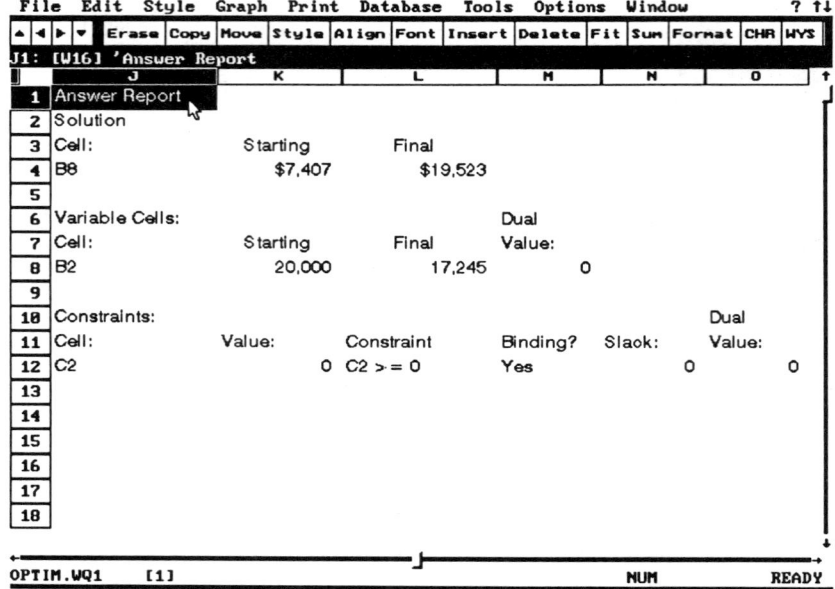

Figure 9.22   Answer Report Created with the Optimizer

cell in the spreadsheet where you want Quattro Pro to start placing the information. The bottom of Figure 9.21 shows a model added to a spreadsheet. When you want to use the optimization settings that are stored on a worksheet, select /Tools Optimizer Model Load, and select the block containing the optimization model.

Optimizer Options

The Optimizer has several option settings you can change that change how the Optimizer finds the best solution for your spreadsheet model. While you may not need to change these settings when you use the Optimizer, other times you might so you will want to know about the settings you can change. These are the following options you can change after you select **Options**.

- Max Time—This sets the maximum number of seconds the Optimizer can work on your problem. If the Optimizer does not find the solution within the time specified, Quattro Pro displays the message Maximum time exceeded. You can change the maximum time by typing a number between 1 and 1000 for the maximum number of seconds and pressing ENTER. The default is 100 seconds.
- Max Iterations—This sets the maximum number of iterations the Optimizer can work on your problem. If the Optimizer does not find the solution within the number of iterations specified, Quattro Pro displays the message

Advanced Analytical and File Features 483

Maximum iterations reached. You can change the maximum number of iterations by typing a number between 1 and 1000 and pressing ENTER. The default is 100 iterations.
- Precision—This sets how close a constraint cell value can be to its limit and still satisfy. For example, if a constraint limits a cell to being no more than 100 and precision is set to .5, then the number can be as high as 100.5 and still be within its limit. If the Optimizer does not find the solution that fulfills the constraints within the precision selected, Quattro Pro displays the message Maximum iterations reached or No feasible solution can be found. You can change the precision from the default of .0005 to any number between 0 and 1 by typing the number and pressing ENTER.
- Linear or Nonlinear—This selects whether the problem you are solving should be solved by linear or nonlinear problem solving techniques. Linear problems are solved faster, but nonlinear approaches can solve more types of problems. You can try selecting Linear to speed up the Optimizer. If the problem is nonlinear, Quattro Pro will display the message Linear model is not a valid assumption. If you get this message, select this option again, and choose Nonlinear.
- Show Iteration Results—This selects whether Quattro Pro pauses after each iteration so you can see how each iteration changed each cell. When you select Yes, Quattro Pro performs the first optimization iteration and then displays a menu box prompting Continue solution. Select Yes to continue with the next iteration or No to stop the optimization.
- Estimates—This sets how the Optimizer finds the initial estimates of the variable cells. The default of Tangent uses linear extrapolation from a tangent vector. You may want to choose the other option, Quadratic, if you are working with highly nonlinear problems.
- Derivatives—This sets how the Optimizer calculates partial derivatives, which are used in solving the problem. Most of the time you will want to leave this setting at the default of Forward; but if you get the message All remedies failed to find better point, then change this setting to Central.
- Search—This sets the direction the Optimizer pursues as it determines the best values for the optimization problem. Most of the time you will want to leave this setting at the default of Newton; but if you get the message Objective function changing too slowly, then change this setting to Conjugate.

As you modify these settings, you can also return all of them to the defaults with the /Tools Optimizer Reset Options command.

AUDITING SPREADSHEETS

When you are creating a new spreadsheet, you will want to test it to confirm that you have created it correctly. Quattro Pro 4 has new auditing features that make checking how a spreadsheet's formulas and values are dependent upon each other easier. You can use Quattro Pro's auditor to trace through formulas to see where

484 *Quattro Pro 4.0 Handbook*

values in one cell are used in other calculations or to see other cells that a cell's formula uses. You can also use Quattro Pro to find the spreadsheet formulas that reference blank cells, labels, cells that equal ERR, or reference data in other spreadsheets.

The information that Quattro provides with its /Tools Audit command can be displayed on the screen or printed. You can change where the output is sent by selecting /Tools Audit Destination and then selecting Screen or Print. When you print the output of another selection from the Audit menu, Quattro Pro uses the same print destination set by the /Print Destination command. When you are finished using the auditing features, select Quit to return to READY mode.

If you need to know all the formulas in a spreadsheet that depend on a value or another formula, you can use Quattro Pro's auditor. In prior releases, you would use the /Window Options Map View command to find all the cells with formulas and then look at them individually, or you would use the /Edit Search & Replace command. To see how a spreadsheet cell uses other cell entries and is used by other cell entries, select /Tools Audit Dependency, select a cell or a block of cells, and press ENTER. Then for each cell you have selected, Quattro Pro displays or prints a tree diagram of the cells that contain formulas that use that cell and the cells that the current cell, or *audited cell*, uses. If you are displaying it on the screen it will look like the one in Figure 9.23. Any cells on the left are formulas

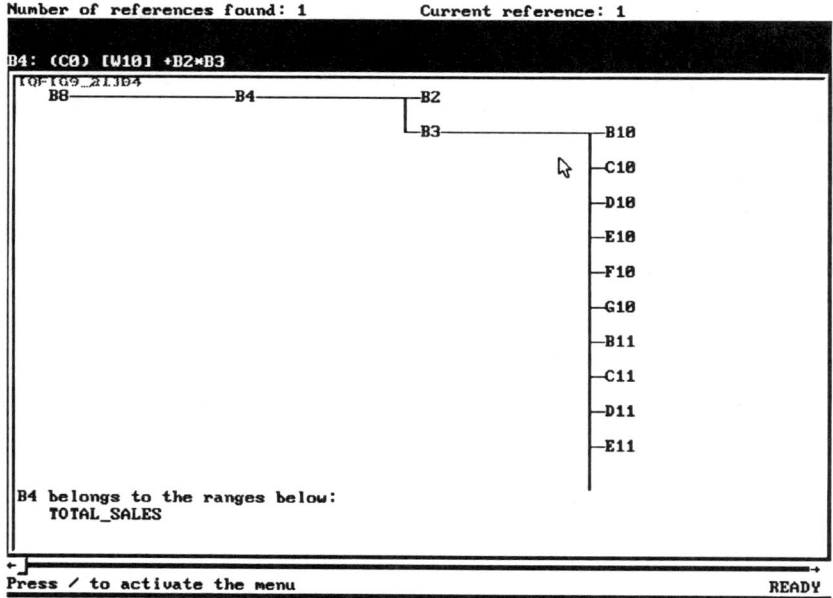

Figure 9.23 /Tools Audit Showing Formula Dependencies

that use the audited cell, and any cells on the right are cells that are used by the audited cell. If the audited cell is used by or uses cells on other spreadsheets, they will be included in the tree diagram if the other spreadsheets are open at the time. When you are displaying the tree diagram on the screen, you will have several options for using the tree that are not available if you print the tree diagram. You can move through this diagram by pressing the arrow keys or clicking a cell in the diagram. When you select another cell in the diagram, the top of the input line contains the cell's formula just as if you moved the selector to the cell. The Number of references found indicates the numbers of cells containing entries in the block you have selected for the command. To show the tree diagram of the next cell in the block you selected, press PGDN or type / for the menu, and select Next. You can also make a previous cell in the block the audited cell by pressing PGUP or selecting /Previous. You can also make the cell you are currently highlighting in the tree diagram the audited cell by pressing ENTER or selecting /Begin. When you want to leave the tree diagram, press ESC or select /Quit. Another option for leaving the tree diagram is to move to a cell in the diagram and then press F5 (GOTO) or select /GoTo.

A spreadsheet error that may cause problems is when the spreadsheet has a formula that references itself. This is called a *circular reference*. For example, you may be typing a formula in B2 that adds 100 to A2 and accidentally type B2. The formula, +B2+100 will increase by 100 every time the spreadsheet is recalculated regardless of whether the value in A2 changes. While you can display circular references as c's with the /Window Options Map View command, you can also display or print a tree diagram like the one you created with the /Tools Audit Dependency that focuses on circular references in the spreadsheet. Using the /Tools Audit Circular command instead lets you focus on multiple formulas that are part of the circular reference. When you have more than one circular reference, which you can tell by the number after "Number of references found," remember to use PGDN and PGUP or /Next and /Previous to see the other circular references.

You can also test out a spreadsheet to find which spreadsheet formulas refer to blank cells, labels, cells equaling ERR, or data in other spreadsheets. Selecting the /Tools Audit and then Blank References, Label References, ERR, or External Links creates a display like the one in Figure 9.24. The screen displays the file name and the cell that references the blank cell, label, ERR value, or external link formula. After Cell is the formula in the cell. If you selected Blank or External Links, the line below that is the cell address that the formula uses that is blank or refers to data in another spreadsheet. If the empty cell is part of a block used by the formula, then the line contains the block address that includes the blank cell. If you selected Label References or ERR, the second line contains the formula that contains the label or ERR reference. When you have more than one circular reference, which you can tell by the number after "Number of references found," remember to use PGDN and PGUP or /Next and /Previous to see the other blank, label, or ERR references. The features this command provides offer more information than if you used the /Window Options Map View to see which cells contain l or +.

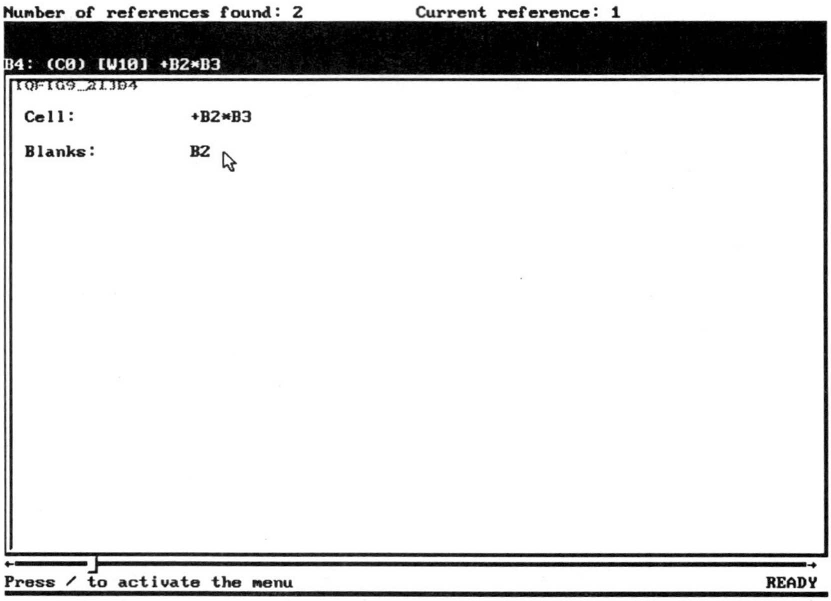

Figure 9.24 Audit Screen for Blank Cells

SAVING PART OF A FILE

When you use Quattro's /File Save command, you are saving the entire file. Quattro has another command that allows you to save only a portion of the file. This command is normally used to copy a section of a spreadsheet to another file, like copying the end-of-the-year totals in Figure 9.25 to the file YEAR_END. To save only a portion of a file, follow these steps:

1. Press / to activate the menu.
2. Select Tools Xtract.
3. Choose Formulas or Values to be extracted. If you select Formulas, Quattro saves the formulas in the extract block. As Quattro creates the extract file, absolute reference cells are adjusted as if you had moved them to the new spreadsheet. Formulas that reference cells outside the extract block can result in erroneous formulas or ERR in the extract file. If you choose Values, Quattro saves the formula's results (rather than the formulas) in the extract file.

   In the example in Figure 9.25, if the Year End column is extracted, the formula in F16, which adds the contents of F4 and F10, is copied to the new file if Formulas is chosen. If Values is chosen, the value 41,231 is extracted to the new file.

4. Select an existing file name (or type a new one), and press ENTER. In the example in Figure 9.25, the file name YEAR_END is typed.

```
 File   Edit   Style   Graph   Print   Database   Tools   Options   Window              ?  ↑↓
 ▲ ◀ ▶ ▼  Erase Copy Move Style Align Font Insert Delete Fit Sum Format CHR WYS
E1:  [W9]  "4th
              A                  B          C          D          E          F
  1                             1st        2nd        3rd        4th      Year End
  2                           Quarter    Quarter    Quarter    Quarter     Totals
  3   Product 1
  4   Number of Units Sold     4,210      4,125      4,275      4,464     17,074
  5   Average Cost Per Unit      3          3          3          3          3
  6   Cost of Units Sold       13,430     12,416     12,697     14,240     52,783
  7   Price of Units Sold      17,514     15,469     16,117     18,302     67,402
  8
  9   Product 2
 10   Number of Units Sold     5,732      6,120      6,555      5,750     24,157
 11   Average Cost Per Unit      6          6          6          6          6
 12   Cost of Units Sold       35,023     39,719     40,510     33,350    148,601
 13   Price of Units Sold      39,322     47,002     53,685     46,978    186,986
 14
 15   Total For All Products
 16   Number of Units Sold     9,942     10,245     10,830     10,214     41,231
 17   Average Cost Per Unit      5          5          5          5          5
 18   Cost of Units Sold       48,452    52,135     53,207     47,590    201,384
 19   Price of Units Sold      56,835    62,470     69,802     65,280    254,388

QFIG9_25.WQ1 [1]                                              NUM           READY
```

Figure 9.25 Computing Year-End Totals for Products

5. Select the block that you want to extract by typing a block address or a block name (or by highlighting the block using the arrow keys). For the spreadsheet in Figure 9.25, the block F1..F19 is selected. If the block contains any hidden columns, the hidden data is also extracted, and that column is hidden in the extracted file.

6. Press ENTER. If you select an existing file in step 4, you have the options of canceling the command, replacing the existing file with the block that you chose, or backing up the existing file before replacing it with the block that you chose. The block of extracted data begins at A1 in the new file regardless of its location in the original file. To use the new file, save the current spreadsheet and use the /File Open command using the file name you provided in step 4. The extract file YEAR_END looks like Figure 9.26.

Extract files have many of the characteristics of their original files. The extract file has all the original file's block names, even though the block names are meaningless if they refer to cells that are not part of the extract file. The extract file has the original file's settings for features such as numeric formats, column widths, and print settings.

THE COMBINING FILES COMMAND

Transferring totals from one report to another and producing consolidated reports by product line or division are tasks that must be handled by any business reporting

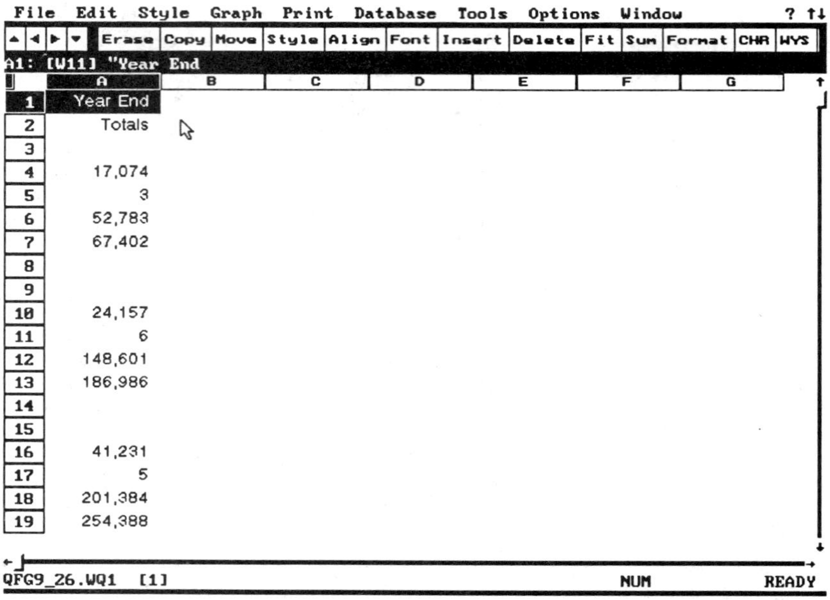

Figure 9.26 Year-End Totals Extracted to Another File as Values

package. Chapter 5 showed how to create formulas that use data in other spreadsheets. Quattro has another option for combining the data in spreadsheets. Before Quattro Pro, combining files though menu commands was the only way you could combine data from multiple spreadsheets. Quattro's /Tools Combine commands allow Quattro to meet this challenge with commands that are easy to use and flexible enough to work in a variety of situations. As you develop new spreadsheets, you may want to move information from another spreadsheet into the new spreadsheet. Also, you may want to combine several similar spreadsheets to produce a consolidated summary sheet of the information in each detailed spreadsheet.

The /Tools Xtract command covered earlier in the chapter allowed you to save part of a spreadsheet as a file on the disk. The /Tools Combine command produces the opposite effect by taking two spreadsheets or blocks within spreadsheets and combining them into one spreadsheet. When you combine spreadsheets, Quattro provides the options for copying, adding, and subtracting.

Copying Spreadsheets

The /Tools Combine Copy command is used to copy one spreadsheet to another spreadsheet. You can use the copy feature to transfer totals from one spreadsheet to another or to copy text entries stored in one sheet to another.

Quattro allows you to copy the contents of an entire file to the current spreadsheet. If you prefer to be more selective in copying information, you can copy a block from a spreadsheet file.

Advanced Analytical and File Features 489

Regardless of whether you use the contents of a block or an entire file, the replacement of the cells in the current spreadsheet begins at the location of the selector. The extent of the replacement is determined by the number of cells you are copying from the spreadsheet file. Each cell from the spreadsheet file that you select replaces a cell in the current spreadsheet with a number, label, or formula.

Figure 9.27 displays a template for computing an income statement with the income from operations for all four product lines. Figure 9.28 displays the spreadsheet for computing the income from operations for the first product line in column B. The /Tools Combine Copy command can be used to combine data in these two spreadsheets by following these steps:

1. Retrieve the spreadsheet that displays the income from operations for Product 1. Since you only need the actual figures for Product 1, the block containing the required data is named in preparation for the combine operation.

▼ **TIP: Use block names with the /Tools Combine commands.**

When you use the /Tools Combine commands with blocks, name the blocks you are using, since block names are easier to remember.

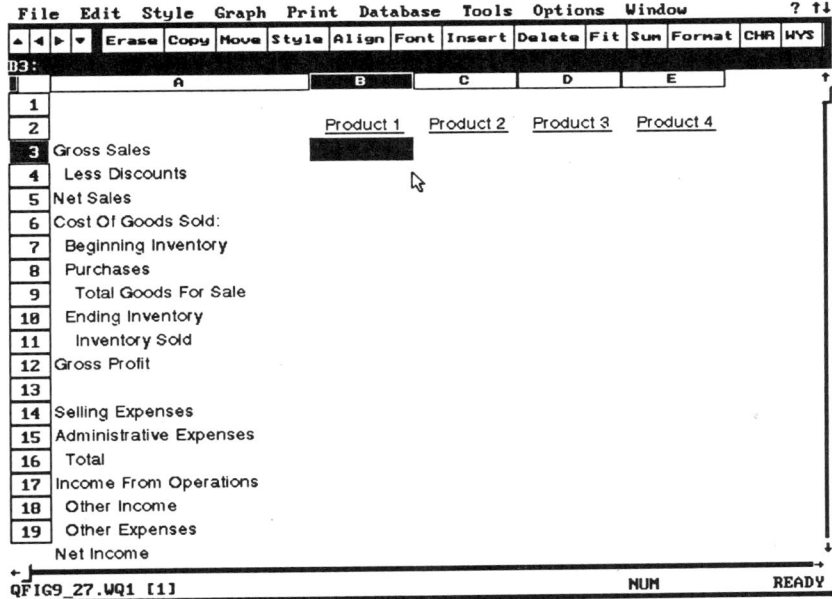

Figure 9.27 Template for Computing Net Income

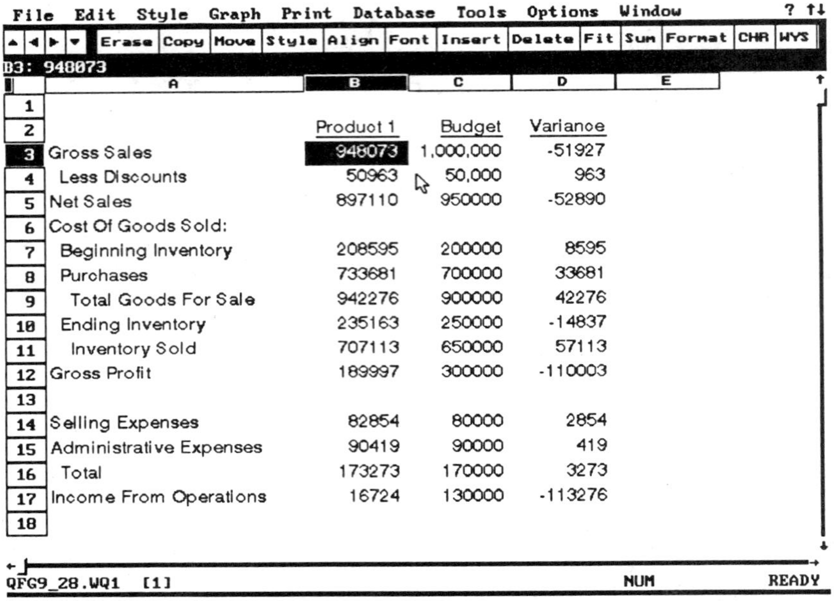

```
    File  Edit  Style  Graph  Print  Database  Tools  Options  Window        ? ↑↓
    ▲ ◄ ► ▼  Erase Copy Move Style Align Font Insert Delete Fit Sum Format CHR WYS
    B3: 948073
                  A              B           C           D          E
    1
    2                        Product 1    Budget    Variance
    3   Gross Sales           948073    1,000,000   -51927
    4     Less Discounts        50963       50,000      963
    5   Net Sales              897110      950000   -52890
    6   Cost Of Goods Sold:
    7     Beginning Inventory  208595      200000     8595
    8     Purchases            733681      700000    33681
    9     Total Goods For Sale 942276      900000    42276
   10     Ending Inventory     235163      250000   -14837
   11     Inventory Sold       707113      650000    57113
   12   Gross Profit           189997      300000  -110003
   13
   14  Selling Expenses         82854       80000     2854
   15  Administrative Expenses  90419       90000      419
   16     Total                173273      170000     3273
   17  Income From Operations   16724      130000  -113276
   18

    QFG9_28.WQ1  [1]                                      NUM        READY
```

Figure 9.28 Spreadsheet Showing Net Income for Product 1

2. Move the selector to the number for gross sales in B3.
3. Type / to activate the menu, and select **Edit Names Create**.
4. Type a name for the block that you are about to create using a maximum of 15 characters (PRODUCT1 in this example).
5. Move the selector to cover the entire area that you are going to combine into another file (B3..B17 for the Product 1 example).
6. Press ENTER. Although steps 2 through 6 can be replaced by typing the address of the block that you want to combine, using a block name helps reduce errors.
7. Save your file by typing / and selecting **File** and **Save** or by pressing CTRL-S.
8. Retrieve the file that contains the consolidated income template for all product lines by typing / and selecting **File** and **Retrieve**.
9. Move the selector to the location for the Product 1 information, B3.
10. Activate the menu by typing / and select **Tools Combine Copy**.
11. Select **Block** from the selection box shown in Figure 9.29. If you choose File, Quattro blocks off the data in the other file and places it at the location of the selector. When you select Block, Quattro inserts only the block that you specify at the selector's location.
12. Type the name that you assigned to the block in step 4 (PRODUCT1), and press ENTER. You can also specify the block to combine by entering the

Advanced Analytical and File Features 491

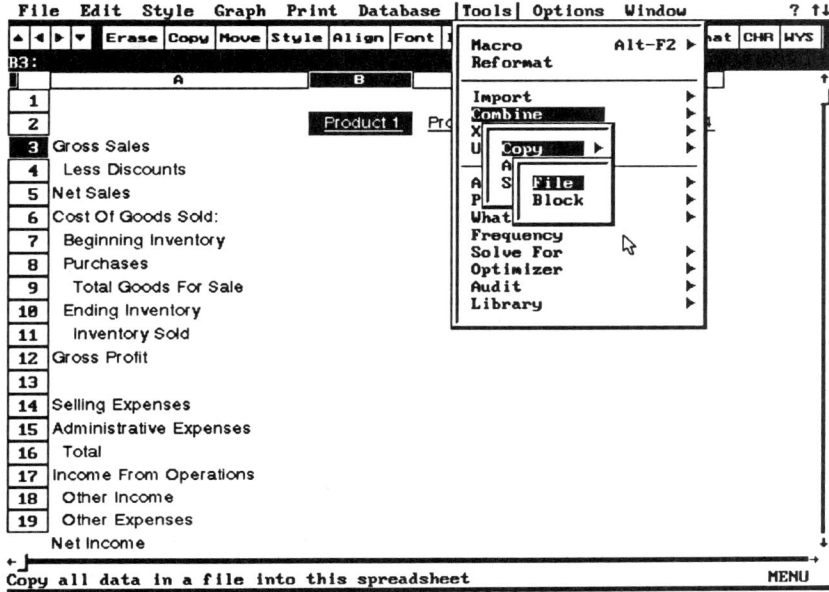

Figure 9.29 Menu for Selecting Whether to Copy a File or Block

address of the block. However, block names are easier to remember and should be used whenever possible.

13. Type the name of the disk file that contains the block, and press ENTER. Quattro copies the block into the spreadsheet, as shown in Figure 9.30. To add the numbers for the other three product lines, save the new file and repeat the process starting from step 1 for each of the other product files.

Whether Quattro copies a block or an entire file, it leaves all formulas intact. For example, in the spreadsheet in Figure 9.30, the formula in B5 subtracts the discounts for Product 1 in B4 from the gross sales for Product 1 in B3. This formula was present in the Product 1 file in Figure 9.28. If a block that you copy contains formula references that refer to an area outside the block being copied, frequently the formulas no longer provide accurate results in the new model. One way of copying values without formulas is to choose **Add** instead of **Copy**. However, this solution is only effective if the area that the block is combined with is blank. Another option is to use the **/Tools Xtract** command on the block that you want to transfer and choose **Values** instead of **Formulas**.

Adding Spreadsheets

Adding entries from one spreadsheet to another combines the values from two spreadsheets. The **/Tools Combine Add** command adds the values from a disk file

```
B3: 948073
                                      A                          B           C          D          E
   1
   2                                                         Product 1   Product 2  Product 3  Product 4
   3   Gross Sales                                             948073
   4      Less Discounts                                        50963
   5   Net Sales                                               897110
   6   Cost Of Goods Sold:
   7      Beginning Inventory                                  208595
   8      Purchases                                            733681
   9      Total Goods For Sale                                 942276
  10      Ending Inventory                                     235163
  11      Inventory Sold                                       707113
  12   Gross Profit                                            189997
  13
  14   Selling Expenses                                         82854
  15   Administrative Expenses                                  90419
  16      Total                                                173273
  17   Income From Operations                                   16724
  18      Other Income
  19      Other Expenses
         Net Income
```

Figure 9.30 Product 1's Information Copied to Template Spreadsheet

to the current spreadsheet by using either the entire disk file or a block of entries. This command provides the perfect solution for budget consolidations and all types of hierarchical rollups. The addition is determined by the location of the selector in the current spreadsheet. The first cell in the disk file is added to the cell containing the selector. Subsequent additions are based on the offset on the disk and the current spreadsheet. Cells on the disk containing labels and formulas are ignored. Adding spreadsheets copies and combines the values instead of copying the formulas that create the values.

You can choose to add an entire file or a block. If you elect to combine a block, you can specify your selection with a block address or a block name.

Figure 9.31 shows the income from operations computed for Product 1 for the first four months of the year. Figure 9.32 shows the income from operations computed for Product 2 for the first four months of the year. To produce a model containing the combined total for the two products, follow these steps:

1. Retrieve the spreadsheet that contains the income from operations for Product 1 by typing /, selecting **File Retrieve**, and typing the name of the file.

2. Save the file under another name by typing / and selecting **File Save As** and typing a new name. In this example, TOTALS is used, since the model for Product 1 will be modified to show the total of the two products.

3. Move to A1, which is where you want Quattro to begin adding information. In this example, you are adding the entire file. When you add a file, the order of the spreadsheet entries must be identical.

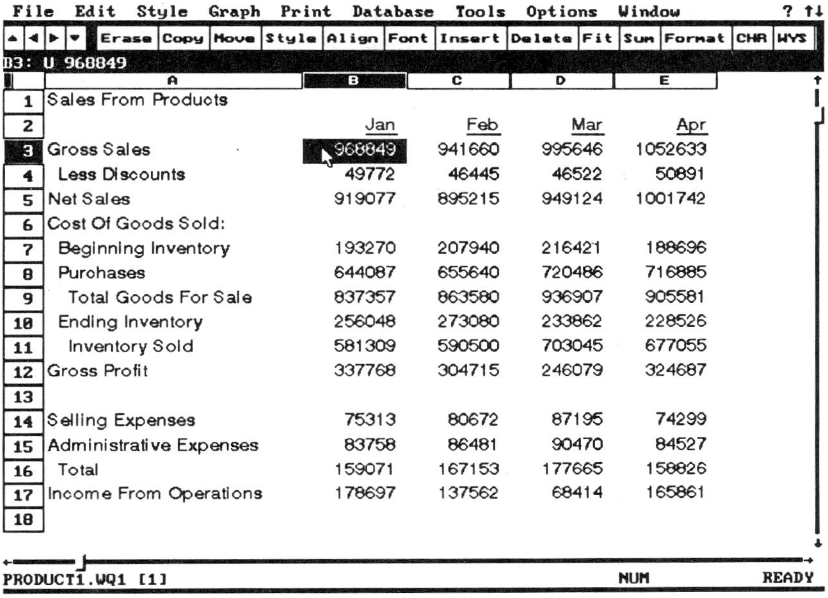

Advanced Analytical and File Features 493

	A	B	C	D	E
1	Sales From Products				
2		Jan	Feb	Mar	Apr
3	Gross Sales	968849	941660	995646	1052633
4	Less Discounts	49772	46445	46522	50891
5	Net Sales	919077	895215	949124	1001742
6	Cost Of Goods Sold:				
7	Beginning Inventory	193270	207940	216421	188696
8	Purchases	644087	655640	720486	716885
9	Total Goods For Sale	837357	863580	936907	905581
10	Ending Inventory	256048	273080	233862	228526
11	Inventory Sold	581309	590500	703045	677055
12	Gross Profit	337768	304715	246079	324687
13					
14	Selling Expenses	75313	80672	87195	74299
15	Administrative Expenses	83758	86481	90470	84527
16	Total	159071	167153	177665	158826
17	Income From Operations	178697	137562	68414	165861
18					

Figure 9.31 Spreadsheet showing Income for Product 1 for Four Months

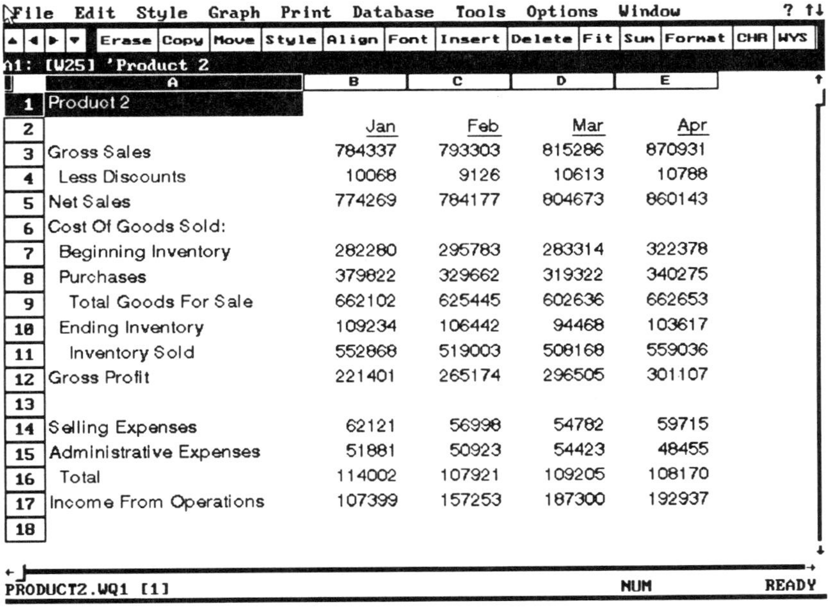

	A	B	C	D	E
1	Product 2				
2		Jan	Feb	Mar	Apr
3	Gross Sales	784337	793303	815286	870931
4	Less Discounts	10068	9126	10613	10788
5	Net Sales	774269	784177	804673	860143
6	Cost Of Goods Sold:				
7	Beginning Inventory	282280	295783	283314	322378
8	Purchases	379822	329662	319322	340275
9	Total Goods For Sale	662102	625445	602636	662653
10	Ending Inventory	109234	106442	94468	103617
11	Inventory Sold	552868	519003	508168	559036
12	Gross Profit	221401	265174	296505	301107
13					
14	Selling Expenses	62121	56998	54782	59715
15	Administrative Expenses	51881	50923	54423	48455
16	Total	114002	107921	109205	108170
17	Income From Operations	107399	157253	187300	192937
18					

Figure 9.32 Spreadsheet Showing Income for Product 2 for Four Months

4. Activate the menu by typing / and select **Tools Combine Add**.
5. Select **File** from the selection box like the one shown in Figure 9.29. This setting adds the contents of both files. If you choose **Block**, you have to specify the block as described in the previous section for copying a block of data from one spreadsheet to another.
6. Type the name of the file used to store the data that you want to add to the current spreadsheet, and press ENTER. In this example, it is PRODUCT2.
7. Type a new description for the spreadsheet in A1. The final result looks like Figure 9.33. If you have more product spreadsheets to add, repeat the process starting from step 3.

When Quattro adds a block or file into another spreadsheet, it changes all the incoming formulas into values; however, formulas in the first spreadsheet remain intact. For example, after the two spreadsheets in the example are combined, B5 still contains the formula which subtracts the discounts in B4 from the gross sales in B3. When you add two spreadsheets together, you must make sure that they have the numbers in the same cells. For example, if you had added the spreadsheet in Figure 9.34 to the one in Figure 9.31, you would get meaningless results. Figure 9.34 has an extra row at the top for describing the spreadsheet. When these two spreadsheets are added, Figure 9.35 results.

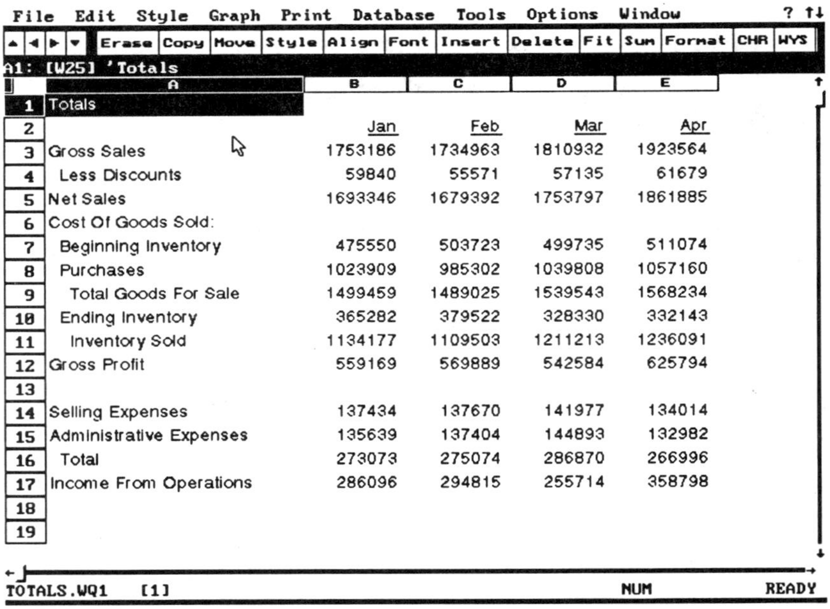

	A	B	C	D	E
1	Totals				
2		Jan	Feb	Mar	Apr
3	Gross Sales	1753186	1734963	1810932	1923564
4	Less Discounts	59840	55571	57135	61679
5	Net Sales	1693346	1679392	1753797	1861885
6	Cost Of Goods Sold:				
7	Beginning Inventory	475550	503723	499735	511074
8	Purchases	1023909	985302	1039808	1057160
9	Total Goods For Sale	1499459	1489025	1539543	1568234
10	Ending Inventory	365282	379522	328330	332143
11	Inventory Sold	1134177	1109503	1211213	1236091
12	Gross Profit	559169	569889	542584	625794
13					
14	Selling Expenses	137434	137670	141977	134014
15	Administrative Expenses	135639	137404	144893	132982
16	Total	273073	275074	286870	266996
17	Income From Operations	286096	294815	255714	358798

Figure 9.33 Spreadsheet Showing Combined Income for Products 1 and 2

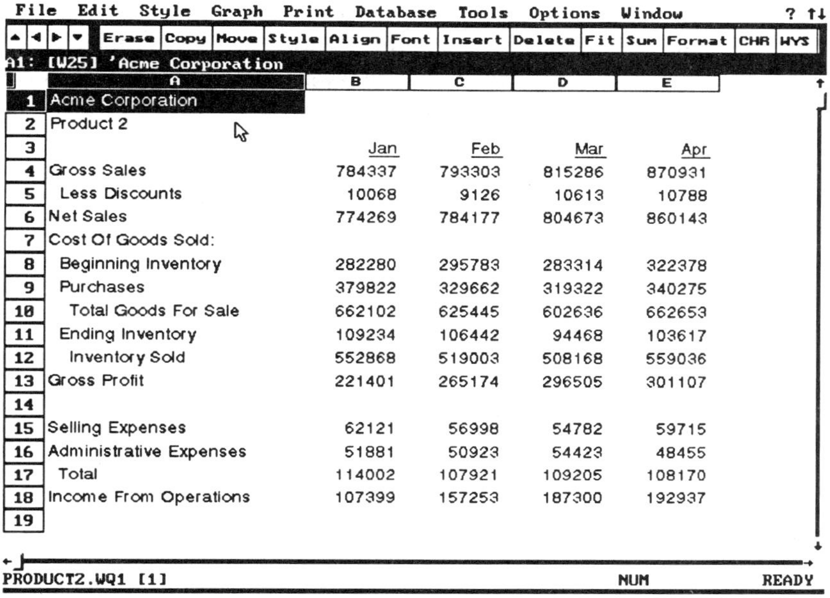

Advanced Analytical and File Features 495

```
File   Edit   Style   Graph   Print   Database   Tools   Options   Window         ? ↑↓
 ▲ ◄ ► ▼  Erase|Copy|Move|Style|Align|Font|Insert|Delete|Fit|Sum|Format|CHR|WYS
A1: [W25] 'Acme Corporation
```

	A	B	C	D	E
1	Acme Corporation				
2	Product 2				
3		Jan	Feb	Mar	Apr
4	Gross Sales	784337	793303	815286	870931
5	Less Discounts	10068	9126	10613	10788
6	Net Sales	774269	784177	804673	860143
7	Cost Of Goods Sold:				
8	Beginning Inventory	282280	295783	283314	322378
9	Purchases	379822	329662	319322	340275
10	Total Goods For Sale	662102	625445	602636	662653
11	Ending Inventory	109234	106442	94468	103617
12	Inventory Sold	552868	519003	508168	559036
13	Gross Profit	221401	265174	296505	301107
14					
15	Selling Expenses	62121	56998	54782	59715
16	Administrative Expenses	51881	50923	54423	48455
17	Total	114002	107921	109205	108170
18	Income From Operations	107399	157253	187300	192937
19					

PRODUCT2.WQ1 [1]   NUM   READY

Figure 9.34 Income for Product 2 in a Different Format

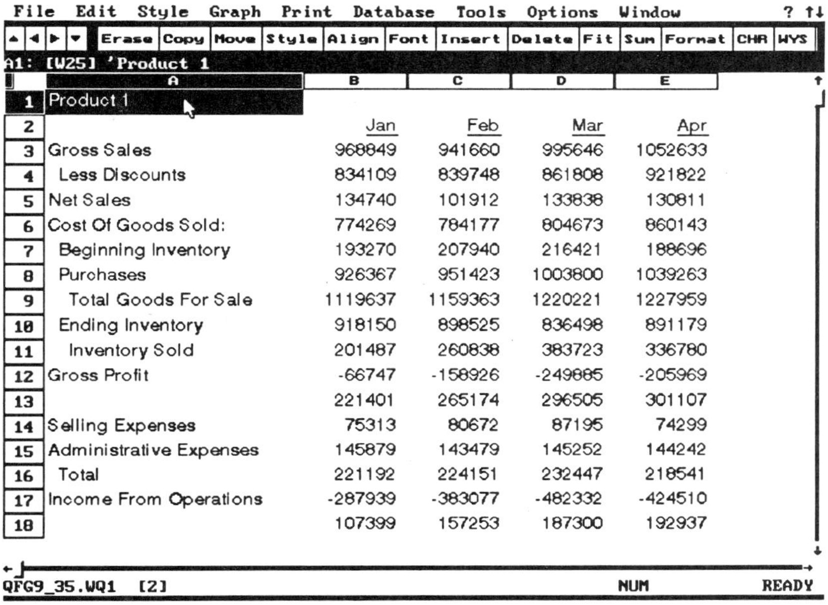

```
File   Edit   Style   Graph   Print   Database   Tools   Options   Window         ? ↑↓
 ▲ ◄ ► ▼  Erase|Copy|Move|Style|Align|Font|Insert|Delete|Fit|Sum|Format|CHR|WYS
A1: [W25] 'Product 1
```

	A	B	C	D	E
1	Product 1				
2		Jan	Feb	Mar	Apr
3	Gross Sales	968849	941660	995646	1052633
4	Less Discounts	834109	839748	861808	921822
5	Net Sales	134740	101912	133838	130811
6	Cost Of Goods Sold:	774269	784177	804673	860143
7	Beginning Inventory	193270	207940	216421	188696
8	Purchases	926367	951423	1003800	1039263
9	Total Goods For Sale	1119637	1159363	1220221	1227959
10	Ending Inventory	918150	898525	836498	891179
11	Inventory Sold	201487	260838	383723	336780
12	Gross Profit	-66747	-158926	-249885	-205969
13		221401	265174	296505	301107
14	Selling Expenses	75313	80672	87195	74299
15	Administrative Expenses	145879	143479	145252	144242
16	Total	221192	224151	232447	218541
17	Income From Operations	-287939	-383077	-482332	-424510
18		107399	157253	187300	192937

QFG9_35.WQ1 [2]   NUM   READY

Figure 9.35 Result of Combining Spreadsheets That Are in Different Formats

When Quattro adds spreadsheets, it replaces values in the first spreadsheet with the sum of the original value and the value in the incoming spreadsheet. Quattro assumes that labels and blank cells have a value of zero when they are added to a number. Also, any incoming values or formulas with a value of @NA or @ERR are changed to 0. Entries of @NA or @ERR in the current spreadsheet are not changed. When you add two labels together, Quattro uses the label from the current spreadsheet and ignores the label from the spreadsheet on disk. Also, Quattro uses the cell formats of the first spreadsheet.

Subtracting Spreadsheets

The /Tools Combine Subtract command allows you to subtract information on a disk from cells on the current spreadsheet. Like the Combine Add and Copy commands, the position of the selector controls the operation of subtract. The command uses values in the disk file, subtracting them from current spreadsheet cells with an identical offset.

You can choose either one block or the entire disk file as the extent of this command. In either case, label and formula entries are ignored.

Subtracting one spreadsheet from another is often used after producing a consolidation to look at the impact of discontinuing a portion of a business. The result of the /Tools Combine Subtract command tells you how the rest of the business would perform without the discontinued segment. If you discontinue a segment, the base that you use to allocate your fixed costs shrinks and the remaining business must compensate for these costs; the /Tools Combine Subtract command can show you this. Figure 9.33 contains the totals for all stores for the company's two product lines. Figure 9.36 shows the items in the income from operations that are eliminated by discontinuing Store 1 for the first four months of the year. By subtracting the two spreadsheets, you can compute what the performance of the company is when Store 1 is discontinued. To subtract the numbers in two spreadsheets, follow these steps:

1. Retrieve the spreadsheet containing the total income from operations for all products by typing /, selecting File Retrieve, typing the name of the file, and pressing ENTER.

2. Save the file under another name by typing / and selecting File Save As and typing a new name. In this example, DIFFER is used. Saving the file is not necessary, but it is a good idea to leave your original intact in the event that you need to return to it.

3. Move to A1, which is where you want Quattro to begin subtracting information. Just as when you add files, the two spreadsheets must be in the same format to produce correct results.

4. Activate the menu by typing / and selecting Tools Combine Subtract.

5. Select File, since you are subtracting the entire file. If you had chosen Block,

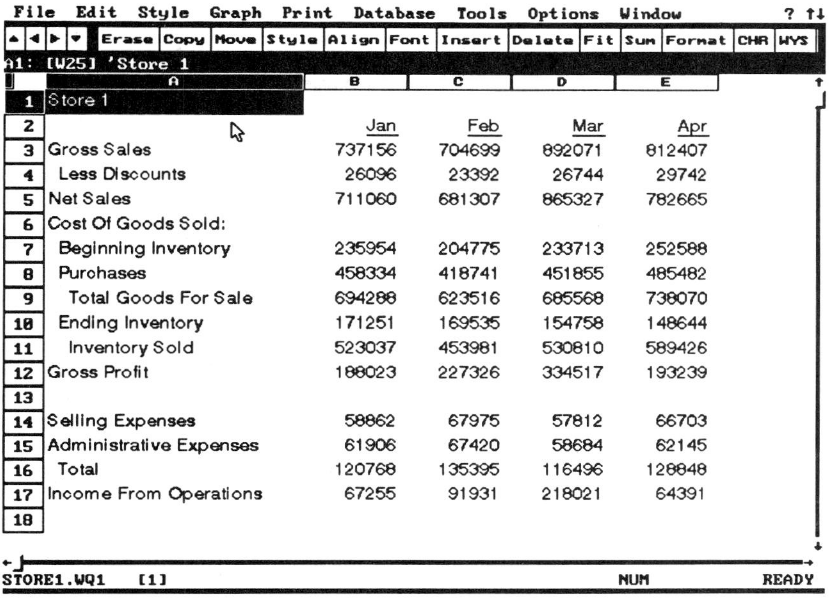

```
File   Edit   Style   Graph   Print   Database   Tools   Options   Window        ? ↑↓
▲ ◀ ▶ ▼  Erase Copy Move Style Align Font Insert Delete Fit Sum Format CHR WYS
A1:  [W25]  'Store 1
           A              B        C        D        E
 1  Store 1
 2                       Jan      Feb      Mar      Apr
 3  Gross Sales        737156   704699   892071   812407
 4    Less Discounts    26096    23392    26744    29742
 5  Net Sales          711060   681307   865327   782665
 6  Cost Of Goods Sold:
 7    Beginning Inventory 235954  204775   233713   252588
 8    Purchases         458334   418741   451855   485482
 9    Total Goods For Sale 694288 623516  685568   738070
10    Ending Inventory  171251   169535   154758   148644
11    Inventory Sold    523037   453981   530810   589426
12  Gross Profit       188023   227326   334517   193239
13
14  Selling Expenses    58862    67975    57812    66703
15  Administrative Expenses 61906 67420   58684    62145
16    Total            120768   135395   116496   128848
17  Income From Operations 67255  91931   218021   64391
18

STORE1.WQ1  [1]                              NUM        READY
```

Figure 9.36 Income for Store 1 for Four Months

you would have had to specify the block (as described in the earlier section for copying one spreadsheet into another).

6. Type the name of the spreadsheet that you want to subtract from the current spreadsheet, and press ENTER. In this example, it is **STORE_1**. When Quattro has subtracted the two spreadsheets, the final result looks like Figure 9.37.

When Quattro subtracts a block or spreadsheet from another, it changes all the incoming formulas into values; however, formulas in the first spreadsheet remain intact. For example, after the two spreadsheets in the example are subtracted, B5 still contains the formula that subtracts the discounts in B4 from the gross sales in B3. As for adding spreadsheets, subtracting spreadsheets requires that the two spreadsheets have the same format (the example for adding files in Figure 9.35 shows what happens when the formats do not match).

When Quattro subtracts spreadsheets, it replaces values in the current spreadsheet with the difference between the current values and the values in the spreadsheet on disk. Quattro assumes that labels and blank cells have a value of zero when they are subtracted from a number. Also, any incoming values equal to @NA or @ERR are changed to 0. Entries of @NA or @ERR in the current spreadsheet are not changed. When you subtract two labels, Quattro uses the label from the current spreadsheet and ignores the label from the spreadsheet on disk. Also, Quattro keeps the cell formats of the current spreadsheet.

IMPORTING DATA

When you bring data from another package into Quattro, you are *importing* data. Quattro provides automatic translation features for importing data from packages like 1-2-3 and dBASE (as discussed in Chapter 5) with the **/File Retrieve** or the **/File Open** command. For data in different format, you have several options. One popular one is to bring in text files as Quattro labels. For this method of importing data, Quattro has a command that breaks the imported long-label entries into individual cell entries.

Quattro can also import data in which the data are separated by commas on each line and labels are enclosed in quotes. When you import this type of a file, Quattro splits the information into cells for you. Sometimes you want to bring data into Quattro, but Quattro cannot translate the data with the **File Retrieve** or the **/File Open** command. Then you must use the **/Tools Import** command.

If your data are not in one of the formats that Quattro can automatically translate, it needs to be in one of three other formats. Quattro can import data that are in an ASCII text file. A sample ASCII text file is shown in Figure 9.38. Most word processors can create files like this with a special menu command or a utility program. The word processor files themselves often contain special characters used for features such as word wrapping and special fonts. Some packages can also create these types of files by printing the data you want to import to a file.

Another type of format that Quattro can import is *delimited* files. Delimited files

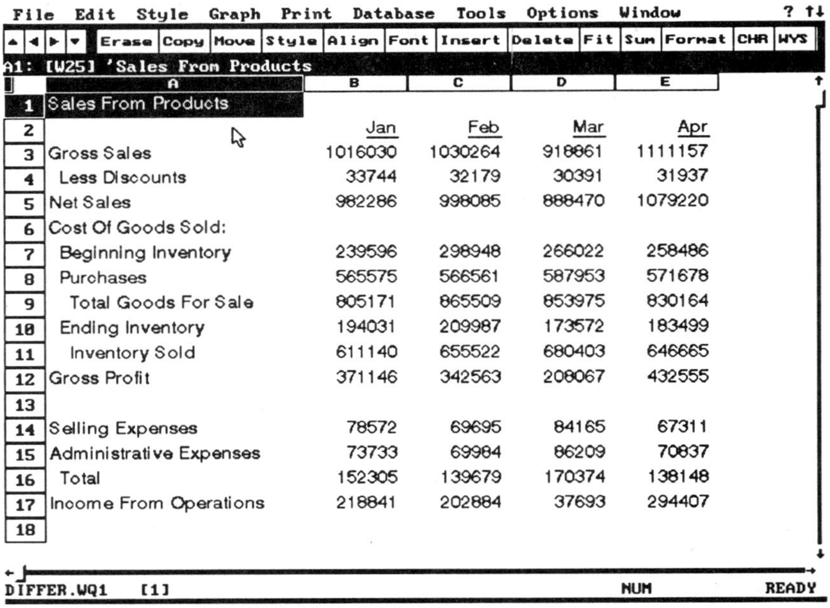

	A	B	C	D	E
1	Sales From Products				
2		Jan	Feb	Mar	Apr
3	Gross Sales	1016030	1030264	918861	1111157
4	Less Discounts	33744	32179	30391	31937
5	Net Sales	982286	998085	888470	1079220
6	Cost Of Goods Sold:				
7	Beginning Inventory	239596	298948	266022	258486
8	Purchases	565575	566561	587953	571678
9	Total Goods For Sale	805171	865509	853975	830164
10	Ending Inventory	194031	209987	173572	183499
11	Inventory Sold	611140	655522	680403	646665
12	Gross Profit	371146	342563	208067	432555
13					
14	Selling Expenses	78572	69695	84165	67311
15	Administrative Expenses	73733	69984	86209	70837
16	Total	152305	139679	170374	138148
17	Income From Operations	218841	202884	37693	294407
18					

Figure 9.37 Company's Performance Without Store 1

```
C:\QPRO\CH9>type qfig_38.prn
42124 Smith, Eliza        Mutual Insurance       500  04/28/88  08:30 AM
25939 Von Steiner, John   Healthcare Systems     500  02/24/88  08:40 AM
42141 Bond, Greg          Blue Cross             500  05/04/88  08:50 AM
58631 Ostrosky, Joan      Blue Shield            200  01/09/88  09:00 AM
22621 Hull, Mary          Acme Inc. Trust Fund   250  02/01/88  09:10 AM
99512 Larson, Karen       Blue Shield            250  10/11/87  09:20 AM
15338 Doe, Dave           Monumental Life        100  10/23/87  09:30 AM
23835 Winchester, Sue     USF&G                  500  12/23/87  09:40 AM
91189 Campbell, Keith     Blue Cross             500  12/01/87  09:50 AM
74466 Grant, Frank        Travelers Insurance    100  11/05/87  10:00 AM
15982 Petrowski, Heather  Monumental Life        500  01/16/88  10:10 AM
89350 Demoura, Liza       Mutual Insurance       500  01/23/88  10:20 AM
63158 Lawrence, Mike      Maryland Casualty      500  02/23/88  10:30 AM
44871 Martin, Amy         USF&G                   50  06/14/87  10:40 AM
82423 Ventzke, Blair      Blue Cross             200  03/10/88  10:50 AM
28627 Watts, Peg          Prudential Insurance   250  10/16/87  11:00 AM
41263 Medici, George      Blue Cross             200  11/20/87  11:10 AM
56464 Perez, Steve        USF&G                  200  03/15/88  11:20 AM
58810 Stevens, Melissa    Healthcare Systems     100  03/08/88  11:30 AM
63678 George, Charles     Blue Shield            100  11/11/87  11:40 AM

C:\QPRO\CH9>
```

Figure 9.38 Sample ASCII Text File

have the different items of data separated by commas. Some delimited files have all the information between the commas in double quotes. Quattro can accept a delimited file either with quotes or without quotes. The advantage of enclosing character data in quotes is that the character data can include commas such as "LJM Partners, LTD". In a delimited file that does not use the double quotes, the comma after Partners makes LTD the next data entry—shifting the remaining entries by one column. A sample file of delimited data with character text enclosed in double quotes is shown in Figure 9.39, and the same file delimited without double quotes is shown in Figure 9.40.

When you import an ASCII text file, Quattro puts all the text in each line in one cell and then moves to the cell below it to import the next line of text. When you import a delimited file, Quattro puts each piece of information between the commas in a cell going from left to right and moves to the next line below for the next line in the delimited file. To import a file in one of these formats, follow these steps:

1. Retrieve the spreadsheet into which you want to import data or erase the current spreadsheet after saving it.
2. Press /, and select Tools and Import.
3. Select either (1) ASCII Text File, (2) Comma & "" Delimited File, or (3) Only Commas. If your file looks like Figure 9.38 with lines of text and no separator characters, choose ASCII Text File. If your file looks like Figure 9.39 with commas separating the different pieces of information and quotes surrounding labels, choose Comma & "" Delimited File. If your file looks

```
C:\QPRO\CH9>type qfig_39.prn
"Eliza Smith","842 Euclid Avenue","Elyria","OH","44136"
"John Von Steiner","2507 E. 115 Street","Pompano","OH","44192"
"Greg Bond","4602 Lorain Avenue","Elyria","OH","44130"
"Joan Ostrosky","9114 Chester Avenue","Painesville","OH","44157"
"Mary Hull","2766 Ivanhoe","Gates Mills","OH","44196"
"Karen Larson","6002 W. 107th Street","Elyria","OH","44196"
"Dave Doe","9629 East Blvd","Cleveland","OH","44116"
"Sue Winchester","2918 Snow Road","Gates Mills","OH","44108"
"Keith Campbell","9727 Riverside Street","Shaker Heights","OH","44189"
"Frank Grant","3442 Cornell Road","Shaker Heights","OH","44198"
"Heather Petrowski","4772 Jefferson Avenue","Gates Mills","OH","44163"
"Liza Demoura","2083 Commercial Blvd","Elyria","OH","44180"
"Mike Lawrence","1445 White Road","Elyria","OH","44146"
"Amy Martin","4782 Kippling","Elyria","OH","44146"
"Blair Ventzke","1522 Cedar Avenue","Elyria","OH","44170"
"Peg Watts","7631 County Line Road","Gates Mills","OH","44163"
"George Medici","5891 Sunrise Boulevard","Painesville","OH","44166"
"Steve Perez","9105 W. 13th Street","Painesville","OH","44107"
"Melissa Stevens","6463 Juniper Road","Parma","OH","44158"
"Charles George","3317 Westminister Avenue","Shaker Heights","OH","44199"

C:\QPRO\CH9>
```

Figure 9.39   Sample Comma and Double Quote Delimited File

```
C:\QPRO\CH9>Type qfig_40.prn
Eliza Smith,842 Euclid Avenue,Elyria,OH,44136
John Von Steiner,2507 E. 115 Street,Pompano,OH,44192
Greg Bond,4602 Lorain Avenue,Elyria,OH,44130
Joan Ostrosky,9114 Chester Avenue,Painesville,OH,44157
Mary Hull,2766 Ivanhoe,Gates Mills,OH,44196
Karen Larson,6002 W. 107th Street,Elyria,OH,44196
Dave Doe,9629 East Blvd,Cleveland,OH,44116
Sue Winchester,2918 Snow Road,Gates Mills,OH,44108
Keith Campbell,9727 Riverside Street,Shaker Heights,OH,44189
Frank Grant,3442 Cornell Road,Shaker Heights,OH,44198
Heather Petrowski,4772 Jefferson Avenue,Gates Mills,OH,44163
Liza Demoura,2083 Commercial Blvd,Elyria,OH,44180
Mike Lawrence,1445 White Road,Elyria,OH,44146
Amy Martin,4782 Kippling,Elyria,OH,44146
Blair Ventzke,1522 Cedar Avenue,Elyria,OH,44170
Peg Watts,7631 County Line Road,Gates Mills,OH,44163
George Medici,5891 Sunrise Boulevard,Painesville,OH,44166
Steve Perez,9105 W. 13th Street,Painesville,OH,44107
Melissa Stevens,6463 Juniper Road,Parma,OH,44158
Charles George,3317 Westminister Avenue,Shaker Heights,OH,44199

C:\QPRO\CH9>
```

Figure 9.40   Sample Comma Delimited File

like Figure 9.40 with commas separating the different pieces of information, choose **O**nly Commas.

4. Choose the name of the file that you want to import by typing the name or by moving in the file selection box to the file that you want and pressing ENTER. Quattro lists all the files in the current directory with a .PRN file extension. If your file does not have a .PRN file extension, press ESC, type ***.***, and press ENTER to list all possible files in the current subdirectory. You can use the same keys and buttons you use with the **/F**ile **R**etrieve commands.

When the data in Figure 9.39 are imported, the results look like Figure 9.41. In this example, each person's name is in column A, the address is in column B, the city is in column C, the state is in column D, and the zip code is in column E. Each row contains the information about a different person. Since each column is in the default width, the information looks congested. A sample of a ASCII text file imported is shown in Figure 9.42. In this example, all the information for each person is contained in column A. However, you can break the information up into cells with the **/T**ools **P**arse command discussed below.

EXPORTING DATA

When you send data from Quattro to another package, you are *exporting* data. Quattro provides automatic translation features with the **/F**ile **S**ave and **/F**ile **S**ave

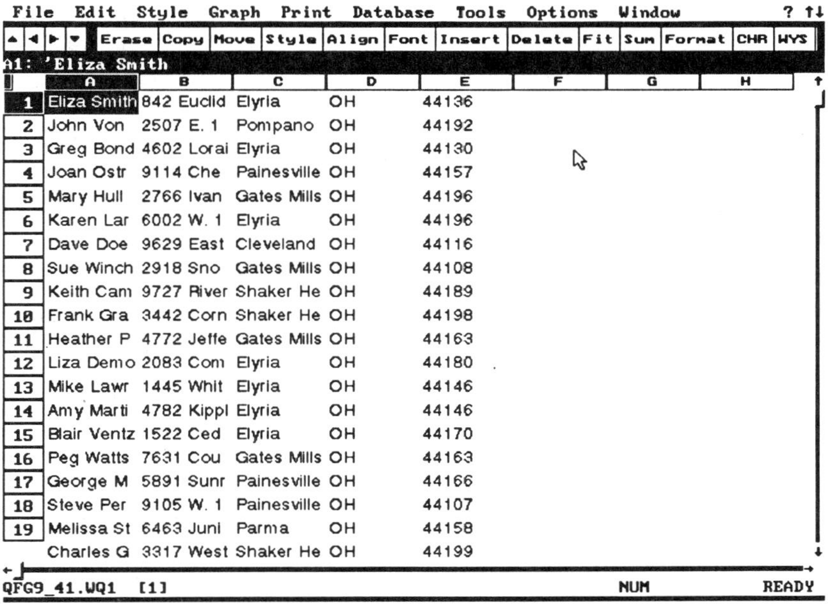

	A	B	C	D	E	F	G	H
1	Eliza Smith	842 Euclid	Elyria	OH	44136			
2	John Von	2507 E. 1	Pompano	OH	44192			
3	Greg Bond	4602 Lorai	Elyria	OH	44130			
4	Joan Ostr	9114 Che	Painesville	OH	44157			
5	Mary Hull	2766 Ivan	Gates Mills	OH	44196			
6	Karen Lar	6002 W. 1	Elyria	OH	44196			
7	Dave Doe	9629 East	Cleveland	OH	44116			
8	Sue Winch	2918 Sno	Gates Mills	OH	44108			
9	Keith Cam	9727 River	Shaker He	OH	44189			
10	Frank Gra	3442 Corn	Shaker He	OH	44198			
11	Heather P	4772 Jeffe	Gates Mills	OH	44163			
12	Liza Demo	2083 Com	Elyria	OH	44180			
13	Mike Lawr	1445 Whit	Elyria	OH	44146			
14	Amy Marti	4782 Kippl	Elyria	OH	44146			
15	Blair Ventz	1522 Ced	Elyria	OH	44170			
16	Peg Watts	7631 Cou	Gates Mills	OH	44163			
17	George M	5891 Sunr	Painesville	OH	44166			
18	Steve Per	9105 W. 1	Painesville	OH	44107			
19	Melissa St	6463 Juni	Parma	OH	44158			
	Charles G	3317 West	Shaker He	OH	44199			

Figure 9.41 Sample Comma and Double Quote Delimited File Imported into Quattro

```
File  Edit  Style  Graph  Print  Database  Tools  Options  Window            ?  ↑↓
A1: '42124 Smith, Eliza         Mutual Insurance        500   04/28/92  08:30
     A          B         C          D       E         F        G        H    ↑End
1   42124 Smith, Eliza         Mutual Insurance       500    04/28/92  08:30  ■ ▲
2   25939 Von Steiner, John    Healthcare Systems     500    02/24/92  08:40  ◄ ►
3   42141 Bond, Greg           Blue Cross             500    05/04/92  08:50  ▼
4   58631 Ostrosky, Joan       Blue Shield            200    01/09/92  09:00
5   22621 Hull, Mary           Acme Inc. Trust Fund   250    02/01/92  09:10  ERS
6   99512 Larson, Karen        Blue Shield            250    10/11/91  09:20
7   15338 Doe, Dave            Monumental Life        100    10/23/91  09:30  CPY
8   23835 Winchester, Sue      USF&G                  500    12/23/91  09:40
9   91189 Campbell, Keith      Blue Cross             500    12/01/91  09:50  MOV
10  74466 Grant, Frank         Travelers Insurance    100    11/05/91  10:00
11  15982 Petrowski, Heather   Monumental Life        500    01/16/92  10:10  STY
12  89350 Demoura, Liza        Mutual Insurance       500    01/23/92  10:20
13  63158 Lawrence, Mike       Maryland Casualty      500    02/23/92  10:30  ALN
14  44871 Martin, Amy          USF&G                   50    06/14/91  10:40
15  82423 Ventzke, Blair       Blue Cross             200    03/10/92  10:50  FNT
16  28627 Watts, Peg           Prudential Insurance   250    10/16/91  11:00
17  41263 Medici, George       Blue Cross             200    11/20/91  11:10  INS
18  56464 Perez, Steve         USF&G                  200    03/15/92  11:20
19  58810 Stevens, Melissa     Healthcare Systems     100    03/08/92  11:30  BAR
20  63678 George, Charles      Blue Shield            100    11/11/91  11:40
QFG9_42.WQ1  [1]                                             NUM          READY
```

Figure 9.42 Sample ASCII Text File Imported into Quattro

As commands for packages like 1-2-3, Reflex, Paradox, and dBASE. When you need to send data to a package for which Quattro does not provide automatic translation, you can capture the data in an ASCII text file using the /Print commands.

When you need to transfer your spreadsheet to a software package that Quattro does not automatically translate as it saves, you must print your spreadsheet to a file. When you print to a file, you must make some minor adjustments before printing the information. These changes make the conversion process easier by excluding information that is used when you print your spreadsheet to the printer. To print your spreadsheet to a file, follow these steps:

1. Change the display mode to text mode if you are displaying the spreadsheet in a graphics mode by selecting /Options Display Mode and selecting an appropriate display mode. Then select Quit to return to READY mode. Since characters take less room in a cell in a graphics display mode, you will want to use a text display mode to insure that the file you will create has all the data.

2. Enlarge the columns to display their contents by moving the selector to the first column, entering /Style Block Size Auto Width or clicking Fit in the SpeedBar, and selecting all data you want to export. This sets each column to be as wide as necessary to export the data. Since the printed file only contains the information that is visible, you must make sure the spreadsheet displays all the information that you want in the file.

Advanced Analytical and File Features

3. Remove all page breaks and setup strings in the block that you are exporting.
4. Press /, and select **Print Destination** and **File**.
5. Type the name of the file that you want the information sent to or move the selector to an existing .PRN file that Quattro lists in the superimposed box, and press ENTER. Do not add an extension unless you want something other than Quattro's .PRN default.
6. Press ENTER.
7. If the file already exists, you can cancel your request, replace the old file with the new one, save the old file with a .BAK extension before replacing the file with the new one, or append the new data to the existing file.
8. Select **Block** and select the block address or name that you want to export.
9. Select **Layout** (and **Margins** if you do not see the Print Layout Options dialog box). Set the Left, the Top, and the Bottom margins to 0. Also, set the Right margin to 511 characters (240 in earlier releases). Even if your spreadsheet is less than 511 characters wide, setting the right margin at the maximum prevents your spreadsheet from being divided into sections. Eliminating the other margins removes the blank space that the margins would add.
10. Select **Quit** to return to the Layout menu.
11. Eliminate automatic page breaks by selecting **Break Pages** from the Page Layout menu and choosing **No**. Changing this setting eliminates page breaks, headers, and footers.
12. Remove any setup strings by selecting **Setup String**, pressing ESC, and pressing ENTER.
13. Select **Quit** to return to the Print menu, and select **Spreadsheet Print**.
14. Select **Quit** to return to the READY mode and close the print file. Quattro prints your information to the disk file.

To use the file that you have just printed, quit the Print menu, save your spreadsheet, use the package into which you want to import the spreadsheet data, and import the ASCII file that the print command creates.

SPLITTING THE LONG LABELS

When you import ASCII files, Quattro combines the information in one line into a long label. Although you can use the @LEFT, @RIGHT, and @MID function to break up these labels, the /Tools Parse command is quicker and more effective when the information is in column format. Like exporting to a file, you will want to use the /Tools Parse command after setting the display mode to something other than graphics mode. This allows you to see how your data align in columns. To break up long labels, follow these steps.

1. Move the selector to the first label that you want to split up. Using the example in Figure 9.42, move the selector to cell A1.

2. Press **/**, and select **Tools Parse**.

3. Select **Create**. This inserts a row above your data and fills that row with a format line. The format line represents Quattro's best guess for how the labels should be split. Figure 9.43 shows a sample line created by this command. Each of the characters in a format line has a special meaning.

4. Select **Edit**. By changing this format line, you change how Quattro splits your data. When you edit the format line, whatever you type replaces the character underneath it unless you press the INS key to switch from the Overwrite mode into Insert mode. Also, Quattro does not let you type a character that it does not understand as part of the format line. The characters that Quattro uses as part of a format line are shown in Table 9.1.

For this example, you need to make the following changes:

- Replace the second L and the asterisk before it with greater than symbols (>).
- Replace the asterisks above the names with greater than symbols (>).
- Replace the asterisks above the insurance companies with greater than symbols (>).

When you have finished, press ENTER. Your format line should look like the one in Figure 9.44.

5. Select **Input** and select the labels that you are parsing. In this example, you are parsing A1 to A21. You must include the format line; otherwise, Quattro

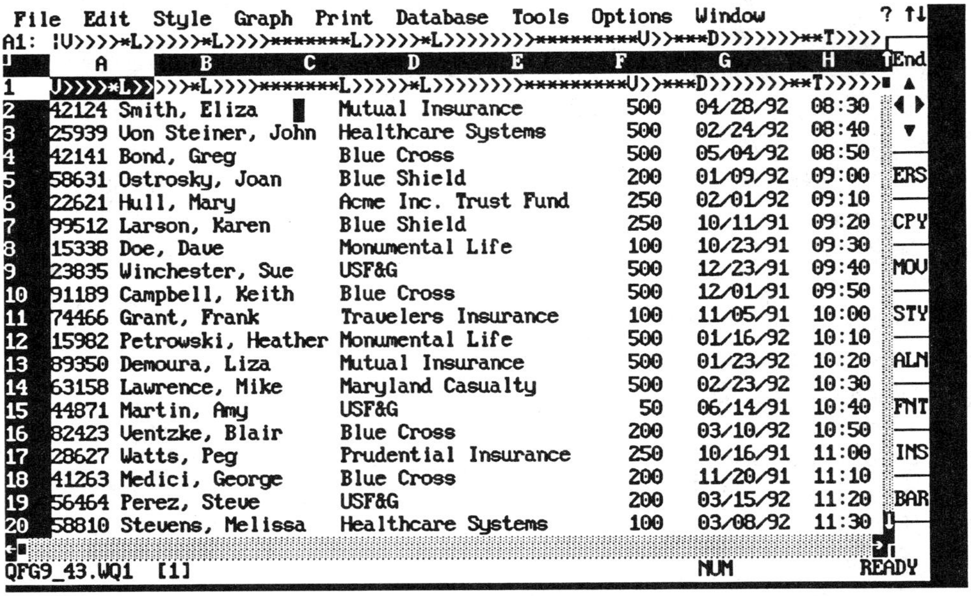

Figure 9.43 Format Line Created by Quattro for Parsing Labels

Advanced Analytical and File Features 505

Table 9.1 Characters Used in a Command Line for /File Parse

Character	Usage
|	Marks the beginning of the format line. This only appears when you edit the line from the Ready mode similarly to how the alignment characters only appear in cell labels when the labels are edited.
V	Marks the beginning of a value entry.
L	Marks the beginning of a label entry.
D	Marks the beginning of a date. Quattro can convert the date label into a date serial number.
T	Marks the beginning of a time. Quattro can convert the time label into a time serial number.
S	Marks a column position that Quattro should skip over when parsing the data.
>	Continues an entry started by a V, L, D, or T.
*	Indicates a blank space.

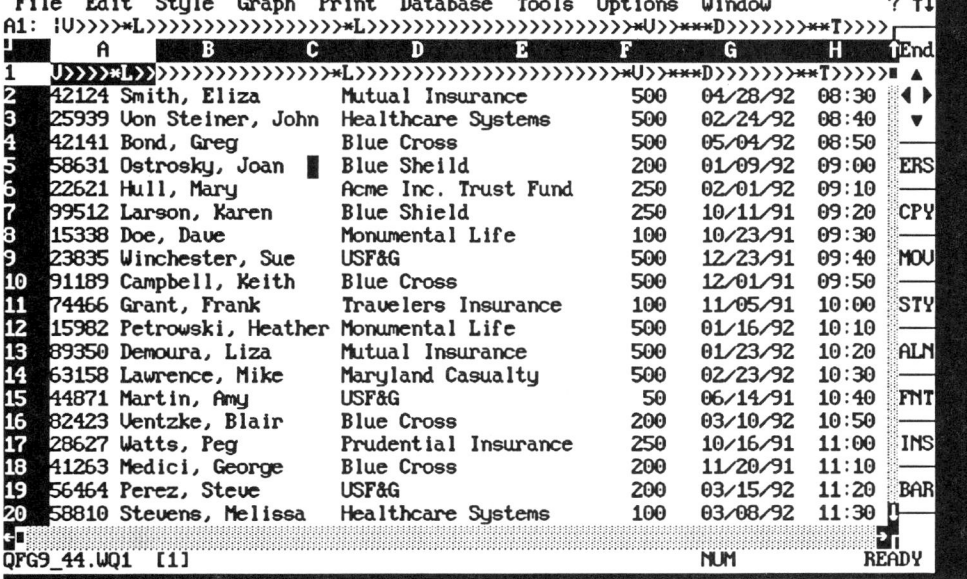

Figure 9.44 Format Line Edited to Parse Data Correctly

displays an error message when you start parsing. Since all the labels are in column A, you only have to select that column and do not have to include the columns used to display the long-label entries.

6. Select **Output** and move the selector to where you want Quattro to put the parsed information. You need to select an area that has adequate space. In this example, A25 is selected, since this spreadsheet does not contain entries beyond row 21.

7. Select **Go**. Quattro parses the data and places the output where you have indicated. When you look at the output (see Figure 9.45), the data appear to be truncated due to the current cell widths. However, all the data are present. You can change the formats and widths to display the parsed data in a more readable format. Columns representing date and time entries always require formatting since the default display shows the data and time serial numbers. Figure 9.46 shows the data after it has been parsed, the columns have been widened, and the date and time columns have been formatted properly and the display mode has returned to WYSIWYG.

If you are missing part of your data, you may need to edit the format line and reparse the data. When you reparse the data, you do not need to redefine the input, output, or create a new format line.

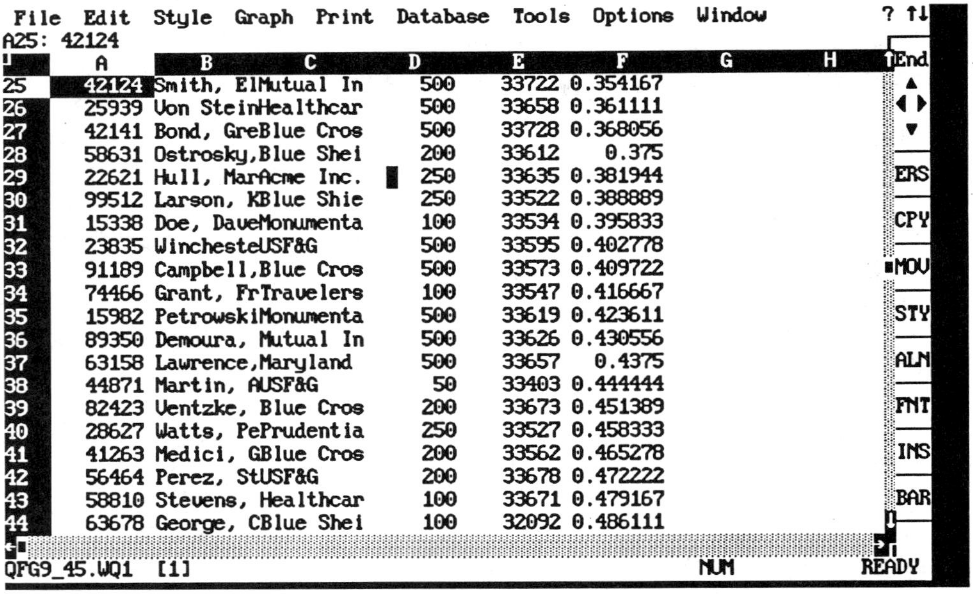

Figure 9.45 Parsed Data

Advanced Analytical and File Features 507

```
File  Edit  Style  Graph  Print  Database  Tools  Options  Window        ? ↑↓
▲ ◀ ▶ ▼  Erase Copy Move Style Align Font Insert Delete Fit Sum Format CHR WYS
A25: [W7] 42124
```

	A	B	C	D	E	F
25	42124	Smith, Eliza	Mutual Insurance	500	04/28/92	08:03 AM
26	25939	Von Steiner, John	Healthcare Systems	500	02/24/92	08:04 AM
27	42141	Bond, Greg	Blue Cross	500	05/04/92	08:05 AM
28	58631	Ostrosky, Joan	Blue Shield	200	01/09/92	09:00 AM
29	22621	Hull, Mary	Acme Inc. Trust Fund	250	02/01/92	09:01 AM
30	99512	Larson, Karen	Blue Shield	250	10/11/91	09:02 AM
31	15338	Doe, Dave	Monumental Life	100	10/23/91	09:03 AM
32	23835	Winchester, Sue	USF&G	500	12/23/91	09:04 AM
33	91189	Campbell, Keith	Blue Cross	500	12/01/91	09:05 AM
34	74466	Grant, Frank	Travelers Insurance	100	11/05/91	10:00 AM
35	15982	Petrowski, Heather	Monumental Life	500	01/16/92	10:01 AM
36	89350	Demoura, Liza	Mutual Insurance	500	01/23/92	10:02 AM
37	63158	Lawrence, Mike	Maryland Casualty	500	02/23/92	10:03 AM
38	44871	Martin, Amy	USF&G	50	06/14/91	10:04 AM
39	82423	Ventzke, Blair	Blue Cross	200	03/10/92	10:05 AM
40	28627	Watts, Peg	Prudential Insurance	250	10/16/91	11:00 AM
41	41263	Medici, George	Blue Cross	200	11/20/91	11:01 AM
42	56464	Perez, Steve	USF&G	200	03/15/92	11:02 AM
43	58810	Stevens, Melissa	Healthcare Systems	100	03/08/92	11:03 AM
	63678	George, Charles	Blue Shield	100	11/11/91	11:04 AM

```
QFG9_46.WQ1  [1]                                        NUM          READY
```

Figure 9.46 Parsed Data with Columns Widened and the Date and Time Columns Formatted Properly

GETTING STARTED

This chapter covered the more complex analytical and file manipulation commands. You should review the section for any feature covered in this chapter before using it for your own applications. However, you can try two of these features (a sensitivity analysis and a frequency distribution) by following these steps to create the spreadsheet in Figure 9.47:

1. Make the following entries:

   B1: "**Last Year**
   C1: "**% Change**
   D1: "**Forecast**
   A2: **Sales**
   B2: **1000000**
   D2: **+B2*(1+C2)**
   A3: **COGS**
   B3: **600000**
   D3: **+B3*(1+C3)**
   A4: **Profit**
   B4: **+B2-B3**
   D4: **+D2-D3**

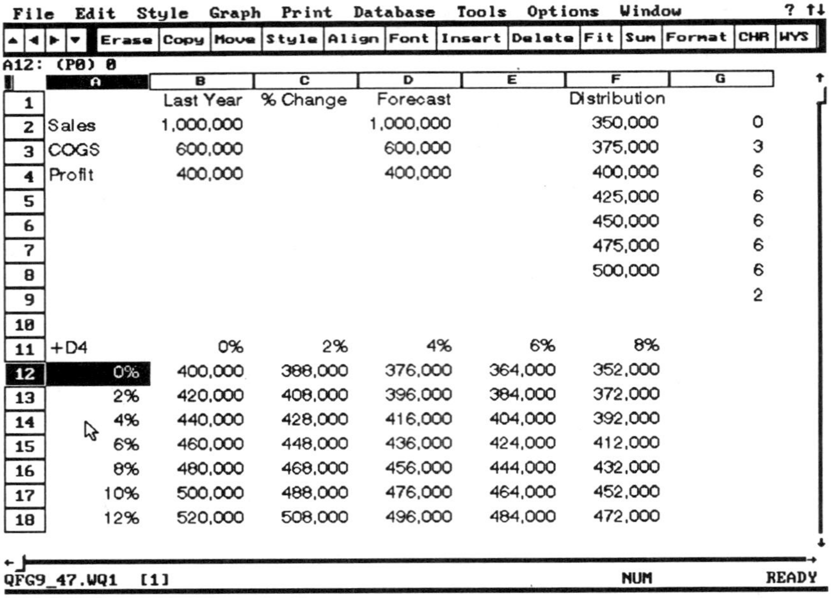

```
File   Edit   Style   Graph   Print   Database   Tools   Options   Window          ? ↑↓
▲ ◀ ▶ ▼ │Erase│Copy│Move│Style│Align│Font│Insert│Delete│Fit│Sum│Format│CHR│WYS│
A12: (P0) 0
```

	A	B	C	D	E	F	G
1		Last Year	% Change	Forecast		Distribution	
2	Sales	1,000,000		1,000,000		350,000	0
3	COGS	600,000		600,000		375,000	3
4	Profit	400,000		400,000		400,000	6
5						425,000	6
6						450,000	6
7						475,000	6
8						500,000	6
9							2
10							
11	+D4		0%	2%	4%	6%	8%
12		0%	400,000	388,000	376,000	364,000	352,000
13		2%	420,000	408,000	396,000	384,000	372,000
14		4%	440,000	428,000	416,000	404,000	392,000
15		6%	460,000	448,000	436,000	424,000	412,000
16		8%	480,000	468,000	456,000	444,000	432,000
17		10%	500,000	488,000	476,000	464,000	452,000
18		12%	520,000	508,000	496,000	484,000	472,000

```
QFG9_47.WQ1  [1]                                          NUM              READY
```

Figure 9.47   Spreadsheet Created in Getting Started Section

2. Create a shell for a two-way table that computes the profits for different rates of growth in sales and cost of goods sold. Move to A11. Type +D4, and press the DOWN ARROW or click A12. Enter /Edit Fill. When Quattro prompts for a block, select A12..A18, and press ENTER (or click [Enter] in the input line). When Quattro prompts for a start value, press ENTER (or click Enter in the box) to select the default of 0. When Quattro prompts for a step value, type .02 and either press ENTER or click Enter in the box. When Quattro prompts for a stop value, press ENTER (or click Enter in the box) to accept the default of 8,191. Move to B6. Enter /Edit Fill. When Quattro prompts for a block, press BACKSPACE, type a period, select B11..F11, and either press ENTER or click [Enter] in the input line. When Quattro prompts for a start value, press ENTER (or click Enter in the box) to select the default of 0. When Quattro prompts for a step value, press ENTER (or click Enter in the box) to accept the previous value of 0.02. When Quattro prompts for a stop value, press ENTER (or click Enter in the box) to accept the default of 8,191.

3. Fill the shell with the profits that would result from different growth rates for cost of goods sold and sales. Enter /Tools What-If 2 Variables. When Quattro prompts for a block, select A11..F18 and either press ENTER or click [Enter] in the input line. When Quattro prompts for the input cell for the column values, select C2 and either press ENTER or click [Enter] in the input line. When Quattro prompts for the input cell for the row values,

Advanced Analytical and File Features 509

select C3 and either press ENTER or click [Enter] in the input line. Quattro fills the table with the profit that would be returned for each combination of sales and cost of goods sold growth. Select **Q**uit to return to READY mode.

4. Create a frequency table. Move to F1. Type **Distribution** and press the DOWN ARROW (or click F1). Enter /**E**dit **F**ill. When Quattro prompts for a block, press BACKSPACE, type a period, select F2..F8, and either press ENTER or click [Enter] in the input line. When Quattro prompts for a start value, type **350000** and either press ENTER or click Enter in the box. When Quattro prompts for a step value, type **25000** and either press ENTER or click Enter in the box. When Quattro prompts for a stop value, type **500000** and either press ENTER or click Enter in the box. Enter /**T**ools **F**requency. When Quattro prompts for a block containing the values, select B12..F18 and either press ENTER or click Enter in the input line. When Quattro prompts for a block containing the bin values, select F2..F8 and either press ENTER or click [Enter] in the input line. Quattro fills column G with the distribution of the values you generated with the two-variable table.

5. Format the cells and widen the column. Enter /**O**ptions **F**ormats **N**umeric **F**ormat **,** (financial). Type **0** and either press ENTER or click Enter in the box.

6. Widen the columns, since some of the cells appear as asterisks. Select **G**lobal **W**idth. Press the RIGHT ARROW to expand the column widths to 10 and press ENTER or click [Enter] in the input line. Select **Q**uit twice to return to the READY mode.

7. Format the formula in A11 as text. Move to A11. Press CTRL-F or click Format in the SpeedBar to enter /**S**tyle **N**umeric **F**ormat. Select **T**ext. When Quattro prompts for a block to format, press ENTER (or click [Enter] in the input line).

8. Format the percentages. Move to B11. Press CTRL-F or click Format in the SpeedBar to enter /**S**tyle **N**umeric **F**ormat. Select **P**ercent. Type **0**, and either press ENTER or click the Enter button in the box. When Quattro prompts for a block to format, select B11..F11. Press ENTER or click [Enter] in the input line. Move to A12. Press CTRL-F or click Format in the SpeedBar to enter /**S**tyle **N**umeric **F**ormat. Select **P**ercent. Type **0** and either press ENTER or click the Enter button in the box. When Quattro prompts for a block to format, select A12..A18. Press ENTER or click [Enter] in the input line. The spreadsheet now looks like Figure 9.47.

10
Customizing Quattro Pro

Once you have mastered Quattro's basic features, you can consider customizing some of Quattro's settings. Customizing Quattro's settings increases your performance with Quattro by eliminating some of the changes that you make for each session and by allowing you to set up the menus, which offer the package's features, to meet your specific needs. Quattro is customized by changing the default settings and by changing the menu structure with its Menu Builder.

Several of the customization commands were covered in earlier chapters along with the specific features they affect. This chapter summarizes the commands covered earlier and includes others that have not been discussed, thus providing a one-stop reference for customizing Quattro. This chapter also covers Quattro's Menu Builder, which lets you customize Quattro's menu.

While a few commands have their own defaults and methods to change them, most of the customizing commands are found in the Options menu shown in Figure 10.1. This menu is accessed by typing a/ and selecting **Options**. The Options menu lets you change the settings for the hardware, the spreadsheet colors, the currency and punctuation symbols, the format settings, the directories, how the spreadsheet is recalculated, the protection status, and the information that Quattro uses when the program is loaded. These default settings can be altered for the current spreadsheet or all spreadsheets. When you have finished selecting the customization options, select **Quit** to return to the READY mode. All menus either return you to the previous menu or provide a **Quit** option for you to select when you have finished with the menu.

Quattro has two types of customization options. System customization options affect how Quattro performs. These options include the spreadsheet colors, the number of lines on the screen, and the buttons available on the SpeedBar. These options are available using the menu selections above Update in the Options menu. In Quattro Pro 3 and 4, you can see many of these settings by selecting **Values** from the Options menu to create a display like the one in Figure 10.2, which

512 *Quattro Pro 4.0 Handbook*

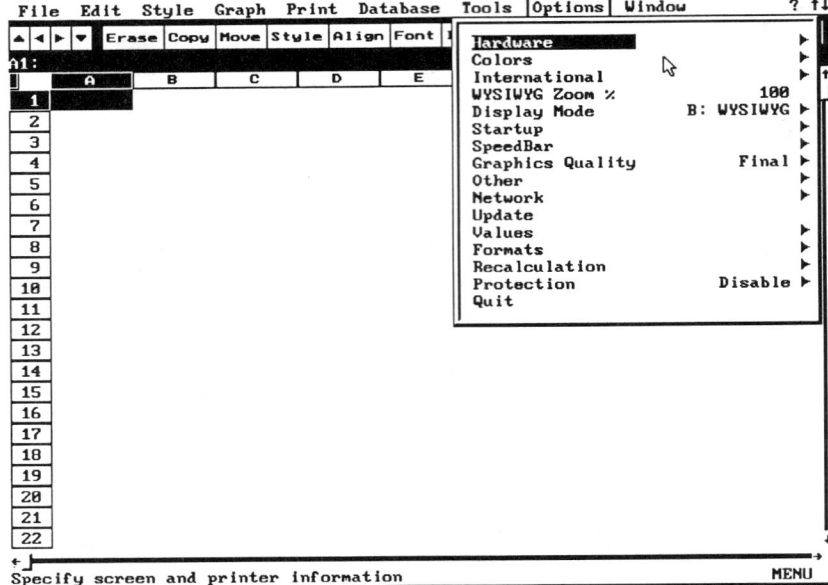

Figure 10.1 Options Menu

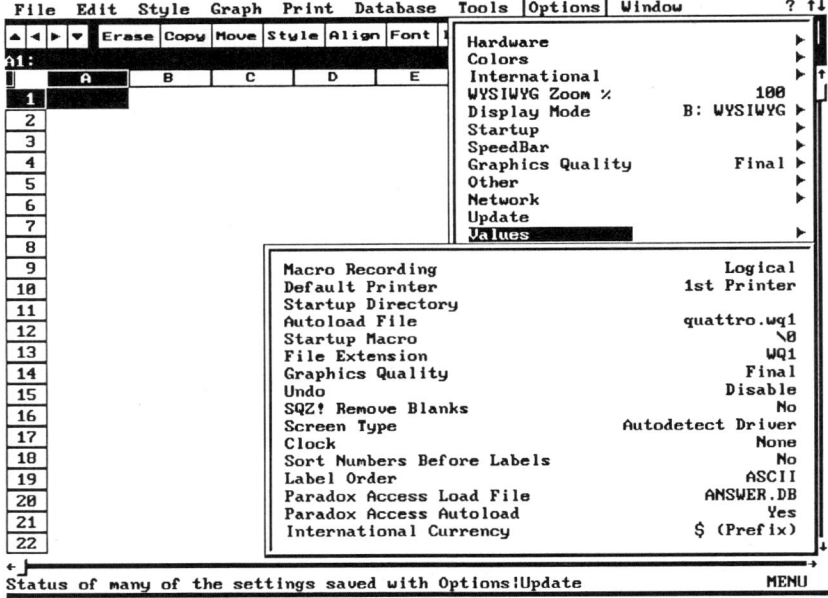

Figure 10.2 /Options Values Displays Spreadsheet Settings

disappears when you press any key. Changes made to these options can be saved for the next Quattro session. Global customization options affect how the current spreadsheet performs. These options include global column width, global numeric format, and global label alignment. These options are available using the menu selections below Update in the Options menu. These options are saved with the spreadsheet and cannot be saved with Quattro's system defaults.

SELECTING AN OPTIONS SET

Quattro stores all of the default settings in a resource file. When you load Quattro by typing **Q** and pressing ENTER, Quattro uses the resource file RSC.RF. When you save changes to the default settings, Quattro updates this file. Part of this file stores which menu Quattro uses, since Quattro lets you use one of two it provides or use one that you build with the Menu Builder described at the end of this chapter. If you are typing Q123 to load Quattro, Quattro uses the file 123.RF for the resource file, which tells it to use the menu tree stored in 123.MU.

You can create additional resource files. For example, if you want to create a custom menu tree and option settings file for yourself while leaving RSC.RF intact for other users, copy an existing default file (RSC.RF or 123.RF) to a new file name using the DOS COPY command. The new file should have the .RF file extension. Once you have created a new resource settings file, tell Quattro which resource file to use by typing: **Q /dRESOURCE.RF**, where RESOURCE.RF represents the name of the resource file you want to use. An example is entering **Q/dMYFILE.RF**, assuming MYFILE.RF represents the file name for existing resource file. If you want a specific file loaded after Quattro is loaded, type the file name after the default file specification, as in **Q /DMYFILE.RF TEMPLATE**. After you press ENTER, Quattro is loaded using the default settings in MYFILE.RF. Once Quattro is loaded, Quattro retrieves the file TEMPLATE.

If you want a resource file to be used every time you start Quattro Pro 3 or 4, or if you want to use a group of settings in the command line to start Quattro Pro every time you start Quattro Pro 3 or 4, you can use the DOS environment variable QARGS. Every time Quattro Pro is loaded, Quattro Pro checks if DOS has QARGS. A DOS environment variable is a variable DOS maintains in its memory throughout the current session and can be accessed by any application. If there is a QARGS DOS environment variable, Quattro Pro is loaded as if the contents of the QARGS DOS environment variable were entered after the Q. For example, If QARGS equals /dMYFILE.RF, by default, when you load Quattro Pro, Quattro Pro is loaded using MYFILE.RF resource file. You can use the QARGS DOS environment varable to start Quattro Pro with any information that you would normally enter after the Q to start Quattro Pro. For example, you can set QARGS to equal /X /E16 /DMYFILES.RF MY_DATA.WQ1 MY_MACRO (the /E selection is described later). To set a DOS environment variable, enter the DOS command SET followed by the variable name (QARGS), an equals sign, and the value you want the environment variable to equal as in SET QARGS=/X /E16 /DMYFILES.RF

MY_DATA.WQ1.MY_MACRO. The environment variable remains assigned until you enter SET and the variable name without following it with a value or you restart your system. If you want the value of QARGS to be used every time you start Quattro Pro, you will want to add the SET command that assigns QARGS to your AUTOEXEC.BAT file.

UPDATING DEFAULTS

Changes to the default settings are not incorporated into the resource file until the resource file is updated. Updating the resource file takes all current option settings and stores them in the current resource file, which is RSC.RF unless another resource file is used when you load Quattro. As you review each of the setting changes that Quattro supports, you must use the /Options Update command if you want your option settings changes to be in effect beyond the current session. While the /Options Update command can update the resource file, several of Quattro's menus also have an Update option that also updates the resource file, including the menu selections not covered in the menu from which you selected Update. For example, selecting Update from the Print Layout menu updates the changes made in the Options menu as well.

CHANGING HARDWARE DEFAULTS

Quattro makes several simple assumptions about your computer's peripheral equipment. Peripheral equipment includes the monitor (or screen) and the printer. Quattro automatically detects the type of display that you are using and loads the appropriate screen driver. A driver contains information telling the computer how it should send data to the peripheral equipment. For the printer, Quattro makes assumptions about how the printer is connected to the computer. All this information can be changed with the /Options Hardware commands. The settings also provide information that Quattro uses to display graphs. The settings are changed through the Hardware menu shown in Figure 10.3. In this menu, Quattro also displays information about the mouse, the memory in the computer, and whether the computer has a math coprocessor. These settings cover printing and displaying spreadsheets.

Changing the Screen

Quattro makes assumptions about the screen. Quattro checks the computer's hardware to determine the proper screen driver to use depending on the display adapter in the computer. If you are using a nonstandard screen type or Quattro is not displaying a spreadsheet properly, you may need to change some of the screen settings.

Once you select **Screen** from the Hardware menu, Quattro displays a menu containing **Screen Type**, **Resolution**, **Aspect Ratio**, **CGA Snow Suppression**, and **Quit**. Quattro initially detects the screen type automatically based on the display adapter in the computer. The other settings control the resolution and the height-to-width ratios. These settings should only be changed when Quattro is not properly displaying spreadsheets and graphs. Quattro provides the following options:

- **Screen Type**—This option determines which screen driver Quattro uses to tell the screen how to display spreadsheet and graph information. Most of the time, selecting Autodetect Driver will provide the most appropriate selection. If you cannot find a suitable driver, select MDA, which does not display graphs, inset graphs or the spreadsheet in WYSIWYG mode.

- **Resolution**—This option determines the setting for graphics resolution. The resolution is a measurement of its clarity. Quattro measures resolution as the number of pixels that fit on a screen. A pixel is a point of light or color on a screen. Quattro has this set for the best resolution with which your current monitor can display graphs. This option also affects the colors that are available for the graphs. The specific options available are determined by the type of monitor that you are using. When you select **Resolution**, Quattro displays a selection box listing the available selections that are appropriate for the selection made with **Screen Type**.

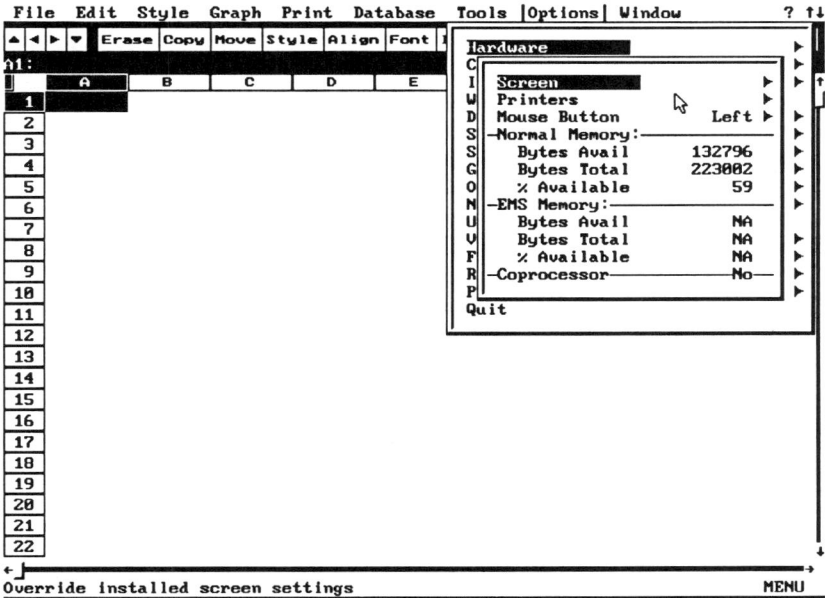

Figure 10.3 Hardware Menu

- **Aspect Ratio**—This option determines the ratio between the height and the width of a pie chart. This option should only be adjusted if the circle in a flat pie graph does not appear or print round, or if you want to change the angle of the pie in a three-dimensional pie chart. If you use this option, the screen appears like Figure 10.4. Use the UP and DOWN ARROWS until the circle appears perfect, and press ENTER. This option does not affect other graph types.
- **CGA Snow Suppression**—This option is used only if you have a CGA monitor and you have flecks of white apearing on your screen (called snow). Select Yes if this happens to remove the snow effect. Since CGA snow suppression makes Quattro Pro run slower, you want this option set to No if you do not have a CGA monitor or it does not display snow.

Changing the Printer

When you print to a printer, you can select printing to a text printer or printing to a graph printer. When you select Printer, Quattro sends just the spreadsheet data without embellishments like fonts, lines, and shading. When you select Graphics Printer, Quattro includes these embellishments as well as printing graphs because Quattro uses a printer driver file that provides Quattro the information needed to print graphs and other enhancements. You need to change Quattro's settings for

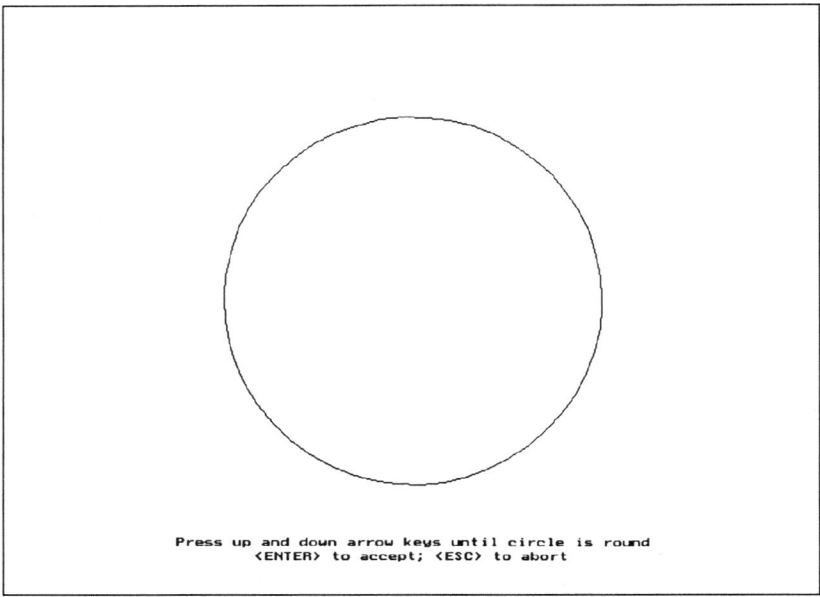

Figure 10.4 Aspect Ratio Screen

the printer if the settings for how your printer is connected to your computer system are incorrect or if you want to change which printers Quattro loads the printer driver files. Quattro assumes that the printer is connected to the computer's first parallel slot using a parallel interface, does not have automatic linefeed, and uses continuous paper. The last assumption also applies for many laser printers that do not use continuous-feed paper but behave as if they do because of their automatic tray-feed mechanisms. The printer Quattro uses when you select **Graphics Printer** is selected when you install Quattro as described in Appendix A. To change one of these assumptions or to select the printer to which Quattro loads the printer driver file, use the **/O**ptions **H**ardware **P**rinters command. This presents the Printers menu like the one in Figure 10.5. From this menu, you can change the printers for which Quattro remembers the settings, the default printer, the plotter speed, the font settings, and other printer settings. In Quattro Pro 4, you can also use background printing, which prints in the background while you continue using Quattro Pro. Using Background printing with the Borland Print Spooler is described in Chapter 4. You will use the menu shown in Figure 10.5 with background printing by selecting **B**ackground and **Y**es. Making these selections tells Quattro Pro to use the Borland Print Spooler to print in the background if it is loaded.

SELECTING A PRINTER Quattro remembers the printer driver files for two printers at a time. You can select which two Quattro remembers. To select a printer to which Quattro will load the printer driver file, select **1**st Printer or **2**nd Printer. When Quattro displays the menu for the printer, you have the following options:

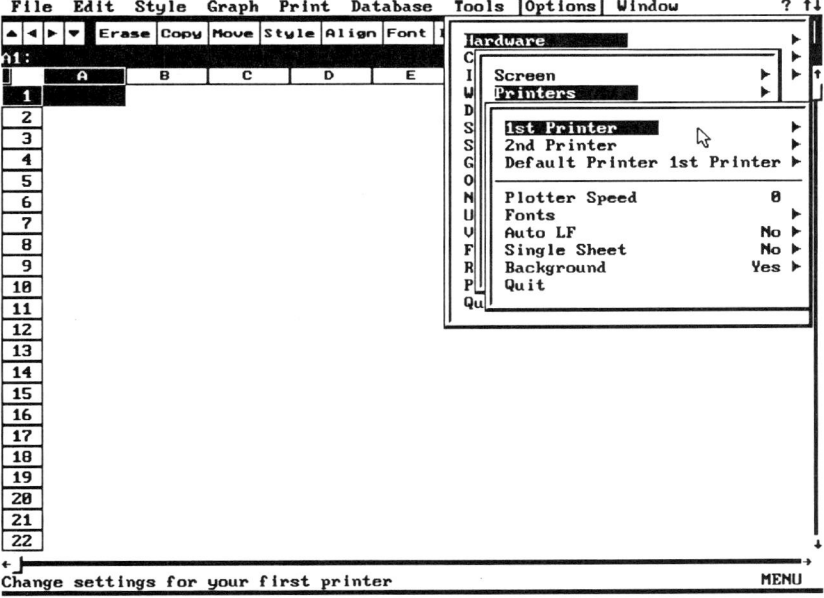

Figure 10.5 Printers Menu

- Type of Printer—This option sets the printer that Quattro remembers. When you select this, you must select the printer manufacturer, the model, and the mode. The mode represents available printing features for your printer. If you choose a laser or dot-matrix printer, the choices for mode list the possible dots per inch (dpi) that can be used for printing. If you select a plotter, the choices for mode are Automatic, Manual, and Monochrome. Automatic uses the current color pins to print the graph. Manual pauses the printer for each color change to allow you to change the color pins. Monochrome prints the graph in one color. For each selection box, select the choice that is appropriate for your printer.

- Device—This option determines the communications port that the printer uses on the computer. The choices are Parallel-1, Serial-1, Parallel-2, Serial-2, LPT1, LPT2, LPT3, LPT4, EPT, PRN, and Network Queue. Move to the one that you want or type the number to the left of your choice, and press ENTER. Use EPT when you are using the IBM Pageprinter.

- Baud Rate—This option sets the speed that Quattro sends information to a serial printer. The correct baud rate is listed in your printer manual. The Leave as is setting uses the baud rate set by DOS with the MODE command.

- Parity—This option sets whether Quattro uses odd or even parity to send information to a serial printer. The serial printer uses the parity information to check that each character is sent correctly. Your choices are Leave as is, No, Odd, or Even. Choose one by typing the first letter of your choice or moving to your choice and pressing ENTER. If you choose Leave as is, Quattro uses the parity set by DOS.

- Stop Bits—This option sets the signal that Quattro sends to a serial printer to instruct it that a character has been sent. Your choices are Leave as is, 1 Bit, or 2 Bits. If it is set to Leave as is, Quattro uses the number of stop bits set by DOS with the MODE command.

- Quit—This option returns to the Printers menu.

SETTING THE DEFAULT PRINTER Once you have selected the printers to which Quattro loads the printer driver files, you can tell Quattro the printer that you want to use by selecting Default Printer. Next select 1st Printer or 2nd Printer. Quattro uses the setting of the default printer every time you print.

SETTING THE PLOTTER SPEED Quattro sends the data to the printer or plotter as quickly as the printer or plotter can accept it. When you are using a plotter, you may want Quattro to send information to the plotter slower so the plotter can draw slower. For example, you will want to draw slower if your pens are old or if the plotter is drawing the lines so quickly that they appear thin (especially on transparencies). To set how quickly Quattro sends information to the plotter, select Plotter Speed from the Printers menu and enter a number between 1 and 9, where 1 represents slowest. If you enter 0, Quattro sends information to the plotter as quickly as the plotter can accept it.

> ▼ TIP: Update default settings after selecting cartridges.
>
> Once you select the LaserJet cartridges, update the default settings so you have the font available for all of your spreadsheets.

SETTING FONT CARTRIDGES AND SCALING When you are using the printer to print high-quality spreadsheets and graphs, you can take advantage of Quattro's font features, such as accepting Hewlett-Packard LaserJet printer cartridges, setting the shading level, and adjusting font size to reflect the graph's overall size. To use Hewlett-Packard LaserJet printer cartridges, you must tell Quattro which fonts are in the printer. To tell Quattro which font cartridges you are using, select **Fonts** from the Printers menu and **Cartridge Fonts** (LaserJet Fonts in prior releases). Then select either the **Left Cartridge** or **Right Cartridge** to match the cartridge slot you want to identify to Quattro. Quattro displays a list of the available cartridge fonts. Select the one appropriate for your cartridge. The letters that represent the cartridge such as E for Letter Gothic or P for Times Roman P&L are on the font cartridge as well as the documentation. You can also select 25 in One if you have a Pacific Data Products 25-in-One font cartridge which provides twenty-five fonts in a single cartridge. Once you have selected a font cartridge it is available the next time you select a font for spreadsheet or graph text.

For some Hewlett Packard LaserJet and Canon printers, you can also select the intensity of the shading for blocks shaded with the **/Style Shading Gray** command, since this printer has seven shading levels. To select the shading level, select **Fonts** from the Printer menu, **Cartridge Fonts** (LaserJet Fonts in prior releases), and **Shading Level**. Enter a percentage representing how dark you want the shading.

By default, when you insert a graph into a spreadsheet, Quattro adjusts the size of the text to reflect the size of the graph in the spreadsheet. For example, if the inserted graph is smaller than the area it occupies when you press F10 (GRAPH), Quattro reduces the actual point size of the graph text to match the reduction in graph size. Another possibility is to display the text graph using the exact point size you selected with the font menus. To set Quattro to keep the graph text point size regardless of the size of the graph, enter **Fonts** from the Printers menu and select **Autoscale Fonts** and **No**. In any subsequently inserted graph, the text is in

> ▼ TIP: Removing cartridge too often wears it out.
>
> Only remove the font cartridge from the laser printer when necessary, since it quickly wears out the cartridge.

the point size selected when the font is chosen. If you want Quattro to scale the text size, enter **Fonts Autoscale Fonts Yes**.

TELLING QUATTRO WHEN TO ADVANCE A LINE Quattro needs to know how the selected printer reacts to moving to the beginning of the line. Some printers automatically advance the paper in the printer to the next line. Other printers do not advance the paper in the printer to the next line, so they need to be told to advance the paper. Quattro assumes that it must tell the printer to advance a line when it moves to the beginning of a line.

You can tell if this setting is correct by printing a spreadsheet block. If all the rows are on the same line, Quattro must supply the line feeds to the printer; you can tell Quattro to do this by entering **/Options Hardware Printers Auto LF No**. If the rows are printing double spaced, Quattro is supplying line feeds when it should not—the printer already supplies them. In this case, enter **/Options Hardware Printers Auto LF Yes**.

TELLING QUATTRO IF THE PRINTER PAUSES BETWEEN PAGES Printers and plotters provide various options for inserting sheets to print a graph or spreadsheet. A printer can use continuous-feed paper, such as the computer paper with sprocket holes on the side that the printer can feed through or it can use single sheets of paper that you must insert before the next page is printed. Laser printers do not use continuous-feed paper but behave as if they do because of their automatic tray-feed mechanisms. Plotters can only print one page at a time. If you are printing to a printer that accepts only one page at a time, you must tell Quattro to pause between pages by entering **/Options Hardware Printers Single Sheet Yes**. Quattro will pause between each page it prints so you can insert the next sheet. When you want to print using continuous feed, enter **/Options Hardware Printers Single Sheet No**.

Setting the Mouse Button

You can tell Quattro Pro which button on the mouse you will use to make selections. The default of Left is appropriate if you are holding the mouse in your right hand. If you will be using your left hand for moving the mouse, you will want to select **Mouse Button** and **Right**; so you must press the right button on the mouse to select what you are pointing to.

Information About the Computer's Memory

The Hardware menu also displays information about the computer's memory and the existence of a math coprocessor. The Normal Memory line in the Hardware menu displays the number of bytes of memory remaining in normal memory (or conventional memory). This number is close to the results of the @MEMAVAIL function. Since entering /Options Hardware uses some memory as Quattro displays the menus, the value displayed after Normal Memory is less than the result of the @MEMAVAIL function. The EMS line displays the number of bytes of expanded memory available. This number is close to the results of the @MEMEMSAVAIL function. Since entering /Options Hardware uses some memory as Quattro displays the menus, the value displayed after EMS is less than the result of the @MEMEMSAVAIL function. As Figure 10.2 shows, Quattro also indicates whether the computer has a coprocessor. These are options that you cannot change.

CHANGING COLOR OPTIONS

As with all other Quattro settings, you can customize the colors used in the spreadsheets by changing the color for each of the spreadsheet's attributes. To change a color, type / and select Options Colors for the menu shown in Figure 10.6. Then make a selection from the Colors menu, which lists areas of Quattro for which you can select an attribute. You need to select the group of attributes followed by the specific attribute to change. After Quattro knows which attribute you want to alter, it displays the colors from which you can choose. For color monitors, Quattro displays a palette box with samples of the different colors, like the palette shown in Figure 10.7. The solid colors represent the background color,

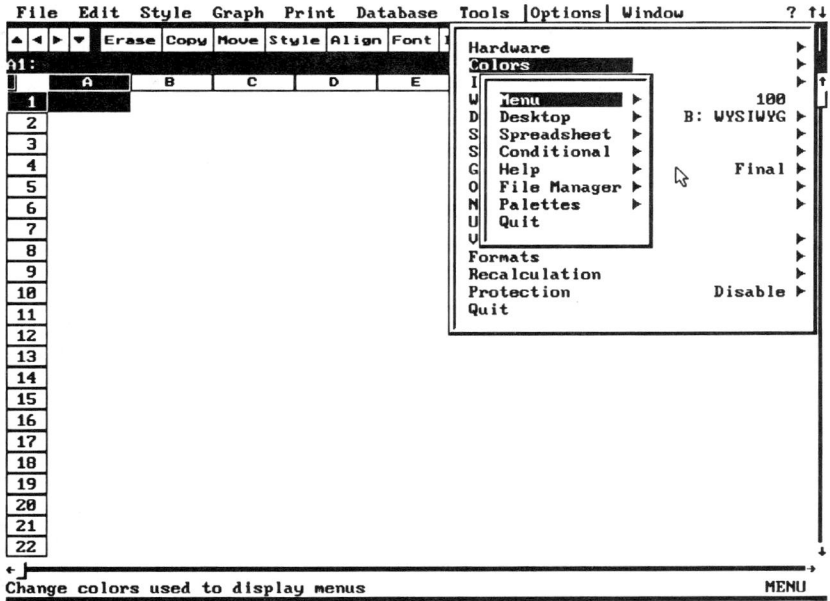

Figure 10.6 Colors Menu

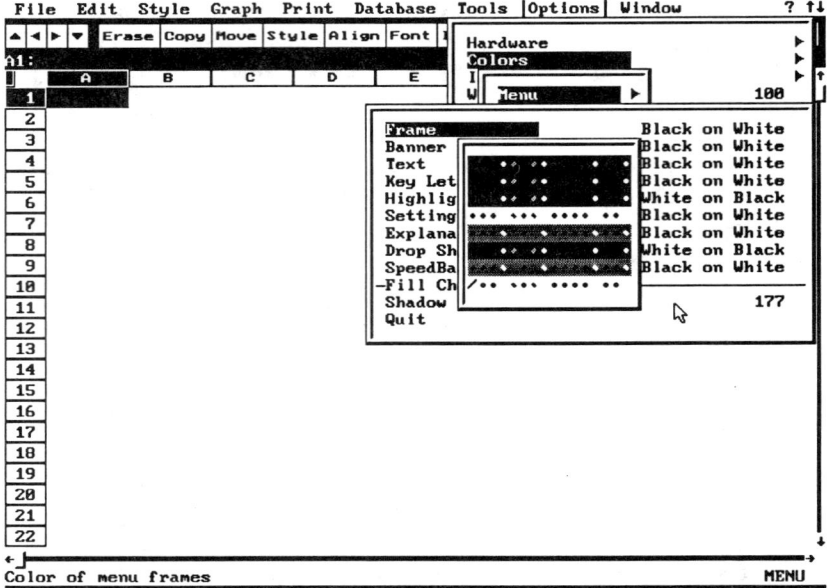

Figure 10.7 Palette of Color Selections

and the dots represent the color of the text. For monochrome monitors, Quattro displays the selection box listing Normal, Bold, Underline, Inverse, and Empty. Once you have selected the color, Quattro returns you to the menu from which you selected the specific attribute and displays the appropriate attribute in the newly selected color. Selecting Quit returns you to the previous menu. To hide the current colors for any group of attributes, press the GRAY MINUS key. Later, you can press the GRAY PLUS key to return the current selections to the menu.

Changing the Menu Colors

Executing the /Options Colors Menu command lists the different portions of the menu for which you can change the color. From the menu shown in Figure 10.7 (which displays the defaults for color monitors), you have these options:

- Frame—This sets the color for the border of the menu.
- Banner—This sets the color for the name of the menu.
- Text—This sets the color for all the letters of the menu items except for the key letter.
- Key Letter—This sets the color for the letter of every menu item that you can type to select it.
- Highlight—This sets the color for the highlight bar and text of selected menu items.

- Settings—This sets the color for the settings of the menu items when you press the GRAY PLUS key in a menu.
- Explanation—This sets the color of the text in the status line that describes the highlighted menu item.
- Drop Shadow—This sets the color for the shadow under the menu. If the color palette is set to Monochrome, you can select Empty so the shadow will not appear.
- SpeedBar—This sets the color of the SpeedBar and its buttons.
- Shadow—This sets the ASCII character Quattro displays as the shadow. Frequently used ASCII codes are 32 (space), 177 (lightly shaded box), 178 (darkly shaded box), and 219 (solid box). You must provide the ASCII code of the character you want (rather than typing the character).

Changing the Desktop Colors

The /Options Colors Desktop command sets the colors Quattro uses to display parts of the screen that do not belong to the menu or a window. For each attribute, you set the color of the attribute and the background color of the attribute. From the menu shown in Figure 10.8 (which displays the defaults for color monitors), you have the following choices:

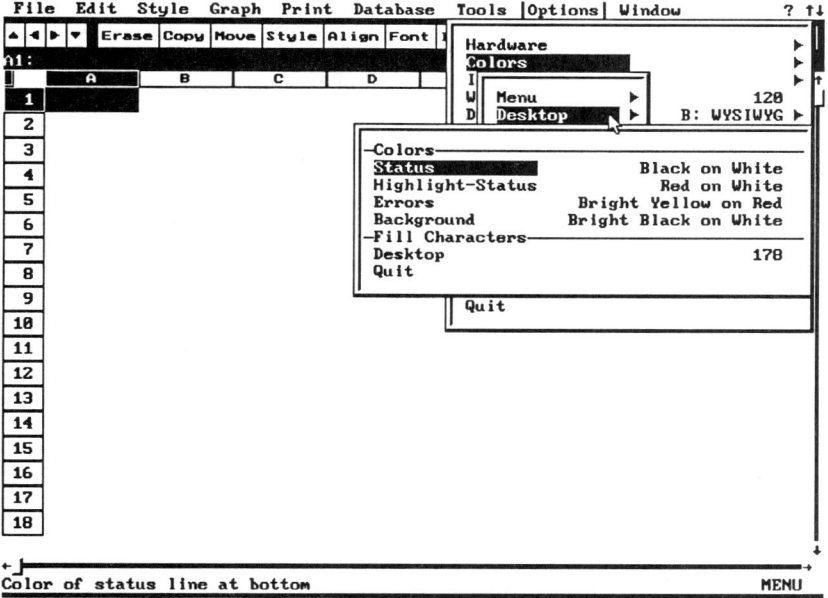

Figure 10.8 Menu Box for Selecting Desktop Colors

- Status—This sets the color of the settings for the mode indicator, file name, current cell contents during EDIT mode, and time and date displayed in the status line.
- Highlight-Status—This sets the color of indicators such as READY and EDIT that appears in the status line.
- Errors—This sets the color of the messages Quattro displays when you attempt an entry or command that Quattro cannot accept or perform.
- Background—This sets the color of the desktop that appears when spreadsheet and File Manager windows do not cover the desktop.
- Desktop—This sets the ASCII character that Quattro displays in the desktop when a portion is not covered by a spreadsheet or File Manager window. Frequently used ASCII codes are 32 (space), 177 (lightly shaded box), 178 (darkly shaded box), and 219 (solid box). You must provide the ASCII code of the character you want (rather than typing the character).

Changing Spreadsheet Window Colors

The /Options Colors Spreadsheet command sets the colors Quattro uses to display parts of the spreadsheet screen. For each attribute, you set the color of the text and the background for the text. Several of the options only change the color of the spreadsheet when you are using a text display and have no effect in WYSIWYG display mode. From the menu shown in Figure 10.9 (which displays the defaults for color monitors), you have the following choices:

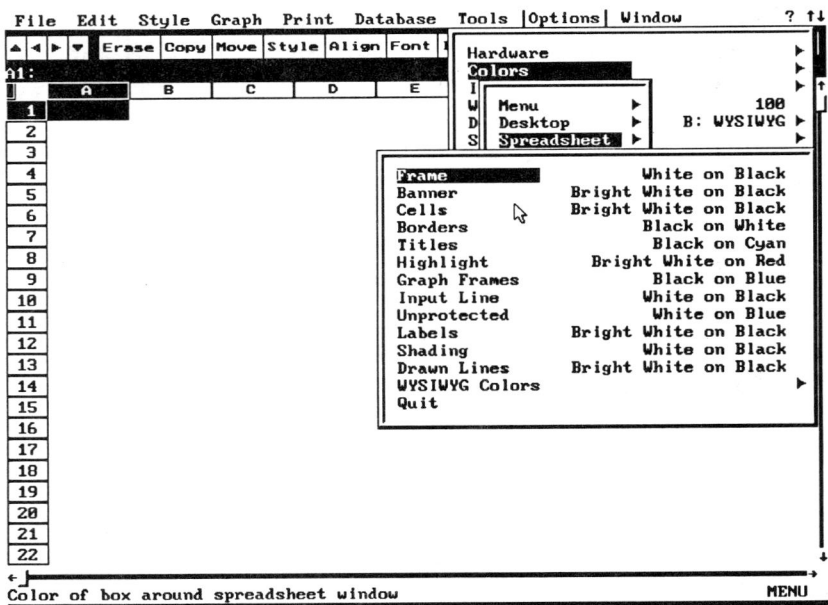

Figure 10.9 Menu Box for Selecting Spreadsheet Colors

- **Frame**—This sets the color of the box around a spreadsheet window if more than one window is shown. This option also sets the color of the horizontal and vertical scroll bars.
- **Banner**—This selects the color of the file name and window number that appears at the top of a spreadsheet window.
- **Cells**—This sets the color for all nonlabel cells.
- **Borders**—This sets the color for the row and column border of the spreadsheet.
- **Titles**—This sets the color for frozen titles.
- **Highlight**—This sets the color for the selector on the current cell.
- **Graph Frames**—This sets the color of the box drawn around inserted graphs.
- **Input Line**—This sets the color of the data at the top of the screen as they are entered and edited and the color of the cell information when the selector points to a cell.
- **Unprotected**—This sets the color for unprotected cells in the spreadsheet.
- **Labels**—This sets the color for label entries.
- **Shading**—This sets the color of the cells shaded with /Style Shading.
- **Drawn Lines**—This sets the color of the cells shaded with /Style Line Drawing.
- **WYSIWYG Colors**—This sets the colors Quattro Pro uses for the WYSIWYG display mode. After selecting this option, Quattro Pro displays the menu shown in Figure 10.10. Background sets the underlying color of the cells, Cursor sets the color of the selector, Grid Lines sets the color of the grid lines added with the /Windows Options Grid Lines command, Unprotected sets the color of the text of unprotected cells, Drawn Lines sets the color of lines added with /Style Line Drawing, Shaded Cells sets the color of shading added with /Style Shading, and Locked Titles Text and Titles Background sets the text and background color of titles added with the /Window Options Locked Titles command. Selecting Row and Column Labels provides an additional menu that lets you select the colors of the sculpted row and column borders.

Setting Conditional Colors

Quattro can display cells in different colors depending on the entries the cells contain. The /Options Colors Conditional command allows you to set the conditions under which the different colors are used. The conditions affect value cell entries and can be used to emphasize spreadsheet values within certain limits.

When you use conditional colors, your selections override the colors selected with the /Options Colors Spreadsheet Cells command. From the menu shown in Figure 10.11 (which displays the defaults for color monitors), you have the following choices:

526   *Quattro Pro 4.0 Handbook*

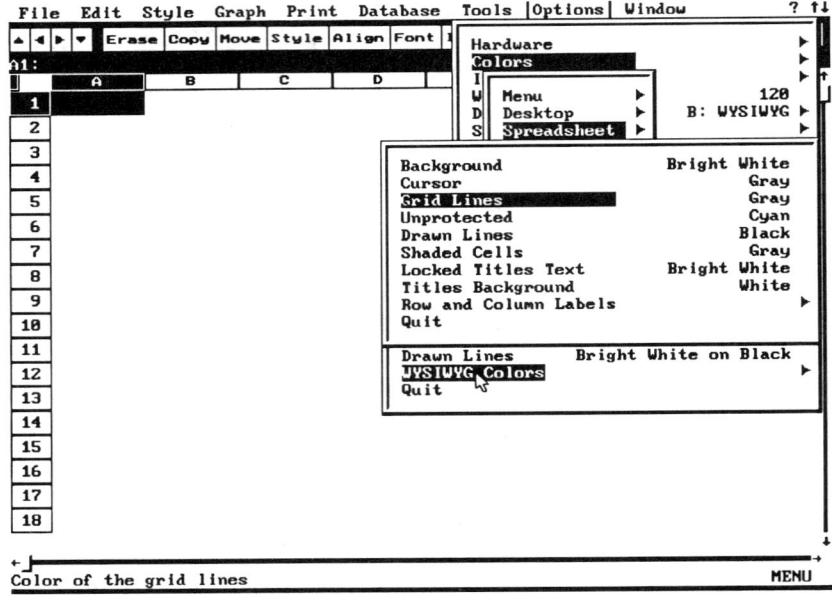

Figure 10.10   Menu for Selecting WYSIWYG Display Colors

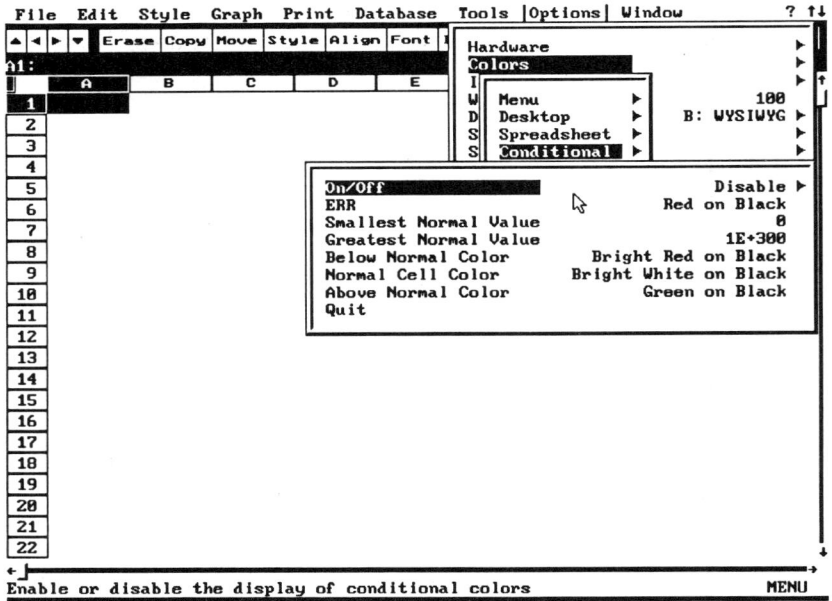

Figure 10.11   Menu Box for Selecting Conditional Colors

- **On/Off**—This enables or disables use of the conditional colors. Quattro initially has this setting at Disable. Until this setting is set to Enable, none of the other settings affect the spreadsheet.
- **ERR**—This sets the color for cells equaling ERR.
- **Smallest Normal Value**—This sets a value and allows you to display cells with values lower than this entry in a special color. This is the lowest value of the normal range. You can use this feature to highlight production run times that are below the standard time or to highlight hourly wage rates that are below the established minimum.
- **Greatest Normal Value**—This sets a value and causes all cells with values above this entry to be displayed in a special color. This is the highest value of the normal range. For example, if a salary exceeds the highest acceptable level, you can elect to show the salary amount in red.
- **Below Normal Color**—This sets the color for cell values that are lower than the smallest normal value.
- **Normal Cell Color**—This sets the color for cell values that are greater than or equal to the smallest normal value and less than or equal to the highest normal value.
- **Above Normal Color**—This sets the color for cell values that are greater than the highest normal value.

Changing the Help Information Colors

The **/O**ptions **C**olors **H**elp command sets the colors Quattro uses to display the help screens. From the Help menu, you have these choices:

- **Frame**—This sets the color of the box around the help screens.
- **Banner**—This sets the color for the name of the help screen.
- **Text**—This sets the color for all help screen text except the keywords.
- **Keywords**—This sets the color for the keywords in the help screens. The keywords are the topics that you can select for further information.
- **Highlight**—This sets the color for the highlight that selects keywords.

Changing the File Manager Window Colors

The **/O**ptions **C**olors **F**ile Manager command sets the colors Quattro uses in a File Manager window. For each attribute, you set the color of the text and the background for the text. Frame and Banner have no effect in the WYSIWYG display mode. From the menu shown in Figure 10.12 (which displays the defaults for color monitors), you have the following choices:

- **Frame**—This sets the color of the box around a File Manager window. This option also sets the color of the horizontal scroll bar.

528 *Quattro Pro 4.0 Handbook*

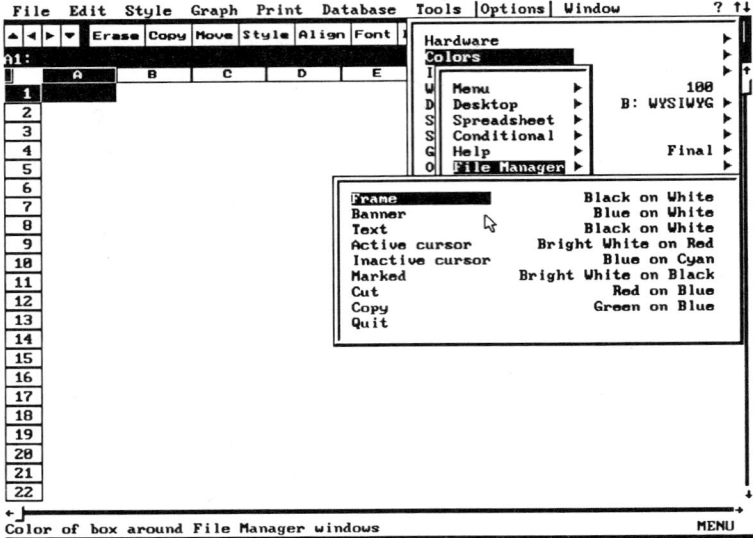

Figure 10.12 Menu Box for Selecting File Manager Colors

- **Banner**—This selects the color of the drive and directory that appears at the top of a File Manager window.
- **Text**—This sets the color for the text in a File Manager window.
- **Active Cursor**—This sets the color of the cursor or highlight in the active pane.
- **Inactive Cursor**—This sets the color of the cursor or highlight in a nonactive pane.
- **Marked**—This sets the color of marked files.
- **Cut**—This sets the color of files marked for moving by cutting from one directory and pasting to another.
- **Copy**—This sets the color of files marked for copying.

Using the Palette Colors

The /Options Colors Palette command returns the color selections to the default settings. You can return the color settings to the default settings under black and white, monochrome, or color. From the menu you have the following choices:

- **Color**—This restores the colors to the defaults for color screens.
- **Monochrome**—This sets the current colors to the defaults for monochrome screens. This does not use the different hues that the black and white palette uses.

- **B**lack & White—This restores the colors to the defaults for the monochrome screens with the color palettes that appear as hues of black and white.
- Gray Scale—This sets the colors of the screen for monitors that can display shades of grey.
- Version 3 Color—This sets the screen colors to match the default colors that Quattro Pro 3 used.

INTERNATIONAL CURRENCY AND PUNCTUATION

Quattro has several initial settings that are standard for currency, dates, times, sort order, and punctuation usage in the United States. This includes the dollar sign used as a prefix for the currency-formatted cells, the date and time formats, and the punctuation symbols. These settings can be changed if you are creating a spreadsheet that is intended for foreign use. The /Options International command allows you to change the default settings of punctuation, currency symbols, display of negative numbers, sort order, and date and time formats. These changes also affect the date and time in the status line and the method for entering the function arguments. In addition, you can select the order that Quattro includes foreign characters in the alphabet, how extended characters are transferred from 1-2-3 files to Quattro, and whether the printer can print foreign characters by overstriking. Foreign characters are those characters that languages other than English use. When you use this command, Quattro displays the International menu shown in Figure 10.13. From this menu, you can select international default settings.

Changing the Currency Symbol

The /Options International Currency command allows you to change the default format of the dollar ($) to another currency symbol. For example, you may want to prepare financial statements in pounds (£). When you select this command, Quattro prompts you for the desired symbol. Type the new currency symbol and press ENTER. If the desired symbol cannot be found on the regular keyboard, you can create an ASCII character by holding down the ALT key and typing in the appropriate ASCII code on the numeric keypad, such as ALT-156 for £. After you have typed the currency symbol, Quattro prompts you for the location of the currency symbol in relation to the value. Choose **P**refix from the submenu if you want the currency symbol placed at the beginning of numbers or **S**uffix if you want the currency symbol to be placed at the end of numbers, and press ENTER.

Displaying Negative Numbers

The currency and financial formats initially display negative numbers enclosed in parentheses. You can change how Quattro Pro 4 shows negative numbers by

530   *Quattro Pro 4.0 Handbook*

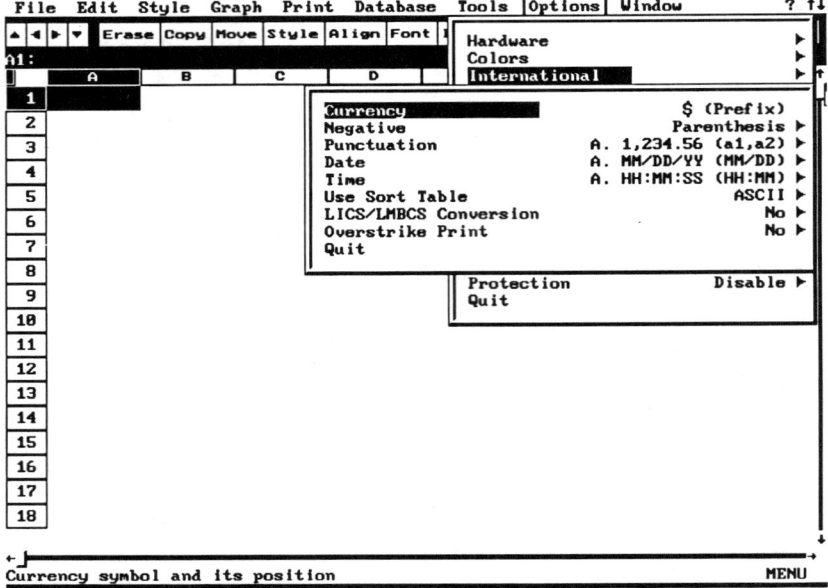

Figure 10.13   International Menu

selecting **Negative** and then either **Parentheses** or **Sign**. The default, **Parentheses**, displays the negative numbers enclosed in parentheses and **Sign** displays negative numbers preceded by a minus sign. Changing this international option only changes how negative numbers are displayed when you use the currency or financial formats.

Changing the Punctuation

Quattro Pro allows you to change the punctuation style that Quattro Pro uses to conform to the standards used in different countries. The choice of punctuation also affects how function and macro arguments are separated. When you execute the /Options International Punctuation command, Quattro displays the menu shown

---

▼ **TIP: Change all macro instructions if you change punctuation.**

If you change the punctuation used, use the /Edit Search and Replace to change the punctuation in macro instructions.

Customizing Quattro Pro 531

in Figure 10.14. For each of these options, Quattro shows how the thousands are separated as the character between the 1 and the 2, the decimal point as the character between the 4 and the 5, and the function and macro argument separator as the character between a1 and a2. When you change the punctuation, Quattro adjusts all existing functions and display formats for the new punctuation. Quattro does not automatically change the macro argument separators.

Changing the Date Format

The /Options International Date command allows you to change the international date formats. The international formats for dates are choices 4 and 5 from the Date menu in the /Style Numeric Format Date command and the /Options Formats Numeric Format Date command. When you select this command, Quattro displays a selection box. You have the following formats to choose from:

	Long Form	Short Form
A.	MM/DD/YY	MM/DD
B.	DD/MM/YY	DD/MM
C.	DD.MM.YY	DD.MM
D.	YY-MM-DD	MM-DD

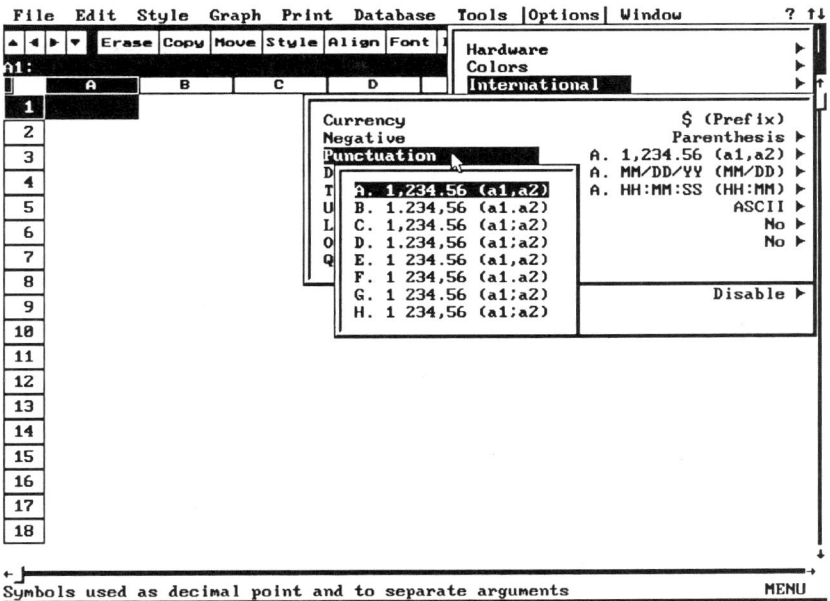

Figure 10.14 Punctuation Selections

The long format of the international dates format is the fourth selection for the date numeric format. The short form of the international date format is the fifth selection for dates.

Changing the international date format does not change the spreadsheet display unless it contains date entries formatted with choice 4 or 5 from the Date menu. Initially, Quattro has the initial international date formats set to MM/DD/YY and MM/DD.

Changing the Time Format

The /Options International Time command allows you to change the international time formats. The international time formats are the last two choices from the Time menu in the /Style Numeric Format Date Time command and the /Options Formats Numeric Format Date Time command. When you select this command, Quattro displays a selection box with the following formats to choose from:

Long Form	Short Form
A. HH:MM:SS	HH:MM
B. HH.MM.SS	HH.MM
C. HH,MM,SS	HH,MM
D. HHhMMmSSs	HHhMMm

The long form of the international time format is the third selection for times. The short form of the international time format is the fourth selection for times.

This command does not use the different international formats unless the spreadsheet already has time entries formatted with one of the international time formats. Initially, Quattro has the initial formats set to HH:MM:SS and HH:MM.

All international time formats use a 24-hour clock. A 24-hour clock does not use A.M. or P.M. to designate whether a time is before noon or after noon. Instead, a 24-hour clock shows time before noon without any special designation. Times after noon have 12 added to the hour. For example, 9:00 A.M. is displayed as 9:00, and 9:00 P.M. is displayed as 21:00 (9 + 12 = 21).

Changing the Sort Order

If you are using foreign characters in a range that you are sorting, you will want to change the order of the alphabet that Quattro uses during sorting to include the foreign characters in their proper sequence. After selecting /Options International Use Sort Table, select INTL.SOR to use the alphabet order that includes most foreign characters used by most European languages, NORDAN.SOR to use the alphabet order used by Norway and Denmark, or SWEDFIN.SOR to use the alphabet order used by Sweden and Finland. You can also select ASCII.SOR to return to the alphabet order that includes all foreign characters after the letters A-Z.

Changing Conversion of LICS Characters

If you are using Quattro Pro with 1-2-3 files that include foreign characters and other characters that the @CHAR function in 1-2-3 returns a number greater that 127, you will need to change the /Options International LICS/LMBCS Conversion command. When this is set to Yes, Quattro Pro retrieves LICS or LMBCS characters and converts them to their ASCII equivalents. When the file is saved, Quattro Pro saves all characters using the LICS or LMBCS character set that 1-2-3 uses (depending on the release). When this is set to No, Quattro Pro retrieves 1-2-3 files and treats the character numbers as ASCII character numbers so no conversion is performed. When the file is saved, Quattro Pro does not convert the characters to the LICS or LMBCS character set.

Printing Foreign Characters by Overstriking

If you are using Quattro Pro with files that contain foreign characters and your printer cannot print them, it may be able to print them by having Quattro direct the printer to print one character, backup one character and print another character over it. This is called overstriking. For example, to print the character, â, the printer would print an a, backup one space and type a caret (^). Some printers can do this while some cannot. If your printer cannot print foreign characters that you have on your spreadsheet, you may want to print them by directing Quattro Pro to overstrike the character. You can do this by selecting /Options International Overstrike Yes. If you find that you cannot print using overstrike or do not need to, select /Options International Overstrike No.

CHANGING THE DISPLAY MODE

Quattro can display the screen using character or graphics mode. A character mode screen can display only ASCII characters. A graphics mode screen can display any type of information, including graphs or pictures, since Quattro (or any other software) dictates what to put in each dot on the screen. Quattro always displays full-screen graphs, the graph annotator, and the screen preview for printing using a graphics screen mode. Quattro lets you choose the mode used to display the spreadsheets. In releases before Quattro Pro 3, Quattro Pro initially displayed the spreadsheet in character mode. In Quattro Pro 3 and 4, you can select during or after installation whether Quattro Pro displays the spreadsheet in either text or graphics mode, called WYSIWYG for what-you-see-is-what-you-get. This graphics mode displays the spreadsheet as it will appear when you print it using the graphics printer. In the WYSIWYG display mode, Quattro Pro 4's SpeedBar will always appear across the top. In a text display mode, the SpeedBar will be on the right side, which is where the mouse palette was in prior releases.

In other releases you can display the spreadsheet in a graphics mode, which allows you to see how the inserted graphs appear in the spreadsheet. Also, when you display a spreadsheet in graphics mode, the mouse pointer changes from a small rectangle to an arrow. With graph menus, some of the selections display galleries, which consist of pictures showing how the selection will appear (as in the /Graph Graph Type). Since Quattro must tell the computer and the screen more information when graphics screen is being used, the cursor movement is slower. Quattro also has other options for displaying the spreadsheet screen in text mode (such as 43 or 50 lines on the screen). This is available with the higher resolution screens like EGA and VGA. To change how Quattro displays the spreadsheet screens, enter /Options Display Mode. Selecting **B**: WYSIWYG (Graphics Mode in prior releases) changes any inserted graphs from shaded areas to the actual graphs. The other options change how the text screen appears. Some of the options let you display 132 columns on the text screen. You can only use these options if your hardware is capable of it. Using a text screen with 132 columns lets you display more Quattro columns on your screen at once. If you select one of the 132 column options and your hardware is incapable of this type of display, your screen will be garbled. If this happens, press CTRL-BREAK and type **/ODA** to select /Options Display Mode **A**: 80 X 25.

If you are using a mouse, changing to a text screen that has more lines on the screen may cause the mouse pointer to disappear. Some mouse drivers are not capable of using the 43- and 50-line displays available with EGA and VGA displays. If this happens, you will want to change to a lower number of lines or change to the graphics mode display. As a long-term solution, you may want to contact the mouse manufacturer to obtain another mouse driver that works with these screens. If you are using a TSR (terminate and stay resident) program, you will want to set the TSR to use the same screen mode as Quattro. If you are using a Microsoft mouse using version 7.04 of the software, you will need to use the /Y switch as in DEVICE=MOUSE.SYS /Y in your CONFIG.SYS file.

With WYSIWYG, Quattro Pro displays the spreadsheet as it will print. You can expand or contract the display to see how the printed spreadsheet will appear from nearer or further away. To change how the WYSIWYG display is expanded or compressed, select /Options WYSIWYG Zoom %, and enter a percentage between 25 and 200. Numbers below 100 display the spreadsheet smaller than it will print and numbers above 100 display the spreadsheet larger than it will print. Figure 10.15 shows a spreadsheet expanded to 150% of its original size.

DEFAULTS AT STARTUP

Quattro's startup default settings provide information that Quattro looks for each time the program is loaded. This information includes loading a predesignated spreadsheet, starting a macro, using a specified menu, and editing menus. All these startup options are in the Startup menu, which is shown in Figure 10.16 and which you can access by typing / and selecting Options Startup. The Menu Builder, available by selecting Edit Menus from the Startup menu, is covered at the end of the chapter.

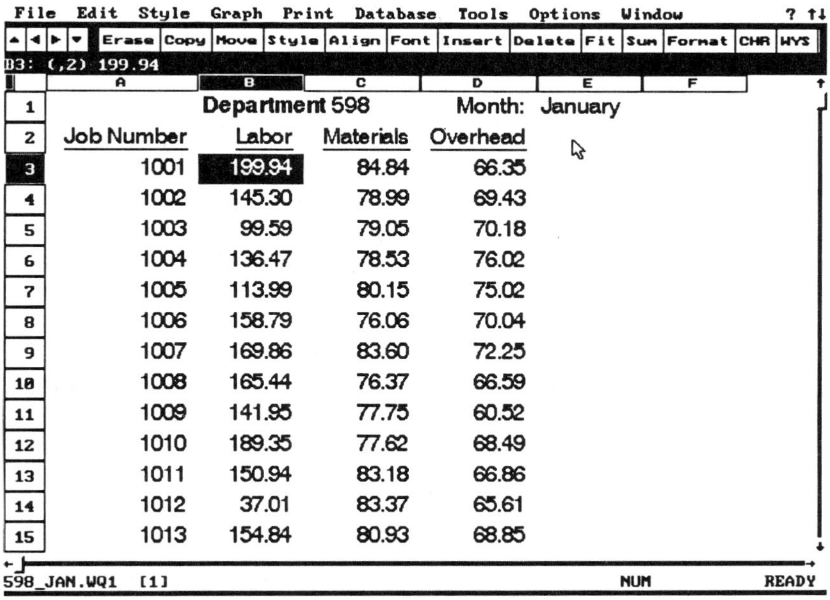

Customizing Quattro Pro

```
File   Edit  Style  Graph  Print  Database  Tools  Options  Window        ? ↑↓
▲ ◄ ► ▼  Erase Copy Move Style Align Font Insert Delete Fit Sum Format CHR WYS
B3: (,2) 199.94
```

	A	B	C	D	E	F
1		Department 598		Month:	January	
2	Job Number	Labor	Materials	Overhead		
3	1001	199.94	84.84	66.35		
4	1002	145.30	78.99	69.43		
5	1003	99.59	79.05	70.18		
6	1004	136.47	78.53	76.02		
7	1005	113.99	80.15	75.02		
8	1006	158.79	76.06	70.04		
9	1007	169.86	83.60	72.25		
10	1008	165.44	76.37	66.59		
11	1009	141.95	77.75	60.52		
12	1010	189.35	77.62	68.49		
13	1011	150.94	83.18	66.86		
14	1012	37.01	83.37	65.61		
15	1013	154.84	80.93	68.85		

```
598_JAN.WQ1  [1]                                         NUM       READY
```

Figure 10.15 Spreadsheet Expanded to 150% of Its Original Size

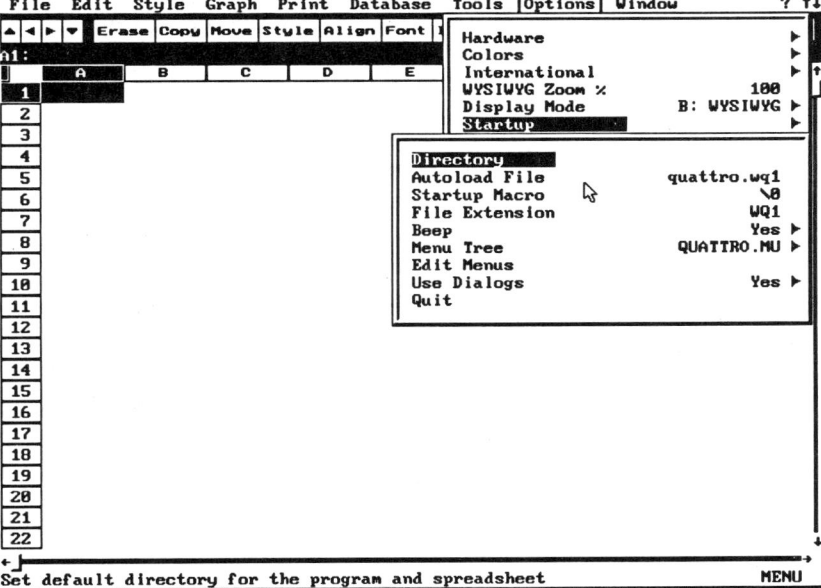

Figure 10.16 Startup Menu

Setting the Default Directory

Every time you use a command that uses an external data file, such as /File Retrieve or /Graph Save, Quattro uses the current directory. This is usually the default directory selected with /Options Startup Directory although it can be temporarily changed with the /File Directory command. Initially, the default directory is the same drive and directory containing the Quattro program files. When you enter /Options Startup Directory, Quattro displays the current setting as it prompts for the new one. The path must include the drive and directories, such as **C:\QPRO\FILES.** Until you select Update from the Options menu, the effect of the /Options Startup Directory command is as temporary as the /File Directory command, which only lasts as long as the current Quattro session. You can continue to specify a different directory for the commands that list or select files by entering a different directory path when you enter the command that uses the files.

Automatically Loading a Spreadsheet File

Quattro allows you to automatically retrieve a particular file each time you load Quattro. When you use the command /Options Startup Autoload File, Quattro prompts you for the name of the file to be loaded automatically. Type in the name of the desired file, and press ENTER. A practical application for this feature is when you use Quattro primarily for one application and want to automatically load the spreadsheet for that application every time you load Quattro. This file name is initially set to QUATTRO.WQ1, but you can change it to any file that Quattro can load with the /File Retrieve or /File Open command. If you remove the file name, Quattro does not try to retrieve any file when you load Quattro. Also, if you provide a file name after the Q to load Quattro, the file name you enter after the Q is loaded instead of the autoload file.

Automatically Starting a Macro

When you use macros to automate applications, you may want a macro to take control of the spreadsheet immediately. This prevents a user from making any changes to the spreadsheet that are not done under the control of the macro. For example, in a spreadsheet with a macro that prompts for the monthly sales figures and creates graphs using the cumulative sales information, having a macro control the spreadsheet immediately reduces potential errors.

Quattro allows you to specify the macro name that is automatically executed when a file containing the macro name is loaded. This autoload macro, initially called \0, can be changed to another valid macro name. To enable this option, use the /Options Startup Startup Macro command. Quattro prompts for the name of the macro to be run when the spreadsheet is loaded. Type the macro name, and press ENTER.

Changing the Default Extension

Quattro allows you to specify the default file extension. Quattro initially assumes that you are working with Quattro spreadsheets and uses the default extension of

.WQ1. To change the default extension, type /, select **Options Startup File Extension**, type in the default extension, and press ENTER. This option should only be changed if you are using Quattro primarily for non-Quattro data files such as 1-2-3, dBASE III, or Paradox, since it will permit you to read and write these file types without supplying the file name extension each time.

Setting the Error Beeps

Quattro beeps when you make a mistake, such as trying to move beyond the edge of a spreadsheet. Although these beeps are informative, you may find them annoying. Quattro allows you to turn off the beep that sounds whenever you make an error with the **/Options Startup Beep No** command. You can use the **/Options Startup Beep Yes** command to reinstate the beeping sound for errors. If you only want to disable the beep for the current session, do not use the **/Options Update** command.

Using a Different Menu Tree

Quattro lets you select the menu tree that you want to use. Each menu tree can have a different structure. Quattro initially provides two menu structures. One is Quattro Pro's menu tree, which is the basis for all the command descriptions in this book. Quattro also has another menu tree that is identical to 1-2-3's menu with bullets (■) marking Quattro commands that do not have a 1-2-3 equivalent. Prior releases of Quattro Pro had a third menu, which was identical to the Quattro 1.X menu. In addition to the two menus provided, you can create your own menus using Quattro's Menu Builder. To specify the menu you want, use the **/Options Startup Menu Tree** command. Quattro displays a list of the available menus. Select one of these menus, and press ENTER.

The use of different menu structures is one reason why you may want to use different resource files. Each of your resource files may use a different menu structure. If you want to use a 1-2-3 style menu, use the special file, Q123, that allows you to configure Quattro to look like 1-2-3. Using Q123 also sets other default settings besides the menu structure. These other settings make Quattro more compatible with 1-2-3. For example, if you are using 1-2-3 macros in Quattro, using Q123 is a good idea.

Using Dialog Boxes

Quattro Pro 4 can display dialog boxes in place of menus for several commands. These commands include **/Print Layout, /Graph Customize Series, /Graph X-Axis, /Graph Y-Axis, /Graph Overall**. The dialog boxes do not provide additional options but rather they condense several menu levels into a single dialog box. Also, with the **/Graph Customize Series** command, the dialog box only presents the options that are applicable to the graph type you are using. To use these dialog boxes, select **/Options Startup Use Dialogs Yes**. If you do not want to use the dialog boxes and want to use the menus instead, select **/Options Startup Use Dialogs No**. Chapter 4 described how you can use the dialog box when you learned about the Print Layout Options dialog box.

SETTING THE SPEEDBAR

Quattro initially decides the function each button in the SpeedBar will perform. You can reassign any of these except for the END-arrow key combination. Quattro Pro 4 can have up to 15 buttons on its SpeedBar but will only display in WYSIWYG mode the buttons that have been assigned. To reassign a button, select SpeedBar from the Options menu and select either READY mode SpeedBar or EDIT mode SpeedBar to select which speedBar you want to change. Next, select the button that you want to change. Quattro then displays a menu containing **Short name** to enter up to three characters that appear in the button in a text display mode, **Long name** to enter up to ten characters that appear in the button in a WYSIWYG display mode, and **Macro** to select the macro the button performs. When you select **Short name** or **Long name** Quattro prompts you to indicate the characters you want to appear in the button. You can either edit the current entry or press ESC and type a new one. When you select **Macro**, Quattro prompts you to indicate the macro instructions you want the button to perform. You can enter keyboard alternative macros as well as use the macro commands and menu equivalents. You can also enter a macro name to have Quattro Pro execute a macro stored on the worksheet when the button is selected. You can edit the current macro, or press ESC and type a new one. You can continue altering the SpeedBar buttons, and then select **Quit** when you are finished. From this menu, you can select another mouse button to modify or **Quit** to return to the Options menu. The SpeedBar always will appear across the top in WYSIWYG mode and on the right in other display modes.

TELLING QUATTRO PRO WHEN TO BUILD BITSTREAM FONTS

When you use a Bitstream font to display the graph or preview the spreadsheet, Quattro checks the INDEX.FON file to check if Quattro has already built the Bitstream font. If Quattro has not built the font file, Quattro builds it. If your hard disk is near capacity or you do not want to wait for Quattro to build a font to display the graph or spreadsheet, you should disable Quattro from building Bitstream fonts. To halt the creation of fonts, enter **/Options Graphics Quality** and select **Draft**. The next time Quattro wants a Bitstream font that is not built yet, it substitutes a Hershey font in its place. When you want to return building fonts, enter **/Options Graphics Quality Final**. After this command, Quattro builds a font whenever you specify one that is not built yet.

> ▼ **TIP:** Test any modified SpeedBar button.
>
> Do not update the resource file until you have tested the modified SpeedBar button to check that it works as planned.

SETTING OTHER SYSTEM OPTIONS

The remaining system options that do not apply to networks are found in the Other menu, since they apply to settings that do not belong to the selections in the Options menu. From the Other menu, you can set whether undo is enabled, which portions of the screen a macro updates, what type of data Quattro stores in the expanded memory, which format of date and time appears in the status line, and settings to use Quattro Pro and Paradox simultaneously. After you have selected one of the options in the Other menu, Quattro returns you to the Options menu.

Setting Undo

Quattro's Undo feature, when it is enabled, allows you to remove the effect of a command you performed. To enable Undo, enter /Options Other Undo Enable. Once Undo is enabled, you can use /Edit Undo or ALT-F5 (UNDO) to remove the effect of the last command.

When Undo is enabled, there are only some changes Quattro can undo. A summary of these changes is shown in Table 10.1. /Edit Undo undoes the effect of the last operation that can be affected by Undo. If you make several changes that Quattro cannot undo and then enter /Edit Undo, Quattro undoes the effect of the last change that Undo can change. Each time you enter /Edit Undo or press ALT-F5 (UNDO), Quattro toggles between the spreadsheet before and after the operation that Undo is changing.

When Undo is enabled, Quattro runs slower, since it must spend some of your computer's computing power storing the effect of the changes you make. Undo also uses your computer's memory. If you want to disable undo, enter /Options Other Undo Disable. Another possible way to recover the spreadsheet from the effect of your actions is to use the Transcript utility covered in Chapter 11.

Table 10.1 Undo's Effect on Spreadsheet Changes

Changes Quattro Can Undo	Changes Quattro Cannot Undo
Changes to spreadsheet entries	Changes to command settings
Deletion of named blocks	Changes to format settings
Deletion of named graphs	File manipulations in File Manager
Retrieval of a file over another file	Style commands except /Style Insert Break
Erasing of a spreadsheet	
Sorting of database records	

Setting How a Macro Updates the Screen

When Quattro performs a macro, Quattro performs the macro instructions very quickly, much more quickly than you can enter the keystrokes. Quattro must spend part of the computer's capacity updating the screen to reflect the most current changes. The updating process is called redrawing the screen. The macro can perform more quickly if Quattro does not constantly redraw the screen. To set when Quattro redraws the screen, select Macro from the Other menu. You can select Both to suppress redrawing the entire screen while Quattro performs the macro, Panel to suppress redrawing the screen except for the spreadsheet windows, Window to suppress redrawing the spreadsheet windows, and None to remove suppression. You should remove redrawing suppression when you are checking your macros for errors. Once the macro performs as expected, you can suppress the redrawing so the macro performs quickly. If part or all of the screen is not redrawn when you perform a macro, Quattro redraws the entire screen when the macro is finished.

Setting How Quattro Uses Expanded Memory

When your computer has expanded memory, Quattro can use this memory to store larger spreadsheets. Quattro automatically detects if the computer has expanded memory. With expanded memory, you can have more and larger spreadsheets. On the other hand, the response to Quattro commands is quicker if you do not use expanded memory. Initially, with expanded memory, Quattro stores a cell format information in conventional memory and spreadsheet data in the expanded memory. You can change how Quattro uses expanded memory by entering /Options Other Expanded Memory. From the selection box Quattro presents, you can select Both to store cell contents and format information in expanded memory, Spreadsheet Data to store spreadsheet labels and formulas in extended memory, Format to store format information in expanded memory and spreadsheet data in conventional memory, or None to not use expanded memory.

You can also change how much of the expanded memory Quattro Pro 3 or 4 uses. When you start Quattro Pro, follow the Q with /E and the number of expanded memory pages (a number ranging from 1 to 65355). An example is Q /E16, which limits Quattro Pro to 16 pages of expanded memory or 262144 bytes. You will want to limit how much expanded memory Quattro Pro uses if you are using a TSR (terminate and stay resident program) that uses expanded memory.

Formatting and Setting the Clock Display in the Status Line

Quattro uses the status line to display information about the current session. One possibility is a display of the date and time. Quattro displays the date and time to the right of the window number on the status line if you enter /Options Other Clock Standard or /Options Other Clock International. If you select Standard, the date is shown in the DD-MMM-YY format and the time is shown in the HH:MM AM/PM format. If you select International, the date and time are shown in the long format of the /Options International Date setting and in the short format of the /Options International Time setting. If you select None, the date and time disappear from the status line.

If the date or time is incorrect, use the DOS TIME or DATE commands after selecting /File Utilities DOS Shell. When you use either of these commands, DOS displays the date or time currently on the system and then prompts for the new date or time.

Using Paradox Databases on a Network

In Chapter 8, you learned how you can use Paradox databases without translating them into a Quattro spreadsheet. One application for using the file without bringing the file into Quattro is network use. If you are using Quattro with Paradox files stored on a network, you must tell Quattro some information about the network. If you are planning to use Paradox and Quattro Pro together, you will need to use some of the following commands. To tell Quattro about the network for the Paradox databases, enter /Options Other Paradox. First select Network Type, and select the type of network. If you are using Quattro Pro and Paradox together not on a network, you will select Other. Then select Directory, and type the drive and directory that contains the PARADOX.NET file, a Paradox file used in network environments. If you are unsure about the network type or the directory containing the PARADOX.NET file, ask your network administrator for this information. If you are not working with Quattro Pro on a network, you still must specify the location of PARADOX.NET, which should be in your Paradox directory. Quattro Pro includes another option called Retries, which sets how often Quattro Pro will attempt to get the file reservation of the Paradox file you wanted to use. Type a number between 0 and 65000 and press ENTER. Select Quit to return to the Options menu.

QUATTRO PRO SETTINGS FOR USING QUATTRO PRO 4 ON A NETWORK

When you are using Quattro Pro 4 on a network, you will want to use the /Options Network command to make working on a network easier. Most of these commands are designed for Novell Netware, so some of these features may not be available with other network systems. Quattro Pro will let you log on to any Netware file server that you are allowed to, using one user name at a time. The permission to access file servers and files in them are granted as rights, which are given by the network administrator. You need to supply Quattro Pro with information about that network. In Quattro Pro 4, you tell Quattro about the network environment by selecting Network.

Since the files you are using from the network are possibly located in various servers, volumes, drives, and directories, you can map drives. This allows you to easily open files from a network Quattro Pro location by selecting a drive letter without having to supply server, volume, drive, path, and user information. To create a drive mapping, select **Drive mappings**, and then select one of the eight slots Quattro Pro has for drive mappings. Next, you are prompted for the drive letter to map, the server name, the volume name, drive and path information, and the user name. For each of these, type the appropriate information, and press ENTER or click the Enter button. For some of the prompts you may be provided a list of possible selections to choose from. You can also change a network mapping by following the steps of creating one but selecting the number you want to alter. If you want to use the same user name for all of your drive mappings, select **User Name**, type your user name, and press ENTER or click the Enter button. Once the drive is mapped, you can select the drive letter you have mapped for a file command and Quattro will display the files in that location.

When you are printing through a network printer, you may want to print a banner page as the first page of your document. A banner page is an additional page that often includes information like your name so you can easily separate the different printouts from the network printer. The banner page is printed when you select **Banner** and **Yes** or omitted when you select **Banner** and **No**. Another setting to change when you are printing through your network is Refresh Interval. This interval selects the number of seconds that the Borland Print Spooler Print Manager or Netware print queue updates the information about the files that you are printing over the network. Type a number between 1 and 300, and then press ENTER or click the Enter button. To have this information displayed in the Borland Print Spooler Print Manager, the setting for Queue Monitor must be set to Yes. If it is set to **No**, the Borland Print Spooler Print Manager will no longer monitor your printing tasks.

FORMAT DEFAULTS

Quattro uses default format options that make assumptions about how you want your data displayed. For instance, Quattro assumes that you want all labels left-aligned. Also, Quattro assumes that all numbers should be displayed in the General format. Quattro makes the assumption that all zero values should be displayed and the default width of the columns is nine. All these assumptions can be changed to new default values through the Formats menu shown in Figure 10.17. The /Options Formats command accesses this menu. Unlike the customization options discussed so far, these options are saved with the spreadsheet and only affect the current spreadsheet.

Customizing Quattro Pro 543

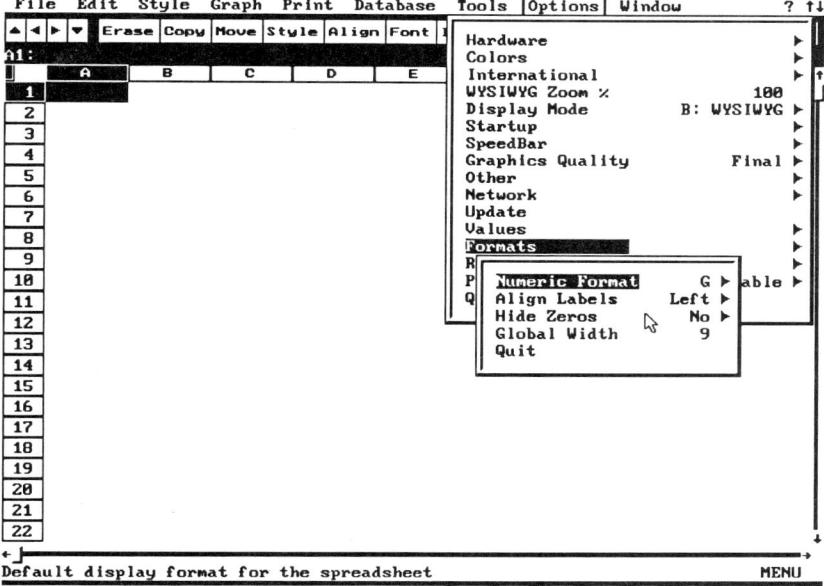

Figure 10.17 Formats Menu

Setting the Default Numeric Format

Quattro allows you to change the default numeric format of values in a spreadsheet. This is the format of values that have not been formatted with the /Style Numeric Format command or assigned a named style. The setting is saved with the spreadsheet. This setting should be changed to match the format of the largest group of values. For example, if you are performing a financial analysis, you probably want to set the default format to Currency to reduce the number of times you use the /Style Numeric Format command. The /Options Formats Numeric Format command has the following options:

- Fixed—This option displays values with a fixed number of decimal places. Examples of numbers formatted with this setting are 32.6, 5000, or -.333.

- Scientific—This option displays values in exponential notation. This expression takes the form of 'x.xxE+06'. The number of decimal places is user defined. For example, 236 could be shown as 2.36E+02.

- Currency—This option displays values in currency terms. A currency symbol is added, commas are inserted every three digits to the left or right of the decimal point, negative values are shown in parentheses, and the number of decimal places is defined by the user (the default setting is two decimal places). An example is $1,000.11.

- **, (Financial)**—This option displays values with commas as separators after the thousand position. The negative values are expressed in parentheses. The desired number of decimal places must be defined. An example is 1,000.11.
- **General**—This option displays values in their normal form, that is the values appear as they were entered without any other formatting. This results in varying numbers of decimal digits and use of scientific notation for very large and very small values.
- **+/-** —This option allows you to create simple horizontal bar charts. It transforms positive values into + signs for each positive integer and negative values into - signs for each negative integer.
- **Percent**—This option displays values as percentages by showing the decimal place two spaces to the right and adding a percent symbol after the number. The number of digits shown after the decimal point is user defined. For example, 0.95 can be displayed as 95.00%, and .012 can be displayed as 1.2%.
- **Date**—This option displays values as dates or times. You have several options within this selection. These options allow you to display dates in the form of DD-MMM-YY, DD-MMM, MMM-YY, Long intl., and Short intl. The long international and short international date formats are determined by the /Options International Date command. By selecting Time from the Date menu, you can select from HH:MM:SS AM/PM, HH:MM AM/PM, Long intl., and Short intl. to set the default display format to display times. The long and short international time formats are set with the /Options International Time command.
- **Text**—This option displays formulas in the cells, rather than the values resulting from the formulas. Cells containing numbers are displayed in General format.
- **Hidden**—This option hides unformatted cells. The cell contents only appear on the input line. This format affects labels as well as values.

When you use the /Options Formats Numeric Format command in a pane, it only affects the current pane. When the pane is later closed, the setting with this command is retained only if the command was used in the upper or left pane. Any format changes made with the /Style Numeric Format command are retained regardless of the pane in which you executed the command.

Unlike the /Style Numeric Format command, you do not have to specify a block for the /Options Formats Numeric Format command. The default display format settings affect all cells except cells formatted with the /Style Numeric Format command.

Setting the Default Label Alignment

Quattro allows you to change the default alignment for labels in a spreadsheet with the /Options Formats Align Labels command. Initially, the default label alignment is set to left-align all labels. This command establishes the alignment for new label entries that are entered without a label prefix. This command does not affect existing label entries. The default alignment setting is saved with the spreadsheet. This setting should be changed if you want most of the labels in a spreadsheet to be right-aligned or centered.

Hiding Zero Values

Quattro allows you to display cells containing zeros as blank, effectively hiding the zeros. For example, Figure 10.18 shows several cells with zero values. The nonzero numbers in column E are the ones that require further analysis, and hiding the zero values emphasizes the other numbers. Figure 10.19 shows the same spreadsheet with the zero values hidden. Hiding zero values is similar to using a hidden format for cells: the contents are still displayed on the input line when the selector is on the cell. To hide zero values, use the /Options Formats Hide Zeros Yes command. To display hidden zero values, use the /Options Formats Hide Zeros No command. This command affects the entire spreadsheet. Quattro does not have a command that hides zeros for a spreadsheet block. Also, remember that it is easy to accidentally type over hidden zeros, since they appear as blank cells.

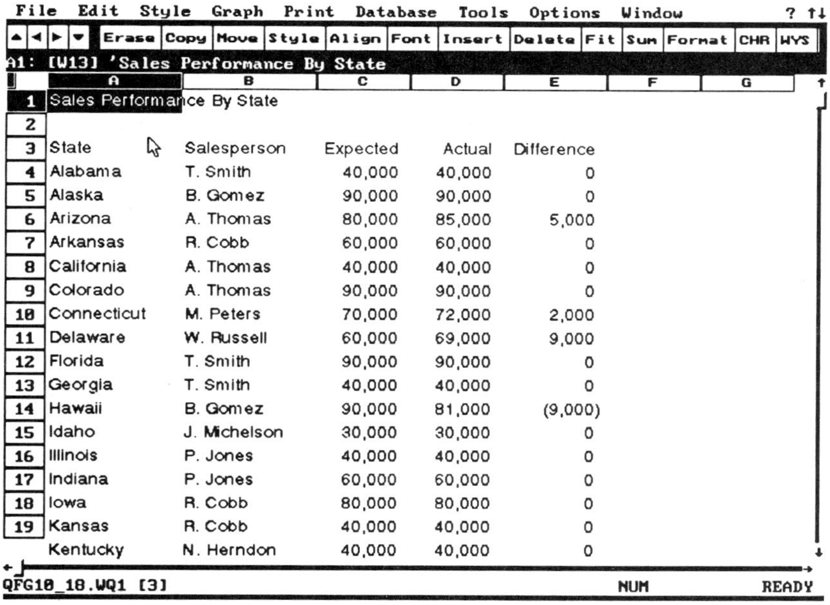

	A	B	C	D	E
1	Sales Performance By State				
2					
3	State	Salesperson	Expected	Actual	Difference
4	Alabama	T. Smith	40,000	40,000	0
5	Alaska	B. Gomez	90,000	90,000	0
6	Arizona	A. Thomas	80,000	85,000	5,000
7	Arkansas	R. Cobb	60,000	60,000	0
8	California	A. Thomas	40,000	40,000	0
9	Colorado	A. Thomas	90,000	90,000	0
10	Connecticut	M. Peters	70,000	72,000	2,000
11	Delaware	W. Russell	60,000	69,000	9,000
12	Florida	T. Smith	90,000	90,000	0
13	Georgia	T. Smith	40,000	40,000	0
14	Hawaii	B. Gomez	90,000	81,000	(9,000)
15	Idaho	J. Michelson	30,000	30,000	0
16	Illinois	P. Jones	40,000	40,000	0
17	Indiana	P. Jones	60,000	60,000	0
18	Iowa	R. Cobb	80,000	80,000	0
19	Kansas	R. Cobb	40,000	40,000	0
	Kentucky	N. Herndon	40,000	40,000	0

Figure 10.18 Spreadsheet with Several Zero Value Cells

```
 File   Edit   Style   Graph   Print   Database   Tools   Options   Window        ?  ↑↓
 ▲ ◀ ▶ ▼  Erase Copy Move Style Align Font Insert Delete Fit Sum Format CHR WYS
 A1: [W13] 'Sales Performance By State
```

	A	B	C	D	E	F	G
1	Sales Performance By State						
2							
3	State	Salesperson	Expected	Actual	Difference		
4	Alabama	T. Smith	40,000	40,000			
5	Alaska	B. Gomez	90,000	90,000			
6	Arizona	A. Thomas	80,000	85,000	5,000		
7	Arkansas	R. Cobb	60,000	60,000			
8	California	A. Thomas	40,000	40,000			
9	Colorado	A. Thomas	90,000	90,000			
10	Connecticut	M. Peters	70,000	72,000	2,000		
11	Delaware	W. Russell	60,000	69,000	9,000		
12	Florida	T. Smith	90,000	90,000			
13	Georgia	T. Smith	40,000	40,000			
14	Hawaii	B. Gomez	90,000	81,000	(9,000)		
15	Idaho	J. Michelson	30,000	30,000			
16	Illinois	P. Jones	40,000	40,000			
17	Indiana	P. Jones	60,000	60,000			
18	Iowa	R. Cobb	80,000	80,000			
19	Kansas	R. Cobb	40,000	40,000			
	Kentucky	N. Herndon	40,000	40,000			

```
 QFG10_19.WQ1 [3]                                       NUM            READY
```

Figure 10.19 Spreadsheet with Zeros Hidden

Setting Default Column Width

Quattro allows you to change the global column width in a spreadsheet. The /Options Formats Global Width command sets all column widths that have not been set with the /Style Column Width, /Style Block Size Auto Width, or /Style Block Size Set Width command. The setting is saved with the spreadsheet. Change this setting if you are changing many of the columns of your spreadsheet to another column width. For example, if a spreadsheet is mostly filled with percentages, changing the default column width to a smaller number displays more columns on the screen. When you execute this command, Quattro prompts for a new column width. You can type in a new number or use the arrow keys before pressing ENTER to set the new default column width. The column width may range from one to 254 characters.

When you use this command in a pane, it only affects the current pane. When the pane is later closed, the default column width is retained only if the command was entered in the upper or left pane.

RECALCULATION DEFAULTS

Initially Quattro keeps the spreadsheet up to date through automatic recalculation every time an entry is made on the spreadsheet. Quattro can assess the impact of every change on the spreadsheet and recalculate only those entries that are affected by the change. This process of assessing the need for recalculating a cell is referred to as minimal recalculation. It can save a significant amount of time if most of your changes affect only a small percentage of spreadsheet cells. Since Quattro does this in the background in between your entries, you do not have to wait for Quattro to finish recalculating before you make the next entry.

Quattro can monitor the need for recalculation through a table it maintains to track all cells that are referenced by another cell. When a cell's contents change, Quattro refers to the table and determines which formulas need to be recalculated. This procedure may seem complex; but in situations where most cells are unaffected by a change, the overhead of table maintenance is more than offset by the quick recalculation that is possible due to Quattro's selective recalculation.

While minimal recalculation is an integral part of Quattro that does not require any effort on your part, Quattro has other settings that affect how the recalculations are performed. You can disable the automatic recalculation, eliminating the immediacy of recalculation. You can change the order in which Quattro recalculates the spreadsheet. You can change the number of iterations that Quattro performs for circular calculations. All of these options are available in the Recalculation menu shown in Figure 10.20 and accessed by typing / and selecting Options Recalculation.

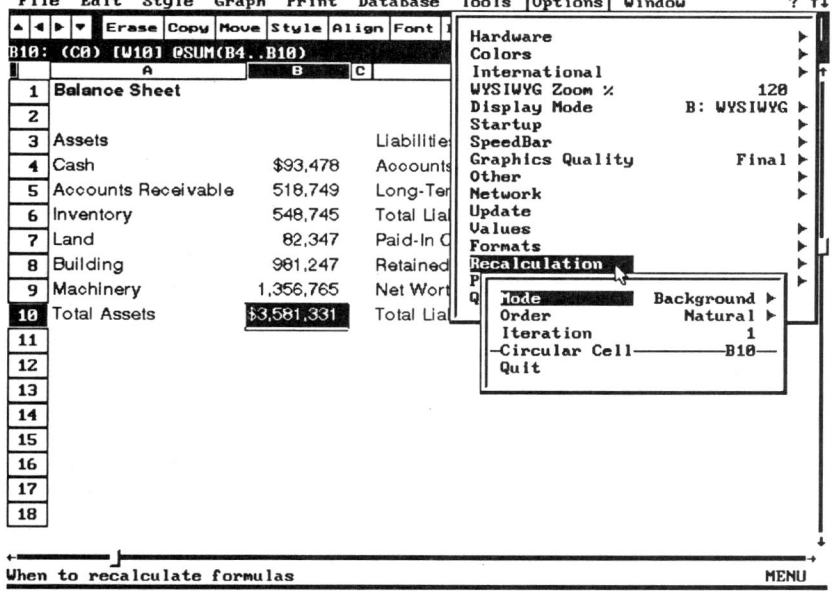

Figure 10.20 Recalculation Menu

Specifying Manual or Automatic Calculation

Although Quattro uses minimal and background recalculation to reduce the amount of time needed to recalculate the spreadsheet, other recalculation options can change the time at which Quattro recalculates a spreadsheet. For instance, you can change Quattro to only recalculate when you press F9 (CALC) by entering /Options Recalculation Mode Manual command. Once the spreadsheet is set to recalculate manually, Quattro only calculates formulas that are entered or edited. The formulas that reference the changed cells are not recalculated. Quattro only recalculates when you press F9 (CALC). Since Quattro must still keep track of the formulas that need to be recalculated, you should press F9 (CALC) whenever Quattro's performance slows. Quattro displays CALC in the status line to remind you that the spreadsheet needs to be recalculated.

Another option is to recalculate the spreadsheet automatically but cause the user to pause until Quattro has finished recalculating the necessary entries. You can use this automatic, but not background, recalculation by entering /Options Recalculation Mode Automatic. This is how Quattro 1.0 recalculated spreadsheets. When you want to return to the default of background and automatic recalculation, enter /Options Recalculation Mode Background. When you change to automatic or background recalculation, Quattro begins the new method of recalculation whenever you press F9 (CALC) or edit a cell.

Changing the Order of Spreadsheet Calculation

Quattro recalculates a spreadsheet based on the dependencies within the formulas. This means that Quattro determines that cells need to be calculated first in order for their results to be available for subsequent calculations. This is referred to as the natural order of calculation.

A look at natural recalculation order in practice helps clarify the process. For example, when Quattro recalculates cell B3 in Figure 10.21, Quattro first checks if the formula in B7 or in G7 needs to be recalculated before computing a result for B3. If cells B7 or G7 contain formulas that refer to other cells, Quattro continues this checking process. In summary, Quattro intelligently chooses the order in which it evaluates the spreadsheet so that all formulas that are affected by a change are properly evaluated.

Quattro provides two alternative orders for calculation: Column-wise and Row-wise. These options offer compatibility with older spreadsheet models that used these methods. These older models are seldom used now because their recalculation methods require the user to enter formulas in certain locations on the spreadsheet. Understanding how they work will motivate you to check periodically to insure that this setting has not been altered inadvertently for any of your models.

A spreadsheet calculated with the row-wise order has every cell in row 1

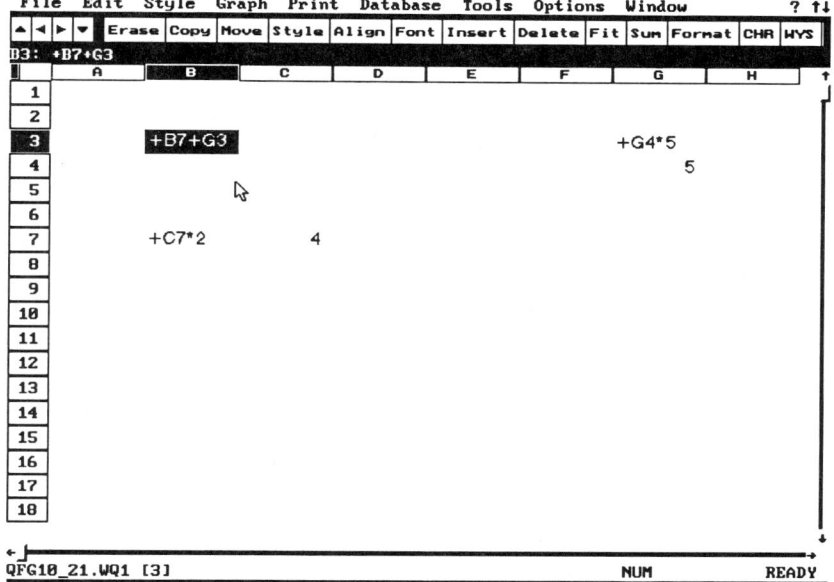

Figure 10.21 Spreadsheet Illustrating Different Recalculation Methods

calculated before calculations are performed in row 2. This progression from row to row continues down the spreadsheet. For example, using the spreadsheet in Figure 10.21, if you changed C7 to 5 and recalculated the spreadsheet, B3 would be evaluated before B7. The formula in B3 would use the old value of B7. This problem can only be remedied by recalculating the spreadsheet multiple times.

Calculating a spreadsheet in column-wise order can present the same problem as row-wise recalculation. A spreadsheet calculated in column-wise order has each cell in columns to the left calculated before columns to the right. For example, using the spreadsheet in Figure 10.21, if you changed G4 to 4 and recalculated the spreadsheet, B3 would be evaluated before G3. The formula in B3 would use the old value of G3. Like row-wise calculation, this problem can only be remedied by recalculating the spreadsheet multiple times.

Quattro allows you to change the order in which the spreadsheet is calculated with the /Options Recalculation Order command. When you execute this command, Quattro displays a selection box listing Natural, Column-wise, and Row-wise. After you have selected the order you want, press ENTER and Quattro changes to the order that you have selected. Since Column-wise and Row-wise can produce incorrect results, they should not be used without a valid reason (such as a need for compatibility with older VISICALC models). If you must use row-wise or column-wise calculation order, check that the spreadsheet is recalculated several times before relying on the spreadsheet data.

> ▼ **TIP: Check for the CALC indicator before printing.**
>
> Before printing data, check that the CALC indicator does not appear in the status line so you know you are printing the most up-to-date values.

Changing the Number of Iterations

The iteration count is the number of times Quattro recalculates formulas in a circular reference. The iteration count should be increased when you have purposely created a circular reference. For example, Figure 10.22 displays a spreadsheet designed to solve a polynomial equation (that is, finding a value of x that makes the equation equal to 0). The formula in B5 evaluates the polynomial using the value in B3 as x. The formula in B3 compares the results of the polynomial to zero and adjusts the value of B3 if B5 does not equal 0. When the value in B5 is 0, the first @IF function stops any further adjustments to B3. If the iteration count is 1, you must press F9 (CALC) repeatedly until the formula is evaluated a sufficient number of times to reach the correct value. By increasing the iteration count,

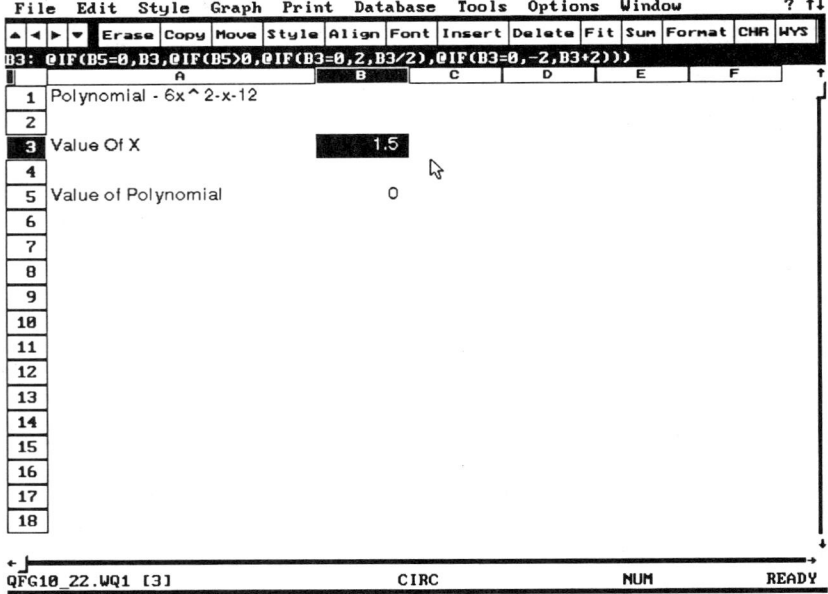

Figure 10.22 Iterative Formula Used to Solve Polynomial

Quattro reevaluates B3 the number of times specified by the iteration count or until B5 equals 0, whichever is less. To change the iteration count, use the /Options Recalculation Iteration command, type the number of iterations (up to 255), and press ENTER.

When a spreadsheet contains a circular reference, Quattro displays CIRC in the status line. Quattro also displays the first cell in the circular reference in the Recalculation menu, as shown in Figure 10.20. This cell reference informs you where to begin searching for a circular reference. Another possible way to find a circular reference is with the /Window Options Map View Yes command, which displays a c for each cell containing a circular reference or use the /Tools Audit Circular command.

PROTECTION DEFAULTS

Once you have created a spreadsheet, you should insure that formulas and other entries that you want to remain unchanged are not inadvertently damaged. To have Quattro protect the spreadsheet cells, use the /Options Protection Enable command. Whenever you attempt to make an entry in a cell that is protected, Quattro displays an error message. Once the protection status is enabled, a protected cell cannot be edited, replaced, or deleted. Also, a column or row containing protected cells cannot be deleted. The only method of erasing a protected cell is by erasing the entire spreadsheet. To disable a spreadsheet's protection, use the /Options Protection Disable command.

Quattro assumes that all cells are protected unless otherwise designated. To designate a block of cells as unprotected, use the /Style Protection Unprotect command. To protect unprotected cells use the /Style Protection Protect command. Unprotected cells appear in a different color from the value and label colors. Unprotected cells display a U between the cell width and format descriptors in the input line. When a spreadsheet is protected, protected cells have a PR between the cell width and format descriptors.

A special type of protection is protecting just the formulas in a spreadsheet. When a spreadsheet's formulas are protected, you cannot modify any formulas in the spreadsheet even if the cell containing the formula you want to edit is unprotected. To protect a spreadsheet's formulas, use the /Options Protection Formulas Enable command. Then like adding a password when you save a file, you must type the password twice pressing ENTER after each time. This formula protection is saved with the file. The only way you can modify the formulas at this point is to select /Options Protection Formulas Disable, type the correct password, and press ENTER.

The protection status is saved with the spreadsheet and is not saved as part of the system settings. Enabling protection for a spreadsheet is not equivalent to password-protecting it. A password prevents retrieval of the file without the password. A protected spreadsheet can be unprotected and modified by anyone able to supply a few Quattro commands.

ASSIGNING SHORTCUT KEYSTROKES TO QUATTRO PRO COMMANDS

As you have learned how to use the Quattro menu, you have been introduced to several shortcut keystrokes. For example, you can press CTRL-C to enter /Edit Copy. Table 10.2 lists the shortcut keystrokes that the initial Quattro menu has assigned to different commands. You can assign any of the 25 letters to any command. To assign a keystroke to a command, enter the command until the highlight is on the menu item to which you want to assign a shortcut keystroke. For example, if you solve linear optimization problems frequently, you might enter /Tools and highlight Optimizer. Next, press CTRL-ENTER. Quattro displays a message in the status line to press CTRL and type the letter you want to assign to the highlighted menu item. Hold down the CTRL key, and type the letter you want to assign. In the linear programming example, you can assign the letter O to the /Tools Optimizer

Table 10.2 Shortcut Keystrokes Assigned to Quattro Commands

Keystroke	Quattro Command
CTRL-A	/ Style Alignment
CTRL-C	/ Edit Copy
CTRL-D	/ Database Data Entry Dates Only
CTRL-E	/ Edit Erase Block
CTRL-F	/ Style Numeric Format
CTRL-G	/ Graph Fast Graph
CTRL-I	/ Edit Insert
CTRL-M	/ Edit Move
CTRL-N	/ Edit Search & Replace Next
CTRL-P	/ Edit Search & Replace Previous
CTRL-R	/Window Move/ Size
CTRL-S	/ File Save
CTRL-T	/Window Tile
CTRL-W	/ Style Column Width
CTRL-X	/ File Exit
CTRL-F10	/ Database Paradox Access Go

command by pressing CTRL-O. After you assign a shortcut keystroke to a command, Quattro displays the shortcut next to the menu item to which it is assigned. If you want to remove a shortcut keystroke, highlight the menu item with the assigned shortcut keystroke and press CTRL-ENTER. When Quattro displays a message in the status line, press DEL. Quattro prompts you to press DEL a second time to confirm that you want to remove the shortcut keystroke. Once you press DEL a second time, the shortcut keystroke disappears from the menu. You cannot assign CTRL-D or CTRL-F10, which are permanently assigned for entering dates or times and switching between Quattro Pro and Paradox.

QUATTRO PRO'S MENU BUILDER

The Menu Builder allows you to customize the menu structure. With the Menu Builder, you can rearrange commands, rename commands, have a command execute a macro, and change existing commands. You can change the menu to make the commands that you use most often quickly accessible.

Each of Quattro's default menu options performs a specific task within Quattro. Although these tasks are defined by Borland and cannot be supplemented by changes in the command structure, you can use the Menu Builder to assign any or all of these tasks to any menu command that you wish. The Menu Builder uses the menu-equivalent command for any action to define the commands in a menu structure.

Using the Menu Builder

To change the current menu structure, check that the menu you want to change is the current menu. Then use the **/O**ptions **S**tartup **E**dit **M**enus command. If you enter this command from a File Manager window, you edit the menu for File Manager windows. Quattro loads the current menu into memory and displays the screen shown in Figure 10.23. From this screen, you can modify the current menu. This screen is divided into three panes. The top pane is the current item pane, which displays information about the menu item highlighted in the menu tree pane. Use the current item pane to define the task that a menu item performs (by using menu-equivalent commands, as discussed later in the chapter and in Chapters 11 and 12).

The menu tree pane contains the current menu tree. In this pane, you select the menu items for change, insert menu items, and delete menu items. All menu items in the menu bar are in the same column. When you expand the menu tree to include the menu items below the menu bar items, each submenu is indented farther to the right (as is shown in Figure 10.24). The menu items indented are child menu items to the parent menu item to the left and above the first child menu item. You can display the child menu items by highlighting the parent and press the GRAY PLUS key. You can also hide them by pressing the GRAY MINUS key. All

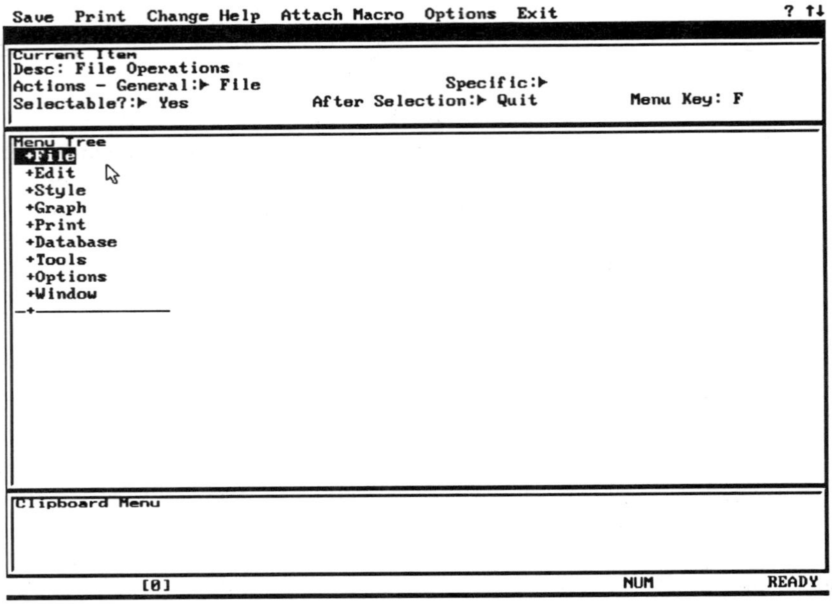

554 *Quattro Pro 4.0 Handbook*

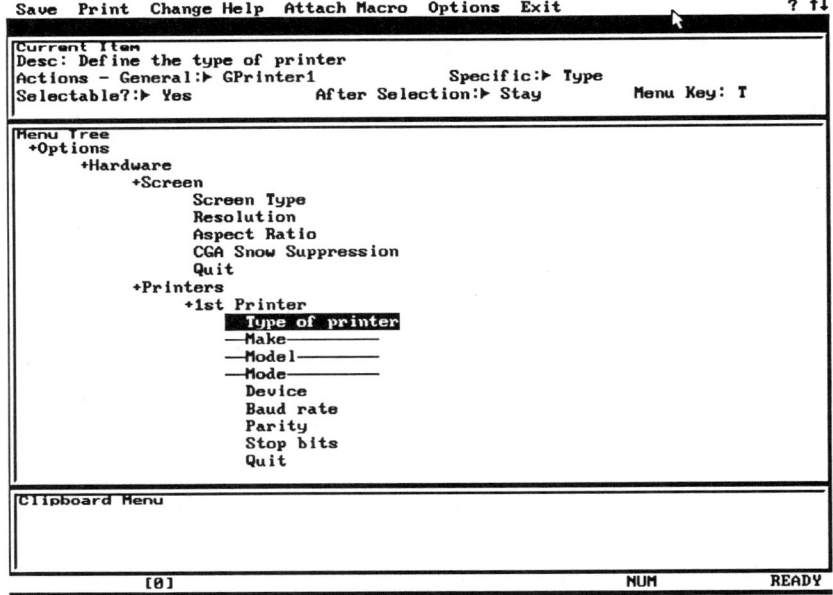

Figure 10.23 Initial Menu Builder Screen

Figure 10.24 Menu Tree Expanded to Show Child Menu Items

menu items in a box are siblings, as are all menu items that appear in the menu bar. All menu items that can be selected by selecting a menu item are its descendants. This includes the child menu items and the child menu items belonging to the children.

To change the highlighted menu item to another sibling menu item, use the UP ARROW and DOWN ARROW keys. To move to a child menu item of the highlighted menu item, press the RIGHT ARROW. To move to a parent menu item from a child menu item, press the LEFT ARROW. You can tell when a menu item has child menu items, since it has a plus sign before the menu item. Table 10.3 describes the keys to use in the Menu Builder. If you are using a mouse, you can also select a menu item or a pane by clicking it.

The bottom pane is the clipboard pane, which temporarily contains menu items that you have deleted in the order you deleted them. Quattro stores both the menu item and the settings assigned to the menu item in the clipboard.

Menu-Equivalent Commands

Quattro has a set of menu-equivalent commands that are primarily used for the Menu Builder and macros. These commands are different from Quattro's normal commands; they are easier to understand than recorded keystrokes in macros and can also be used for defining menu structures. The menu-equivalent commands operate regardless of the current menu structure chosen.

Quattro divides its commands into 80 groups. Each group is a *general action*. This action describes the generic feature that you are using such as Print for printing or File for file commands. Within each group, each command has a *specific action*. The specific action describes the specific command that you want Quattro to perform. These two types of actions can describe any Quattro command. For example, the menu-equivalent command for protecting your spreadsheet (/Options Protection Enable) is **{/ Protection;Enable}**. The Quattro commands and their menu-equivalent commands are listed in Appendix C.

The menu-equivalent commands are also used for the function @CURVALUE to display the current value of any menu command's settings. In this function, the general action is the first function argument, and the specific action is the second function argument, as in **@CURVALUE("Protection","Enable")**.

When the menu-equivalent commands are used in the Menu Builder, Quattro lets you give any name to a command. However, you must define the command in terms of its menu-equivalent command before it can perform an action. Even if a macro is assigned to a command in the menu, the Quattro commands that the macro performs must be defined in terms of menu-equivalent commands.

Editing a Menu Item

To change a menu item, make that menu item current. If you want to change the text of the menu item, you can type the new text or press F2 (EDIT) and edit the

Table 10.3 Keys in Menu Builder's Menu Tree Pane

Key	Action Key Performs
UP ARROW	Moves to the sibling menu item above the current one
DOWN ARROW	Moves to the sibling menu item below the current one
LEFT ARROW	Moves to the parent menu item above the current one
RIGHT ARROW	Moves to the child menu item below the current one
GRAY +	Displays child menu items of current menu item
GRAY -	Hides child menu items of current menu item
PGUP	Scrolls menu tree one screen up
PGDN	Scrolls menu tree one screen down
CTRL-PGUP	Moves to the parent menu of the current menu item
CTRL-PGDN	Moves to the last child menu item of the current parent menu item
CTRL-END	Moves to the last menu item displayed
CTRL-HOME	Moves to the first menu item displayed
TAB	Makes the current menu item (and its descendant menu items) a child of the sibling above it
SHIFT-TAB	Makes the current menu item (and its descendant menu items) a sibling of its parent menu item
ENTER	Inserts new menu item at same level as the current menu item
DEL	Moves menu item out of the menu tree and into the clipboard pane
INS	Moves menu item from clipboard pane to menu tree as sibling of current menu item
F2 (EDIT)	Allows you to edit the text of the current menu item
F6 (PANE)	Alternates among the menu tree pane, the clipboard pane, and the current item pane

existing menu item text. Once the menu item you want to change is highlighted, press F6 (PANE) to switch to the current item pane. This places a second highlight on the current item's description. From the current menu pane, you can make the following changes.

- Desc—This is the text that Quattro displays in the status line that describes the task that the menu item performs. Although this is not necessary, it is helpful.

- Actions-General—This is the general action that the menu performs. This must be one of the general actions used in menu-equivalent commands. When you press ENTER with the highlight on this item, Quattro displays a list of the available actions.

- Actions-Specific—This is the specific action that the menu performs. This must be one of the specific actions used for menu-equivalent commands that is appropriate for the general command. When you press ENTER with the highlight on this item, Quattro displays a list of the available actions. This should be left blank if Quattro displays a submenu when this menu item is selected. If a specific action is listed and you want to remove it, select the same general action again and the specific action will disappear.

- Selectable?—This determines whether you can select this menu item. For example, in the Hardware menu, you can select Printers but you cannot select Normal Memory. Set this to Yes for selectable items like Printers or items with child menus, or No for unselectable items like Normal Memory. When an item is unselectable, Quattro puts lines to the left and right of the menu item. This type of menu item subdivides a menu.

- After Selection—This is what Quattro does after you select this item and Quattro finishes executing it. To choose the action Quattro takes after performing the task assigned to the menu item, press ENTER and select one from the selection box Quattro displays. Your choices for what to do after an item is selected are Stay, Go to Parent, or Quit. For menu items with a submenu, this selection is automatically Quit. Selecting Quit branches to a submenu if the menu item has one or returns to READY mode if the menu item has a general and specific task assigned to it.

  If the menu item's choice is Stay, Quattro stays in the menu containing the menu item after the task is completed. For example, when you execute the /Options Update command, Quattro stays in the Options box after updating the resource file.

- If the menu selection for an item is Go to Parent, Quattro returns control to the menu that lists the menu item's parent. An example is /Graph Customize Series Reset Graph command, which returns to the customize series menu.

- Menu Key—This is the key letter that you must type to select the menu item. Quattro displays the letter in the color selected by the /Options Colors Menu Key Letter command.

CHANGING THE RELATION OF MENU ITEMS When you add a menu item, it is a sibling of the menu item above it. If you want the menu item to be a child of the menu item above it, you must tell Quattro to make the menu item a child by pressing TAB. If you want a menu item to become a parent menu item of the menu items below it, press SHIFT-TAB. Changing the level that a menu item belongs to also changes its children menu items, since they are moved with their parent menu item.

Inserting a New Menu Item

Although Quattro's menu structure contains all available Quattro commands, you may want to insert new menu items. For example, you can create a macro that Quattro can treat as a menu item and execute that macro whenever the menu item is selected. Also, you may want a menu item to be available in different menus or may wish to rearrange its presentation. To insert a new menu item, follow these steps:

1. Move the highlight to the menu where you want the new menu item.
2. Move the highlight to the menu item above where you wish to add the menu item.
3. Press ENTER, and type the name of the command that you want to use for the menu item.
4. Press ENTER to finalize the menu item text.
5. Press F6 (PANE) to move to Desc in the current item pane.
6. Press F2 (EDIT), and edit the description or type a new description before pressing ENTER to finalize it.
7. Press the RIGHT ARROW to move to the General prompt and select the appropriate general action for the task that you want the menu item to perform. Press ENTER to display a list of the available choices.
8. Press the RIGHT ARROW, and select the appropriate specific action you want the menu item to perform. If this menu item has a submenu, leave the specific action blank.
9. Press the RIGHT ARROW to move to Selectable. If the menu item should not be selected, type an **N** for No.
10. Press the RIGHT ARROW and select the menu item's action after it is completed. If the menu item leads to another menu, leave **Quit**.
11. Press the RIGHT ARROW and select the letter that the user must type to select the menu item. The letter should be part of the menu item and should be unique in its menu.

After the menu is saved, the new menu item is available.

Attaching a Macro to a Menu Item

Besides assigning a Quattro command to a menu item, you can also assign a macro to a menu item. When you select the menu item with a macro assigned, Quattro executes the macro. Since the macro must be in an open file, you should store all macros invoked with menus in the file name selected with /Options Startup Autoload File. To insert a macro in a menu, follow these steps:

1. Move the highlight to the menu item above where you want to add the menu item with a macro assigned to it.
2. Press ENTER, and type the name of the command that you want to use for the macro.
3. Type / to invoke the Menu Builder menu, and type A for Attach Macro.
4. Type the macro name, and press ENTER. You should include the file name in square brackets.
5. Press ENTER. Quattro immediately changes the general action to Name and the specific action to Attach.
6. Press F6 (PANE) to switch to the current item pane.
7. Enter the description to appear in the status line when the menu item is highlighted and press ENTER.
8. Move with the RIGHT ARROW to Menu key if you want to change the letter that selects the menu item.

An example of the macro as a menu item is shown in Figure 10.25. In this example, the macro Save & Print is a menu item. When this menu item is chosen by typing the ampersand (&), Quattro performs the macro Save & Print if it exists on an open spreadsheet. On the screen, the ampersand appears in red while the remaining letters appear in black (in Figure 10.25, of course, all the characters appear black). Since Quattro performs the macro only from open files, it is a good idea to name the macro file QUATTRO.WQ1 or change the name of the file of the /Options Startup Autoload File command.

Deleting and Inserting a Menu Item

When you have a menu item you do not want, you can remove it by deleting it from the menu tree. To delete a menu item, highlight it and press DEL. Quattro stores the deleted menu item in the clipboard pane. When you delete a menu item, you are also deleting all child menu items assigned to the deleted menu item and their child menu items. When a menu item is in the clipboard pane, Quattro retains all menu item settings with the menu item. Each time you press DEL, Quattro deletes another menu item and stores it above the previously deleted menu items. The order of the deleted items becomes important if you want to insert one or more

Figure 10.25 Menu Item Representing a Macro

of the menu items into the current menu tree. Once an item is in the clipboard pane, pressing F6 (PANE) selects the clipboard pane every third time. The menu items remain in the clipboard until you insert them into the menu tree or you exit the Menu Builder. When you exit the Menu Builder, Quattro erases the contents of the clipboard. When you want to insert the last item on the Clipboard into the menu as a sibling of the currently highlighted menu item, press INS. The inserted item is removed from the Clipboard and has all the same settings in the top pane that it had when you deleted the menu item.

Moving a Menu Item

Moving a command is as simple as deleting the command from its current position, moving to another position and placing the command into the menu tree from the clipboard. You can move menu items from one level to another simply by changing the menu level where you enter the removed command. To delete a command, press the DEL key. Once a menu item is removed, move to the menu item that you want to be above the moved menu item. It does not have to be in the same menu or the same level of menus. To put the command in the clipboard into the menu at this location, press the INS. When you press INS, the Menu Builder places the last deleted command below the current highlighted menu item. If the menu item you want to add from the clipboard is not the first menu item on the clipboard, press F6 (PANE) twice so the clipboard pane is active. Then highlight the menu item you want to insert, press F6 (PANE) so the menu tree pane is active and press INS. Moving a menu item moves all menu items in its child menu with it.

Setting Compatibility Options

The Menu Builder allows you to change several settings that affect how the menus behave. These settings make the menus more compatible with other spreadsheet packages. These settings are available by typing / to invoke the Menu Builder menu and by selecting **Options**. When you have finished changing the options, you can select **Quit** to return to the READY mode of the Menu Builder. When you enter /Options, you have the following options:

- Autoload File—This option determines the file Quattro loads automatically when Quattro is loaded with the menu tree. This is the same as the /**O**ptions **S**tartup **A**utoload File command.

- File Extension—This option determines the file extension Quattro uses as the default for file commands. This is the same as the /**O**ptions **S**tartup **F**ile **E**xtension command.

- Macro Recording—This option determines how Quattro records commands in macros. This is the same as the /**T**ools **M**acro **M**acro **R**ecording command. You can select **Logical** to record commands using the menu equivalents or select **Keystroke** to record the commands using keystrokes.

- Use Menu Bar—This option determines whether Quattro displays the initial menu as a menu bar along the top of the screen. If this option is set to **Yes**, Quattro displays a menu bar. When you select a menu item from the menu bar, Quattro displays the pull-down menu assigned to that menu item. If you press ESC from one of these pull-down menus, Quattro returns to the READY mode. If this option is set to **No**, Quattro only uses pop-up menus with no menu bar. Pressing ESC always returns you to the previous menu. If this option is set to **Compatible**, the initial menu appears as a menu bar, and pull-down menus are displayed when a menu item from the menu bar is selected. Unlike the **Yes** option, pressing ESC from a pull-down menu removes the pull-down menu but leaves the menu item highlighted in the menu bar. This option is used for the 123 compatible menu.

- Borland Style—This option determines when confirmation boxes are displayed. If this option is set to **No**, Quattro automatically displays confirmation boxes when you erase a spreadsheet or quit the program. If this option is set to **Yes**, Quattro displays confirmation boxes whenever you reset block or graph names. It also displays the boxes if you will lose data when you erase a spreadsheet or quit the program (for example, if your file is not saved).

- **During Macros**—This option determines whether confirmation boxes are displayed during macro execution. If set to **Yes**, Quattro displays all confirmation boxes as if you were performing the commands yourself. If set to **No**, Quattro suspends all confirmation boxes.
- **Quit**—This option returns you to the READY mode in the Menu Builder screen.

Quattro has two other compatibility options. One is whether the menus are displayed with their settings as in Figure 10.26 (the default) or whether the menus do not display the settings as in Figure 10.27. The other is whether Quattro remembers your position on a menu the next time you use it. The menu width compatibility setting is set by executing the menu equivalent command {/ Startup;WideMenus}. Determining whether Quattro remembers your last position on a menu is set by executing the menu equivalent command {/ Startup;Remember}. After performing either menu command you must select Yes or No. To make the change to the menu complete, you must use the /Options Update command. With the menu width, you can always override it by pressing the GRAY PLUS key or the GRAY MINUS key. With remembering the last menu chosen, No is the default for the QUATTRO.MU and 123.MU menu trees, and if you are using Quattro Pro on a network.

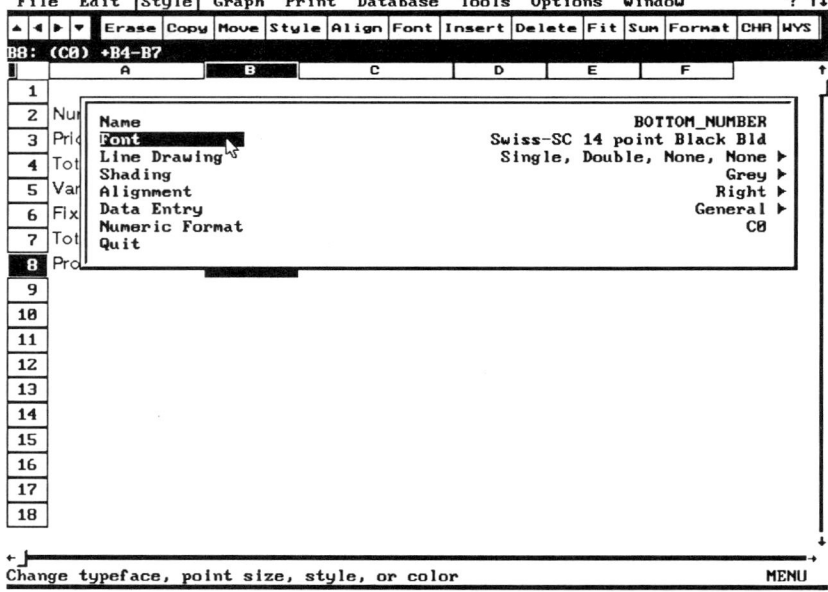

Figure 10.26 Menu with Settings Shown

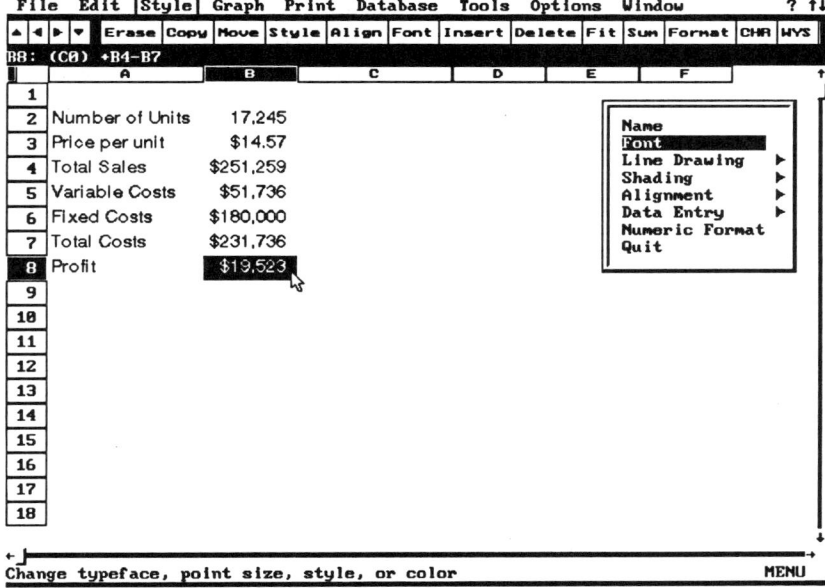

Figure 10.27 Menu without Settings Shown

Setting the Help Screen

Quattro initially has set which help screen appears when you press F1 (HELP) based on the menu item highlighted at the time. When you are building your own menu or modifying an existing one, you should change the help screen that Quattro displays when you press F1 (HELP). To set the help screen Quattro displays when a menu item is highlighted, type / and select Change Help. Quattro displays the currently assigned help screen. Since the help screens are interrelated, you can switch from one to another as you find a help topic that interests you. When you find the help screen you want to attach to the menu item, press ESC. Quattro prompts you between attaching the last help screen and canceling the change in the help screen. If you select Attach To Last Screen Shown, Quattro displays that help screen whenever a user presses F1 (HELP) with the current menu highlighted.

Printing the Menu Tree

While you are working on modifying a menu, it is difficult to remember all menu items contained in the menu tree. You can print out the menu tree so you have an up-to-date complete diagram of the menu tree. This printout also creates documentation for other people who use this menu. To print the current menu tree, enter /Print. Quattro prompts you with two options. Selecting **Printer** prints the menu tree immediately. Selecting **File** makes Quattro prompt for the name of a file in which the information can be saved. The file will have an .MNU extension unless you provide a different one. You can use the file option if you want to incorporate the menu tree into documentation that you are creating for other users. Figure 10.28 shows the first page of the printout from the Quattro default menu tree printed with this menu option.

Saving a Menu

After making the changes to the menu, you can save the menu by entering /**S**ave. Quattro displays a list of the existing menu files. You can either select one from the list or enter a new file name before pressing ENTER. You cannot save it to the same file name as the current menu tree. If you select an existing menu file name, Quattro displays the Cancel, Backup, and Replace selection box. Since Quattro adds an .MU file extension, you do not need to provide one. When Quattro has finished saving the file, Quattro returns to the pane in the Menu Builder you were in before you entered /**S**ave.

Exiting the Menu Builder

When you have finished modifying the menu or you have changed your mind and do not want to save your changes, enter /Exit. If the menu has changes, which have not been saved, Quattro asks you if you want to save the changes. If you select **No**, Quattro does not save the changes to the menu and returns you to the spreadsheet. If you select Yes, Quattro displays the list of existing menu tree file names and prompts for the file name under which the menu should be saved. Once you select or type a file name, Quattro saves the menu tree and leaves the Menu Builder.

The menu you have just modified does not appear when you type /. Quattro is still set to use the menu that you used before you entered the Menu Builder. To use the new menu, enter /Options Startup Menu Tree, and select the menu tree name from the list.

Using a Menu Tree From an Earlier Version of Quattro Pro

If you have created a menu tree with an earlier version of Quattro Pro, you must translate it to the format that Quattro Pro uses. This is done by using the NEWMU command from DOS, which you can access by quitting Quattro or by using the /File Utilities DOS Shell command. At the DOS command prompt, type **NEWMU** followed by the old menu name and the name you want for the updated menu (they must be different). You do not need to provide file extensions, since the

```
+File: File Operations
   New: Open a new blank spreadsheet window
   Open: Load a file into a new spreadsheet window
   Retrieve: Load a spreadsheet into the current window
   ---------------:
   Save: Save the current spreadsheet on disk
   Save As: Save the current spreadsheet under a new name
   Save All: Save all currently open spreadsheets
   Close: Close the current spreadsheet window
   Close All: Close all open windows
   Erase: Erase the contents of the current spreadsheet
   ---------------:
   Directory: Set a temporary data directory
   +Workspace: Save or load a setup of windows and files
      Save: Save the current arrangement of windows and files
      Restore: Load a saved workspace
   +Utilities: Access DOS, the file manager, or SQZ! settings
      DOS Shell: Execute DOS commands
      File Manager: Open a file manager window
      +SQZ!: Set SQZ! file compression options
         Remove Blanks: Remove empty cells before saving
         Storage of Values: Store exact values, approximate values, or formulas only
         Version: Save as SQZ! or SQZ! Plus file
         Quit: Return to the spreadsheet
   Exit: Close all windows & exit to DOS
+Edit: Copy, move, insert, delete data; block names; search & replace
   Copy: Copy a block of data
   +Copy Special: Copy cell contents only or format only in a block of data
```

Figure 10.28 Printout of Menu Tree

program automatically uses MU. You may need to provide path information (drive and directory) if the menu tree files are not in the current path. After you translate the menu, you can start using the menu using the /Options Startup Menu Tree command. You will want to add the new Quattro Pro commands, which includes /Edit Copy Special, /Graph Series Analyze, /Tools Audit, and /Tools

Optimizer. You may also need to alter the menu compatibility options and shortcut keys (commands performed by pressing CTRL and a letter), since the menu compatibility options are erased and the shortcut keys may be assigned to different commands.

GETTING STARTED

In this chapter you learned how to make changes to Quattro's settings and to other settings in the spreadsheet. You can try some of these features by following these steps to create the spreadsheet in Figure 10.29.

1. Make the following entries:

    A1: **Sales**
    B1: **1100000**
    A2: **Cost of Goods Sold**
    B2: **700000**
    A3: **Gross Profit**
    B3: **+B1-B2**
    A4: **Operating Expenses**
    B4: **500000**
    A5: **Net Profit**
    B5: **+B3-B4**

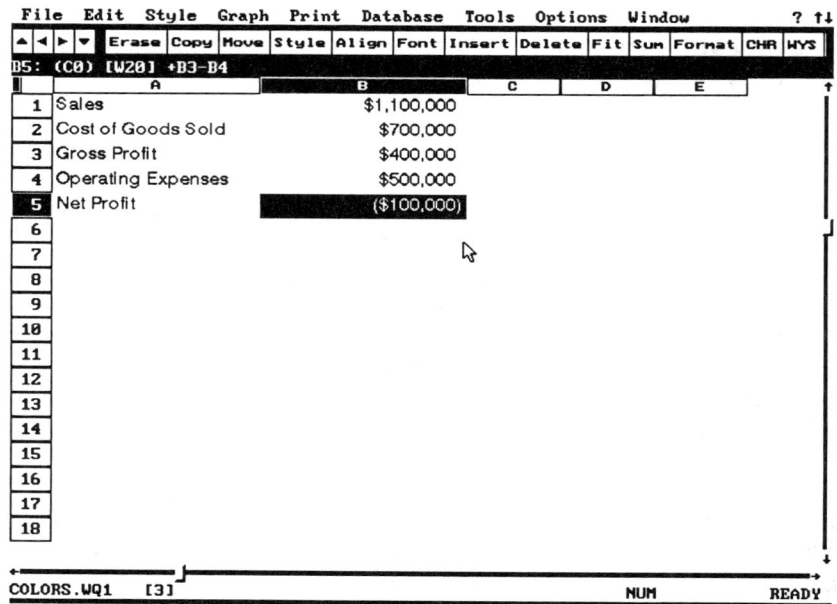

Figure 10.29 Spreadsheet Created with Getting Started Section

Customizing Quattro Pro 567

2. Make all columns wider so the labels in column A fit within the width of the column. Enter /Options Formats Global Width. When Quattro prompts for the default column width, type **20** or press the RIGHT ARROW until the column widths are 20. Press ENTER (or click [Enter] in the input line).
3. Since these numbers are currency values, set the default format for numbers to currency with no digits after the decimal point. Enter **Numeric Format** from the Formats menu, and select **Currency**. When Quattro prompts for the number of decimal places, type **0** and either press ENTER or click the Enter button in the box. Select **Q**uit to return to the Options menu.
4. Set Quattro to display the date and time in the status line. Select **Other**, **Clock**, and **Standard**. This displays the clock in the status line with the first date and second time format.
5. Set Quattro to use conditional colors. Enter Colors Conditional. Select **On/Off** and **Enable** to use the conditional colors. Select **Smallest Normal Value**. When Quattro prompts for the lowest value to display using the normal color, type **0** and either press ENTER or point to the ENTER button in the box and press the mouse button. This emphasizes negative values such as the net loss in the spreadsheet. Select **Greatest Normal Value**. When Quattro prompts for the highest value to display using the normal color, type **1000000** and either press ENTER or point to the ENTER button in the box and press the mouse button. This emphasizes large numbers such as the high sales value. Select **Q**uit three times to return to the spreadsheet to display the spreadsheet shown in Figure 10.29.
6. Save this spreadsheet. Press CTRL-S to enter /File Save, and type a file name such as **COLORS**, then press ENTER.
7. Exit Quattro. Press CTRL-X to enter /File Exit. Since you did not select **U**pdate from the Options menu, the changes you made to the top portion of the Options menu were not saved.
8. Check that your changes to Quattro's options are not maintained. Type **Q** and press ENTER to start Quattro again. When the initial spreadsheet appears, you will notice that the date and time do not appear in the status line. Enter /Options Colors Conditional. Notice that the changes you have made in this menu before are not present. Select **Q**uit three times to return to the READY mode.
9. Retrieve the spreadsheet you saved in step 6. Enter /File Retrieve and select the file name you entered in step 6. Notice that the spreadsheet does not display the date and time in the status line. On the other hand, notice how the columns have a width of 20 and the spreadsheet uses the default numeric format of currency with no digits after the decimal. These settings are saved with the spreadsheet.

11

Automating Quattro Pro Tasks

Macros can save you time by recording frequently needed tasks for repeated use. You will find much that is familiar in macros but will also need to master new terminology and concepts. This chapter focuses on the simplest type of macro—the keyboard alternative. You will learn all the basics of macro creation in this chapter. In addition, you will learn how to use Quattro's transcript features to make your work even easier.

MACRO BASICS

A *macro* is a recording of Quattro commands that can be executed at a later time. This recording of commands is stored as ordinary labels. The labels do not perform any function until you execute them. When you execute a macro, Quattro performs each step in the macro exactly as it would if you were typing each command from the keyboard.

Figure 11.1 displays a macro. When this macro is executed, Quattro performs the commands represented in each cell in column I. Quattro continues executing the requests represented by these labels until it encounters a blank cell or a cell containing a value.

A macro is stored with the spreadsheet in which you created it. This allows each spreadsheet to have unique macros. You can share macros between spreadsheets, since Quattro executes a macro on the current spreadsheet regardless of which open spreadsheet contains the macro.

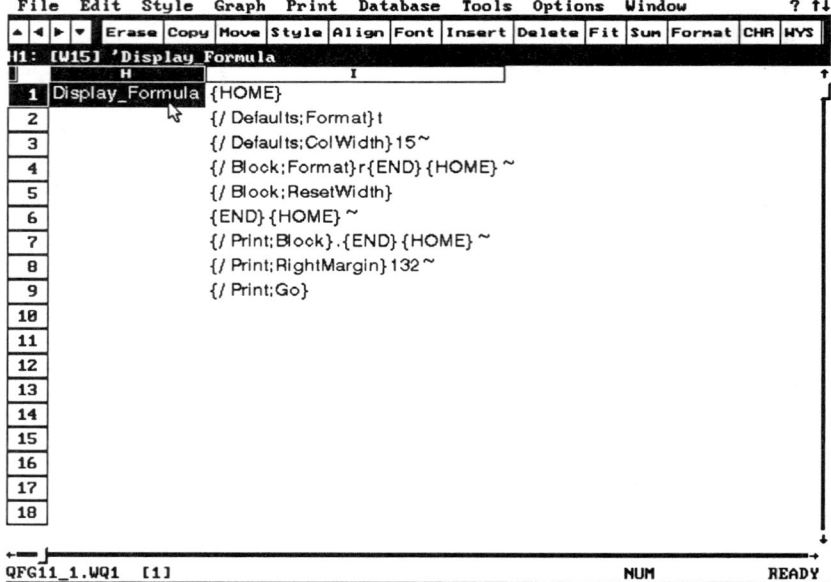

Figure 11.1 Macro in column I

Types of Macros

Quattro has two types of macros. One type is a keyboard macro. Keyboard macros are nothing more than a set of keystrokes. When you execute one of these macros, it is as if you are typing yourself. A keyboard macro provides efficiency for repetitive tasks and reduces errors. Once you have created and tested a macro, you do not have to worry about typing mistakes.

Quattro's other type of macro is more advanced and uses macro commands. Macro commands perform functions unavailable from Quattro's menu like repetitive processing, condition checking, and specialized file input and output options. The macro commands provide programming features that you would expect in a programming language within Quattro's easy-to-use framework. These are covered in Chapter 12.

Picking a Location for a Macro

Before creating a macro, you need to select a location on the spreadsheet. If a macro is in a good location, it will not affect the spreadsheet's other entries and it will be protected from changes in other spreadsheet entries. Since Quattro has efficient memory management, you do not have to consider memory allocation in your decision of where you place the macro.

If the macro is in the same spreadsheet as other spreadsheet data, the location selected should allow room for spreadsheet or macro expansion. For example, if your spreadsheet is likely to expand to the right but not downward, you may want to put the macros below the spreadsheet. Grouping the macros within one area is a good idea to make location of any macro easy. If your spreadsheet has rows or columns that you expect to delete, do not put macros in those rows or columns. Protecting a macro after you have tested it eliminates accidental deletion later. Reserving a blank column to the left and right of the macro is useful for documenting the macro. You must have a blank cell or use the macro command {QUIT} to end each macro.

You can place a macro on a spreadsheet outside the spreadsheet of the data on which the macro is used. Quattro uses the current spreadsheet when it executes a macro even if the macro is in a separate spreadsheet. You can use this feature to create spreadsheets that contain only macros. You can also use this feature to create macros for use with data files that are not stored in a spreadsheet. For example, you can use macros in a spreadsheet to use the data in a dBASE III database.

Another approach for macro organization is to create a macro spreadsheet. A macro spreadsheet contains the macros that you use most frequently and is sometimes referred to as a macro library. When you create a new spreadsheet model, you can use the macro library to obtain the macros for your new model.

Recording a Macro

Since macros are a column of labels containing instructions, you must convert the Quattro task requests into labels. When you want the macro to type text, you type the text into the macro labels. When you want the macro to invoke Quattro's menu, type / in the macro instruction. If the slash is the first character for the label, precede it with an apostrophe to have Quattro store the slash rather than invoke the menu. Do not use the mouse when you are recording a macro, since Quattro will not record the macro instructions for the steps you perform with a mouse.

Some special keys like ESC and ENTER require a different approach. Quattro uses key-equivalent commands to represent these special keys. These key-equivalent commands are displayed in Table 11.1 and can be included in a macro exactly as shown there. For many of the macro instructions that represent direction keys, you can put a number in them to indicate the number of times the key should be performed as in {DOWN 10}. With {ABS} and {NEXTWIN}, you can also use numbers as in {ABS 4} and {NEXTWIN 2}. {ABS} with a number will change an address into a relative, mixed, or absolute address as if you pressed F4 (ABS) after moving to the address. {NEXTWIN} with a number moves through the list of open windows by the number of times selected by the number.

Quattro provides two ways to record menu commands. In addition to the keystroke approach, you have the option of using special menu-equivalent commands. The menu-equivalent commands are easier to understand, and they work

Table 11.1 Special Key Equivalents Used in Macro

Special Key	Key Equivalent Command
F2 (EDIT)	{EDIT}
F3 (CHOICES)	{NAME}
F4 (ABSOLUTE)	{ABS}
F5 (GOTO)	{GOTO}
F6 (PANE)	{WINDOW}
F7 (QUERY)	{QUERY}
F8 (TABLE)	{TABLE}
F9 (CALC)	{CALC} or {READDIR} in File Manager
F10 (GRAPH)	{GRAPH}
SHIFT-F2 (DEBUG)	{STEP}
SHIFT-F3 (MACROS)	{MACROS}
SHIFT-F5 or ALT-0 (PICK WINDOW)	{CHOOSE}
SHIFT-F6 (NEXT WINDOW)	{NEXTWIN}
SHIFT-F7 (MARK)	{MARK}
SHIFT-F8 (MOVE)	{MOVE}
SHIFT-F9 (COPY)	{COPY}
SHIFT-F10 (PASTE)	{PASTE}
ALT-F3 (FUNCTIONS)	{FUNCTIONS}
ALT-F5 (UNDO)	{UNDO}
ALT-F6 (ZOOM WINDOW)	{ZOOM}
ALT-F7 (MARK ALL)	{MARKALL}
CTRL-F10	{PDXGO}
ALT-1 to ALT-9	{WINDOW1} to {WINDOW9}
UP ARROW	{UP} or {U}
DOWN ARROW	{DOWN} or {D}
RIGHT ARROW	{RIGHT} or {R}
LEFT ARROW	{LEFT} or {L}

Table 11.1 Special Key Equivalents Used in Macro

Special Key	Key Equivalent Command
CTRL-RIGHT ARROW or TAB	{BIGRIGHT} or {TAB}
CTRL-BREAK	{BREAK}
CTRL-LEFT ARROW or SHIFT-TAB	{BIGLEFT} or {BACKTAB}
PGUP	{PGUP}
PGDN	{PGDN}
HOME	{HOME}
END	{END}
ENTER	{CR} or <~>
ESC	{ESC} or {ESCAPE}
INS	{INS}, {INSERT}, {INSOFF}, or {INSON}
DEL	{DEL} or {DELETE}
BACKSPACE	{BS} or {BACKSPACE}
CTRL-BACKSPACE	{CLEAR}
CTRL-\	{DELEOL}
CTRL-D	{DATE}
NUM LOCK	{NUMON} or {NUMOFF}
CAPS LOCK	{CAPON} or {CAPOFF}
SCROLL LOCK	{SCROLLON} or {SCROLLOFF}

with any menu tree. The fact that your macros will not be compatible with 1-2-3 is a potential disadvantage of the menu-equivalent commands. The menu-equivalent commands are listed fully in Appendix C.

USING QUATTRO'S RECORD MODE Quattro has a RECORD mode that allows you to monitor the effect of your menu selections as they are recorded on your spreadsheet. Quattro records every key you type and stores it in a block that you name. To use this recording feature, follow these steps:

1. Enter **/T**ools **M**acro or press ALT-F2 (MACRO MENU).
2. Select **R**ecord. Quattro returns you to the READY mode and displays REC in the status line.
3. Enter the keystrokes and commands that you want to record.

Quattro can record your keystrokes and commands using either the literal keystrokes as in /EC for /Edit Copy or it can record the menu-equivalent command as in {/ Block;Copy}. Menu-equivalent commands provide built-in explanations of the macro instructions. If you are recording the commands by their literal keystrokes, make your menu selections by typing the first letter of the command rather than by using the arrow keys to move to your selection and pressing ENTER to make a selection. Figure 11.2 shows the macro from Figure 11.1 recorded as keystrokes using the arrow keys and ENTER to select the menu choices. Figure 11.3 shows the same macro recorded with the first letter of the menu choices. As the two figures illustrate, using the first letter makes the macro easier to understand.

4. Enter /Tools Macro or press ALT-F2 (MACRO MENU), and select Record. Selecting this option a second time discontinues the macro recording.

Testing the Macro Before Copying It to the Spreadsheet Quattro stores the macro you have recorded in its memory until you enter /Tools Macro Record again. You can use the macro instructions stored in Quattro's memory two ways. You can copy the macro to a spreadsheet by entering /Tools Macro Paste as described in the next paragraph. You can also execute these macro instructions. To execute the macro stored in memory, enter /Tools Macro Instant Replay. Quattro performs the macro you have just recorded. You can use this command to test the macro before you copy the macro to the spreadsheet. You can also use this command to create a

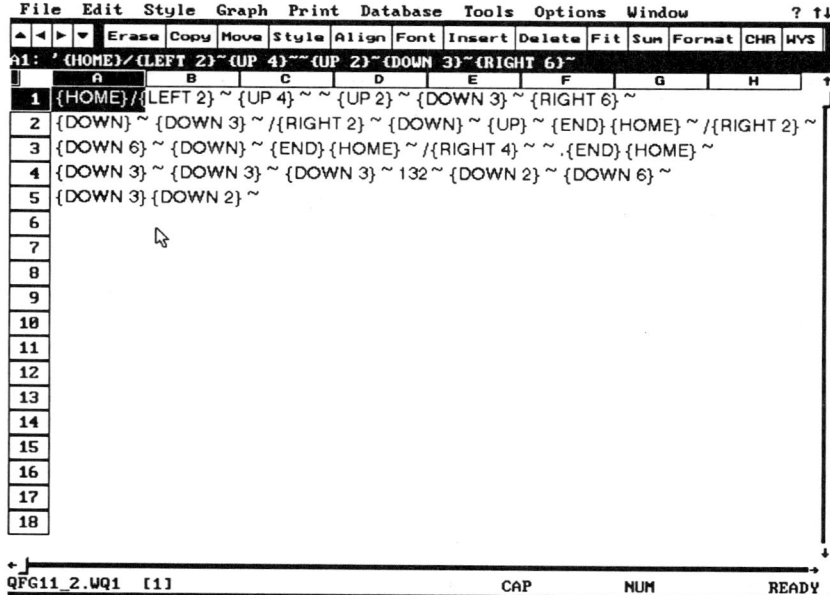

Figure 11.2 Macro Recorded Using Arrow Keys

Automating Quattro Pro Tasks 575

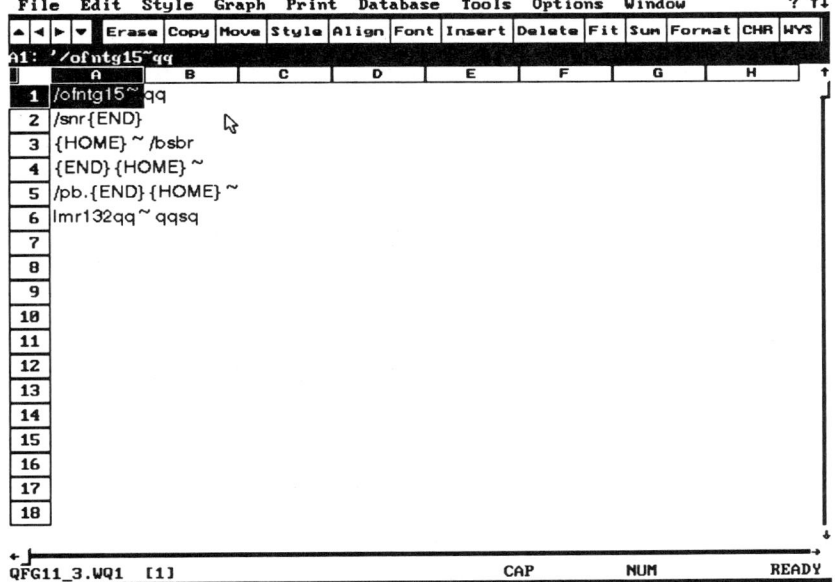

Figure 11.3 Macro Recorded Using First Letters

temporary macro that you do not want to store permanently in a spreadsheet. By executing the temporary copy instead of a copy of the macro in a spreadsheet, you can delete the temporary macro by recording a new macro or by exiting Quattro.

Copying the Macro to the Spreadsheet After you have finished recording the macro and tested that it works, you can copy the macro to the spreadsheet so that it is available for later use. Also you can modify the macro to change how it performs or to delete keystrokes that you pressed accidentally. To copy a recorded macro to the spreadsheet, follow these steps:

1. Enter /Tools Macro or press ALT-F2 (MACRO MENU), and select Paste. This option copies the recorded keystrokes to the spreadsheet. Quattro displays a list of the defined block names and prompts you for a name of the macro.

2. Type the macro name, and press ENTER. If you want this to be an instant macro that you can invoke with a single keystroke, type a backslash (\) and a letter. If the macro you are creating is not an instant macro, you must follow Quattro's block name rules when entering a macro name. These rules include a 15-character limit. The name you select must consist of letters, numbers, punctuation marks, spaces, and special characters, although the last three may create problems and are best avoided. Quattro prompts you for the location of the block you are naming. This is the block in which Quattro places the macro instructions.

3. Type a block address or select one with the arrow keys or mouse, and press ENTER. You only need to supply the upper-left corner of the block; Quattro places all your entries in the same column. If you specify more than one row in the block, Quattro only uses the number of rows specified to record the macro. If Quattro cannot fit all the keystrokes or instructions in the specified block, Quattro displays an error message. Quattro also uses the number of columns in the specified block to determine the width of the recorded keystrokes Quattro fits into each cell. Quattro overwrites any cells below the selected block unless you select a block of more than one row. When Quattro pastes the keystrokes that it has recorded into the spreadsheet, it then turns the macro recorder off. If you want to record more macros, you need to enter /Tools Macros Record again. Since the pasted macro instructions are still in Quattro's memory for the macro recorder, you can enter /Tools Macros Paste again if you want to make an additional copy of the macro.

When you record a macro with Quattro's RECORD mode, Quattro stores all the menu commands by their menu-equivalent commands. However, Quattro records a macro by using the keystrokes if the /Tools Macro Macro Recording Keystroke command is used. If you are creating macros to be used with 1-2-3, you should use keystrokes because menu-equivalent commands are not compatible with 1-2-3.

RECORDING A MACRO BY TYPING THE TEXT You can also record a macro by typing the keystrokes as label entries. To enter a macro by typing the text, follow these steps:

1. Plan the tasks that the macro should perform. For each task, you must consider all the steps that Quattro must perform. This includes the menu command the macro will use, the special keys the macro will have to select, and other information that the commands and functions will need. If the macro consists of several tasks, divide the tasks into steps. With small steps, both creation of the macro and subsequent error corrections are simpler. A macro entered by typing the instructions into the macro block is more likely to have errors due to typing mistakes or an omitted character. A missing or incorrect character can cause the entire macro to be incorrect.
2. Move the selector to the cell where the macro should begin.
3. Type an apostrophe to insure that the subsequent characters are treated as a label.
4. Type the instructions for the step.
5. Press ENTER to finalize the macro instruction.
6. Press the DOWN ARROW key to where you want the next macro instruction placed. Store each step of the macro in a different cell in the column. Do not skip any cells between macro instructions, since Quattro terminates the macro's execution when it encounters a blank cell or a value cell.
7. Repeat steps 3 through 6 for each step of the macro.

> ▼ **TIP: Position the selector to start a macro.**
>
> Start a macro by positioning the selector so you will always know where it is.
>
> ▼ **TIP: Some commands use confirmation keystrokes.**
>
> Remember confirmation keystrokes that some Quattro commands use (such as Backup, Cancel, or Replace when you save a file a second time).

8. Type / and select **Tools Macro Name** (or press ALT-F2 (MACRO MENU) and select **Name**). When you use this command, Quattro prompts you for the name of the macro. The name must follow all the conventions for named blocks.
9. Type the name of the macro and press ENTER. Quattro prompts you for the location of the macro. Specify the location of the first cell in the block and press ENTER. (Since Quattro starts macro execution from this cell and continues execution until it encounters a blank cell, a {RETURN}, or a {QUIT}, the first cell is sufficient).

When you enter the macro instructions as labels, you can use SHIFT-F3 (MACROS) to list the menu-equivalent commands. Quattro displays a box listing the different types of macro commands. The last choice, / Commands, presents a list of the general actions for all the menu-equivalent commands. Once a general action is selected, Quattro displays the specific actions that are available.

When you create a macro by typing the macro instructions into cells, you must follow the rules Quattro has for cell entries. For example, each cell can contain up to 254 characters. While storing the maximum number of characters in each cell may seem quicker, it makes the macro difficult to understand, since you can only see a small portion of the macro's instructions on the screen.

Naming a Macro

The name that you assign to a macro determines how you can execute it. Quattro has three types of names that you can assign to a macro. All three types of macro names are assigned as a block name to the top cell in the macro.

The first type is an auto-execute macro. This type of macro is executed immediately when the file containing the macro is retrieved. Initially, Quattro expects this type of a macro to be named \0. This macro name can be changed to another macro name with the /Options Startup Startup Macro command. You can only have one auto-execute macro on each spreadsheet.

The second type of macro name is an instant macro. Instant macro names have a single letter preceded by a backslash. These macros are executed by holding the ALT key and pressing the letter of their name. The macros that you frequently use should be named as instant macros. With this approach, Quattro supports 26 instant macros.

The third type of macro name can have up to 15 characters. The additional character limit allows you to provide a short description relating to the task the macro performs. Since Quattro treats these macro names as block names, they must be unique from existing block names.

Several of Quattro's features for named blocks have useful applications for macros. For example, to display the macro address of all the macros, you can press the GRAY PLUS key when you press F3 (CHOICES) to list all named blocks and macros. When you use the /Edit Names Create or the Make Table command, the resulting table lists all the macros and named blocks and their addresses.

To name the macros, you can use the /Edit Names Create or the /Tools Macro Name Create command. Once you enter either command, Quattro displays a list of macro and block names and then prompts you for a block to assign. Either select an existing block name or type a new block name. Then you must supply the address to be represented by the block name. If you have selected an existing block name, Quattro suggests the block address currently assigned to the name. For macros, you only need to assign the first cell in the macro, since the macro continues executing until it reaches a command that tells the macro to stop executing or until the macro reaches a blank cell or a cell containing a value.

Executing a Macro

Quattro provides several methods for executing a macro. The method you use to execute a specific macro depends on the name type. For example, Quattro can execute an instant macro automatically when you press the ALT key and the appropriate letter key.

EXECUTING A MACRO AUTOMATICALLY As Chapter 10 describes, you can direct Quattro to execute a macro after it has loaded a spreadsheet with a macro of a specific name. The /Options Startup Startup Macro command lets you specify the name of the macro that Quattro should execute once a file is opened. When the file is opened, if it has a macro with the specified name, the macro is executed immediately. Quattro initially has the default startup macro set to \0. This default setting can be changed to any macro name, including the names that do not qualify as instant macros.

EXECUTING AN INSTANT MACRO Quattro can have up to 26 instant macros. The names of instant macros are each composed of a single letter preceded by a backslash. These macros are executed by holding down the ALT key and pressing their single letter name.

EXECUTING A MACRO USING THE /TOOLS MACRO EXECUTE COMMAND Quattro's /Tools Macro Execute command lets you execute a macro. When you use this command, Quattro prompts for the macro name or cell address containing the first macro instruction to perform. You can type a name or press F3 (CHOICES) to select one from the list. If the macro you want to execute is in a macro library, which is discussed later, you can enter the macro name directly. If the macro you want to execute is in a different spreadsheet that is not a macro library, you must include the file name in square brackets before the macro name. You can also point to the first cell in a macro to execute, which works well if you want to use ALT-0 through ALT-9 to switch to another spreadsheet that contains the macro to execute. Once you select a macro and press ENTER, Quattro begins executing the selected macro.

Executing a 1-2-3 Macro in Quattro

If you are running a macro that uses the 1-2-3 menu and you are using the Quattro menu, you can easily run the macros without changing the menu tree you are using. The /Tools Macro Key Reader command sets whether Quattro checks if a running macro uses 1-2-3 menus. When you select /Tools Macro Key Reader Yes, Quattro interprets all keystrokes for menu commands as applying to the 1-2-3 menu. When you select /Tools Macro Key Reader No, Quattro interprets all keystrokes for menu commands as applying to the currently selected menu tree. The setting of the /Tools Macro Key Reader command is saved with the default settings which means to make a change with the /Tools Macro Key Reader command permanent, you must use the /Options Update command. You will want to change this command to Yes when you are using macros in 1-2-3 worksheet files.

Changing a Macro

When you want to change the tasks a macro performs, you edit the cells that contain the macro instructions. A macro may need to be changed if it is not performing properly. Also, you may want to alter the task a macro performs. If you are building a long macro in steps, you may want to enter the next set of steps after testing and error checking the first set of instructions.

Quattro provides a debugger that assists the editing process. Since the debugger is designed for complex macros, it is discussed in Chapter 12. To edit a simpler macro, move the selector to the macro instruction that you want to change and press F2 (EDIT) or click the entry in the input line. This action places you in EDIT mode. You can use the same techniques used for editing any spreadsheet cell. After you make your changes, press ENTER.

When you edit a macro, you must follow the rules for macros. This includes using the special key equivalents. If you use the menu-equivalent commands, you must make sure to include the proper command arguments. For example, to use the /Edit Fill command in a macro, you would use the menu-equivalent command {/ Math;Fill} followed by four arguments (block, start value, step value, stop value) with a {CR} or tilde (~) following each argument. You can press SHIFT-F3 (MACROS) and select /Commands, or click Macro in the SpeedBar to select a menu-equivalent command while editing a cell.

Documenting a Macro

Documentation records descriptive information that helps you remember the reasons for your actions. When you document a macro, you record text next to the macro that describes how the macro works. Although you know the macro's name and function when you create it, you may not remember it when you have to change it a month later. Documenting a macro provides explanatory text that can describe the macro's name and an explanation of the different steps.

The style that you use to document your macros is something you can decide with time and practice. However, a few simple rules can get you started. A good method of documenting macros is to put the macro name to the left of the first macro cell and the description of each macro step to the right of the step. Figure 11.4 shows an example of a well-documented macro. On that figure you can see clearly the macro's name and the various steps that it performs. If you are typing the macro instead of using Quattro's recorder and you type the macro name next to the macro, you can use the /Edit Names Labels command to define the macro so that you do not have to type the macro name a second time.

Deleting a Macro

Deleting a macro is an easy process that should be performed when the macro is no longer needed in the spreadsheet. Since a macro is a named block, the process for deleting a macro is the same as deleting a named block. Quattro's /Tools Macro Name Delete command removes a macro name without destroying its contents. You can also use the /Edit Names Delete command. When you execute either command, Quattro lists all named blocks and prompts for the one that you want to delete. After you select one and press ENTER, Quattro removes the macro name from the spreadsheet and leaves the macro's contents intact. These macro instructions remain on the spreadsheet until the cells are erased with the /Edit Erase Block command or the DEL key.

To remove an auto-execute macro, you have several options. You can erase the cells containing the macro instructions. You can erase the macro name with the /Tools Macro Name Delete or /Edit Names Delete command. You can change the auto-execute macro name by using the /Options Startup Startup Macro command.

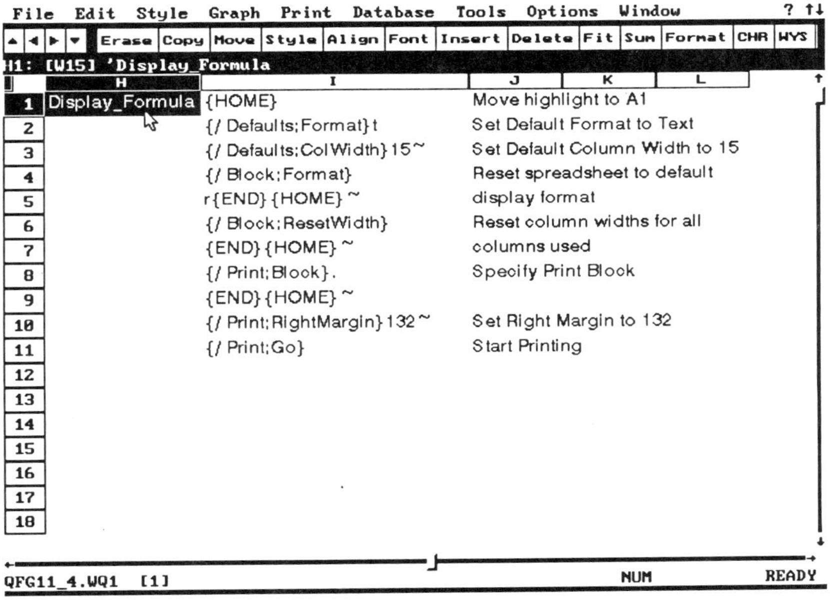

```
  File  Edit  Style  Graph  Print  Database  Tools  Options  Window        ? ↑↓
  ▲ ◀ ▶ ▼  Erase Copy Move Style Align Font Insert Delete Fit Sum Format CHR WYS
  H1: [W15] 'Display_Formula
           H              I                      J         K         L
   1 Display_Formula {HOME}              Move highlight to A1
   2                 {/ Defaults;Format}t   Set Default Format to Text
   3                 {/ Defaults;ColWidth}15~ Set Default Column Width to 15
   4                 {/ Block;Format}     Reset spreadsheet to default
   5                 r{END}{HOME}~         display format
   6                 {/ Block;ResetWidth}  Reset column widths for all
   7                 {END}{HOME}~          columns used
   8                 {/ Print;Block}.      Specify Print Block
   9                 {END}{HOME}~
  10                 {/ Print;RightMargin}132~ Set Right Margin to 132
  11                 {/ Print;Go}          Start Printing
  12
  13
  14
  15
  16
  17
  18

  QFG11_4.WQ1  [1]                                     NUM         READY
```

Figure 11.4 Documented Macro

Macro Libraries

Since Quattro can perform a macro from a spreadsheet in any open spreadsheet, you can reduce the size of your spreadsheets by consolidating the macros for the individual spreadsheets into one spreadsheet. This spreadsheet that contains the macros designed for other spreadsheets is a macro library. You can benefit from macro libraries when the macros stored in a macro library are used in more than one spreadsheet. A macro library also provides a storage area for your macros that cannot interfere with other spreadsheet data. To tell Quattro that you want to use a spreadsheet as a macro library, enter /Tools Macro Library Yes. The next time you enter a macro name to execute, Quattro first looks in the active spreadsheet, then it looks in the open macro libraries. If you decide that you do not want to use a spreadsheet as a macro library, enter /Tools Macro Library No.

When you use a macro from a macro library, Quattro treats the cell and block addresses differently than it treats the block names. All cell and block addresses are assumed to come from the current spreadsheet. Any named block addresses are assumed to come from the macro library unless the block name is preceded by square brackets as in {/ Math;Fill}[]DATES~10~5~100~.

> ▼ **TIP: Name the macro library so it is always available.**
>
> If you are using only one macro library, name the file the same name as the file for the /Options Startup Autoload File so the macro library is always available for you.
>
> ▼ **TIP: Only one macro library should be open at any one time.**
>
> Only have one macro library open at a time; Quattro will provide inconsistent results if you execute a macro contained in both macro libraries when both macro libraries are open.

SAMPLE KEYBOARD MACROS

The following section presents sample macros for you to use. Each of the macros has been tested and performs a specific task. Each macro has a description of the macro instructions and directions for its use. Since your spreadsheet is probably designed differently than these examples are, you need to modify the macros before adapting them to your own use. Each macro includes suggestions for customizing it to your use. Once you have adapted the macros for your own use, you can broaden the macro's application to perform other tasks for you.

The macros follow several conventions. Instead of using cell and block addresses, the macros use block names. The cells referenced by the block names are stated in the accompanying text or in the macro's documentation. The macro is documented in the style described earlier in this chapter (the macro name is at the left of the macro, and the macro documentation is at the right). The macros use menu-equivalent commands instead of keystrokes. Appendix C contains a full list of the menu-equivalent commands. The menu-equivalent commands and block names are in proper case. Special key equivalents are shown in uppercase.

Macro for Copying a Block

Although copying cells from one location to another is already a simple operation, creating a macro to perform this task saves time if you are copying the same block repeatedly. For example, if a spreadsheet is tracking the progress of several contracts, the spreadsheet may look like Figure 11.5. Every time a new contract is added, the formulas that total the costs incurred to date and compute the percent-

```
File   Edit   Style   Graph   Print   Database   Tools   Options   Window         ?  ↕
▲ ◄ ► ▼  Erase  Copy  Move  Style  Align  Font  Insert  Delete  Fit  Sum  Format  CHR  WYS
B17:  '{/ Block;Copy}Dummy Contract~~
```

	A	B	C	D	E
1	Contract Number		213-593	951-222	215-286
2	Client Name		Steak N' Cake	Tom Doe	Holey Donuts
3	Project		Kitchen Expansion	House	Remodeling
4					
5	Expected Cost		60,000	75,000	100,000
6	Cost To Date:				
7	Labor		25,000	10,000	30,000
8	Materials		29,500	35,000	40,000
9	Other		4,000	2,000	5,000
10	Total	0	58,500	47,000	75,000
11					
12	% Completed	0%	98%	63%	75%
13	Contract Price		80,000	90,000	125,000
14	Profit Earned	0	19,500	9,400	18,750
15					
16					
17	\z	{/ Block,Copy}Dummy Contract~ ~			
18			copies column B to current column		
19			Dummy Contract is B1..B14		

```
QFG11_5.WQ1  [1]                           CAP         NUM          READY
```

Figure 11.5 Spreadsheet Displaying Contracts

age of completion and the percentage of profit earned must be copied to the column for the new contract. Since a construction company may have many projects at once, a spreadsheet like this uses many columns. It is cumbersome to move the selector to the column with the blank formulas every time a new contract is entered. The macro in the spreadsheet copies the formulas to the column highlighted at the time that the macro is executed. When the dummy column is copied, it also erases any numbers that were in the column previously. Thus, this macro can remove the data for a contract when the contract is completed. In this macro, the selector must be in row 1 so the copied formulas are in the proper row. With a macro like this, you may want to hide column B to display more contracts on the screen. The block name Dummy Contract is copied to the current location whenever ALT-Z is pressed or /Tools Macro Execute is executed and \Z is selected.

SUGGESTIONS FOR CUSTOMIZATION This macro can be modified for copying blocks of any size. This macro only makes one copy at a time but can be modified to create multiple copies. In the example using the construction company contracts, a mixture of absolute, relative, and mixed references may be the best solution to insure that Quattro uses the correct rows. For example, if you are in row 2 when you use this macro, all formulas are one column below the other contracts. Depending on your spreadsheet, the END-UP ARROW key sequence may be sufficient. You can also modify the macro to be on a different spreadsheet so you can modify the spreadsheet without affecting the macro. In the above example, you could also add a second macro to set the column widths to fit the project descriptions in rows 2 and 3.

Macro for Displaying and Printing Formulas

The process of displaying formulas and printing the spreadsheet with the formulas displayed requires many steps. If you frequently modify a spreadsheet to display the formulas, using the macro shown in Figure 11.6 can make the task simpler. This macro sets the default display format to Text. Once the new default format is set, the macro undoes the formats specified with the /Style Numeric Format command and sets all the columns to one character wider than the contents of the column. Once the formatting is complete, the macro prints the entire spreadsheet.

SUGGESTIONS FOR CUSTOMIZATION To use this macro in another spreadsheet, you may want to change the print block specified in I7 to print a smaller section of your spreadsheet. It is also a good idea to save the altered spreadsheet to a temporary file either before executing the macro or as a macro command to prevent you from accidentally saving this version over your copy of the file with the original formatting. You may also want to change other print settings (such as margins and header). You can place this type of a macro in a macro library spreadsheet since this macro is not specific to a particular spreadsheet.

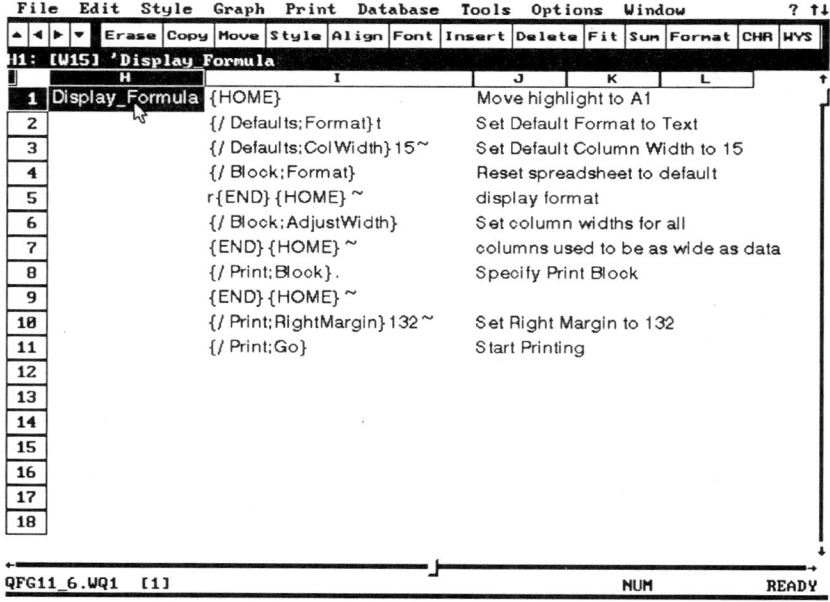

Figure 11.6 Macro That Displays and Prints Formulas

Macro for Printing Files

When a spreadsheet contains several reports, it can be troublesome to modify the settings to print each report. Rather than repeat the print commands for each report, you can use a macro to set the print settings and start the print operation. Figure 11.7 shows a spreadsheet that contains three print macros. Each macro prints a different portion of the spreadsheet with a different header and footer. To use this macro, the three blocks Income, Balance, and Aging must be defined as areas of the spreadsheet. The {CLEAR} after {/Print;Footer} and {/ Print;Header} removes the existing entry before entering a new footer or header. {CLEAR} is the same as CTRL-BACKSPACE. Unlike {ESC}, which can also remove an existing entry, {CLEAR} does not return to the prior menu if a menu option does not have a setting. These macros assume that the current spreadsheet contains named blocks called Income, Balance, and Aging. When entering these macros, you must be careful to type an apostrophe in cells B5, B12, and B19 before typing the first vertical bar so the entry is not treated as a printer control label.

SUGGESTIONS FOR CUSTOMIZATION You can use macros to further customize the print selections. Each macro can have commands added that change the page layout or the block destination. Another possible addition to a print macro is the choice of printer. For example, if you have an extra wide printer connected to the computer's first serial port, you must make several changes before you can print a spreadsheet. The commands that change the default settings of the printer

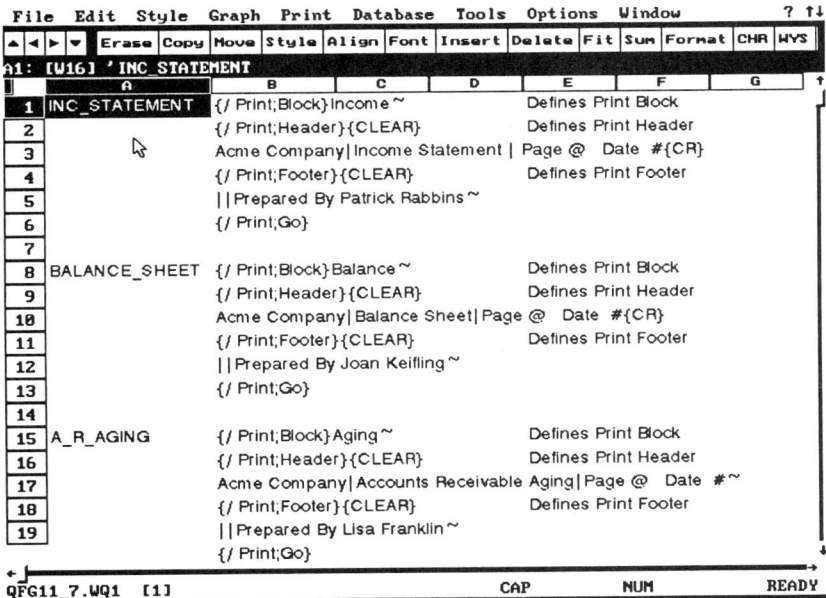

Figure 11.7 Print Macros

can be updated before the spreadsheet is printed. If the default settings are not updated, the changes to the printer settings are not saved. If this macro is in a macro library spreadsheet, the cells in B1, B8, and B15 would need to include [ ] before the block name to tell Quattro to look for the named block in the current spreadsheet.

Macro for Combining Files

Combining spreadsheets allows you to summarize the results of several spreadsheets. However, this process requires many steps. The macro in Figure 11.8 copies values from four other spreadsheets. Since this macro is named \0, the macro is executed whenever the file is retrieved. Making the macro an auto-execute macro insures that the spreadsheet always has the most up-to-date information. This macro copies data from the DIVISN_1, DIVISN_2, DIVISN_3, and DIVISN_4 spreadsheet files. This macro presumes that in each of the division's subsidiary spreadsheets, the summary information is a named block called Division 1, Division 2, Division 3, or Division 4. Using the block names prevents potential errors (for example, if the block containing the values you want to copy into this file is moved, its address may change, but its name remains the same).

SUGGESTIONS FOR CUSTOMIZATION When you are using this macro for your own spreadsheets, you must modify the block names and file names to correspond to your application.

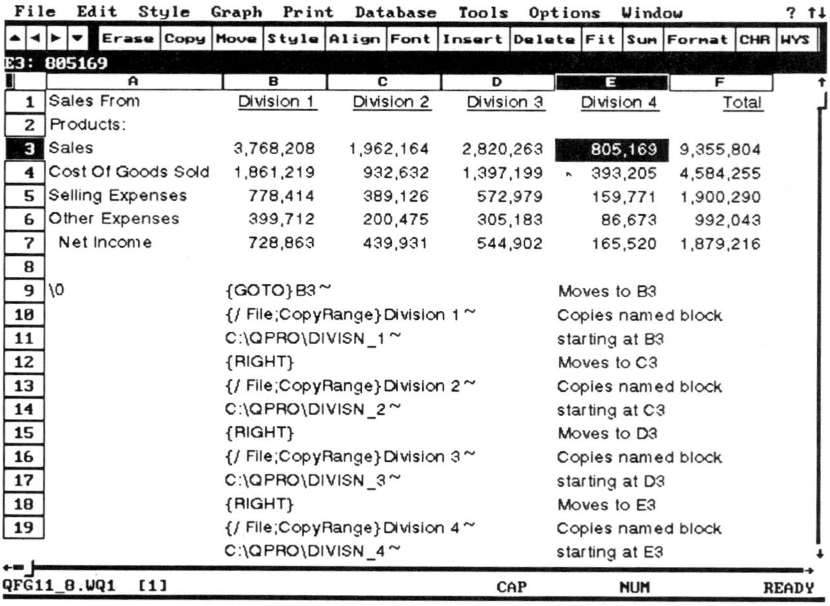
File Edit Style Graph Print Database Tools Options Window ? ↑↓
Erase Copy Move Style Align Font Insert Delete Fit Sum Format CHR WYS
E3: 805169

	A	B	C	D	E	F
1	Sales From	Division 1	Division 2	Division 3	Division 4	Total
2	Products:					
3	Sales	3,768,208	1,962,164	2,820,263	805,169	9,355,804
4	Cost Of Goods Sold	1,861,219	932,632	1,397,199	393,205	4,584,255
5	Selling Expenses	778,414	389,126	572,979	159,771	1,900,290
6	Other Expenses	399,712	200,475	305,183	86,673	992,043
7	Net Income	728,863	439,931	544,902	165,520	1,879,216
8						
9	\0	{GOTO}B3~			Moves to B3	
10		{/ File;CopyRange}Division 1~			Copies named block	
11		C:\QPRO\DIVISN_1~			starting at B3	
12		{RIGHT}			Moves to C3	
13		{/ File;CopyRange}Division 2~			Copies named block	
14		C:\QPRO\DIVISN_2~			starting at C3	
15		{RIGHT}			Moves to D3	
16		{/ File;CopyRange}Division 3~			Copies named block	
17		C:\QPRO\DIVISN_3~			starting at D3	
18		{RIGHT}			Moves to E3	
19		{/ File;CopyRange}Division 4~			Copies named block	
		C:\QPRO\DIVISN_4~			starting at E3	

QFG11_8.WQ1 [1] CAP NUM READY

Figure 11.8 Macro That Combines Spreadsheets

Although this example copies only four numbers from four spreadsheets, the macro can be expanded to provide additional consolidation information. For example, this macro can be expanded to consolidate information for several product lines or for all stores in a chain. The macro can also be changed to copy multiple blocks from each spreadsheet. For example, you can design the macro to copy one block containing income information and another block containing balance sheet information.

A Macro for Product Costing

Chapter 9 described the /Tools Advanced Math Multiply command and Quattro's advanced features to compute the product costs. The disadvantage of Quattro's advanced commands is that the results are not updated when spreadsheet numbers change. Figure 11.9 contains the same spreadsheet used in Chapter 9 to illustrate Quattro's matrix multiply features. This spreadsheet has a macro added that executes Quattro's /Tools Advanced Math Multiply command. In this spreadsheet, the matrices are the block names Matrix1 (B2..D3) and Matrix2 (B6..C8). The resulting matrix is stored in the Output named block (B12..C13). The results of the multiplied matrices are recalculated whenever ALT-F2 (MACRO MENU) is pressed, Execute is selected, and MULT_MTR is selected. You can also enter /Tools Macro Execute and type MULT_MTR or B15.

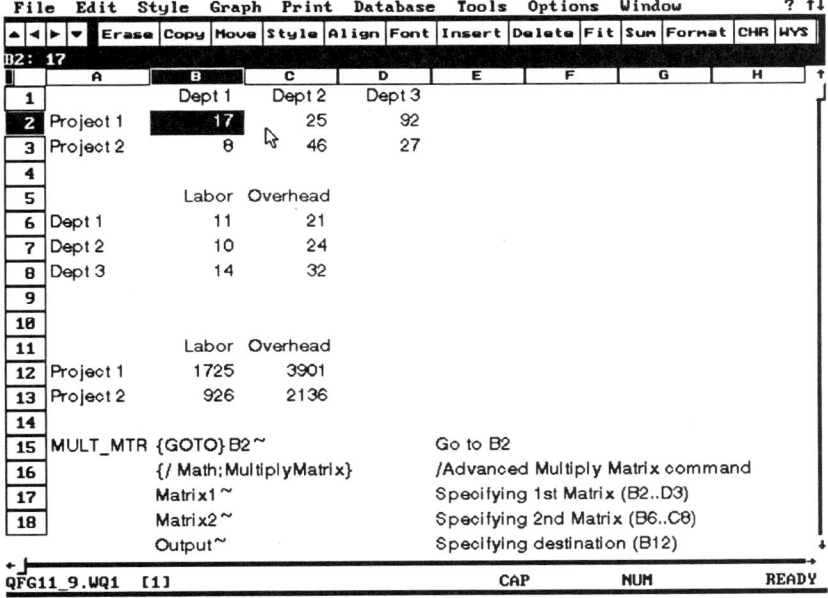

Figure 11.9 Macro That Performs Matrix Multiplication

SUGGESTIONS FOR CUSTOMIZATION This macro for multiplying matrices can be quickly modified to solve linear equations. Figure 11.10 shows a macro that solves the linear equations for the capacity-requirement problem that illustrated the /Tools Advanced Math Invert command in Chapter 9. In this example, the macro first inverts the first matrix and then multiplies the inverted matrix by the second matrix. The macro for the multiplication of these two matrices follows the same steps as the macro shown in Figure 11.9, except that the address and name for the first matrix multiplied belongs to the inverted matrix rather than the original one. In this spreadsheet, InvertMatrix represents E7..G9, Matrix1 represents B2..D4, Matrix2 represents B8..B10, and Output represents B13..B15.

Macro for Creating a What-If Analysis

Like the matrix operations, several other advanced analytical features create blocks of numbers that are not updated if you change the numbers that they rely on. Updating what-if analysis tables is another application for a macro. Figure 11.11 shows a company's schedule of short-term investments. For each of the investments, the schedule shows the type of investment, the company, the maturity date, the amount, and the rate. Although the /Database Sort command lets you sort the investments in order of their maturity dates and rates of interest, using the database statistical functions with the two-variable what-if table provides important information like the amount of securities for each interest rate and term. Figure 11.12

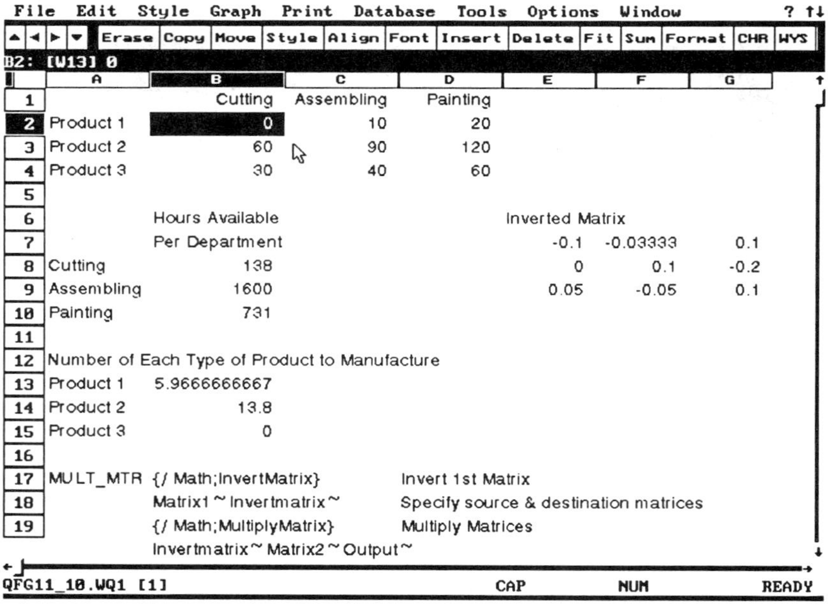

	A	B	C	D	E	F	G
1		Cutting	Assembling	Painting			
2	Product 1	0	10	20			
3	Product 2	60	90	120			
4	Product 3	30	40	60			
5							
6		Hours Available			Inverted Matrix		
7		Per Department			-0.1	-0.03333	0.1
8	Cutting	138			0	0.1	-0.2
9	Assembling	1600			0.05	-0.05	0.1
10	Painting	731					
11							
12	Number of Each Type of Product to Manufacture						
13	Product 1	5.9666666667					
14	Product 2	13.8					
15	Product 3	0					
16							
17	MULT_MTR	{/ Math;InvertMatrix}		Invert 1st Matrix			
18		Matrix1 ~ Invertmatrix ~		Specify source & destination matrices			
19		{/ Math;MultiplyMatrix}		Multiply Matrices			
		Invertmatrix ~ Matrix2 ~ Output ~					

Figure 11.10 Macro That Performs Matrix Inversion and Multiplication

```
    File   Edit   Style   Graph   Print   Database   Tools   Options   Window             ?  ↑↓
   ▲ ◄ ► ▼  Erase Copy Move Style Align Font Insert Delete Fit Sum Format CHR WYS
  A1: [W18]
                    A                  B                    C           D       E       ↑
   1                         Schedule of Company's Short Term Investments
   2            ▷
   3    Type                   Name                      Maturity   Amount   Rate
   4    Options                B. P. Smith & Co.         06/30/92   161,776  11%
   5    Convertible Bonds      Walkers Cane Distributors 06/30/92   499,025  11%
   6    Options                Brownstone, LTD           12/31/93   302,981  12%
   7    Tax Free Bonds         Billington County         03/31/94   452,130  11%
   8    Convertible Bonds      Nace Electric             12/31/92   548,813  12%
   9    Convertible Bonds      Acme Inc.                 09/30/92   507,447  12%
  10    Bond                   Crooked Towers            03/31/93   279,236   9%
  11    Common Stock           York Tailor               12/31/92   243,972   8%
  12    Preferred Stock        Rusty's Automotive Parts  12/31/92   260,095  12%
  13    Convertible Bonds      Helm Plating Inc.         09/30/92   420,308  10%
  14    Tax Free Bonds         Fordman City              12/31/92   206,261  11%
  15    Preferred Stock        Bargain Basement Discounters 03/31/92 395,052 11%
  16    Options                Crystal Ball Glass Makers 01/01/92   306,982  12%
  17    Options                Software Unlimited        06/30/93   270,774  11%
  18    Preferred Stock        Birdfeeders Inc.          01/01/92   531,728  10%
  19    Tax Free Bonds         State of Hawaii           03/31/92   352,905  10%
          Tax Free Bonds       Sanibel Island Water Dept 06/30/92   173,053  12%  ↓
  ◄
  QFG11_11.WQ1 [1]                       .         CAP           NUM            READY
```

Figure 11.11 Spreadsheet Showing Short Term Investments

shows a macro that creates a two-way table and the table that it produces. The hidden formula in I3 is **@DSUM($Invest,3,$Criteria)**, which computes the investment in securities for each possible interest rate and maturity date. The block name **Mat_date** used in the macro is I16, representing the input cell for the table's column data. The block name **Inv_rate** used in the macro is J16, representing the input cell for the table's row data. The block name Table is assigned to the block I3..N13. The block name Criteria is assigned to I15..J16. The Invest block name is assigned to the block containing the investments partially shown in Figure 11.11.

SUGGESTIONS FOR CUSTOMIZATION The macro for creating a two-variable table can be modified to accept additional interest rates and maturity dates. For example, you can add the /Edit Fill command to the macro to generate the interest rates and maturity dates. An even better solution is to use the /Database Query Unique command to list all the unique maturity dates and interest rates in the schedule. Once you have the unique maturity dates and interest rates, you can sort them and copy them to the table with the /Edit Copy and /Edit Transpose commands. When these steps are combined, the result is a macro like the one in Figure 11.13. This macro uses the schedule of investments to list the unique maturity dates and interest rates and then copies them to the table. Once the dates and rates are copied, the same {/ Math;2CellWhat-If} command creates the same two-variable what-if table. The difference between this macro and the macro shown at the bottom of Figure 11.12 is that, as the investments in the investment database change, the macro in Figure 11.13 includes the new dates and rates in the table. In this figure, the two-way table is moved farther to the right so the macro

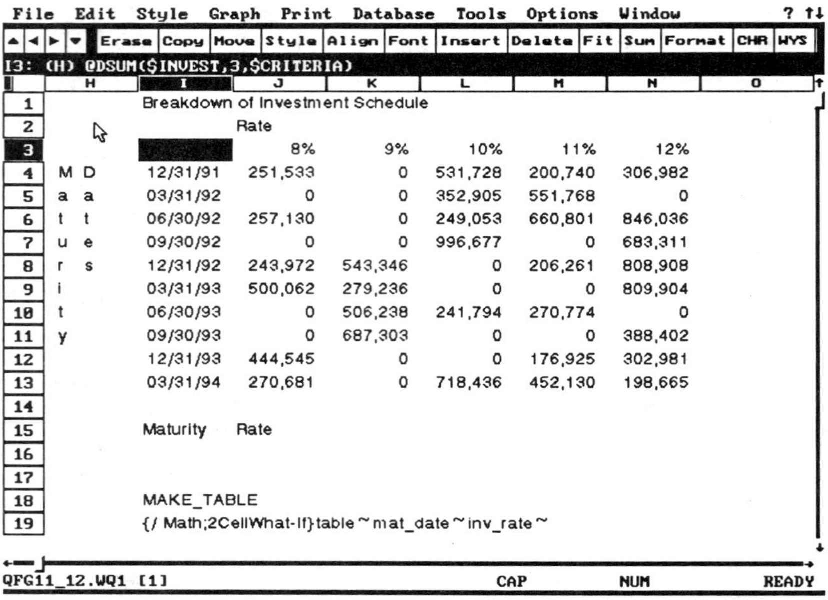

Figure 11.12 — Spreadsheet 1

Cell reference: `I3: (H) @DSUM($INVEST,3,$CRITERIA)`

	H	I	J	K	L	M	N	O
1			Breakdown of Investment Schedule					
2				Rate				
3				8%	9%	10%	11%	12%
4	M	D	12/31/91	251,533	0	531,728	200,740	306,982
5	a	a	03/31/92	0	0	352,905	551,768	0
6	t	t	06/30/92	257,130	0	249,053	660,801	846,036
7	u	e	09/30/92	0	0	996,677	0	683,311
8	r	s	12/31/92	243,972	543,346	0	206,261	808,908
9	i		03/31/93	500,062	279,236	0	0	809,904
10	t		06/30/93	0	506,238	241,794	270,774	0
11	y		09/30/93	0	687,303	0	0	388,402
12			12/31/93	444,545	0	0	176,925	302,981
13			03/31/94	270,681	0	718,436	452,130	198,665
14								
15			Maturity	Rate				
16								
17								
18			MAKE_TABLE					
19			{/ Math;2CellWhat-If}table ~ mat_date ~ inv_rate ~					

File: QFG11_12.WQ1 [1]   CAP NUM READY

Figure 11.12   Macro That Generates Two-Variable Analysis

Figure 11.13 — Spreadsheet 2

Cell reference: `J1: (D4) [W14] 'MAKE_TABLE`

	J	K	L
1	MAKE_TABLE	{/ Query;Block}Invest ~	Set database to search
2		{/ Query;CriteriaBlock}Criteria_1 ~	Find unique maturity dates
3		{/ Query;Output}H6 ~ {/ Query;Unique}	using criteria in H2..H3
4		{/ Query;CriteriaBlock}Criteria_2 ~	Find unique interest rates
5		{/ Query;Output}I6 ~ {/ Query;Unique}	using criteria in I2..I3
6		{GOTO}H7 ~	Go to first maturity date
7		{/ Sort;Reset}{/ Sort;Block}.{END}	Sort maturity dates
8		{DOWN} ~ {/ Sort;Key1} ~ a ~ {/ Sort;Go}	in ascending order
9		{/ Block;Copy}.{END}{DOWN} ~ P4 ~	Copies dates to table
10		{GOTO}I7 ~	Go to first rate
11		{/ Sort;Reset}{/ Sort;Block}.{END}	Sort all maturity dates
12		{DOWN} ~ {/ Sort;Key1} ~ a ~ {/ Sort;Go}	in ascending order
13		{/ Block;Transpose}{END}{DOWN} ~	Copies rates to table
14		Q3 ~ {GOTO}Table ~	Move to Table (P2)
15		{/ Math;2CellWhat-If}{BS}.	Create two variable table
16		{END}{RIGHT}{PGDN} ~ Mat_date ~ Inv_rate ~	
17		{END}{DOWN 2}{RIGHT}	Move to extra table data
18		{/ Block;Erase}	Erase extra table data
19		{END}{DOWN}{END}{RIGHT} ~	
		{GOTO}O1 ~	Return to top of table

File: QFG11_13.WQ1 [1]   CAP NUM READY

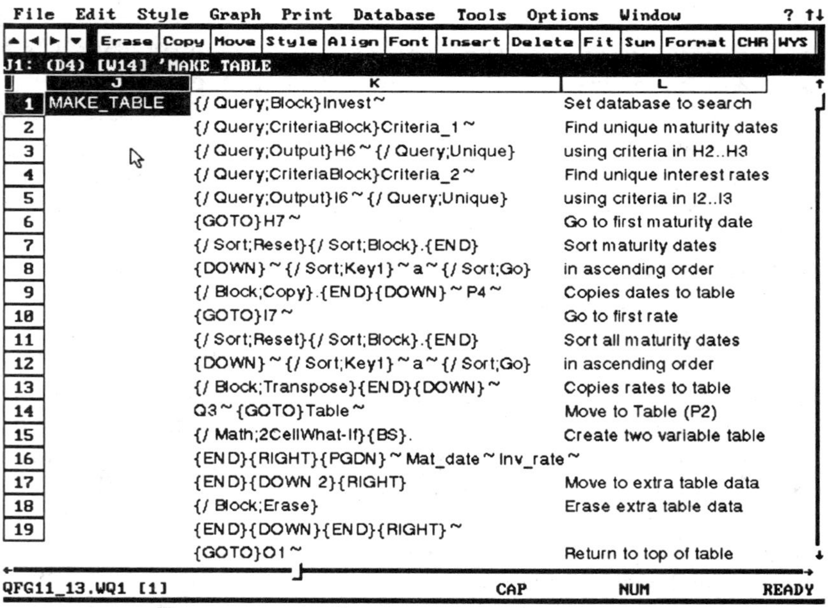

Figure 11.13   Macro That Generates Two-Variable Analysis Using Other Advanced Features

can be on the table's left side. This provides extra room for the table to expand without interfering with the macro.

The first line in Figure 11.13 uses the /Database Query Block command to specify Invest as the database that later queries will use. In K2 and K3, the menu-equivalent commands query the database for all unique maturity dates. Then in K4 and K5, the menu-equivalent commands query the database for all maturity dates. The two database queries use Criteria_1, which is H2..H3, and Criteria_2, which is I2..I3 as shown in Figure 11.14. The output data for both of these queries are shown in Figure 11.14. Once the two queries are performed, the macro moves to H7, sorts the dates (K7..K8), and then copies them to the table (K9). Next, the macro moves to I7, sorts the rates (K11..K12), and then copies them to the table. Since the interest rates must be rotated as they are put into the table, the /Edit Transpose command is used. Once the two sides of the table are copied, the macro performs the {/Math;2CellWhat-If} command in K15..K16. The macro assumes that there are no more than 19 maturity dates. If there are more, the table computes the two-variable table for the first 19 maturity dates and ignores the others. If there are fewer, the table creates additional entries that are removed by the macro instructions in K17..K19. If the table uses all 19 rows, the {/ Block;Erase} command removes an empty block on the spreadsheet, which is no longer needed. The final line returns the display to the beginning of the two-variable table that the macro has just created. This macro works best when the cells below and to the right of the table

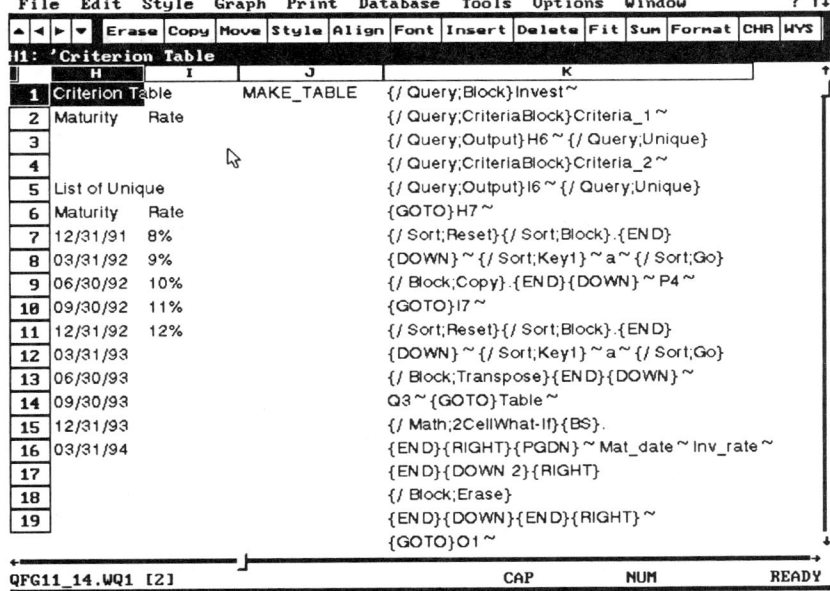

Figure 11.14 Spreadsheet Area Used to Store Information Used by Macro

are blank, which is why the macro instructions and the criteria cells are inserted to the left of the table. This macro also assumes that the entries in P1, P2, P3 (table formula), and O4..O11 are entered before the macro is executed. When this macro is executed using the same data that the macro in Figure 11.12 used, the same results shown in the top of Figure 11.12 are produced (although the table is at a different location). However, these results change as new investments are added to the table with either new maturity dates or new interest rates.

USING QUATTRO PRO'S TRANSCRIPT FEATURES

Quattro provides a Transcript utility that records the actions you have performed. Transcript is like the macro recorder, since it records every step you perform. Unlike the macro recorder, Transcript saves the keystrokes to a log file instead of to a spreadsheet block. While Transcript is an effective tool for creating macros, it also provides other features. Transcript can also undo steps that you have executed. It can also restore a spreadsheet that you have updated but not saved if something happens to the current spreadsheet. Also, it can audit the changes that you make to a spreadsheet. Transcript is an integral component that automatically records your keystrokes.

Activating Transcript

Transcript is activated by using the Macro menu box (just as the macro recorder is). To activate Transcript, type /, and select Tools Macro Transcript. Once Transcript is activated, it displays a log of all steps that it has recorded. A sample of potential entries is shown in the window area in Figure 11.15. Transcript's record of the steps you have performed resembles a macro, since the menu commands are shown using the menu-equivalent commands or the keystrokes depending on whether /Tools Macro Macro Recording is set to Logical or Keystroke. The highlight is on the last step that you performed. Transcript stores these steps in the file QUATTRO.LOG in the directory containing the program files. As Figure 11.15 shows, Transcript places a bracket around the steps that it has not yet saved to QUATTRO.LOG.

Transcript treats the /File Save, the /File Save As, the /File Retrieve, and the /File Erase commands as checkpoints. Quattro can restore the current spreadsheet from the last checkpoint but cannot restore spreadsheets between previous checkpoints.

The Transcript record of the steps performed usually extends beyond what is displayed in the window. To view the remaining contents, use the UP and DOWN ARROW keys to move the window's display up and down a line at a time. The PGUP and PGDN keys move the window's display up or down fourteen lines at a time. Pressing HOME moves the highlight to the top of the log and pressing END moves the highlight to the bottom of the log.

Automating Quattro Pro Tasks 593

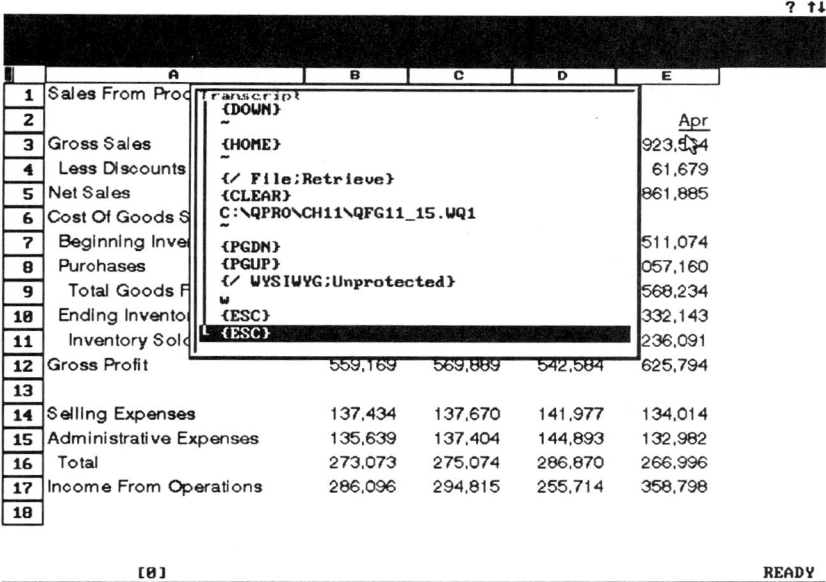

Figure 11.15 Transcript's Window

Replaying Transcript Entries

Quattro and Transcript can interact to play back portions of the recording. When Transcript is active, you can instruct Transcript to execute a set of instructions that you specify. To define which instructions in the log you want Quattro to perform, press the / while the Transcript window appears on the screen. The Transcript menu box is shown in Figure 11.16. This menu box provides several options for replaying portions of the log file and copying portions of the log to a spreadsheet block.

UNDOING THE LAST COMMAND Transcript provides an undo feature that lets you negate the last command. When you press / and select Undo Last Command, Transcript retrieves the file as it existed from the last checkpoint (retrieving the last saved version or erasing the spreadsheet) and instructs Quattro to execute all steps that you have performed except the last one. As Quattro performs these steps, Transcript displays WAIT in the bottom-right corner of the spreadsheet. This is similar to the Undo feature, except there are certain commands that the Undo feature cannot change back, but the Transcript utility can (for example, font selections). When Transcript finishes, Quattro returns to the READY mode of the current spreadsheet.

RESTORING ACTIONS TO A POINT Transcript allows you to undo multiple commands. To restore a spreadsheet to a specific point, move the highlight to the

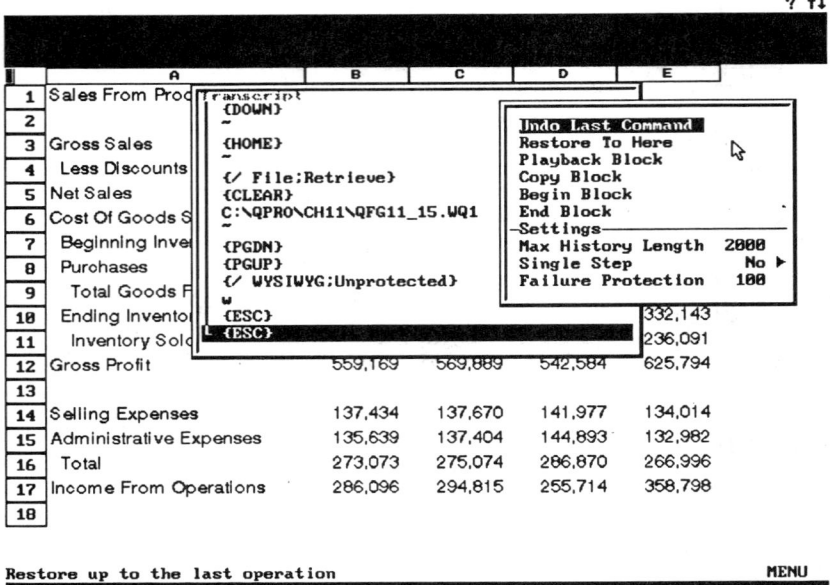

Figure 11.16 Transcript's Menu Box

last command that you want Transcript to perform and use the /Restore To Here command. Transcript retrieves the file as it existed from the last checkpoint (retrieving the last saved version or erasing the spreadsheet). Transcript then instructs Quattro to execute all steps that you performed up to the highlighted command. As Quattro performs all these steps, Transcript displays WAIT in the status line. When Transcript is finished, Quattro returns to the READY mode in the current spreadsheet.

PLAYING BACK A BLOCK OF COMMANDS Transcript lets you play back a block of commands in the log. To do this, move the highlight to the first command of the log that you want Transcript to play back, type / and select **Begin Block**. Once the beginning of the block is marked, move the highlight to the last command of the log that you want Transcript to play back, type / and select End Block commands. When both ends of the block are marked, Transcript displays pointers next to the steps in the block like the ones shown in Figure 11.17. To play back this block of commands use the /Playback Block command. Transcript's window disappears and Transcript directs Quattro to perform all steps in the block using the current spreadsheet. When Transcript is finished, Quattro returns to the READY mode.

Transcript's /Playback Block command is like a macro since it instructs Quattro to perform certain steps and the steps can be repeatedly performed. The playback block does not have to originate from the spreadsheet in which the steps were originally performed. This command can also play back a block to restore a

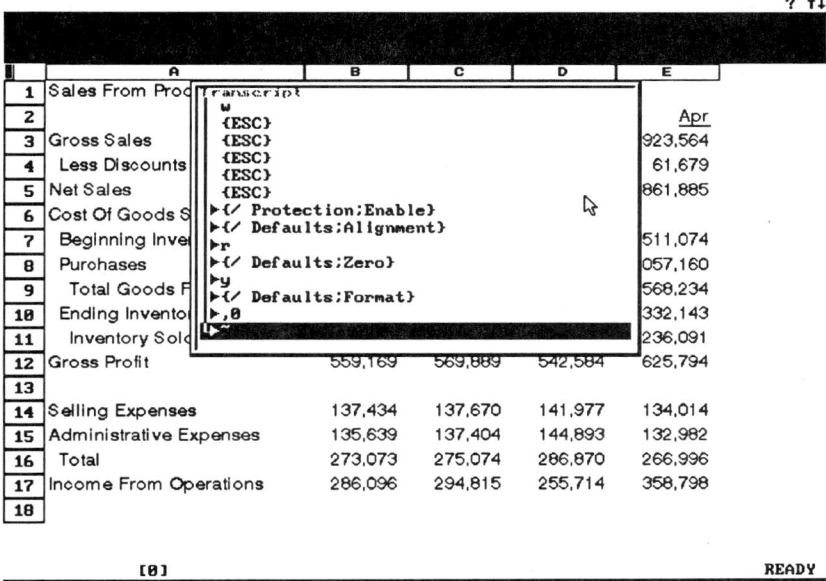

Figure 11.17 Block Marked in Transcript

spreadsheet that you have previously abandoned. You can restore the changes you have made to the spreadsheet. If you want to edit the steps that are performed, copy the block to the spreadsheet and execute it as a macro. The block remains marked so you can perform the commands in the block again by entering /Tools Macro Transcript and /Playback Block.

COPYING A BLOCK TO THE SPREADSHEET Transcript lets you take a block of commands in the log and place them in a spreadsheet. To do this, mark the block that you want to copy with the /Begin Block and /End Block commands and use the /Copy Block command. Transcript's window disappears, and you are prompted for the name of the macro. Quattro lists the existing macro and block names so you can check if the name you want is already in use. Then Quattro prompts for the location of the copied block. Move the highlight to the destination location for the first line from the block and press ENTER. If you want the block in a separate spreadsheet use ALT-0 (PICK) or the ALT-number combination to point to another spreadsheet. This is an excellent method for creating a macro. Also, the spreadsheet into which you entered the commands does not have to be the same spreadsheet that contains the copied block. Quattro names the block for you so it is ready to use as a macro name.

One use of copying a block is to restore a spreadsheet when Transcript does not play back the instructions the way you had intended. By copying a block and using it as a macro, you can modify the steps that Transcript recorded. For example, if the macro instructions edit cells that you do not want to change, you can delete the cells containing the editing instructions. When you delete instructions from the block in the spreadsheet, you may need to move the remaining instructions to take the places of the deleted instructions.

Another reason for copying a Transcript block to your spreadsheet is to print it. The only way to print Transcript's log is to block the log, copy it to a spreadsheet, and print the spreadsheet using the block that contains the Transcript instructions as the print block.

Transcript's Limitations

Some features of Quattro cannot be replicated by Transcript. Most of these features involve files. For example, Transcript cannot undo the changes you make to a menu tree with the Menu Builder. Transcript cannot replicate steps performed at the DOS level after you have used the **/File Utilities DOS Shell** command.

Other Transcript Options

Transcript has other options that affect how Transcript maintains the log file. These settings determine Transcript's playback speed, the number of steps the log file remembers, and the number of steps that are performed before Transcript saves the performed steps in the log file.

SETTING TRANSCRIPT'S PLAYBACK SPEED Transcript has three speeds that it can use for playbacks. The playback speed is controlled by entering **/Single Step**. One speed is the *regular* speed. This is the quickest speed at which Quattro can perform the commands. The other is a *single-step* mode. The single-step mode performs one step or keystroke at a time. The single-step mode is useful when you are playing back a block, but the block is not performing as you intended. The third speed is *timed*, which makes Transcript wait a moment after performing a keystroke or command before performing the next command. Although this setting is usually set to Yes (Transcript's fastest speed), the setting can be changed with the **/Single Step** command. When this setting is No, Transcript directs Quattro to perform a step or keystroke every time the SPACEBAR is pressed. When ENTER is pressed, Transcript resumes to normal speed. When this setting is set to Timed, Transcript performs a step or keystroke and waits a moment before performing the next step or keystroke. This approach is slow enough that you can see the steps Quattro is performing, yet you do not have to press a key each time for Quattro to continue. You can look at the impact of each individual step with either the single-step or timed approach.

SETTING THE LOG FILE'S SIZE LIMIT When you use Transcript, Quattro opens the file QUATTRO.LOG and appends your keystrokes and menu commands to the log file. This file contains all steps that you have performed in Quattro. This file can become very large if it saves every step you have performed since you loaded Quattro. To make the log file more manageable, Quattro limits its size. When the log file reaches a checkpoint after storing a predetermined number of keystrokes, Transcript copies the current log file to QUATTRO.BAK and starts a new QUATTRO.LOG. Every time Transcript does this, it writes over the existing QUATTRO.BAK. Transcript initially starts a new log file when the current log file reaches 2,000 keystrokes. By typing / and selecting **Max History Length**, you can select a different maximum size for QUATTRO.LOG. When you use this command, you must provide a number between 1 and 25,000 representing the number of keystrokes the log file may occupy before it is renamed to QUATTRO.BAK. If you enter 0 for the number of keystrokes, the Transcript utility is disabled and Quattro uses the memory that was used by Transcript for other parts of the Quattro program.

SETTING THE NUMBER OF STEPS PERFORMED BETWEEN SAVES Transcript initially waits until 100 keystrokes are performed before it groups these steps together and appends them to QUATTRO.LOG. Until it saves these steps, they are stored in a memory buffer. If a power failure should occur before these steps are written to a log file, the last few steps would not yet be part of QUATTRO.LOG, and you would have to execute them again. You can change the number of steps that Transcript stores in a memory buffer by typing / and selecting **Failure Protection**. When you use this command, Transcript prompts for a number between 1 and 25,000 for the number of steps that are performed between saves. If the number is low, few steps will have to be repeated in case of a power failure. However, if the number is high, less time is required for disk access.

Leaving Transcript

To exit from Transcript's boxes, press ESC. While you are in READY mode, Transcript continues to record all steps that you perform. The Transcript window also disappears when Transcript has finished performing the /Undo Last Command, /Restore to Here, /Playback Block, or /Copy Block command.

GETTING STARTED

In this chapter, you learned how you can create macros that perform a variety of tasks. You can use these features to create the macro in Figure 11.18, which hides the row and column borders, waits for data entries, and prints the spreadsheet. To create this macro, follow these steps:

1. Make the following entries:

A1: **Yearly Sales**
A2: **Division A**
A3: **Division B**
A4: **Division C**

2. Change the default column width and format. Enter /Options Formats Global Width. When Quattro prompts for the new default column width, press the RIGHT ARROW three times, and either press ENTER or click [Enter] in the input line. Select **N**umeric Format. Select **C**urrency. When Quattro prompts for the number of decimal digits, type **0**, and either press ENTER or click Enter in the box. Select **Q**uit twice to return to the spreadsheet.

3. Unprotect the cells in which you will enter values for the yearly sales of the different divisions. Enter /**S**tyle **P**rotection **U**nprotect. When Quattro prompts for a block to unprotect, select B2..B4.

4. Press ALT-F2 (MACRO) to display the Macro menu, and select **R**ecord to start recording your keystrokes. You will use these keystrokes as the basis for the macro.

5. Hide the column and row borders. Enter /**W**indow **O**ptions **R**ow & Col **B**orders **H**ide.

6. Enable protection so the macro user will only be able to edit cells you want to change. Enter /**O**ptions **P**rotection **E**nable to enable protection and **Q**uit to return to the spreadsheet.

7. Press HOME, the DOWN ARROW, and the RIGHT ARROW so you are sure the macro will position the selector correctly. Make the following entries:

B2: **650000**
B3: **800000**
B4: **450000**

8. Print the spreadsheet. Enter /**P**rint **B**lock, and select the block A1..B4. Select **S**preadsheet Print to print the spreadsheet and **Q**uit to return to the spreadsheet. Since this spreadsheet is using the destination of Printer, the printer will use its own default font to print the spreadsheet data.

9. Finish recording the macro. Press ALT-F2 (MACRO) to display the Macro menu and select **R**ecord to stop recording your keystrokes.

10. Enable protection so you can copy the macro instructions to the spreadsheet. Enter /**O**ptions **P**rotection **D**isable and **Q**uit to return to the spreadsheet.

11. Copy the macro instructions you have recorded to the spreadsheet. Press ALT-F2 (MACRO) and select **P**aste. When Quattro prompts for a macro name, type **\0** so this macro will execute the commands when the spreadsheet is retrieved. Then press ENTER or click the ENTER button in the box. When Quattro prompts for an address for the macro, select I1. By selecting this out-of-the-way location, the macro user will not see the macro instructions as the macro is performed. Press TAB to see if the macro looks like Figure 11.18. You will want to change your macro so it looks like the

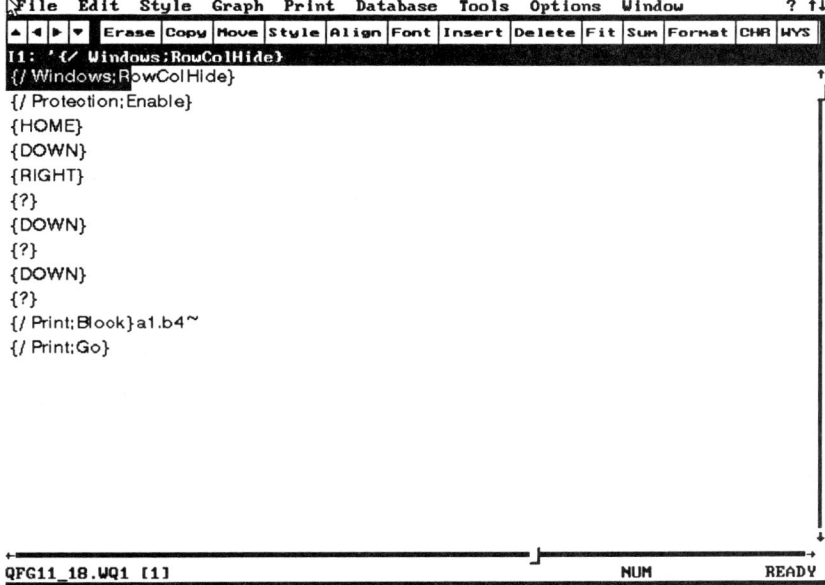

Figure 11.18 Macro Created in Getting Started Section

one in the figure. (See step 12 for changes to G6, G8, and G10.) For example, if you made any typing mistakes, remove from the pasted macro both the instructions containing the mistakes and the keystrokes you used to fix the mistakes.

12. Replace the values in the macro instructions in G6, G8, and G10 with the {?} macro instruction so the macro waits for the user to input the sales for the divisions. Move to G6, G8, and G10 and type {?}.

13. Save this macro by pressing CTRL-S to enter /File Save. Type **MACRO** as the file name, and either press ENTER or click the ENTER button in the box.

14. Retrieve this spreadsheet so your startup macro will execute the commands. Enter /File Retrieve and select MACRO from the list. The \0 macro will start executing the commands. If it does not, press ALT-0.

15. When the macro stops executing commands, it is waiting for you to enter the sales for Division A. Type **700000**, and either press ENTER or click [Enter] in the input line. When the macro stops again and waits for your entry, type **350000**, and either press ENTER or click [Enter] in the input line. When the macro stops a third time, type **600000**, and either press ENTER or click [Enter] in the input line. The printed output from your macro shows the new data.

12

Advanced Macro Options

In Chapter 11 you were introduced to macro basics. Although there are some time-saving applications that can be developed with the exclusive use of these techniques, Quattro offers much more. Quattro's macro command language provides a full-fledged programming language for the Quattro user who wants to develop customized applications. Whether you want to develop full-scale custom applications with menus and security features or just want to add a little sophistication to basic keyboard alternative macros, you will find the instructions you need within Quattro's command set. You can build custom menus that perform separate macros allowing a user to select an option from a custom menu to accomplish a complete series of actions. The complete set of command language instructions is covered in this chapter.

Quattro's command language instructions are used in the same manner as macro menu-equivalent commands except that Quattro cannot automatically record them as you try out a new application. You can intersperse menu abbreviations, special key representations, and menu-equivalent commands with Quattro's command language instructions. Most of Quattro's command instructions are enclosed in a set of braces ({ }). For complete compatibility with 1-2-3 Release 1A, Quattro also supports the /X commands introduced in that package.

Most of the macro language commands that are not menu-equivalent commands allow you to add iterative processing and condition checking to a macro. Others let you display a prompt on the screen and accept appropriate information from the keyboard. Still others allow you to read information stored in a disk file or to write information to a disk file. You can even assign macro instructions such as the ones covered in this chapter to buttons on the SpeedBar.

ADVANCED MACRO FEATURES

Quattro's advanced macro features require a little planning and attention to detail for successful application. Because they afford you all the opportunities of a programming language, you should invest some time planning the best solution for your problem before you begin coding these instructions. This planning parallels the process used by a programmer with any programming language.

Entering Menu Instructions as Labels

Once you have determined the set of macro instructions that are required to solve your problem, you can enter these instructions in the spreadsheet as a label. You must follow the unique syntax requirements for the particular command as you make these entries since most command language instructions use arguments in a manner similar to @ functions. Just as you can list the functions by pressing ALT-F3 (FUNCTIONS) or clicking @ in the EDIT mode SpeedBar, you can list the macro commands by pressing SHIFT-F3 (MACRO LIST) or clicking Macro in the EDIT SpeedBar. When you press SHIFT-F3 (MACRO LIST) or click Macro in the EDIT SpeedBar, Quattro displays a selection box from which you can choose the type of macro command from Keyboard, Screen, Interactive, Program flow, Cells, File, or / Commands. Once the general type is selected, you can select the specific macro command from the list. The last selection in the selection box, / Commands, lets you select menu-equivalent commands.

Incorporating Macro Commands

Since command language instructions can add logic for iterative processing or condition checking, they are often useful in a macro that consists of menu-equivalent instructions. The best strategy to use for constructing these combination macros is to record the menu-equivalent selections with Quattro's recorder and to add the other instructions after testing the recorded macro.

Figure 12.1 shows a macro that widens a column to 12 and formats the first 25 entries in the column as currency with 0 decimal places. The addition of a few block names and one or two instructions changes this macro into one that can make the same change to 10 consecutive columns. Figure 12.2 shows the macro with the addition of the command language instruction FOR, along with other changes required to insure a successful application. Some of these changes include naming blocks Counter and Loop.

Debugging Strategies

Since you cannot record command language instructions as you try out a new command, debugging requires a little more effort than is required for a macro

Advanced Macro Options 603

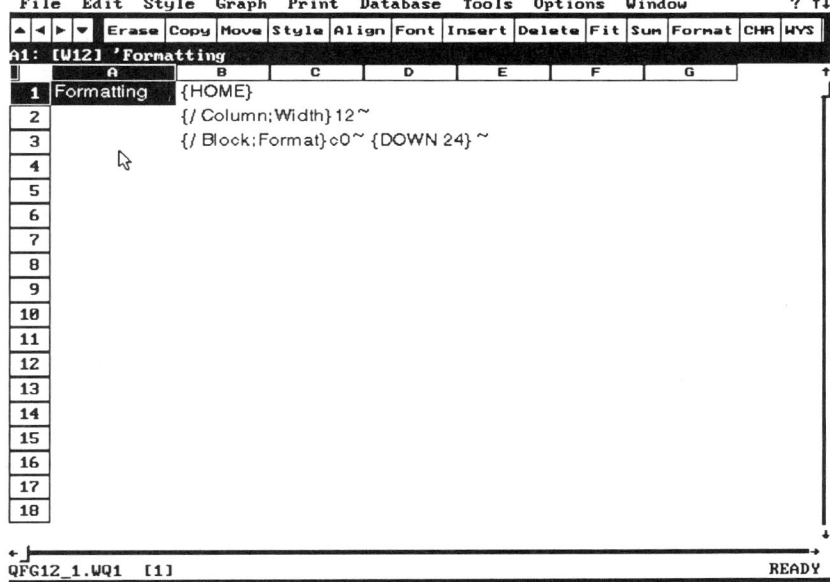

Figure 12.1 Keyboard Alternative Macro

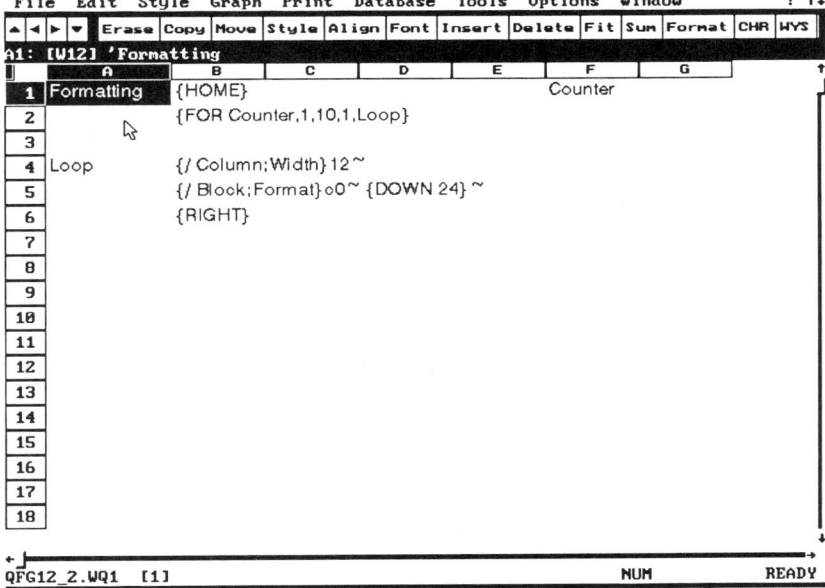

Figure 12.2 Keyboard Alternative Macro with Macro Commands Added

composed of menu-equivalent commands. Also, a macro's execution speed can prevent you from seeing where the error occurs as it is executed. Quattro's Single Step mode and breakpoint options make this process a little easier. These debugging features are available by pressing SHIFT-F2. You can also activate the DEBUG mode by entering the /Tools Macro Debugger Yes command or the shortcut of ALT-F2 and Debugger Yes. When you press SHIFT-F2, Quattro displays DEBUG in the status line. Any macro that is executed afterward uses Quattro's debugger.

USING STEP MODE When you execute a macro with DEBUG in the status line, the macro executes in Single Step mode. In Single Step mode, Quattro executes the macro one keystroke at a time, waiting until you press the SPACEBAR or click the mouse before executing the next macro keystroke. As the macro is executed, Quattro displays the Debug Window like the one shown in Figure 12.3. In the top half of the window, Quattro displays three lines of the macro. The top line contains the previous macro instruction. The middle line contains the macro instruction that Quattro is currently executing; the highlight is on the next step or keystroke that Quattro will perform. The third line is the cell below. Quattro uses the bottom half of the Debug Window for trace cells, which are discussed later in the chapter.

While the DEBUG mode is on, you instruct Quattro to perform the next step or keystroke by pressing the SPACEBAR or clicking the mouse. Pressing ENTER returns the macro's execution speed to normal until either the macro ends or Quattro reaches a breakpoint created with the debugger (discussed in the next section).

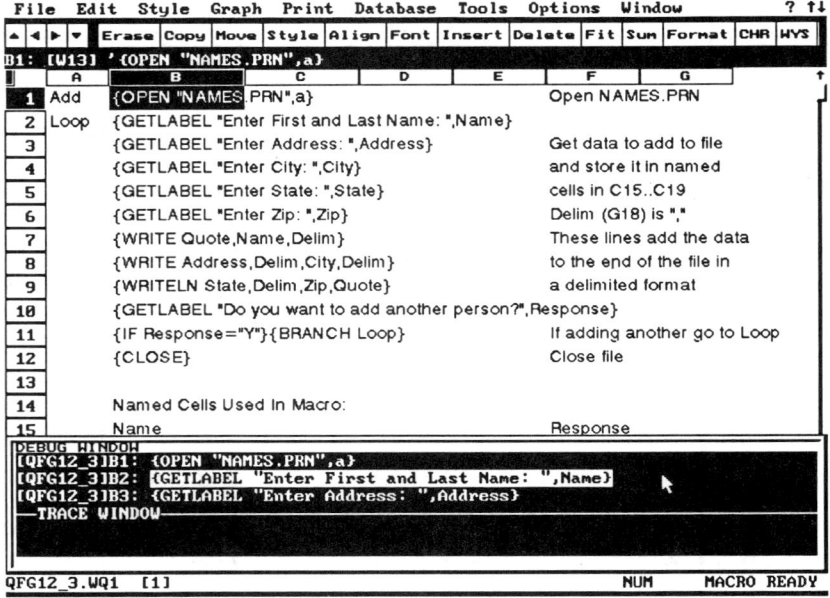

Figure 12.3 Debug Window

SETTING BREAKPOINTS Once you have narrowed the location of a problem in a macro to a specific area, you can use breakpoints to limit the Single Step mode to the area of the problem. Quattro has two types of breakpoints. The first type, a standard breakpoint, sets the macro's execution speed to Single Step mode when Quattro reaches a designated macro instruction. The second type, a conditional breakpoint, changes the macro's execution speed when a cell containing a logical formula is true.

Using a Standard Breakpoint When a macro contains standard breakpoints, you can execute portions of a macro at normal speed and other portions in Single Step mode. When Quattro reaches a breakpoint, Quattro changes the macro's execution speed to Single Step mode. If you want to execute the macro's instructions until the next breakpoint at normal speed, press ENTER. To execute the macro in Single Step mode, continue to press the SPACEBAR or click the mouse. To set a breakpoint, type **/** from the Debug Window to display the menu in Figure 12.4. From this menu, select **B**reakpoints to display the Macro Breakpoints menu box shown in Figure 12.5. As this menu box shows, you may have up to four standard breakpoints in a macro. When you have selected one of the breakpoints, Quattro displays the menu box in Figure 12.6. If you select **B**lock, Quattro hides the Debug Window so you can point to the cells you want and prompts you for a cell that will be a breakpoint. You can either point to the cell or type the address or block name directly. Once the cell is selected, you can set select **Q**uit to return to the menu box in Figure 12.6. From this menu, you can set another standard breakpoint or select

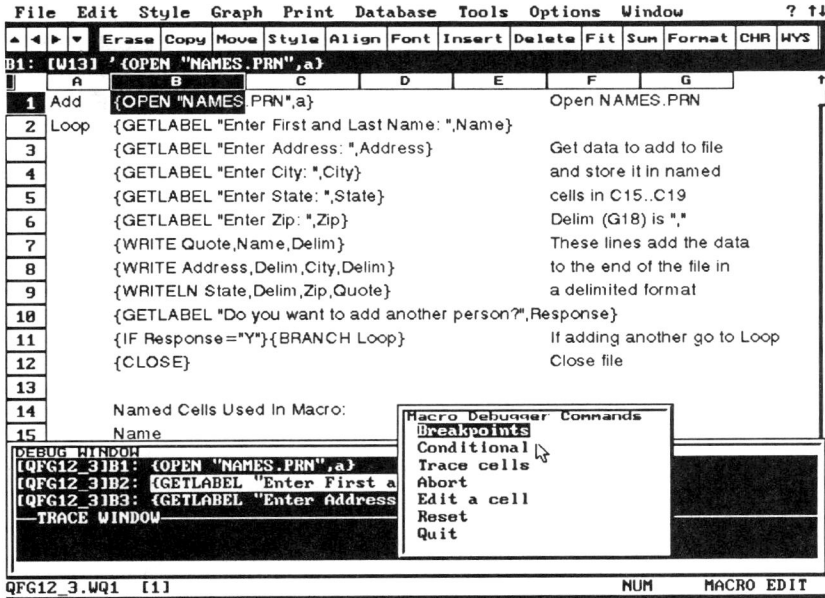

Figure 12.4   The Debug Window Menu

606 Quattro Pro 4.0 Handbook

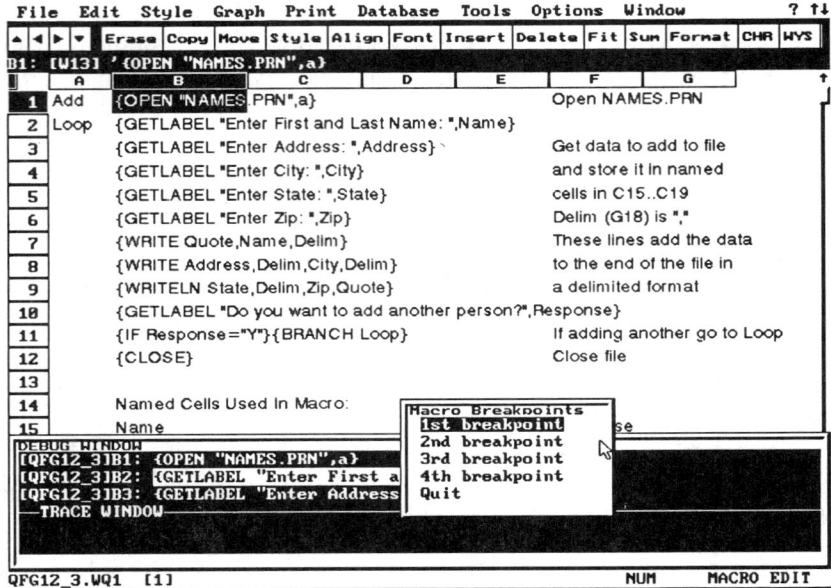

Figure 12.5   Macro Breakpoints Menu Box

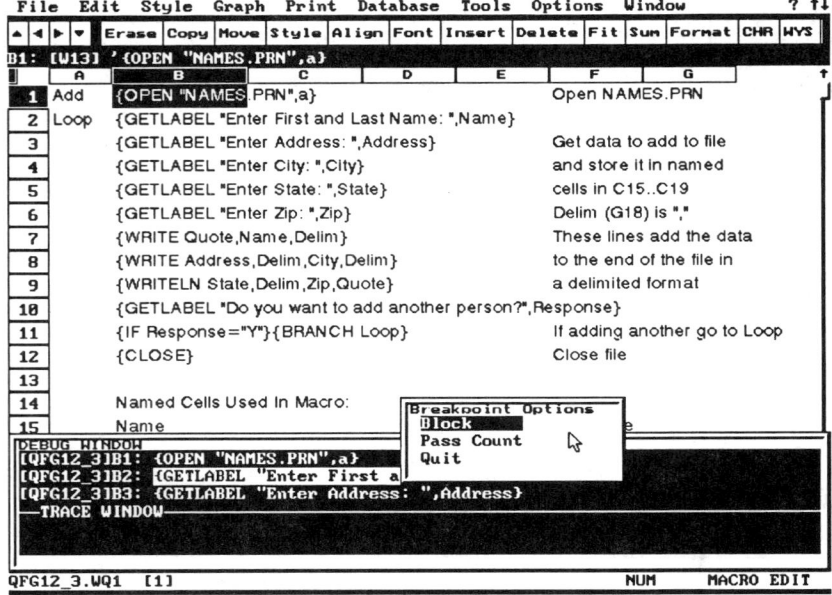

Figure 12.6   1st Breakpoint Menu

Quit to return to the Macro Breakpoints menu in Figure 12.5. When the macro reaches the first instruction in the block, the macro starts executing commands in Single Step mode. The next time you press ENTER, Quattro continues executing the macro at normal speed.

In macros that contain loops, a particular section may not be a problem the first time it is executed. On subsequent executions, the same macro can result in an error. If you select Pass Count from the menu box in Figure 12.6, you may select the number of times that Quattro passes by the macro instruction before treating it as a breakpoint. For example, if you set the Pass Count for a breakpoint of 2, the macro starts in Single Step mode every other time the macro reaches the designated breakpoint. Selecting Quit returns you to the menu box shown in Figure 12.5. From this menu box, you can select another breakpoint or Quit to return to the initial Debug menu.

Using a Conditional Breakpoint When a macro contains conditional breakpoints, you can alter the macro's execution speed depending on a cell's value. A conditional breakpoint sets the macro execution to Single Step mode when a cell that contains a logical formula is true. For example, if you have a macro that is returning information that you know is incorrect, using a conditional breakpoint can help locate the macro instruction that is causing the problem. Once the logical formula checking for invalid entries is true, the breakpoint is in effect and Quattro changes the macro's execution speed to Single Step mode. To return the macro's execution speed to normal, press ENTER. To continue to execute the macro in Single Step mode, continue to press the SPACEBAR or click the mouse.

To set a conditional breakpoint, type / and select Conditional to display the menu box shown in Figure 12.7. As this menu box shows, you can have up to four conditional breakpoints in your macro. When you have selected one of the breakpoints, Quattro prompts you for the cell with the logical formula. Indicate the cell with the logical formula by typing the cell address or name, or by pointing to the cell and pressing ENTER. The cell can be in the current spreadsheet or in another one. If it is in another spreadsheet, it must include the file name in square brackets. Once the cell is selected, you can select another conditional breakpoint or select Quit to return to the Debug menu.

USING TRACE CELLS The top half of the Debug Window monitors the macro instructions as Quattro performs them. The bottom half can monitor cell contents as Quattro executes the macro. The cells monitored in the Debug Window are called trace cells. Quattro allows up to four trace cells. To set a trace cell, type / and select Trace cells and the number of the trace cell that you want to select. Quattro prompts for the cell address to be traced during the macro's execution. You can type the cell name or address, or you can point to the cell using the ARROW keys or the mouse. The trace cell can be in the current spreadsheet or in another one. Once the trace cell is selected, you can select another trace cell or select Quit to return to the Macro Debug Window menu. After you select Quit to leave this Debug menu, Quattro displays the cell address and its value as it appears in the cell. As the

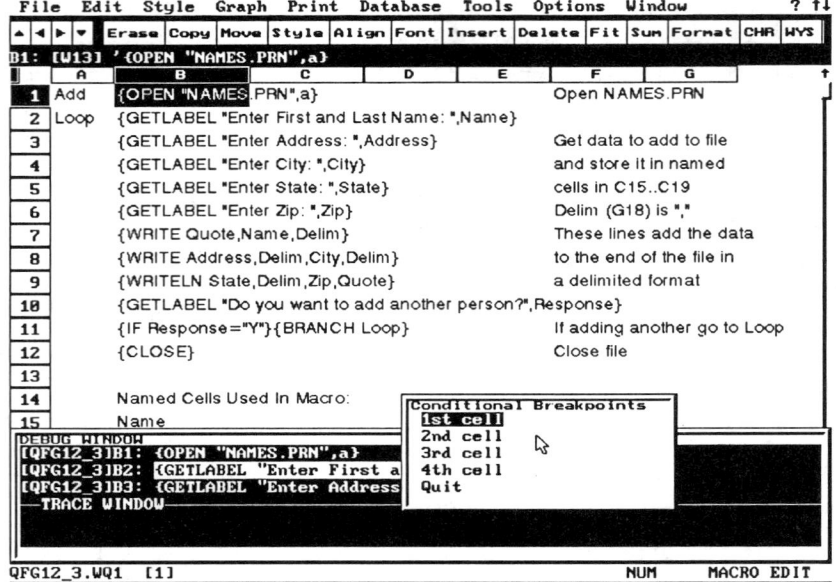

Figure 12.7 Conditional Breakpoints Menu

macro instructions change the value of the trace cells, Quattro updates the values displayed in the lower half of the Debug Window—even when the macro does not update the spreadsheet screen. Figure 12.8 shows a Debug Window with four trace cells.

REMOVING BREAKPOINTS AND TRACE CELLS As you edit your macro, you may need to specify new breakpoints and trace cells or remove them altogether. To remove breakpoints and trace cells while in the Debug Window, type / and select Reset. Quattro's /Tools Macro Clear Breakpoints command also removes all the breakpoints and trace cells.

EDITING A CELL USING QUATTRO'S DEBUGGER While you are executing a macro within the Debug Window, you may realize that macro instruction needs to be edited before Quattro executes it. Rather than aborting the macro, you can edit while the Debug Window is displayed. You can also use this editing feature to change other cells that are not part of the macro. To edit a cell's contents from the Debug Window, type / and select Edit a cell. When you use this command, Quattro updates the screen and prompts for the cell that you want to edit. You can point to the cell (or type the cell address or name), and then press ENTER. When you have specified the cell, Quattro displays the current cell's contents in the input line. Like editing a cell from the EDIT mode, you can use all Quattro's editing keys and SpeedBar buttons to change the cell's contents. When you have finished

Advanced Macro Options 609

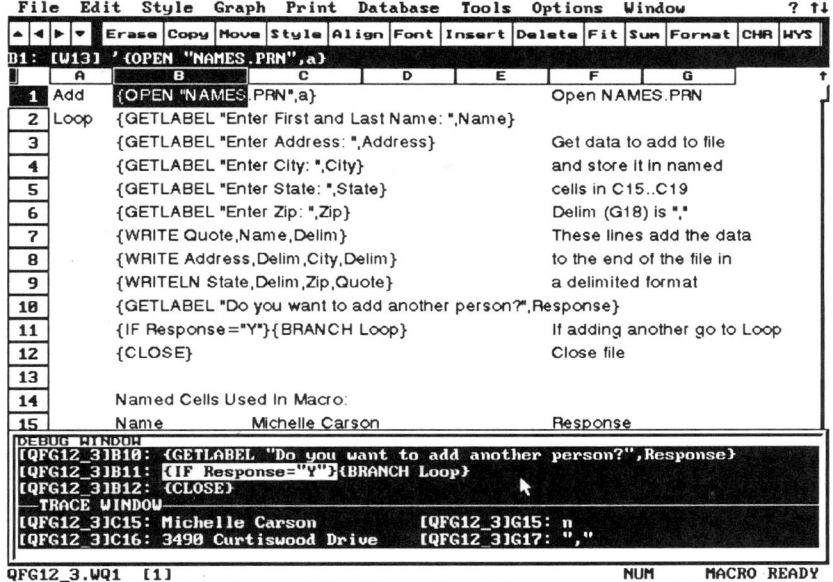

Figure 12.8 Debug Window with Trace Cells

editing the cell, press ENTER. You can select another menu item from the Debug menu or select Quit to return to the Debug Window and continue executing the macro. If you are editing a macro instruction, Quattro uses the edited macro instruction if it comes after the current macro instruction. For example, Figure 12.9 shows a macro in the middle of execution. The macro instruction in F18 contains a mistake (the general action should be Defaults, not Default). By using the /Edit a cell command, editing the cell, inserting an s after Default, pressing ENTER, and selecting Quit to leave the menu, the macro instruction is corrected. When Quattro continues executing the macro, it uses the corrected version of F18.

STOPPING THE MACRO'S EXECUTION While you are executing a macro, you may decide that you want to stop. To stop a macro from the Debug Window, type / to activate the Debug menu, and select Abort. This terminates the macro just as if you pressed CTRL-BREAK. Also, the /Abort Debug command works even when the {BREAKOFF} macro command has disabled the CTRL-BREAK sequence.

LEAVING QUATTRO'S DEBUGGER To remove Quattro's debugger from the READY mode, press SHIFT-F2. You can also deactivate the DEBUG mode by entering the /Tools Macro Debugger No command (or the shortcut of ALT-F2 and Debugger No). Any macros that are executed afterward are executed at the normal speed. If you are executing a macro when you press SHIFT-F2, the Debug Window disappears and the macro is executed at its normal speed. You can temporarily

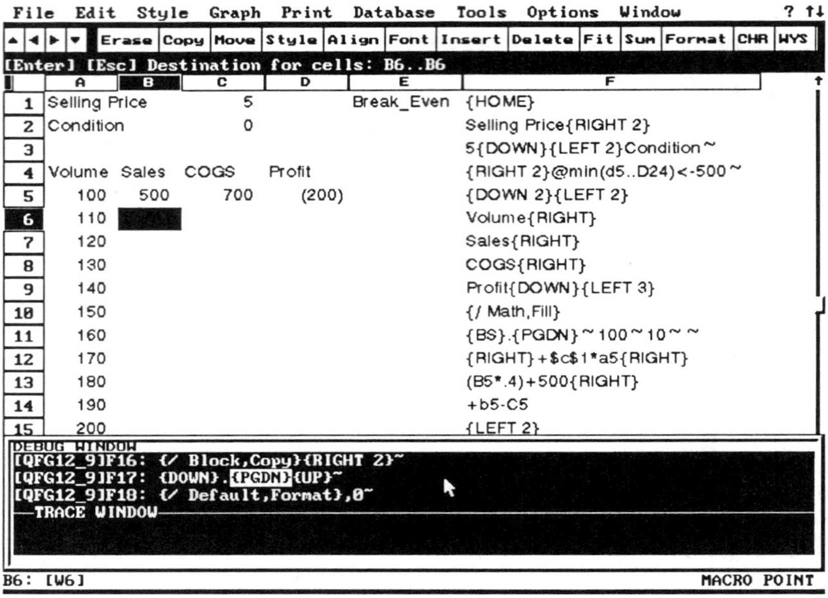

Figure 12.9   Macro with Mistake in the Middle of Execution

disable the Debugger by pressing ENTER instead of the SPACEBAR to continue performing the macro at normal speed until the next breakpoint.

COMMAND LANGUAGE OPTIONS

The macro instructions in the sections that follow are grouped according to the categories that Quattro's documentation uses. (These categories and their commands are shown in Table 12.1.) In addition to a description of each command language instruction, an example of its use is provided. The macro arguments, which are optional, are enclosed in brackets (<>). As you duplicate these examples, remember to assign block names to the appropriate fields so that the macros function properly. These names appear in proper case to make it easy to distinguish them from command language instructions, which appear in uppercase.

CELLS COMMANDS

The cell contents macro commands change the contents of spreadsheet cells. These commands can delete a group of cells, assign values to cells, and recalculate cells.

Table 12.1 Macro Commands by Category

Cell Contents

{BLANK}
{CONTENTS}
{LET}
{PUT}
{RECALC}
{RECALCCOL}

Program Flow

{BRANCH}
{DEFINE}
{DISPATCH}
{FOR}
{FORBREAK}
{IF}
{ONERROR}
{QUIT}
{RESTART}
{RETURN}
{SubRoutine}

Interactive

{?}
{BREAKOFF}
{BREAKON}
{GET}
{GETLABEL}
{GETNUMBER}
{GRAPHCHAR}
{IFKEY}
{LOOK}
{MENUBRANCH}
{MENUCALL}
{MESSAGE}
{STEPOFF}

{STEPON}
{WAIT}

File

{CLOSE}
{FILESIZE}
{GETPOS}
{OPEN}
{READ}
{READLN}
{SETPOS}
{WRITE}
{WRITELN}

Screen

{BEEP}
{INDICATE}
{PANELOFF}
{PANELON}
{PLAY}
{WINDOWSOFF}
{WINDOWSON}

Miscellaneous

{}
{;}

/X for Compatibility with 1-2-3

/XC={Subroutine}
/XG={BRANCH}
/XI={IF}
/XL={GETLABEL}
/XM={MENUBRANCH}
/XN={GETNUMBER}
/XQ={QUIT}
/XR={RETURN}

{BLANK} The {BLANK} command deletes the contents of the cell or block that you specify. This command is equivalent to using the DEL key or using the /Edit Erase Block command to erase cell contents.

Format {BLANK Location} is the format of the {BLANK} command.

Location is the cell address, block address, or block name whose contents are to be deleted.

Use The {BLANK} command can replace a {/ Block;Erase} menu-equivalent command or the {DEL} special-key equivalent in a macro to erase one or more cells. Unlike the /Edit Erase Block command, Quattro can execute this command while in the middle of another command.

Example Figure 12.10 shows a macro that uses the {BLANK} command. This macro gives the user the option of including notes with the budget. If the user wants to include notes, the macro lets the user type them and then prints the budget and the notes. If the user does not want notes, the macro prints only the budget. The {BLANK} command at the beginning of the macro removes the contents of the block named Notes (which is B11..H20) to prevent notes from a prior budget from appearing with the notes for the new budget.

{CONTENTS} The {CONTENTS} command copies the contents from one location to another. If the original location contains a numeric value, you can specify a format and width to store the value as a string.

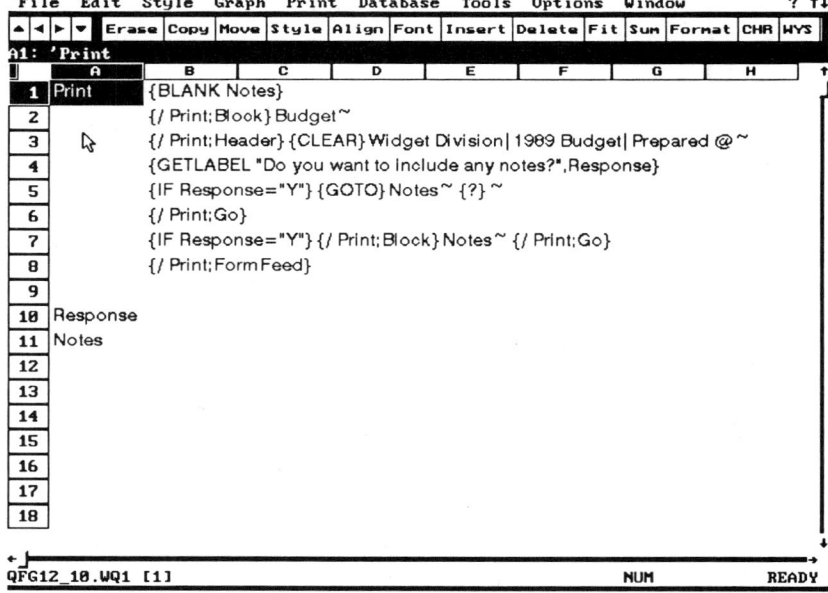

Figure 12.10 Macro Using {BLANK} Command

Format {CONTENTS Destination,Source<,Width<,Format>>} is the format for the {CONTENTS} command.

Destination is the location in which you want to store the Source value as a left-aligned label. It is a block name or cell address.

Source is the location of the entry you want copied to the destination. It is specified as a cell address or block name.

Width is the column width of the left-aligned label used when the value of the source is a number. It must be a number between 1 and 254. This argument is optional, but if you use the Format argument, you must use this argument. If the width is missing, Quattro uses the width of the source column. This command does not change the column width. This command puts the value of Source into Destination as the number would appear in a column of the specified width. For example, if the column width is 5 for a number that needs a width of at least 7, Quattro stores the label '***** in the Destination. If the width is greater than the number needs, Quattro adds spaces to the beginning so the length of the resulting label is the same as the width.

Format is a number corresponding to the format used in the Destination. Table 12.2 lists the numbers you can use as the Format argument. Like the Width argument, this argument is optional. If the Format argument is missing, Quattro uses the format of the Source cell.

Use This command changes the spacing and format of cells. For writing to files that are in a structured format, this command changes the appearance so the information lines up with the information in other records of the file.

Example Figure 12.11 shows a template designed for costing the production of gas pump hoses. In this template, the macro updates the amount in stock in the inventory file after the gas pump hoses are produced. After another macro determines the parts' prices and initial quantity information, the \Y macro updates inventory quantity from the quantity in stock to the amount that remains after the gas pumps hoses are produced. This macro opens the inventory file and searches for the information for each part. Once the Loop_Out macro finds the record for each part, the Write_Out macro moves the selector to the Remaining column for the part number. The {LET} command transfers the contents to the cell Remain in H28. The {CONTENTS} command converts the number to a label with a width of 7. The new value of Remain is a label with two spaces to the right of the number and one space to the left. The {WRITE} command in B33 replaces the old inventory quantity with the new quantity. Since the part number and price have not changed, the macro leaves this information intact. Since the {CONTENTS} command cannot use functions or formulas as a Source argument, the macro uses the {LET} command to convert a formula result to a cell's contents. The {CONTENTS} command ensures that the value of the remaining inventory written to the file aligns with the other inventory values.

{LET} The {LET} command allows you to enter value or string entries in a cell during macro execution without having to move the selector to the location of the cell.

Table 12.2 Format Codes for {CONTENTS} Macro Command

Code	Numeric Format
0-15	Fixed with 0-15 decimals
16-31	Scientific with 0-15 decimals
32-47	Currency with 0-15 decimals
48-63	Percentage with 0-15 decimals
64-79	, (Financial) with 0-15 decimals
112	Plus/Minus
113	General
114	Date Format 1 = DD-MMM-YY
115	Date Format 2 = DD-MMM
116	Date Format 3 = MMM-YY
117	Text
118	Hidden
119	Time Format 1 = HH:MM:SS AM/PM
120	Time Format 2 = HH:MM AM/PM
121	Date Format 4 = Long International
122	Date Format 5 = Short International
123	Time Format 3 = Long International
124	Time Format 4 = Short International
127	Default set with /Options Formats Numeric Format command

Format {LET Location,Value<:Type>} is the format of the {LET} command.

Location is the address or name of the cell or block in which the Value is to be stored.

Value is the numeric or string entry you want stored in the cell or block specified by Location. This is a cell address or block name, a formula, a string enclosed in quotes, or a value.

Type is either string or value. Using string stores the argument Value as a left-aligned label. If Value contains a formula, a type of string stores the formula as a left-justified label. A type of value stores the Value argument as the value entered. If you omit this optional argument, Quattro attempts to store Value as a numeric value. If Quattro is unsuccessful, Quattro stores Value as string.

Advanced Macro Options 615

```
 File   Edit   Style   Graph   Print   Database   Tools   Options   Window          ? ↑↓
 ▲ ◄ ► ▼  Erase Copy Move Style Align Font Insert Delete Fit Sum Format CHR WYS
 B5: [W8]
         A              B         C      D       E       F         G
  2  Hose (in feet)   YNCEED      7    8899    0.75    1899
  3  Nozzle           EPDAPY      1    6797   10.51    5797
  4  Pump Attachment  NHIXYD      1    9669    2.98    8669
  5  Number of Gas Pumps To Be Produced                        1000
         A              B         C      D       E       F         G
 22  \Y               {GOTO}Hose~ {OPEN "Out.prn",M}        Size_Out
 23                   {FILESIZE Size_Out}                    Count
 24  Next_Part        {FOR Count,0,Size_Out-20,20,Loop_Out}
 25                   {DOWN} {IF @CELLPOINTER("Type")< >"b"} {BRANCH Next_Part}
 26                   {CLOSE}
 27                                                          Part
 28  Loop_Out         {SETPOS Count}                         Remain
 29                   {READ 6,Part}
 30                   {IF Part=@CELLPOINTER("Contents")} {BRANCH Write_Out}
 31
 32  Write_Out        {RIGHT 4} {CALC} {LET Remain,@CELLPOINTER("Contents")}
 33                   {CONTENTS Remain,Remain,7} {WRITE Remain}
 34                   {LEFT 4} {FORBREAK}
 35
 QFG12_11.WQ1 [1]                                        NUM         READY
```

Figure 12.11   Macro Using {CONTENTS} Command

Use This command is very flexible, since you can specify either string or value entries. It is very useful in a loop that executes a section of code. You can use this command to increment a counter. Some examples follow:

{LET C1,12} This stores the value 12 in C1.
{LET C1,+C1+5} This increases C1 by 5.
{LET C1,+C1+5:string} This stores the label '+C1+5 in C1.

Example Figure 12.12 shows a macro using several {LET} commands. This macro lists all possible account numbers. Using the file instead of typing the numbers directly into the spreadsheet reduces the number of typing errors. Table is the block name for G5..G41, the location where the {PUT} command places the account numbers that are read from a file. The {LET} command in B3 stores the value of Size divided by 12 in Records. The {LET} command in B4 stores a value in Counter. The {LET} command in B8 increments the value of Counter by 1. This macro uses the {LET} command to change spreadsheet values without the need for positioning the selector on the cell to be changed.

{PUT} Like the {LET} command, the {PUT} command allows you to copy a value or string from a specified cell to another cell. Instead of specifying a cell address or block name to which the value is to be copied, you need to specify the destination as the block name and the offset in the block. The offset is the number of columns to the right and number of rows down from the upper-left corner of the block. The {PUT} command creates an array of data in a spreadsheet block.

616 *Quattro Pro 4.0 Handbook*

```
File   Edit   Style   Graph   Print   Database   Tools   Options   Window          ? ↑↓
▲ ◄ ► ▼  Erase Copy Move Style Align Font Insert Delete Fit Sum Format CHR WYS
A1: [W10] '\r
        A              B              C              D          E        F            G          H
   1   \r         {OPEN "Accounts.prn",R} {OpenErr}                   Size          144
   2              {FILESIZE Size}                                     Records        12
   3              {LET Records,@int(Size/12)}                         Counter        11
   4              {LET Counter,0}                                     Data      1734505404
   5   Top        {READLN Data}                                       Table     4586022383
   6              {PUT Table,0,Counter,Data}                                    4917185960
   7              {IF Counter=Records-1} {BRANCH End}                           7676989700
   8              {LET Counter,Counter+1}                                       8828409516
   9              {BRANCH Top}                                                  8232365752
  10   End        {CLOSE "Accounts.prn"}                                        8835694055
  11                                                                            8901184605
  12   OpenErr    {Message Open_Msg,5,5,0} {QUIT}                               9114757112
  13                                                                            5759661467
  14   Open_Msg   Cannot find the file. Use the File                            3127383703
  15              Manager to confirm the file's location.                       1573424138
  16                                                                            1734505404
  17
  18

QFG12_12.WQ1 [1]                                                    NUM              READY
```

Figure 12.12 Macro Using {LET} and {PUT} Commands

Format {PUT Location,Column#,Row#,Value<:Type>} is the format for the {PUT} command.

Location is a block in which the command stores the value. This block must contain all the columns and rows that the {PUT} command uses. This argument is either a block address or block name.

Column# is the number of columns to the right of the first column of the block where Quattro stores the value. This argument is a number, cell address, block name containing a value, or a formula that returns a value. Quattro starts counting the columns with 0. The first column of a block has a Column# of 0, and the second column of a block has a Column# of 1. The identifying number is always one less than the number of columns in the block.

Row# is the number of rows below the top row of the location block where Quattro stores the Value. This argument is a number, cell address, or block name containing either a value or a formula that returns a value. Quattro starts counting the rows with 0. The first row of a block has a Row# of 0 and the second row of a block has a Row# of 1. This identifying number is always one less than the number of rows in the block.

Value is the value that Quattro places in the cell specified by the column and row offset of the block. It is a string, numeric value, formula, cell address, or block name.

Type is string or value. If Type is string, Quattro stores Value as a label. If Value is a block name or formula, the name or formula is stored in the specified location as a left-aligned label. If this argument is a value, Quattro determines the value of Value before storing the value in the specified location. This argument is optional. If this argument is omitted, Quattro attempts to store Value as a numeric value. If Quattro is unsuccessful, Quattro stores Value as a string.

Use This command stores values in spreadsheet cells. Unlike the {LET} command, the {PUT} command uses an offset to determine the location. The argument Value is placed a specified number of rows and columns into the block. If the Column# or Row# argument is too high the macro aborts, since this is not an error that {ONERROR} can trap.

Example Figure 12.12 provides an example of the {PUT} command. This macro lists all possible account numbers. Using the file instead of typing the numbers directly into the spreadsheet reduces the number of typing errors. Table is the block name for G5..G41, the location where the {PUT} command places the account numbers that are read from a file. The macro reads one line at a time and stores the information in Data, G4. The {PUT} command copies this information from Data to the next blank row in Table. The {PUT} command uses the value of Counter in G3 for Row#. Since 0 is the Column#, the {PUT} command copies the data into column G.

{RECALC} The {RECALC} command recalculates a specified block of the spreadsheet. Quattro recalculates row by row within the block.

Format {RECALC Location<,Condition<,Iteration#>>} is the format for the {RECALC} command.

Location is the block of cells you want recalculated.

Condition is an optional argument that halts the recalculation process when the condition this argument represents is true. The recalculation process continues as long as this condition is false.

Iteration# is also an optional argument. This argument is used in conjunction with the condition. It allows you to specify the maximum number of times Quattro recalculates the formulas within the block while the condition is false.

Use The {RECALC} command recalculates an area of a spreadsheet while leaving the remainder of the spreadsheet uncalculated. This command speeds up macro execution by limiting the area in which Quattro calculates the formulas. If the cells that the formulas in Location reference are not above or to the left of the formulas and in the Location block, you should use either {RECALCCOL} or {CALC}. You may want to increase the iteration count to confirm that the cells in Location have been correctly computed. The number of iterations can be increased by using @FALSE for the condition and a number of iterations as parameters for the macro command.

Example Figure 12.13 provides an example of the {RECALC} command. The projected figures in column E are formulas that use current figures increased by a

```
    File    Edit    Style    Graph    Print    Database    Tools    Options    Window        ? ↑↓
    ◄ ► ▼  Erase Copy Move Style Align Font Insert Delete Fit Sum Format CHR WYS
    B10:   '{GETNUMBER "Enter the Rate of Sales Increase ",Increase}~
           A        B           C         D          E       F       G      H      ↑
     1                                    Current  Projected
     2                                    -------  ---------
     3    Sales                             1,000    1,200
     4    Variable Cost                       400      480
     5    Contribution Margin                 600      720
     6
     7              Sales Growth Percentage            20%
     8
     9
    10    PROJECT  {GETNUMBER "Enter the Rate of Sales Increase ",Increase} ~
    11             {/ Defaults;RecalcMode}m
    12             {LET Growth,Increase}
    13             {RECALC Forecast}
    14             {/ Defaults;RecalcMode}a
    15
    16                        Increase     0.2
    17
    18
    QFG12_13.WQ1 [1]                                        NUM         READY
```

Figure 12.13   Macro Using {RECALC} Command

specified sales growth rate. The block D3..E5 is named Forecast. The sales growth rate in E7 is named Growth. When the macro begins, Quattro prompts you for the sales growth rate. The formula in E7 (which is +E15) duplicates the value in E7. After entering the rate, the {/Defaults;RecalcMode}m command switches the recalculation mode from automatic to manual to reduce the macro execution time. When Quattro executes the {RECALC} command, Quattro recalculates the formulas in the block Forecast. In this example, the growth rate is 20%. Unless the recalculation mode is set to manual, Quattro automatically recalculates the spreadsheet, which makes the {RECALC} command unnecessary. Since recalculation is set to manual, Quattro only recalculates a part of the spreadsheet when Quattro executes the {RECALC} command. This macro instruction is primarily used for long macros and for macros that use large spreadsheets containing many formulas.

{RECALCCOL} The {RECALCCOL} command recalculates the specified block column by column.

Format {RECALCCOL Location,<Condition,<Iteration#>>} is the format for the {RECALCCOL} command.
   Location is the specified block of cells that you want recalculated.
   Condition is a logical condition that stops the recalculation process when the condition is true. As long as the condition is false, the recalculation takes place. This argument is optional. If the command uses the Iteration# argument, Condition is a required argument.

Advanced Macro Options 619

Iteration# is the maximum number of times the formulas are recalculated in the block while the condition remains false. As long as the condition is false, Quattro recalculates the block the number of times specified by Iteration#. However, when the condition is true, recalculation stops even though Quattro has not recalculated the formulas the number of times specified by Iteration#.

Use The {RECALCCOL} command is used when the area to be recalculated is to the right of and above the cells that the formulas in this area reference. This command speeds up macro execution by limiting the area in which Quattro calculates the formulas. If the area that the formulas reference are to the left of and below the block, you should use either {RECALC} or {CALC}. If the block contains several formulas that refer to values within the block, the formulas should be recalculated at least twice to insure that the formulas reflect the current values. The number of iterations is increased by including @FALSE for the condition and the number of iterations as parameters for the macro command.

Example Figure 12.14 provides an example of the {RECALCCOL} command. The figures in column E are formulas that use current figures increased by a specified sales growth rate. The block D3..E5 is named Forecast. The sales growth rate in E7 is named Growth. When macro begins, Quattro prompts you for the sales growth rate. After entering the rate, the {/ Defaults;RecalcMode}m command switches the recalculation mode from automatic to manual to reduce the macro execution time. When Quattro executes the {RECALCCOL} command, Quattro recalculates the

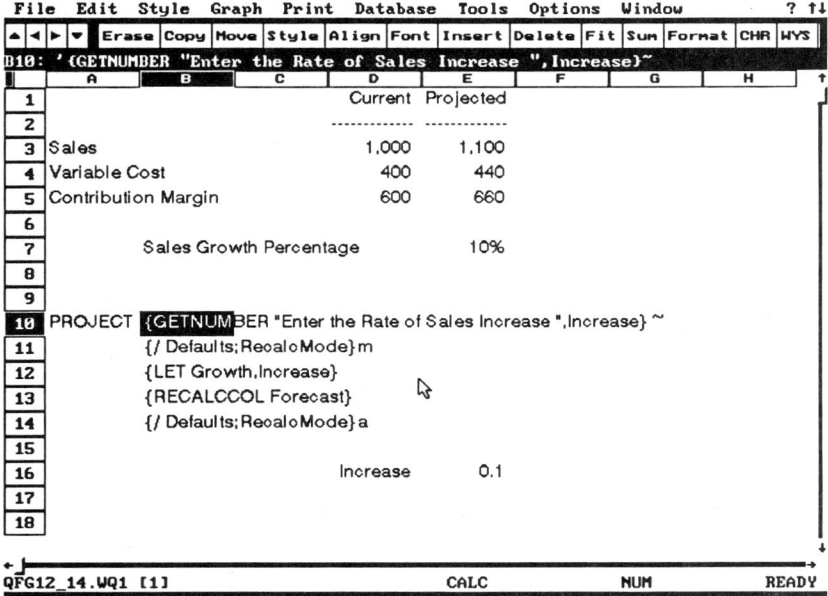

Figure 12.14 Macro Using {RECALCCOL} Command

formulas in the block Forecast. In this example, the growth rate is 10%. Unless the recalculation mode is set to manual, Quattro automatically recalculates the spreadsheet, which makes the {RECALCCOL} command unnecessary. Since recalculation is set to manual, Quattro only recalculates a part of the spreadsheet when Quattro executes the {RECALCCOL} command.

Program Flow Commands

Quattro has several commands that allow you to change the macro instructions that Quattro performs as the macro executes. Quattro has several other commands that create loops; this allows you to repeat a group of macro instructions. Yet another set of commands lets you redirect Quattro to another group of macro instructions. Quattro can branch to a second group of instructions, thereby changing the execution flow of the macro. A macro that branches does not return to the first area of the macro after completing the instructions in the area where the macro instruction branches. However, Quattro can treat a group of instructions as a subroutine. When a subroutine is used, Quattro returns to the original macro location and continues with the next instruction after completing the subroutine.

Some of the program flow commands change the ending point of a macro or subroutine. These let you omit a group of instructions. One of the more important program flow commands is the {IF} command, which allows you to execute another set of instructions if a condition is true.

{BRANCH} The {BRANCH} macro command switches to a series of macro commands that begin in another location. When Quattro alters the execution flow to the new location, Quattro does not return to the original set of macro instructions. If the original set has additional instructions, the additional instructions will not be executed unless another branch instruction returns to them. This command is equivalent to /XG in 1-2-3 Release 1A.

Format {BRANCH Location} is the format of the {BRANCH} command.

Location can be a block name or a cell address containing the first macro instruction that Quattro performs after executing the {BRANCH} command. If Location is a block name, Quattro starts with the macro instruction commands in the upper-left cell. If Location is in another spreadsheet, the spreadsheet filename must be included in square brackets before the cell address or block name. From the new location, Quattro continues performing macro instructions until Quattro reaches an empty cell, a {QUIT} command, or another command that redirects control to another macro.

Use The {BRANCH} command is often the macro instruction following an {IF} command. If the condition in a {IF} command is true, you may want macro execution to continue at another location. If the condition is false, the macro execution continues with the instruction in the cell below.

Example Figure 12.15 shows two examples of the {BRANCH} command. In B7, when the value of Counter reaches the value of Records less one, the macro branches execution to the End macro. In this case, the {BRANCH} command only executes when the value of the condition in the {IF} command is true. The {BRANCH} command in B9 behaves differently. This macro instruction always branches macro execution back to the Top macro. This {BRANCH} command is always executed when the macro execution reaches this cell.

{DEFINE} The {DEFINE} command defines all arguments that a macro passes to a subroutine. This command must be the first macro instruction in a subroutine that uses arguments.

Format {DEFINE Location1<:Type1>,Location2<:Type2>,...LocationN<:TypeN>} is the format of the {DEFINE} function.

Location1 through LocationN are the locations from which Quattro copies arguments. These can be block names or cell addresses. This command defines the arguments sequentially. For example, Location1 and Type1 define the first argument.

Type1 through TypeN are the data types for the different arguments. The types may be either value or string. Value stores the value of a formula or block name passed to a subroutine. String treats the argument as a literal string and stores the

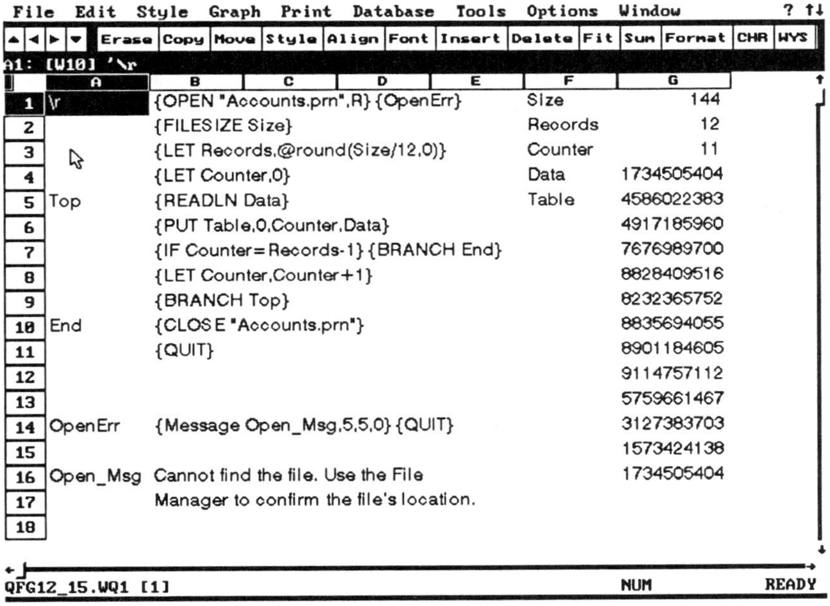

	A	B	C	D	E	F	G
1	\r	{OPEN "Accounts.prn",R} {OpenErr}				Size	144
2		{FILESIZE Size}				Records	12
3		{LET Records,@round(Size/12,0)}				Counter	11
4		{LET Counter,0}				Data	1734505404
5	Top	{READLN Data}				Table	4586022383
6		{PUT Table,0,Counter,Data}					4917185960
7		{IF Counter=Records-1} {BRANCH End}					7676989700
8		{LET Counter,Counter+1}					8828409516
9		{BRANCH Top}					8232365752
10	End	{CLOSE "Accounts.prn"}					8835694055
11		{QUIT}					8901184605
12							9114757112
13							5759661467
14	OpenErr	{Message Open_Msg,5,5,0} {QUIT}					3127383703
15							1573424138
16	Open_Msg	Cannot find the file. Use the File					1734505404
17		Manager to confirm the file's location.					
18							

Figure 12.15 Macro Using {BRANCH} Command

string in the specified location. This argument is optional. If this argument is omitted, Quattro assumes that the argument is a literal string.

Use This command defines the location and types of variables. This command stores the values used by one macro separate from the values used by other macros.

If the number of arguments exceeds the number of locations, the subroutine ignores the extra arguments. If the number of locations exceeds the number of arguments, Quattro aborts the macro and displays an error message.

Example Figure 12.16 shows the second and third macros that operate a spreadsheet containing inventory information. As described in the {Subroutine} command, control passes to the Invent macro when the user types a **Y** in response to the first question in the /0 macro. From this macro, Invent, control passes to the Add, Remove, or Change macro or returns to the initial macro, depending on the letter provided for the {GETLABEL} command in B14. If the user types **A**, control passes to the Add macro starting in B20. This {Subroutine} command passes the part number as an argument. The first macro instruction defines the location in which Quattro should place a copy of the value of Part_No and the type. The type value evaluates the argument passed to the macro and places the value of Part_No into Part_Add. If the type is string, Quattro places the left-aligned label "Part_No" in the block Part_Add. This {DEFINE} statement is required; otherwise, Quattro terminates the macro and displays an error message.

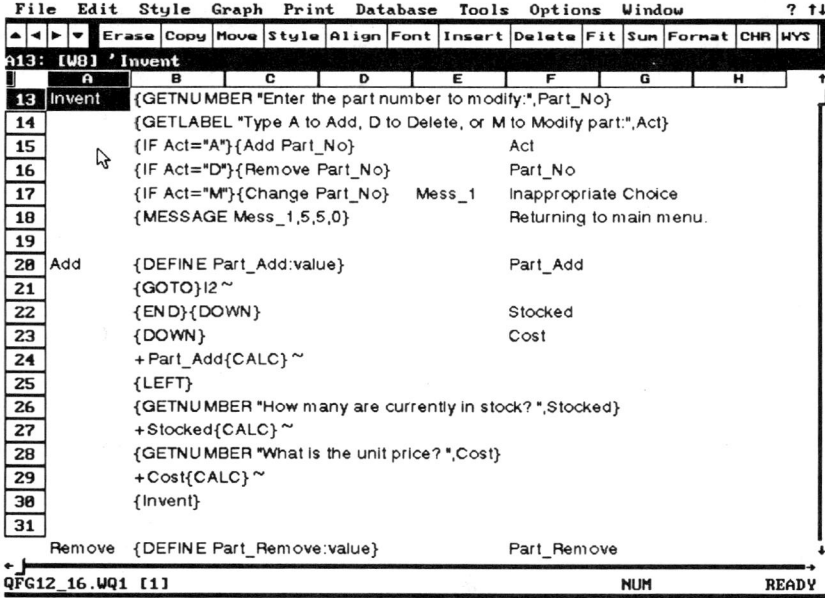

Figure 12.16 Macro Using {DEFINE} Command

{DISPATCH} The {DISPATCH} macro command switches macro execution to a series of macro commands stored in another location. Unlike the {BRANCH} command, by which you specify the location of the first macro instruction, the {DISPATCH} command specifies a location of a cell containing the address of the branch location. The {DISPATCH} command indirectly references the new macro's location while the {BRANCH} command directly references it. When Quattro switches execution flow to the new location, Quattro does not return to the original set of macro instructions.

Format {DISPATCH Location} is the format of the {DISPATCH} command.

Location can be a block name or a cell address that contains the address or block name of the first macro instruction that Quattro performs after executing the {DISPATCH} command. Quattro continues executing macro instructions starting from the location specified in the Location argument until Quattro reaches a blank cell, a {QUIT} command, or another command that redirects control to another macro. If you use a block name as the location, Quattro uses the cell address in the upper-left cell.

Use The {DISPATCH} command is used when you want the macro to branch to different macros depending on criteria that you have established elsewhere in the macro. You can use your criteria to control the address placed in the location argument.

Example Figure 12.17 shows an example of the {DISPATCH} command. This macro creates a form letter to inform subscribers when their subscription is about to

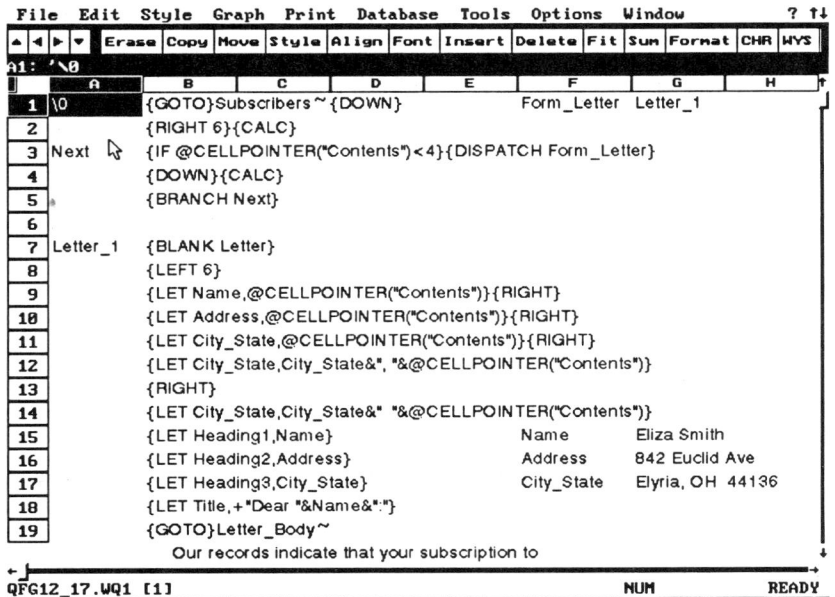

Figure 12.17 Macro Using {DISPATCH} Command

expire. The formula in G1 converts the number of months until the subscription expires into one of several form letter names. When Quattro executes the {DISPATCH} command, Quattro looks at the block name specified by the block Form_Letter (which is G1). In the example shown in the figure, Quattro uses the block name Letter_1 and begins executing the macro starting at B7. This macro prepares the form letter. Since the form letter depends on the number of months until a subscription lapses, the macro executes different subroutines for the subscribers in the database. The macros that create the form letters use the information from the subscription database to personalize the form letters sent.

{FOR} The {FOR} command establishes a loop, which causes a set of instructions to be executed repeatedly. You can control the number of instructions executed as well as the number of iterations.

Format {FOR Counter,Start#,Stop#,Step#,StartLocation} is the format of the {FOR} command.

The Counter argument is a cell address or block name used to count the number of iterations. The {FOR} command initializes this location with the value specified in the Start# argument.

The Start# argument is the initial value for the Counter that is either a value or a cell address or block name referencing a value.

The Stop# argument ends the execution of the {FOR} command when the value of Counter exceeds this value. It is either a value or a cell address or block name referencing a value.

The Step# argument is the number that Quattro adds to the value in Counter each time Quattro executes the loop. It is either a value or a cell address or block name referencing a value.

The StartLocation is a cell address or a block name that contains the first instruction of the subroutine to be executed repeatedly.

If you alter the Counter or Step# arguments while the {FOR} command is executing, you change how many times Quattro repeats the subroutine starting in StartLocation.

Use The {FOR} loop performs repetitive tasks efficiently. Quattro carries out the subroutine a specified number of times without the need to activate the routine each time.

Example Figure 12.18 provides an example of the {FOR} command. Counter is the block name given to the Counter argument. The 1 is the Start# value placed in Counter. Stop is the block name given to the Stop# argument. When the value in Counter exceeds the value in Stop, the loop execution stops. The 1 after the Stop# argument is the increment added to the value in Counter every time the loop executes. Enter_Data is the macro name of the subroutine that Quattro performs when Quattro executes the {FOR} command.

Advanced Macro Options

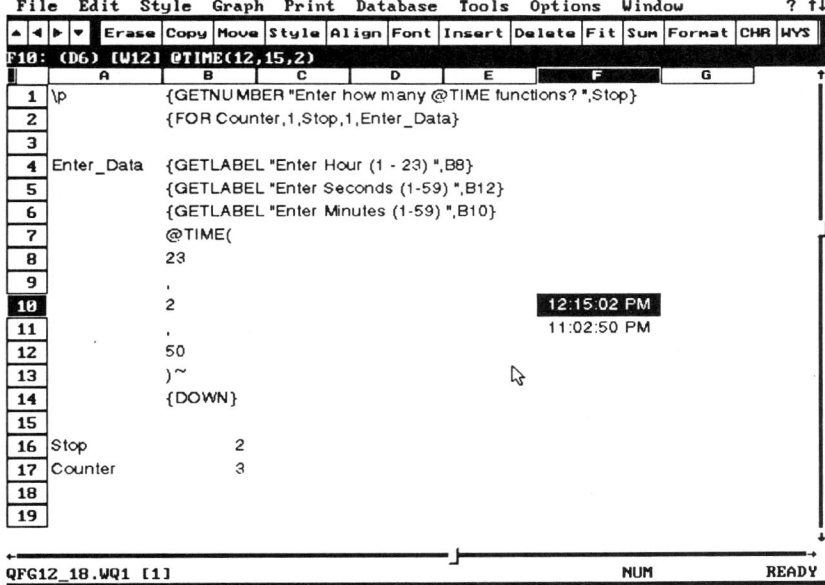

Figure 12.18 Macro Using {FOR} Command

{FORBREAK} The {FORBREAK} command stops the execution of a {FOR} loop before Quattro reaches the stop value specified in the {FOR} loop.

Format {FORBREAK} is the format of the {FORBREAK} command.
 This command has no arguments.

Use This command is often combined with an {IF} command to check for a specific condition. If the condition is true, a {FORBREAK} instruction can be used to stop the {FOR} loop from further execution. For example, you may want to use the {FORBREAK} command to stop a {FOR} loop from further execution when a variable (like inventory), is depleted. When Quattro executes the {FORBREAK} command, the next command Quattro performs is the command below the {FOR} command that the {FORBREAK} command is breaking.

Example Figure 12.19 shows a template designed for costing the production of gas pump hoses. The macro that updates the amount in stock in the inventory file after producing the gas pump hoses is also shown. The macros shown update the inventory file for the new inventory quantity that remains after the gas pumps hoses are produced. The \Y macro opens the inventory file and the Loop_Out macro searches for the information for each part. Once the information for each part is located, the Write_Out macro moves the selector to the Remaining column

626 *Quattro Pro 4.0 Handbook*

```
File  Edit  Style  Graph  Print  Database  Tools  Options  Window       ? ↑↓
◄ ► ▼  Erase Copy Move Style Align Font Insert Delete Fit Sum Format CHR WYS
B5: [W9]
         A                B          C     D       E       F        G
 2  Hose (in feet)      YNCEED       7    8899   0.75    1899
 3  Nozzle              EPDAPY       1    6797   10.51   5797
 4  Pump Attachment     NHIXYD       1    9669   2.98    8669
 5  Number of Gas Pumps To Be Produced                            1000

         A                B           C        D       E       F        G
22  \Y                {GOTO}Hose ~ {OPEN "Out.prn",M}          Size_Out
23                    {FILESIZE Size_Out}                      Count
24  Next_Part         {FOR Count,0,Size_Out-20,20,Loop_Out}
25                    {DOWN}{IF @CELLPOINTER("Type")<>"b"}{BRANCH Next_Part}
26                    {CLOSE}
27                                                             Part
28  Loop_Out          {SETPOS Count}                           Remain
29                    {READ 6,Part}
30                    {IF Part=@CELLPOINTER("Contents")}{BRANCH Write_Out}
31
32  Write_Out         {RIGHT 4}{CALC}{LET Remain,@CELLPOINTER("Contents")}
33                    {CONTENTS Remain,Remain,7}{WRITE Remain}
34                    {LEFT 4}{FORBREAK}
35

QFG12_19.WQ1 [1]                                          NUM       READY
```

Figure 12.19 Macro Using {FORBREAK} Command

for the part number. The {LET} command transfers the contents to the cell Remain in H28. The {CONTENTS} command converts the number to a label with a width of 7. The {WRITE} command in B33 replaces the old inventory quantity with the new quantity. The macro leaves the part number and price information intact. Since the {FOR} command does not need to search the rest of the inventory file after finding the part's data and writing the new inventory amount, the {FORBREAK} command ends the {FOR} command and execution continues at B25.

{IF} The {IF} command evaluates a condition and executes the macro instructions following the {IF} command in the same cell if the condition is true. The {IF} command operates as the @IF function does. The {IF} command is equivalent to the 1-2-3 Release 1A command /XI.

Format {IF Condition} is the format of the {IF} command.

Condition is a statement that Quattro can evaluate as either true or false. A true condition has a value of 1 and a false condition has a value of 0. Conditions can include functions, block names, cell addresses, strings, values, and operators. When the {IF} command compares strings, the comparison does not consider case differences. {IF @CELLPOINTER("Contents")=9999} and {IF PASSWORD=OK} are sample {IF} commands.

Use The {IF} command performs a condition test within a macro. The {IF} command is often combined with the {BRANCH} command. The macro can perform

Advanced Macro Options 627

one set of macro instructions if a condition is true and another set if the condition is false. The {IF} command can also be combined with {QUIT} to provide criteria for when the macro should be ended. Unlike the @IF function, {IF} commands cannot be nested, nor can the condition include other macro commands. If the macro instructions that follow the {IF} command do not branch the macro to another location, the macro proceeds with the macro instruction in the cell below the {IF} command.

Example Figure 12.20 shows a table listing names, departments, and phone numbers. Figure 12.21 shows the macro that uses the {IF} command to determine when the user is finished with data input into this table. When Quattro executes this macro, the macro moves to the first blank line at the bottom of the table and accepts the information for another person by using the {?} command. After the name is entered, the {IF} command compares the entry to AAA to determine if the user has finished making entries. As long as the name does not equal AAA, the condition for the {IF} command is false and the macro does not execute the {BRANCH} command after the {IF} command. After the user enters each type of information, the macro finalizes the entry and moves to the next column. When all entries for a person are complete, the macro moves to the beginning of the next blank line. After all entries are made, the user types AAA to indicate that the user has finished entering information. The AAA in the current cell makes the condition in the {IF} command true, and the macro branches to Sort, causing the macro to sort the data in alphabetical order after deleting the AAA.

```
 File  Edit  Style  Graph  Print  Database  Tools  Options  Window        ? ↑↓
 ▲ ◄ ► ▼  Erase Copy Move Style Align Font Insert Delete Fit Sum Format CHR WYS
A1: [W20] 'Name
            A            B         C         D        E        F
   1  Name           Dept      Phone
   2  Borris, Jane   TREAS.    EXT-441
   3  Garrison, Jim  FIN.      EXT-786
   4  Harris, Bill   ACCT.     EXT-832
   5  Lavers, Mary   ACCT.     EXT-789
   6  Walker, John   ACCT.     EXT-982
   7  Williams, Nancy FIN.     EXT-231
   8
   9
  10
  11
  12
  13
  14
  15
  16
  17
  18
QFG12_20.WQ1 [1]                                    NUM            READY
```

Figure 12.20 Table Listing Names, Departments, and Phone Numbers

	G	H	I	J	K	L	M
1	\d	{HOME}			Moves to A1		
2		{END}{DOWN}			Moves to the last name on the list		
3	Enter	{DOWN}			Moves to the next blank line		
4		{?}~			Accepts the name		
5		{IF @CELLPOINTER("Contents")="AAA"}{BRANCH Sort}					
6		{}			Tests if name is AAA;if so, breaks loop		
7		{RIGHT}			Moves to Dept column		
8		{?}~			Accepts Department		
9		{RIGHT}			Moves to Phone column		
10		{?}~			Accepts Phone number		
11		{LEFT 2}			Moves to the first column		
12		{BRANCH Enter}			Repeats loop for next person		
13	Sort	{DEL}			Removes the AAA typed to end the loop		
14		{HOME}{DOWN}			Moves to the first person on the list		
15		{/ Sort;Block}{BS}.{END}{DOWN}{END}{RIGHT}~					
16		{/ Sort;Key1}~ ~			Sorts by Name		
17		{/ Sort;Go}					
18							

Figure 12.21 Macro Using {IF} Command for Use with List in Figure 12.20

{ONERROR} The {ONERROR} command redirects macro execution when Quattro encounters an error. This command can store the error message in a cell that Quattro would display.

Format {ONERROR BranchLocation<,MessageLocation<,ErrorLocation>>} is the format of the {ONERROR} command.

BranchLocation is the location of the next macro instruction that Quattro performs when Quattro encounters an error. The location should be either a cell address or a block name. If location is a block name, Quattro executes the macro command in the upper-left corner of the block.

The optional MessageLocation is the location in which you want the error message. If MessageLocation is provided, Quattro stores the message rather than displays the message. Like the BranchLocation, the MessageLocation is a cell address or block name. If MessageLocation is a block name, Quattro places the error message in the upper-left corner of the block.

The optional ErrorLocation is the location in which you want Quattro to place the address of the cell containing the macro instruction that includes the error. Like the BranchLocation, the ErrorLocation is a cell address or block name. If ErrorLocation is a block name, Quattro places the error message in the upper-left corner of the block.

Advanced Macro Options 629

Use When a macro contains a {ONERROR} command, the command is in effect until either Quattro reaches another {ONERROR} command or the macro ends. The exception is when a {ONERROR} is to the right of another command that prevents {ONERROR} from executing unless a condition is met. For example, if {WRITE} or {CLOSE} in the same cell precedes {ONERROR}, the {ONERROR} command is only evaluated if the file cannot be opened or closed.

An evaluated {ONERROR} command is used once. Once Quattro performs the macro instructions at the branch location, Quattro treats the macro as if the macro does not contain {ONERROR} commands until another one is executed.

The {ONERROR} command applies only to certain errors. For example, the {ONERROR} command executes when there are disk read and write errors, when you press CTRL-BREAK, or when you try editing a protected cell. The {ONERROR} command is not executed for other errors, such as a macro command that has incorrect arguments. If Quattro encounters an error from the second group, the macro aborts or continues with the next macro instruction depending on the type of error.

Example Figure 12.22 shows a macro that positions the selector in the cell where the user should make data entries. Once the user has made the entries, the macro prints and saves the file before erasing the spreadsheet. When a macro uses {?} to get user entries, the user has control over the spreadsheet until ENTER is pressed. In this example, the user can move the selector to another cell before making an

	A	B	C	D	E	F
1	1990 Budget				Open_Msg	Enter each actual number &
2		Actual	Planned	Variance		press ENTER after each one.
3	Sales	98475	100000	1525		Press a key to continue.
4	COGS	49580	50000	420		
5	Gross	48895	50000	1105	\0	{MESSAGE Open_Msg,5,5,0}
6	Expenses	23896	25000	1104		{ONERROR Err_Occur}
7	Net	24999	25000	1		{GOTO}B3~{?}{DOWN}
8						{?}{DOWN}{DOWN}{?}~
9						{/ Print;Block}A1.D7~
10						{/ Print;Go}
11						{/ File;SaveNow}r
12						{/ Basics;Erase}
13						
14					Err_Occur	{MESSAGE Err_Msg,5,5,0}
15						{\0}
16						
17					Err_Msg	You have entered data in a
18						protected cell. Try entering
19						the data again.

Figure 12.22 Macro Using {ONERROR} Command

entry. To protect the spreadsheet against this possibility, the spreadsheet has protection enabled (only the cells in B3, B4, and B6 are unprotected). The macro contains the {ONERROR} command that displays an error message and then starts the macro over. If the user tries to enter data in a protected cell or presses CTRL-BREAK, the message in F17..H19 appears. The macro starts over as soon as the user presses a key.

{QUIT} The {QUIT} command ends the macro's execution and returns to the READY mode. If Quattro is executing a subroutine, Quattro does not return to the macro that called it. This command is equivalent to /XQ.

Format {QUIT} is the format of the {QUIT} command.
This command does not have any arguments.

Use The {QUIT} macro command can end a macro before the last macro instruction. It is used in subroutines and within loops.

Example Figure 12.23 is an example of the {QUIT} command. This macro displays an opening message and then displays several previously created graphs. The user can quit at any time by typing **Q** while a graph is on screen. The {IF} commands in I11, I14, I17, and I20 determine if the key the user pressed is either Q or q. If the user typed either Q or q, Quattro executes the macro instruction {QUIT} to the right of the {IF} command. This stops the macro's execution.

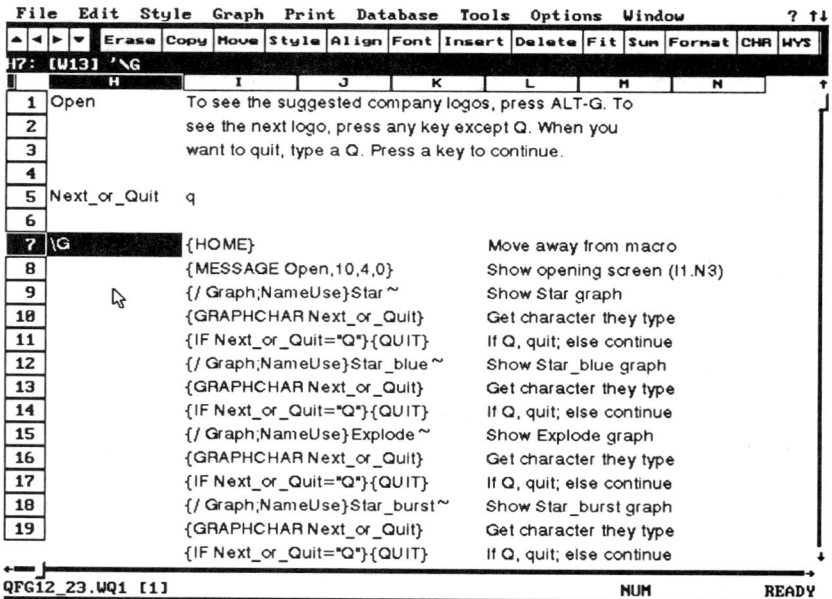

Figure 12.23 Macro Using {QUIT} Command

{RESTART} The {RESTART} command terminates the macro execution when Quattro executes the last macro instruction in the current subroutine. Quattro does not return control to the macro that called the subroutine and returns the spreadsheet to READY mode. This command causes Quattro to treat the subroutine as if the subroutine is the initial macro that Quattro executes.

Format {RESTART} is the format of this command.
This command does not use any arguments.

Use This command is for error handling.

Example Figure 12.24 displays a group of macros that modify an employee database. In this example, the macro prompts for the person's name that you want to modify. Once the macro has the name, Quattro executes the Find_Name subroutine to search for the name. If Quattro cannot find the name, Quattro executes the subroutine Not_Found. In this subroutine, with the execution of the {RESTART} command, the flow of execution is changed so that when the subroutine is finished, Quattro returns to the READY mode.

{RETURN} The {RETURN} command returns the macro execution to the macro that called the subroutine. This command is equivalent to /XR.

Format {RETURN} is the format of this command.
This command does not use any arguments.

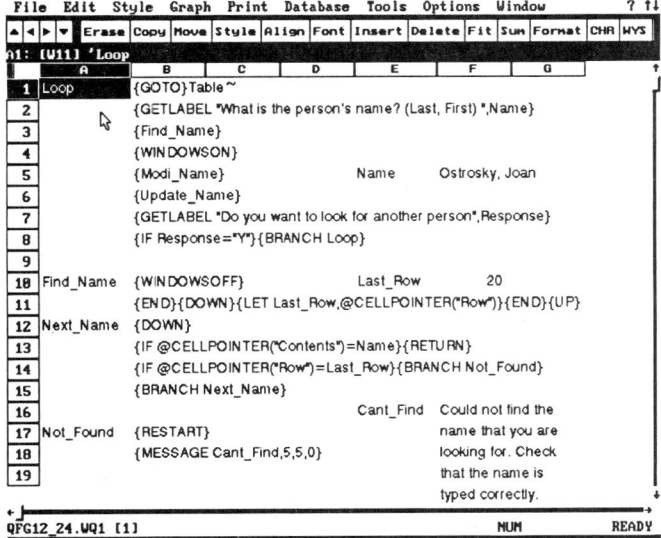

Figure 12.24 Macro Using {RESTART} and {RETURN} Command

Use This command ends a subroutine's execution at a location different from that of its last macro command. Since Quattro automatically returns to a macro that calls a subroutine when Quattro finishes executing the subroutine, a {RETURN} at the end of a subroutine is optional and shows that the instructions are a subroutine. This command often follows an {IF} command to return to the initial macro when a condition is true.

Example The Find_Name subroutine in Figure 12.24 has a {RETURN} command to return the flow of the macro execution to the Loop macro once the macro instructions find the record in the database that matches the label stored in Name. Quattro Pro moves through the database, comparing the names with the label stored in Name. When Quattro Pro finds a match and the condition for the {IF} command in B13 is true, Quattro Pro executes the {RETURN} command. The next macro instruction Quattro Pro performs is the {WINDOWSON} command in B4. Quattro Pro executes this command next, because it is the command after the {Find_Name} subroutine command.

{Subroutine} The {Subroutine} command transfers the macro's execution to a second macro. Once Quattro completes the second macro, Quattro returns execution to the first macro (starting with the macro instruction after the {Subroutine} command). This command is equivalent to /XC.

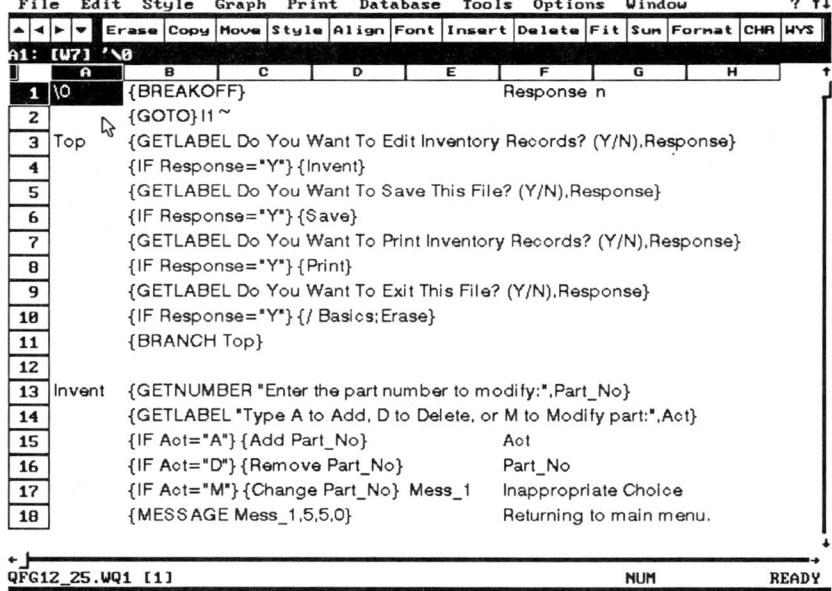

Figure 12.25 Macro Using {Subroutine} Command

Format {Subroutine <ArgumentList>} is the format of this command.

Subroutine is a valid macro name. The upper-left corner of the named block contains the first macro instruction of the subroutine. The subroutine name must follow the rules of macro names. If Subroutine is in another spreadsheet, the spreadsheet file name must be included in square braces before the cell address or block name.

ArgumentList is a list of arguments that Quattro passes to the subroutine. These arguments are optional, but if they are included, the first macro instruction in the subroutine must be the {DEFINE} command. The arguments must be separated by commas or semicolons.

Use The {Subroutine} command allows the macro to execute another macro before competing the current macro. Subroutines are used for macro instructions that are executed repeatedly through a macro. Subroutines are also used when you want Quattro to perform multiple macro instructions when the condition in an {IF} command is true.

A subroutine may contain other subroutines. Quattro treats each subroutine as a level. Quattro can accept up to 32 levels.

When a subroutine is called, Quattro continues executing the subroutine until Quattro reaches a blank cell, {RETURN}, or {QUIT}. If Quattro reaches a blank cell or {RETURN}, Quattro executes the next macro instruction after the {Subroutine} command. If Quattro executes a {QUIT} command, the macro is terminated and Quattro returns to READY mode. If Quattro executes a {RESTART} command, Quattro Pro does not return to the macro containing the {Subroutine} command.

Quattro allows a macro to call itself and refers to the macro as a recursive macro. Recursive macros are not recommended, since they are more complicated to debug.

Example Figure 12.25 shows two of the macros that operate a spreadsheet containing inventory information. This macro executes automatically when the spreadsheet is loaded as long as the default startup macro is \0 since the first macro is named \0. The \0 macro prompts the user with several questions to determine the next macro to execute. One of these selections executes the Invent macro. When

---

▼ **TIP: Use \ and a letter to call an instant macro for a subroutine.**

To call an instant macro (a macro that executes by pressing ALT and a letter) as a subroutine, use the backslash and letter in braces (for example, {\A} for an ALT-A macro and {\0} for an automatic macro).

634 *Quattro Pro 4.0 Handbook*

Quattro executes the Invent macro, it prompts for a part number and then prompts for the user to type **A**, **D**, or **M** to indicate which macro to perform next. Depending on the user's entry, the macro performs the Add, Change, or Remove macro. If the user types an inappropriate character, the Invent macro displays a message and when the user presses a key to continue, the macro execution returns to the macro that called the Invent macro. For the Add, Change, or Remove macros, Quattro passes the part number to the macro. In the Add, Change, and Remove macros, the macro starts with a {DEFINE} command to define the argument. With the Add, Change, and Remove macros, Quattro continues executing the macros until it either reaches a {RETURN} or executes the last macro instruction. When Quattro finishes executing one of these macros, Quattro Pro returns to the Invent macro.

Interactive Commands

Quattro's interactive macro commands take information from sources outside of the macro. These commands prompt the user for different types of input. Other interactive macro commands prevent a macro from being prematurely terminated or force macro execution to temporarily stop. Another group of interactive macro commands temporarily switch control to a custom menu. Finally, Quattro has program flow commands that activate and deactivate the Debug Window from within a macro.

{?} The {?} command returns control of Quattro to the user temporarily until the ENTER key is pressed.

Format {?} is the format of this command.
  This command does not use any arguments.

Use This command accepts input from the keyboard. Like the {GET} command, this command does not display a prompt. Also, this command can accept numbers as well as labels. Unlike the {GET} command, the {?} accepts multiple characters. Also, the {?} command does not store the keyboard input in a cell. The keyboard input functions exactly as if the macro was typing the keys in. The user can use any keys except ENTER. The keys perform the same function that they provide when the macro is not running. For example, the user can either access Quattro's menu or move to another cell. The {?} macro command cannot be used in graph buttons, the SpeedBar, or menu trees.
  The {?} command is often followed by a tilde (~), since the ENTER key that the user types to end this command does not finalize the entry. When the user presses ENTER, the user relinquishes control to the macro.

Example Figure 12.26 shows a table listing names, departments, and phone numbers. Figure 12.27 shows the macro that uses the {?} command to input data into a table. When this macro is executed, the macro moves to the first blank line at the

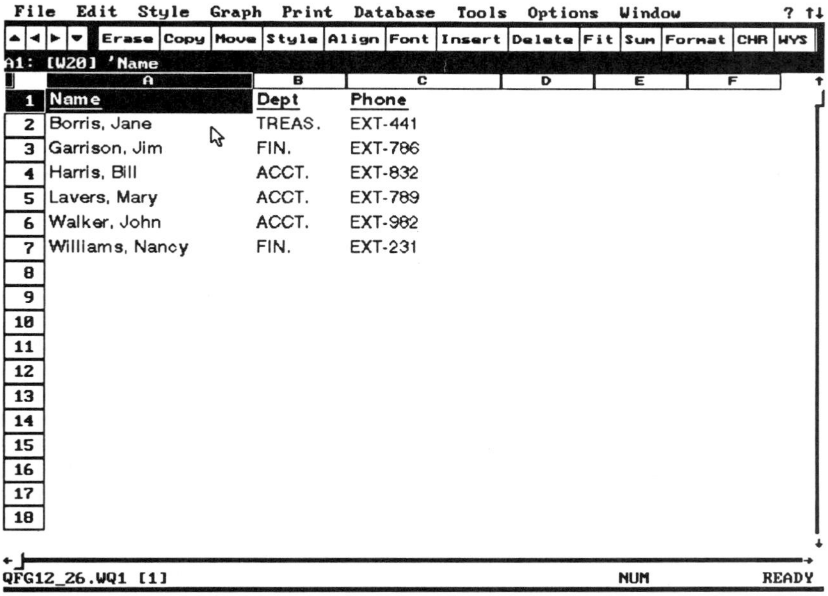

Advanced Macro Options 635

```
File   Edit   Style   Graph   Print   Database   Tools   Options   Window   ?
      Erase Copy Move Style Align Font Insert Delete Fit Sum Format CHR HYS
A1: [W20] 'Name
       A            B        C           D       E       F
  1  Name         Dept    Phone
  2  Borris, Jane  TREAS.  EXT-441
  3  Garrison, Jim FIN.    EXT-786
  4  Harris, Bill  ACCT.   EXT-832
  5  Lavers, Mary  ACCT.   EXT-789
  6  Walker, John  ACCT.   EXT-982
  7  Williams, Nancy FIN.  EXT-231
  8
  ...
 18
QFG12_26.WQ1 [1]                                 NUM      READY
```

Figure 12.26 Table Listing Names, Departments, and Phone Numbers

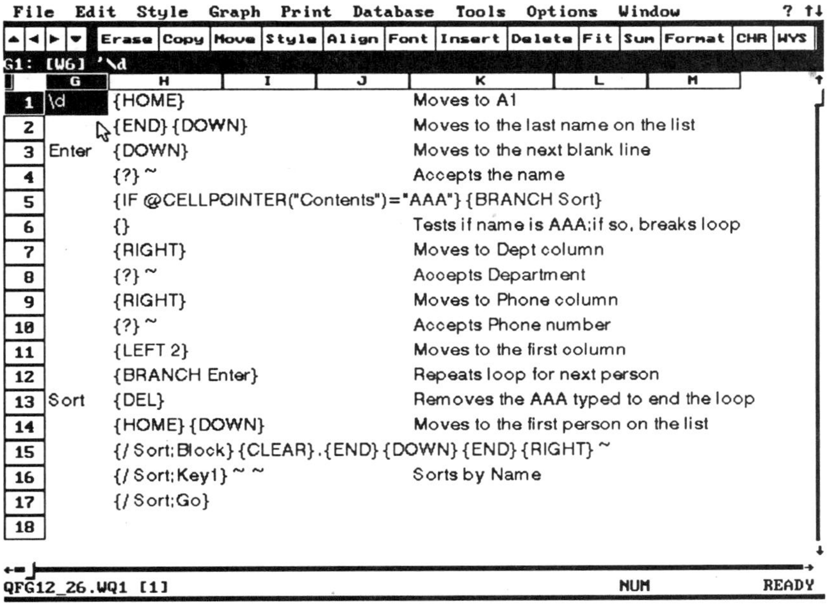

```
File   Edit   Style   Graph   Print   Database   Tools   Options   Window   ?
      Erase Copy Move Style Align Font Insert Delete Fit Sum Format CHR HYS
G1: [W6] '\d
    G      H                   I        J        K                L       M
 1 \d     {HOME}                                 Moves to A1
 2        {END}{DOWN}                             Moves to the last name on the list
 3 Enter  {DOWN}                                  Moves to the next blank line
 4        {?}~                                    Accepts the name
 5        {IF @CELLPOINTER("Contents")="AAA"}{BRANCH Sort}
 6        {}                                      Tests if name is AAA;if so, breaks loop
 7        {RIGHT}                                 Moves to Dept column
 8        {?}~                                    Accepts Department
 9        {RIGHT}                                 Moves to Phone column
10        {?}~                                    Accepts Phone number
11        {LEFT 2}                                Moves to the first column
12        {BRANCH Enter}                          Repeats loop for next person
13 Sort   {DEL}                                   Removes the AAA typed to end the loop
14        {HOME}{DOWN}                            Moves to the first person on the list
15        {/ Sort;Block}{CLEAR}.{END}{DOWN}{END}{RIGHT}~
16        {/ Sort;Key1}~ ~                        Sorts by Name
17        {/ Sort;Go}
18
QFG12_26.WQ1 [1]                                 NUM      READY
```

Figure 12.27 Macro Using {?} Command for Use with List in Figure 12.26

bottom of the table and accepts the information for another person using the {?} command. The {?} commands in H4, H8, and H10 are followed by tildes, since the user does not finalize the entry by pressing ENTER. Pressing ENTER merely transfers control to the macro, and the tilde characters are needed to finalize the entries. After the user enters each type of information, the macro finalizes the entry and moves to the next column. When all entries for one person have been completed, the macro moves to the beginning of the next blank line. After all entries are made, typing AAA indicates that the user has finished entering information. The AAA in the current cell makes the condition in the {IF} command true and the macro branches to Sort.

{BREAKOFF} The {BREAKOFF} command disables CTRL-BREAK. If CTRL-BREAK is disabled, the only way to terminate a macro before the macro is finished is by rebooting the computer (turning it off and on). CTRL-BREAK is enabled with the {BREAKON} command. The {BREAKOFF} command only affects the current macro. Any macros that are executed subsequently are not affected by this command.

Format {BREAKOFF} is the format of the {BREAKOFF} command.
This command does not use any arguments.

Use This command prevents a user from prematurely terminating a macro. For example, a macro may use {BREAKOFF} in a macro that reads and writes to files to prevent the file from being corrupted if the file is not properly closed.

Example Figure 12.28 shows a macro that uses the {BREAKOFF} command to prevent the user from accidentally or intentionally terminating the macro. After Quattro performs this command, Quattro executes the {MENUBRANCH} command and displays the custom menu defined starting in row 4. As Quattro executes the macro instructions for the menu items selected, the CTRL-BREAK is disabled until either the macro ends or Quattro executes the {BREAKON} command.

{BREAKON} The {BREAKON} command enables the CTRL-BREAK key that has been disabled with the {BREAKOFF} command. This allows a macro to be terminated by pressing CTRL-BREAK.

Format {BREAKON} is the format of the {BREAKON} command.
This command does not use any arguments.

▼ **TIP: Test the macro before including {BREAKOFF}.**

Do not include {BREAKOFF} in a macro until the macro runs correctly. This avoids the need for rebooting the computer if it is locked by the macro.

Advanced Macro Options

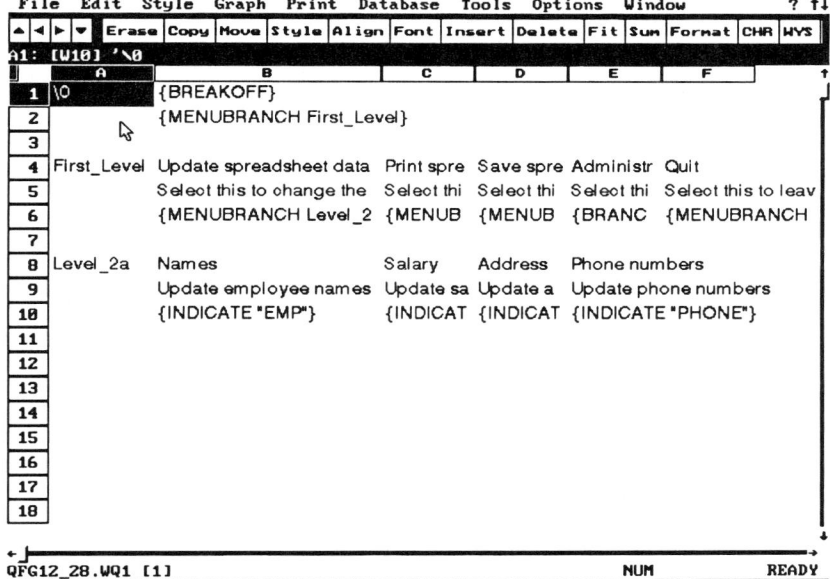

Figure 12.28 Macro Using {BREAKOFF} Command

Use This command allows a user to terminate a macro with CTRL-BREAK before the macro is finished.

Example Figure 12.29 shows a macro that uses the {BREAKON} command to allow the user to terminate the macro after a correct password is provided. At the beginning of the macro in Figure 12.28, Quattro executes a {BREAKOFF} command to insure that the user does not terminate the macro. After this command, Quattro executes the {MENUBRANCH} command and displays the custom menu defined starting in row 4. If the menu item Administration (defined in column E) is selected, Quattro branches to the macro commands starting in cell B20 (Figure 12.29). After the password prompt and a user-typed entry, Quattro compares the entry in Password with the entry stored in the block Ok. If the two labels are not the same, Quattro saves the file and erases the spreadsheet. If the two labels are the same, Quattro executes the macro instructions at BrkOn, which is at B26. At BrkOn, CTRL-BREAK is restored with the {BREAKON} command and the macro transfers control to Admin_Work. Before the break feature was restored, the only method available to stop the macro's execution is to turn off the computer.

{GET} The {GET} command halts the macro's execution until a key is typed. The first character typed is stored in a cell.

Format {GET Location} is the format of the {GET} command.

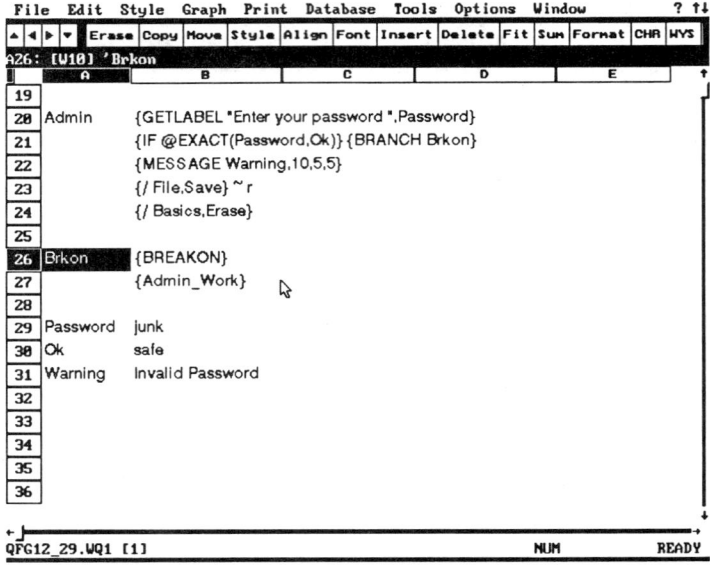

Figure 12.29 Macro Using {BREAKON} Command

Location is the spreadsheet location in which Quattro stores the cell typed. It can be a cell address or a block name.

Use The {GET} command captures the first character typed after Quattro executes this command. If the character typed is a character that Quattro represents with keyword equivalents, such as {DOWN} or {DEL}, the keystroke equivalent is stored in Location. This command does not provide a prompt as do the {GETLABEL} and {GETNUMBER} commands. This command is often used when the information on the screen directs the user to press a key. This command limits the input to one character; that character may be any key on the keyboard except for F1 or CTRL-BREAK. If CTRL-BREAK is pressed, the macro is terminated (unless Quattro has executed the {BREAKOFF} command).

Example One use of the {GET} command is the creation of full-screen menus. Although {MENUBRANCH} and {MENUCALL} are for menus, the {GET} command may be preferable when the menu has more selections than {MENUBRANCH} or {MENUCALL} can display. Figure 12.30 shows a menu that has more selections than the {MENUBRANCH} or {MENUCALL} commands can display. In this menu, the text is in the spreadsheet. The macro that uses this menu is displayed in Figure 12.31. Using the key typed for the {GET} command, the macro determines the location to which to move in the spreadsheet. The macro is created to move the user to the data to be manipulated since the spreadsheet is so large. The {LOOK}

Advanced Macro Options   639

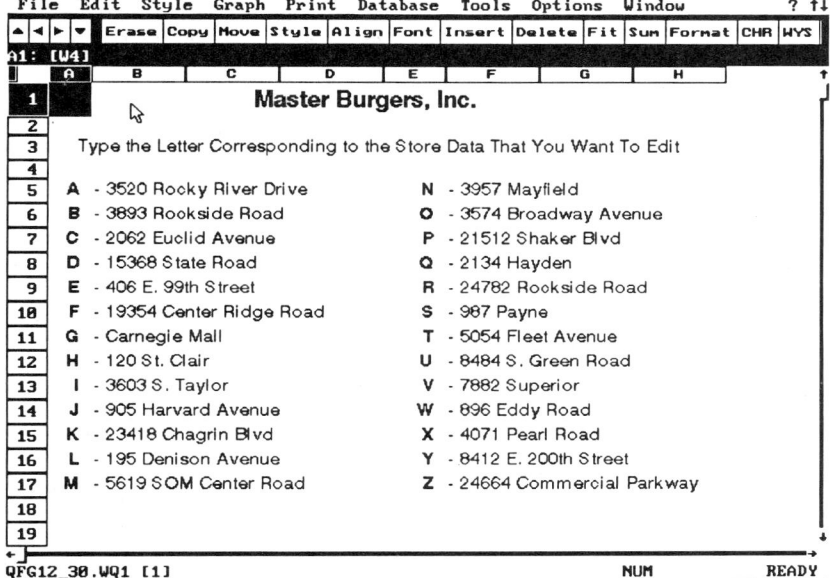

Figure 12.30   Menu Using {GET} Command

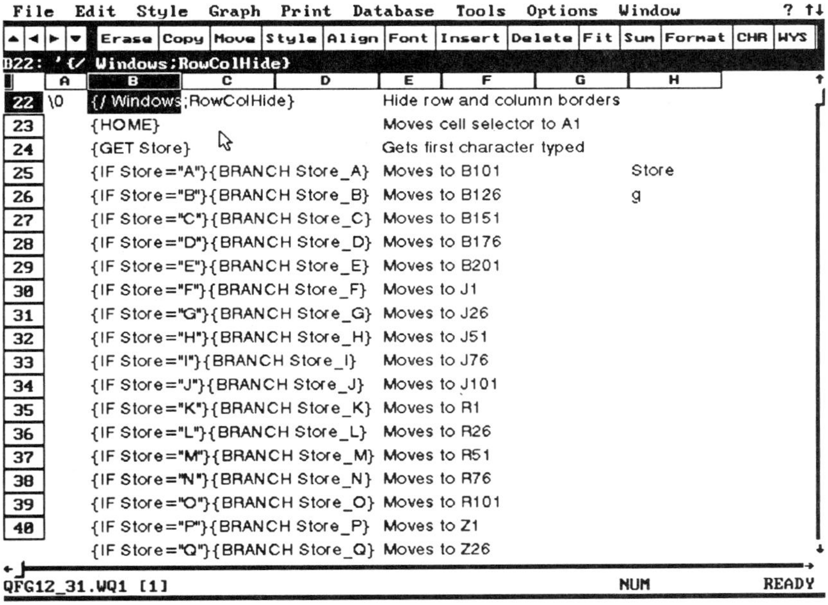

	A	B	C	D	E	F	G	H
22	\0	{/ Windows;RowColHide}			Hide row and column borders			
23		{HOME}			Moves cell selector to A1			
24		{GET Store}			Gets first character typed			
25		{IF Store="A"}{BRANCH Store_A}			Moves to B101		Store	
26		{IF Store="B"}{BRANCH Store_B}			Moves to B126		g	
27		{IF Store="C"}{BRANCH Store_C}			Moves to B151			
28		{IF Store="D"}{BRANCH Store_D}			Moves to B176			
29		{IF Store="E"}{BRANCH Store_E}			Moves to B201			
30		{IF Store="F"}{BRANCH Store_F}			Moves to J1			
31		{IF Store="G"}{BRANCH Store_G}			Moves to J26			
32		{IF Store="H"}{BRANCH Store_H}			Moves to J51			
33		{IF Store="I"}{BRANCH Store_I}			Moves to J76			
34		{IF Store="J"}{BRANCH Store_J}			Moves to J101			
35		{IF Store="K"}{BRANCH Store_K}			Moves to R1			
36		{IF Store="L"}{BRANCH Store_L}			Moves to R26			
37		{IF Store="M"}{BRANCH Store_M}			Moves to R51			
38		{IF Store="N"}{BRANCH Store_N}			Moves to R76			
39		{IF Store="O"}{BRANCH Store_O}			Moves to R101			
40		{IF Store="P"}{BRANCH Store_P}			Moves to Z1			
		{IF Store="Q"}{BRANCH Store_Q}			Moves to Z26			

Figure 12.31   Macro Using {GET} Command for Use with Figure 12.30

command (discussed later) is not appropriate since the user may type keys accidentally or intentionally that do not reflect the intended response for the menu.

{GETLABEL} The {GETLABEL} command prompts the user to enter information and accepts a string of characters from the keyboard. Unlike the {GET} command, the {GETLABEL} command cannot accept nonprintable characters as input. {GETLABEL} is not affected by {PANELOFF}. This command is equivalent to /XL.

Format {GETLABEL Prompt,Location} is the format for this command.

The Prompt argument allows you to display instructions on the screen to guide the user to enter the desired data. When the macro is executed, Quattro displays the first 70 characters of the Prompt in the input line. The string may be enclosed in double quotes; these are optional unless the string includes commas, colons, or semicolons. If the Prompt is stored in another cell, it must be followed by a colon and a v, which tell Quattro to use the value of the cell referenced by the block name or cell address as shown in the example for {GETNUMBER}.

The Location argument is the address of a cell or block or the name of a block into which Quattro places the typed input as a left-aligned label. Whenever you specify a block of cells as the Location argument, Quattro stores the typed entries in the upper-left corner of the block. A maximum of 79 characters can be stored.

Use Since this command stores your entry as a left-justified label, you can use it to store numeric values that need to be placed at the left edge of the cell for use as macro keystrokes.

Example Figure 12.32 displays a macro that uses the {GETLABEL} command extensively. The macro instructions prompt the user for information pertaining to the specified person and store the information in the respective named block specified as the Location argument.

{GETNUMBER} The {GETNUMBER} command allows you to enter numeric entries in a specified area in your spreadsheet in response to a prompt instruction. This command is equivalent to /XN.

Format {GETNUMBER Prompt,Location} is the format for the {GETNUMBER} command.

The Prompt argument allows you to display instructions on the screen to guide the user to enter the desired data. When the macro is executed, Quattro displays the first 70 characters of the Prompt in the input line. The string may be enclosed in double quotes; these are optional unless the string includes commas, semicolons, or colons. If the Prompt is stored in another cell, it must be followed by a colon and a v, which tell Quattro to use the value of the cell referenced by the block name or cell address.

The Location argument is the address of a cell or a block address or the name of a block into which the numbers entered through the keyboard are stored. You

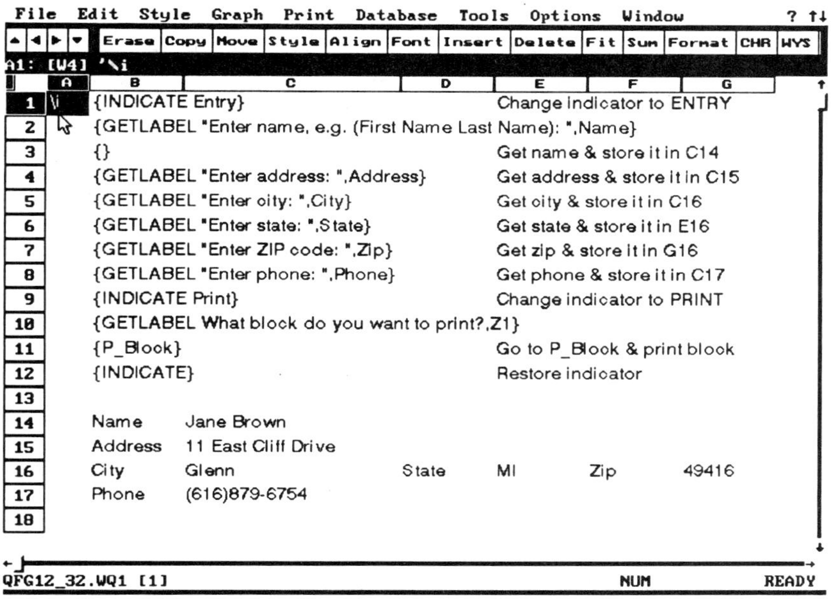

Figure 12.32 Macro Using {GETLABEL} Command

```
File  Edit  Style  Graph  Print  Database  Tools  Options  Window    ? ↑↓
Erase Copy Move Style Align Font Insert Delete Fit Sum Format CHR HYS
A1: [W4] '\i
        A   B                    C                       D       E         F          G
    1   \i  {INDICATE Entry}                                  Change indicator to ENTRY
    2       {GETLABEL "Enter name, e.g. (First Name Last Name): ",Name}
    3       {}                                                Get name & store it in C14
    4       {GETLABEL "Enter address: ",Address}              Get address & store it in C15
    5       {GETLABEL "Enter city: ",City}                    Get city & store it in C16
    6       {GETLABEL "Enter state: ",State}                  Get state & store it in E16
    7       {GETLABEL "Enter ZIP code: ",Zip}                 Get zip & store it in G16
    8       {GETLABEL "Enter phone: ",Phone}                  Get phone & store it in C17
    9       {INDICATE Print}                                  Change indicator to PRINT
   10       {GETLABEL What block do you want to print?,Z1}
   11       {P_Block}                                         Go to P_Block & print block
   12       {INDICATE}                                        Restore indicator
   13
   14       Name      Jane Brown
   15       Address   11 East Cliff Drive
   16       City      Glenn                        State  MI        Zip        49416
   17       Phone     (616)879-6754
   18
QFG12_32.WQ1 [1]                                                       NUM        READY
```

can specify a formula, a value, or a block name as the Location argument. If you supply a block for this argument, Quattro stores the entry in the upper-left cell of the block.

Use The {GETNUMBER} command is useful whenever you want a numeric value stored in a particular cell or block of cells. For example, you might want to store the price of a product or the salary of an employee in a specified location for further computations. Since this macro command expects a number or formula as input, Quattro stores ERR in the cell specified by Location if you enter a string.

Example Figure 12.33 shows a macro that uses the {GETNUMBER} command. In this example, the macro instructions in B9 and B10 prompt the user to enter the amount that the user wants to borrow and the number of years of the loan. Quattro stores these values in B17 and B18. The {GETNUMBER} commands use prompts stored in the named cells Prompt_1 and Prompt_2. Quattro knows to use the contents of these named cells since the {GETNUMBER} command includes :v.

{GRAPHCHAR} The {GRAPHCHAR} command halts the macro's execution until a key is typed to remove a graph or message from the screen. The first character typed is stored in a cell.

Format {GRAPHCHAR Location} is the format of the {GRAPHCHAR} command.

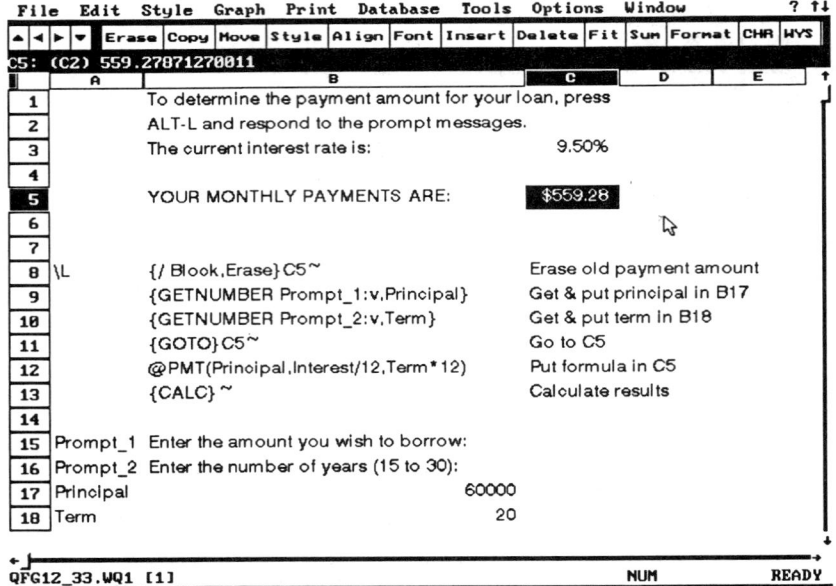

Figure 12.33 Macro Using {GETNUMBER} Command

Location is the spreadsheet location at which Quattro stores the key typed. It can be a cell address or a block name.

Use The {GRAPHCHAR} command captures the first character typed after a macro displays a graph or message. This command does not provide a prompt as do the {GETLABEL} and {GETNUMBER} commands. This command is an alternative to {GET} and lets the users indicate that they have finished using the graph or viewing the message. You can use the entry stored in Location in place of a graph button where the character typed selects one of the topics described in a graph. In this case, you would follow the {GRAPHCHAR} command with {IF} commands to process the character stored in Location.

Example The \G macro in Figure 12.34 shows how you can use {GRAPHCHAR}. The macro displays a graph and then waits until the user presses a key to continue. If the user types **Q**, the macro stops; otherwise, the macro continues to show the next graph. The macro stores the key pressed by the user in the cell named Next_or_Quit. An alternative to the {GRAPHCHAR} command in this application is use of the {/ Graph;NameSlide} menu-equivalent command or add a graph button.

IFKEY The {IFKEY} command performs macro commands if it is given a valid macro key name as an argument. This command is for checking if a user has

Advanced Macro Options 643

```
File   Edit   Style   Graph   Print   Database   Tools   Options   Window           ? ↑↓
 ▲ ◄ ► ▼  Erase Copy Move Style Align Font Insert Delete Fit Sum Format CHR WYS
 I7:  [W13]  '\G
         H              I              J           K          L              M           N
 1   Open             To see the suggested company logos, press ALT-G. To
 2                    see the next logo, press any key except Q. When you
 3                    want to quit, type a Q. Press a key to continue.
 4
 5   Next_or_Quit     q
 6
 7   \G               {HOME}                          Move away from macro
 8                    {MESSAGE Open,10,4,0}           Show opening screen (I1.N3)
 9                    {/ Graph;NameUse}Star ~         Show Star graph
10                    {GRAPHCHAR Next_or_Quit}        Get character they type
11                    {IF Next_or_Quit="Q"}{QUIT}     If Q, quit; else continue
12                    {/ Graph;NameUse}Star_blue ~    Show Star_blue graph
13                    {GRAPHCHAR Next_or_Quit}        Get character they type
14                    {IF Next_or_Quit="Q"}{QUIT}     If Q, quit; else continue
15                    {/ Graph;NameUse}Explode ~      Show Explode graph
16                    {GRAPHCHAR Next_or_Quit}        Get character they type
17                    {IF Next_or_Quit="Q"}{QUIT}     If Q, quit; else continue
18                    {/ Graph;NameUse}Star_burst~    Show Star_burst graph
19                    {GRAPHCHAR Next_or_Quit}        Get character they type
                      {IF Next_or_Quit="Q"}{QUIT}     If Q, quit; else continue
QFG12_34.WQ1 [1]                                                   NUM            READY
```

Figure 12.34 Macro Using {GRAPHCHAR} Command

pressed a key such as a function key or an arrow key. If {IFKEY} does not accept the entry as a valid macro key name, it skips the macro instructions in the rest of the cell and continues executing macro instruction in the cell below.

Format {IFKEY String} is the format of the {IFKEY} command. String is the text that you want {IFKEY} to determine if it is a valid macro key name. This must be the literal key name as in HOME. {IFKEY} cannot use the key name with braces as in {IFKEY {HOME}}, nor can it accept a block name that contains the key name. If the key name you want to test is in a block name, make the cell containing the {IFKEY} command a string formula that combines {IFKEY}, the key name, and the remaining macro instructions.

Use The {IFKEY} command is used for testing if a macro has pressed a key such as a function key or a directional key.

Example In Figure 12.35, the \0 macro uses the {IFKEY} command to test if the user has pressed a key to indicate that they want help information. The macro first displays the spreadsheet information stored at Open_Screen. This opening screen might include information such as pressing F10 for assistance or pressing the SPACEBAR to continue. After waiting 20 seconds, the {GET} command puts their entry in the block named Answer. The {GET} command is useful for this purpose, since it captures keystrokes like function keys that other interactive macro commands ignore. The tilde calculates the formula in No_Braces, which removes the

```
File   Edit   Style   Graph   Print   Database   Tools   Options   Window              ? ↑↓
▲ ◄ ► ▼  Erase Copy Move Style Align Font Insert Delete Fit Sum Format CHR WYS
B4:  +"{IFKEY "&NO_BRACES&"}{MESSAGE Help,5,5,0}"
         A          B                  C          D          E              F           G         H
  1   \0          {GOTO}Open_Screen~                Display initial screen
  2               {WAIT @NOW+@TIME(0,0,20)          Wait twenty seconds
  3               {GET Answer}~                     Get the key user presses
  4               {IFKEY HOME}{MESSAGE Help,5,5,0}
  5               {}                                 If they press a direction key, display help
  6               {BRANCH Main_Routine}              Start main macro routine
  7
  8   Answer      {HOME}
  9   No_Brace    HOME
 10                                                  Done macro is called by Main_Routine
 11   Done        {/ Print;Block}Consolidation~      Selects print block
 12               {/ Print;Go}                       Starts printing
 13               {LOOK Password}                    Checks if the password is pressed
 14               {IF Password="\"}{QUIT}            If password is correct, quits macro
 15               {/ File;Save}~ r                   Otherwise, saves the file and exits
 16               {/ Basics;Erase}
 17
 18   Password

QFG12_35.WQ1 [1]                                                      NUM              READY
```

Figure 12.35 Macro Using {IFKEY} and {LOOK} Command

braces from the key stored in Answer. The formula that is entered in B4, +"{IFKEY "&NO_BRACES&"}{MESSAGE Help,5,5,0}" displays a help screen if the user has pressed a key like one of the function keys, which the text shown in Open_Screen may direct them to press if they require more help. If the user has not pressed a valid macro key, Quattro Pro ignores the {MESSAGE} command and branches to Main_Routine.

{LOOK} The {LOOK} command checks the first character from the keyboard buffer and stores the character in a spreadsheet cell. This command is similar to {GET}, except that the {LOOK} command does not remove the keystroke from the keyboard buffer so the keystroke is available for other macro commands or to affect the current spreadsheet when the macro ends.

Format {LOOK Location} is the format of the {LOOK} command.
Location is the cell address or block name where Quattro stores the first keystroke in the keyboard buffer when Quattro executes this command.

Use This command uses the keyboard buffer. When you type keystrokes that Quattro does not immediately use because it is executing another command, Quattro stores the keystrokes in a keyboard buffer. Normally, when Quattro finishes the task that caused the keystroke be stored in the buffer, Quattro types that keystroke as if you were typing the character. This allows you to type ahead.

The {LOOK} command takes the first keystroke and places the keystroke in the location that you have specified.

Example The {LOOK} command can be used for a password that determines whether a particular user is authorized to update the spreadsheet. For example, in a macro that controls the user's access to the spreadsheet, the user can only perform certain steps. However, the person who wrote the macro may need to modify the macro. One method of allowing the macro to be edited is the addition of a special password. By using a password that the user is not aware of, the security of the system is further enhanced. This secret password could be an undocumented feature that the macro's author would use. Even a person who uses the spreadsheet frequently may be unaware of this password. Figure 12.35 shows a portion of a larger macro that has this type of a password. When the user is finished, the initial macro sends control to the Done macro. This macro prints, saves, and erases the file. However, if the macro needs to be modified, typing a backslash (\) while the macro prints part of the spreadsheet allows the user to edit the file by exiting the macro at that point. The {LOOK} command in B12 takes the first character typed and stores the character in the block Password. The {IF} command in B4 compares this character to the backslash. If the characters are not the same, the macro saves and then erases the spreadsheet.

Since this feature would not be known by the person who uses the spreadsheet to produce the consolidated information, the macro would not be inappropriately terminated. The initial macro that uses the Done macro would also use the {BREAKOFF} command. This type of password protection is only effective if the user does not see the macro instructions that perform the tasks.

{MENUBRANCH} The {MENUBRANCH} command displays a custom menu that you have previously created and lets you select one of the menu items. The menu item that you select determines the next macro instruction that Quattro performs. The {MENUBRANCH} command is different from the {MENUCALL} macro command, since the {MENUBRANCH} command permanently alters the execution flow of the macro. The {MENUBRANCH} command is equivalent to the 1-2-3 Release 1A /XM command.

Format {MENUBRANCH Location} is the format of the {MENUBRANCH} command.

Location is the first cell that defines the custom menu. It is either a cell address or a block name.

The custom menu that this macro creates must be defined before the macro is executed. The custom menu has the different menu choices on the first line, as in row 4 in Figure 12.36. The custom menu called First_Level has five choices. Each of these choices is in a different cell in row 4. Your menus can have up to 256 menu items. A menu created with the {MENUBRANCH} command behaves as does one of Quattro's menus. The only difference is if the macro user presses ESC, the macro execution continues with the macro instructions after the {MENUBRANCH} command.

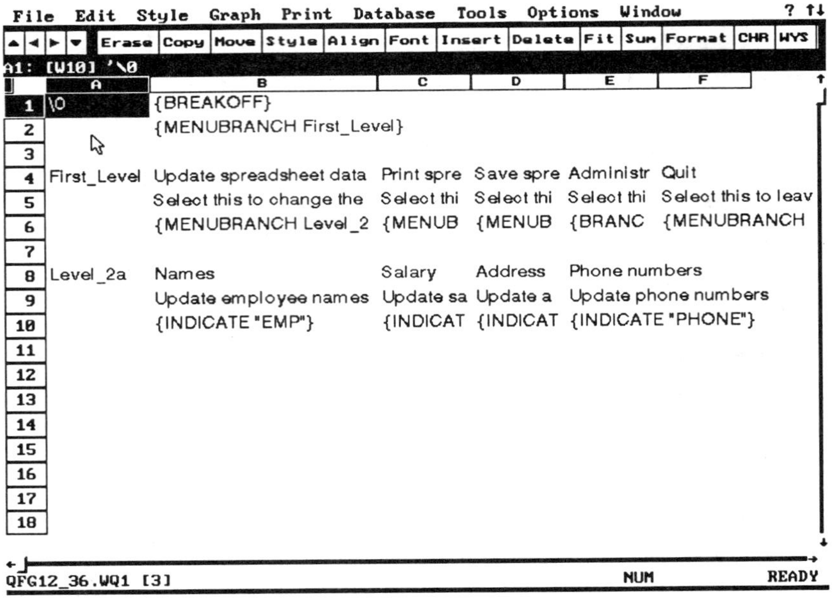

```
 File   Edit   Style   Graph   Print   Database   Tools   Options   Window                    ? ↑↓
 ▲ ◄ ► ▼  Erase Copy Move Style Align Font Insert Delete Fit Sum Format CHR WYS
 A1: [W10] '\0
              A              B              C        D        E        F
   1  \0            {BREAKOFF}
   2                {MENUBRANCH First_Level}
   3
   4  First_Level  Update spreadsheet data  Print spre  Save spre  Administr  Quit
   5               Select this to change the  Select thi  Select thi  Select thi  Select this to leav
   6               {MENUBRANCH Level_2   {MENUB    {MENUB    {BRANC   {MENUBRANCH
   7
   8  Level_2a    Names                    Salary     Address    Phone numbers
   9               Update employee names  Update sa  Update a   Update phone numbers
  10               {INDICATE "EMP"}         {INDICAT   {INDICAT  {INDICATE "PHONE"}
  11
  12
  ...
  18

 QFG12_36.WQ1 [3]                                              NUM          READY
```

Figure 12.36 Macro Using {MENUBRANCH} Command

Since Quattro uses as much room as needed to display the menu items, the column width of the cells that display the menu item text is not important.

Underneath each menu choice is the description that is displayed when the highlight is on the menu choice. This feature allows you to create menu descriptions that are identical to Quattro's menu. You can put a brief description of the menu item's function for the menu item text and a more detailed description for the custom menu item description. The description is limited to 63 characters. Since Quattro displays the entire cell contents of the descriptions in the status line, the column width of the custom menu columns are not important.

The row below each of the descriptions contains the macro instructions that Quattro performs when a menu item is selected. Quattro does not limit the number of macro instructions that you can put below each of the menu items. If you have many instructions, you may want to place them in another location and have the macro instruction below the menu item's description branch to the additional instructions. For many macros using the {MENUBRANCH}, the macro commands

▼ **TIP:** Start each menu choice with a unique first letter.

Make all menu choices start with a unique first letter so that the user can make a menu selection by typing the first letter.

Advanced Macro Options 647

> ▼ TIP: Include a Quite (or Exit) option.
>
> Include a Quit or Exit option so the user knows how to leave the macro when desired for a more user-friendly interface.

below the description are another {MENUBRANCH} to display a submenu of more specific options.

Use The {MENUBRANCH} command creates custom menus that look and function as Quattro menus do. Instead of offering Quattro features, these menus can be designed to meet the needs of specific business applications.

Example Figure 12.36 shows a macro that displays the custom menu that starts at First_Level whenever the spreadsheet is retrieved. Figure 12.37 shows this custom menu. As the menu box displays, the menu items are described in different cells in row 4 starting with B4. The text for each of the menu items is below the appropriate menu item in row 5. When one menu item is selected, the next macro instruction that is performed is the macro instruction for the appropriate menu item in row 6. For each menu item, the macro branches to another menu. For example, if you select Update from the menu box, Quattro executes the macro

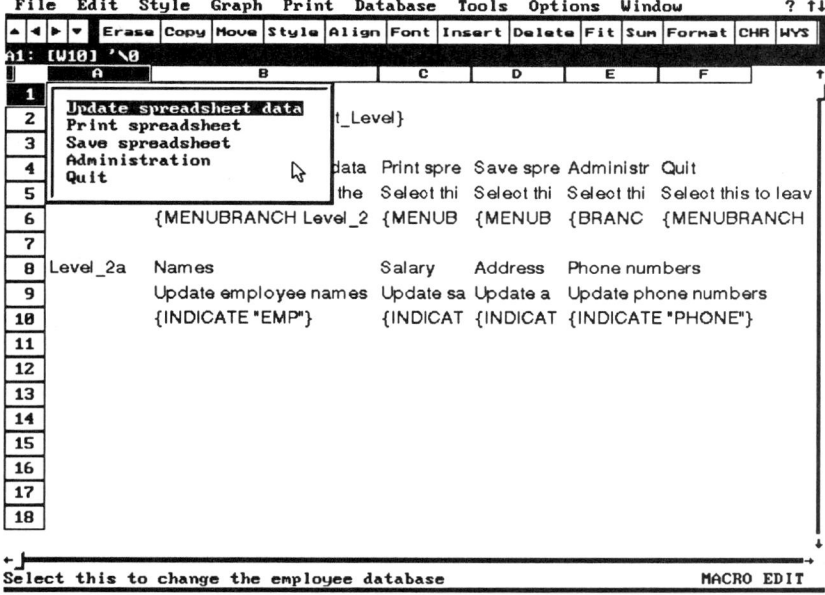

Figure 12.37   Menu generated with {MENUBRANCH} Command

command in B6 and displays the menu located at Level_2a as shown in Figure 12.38. When one menu item is selected, Quattro executes the appropriate macro command in row 10.

{MENUCALL} The {MENUCALL} command displays a custom menu and performs the tasks related to the selected menu item. This command differs from {MENUBRANCH} in that this command returns control to the instruction following the {MENUCALL} command after executing the menu instructions. In essence, this command treats the menu as a subroutine and returns to the main macro routine once a menu item is selected and the macro commands below the appropriate menu item's description are executed. The {MENUBRANCH} command does not return to the macro containing the {MENUBRANCH} command unless the user presses ESC.

Format {MENUCALL Location} is the format of the {MENUCALL} command.

Location is the location of the first cell of a block containing a custom menu. It can be a block name or cell address. The custom menu that this macro command expects is identical to the menu defined for the {MENUBRANCH} command. See the instructions for how to create a menu in the {MENUBRANCH} instruction for further detail.

Use This command creates custom menus. Since this command returns to the original macro, you can have many {MENUCALL} instructions in a macro and still maintain a logical flow within the macro.

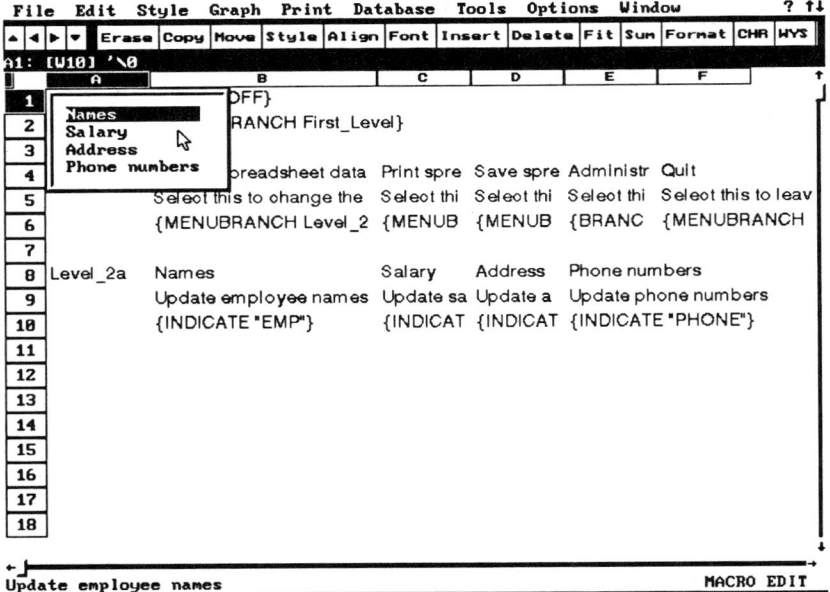

Figure 12.38 {MENUBRANCH} Command Generation of a Submenu of the Menu in Figure 12.37

Advanced Macro Options 649

Example One use of the {MENUCALL} command is to have the user make selections from predefined choices. An example is a spreadsheet containing several reports. To print one report, several choices must be made. Chapter 11 contains a group of ready-made macros that allows you to select the report that you want to print by using the macro name. The macros do not provide you with the ability to change the name of the person preparing the report. Figure 12.39 shows a macro that prints any of the three reports, with unlimited options for the preparer's name. This macro uses two {MENUCALL} commands. The first one creates the menu box shown in Figure 12.40. This menu box prompts for the report to be printed. The macro instructions listed below each menu item's description define the appropriate print block and header. The second {MENUCALL} command displays the menu box shown in Figure 12.41, which prompts for the name of the preparer. As the entries in row 14 indicate, the descriptions display the position of the person's name that is highlighted. The last selection (Other) allows the user to provide a name that is not one of the menu selections. The macro instructions below the menu item description define the footer for each name selected. As the Other menu item indicates, the different macro selections can have various amounts of macro instructions. Once a menu item is selected from the second menu, the macro provides a footer and starts printing.

{MESSAGE} The {MESSAGE} command displays a block in a box on the screen either for a specified time or until the user presses a key.

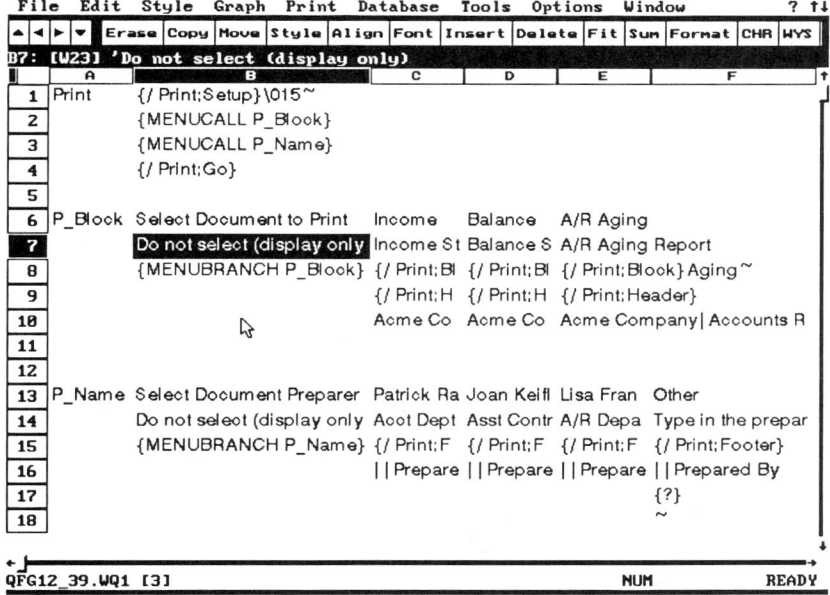

Figure 12.39 Macro using {MENUCALL} Command

650 *Quattro Pro 4.0 Handbook*

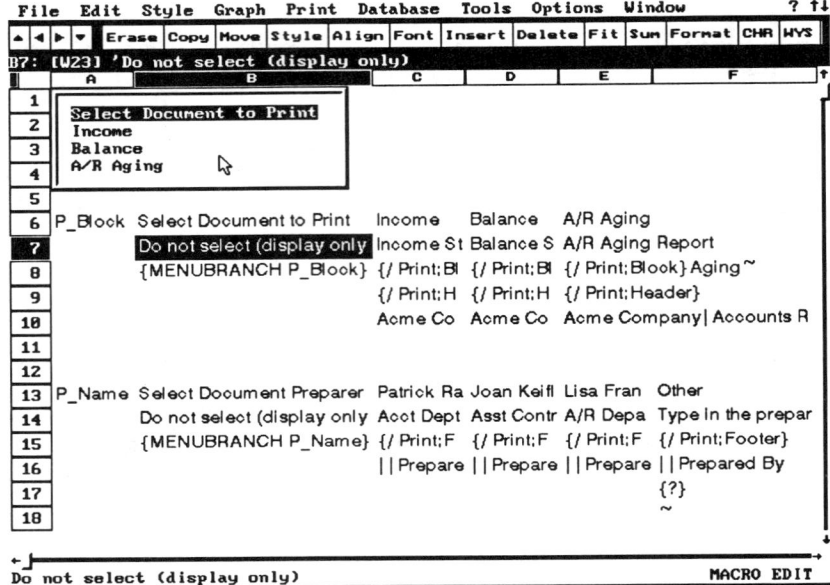

Figure 12.40 Menu Generated with {MENUCALL} Command

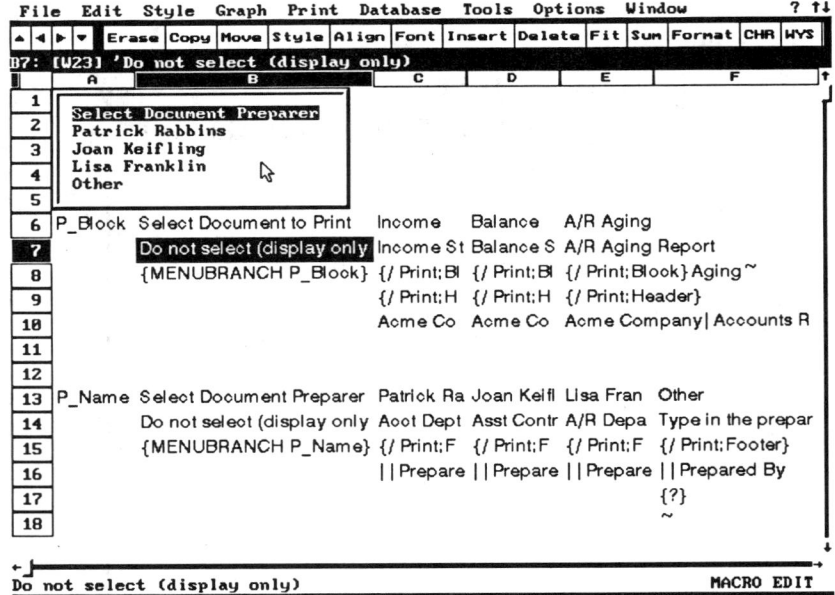

Figure 12.41 Another Menu Generated with {MENUCALL} Command

Format {MESSAGE Block,Left,Top,Time} is the format of the {MESSAGE} command.

Block represents the block address or name containing the information you want in the message box. Since Quattro uses the block size to determine the message box size, you must include the cells from which labels borrow display space.

Left represents the first column of the message box on the screen. The default is 0, which displays the box in the leftmost column. This number can range from 0 to 79 but must be enough to the left so Quattro has room to display the block.

Top represents the first row of the message box on the screen. The default is 0, which displays the box in the top row (the same as the menu bar row). This number can range from 0 to the number of rows in the screen, but the row number must be high enough to display the block.

Time represents at which time the message box disappears from the screen. The default of 0 indicates that the message box remains on the screen until the user presses a key. Time can either be the number of seconds, such as 5, or the time the message box should disappear, such as @NOW+@TIME(0,0,5).

Use The {MESSAGE} command displays a message in the middle of a macro. A macro can use the message box to display any kind of message. This is unlike the {GETLABEL} and {GETNUMBER} commands, which prompt for information. This command can be used to tell the user an error has occurred, display an opening screen, or display a message telling the user the macro is performing a task (especially when the macro takes a long time to execute a command).

You can also combine the {GRAPHCHAR} command with the {MESSAGE} command to display a message and then capture the keystroke. Combining the {GRAPHCHAR} and {MESSAGE} commands this way lets you display the prompt to press a key in a customized box and then use {GRAPHCHAR} to store the keystroke used to remove the message box. You must use {GRAPHCHAR} instead of the {GET} command, because the {MESSAGE} command without a Time argument assumes that the first key you press is the one to remove the message. The {GRAPHCHAR} captures this keystroke while {GET} will capture the second keystroke after the message is displayed.

Example Figure 12.42 shows a macro that uses the {MESSAGE} command as an opening screen. This macro moves the selector to A1, so the macro does not appear behind the message box. Then it displays the block I1..N3 in a message box like the one shown in Figure 12.43. Since the {MESSAGE} command uses 0 for the time, the message box appears until the user presses any key to continue.

{STEPOFF} The {STEPOFF} command returns the macro execution speed to normal and removes the Debug Window from the screen. This macro command works the same as pressing SHIFT-F2 when the DEBUG indicator is on the screen. If Quattro executes this command when the DEBUG indicator does not appear on the status line, Quattro ignores this command.

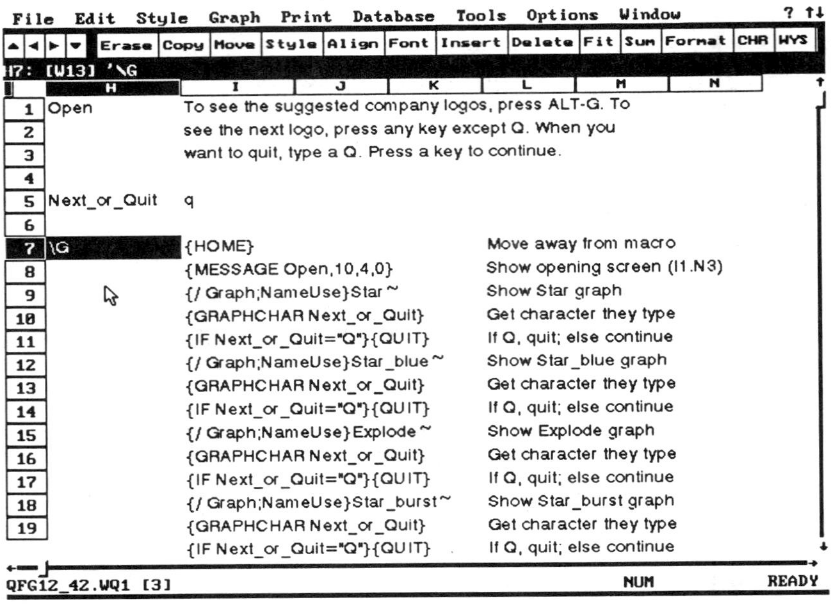

652 Quattro Pro 4.0 Handbook

```
H7: [W13] '\G
          H                    I                   J                K                L               M            N
  1  Open              To see the suggested company logos, press ALT-G. To
  2                    see the next logo, press any key except Q. When you
  3                    want to quit, type a Q. Press a key to continue.
  4
  5  Next_or_Quit      q
  6
  7  \G                {HOME}                                  Move away from macro
  8                    {MESSAGE Open,10,4,0}                   Show opening screen (I1..N3)
  9                    {/ Graph;NameUse}Star~                  Show Star graph
 10                    {GRAPHCHAR Next_or_Quit}                Get character they type
 11                    {IF Next_or_Quit="Q"}{QUIT}             If Q, quit; else continue
 12                    {/ Graph;NameUse}Star_blue~             Show Star_blue graph
 13                    {GRAPHCHAR Next_or_Quit}                Get character they type
 14                    {IF Next_or_Quit="Q"}{QUIT}             If Q, quit; else continue
 15                    {/ Graph;NameUse}Explode~               Show Explode graph
 16                    {GRAPHCHAR Next_or_Quit}                Get character they type
 17                    {IF Next_or_Quit="Q"}{QUIT}             If Q, quit; else continue
 18                    {/ Graph;NameUse}Star_burst~            Show Star_burst graph
 19                    {GRAPHCHAR Next_or_Quit}                Get character they type
                       {IF Next_or_Quit="Q"}{QUIT}             If Q, quit; else continue
```

Figure 12.42 Macro Using {MESSAGE} Command

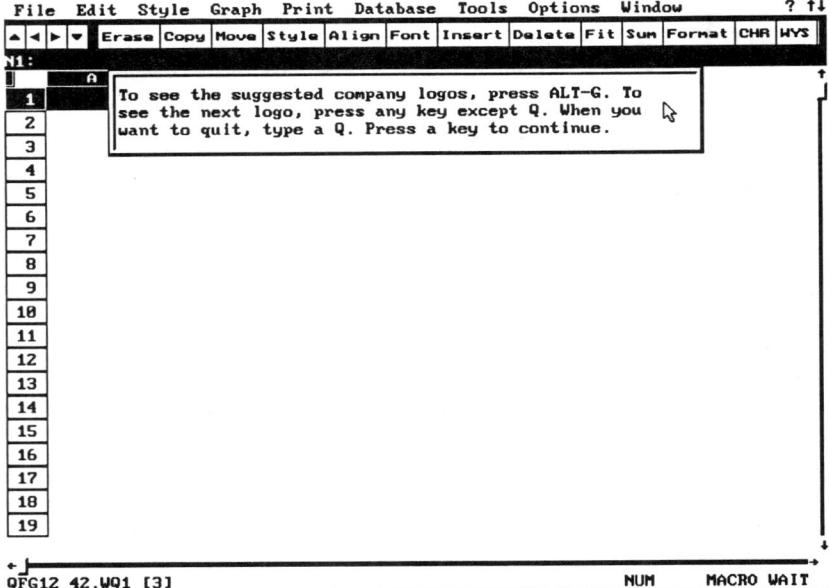

Figure 12.43 Message Displayed with {MESSAGE} Command Shown in Figure 12.42

Format {STEPOFF} is the format for this command.
This command does not have any arguments.

Use This command is a debugging tool to remove the effects of the {STEPON} command.

Example Once you isolate the general area of an error in a macro, you should observe this area of the macro closely. It is inefficient to execute the other parts of the macro in Single Step mode. Figure 12.44 shows a macro with the second and third arguments for the PUT command reversed. Since the error occurs in the loop, the {STEPON} command is the last command executed before the loop starts and the {STEPOFF} command is the first command after the loop.

{STEPON} The {STEPON} command changes the macro execution speed to Single Step mode. The effect of this macro command is the same as pressing SHIFT-F2 to activate DEBUG mode. The macro execution speed is returned to normal either with the {STEPOFF} command or by pressing ENTER instead of the SPACEBAR. Since this command is equivalent to pressing SHIFT-F2, once Quattro executes this command, all macros executed after the current one also execute in Single Step mode until Quattro executes a {STEPOFF} command or until the user presses either SHIFT-F2 or ENTER.

```
File   Edit   Style   Graph   Print   Database   Tools   Options   Window        ? ↑↓
▲ ◄ ► ▼  Erase Copy Move Style Align Font Insert Delete Fit Sum Format CHR WYS
A1: [W10] '\r
        A          B                    C              D          E       F              G          H    ↑
  1  \r           {OPEN "Accounts.prn",R} {OpenErr}          Size            144
  2                {FILESIZE Size}                            Records         12
  3                {LET Records,@int(Size/12)}                Counter         11
  4                {LET Counter,0}                            Data         1734505404
  5                {STEPON}                                   Table        4586022383
  6  Top          {READLN Data}                                            4917185960
  7                {PUT Table,Counter,0,Data}                              7676989700
  8                {IF Counter=Records-1}{BRANCH End}                      8828409516
  9                {LET Counter,Counter+1}                                 8232365752
 10                {BRANCH Top}                                            8835694055
 11                {STEPOFF}                                               8901184605
 12  End          {CLOSE "Accounts.prn"}                                   9114757112
 13                                                                        5759661467
 14  OpenErr      {Message Open_Msg,5,5,0}{QUIT}                           3127383703
 15                                                                        1573424138
 16  Open_Msg   Cannot find the file. Use the File                         1734505404
 17                Manager to confirm the file's location.
 18
QFG12_44.WQ1 [3]                                                NUM        READY
```

Figure 12.44 Macro Using {STEPON} and {STEFOFF} Command

Format {STEPON} is the format for this command.
This command does not have any arguments.

Use This command is a debugging tool. When Quattro executes this command, Quattro displays the Debug Window. All other options available through the Debug Window are available with the {STEPON} command.

Example Figure 12.44 shows a macro with the second and third arguments for the PUT command in B7 reversed. Since the error occurs in the loop, the {STEPON} command is the last command executed before the loop starts. Single Step mode continues until Quattro executes the {STEPOFF} command. Since this command starts Quattro's debugger, you can specify trace cells once the Debug Window appears.

{WAIT} The {WAIT} command halts the macro execution for a specific date and time serial number.

Format {WAIT DateTimeNumber} is the format of the {WAIT} command.
DateTimeNumber is the date and time serial number at which the macro execution continues. You can use functions such as @DATE and @NOW to specify the date and time serial numbers. The DateTimeNumber can also refer to a cell, which contains a date and time serial number. You can create a fixed delay by using the @NOW and @TIME function with this macro.

Use The {WAIT} command temporarily halts a macro's execution. This command often provides the user sufficient time to view a screen display. While the {WAIT} command is in effect, Quattro does not process anything. While Quattro is postponing the macro's execution, Quattro displays a WAIT indicator, or the indicator set with the {INDICATE} command (see later section). If the DateTimeNumber has already passed, Quattro ignores this command.

Example The most common use of the {WAIT} command is freezing the screen for a time so that the user has a chance to read the screen. Figure 12.45 shows a macro with this command. A {MENUBRANCH} command in another macro will transfer to the Admin macro when Administration is selected. If Administration is selected, the macro prompts for a password. If the password is incorrect, the macro puts the message "Invalid password" in Message and moves to the cell Message. The {WAIT} command halts the macro for a 0.0001th of a day (approximately ten seconds) from the current time before the spreadsheet is saved and erased.

File Commands

Quattro has several macro commands that can manipulate files. These commands can open and close files, write to them, and read from them. Quattro allows only one file open at a time. These commands operate on a file in sequential order.

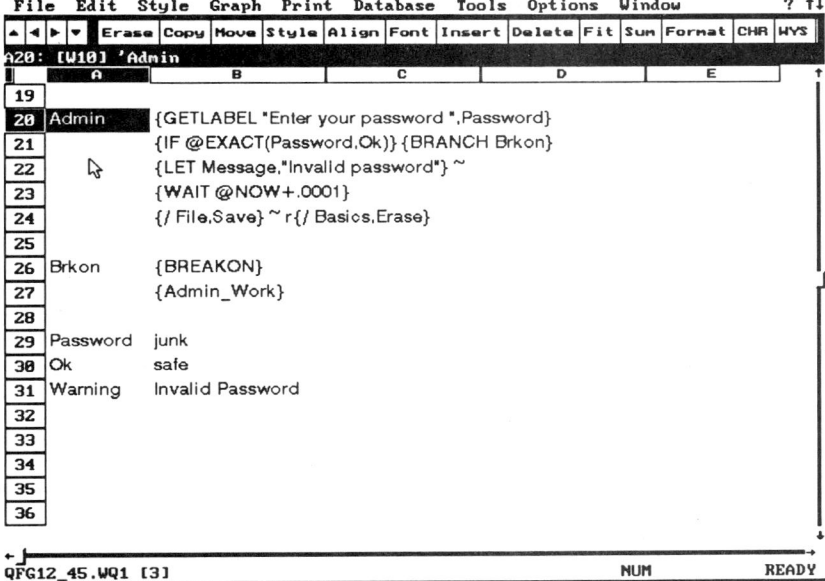

Figure 12.45 Macro Using {WAIT} Command

While Quattro's file macro commands can operate on any file, the commands work best with ASCII text files. An example of this type of file is the file you create when you select File as the destination for printing. Other file types may store their data in a format that is impossible to understand. Until a file is opened with the {OPEN} command, no other file macro command operates as designed. Once a file is opened, Quattro monitors its position within the file with a file pointer.

FILE POINTERS Quattro uses file pointers to mark its position in the file. A file pointer is the number of bytes from the beginning of the file. When the file pointer is at the beginning of a file, the file pointer's value is 0 (not 1). A byte equals one letter, number, space, or symbol (the exception is a carriage return which consists of two bytes). An example of how Quattro counts bytes is illustrated by the phrase "A stitch in time saves nine." This phrase consists of 30 bytes—22 letters, 5 spaces, 1 symbol (the period), and a carriage return (2 bytes).

When you open a file, Quattro puts the file pointer at position 0. For example, when the ASCII text file shown in Figure 12.46 is opened, the pointer is just before the first 4 in 42124. The file pointer is increased every time you read or write information by the number of characters read or written. For example, if you read six characters from the beginning of the file shown in Figure 12.46, the file pointer points to the S in Smith after reading the characters (remember, start counting at 0). You can also change the file pointer's position with the {SETPOS} command (explained later). At any point in time, you can assign a spreadsheet's cell value to the file pointer position with the {GETPOS} command (explained later). When you

```
42124  Smith, Eliza          Mutual Insurance         500    04/28/88    08:30 AM
25939  Von Steiner, John     Healthcare Systems       500    02/24/88    08:40 AM
42141  Bond, Greg            Blue Cross               500    05/04/88    08:50 AM
58631  Ostrosky, Joan        Blue Shield              200    01/09/88    09:00 AM
22621  Hull, Mary            Acme Inc. Trust Fund     250    02/01/88    09:10 AM
99512  Larson, Karen         Blue Shield              250    10/11/87    09:20 AM
15338  Doe, Dave             Monumental Life          100    10/23/87    09:30 AM
23835  Winchester, Sue       USF&G                    500    12/23/87    09:40 AM
91189  Campbell, Keith       Blue Cross               500    12/01/87    09:50 AM
74466  Grant, Frank          Travelers Insurance      100    11/05/87    10:00 AM
15982  Petrowski, Heather    Monumental Life          500    01/16/88    10:10 AM
89350  Demoura, Liza         Mutual Insurance         500    01/23/88    10:20 AM
63158  Lawrence, Mike        Maryland Casualty        500    02/23/88    10:30 AM
44871  Martin, Amy           USF&G                     50    06/14/87    10:40 AM
82423  Ventzke, Blair        Blue Cross               200    03/10/88    10:50 AM
28627  Watts, Peg            Prudential Insurance     250    10/16/87    11:00 AM
41263  Medici, George        Blue Cross               200    11/20/87    11:10 AM
56464  Perez, Steve          USF&G                    200    03/15/88    11:20 AM
58810  Stevens, Melissa      Healthcare Systems       100    03/08/88    11:30 AM
63678  George, Charles       Blue Shield              100    11/11/87    11:40 AM
```

Figure 12.46 ASCII Text File

append to a file, the file pointer is positioned at the end instead of the beginning so you can quickly add data.

Within an ASCII text file like the one in Figure 12.46, moving the file pointer is simple since each line or record has the same number of characters. To move from one record to the next, change the file pointer by the same number of characters. Also, each type of data or field is the same number of characters away from the beginning of a line. For example, the names are all six characters from the start of the line. Most macros that use the file macro commands use files that have their data arranged in a fixed format like this because it is easier to find specific pieces of information.

{CLOSE} The {CLOSE} command closes a file opened with the {OPEN} command. It allows another file to be opened since Quattro only permits one open file at a time. This command adds an end-of-file character to the open file and updates the disk directory to include the date and time that the file is closed and saved, as well as the new size of this file. If the computer is turned off before the {CLOSE} command is executed, data may be lost. If there are no open files when Quattro reaches this command, the command is ignored.

Format {CLOSE} is the format of the {CLOSE} command.

This command does not have any arguments. If you are opening and closing many files, you should put the filename in quotes between CLOSE and the right brace.

Advanced Macro Options 657

> ▼ **Tip: Use {ONERROR} with file commands.**
>
> Always include an {ONERROR} command after file commands so you are notified if they do not execute as expected. Remember that the macro does continue executing even if a file macro command does not perform as expected.

Use This command closes an open file. It is necessary to use {CLOSE} to finalize changes made to a file. If Quattro executes this command successfully, Quattro executes the macro instruction in the line below the {CLOSE} command. If Quattro cannot execute this command, Quattro performs the macro instructions following the {CLOSE} command in the same cell, allowing you to use the {ONERROR} command in case the command fails. The usual cause of the command's failure is removal of the disk with the data file in a floppy disk system.

Example Figure 12.47 shows a spreadsheet that lists all accounts from the ACCOUNTS.PRN file. The first macro instruction opens the file. The macro instruction in B10 closes this file. As a reminder of which file is being closed, the {CLOSE} command includes the file name in quotes. Quattro ignores anything between CLOSE and the right closing brace.

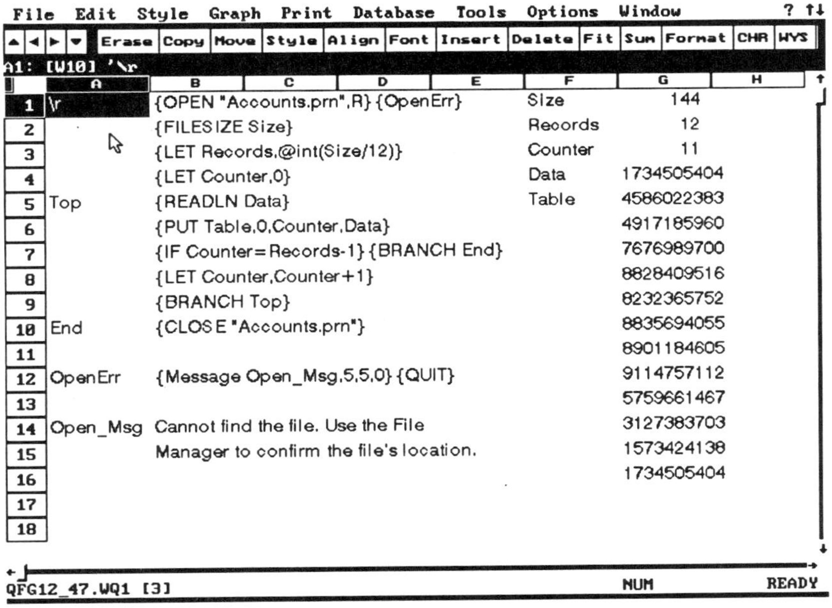

	A	B	C	D	E	F	G	H
1	\r	{OPEN "Accounts.prn",R}{OpenErr}				Size	144	
2		{FILESIZE Size}				Records	12	
3		{LET Records,@int(Size/12)}				Counter	11	
4		{LET Counter,0}				Data	1734505404	
5	Top	{READLN Data}				Table	4586022383	
6		{PUT Table,0,Counter,Data}					4917185960	
7		{IF Counter=Records-1}{BRANCH End}					7676989700	
8		{LET Counter,Counter+1}					8828409516	
9		{BRANCH Top}					8232365752	
10	End	{CLOSE "Accounts.prn"}					8835694055	
11							8901184605	
12	OpenErr	{Message Open_Msg,5,5,0}{QUIT}					9114757112	
13							5759661467	
14	Open_Msg	Cannot find the file. Use the File					3127383703	
15		Manager to confirm the file's location.					1573424138	
16							1734505404	

Figure 12.47 Macro Using {CLOSE} and {FILESIZE} Commands in Figure 12.46

{FILESIZE} The {FILESIZE} command determines the number of bytes in the file that is open and stores the number in a spreadsheet cell. If a file is not open when the command is reached, the command is ignored.

Format {FILESIZE Location} is the format of the {FILESIZE} command.

Location is a cell address or block name in which Quattro stores the file size information. If the location is a block name, the number of bytes is stored in the upper-left cell of the block.

Use This command determines the size of a file. It is often combined with the {SETPOS} command (covered later). This command is used with the {FOR} command to determine the number of times a loop should be repeated.

Example Figure 12.47 shows a macro that lists all possible accounts starting with the block name Table. The {FILESIZE} command in B2 puts the number of bytes in the block Size (which is the cell G1). The {LET} command in B3 uses this number to determine the number of records in the file. This macro assumes that each record contains 10 characters and a carriage return. In B7, the macro uses the value of Records to determine when the macro should break out of the loop.

{GETPOS} The {GETPOS} command determines the file pointer location and stores this value in a cell.

Format {GETPOS Location} is the format of the {GETPOS} command.

Location is a cell address or block name in which Quattro stores the value of the file pointer.

Use This command is primarily used to determine the position of the file pointer before reading from or writing to a file. Quattro ignores this command if a file is not open. Macros frequently use this command when the macros use files that have a different number of characters per line.

Example Figure 12.48 shows a spreadsheet that reads the first twenty records of a file and stores the data and the length of each record in the block Output. The Loop_1 macro uses the {GETPOS} macro command before and after each {READLN} command. By subtracting the two values and subtracting two more for the end-of-line characters, the macro computes the length of each line. The macro shown in this example could be used as part of a larger macro that further processes the data in the Output block.

{OPEN} The {OPEN} command opens a file for reading, writing, appending, or modifying data and places the file pointer at the beginning of the file. A macro with this command should also have a {CLOSE} command.

Format {OPEN Filename,AccessMode} is the format of the {OPEN} command.

```
File  Edit  Style  Graph  Print  Database  Tools  Options  Window        ? ↑↓
  Erase Copy Move Style Align Font Insert Delete Fit Sum Format CHR WYS
A1: [W10] 'Start
         A              B                         C    D    E         F
 1  Start          {OPEN "Names.prn",r}{OpenErr}  Output 54 "Eliza Smith","842 Euclid Aven
 2                 {FOR Count,0,19,1,Loop_1}            62 "John Von Steiner","2507 E. 1
 3                 {CLOSE "Names.prn"}                  54 "Greg Bond","4602 Lorain Ave
 4                                                      64 "Joan Ostrosky","9114 Cheste
 5  Loop_1         {GETPOS Pos_1}                       53 "Mary Hull","2766 Ivanhoe","G
 6                 {READLN Data}                        59 "Karen Larson","6002 W. 107t
 7                 {GETPOS Pos_2}                       52 "Dave Doe","9629 East Blvd","
 8                 {LET Length,Pos_2-Pos_1-2}           60 "Sue Winchester","2918 Snow
 9                 {PUT Output,0,Count,Length}          70 "Keith Campbell","9727 Riversi
10                 {PUT Output,1,Count,Data}            63 "Frank Grant","3442 Cornell R
11                                                      70 "Heather Petrowski","4772 Jeff
12  OpenErr        {Message Open_Msg,5,5,0}{QUIT}       59 "Liza Demoura","2083 Comme
13  Open_Msg       Cannot find the file. Use the File   55 "Mike Lawrence","1445 White
14                 Manager to confirm the file's location. 50 "Amy Martin","4782 Kippling","
15                                                      57 "Blair Ventzke","1522 Cedar A
16  Pos_1                             1168              62 "Peg Watts","7631 County Lin
17  Pos_2                             1243              67 "George Medici","5891 Sunrise
18  Count                               20              62 "Steve Perez","9105 W. 13th S
19  Length                              73              57 "Melissa Stevens","6463 Junip
    Data           "Charles George","3317 Westminister Avenue", 73 "Charles George","3317 West
QFG12_48.WQ1 [3]                                        NUM              READY
```

Figure 12.48 Macro Using {GETPOS} Command

The Filename is either a string enclosed in quotes or a cell address or block name that contains the file name. The file name must include the file name extension. The directory must be included if the directory is not the default directory.

The AccessMode is a single-letter description of the actions to be performed on the file. The letter can be uppercase or lowercase and is not enclosed in quotes. Quattro has four options for the AccessMode argument:

A—Append lets you modify an existing file. The difference between this and the other access modes is that Append positions the file pointer at the end of the file instead of at the beginning.

R—Read only does not permit you to change the file. The {WRITE} and {WRITELN} commands (see later sections) are invalid if the file is opened with this AccessMode.

M—Modify permits changes to be made to an existing file. All file macro commands can be used on a file opened with this AccessMode.

W—Write only creates and opens a file with the name specified as the Filename argument. If a file already exists with that name, that file is erased before the new file is created. While all file macro commands operate on a file opened with this AccessMode, the {READ} and {READLN} commands (see next two sections) cannot be used until data is written to the file.

> ▼ **Tip:** Macro file commands are not appropriate for editing spreadsheet or program files.
>
> Do not use the macro file commands to edit spreadsheet or program files, since these files contain information in a specialized format that you cannot use.

Use The {OPEN} command provides access to data in a file. When Quattro executes this command successfully, Quattro performs the next macro instruction in the line below the {OPEN} command. If Quattro cannot open the file, Quattro performs the macro instructions following the {OPEN} command in the same cell, allowing you to use the {BRANCH} or {ONERROR} command to adjust the macro's execution if the {OPEN} command fails. Quattro only allows one open file at a time.

Example Figure 12.47 displays a macro that retrieves and lists all the accounts. This information is kept in the file ACCOUNTS.PRN. This file is in the default directory. The first macro instruction opens the file as a read-only file. The {OpenErr} after the {OPEN} branches the control of the macro to OpenErr if Quattro cannot open the file.

{READ} The {READ} command reads information from a file starting at the current file pointer position.

Format {READ #Bytes,Location} is the format of the {READ} command.
#Bytes is the number of characters to be read.
Location is the location in which Quattro stores the information that Quattro reads from the file. This may be specified as a cell address or a block name.

Use This command retrieves information from a file. When this command is executed, Quattro starts at the file pointer's current location.
Two aspects of this command are different from {READLN} (see next section). {READLN} removes the two-byte carriage return at the end of a line. If you read a carriage return with the {READ} command, Quattro displays two symbols (a musical note and a highlighted circle in text mode or as two question marks in the WYSIWYG display mode) to represent these two bytes. Also, {READLN} reads characters until the command reaches a carriage return. The {READ} command reads only the number of characters specified. {READ} is used more frequently when the file is well-structured. {READLN} is used more often when the file has a varying format. For example, the {READ} command can read different types of

Advanced Macro Options 661

information stored in one line. If you used {READLN}, you would have to use Quattro's string functions or the /Tools Parse command to extract the data contained within a line. On the other hand, if you do not know the position of the data that you are looking for, you should use the {READLN} command.

After this command is executed, the file pointer points to the character following the last character read. After this command is executed, Quattro executes the next macro instruction in the cell below the {READ} command. If Quattro cannot perform the command, Quattro performs the macro instructions following the {READ} command in the same cell, allowing you to use the {ONERROR} command to adjust the macro's execution if the command fails.

Example Figure 12.49 shows a template that determines the production cost of gas pump hoses. This figure also shows the macros that retrieve the quantity and price information. The macros determine the inventory quantity and price for each part required to make a gas pump hose. For each component that makes up a gas pump hose, you have more than one part that you can use. For example, if you were making gas pump hoses for leaded gas, you would use a nozzle with a wide spout to prevent someone from putting leaded gas into a car that uses unleaded. Each component has a unique part number. Before you use this macro, you must provide the part number of the components to be used, the quantity of each component required for each gas pump hose, and the number of gas pump hoses that you are assembling, as shown in Figure 12.50. The macro \Z moves to the first

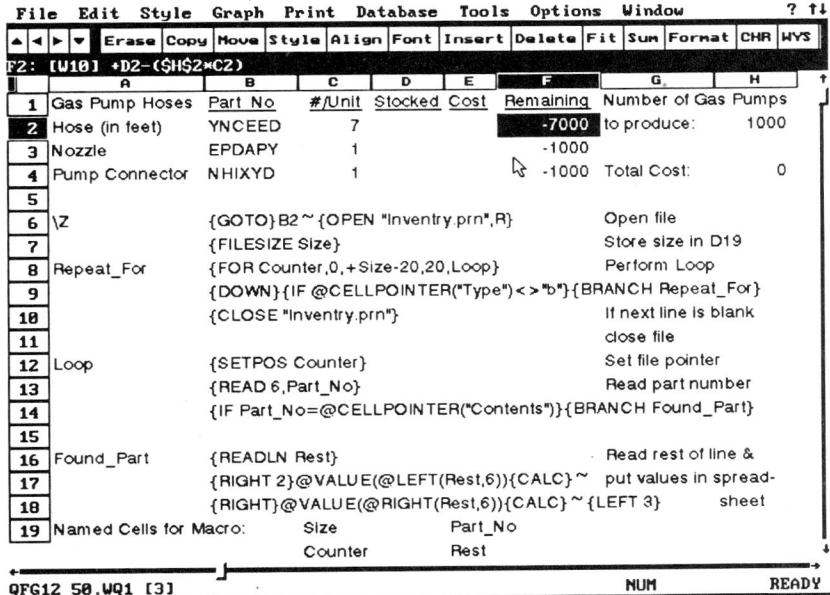

Figure 12.49 Macro Using {READ} and {SETPOS} Commands

```
File   Edit   Style   Graph   Print   Database   Tools   Options   Window            ? ↑↓
▲ ◀ ▶ ▼  Erase Copy Move Style Align Font Insert Delete Fit Sum Format CHR WYS
B5: [W9]
        A               B           C      D      E        F            G              H
  1  Gas Pump Hoses   Part No      #/Unit Stocked Cost  Remaining   Number of Gas Pumps
  2  Hose (in feet)   YNCEED         7     8899   0.75    1899      to produce:       1000
  3  Nozzle           EPDAPY         1     6797   10.5    5797
  4  Pump Connector   NHIXYD         1     9669   2.98    8669      Total Cost:      18740
  5
  6  \Z               {GOTO}B2~{OPEN "Inventry.prn",R}         Open file
  7                   {FILESIZE Size}                          Store size in D19
  8  Repeat_For       {FOR Counter,0,+Size-20,20,Loop}         Perform Loop
  9                   {DOWN}{IF @CELLPOINTER("Type")<>"b"}{BRANCH Repeat_For}
 10                   {CLOSE "Inventry.prn"}                   If next line is blank
 11                                                            close file
 12  Loop             {SETPOS Counter}                         Set file pointer
 13                   {READ 6,Part_No}                         Read part number
 14                   {IF Part_No=@CELLPOINTER("Contents")}{BRANCH Found_Part}
 15
 16  Found_Part       {READLN Rest}                            Read rest of line &
 17                   {RIGHT 2}@VALUE(@LEFT(Rest,6)){CALC}~    put values in spread-
 18                   {RIGHT}@VALUE(@RIGHT(Rest,6)){CALC}~{LEFT 3}   sheet
 19  Named Cells for Macro:    Size            Part_No
                               Counter    0    Rest
QFG12_50.WQ1 [3]                                        NUM           READY
```

Figure 12.50 Template After Executing Macro Shown in Figure 12.49

part number and opens the file INVENTRY.PRN, which contains all available inventory parts and their quantity and price information. Once the file is opened, the {FOR} loop starts the Loop branch, which moves the file pointer to the part number that the macro is looking for. In Loop, the {SETPOS} command moves the file pointer to every twentieth place, since 20 is the length of each record. The {READ} command in B13 reads the first six characters of every line. If the part number read by the {READ} command agrees with the current part number, the macro switches to Found_Part. If the part numbers do not agree, the macro moves the file pointer to the beginning of the next record and reads that part number. When the macro branches to Found_Part after finding the correct part number, the macro reads the remaining information and stores the information in Rest. The next two macro instructions direct Quattro to put the value of the first six characters of Rest into the Stocked column and the value of the last six characters in the Cost column. After the macro provides this information for a part number, the macro moves to the cell below the current part number. The {IF} command in B9 repeats the {FOR} command if this cell is not blank. If this cell is blank, as cell B5 is, the macro closes the file and stops. Figure 12.50 shows the template after the macros have been executed.

{READLN} The {READLN} command reads characters from an input file until the command reaches the end-of-line character. The characters read by this command are stored in a spreadsheet cell.

Advanced Macro Options **663**

Format {READLN Location} is the format of the {READLN} command.
Location is the storage area in which Quattro places the characters that have been read. This may be a cell address or block name.

Use This command retrieves information from a file. When Quattro executes the {READLN} command, Quattro starts at the current file pointer's location and reads characters until the end-of-line character is reached. Quattro stores the information in a spreadsheet cell specified by the command's argument and removes the end-of-line character from the string stored in the cell. Once Quattro executes this command, the file pointer is at the beginning of the next line. When this command has been executed successfully, Quattro moves to the next macro instruction in the line below the {READLN} command. If Quattro cannot read the line, it executes the macro instructions following the {READLN} command in the same cell, so that you can use the {ONERROR} or {BRANCH} command to adjust the macro's execution if the {READLN} command fails.

Example Figure 12.50 shows a template that determines the production cost of gas pump hoses and also shows the macros that retrieve the quantity and price information. The macros provide the inventory quantity and price for each part required to make a gas pump hose. For each component that makes up a gas pump hose, there are different parts that can be used. For example, if you are making gas pump hoses for leaded gas, you would use a nozzle with a wide spout to prevent someone from putting leaded gas into a car that uses unleaded gas. Each part has a unique part number. To use this macro, you must provide the part number of the components that you are using, the number of each component required for each gas pump hose, and the number of gas pump hoses that you are assembling, as shown in Figure 12.49. The macro \Z moves to the first part number and opens the file INVENTRY.PRN, which contains all available inventory parts and their quantity and price information. Once the file is opened, the {FOR} loop starts the Loop branch, which moves the file pointer to the part number that the macro is looking for. In Loop, the {SETPOS} command moves the file pointer to every twentieth place (each record contains 20 characters). The {READ} command in B13 reads the first six characters of every line. If the part number read by the {READ} command agrees with the current part number, the macro switches to Found_Part. If the part numbers do not agree, the macro moves the file pointer to the beginning of the next record and reads that part number. When the macro branches to Found_Part, the macro uses {READLN} to read the remaining information and to store the information in Rest. The next two macro instructions direct Quattro to put the value of the first six characters of Rest into the Stocked column and the value of the last six characters in the Cost column. After Quattro has found this information for a part number, the macro moves to the cell below the current part number. The {IF} command in B9 checks if the next cell is blank. If this cell contains a part number, the macro branches to Repeat_For. If this cell is blank, the macro closes the file and quits. Figure 12.50 shows the macros and template after the macros have been executed.

{SETPOS} The {SETPOS} command specifies the location for the file pointer.

Format {SETPOS FilePosition} is the format of the {SETPOS} command.

FilePosition is a value between 0 and the number of bytes in the file. This can either be a number, or it can be a cell address or block name that refers to a number.

Use This command positions the file pointer before reading from or writing to a file. If the value specified for the FilePosition is larger than the file size, Quattro moves the file pointer to the end of the file. If Quattro can move the file pointer to the position specified, the macro instruction in the next cell is executed and any macro instructions that follow the {SETPOS} command in its cell are ignored. If a file is not open when Quattro tries executing this command, Quattro executes the macro instructions following the {SETPOS} command in its cell. This allows you to trap errors with the {BRANCH} or {ONERROR} command.

Example Figure 12.49 shows a template that determines the production cost of gas pump hoses and also shows the macros that retrieve the quantity and price information. The macros provide the inventory quantity and price for each part required to make a gas pump hose. For each component in a gas pump hose, you can choose from more than one part. For example, you may use a different type of hose depending on the chemical that the hose contains. Each part has a unique part number. Before using this macro, you must provide the part number of the components you want, the number of each component required for each gas pump hose, and the number of gas pump hoses that you are assembling, as shown in rows 1 through 4 of Figure 12.49. The macro \Z moves to the first part number and opens the file INVENTRY.PRN, which contains all available inventory parts and their quantity and price information. Once the file is opened, the {FOR} loop performs the Loop branch, which moves the file pointer to the part number that the macro is looking for. In Loop, the {SETPOS} command moves the file pointer to every twentieth place (each record contains 20 characters). The {READ} command in B13 reads the first six characters of every line. If the part number read by the {READ} command agrees with the current part number, the macro switches to Found_Part, which enters the data from the file into the spreadsheet. If the part number read from the file does not agree with the current part number, the Loop branch repeats because of the {FOR} command, and the {SETPOS} command uses the value of Counter from the {FOR} command to read the next part number from the file.

{WRITE} The {WRITE} command writes information to a file starting at the current file pointer position.

Format {WRITE String} is the format of the {WRITE} command.

String is the characters to be written as a single line. This information may be a string enclosed in quotes, a cell address, a block name, or a formula. You can combine strings by separating them by commas.

Advanced Macro Options 665

Use This command appends and replaces information in a file. When this command is executed, Quattro starts at the file pointer's current location. If the file already has data stored at this location, the {WRITE} command replaces the information. If the file pointer is at the end of the file, the information is added to the end of the file. After this command is executed, the file pointer points to the character following the last character written. When Quattro executes this command, Quattro executes the next macro instruction in the cell below the {WRITE} command. If Quattro cannot perform the command (for example, if there is a disk error), Quattro performs the macro instructions following the {WRITE} command in the same cell, which allows you to use the {ONERROR} command to adjust the macro's execution if the command fails.

Example Figure 12.51 shows a macro that prompts for various types of information and converts the entered information into delimited format that other programs can import easily. This macro moves to the end of an ASCII file and adds the data that you provide through the {GETLABEL} commands. The {WRITE} commands in B7 and B8 write the sections of the data that the macro adds. Since the data file is delimited with commas and double quotes, the macro instructions in B7, B8, and B9 use both the double quote stored in Quote and also the double quote, comma, and double-quote combination stored in Delim. Rather than entering the characters directly, the macro uses these named cells to make the macro easier to read. Double quotes must be added by using a named block (as in this example) or by using @CHAR(34) (when you enter a double quote, Quattro assumes it is the

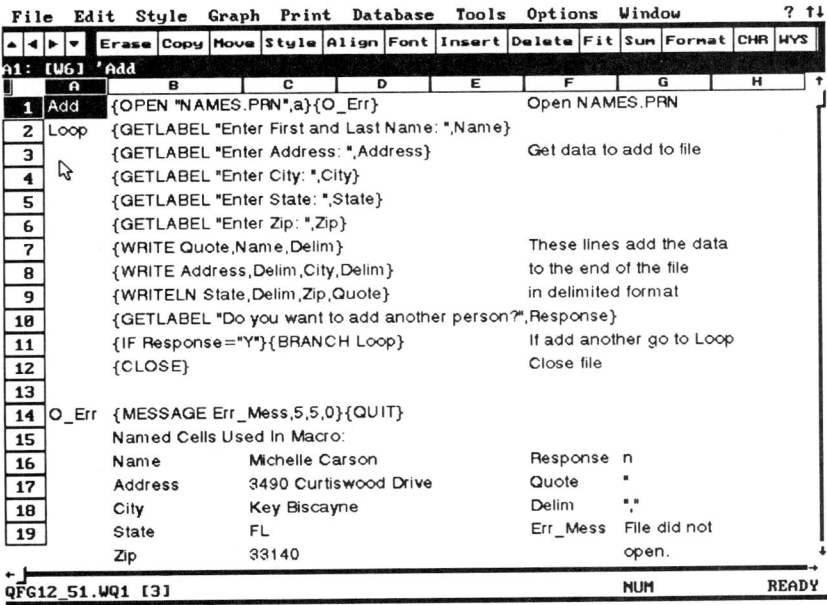

Figure 12.51 Macro Using {WRITE} and {WRITELN} Commands

beginning or end of a string). In order to omit the end-of-line characters, the {WRITE} command is used in B7 and B8 instead of {WRITELN}. When the last information for a record is entered, the {WRITELN} command ends the line as it adds the state and zip code to the file.

{WRITELN} The {WRITELN} command writes information to a file and adds end-of-line characters. The information is written at the current file pointer position.

Format {WRITELN String} is the format of the {WRITELN} command.

String is the characters to be written as a single line. This information may be a string enclosed in quotes, or it may be a cell address, a block name, or a formula. You can combine strings in the {WRITELN} command by separating the strings by commas. If the string "" is specified, Quattro writes an end-of-line character. This puts a blank line in the file or ends a line started with the {WRITE} command.

Use This command appends and replaces information in a file. When the {WRITELN} command is executed, Quattro starts at the current file pointer location. If the file has information at the current location, the information is written over. If the file pointer is at the end of the file, the information is added to the end of the file. After this command has written the characters in the specified string, this command writes the two-byte character for the end-of-line marker. After this command is executed, the file pointer points to the character following the end-of-line character. When this command has been executed successfully, Quattro moves to the next macro instruction in the line below the {WRITELN} command. If Quattro cannot write the string (for example, if the disk is full), Quattro performs the macro instructions following the {WRITELN} command in its cell, which allows you to use the {ONERROR} command to adjust the macro's execution if the {WRITELN} command fails.

Example Figure 12.51 shows a macro that prompts for various types of information and converts the entered information into delimited format that other programs can import easily. This macro moves to the end of an ASCII file and adds the data that you provide through the {GETLABEL} commands. The {WRITE} commands in B7 and B8 write the sections of the data that the macro adds. Since the data file is delimited with commas and double quotes, the macro instructions in B7, B8, and B9 use both the double quote stored in Quote and also the double quote, comma, and double-quote combination stored in Delim. Rather than entering the characters directly, the macro uses these named cells to make the macro easier to read. Double quotes must be added by using a named block as in this example or by using @CHAR(34) (when you enter a double quote, Quattro assumes it is the beginning or end of a string). In order to omit the end-of-line characters, the {WRITE} command is used in B7 and B8 instead of {WRITELN}. When the last information for a record is entered, the {WRITELN} command ends the line as it adds the state and zip code to the file.

Advanced Macro Options 667

Screen Commands

Quattro's screen macro commands customize the screen's appearance during macro execution and ring the computer's bell. During a macro's execution, Quattro displays all menu boxes, confirmation boxes, and prompts as if you were performing the steps yourself. The screen macro commands let you change the display of these features. While these features provide information about the macro's progress, the features can cause the screen to flicker as Quattro performs the macro steps faster than the screen can update the display.

{BEEP} The {BEEP} command sounds the computer bell.

Format {BEEP Number} is the format for this command.
    The Number argument can have any value from 1 to 4, with a default setting of 1. The argument number selected affects the tone of your computer's bell: 1 represents the lowest pitch, and 4 represents the highest pitch.

Use The {BEEP} command can alert the user to an error that has occurred, prompt the user to provide input, give the user some assurance that a long-running macro is still functioning while running, and inform the user that a step has been finished.

Example Figure 12.52 shows a set of macro instructions that use the {BEEP}

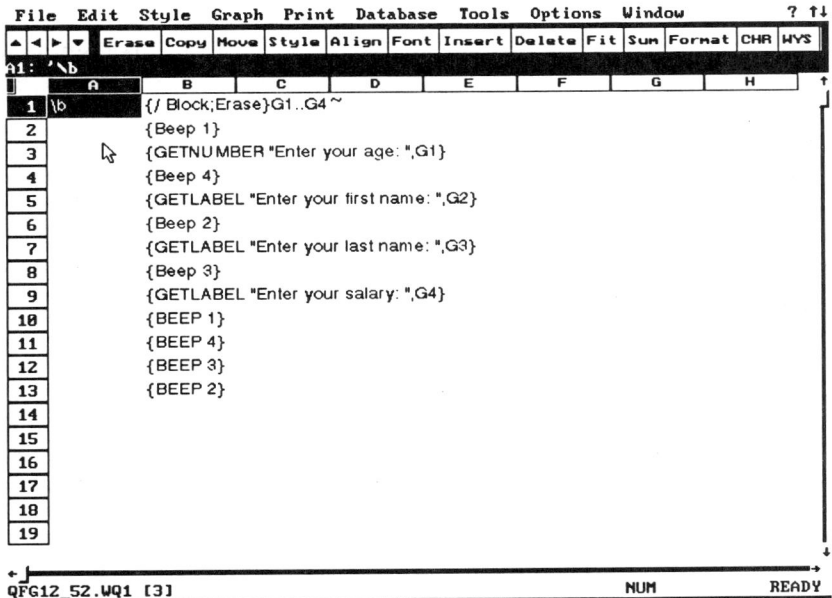

Figure 12.52 Macro Using {BEEP} Command

command. The purpose of the macro instructions is to prompt the user to input his/her age, first and last name, and salary level. When the macro is executed, the first line of the macro erases the block G1..G4. The {BEEP 1} command on the second line causes the computer to make a low-pitched beeping sound. The user is then prompted to enter age. Quattro stores the number typed in cell G1. This is followed by the {BEEP 4} command, which creates a high-pitched beep. Quattro then prompts the user to enter a first name. The computer bell beeps with another pitch {BEEP 2}. A prompt asking for a last name appears next. This is followed by a different pitched beep {BEEP 3}. After this beep, a prompt requesting salary appears. When the salary has been entered, the macro generates four different-pitched beeps, which conclude the macro.

{INDICATE} The {INDICATE} command allows you to change the mode indicator (which appears in the lower right corner of your screen) to some specified string.

Format {INDICATE String} is the format for this command.

String is any string of characters. However, only the first five characters of the String argument are shown. You can use an empty string {INDICATE ""} to remove the indicator from the status line. If you want spaces in the mode indicator string, enclose the string in quotes. The command {INDICATE} by itself returns the indicator to Quattro's default.

Use You can use the {INDICATE} command in several situations. When you have a menu selection in a set of macro instructions, you can use this command to indicate which type of menu item the user has selected. You can also use this command to test macro shells. A subroutine within a macro can be represented initially by just an {INDICATE} command with an appropriate string of characters to check the flow of the macro.

Example Figure 12.53 provides an example of the {INDICATE} command. The first line of the macro (B1) changes the mode descriptor at the lower right corner of the screen from READY to ENTRY. The second {INDICATE} command (B9) changes the mode descriptor from ENTRY to PRINT. Finally, the last line of the macro (B12) returns the mode descriptor to READY.

{PANELOFF} The {PANELOFF} command disables the display of the menu and prompts during menu execution. The menu and prompts are restored when the {PANELON} command is used (see next section) or when Quattro has finished executing the macro.

Format {PANELOFF} is the format for the {PANELOFF} command.
This command has no arguments.

Use This command hides the display of Quattro's menus and prompts. During macro execution, the menus change so quickly that they cannot be read. Also, since

Advanced Macro Options 669

```
File   Edit   Style   Graph   Print   Database   Tools   Options   Window         ? ↑↓
 ▲ ◀ ▶ ▼  Erase Copy Move Style Align Font Insert Delete Fit Sum Format CHR WYS
A1: [W4] '\i
       A        B                   C                  D         E              F            G       ↑
  1   \i    {INDICATE Entry}                                Change Indicator to ENTRY
  2         {GETLABEL "Enter name, e.g. (First Name Last Name): ",Name}
  3         {}                                              Get name & store it in C14
  4         {GETLABEL "Enter address: ",Address}            Get address & store it in C16
  5         {GETLABEL "Enter city: ",City}                  Get city & store it in C18
  6         {GETLABEL "Enter state: ",State}                Get state & store it in E18
  7         {GETLABEL "Enter ZIP code: ",Zip}               Get zip & store it in G18
  8         {GETLABEL "Enter phone: ",Phone}                Get phone & store it in C20
  9         {INDICATE Print}                                Change indicator to PRINT
 10         {GETLABEL What block do you want to print?,Z1}
 11         {P_Block}                                       Go to P_Block & print block
 12         {INDICATE}                                      Restore indicator
 13
 14         Name       Jane Brown
 15
 16         Address    11 East Cliff Drive
 17
 18         City       Glenn                 State     MI          Zip          49416
 19
            Phone      (616)879-6754
QFG12_53.WQ1 [3]                                                        NUM             READY
```

Figure 12.53 Macro Using {INDICATE} Command

Quattro must update the screen for every new menu and prompt, disabling their display speeds up macro execution.

Example Figure 12.54 provides an example of the {PANELOFF} command. The {PANELOFF} command in the first line of the macro (F1) instructs Quattro not to update the control panel during the macro execution. The {PANELON} command in F10 enables the menu's display for the font change made with the macro instructions in F12..F13.

{PANELON} The {PANELON} command restores the menus and prompts that have been hidden with the {PANELOFF} command. {PANELON} cannot perform any action without a prior {PANELOFF}, so using this command without a prior {PANELOFF} has no effect.

Format {PANELON} is the format of the {PANELON} command.
   This command has no arguments.

Use This command is used when you have hidden the menus and prompts with the {PANELOFF} command. Quattro automatically performs {PANELON} when it reaches the end of a macro.

Example Figure 12.54 provides an example of the {PANELON} command. The {PANELOFF} command in F1 instructs Quattro not to display the menus and

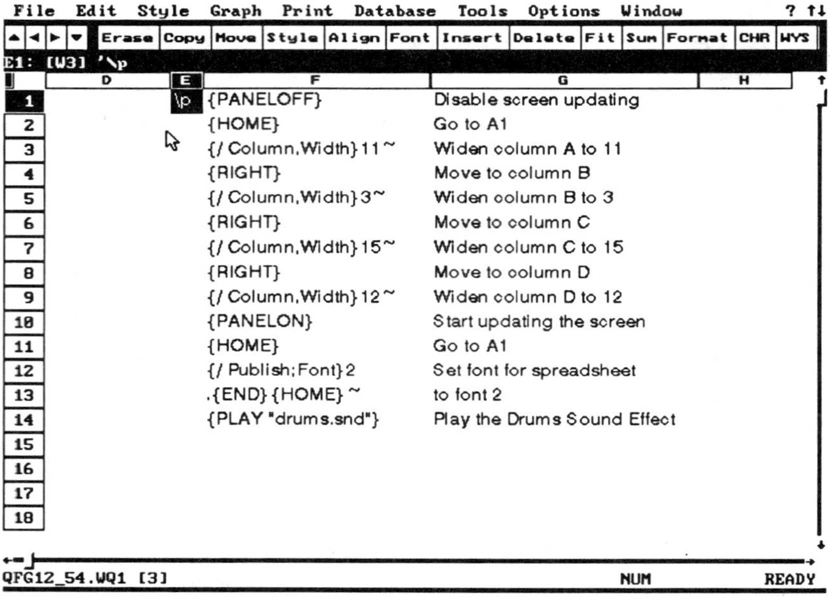

```
File  Edit  Style  Graph  Print  Database  Tools  Options  Window        ? ↑↓
▲ ◄ ► ▼  Erase Copy Move Style Align Font Insert Delete Fit Sum Format CHR WYS
E1: [W3] '\p
        D           E         F                    G                H
  1                 \p   {PANELOFF}         Disable screen updating
  2                      {HOME}             Go to A1
  3                      {/ Column,Width}11~ Widen column A to 11
  4                      {RIGHT}            Move to column B
  5                      {/ Column,Width}3~ Widen column B to 3
  6                      {RIGHT}            Move to column C
  7                      {/ Column,Width}15~ Widen column C to 15
  8                      {RIGHT}            Move to column D
  9                      {/ Column,Width}12~ Widen column D to 12
 10                      {PANELON}          Start updating the screen
 11                      {HOME}             Go to A1
 12                      {/ Publish;Font}2  Set font for spreadsheet
 13                      .{END}{HOME}~      to font 2
 14                      {PLAY "drums.snd"} Play the Drums Sound Effect
 15
 16
 17
 18
QFG12_54.WQ1 [3]                                         NUM       READY
```

Figure 12.54 Macro Using {PANELOFF}, {PANELON}, and {PLAY} Commands

prompts during the macro execution. The {PANELON} command in F10 restores the menus and prompts to display so that the font-selection macro instructions in F12..F13 display the menu boxes and prompts.

{PLAY} The {PLAY} command plays a sound file that provides various sound effects that Quattro Pro can perform.

Format {PLAY "filename"} is the format of the {PLAY} command.

Filename is the name of the sound effect file with a .SND file extension that is available with Quattro Pro, in Quattro Pro's Power Pack or is available separately. The sound files are the same sound files that you can use in graph slide shows and buttons.

Use You can use this command for adding sound effects to a macro such as having the macro say "Thank You" or indicating that the macro is finished.

Example Figure 12.54 shows a macro that uses the {PLAY} command to indicate that the macro has finished by performing the sounds stored in the DRUMS.SND sound file.

{WINDOWSOFF} The {WINDOWSOFF} command disables the automatic updating of the spreadsheet display. The display is automatically updated when the {WINDOWSON} command is used (see next section) or when the macro execution is finished.

Format {WINDOWSOFF} is the format for the {WINDOWSOFF} command.
This command has no arguments.

Use This command is used when you want to speed up the macro execution. Since Quattro automatically updates the screen as changes are made, the amount of time consumed by the updating can slow down a macro significantly. Disabling window updating reduces the flickering that appears on the screen. Also, it is useful when you do not want the operator to see the execution of each instruction or be aware of each activity that takes place. This command does not affect trace cells.

Example Figure 12.55 provides an example of the {WINDOWSOFF} command. The {WINDOWSOFF} command in the Find_Name macro (B10) instructs Quattro not to update the spreadsheet display until Quattro reaches the {WINDOWSON} command after it has found the name. The {WINDOWSOFF} and {WINDOWSON} commands hide the steps the Find_Name macro performs to find the name.

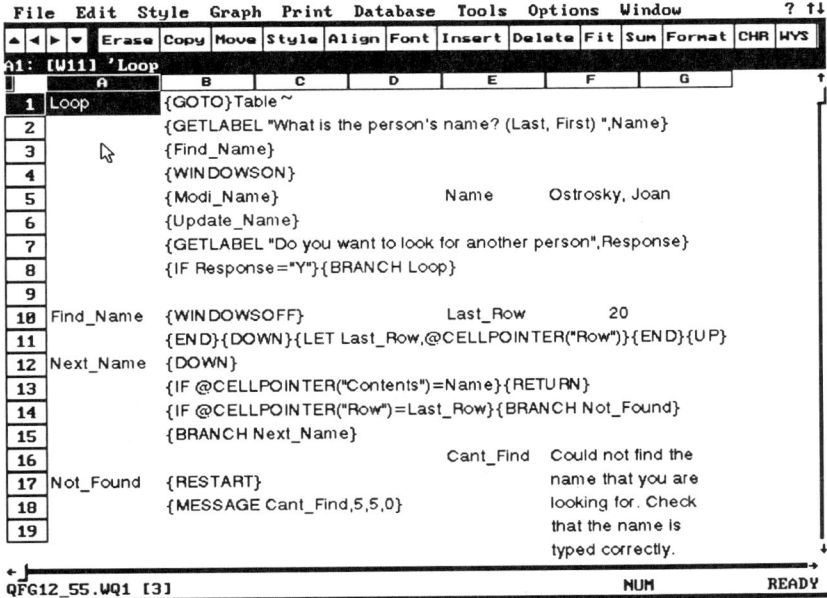

Figure 12.55 Macro Using {WINDOWSOFF} and {WINDOWSON} Commands

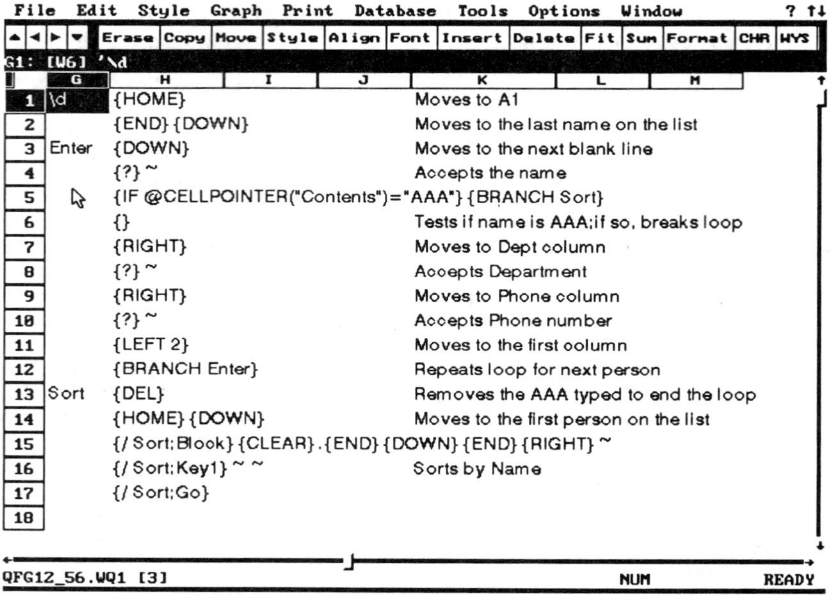

```
File   Edit   Style   Graph   Print   Database   Tools   Options   Window                ? ↑↓
    Erase Copy Move Style Align Font Insert Delete Fit Sum Format CHR HYS
G1: [W6] '\d
      G         H              I         J              K              L         M
 1   \d    {HOME}                             Moves to A1
 2         {END}{DOWN}                        Moves to the last name on the list
 3   Enter {DOWN}                             Moves to the next blank line
 4         {?}~                               Accepts the name
 5         {IF @CELLPOINTER("Contents")="AAA"}{BRANCH Sort}
 6         {}                                 Tests if name is AAA; if so, breaks loop
 7         {RIGHT}                            Moves to Dept column
 8         {?}~                               Accepts Department
 9         {RIGHT}                            Moves to Phone column
10         {?}~                               Accepts Phone number
11         {LEFT 2}                           Moves to the first column
12         {BRANCH Enter}                     Repeats loop for next person
13   Sort  {DEL}                              Removes the AAA typed to end the loop
14         {HOME}{DOWN}                       Moves to the first person on the list
15         {/ Sort;Block}{CLEAR}.{END}{DOWN}{END}{RIGHT}~
16         {/ Sort;Key1}~ ~                   Sorts by Name
17         {/ Sort;Go}
18

QFG12_56.WQ1 [3]                                                NUM            READY
```

Figure 12.56 Macro Using { } Command

{WINDOWSON} The {WINDOWSON} command re-enables the updating of the spreadsheet display. Since {WINDOWSON} does not perform any action without a prior {WINDOWSOFF}, using this command without a prior {WINDOWSOFF} does not have any effect.

Format {WINDOWSON} is the format of the {WINDOWSON} command.
This command has no arguments.

Use This command is used when you have disabled the automatic display updating with the {WINDOWSOFF} command and then want the display to be updated.

Example Figure 12.56 provides an example of the {WINDOWSON} command. The {WINDOWSON} command after the {Find_Name} macro instruction directs Quattro to refresh the spreadsheet display that was disabled with the {WINDOWSOFF} command. The {WINDOWSOFF} and {WINDOWSON} commands hide the steps the Find_Name macro performs to find the name.

Miscellaneous Commands

Quattro has two miscellaneous commands. These commands do not perform actions but are designed for documenting and editing a macro.

{ } The { } command performs no actions but acts as a connector between the macro instruction in the line above and the macro instruction in the line below.

Format { } is the format of this function.
This function does not use any arguments.

Use This macro often appears within other macros to provide additional rows for the documentation. You may want to use this macro command if you have deleted a macro instruction in a cell, but you want the macro execution flow to continue to the macro instructions below the deleted macro instruction.

Example Many of the macros in this chapter have not included the macro's documentation to the right of the macro instructions due to screen width limitations. Figure 12.56 shows a macro with this spacing problem. For the macro instruction in H5, the display does not have enough space for the user to see the documentation. Therefore, the row below the {IF} command has the { } command (H6). This blank macro instruction provides the room in the documentation column to document the {IF} command without disrupting the macro's flow.

{;} The {;} command causes Quattro to ignore the text between the semicolon and the right brace. When Quattro reaches this command, it continues to the next instruction.

Format {;String} is the format of this function.
String is any set of characters. This string may be up to 251 characters. This information may be a string enclosed in quotes, a cell address, a block name, or a formula.

Use This macro command often appears in macros to document the macro. During macro debugging, other macro instructions are converted to this macro instruction by entering a semicolon after the opening brace to temporarily disable a macro instruction. For example, if you place a semicolon in a {WRITELN} command, Quattro ignores the {;WRITELN} command and performs the next macro instruction.

Example Figure 12.57 shows a macro that uses the {;} command to document the macro and to temporarily disable a {BRANCH} command. When this macro is executed, Quattro skips over the documentation comment in B7. When the {IF} command in B12 is reached, Quattro executes the macro instruction below the {IF} whether the {IF} command's condition is true or not (the macro instruction to be performed if the condition is true is a {;} command).

/X Commands for Compatibility

Quattro also supports the /X commands used by Lotus 1-2-3 Release 1A. Quattro supports these commands so that macros created in 1-2-3 Release 1A work in

```
  File  Edit  Style  Graph  Print  Database  Tools  Options  Window        ? ↑↓
 ▲ ◄ ► ▼  Erase Copy Move Style Align Font Insert Delete Fit Sum Format CHR WYS
A1: [W6] 'Add
        A        B              C            D        E        F         G        H
  1   Add      {OPEN "Names.prn",a}{O_Err}                Open NAMES.PRN
  2   Loop     {GETLABEL "Enter First and Last Name: ",Name}
  3            {GETLABEL "Enter Address: ",Address}       Get data to add to file
  4            {GETLABEL "Enter City: ",City}             and store it in named
  5            {GETLABEL "Enter State: ",State}           cells in C15..C19
  6            {GETLABEL "Enter Zip: ",Zip}               Delim (G18) is ","
  7            {;macro delimits data as the macro writes the data}
  8            {WRITE Quote,Name,Delim}                   These lines add the data
  9            {WRITE Address,Delim,City,Delim}           to the end of the file
 10            {WRITELN State,Delim,Zip,Quote}            in delimited format
 11            {GETLABEL "Do you want to add another person?",Response}
 12            {IF Response="Y"}{;BRANCH Loop}            If add another go to Loop
 13            {CLOSE "Names.prn"}                        Close file
 14
 15   O_Err   {MESSAGE Err_Mess,5,5,0}{QUIT}
 16
 17           Named Cells Used In Macro:
 18           Name         Michelle Carson                Response   n
 19           Address      3490 Curtiswood Drive          Quote      "
              City         Key Biscayne                   Delim      ","
QFG12_57.WQ1 [3]                                                    NUM         READY
```

Figure 12.57 Macro Using {;} Command

Quattro. The /X commands do not have braces and do not have a space between the command and the argument. These commands have fewer options than Quattro's other macro commands and have macro-command equivalents. Unless you are creating macros for 1-2-3 Release 1A, use the Quattro macro commands.

/XC The /XC command transfers the macro's execution to a second macro. Once the second macro has been executed, Quattro returns to the first macro. It begins executing commands with the instruction after the /XC command. This command is equivalent to {Subroutine}. However, unlike the {Subroutine} command, the /XC command cannot pass arguments to the subroutine.

Format /XCLocation~ is the format of this command.
   Location is a block name or cell address that contains the first macro instruction of the subroutine.

Use This command transfers control to another macro. It is often helpful for instructions used several times.
   A subroutine may contain other subroutines. When the /XC command is executed, Quattro executes the subroutine until Quattro reaches a blank cell, /XR, or /XQ. If Quattro reaches a blank cell or /XR, the next macro instruction is executed after the /XC command. If Quattro executes a /XQ command, the macro is terminated and Quattro returns to the READY mode.

Advanced Macro Options

Example Figure 12.58 displays two macros that are part of the macros that operate an inventory database. These macros have been modified to work for Lotus 1-2-3 Release 1A and to use the 1-2-3 menu tree. When the top macro is executed, if the user types a Y in response to the first /XL command (which acts as a {GETLABEL} command), the menu executes the subroutine Invent. Depending on the answer to the first question, Invent branches to another subroutine. As Quattro completes each subroutine, it returns to the macro that called the subroutine and executes the macro instruction below the /XC command.

/XG The /XG command switches macro execution to another series of macro instructions that are stored in a different location. This command is different from the /XC command because the /XG command does not return to the macro with the /XG command. This command is equivalent to the {BRANCH} macro command.

Format /XGLocation~ is the format of the /XG command.

Location is a block name or a cell address that contains the first macro instruction that Quattro performs after executing the /XG command.

Use The /XG command is often the true condition for the /XI command.

Example Figure 12.58 shows an example of the /XG command. The \0 macro asks the user several questions and uses the /XL command to determine the actions to

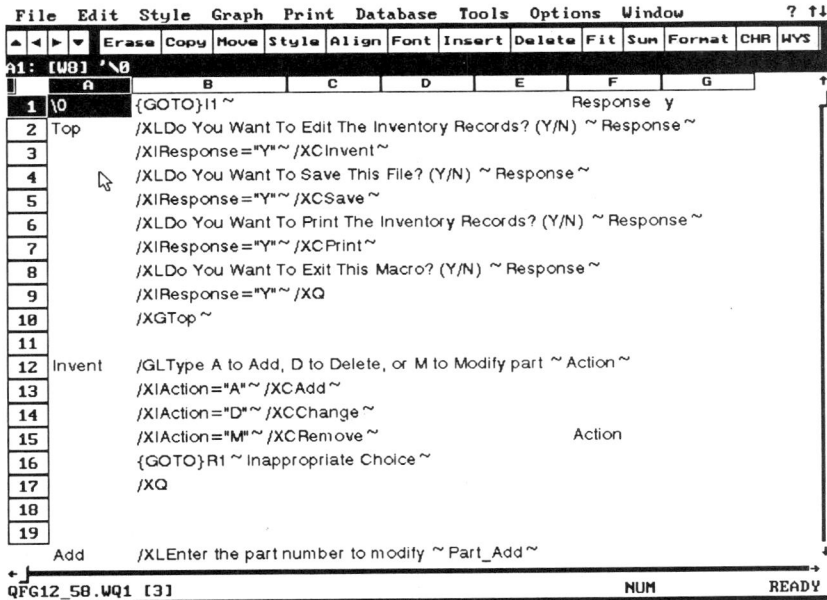

Figure 12.58 Macros Using /CX, /XL, /XG, /XI, and /XQ Commands

be taken. After all the actions are taken, the macro branches back to B2 and executes the macro again. The other macros use this command to redirect the macro instructions that Quattro performs.

/XI The /XI command evaluates a condition and executes the macro instructions following the condition if the condition is true. The /XI command operates like the {IF} function.

Format /XICondition~True_Instructions~ is the format of the /XI command.

Condition is a statement that Quattro evaluates as true or false. A true condition has a value of 1, and a false condition has a value of 0. Conditions can be composed of @ functions, block names, cell addresses, strings, values, and operators.

True_Instructions are the macro instructions that Quattro performs if the Condition is true. They can be any macro instructions.

Use The /XI command changes the macro instructions that Quattro performs depending on a condition. Often, the True_Instructions are an /XG, /XR, or /XQ command.

Example Figure 12.58 shows macros that use the /XI command in B3, B5, B7, and B9 to determine the actions the user wants the macro to perform. For each of these /XI commands, the /XI command compares the label in Response to a Y. If Response is a Y, the macro goes to the subroutine listed after the /XC command.

/XL The /XL command prompts the user for information and stores the entry as a label. This command is equivalent to the {GETLABEL} command. However, unlike the {GETLABEL} command, the prompt cannot be stored in a separate cell.

Format /XLPrompt~Location~ is the format for this command.

The Prompt argument is the string that the macro displays as the /XL command prompts the user for input. This string allows the display of instructions on the screen to guide the user to enter the desired data. While Lotus 1-2-3 Release 1A has a limit of 39 characters, Quattro displays up to 63 characters for the prompt in the input line.

The Location argument is a location (a cell address, a block address, or a block name) where Quattro stores the typed input as a left-aligned label. When the Location is a block of cells, Quattro uses the upper-left cell of the block. A maximum of 254 characters can be stored.

Use This command accepts information from the keyboard while the macro is still executing.

Example Figure 12.58 contains several /XL commands. The /XL commands get input from the user.

Advanced Macro Options 677

/XM The /XM command displays a custom menu, allows selection of one of the menu items, and executes the menu item's macro instructions. This command branches to the macro instructions below the menu item and does not return to the macro with the /XM command. This command is equivalent to the {MENUBRANCH} command.

Format /XMLocation~ is the format of the /XM command.

Location is the first cell that defines the custom menu. It is either a cell address or a block name. The custom menu is identical to the one for {MENUBRANCH} and is described with that menu command.

Use The /XM command lets the user select the tasks that the macro performs. If the user presses ESC, the macro continues in the initial macro, starting with the instruction following the /XM command.

Example Figure 12.59 shows an alternative for the Invent macro described earlier. In this macro, the choices for editing the inventory database are menu items. This menu is defined starting at Menu. When one menu item is selected, Quattro executes the appropriate macro instructions starting in row 15. If ESC is pressed, the macro goes to R1 and displays Inappropriate Choice.

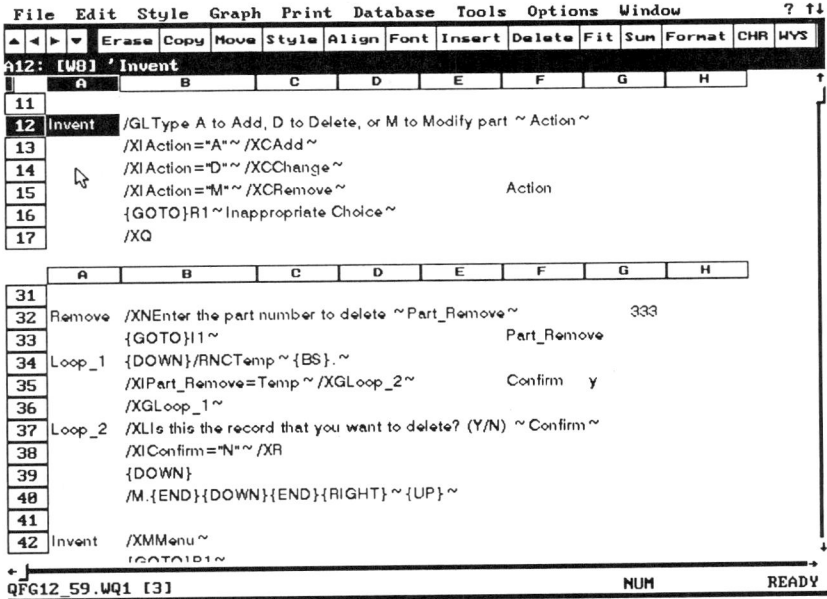

Figure 12.59 Alternative Invent Subroutine Using the /XM Command

678   *Quattro Pro 4.0 Handbook*

/XN   The /XN command prompts the user to enter a numeric entry that is stored in a spreadsheet cell. This command is equivalent to the {GETNUMBER} command. However, unlike the {GETNUMBER} command, the prompt cannot be stored in a separate cell.

Format   /XNPrompt~Location~ is the format for the /XN command.

Prompt is the string that Quattro displays in the input line, which allows you to display instructions on the screen to guide the user to enter the desired data. Like the /XL command, Quattro displays up to 63 characters for a prompt in the input line (although if you are using this macro with 1-2-3 Release 1A, use its limit of 39 characters).

The Location argument is a cell address, a block address, or a block name of the place where Quattro stores the user's entry. Location is a cell address or block name.

Use   The /XN command is useful whenever you want a numeric value stored in a particular cell or block of cells.

Example   Figure 12.60 contains an /XN command to determine the part number that the user wants to delete in the subroutine Remove.

/XQ   The /XQ command terminates the macro's execution and returns to the READY mode. This command is equivalent to {QUIT}.

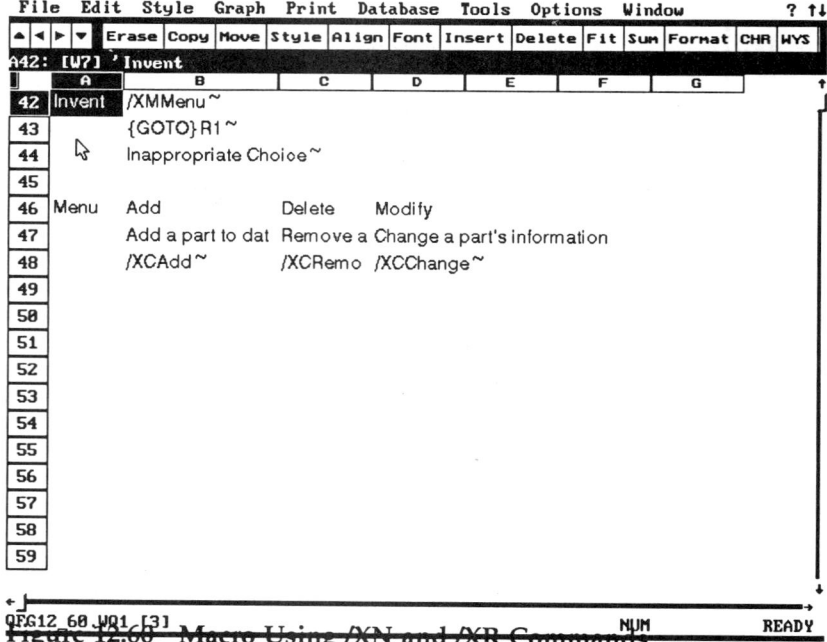

Figure 12.60   Macro Using /XN and /XR Commands

Format /XQ is the format of the /XQ command.

Use The /XQ macro command terminates a macro at a position different from the macro's end position.

Example The first macro in Figure 12.58 allows the user to determine the actions that the macro performs. The last question (B9) allows the user to leave the macro. If you type a Y for the last question, Quattro stops the macro's execution instead of branching to Top because of the /XQ command.

/XR The /XR command returns the macro execution to the macro that called the subroutine containing the /XR command. This is equivalent to the {RETURN} command.

Format /XR is the format of this command.

Use This command ends a subroutine's execution at a location other than its last macro command.

Example The macro in the bottom half of Figure 12.59 contains one of the subroutines that the Invent subroutine calls. This macro looks for the part number to delete and requests a confirmation. If the response to the /XL command is N, the subroutine ends and control returns to the Invent subroutine (because of the /XR command, which is the true condition of the /XI command).

GETTING STARTED

In this chapter, you learned how you can create macros using macro command instructions to provide advanced programming features that you might expect more in a programming language than in a spreadsheet. You can use these features to create the macro in Figure 12.61, which formats columns of numbers to currency with 0 decimals. To create this macro, follow these steps:

1. Make the following entries to enter the steps that the macro will perform. You can make these entries using uppercase or lowercase.

    A1: **Format**
    A4: **Col_form**
    A7: **Counter**
    A8: **Num_Col**
    B1: {GETNUMBER How many columns do you want to format?;Num_Col}
    B2: {FOR Counter,1,Num_Col,1,Col_Form}
    B4: {/ Block;Format}c0~{END}{DOWN}~
    B5: {RIGHT}

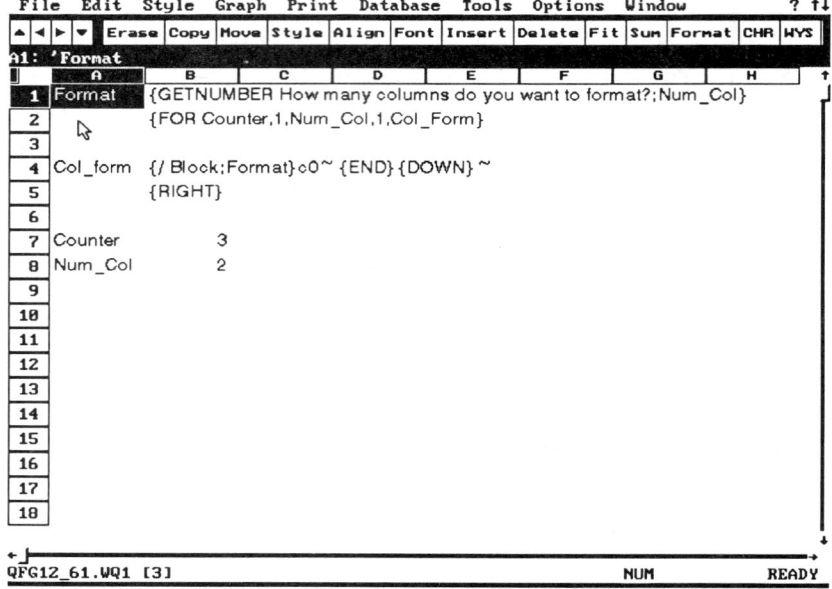

Figure 12.61 Macros Created in Getting Started Section

2. Name the cells used in the macro. Since the labels for the named blocks are all in column A, you can use the /Edit Names Labels command to name the blocks. Enter /Edit Names Labels Right. When Quattro prompts for a block, press PGDN to select the block A1..A21 and press ENTER. Quattro does not care that some of the cells are blank, since this command only uses the cells in the block that contains labels. Entering this command names B1 as Format, B4 as Col_Form, B7 as Counter, and B8 as Num_Col.

3. Save this macro by pressing CTRL-S to enter /File Save. Type **MAC_FORM** as the file name, and press ENTER or click Enter in the box.

4. Open a new spreadsheet by entering /File New. This new spreadsheet is assigned the next highest unused window number.

5. Make the following entries:

   A1: **Yearly Sales**
   A2: **Division A**
   A3: **Division B**
   A4: **Division C**
   B1: **1991**
   B2: **650000**
   B3: **800000**
   B4: **450000**
   C1: **1992**

C2: **700000**
C3: **350000**
C4: **600000**

6. Execute the macro you have created. Move to B2 in the new spreadsheet. Press ALT-F2 (MACRO) to display the Macro menu and select Execute. When Quattro prompts for a macro name, press ALT-1 to select the MAC_FORM spreadsheet. Then press F3 (CHOICES), and select FORMAT from the list. When the {GETLABEL} command prompts you for the number of columns you want to format, type **2** and press ENTER. This macro first formats B2..B4 then formats C2..C4. You can use this macro to format varying number of columns of values, since the {FOR} command only repeats the macro commands in Col_Form the number of times you enter with the {GETNUMBER} command.

Appendix A

Installing Quattro Pro

Installing Quattro Pro is a simple process. Quattro has an installation utility that performs most of the installation for you. That utility copies the program files from the disks to your hard drive. Once the files are copied, you are asked questions that determine how Quattro will appear, the initial printer you plan to use, and if you will use Quattro Pro with Windows. After the installation utility is finished, you are ready to use Quattro. If you already have a previous version of Quattro installed on your machine, you will first need to copy your worksheet, clip art, and customized menu tree files to another directory and then erase the files in the Quattro Pro directory and in the FONTS directory in the Quattro Pro directory. If you are installing a previous version of Quattro Pro, you will find that the steps are similar but slightly different.

THE INSTALLATION PROCEDURE

When you install Quattro, you execute an installation utility. This utility creates a directory for your Quattro program files. Next, it copies the program files from the diskettes. Finally, the installation utility prompts for several settings.

To install Quattro to your hard disk, follow these steps:

1. Insert Disk 1 of the Quattro disks in a floppy disk drive, and close the door (if any).

2. Start the installation program. If you inserted the first disk in drive A, type **A:INSTALL** and press ENTER. The installation utility displays an opening screen. If you are using an LCD monitor or your computer has a color graphics adapter card and a monochrome or composite monitor, type **A:INSTALL/B** and press ENTER to use a black-and-white display for the installation program.

3. Press ENTER to continue. Quattro prompts for the source drive to use. This is the drive containing the program files. Although the default is the floppy disk drive you started from or drive A, you can change it to any valid drive.
4. Type the new source drive letter or leave the existing setting and press ENTER. Quattro displays a menu box to select the Quattro Pro Directory.
5. If you want to change the directory from the default of C:\QPRO, press F2. Quattro prompts for the directory, displaying the current selection. You can edit this and finalize the entry by pressing ENTER.
6. Start installing Quattro by pressing ENTER. At this point, the installation utility checks if you have enough space on the disk. If you have approximately 6MB of space, the installation utility continues. If you have less than 6MB, the installation utility displays a message box. If this happens, you can press ESC until you return to DOS and remove unneeded files to free disk space before you install Quattro Pro. Quattro starts reading the files on the diskette and writing them to the hard drive. The box in the bottom of the screen lets you monitor the progress.
7. Each time the installation utility displays a message prompting for the next disk, remove the current disk and insert the next disk in the same drive. Once the disk is inserted and any door or latch is closed, press a key to direct the installation utility to start reading and writing the files. When all the files have been copied, a box is displayed telling you that you will be asked a few questions. These questions register your copy of Quattro Pro and make some initial setting selections. You can change the settings later in Quattro if you find that you have made an incorrect selection or you have changed your equipment. At any point, you can press CTRL-X to terminate the installation utility without answering all the questions.
8. Press any key to continue.
9. The installation utility can detect what type of display adapter you have, but it cannot detect if your monitor is color, black and white, or can display shades as laptops do. If the current selection is inappropriate for your monitor, press F2 and select the appropriate choice. When the correct monitor type appears after the prompt, press ENTER.
10. The installation program prompts you for product registration information which will appear every time you load Quattro Pro. You must provide the registration information to complete the installation process. At the Company Name prompt, press F2, type your company name (or your own name if this is your personal copy) and press ENTER. Press ENTER again for confirmation. At the Name prompt, press F2, type your name (or your company name) and press ENTER. Press ENTER again for confirmation. At the Serial # prompt, press F2, type the serial number that appears on Disk 1, and press ENTER. Press ENTER again for confirmation.
11. The installation program prompts if you are installing Quattro Pro on a network server. Press ENTER to select No unless you are installing Quattro Pro on a network server.

12. If you do not have a CONFIG.SYS file or it does not include a FILES= command followed by a number greater than 20, the installation program prompts if you want your CONFIG.SYS file edited. To tell the installation utility not to modify or create the CONFIG.SYS file, press F2, highlight No and press ENTER. If you want the utility to edit the CONFIG.SYS file for you, leave the Edit CONFIG.SYS File setting at Yes. At the preferred setting, press ENTER. If you select Yes, the installation utility will create a CONFIG.SYS file or edit the existing one for you on drive C containing a FILES=20 statement.

13. If the AUTOEXEC.BAT file on your hard drive does not contain C:\QPRO (or the appropriate path to Quattro) in a PATH command, the installation utility displays a message telling you that to run Quattro from any drive or directory, you must include the drive and directory in a PATH command stored in the AUTOEXEC.BAT file. To tell the Quattro Pro installation utility not to modify or create the AUTOEXEC.BAT file, press F2, highlight No, and press ENTER. If you want the utility to create or edit the AUTOEXEC.BAT file for you, leave the setting at Yes. When this setting is the way you want it, press ENTER. If you select Yes, the installation utility will create or edit the AUTOEXEC.BAT file for you to include the PATH command followed by the drive and directory containing the Quattro files.

14. The Quattro Pro installation utility prompts you to select your printer manufacturer. You can skip over selecting the printer by pressing ESC although you must select the printer to print using enhanced printing features such as fonts or bullets, or to print graphs. To select the printer manufacturer, press F2, highlight the manufacturer appropriate for your printer, and press ENTER. When the correct printer manufacturer appears after the Printer Manufacturer prompt, press ENTER. Next, you must choose the printer model by pressing F2, highlighting your printer model, and pressing ENTER. When the printer model appears after the Printer Model prompt, press ENTER. Finally, you must choose the printing mode. Most printers can print in more than one mode. For example, the Hewlett-Packard LaserJet series II can print in high (300 x 300 dpi) or medium (150 x 150 dpi) modes. The higher the dpi (dots per inch), the sharper the image and the longer the printing process takes. To select a mode, press F2, highlight your choice, and press ENTER. When the printing mode you want appears after the Printer Mode prompt, press ENTER.

15. The installation program prompts if you want the WYSIWYG display which displays the spreadsheet as Quattro Pro will print it when you print to a graphics printer. When you print using a graphics printer, you can print graphs, multiple fonts, lines, and shading. Press ENTER to select Yes or press F2, the DOWN ARROW and ENTER twice to use the text display.

16. The installation program prompts if you want to install Quattro Pro for Windows version 3.0 or above. To install Quattro without using Windows, press ENTER to select No. To install Quattro Pro 4 for Windows, press F2, the DOWN ARROW, and ENTER twice to change the No to Yes. If you

select Yes, you must then provide the path to the Windows program files. Press F2 and enter the drive and directory that contains Windows. Press ENTER twice. When you run Quattro Pro in Windows, you must run it full screen mode.

17. The installation program prompts you for the character set you are using. Using the default of Standard U.S. is quicker for printing with Bitstream fonts. You may want to change to Standard European by pressing F2, highlighting Standard European and pressing ENTER if you plan to use foreign characters with Bitstream fonts. Press ENTER again as confirmation.

When Quattro Pro has finished, it displays a message that the installation is completed and recommends that you reboot the computer to execute changes made to the CONFIG.SYS or AUTOEXEC.BAT files. After reading the message, press a key to leave Quattro. At this point, you are ready to use Quattro.

USING QUATTRO PRO WITH EXTENDED MEMORY

Many of the newer machines, such as the PC AT and the PS/2, use extended memory. While Quattro 1.x was initially designed to use the computer's conventional RAM and any expanded memory, Quattro Pro can use up to 512K of extended memory to store program modules. Program modules are parts of the Quattro Pro program. By only loading the modules of the Quattro Pro program that you need, you have more room for your spreadsheets. Using extended memory for program modules will make Quattro execute faster. To use Quattro and extended memory, type **Q/X** to load and start the macro. Quattro will continue using any expanded memory but as you add more data and open more windows, you will notice an increase in performance.

If you aren't sure if you have extended memory, try running Quattro and loading as many spreadsheets as possible. As you add more spreadsheets, you will notice that Quattro's performance slows. Exit Quattro and load it again using **Q/X**. Then try loading the spreadsheets again. If you notice an increase of speed, you have extended memory. Quattro cannot recognize other programs that use extended memory such as disk cache drivers, RAM disk drivers, or TSR programs (programs that remain in memory even when they do not appear). If you are using one of these products, you should check the documentation to see if the product uses any extended memory. If you are using one of the products that use extended memory, either do not use **Q/X** to load Quattro or remove these programs from memory before using **Q/X** to load Quattro.

USING QUATTRO PRO WITH EXPANDED MEMORY

If your computer has expanded memory but Quattro does not recognize it, run a special utility program provided with Quattro. The EMSTEST utility verifies that your expanded memory is working correctly. To run this utility, type **EMSTEST** from the DOS prompt and press ENTER. The utility will provide instructions for you to follow.

Appendix B

Command Reference

This appendix defines all the Quattro commands. It lists the Quattro commands available in a spreadsheet window and in a File Manager window, each in separate sections. While the description of each command is brief, the major points are covered, including the options available with the command. The commands are listed in alphabetical order, for example, /File Close All is listed after /File Close. Most of the commands that use spreadsheet blocks can have their spreadsheet blocks selected before you select the command, although the command reference mentions selecting the blocks after the command. If you preselect a block, you are not prompted to select a block after you select a command. Notes that point out unusual features, shortcuts, or special uses are provided for some commands.

Quattro Spreadsheet Commands

/DATABASE DATA ENTRY

This command limits the type of entries accepted in a block.

OPTIONS

General—This option removes the data entry restrictions placed by the other two options (see below). When Quattro prompts for a block, you can either type a block address or name or point to a block before pressing ENTER.

Labels Only—This option accepts entries in the block that you specify as a label. When Quattro prompts for a block, you can either type a block address or name or point to a block before pressing ENTER. Quattro treats any entry as a label, allowing you to enter Social Security numbers and phone numbers without preceding the entry with a label indicator. A cell using this option has Label before the cell address in the input line.

Dates Only—This option only accepts dates or times in the block that you specify when Quattro prompts for a block. You can either type a block address or name or point to the block before pressing ENTER. When you make an entry in one of these cells, Quattro interprets the entry as a date or time. If the entry is not a valid date or time, Quattro displays an error message. This is equivalent to pressing CTRL-D before entering the dates or times in the cells. A cell using this option has Date before the cell address in the input line.

/DATABASE PARADOX ACCESS

This command makes several selections that Quattro uses when you use Paradox Access and Quattro together. With this command, you can switch to Paradox, set the file Quattro loads when you switch from Paradox to Quattro, and select whether Quattro loads this file every time you switch from Paradox to Quattro.

OPTIONS

Go—This option switches to Paradox. Any Quattro data remains in memory so you can return to the Quattro data where you left it. You can also switch to Paradox by pressing CTRL-F10.

Load File—This option selects the name of the file that Quattro loads every time you switch from Paradox to Quattro. This can be one of the temporary tables Paradox uses or another file that Quattro will accept. The file must be in a path Quattro can find such as the Paradox temporary directory or the current directory Quattro is set to use. This setting is only important if the Autoload option is set to Yes. The default for this option is ANSWER.DB, which is the temporary file Paradox creates every time you create a query. By using the default file, the results of the query are immediately available to you in Quattro.

Autoload—This option sets whether Quattro loads the file set with the Load File option every time you switch from Paradox to Quattro. This is initially set to Yes to load the file every time, but you can select No to discontinue loading the selected file.

Quit—This option returns you to the spreadsheet in READY mode.

/DATABASE QUERY

This command searches through a database and locates records that meet specified criteria. To use this command, you must specify the block of cells that contains the data entries you wish to search. Quattro also needs the specific criteria to use in searching through your database records.

OPTIONS

Block—This option specifies the location of the database. You can specify the desired block by pointing or typing the desired block address or name. If the block is in another spreadsheet, you must precede the block address or name with the file name enclosed in brackets. In either case, you need to include the field names as part of your specification before pressing ENTER. The block does not have to contain all the database's fields, but the block must contain all the fields used by the criteria and the output block (if any). If you want to use a dBASE, Paradox, or Reflex database as the block, enter the file name in brackets followed by a block address. Since the block address prevents a Quattro syntax error, the actual address is irrelevant.

Criteria Table—This option specifies your criteria in a table format. You must enter your criteria on the spreadsheet in an acceptable tabular form before selecting this command. Enter the block address or name, or point to the block and press ENTER. If the block is in a different spreadsheet, include the file name in brackets before the block address or name.

Output Block—Before you use the Extract and Unique options, you must specify the area of the spreadsheet where Quattro will store the selected records. When you select this option, highlight or type the address of the output area. The output area must contain the field names you wish to extract. If the block is in a different spreadsheet, you must include the file name in brackets before the block address or name. If the output block contains only one row, Quattro uses as many rows below the output block as Quattro needs to copy the extracted records after deleting all the data below the field names. If the output block contains more than one row, Quattro only uses the output block. When Quattro fills the output block and more room is needed for extracted records, Quattro displays an error message.

Assign Names—This option automatically assigns field names to the cells in the first record of the specified block. This option allows you to use the field names when specifying your criteria instead of referring to the cell addresses. You must specify the database block before assigning the names.

Locate—This command instructs Quattro to highlight the records that meet your specified criteria. You must select a database block and a criteria table before using this option. You can use the DOWN and UP ARROW keys to view other records that meet the specified criteria. You can also edit highlighted records by using F2 (EDIT) and the LEFT and RIGHT ARROW keys.

Extract—This option copies the selected records to the specified output area. You need to select a database block and a criteria table before you use this option. You also must specify an output block where you want the copy of the extracted records before executing this request.

Unique—This option instructs Quattro to copy only records that are unique to the specified output area. Quattro determines uniqueness to the fields in the output block. You need to specify a database block, criteria, and the output block before you use this option.

Delete—This option deletes records that meet specified criteria. Before you use this option, you need to select a database block and a criteria table. Quattro prompts for confirmation that you want to delete the records. Enter Cancel to keep the records or Delete to remove the records from the database.

Reset—This option removes the block addresses selected for the Block, Criteria Table, and Output Block.

Quit—This option returns you to the spreadsheet in READY mode.

NOTE

You can reexecute the last /Database Query command using the same settings by pressing F7 (QUERY). Use this shortcut when you are changing the entries in the criteria table and want to see the effect.

/DATABASE RESTRICT INPUT

This command restricts data entry to a specific block as if you were entering data in an entry form. After you execute this command, the selector moves only to unprotected cells in the block. Even though the other cells are visible, they are inaccessible. When you are in this mode, Quattro does not allow you to use the menu.

You first need to unprotect all the cells where you will want to make entries with the /Style Protection Unprotect command. Activate the Restrict Input mode by typing /Database Restrict Input and then specifying the block for data entry. To end this mode, simply press the ESC key or press ENTER without typing an entry.

OPTIONS

None.

/DATABASE SORT

The /Database Sort command sorts your database records and your columns in any sequence that you specify. The data to sort must be in the spreadsheet before you issue this command. You can sort your records using up to five keys. The first key is the primary key. Quattro allows as many as four additional keys to serve as tie-breakers in the event of duplicate entries in keys with a higher priority.

Quattro does not adjust formulas when it sorts data. If you have formulas in the sort block, change them to use absolute addresses or convert them to values before sorting. If you have formulas outside the sort block that use values in the sort block, change them to values or reenter them after sorting.

OPTIONS

Block—The **B**lock option specifies the block of cells you wish to sort. You can type the block address of the data or highlight the specified block of cells. Do not include any database field names when using this option, since Quattro will sort these entries. You must include all the fields of the database. If you do not include all the fields, the database losses its integrity after sorting, since Quattro sorts some fields in the database but not all.

1st Key—This option specifies the primary key or controlling sequence for the sort. The first key is selected by pointing to a cell in a column that you wish to control the sort and pressing ENTER. If you are sorting columns, you must select a cell in the row you want to use to sort the columns. You also need to specify whether you want to sort the data in ascending or descending order.

2nd, 3rd, 4th, 5th Key—These options allow you to select additional sort keys. For each key selected, choose a cell from the column or row of entries and either ascending or descending order.

Go—This option performs the sort after you have set the other options.

Reset—This option removes the specifications made by the other menu options.

Sort Rules—This option has three selections that affect how Quattro sorts the block. The **Numbers Before Labels** selection determines whether Quattro places numbers before or after labels. If you select **Yes**, Quattro puts the numbers at the beginning if it is sorting in ascending order and at the end if it is sorting in descending order. If you select **No**, Quattro puts the numbers at the end if it is sorting in ascending order and at the beginning if it is sorting in descending order. This selection affects labels with numbers but not cells containing values which are always last. The new Quattro Pro 4 **Sort Rows/Columns** option selects whether Quattro Pro will sort the columns or the rows in the selected block. The default of **Rows** sorts the database by rows as you would use to sort a database. You can also select **Columns** to sort the block by columns according to the values in the rows you select for sort keys. The selection, **Label Order**, determines how Quattro sorts labels. You choose the label order by selecting **Dictionary** or **ASCII**. The **Dictionary** option sorts the labels in alphabetical order ignoring upper- and lowercase differences. The **ASCII** selection puts uppercase letters in alphabetical order and then puts lowercase letters in alphabetical order. This option uses the ASCII values of the letters. Selecting **Quit** returns you to the **/Database Sort** menu.

Quit—This option returns you to the spreadsheet in READY mode.

/EDIT COPY

The **/Edit Copy** command copies numbers, labels, and formulas to other cells in a spreadsheet. You must tell Quattro two things every time you use this command. First, you need to tell Quattro the cells to copy when Quattro prompts you for the Source block. This block can consist of one or many cells. If the Source block consists of multiple cells, they can be in the form of a row, column, or rectangle. You can supply the Source block as a cell address, a block name, or an address. You can point to the block using the arrow keys or mouse if you prefer.

The second piece of information that Quattro needs is the destination of the information that Quattro is copying. The Destination block specifies the location for the copied information. The size of the Destination block determines whether Quattro makes one or several copies of the source block. To specify the Destination block, you only need to include the top left cell address of the desired location in the spreadsheet for each copy that Quattro makes. For example, if you want to copy the contents of A1..A5 to C1..E5, the Destination block is specified as C1..E1. You can copy cells to another location in the same spreadsheet or in a different open spreadsheet. If you are copying between spreadsheets, you must include the file name in brackets ([ ]) when you reference an open but inactive spreadsheet. The source block does not have to be in an open spreadsheet but the destination one does. Quattro automatically adds the file name for you if you point to a block in another spreadsheet.

OPTIONS

The /Edit Copy command can copy in four different situations:

1. One cell to one cell.
2. One cell to many cells.
3. A block of cells to another block of cells whose block size is the same as the original block.
4. A block of cells to another block in the same shape and size as the original block. For example, Quattro can copy a row of 10 cells to several rows of 10 cells.

NOTE

You can copy cells to only one spreadsheet at a time. This command has two shortcuts—pressing CTRL-C and clicking Copy in the SpeedBar, which you can use instead of entering /Edit Copy.

/EDIT COPY SPECIAL

This command copies either the format or the entries from one location to another. Use this command instead of /Edit Copy to copy entries without copying the formats of the entries. You can also use this command to copy the formats and styles from one location to another and have the formats and styles applied to a different set of entries.

OPTIONS

This command has two options, but after you select one of these options, you must select the block to copy and the block where you want the original block copied. The cell or blocks you select choose the extent of your copy operation just as with the /Edit Copy command. The two options are:

Contents—This option copies the cell entries from one location to one or more other locations without including formatting information such as font, shading, lines, numerical format, and protection status.

Formats—This option copies the cell formatting from one location to one or more other locations without replacing the cell entries in the new location. The cell formatting includes font, shading, lines, numerical format, and protection status.

/EDIT DELETE COLUMN BLOCK

This command deletes the columns of a spreadsheet only in the rows you select. Rows that you do not include in the block you use with this command do not change. You can also select this command by clicking the Delete button in the SpeedBar and then selecting Column Block.

OPTIONS

You must select a block for this command that includes the specific columns you want to delete and the rows where you want these columns deleted. Select the block with the arrow keys or the mouse. When you press ENTER or click [Enter] in the input line, Quattro Pro will partially delete the selected columns.

/EDIT DELETE COLUMNS

This command deletes columns from your spreadsheet. You can also select this command by clicking the Delete button in the SpeedBar and then selecting Columns.

OPTIONS

When selecting this option, you must specify a block containing at least one cell from each column you want to delete. You can specify the block by pointing to it or by typing a block address. When you press ENTER, Quattro removes the columns from the spreadsheet and adjusts all the formulas accordingly. You cannot delete a column that contains protected cells.

/EDIT DELETE ROW BLOCK

This command deletes the rows of a spreadsheet only in the columns you select. Columns that you do not include in the block you use with this command do not change. You can also select this command by clicking the Delete button in the SpeedBar and then selecting Row Block.

OPTIONS

You must select a block for this command that includes the specific columns you want to delete and the rows where you want these columns deleted. Select the block with the arrow keys or the mouse. When you press ENTER or click [Enter] in the input line, Quattro Pro will partially delete the selected columns.

/EDIT DELETE ROWS

This command removes one or more rows from the spreadsheet. You can also select this command by clicking the Delete button in the SpeedBar and then selecting Rows.

OPTIONS

Quattro prompts you for the rows you want to delete. If you want to delete the current row, press ENTER. If you want to delete more than one row, use the DOWN ARROW key to highlight the rows to delete. Press ENTER after all the rows to be deleted are highlighted. You cannot delete rows containing protected cells.

/EDIT ERASE BLOCK

The /Edit Erase Block command erases entries in one or more cells on the spreadsheet. Quattro prompts you for the cells you wish to erase. The /Edit Erase Block command does not affect the cell format or the column width. Therefore, a cell with a currency format and a column width of 16 retains the column width and the currency format after you erase the cell. Quattro will not let you erase protected cells while protection is enabled. Quattro displays an error message if you attempt to erase a protected cell.

OPTIONS

You can enter the block to erase by typing the block address, entering a block name, or pointing to the block you wish to erase. If you use the pointing method, Quattro highlights the cells to erase.

NOTE

If you want to erase a single cell or a block selected with a mouse or the SHIFT-F7 (SELECT) key, you can erase it by moving to that cell or block and pressing the DEL key. You cannot use the SPACEBAR to erase a cell, since Quattro will place a label indicator in the blank cell. This command has two shortcuts—pressing CTRL-E and clicking Erase in the SpeedBar, which you can use instead.

/EDIT FILL

This command directs Quattro to enter a series of numbers in a row or column.

OPTIONS

When you select the /Edit Fill command, Quattro prompts you for the block of cells where the series of numbers will be placed. Next, Quattro prompts you for the Start value, the Step value, and the Stop value. The Start value is the first number in the series. The Step value is the specified increment between consecutive numbers in series. The Stop value causes Quattro to stop generating numbers even if the block is not filled when Quattro reaches the Stop value. If you want Quattro to fill the block selected, you must enter a Stop value that is high enough to allow Quattro to generate values for the entire block. The start, step, and stop values accept numbers, formulas, and block names referencing values as input.

/EDIT INSERT COLUMN BLOCK

This command inserts columns into a spreadsheet only in the rows you select. Rows that are not included in the block you use with this command do not change. You can also select this command by clicking the Insert button in the SpeedBar or pressing CTRL-I and then selecting Column Block.

OPTIONS

You must select a block for this command that includes the specific columns you want to insert and the rows where you want these columns inserted. Select the block with the arrow keys or the mouse. When you press ENTER or click [Enter] in the input line, Quattro Pro will partially insert the selected columns.

/EDIT INSERT COLUMNS

This command inserts columns at any location in the spreadsheet. You can also select this command by clicking the Insert button in the SpeedBar or pressing CTRL-I and then selecting Columns.

OPTIONS

When you select this command, Quattro prompts for the column(s) to insert. You can point to the columns and press ENTER. Quattro also adjusts all the formulas accordingly.

/EDIT INSERT ROW BLOCK

This command inserts rows into a spreadsheet only in the columns you select. Columns that are not included in the block you use with this command do not change. You can also select this command by clicking the Insert button in the SpeedBar or pressing CTRL-I and then selecting Row Block.

OPTIONS

You must select a block for this command that includes the specific columns you want to insert and the rows where you want these columns inserted. Select the block with the arrow keys or the mouse. When you press ENTER or click [Enter] in the input line, Quattro Pro will partially insert the selected columns.

/EDIT INSERT ROWS

This command inserts one or more rows in the spreadsheet at any location you specify. You can also select this command by clicking the Insert button in the SpeedBar or pressing CTRL-I and then selecting Rows.

OPTIONS

To use this command, move the selector to the row below where you want to insert rows, press /, and select Edit Insert Rows. When Quattro prompts for the rows to insert, press ENTER if you want to insert one row. If you want to insert more than one row, press the DOWN ARROW key once for each row beyond the first that you wish to insert. Once the desired rows are highlighted, press ENTER.

/EDIT MOVE

The /Edit Move command relocates a block of cell entries to any part of the spreadsheet. This command adjusts the formulas within the block that Quattro moves to correspond to the new location. The adjustment occurs whether the formula in the cell contains relative (A1), mixed ($A1,A$1), or absolute (A1) addresses. Also, Quattro adjusts formulas not in the block that reference cells in the moved block that's being moved regardless of the type of cell references these formulas contain.

OPTIONS

To execute this command, Quattro requires two pieces of information. Quattro needs to know the Source block that contains the data to move as well as the Destination block that tells Quattro the new location. Quattro prompts you for these two pieces of information. You can enter the information by typing the cell address or block address. You can also enter the information by referencing its assigned block name or pointing to the block with the arrow keys or mouse. The Source block and the Destination block can be in different spreadsheets as long as both spreadsheets are open.

NOTE

This command has two shortcuts—pressing CTRL-M and clicking Move in the SpeedBar, which you can use instead of entering /Edit Move.

/EDIT NAMES CREATE

This command assigns names to blocks of cells. This allows you to refer to cells with the assigned names rather than cell addresses. Formulas are easier to understand when they use the formula names rather than the cell addresses. These assigned names can replace cell or block addresses in any of Quattro's commands. Once you name a block, Quattro Pro will change any spreadsheet formulas that use the block to using the name. You can subsequently select block names to use in formulas by pressing F3 (CHOICES) or clicking Name in the EDIT mode SpeedBar. For commands that use blocks, you can select a named block for the command to use by pressing F3 (CHOICES) and selecting a block name. You can also use more than one name for the same block or an overlapping one.

OPTIONS

You can use an existing block name or you can specify a new name for a block. If you choose an existing block name, you can select one of the names listed in the menu. Quattro highlights the cells that are currently assigned this name. Press ESC or BACKSPACE to undo the block name assignment. With the old assignment removed, you can specify a new block of cells to assign this name.

If you choose to create a new block name, type a new block name and press ENTER. The name should not exceed 15 characters. Quattro prompts you for the block of cells that are to be assigned the new name. You can respond by pointing to the block address or by typing the block address.

NOTE

In Quattro Pro 4, you can add block notes to block names. You can add block names any time from a block name selection box such as the one Quattro Pro displays when you use the /Edit Names Create command and the spreadsheet already has one named block, or when you click Name in the SpeedBar. To add a block note, highlight the block name you want to add a note in the block name selection box and press F6 (PANE). Next, type the block note and press ENTER or click the Enter button to finalize the note and return to the block name selection box. The block note will appear in the block name selection box when you highlight the block name. The block note is also included when you create a block name table with the /Edit Names Make Table command.

/EDIT NAMES DELETE

This command removes block names that are no longer needed. Each time you use this command you can delete one block name.

OPTIONS
Type in the block name, or select one from the box of block names.

/EDIT NAMES LABELS

This command assigns names from labels in the spreadsheet to adjacent cells as block names. This command assigns each label to a single cell. Also, the cell to be assigned the block names must be adjacent to the cell that contains the labels for the named blocks. Quattro has a 15-character limit for the block name assignment, after which it truncates the label.

OPTIONS
The four options for this command are **Right**, **Left**, **Down**, and **Up**. These options tell Quattro the direction in which the assignment is to be made. After selecting one of these options, you need to specify the block containing the label names to assign.

/EDIT NAMES MAKE TABLE

This command creates a table of block names in the current spreadsheet and the addresses to which these names are assigned. Quattro uses the upper-left cell of the address you provide as the upper-left corner of the table. The table uses three columns and as many rows as the spreadsheet has block names. The first column of the table contains the block names, the second column contains the block addresses, and the third column contains any block notes that you can add to block names in Quattro Pro 4.

OPTIONS
You must specify an area of the spreadsheet for the table. You can do so by pointing to the block address or by typing a cell address when Quattro prompts you to.

/EDIT NAMES RESET

This command deletes all the assigned block names at once. You can select this command instead of deleting each assigned block name individually with the /Edit Names Delete command. This command only affects the current spreadsheet.

OPTIONS

Quattro prompts for confirmation before removing all block names. Select Yes to remove all the block names or No to cancel the command.

/EDIT SEARCH & REPLACE

This command searches for and replaces entries that meet certain criteria. To use this command, type / and select Edit Search & Replace.

OPTIONS

Block—This option specifies the block of cells you want to search. When Quattro prompts for the block, you can type a block address, block name, or point to the block of cells.

Search String—This option specifies the string, such as Sales, or the condition, such as ? >100000, that Quattro will search for. Type an entry and press ENTER. If you enter a condition, you must change the Look In option to Condition.

Replace String—This option specifies the data that will replace the searched for entry when this command finds it. Quattro prompts for the replacement entry when you select this option. Type an entry, and press ENTER.

Look In—This option determines the part of formulas that Quattro searches to find the search string. The choices are Formula, which looks at the characters in the formula; Value, which looks at the value of the formula; and Condition, which evaluates the formula's result using the condition entered as the search string.

Direction—This option determines whether Quattro searches the block on a row-by-row basis or on a column-by-column basis. The two choices are Row and Column.

Match—This option determines if a cell containing the search string can have additional characters before or after the string. If this option is set to Part, Quattro will find cells that contain the search string even if the cell contains additional information before or after the search string. If this option is set to Whole, Quattro will only find cells that contain the search string but do not contain additional characters.

Case Sensitive—This option determines whether a potential match must have the same case as the search string. If you select Exact Case, the string in the block must have the same case as the search string. If you select Any Case, the string in the block must have the same letters as the search string but they can be in upper- or lowercase.

Options Reset—This option removes the search and replace string and resets the other options to the defaults of Formula for Look In, Row for Direction, Part for Match, and Any Case for Case Sensitive.

Next—This option performs the search and replace using the options specified with the other selections. This option starts at the selector's position and works toward the end of the block before starting at the beginning of the block and working to the selector's position. As Quattro finds the search string, it prompts for the action to take. The choices are Yes, No, All, Edit, and Quit. Selecting Yes replaces the search string with the replace string and moves to the next occurrence of the search string. Selecting No moves to the next occurrence of the search string. Selecting All replaces all occurrences of the search string with the replacement string without prompting for confirmation. Selecting Edit lets you edit the current cell without replacing the search string or disrupting the /Edit Search & Replace command. Selecting Quit aborts the command and returns to the READY mode. This option has a shortcut, CTRL-N, which you can press from the READY mode.

Previous—This option performs the search and replace using the options specified with the other selections. This option starts at the selector's position and works toward the beginning of the block before starting at the end of the block and working to the selector's position. As Quattro finds the search string, it prompts for the action to take. The selections to choose from are the same as for the Next option. This option has a shortcut, CTRL-P, which you can press from the READY mode.

Quit—This option leaves the Search & Replace menu and returns to the READY mode without performing a search and replace.

/EDIT TRANSPOSE

This command copies entries stored in a row or column to the reverse orientation. When you select this command, you need to specify the Source block you are copying from and the Destination block you are copying to. The Source and Destination blocks do not have to be in the same spreadsheets although the Destination block must be in an open spreadsheet.

OPTIONS
None.

NOTE
This command cannot copy formulas containing relative references because Quattro does not correctly adjust relative cell references in the formulas. However you can edit the formulas and change all the relative address references to absolute references before invoking the command.

/EDIT UNDO

This command removes the effect of the last "undo-able" command that you performed. This command only works after you enable undo with the /Options Other Undo Enable command. The /Edit Undo command cannot undo all of the actions you perform with Quattro.

This command acts as a toggle switch. The first time you execute the command, Quattro shows the spreadsheet without the effect of the last undo-able command. When you execute this command or press ALT-F5 (UNDO), Quattro shows the spreadsheet with the effect of the last undo-able command.

OPTIONS
None.

NOTE
This command has a shortcut, ALT-F5 (UNDO), which you can press instead of entering /Edit Undo. Another method of removing the effects of previous actions is with the Transcript utility.

/EDIT VALUES

This command converts the formulas in a block of cells to values in the same block of cells or to different block of cells. The converted entries contain values rather than formulas.

OPTIONS
When you select this command, Quattro prompts you for the Source block containing the formulas. You can specify this block of cells by typing the cell addresses or by pointing to the block that Quattro highlights. You specify the Destination block that will contain the converted entries using the same methods. The Source and Destination blocks do not have to be in the same spreadsheets although the Destination block must be in an open spreadsheet.

NOTE
If you want to convert a formula to a value for a single cell, press F2 (EDIT) to enter Edit mode, F9 (CALC) to calculate the results, and ENTER to finalize the value. You can also click Calc in the SpeedBar instead of pressing F9 (CALC).

/FILE CLOSE

This command closes the current window and moves the selector to another window. If the spreadsheet contains changes that you have not saved, Quattro will prompt you to confirm that you want to close the window. Closing a window does not affect the size or position of the remaining windows. If the window that you are closing is the last remaining window, the desktop area will be blank and only File will appear in the Menu bar with only a few of the menu options listed. If you are using a mouse, you can also close a window by clicking the upper-left corner of the window.

OPTIONS
None.

/FILE CLOSE ALL

This command closes all windows. If any spreadsheet windows contain unsaved changes, Quattro prompts you to confirm that you want to close the window. Once the windows are closed, the desktop area will be blank and only File will appear in the Menu bar with only a few of the menu options listed.

OPTIONS
None.

/FILE DIRECTORY

This command specifies the disk directory that Quattro uses when saving and retrieving files. Quattro uses this directory only during the current session. To permanently change the directory in which Quattro looks for your files, use the /Options Startup Directory and the /Options Update commands. You can override this command setting by supplying a different drive and directory when you save or create this.

OPTIONS
Type the drive and directory to use, and press ENTER.

/FILE ERASE

This command erases the entire current spreadsheet from memory without affecting any files on disk.

OPTIONS
If the spreadsheet has unsaved changes, Quattro prompts you to confirm whether you want to erase the spreadsheet and lose the changes. If you select Yes, Quattro erases the entire spreadsheet. If you select No, Quattro cancels the command.

/FILE EXIT

This command closes the open windows and then exits from Quattro into DOS. As Quattro closes spreadsheet windows, Quattro will prompt for an action to take if the current spreadsheet window contains unsaved changes.

OPTIONS
You have three choices when a spreadsheet window has unsaved changes.

Yes—This option closes the window without saving the current spreadsheet window.

No—This option cancels the /File Exit command. Any windows that are closed before you select No remain closed.

Save & Exit—This option performs the /**File** **S**ave command for the current spreadsheet and then closes it before closing the next open window.

NOTE

You can also perform this command by pressing CTRL-X.

/FILE NEW

This command opens a new spreadsheet window with an empty unnamed spreadsheet in the window. To activate this command press / and select **File** **N**ew. The new file is named SHEET followed by the next lowest unused sheet number until you save or erase the file. Quattro will assign the new spreadsheet window an unused window number. Quattro can have up to 32 windows open at once although your computer's memory may lower that limit.

OPTIONS

None.

NOTE

Be sure to save any unnamed spreadsheets before you save the spreadsheets that contain formulas to those spreadsheets so Quattro can replace the SHEET# references with the correct file name.

/FILE OPEN

This command opens a new spreadsheet window and loads a file into the window. This command is different from / **File** **R**etrieve, since it adds the spreadsheet window to the windows open in Quattro Pro rather than replacing the spreadsheet in the spreadsheet window with another spreadsheet. Quattro can have up to 32 windows open at once, although your computer's memory may lower that limit.

OPTIONS

After you select this command, you must select the file you want to use. If the file is not stored in Quattro's format, you must include the file extension with the file name. By specifying a different extension, Quattro can retrieve compressed, 1-2-3, dBASE, Multiplan, Paradox, Reflex, Surpass, and Symphony files. If the file is a Release 2.2 file that contains links to other spreadsheets, Quattro converts it to its own format.

From the file selection box Quattro Pro displays, you can highlight the file you want and press ENTER, or you can click the file. You can use the arrow keys, PGUP, PGDN, HOME, and END to move through the file list as well as using the mouse with the scroll bar. You can use key combinations and the buttons in the file selection box to make selecting the file easier. Pressing BACKSPACE or selecting the ..\ button displays the files in the parent directory. Pressing the GRAY + or selecting the +/- button adds the file sizes, times, and dates to the display. You can press the GRAY - or select the +/- button again to remove this information.

Pressing F3 (CHOICES) or selecting the ↑/↓ button expands the box to fill more of the screen. Repeating this shrinks the box to its original size. The remaining three buttons do not have key equivalents, but you can select these buttons as well as the three previously mentioned ones by typing /, using the arrow keys to select a button, and pressing ENTER. You can choose the DRV button to change the drive of the files listed in the file selection box. You can select PRV and select one of the nine previously selected files. You can select the NET button to select one of the mapped network drives.

You can also press F2 (EDIT), and Quattro displays a Search for prompt. You can type one or more characters and press ENTER to have Quattro Pro search for files that start with those characters. Once you select the file, Quattro Pro opens the file, converting it from its current format if necessary. If the spreadsheet file has an attached Allways, WYSIWYG, or Impress format file, Quattro Pro will prompt if you want to bring the file into Quattro Pro and format the selected spreadsheet. If you open a 1-2-3 Release 3 (and 1-2-3 for Windows) spreadsheet that has multiple sheets, Quattro Pro will let you open the spreadsheet but it will split each sheet in the file to a separate spreadsheet in Quattro Pro. Each file uses up to the first six characters of the spreadsheet name and then adds letters A through Z and AA through AF for each sheet that Quattro Pro splits into a different file.

NOTE

You can also open a file from the File Manager window by moving the active cursor to a file and pressing ENTER. When you do this, Quattro opens a new spreadsheet window containing the file you selected.

/FILE RETRIEVE

This command retrieves a file that you have saved before and places the file in the current spreadsheet window. This command leaves the files in the other spreadsheet windows intact.

OPTIONS

The options for this command are the same as the /File Open command except if the current spreadsheet has unsaved changes. If so, you are prompted for whether you want to lose your changes. You can select Yes to lose your changes and display the file selection box or select No to cancel the command.

/FILE SAVE

This command saves a file. If the file is unnamed, Quattro prompts for a file name. If the file has been saved before, Quattro uses the same file name to save the file again. To use this command, press / and select File Save. If the file has not been saved before, Quattro displays a menu of file names. You can type a name or select one of the existing names using the arrow keys or a mouse before pressing ENTER.

If the file has not been saved before and you type a new file name, Quattro saves the file. If the file has not been saved before and you selected an existing file name or you are saving a file you have saved before, Quattro prompts if you want to Cancel, Replace, or Backup. Selecting Cancel cancels the /File Save command. Selecting Replace saves the current spreadsheet using the selected name. Selecting Backup renames the spreadsheet saved in the file to have a .BAK extension and then saves the current spreadsheet using the selected name. Quattro automatically adds a .WQ1 extension to a new file name if you do not provide one.

OPTIONS

By specifying an extension other than .WQ1, Quattro saves the file in another format. This feature allows Quattro to save files for 1-2-3, dBASE, Harvard Graphics Multiplan, Paradox, Reflex, Surpass, and Symphony as well as a compressed file for these formats. If you use a .DB, .DB2, .DBF, .R2D, or .RXD extension, Quattro prompts you for the information it needs to convert the spreadsheet into a database file.

You can also make a new spreadsheet password-protected by putting a space and a P at the end of the file name. If you add these two characters, Quattro prompts you for the password twice to verify that you typed it correctly. To password protect a spreadsheet you have saved before, use the /File Save As command.

If you are saving a file with a .WK1 extension and the file has formulas that contain references to other files, Quattro displays an additional prompt asking for how you want the cells containing links saved. You can select No to cancel the command, Yes to save the file and save the formulas with links as their values instead of their formula, or Use 2.2 Syntax. This last option converts formulas that only contain a link reference to a cell in another spreadsheet to use the 1-2-3 Release 2.2 syntax. Other formulas that are more complex than 1-2-3 Release 2.2 uses are saved as their values rather than the formulas.

NOTE

This command's shortcut is CTRL-S, which is equivalent to entering /File Save.

/FILE SAVE ALL

This Quattro Pro 3 and 4 command saves all open files as if you selected the /File Save command for each open spreadsheet.

OPTIONS

This command has the same options as the /File Save command described above, except they are repeated for each open spreadsheet.

/FILE SAVE AS

This command saves a file after letting you alter the file name if you have saved the file before. If the file has not been saved before, Quattro prompts for a file name. If the file has been saved before, Quattro uses the same file name to save the file again. Pressing ESC changes these prompts to list all of the spreadsheet files in the current directory. If the file has been saved before, you can alter the file name by pressing F2 (EDIT) and making changes to the file name. You can type a name or select one of the existing names using the arrow keys or a mouse before pressing ENTER. If the file has not been saved before and you type a new file name, Quattro saves the file. If the file has not been saved before and you select an existing file name or you are saving a file you have saved before, Quattro prompts if you want to Cancel, Replace, or Backup. Selecting Cancel cancels the /File Save As command. Selecting Replace saves the current spreadsheet using the selected name. Selecting Backup renames the spreadsheet saved in the file to have a .BAK extension and then saves the current spreadsheet using the selected name. Quattro automatically adds a .WQ1 extension to a new file name if you do not provide one.

OPTIONS

This command has the same options as the /File Save command described above.

/FILE UTILITIES DOS SHELL

This command allows you to use DOS temporarily without exiting from Quattro. Your Quattro spreadsheet remains in memory while you are executing DOS commands or running another program. When you select the /File Utilities DOS Shell command, an operating system prompt appears. To return to the spreadsheet, type **Exit** and press ENTER. Quattro returns you to the spreadsheet that was current before the temporary DOS exit.

OPTIONS
None.

NOTE
Many of the file commands that were performed using a temporary exit to the operating system in other spreadsheet packages can be performed using Quattro's File Manager. In Quattro Pro 3 and 4, you have the additional option of performing a single command and then returning to Quattro Pro by entering the DOS command to perform rather than just pressing ENTER to use the full DOS Shell.

/FILE UTILITIES FILE MANAGER

This command opens a File Manager window that you can use to perform file manipulations. A File Manager window is assigned the next unused window number.

OPTIONS

The File Manager menu is similar to Quattro's and is covered after the spreadsheet window commands.

/FILE UTILITIES SQZ!

This command defines several settings Quattro uses when it saves files in the compressed SQZ! format.

OPTIONS

Remove Blanks—This option determines whether Quattro saves blank labels and format settings for blank cells. The choices for this option are Yes and No.

Storage of Values—This option determines whether Quattro saves the values of formulas with the formulas. Since Quattro recalculates formulas when it retrieves a file, omitting the values from the squeezed file does not damage the spreadsheet. The choices for this option are Exact, Approximate, and Remove. Exact stores the value with the formula, up to 15 places. Approximate stores the value with the formula, up to seven places. Remove stores the formula but does not store the value.

Version—This option determines whether Quattro saves a squeezed file using SQZ! or SQZ! Plus. While SQZ! Plus is more efficient and works with many packages, use SQZ! if you are using the squeezed file in 1-2-3 or Symphony.

Quit—This option returns you to the READY mode.

/FILE WORKSPACE RESTORE

This command opens spreadsheet and File Manager windows and puts the spreadsheets and File Manager window settings in the appropriate windows. This command quickly positions all the windows you had open when you saved the workspace with /File Workspace Save.

OPTIONS

When you enter this command, Quattro lists the workspace names that you can select; or you can type a workspace name, and press ENTER.

/FILE WORKSPACE SAVE

This command saves the size and position of all open windows as well as the file names of the spreadsheet windows and the control pane settings of the File Manager windows. This treats a set of spreadsheets and File Manager windows that you can use as a group instead of retrieving and adding each window separately.

OPTIONS

When you enter this command, Quattro prompts for a workspace name. You can select an existing workspace name or type a new file name and press ENTER. Do not include an extension, since Quattro adds a .WSP extension to the file name.

/GRAPH ANNOTATE

This command activates the Graph Annotator. The Graph Annotator lets you customize the graph by modifying any element on the graph and by adding new ones.

OPTIONS

The Graph Annotator has its own menu options. The menu is primarily icon-based, and provides a visual image of each menu option's function. Chapter 7 covers the different options you can use with the Graph Annotator.

NOTE

You can also activate the Graph Annotator when you are viewing a graph by typing /.

/GRAPH CUSTOMIZE SERIES BAR WIDTH

This command determines the portion of the x-axis that Quattro uses for bars in a bar, stacked bar, rotated bar, 3-D bar, 3-D ribbon, or 3-D step graph, leaving the remaining area of the x-axis to separate the data points. You can also select the bar width from the Graph Customize dialog box by selecting **B**ar width when that option appears (it only appears for graph types that use the setting).

OPTION

The only option for this command is the percentage you enter when you enter this command. The percentage you enter must be between 20 and 90 percent. This is the percentage of the x-axis that Quattro uses for bars in bar, stacked bar, and rotated bar graphs. The difference between this percentage and 100 percent is the portion of the x-axis Quattro uses to separate the bars.

/GRAPH CUSTOMIZE SERIES BUBBLES

This Quattro Pro 4 command sets customization options, which apply solely to bubble graphs.

OPTIONS

Colors—This option sets the colors used for the bubbles. Quattro Pro automatically assigns the first nine bubbles different colors, but you can change the color assignments. Quattro uses these selections for the second nine slices and so forth. First, select **1**st Bubble through **9**th Bubble to select the bubble to change, and then select a color from the list of colors or color palette Quattro Pro displays. Repeat this step for each bubble color you want to change, and then select **Q**uit to return to this command's list of options. To set the color from the Graph Customize dialog box (only when the graph type is already Bubble), select **B**ubble, then **1** through **9** for the bubble to change, and then select a color from the list below **C**olor.

Patterns—This option sets the fill patterns used for the bubbles. Quattro Pro automatically assigns the first nine fill patterns, but you can change them. Quattro uses these selections for the second nine bubbles and so forth. First, select **1**st Bubble through **9**th Bubble to select the bubble to change, and then select a pattern from the list or palette Quattro Pro displays. Repeat this step for each bubble you want to change, and then select **Q**uit to return to this command's list of options. To set the fill pattern from the Graph Customize dialog box, select **B**ubble, then **1** through 9 for the bubble to change, and then select a pattern from the list below Fill Pattern.

Max Bubble Size—This option sets the maximum percentage of the x-axis that a bubble may be. You can set the size of the largest bubble, and Quattro Pro will proportionally size the other bubbles in the graph. Type a number between 1 and 25 for the maximum percentage of the x-axis the bubble may occupy, and press ENTER. To set the maximum bubble size in the Graph Customize dialog box, select **Max Bubble Size** and type the percentage for the bubble size.

Quit—This option returns to the Customize Series menu.

/GRAPH CUSTOMIZE SERIES COLORS

This command sets the color Quattro uses to represent each series for all graphs except text, pie, column, and bubble. This command presents a menu to select the data series whose color you want to change. When you have chosen the series to change, Quattro lists in a selection box or displays the available colors in a gallery. The appearance of the colors you select depends on the hardware you are using. Select the color that you want and press ENTER. You can also select the colors for a series when you see the Graph Customize dialog box after selecting /Graph Customize Series. First, select **Series** and the series you want to set the color. Next, select one of the colors named under **Color**.

OPTIONS

1st Series—This option sets the color for the first series.
2nd Series—This option sets the color for the second series.
3rd Series—This option sets the color for the third series.
4th Series—This option sets the color for the fourth series.
5th Series—This option sets the color for the fifth series.
6th Series—This option sets the color for the sixth series.
Quit—This option returns you to the Customize Series menu.

/GRAPH CUSTOMIZE SERIES FILL PATTERNS

This command sets the fill pattern Quattro uses to represent the data points for each series in area, bar, rotated bar, stacked bar, and 3-D graphs. This command presents a menu from which to select the data series whose pattern you want to change. When you have chosen the series that you want to change, Quattro lists in a selection box or displays in a gallery the 16 types of fill patterns available. Select the fill pattern that you want to use, and press ENTER. You also can select the fill patterns for a series when you see the Graph Customize dialog box after selecting /Graph Customize Series. First, select **Series** and the series you want to set the fill pattern. Next, select one of the pattern descriptions listed under **Fill Pattern**.

OPTIONS
1st Series—This option sets the fill patterns for the first series.
2nd Series—This option sets the fill patterns for the second series.
3rd Series—This option sets the fill patterns for the third series.
4th Series—This option sets the fill patterns for the fourth series.
5th Series—This option sets the fill patterns for the fifth series.
6th Series—This option sets the fill patterns for the sixth series.
Quit—This option returns you to the Customize Series menu.

/GRAPH CUSTOMIZE SERIES INTERIOR LABELS

This command labels the data points in a graph. These labels can be labels or numbers. Quattro assigns the block defined for a series' labels sequentially to the data points. Quattro displays the labels as they appear on the spreadsheet. This command controls the placement of the labels in relation to the data points. If the graph has many data points, the data point labels can overlap causing a blurred image. This command does not affect area and 3-D area graphs that cannot display labels. It also does not affect pie and column graphs. For bar and three-dimensional bar graphs, Quattro places the labels above the data points. For rotated bar graphs, Quattro places the labels to the right of the data points. For stacked bar graphs, Quattro can only display the labels for the top series of data. You also can add interior labels to a series from the Graph Customize dialog box available after selecting /Graph Customize Series. Select Series and the series you want to add or change the interior labels. Next, choose Interior Label Block.

OPTIONS
1st Series—This option defines the labels for the first series.
2nd Series—This option defines the labels for the second series.
3rd Series—This option defines the labels for the third series.
4th Series—This option defines the labels for the fourth series.
5th Series—This option defines the labels for the fifth series.
6th Series—This option defines the labels for the sixth series.
Quit—This option returns you to the Customize Series menu.
Each of these options (except Quit) has the following options:
Center—This option places the labels on the data points.
Left—This option places the labels to the left of the data points.
Above—This option places the labels above the data points.
Right—This option places the labels to the right of the data points.
Below—This option places the labels below the data points.
None—This option removes the data labels from the graph. It does not remove the setting for the current labels selected for the series.

NOTE
If your graph uses the /Graph Series Analyze command and you want to label the graphed data points with their values, you will want to use the Table option

(available after you select a series) to copy the calculated values to the spreadsheet. Then you can use this command to choose the block created with **/Graph Series Analyze** as the block for interior labels.

/GRAPH CUSTOMIZE SERIES MARKERS & LINES FORMATS

This command determines how Quattro represents each data series. This command first presents a menu from which to select the data series whose format you want to change. When you have chosen a series, Quattro displays a menu to select **Lines, Symbols, Both,** or **Neither.** A series using only lines has lines connecting the data points. A series using symbols marks each data point with a symbol. A series using both marks each data point with a symbol and connects the data points with a line. A series using Neither does not use symbols or lines. This option can be combined with the **/Graph Customize Series Interior Labels** to display the data points as their values instead of symbols. To set the format of a series using the Graph Customize dialog box, select **Series** and the series number. Next, choose Format and then from Lines, Symbols, Both, or Neither.

OPTIONS

1st Series—This option sets the format for the first series.
2nd Series—This option sets the format for the second series.
3rd Series—This option sets the format for the third series.
4th Series—This option sets the format for the fourth series.
5th Series—This option sets the format for the fifth series.
6th Series—This option sets the format for the sixth series.
Quit—This option exits the menu and returns you to the Markers & Lines menu.

/GRAPH CUSTOMIZE SERIES MARKERS & LINES LINE STYLES

This command changes the style of the lines Quattro uses to connect the data points for each series. This command presents a menu from which to select the data series for which you want to change the marker. When you have chosen the series to change, Quattro lists descriptions or displays the eight types of line styles. Select the marker that you want, and press ENTER. To set the line style of a series using the Graph Customize dialog box, select the series by choosing **Series** and the series number. Next, choose Line Style and one of the line styles listed below.

OPTIONS

1st Series—This option sets the line styles for the first series.
2nd Series—This option sets the line styles for the second series.
3rd Series—This option sets the line styles for the third series.
4th Series—This option sets the line styles for the fourth series.

5th Series—This option sets the line styles for the fifth series.
6th Series—This option sets the line styles for the sixth series.
Quit—This option exits the menu and returns you to the Markers & Lines menu.

/GRAPH CUSTOMIZE SERIES MARKERS & LINES MARKERS

This command changes the symbol Quattro uses to represent the data points for each series. This command presents a menu to select the data series for which you want to change the marker. When you have chosen the series that you want to change, Quattro lists the 10 types of markers available or displays them in a gallery of styles to select from. Select the marker that you want to use, and press ENTER. To set a series' marker using the Graph Customize dialog box, select **Series** and the series number. Next, choose **Marker** and one of the markers listed below.

OPTIONS
1st Series—This option sets the markers for the first series.
2nd Series—This option sets the markers for the second series.
3rd Series—This option sets the markers for the third series.
4th Series—This option sets the markers for the fourth series.
5th Series—This option sets the markers for the fifth series.
6th Series—This option sets the markers for the sixth series.
Quit—This option exits the menu and returns you to the Markers & Lines menu.

/GRAPH CUSTOMIZE SERIES MARKERS & LINES QUIT

This command returns Quattro to the Customize Series menu from the Markers & Lines menu.

OPTIONS
None.

/GRAPH CUSTOMIZE SERIES OVERRIDE TYPE

This command lets you graph a series on top of the graph selected by the /Graph Graph Type command. You can use this command to produce a combination graph of up to three graphs. The types of graphs that Quattro can combine are line, bar, and XY graph types. First, the /Graph Graph Type command must select one of these graph types. To create an overriding graph, type /, select **Graph Customize Series Override Type**, select the series that you want graphed separately, and select bar, line, or default to represent the type of graph. If you are using dialog boxes, select /**Graph Customize**, then **Series** and the graph that you want to assign to a different graph type. Next select Override and overriding type of graph that series will use. For each series for which you do not override the default graph type, Quattro continues to use the graph type selected with the /Graph Graph Type command. To remove the overriding graph, enter /Graph Customize Series Override Type, select the series that uses an overriding graph type, and select Default.

OPTIONS

1st Series—This option sets the graph type for the first series as an overriding graph.

2nd Series—This option sets the graph type for the second series as an overriding graph.

3rd Series—This option sets the graph type for the third series as an overriding graph.

4th Series—This option sets the graph type for the fourth series as an overriding graph.

5th Series—This option sets the graph type for the fifth series as an overriding graph.

6th Series—This option sets the graph type for the sixth series as an overriding graph.

Quit—This option returns you to the Customize Series menu.

NOTE

If an XY graph is to be one of the graph types, this must be the default graph type. If you are using the Graph Customize dialog box, you can customize the overriding graph type by temporarily changing the default graph to the overriding graph type, customizing the overriding graph, and then returning the default graph type to its previous setting.

/GRAPH CUSTOMIZE SERIES PIES COLORS

This command determines the colors used for pie slices and column sections. Quattro automatically assigns the first nine slices different colors. Quattro uses the same colors for the second nine slices, and so on.

OPTIONS

When you select this option, you must select the slice or section whose color you want to change. Once you have selected a slice or section, you must select the color from the list or gallery. When you have finished selecting colors, select Quit to return to the Pies menu. To set the color of a pie slice from the Graph Customize dialog box available by selecting /Graph Customize Series, select Slice, the slice you want to change, and one of the colors listed below Color.

/GRAPH CUSTOMIZE SERIES PIES EXPLODE

This command determines if Quattro explodes any of the pie slices. Quattro moves exploded pie slices away from the center of the pie to emphasize them. Quattro can only explode the first nine pie slices using the menu. Once you have selected a pie slice, you must select between Don't Explode and Explode. This command does not affect column graphs.

OPTIONS

With this command, your options are which pie slice you select and whether that pie slice is exploded. Select Explode to explode the chosen pie slice or Don't Explode to return the pie slice to the center. When you have finished selecting pie slices, select Quit to return to the Pies menu. To explode a pie slice using the Graph Customize dialog box, select Slice, the slice you want to explode, Explode, and Explode or Don't Explode.

NOTE

You can also explode pie slices by assigning a second series of data. The slices that have corresponding values in the second series greater than 100 will be exploded.

/GRAPH CUSTOMIZE SERIES PIES LABEL FORMAT

This command sets the format of the first series values that labels each slice of the pie chart or each section of the column graph. Quattro displays the label in parenthesis between the pie slice or column section and the appropriate X series label. To set the label format using the Graph Customize dialog box, select Label Format.

OPTIONS

The options for this command determine how the first series values display. The choices are Value, %, $, and None. Value displays the value of each point in the data series as it would display with a general format. % displays the percentage of the value in relation to the total rounded to the nearest percent. $ displays the values rounded to the nearest integer. None hides the labels.

/GRAPH CUSTOMIZE SERIES PIES PATTERNS

This command determines the fill patterns used for the pie slices or column segments. The patterns selected for the first nine slices or sections also apply to the second nine slices or sections.

OPTIONS

When you enter this command, you must select the slice or segment whose fill pattern you want to change. Once you have selected a pie slice, you must select the fill pattern from the list or gallery. When you have finished selecting fill patterns, select Quit to return to the Pies menu. To set the pattern of a pie slice from the Graph Customize dialog box available by selecting /Graph Customize Series, select Slice, the slice you want to change, and one of the patterns listed below Fill Pattern.

/GRAPH CUSTOMIZE SERIES PIES QUIT

This command returns you to the Customize Series menu from the Pies menu.

OPTIONS
None.

/GRAPH CUSTOMIZE SERIES PIES TICK MARKS

This command hides or displays the connecting lines between the pie slices or column sections and their descriptive labels. To add or remove tick marks using the Graph Customize dialog box, select **Tick Marks**.

OPTIONS
The options for this command determine if the tick marks appear. If you select **Yes**, the lines connecting the slice or section labels to the slice or section will appear. If you select **No**, the lines connecting the slice or section labels to the slice or section will disappear.

/GRAPH CUSTOMIZE SERIES QUIT

This command leaves the Customize Series menu and returns you to the Graph menu. The Graph Customize dialog box has **Q**uit to perform this function.

/GRAPH CUSTOMIZE SERIES RESET

This command resets graph settings to their default settings. You can select between the entire graph or any one of the series. You can also reset part or all of the graph settings when you are using dialog boxes by selecting **Reset** in the Graph Customize dialog box.

OPTIONS
1st Series—This option resets all graph settings for the first series and other settings that the first series uses.

2nd Series—This option resets all graph settings for the second series and other settings that the second series uses.

3rd Series—This option resets all graph settings for the third series and other settings that the third series uses.

4th Series—This option resets all graph settings for the fourth series and other settings that the fourth series uses.

5th Series—This option resets all graph settings for the fifth series and other settings that the fifth series uses.

6th Series—This option resets all graph settings for the sixth series and other settings that the sixth series uses.

X-Axis Series—This option resets the graph settings and block assigned to the x-axis.

Graph—This option resets all graph settings to their defaults, removes the block addresses of the series, and removes the graph's text.

Quit—This option leaves the Reset menu and returns you to the Customize Series menu or Graph Customize dialog box.

/GRAPH CUSTOMIZE SERIES UPDATE

This command saves the graph customization settings. Since this command is also equivalent to the /Options Update command, it also saves the settings made in the top half of the Options menu. You can also update the graph settings when you are using dialog boxes by selecting Update in the Graph Customize dialog box.

OPTIONS
None.

/GRAPH CUSTOMIZE SERIES Y-AXIS

This command assigns which data series use the primary y-axis and which data series use the secondary y-axis. When you enter this command, Quattro prompts you for the data series you want to assign to an axis. Once you select the data series, Quattro prompts for which y-axis you want the selected data series to use. To set which y-axis a series uses from the Graph Customize dialog box, choose Series and the series you want to set the y-axis. Next, select Y-Axis and then either Primary or Secondary.

OPTIONS

1st Series—This option selects which y-axis the first series uses.
2nd Series—This option selects which y-axis the second series uses.
3rd Series—This option selects which y-axis the third series uses.
4th Series—This option selects which y-axis the fourth series uses.
5th Series—This option selects which y-axis the fifth series uses.
6th Series—This option selects which y-axis the sixth series uses.
Quit—This option returns you to the Customize Series menu.

/GRAPH FAST GRAPH

This command creates a quick graph using data in a spreadsheet block. The fast graph uses the current graph settings including graph type and legend position. When you enter this command, Quattro prompts for the block containing the data to graph. Quattro analyzes the block to determine how to divide the data into the information the graph will use.

If the block uses more columns than rows, Quattro divides the data according to rows. If the first row contains labels, the row of labels becomes the x-axis data. If the first column contains labels, the first column of labels becomes the legend text. When the block contains data that Quattro uses as legends or x-axis labels, Quattro divides the remainder of the block into the first through sixth series according to rows. If the block does not contain text that Quattro uses as legends or x-axis labels, Quattro uses the entire block for the data series divided according to rows.

If the block uses more rows than columns, Quattro divides the data according to columns. If the first column contains labels, the first column of labels becomes the x-axis data. If the first row contains labels, the first row of labels becomes the legend text. When the block contains data that Quattro uses as legends or x-axis labels, Quattro divides the remainder of the block into the first through sixth series according to columns. If the block does not contain text that Quattro uses as legends or x-axis labels, Quattro uses the entire block for the data series divided according to columns.

OPTIONS

The only option for this command is the block you select to graph.

NOTE

You can also perform this command by pressing CTRL-G and selecting the block to graph.

/GRAPH GRAPH TYPE

The /Graph Graph Type command selects the type of graph Quattro uses when it displays your spreadsheet data. Quattro has 11 graph types. The default is a stacked bar graph. Quattro lets you change from one type of graph to another. If you are using dialog boxes (/Options Startup Use Dialogs is set to Yes), when you select /Graph Customize Series, Quattro Pro will display the dialog box that contains the customization options that are appropriate for the graph type you select.

OPTIONS

Line—A line graph consists of a line that connects the points for each series of data on the graph. Quattro can plot up to six series values against the y-axis.

Bar—A bar graph has horizontal bars whose height is determined by the value of the data points in the series measured against the y-axis scale. Each series, up to six, has a different fill pattern or color. The series are placed next to each other for each point on the x-axis.

XY—An XY graph plots the values in up to six series against the values in a one series. Both the x-axis and y-axis are numeric values. Markers indicate each data point and lines connect the points in each series.

Stacked Bar—The stacked bar graph places each value of up to six series on top of the values from other series for each point on the x-axis. Each series has a different fill pattern or color.

Pie—A pie chart shows one series of values with each value in the series represented as a wedge in the pie. Each wedge is in proportion to the percentage each value is of the total of all the values in the series. If you select this option, Quattro only graphs the first series of data. Pie charts have different customization options than other graph types.

Area—The area graph uses lines to graph up to six series on top of another and fills the area between the lines with a different fill pattern or color. The first series is on the bottom, and the graph works upward for the succeeding series.

Rotated Bar—The rotated bar graph is a bar graph that has the x-axis as the vertical axis and the y-axis as the horizontal.

Column—The column graph is like a pie chart since it shows each value's proportion to the total. Instead of a circle the column graph uses a column with the entire column representing the total of the column sections. This graph type only graphs the first data series. Column graphs use the same customization options as pie graphs.

High-Low—The High-Low-Open-Close graph creates a graph that is frequently used for financial commodities and statistical data. For each data point, the first data series represents the high value, the second series represents the low value, the third data series represents the open value, and the fourth series represents the close value. Quattro draws a line from the high value to the low value with a line branching to the left for the open value and a line branching to the right for the close value. The fifth and sixth data series are plotted as line graphs.

Text—The text graph is a blank graph that does not use most of the options in the Graph menu. The text graph is primarily for creating custom drawings or text screens with the Graph Annotator.

Bubble—A bubble graph creates bubbles of different sizes in different places of the x-axis and y-axis to represent the combination of each of the values in the x-axis, first and second series. This graph type is new to Quattro Pro 4 and does not use the third through sixth series. For each bubble, the x-axis value determines its horizontal position, the first series value determines the vertical position of the bubble's center, and the second series value determines the bubble's size.

3-D Graphs—The 3-D Graphs is a collection of four graph types, which are three-dimensional enhancements of other graph types. After selecting 3-D Graphs, select Bar, Ribbon, Step, or Area. These graph types put the different series in front of each other instead of side by side (or on top of each other as in line graphs). **Bar** creates a three-dimensional bar graph. Ribbon creates a three-dimensional line graph. Step is like bar, except the bars for each series are adjoining. Area creates a three-dimensional area graph.

/GRAPH HIDE

This command removes an inserted graph from the spreadsheet. When you enter this command, Quattro displays a list of the graphs inserted into the spreadsheet. Once you select the name of the graph or <Current Graph> to remove the current graph and press ENTER, Quattro removes the graph from the spreadsheet and displays any information that the inserted graph hid.

OPTIONS

The only option for this command is the name of the graph to hide.

/GRAPH INSERT

This command inserts a graph into the spreadsheet. When you enter this command, Quattro prompts you for the graph name to insert into the spreadsheet. You can select a named graph or <Current Graph> to insert the current graph. A graph can only be in a spreadsheet in one position. Once you select a graph, Quattro prompts for a block to place the graph. Enter a block name or address where Quattro will place the graph. When a spreadsheet contains an inserted graph and the selector is on a cell containing the inserted graph, the graph name appears in the input line. If Quattro is set to display in WYSIWYG mode, the graph will appear. If Quattro is displaying the spreadsheet using a text mode, the block containing the graph will appear in a different color or attribute. When the print block for the /Print Block command contains an inserted graph, Quattro will print the graph if the destination is a binary file or a graphics printer. Quattro rescales the text in the graph to fit the dimensions of the block if /Options Hardware Printers Fonts Autoscale is set to Yes. If this command is set to No, the text in the graph uses the literal size selected with the /Graph Text Font command.

To change the block containing the graph, enter the /Graph Insert command and select the named graph that you want to resize. When Quattro highlights the block containing the graph, you can enter a new block address or name, or change the current block dimensions using the arrow keys.

OPTIONS

The only option for this command is the name of the graph inserted and the location of the graph.

/GRAPH NAME AUTOSAVE EDITS

This command sets Quattro Pro 3 and above to save all changes made to the currently named graph or to only save a named graph and its settings when the /Graph Name Create command is used.

OPTIONS

This command has two options. Yes sets Quattro Pro to save all graph changes to the currently named graph whenever you execute the /Graph Name Display, /Graph Name Autosave Edits, /Graph Name Erase, /Graph Name Slide, /Graph Name Graph Copy, /Graph View, or /Print Graph Print Name commands. No, the default, sets Quattro Pro to only save named graphs when you use the /Graph Name Create command.

/GRAPH NAME CREATE

This command assigns a name to the current set of graph specifications. It allows a spreadsheet to store multiple graphs. When you use this command, you must provide a graph name or select one from the box that Quattro displays. If you select an existing graph name, Quattro replaces the graph specifications referenced by this name with the current graph specifications. When the spreadsheet is saved, Quattro saves the named graphs and the related settings with the spreadsheet.

OPTIONS

The graph name that you provide for the named graph must follow the rules of block names.

NOTE

The named graph can only be used in the spreadsheet that named the graph. If you want a graph in another spreadsheet, you can copy a named graph to another spreadsheet with the /Graph Name Graph Copy command.

/GRAPH NAME DISPLAY

This command sets the current graph settings to one of the graphs named with the /Graph Name Create command. After activating a named graph, any changes made to the graph settings are not stored under the graph's name until you use the /Graph Name Create command again.

OPTIONS

When you use this command, you must type the name of the graph or point to it in the selection box. The named graph must be stored in the current spreadsheet. When you press ENTER, Quattro displays the graph.

/GRAPH NAME ERASE

This command removes one of the named graph settings from the current spreadsheet.

OPTIONS

When you use this command, Quattro prompts for the name of the graph to remove. Type the name of the graph, or point to it in the box that Quattro displays. When you press ENTER, Quattro deletes the graph.

/GRAPH NAME GRAPH COPY

This command copies a graph to another file. Both the file that contains the original graph and the file where the graph will be copied must be open before you use this command. Copying a graph copies the graph name, all the settings, and all objects added with the annotator. The ranges that the copied graph uses will refer to the original graph data used by the original graph which is normally in the same spreadsheet as the original graph.

OPTIONS

After selecting this command, you must select the named graph that you want to copy and then the file where you want it copied.

/GRAPH NAME RESET

This command removes all named graphs from a spreadsheet. It does not affect the data stored in the spreadsheet.

OPTIONS

When you execute this command, Quattro prompts for confirmation before removing all named graphs. Select **Yes** to remove the named graphs or **No** to cancel the command.

/GRAPH NAME SLIDE

This command creates a slide show. The slide show can include special effects such as transition between graphs, timed graph display, and sound effects.

OPTIONS

When you enter this command, Quattro prompts for a block containing graph names in the first column and the number of seconds the graph should appear in the second column. In Quattro Pro 3 and above, you can add a third column for a transition effect, a fourth column for the transition effect's speed, and a fifth column for the audio effect. Quattro displays each graph named in the block for the number of seconds specified in the adjacent cell. If a graph does not use the second column, Quattro displays the graph named in the first column until the user presses a key.

/GRAPH OVERALL BACKGROUND COLOR

This command sets the color that Quattro uses for the graph's background. The actual appearance on the graph will depend on the colors your screen can display or your printer can print.

OPTIONS

When you enter this command you must select a color from the list or from the gallery of colors. You can also set the background color by selecting a color under **Background** in the Graph Overall dialog box.

/GRAPH OVERALL COLOR/B&W

This command specifies whether the graph uses colors.

OPTIONS

Color—This option displays the graph in color using different colors to distinguish each series. This option is also selected when you choose Yes under Use Colors in the Graph Overall dialog box.

B&W—This option displays the graphs in monochrome, usually white lines on a black background. This option is also selected when you choose No under Use Colors in the Graph Overall dialog box.

/GRAPH OVERALL DROP SHADOW COLOR

This Quattro Pro 3 and 4 command sets the colors used as shadows for graph text that use the Drop Shadow font style added with the /Graph Text Font command. In the Graph Overall dialog box, you can select Drop Shadow to display the choices for drop shadow selections.

OPTIONS

This command has two sets of options. First, select the color that you want to set the drop shadow color for. Next, select the color that you want to be used as a shadow for graph text that displays in the first color you selected. Press ESC when you are finished selecting drop shadow colors.

/GRAPH OVERALL GRID

This command determines the type of grid Quattro adds to a graph and the colors Quattro uses for the graph.

OPTIONS

Horizontal—This option creates horizontal grid lines starting from the major tick marks on the y-axis. You can add these types of grid lines in the Graph Overall dialog box by selecting Grid and Horizontal.

Vertical—This option creates vertical grid lines starting from the major tick marks on the x-axis. You can add these types of grid lines in the Graph Overall dialog box by selecting Grid and Vertical.

Both—This option creates horizontal and vertical grid lines starting from the major tick marks on the y- and x-axes. You can add these types of grid lines in the Graph Overall dialog box by selecting Grid and Both.

Clear—This option removes existing grid lines. You can remove the grid lines in the Graph Overall dialog box by selecting Grid and Clear.

Grid Color—This option sets the color of the grid lines. You must select a color from the selection box or gallery. You can also set the Grid color by selecting a color under Grid in the Graph Overall dialog box.

Line Style—This option sets the line style of the grid lines. You must select a line style from the selection box or gallery. You can also set the line style by selecting one of the line options under Grid Line Style in the Graph Overall dialog box.

Fill Color—This option sets the color of the box containing the graph. You must select a color from the selection box or gallery. You can also set the fill color by selecting a color under Fill in the Graph Overall dialog box.

Quit—This option returns you to the Graph menu.

/GRAPH OVERALL OUTLINES

This command adds and removes outlines around the legend, the titles, or the entire graph. For each type of outline, you can select the type of line Quattro draws (Box, Double-line, Thick-line, Shadow, 3D, Rnd Rectangle or, in Quattro Pro 3 and above, Sculpted), or select None to remove the outline.

OPTIONS

Titles—This option determines the type of outline around the first and second line titles of the graph. You can also select the outline around the titles by selecting a line type under Titles in the Graph Overall dialog box.

Legend—This option determines the type of outline around the legend. You can also select the outline around the legend by selecting a line type under Legend in the Graph Overall dialog box.

Graph—This option determines the type of outline around the graph. You can also select the outline around the graph by selecting a line type under Graph in the Graph Overall dialog box.

Quit—This option returns you to the Graph menu.

/GRAPH OVERALL THREE-D

This command displays graphs with a three-dimensional effect or as a flat graph. This option affects bar, stacked bar, pie, rotated bar, and column graphs. The change made by this command creates different graphs from those created using the 3-D graph type. You can use this command with the 3-D graph types to produce a flat or 3-D appearance with these graphs.

OPTIONS

Yes—This option creates graphs with a three-dimensional effect. This is the same as selecting Add Depth and Yes in the Graph Overall dialog box.

No—This option creates graphs without a three-dimensional effect. This is the same as selecting Add Depth and No in the Graph Overall dialog box.

/GRAPH QUIT

This command leaves Quattro's Graph menu and returns you to the spreadsheet in the READY mode.

OPTIONS
None.

/GRAPH SERIES

This command defines the spreadsheet values to graph for each of the different series. For pie and column graphs, Quattro only uses the first series values. Bubble graphs only use the X-Axis Series and the 1st and 2nd Series. Text graphs do not use any of the series. Other graph types can use the X-Axis Series and the 1st through 6th Series. The values are specified as a block address or a block name. If the data for a graph series is in another spreadsheet, the file name of the spreadsheet containing the values must be included in brackets ([]).

OPTIONS

1st Series—This defines the spreadsheet values to use for the first series of data.

2nd Series—This defines the spreadsheet values to use for the second series of data.

3rd Series—This defines the spreadsheet values to use for the third series of data.

4th Series—This defines the spreadsheet values to use for the fourth series of data.

5th Series—This defines the spreadsheet values to use for the fifth series of data.

6th Series—This defines the spreadsheet values to use for the sixth series of data.

X-Axis Series—This defines the spreadsheet values to use for the x-axis. For pie charts and column graphs, the x-axis values are labels for the pie slices and column sections. For other graph types, these values label the x-axis.

Group—This defines the spreadsheet values for one or more series of data. When you select this option, Quattro prompts if you want to divide the block by **Columns** or **Rows**. After selecting how you want the block divided, Quattro prompts for a block containing graph data. Type the block address or name or point to the block and press ENTER. The first column or row is the first series, the second column or row is the second series and so on until Quattro assigns the sixth series or assigns all the data in the block. Selecting this option removes the previous settings for the other series.

Analyze—This option, new in Quattro Pro 4, processes the values you use in a series and uses the results of the calculations you perform on a series' values for the data values to graph. Once you select **Analyze**, you must select **X-Axis Series** or **1st Series** through **6th Series** for the series to set how the series values are analyzed to determine the data points in the graph. You can also select **All Series** to process all the graph's series in the same way (if the x-axis series contains text, it is ignored). When you finish selecting how you want the data analyzed, select Quit to return to the /Graph Series menu. After you select the series to process, you will have a menu containing Aggregation, Moving Average, Linear Fit, Exponential Fit, Reset, and Table (if you select All Series you will not have the Table option). These selections choose how you want to analyze the data. Select Aggregation to perform simple statistical calculations on the data, Moving Average to calculate moving averages, Linear Fit to calculate a straight line that best fits the data points, and Exponential Fit to calculate a curved line that best fits the data points. When you no longer want to graph the analytical data and want to return to graphing the individual points in the series, select Reset.

If you select Aggregation, choose Function and select the statistical function Quattro Pro will perform on each group of values in the series from SUM, AVG, STD, STDS, MIN, and MAX. Next, select Series Period and select from Days, Weeks, Months, Quarters, and Years for the time intervals between each value in the series. Next, select Aggregation Period and select from Weeks, Months, Quarters, Years, or Arbitrary for how you want to divide the periods into groups. If you select Arbitrary, type a number between 2 and 1000 for the number of values that are in each group, and press ENTER or click Enter in the box. If you use Arbitrary, set the Series Period to Days. Select Quit when you finish making the selections.

If you select Moving Average, select Period, type the number of values Quattro Pro will use to calculate the average, and press ENTER or click Enter in the box. If you want the different values in the moving average calculations to have different weights, select Weighted and Yes. To return to not using weighted values in the moving average, select Weighted and No. Select Quit when you finish making selections for displaying the series data as a moving average.

If you select Table to put the calculated values that Quattro Pro computed for the series data points on the spreadsheet, select a cell in the spreadsheet where Quattro Pro will put the values. Press ENTER or click [Enter] in the input line. Quattro places all the calculated values in the spreadsheet that it uses to graph the series starting in the cell's location you choose.

Quit—This option returns you to the main Graph menu.

/GRAPH TEXT FONT

This command provides options that control the appearance of the text in the graph. With this command, you can select the typeface, size, style, and color of the graph text.

OPTIONS

This command has two sets of options. The first set determines which text this command will affect.

1st Line—This option changes the appearance of the first title line in the graph.

2nd Line—This option changes the appearance of the second title line in the graph.

X-Title—This option changes the appearance of the x-axis title.

Y-Title—This option changes the appearance of the y-axis title.

Legends—This option changes the appearance of the legend text entered with the **/**Graph Text **L**egends command.

Data & Tick Labels—This option changes the appearance of all text not controlled by the previous options.

Quit—This option returns you to the Text menu.

The second set of options controls how the appearance of the text selected above will appear.

Typeface—This option determines the typeface of the text selected with the first set of options. The typeface is the basic appearance of a font. Quattro comes with several Bitstream fonts and Hershey fonts. Quattro also supports the internal fonts supported by a PostScript or Hewlett-Packard LaserJet printer. Plotters cannot print Bitstream fonts. Highlight one of the typefaces and press ENTER or click the typeface you want.

Point Size—This option selects the height of the text selected with the first set of options. The size is measured in points from 8 to 72 with the larger point size representing the larger characters. A point is 1/72 of an inch. Highlight the size you want and press ENTER or click the size you want.

Style—This option presents a second menu that lets you boldface, italicize, underline, or, in Quattro Pro 3 and 4, add drop shadows to the text selected with the first set of options. To add or remove a style option, select the letter of the option you want to add or remove. Quattro displays On next to the option that is currently in use. To remove the style options, select **Reset**. To return to the previous menu, select **Quit**.

Color—This option determines the color of the text selected with the first set of options. Highlight the color you want from the list or gallery of colors, and press ENTER.

Quit—This option returns you to the Font menu.

/GRAPH TEXT LEGENDS

This command provides options for the legends that appear on the right side or the bottom of the graph. The legend can also include descriptive text. You can enter the legend text directly at Quattro's prompt or you can use the contents of a cell as a legend by typing a backslash followed by the cell address or block name. When you enter the legend text at Quattro's prompt, you can enter up to 19 characters. When you reference a cell for the legend text, Quattro uses the entire cell, even if the cell contains more than 19 characters. Since Quattro does not adjust legend cell addresses if you move the cells, it is better to use block names. One of this command's options hides the legends.

OPTIONS

1st Series—This option sets the text for the first series' legend.

2nd Series—This option sets the text for the second series' legend.

3rd Series—This option sets the text for the third series' legend.
4th Series—This option sets the text for the fourth series' legend.
5th Series—This option sets the text for the fifth series' legend.
6th Series—This option sets the text for the sixth series' legend.

Position—This option sets the position of the legend relative to the graph. The choices are **B**ottom, which places the legend below the graph; **R**ight, which places the legend to the right of the graph; and **N**one, which removes the legend from the graph. 3-D graph legends always appear in the same location regardless of whether you select **R**ight or **B**ottom.

Quit—This option returns you to the Text menu.

NOTE

Since Quattro reduces the size of the graph to fit the legend and the legend text, you should make the legend text as short as possible.

/GRAPH TEXT QUIT

This command returns you to the Graph menu.

OPTIONS
None.

/GRAPH TEXT SECONDARY Y-AXIS

This command defines the text that appears to the right of the secondary y-axis on the graph. The text entered with this command only appears if one or more graph series is assigned to the secondary y-axis with the **/Graph Customize Series Y-Axis** command.

OPTIONS

You can type up to 39 characters directly or enter a backslash followed by a cell address or block name that contains the text you want to use. Since Quattro does not adjust cell addresses if you move the cell's contents, you should use a block name. To remove this title, enter this command, press ESC, then press ENTER.

/GRAPH TEXT X-TITLE

This command defines the text that appears below the x-axis on the graph.

OPTIONS

You can type up to 39 characters directly or enter a backslash followed by a cell address or block name that contains the text you want to use. Since Quattro does not adjust cell addresses if you move the cell's contents, you should use a block name. To remove this title, enter this command, press ESC, then press ENTER.

/GRAPH TEXT Y-TITLE

This command defines the text that appears to the left of the y-axis on the graph.

OPTIONS

You can type up to 39 characters directly or enter a backslash followed by a cell address or block name that contains the text you want to use. Since Quattro does not adjust cell addresses if you move the cell's contents, you should use a block name. To remove this title, enter this command, press ESC, then press ENTER.

/GRAPH TEXT 1ST LINE

This command defines the first line title that appears on the graph.

OPTIONS

You can type the text directly or enter a backslash followed by a cell address or block name to use the contents of a cell. The title can be up to 39 characters if entered directly or more if in a cell. Since Quattro does not adjust cell addresses if you move the cell's contents, you should use a block name. To remove this title, enter this command, press ESC, then press ENTER.

/GRAPH TEXT 2ND LINE

This command defines the second line title that appears on the graph below the first title.

OPTIONS

You can type the text directly or enter a backslash followed by a cell address or block name to use the contents of a cell. The title can be up to 39 characters if entered directly or more if in a cell. Since Quattro does not adjust cell addresses if you move the cell's contents, you should use a block name. To remove this title, enter this command, press ESC, then press ENTER.

/GRAPH VIEW

This command displays the graph using all the current graph settings. Any graph buttons, slide show transitions, and audio effects are in effect. Pressing any key except a slash returns you to the Graph menu.

OPTIONS

If you type a slash, you will activate the Graph Annotator. While you are viewing the graph in Quattro Pro 4, you can look at it more closely using a mouse. When the graph is on the screen, press both mouse buttons simultaneously. Quattro Pro adds a Zoom and Pan palette to the top of the screen that contains buttons labeled ++, ==, --, <<, and >> as well as a position bar that shows your relative position in the graph. Clicking ++ enlarges the graph so you see less of it on the screen but in greater detail. Clicking -- reduces the graph to see it at a smaller magnification. Clicking == displays the graph at its actual size. When you are looking at the graph closely, you can pan or shift which section of the graph appears on the screen by clicking the << or >> buttons. These buttons shift the displayed graph left or right (or in a rotated bar graph, up and down). You can also click a section of the position bar to display that relative location of the graph. Pressing the right mouse button will remove the Zoom and Pan palette.

NOTE

This command's shortcut is pressing F10 (GRAPH). The difference between entering the command and pressing F10 is that you can press F10 at any time, including while you are in the middle of another command.

If you cannot see the graph when you press F10 or use the /Graph View from one of the graph menus, you may have a monitor that cannot display graphs. You can still create them, save them, and print them although you will not be able to monitor their creation on the screen.

/GRAPH X-AXIS

This command changes how Quattro displays the x-axis. The type of changes you can make include how Quattro scales the axis, the number of minor ticks, whether the axis displays scaling, and if the axis uses alternating ticks. All the settings apply to XY graphs and bubble graphs when the X Series contains numeric data. Other graph types only use the No. of Minor Ticks and Alternate Ticks options. If /Options Startup Use Dialogs is set to Yes, the options for this command will appear in a x-Axis options dialog box.

OPTIONS

Scale—This option has two choices: Automatic and Manual. If you select Automatic, Quattro automatically sets the scale. If you select Manual, Quattro uses the information you provide with this command's other options to set the scale. Until you select Manual, Quattro ignores the information provided for the Low, High, and Increment options.

Low—This option is the lowest number that appears in the x-axis scale. The number you provide should be as small or smaller than the lowest number in the data series. If you are graphing negative numbers, make sure that this number has a minus sign before it.

High—This option is the highest number that appears in the x-axis. The number you enter should be as large or larger than the largest value in the graph.

Increment—This option is a number representing the interval between each tick mark. If this number is too small, the grid lines and tick marks become indistinguishable. If you enter 0, Quattro creates tick marks at regular intervals.

Format of Ticks—This option sets the display format of the numbers marking the tick marks. This option displays a box listing all the formats available with the

/Options Formats Numeric Format command and prompts for the number of digits after the decimal point.

No. of Minor Ticks—This option sets the number of minor tick marks between the regular tick marks. Minor tick marks do not have labels below them and do not connect with grid lines.

Alternate Ticks—This option determines whether Quattro alternates the labels placement between the two lines. If you choose Yes, Quattro alternates the labels between two lines. If you choose No, all the labels are on the same line.

Display Scaling—This option has two choices. If you select Yes, Quattro displays a scale measurement next to the axis. If you select No, Quattro hides this information.

Mode—This option determines whether the x-axis uses standard scaling or logarithmic scaling. Select Normal for standard scaling (the interval between each tick mark is the same), or Log for logarithmic scaling (the interval between each tick mark is an increasing power of 10).

Quit—This option returns you to the Graph menu.

/GRAPH Y-AXIS

This command sets how Quattro displays the y-axis. The type of changes you can make includes how Quattro scales the axis, the number of minor ticks, whether scaling is displayed, whether the axis uses alternating ticks and how the second y-axis is displayed. If /Options Startup Use Dialogs is set to Yes, the options for this command will appear in a Y-Axis options dialog box.

OPTIONS

Scale—This option has two choices: Automatic and Manual. If you select Automatic, Quattro automatically sets the scale. If you select Manual, Quattro uses the information you provide with this command's other options to set the scale. Until this option is set to Manual, Quattro ignores the information provided for the Low, High, and Increment options.

Low—This option sets the lowest number that appears in the y-axis. The number you enter should be as small or smaller than the lowest number in the data series. If the series contains negative numbers, make sure that the low value has a minus sign before it.

High—This option is the highest number that appears in the y-axis. The number you type should be as large or larger than the largest number in the series.

Increment—This option is a number representing the interval between each tick mark. If this number is too small, the grid lines and tick marks become indistinguishable. If you enter 0, Quattro creates tick marks at regular intervals.

Format of Ticks—This option sets the display format of the numbers marking the tick marks. This option displays a box listing all the formats available with the /Options Formats Numeric Format command and prompts for the number of digits after the decimal point.

No. of Minor Ticks—This option sets the number of minor tick marks between the regular tick marks. Minor tick marks do not have numeric labels and do not connect with grid lines.

Display Scaling—This option has two choices. If you select **Yes**, Quattro displays a scale measurement next to the axis. If you select **No**, Quattro hides this information.

Mode—This option determines whether the y-axis uses standard scaling or logarithmic scaling. Select **Normal** for standard scaling (The interval between each tick mark is the same), or **Log** for logarithmic scaling (the interval between each tick mark is an increasing power of 10).

2nd Y-Axis—This option presents the menu to select how Quattro displays the second y-axis. If **/O**ptions **S**tartup **U**se **D**ialogs is set to **Yes**, when you select **2**nd **Y**-Axis, Quattro Pro will display the 2nd Y-Axis options dialog box for you to make your selections. From this menu or dialog box, you can change how Quattro scales the axis, the number of minor ticks, whether scaling is displayed, whether the axis uses alternating ticks, and how the second y-axis is displayed. The options for this menu are identical to the menu to change the y-axis.

Quit—This option returns you to the Graph menu.

/OPTIONS COLORS CONDITIONAL

This command sets the colors Quattro uses to display cells if the cell's contents meet certain conditions. The conditions affect value entries. When you use conditional colors, the conditional colors selected override the colors selected with the **/O**ptions **C**olors **S**preadsheet **C**ells command.

OPTIONS

On/Off—This option enables or disables Quattro's use of conditional colors. Quattro initially has this setting at **Disable**, which does not use the conditional colors. If you set this option to **Enable**, Quattro uses the colors set with the other options.

ERR—This option sets the color for cells equaling ERR.

Smallest Normal Value—This option sets the lowest value of the normal range. All cells with values below this value display in the color chosen for the **B**elow Normal Color option.

Greatest Normal Value—This option sets the highest value in the normal range. All cells with values above this value display in the color chosen for the **A**bove Normal Color option.

Below Normal Color—This option sets the color for cell values that are less than the **S**mallest Normal Value option.

Normal Cell Color—This option sets the color for cell values that are between the **S**mallest Normal Value and the **G**reatest Normal Value option.

Above Normal Color—This option sets the color for cell values that are greater than the **G**reatest Normal Value option.

Quit—This option exits the Conditional menu and returns you to the Colors menu.

/OPTIONS COLORS DESKTOP

This command sets the colors that Quattro uses for the desktop (the area of the screen not used by the menu or by the windows). After you select the option representing the menu characteristic that you want to change, Quattro either displays a color palette or a selection box with the choices.

OPTIONS

Status—This option sets the color of the status line.

Highlight-Status—This option sets the color of the indicators that appear on the status line.

Errors—This option sets the colors of the error messages Quattro displays when an error occurs.

Background—This sets the color of the area of the desktop in which the spreadsheet and File Manager windows do not appear.

Desktop—This option sets the ASCII character Quattro displays in the desktop background.

Quit—This option leaves the Desktop menu and returns you to the Colors menu.

/OPTIONS COLORS FILE MANAGER

This command sets the colors Quattro uses to display File Manager windows. For each attribute, you set the color of the text and the text's background. After you select the option representing the menu characteristic you want to change, Quattro displays either a color palette or a selection box with the choices.

OPTIONS

Frame—This option sets the color of the frame around a File Manager window. This option has no effect in the WYSIWYG display mode.

Banner—This option sets the color of the drive and directory designation that appear at the top of a File Manager window. This option has no effect in the WYSIWYG display mode.

Text—This option sets the color of the text in a File Manager window.

Active Cursor—This option sets the color of the cursor in the active pane.

Inactive Cursor—This option sets the color of the cursor in an inactive pane.

Marked—This option sets the color of marked files in the file list pane.

Cut—This option sets the color of files marked for moving by cutting from one directory and pasting to another.

Copy—This option sets the color of files marked for copying.

Quit—This option exits the File Manager menu and returns you to the Colors menu.

/OPTIONS COLORS HELP

This command sets the colors Quattro uses to display the help screens.

OPTIONS

Frame—This option sets the color of the box around the help screen text.

Banner—This option sets the color for the name of the help screen.

Text—This option sets the color for all text except keywords.

Keywords—This option sets the color for the keywords in the help screens. The keywords are the topics that you can select for further information.

Highlight—This option sets the color for the highlight that selects keywords.

Quit—This option exits the Help menu and returns you to the Colors menu.

/OPTIONS COLORS MENU

This command sets the colors that Quattro uses for the different portions of the menu. After you select the option representing the menu characteristic that you want to change, Quattro either displays a color palette or a selection box with the choices.

OPTIONS

Frame—This option sets the color for the border of the menu.

Banner—This option sets the color for the name of the menu.

Text—This option sets the color for the text of the menu items except for the key letter.

Key Letter—This option sets the color for the letter of every menu item that you can type to select it.

Highlight—This option sets the color for the highlight bar and text that selects menu items.

Settings—This option sets the color for the settings of the menu items that appear when you press the GRAY + key in a menu.

Explanation—This option sets the color of the text in the status line that describes the highlighted menu item.

Drop Shadow—This option sets the color for the shadow under the menu.

SpeedBar—This option sets the color of the SpeedBar.

Shadow—This option sets the ASCII character Quattro displays for the shadow.

Quit—This option exits the menu and returns you to the Colors menu.

/OPTIONS COLORS PALETTES

This command returns the color selections to the default settings. You can return the color settings to the default settings under black and white, monochrome, or color.

OPTIONS

Color—This restores the colors to the defaults for color screens.

Monochrome—This sets the current colors to the defaults for monochrome screens. This does not use the same hues used by the black and white palette.

Black & White—This restores the colors to the defaults for the monochrome screens that use the color palettes that appear as hues.

Gray Scale—This Quattro Pro 3 and 4 option sets the current colors to the default for monochrome screens that can display shades.

Version 3 Color—This Quattro Pro 4 option uses the default color set that Quattro Pro 3 and earlier used for text screens.

Quit—This option exits the Palettes menu and returns you to the Colors menu.

/OPTIONS COLORS QUIT

This command exits the Colors menu and returns you to the Options menu.

OPTIONS
None.

/OPTIONS COLORS SPREADSHEET

This command sets the colors Quattro uses to display spreadsheet windows. For each attribute, you set the color of the text and the text's background. After you select the option representing the menu characteristic that you want to change, Quattro displays either a color palette or a selection box with the choices. Some of the options like **Frame** and **Banner** only apply to the spreadsheet display in text mode.

OPTIONS

Frame—This option sets the color of the frame around a spreadsheet window.

Banner—This option sets the color of the file name and window number that appear at the top of a spreadsheet window.

Cells—This option sets the color for all blank and value cells.

Borders—This option sets the color for the row and column borders of the spreadsheet.

Titles—This option sets the color for locked titles.

Highlight—This option sets the color of the selector.

Graph Frames—This option sets the color of the boxes drawn around inserted graphs.

Input Line—This option sets the color for cell information displayed in the input line and cell data as it is edited.

Unprotected—This option sets the color for unprotected cells.

Labels—This option sets the color for label entries.

Shading—This option sets the color of cells shaded with the /Style Shading command.

Drawn Lines—This option sets the color of lines drawn with **/Style Line Drawing**.

WYSIWYG Colors—This Quattro Pro 3 and 4 option sets the WYSIWYG display colors. This option displays another menu that lets you set the background color of the cells (Background), the selector color (Cursor), the grid line color (Grid Lines), the background color of unprotected cells (Unprotected), color of lines added with **/Style Line Drawing** (Drawn Lines), background color of cells shaded with **/Style Shading** (Shaded Cells), the colors of the text and background of spreadsheet titles (Locked Titles Text and Titles Background), and the colors used by the sculpted row and column borders (Row and Column Labels).

Quit—This option exits the Spreadsheet menu and returns you to the Colors menu.

/OPTIONS DISPLAY MODE

This command sets how Quattro displays the spreadsheet. Some monitors can display in more than one mode. For example, VGA screens can display 25, 43, or 50 lines on the screen. While many monitors can display up to 80 columns, some monitors can display 132 columns, which let you see more columns of your worksheet. Another option of this command is **B**: WYSIWYG (**B**: Graphics Mode in prior releases). When a spreadsheet appears in graphics mode, Quattro displays the inserted graphs instead of a highlighted area. You can use this command to change how Quattro displays the spreadsheet.

With Quattro Pro 4, when you use the WYSIWYG display mode, the SpeedBar appears below the menu bar and when you use a text display mode, the buttons will be on the right side and have shorter descriptions. If not all the buttons fit, the last button displayed is BAR so you can switch between which set of buttons to display. Quattro Pro 4 also has two buttons on the SpeedBar, CHR, and WYS that you can use to switch between the text display and WYSIWYG mode.

OPTIONS

The specific options depend on the type of monitor and graphics adapter card you are using.

NOTE

If you are displaying the spreadsheet in graphics mode, Quattro will perform slower. Graphics display mode is only available for EGA and VGA screens. If you select a 132-column display mode and your hardware is not capable of displaying 132 columns, you will want to press CTRL-BREAK and type **/ODA** to set the display mode to 25 rows and 80 columns.

/OPTIONS FORMATS ALIGN LABELS

This command aligns all new label entries in the current spreadsheet according to your specification. This command does not affect existing spreadsheet entries.

OPTIONS

Left—This option aligns labels subsequently entered at the left side of the cell.

Right—This option aligns labels subsequently entered at the right side of the cell.

Center—This option centers labels subsequently entered within the cell.

/OPTIONS FORMATS GLOBAL WIDTH

This command changes the width of all the columns in the spreadsheet that have not had their column widths set with **/Style** Column Width or **/Style** Block Size.

OPTIONS

Quattro prompts for the new column width. You can type a new number for a column width or you can use the RIGHT and LEFT ARROW keys to adjust the width of all the columns visually. After you have selected the desired column width, press ENTER. This setting only applies to the current spreadsheet.

/OPTIONS FORMATS HIDE ZEROS

This command hides zero values in your spreadsheet.

OPTIONS

When you select this option, Quattro displays a menu with Yes/No options. Select **Yes** from the menu option if you want to hide zeros and **No** if you want to display zero values.

/OPTIONS FORMATS NUMERIC FORMAT

This command changes the default display format of values in your spreadsheet. This command only affects the current spreadsheet and only the cells in the current spreadsheet that have not had their format set with the **/Style** Numeric Format or the **/Style** Use Style command.

OPTIONS

Fixed—This option displays a fixed number of decimal places for the values in your spreadsheet, for example, 1000.11.

Scientific—This option expresses your values in scientific exponential notation, for example, 1.00011E+03.

Currency—This option displays values in currency terms. Commas are added as thousand separators, negative values are enclosed in parentheses and the number of decimal places is defined by the user. The default setting is two decimal places. An example of a positive is $1,000.11. A negative value of the same magnitude would appear as ($1,000.11).

,(Financial)—This option displays values with commas as separators after the

thousand position, for example, 1,000.11. The negative values are enclosed in parentheses. Quattro prompts for the desired number of decimal places.

General—This option expresses values in their normal form, that is, the values appear without any of the selectable display options. This results in a display with varying numbers of decimal digits and scientific notation for very large and very small values.

+/- —This option creates simple horizontal bar charts. It transforms positive values into + signs for each positive integer and negative values into - signs for each negative integer.

Percent—This option multiplies values by 100 and adds a percent symbol after the number. For example, 0.95 appears as 95.00%, and 1.2 appears as 120.00%.

Date—This option displays your values as dates or times. There are several suboptions, which allow you to display dates in the form of DD-MMM-YY, DD-MMM, MMM-YY, Long intl., and Short intl. You can also select the Time suboption, which is further divided into time format selections. The time options display times in the format HH:MM:SS AM/PM, HH:MM AM/PM, Long intl., and Short intl.

Text—This option displays formulas in the cells rather than the values resulting from the formulas.

Hidden—This option hides the cell contents from the screen. The cell contents only show on the input line.

/OPTIONS FORMATS QUIT

This command leaves the Formats menu and returns you to the Options menu.

OPTIONS
None.

/OPTIONS GRAPHICS QUALITY

This command controls when Quattro creates Bitstream fonts. Quattro builds a Bitstream font that it must use but has not built before. This command does not affect Hershey and internal printer fonts.

OPTIONS

Draft—This option directs Quattro not to build Bitstream fonts. If Quattro needs a Bitstream font for displaying or printing a spreadsheet or graph, Quattro substitutes a Hershey font in its place.

Final—This option directs Quattro to build Bitstream fonts whenever it needs one. This option means that Quattro will always use the selected Bitstream fonts for viewing and printing.

/OPTIONS HARDWARE COPROCESSOR

This command displays whether Quattro Pro detects a math coprocessor.
OPTIONS
None.

/OPTIONS HARDWARE EMS MEMORY

This command displays the number of bytes of expanded memory available. In Quattro Pro 4, the displayed information includes the amount available, the total, and the percentage used. This information helps you assess if you have enough memory to expand your spreadsheet. This number is approximately the same number provided by the @MEMEMSAVAIL function.
OPTIONS
None.

/OPTIONS HARDWARE MOUSE BUTTON

This Quattro Pro 3 and 4 command lets you change the mouse button that you use with Quattro Pro to make selections.
OPTIONS
This command has two options that select the mouse button—Left, the default, uses the left mouse button to make selections, and Right uses the right mouse buttons to make selections.

/OPTIONS HARDWARE NORMAL MEMORY

This command displays the number of bytes of memory available. In Quattro Pro 4, the displayed information includes the amount available, the total, and the percentage used. This enables you to assess if you have enough memory to expand your spreadsheet. The available memory shown is approximately the same number returned by the @MEMAVAIL function.
OPTIONS
None.

/OPTIONS HARDWARE PRINTERS AUTO LF

This command determines whether Quattro must send a line feed at the end of every line. You should execute this command only if the printer is not advancing the paper or if the printout is double-spaced.

OPTIONS
This command has two options. Select **No** if the document is printing double-spaced. Select **Yes** if the printer is not advancing to the next line.

/OPTIONS HARDWARE PRINTERS BACKGROUND

This Quattro Pro 4 command sets whether Quattro Pro prints in the background. Printing in the background allows you to continue to use Quattro Pro while part of Quattro Pro prints your data. Before you can use background printing, you must load the Borland Print Spooler. To load the Borland Print Spooler from DOS, type **BPS** in the Quattro Pro directory and press ENTER. Once the Borland Print Spooler is loaded, you can use this command to tell Quattro Pro to use the print spooler rather than having to wait when you print data until all the data is printed.

OPTIONS
The two selections you can make for this command are **Yes** to use the background printing or **No** to not use it. Selecting **Yes** will not have any effect unless the Borland Print Spooler is loaded. With **Yes** selected and the Borland Print Spooler loaded, you can use background printing and control the background printing with the **/P**rint Print Manager command.

/OPTIONS HARDWARE PRINTERS DEFAULT PRINTER

This command sets whether the printer selected with the **/O**ptions Hardware Printers 1st Printer or **/O**ptions Hardware Printer 2nd Printer command will be used. The printer selected with the **/O**ptions Hardware Printer Default Printer is used when the destination for printing a spreadsheet or graph is the graphics printer, a binary file, or the screen previewer.

OPTIONS
The only options for this command are **1st Printer**, which selects the printer defined with **/O**ptions Hardware Printers 1st Printer command or **2nd Printer**, which selects the printer defined with **/O**ptions Hardware Printers 2nd Printer command.

/OPTIONS HARDWARE PRINTERS FONTS

This command defines the Hewlett-Packard LaserJet printer cartridges attached and determines if Quattro adjusts the size of text in graphs to the size of the graph area.

OPTIONS
Cartridge Fonts—This option tells Quattro which Hewlett-Packard LaserJet (or

Pacific Data Products 25-in-One) printer cartridges are attached to your printer or shading level to print. When you select this option, you must select **Left Cartridge** or **Right Cartridge**. Then, for the cartridge position selected, select the cartridge name contained in the cartridge slot. Quattro Pro 3 and 4 have an additional option, **Shading Level**, which selects the shading level that a Hewlett-Packard LaserJet III or Canon LBP printer prints shading added with the **/Style Shading Grey** command. After selecting **Shading Level**, you can select the percentage of shading to print the shaded cells. 1 to 2 percent uses the first shading level, 3 to 10 percent uses the second shading level, 11 to 20 percent uses the third shading level, 21 to 35 percent uses the fourth shading level, 36 to 55 uses the fifth shading level, 56 to 80 percent uses the sixth shading level, 81 to 99 percent uses the seventh shading level, and 100 percent uses solid black. In Quattro Pro 2 and 3 this option was called **LaserJet Fonts**.

Autoscale Fonts—This option determines whether Quattro treats the point size of the text in a graph as relative or absolute. If this option is set to **Yes**, Quattro treats the text point size as relative and adjusts the text size in relation to the graph size. If this option is set to **No**, Quattro treats the text point size as absolute. In this case, the text will be the same size regardless of the graph size.

/OPTIONS HARDWARE PRINTERS PLOTTER SPEED

This command sets the plotter speed. You may want to adjust this if the plotter is printing too quickly and the lines are not firm and steady. This should also be changed if you are changing from printing on paper to transparencies or if you are using old plotter pens. 0 represents the fastest speed that Quattro supports. 1 through 9 represent increasing speeds that Quattro can send information to the plotter.

OPTIONS
None.

/OPTIONS HARDWARE PRINTERS QUIT

This command leaves the Printers menu and returns you to the Options menu.
OPTIONS
None.

/OPTIONS HARDWARE PRINTERS SINGLE SHEET

This command tells Quattro if the printer is using continuous-feed paper. Laser printers behave like continuous-feeding printers because of their paper-feeding mechanisms.

OPTIONS

This option is set to Yes for printers using continuous feed paper. This option is set to No for printers that must stop after every page and wait for another page to be manually inserted.

/OPTIONS HARDWARE PRINTERS 1ST PRINTER

This command specifies the graphics printers that Quattro uses when the default printer is the first graphics printer. The printer selected with this command can print graphs and spreadsheets. This printer should be the one that you are planning to use most often. The printer is initially selected when you install Quattro.

OPTIONS

Type of printer/Make—This option lists the printer manufacturers that Quattro supports. Select one from the list.

Type of printer/Model—This option lists the models of the selected manufacturer that Quattro supports. Select one from the list.

Type of printer/Mode—This option lists the modes that your printer can support. This option lets you select whether to print quickly or slower but with a more finished quality. The actual options available depend upon the printer make and model selected.

Device—This option specifies where the printer connects to the computer. The choices are Parallel-1, Parallel-2, Serial-1, Serial-2, LPT1, LPT2, LPT3, LPT4, EPT, PRN, and Network Queue. Quattro initially sets this option to Parallel-1.

Baud rate—This option specifies the baud rate at which Quattro sends information to the printer. Quattro initially sets this option to Leave as is, which uses the baud rate set by the last DOS MODE command.

Parity—This option specifies the parity at which Quattro sends information to the printer. Quattro initially sets this option to Leave as is, which uses the parity setting set by the last DOS MODE command.

Stop bits—This option specifies the stop bits that Quattro uses to send information to the printer. Quattro initially sets this option to Leave as is, which uses the stop bit setting set by the last DOS MODE command.

Quit—This option exits the menu and returns you to the Printers menu.

/OPTIONS HARDWARE PRINTERS 2ND PRINTER

This command specifies the graphics printer that Quattro uses when the default printer is the second graphics printer. The printer selected with this command can print graphs and spreadsheets.

OPTIONS

The options for this command are identical to the /Options Hardware Printers 1st Printer command.

/OPTIONS HARDWARE SCREEN

This command changes the settings Quattro uses to send information to the monitor. Quattro uses default settings for the text screen, and does not need to know the type of screen you are using. For graphics screens such as graphs, the Screen Preview, and displaying a spreadsheet in WYSIWYG mode, Quattro uses information called a screen driver to tell the screen the information it wants to show. Quattro checks the computer's hardware to determine the proper screen driver to use. If you are using a nonstandard screen type or Quattro is not displaying graphics screens properly, you may need to change some of the screen settings.

OPTIONS

Screen Type—This option determines the screen type. Quattro uses this setting to determine which screen driver file it should use. This option is initially set to **Autodetect Driver**, which allows Quattro to determine the proper screen driver. You should only change this setting if Quattro is not displaying graphic screens properly. If your screen type is not listed, select **L** for MDA, which cannot display graphic images. You cannot change the screen type in the WYSIWYG display mode.

Resolution—This option sets the resolution for graphics screens. This option can affect the colors that are available and the clarity of the image. For example, in monitors using VGA boards, you can choose between displaying graphs using two EGA settings or one VGA setting. The specific options displayed for this command depend upon the monitor and the graphics adapter card in use. You cannot change the resolution in the WYSIWYG display mode.

Aspect Ratio—This option determines the ratio between the height and the width of a circle in a pie chart. Use this option only if the circle in a flat pie chart is not round or to change the angle of a three-dimensional pie chart. When you select this option, Quattro clears the screen and displays a circle with two axes. Use the UP and DOWN ARROWS until the circle appears perfect, and press ENTER. This option does not affect other graphic images.

CGA Snow Suppression—This option is used if you have a CGA screen that flickers when you scroll. Quattro is normally able to determine if it needs to suppress the screen snow. Select **Yes** if it displays too much snow.

Quit—This option exits the Screen menu and returns you to the Options menu.

/OPTIONS INTERNATIONAL

This command establishes the default settings for punctuation, currency symbol, dates, and times to match the options customary in other countries.

OPTIONS

Currency—This options sets the default currency symbol. When you select this command, Quattro prompts you for the desired symbol. If the desired symbol cannot be found on the regular keyboard, you still are able to use certain special ASCII characters. When Quattro prompts you for the currency symbol, simply hold down the ALT keys and type in the corresponding numbers on the numeric keypad for the special ASCII character and press ENTER. Quattro prompts you for the location of the currency symbol. Choose **Prefix** from the submenu if you want the currency symbol placed in front of numbers, or **Suffix** if you want the currency symbol placed after numbers, and press ENTER.

Negative—This option sets how negative values display with the Currency and , (Financial) formats. You can select either **Parentheses** to put parentheses around a negative number or **Sign** to put a minus sign before the number. This option does not affect other numerical formats.

Punctuation—This option sets the punctuation displayed in your spreadsheets to conform with the conventions used by other countries. Quattro provides you with a submenu of display formats from which to choose. Highlight the punctuation option desired, and press ENTER.

Date—This option sets the display of date entries. Quattro provides you with a choice of four different date display options. When you select **/Options International Date**, Quattro provides a submenu of display formats:

- MM/DD/YY (MM/DD)
- DD/MM/YY (DD/MM)
- DD.MM.YY (DD.MM)
- YY-MM-DD (MM-DD)

Highlight the date display format of your choice and press ENTER. Quattro uses the date format selected when you use the **/Style Numeric Format Date 4-(Long intl.)** command. Quattro truncates the year from the option you selected for the **/Style Numeric Format Date 5-(Short intl.)** command.

Time—This option sets the display of times entries. When you select **/Options International Time**, Quattro provides a submenu of the following options:

- HH:MM:SS (HH:MM)
- HH.MM.SS (HH.MM)
- HH,MM,SS (HH,MM)
- HHhMMmSSs (HHhMMm)

Highlight the desired selection, and press ENTER. Quattro uses the first time format selected with the **/Style Numeric Format Date Time 3-(Long intl.)** command. Quattro truncates the seconds from the option you selected for the **/Style Numeric Format Date Time 4-(Short intl.)** command.

Use Sort Table—This option selects the alphabet Quattro uses while sorting. You can select ASCII.SOR to have the letters A-Z followed by other characters, including letters used by other foreign languages. You can select INTL.SOR to have the letters A-Z with letters used by other foreign languages included in their proper order. You can select SWEDFIN.SOR to use the alphabet order used by Sweden and Finland. You can select NORDAN.SOR to use the alphabet order used by Norway and Denmark.

LICS/LMBCS Conversion—This option selects how Quattro Pro converts characters in 1-2-3 spreadsheet files. Selecting **No**, the default, translates all characters in 1-2-3 spreadsheet files using the ASCII character set. Selecting **Yes** translates characters in a .WK1 spreadsheet file to use the characters used by the LICS or LMBCS character set. The translation is done when the file is opened and saved.

Overstrike Print—This option selects whether or not the printer can create foreign characters by overstriking which is printing one character, backing up and printing another on top of it. Selecting **Yes** creates foreign characters the printer cannot directly print by overstriking them. Selecting **No**, the default prevents this from occurring. Not all printers can overstrike.

Quit—This option exits the International menu and returns you to the Options menu.

/OPTIONS NETWORK

This command makes selections that make using Quattro Pro on a network or with network files easier.

OPTIONS

Drive mappings—This option assigns drive letters to network servers, volumes, and directories. Once a network directory is mapped to a drive, you can easily select the network files by selecting the mapped drive rather than specifying the network information such as server and volume each time. To map a drive, select a number **1** through **8** for the drive you want to map. Next, type the letter (usually H or above) that you want to use for the mapped drive, and press ENTER. Type the server name, and press ENTER; then type the volume name, and press ENTER. Next, type the drive and directory on the network file server the mapped drive will represent, and press ENTER. Finally type the user name (or leave the default user name supplied by the User Name option below), and press ENTER. You can repeat this for up to eight drive mappings. To change a drive's mapping, select the mapped drive to change and review each of the server, volume, drive and directory, and user name prompts, changing them if necessary. When you are finished, select **Quit** to return to the Options menu.

Banner—This option sets, when you print in Quattro to a network printer, whether Quattro prints a banner page that you can use to identify the printed output when you are sharing the network printer with many users. Select **Yes** to have a banner page printed or **No** to omit a banner page.

Refresh Interval—This option sets how frequently Quattro Pro checks on the status of network or background print jobs. Type a number from 1 to 300, and press ENTER.

Queue Monitor—This option sets whether Quattro Pro monitors the print jobs that you have sent to a network printer and displays their progress on the status line. You can select **Yes** to have Quattro Pro monitor your print jobs or **No** to omit this.

User Name—This option sets the default user name that you are using for drive mappings to make creating drive mappings easier. After you select User Name, type your user name and press ENTER. You can always override the user name when you are logging into a network or creating a drive mapping.

/OPTIONS OTHER CLOCK

This command establishes or removes the date and time display in the status line. After you select /Options Other Clock, Quattro displays a submenu of three options.

OPTIONS

Standard—This option is the default setting in Quattro. Choosing this option causes the date and time to be displayed as 06-Jun-92 and 11:08 AM.

International—This option sets the date and time display to the current international date and time formats.

None—This option removes the date and time displays from the status line.

/OPTIONS OTHER EXPANDED MEMORY

This command determines how Quattro uses expanded memory. Quattro can use expanded memory to store cell formats and cell entries. Although expanded memory is slightly slower than normal memory, it does allow you to create larger spreadsheets. Setting the type of information Quattro stores in expanded memory will affect Quattro's speed and storage of the spreadsheet in memory.

OPTIONS

Both—This option stores both cell formats and cell entries in expanded memory.

Spreadsheet Data—This option stores cell entries in expanded memory and cell formats in normal memory.

Format—This option stores cell format information in expanded memory and cell entries in normal memory.

None—This option stores cell formats and cell entries in normal memory. It prevents Quattro from using expanded memory.

/OPTIONS OTHER MACRO

This command determines whether Quattro updates the screen to show all the steps a macro is performing. Since Quattro can perform the macro instructions quickly, constantly updating the screen slows down a macro's execution. By updating less of the screen, Quattro can execute the macro quicker. Changing when Quattro updates the screen does not change the spreadsheet's values since Quattro updates the screen does not change the spreadsheet's values since Quattro internally keeps track of the spreadsheet values even if they do not appear on the

screen. The command only affects the screen during macro execution since Quattro automatically updates the screen when Quattro has finished executing a macro.
OPTIONS
Both—This option causes Quattro not to update the screen during macro execution. Macros execute fastest with this option.

Panel—This option causes Quattro to date the spreadsheet windows during macro execution and ignore the other parts of the screen.

Window—This option causes Quattro to update all parts of the screen except spreadsheet windows during macro execution and to ignore the spreadsheet windows.

None—This option causes Quattro to update the screen during macro execution. Macros execute slowest with this option.

/OPTIONS OTHER PARADOX

This command provides information that Quattro uses to query Paradox databases on a network without reading the file into a Quattro spreadsheet. This command must be performed before you use the /Database Query commands to query an external Paradox database stored on a network. You may also need to use this command if you are using Quattro Pro and Paradox simultaneously.
OPTIONS
Network Type—This option selects the network type that operates the network containing the Paradox databases. Pick the appropriate choice from the displayed list.

Directory—This option sets the network directory that contains the PARADOX.NET file. Type this entry and press ENTER.

Retries—This option sets the number of milliseconds between retries that Quattro attempts to obtain a file reservation if it does not have the file reservation already. Type a number between 0 and 65000 and then press ENTER.

Quit—This option returns you to the Options menu.

/OPTIONS OTHER UNDO

This command enables the undo function so you can use the ALT-F5 (UNDO) key or /Edit Undo to remove the effect of an undo-able action.
OPTIONS
Select Enable or Disable to turn the undo function on or off.

/OPTIONS PROTECTION

This command allows you to prevent the data in your spreadsheet from being overwritten accidentally. When you use this command to enable spreadsheet protection, you cannot delete, edit, or replace the entries in protected cells. When

748 *Quattro Pro 4.0 Handbook*

you enable protection, you will see a PR or U in the input line indicating whether the current cell is protected or unprotected. Even though individual cells have a protection attribute, Disable causes Quattro to ignore this attribute. Quattro Pro 4 also has formula protection that prevents you from making changes to formulas in any cell in the spreadsheet while letting you alter empty cells and cells containing values and labels.

OPTIONS

Enable—This option enables protection for the protected cells in your spreadsheet.

Disable—This option disables protection for all the cells in your spreadsheet.

Formulas—This option adds or removes formula protection to the current spreadsheet. Select Protect to add the formula protection and then type the password to assign to the spreadsheet twice, pressing ENTER after each time. To remove formula protection, use this command and option then select Unprotect, type the password, and press ENTER. Like the password you add to a file, the password that protects spreadsheet formulas is case sensitive.

/OPTIONS QUIT

This command leaves the Options menu and returns you to the READY mode.

OPTIONS
None.

/OPTIONS RECALCULATION

This command sets the defaults that Quattro uses to recalculate the spreadsheet. These default settings include the order in which Quattro recalculates the formulas, the number of times Quattro recalculates the formulas, and the timing of formula recalculation. This command also describes the first circular cell if the spreadsheet has one.

OPTIONS

Mode—This option determines when Quattro recalculates the formulas. Its three selections are Automatic, Manual, and Background. If you select Manual, Quattro recalculates the spreadsheet when you press F9 (CALC). If you select Automatic, Quattro recalculates formulas as the values that they depend on change. If you select Background, Quattro recalculates formulas as the values they depend on change but Quattro only performs the recalculations when you are not using the spreadsheet for other operations.

Order—This option determines the order in which Quattro calculates the formulas. Its three selections are Natural, Column-wise, and Row-wise. If you select Natural, Quattro recalculates the cells referenced by a formula before it recalculates the formula. The other two methods are for compatibility with other spreadsheet programs. **Column-wise** recalculates formulas a column at a time. **Row-wise** recalculates formulas a row at a time.

Iteration—This option determines the number of times Quattro recalculates a circular reference before Quattro completes the recalculation process. Quattro's default is 1 but this number should be increased if the spreadsheet contains intentional circular references.

Circular Cell—This option provides the cell address of the first circular reference that Quattro finds when it recalculates the spreadsheet.

Quit—This option exits the Recalculation menu and returns you to the Options menu.

/OPTIONS SPEEDBAR

This command sets the buttons that appear on the SpeedBar at the top or right side of the screen depending on the display mode. You can change all the buttons except for the END and arrow key combinations. Each of the up to 15 buttons can perform any menu command, macro instructions, or combination of both. Quattro Pro 4 has two SpeedBars—one for READY mode and one for EDIT mode, which also appears in LABEL, VALUE, and POINT mode. In prior releases, Quattro Pro had a mouse palette instead of a SpeedBar that only had eight buttons and was changed with the /Options Mouse Palette command.

OPTIONS

Once you select this command, you must select READY mode SpeedBar or EDIT mode SpeedBar for the SpeedBar you want to change. Next, select **A** Button through **O** Button to select the button you want to assign or change. Then after selecting the button, select **Short** name, **Long** name, or **Macro** for the button feature you want to change. If you select **Short** name, type the three letters that appear in the button when the SpeedBar appears on the right side of the screen, and press ENTER or click Enter in the box. If you select **Long** name, type up to 10 characters that appears in the button when the SpeedBar appears below the menu bar and press ENTER or click Enter in the box. If you select **Macro**, type the macro instructions and/or menu-equivalent commands you want performed when the button is selected, and press ENTER or click Enter in the box. When you have finished modifying the button, select **Quit** to return to the button to change. At this point, you can select another button to modify. When you select **Quit** from this menu, you are returned to the menu to select the SpeedBar to change. From this point, you can select another SpeedBar or **Quit** to return to the Options menu. While you are editing a SpeedBar's buttons, you must use consecutively numbered buttons, which means that you cannot assign the fifteenth button until you have assigned tasks to the first fourteen. To make these changes applicable to subsequent times that you use Quattro Pro, use the /Options Update command.

/OPTIONS STARTUP AUTOLOAD FILE

This command instructs Quattro to retrieve automatically a particular file each time you load Quattro. Initially, Quattro automatically loads any file named QUATTRO.WQ1.

OPTIONS

When you use this command, Quattro prompts for the name of the file to load automatically. Type the name of the desired file, and press ENTER. After you execute this command, Quattro displays the file name listed at the right of the Autoload File option in the Startup menu. You must use the /Options Update command so the autoload feature is effective the next time you load Quattro.

/OPTIONS STARTUP BEEP

This command allows you to turn off the beep that sounds when you make an error. Although most people find the beep helpful because it alerts them to an error, some find it annoying.

OPTIONS

You can turn off this beeping sound by selecting **No** when Quattro provides you with the Yes/No choices. If you want to make this change permanent, use the /Options Update command. When you want to hear the beep again, select **Yes**.

/OPTIONS STARTUP DIRECTORY

This command sets the directory that Quattro uses to search for your files. Initially, the default directory setting is the same as the directory used to load Quattro. You can change this directory to any valid drive and directory. After using this command, you must use the /Options Update command, if you want the directory to be the default the next time you load Quattro. If you want to change the directory for only the current session, use the /File Directory command.

OPTIONS

The only option for this command is the drive and directory designation you provide. It must be a valid drive and directory for the system you are using. After entering the drive and directory, press ENTER.

/OPTIONS STARTUP EDIT MENUS

This command loads the Menu Builder and runs it. The Menu Builder lets you create and modify menu trees.

OPTIONS

From the Menu Builder, you can make extensive changes to the current menu. The Menu Builder is covered in detail in Chapter 10.

/OPTIONS STARTUP FILE EXTENSION

This command sets the default file extension Quattro assigns when you use the **/File Save, /File Save As,** or **/Tools Xtract**. The default of .WQ1 is for Quattro Pro files but it can be changed to any valid extension that Quattro can save and retrieve. You can change this extension to use different types of file formats. When you execute this command, Quattro prompts you for the default extension. Type in the default extension, and press ENTER. You must also use the **/Options Update** command if you want Quattro to use this setting permanently.

OPTIONS
None.

/OPTIONS STARTUP MENU TREE

This command lets you select the desired menu tree. Menus can be created and modified using the Menu Builder. To work with the Menu Builder, use the **/Options Edit Menus** command.

OPTIONS
The only option for this command is the menu you select. When you enter this command, Quattro displays a list of the .MU menu tree files in Quattro's directory. Highlight one of them, and press ENTER.

/OPTIONS STARTUP QUIT

This command leaves the Startup menu and returns you to the Options menu.

OPTIONS
None.

/OPTIONS STARTUP STARTUP MACRO

This command sets the macro name that Quattro tries to execute every time a file is loaded. You can change the macro name from the default of \0 to another valid macro name. When you use this command, Quattro prompts for the name of the macro to run when a spreadsheet is loaded. Type the macro name, and press ENTER. The macro name appears on the right of the Startup Macro option in the Startup menu. You must use the **/Options Update** command so that Quattro executes this default macro in the next Quattro session. If you want to eliminate any startup macro, execute this command, press ESC to remove the existing entry, and then press ENTER to finalize the new setting.

OPTIONS
None.

/OPTIONS STARTUP USE DIALOGS

This command sets whether you will use dialog boxes with commands such as /Print Layout and /Graph Customize Series.

OPTIONS

Your two options for this command are Yes, which uses dialog boxes, and No, which does not.

/OPTIONS UPDATE

This command saves the default changes that you make. Quattro saves all the settings made with the menu items in the Options menu above the Update menu item. Quattro uses these default settings the next time you begin a Quattro session. Since this command is also equivalent to the /Graph Customize Series Update, /Print Layout Update, and /Print Graph Print Layout Update commands, this command also saves the graph and printing customization settings. This command also saves settings made with /Tools Macro and /Database Sort Sort Rules, as well as libraries loaded with /Tools Library Load.

OPTIONS

None.

/OPTIONS VALUES

This Quattro Pro 3 and 4 command displays some of the spreadsheet settings that will be saved if you select the /Options Update command. The settings include how commands are recorded by the macro recorder, the default printer, the startup directory, the spreadsheet that Quattro Pro will automatically load, the macro that Quattro Pro will automatically execute, the default file extension, the graphics quality, whether undo is enabled, SQZ file compression settings, the screen type, the clock display, whether numbers are sorted before or after labels, the label order, the Paradox file that Quattro will automatically load when you switch between Quattro and Paradox and whether the file is loaded, and the international currency symbol and placement.

OPTIONS

This command does not have any options and the box this command displays will disappear once you press a key or press the mouse button.

/OPTIONS WYSIWYG ZOOM %

This Quattro Pro 3 and 4 command enlarges or reduces the spreadsheet display to be larger or smaller than it will appear when you print it. You can use this option to quickly see more or less of the spreadsheet data.

OPTIONS

The only option for this command is to enter the percentage of the original size that you want the spreadsheet to appear. Numbers less than 100 reduce the spreadsheet size so you see more of it on the screen, and numbers more than 100 expand the spreadsheet size so you can see less of it on the screen.

/PRINT ADJUST PRINTER

This command adjusts the printer. The options for this command move the paper in the printer and tell Quattro that the printer is at the top of the page. Quattro keeps track of the top of the page by using an internal counter and the number of lines per page set by the /Print Layout Margins Page Length command. Since Quattro keeps track of the top of the page, manually moving the paper makes Quattro's record of the location of the top of the page incorrect and causes Quattro to page break incorrectly. Using this command ensures that Quattro breaks the spreadsheet into pages correctly. When Quattro is loaded, it assumes that the printer is at the top of the page.

OPTIONS

Skip Line—This option moves the paper in the printer forward one line. Use this option to create space between two printed blocks.

Form Feed—This option moves the paper in the printer forward one page.

Align—This option tells Quattro that the printer is currently positioned at the top of the page. This resets Quattro's internal counter. This command also sets the page counter to zero.

/PRINT BLOCK

This command defines the block of the spreadsheet that Quattro prints when you use the /Print Spreadsheet Print command.

OPTIONS

This command prompts for the block to print. Type a block address or a name, and press ENTER. You can also use the Arrow keys to specify the block by pointing to the first cell in the block, typing a period, and using the Arrow keys to highlight the rest of the block. If a block is already highlighted, you can redefine it by pressing the ESC key to return to the specified block's upper-left corner or the BACKSPACE key to return to the selector's position when you entered Quattro's menu. You can also modify the current block by using the Arrow keys to move the block's lower-right corner. You can also use the period to rotate which block corner you can modify. The print block is marked with a dashed line when /Window Options Print Block is set to Display, and the print destination is the graphics printer, binary file, or Screen Preview.

If the contents of a cell within the print block borrows display space from cells outside of the print block, Quattro does not print the portion of these entries that borrow space. To print these entries in full, change the column width to allow the entire cell contents to display in its own column or expand the print block to include the borrowed space. If the print block exceeds the page in width or length, Quattro prints the data on multiple pages, automatically breaking the pages at appropriate locations.

A print block must consist of a contiguous block of cells. If you do not want to print some of the columns, use the **/Style Hide Column Hide** command on those columns.

NOTE

If the print block includes inserted graphs, Quattro will print them if the destination is a graphics printer, a binary file, or the Screen Preview.

/PRINT COPIES

This Quattro Pro 3 and 4 command specifies how many copies will print when you select **S**preadsheet Print or Print-to-Fit in the Print menu.

OPTIONS

The only option for this command is the number of copies you wish to print. By default this is 1 but you can enter a number between 1 and 1000. This reverts to 1 after you select **S**preadsheet Print or Print-To-Fit.

/PRINT DESTINATION

This command specifies where Quattro prints the file. Quattro lets you choose to print the spreadsheet to a printer or a file, or to display the spreadsheet as it will look printed using the Screen Preview. For all the options, Quattro does not start printing until you enter **/P**rint **S**preadsheet **/P**rint or Print-To-Fit.

OPTIONS

Printer—This option directs the print output to the printer. This is the default if a destination is not specified. The printer selection cannot print graphic features such as shading, fonts, and graphs.

File—This option sends the printed spreadsheet to a file without including graphics formatting such as fonts, shading, and graphs. When you select this option, Quattro lists the .PRN files in the current directory. Select one, or type a new name. Do not include an extension, since Quattro automatically adds .PRN. If you select an existing .PRN file, Quattro prompts for you to select between appending the new printed spreadsheet to the old one, backing up the old printed spreadsheet before printing the new one, canceling the command, or replacing the old printed spreadsheet with the new one.

Use the file destination option if you are importing the data into another file and need the file in an ASCII text file. If you are importing the file into another program, you should remove setup strings and execute the **/P**rint Layout Break Pages **N**o command. You can print a .PRN file with the DOS COPY command.

Graphics Printer—This option directs the print output to the printer. This option uses the printer selected with the /Options Hardware Printers Default Printer command. This printer selection can print graphic features such as shading, fonts, and graphs.

Binary File—This option sends the printed spreadsheet to a file. Unlike the File option, this option includes printer specific information that Quattro must supply to print using the default graphics printer. This destination will include graphic features such as shading, fonts, and graphs. When you select this option, Quattro lists the .PRN files in the current directory. Select one, or type a new name. Do not include an extension, since Quattro automatically adds .PRN. If you select an existing .PRN file, Quattro prompts for you to select between backing up the old printed spreadsheet before printing the new one, canceling the command, or replacing the old printed spreadsheet with the new one. Use this destination option if you are printing the spreadsheet at another time. You can print this file with the DOS COPY command.

Screen Preview—This option displays the print block on the screen as Quattro would print the print block using the current settings and the graphics printer as the destination. This option lets you visually confirm the output before you actually print it.

/PRINT FORMAT

This command determines the format that Quattro uses to print the block.

OPTIONS

As Displayed—This option causes Quattro to print the spreadsheet in the format displayed on the screen. When you select this option, Quattro prints the cells using their display format and column widths. This option prints the formulas' results rather than the formula, unless a format of text is selected. This option is Quattro's default.

Cell-Formulas—This option causes Quattro to print the cell contents. When you select this option, Quattro prints the cell addresses followed by font, format, and column width information and the cell's contents. This option prints formulas as the formula entered rather than the formula result. This format also prints cells comments.

/PRINT GRAPH PRINT DESTINATION

This command specifies the destination for the printed graph as the default printer, a file or the screen preview. You must perform this command before the /Print Graph Print Go command is executed if you want to print the graph to a device other than the printer.

OPTIONS

File—This option directs Quattro to print the graph to a file. This file contains the same information that Quattro would send to the printer if you selected **Graph Printer**. When you select this option, you must provide a file name. Quattro will add a .PRN extension if you do not provide one.

Graph Printer—This option directs Quattro to print the graph to the printer specified with the /Options Hardware Printers Default Printer command.

Screen Preview—This option displays the graph as it will appear if you select **Graph Printer** as the destination. Quattro will not display the graph until you use the /Print Graph Print Go command.

/PRINT GRAPH PRINT GO

This command directs Quattro to print the current graph or the graph specified with the /Print Graph Print Name command using the current settings. If the destination is Screen Preview, Quattro displays the Screen Preview screen with the graph as Quattro would print it if the destination is the default graphics printer. If the destination is a file, Quattro writes the information to the file. If the selector is on an inserted graph this command will print the inserted graph.

OPTIONS
None.

/PRINT GRAPH PRINT LAYOUT

This command allows you to describe how you want your graph printed on the page. You can specify the size of the area used to print the graph. Quattro then automatically sizes the graph to use the space available.

OPTIONS

Left Edge—This option determines the distance between the left edge of the paper and the graph.

Top Edge—This option determines the distance between the top edge of the paper and the graph.

Height—This option determines the distance between the top and the bottom of the graph. If this option equals 0, Quattro uses a default setting of 10 inches.

Width—This option determines the distance between the left and the right side of the graph. If this option equals 0, Quattro uses a default setting of 7.5 inches.

Dimensions—This option determines whether the measurements for **Left Edge**, **Top Edge**, **Height**, and **Width** are measured in centimeters or inches.

Orientation—This option determines the rotation of the graph. If you set this option to **Portrait**, Quattro prints the graph vertically. If you set this option to **Landscape**, Quattro prints the graph horizontally.

4:3 Aspect—This option determines if Quattro maintains the 4:3 ratio between width and height as the graph expands to fill the largest available area. If you select **Yes**, Quattro only expands the graph to fit the largest area while maintaining the

4:3 ratio. If you select No, Quattro expands the graph to fit the largest area even if it changes the ratio between width and height.

Reset—This option returns the other settings in the Layout menu to the default settings.

Update—This option makes the current printing settings the new defaults. This saves both the settings made in the Graph Print Layout menu and in the Print Layout menu. This is the same as using the /Options Update command.

Quit—This option leaves the Layout menu and returns you to the Graph Print menu.

/PRINT GRAPH PRINT NAME

This command instructs Quattro to print a named graph rather than the current one.

OPTIONS

When you execute this command, Quattro prompts for a graph name and displays a list of the current named graphs. Type a graph name or select one from the box that Quattro displays.

/PRINT GRAPH PRINT QUIT

This command leaves the Graph Print menu and returns you to the Print menu.

/PRINT GRAPH PRINT WRITE GRAPH FILE

This command prints the current or named graph to a file in a PC Paintbrush, PostScript, or 1-2-3 .PIC format. Several word processors and desktop publishing packages can combine graphs saved in one of these formats with text.

OPTIONS

.EPS File—This prints the current graph to a file in PostScript format. When you select this option, Quattro prompts you for a file name. Select a file from the box, or type a file name. Quattro automatically adds an .EPS extension. When you press ENTER, Quattro immediately saves the graph to a file.

.PIC File—This prints the current graph to a file in 1-2-3's PrintGraph format. When you select this option, Quattro prompts you for a file name. Select a file from the box, or type a file name. Quattro automatically adds a .PIC extension. When you press ENTER, Quattro immediately saves it to a file.

Slide EPS—This prints the current graph to a file in a .EPS file that slide production services can use to create slides with greater clarity than the .PCX files. When you select this option, Quattro prompts you for a file name. Select a file from the box, or type a file name. Quattro automatically adds an .EPS extension. When you press ENTER, Quattro immediately saves the graph to a file.

.PCX File—This prints the current graph to a file in a .PCX file that graphics programs such as PC Paintbrush can use. When you select this option, Quattro prompts you for a file name. Select a file from the box, or type a file name. Quattro automatically adds .PCX extension. When you press ENTER, Quattro immediately saves the graph to a file.

Quit—This option exits the menu and returns you to the Graph Print menu.

/PRINT HEADINGS

This command specifies the columns that Quattro prints at the left side of every page or the rows that Quattro prints at the top of every page. The /Print Layout Reset Headings command removes both the top and left headings.

OPTIONS

Your options for this command are Left Heading, which specifies the columns that will appear to the left of the print block and Top Heading, which specifies the rows that will appear above the print block. You do not have to specify the entire block that you want to use as a heading; you only have to include one cell in a column or row to use the entire column or row. Do not include the columns or rows of the headings as part of the print block to prevent the columns or rows from printing twice. The rows in the left heading match the rows selected in the print block. The columns in the top heading match the columns selected in the print block. A heading cannot include any setup strings.

/PRINT LAYOUT BREAK PAGES

This command determines whether Quattro breaks a spreadsheet into pages.

OPTIONS

If you select **Yes**, Quattro uses the number of lines per page provided by the /Print Layout Margins Page Length command. If you select **No**, Quattro does not separate the spreadsheet into pages. Quattro also does not print the header and footer. You can also set whether Quattro Pro breaks pages by selecting /Print Layout and choosing Yes or No after Break Pages in the Print Layout Options dialog box.

/PRINT LAYOUT DIMENSIONS

This command determines whether Quattro measures the margins and page length in lines and characters, centimeters, or inches. When you change from one measurement type to another, Quattro automatically converts the current settings for you. When you enter the page length and margins, Quattro displays the range of the valid settings using the current measurement setting. If you are printing in WYSIWYG, you will want to work with margins measured in inches or centimeters rather than in Lines/Characters, since this is a more meaningful method of measurement as you use fonts of different sizes. You can also set the printing dimensions by selecting **/Print Layout** and choosing one of the options below Dimensions in the Print Layout Options dialog box.

OPTIONS

Lines/Characters—This option measures the page length, top margin, and bottom margins by the number of lines and the left and right margins by the number of characters. This is Quattro's default.

Inches—This option measures the page length and margins using inches.

Centimeters—This option measures the page length and margins using centimeters.

/PRINT LAYOUT FOOTER

This command defines the text that Quattro prints at the bottom of each page. The footer can consist of up to 511 characters. The footer usually displays information that does not appear in the spreadsheet. Quattro uses three lines on each page for the footer: one for the footer and two blank lines to separate it from the spreadsheet data. You can add or alter the footer using the Print Layout Options dialog box by selecting Footer Text and then typing or editing the footer text.

OPTIONS

Quattro uses three characters to provide additional features in a footer. The pound sign (#) is replaced by the current page number on every page. Quattro converts the commercial at sign (@) to the current system date when it prints the spreadsheet. The vertical bar (|) changes the alignment of the header text. Left-aligned text must appear before any vertical bars. Centered text follows the first vertical bar. Right-aligned text follows the second vertical bar. If you want to use a spreadsheet cell for the footer, enter a backslash followed by the cell address or block name that you want to use.

/PRINT LAYOUT HEADER

This command defines the text that Quattro puts at the top of each page. A header entry can consist of up to 511 characters. The header usually presents information that does not appear in the print block. Quattro uses three lines on each page for the header: one for the header and two blank lines to separate it from the spreadsheet data. You can add or alter the header using the Print Layout Options dialog box by selecting Header Text and then typing or editing the header text.

OPTIONS

Quattro uses three characters to provide additional features for the headers. The pound sign (#) is replaced by the current page number on every page. Quattro replaces the commercial at sign (@) with the current system date when the spreadsheet is printed. The vertical bar (|) changes the alignment of the header text. Left-aligned text must appear before any vertical bars. Centered text follows the first vertical bar in the header. Right-aligned text follows the second vertical bar in the header. If you want to use a spreadsheet cell for the header, enter a backslash followed by the cell address or block name that you want to use.

/PRINT LAYOUT MARGINS

This command specifies the settings Quattro uses for margins and page length. These measurements will be in lines and characters, inches, or centimeters depending on the setting of /Print Layout Dimensions. When you are printing to a graphics printer or binary file, Quattro Pro will convert the page length and margins into the appropriate measurements. Then Quattro Pro will fit as many characters and lines as possible on the page depending on the fonts and row heights of the selected block. You can set the page length and margins using the Print Layout Options dialog box by selecting **Page Length**, **Left**, **Top**, **Right**, or **Bottom** and then typing a new number.

OPTIONS

Page Length—This option is the length of the page. Using line numbers, it can be any number between 0 and 100. Quattro uses this number to determine when it should break a spreadsheet into pages and to count the number of lines it has printed to determine the beginning of the page. Quattro's initial default is 66 lines per page which equals 11 inches or 28 centimeters (cm). To change the page size to another preset size, use the **/Options Hardware 1st Printers** (or **2nd Printer**) **Type of printer/Mode** command instead of changing the page length.

Left—This option determines the space between the left edge of the paper and the printed spreadsheet. Using the number of characters, this number ranges between 0 and 254. Quattro's initial default of 4 characters creates a .4 inch margin or 1 cm.

Top—This option specifies the space between the top edge of the paper and the printed spreadsheet. Using the number of lines, this number ranges between 0 and 32. Quattro's initial default of 2 lines creates a one-third-inch margin or .85 cm.

Right—This option is the space allowed for printing the right margin and the spreadsheet. Quattro's initial default of 76 characters creates a right .4 inch or 1 cm margin. This number is between 0 and 254 characters.

Bottom—This option specifies the space between the bottom edge of the paper and the printed spreadsheet. Quattro's initial default of 2 lines creates a one-third-inch or .85 cm margin. Using the line number dimensions, this number is between 0 and 32.

Quit—This option exits the Margins menu and returns you to the Layout menu.

/PRINT LAYOUT ORIENTATION

This command determines the rotation of the spreadsheet. You can use this command to print your spreadsheet sideways.

OPTIONS

The options for this command are Portrait, which prints the spreadsheet vertically and Landscape, which prints the spreadsheet horizontally. Quattro Pro 3 and 4 have a third option, Banner, which prints the output sideways. But unlike Landscape, Quattro Pro does not split the output into pages so it can print over several separate pages. This last option is not available for daisy wheel and laser printers. Since banner printing prints as if the output is on one page, headers, footers, and top and left headings are only printed once. You can also change the orientation by selecting Portrait, Landscape, or Banner under Orientation in the Print Layout Options dialog box.

/PRINT LAYOUT PERCENT SCALING

This Quattro Pro 3 and 4 command expands or compresses the output by a percentage of the original size. If you use this command, do not use the /Print Print-To-Fit command to start printing the spreadsheet. /Print Print-To-Fit will ignore this setting. You can also select this command by selecting /Print Layout to display the Print Layout Options dialog box and then selecting % Scaling.

OPTIONS

The only option for this command is the percentage of the original size. Numbers from 1 to 99 decrease the size of the output, and numbers from 101 to 1000 increase the size of the output. Shrinking or expanding the printed output only affects the printed material—settings made with the /Print Layout Margins command are not affected. If you change the scaling, certain hardware fonts that the spreadsheet has selected may print differently, since Quattro Pro may need to substitute a font that is the rescaled size.

/PRINT LAYOUT QUIT

This command exits the Layout menu or Print Layout Options dialog box and returns you to the Print menu.

OPTIONS
None.

/PRINT LAYOUT RESET

This command resets some or all of the print settings to their default values. For certain print settings like the print block, this command removes the current settings. For other settings, this command returns the settings to Quattro's initial defaults or the settings established with the last /Print Layout Update command. You can also perform this command by selecting Reset from the Print Layout Options dialog box.

OPTIONS

All—This option removes all the current print settings.

Print Block—This option removes the block setting created with the /Print Block command.

Headings—This option removes the settings created with the /Print Headings command.

Layout—This option returns the page layout settings to their values when the /Print Layout Update command was last executed.

/PRINT LAYOUT SETUP STRING

This command specifies the setup string that Quattro sends to the printer before printing a spreadsheet. The setup string is a printer control code that accesses special printer features, such as compressed print. You can also incorporate setup strings into your spreadsheet by inserting a blank row and placing two vertical bars (| |) and the setup string in the first column of the print block. Quattro will not print any other information that appears in the row with the setup string. The feature invoked by a setup string continues until another setup string undoes the first setup string or the printer is reset. The setup string that creates special printer features varies from printer to printer. You can find the correct setup strings in your printer manual under printer codes or printer commands. Decimal values must be preceded by a backslash (\). For example, ESC is \027. Setup strings may be up to 39 characters.

OPTIONS

Type in the setup string, and press ENTER. You also can enter a setup string by selecting Printer Setup string in the Print Layout Options dialog box.

NOTE

You can execute many of the printer features that other spreadsheet packages use setup strings to create through Quattro's menus.

/PRINT LAYOUT UPDATE

This command makes the current print settings the default settings that Quattro uses for the page layout. Quattro returns the page layout settings to their defaults whenever you execute the /Print Layout Reset command. Quattro also uses these defaults as the settings for all new spreadsheets. This command saves the layout settings shown with the /Print Layout and the /Print Graph Layout command. This command saves all of Quattro Pro's default settings as well and so performs the same action as the /Options Update command. You can also update the settings with the Print Layout Options dialog box by selecting Update.

OPTIONS
None.

/PRINT LAYOUT VALUES

This Quattro Pro 3 and 4 command displays the printing settings that have been made with other /Print Layout commands. The information displayed includes the printing destination, whether Quattro Pro will break the output into pages, how dimensions are measured, the page length, the margins, the setup string, and the orientation. This command is not available when Quattro Pro 4 is showing dialog boxes (/Options Startup Use Dialogs is set to Yes), because these values already appear in the Print Layout Options dialog box.

OPTIONS
This command does not have any options and the box this command displays will disappear once you press a key.

/PRINT PRINT MANAGER

This Quattro Pro 4 command opens a Print Manager window. From a Print Manager window, you can look at the print queue and change the printing tasks handled by a Novell print spooler or the Borland Print Spooler that comes with Quattro Pro 4. If you are using background printing, you must first load the Borland Print Spooler and then select /Options Hardware Printers Background Yes. Each printing task that the Print Manager monitors is called a *print job*.

OPTIONS
The Print Manager window initially displays the print jobs it is currently monitoring. For background printing with the Borland Print Spooler, the Print Manager window lists for each print job the sequence, the name of the temporary file containing the information to send to the printer, its status, its port, the temporary file's size, and the number of copies. For Novell network printing, the Print Manager window lists for each print job the sequence it will be printed, the user name for the server, the name of the print job, the status, the job number assigned to it by the network print spooler, the size of the temporary file, and the number of copies. The Print Manager window also has its own menu that includes the following selections:

File—The choices, Close and Close All, from the File pull-down menu are identical to the **/File Close** and **/File Close All** commands available in spreadsheet and File Manager windows.

Queue—This selects the print queue that is monitored in the Print Manager window. Select **B**ackground to monitor the background printing controlled by the Borland Print Spooler or **N**etwork to monitor the printing to a network printer on a Novell network.

Job—This changes when and whether a print job selected in the list is printed. You can select **S**uspend to postpone a selected print job until you later select **/J**ob **R**esume. You can also remove a selected print job by selecting **D**elete.

Window—The choices **Z**oom, **T**ile, **S**tack, **M**ove/Size, and **P**ick from the Window pull-down menu are identical to the **/W**indow **Z**oom, **/W**indow **T**ile, **/W**indow **S**tack, **/W**indow **M**ove/Size, and **/W**indow **P**ick commands available in spreadsheet and File Manager windows.

/PRINT PRINT-TO-FIT

This command in Quattro Pro 3 and 4 automatically contracts printed output to fit on one page, or on as few pages as possible. Quattro Pro makes the determination of the smallest it can compress the printed output while still making it legible based on the printer and its resolution. All the information on the page is scaled down although Quattro Pro uses the margins as set with **/P**rint **L**ayout **M**argins command. This command is like the **/P**rint **L**ayout **P**ercent Scaling command, except Quattro Pro determines how much to compress the output. If the spreadsheet uses hardware fonts, they may print differently since Quattro Pro may need to substitute a font that is the rescaled size.

OPTIONS

This command does not have any options, since it immediately prints the spreadsheet using all of the settings you have made up to this point. Once Quattro Pro has finished printing the spreadsheet, Quattro Pro returns to the Print menu.

/PRINT QUIT

This command exits the Print menu and returns you to the READY mode.

/PRINT SPREADSHEET PRINT

This command begins printing using the settings established with other print commands. If the destination is a file or a binary file, Quattro writes the information to that file. If the destination is Screen Preview, Quattro displays the spread-

sheet as Quattro would print it if Graphics Printer is chosen as the destination. To leave Screen Preview, press ESC or enter **/Q**uit.
OPTIONS
None.

/STYLE ALIGNMENT

This command aligns entries in a block of cells according to your specification. This setting affects both numbers and labels. However, this command does not affect blank cells within the block. Blank cells use the default label alignment setting when you make entries into them.

OPTIONS
General—This option aligns label entries according to the setting of **/O**ptions Formats Align Labels command and right-aligns numeric entries.
Left—This option aligns entries at the left of the cell.
Right—This option aligns entries at the right of a cell.
Center—This option centers entries within a cell.

NOTE
You can also perform this command by pressing CTRL-A or clicking Align in the SpeedBar and selecting between **G**eneral, **L**eft, **R**ight, and **C**enter and then selecting the block to align.

/STYLE BLOCK SIZE

This command (called **/S**tyle **B**lock Widths in earlier releases) sets the widths for multiple columns and heights for one or more rows. The options for this command let you set the column widths to a new value, reset the widths to the default, set the widths to be as wide as the data contained in the block, set a new row height, or return the row heights to the default. Once you select one of the options, Quattro prompts you for a block. You can type the block address or name or point to it using the arrow keys or a mouse. With the **S**et Width, **R**eset Width or **H**eight options, the block should include one cell from each column or row you want to affect. With the **A**uto Width option, the block should include all cells that you want Quattro to use to adjust the column width.

OPTIONS
Set Width—This option sets the widths of the columns in a block to a new value. When Quattro asks for the new column width, you can type in the new number, or you can press the RIGHT and LEFT ARROW keys to see the change. After entering the desired column width, press ENTER.
Reset Width—This option changes the column widths of a block to the default column width set with **/O**ptions Formats **G**lobal Width.

Auto Width—This option sets each column width in the block to a width sufficient to display the longest entry in each column of the block plus the number of extra characters specified when you select Auto Width.

Height—This option, introduced in Quattro Pro 3, sets row heights or returns row heights to their default. The default row height is based on the height of the largest characters in the row. After you select this option, you must select **Set Row Height** to select new row heights or **Reset Row Height** to return rows in a block to their default height. Next select a block containing the rows that you want to change. If you selected **Set Row Height**, you must enter the number of points tall (1 to 240) you want the rows. In the WYSIWYG display mode, you will see the new row size on the screen but in a text display mode, you will not see the changed row height until you print it. You can also change a row's height with a mouse, by dragging the row number up or down.

/STYLE COLUMN WIDTH

This command changes the width of a single column. To use it, move to the column whose width you want to change.

OPTIONS

When Quattro asks for the new column width, you can type in the new number or you can press the RIGHT and LEFT ARROW keys. When you press the RIGHT ARROW key, the number at the top of the screen for the current width increases by one and the column widens by one space. If you press the LEFT ARROW key, the number for the current width at the top of the screen decreases by one and the column becomes one space narrower. After entering the desired column width, press ENTER.

NOTE

This command has a shortcut, CTRL-W, which you can press instead of entering /Style Column Width. If you are using a mouse, you can widen a column by pointing to the column letter, holding down the mouse button and moving the mouse to the left to reduce the column width or to the right to expand the column width. If a block is selected before you do this, you will change the column widths of all columns in the selected block.

/STYLE DEFINE STYLE CREATE

This command creates and alters the named styles that you use in a spreadsheet. A named style is a group of formatting settings that includes alignment, data entry limitations, font, line drawing, numeric format, and shading. All cells that do not have a named style assigned to it automatically use the NORMAL named style; so changing that named style changes all entries you have not assigned to other style names.

OPTIONS

After selecting this command, type the name of the style definition you want to create or select one from the list of existing named styles Quattro Pro presents if you want to alter an existing one. Next, Quattro Pro displays a menu containing these options:

Font—This option sets the font of the selected named style. The menu that appears is identical to the menu selections you have with the /Style Font command.

Line Drawing—This option sets the lines drawn around the cells in the spreadsheet block that uses the selected named style. After selecting this option, select from Top, Bottom, Left, Right, or Quit. When you select one of the first four choices, you can select from None, Single, Double, or Thick.

Shading—This option sets the shading for the cells using the named style. Select from None, Gray, or Black.

Alignment—This option sets the alignment for the cells using the named style. Select from General, Left, Right, or Center.

Data Entry—This option sets any data limitations that apply to the cells using the named style. Select from General, Labels Only, or Dates Only. These are the same data limitations you can add to a block with the /Database Data Entry command.

Numeric Format—This option sets the numeric format for the cells using the named style. You have all the formatting options that are available through the /Style Numeric Format command with the addition of User Defined. If you select User Defined, you must type the definition of the custom format in response to Quattro Pro's prompt. This lets you create formats for numbers and dates that are not available through the /Options Formats Numeric Format or Style Numeric Format command.

Quit—This option finalizes the style changes and returns to the /Style Define Style menu.

/STYLE DEFINE STYLE ERASE

This command removes a named style from a spreadsheet block so the block uses the default NORMAL named style.

OPTIONS

The first option you have for this command is the named style you want to delete. Select one from the list that Quattro Pro displays, or type the style name. The second option for this command is selecting the block that contains the name style you want to erase.

/STYLE DEFINE STYLE FILE

This command stores named styles in a file and add named styles from a file to the current spreadsheet. This command is used to share named styles between files.

OPTIONS

Retrieve—This option adds style names and definitions saved in a file to the current spreadsheet. The style names and definitions are combined with the style names and definitions in the current spreadsheet. Select one of the style file with a .STY extension, or type the style file name and press ENTER or click the Enter button.

Save—This option puts the style names and their style definitions in a file that you can later bring into other spreadsheets. Type a name for the file, and press ENTER or click the Enter button. If you name the file QUATTRO.STY (you must select **Replace** when you save it), Quattro Pro will use the style file for all new spreadsheets.

/STYLE DEFINE STYLE QUIT

This command leaves the /Style Define Style menu and returns to READY mode.
OPTIONS
None.

/STYLE DEFINE STYLE REMOVE

This command removes a named style that you created with the /Style Define Style Create command from the spreadsheet. You cannot erase the NORMAL named style. When you remove a named style that spreadsheet blocks use, the spreadsheet blocks continue to have the formatting information but without the style name connected to it as if you used separate /Style and /Database commands to add the formatting to the cells.

OPTIONS

The only option you have for this command is the named style you want to delete. Select one from the list that Quattro Pro displays, or type the style name. If spreadsheet cells use that named style, you have an additional confirmation to delete the style name. Select **Yes** to delete the style name or **No** to cancel the command.

/STYLE FONT

This command sets the fonts a spreadsheet uses and the cells that the current spreadsheet uses. This command is different in Quattro Pro 4 and in prior releases. For Quattro Pro 3 and earlier, the /Style Font command is identical to the /Style FontTable command described below. The fonts only appear in WYSIWYG display mode or when you print the spreadsheet choosing **Binary File**, **Graphics Printer**, or **Screen Preview** as the destination. Quattro provides several Bitstream typefaces and Hershey fonts. Quattro can also use the fonts a Postscript or Hewlett-Packard LaserJet printer automatically supplies as long as you select one of these printers with the /Options Hardware Printers Default Printer command.

OPTIONS

The first option for this command is the block you want to set the font for. Select the block by pointing or typing, and then press ENTER or click [Enter] in the input line. Next, Quattro Pro displays a menu with the following options:

Typeface—This option sets the typeface of the font the block uses. Select one of the fonts from the box Quattro Pro displays. The displayed fonts include Bitstream, Hershey, and any printer defined fonts that Quattro Pro can use. Bitstream fonts followed by an -SC are faster fonts to use than the same Bitstream fonts without the -SC.

Point Size—This option sets the size of the font for the block. Select a point size from the ones listed.

Color—This option sets the color of the font for the block. Select one of the colors from the palette or list of color names Quattro Pro displays. The way the colored text will print depends on your printer.

Bold—This options sets whether the block uses boldfaced characters. Selecting this option toggles this option on or off. When On is displayed the block is boldfaced, and when Off is displayed the block is not.

Italic—This option sets whether the block uses italicized characters. Selecting this option toggles this option on or off. When On is displayed the block is italicized, and when Off is displayed the block is not.

Underlined—This option sets whether the block uses underlined characters. Selecting this option toggles this option on or off. When On is displayed the block is underlined and when Off is displayed the block is not.

Reset—This option resets the Bold, Italic, and Underlined options to Off.

Quit—This option leaves the menu of options and applies the font selections you have made to the block.

NOTE

You can also select this command by clicking Font in the SpeedBar.

/STYLE FONTTABLE

This command sets the fonts of a spreadsheet using a font table. This command is identical to the /Style Font command in Quattro Pro 3 and earlier. With a font table, the spreadsheet uses one of eight fonts in the table using font 1 as the default. To change a font a block uses, set the block to use another font table entry and then change that font table entry's characteristics to match the font you want the block to use. You can change the font characteristics of any or all of the eight font table entries. Each spreadsheet can have different font table characteristics.

OPTIONS

This command has two types of options. The first type selects which font table entry a spreadsheet block will use. The second type of options selects the font attributes that each of the entries in the font table has. These options are:

1 Font 1 through *8 Font 8*—These options set which of the eight entries in the font table a spreadsheet block uses. The font characteristics for each of the font table entries are described after each of the eight font table options. After selecting one of the eight spreadsheet font table entries, select the block that uses the font represented by the font table entry.

Edit Fonts—This options lets you change the font assigned to the font table entries. After selecting Edit Fonts, select **1 Font 1** through **8 Font 8** for the font table entry you want to change. Next, you have a menu containing **Typeface**, **Point Size**, **Style**, **Color**, and **Quit**. Select **Typeface** and one of the typefaces listed to select the font style the font table entry uses. Select **Point Size** and one of the sizes listed to select the size of the font table entry. Select **Style** and then from **Bold**, **Italic**, **Underlined**, or **Reset** to add or remove one of the font styles from the font table entry. Select **Color** and one of the colors shown to select the color for the font table entry. Select **Quit** when you have finished changing the font table entry and return to the list of selections you saw when you selected Edit Fonts. Any spreadsheet cells assigned to the font table entry change to use the modified font entry settings. The **Reset** and **Update** selections from the menu that you see when you select Edit Fonts have the same effect as the Reset and Update options described below. The **Quit** selection from the menu that you see when you select Edit Fonts leaves the menu and returns you to READY mode.

Reset—This option returns the font table entries to the default font table entries saved when you select Update.

Update—This option saves the current font table entry settings as the defaults to be used by later spreadsheets or when you select the Reset option.

/STYLE HIDE COLUMN

This command hides and displays columns. You can hide columns to temporarily remove them from display or to hide them so you can print data in noncontiguous columns. When columns are hidden, Quattro constructs the display from the remaining columns, effectively moving columns from the right to the left to fill in the space vacated by the hidden columns. Quattro does not reletter the exposed columns as it would if you deleted columns. The information in the hidden columns is still in memory. This information can be referenced in formulas. The hidden columns will temporarily reappear in POINT mode. When a hidden column temporarily reappears, the column letter will have an asterisk next to it.

OPTIONS

Expose—This option displays columns that you have previously hidden. When you select this option, Quattro displays all the columns and marks hidden columns with an asterisk (*) next to the column letter. Move the selector to the column you want to expose, and press ENTER. To expose more than one column, move the selector to the first column you want exposed, and select a block that contains the hidden columns you want to expose. If you want to expose columns that are not adjoining, include the currently exposed columns between the hidden columns in the block you select. When all columns that you want exposed are highlighted, press ENTER.

Hide—This option hides columns from the screen. When you select this option, move the selector to the first column you wish to hide. To hide more than the current column, press a period, select a block containing the columns you wish to hide, and press ENTER.

/STYLE INSERT BREAK

This command inserts a page break into the spreadsheet at the selector's position. This command inserts a row and puts a vertical bar and two colons (|::) into the first column. Quattro does not print any cell contents that appear in this row. You can also add page breaks by putting the page break indicator (|::) into the first column of a blank row. This command directs where Quattro should insert page breaks.

OPTIONS
None.

NOTE
The page break indicator must be in the first column of the print block. If the print block does not include the column with the page break, you will want to copy the page break symbol to the appropriate column before printing the block.

/STYLE LINE DRAWING

This command draws lines in a spreadsheet. You can select where the lines are drawn and the types of lines Quattro draws. As Quattro draws the lines, the line spacing and column spacing are adjusted to display the lines without affecting the column widths or inserting rows. Quattro will join lines where they meet. When you enter this command, Quattro prompts for the block you want to use to draw lines. Enter the block address or point to the block and press ENTER.

OPTIONS
The first set of options selects the placement of the lines:

All—This option draws a line around all four sides of each cell in the block.

Outside—This option draws a line around all four sides of the block.

Top—This option draws a line above the block.

Bottom—This option draws a line below the block.

Left—This option draws a line on the left side of the block.

Right—This option draws a line on the right side of the block.

Inside—This option draws horizontal and vertical lines between the cells in the block.

Horizontal—This option draws horizontal lines between the cells in the block.

Vertical—This option draws vertical lines between the cells in the block.

Quit—This option returns you to the READY mode.
The second set of options determines the type of line drawn:
None—This option removes the lines added with **Single**, **Double**, or **Thick**.
Single—This option draws a single line.
Double—This option draws a double line.
Thick—This option draws a single thick line.

/STYLE NUMERIC FORMAT

This command changes the appearance of value entries. You need to specify the block whose format you wish to change by typing the address and pointing to the cell addresses, or by entering an assigned block name. Quattro provides a wide variety of formatting options. This command only changes the cell's appearance, never the value of the entry.

OPTIONS

Fixed—This option displays a fixed number of decimal places for all the values in a block, for example, 1000.11.

Scientific—This option displays values in scientific exponential notation, for example, 1.00011E+03. The number of decimal places is user-defined.

Currency—This option displays values as currency. Quattro displays the currency symbol next to the number, for example, $1,000.11. Quattro adds commas as thousand separators and shows negative values in parentheses. The number of decimal places are user-defined to override the default setting of two decimal places.

,(Financial)—This format selection displays values with commas for thousand separators, for example, 1,000.11. Quattro encloses negative values in parentheses. The number of decimal places ar user-defined to override the default setting of two decimal places.

General—This option is the default display format. When you first load Quattro, the general format displays whole numbers, decimal fractions, and scientific notation depending on the magnitude of the cell entry.

+/- —This option creates simple horizontal bar charts. It transforms positive values into + signs with one + for each positive integer in the cell value. Quattro displays negative values as - signs with one minus sign generated for each negative integer.

Percent—This option multiplies the cell entry by 100 and places a percent symbol after the entry. For example, Quattro displays 0.95 as 95.00% and 1.2 as 120.00%.

Date—This option displays your values as dates. With a display format of Date, you can display date entries in the form of DD-MMM-YY, DD-MMM, MMM-YY, Long intl., and Short intl. The Time suboptions offer additional choices to display time serial numbers The time options display times in the format HH:MM:SS AM/PM, HH:MM AM/PM, Long intl., and Short intl.

Text—This option displays the formulas in the cells rather than their values. Numeric values appear in the General format.

Hidden—This option hides the cell contents from the screen. The contents of cells formatted as hidden show only on the input line.

Reset—This option displays the values in the block using the default numeric format selected with **/O**ptions Formats Numeric Format.

NOTE

This command's two shortcuts, pressing CTRL-E or clicking Format in the SpeedBar, can be pressed instead of entering **/**Style Numeric Format. You also can format cells for dates and times and convert any entries to dates or times with the **/D**atabase Data Entry Dates Only command.

/STYLE PROTECTION PROTECT

This command reprotects cells that you have unprotected with the /Style Protection Unprotect command. Once you enable protection, protected cells do not accept entries of any type. Cell protection has no effect until you execute the /Options Protection Enable command to enable protection. If you wish to protect cells that you previously unprotected, you can use this command.

OPTIONS

When you activate this command, specify the block of cells you wish to protect. You can type the cell addresses or the assigned name given to the block or point to the cell addresses of the desired block when Quattro prompts you for this entry.

/STYLE PROTECTION UNPROTECT

This command unprotects cells. You can remove the default protection with this command or you can unprotect cells that you reprotected.

OPTIONS

When you use this command, specify the block of cells that is to be unprotected. You can do so by typing in the cell addresses, pointing to the block of cells, or typing in the assigned name of the block when Quattro prompts you to do so.

/STYLE RESET WIDTH

This command changes the width of a column to the default column width set with **/O**ptions Formats Global Width. Press **/**, and select Style Reset Width. Quattro resets the column width of the column containing the selector.

OPTIONS

None.

/STYLE SHADING

This command adds shading to cells. The options for this command select the type of shading Quattro adds. When you enter this command, Quattro prompts for the type of shading you want. Select one of the options listed below. Then Quattro prompts for the block you want to shade. Enter the block address or point to the block, and press ENTER.

OPTIONS
None—This option removes the shading added with the other two options.
Gray—This option adds light shading to the selected cells.
Black—This option adds solid shading to the selected cells.

/STYLE USE STYLE

This command applies a style that is defined with the **/Style Define Style Create** command to a spreadsheet block. The block you select with this command sets the alignment, data entry limitations, font, line drawing, numeric format, and shading defined by the named style. When a cell uses a named style (except for the Normal named style), the style name appears in the input line when the selector is on the cell.

OPTIONS
The two options you have for this command are selecting the named style and selecting the spreadsheet block. For the named style, select one of the named styles from the list Quattro Pro provides. Next, select the spreadsheet block, and press ENTER or click [Enter] on the input line.

NOTE
You can also assign a named style to a block by clicking the Style button in the SpeedBar.

/TOOLS ADVANCED MATH INVERT

This command creates an inverted matrix. Matrix inversion is used in solving simultaneous equations. A matrix is a group of numbers arranged in tabular form. For example, a matrix consisting of eight rows and four columns of numbers is an eight by four matrix. To invert a matrix, the matrix must have the same number of rows and columns.

OPTIONS
When you select this option, Quattro prompts for the source matrix. Highlight the matrix or type the address or block name. Next Quattro prompts for the destination matrix. Move the cell selector to a blank area of a spreadsheet, and press ENTER. Quattro computes the inverted matrix and stores it starting in the cell that you selected for the matrix's destination.

/TOOLS ADVANCED MATH MULTIPLY

This command multiplies two matrices. A matrix is a group of numbers arranged in tabular form. For example, a matrix consisting of eight rows and four columns of numbers is an eight by four matrix. The order of the matrices is important, since the first matrix must have the same number of columns as the number of rows in the second matrix.

OPTIONS

When you use this command, Quattro prompts for the first matrix. Highlight the matrix or type the address and press ENTER. Next Quattro prompts for the second matrix. Highlight the matrix or type the address, and press ENTER. Finally, Quattro prompts for the destination block. Highlight the first cell at which you want the resulting matrix placed or type the address, and press ENTER. Quattro computes and puts the resulting matrix starting in the cell that you selected for the matrix's destination. The resulting matrix has the same number of rows as the first matrix and the same number of columns as the second matrix. Matrix multiplication is used with product costing and is combined with matrix inversion to solve simultaneous equations.

/TOOLS ADVANCED MATH REGRESSION

This command performs regression analysis to estimate the relationship between two or more variables. It estimates the correlation between one or more sets of independent variables and a dependent variable. The command calculates estimated coefficients of the independent variables and evaluates how well the independent variables predict the value of the dependent variable.

To use this command, you must perform a few preliminary steps. First, enter your dependent and independent data into their respective columns. Each column used in the regression analysis should contain only numeric values and should have the same number of entries. After entering the data, select the regression analysis command by pressing / and selecting **Tools Advanced Math Regression**.

OPTIONS

Independent—This option specifies the independent variables used in the regression analysis. Highlight the column containing the independent variables' values or type in the block address that contains the independent variables, and press ENTER.

Dependent—This option specifies the column containing the dependent variables' values. Highlight the columns containing the dependent variable or type in the block address, and press ENTER.

Output—This option specifies the output location. Point to the cell or type the address of the cell that will be the upper-left corner of the block containing the regression analysis output, and press ENTER. The output overwrites any existing data.

Y Intercept—This option instructs Quattro to either calculate the Y intercept or to set the value of the Y intercept to zero. Highlight the desired option, and press ENTER.

Go—This option commands Quattro to perform the necessary statistical computations.

Reset—This option removes the settings of the other options.

Quit—This option returns you to the spreadsheet in READY mode.

/TOOLS AUDIT

This command provides auditing features for the spreadsheet. With the features this command provides, you can trace the formulas that use a selected cell, the cells used by a selected formula, circular references, and the formulas that reference cells containing labels, cells equaling ERR, empty cells, and cells in other spreadsheets. This command provides more detailed information than you see in the map view available with /Window Options Map View Yes.

OPTIONS

Dependency—This option shows the relationship between the cells a formula uses and the other formulas that use the selected cell. For this option you must select a block in the spreadsheet. For each cell containing an entry in the block, Quattro Pro creates a dependency diagram. Cell addresses to the left of the diagrammed cell are formulas that reference the diagrammed cell or reference a formula that uses the diagrammed cell. Cell addresses to the right of the diagrammed cell are cells that the diagrammed cell uses or are used by formulas in the cells it references.

Circular—This option shows the relationship between circular reference formulas. Quattro Pro creates a diagram of the formula involved in the circular reference. As you move to each cell you can see the formula in the input line. The diagram includes CIRC after a cell is referenced twice.

Label References—This option finds cells and their formulas in the spreadsheet that reference cells in the spreadsheet that contain labels. This option displays the cell address, its formula, and the part of the formula that references a label for each formula that Quattro Pro finds.

ERR—This option finds cells and their formula in the spreadsheet that contain references to cells in the spreadsheet that equal ERR. This option displays the cell address, its formula, and the part of the formula that references a cell equaling ERR for each formula that Quattro Pro finds.

Blank References—This option finds cells and their formulas in the spreadsheet that contain references to empty cells in the spreadsheet. This option displays the cell address, its formula, and the cell that the formula references that is empty for each formula that Quattro Pro finds.

External Links—This option finds cells and their formulas in the spreadsheet that contain links to other spreadsheets. The information displayed contains the cell address, its formula, and the part of the formula that is linked to another spreadsheet for each formula that contains an external link.

Destination—This option selects where Quattro Pro puts the results of choosing one of the other options. Select **Screen** to display the auditing information on the screen or **Print** to print it to the print location selected with the /Print Destination command. When the destination is the screen and Quattro Pro has auditing information on more than one cell, you can display the next one by pressing PGDN or selecting /Next. You can display the previous one by pressing PGDN or selecting /Previous. You can press F5 (GOTO) or select /GoTo to leave the /Tools Audit command and go to the cell highlighted in the display. With the Dependency option of the /Tools Audit command you can select /Begin or press ENTER to change the cell that the dependency information displayed to the selected cell. When you are finished looking at the information, you can press ESC or select /Quit to return to the /Tools Audit menu. If the destination is the printer and you select **Dependency** or **Circular**, Quattro Pro creates a dependency diagram for each cell in the block you select or each cell in the circular reference. If you select **Label References**, **ERR**, **Blank References**, and **External Links**, each cell that Quattro Pro finds and the information for the cell is on a separate page.

Quit—This option leaves the /Tools Audit menu and returns to READY mode.

/TOOLS COMBINE ADD

This command adds some or all of the values from a spreadsheet file to the current spreadsheet values. When you use this command, Quattro uses the current cell in the current spreadsheet as the left uppermost cell that is added with data from disk. This operation affects blank cells and cells that contain values. Cells that contain labels or formulas are unaffected by this command.

OPTIONS

This command can add an entire file or a block of cells.

File—This option adds every value stored in a spreadsheet file to the corresponding cell in the current spreadsheet. The contents of cell A1 in the spreadsheet file are added to the current cell in the spreadsheet in memory.

When this option is selected from the Add submenu, Quattro displays a list of file names on the screen. Choose the name of the file containing the data to be added by typing the file name or by highlighting the file name with the arrow keys. After you have selected the file name, press ENTER so Quattro can add the two files.

Block—This option adds a block of cells stored in a spreadsheet file to the current spreadsheet. Quattro prompts you for the block address or name to use in the addition process. You can type the address or the assigned block name. Note that the assigned block name that you enter must have been previously assigned before the spreadsheet was stored on disk. Quattro prompts for the name of the spreadsheet file. The process for specifying the file name is identical to the instructions under the **File** option.

/TOOLS COMBINE COPY

This command replaces some or all the entries from the current spreadsheet with entries from a spreadsheet stored on a disk. When you select this command, Quattro uses the current cell as the upper-left cell replaced with entries from the spreadsheet file.

OPTIONS

Like the /Tools Combine Add command, the /Tools Combine Copy command has two options.

File—This option copies an entire spreadsheet from a disk file to the current spreadsheet. Cell A1 of the spreadsheet on disk is copied to the current cell on the spreadsheet in memory. When you select this option, Quattro prompts you for the file to be copied from and displays a menu of file names on the screen. You can specify a file name by typing the file name or by pointing to the file name with the arrow keys. After you have selected the desired file, press ENTER.

Block—This option copies a block of cells from a spreadsheet on disk to the current spreadsheet. When you choose this option, Quattro prompts for the block address or the assigned block name in the spreadsheet file. If you provide a block name, it must have been defined in the disk file. Next, you must specify the file containing the block. You can use the same options for this specification as were used with the File option discussed earlier.

NOTE

The results you produce with this command can also be achieved by copying the data you want from one spreadsheet to the spreadsheet in which you want the data.

/TOOLS COMBINE SUBTRACT

This command subtracts some or all the values in a spreadsheet file from the values in the current spreadsheet. When you use this command, Quattro uses the current location of the selector as the left uppermost cell affected by the subtract operation. The first cell in the spreadsheet file or selected block is subtracted from this location. When using this command, only blank cells and cells with value entries are affected. Cells containing formulas or label entries are unaffected.

OPTIONS

File—This option subtracts every value in a spreadsheet file from the cells in the current spreadsheet. The value of the cell that contains the selector in the current spreadsheet is used to subtract the value of cell A1 from the spreadsheet file. The value of cell B1 from the spreadsheet file is subtracted from the value of the cell to the right of the current selector location. When you select this option, Quattro prompts you for the name of the file. You can type the file name or use the arrow keys to point to the desired file name from the list that appears on the screen. Pressing ENTER is the last step required.

Block—This option subtracts a block of entries stored in a spreadsheet file from entries in the current spreadsheet. When you choose this option, Quattro prompts you for the block address in the spreadsheet file. You can specify the block by typing the address or the block name. Note that the block names must correspond with the file that you intend to use. After specifying the block, Quattro prompts for the file you want to use in the subtraction process. The rules for specifying the file name are the same as the rules described for the **File** option.

/TOOLS FREQUENCY

This command constructs a frequency distribution of values in a block. It tells you the number of times values fall within specified preestablished intervals. Before you use this command, you must create a column of value entries in a spreadsheet to record the specified frequency intervals (bins). These entries must be in ascending sequence from the top to the bottom of the columns. The column next to the frequency intervals must be empty. The row below the last frequency interval must be empty. Quattro analyzes your data against these bins.

OPTIONS

Quattro prompts you for the block containing the values for which you want to compute a frequency distribution. Highlight this block or type the block address of this column and press ENTER. Quattro prompts you for the bin's block. Highlight this block or type in the block address for this column. Press ENTER. If either the value's block or the bin's block is in a different spreadsheet, include the file name in square brackets before the block address or name. Quattro enters the frequency numbers in the column to the right of the bin numbers. Quattro uses the row immediately below the last bin to record the frequency number of all the values that exceed the last bin value.

/TOOLS IMPORT

This command imports data from another file. This command can import ASCII text files and delimited files. This command is often used to import data from sources that Quattro cannot automatically use with the **/File O**pen or **/File R**etrieve command. In these other types of programs, printing the information to a file often puts the information in a format that Quattro can import with this command.

OPTIONS

ASCII Text File—This option is selected when the information you want to export is not a delimited file. Often, the data imported with this option has each field of data in columns. When Quattro imports this type of file, each line in the import file is stored in a spreadsheet cell, starting with the current cell and working downward. After this option is selected, Quattro prompts for the name of the file to import. Quattro displays all of the .PRN files on the current directory. Either type a file name and extension or select one of the file names displayed. Once

Quattro imports the data, it can be broken into smaller fields using the /Tools Parse command.

Comma & "" Delimited File—This option is selected when each record is on a different line and the fields belonging to each record are separated by commas. If any of the fields contain labels, the labels are encased in quotes. When Quattro imports this type of file, each record is stored in a row. Each of the fields in a record is stored in a different column. After this option is selected, Quattro prompts for the name of the file to import. Quattro displays all the .PRN files on the current directory. Either type a file name and extension, or select one of the files displayed.

Only Commas—This option is selected when each record is on a different line and the fields belonging to each record are separated by commas. Unlike the comma-and-quote-delimited files, the text data is not enclosed in quotes. When Quattro imports this type of file, each record is stored in a row. Each of the fields in a record is stored in a different column. After this option is selected, Quattro prompts for the name of the file to import. Quattro displays all the .PRN files on the current directory. Either type a file name and extension, or select one of the files displayed.

/TOOLS LIBRARY

This command loads or unloads a library file that contains additional @functions. Quattro Pro library files have a .QLL extension. Once a library file is loaded, you can use the add-in functions provided in the library by putting the library name and a period before the function name. An example is @SAMPLE.SINH(5) where SAMPLE is the library file, SINH is the function name, and 5 is the argument the function uses. If you want a library file loaded every time you use Quattro Pro, load the library file and select /Options Update.

OPTIONS

Load—This option loads a library file. Select one form the file selection box. You can use the buttons and keys described with the /File Open command to change the location of the files listed.

Unload—This option unloads a library file. Select one from the list.

/TOOLS MACRO CLEAR BREAKPOINTS

This command removes breakpoints and trace cells inserted in a macro through the Debug Window. This command is equivalent to the /Reset command in the Debug Window.

OPTIONS

None.

NOTE

You can also perform this command by pressing ALT-F2 (MACRO) and selecting **Clear Breakpoints**.

/TOOLS MACRO DEBUGGER

This command executes macros using the macro debugger. The macro debugger offers several options for you to monitor the progress of a macro as it executes. When you enter this command, your choices are Yes or No. Selecting Yes activates the macro debugger when you execute a macro. Selecting No prevents the macro debugger from running when a macro executes. When the debugger is used, macros will execute in Single Step mode. Quattro displays the macro instructions it is performing in a Debug Window. When you execute a macro, you must press a key to tell the macro debugger to execute the next step. If you press ENTER, the macro will continue to execute at full speed until it reaches the end of the macro or one of the breakpoints set with the debugger menu options.

OPTIONS

Besides the Yes and No options that activate or deactivate the macro debugger, the macro debugger also has the following options, which appear when you type /:

Breakpoints—This option instructs Quattro to start executing macro instructions at a specific cell in Single Step mode. When you select this option, you must select which of four standard breakpoints you want to set. Then you must select **Block**, type the cell address or block name or point to the cell containing the breakpoint, and press ENTER. If the cell for the breakpoint is part of a loop, you may want to select **Pass Count** and enter the number of times the loop performs until the cell becomes a breakpoint. When you have finished selecting the breakpoint, select **Quit** to return to the menu to choose another breakpoint or select **Quit** to return to the Debugger menu.

Conditional—This option instructs Quattro to start executing macro instructions in Single Step mode when a condition becomes true. When you select this option, you must select which of four conditional breakpoints you want to set. Then you must type the cell address or block name or point to the cell containing the conditional breakpoint, and press ENTER. When you return to the Conditional menu, you can select another conditional breakpoint or select **Quit** to return to the Debugger menu.

Trace cells—This option displays the value of one to four cells displayed in the lower half of the Debug Window. When you select this option, you must select which of the four trace cells you want to set. Then you must type the cell address or block name or point to the cell you want, and press ENTER. When you return to the Trace Cells menu, you can select another trace cell or select **Quit** to return to the Debugger menu.

Abort—This option halts a macro's execution. This is the same as pressing CTRL-BREAK.

Edit a cell—This option edits a cell. When you select this option, you must select which cell you want to edit by typing the cell address or block name or pointing to the cell and pressing ENTER. After you have finished editing the cell, press ENTER. This option is for editing a cell during macro execution.

Reset—This option removes the settings for the standard breakpoints, conditional breakpoints and trace cells. This option is equivalent to /Tools Macro Clear Breakpoints.

Quit—This option returns control to the Debug Window so you can continue executing the macro.

NOTE

You can also execute this command by pressing ALT-F2 (MACRO) and selecting Debugger or by pressing SHIFT-F2 (DEBUG).

/TOOLS MACRO EXECUTE

This command executes a set of macro instructions.

OPTIONS

After selecting /Tools Macro Execute, Quattro prompts you for the block address that contains the macro instructions. Type the block address or highlight these cells and press ENTER. If you have named the cell containing the first macro instruction, press F3 (CHOICES) and select the block name from the list. Quattro only needs to know the location of the first macro instruction.

NOTE

You can also perform this command by pressing ALT-F2 (MACRO) and selecting Execute. If it is an instant macro you can press ALT and type the letter to execute the macro.

/TOOLS MACRO INSTANT REPLAY

This command replays the macro instructions Quattro has recorded with the macro recorder. This lets you test the macro before you copy it to the spreadsheet. It also lets you create a temporary macro that you want to execute at the moment but do not want to store in a spreadsheet.

OPTIONS

None.

NOTE

You can also perform this command by pressing ALT-F2 (MACRO) and selecting Instant Replay.

/TOOLS MACRO KEY READER

This command selects whether Quattro treats keys after / or {MENU} as using the 1-2-3 menu tree or the currently selected menu tree. This command lets you run macros created for 1-2-3 in Quattro without changing the currently selected menu tree. Menu equivalent commands will continue executing the same way regardless of this command's setting.

OPTIONS

The available options are Yes to have Quattro treat keys after / or {MENU} as using the 1-2-3 menu tree or No to have Quattro treat keys after / or {MENU} as using the current tree.

NOTE

If you want to make the change to this command permanent for future Quattro Pro sessions, use the /Options Update command.

/TOOLS MACRO LIBRARY

This command makes the current spreadsheet a macro library file or removes the macro library file setting from an existing macro library file. Quattro searches open macro libraries when you try to execute a macro that is not in the current spreadsheet. A macro library spreadsheet lets you gather your most frequently used macros into one spreadsheet.

OPTIONS

Your options for this command are Yes, which makes the current spreadsheet a macro library and No, which removes any macro library setting from the current spreadsheet.

NOTE

You can also perform this command by pressing ALT-F2 (MACRO) and selecting Library.

/TOOLS MACRO MACRO RECORDING

This command determines whether Quattro stores menu commands in macros generated by the macro recorder as the keystrokes or by their menu-equivalent commands. You should store macros using the actual keystrokes pressed if you are creating macros designed for another package, such as 1-2-3. You should store macros using the logical menu-equivalent commands if you are creating macros to execute in Quattro and you want users to choose the menu tree they want to use. Making a change with this command affects how Quattro Pro records your menu selections when it records macros for you with /Tools Macro Record and when you display the Transcript window with /Tools Macro Transcript. You can change this command's settings, and Quattro Pro retroactively applies it to the macro instructions in its macro buffer and Transcript log.

OPTIONS

Your options for this command are Keystroke, which records menu actions as the keystrokes you enter and Logical, which records menu actions as menu-equivalent commands.

NOTE
You can also perform this command by pressing ALT-F2 (MACRO) and selecting **Macro Recording**.

/TOOLS MACRO NAME

This command names or removes the name assigned to a block of cells that contain a set of macro instructions. This command is for naming macros and removing the macro names without affecting the macro's contents.

OPTIONS

Create—After selecting this option, Quattro displays the existing block and macro names and prompts you for the name you wish to give the macro. Select one from the list or type the desired macro name, and press ENTER. The macro name may consist of up to 15 characters. If it is a backslash (\) followed by a letter, it becomes an instant macro, which you can execute by holding down the ALT key and typing the letter. If it is \0, Quattro executes the macro whenever the file is retrieved if \0 is the setting of the /Options Startup Startup Macro. Quattro then prompts for the block of cells that contains the macro instructions. You can designate the block by either typing the block address or by highlighting the block. This block may contain as much or as little of the macro as you desire as long as the upper-left corner of the block contains the first macro instruction. This command is equivalent to the /Edit Names Create command. In Quattro Pro 4, you can add notes to the block and macro names as described in the /Edit Names Create command.

Delete—After selecting this option, Quattro prompts you for the block name you want to delete and displays the existing block and macro names. Select one from the list, and press ENTER; or point to it, and press the mouse button. This option is equivalent to the /Edit Names Delete command.

NOTE
You can also perform this command by pressing ALT-F2 (MACRO) and selecting **Name**.

/TOOLS MACRO PASTE

This command copies the commands and keystrokes that Quattro has recorded to the spreadsheet. When you use this command, you must provide a macro name. This command performs the /Tools Macro Name Create command as it copies the macro commands to the spreadsheet.

OPTIONS

When you enter this command, you must provide a macro name and then a block address where Quattro will copy the commands and keystrokes. When Quattro prompts for the macro name, you can select one from the list of existing block and macro names Quattro provides or you can type a new name. If you select an existing block or macro name, you may want to press ESC or BACKSPACE if you want the commands and keystrokes copied to a different location. When you specify the block, you can specify either one row or multiple rows. If you specify only one row, Quattro stores the commands and keystrokes using as many rows as necessary. If you specify multiple rows, Quattro only uses the cells indicated to store the keystrokes and commands.

NOTE

You can also perform this command by pressing ALT-F2 (MACRO) and selecting Paste. This command by default uses menu equivalent commands to record the choices made with Quattro's menus. If you want to record the actual keystrokes, you must use the /Tools Macro Macro Recording command first.

/TOOLS MACRO RECORD

This command turns the macro recorder on. Once you execute this command, Quattro records the commands and keystrokes you perform until you select another menu item from the Macro menu. Once Quattro records the commands and keystrokes, Quattro remembers the commands and keystrokes until you exit Quattro or you enter this command again to record a new set of commands and keystrokes. Once the macro instructions are recorded, you can copy them to the spreadsheet with the /Tools Macro Paste command.

OPTIONS
None.

NOTE
You can also perform this command by pressing ALT-F2 (MACRO) and selecting Record.

/TOOLS MACRO TRANSCRIPT

This command activates the Transcript utility. You can use the Transcript utility to create macros and to recover from errors. Transcript stores a record of the commands and keystrokes you have performed. Transcript encloses the commands and keystrokes that you have performed from the last checkpoint. (a checkpoint is a command like /File Erase, /File Save, /File Save As, or /File Retrieve, which Quattro cannot undo the effects of.)

OPTIONS

Undo Last Command—This option performs all the commands from the last checkpoint except the last command executed. Select this option when you want to undo the effect of a command Quattro cannot undo with ALT-F5 (UNDO) or if Undo is not enabled.

Restore to Here—This option performs all the commands from the last checkpoint to the highlighted position. Before you can select this option, you must position the highlight to the last command you want Quattro to perform. This is the option to select when you want to undo the effects of more than one command.

Playback Block—This option performs all the marked commands in the Transcript log.

Copy Block—This option copies the marked commands to the current spreadsheet. Like the /Tools Macro Paste command, you must type a block name that this command will assign to the first cell in the block of copied macro instructions this option will place on the spreadsheet. Next, you must enter the cell address or point to the first cell where you want Quattro to copy the marked commands and keystrokes in the Transcript log.

Begin Block—This option marks the first command that will be used by the Playback Block or Copy Block option. All the commands between the command marked with this option and marked with the End Block option have a mark on the left side.

End Block—This option marks the last command that will be used by the Playback Block or Copy Block option. All the commands between the command marked with the Begin Block option and this option have a mark on the left side.

Max History Length—This option determines the number of commands and keystrokes Quattro stores in the Transcript log. This number can range between 0 (which disables the Transcript utility) and 25000. The next time Quattro reaches a checkpoint after the log file reaches the maximum history length, Quattro renames the log file from QUATTRO.LOG to QUATTRO.BAK and creates a new QUATTRO.LOG file for the commands and keystrokes entered after the last checkpoint.

Single Step—This option determines the speed that Quattro plays back the commands and keystrokes stored in the Transcript utility. The default, **No**, performs the commands and keystrokes as quickly as possible. **Yes** plays back the commands and keystrokes using Single Step mode. **Timed** plays back the commands and keystrokes with a few second intervals between keystrokes and commands. You can use this option to watch the steps Quattro performs without continually pressing the SPACEBAR or clicking the mouse as you do with Single Step mode.

Failure Protection—This option determines how frequently Quattro copies the newest keystrokes from the Transcript log to the QUATTRO.LOG file. The default is 100 commands and keystrokes.

NOTE

You can also perform this command by pressing ALT-F2 (MACRO) and selecting Transcript.

/TOOLS OPTIMIZER

This Quattro Pro 4 command starts the Optimizer to find the best values for selected spreadsheet cells that produce the results you want in other cells. This command can be used for linear and nonlinear problem solving. You want to use this when you want to find the values you can use in one set of cells that through the calculations in the spreadsheet produces other results. The options for this command describe the cells you want to change, how you want them changed, and the limits that you place on the cells used by the model. Before you use this command, you must create the model that the Optimizer will try to find the best solution for. In the initial cells that you want the Optimizer to find the best values for, put values in these cells that are the best estimate of what you expect the results to be, since it reduces time the Optimizer needs to find a solution, and in nonlinear problems, the problem may have more than one solution and the initial values select which of the solutions it finds are put into the spreadsheet cells.

OPTIONS

Solution Cell—This option selects the cell that contains the final result or the calculations and the value you want the cell to be. Select Cell, and choose the cell that contains the formula that you want to set to be another value when the Optimizer is finished finding new values for the cells you select with Variable Cell(s). Next, select Max, Min, Equal and choose whether you want the selected cell to be as large as possible (Maximize), small as possible (Minimize), equal to the value that you subsequently enter (Equal), or not used (None).

Variable Cell(s)—This option selects the cells that the Optimizer can change to make the solution cell equal its solution while staying within the limits set by Constraints. Select the block of up to 200 cells to use as the cells the Optimizer can change. If spreadsheet protection is enabled, these cells must be unprotected. These cells must contain numbers and cannot contain dates, formulas, or labels. If the cell you select with Solution Cell is a value, it must be included in the block you select with this option so the Optimizer can change it.

Constraints—This option places limits on cells in the spreadsheet model that must be met when the Optimizer searches for the best solution. One constraint must be created for each cell you want to place a limit. The limits you can put on cell formulas and numbers include having a cell less than or equal to, greater than or equal to, or equal to another value. To create a constraint, select Constraints and then select <Add New Constraint>. Next, select the cell that contains the formula result or value that you want to place a limit on called the constraint cell. Now choose from <=, >=, or = for the relationship you want between the constraint cell and its constraint value. Finally, type the number you want the constraint cell to equal. If you want a constraint that causes two cells to have the same value, put a formula that subtracts the two cells, and then have that cell with the subtraction formula equal to zero. To alter an existing constraint, select Constraints and the constraint you want to modify from the list. Then for each prompt, select the same entry or choose a different one.

Options—This option changes settings the Optimizer uses to find the values for the variable cells. You do not have to change any of the Optimizer options to use the Optimizer—only the ones you want. Once you select Options, you have another menu that includes Max Time, Max Iterations, Precision, Linear or Nonlinear, Show Iteration Results, Estimates, Derivatives, Search, and Quit. Choose Max Time and type a number between 1 and 1000 to set how many seconds that the Optimizer can spend looking for a solution. Choose Max Iterations and type a number between 1 and 1000 to set the maximum number of iterations (cycles through potential values for the variable cells) the Optimizer can try. Choose **Precision** and type a number between 0 and 1 for the decimal precision a constraint cell must equal or be relative to its constraint value. Choose Linear or Nonlinear and then select **Linear** or **Nonlinear** to select the type of problem the Optimizer will solve, since the Optimizer can solve linear problems quicker than nonlinear ones. But if you problem is nonlinear, you must select **Nonlinear** for the Optimizer to find the best results. Choose Show Iteration Results and then **Yes** to have Quattro Pro pause after each Optimizer Iteration once you select **Go**. Choose Show Iteration Results and **No** to omit this pause. You can also list the values of each iteration by creating a detail report. Choose Estimates and then either **Tangent** or **Quadratic** to set how the Optimizer finds the initial estimates of the variable cells. Tangent works better in linear problems and **Quadratic** works better in highly nonlinear ones. If you see the message "All remedies failed to find better solution," choose Derivatives and **Central**, which sets how the Optimizer finds the estimates of partial derivatives. You can select Derivatives and **Forward** to return to the default, which requires less calculations. If you see the message "Objective function changing too slowly," choose Search and **Conjugate**, which sets the search direction. You can select Search and **Newton** to return to the default, which is faster. Select **Quit** to return to the /Tools Optimizer menu.

Answer Report—This option sets where the Optimizer places an answer report on the spreadsheet. This report lists the variable cells with their original and final values, the solution cell, the constraints, the variable dual values, and the constraint dual values. Select a cell in an empty area of the spreadsheet where Quattro Pro should start placing the report.

Detail Report—This option sets where the Optimizer places a detail report on the spreadsheet. This report lists the values of the variable cells and the solution cell for each iteration the Optimizer performs. Select a cell in an empty area of the spreadsheet where Quattro Pro should start placing the report.

Go—This option starts the Optimizer and calculates the best values for the variable cells that meet all of the constraint limitations and returns the desired result for the solution cell if any is used. The new values are placed in the spreadsheet and you are returned the /Tools Optimizer menu.

Restore—This option returns the variable cells to their value before you selected **Go** the last time. If spreadsheet recalculation is set to manual, the other spreadsheet formulas that use the variable cells will not be updated until you press F9 (CALC).

Model—This option stores Optimizer problem definitions in the spreadsheet or sets the /Tool Optimizer command options to match an Optimizer problem definition stored on the spreadsheet. This option is for putting more than one Optimizer problem definition in a spreadsheet. Select **Load** and the spreadsheet block containing an Optimizer problem definition to set the Optimizer to use the problem definition described in the spreadsheet block. Select **Save** and a cell where the Optimizer will start putting the Optimizer problem definition in the spreadsheet. You can also select a block after selecting **Save** if you want to be sure that the problem definition does not overwrite other spreadsheet data.

Reset—This option removes the settings made with other options of the /Tool

Optimizer command. Choose from Solution Cell, Variable Cell(s), Constraints, Options, Answer Report, Detail Report, or All.

Quit—This option leaves the menu and returns to READY mode.

/TOOLS PARSE

The /Tools Parse command divides labels into smaller spreadsheet cells. This command is primarily used on data imported as an ASCII text file. This command can divide the long labels into labels, numeric values, and date and time serial numbers. This command assumes that the data it is parsing is in a consistent format.

OPTIONS

Create—This option inserts a row above the selector, places a format line in the cell above the cell selector and moves the selector to the format line. The format line is Quattro's description of how it thinks the labels below should be broken into cells. A format line uses these characters to indicate the data type:

L - Character below this letter is the first character of a label entry.

V - Character below this letter is the first character of a value entry.

D - Character below this letter is the first character of a date serial number.

T - Character below this letter is the first character of a time serial number.

> - Character below this letter is a continuation of a label, value, date, or time entry.

* - Character below this letter is blank but may be used by the other data that will be parsed as a continuation of an entry.

S - Characters in the column below this letter are ignored in the parsing process.

Edit—This option edits the format line. When you are editing the format line, you may only type the characters acceptable for format lines.

Input—This option defines the spreadsheet cells that Quattro will parse. The input is a block address or name. You can specify it by pointing. The format line must be the first line of this block.

Output—This option defines where Quattro puts the parsed data. Quattro only needs to know the upper-left corner of the block where it will place the parsed data. Either type a cell address or point to it. Since Quattro writes over any existing information in the output area, the output area should be a blank area of the spreadsheet.

Go—This option tells Quattro to start parsing.

Reset—This option removes the setting for the input and output settings.

Quit—This option returns you to the spreadsheet in the READY mode.

/TOOLS REFORMAT

This command reformats lengthy text entries into shorter text entries within a block. When you select this option, Quattro prompts you for the block of cells to reformat. You can type the cell addresses or highlight the desired block by pointing. If you select only one row in the block to reformat, Quattro uses as many rows as necessary and moves the remaining entries in the first column down as the reformatted block uses more rows. If you select more than one row in the block to reformat, Quattro only uses the selected block to reformat the text. The number of columns in the block indicates the width of the resulting reformatted text. If the block is too small, Quattro displays an error message and stores the extra text in the last cell. The reformatted block only contains entries in the first column—the remaining columns are used only for display space.

OPTIONS
None.

/TOOLS SOLVE FOR

This command alters the number stored in a cell so another cell that contains a formula equals a predefined value. This command lets you work backward through calculations to find the initial value that will produce the desired result.

OPTIONS

Formula Cell—This is the cell containing a formula that will afterward equal the value set with the Target Value option. You must provide a cell address or block name of the cell containing the formula.

Target Value—This is the value that the cell selected with the Formula Cell option will equal after you select Go. You must enter a number.

Variable Cell—This is the cell that Quattro can change the value stored in the cell so that the cell selected with the Formula Cell option will equal the number selected with the Target Value option. You must provide a cell address or block name of the cell to change. It can contain any entry although after you select Go it will contain a number.

Parameters—This selects the parameters Quattro uses to find the answer. After selecting Parameters, you can select Max Iterations and enter a number between 1 and 99 for the number of attempts Quattro performs to find the answer. You can select Accuracy and enter a number that the result of the cell selected with Formula Cell must be within the value selected with Target Value for Quattro to consider the answer of the current iteration to be a solution. For example, entering 1 for this option and 100 for the target value means that an answer where the formula cell is between 99 and 101 is used.

Go—This option finds an answer using the entries provided by the options described above.

Reset—This option removes the current settings of Formula Cell, Target Value, and Variable Cell as well as returning the number of iterations to 5 and the accuracy to within .0005.

Quit—This option returns to the READY mode.

/TOOLS UPDATE LINKS

This command manipulates files with external links. The options for this command opens files that the current spreadsheet contains external links to, updates the values of formulas with external links, changes the file name used in external links, and deletes external links.

OPTIONS

Open—This option opens spreadsheets that formulas in the current spreadsheet contain links to. When you select this option, Quattro lists the spreadsheets that the current spreadsheet uses in linked formulas. Select the ones you want to open, and press ENTER. To open one, highlight each spreadsheet to open and press SHIFT-F7 (SELECT). You can also press ALT-F7 (SELECT ALL) and ENTER to open all supporting spreadsheets.

Refresh—This option recalculates formula with external links to check if the values in the other spreadsheets have changed.

Change—This option changes the file name of a spreadsheet used in external links to another spreadsheet. When you select this option, Quattro displays a list of spreadsheets used in external file links. After selecting the file name that you want to replace, Quattro prompts for the replacement file name. You can type a file name or select one from the list. Quattro replaces all instances of the first file name in external link formulas with the second file name.

Delete—This option removes external links to a particular file. When you select this option, Quattro displays a list of spreadsheets used in external file links. You can select one by pressing ENTER. If you want to select more than one, highlight each one you want to delete the external link reference and press SHIFT-F7 (SELECT) before pressing ENTER. Once you select Yes to confirm deleting links, Quattro replaces the external link references with ERR.

NOTE

When you load a file containing external link references, Quattro prompts if you want to load the supporting spreadsheets to update the values, or neither. The first two options are equivalent to the /Tools Update Links Open command and the /Tools Update Links Refresh command.

/TOOLS WHAT-IF

This command performs what-if analysis. You can substitute alternative values in your formulas and record the results of the substitutions in a table. You can create a table showing the results of varying one spreadsheet cell or you can create a table showing the result of varying two spreadsheet cells. In either case, there are rules to follow when making your selection.

OPTIONS

1 Variable—This option constructs a one-way table. The left side of the table contains the input values of the variable. The right side of the table displays the result of one or more computations for each of the different values that the variable assumes. Before using this command, you must set up a table area in the spreadsheet. This table is created by selecting a blank area of a spreadsheet and placing input values for a variable in a column. Next, move the selector to the cell one row above and a column to the right of the first variable value and enter a formula or a reference to a formula you wish computed with the input values provided. If you want the table to include the results of more than one formula, type the additional formulas you want evaluated in the cells to the right of the first formula. These entries create a structure for the what-if table with the input values forming the left edge of the table and the formulas forming the top edge of the table.

Once you have constructed the table shell, you are ready to invoke the command. When you select the **1 Variable** option, Quattro prompts for the location of your table. Move the selector so the entire block is highlighted and press ENTER. Next, type the cell address or point to the cell that the command uses as the input cell and press ENTER. This input cell can be in any open spreadsheet. Quattro evaluates each formula for each of the input values and places the result in the column beneath the formula and on the same row as the input value. The table entries do not contain formulas. The table entries are value entries; and, as such, modifications to the input values or to any other cells that the formulas use will not change the table results.

2 Variables—This command constructs a two-way table. This two-way table is similar to the one-way table; however, the two-way table uses two input values and evaluates only one formula. Before using this command, you must set up a table shell in your spreadsheet. This table records two values for two different input variables. These values are plugged into two input cells. Quattro puts one row and one column input value in two input cells at a time and records the resulting values of a formula in a table. When setting up the table, put the input values of the first variable in a column in a blank area of the spreadsheet. Move to the cell one row above the first input value and one column to the right. Enter the values for the second input variable across the row. Place the formula or cell reference which you want evaluated in the cell above the first variable value. After constructing the table shell, you can invoke the menu command to fill in the table shell. Type /, and select **Tools What-If 2 Variables**. When Quattro prompts for your table's location, highlight the entire table including the formula or cell reference in the upper left corner of the table, all the column input values and all the row input values, and press ENTER. Quattro prompts you for the column spreadsheet cell to be used as the first input cell. Enter the cell address or point to the cell and press ENTER. Quattro then prompts you for the row input cell. Enter the row input cell address or point to the cell, and press ENTER. Both input cells can be in any open spreadsheet. Quattro evaluates the formula using one column and one row input value at a time and places the result in the table where the column input value and the row input value intersect. The table entries are values, not formulas, Modifications to the column or row input cells or to any other cells that are used in the calculations do not change the table results.

Reset—This option removes the block and cell addresses provided with the **1 Variable** or **2 Variable** options.

Quit—This option returns you to the spreadsheet in READY mode.

NOTE

You can reexecute the last /Tools What-If command using the same settings by pressing F8 (TABLE).

/TOOLS XTRACT

This command saves a section of a spreadsheet to a spreadsheet file. To use this command, simply press / and select File Xtract. You can save formulas or values from a block of the spreadsheet.

OPTIONS
This command has two options.

Formulas—This option saves the current spreadsheet formulas, labels, and values into another spreadsheet file. When you select this option, Quattro prompts you for the file name to use when saving the block in the current spreadsheet. You can type the file name or point to the file name from the list of file names Quattro presents. After pressing ENTER, Quattro prompts for the address of the block in the current spreadsheet that you want to save. You can type the block address or highlight the desired block with the arrow keys.

Values—This option converts formulas to values before saving them to a spreadsheet. Note that the formulas are not saved when this option is used. When you choose this option, Quattro prompts you for the name of the file in which you want the current block saved. The steps you need to follow are the same as the procedures used in the Formula option.

NOTE
You can obtain the same results produced with this command by copying the data you want to an empty spreadsheet with the /Edit Copy or /Edit Values commands.

/WINDOW MOVE/SIZE

This command changes the position or size of the current window in text display mode. When you enter this command, Quattro displays MOVE in the upper-left corner of the window. While MOVE appears in the upper-left corner, you can move the window to any position on the desktop. By pressing SCROLL LOCK, Quattro changes the indicator from MOVE to SIZE. While SIZE appears in the upper-left corner, the arrow keys you press will affect the size of the window. You can switch between MOVE and SIZE by pressing the SCROLL LOCK key. This command has no effect in WYSIWYG display mode.

OPTIONS
The only choices offered by this command are changing between positioning the window and sizing the window by pressing the SCROLL LOCK key.

NOTE
You can also perform this command by pressing CTRL-R instead of entering /Window Move/Size. If you are using a mouse, you can size a window by clicking the lower-right corner of the window and dragging it to a new position. You can move a window by clicking one of its four sides and dragging it to a new position.

/WINDOW OPTIONS CLEAR

This command removes the second pane from a spreadsheet window. If the screen was split horizontally, the top window remains. If the window was split vertically, the left window remains. Some settings that are made in the second window are not kept when the two panes are combined. These settings include column width changes, locked titles, or hidden and exposed columns.

OPTIONS
None.

/WINDOW OPTIONS GRID LINES

This Quattro Pro 3 and 4 command adds or removes grid lines that you can display in the WYSIWYG display mode.

OPTIONS
This command has two options. Display makes the grid lines separating the cell borders appear. Hide removes the grid lines from display.

/WINDOW OPTIONS HORIZONTAL

This command lets you view two sections of your spreadsheet at the same time by splitting the current spreadsheet window into two panes. This command is especially useful when you have a large spreadsheet and want to view two areas simultaneously. Before you enter this command, position the selector to where you want the first pane to end. When you enter /Window Options Horizontal, a dividing line replaces one of the rows in your spreadsheet. Your spreadsheet is divided at the position of the selector on the screen when you execute this command. To move from one pane to another, simply press F6 (PANE). This command only affects the current spreadsheet.

OPTIONS
None.

/WINDOW OPTIONS LOCKED TITLES

This command freezes specific columns or rows on the screen. Even when you scroll the screen, the entries in these columns remain visible. The portion of the spreadsheet that is not frozen can still be scrolled. The frozen columns and rows will appear in a different color—either the color set by /Options Colors Spreadsheet Titles in text mode or by the Locked Title Text and Titles Background options of the /Options Colors Spreadsheet WYSIWYG Colors command in WYSIWYG mode.

OPTIONS

Horizontal—This option freezes specific rows on the screen. To use this option, you must first scroll the screen to place the rows you want to freeze at the top of the screen. Next, move the selector to any cell just below the bottom row in the area to be frozen, type /, select Window Options Locked Titles Horizontal. The rows above the cell selector freeze and you cannot move the selector to the frozen area unless you use the GOTO (F5) key or are in POINT mode.

Vertical—This option freezes specific columns on the screen. To freeze columns, first scroll the screen to place the columns you want to freeze at the left side of the screen. Next, move the selector to the column immediately to the right of the last column you want frozen. Type /, select Window Options Locked Titles Vertical, and the columns to the left of the selector are frozen. You cannot access the frozen area unless you use the GOTO (F5) key or are in POINT mode.

Both—This option freezes both rows and columns on the screen. To use this option, scroll the screen until the rows you want frozen are at the top of your screen and the columns you want frozen are at the left side of the screen. Then, move the selector to the cell just below the last row and to the right of the last column you want frozen. Select /Window Options Locked Titles Both and Quattro freezes the designated rows and columns.

Clear—This option clears all the title rows and columns you chose using the other /Window Option Titles command options.

/WINDOW OPTIONS MAP VIEW

This command changes the appearance of the current pane or spreadsheet to show a map view of the type of data contained in each cell. In a map view, l represents label entries, n represents number entries, + represents formula entries, - represents formulas containing link references, g represents an inserted graph, and c represents formulas containing circular references.

OPTIONS

This command has the options Yes, which displays the spreadsheet using map view and No, which displays the spreadsheet using a normal display.

/WINDOWS OPTIONS PRINT BLOCK

This command sets whether Quattro Pro displays a dashed line around the block selected with the /Print Block command when the printer destination is Graphics Printer, Binary File, or Screen Preview and you are using the WYSIWYG display mode.

OPTIONS

The two options for this command are Hide and Display. Hide does not indicate the print block, whereas Display adds the dashed line around the print block.

/WINDOW OPTIONS ROW & COL BORDERS

This command hides or displays the row and column border that appears at the top and left of the current pane or spreadsheet window. When the row and column borders do not appear, Quattro uses the additional space to display the spreadsheet. This command is primarily used in macros to create custom screens for user input.

OPTIONS

This command has two options. Display makes hidden row and column borders reappear. Hide removes the row and column borders from display.

/WINDOW OPTIONS SYNC

This command scrolls both panes in a synchronized manner as you scroll through one pane. This means that scrolling in one pane automatically causes the same rate of scrolling in the other pane. This is the default setting when you set up your second pane.

OPTIONS
None.

/WINDOW OPTIONS UNSYNC

This command removes the synchronized scrolling that occurs when you scroll in one pane and the other pane scrolls. After you enter this command, the inactive pane will remain stationary as you move through the active pane.

OPTIONS
None.

/WINDOW OPTIONS VERTICAL

This command lets you view two sections of your spreadsheet at the same time by splitting the current spreadsheet window into two panes. This command is especially useful when you have a large spreadsheet and want to view two areas simultaneously. Before you enter this command, position the selector to the column at which you want the first pane to end. When you enter /Window Options Vertical, a dividing line splits the spreadsheet vertically. Your spreadsheet is divided at the position of the selector on the screen. To move from one window to another, simply press F6 (PANE).

OPTIONS
None.

/WINDOW PICK

This command selects the current window from all open windows.

OPTIONS

When you enter this command, Quattro displays a list of the open windows. Highlight one from the list, and press ENTER.

NOTE

You can also perform this command by pressing ALT-0 or SHIFT-F5 (PICK WINDOW). To switch to the next window, press SHIFT-F6 (NEXT WINDOW). To make a window from one through nine the current window, press the ALT key and the number of the window you want active.

/WINDOW STACK

This command stacks the open windows on top of each other. The resulting spreadsheet area has the top line from each window visible, showing the file names and the window numbers. This command has no effect in WYSIWYG display mode.

OPTIONS

None.

/WINDOW TILE

This command resizes all open windows so each window occupies approximately the same space. This option lets you show all open windows. The disadvantage with this command is that as the number of open windows increases, the amount you see of any particular window decreases.

OPTIONS

None.

NOTE

You can also perform this command by pressing CTRL-T.

/WINDOW ZOOM

This command enlarges the current window so it occupies the entire spreadsheet area. If the current window already occupies the entire spreadsheet area, this command reduces the window to the size it was before the window was last expanded. In WYSIWYG mode, you can only use this command once. If you want to return a zoomed window to its tiled size, you must reuse the /Window Tile command.

OPTIONS
None.

NOTE
You can also perform this command by pressing ALT-F6 (ZOOM) or by clicking the up and down arrows in the upper right corner of the window.

File Manager Command Reference

/EDIT ALL SELECT

This command selects all files in the File Manager window to be included in a /Edit Copy, /Edit Move, /Edit Erase, or /Edit Paste command. If any files are already selected, this command unselects all files. Quattro marks the selected files using the color or attribute selected with the /Options Colors File Manager Marked command.

OPTIONS
None.

NOTE
You can also perform this command by pressing ALT-F7 (ALL SELECT).

/EDIT COPY

This command copies the marked files to the paste buffer. The paste buffer temporarily stores files that you want to move or copy to another drive and directory. Once the files are copied to the paste buffer, you can copy them elsewhere using the /Edit Paste command.

OPTIONS
None.

NOTE
You can also perform this command by pressing SHIFT-F9 (COPY).

/EDIT DUPLICATE

This command copies a file with the option to provide a different name for the copy. Before you enter this command, you must move the active cursor to the file in the file list you want to duplicate. When you enter /Edit Duplicate, Quattro prompts you for the file name that you want to copy to. If you want the copy of the file to be on a different drive or directory, you must provide this information. When you press ENTER, Quattro copies the file.

OPTIONS

The only options for this command are the file name, extension, drive, and directory that you specify for the new file.

/EDIT ERASE

This command removes the marked files from the disk. If no files are marked when you enter this command, this command erases the current file. You may not be able to delete a file if the file is a spreadsheet file that is open in another window. Once you erase a file, it is no longer available (although DOS 5 and some disk utilities such as the Norton Utilities can recover erased files).

OPTIONS

When you enter this command, you must confirm the deletion by selecting Yes or cancel the command by selecting No.

NOTE

You can also perform this command by pressing DEL.

/EDIT MOVE

This command copies the marked files to the paste buffer. The paste buffer temporarily stores files that you want to move or copy to another drive and directory. Once the files are copied to the paste buffer, you can move them elsewhere using the /Edit Paste command. After Quattro copies the files to the new drive and directory, Quattro erases the original files.

OPTIONS

None.

NOTE

You can also perform this command by pressing SHIFT-F8 (MOVE).

/EDIT PASTE

This command copies files in the paste buffer to the current drive and directory. The files must first be placed in the paste buffer with the /Edit Copy or /Edit Move command. You cannot paste the files in the same directory that you copied them from.

OPTIONS

None.

NOTE

You can also perform this command by pressing SHIFT-F10 (PASTE).

/EDIT RENAME

This command moves a file with the option to provide a different name for the copy. You can also use this command to rename the file without changing the drive or directory. Before you enter this command, you must move the active cursor to the file in the file list you want to move or rename. Then when you enter /Edit Rename, Quattro prompts you for the new file name. If you want the copy of the file to be on a different drive or directory, you must provide this information. When you press ENTER, Quattro renames and moves the file.

OPTIONS

The only options for this command are the file name, drive, and directory that you specify for the new file.

NOTE

You can also perform this command by pressing F2 (EDIT) and supplying the new file name, drive, and directory.

/EDIT SELECT FILE

This command selects the current file to be included in a /Edit Copy, /Edit Move, /Edit Erase, or /Edit Paste command. If the current file is already selected, this command unselects the file. Quattro marks the selected file using the color or attribute selected with the /Options Colors File Manager Marked command.

OPTIONS

None.

NOTE

You can also perform this command by pressing SHIFT-F7 (SELECT).

/FILE CLOSE

This command closes the current window and makes the next window the current window. Closing a window does not affect the size or position of the remaining windows. If the window that you are closing is the only open window, the desktop area will be blank and File will appear by itself in the Menu bar with only a few of the menu options listed. If you are using a mouse, you can also close a window by clicking the upper-left corner of the window.

OPTIONS

None.

/FILE CLOSE ALL

This command closes all windows. If any spreadsheet windows contain changes that have not been saved, Quattro will prompt you to confirm that you want to close the window. If you select Save & Close, Quattro performs the /File Save command for that spreadsheet window. Once the windows are closed, the desktop area will be blank, and File will appear by itself in the Menu bar with only a few of the menu options listed.

OPTIONS
None.

/FILE EXIT

This command closes the open windows and then exits Quattro to DOS. As Quattro closes spreadsheet windows, you are prompted for an action to take if a window contains unsaved changes.

OPTIONS
You have three choices when a spreadsheet window has unsaved changes.

Yes—This option closes the window without saving the current spreadsheet window.

No—This option cancels the /File Exit command. Any windows that are closed before you select No remain closed.

Save & Exit—This option performs the /File Save command for the current spreadsheet and then closes it before moving to the next open window.

NOTE
You can also perform this command by pressing CTRL-X.

/FILE MAKE DIR

This command creates a new directory below the current directory. Before you enter this command, you need to select the directory below which you want to add the new directory using the control pane. When you enter this command, Quattro prompts you for the new directory name. The directory name must comply with DOS's naming conventions for directories. (Briefly, a directory name cannot exceed eight characters plus an extension of three characters, cannot contain spaces, and must be unique to the directory.) Type the name of the directory, and press ENTER.

OPTIONS
The only option for this command is the directory name you supply.

/FILE NEW

This command opens a new spreadsheet window with an empty unnamed spreadsheet in the window. To activate this command press /, and select File New. The new file will have a name SHEET followed by the next lowest unused number until the file is saved. Quattro will assign the new spreadsheet window an unused window number. Quattro can have up to 32 windows open at once, although your computer's memory may lower the limit.

OPTIONS

None.

NOTE

Be sure to save any unnamed spreadsheets before you save the spreadsheets that contain formulas referring to them so Quattro can replace the SHEET# references with the correct file names.

/FILE OPEN

This command opens a new spreadsheet window and loads a file into the window.

OPTIONS

This command is identical to the **/File Open** command in a spreadsheet window and has all the options available that are described under that command description.

NOTE

You can also perform this command by highlighting a file and pressing ENTER. When you do this, Quattro opens a new spreadsheet window containing the file you selected.

/FILE READ DIR

This command reads the current directory and updates the files in the file list pane. This command is for networked and floppy drive systems, on which the files in the directory may change, since Quattro last checked the drive and directory. Quattro automatically checks the drive and directory when you switch the current drive and directory and when you open a File Manager window.

OPTIONS

None.

NOTE

You can also perform this command by pressing F9 (CALC), since this command recalculates the files that appear in the file list pane.

/FILE UTILITIES DOS SHELL

This command temporarily allows you to use DOS without exiting from Quattro. All windows remains in memory while you are executing DOS commands or running another program. When you select the **/File Utilities DOS Shell** command, an operating system prompt appears. To return to Quattro type **Exit**, and press

ENTER. Quattro returns you to the window that was current before the temporary DOS exit.
OPTIONS
None.

/FILE UTILITIES FILE MANAGER

This command opens another File Manager window. The new File Manager window will have a different window number. The window will initially use the same settings as the current File Manager window but you can change these settings. Like spreadsheet windows, you cannot have more than 32 windows open, although your computer's memory may lower this limit.
OPTIONS
None.

/FILE UTILITIES SQZ!

This command defines several settings that Quattro uses when it saves files in the compressed SQZ! format.
OPTIONS
Remove Blanks—This option determines whether Quattro saves blank labels and formats for blank cells. The choices for this option are Yes and No.

Storage of Values—This option determines whether Quattro saves the values of formulas with the formulas. Since Quattro recalculates formulas when it retrieves a file, omitting the values from the squeezed file does not damage the spreadsheet. The choices for this option are Exact, Approximate, and Remove. Exact stores the value with the formula, up to 15 places. Approximate stores the value with the formula, up to 7 places. Remove stores the formulas but does not store the values.

Version—This option determines whether Quattro saves a squeezed file using SQZ! or SQZ! Plus. While SQZ! Plus is more efficient and works with many packages, use SQZ! if you are using the squeezed file in 1-2-3 or Symphony.

Quit—This option returns you to the READY mode.

/FILE WORKSPACE RESTORE

This command opens spreadsheet and File Manager windows and puts the spreadsheets and File Manager window settings in the appropriate windows. This command quickly positions all the windows you had open when you saved the workspace with **/F**ile Workspace **S**ave. When you enter this command Quattro prompts for the workspace name, which you can select from the list or type in, and then you press ENTER.

OPTIONS
None.

/FILE WORKSPACE SAVE

This command saves the size and position of all open windows as well as the file names of the spreadsheet windows and the settings of the File Manager window. This treats a set of spreadsheets and File Manager windows that you can use as a group instead of retrieving and adding each window separately.

OPTIONS
When you enter this command, Quattro prompts for the workspace name. You can select one from the list, or type a file name and press ENTER. Do not include an extension, since Quattro adds a .WSP extension to the file name.

/OPTIONS BEEP

This command allows you to turn off the beep that sounds when you make an error. Although most people find the beep helpful because it alerts them to mistakes, some find it annoying. You can turn off the beep by selecting the Beep option from the Options menu and then selecting **No**. If you want to make this change permanent, use the /Options Update command.

OPTIONS
None.

/OPTIONS COLORS

This command sets the colors Quattro uses to display.

OPTIONS
The options for this command are listed under the /Options Hardware Colors commands listed with the spreadsheet window commands.

/OPTIONS DISPLAY MODE

This command sets how Quattro displays. Some monitors can display in more than one mode. For example, VGA screens can display 25, 43, or 50 lines on the screen. While many monitors can display up to 80 columns, some monitors can display 132 columns. Another option of this command is **B: WYSIWYG**. In prior releases this is called **B:** Graphics Mode. When a spreadsheet appears in graphics mode, Quattro displays the inserted graphs instead of a highlighted area. You can use this command to change how Quattro displays the windows.

OPTIONS

The exact options depend on the type of monitor and graphics adapter card you are using.

NOTE

If you are displaying in graphics mode, Quattro will perform slower. Graphics display mode is only available for EGA and VGA screens. If you select a 132-column display mode and your hardware is not capable of displaying 132 columns, you will want to press CTRL-BREAK and type **/ODA** to set the display mode to 25 rows and 80 columns.

/OPTIONS FILE LIST

This command controls how Quattro displays the files in the file list pane.

OPTIONS

Wide View—This option displays only the file name and extension. Quattro displays as many files on each line as Quattro can fit in the File Manager window. This produces a file list similar to the list produced with the **/File Retrieve** command.

Full View—This option displays each file on a separate line and lists the file name, extension, size, and date and time the file was last saved. This produces a file list similar to the list produced by pressing the GRAY + or selecting the +/− button in the file selection box.

/OPTIONS HARDWARE

This command is identical to the **/Options Hardware** command from a spreadsheet window. You can use this command to set screen and printer attributes as well as to display the amount of normal and expanded memory available and whether Quattro detects a 8087, 20287, or 80387 math coprocessor.

OPTIONS

The options for this command are listed under the **/Options Hardware** commands listed for the spreadsheet window commands.

/OPTIONS STARTUP DIRECTORY

This command determines the directory that Quattro sets the File Manager window to when a new window is open. Your choices are the directory where you started Quattro or the settings of the last File Manager window. After using this command, you should use the /Options Update command to designate the directory as the default the next time you load Quattro.

OPTIONS

Previous—This option sets the new File Manager windows to use the drive and directory settings of the previous File Manager window.

Current—This option sets the new File Manager windows to use the drive and directory that was current when you loaded Quattro.

/OPTIONS STARTUP EDIT MENUS

This command loads the Menu Builder and runs it. The Menu Builder lets you create and modify menu trees. Running the Menu Builder from a File Manager window lets you change the menu available with File Manager windows.

OPTIONS

From the Menu Builder, you can make extensive changes to the current menu. The Menu Builder is covered in detail in Chapter 10.

/OPTIONS STARTUP MENU TREE

This command lets you select the menu tree that you want to use. Menus can be created and modified using the Menu Builder. To use the Menu Builder, use the /Options Startup Edit Menus command.

OPTIONS

The only option for this command is the menu you select. When you enter this command, Quattro displays a list of the .MU menu tree files in Quattro's directory. Highlight one of them, and press ENTER.

/OPTIONS UPDATE

This command saves the default changes that you make in the File Manager window Options menu, the top half of a spreadsheet window Options menu, the print layout settings in a spreadsheet window, and the graph settings in a spreadsheet window. Quattro uses these default settings the next time you begin a Quattro session.

OPTIONS

None.

/PRINT ADJUST PRINTER

This command adjusts the printer. The options for this command move the paper in the printer and tell Quattro that the printer is at the top of the page. Quattro keeps track of the top of the page by using an internal counter and the number of lines per page set by the /Print Page Layout Margins & Length Page Length command. Since Quattro keeps track of the top of the page, manually moving the paper makes Quattro's record of the location of the top of the page incorrect and causes Quattro to page break incorrectly. Using this command ensures that Quattro breaks the output into pages correctly. When Quattro is loaded, it assumes that the printer is at the top of the page.

OPTIONS

Skip Line—This option moves the paper in the printer forward one line.

Form Feed—This option moves the paper in the printer forward one page.

Align—This option tells Quattro that the printer is currently positioned at the top of the page. It resets Quattro's internal counter and sets the page counter to zero.

/PRINT BLOCK

This command defines what part of the File Manager window Quattro will print.

OPTIONS

Files—This option prints a list of the files contained in the file list pane.

Tree—This option prints a diagram of the tree in the tree pane.

Both—This option prints the list of files in the file list pane and the tree in the tree pane.

/PRINT DESTINATION

This command specifies where Quattro prints the file. Quattro lets you select between printing to the printer or to a file. For either option, Quattro does not start printing until you enter /Print Go.

OPTIONS

Printer—This option directs the print output to the printer. This is the default if a destination is not specified.

File—This option sends the output to a file. When you select this option, Quattro lists the .PRN files in the current directory. Select one or type a new name. Do not include an extension, since Quattro automatically adds .PRN. If you select an existing .PRN file, Quattro prompts for you to select between appending the new output to the existing file, backing up the old file before creating the new one, canceling the command, or replacing the old file data with the new data.

Use the file destination option if you are printing the files at another time or you are importing the data into another file and need the file in an ASCII text file. If you are importing the file into another program, you should remove setup strings and execute the /Print Page Layout Break Pages No command. You can print a .PRN file with the DOS PRINT command.

/PRINT GO

This command begins printing using the settings established with other print commands. If the destination is a file, Quattro writes the information to that file.

OPTIONS
None.

/PRINT PAGE LAYOUT

This command describes how you want the File Manager window data printed on the page. It specifies the size of the paper, the margins, the setup strings, the header, the footer, and whether Quattro should break the printout into pages.

OPTIONS

Header—This option defines the text that Quattro puts at the top of each page. A header entry can consist of up to 511 characters. Quattro uses three lines on each page for the header: one for the header and two blank lines to separate it from the File Manager window data. A header can contain three characters to provide additional features. The pound sign (#) prints the current page number on every page in place of this character. The commercial at sign (@) is converted to the current system date when it is printed. The vertical bar (|) changes the alignment of the header text. Left-aligned text must precede any vertical lines. Centered text follows the first vertical bar in the header. Right-aligned text follows the second vertical bar in the header.

Footer—This option defines the text that Quattro prints at the bottom of each page. The footer can consist of up to 511 characters. Quattro uses three lines on each page for the footer: one for the footer and two blank lines to separate it from the File Manager window data. A footer can also use the special characters that are described with the Header option.

Break Pages—This option determines whether Quattro breaks the printed output into pages. If you select Yes, Quattro uses the number of lines per page provided by the **/Print Page Layout Margins & Length Page Length** command. If you select No, Quattro does not separate the data into pages. Quattro also does not print the header and footer.

Margins & Length—This option sets the settings Quattro uses for margins and page length. These measurements are in lines and characters. Page Length sets the length of the page. The default is 66 but it can be any number between 0 and 100. Quattro uses this number to determine when it should insert a page break. Left sets the space between the left edge of the paper and the printed output. The default is four characters but this value can range from zero to 254. Top sets the space between the top edge of the paper and the printed output. The default is two but it can be any number between zero and 32. Right sets the space Quattro uses for the left margin and printing the data. Quattro's initial default of 76 characters creates a right margin of four characters. This number is between zero and 254 characters. Bottom sets the space Quattro puts between the bottom edge of the paper and the printed data. The default is two lines but it can range from zero to 32. Quit exits the submenu and returns you to the Layout menu.

Setup String—This option specifies the setup string that Quattro sends to the printer before printing the data. The setup string is a printer control code that accesses special printer features, such as compressed print. The feature invoked by a setup string continues until another setup string undoes the first setup string or the printer is reset. Setup strings vary from printer to printer. The exact setup string is found in the printer manual under printer codes or printer commands. Decimal values must be preceded by a backslash (\). For example, ESC is \027. Setup strings may be up to 39 characters.

Quit—This option exits the Page Layout menu and returns you to the Print menu.

/PRINT QUIT

This command exits the Print menu and returns you to the READY mode in the current File Manager window.

/PRINT RESET

This command resets some or all of the print settings to their default values. For certain print settings like /Print Block, this command removes the current settings. For other settings, this command returns the settings to Quattro's initial defaults or the settings established when the /Print Layout Update command was last executed in a spreadsheet window.

OPTIONS

All—This option removes all the current print settings.

Print Block—This option returns the setting of the /Print Block command to Files.

Layout—This option returns the page layout settings to their values when the /Print Layout Update command was last executed in a spreadsheet window.

/SORT

This command determines how Quattro lists the files selected by the control pane in the file list pane. The options determine the order of the files. In a File Manager window, Quattro always sorts the files in ascending order.

OPTIONS

Name—This option sorts the files in the file list pane by file name.

Timestamp—This option sorts the files in the file list pane by when they were last saved.

Extension—This option sorts the files in the file list pane by extension.

Size—This option sorts the files in the file list pane by size.

DOS Order—This option does not sort the files but lists them by their order in the directory. This is the same order you would see if you used the DOS DIR command.

/TREE

This command controls the appearance of the tree pane. The tree pane displays the directory structure of the current drive. You can change directories of the file list pane by pointing to another branch in the tree.

OPTIONS

Open—This option adds a tree pane to the File Manager window.

Resize—This option changes the size of the tree pane in relation to the file list pane. When you select this option, Quattro prompts for a percentage of the File Manager window that the tree should occupy. Enter a number between 10 and 100 then press ENTER.

Close—This option removes a tree pane from a File Manager window.

/WINDOW MOVE/SIZE

This command changes the position or size of the current window. When you enter this command, Quattro displays MOVE in the upper-left corner of the window. While MOVE appears in the upper-left corner, you can move the window to any position on the desktop. By pressing SCROLL LOCK, Quattro changes the indicator from MOVE to SIZE. While SIZE appears in the upper-left corner, the arrow keys you press will affect the size of the window. You can switch between MOVE and SIZE by pressing the SCROLL LOCK key. If you are using a mouse, you can size a window by clicking the lower-right corner of the window and dragging it to a new position. You can move a window by clicking one of its four sides and dragging it to a new position. This command has no effect in Quattro Pro's WYSIWYG display mode.

OPTIONS

This command lets you choose between positioning the window and sizing the window by pressing the SCROLL LOCK key.

/WINDOW PICK

This command selects the current window from all open windows.

OPTIONS

When you enter this command, Quattro displays a list of the open windows. Highlight one from the list and press ENTER.

NOTE

You can also perform this command by pressing ALT-0 or SHIFT-F5. To switch to the next window, press SHIFT-F6. To make a window from one through nine the current window press the ALT key and the number of the window you want active. File Manager windows appear as the drive setting in the control pane.

/WINDOW STACK

This command stacks the open windows on top of each other. The resulting spreadsheet area shows the top line from each window displaying the file names and the window numbers for spreadsheet windows and the drive, directory, and window number for File Manager windows.

OPTIONS
None.

/WINDOW TILE

This command resizes all open windows so each window occupies approximately the same space, to let you show all open windows. The disadvantage is that as the number of open windows increases, the amount you see of any particular window decreases.

OPTIONS
None.

/WINDOW ZOOM

This command enlarges the current window so it occupies the entire spreadsheet area. If the current window already occupies the entire spreadsheet area, this command reduces the window to the size it was before it was last expanded. In WYSIWYG mode, you can only use this command once. If you want to return a zoomed window to its tiled size, you must reuse the /Window Tile command.

OPTIONS
None.

NOTE

You can also perform this command by pressing ALT-F6 (ZOOM) or by clicking the up or down arrows in the upper-right corner of the window.

Appendix C

Menu Equivalent Commands

Menu Equivalent commands are used for telling Quattro a menu command to perform without worrying about which menu tree is used. Menu equivalent commands are used to build menu trees, to build macros, in the Transcript utility, and as macro commands in the SpeedBar. Table C.1 lists each default Quattro menu tree command and the menu equivalent command that performs the same task. For menu equivalent commands that you must select from a list of options, you can make these selections by using {EDIT} and the text of the entry you want to select as in using {EDIT}Dutch-SC~ to select the Dutch-SC from a font list.

Table C.1 Quattro Pro Commands and Menu Equivalent Commands

Quattro Commands	Menu Equivalent
/Database Data Entry Dates Only	{/ Publish;DataEntryDate}
/Database Data Entry General	{/ Publish;DataEntryFormula}
/Database Data Entry Labels Only	{/ Publish;DataEntryLabel}
/Database Paradox Access Go	{/ Paradox;SwitchGo}
/Database Paradox Access Load File	{/ Paradox;SwitchFile}
/Database Paradox Access Autoload	{/ Paradox;SwitchAutoLoad}
/Database Query Assign Names	{/ Query;AssignNames}
/Database Query Block	{/ Query;Block}
/Database Query Criteria Table	{/ Query;CriteriaBlock}
/Database Query Delete	{/ Query;Delete}
/Database Query Extract	{/ Query;Extract}
/Database Query Locate	{/ Query;Locate}
/Database Query Output Block	{/ Query;Output}
/Database Query Reset	{/ Query;Reset}
/Database Query Unique	{/ Query;Unique}
/Database Restrict Input	{/ Block;Input}
/Database Sort 1st Key	{/ Sort;Key1}
/Database Sort 2nd Key	{/ Sort;Key2}
/Database Sort 3rd Key	{/ Sort;Key3}
/Database Sort 4th Key	{/ Sort;Key4}
/Database Sort 5th Key	{/ Sort;Key5}
/Database Sort Block	{/ Sort;Block}
/Database Sort Go	{/ Sort;Go}
/Database Sort Reset	{/ Sort;Reset}
/Database Sort Sort Rules Label Order	{/ Startup;LabelOrder}
/Database Sort Sort Rules Numbers Before Labels	{/ Startup;CellOrder}

Table C.1 Quattro Pro Commands and Menu Equivalent Commands *(continued)*

Quattro Commands	Menu Equivalent
/Database Sort Sort Rules Sort Rows/Columns	{/ Startup;SortOrder}
/Edit Copy	{/ Block;Copy}
/Edit Copy Special Contents	{/ Block;CopyContents}
/Edit Copy Special Format	{/ Block;CopyFormat}
/Edit Delete Column Block	{/ Column;Delete Block}
/Edit Delete Columns	{/ Column;Delete}
/Edit Delete Row Block	{/ Row;DeleteBlock}
/Edit Delete Rows	{/ Row;Delete}
/Edit Erase Block	{/ Block;Erase}
/Edit Fill	{/ Math;Fill}
/Edit Insert Column Block	{/ Column;Insert Block}
/Edit Insert Columns	{/ Column;Insert}
/Edit Insert Row Block	{/ Row;InsertBlock}
/Edit Insert Rows	{/ Row;Insert}
/Edit Move	{/ Block;Move}
/Edit Names Create	{/ Name;Create}
/Edit Names Delete	{/ Name;Delete}
/Edit Names Labels Down	{/ Name;UnderCreate}
/Edit Names Labels Left	{/ Name;LeftCreate}
/Edit Names Labels Right	{/ Name;RightCreate}
/Edit Names Labels Up	{/ Name;AboveCreate}
/Edit Names Make Table	{/ Name;Table}
/Edit Names Reset	{/ Name;Reset}
/Edit Search & Replace Block	{/ Audit;ReplaceRange}
/Edit Search & Replace Case Sensitive	{/ Audit;SearchCase}
/Edit Search & Replace Case Sensitive Any Case	{/ Audit;SearchAnyCase}

Table C.1 Quattro Pro Commands and Menu Equivalent Commands *(continued)*

Quattro Commands	Menu Equivalent
/Edit Search & Replace Case Sensitive Exact Case	{/ Audit;SearchExactCase}
/Edit Search & Replace Direction	{/ Audit;SearchDirection}
/Edit Search & Replace Direction Column	{/ Audit;SearchByCol}
/Edit Search & Replace Direction Row	{/ Audit;SearchByRow}
/Edit Search & Replace Look In	{/ Audit;SearchLookIn}
/Edit Search & Replace Look In Condition	{/ Audit;SearchCondition}
/Edit Search & Replace Look In Formula	{/ Audit;SearchFormula}
/Edit Search & Replace Look In Value	{/ Audit;SearchValue}
/Edit Search & Replace Match	{/ Audit;SearchMatch}
/Edit Search & Replace Match Part	{/ Audit;SearchForPart}
/Edit Search & Replace Match Whole	{/ Audit;SearchForWhole}
/Edit Search & Replace Next	{/ Audit;Replace}
/Edit Search & Replace Options Reset	{/ Audit;SearchReset}
/Edit Search & Replace Previous	{/ Audit;SearchPrev}
/Edit Search & Replace Replace String	{/ Audit;ReplaceString}
/Edit Search & Replace Search String	{/ Audit;SearchString}
/Edit Transpose	{/ Block;Transpose}
/Edit Undo	{/ Basics;Undo} or {UNDO}
/Edit Values	{/ Block;Values}
/File Close	{/ Basics;Close}
/File Close All	{/ System;TidyUp}
/File Directory	{/ File;Directory}
/File Erase	{/ Basics;Erase}
/File Exit	{/ System;Exit}
/File New	{/ View;NewWindow}
/File Open	{/ View;OpenWindow}
/File Retrieve	{/ File;Retrieve}

Table C.1 Quattro Pro Commands and Menu Equivalent Commands *(continued)*

Quattro Commands	Menu Equivalent
/File Save	{/ File;SaveNow}
/File Save All	{/ File:SaveAll}
/File Save As	{/ File;Save}
/File Utilities DOS Shell	{/ Basics;OS} or {/Basics;Shell}
/File Utilities File Manager	{/ View;NewFileMgr}
/File Utilities SQZ! Remove Blanks	{/ SQZ;Blanks}
/File Utilities SQZ! Storage of Values	{/ SQZ;Values}
/File Utilities SQZ! Version	{/ SQZ;Version}
/File Workspace Restore	{/ System;RestoreWorkspace}
/File Workspace Save	{/ System;SaveWorkspace}
/Graph Annotate	{/ Graph;Annotate}
/Graph Customize Series	{/ Dialog;GraphCustomize} when Quattro Pro displays dialog boxes
/Graph Customize Series Bar Width	{/ Graph;BarWidth}
/Graph Customize Series Bubbles Colors 1st Bubble through 9th Bubble	{/ BubbleColor;1} through {/ BubbleColor;9}
/Graph Customize Series Bubbles Max Bubble Size	{/ Bubble Size}
/Graph Customize Series Bubbles Patterns 1st Bubble through 9th Bubble	{/ BubblePattern;1} through {/ BubblePattern;9}
/Graph Customize Series Colors 1st Series through 6th Series	{/ 1Series;Color} through {/ 6Series;Color}
/Graph Customize Series Fill Patterns 1st Series through 6th Series	{/ 1Series;Pattern} through {/ 6Series;Pattern}
/Graph Customize Series Interior Label 1st Series through 6th Series	{/ CompGraph;ALabels} through {/ CompGraph;FLabels}
/Graph Customize Series Markers & Lines Formats 1st Series through 6th Series	{/ CompGraph;AFormat} through {/ CompGraph;FFormat}
/Graph Customize Series Markers & Lines Formats Graph	{/ CompGraph;GraphFormat}

Table C.1 Quattro Commands and Menu Equivalent Commands *(continued)*

Quattro Commands	Menu Equivalent
/Graph Customize Series Markers & Lines Line Styles 1st Series through 6th Series	{/ 1Series;LineStyle} through {/ 6Series;LineStyle}
/Graph Customize Series Markers & Lines Markers 1st Series through 6th Series	{/ 1Series;Markers} through {/ 6Series;Markers}
/Graph Customize Series Override Type 1st Series through 6th Series	{/ 1Series;Type} through {/ 6Series;Type}
/Graph Customize Series Pies Colors 1st Slice through 9th Slice	{/ PieColor;1} through {/ PieColor;9}
/Graph Customize Series Pies Explode 1st Slice through 9th Slice	{/ PieExploded;1} through {/ PieExploded;9}
/Graph Customize Series Pies Label Format	{/ Pie;ValueFormat}
/Graph Customize Series Pies Patterns 1st Slice through 9th Slice	{/ PiePattern;1} through {/ PiePattern;9}
/Graph Customize Series Pies Tick Marks	{/ Pie;TickMarks}
/Graph Customize Series Reset 1st Series through 6th Series	{/ Graph;Reset1} through {/ Graph;Reset6}
/Graph Customize Series Reset Graph	{/ Graph;ResetAll}
/Graph Customize Series Reset X-Axis Series	{/ XAxis;Reset}
/Graph Customize Series Update	{/ Graph;UpdateGraph}
/Graph Customize Series Y-Axis 1st Series through 6th Series	{/ 1Series;YAxis} through {/ 6Series;YAxis}
/Graph Fast Graph	{/ Graph;FastGraph}
/Graph Graph Type	{/ Graph;Type}
/Graph Hide	{/ Graph;NameHide}
/Graph Insert	{/ Graph;NameInsert}
/Graph Name Autosave Edits	{/ Graph;NameAutosave}
/Graph Name Create	{/ Graph;NameCreate}
/Graph Name Display	{/ Graph;NameUse}
/Graph Name Erase	{/ Graph;NameDelete}

Table C.1 Quattro Pro Commands and Menu Equivalent Commands (*continued*)

Quattro Commands	Menu Equivalent
/Graph Name Graph Copy	{/ Graph;NameCopy}
/Graph Name Reset	{/ Graph;NameReset}
/Graph Name Slide	{/ Graph;NameSlide}
/Graph Overall Background Color	{/ Graph;BackColor}
/Graph Overall Color/B&W B&W	{/ Graph;BW}
/Graph Overall Color/B&W Color	{/ Graph;Color}
/Graph Overall Drop Shadow Color	{/ Graph;DS*color*}
/Graph Overall Grid Both	{/ CompGraph;GridBoth}
/Graph Overall Grid Clear	{/ CompGraph;GridClear}
/Graph Overall Grid Fill Color	{/ Graph;GridFill}
/Graph Overall Grid Grid Color	{/ Graph;GridColor}
/Graph Overall Grid Horizontal	{/ CompGraph;GridHorz}
/Graph Overall Grid Line Style	{/ Graph;GridLines}
/Graph Overall Grid Vertical	{/ CompGraph;GridVert}
/Graph Overall Outlines Graph	{/ Graph;GraphOtl}
/Graph Overall Outlines Legend	{/ Graph;LegendOtl}
/Graph Overall Outlines Titles	{/ Graph;TitleOtl}
/Graph Overall Three-D	{/ Graph;3D}
/Graph Series 1st Series through 6th Series	{/ 1Series;Block} through {/ 6Series;Block}
/Graph Series Analyze 1st Series through 6th Series	{/ GraphAnalyze1;ShowKind} through {/ GraphAnalyze6;ShowKind}
/Graph Series Analyze 1st Series through 6th Series Aggregation	{/ GraphAnalyze1;Aggregation} through {/ GraphAnalyze6;Aggregation}
/Graph Series Analyze 1st Series through 6th Series Aggregation Aggregation Period	{/ GraphAnalyze1;AgPeriod} through {/ GraphAnalyze6;AgPeriod}

Table C.1 Quattro Pro Commands and Menu Equivalent Commands *(continued)*

Quattro Commands	Menu Equivalent
/Graph Series Analyze 1st Series through 6th Series Aggregation Aggregation Period Weeks	{/ GraphAnalyze1;AgWeeks} through {/ GraphAnalyze6;AgWeeks}
/Graph Series Analyze 1st Series through 6th Series Aggregation Aggregation Period Months	{/ GraphAnalyze1;AgMonths} through {/ GraphAnalyze6;AgMonths}
/Graph Series Analyze 1st Series through 6th Series Aggregation Aggregation Period Quarters	{/ GraphAnalyze1;AgQuarters} through {/ GraphAnalyze6;AgQuarters}
/Graph Series Analyze 1st Series through 6th Series Aggregation Period Years	{/ GraphAnalyze1;AgYears} through {/ GraphAnalyze6;AgYears)
/Graph Series Analyze 1st Series through 6th Series Aggregation Aggregation Period Arbitrary	{/ GraphAnalyze1;AgArbitrary} through {/ GraphAnalyze6;AgArbitrary}
/Graph Series Analyze 1st Series through 6th Series Aggregation Function	{/ GraphAnalyze1;Function} through {/ GraphAnalyze6;Function}
/Graph Series Analyze 1st Series through 6th Series Aggregation Series Period	{/ GraphAnalyze1;AgSeriesPeriod} through {/ GraphAnalyze6;AgSeriesPeriod}
/Graph Series Analyze 1st Series through 6th Series Aggregation Series Period Days	{/ GraphAnalyze1;AgSeriesDays} through {/ GraphAnalyze6;AgSeriesDays}
/Graph Series Analyze 1st Series through 6th Series Aggregation Series Period Weeks	{/ GraphAnalyze1;AgSeriesWeeks} through {/ GraphAnalyze6;AgSeriesWeeks}
/Graph Series Analyze 1st Series through 6th Series Aggregation Series Period Months	{/ GraphAnalyze1;AgSeries Months} through {/ GraphAnalyze6;AgSeriesMonths}
/Graph Series Analyze 1st Series through 6th Series Aggregation Series Period Quarters	{/ GraphAnalyze1;AgSeries Quarters} through {/ GraphAnalyze6; AgSeriesQuarters}

Table C.1 Quattro Pro Commands and Menu Equivalent Commands *(continued)*

Quattro Commands	Menu Equivalent
/Graph Series Analyze 1st Series through 6th Series Aggregation Series Period Years	{/ GraphAnalyze1;AgSeriesYears} through {/ GraphAnalyze6;AgSeriesYears}
/Graph Series Analyze 1st Series through 6th Series Exponential Fit	{/ GraphAnalyze1;ExponFit} through {/ GraphAnalyze6;ExponFit}
/Graph Series Analyze 1st Series through 6th Series Linear Fit	{/ GraphAnalyze1;LinearFit} through {/ GraphAnalyze6;LinearFit}
/Graph Series Analyze 1st Series through 6th Series Moving Average	{/ GraphAnalyze1;MovingAvg} through {/ GraphAnalyze6;MovingAvg}
/Graph Series Analyze 1st Series through 6th Series Moving Average Period	{/ GraphAnalyze1;MovingAvg Periods} through {/ GraphAnalyze6; MovingAvgPeriods}
/Graph Series Analyze 1st Series through 6th Series Moving Average Weighted	{/ GraphAnalyze1;MovingAvg Weighted} through {/ GraphAnalyze6; MovingAvgWeighted}
/Graph Series Analyze 1st Series through 6th Series Reset	{/ GraphAnalyze1;Reset} through {/ GraphAnalyze6;Reset}
/Graph Series Analyze 1st Series through 6th Series Table	{/ GraphAnalyze1;Table} through {/ GraphAnalyze6;Table}
/Graph Series Analyze All	Same as /Graph Series Analyze 1st Series except the general category is GraphAnalyzeAll
/Graph Series Analyze X-Axis Series	Same as /Graph Series Analyze 1st Series except the general category is GraphAnalyzeX
/Graph Series Group Columns	{/ Graph;ColumnSeries}
/Graph Series Group Rows	{/ Graph;Row Series}
/Graph Series X-Axis Series	{/ X-Axis;Labels}

Table C.1 Quattro Pro Commands and Menu Equivalent Commands *(continued)*

Quattro Commands	Menu Equivalent
/Graph Text 1st Line	{/ Graph;Main Title}
/Graph Text 2nd Line	{/ Graph;SubTitle}
/Graph Text Font	{/ GraphPrint;Fonts}
/Graph Text Legends 1st Series through 6th Series	{/ 1Series;Legend} through {/ 6Series;Legend}
/Graph Text Legends Position	{/ Graph;LegendPos}
/Graph Text Secondary Y-Axis	{/ Y2Axis;Title}
/Graph Text X-Title	{/ XAxis;Title}
/Graph Text Y-Title	{/ YAxis;Title}
/Graph View	{/ Graph;View} or {GRAPH}
/Graph X-Axis	{/ Dialog;GraphXAxis} when Quattro Pro displays dialog boxes
/Graph X-Axis Alternate Ticks	{/ XAxis;Alternate}
/Graph X-Axis Display Scaling	{/ XAxis;ShowScale}
/Graph X-Axis Format of Ticks	{/ XAxis;Format}
/Graph X-Axis High	{/ XAxis;Max}
/Graph X-Axis Increment	{/ XAxis;Step}
/Graph X-Axis Low	{/ XAxis;Min}
/Graph X-Axis Mode	{/ XAxis;ScaleType}
/Graph X-Axis No. of Minor Ticks	{/ XAxis;Skip}
/Graph X-Axis Scale	{/ XAxis;ScaleMode}
/Graph Y-Axis	{/ Dialog;GraphYAxis} when Quattro Pro displays dialog boxes
/Graph Y-Axis 2nd Y-Axis	{/ Dialog;Graph2YAxis} when Quattro Pro displays dialog boxes
/Graph Y-Axis 2nd Y-Axis Display Scaling	{/ Y2Axis;ShowScale}
/Graph Y-Axis 2nd Y-Axis Format of Ticks	{/ Y2Axis;Format}
/Graph Y-Axis 2nd Y-Axis High	{/ Y2Axis;Max}

Table C.1 Quattro Pro Commands and Menu Equivalent Commands (*continued*)

Quattro Commands	Menu Equivalent
/Graph Y-Axis 2nd Y-Axis Increment	{/ Y2Axis,Step}
/Graph Y-Axis 2nd Y-Axis Low	{/ Y2Axis;Min}
/Graph Y-Axis 2nd Y-Axis Mode	{/ Y2Axis;ScaleType}
/Graph Y-Axis 2nd Y-Axis No. of Minor Ticks	{/ Y2Axis;Skip}
/Graph Y-Axis 2nd Y-Axis Scale	{/ Y2Axis;ScaleMode}
/Graph Y-Axis Display Scaling	{/ YAxis;ShowScale}
/Graph Y-Axis Format of Ticks	{/ YAxis;Format}
/Graph Y-Axis High	{/ YAxis;Max}
/Graph Y-Axis Increment	{/ YAxis;Step}
/Graph Y-Axis Low	{/ YAxis;Min}
/Graph Y-Axis Mode	{/ YAxis;ScaleType}
/Graph Y-Axis No. of Minor Ticks	{/ YAxis;Skip}
/Graph Y-Axis Scale	{/ YAxis;ScaleMode}
/Options Colors Conditional Above Normal Color	{/ ValueColors;High}
/Options Colors Conditional Below Normal Color	{/ ValueColors;Low}
/Options Colors Conditional ERR	{/ ValueColors;Err}
/Options Colors Conditional Greatest Normal Value	{/ ValueColors;Max}
/Options Colors Conditional Normal Cell Color	{/ ValueColors;Normal}
/Options Colors Conditional On/Off	{/ ValueColors;Enable}
/Options Colors Conditional Smallest Normal Value	{/ ValueColors;Min}
/Options Colors Desktop Background	{/ Startup;DesktopColor}
/Options Colors Desktop Desktop	{/ Startup;DesktopChar}
/Options Colors Desktop Errors	{/ ErrorColor;SetErrorColor}
/Options Colors Desktop Highlight-Status	{/ Color;Indicators}
/Options Colors Desktop Status	{/ Color;Status}

Table C.1 Quattro Pro Commands and Menu Equivalent Commands *(continued)*

Quattro Commands	Menu Equivalent
/Options Colors File Manager Active Cursor	{/ FileMgrColors;ActiveCursor}
/Options Colors File Manager Banner	{/ FileMgrColors;Banner}
/Options Colors File Manager Copy	{/ FileMgrColors;Copy}
/Options Colors File Manager Cut	{/ FileMgrColors;Cut}
/Options Colors File Manager Frame	{/ FileMgrColors;Frame}
/Options Colors File Manager Inactive cursor	{/ FileMgrColors;InactiveCursor}
/Options Colors File Manager Marked	{/ FileMgrColors;Marked}
/Options Colors File Manager Text	{/ FileMgrColors;Text}
/Options Colors Help Banner	{/ HelpColors;Banner}
/Options Colors Help Frame	{/ HelpColors;Frame}
/Options Colors Help Highlight	{/ HelpColors;Highlight}
/Options Colors Help Keywords	{/ HelpColors;Keyword}
/Options Colors Help Text	{/ HelpColors;Text}
/Options Colors Menu Banner	{/ MenuColors;Banner}
/Options Colors Menu Drop Shadow	{/ Startup;Shadow}
/Options Colors Menu Explanation	{/ MenuColors;Explanation}
/Options Colors Menu Frame	{/ MenuColors;Frame}
/Options Colors Menu Highlight	{/ MenuColors;MenuBar}
/Options Colors Menu Key Letter	{/ MenuColors;FirstLetter}
/Options Colors Menu Settings	{/ MenuColors;Settings}
/Options Colors Menu Shadow	{/ Startup;ShadowChar}
/Options Colors Menu SpeedBar	{/ Startup;PaletteCol}
/Options Colors Menu Text	{/ MenuColors;Text}
/Options Colors Palettes Black & White	{/ Color;BWCGAPalette}
/Options Colors Palettes Color	{/ Color;ColorPalette}
/Options Colors Palettes Gray Scale	{/ Color;GSPalette}
/Options Colors Palettes Monochrome	{/ Color;BWPalette}

Table C.1 Quattro Pro Commands and Menu Equivalent Commands (continued)

Quattro Commands	Menu Equivalent
/Options Colors Palettes Version 3 Color	{/ Color;Ver3Palette}
/Options Colors Spreadsheet Banner	{/ Color;Banner}
/Options Colors Spreadsheet Borders	{/ Color;Border}
/Options Colors Spreadsheet Cells	{/ Color;Cells}
/Options Colors Spreadsheet Drawn Lines	{/ Color;LineDrawing}
/Options Colors Spreadsheet Frame	{/ Color;Frame}
/Options Colors Spreadsheet Graph Frames	{/ Color;GraphFrame}
/Options Colors Spreadsheet Highlight	{/ Color;Cursor}
/Options Colors Spreadsheet Input Line	{/ Color;Edit}
/Options Colors Spreadsheet Labels	{/ ValueColors;Labels}
/Options Colors Spreadsheet Shading	{/ Color;Shading}
/Options Colors Spreadsheet Titles	{/ Color;Titles}
/Options Colors Spreadsheet Unprotected	{/ Color;Unprotect}
/Options Colors Spreadsheet WYSIWYG Colors Background	{/ WYSIWYG;Cells}
/Options Colors Spreadsheet WYSIWYG Colors Cursor	{/ WYSIWYG;Cursor}
/Options Colors Spreadsheet WYSIWYG Colors Drawn Lines	{/ WYSIWYG;Lines}
/Options Colors Spreadsheet WYSIWYG Colors Grid Lines	{/ WYSIWYG;Grid}
/Options Colors Spreadsheet WYSIWYG Colors Locked Titles Text	{/ WYSIWYG;TitlesF}
/Options Colors Spreadsheet WYSIWYG Colors Row and Column Labels Face	{/ WYSIWYG;BezelFront}
/Options Colors Spreadsheet WYSIWYG Colors Row and Column Labels Highlight	{/ WYSIWYG;BezelTop}
/Options Colors Spreadsheet WYSIWYG Colors Row and Column Labels Shadow	{/ WYSIWYG;BezelBottom}
/Options Colors Spreadsheet WYSIWYG Colors Row and Column Labels Text	{/ WYSIWYG;BezelText}

Table C.1 Quattro Pro Commands and Menu Equivalent Commands *(continued)*

Quattro Commands	Menu Equivalent
/Options Colors Spreadsheet WYSIWYG Colors Shaded Cells	{/ WYSIWYG;Shading}
/Options Colors Spreadsheet WYSIWYG Colors Titles Background	{/ WYSIWYG;TitlesB}
/Options Colors Spreadsheet WYSIWYG Colors Unprotected	{/ WYSIWYG;Unprotected}
/Options Display Mode	{/ ScreenHardware;TextScreenMode}
/Options Formats Align Labels	{/ Defaults;Alignment}
/Options Formats Global width	{/ Defaults;ColWidth}
/Options Formats Hide Zeros	{/ Defaults;Zero}
/Options Formats Numeric Format	{/ Defaults;Format}
/Options Graphics Quality	{/ Defaults;GraphicsQuality}
/Options Hardware Coprocessor	{/ Basics;ShowCoProc}
/Options Hardware EMS Memory Bytes Available	{/ Basics;ShowEMS}
/Options Hardware EMS Memory Bytes Total	{/ Basics;ShowEMSTotal}
/Options Hardware EMS Memory % Available	{/ Basics;ShowEMSPct}
/Options Hardware Mouse Button	{/ Hardware;MouseButton}
/Options Hardware Normal Memory Bytes Available	{/ Basics;ShowMem}
/Options Hardware Normal Memory Bytes Total	{/ Basics;ShowMemTotal}
/Options Hardware Normal Memory % Available	{/ Basics;ShowMemPct}
/Options Hardware Printers 1st Printer Baud rate	{/ GPrinter1;Baud}
/Options Hardware Printers 1st Printer Device	{/ GPrinter1;Device}
/Options Hardware Printers 1st Printer Make	{/ GPrinter1;ShowMake}
/Options Hardware Printers 1st Printer Mode	{/ GPrinter1;ShowMode}
/Options Hardware Printers 1st Printer Model	{/ GPrinter1;ShowModel}

Table C.1 Quattro Pro Commands and Menu Equivalent Commands *(continued)*

Quattro Commands	Menu Equivalent
/Options Hardware Printers 1st Printer Parity	{/ GPrinter1;Parity}
/Options Hardware Printers 1st Printer Stop bits	{/ GPrinter1;Stop}
/Options Hardware Printers 1st Printer Type of printer	{/ GPrinter1;Type}
/Options Hardware Printers 2nd Printer Baud rate	{/ GPrinter2;Baud}
/Options Hardware Printers 2nd Printer Device	{/ GPrinter2;Device}
/Options Hardware Printers 2nd Printer Make	{/ GPrinter2;ShowMake}
/Options Hardware Printers 2nd Printer Mode	{/ GPrinter2;ShowMode}
/Options Hardware Printers 2nd Printer Model	{/ GPrinter2;ShowModel}
/Options Hardware Printers 2nd Printer Parity	{/ GPrinter2;Parity}
/Options Hardware Printers 2nd Printer Stop bits	{/ GPrinter2;Stop}
/Options Hardware Printers 2nd Printer Type of printer	{/ GPrinter2;Type}
/Options Hardware Printers Auto LF	{/ Hardware;AutoLf}
/Options Hardware Printers Background	{/ Hardware;BackgroundPrint}
/Options Hardware Printers' Default Printer	{/ Defaults;PrinterName}
/Options Hardware Printers Fonts Autoscale Fonts	{/ Hardware;AutoFonts}
/Options Hardware Printers Fonts Cartridge Fonts Left Cartridge	{/ Hardware;LJetLeft}
/Options Hardware Printers Fonts Cartridge Fonts Right Cartridge	{/ Hardware;LJetRight}
/Options Hardware Printers Fonts Cartridge Fonts Shading Level	{/ Hardware;LJShadeLevel}
/Options Hardware Printers Plotter Speed	{/ GraphPrint;PlotSpeed}
/Options Hardware Printers Single Sheet	{/ Hardware;SingleSheet}
/Options Hardware Screen Aspect Ratio	{/ ScreenHardware;AspectRatio}
/Options Hardware Screen CGA Snow Suppression	{/ ScreenHardware;Retrace}

Table C.1 Quattro Pro Commands and Menu Equivalent Commands *(continued)*

Quattro Commands	Menu Equivalent
/Options Hardware Screen Resolution	{/ Graph;ScreenMode}
/Options Hardware Screen Screen Type	{/ ScreenHardware;GraphScreenType}
/Options International Currency	{/ Intnl;Currency}
/Options International Date	{/ FormatChanges;IntlDate}
/Options International LICS/LMBCS Conversion	{/ Intnl;LICS}
/Options International Negative	{/ Intnl;Negative}
/Options International Overstrike Print	{/ Intnl;PrintComposed}
/Options International Punctuation	{/ Intnl;Punctuation}
/Options International Time	{/ FormatChanges;IntnlTime}
/Options International Use Sort Table	{/ Intnl;UseSortTable}
/Options Network Banner	{/ Network;Banner}
/Options Network Drive mappings	{/ Network;DriveMaps}
/Options Network Queue Monitor	{/ Network:MonitorQueue}
/Options Network Refresh Interval	{/ Network;Interval}
/Options Network User Name	{/ Network;UserName}
/Options Other Clock	{/ Defaults;ClockFormat}
/Options Other Expanded Memory	{/ Defaults;ExpMem}
/Options Other Macro	{/ Defaults;Suppress}
/Options Other Paradox Network Type	{/ Paradox;NetType}
/Options Other Paradox Directory	{/ Paradox;NetDir}
/Options Other Paradox Retries	{/ Paradox;NetRetries}
/Options Other Undo	{/ Defaults;Undo}
/Options Protection	{/ Protection;Status}
/Options Protection Disable	{/ Protection;Disable}
/Options Protection Enable	{/ Protection;Enable}
/Options Protection Formulas	{/ Protection;FormStatus}
/Options Protection Formulas Protect	{/ Protection;FormProtect}

Table C.1 Quattro Pro Commands and Menu Equivalent Commands *(continued)*

Quattro Commands	Menu Equivalent
/Options Protection Formulas Unprotect	{/ Protection;FormUnprotect}
/Options Recalculation Circular Cell	{/ Audit;ShowCirc}
/Options Recalculation Iteration	{/ Defaults;RecalcIteration}
/Options Recalculation Mode	{/ Defaults;RecalcMode}
/Options Recalculation Order	{/ Defaults;RecalcOrder}
/Options SpeedBar EDIT mode SpeedBar A Button through O Button Long name	{/ Buttons2;LrgText1} through {/ Buttons2;LgrText15}
/Options SpeedBar EDIT mode SpeedBar A Button through O Button Macro	{/ Buttons2;Macro1} through {/ Buttons2;Macro15}
/Options SpeedBar EDIT mode SpeedBar A Button through O Button Short name	{/ Buttons2;SmlText1} through {/ Buttons2:SmlText15}
/Options SpeedBar READY mode SpeedBar A Button through O Button Long name	{/ Buttons1;LrgText1} through {/ Buttons1;LrgText15}
/Options SpeedBar READY mode SpeedBar A Button throughO Button Macro	{/ Buttons1;Macro1} through {/ Buttons1;Macro15}
/Options SpeedBar READY mode SpeedBar A Button through O Button Short name	{/ Buttons1;SmlText1} through {/ Buttons1;SmlText15}
/Options Startup Autoload File	{/ Startup;File}
/Options Startup Beep	{/ Startup;Beep}
/Options Startup Directory	{/ Defaults;Directory}
/Options Startup Edit Menus	{/ MenuBuilder;Run}
/Options Startup File Extension	{/ Startup;Extension}
/Options Startup Menu Tree	{/ Startup;Menus}
/Options Startup Startup Macro	{/ Startup;Macro}
/Options Startup Use Dialogs	{/ Dialog;Enable}
/Options Update	{/ Defaults;Update}
/Options WYSIWYG Zoom %	{/ WYSIWYG;Zoom}
/Print Adjust Printer Align	{/ Print;Align}
/Print Adjust Printer Form Feed	{/ Print;FormFeed}

Table C.1 Quattro Pro Commands and Menu Equivalent Commands *(continued)*

Quattro Commands	Menu Equivalent
/Print Adjust Printer Skip Line	{/ Print;SkipLine}
/Print Block	{/ Print;Block}
/Print Copies	{/ Print;Copies}
/Print Destination Binary File	{/ Print;OutputHQFile}
/Print Destination File	{/ Print;OutputFile}
/Print Destination Graphics Printer	{/ Print;OutputHQ}
/Print Destination Printer	{/ Print;OutputPrinter}
/Print Destination Screen Preview	{/ Print;OutputPreview}
/Print Format	{/ Print;Format}
/Print Graph Print Destination File	{/ GraphPrint;DestIsFile}
/Print Graph Print Destination Graph Printer	{/ GraphPrint;DestIsPtr}
/Print Graph Print Destination Screen Preview	{/ GraphPrint;DestIsPreview}
/Print Graph Print Go	{/ GraphPrint;Go}
/Print Graph Print Layout 4:3 Aspect	{/ Hardware;Aspect43}
/Print Graph Print Layout Dimensions	{/ GraphPrint;Dimensions}
/Print Graph Print Layout Height	{/ GraphPrint;Height}
/Print Graph Print Layout Left Edge	{/ GraphPrint;Left}
/Print Graph Print Layout Orientation	{/ GraphPrint;Rotated}
/Print Graph Print Layout Reset	{/ Print;ResetAll}
/Print Graph Print Layout Top Edge	{/ GraphPrint;Top}
/Print Graph Print Layout Update	{/ Print;Update}
/Print Graph Print Layout Width	{/ GraphPrint;Width}
/Print Graph Print Name	{/ GraphPrint;Use}
/Print Graph Print Write Graph File EPS File	{/ GraphFile;Postscript}
/Print Graph Print Write Graph File PCX File	{/ GraphFile;PCX}
/Print Graph Print Write Graph File PIC File	{/ GraphFile;PIC}
/Print Graph Print Write Graph File Slide EPS	{/ GraphFile;SlideEPS}

Table C.1 Quattro Pro Commands and Menu Equivalent Commands *(continued)*

Quattro Commands	Menu Equivalent
/Print Headings Left Heading	{/ Print;LeftBorder}
/Print Headings Top Heading	{/ Print;TopBorder}
/Print Layout	{/ Dialog;PrintLayout} when Quattro Pro displays dialog boxes
/Print Layout Break Pages	{/ Print;Breaks}
/Print Layout Dimensions	{/ Print;Dimensions}
/Print Layout Footer	{/ Print;Footer}
/Print Layout Header	{/ Print;Header}
/Print Layout Margins Bottom	{/ Print;BottomMargin}
/Print Layout Margins Left	{/ Print;LeftMargin}
/Print Layout Margins Page Length	{/ Print;PageLength}
/Print Layout Margins Right	{/ Print;RightMargin}
/Print Layout Margins Top	{/ Print;TopMargin}
/Print Layout Orientation	{/ Print;Rotated}
/Print Layout Percent Scaling	{/ Print;PercentScaling}
/Print Layout Reset All	{/ Print;ResetAll}
/Print Layout Reset Headings	{/ Print;ResetBorders}
/Print Layout Reset Layout	{/ Print;ResetDefaults}
/Print Layout Reset Print Block	{/ Print;ResetBlock}
/Print Layout Setup String	{/ Print;Setup}
/Print Layout Update	{/ Print;Update}
/Print Print Manager	{/ View;NewPrintMgr}
/Print Print-To-Fit	{/ Print;PrintToFit}
/Print Spreadsheet Print	{/ Print;Go}
/Style Alignment Center	{/ Publish;AlignCenter}
/Style Alignment General	{/ Publish;AlignDefault}
/Style Alignment Left	{/ Publish;AlignLeft}

Table C.1 Quattro Pro Commands and Menu Equivalent Commands *(continued)*

Quattro Commands	Menu Equivalent
/Style Alignment Right	{/ Publish;AlignRight}
/Style Block Size Auto Width	{/ Block;AdjustWidth}
/Style Block Size Height Set Row Height	{/ Block;SetHeight}
/Style Block Size Height Reset Row Height	{/ Block;ResetHeight}
/Style Block Size Reset Width	{/ Block;ResetWidth}
/Style Block Size Set Width	{/ Block;SetWidth}
/Style Column Width	{/ Column;Width}
/Style Define Style Create	{/ Publish;EditNamedStyle}
/Style Define Style Erase	{/ Publish;EraseNamedStyle}
/Style Define Style File Retrieve	{/ Publish;LoadStyleSheet}
/Style Define Style File Save	{/ Publish;SaveStyleSheet}
/Style Define Style Remove	{/ Publish;DeleteNamedStyle}
/Style Font	{/ Publish;ApplyAnonymousStyle}
/Style FontTable	{/ Publish;Font}
/Style Hide Column Expose	{/ Column;Display}
/Style Hide Column Hide	{/ Column;Hide}
/Style Insert Break	{/ Print;CreatePageBreak}
/Style Line Drawing	{/ Publish;LineDrawing}
/Style Numeric Format	{/ Block;Format}
/Style Protection Protect	{/ Block;Protect}
/Style Protection Unprotect	{/ Block;Unprotect}
/Style Reset Width	{/ Column;Reset}
/Style Shading Black	{/ Publish;ShadingBlack}
/Style Shading Grey	{/ Publish;ShadingGrey}
/Style Shading None	{/ Publish;ShadingNone}
/Style Use Style	{/ Publish;UseNamedStyle}
/Tools Advanced Math Invert	{/ Math;InvertMatrix}

Table C.1 Quattro Pro Commands and Menu Equivalent Commands *(continued)*

Quattro Commands	Menu Equivalent
/Tools Advanced Math Multiply	{/ Math;MultiplyMatrix}
/Tools Advanced Math Regression Dependent	{/ Regression;Dependent}
/Tools Advanced Math Regression Go	{/ Regression;Go}
/Tools Advanced Math Regression Independent	{/ Regression;Independent}
/Tools Advanced Math Regression Output	{/ Regression;Output}
/Tools Advanced Math Regression Reset	{/ Regression;Reset}
/Tools Advanced Math Regression Y Intercept	{/ Regression;Intercept}
/Tools Audit Blank References	{/ Auditor;BlankReference}
/Tools Audit Circular	{/ Auditor;TypeCIRC}
/Tools Audit Dependency	{/ Auditor;TypeDependency}
/Tools Audit Destination	{/ Auditor;Destination}
/Tools Audit ERR	{/ Auditor;TypeERR}
/Tools Audit External Links	{/ Auditor;TypeExternalReference}
/Tools Audit Label References	{/ Auditor;TypeLabelReference}
/Tools Combine Add Block	{/ File;AddRange}
/Tools Combine Add File	{/ File;AddFile}
/Tools Combine Copy Block	{/ File;CopyRange}
/Tools Combine Copy File	{/ File;CopyFile}
/Tools Combine Subtract Block	{/ File;SubtractRange}
/Tools Combine Subtract File	{/ File;SubtractFile}
/Tools Frequency	{/ Math;Distribution}
/Tools Import ASCII Text File	{/ File;ImportText}
/Tools Import Comma & "" Delimited File	{/ File;ImportNumbers}
/Tools Import Only Commas	{/ File;ImportComma}
/Tools Library Load	{/ Library;Load}
/Tools Library Unload	{/ Library;Unload}
/Tools Macro	{/ Macro;Menu}

Table C.1 Quattro Pro Commands and Menu Equivalent Commands *(continued)*

Quattro Commands	Menu Equivalent
/Tools Macro Clear Breakpoints or ALT-F2 Clear Breakpoints	{/ Name;BkptReset}
/Tools Macro Debugger or ALT-F2 Debugger	{/ Macro;Debug}
/Tools Macro Execute or ALT-F2 Execute	{/ Name;Execute}
/Tools Macro Instant Replay or ALT-F2 Instant Replay	{/ Macro;Replay}
/Tools Macro Key Reader or ALT-F2 Key Reader	{/ Macro;Reader}
/Tools Macro Library or ALT-F2 Library	{/ Macro;Library}
/Tools Macro Macro Recording or ALT-F2 Macro Recording	{/ Startup;Record}
/Tools Macro Name Create or ALT-F2 Name Create	{/ Name;Create}
/Tools Macro Name Delete or ALT-F2 Name Delete	{/ Name;Delete}
/Tools Macro Paste or ALT-F2 Paste	{/ Macro;Paste}
/Tools Macro Record or ALT-F2 Record	{/ Macro;Record}
/Tools Macro Transcript or ALT-F2 Transcript	{/ Macro;Transcript}
/Tools Optimizer Answer Report	{/ Solution;Answer}
/Tools Optimizer Constraints	{/ Solution;Constraints}
/Tools Optimizer Detail Report	{/ Solution;Detail}
/Tools Optimizer Go	{/ Solution;Go}
/Tools Optimizer Model	{/ Solution;LoadSave}
/Tools Optimizer Model Load	{/ Solution;Load}
/Tools Optimizer Model Save	{/ Solution;Save}
/Tools Optimizer Options Derivatives	{/ Solution;Derivatives}
/Tools Optimizer Options Derivatives Central	{/ Solution;Central}
/Tools Optimizer Options Derivatives Forward	{/ Solution;Forward}
/Tools Optimizer Options Estimates	{/ Solution;Estimates}
/Tools Optimizer Options Estimates Quadratic	{/ Solution;Quad}

Table C.1 Quattro Pro Commands and Menu Equivalent Commands *(continued)*

Quattro Commands	Menu Equivalent
/Tools Optimizer Options Estimates Tangent	{/ Solution;Tangent}
/Tools Optimizer Options Linear or Nonlinear	{/ Solution;Linear}
/Tools Optimizer Options Linear or Nonlinear Linear	{/ Solution;SetLinear}
/Tools Optimizer Options Linear or Nonlinear Nonlinear	{/ Solution;SetNonLinear}
/Tools Optimizer Options Max Iterations	{/ Solution;MaxIterations}
/Tools Optimizer Options Max Time	{/ Solution;MaxTime}
/Tools Optimizer Options Precision	{/ Solution;Precision}
/Tools Optimizer Options Search	{/ Solution;Search}
/Tools Optimizer Options Search Conjugate	{/ Solution;Conjugate}
/Tools Optimizer Options Search Newton	{/ Solution;Newton}
/Tools Optimizer Options Show Iteration Results	{/ Solution;Show}
/Tools Optimizer Reset All	{/ Solution;Reset}
/Tools Optimizer Reset Answer Report	{/ Solution;ResetAns}
/Tools Optimizer Reset Constraints	{/ Solution;ResetCon}
/Tools Optimizer Reset Detail Report	{/ Solution;ResetDet}
/Tools Optimizer Reset Options	{/ Solution;ResetOpt}
/Tools Optimizer Reset Solution Cell	{/ Solution;ResetSol}
/Tools Optimizer Reset Variable Cell(s)	{/ Solution;ResetVar}
/Tools Optimizer Restore	{/ Solution;Restore}
/Tools Optimizer Solution	{/ Solution;Solution}
/Tools Optimizer Solution Cell	{/ Solution;GoalCell}
/Tools Optimizer Solution Max, Min, Equal	{/ Solution;MinMax}
/Tools Optimizer Solution Max, Min, Equal Maximize	{/ Solution;Maximum}
/Tools Optimizer Solution Max, Min, Equal Minimize	{/ Solution;Minimum}

Table C.1 Quattro Pro Commands and Menu Equivalent Commands *(continued)*

Quattro Commands	Menu Equivalent
/Tools Optimizer Solution Max, Min, Equal Equal	{/ Solution;Equal}
/Tools Optimizer Solution Max, Min, Equal None	{/ Solution;NoGoal}
/Tools Optimizer Variable Cells	{/ Solution;Variable}
/Tools Parse Create	{/ Parse;CreateLine}
/Tools Parse Edit	{/ Parse;EditLine}
/Tools Parse Go	{/ Parse;Go}
/Tools Parse Input	{/ Parse;Input}
/Tools Parse Output	{/ Parse;Output}
/Tools Parse Reset	{/ Parse;Reset}
/Tools Reformat	{/ Block;Justify}
/Tools Solve For Formula Cell	{/ Math;SolveFormula}
/Tools Solve For Go	{/ Math;SolveGo}
/Tools Solve For Parameters Accuracy	{/ Math;SolveAccuracy}
/Tools Solve For Parameters Max Iterations	{/ Math;SolveMaxIt}
/Tools Solve For Reset	{/ Math;SolveReset}
/Tools Solve For Target Value	{/ Math;SolveTarget}
/Tools Solve For Variable Cell	{/ Math;SolveVariable}
/Tools Update Links Change	{/ HotLink;Change}
/Tools Update Links Delete	{/ HotLink;Delete}
/Tools Update Links Open	{/ HotLink;Open}
/Tools Update Links Refresh	{/ HotLink;Update}
/Tools What-If 1 Variable	{/ Math;1CellWhat-If}
/Tools What-If 2 Variables	{/ Math;2CellWhat-If}
/Tools What-If Reset	{/ Math;ResetWhat-If}
/Tools Xtract Formulas	{/ File;ExtractFormulas}
/Tools Xtract Values	{/ File;ExtractValues}

Table C.1 Quattro Pro Commands and Menu Equivalent Commands *(continued)*

Quattro Commands	Menu Equivalent
/Window Move/Size	{/ View;Size}
/Window Options Clear	{/ Windows;Clear}
/Window Options Grid Lines	{/ Windows;GridLines}
/Window Options Horizontal	{/ Windows;Horizontal}
/Window Options Locked Titles Both	{/ Titles;Both}
/Window Options Locked Titles Clear	{/ Titles;Clear}
/Window Options Locked Titles Horizontal	{/ Titles;Horizontal}
/Window Options Locked Titles Vertical	{/ Titles;Vertical}
/Window Options Map View	{/ Windows;MapView}
/Window Options Print Block	{/ Windows;PrintBlock}
/Window Options Row & Col Borders Display	{/ Windows;RowColDisplay}
/Window Options Row & Col Borders Hide	{/ Windows;RowColHide}
/Window Options Sync	{/ Windows;Synch}
/Window Options Unsync	{/ Windows;Unsynch}
/Window Options Vertical	{/ Windows;Vertical}
/Window Pick	{/ View;Choose}
/Window Stack	{/ View;Cascade}
/Window Tile	{/ View;Arrange}
/Window Zoom	{/ View;Zoom}
Gray + key when using the file options	{/ File;List}

File Manager Menu Equivalent Commands

/Edit All Select	{/ FileMgr;AllMark}
/Edit Copy	{/ FileMgr;Copy}
/Edit Duplicate	{/ FileMgr;Duplicate}
/Edit Erase	{/ FileMgr;Erase}
/Edit Move	{/ FileMgr;Cut}
/Edit Paste	{/ FileMgr;Paste}

Table C.1 Quattro Pro Commands and Menu Equivalent Commands *(continued)*

Quattro Commands	Menu Equivalent
/Edit Rename	{/ FileMgr;Rename}
/Edit Select File	{/ File Mgr;Mark}
/File Close	{/ Basics;Close}
/File Close All	{/ System;TidyUp}
/File Exit	{/ System;Exit}
/File Make Dir	{/ FileMgr;MakeDir}
/File New	{/ View;NewWindow}
/File Open	{/ View;OpenWindow}
/File Read Dir	{/ FileMgr;ReadDir}
/File Utilities DOS Shell	{/ Basics;OS} or {/ Basics;Shell}
/File Utilities File Manager	{/ View;NewFileMgr}
/File Utilities SQZ! Remove Blanks	{/ SQZ;Blanks}
/File Utilities SQZ! Storage of Values	{/ SQZ;Values}
/File Utilities SQZ! Version	{/ SQZ;Version}
/File Workspace Restore	{/ System;RestoreWorkspace}
/File Workspace Save	{/ System;SaveWorkspace}
/Options Beep	{/ Startup;Beep}
/Options Colors: Same as /Options Colors for spreadsheets	
/Options Display Mode	{/ ScreenHardware;TextScreenMode}
/Options File List Full View	{/ FileMgr;Narrow}
/Options File List Wide View	{/ FileMgr;Wide}
/Options Hardware: Same as /Option Hardware for spreadsheets	
/Options Startup Directory Current	{/ FileMgr;CurrDir}
/Options Startup Directory Previous	{/ FileMgr;SameDir}
/Options Startup Edit Menus	{/ MenuBuilder;Run}
/Options Startup Menu Tree	{/ Startup;Menus}
/Options Update	{/ Defaults;Update}

Table C.1 Quattro Pro Commands and Menu Equivalent Commands *(continued)*

Quattro Commands	Menu Equivalent
/Print Adjust Printer Align	{/ FileMgrPrint;Align}
/Print Adjust Printer Form Feed	{/ FileMgrPrint;FormFeed}
/Print Adjust Printer Skip Line	{/ FileMgrPrint;SkipLine}
/Print Block	{/ FileMgrPrint;Block}
/Print Destination File	{/ FileMgrPrint;OutputFile}
/Print Destination Printer	{/ FileMgrPrint;OutputPrinter}
/Print Go	{/ FileMgrPrint;Go}
/Print Page Layout Break Pages	{/ FileMgrPrint;Breaks}
/Print Page Layout Footer	{/ FileMgrPrint;Footer}
/Print Page Layout Header	{/ FileMgrPrint;Header}
/Print Page Layout Margins & Length Bottom	{/ FileMgrPrint;BottomMargin}
/Print Page Layout Margins & Length Left	{/ FileMgrPrint;Left Margin}
/Print Page Layout Margins & Length Page Length	{/ FileMgrPrint;PageLength}
/Print Page Layout Margins & Length Right	{/ FileMgrPrint;RightMargin}
/Print Page Layout Margins & Length Top	{/ FileMgrPrint;TopMargin}
/Print Page Layout Setup String	{/ FileMgrPrint;Setup}
/Print Reset All	{/ FileMgrPrint;ResetAll}
/Print Reset Layout	{/ FileMgrPrint;ResetDefaults}
/Print Reset Print Block	{/ FileMgrPrint;ResetBlock}
/Sort DOS Order	{/ FileMgr;SortNone}
/Sort Extension	{/ FileMgr;SortExt}
/Sort Name	{/ FileMgr;SortName}
/Sort Size	{/ FileMgr;SortSize}
/Sort Timestamp	{/ FileMgr;SortDate}
/Tree Close	{/ FileMgr;TreeClear}
/Tree Open	{/ FileMgr;TreeShow}

Table C.1 Quattro Pro Commands and Menu Equivalent Commands *(continued)*

Quattro Commands	Menu Equivalent
/Tree Resize	{/ FileMgr;TreeSize}
/Window Move/Size	{/ View;Size}
/Window Pick	{/ View;Choose}
/Window Stack	{/ View;Cascade}
/Window Tile	{/ View;Arrange}
/Window Zoom	{/ View;Zoom}

Appendix D

Quattro Pro Menus

This appendix shows the Quattro Pro menus for each of the menu items in the menu bar. Next to each command is the chapter number that covers the command in more detail. You can also check Appendix B for a synopsis of the command. You will want to use this appendix to quickly find a command you want to use or to use as a checklist of Quattro Pro commands that you have added to your skills.

Spreadsheet Window Commands

| File | Edit | Style | Graph | Print | Database | Tools | Options | Window |

File Menu

New		5
Open		5
Retrieve		5
Save	Ctrl-S	5
Save As		5
Save All		5
Close		5
Close All		5
Erase		5
Directory		5
Workspace		5
Utilities		5
Exit	Ctrl-X	1

Workspace

Save	5
Restore	5

Utilities

DOS Shell	5
File Manager	5
SQZ!	5

SQZ!

Remove Blanks	
Storage of Values	
Version	
Quit	

Edit Menu

Copy	Ctrl-C	3
Copy Special		3
Move	Ctrl-M	3
Erase Block	Ctrl-E	3
Undo	ALT-F5	3,10
Insert	Ctrl-I	3,8
Delete		3,8
Names		3
Fill		9,3
Values		3
Transpose		3
Search & Replace		3

Copy Special

Contents	3
Format	3

Insert/Delete

Rows	3
Columns	3
Row Block	3
Column Block	3

Search & Replace

Block	3
Search String	3
Replace String	3
—Options—	
Look In	3
Direction	3
Match	3
Case Sensitive	3
Options Reset	3
Next	Ctrl-N	3
Previous	Ctrl-P	3
Quit		3

Names

Create	3,11
Delete	3
Labels	3,11
Reset	3
Make Table	3

Quattro Pro Menus

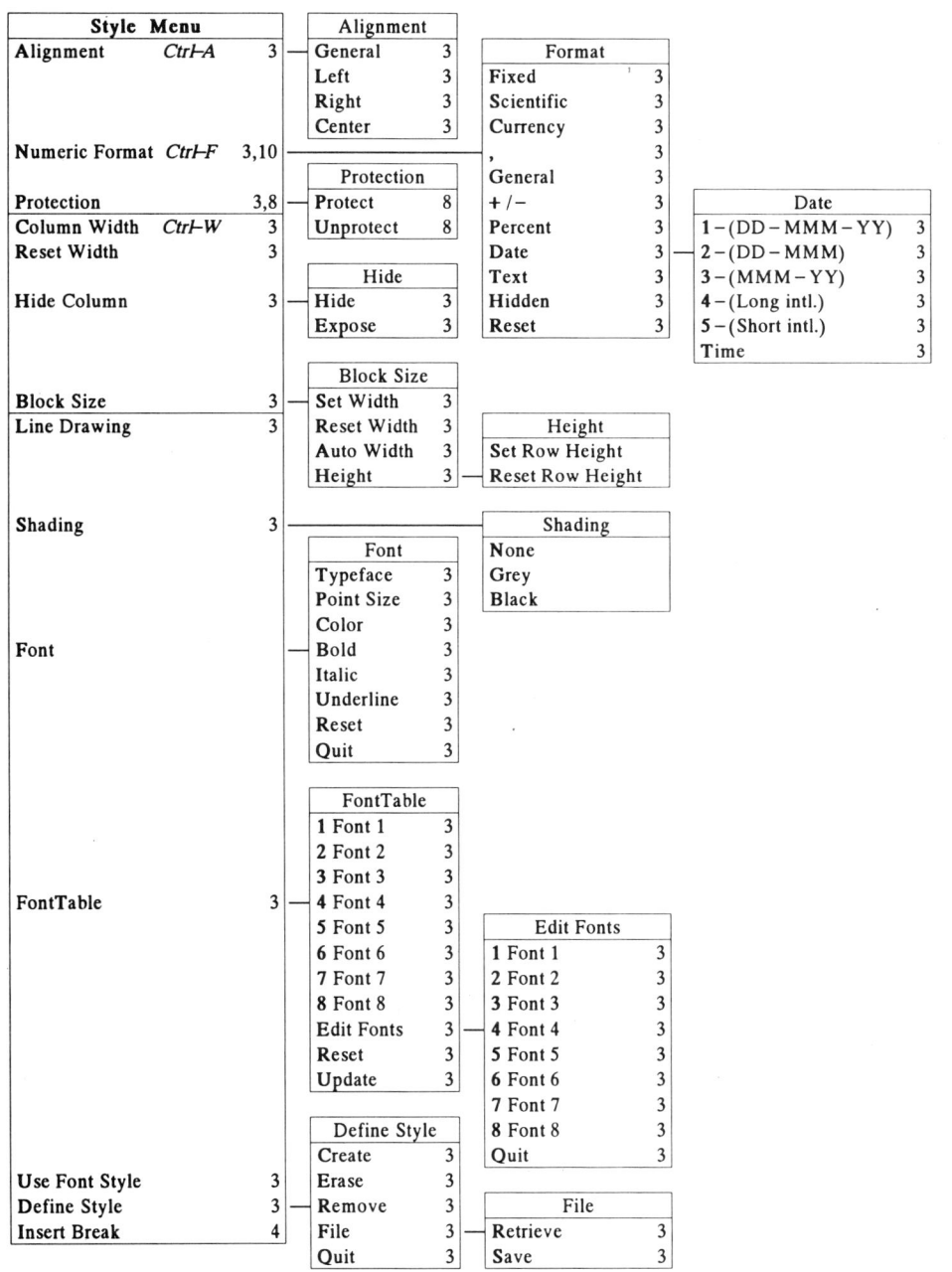

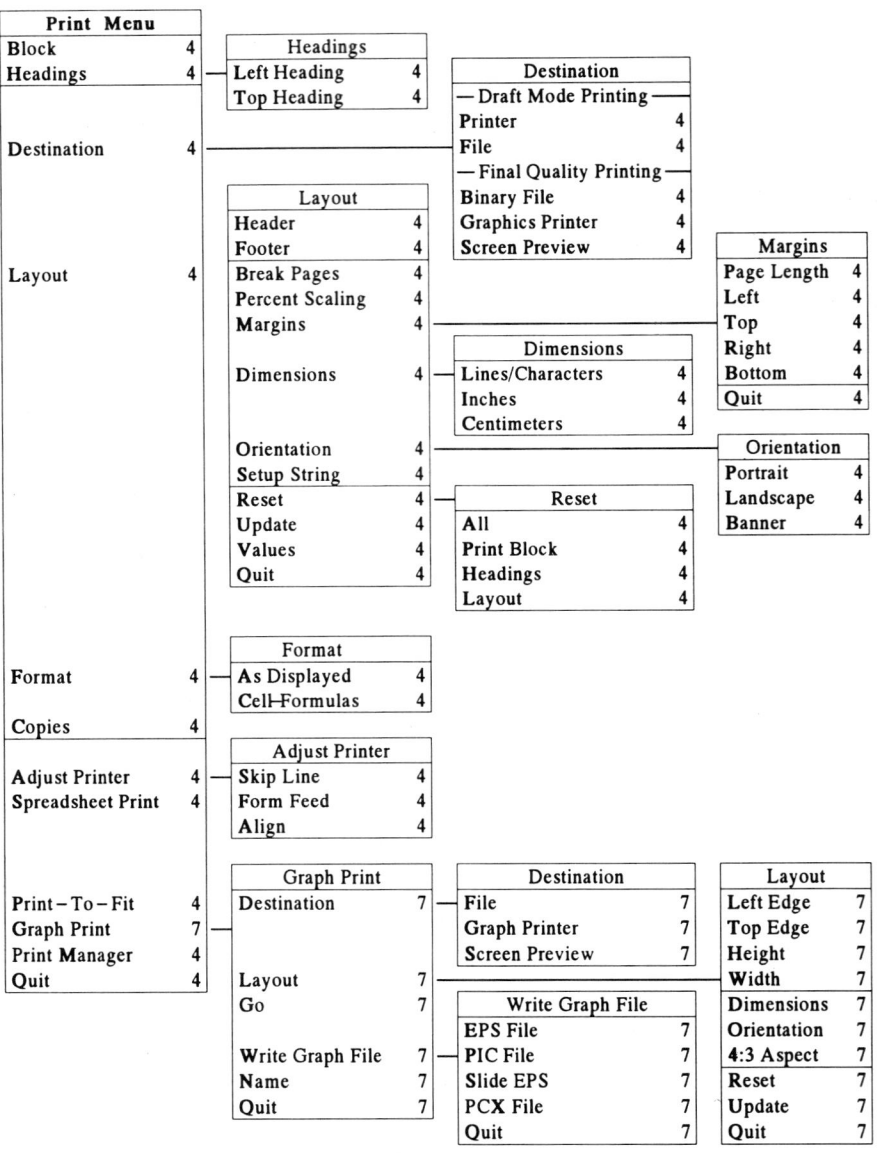

Quattro Pro Menus

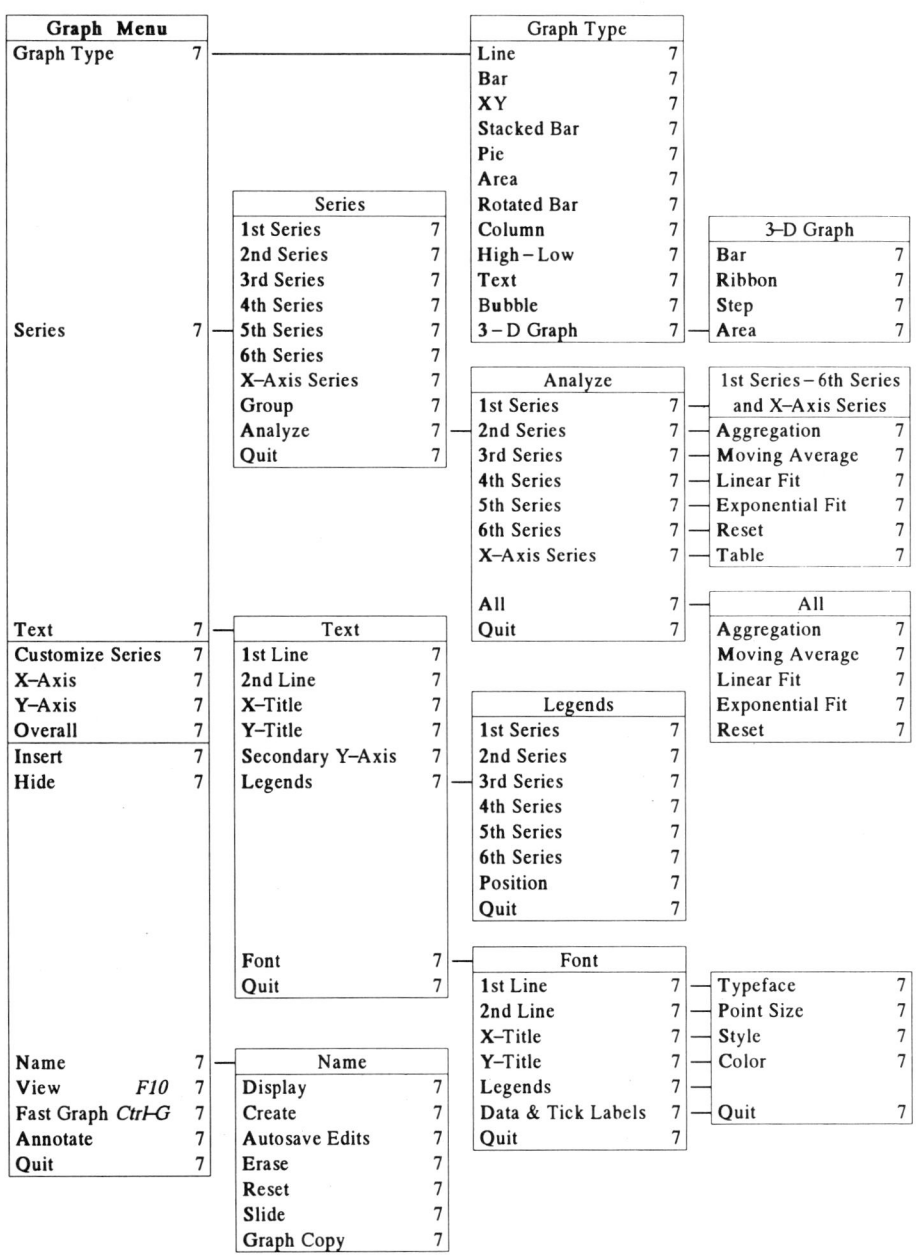

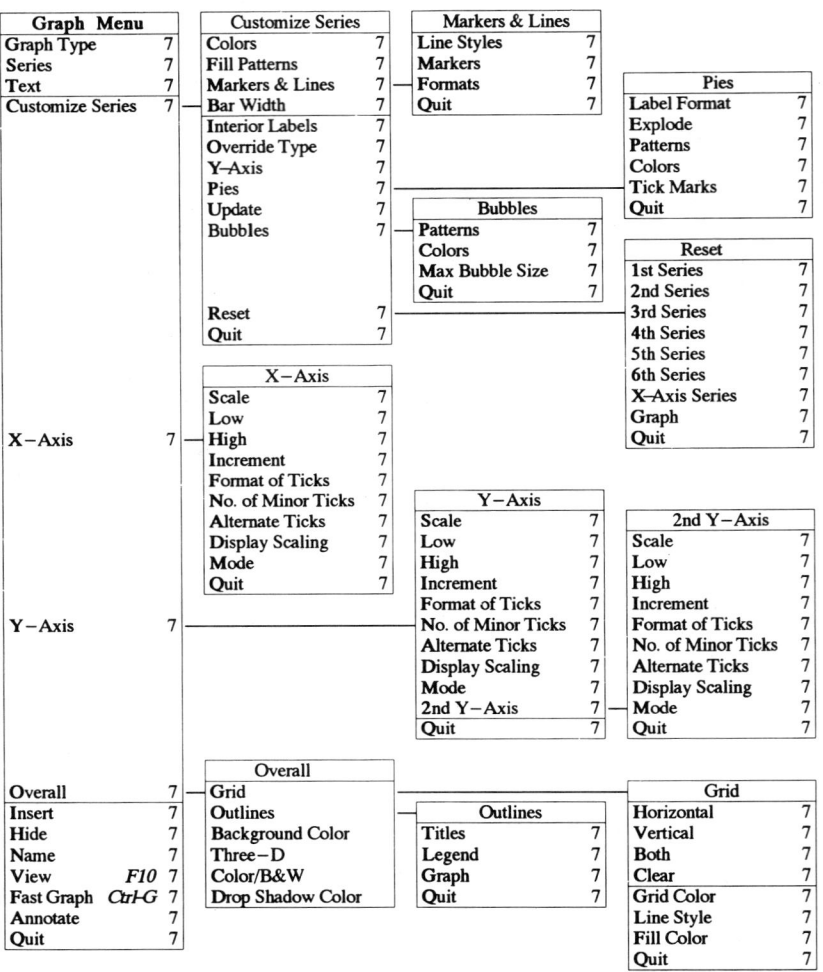

Quattro Pro Menus

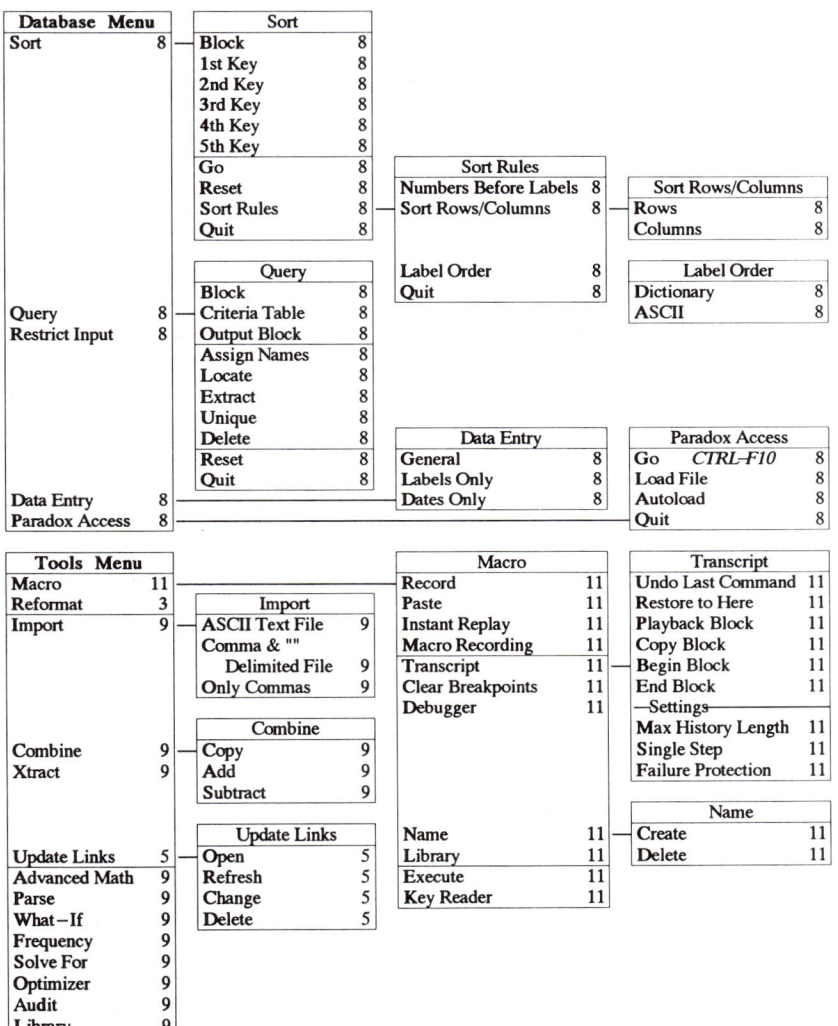

Database Menu		Sort	
Sort	8	Block	8
		1st Key	8
		2nd Key	8
		3rd Key	8
		4th Key	8
		5th Key	8
		Go	8
		Reset	8
		Sort Rules	8
		Quit	8

Sort Rules	
Numbers Before Labels	8
Sort Rows/Columns	8
Label Order	8
Quit	8

Sort Rows/Columns	
Rows	8
Columns	8

Label Order	
Dictionary	8
ASCII	8

Query	
Block	8
Criteria Table	8
Output Block	8
Assign Names	8
Locate	8
Extract	8
Unique	8
Delete	8
Reset	8
Quit	8

| Query | 8 |
| Restrict Input | 8 |

Data Entry	
General	8
Labels Only	8
Dates Only	8

Paradox Access		
Go	CTRL-F10	8
Load File		8
Autoload		8
Quit		8

| Data Entry | 8 |
| Paradox Access | 8 |

Tools Menu	
Macro	11
Reformat	3
Import	9

Import	
ASCII Text File	9
Comma & "" Delimited File	9
Only Commas	9

Macro	
Record	11
Paste	11
Instant Replay	11
Macro Recording	11
Transcript	11
Clear Breakpoints	11
Debugger	11

Transcript	
Undo Last Command	11
Restore to Here	11
Playback Block	11
Copy Block	11
Begin Block	11
End Block	11
—Settings—	
Max History Length	11
Single Step	11
Failure Protection	11

| Combine | 9 |
| Xtract | 9 |

Combine	
Copy	9
Add	9
Subtract	9

Name	
Create	11
Delete	11

Update Links	5
Advanced Math	9
Parse	9
What–If	9
Frequency	9
Solve For	9
Optimizer	9
Audit	9
Library	9

Update Links	
Open	5
Refresh	5
Change	5
Delete	5

Name	
Library	11
Execute	11
Key Reader	11

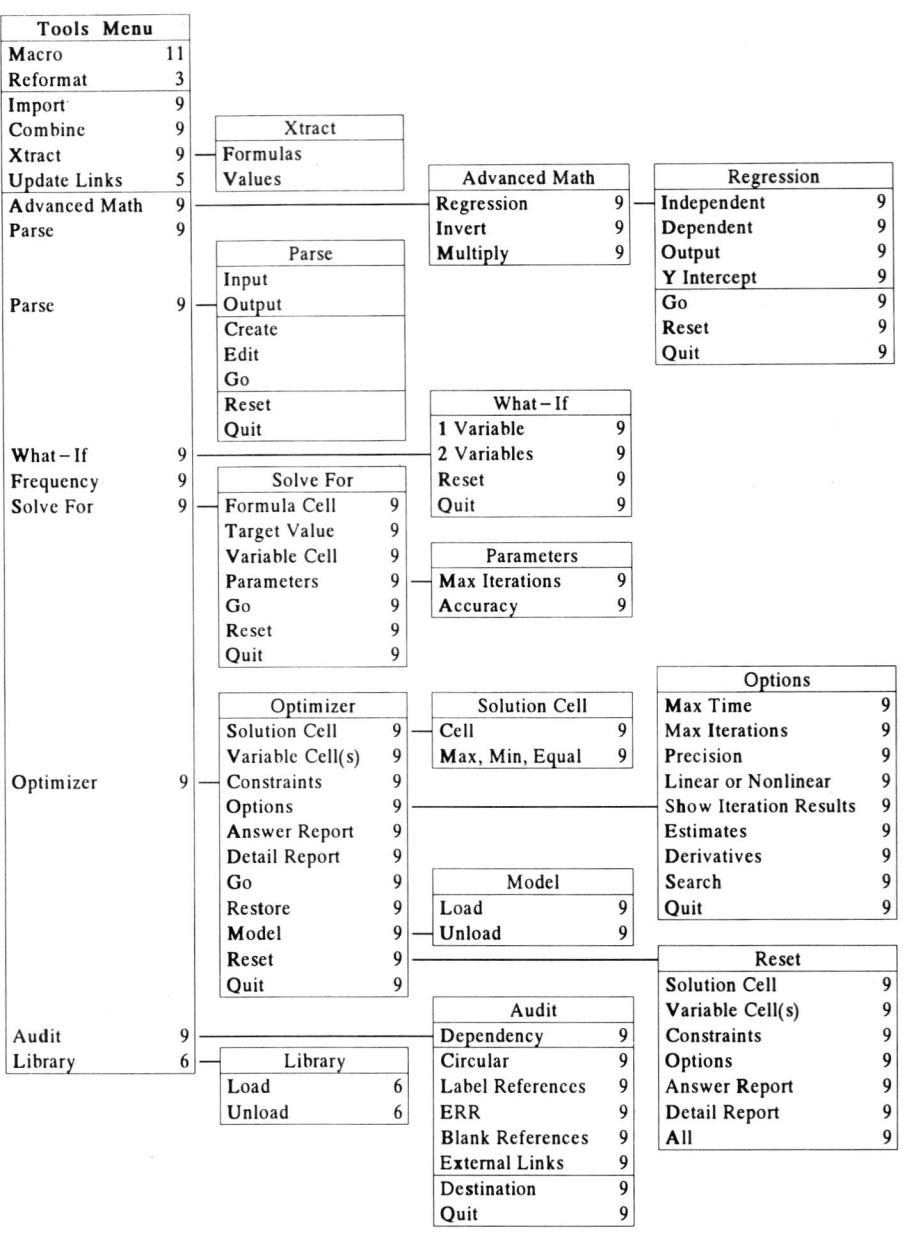

Quattro Pro Menus

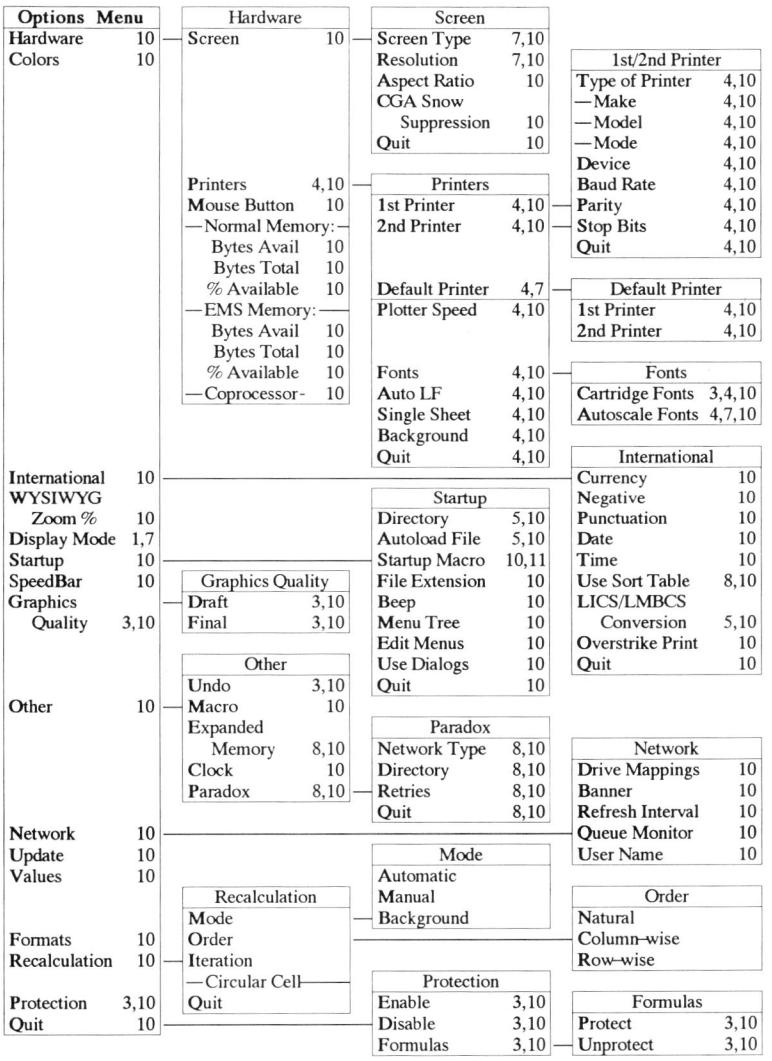

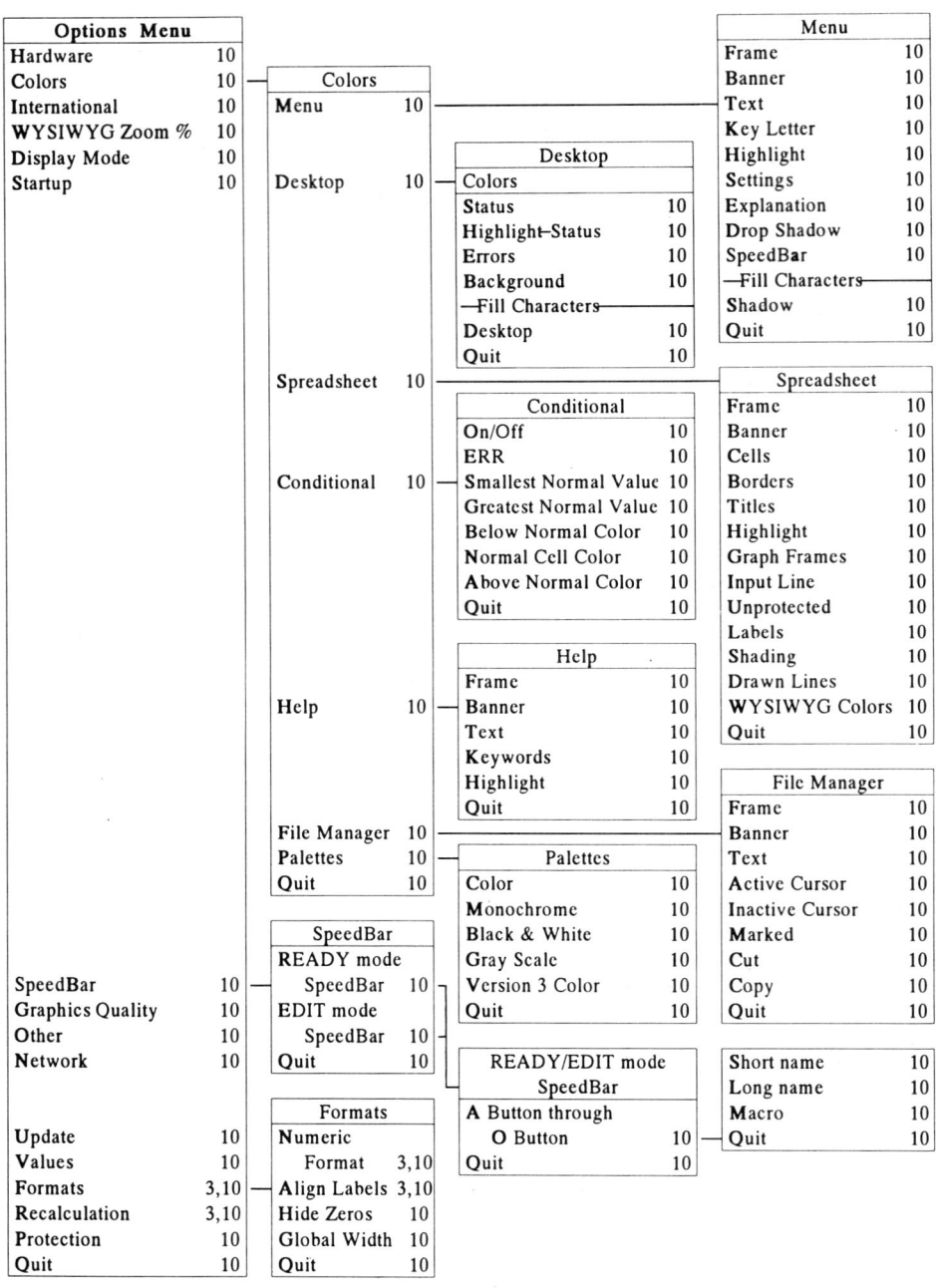

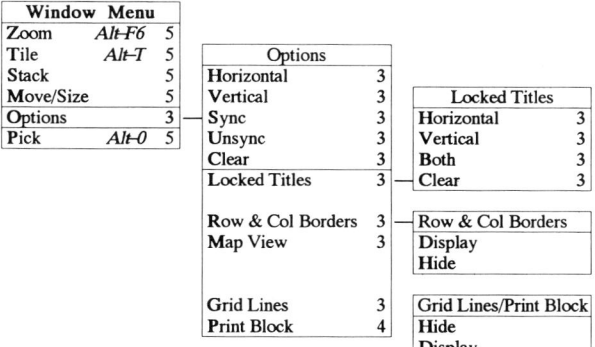

File Manager Commands (Chapter 5)

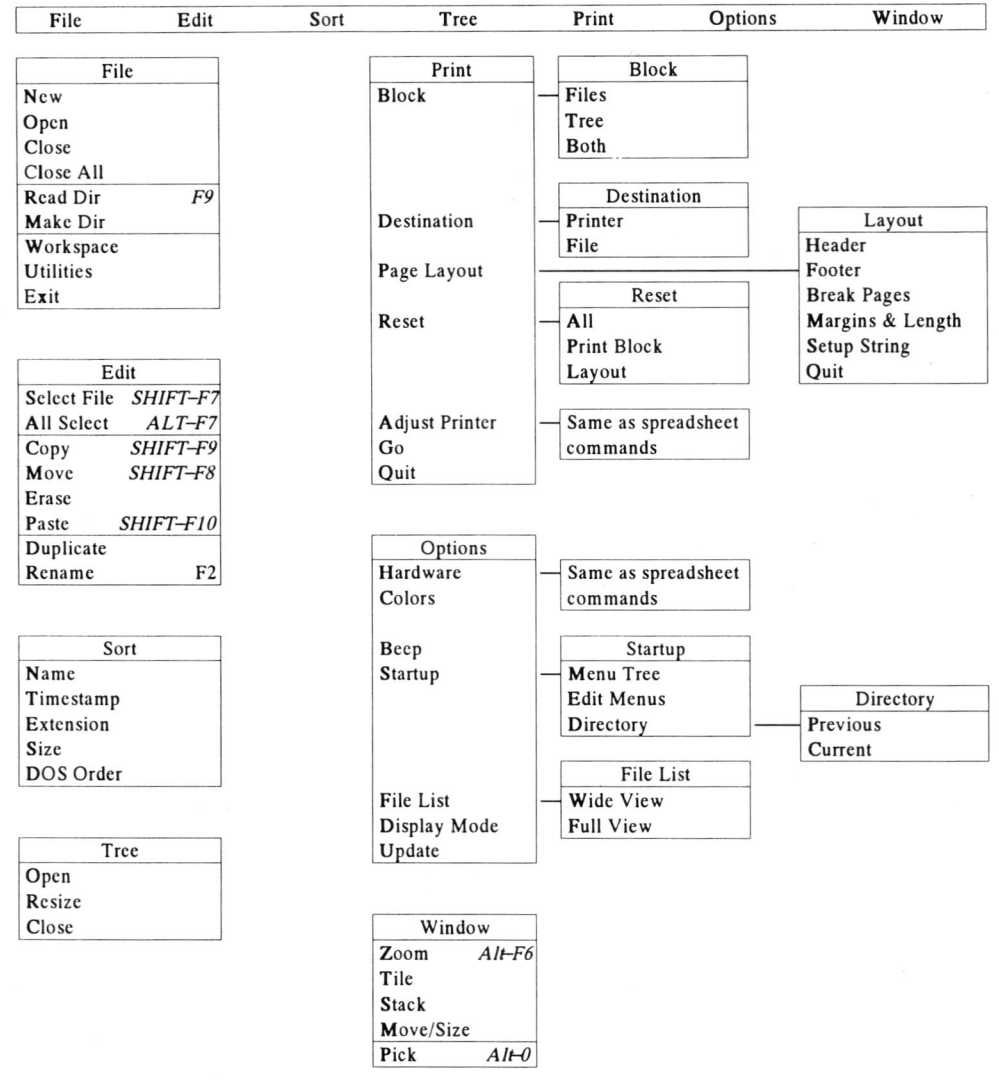

Index

A

Abort Debug, 609
@ABS, 310
Absolute address, 48, 49
   and copied formulas, 73
AccessMode, 659
@ACOS, 316–317
Adding spreadsheets, 491–486
Advanced analytical/file features
   auditing spreadsheet, 483–486
   combining files, 487–497
   exporting data, 501–503
   frequency distribution, 462–464
   importing data, 498–501
   long labels, splitting, 503–506
   matrix math, 464–470
   Optimizer, 476–483
   regression analysis, 471–474
   saving part of file, 486–487
   values, solving for, 474–476
   What-If analysis, 454–462
Alignment
   blocks, 69
      changing alignment, 69
   spreadsheet
      labels, 544–545
      values, 41
ALT-# keys, 20
Area graph, 342, 344
Arithmetic formulas, 42, 43, 48
   @ functions in, 48
   with multiple operators, 44
   order of calculation, 43
   parenthesis, use of, 45
   pointing method, 45–48
   uses of, 42

Arrow icon, 379
ARROW key functions, 16–19, 21, 22
ASCII characters, 193
   Desktop setting, 524
   shadow setting, 523
ASCII text files
   and file pointers, 655–656
   importing, 498–501
@ASIN, 316
Aspect ratio, screen, 516
@ functions, in arithmetic formulas, 48
@@, 321–323
@ATAN2, 317–318
@ATAN, 317
Auditing spreadsheet, 483–485
Audit trail, 158
AUTOEXEC.BAT, 24, 437
Autoload file option, 561
Automatic translation, exporting data, 501–502
@AVG, 243–244
Axis, of graph, 340–341

B

Background color, graphs, 375
Background printing, spreadsheets, 170–172
BACKSPACE key, 18, 19, 30–31
Banner, 525, 527, 528
Bar graph, 342, 361, 363
Baud rate, 518
BEEP, 667–668
Begin Block, 594, 595
Bitstream fonts, 4, 122, 123, 126
   building fonts, 538
   downloading, 169

BKGD, status indicator, 12
BLANK, 612
Block argument, database, 443
Block commands
  Edit and Search & Replace, 96–98
  Edit Copy, 70–81
  Edit Delete Columns Block, 109
  Edit Erase Block, 85, 134
  Edit Fill, 102–104
  Edit Insert Columns Block, 109
  Edit Move, 62, 82–83
  Edit Names Create, 86, 90
  Edit Names Delete, 89
  Edit Names Label, 86
  Edit Names Make Table, 90
  Edit Names Notes Create, 90
  Edit Names Reset, 89
  Edit Search & Replace, 137
  Edit Transpose, 95
  Edit Values, 94–95
  invoking commands, 64
  Options Formats Align Labels, 69
  Options Formats Numeric Format, 68
  Options Protection Disable, 92
  Options Protection Enable, 92, 93
  Style Block Size, 111
  Style Block Size Auto Width, 112
  Style Block Size Height, 115
  Style Numeric Format, 62, 66–69
  Style Numeric Format Reset, 68, 69
  Style Protection Protect, 93
  Style Protection Unprotect, 92, 93
  Tools Reformat, 100
  use of, 62–63
Block name, 237
Block reference, 237
Blocks
  alignment, changing, 69
  appearance of, 63
  copying, 77–82
    one block to another, 77–78
    selectively copying block, 81–82
    to several locations, 78, 80–81
  documentation of, 89–90
  erasing, 85
  formatting, 66–69
  generate series of values, 101–104
  and link references, 215
  macro for copying block, 582–584
  mouse, selecting block with, 65
  moving, 82–85
    cell addresses in moved formulas, 83, 85
  moving block, 82–83
  naming, 85–90
    adding note to block, 89–90
    automatic update of name, 85–86
    block name table, 90
    changing address of block name, 90
    creating name, 86–87
    function key for access to names, 88
    number of characters in, 86
    removing names, 89
    using names, 87–89
  print block
    resetting block, 147–148
    selection of, 146–147
  reformatting text blocks, 99–101
  select key, selecting block with, 65
  specifying block, 63–65
  text blocks, reformatting, 99–101
  values, generation in blocks, 101–104
Borland style option, 561
Boxes
  in graph, 375
  in spreadsheets, 127, 129
BRANCH, 620–621
BREAKOFF, 636
BREAKON, 636–637
Breakpoints, debugger, 605–607
BSINST, and fonts, 126
Bubble graph, 344
  See also Graphs
Bullet characters, spreadsheets, 127

C

CALC, status indicator, 12
CAP, status indicator, 12
CAPS LOCK keys, 19, 20
Cartridge fonts, 127
  setting for, 519
@CELL, 323–324
Cell addresses. *See* Reference types
Cell functions, 321–327
  @@, 321–323
  @CELL, 323–324
  @CELLINDEX, 325–327
  @CELLPOINTER, 324–325
Cell identifier, format abbreviations of, 9
@CELLINDEX, 325–327
@CELLPOINTER, 324–325
Cell reference, nature of, 237
Cells
  copying
    one cell to another, 70, 72
    one cell to several cells, 76–77
  editing cell with debugger, 608–609
  printing contents, 158–160
CGA snow suppression, screen, 516

Index 855

@CHAR, 264
Character mode screen, 533
@CHOOSE, 329–331
CIRC, status indicator, 12
Circular references, 485
@CLEAN, 253
Clicking, mouse, 5
Clipboard. *See* Graph Annotator
Clock display, setting, 540–541
CLOSE, 656–657
@CODE, 263–264
Code, nature of, 264
Color
  customization for, 521–529
    conditional colors, 525, 527
    Desktop colors, 523–524
    File Manager window colors, 527–528
    Help information colors, 527
    menu colors, 522–523
    Palette colors, 528–529
    spreadsheet window colors, 524–525
  for font, 123
  graphs, 359, 366, 375, 377
@COLS, 333
Column argument, database, 443
Column commands
  Edit Delete Columns, 106
  Edit Delete Columns Block, 109
  Edit Insert Columns, 104
  Edit Insert Columns Block, 107
  Options Formats Global Width, 114
  Select Reset Width, 111
  Style Block Size Auto Width, 112
  Style Block Size Set Width, 111–112
  Style Block Widths, 115
  Style Column Width, 110–111, 114, 115
  Style, Hide Column, and Expose, 109
  Style, Hide Column, and Hide, 109
  Style Reset Width, 111
Column graph, 342
  See also Graphs
Columns
  hiding borders of, 121–122
  printing, hiding columns, 157–158
  search of, 99
  spreadsheet
    blocks of columns, 107, 109
    deleting, 106
    hiding, 109
    insertion of, 104, 106
    width, 110–115
  width
    changing for several columns, 111–112, 114
    changing width, 110–111

narrow columns, setting for, 115
resetting for single column, 111
setting default, 546
setting for all columns, 114–115
wider column width, 168
Combining files, 487–497
  adding spreadsheets, 491–486
  copying one spreadsheet to another, 488–491
  subtracting spreadsheets, 496–497
Commands
  general action commands, 555
  menu-equivalent commands, 555
    listing of, 814–840
  shortcut keystrokes, listing of, 552
  specific action commands, 555
  See also File Manager commands; Macros; Spreadsheet commands; individual commands
Compatibility options, Menu Builder, 561–562
Compound criteria, 427–429
Compressing spreadsheet, 164–165
Conditional colors, setting, 525, 527
CONTENTS, 612–613
Copy Block, 595
Copying
  spreadsheet
    block to several locations, 78, 80–81
    one block to another, 77–78
    one cell to another, 70, 72
    one cell to several cells, 76–77
    reference styles in copied formulas, 72–76
    selectively copying block, 81–82
Corrections
  to database, 412
  and EDIT mode, 40, 49
  ERR, 49
  error beeps, setting, 537
  to numeric entries, 40
  to spreadsheet entries, 30–31
  with Undo, 134, 137–138
@COS, 315
@COUNT, 240–241
Courier fonts, 122
Criteria argument, database, 443
Criteria table
  database, 422–429
    compound criteria, 427–429
    exact match criteria, 423–425
    formula criteria, 425–427
    location for criteria, 423
@CTERM, 296–297
CTRL-BACKSPACE keys, 18, 19

CTRL-BREAK keys, 22, 25
CTRL-ENTER keys, 20
CTRL-forward slash keys, 18, 19, 31
CTRL key functions, 16, 17
CTRL-X, 25
{ } command, 673
Currency
    international
        changing symbol, 529
        displaying negative numbers, 529–530
    numeric format, 543
Cursor
    active and inactive, 528
    function of, 18
@CURVALUE, 334
Customizing Quattro Pro
    Bitstream font building, 538
    clock display, setting, 540–541
    display mode, 533–534
    for expanded memory, 540
    format defaults, 542–546
        default column width, 546
        hiding zero values, 545
        for label alignment, 544–545
        for numeric format, 543–544
    global customization options, 513
    for information about computer memory, 521–522
    international formats, 529–533
    mouse button, 520
    and Paradox, 541
    printer, 516–520
    protection defaults, 551
    for Quattro Pro on network, 541–542
    recalculation defaults, 546–551
        changing number of iterations, 550–551
        changing order of spreadsheet calculation, 548–549
        choosing manual or automatic calculation, 548
    screen, 514–516
    selecting an options set, 513–514
    SpeedBar, setting, 538
    startup defaults, 534–537
        automatic loading of spreadsheet, 536
        automatic start-up of macro, 536
        default directory, setting, 536
        default extension, changing, 536–537
        dialog boxes, use of, 537
        error beeps, setting, 537
        menu tree, selection of, 537
    system customization options, 511, 513
Undo
    setting, 539

updating with macros, 540
See also Menu Builder

D

Database
    corrections to, 412
    criteria table, 422–429
        compound criteria, 427–429
        exact match criteria, 423–425
        formula criteria, 425–427
        location for criteria, 423
    data entry, input form for, 440–441
    data types, control of, 441–442
    entering data, 412
    external databases, 435–440
        Paradox, 437–440
        saving file, 436
        specifying file type, 435–436
    Extract feature, 431–435
        extracting matching information, 433–434
        extracting unique records, 434–435
        output area, creating, 431–433
    field names, rules for, 411
    fields of, 410
    matching records, locating, 430–431
    nature of, 410
    query features
        assigning names to fields, 421–422
        defining block for search, 420–421
        deleting matching records, 435
        steps in query, 419
    records of, 410
    sorting
        changing order of, 415
        data integrity during, 417–419
        sort keys, 413–415
        specifying records for, 412–413
    statistical functions, 442–448
        @DAVG, 443–444
        @DCOUNT, 444
        @DMAX, 444–445
        @DMIN, 445
        @DSTD, 446
        @DSTDS, 446
        @DSUM, 445–446
        @DVAR, 446–447
        @DVARS, 447
        management summary report with, 448–449
        syntax of, 443
        and What-If analysis, 460–462

Index   857

Database Data Entry, 130, 133, 441, 689–690
Database Data Entry Dates Only, 442
Database Data Entry Labels Only, 442
Database Paradox Access, 438–439, 690
Database Paradox Access Autoload, 439
Database Paradox Access Go, 439
Database Paradox Access Load File, 439
Database Query, 420, 421, 423, 690–692
Database Query Assign Names, 411, 414, 422, 426, 435
Database Query Block, 419, 421, 422, 435, 591
Database Query Extract, 434
Database Query Unique, 462
Database Restrict Input, 440, 441, 692
Database Sort, 413, 588, 692–693
Database Sort Block, 413, 414, 418
Database Sort Sort Rules, 415
Data management, 2–3
Data point, of graph, 341, 351–352, 389
@DATE, 267
Date
  international, changing format, 531–532
  spreadsheet, 54–56
    date calculations, 55–56
    documentation for, 57
    formats for, 54
  mode indicator, 13
Date and time functions, 265–276
  @DATE, 267
  @DATEVALUE, 274–275
  @DAY, 269, 271
  @HOUR, 272
  @MINUTE, 272–273
  @MONTH, 268–269
  @NOW, 266
  @SECOND, 273–274
  @TIME, 271
  @TIMEVALUE, 275
  @TODAY, 266
  @YEAR, 268
@DATEVALUE, 274–275
@DAVG, 443–444
@DAY, 269, 271
DBase, exporting data to, 185, 187, 189
@DCOUNT, 444
@DDB, 289–290
DEBUG, status indicator, 12
Debugger, 579, 602–609
  breakpoints
    conditional breakpoint, 607
    standard breakpoint, 605, 607
  editing cell with debugger, 608–609
  leaving debugger, 609
  in Step mode, 604
  stopping execution of macro, 609
  trace cells, 607–608
Decimal fractions, format for, 39–40
Defaults
  changing settings, 20
  format defaults, 542–546
    default column width, 546
    hiding zero values, 545
    for label alignment, 544–545
    for numeric format, 543–544
  graphs, 364–365
    resetting, 364–365
  hardware defaults, changing, 514–521
  printing, 144–146, 170
    for page layout, 145–146
    selecting default printer, 518
    updating defaults, 170
  protection defaults, 551
  Quattro Pro, 20
  recalculation defaults, 546–551
    changing number of iterations, 550–551
    changing order of spreadsheet calculation, 548–549
    choosing manual or automatic calculation, 548
  and resource files, 513–514
  startup, 534–537
    automatic loading of spreadsheet file, 536
    automatic start-up of macro, 536
    default directory, setting, 536
    default extension, changing, 536–537
    dialog boxes, use of, 537
    error beeps, setting, 537
    menu tree, selection of, 537
  updating, 514
DEFINE, 621–622
@DEGREES, 314
Deleting files, File Manager, 225–226
Delimited files, importing, 498–499
DEL key, 18, 19
Desktop, colors, changing, 523–524
Dialog boxes, use of, 537
Direction keys, 16–18
  listing of, 16–17
  and mode, 18
  operation of, 18
Directories
  changing directories, 194–195
    for current session, 194
    permanent change to, 195
    for single file, 194
  nature of, 178–179
  path, 179

Disk formatting, DOS, 218
DISPATCH, 623–624
Display, 5–11
  changing modes, 5, 533–534
  input line, 7–8
  menu bar, 7
  spreadsheet area, 5–7
  status line, 8–11
  text mode display, 5
  WYSIWYG display, 5
@DMAX, 444–445
@DMIN, 445
Documentation
  blocks, adding note to, 89–90
  for date/formulas/numeric entries, 57
  of macro, 580
  printing cell contents as, 158–160
  spreadsheets, types of, 158
DOS
  access to in Quattro, 217
  commands to avoid, 218
  disk formatting, 218
  running other programs from, 218
Downloading, fonts, 169
Draft mode, and margins, 152
Dragging mouse, 65
Drawing area, Graph Annotator, 378
Drop shadow, 523
@DSTD, 446
@DSTDS, 446
@DSUM, 445–446
Duplication of files, File Manager, 226
Dutch fonts, 122
@DVAR, 446–447
@DVARS, 447
DVR button, 191–192

E

EDIT, mode indicator, 13
Edit All Select, 224, 798
Edit and Search & Replace, 96–98
Edit Copy, 70–81, 201, 224, 226, 423, 574, 589, 693–694, 798
Edit Copy Special, 565, 694
Edit Delete Column Block, 694–695
Edit Delete Columns, 106, 412, 695
Edit Delete Row Block, 695
Edit Delete Rows, 107, 412, 695
Edit Duplicate, 226, 798–799
Edit Erase, 225, 799
Edit Erase Block, 85, 134, 580, 612, 695–696
Edit Fill, 102–104, 333, 455, 458, 580, 589, 696
Editing keys, 18–19
  listing of, 19
  operation of, 18–19
Edit Insert Columns, 104, 412, 679
Edit Insert Columns Block, 107, 696
Edit Insert Row Block, 107, 679
Edit Insert Rows, 106, 157, 679
EDIT mode
  and error correction, 40, 49
  and status line, 10
Edit Move, 62, 82–83, 104, 225, 250, 253, 697–698, 799
Edit Name Labels Right, 475
Edit Names Create, 86, 90, 215, 578, 698–699
Edit Names Delete, 89, 580, 699
Edit Names Labels, 86, 580, 699
Edit Names Labels Down, 422
Edit Names Make Table, 90, 699
Edit Names Notes Create, 90
Edit Names Reset, 89, 700
Edit Paste, 224, 225, 226, 799
Edit Rename, 226, 800
Edit Search & Replace, 120, 137, 208, 215, 530, 700–701
Edit Select, 222
Edit Select All, 222
Edit Select File, 224, 800
Edit Transpose, 95, 589, 591, 701
Edit Undo, 138, 539, 701–702
Edit Values, 94–95, 250, 251, 253, 702
Element icons, listing of, 379–380
Elements of graph. *See* Graph Annotator
Ellipse icon, 380
END, status indicator, 12
End Block, 594, 595
END key, 16, 17, 18, 19, 22
ENTER key, 21, 22
Entries
  spreadsheet, 27–32
    correcting mistakes, 30–32
    finalizing entries, 30, 31
    label entries, 28–29
    making entries, 29–30
    and memory, 27–28
    and mode indicator, 28, 29
    organization of, 27
    value entries, 29
Equipment requirements
  hard drive, 3
  memory options, 4
  mouse, 4–5
  printing devices, 3–4
  storage capacity, 4
Erasing, blocks, 85
@ERR, 49, 285–286
ERR, 49, 527

ERROR, mode indicator, 13
Error beeps, setting, 537
Error messages
    ERR, 49
    and file retrieval, 190
    help for, 24
    printing, 149
@EXACT, 259-260
@EXP, 320
Expanded memory, 746
    setting for, 540
Exporting data, 501-503
    automatic translation, 501-502
    to dBase or Paradox, 185, 187, 189
    other spreadsheets in formulas, 202
    other spreadsheets in Quattro commands, 201-202
    steps in, 502-503
EXT, status indicator, 12
Extended memory, testing program for, 686
Extract feature
    database, 431-435
        extracting matching information, 433-434
        extracting unique records, 434-435
        output area, creating, 431-433

F

@FALSE, 284-285
Fields
    database
        naming fields, 411
        nature of, 410
File Close, 197, 220, 702, 800
File Close All, 197, 220, 703, 800-801
File Directory, 184, 194, 536, 703
File Erase, 592, 703
@FILEEXISTS, 283
File Exit, 703-704, 801
File extension option, 561
File Make Dir, 227, 801
File Manager
    colors, changing, 527-528
    directory tree pane, 222
    example of use, 228-230
    file list pane
        setting file name, 221
        setting filter, 220-221
        use of, 221-222
    menu commands, 222-227
        changing file list pane display, 223
        copying files, 224-225
        creating subdirectories, 226-227
        deleting files, 225-226
        duplicating files, 226
        moving files, 225
        printing directory information, 224
        printing file list, 224
        renaming files, 226
        sorting files, 223-224
    opening and closing windows, 219-220
    workspaces, creating, 227
File Manager commands
    Edit All Select, 798
    Edit Copy, 798
    Edit Duplicate, 798-799
    Edit Erase, 799
    Edit Move, 799
    Edit Paste, 799
    Edit Rename, 800
    Edit Select File, 800
    File Close, 800
    File Close All, 800-801
    File Exit, 801
    File Make Dir, 801
    File New, 801-802
    File Open, 802
    File Read Dir, 802
    File Utilities DOS Shell, 802-803
    File Utilities File Manager, 803
    File Utilities SQZ!, 803
    File Workspace Restore, 803-804
    File Workspace Save, 804
    Options Beep, 804
    Options Colors, 804
    Options Display Mode, 804-805
    Options File List, 805
    Options Hardware, 805
    Options Startup Directory, 805-806
    Options Startup Edit Menus, 806
    Options Startup Menu Tree, 806
    Options Update, 806
    Print Adjust Printer, 806-807
    Print Block, 807
    Print Destination, 807
    Print Go, 808
    Print Page Layout, 808-809
    Print Quit, 809
    Print Reset, 809
    Sort, 809-810
    Tree, 810
    Window Move/Size, 810
    Window Pick, 810-811
    Window Stack, 811
    Window Tile, 811
    Window Zoom, 811
File mode indicator, 13
File name

File Manager, 221
status line, 10
File New, 196, 704, 801–802
File Open, 195, 196, 487, 498, 536, 704–705, 802
File Read Dir, 222, 226, 802
File Retrieve, 189, 195–196, 223, 498, 536, 592, 705
Files
   directories and subdirectories, 178–179
   file pointers, 655–656
   linking files, 203–216
      block names with link references, 213–215
      linked references in Quattro commands, 208–213
      linking to other spreadsheets, 203–208
      link library, 215
   multiple files
      closing window, 197
      display options for, 197–199, 201
      opening second spreadsheet, 195–196
      opening window with new spreadsheet, 196
   naming of, 179–181
      establishing naming standard, 180–181
      rules for, 180
   retrieving files, 189–194
   saving files, 181–189
File Save, 181, 182, 185, 196, 486, 501, 592, 705–706
File Save All, 196, 706
File Save As, 159, 181, 185, 187, 196, 439, 501–502, 592, 706–707
FILESIZE, 658
File Utilities DOS Shell, 182, 217, 218, 226, 403, 437, 541, 564, 802–803
File Utilities File Manager, 219, 707, 803
File Utilities SQZ!, 184, 707–708, 803
File Workspace Restore, 227, 708, 803–804
File Workspace Save, 227, 708, 804
Fill pattern, graphs, 341, 359–360, 366
Filter, File Manager, setting filter, 220–221
Financial functions, 287–305
   @CTERM, 296–297
   @DDB, 289–290
   @FV, 296
   @FVAL, 303
   @IPAYMT, 293
   @IRATE, 300–301
   @IRR, 305
   @NPER, 298–330
   @NPV, 304–305
   @PAYMT, 291–293
   @PMT, 290–291
   @PPAYMT, 294

   @PV, 301–302
   @PVAL, 302–303
   @RATE, 297–298
   @SLN, 287
   @SYD, 288–289
   @TERM, 294–296
Financial numeric format, 544
@FIND, 260–261
FIND, mode indicator, 13
Fixed numeric format, 543
Fonts
   Bitstream fonts, 4, 126, 538
   cartridges, setting for, 519
   downloading, 169
   graphs, 341, 354–355
   and international characters, 123
   spreadsheets, 122–127
      building fonts, 123, 126
      cartridge fonts, 127
      font table, 125
      loading new fonts, 126–127
      selecting font, 123
      selecting for specific spreadsheet, 126
      types of fonts, 122–123
FOR, 624
FORBREAK, 625–627
FORMAT, DOS command, 218
Format indicator, 68
Formatting
   blocks, 66–69
   numeric entries, 66–69
      choices for formats, 66, 67
   reformatting text blocks, 99–101
Formula criteria, 425–427
Formulas, 38
   formula links
      pointing method, 204–205
      typing method, 205–206
   macro for displaying/printing formulas, 584
   protection for, 93, 551
   search of, 98–99
   spreadsheet, 41–54
      arithmetic formulas, 42, 43–48
      conversion to result of formula, 93–94
      display of, 43–44
      documentation for, 57
      logical formulas, 42, 50–52
      and operators, 43
      printing with formulas displayed, 158–160
      recalculation of, 48–49
      reference types, 48, 49
      special values, 49–50
      string formulas, 42, 52

testing formulas, 53–54
use of other spreadsheets in, 202
Frame, 525, 527
Frequency distribution, 462–464
   steps in, 463–464
FRMT, mode indicator, 13
Function keys, 13, 15–16
   listing of function key assignments, 15
   template for, 16
Functions
   adding other functions, 238
   categories of, 231
   cell functions, 321–327
   choosing functions, 237–238
   date and time functions, 265–276
   example of use, 335–338
   financial functions, 287–305
   function arguments, 232–237
      block name, 237
      block reference, 237
      cell reference, 237
      list, 237
      listing of, 233–236
      number, 232
      string, 232, 237
   logical functions, 276–286
   mathematical functions, 306–321
   nesting functions, 238
   statistical functions, 238–249
   string functions, 249–265
   syntax rules, 232
   system functions, 333–335
   table functions, 327–333
@FV, 296
@FVAL, 303

G

Gallery, Graph Annotator, 378
General format, numeric entries, 39–40
GET, 637–640
GETLABEL, 640
GETNUMBER, 640–641
GETPOS, 658
Global customization options, 513
Graph Annotate, 377, 708–709
Graph Annotator, 377–392
   activation of, 377
   altering graph from Quattro graph menus, 385–387
   Clipboard, 389–392
      copying elements from, 391
      copying elements from Clipboard file, 391
      copying elements to file, 391
      storing elements in, 391
   elements
      adding elements, 380–382
      changing attributes of, 383–384
      changing elements, 382–384
      changing layer of, 387, 389
      linking to data point, 389
      moving elements, 384–385
      removing elements, 385
      resizing elements, 385
   exiting, 392
   icons, listing of, 379–380
   screen, areas of, 377–379
GRAPHCHAR, 641–642
Graph Customize Series, 365, 537
Graph Customize Series Bar Width, 709
Graph Customize Series Bubbles, 709–710
Graph Customize Series Colors, 710
Graph Customize Series Fill Patterns, 710–711
Graph Customize Series Interior Block, 351
Graph Customize Series Interior Labels, 366, 711–712
Graph Customize Series Markers & Lines Formats, 712
Graph Customize Series Markers & Lines Line Styles, 712
Graph Customize Series Markers & Lines Markers, 713
Graph Customize Series Markers & Lines Quit, 713
Graph Customize Series Override Type, 713–714
Graph Customize Series Pies Colors, 714
Graph Customize Series Pies Explode, 714–715
Graph Customize Series Pies Label Format, 715
Graph Customize Series Pies Patterns, 715
Graph Customize Series Pies Quit, 716
Graph Customize Series Pies Tick Marks, 716
Graph Customize Series Quit, 716
Graph Customize Series Reset, 716–717
Graph Customize Series Reset Graph, 365, 392
Graph Customize Series Update, 365, 369, 373, 717
Graph Customize Series Y-Axis, 717
Graph Fast Graph, 356, 717–718
Graph frames, 525
Graph Graph Type, 346, 358, 363, 365, 534, 718–719
Graph Hide, 400, 719–720
Graphics, 2
Graphics mode

graphics mode screen, 533
   and margins, 152
Graph Insert, 399, 400, 720
Graph Name, 392
Graph Name Autosave Edits, 393, 720
Graph Name Create, 721
Graph Name Display, 393, 402, 721
Graph Name Erase, 393, 721
Graph Name Graph Copy, 393, 721–722
Graph Name Reset, 722
Graph Name Slide, 393, 394, 395, 722
Graph Overall, 365, 373, 537
Graph Overall Background Color, 722
Graph Overall Color/B & W, 723
Graph Overall Drop Shadow Colors, 355, 723
Graph Overall Grid, 723–724
Graph Overall Outlines, 724
Graph Overall Three-D, 344, 724
Graph Quit, 725
Graphs
   for analytical data
      data points in spreadsheet, 351
      moving average, 350
      statistics of series, 349–350
      trends, 350–351
   appearance of
      bar width, 361
      color, 359
      fill pattern, 359–360
      interior labels, 361
      line styles, 360–361
      markers, 360
      two graph types, use of, 361, 363
      two y-axes, use of, 363–364
   background color, setting, 375
   boxes, drawing in graph, 375
   choosing type of, 346–348
   colors, settings for, 377
   copying to another spreadsheet, 393
   defaults, resetting, 364–365
   fast graph, creating, 356–357
   grid lines, adding, 373–374
   pie/column/bubble options, 365–368
      color, changing, 366
      displaying/hiding tick marks, 367
      exploding pie slices, 366–367
      fill patterns, 366
      formatting labels, 365–366
      second series, use of, 367–368
      size of bubbles, 368
   printing, 400–406
      fonts, 341, 354–355
      graph layout, 404, 406
      named graph, 402
      preview of graph, 406
      printer requirements, 401
      resetting options, 406
      sending graph to file, 402–403
      sending graph to second printer, 402
   saving
      graphic image, 394
      and naming graph, 392–393
      in other format, 403
      spreadsheet, 393–394
   scaling
      for axis, 372–373
      changing scaling, 369–370
      displaying scaling, 370
   settings, resetting, 365
   slide show, 394–399
   spreadsheets, adding to, 399–400
   terms related to, 340–341
   text in
      legend, 353–354
      setting fonts for, 354–355
      titles, 352–353
   three-dimensional effect, 376
   tick marks, changing, 370–372
   types of, 342–344
   viewing of, 355–356
Graph Save, 536
Graph Series, 725–726
Graph Series Analyze, 349, 565
Graph Series Group, 347, 356
Graph Text 1st Line, 729
Graph Text 2nd Line, 729
Graph Text Font 1st Line Color, 387
Graph Text Font 2nd Line Color, 387
Graph Text Font, 399, 726–727
Graph Text Font Data & Tick Labels, 386
Graph Text Font Legends, 387
Graph Text Font Legends Color, 387
Graph Text Font X-Title, 386
Graph Text Font Y-Title, 386
Graph Text Legends, 727–728
Graph Text Legends Position None, 387
Graph Text Quit, 728
Graph Text Secondary Y-Axis, 728
Graph Text X-Title, 728
Graph Text Y-Title, 729
Graph View, 393, 404, 729–730
Graph X-Axis, 365, 369, 537, 730–731
Graph Y-Axis, 365, 369, 537, 731–732
GRAY MINUS key, 19, 20, 23, 553, 562
GRAY PLUS key, 19, 20, 23, 553, 562
Gray scale setting, 529
Grid lines
   graphs, 341
      adding, 373–374
   hiding/displaying of, 121

Index   863

H

Handles, nature of, 384
Hard drive, and Quattro Pro, 3
Hardware defaults, changing, 514
Headers and footers
    printing defaults for, 146
    spreadsheet
        creating, 155
        printing, 155–156
        special characters for, 155–156
Headings
    printing defaults for, 145–146
    spreadsheet
        printing, 154–155
            at side of page, 154–155
            at top of page, 154
Help, 23–24
    activation of, 23
    colors, changing, 527
    and error messages, 24
    help screen, setting, 563
    keywords of, 24, 25
    and mouse, 23–24
        mode indicator, 13
Hershey fonts, 122
Hewlett-Packard LaserJet Printer, 122, 169
    cartridge fonts, 519
    Series III, 130, 169
    and setup strings, 16
    shading, 169
@HEXTONUM, 264
Hidden format, 69
    exposing hidden cell, 69
    hiding columns, 121–122, 157–158
High-low graph, 344
@HLOOKUP, 328–329
HOME key, 16, 17, 19, 22
Horizontal line icon, 380
@HOUR, 272

I

Icons, of Graph Annotator, 379–380
@IF, 276–278
IFKEY, 642–644
Importing data, 498–501
    formats for, 498–499
    steps in, 499, 501
@INDEX, 331–332
INDICATE, 668
Input line, nature of, 7–8
INS key, 19
Installation of Quattro Pro, 3, 683–686

@INT, 308
International characters
    and file retrieval, 193
    LICS characters, changing conversion of, 533
    printing
        by overstriking, 533
        and fonts, 123
    sorting, changing sort order, 532
International formats, 529–533
    currency
        changing symbol, 529
        displaying negative numbers, 529–530
    date, changing format, 531–532
    punctuation, changing style, 530–531
    time, changing format, 532
Invoice form, creation of, 57–60
@IPAYMT, 293
@IRATE, 300–301
@IRR, 305
@ISAAF, 283
@ISAPP, 283
@ISERR, 280, 282
@ISNA, 282–283
@ISNUMBER, 278–279
@ISSTRING, 279–280
Iterations, spreadsheet, iterations, 550–551

J

Job Delete, 171
Job Resume, 171
Job Suspend, 171

K

Keyboard, 11–20
    direction keys, 16–18
    editing keys, 18–19
    function keys, 13, 15–16
    regular and enhanced IBM keyboard, 14
    special keys, 19–20
    special symbols, 13
    for typing letters and numbers, 12–13
Keyboard macros, 570
Keywords, and help, 24, 25

L

LABEL, mode indicator, 13
Labels
    alignment, setting default, 544–545

entering macro instructions as, 602
entries, 28-29
graphs, 341, 361, 365-366
long labels, splitting, 503-506
spreadsheet, 32-37
    alignment, 34-35
    long labels, 33-34
    with numeric characters, 37
    purposes of, 32
    repeating labels, 35
    rules for, 32
Landscape orientation
    graphs, 404, 405
    spreadsheet, 163-164
@LEFT, 253, 255
Legends, graphs, 341, 353-354
@LENGTH, 249-250
Length of values, values, 39
LET, 613-615
Libraries, macros, 581
LICS characters, 193
    changing conversion of, 533
Line graph, 342, 361, 363
Line icon, 380
Lines
    in spreadsheets, 127, 129
    styles, graphs, 360-361
Linking files, 203-216
    advantages of, 203
    block names with link references, 213-215
    changing link references, 208
    copying and moving files, 211, 213
    deleting link references, 208
    formula links
        pointing method, 204-205
        typing method, 205-206
    linked references in Quattro commands, 208-213
    linking to other spreadsheets, 203-208
    link library, 215
    links to all open files, 206-208
    primary spreadsheet, 203
    recalculation of, 210
    retrieval of file with link references, 209-210
    supporting spreadsheets, 203
List, nature of, 237
@LN, 320-321
@LOG, 319-320
Logarithmic functions
    @EXP, 320
    @LN, 320-321
    @LOG, 319-320
Log file size, setting limit for, 596-597

Logical formulas, 50-52, 52
    logical operators, listing of, 50
    text in, 52
    uses of, 42, 50
Logical functions, 276-286
    @ERR, 285-286
    @FALSE, 284-285
    @FILEEXISTS, 283
    @IF, 276-278
    @ISAAF, 283
    @ISAPP, 283
    @ISERR, 280, 282
    @ISNA, 282-283
    @ISNUMBER, 278-279
    @ISSTRING, 279-280
    @NA, 286
    @TRUE, 284
LOOK, 644-645
Lotus 1-2-3, X commands, 673-679
Lotus/Intel/Microsoft (LIM) expanded memory specification, 4
Lotus International Character Set, 193
Lotus Multibyte Character Set, 193
@LOWER, 250

M

MACRO, status indicator, 12
Macros
    automatic start-up, 536
    by typing text, 576-577
    cells commands
        BLANK, 612
        CONTENTS, 612-613
        LET, 613-615
        PUT, 615-617
        RECALC, 617-618
        RECALCCOL, 618-620
    changing task of, 579-580
    for combining files, 586-587
    commands, uses of, 602
    for copying block, 582-584
    { } command, 673
    debugger, 602-609
    deleting macro, 580
    for displaying/printing formulas, 584
    documentation of, 580
    entering macro instructions as labels, 602
    executing macros, 578-579
        automatic execution of, 578
        instant macros, 578-579
        1-2-3 macro in Quattro, 579
        with Tools Macro Execute Command, 579

Index 865

file commands
   CLOSE, 656–657
   FILESIZE, 658
   GETPOS, 658
   OPEN, 658–660
   READ, 660–662
   READLN, 662–663
   SETPOS, 664
   WRITE, 664–666
   WRITELN, 666
functions of, 569
interactive commands
   BREAKOFF, 636
   BREAKON, 636–637
   GET, 637–640
   GETLABEL, 640
   GETNUMBER, 640–641
   GRAPHCHAR, 641–642
   IFKEY, 642–644
   LOOK, 644–645
   MENUBRANCH, 645–648
   MENUCALL, 648–649
   MESSAGE, 649–651
   ? command, 634–636
   STEPOFF, 651–653
   STEPON, 653–654
   WAIT, 654
keyboard macros, 570
libraries, 581
location for, 570–571
macro commands, 570
macro recorder, Transcript, 592–597
menu items, attaching macro to, 559
naming macros, 577–578
for printing files, 585–586
for product costing, 587–588
program flow commands
   BRANCH, 620–621
   DEFINE, 621–622
   DISPATCH, 623–624
   FOR, 624
   FORBREAK, 625–627
   ONERROR, 628–630
   QUIT, 630
   RESTART, 631
   RETURN, 631–634
recording of, 571, 573–577
   copying macro to spreadsheet, 575–576
   RECORD mode, 573–574
   testing recorded macro, 574–575
recording option, 561
redrawing the screen, 540
screen commands
   BEEP, 667–668
   INDICATE, 668
   PANELOFF, 668–669
   PANELON, 669–670
   PLAY, 670
   WINDOWSOFF, 671
   WINDOWSON, 672
   ; command, 673
special key equivalents used, 572–573
stopping execution, 609
for What-If analysis, 588–592
X commands
   XC command, 674
   XG command, 675
   XI command, 676
   XL command, 676
   XM command, 677
   XN command, 678
   XQ command, 678–679
   XR command, 679
Management summary report, 448–449
Map view, spreadsheet, 120–121
Margins
   and draft mode, 152
   and graphics mode, 152
   printing defaults for, 146
   resetting, 168–169
   right and left, adjustment of, 153
   spreadsheets, 152–153, 168–169
   top and bottom, adjustment of, 153
Markers, graphs, 360
Mathematical functions, 306–321
   @ABS, 310
   @INT, 308
   @MOD, 308, 310
   @PI, 311–312
   @RAND, 312
   @ROUND, 306–308
   @SQRT, 310–311
   See also Logarithmic functions; Trigonometric functions
Matrix math, 464–470
   inverting matrices, 468–470
   multiplying matrices, 465–467
@MAX, 239
@MEMAVAIL, 334–335, 520–521
@MEMEMSAVAIL, 335
Memory
   expanded memory, 540, 687, 746
   extended memory, 686
   information from Quattro Pro about, 521–522
   memory expansion, 4
   Virtual Real Time Object-Oriented Memory Manager (VROOMM), 4

MENU, mode indicator, 13
Menu bar, 7
MENUBRANCH, 645–648
Menu Builder
    changing relation of menu items, 558
    compatibility options, setting, 561–562
    deleting and inserting menu item, 559–560
    editing menu item, 555, 557
    exiting, 564
    function of, 553
    help screen, setting, 563
    macro, attaching to menu item, 559
    menu-equivalent commands, 555
    menu tree
        from earlier version of Quattro, 564–566
        keys in menu tree pane, 556
        printing, 563–564
    moving menu item, 560–561
    new menu item, insertion of, 558
    saving menu, 564
MENUCALL, 648–649
Menu-Equivalent commands, listing of, 814–840
Menus, 20–23
    activation of, 20
    colors, changing, 522–523
    dialog boxes instead of, 537
    listing of, 841–852
    menu tree, selection of, 537
    and mouse, 21, 23
    selecting item from, 21, 22–23
MESSAGE, 649–651
@MID, 256–257
@MIN, 240
@MINUTE, 272–273
Mixed cell address, 48, 49
    and copied formulas, 73–76
    use of, 74, 76
@MOD, 308, 310
Mode indicators
    listing of, 13
    status line, 11
@MONTH, 268–269
Mouse
    and blocks, 65
    customization of, 520
    display position of, 5
    dragging mouse, 65
    and height of rows, 115
    and help, 23–24
    installation of, 4
    and menus, 21, 23
    moving within spreadsheet, 18
    operation of, 4–5
    pointing method, arithmetic formulas, 47

Moving average, graphing, 350
Moving files, File Manager, 225

N

@N, 263
@NA, 49, 209, 286
Named styles, 130–134
    creating, 131–132
    numerical formats, 133–134
    removing, 132–133
    style files for, 133
    uses of, 130–131, 132
Negative numbers
    displaying, 529–530
    display of, 40
Nesting functions, 238
NetWare, and Print Manager, 170–171
Networks
    Paradox on, 437, 541
    Quattro Pro on, settings for, 541–542
Normal values, smallest and greatest, 527
@NOW, 266
@NPER, 298–330
@NPV, 304–305
NUM, status indicator, 12
Numerical formats, 66–69
    choices for formats, 66, 67
    setting default, 543–544
    user-defined formats, 133–134
Numeric entries
    alignment of, 41
    documentation for, 57
    General format, 39–40
    in labels, 37
    values, 38–41
        rules for, 38
NUM LOCK keys, 19, 20
@NUMTOHEX, 265

O

ODA, 5, 534
ODB, 5
ONERROR, 628–630
OPEN, 658–660
Optimizer, 476–483
    options for, 482–483
    setting up problem for, 477–478
    steps in finding solution, 478–482
    uses of, 476–477
Options Beep, 804
Options Colors, 804

Index 867

Options Colors Conditional, 525, 732
Options Colors Desktop, 523, 733
Options Colors File Manager, 733
Options Colors Help, 527, 734
Options Colors Menu, 522, 734
Options Colors Palettes, 528, 734–735
Options Colors Quit, 735
Options Colors Spreadsheet, 524, 525, 735–736
Options Display Mode, 399, 502, 534, 736, 804–805
Options File List, 805
Options File List Full View, 223
Options File List Wide View, 223
Options Formats, 542
Options Formats Align Labels, 69, 544, 736–737
Options Formats Global Width, 114, 546, 737
Options Formats Hide Zeros, 545, 737
Options Formats Numeric Format, 68, 371, 531, 543, 544, 737–738
Options Formats Numeric Format Date Time, 532
Options Formats Quit, 738
Options Graphics Quality, 126, 538, 738
Options Hardware, 514, 805
Options Hardware Coprocessor, 739
Options Hardware EMS memory, 739
Options Hardware Mouse Button, 739
Options Hardware Normal Memory, 739
Options Hardware Printer Fonts Cartridge Fonts Shading Level, 169
Options Hardware Printers 1st Printer, 742
Options Hardware Printers 2nd Printer, 742
Options Hardware Printers, 224, 517
Options Hardware Printers Auto LF, 520, 739
Options Hardware Printers Background, 170, 740
Options Hardware Printers Default Printer 1st Printer, 402
Options Hardware Printers Default Printer 2nd Printer, 402
Options Hardware Printers Default Printer, 740
Options Hardware Printers Fonts, 740–741
Options Hardware Printers Fonts Autoscale Fonts, 399
Options Hardware Printers Fonts Cartridge Fonts, 127
Options Hardware Printers Plotter Speed, 741
Options Hardware Printers Quit, 741
Options Hardware Printers Single Sheet, 520, 741–742
Options Hardware Screen, 359, 375, 743
Options International, 529, 743–745
Options International Currency, 529
Options International Date, 541
Options International LICS/LMBCS Conversion, 193, 533
Options International Overstrike, 533
Options International Punctuation, 232
Options International Use Sort Table, 415, 532
Options Network, 745–746
Options Network Refresh, 172
Options Other Clock, 541, 746
Options Other Clock International, 541
Options Other Expanded Memory, 540, 746
Options Other Macro, 746–747
Options Other Paradox, 437, 541, 747
Options Other Undo, 747
Options Other Undo Disable, 138, 539
Options Other Undo Enable, 137, 539
Options Protection, 747–748
Options Protection Disable, 92
Options Protection Enable, 92, 93, 551
Options Protection Formulas Disable, 551
Options Protection Formulas Enable, 551
Options Protection Formulas Protect, 93
Options Protection Formulas Unprotect, 93
Options Quit, 748
Options Recalculation, 548, 748–749
Options Recalculation Mode Automatic, 548
Options Recalculation Mode Background, 548
Options Recalculation Mode Manual, 548
Options Recalculation Order, 549
Options Speedbar, 749
Options Startup, 534
Options Startup and Directory, 195
Options Startup Autoload File, 193, 439, 536, 559, 750
Options Startup Beep, 537, 750
Options Startup Directory, 536, 750, 805–806
Options Startup Directory Current, 220
Options Startup Directory Previous, 220
Options Startup Edit Menus, 553, 750, 806
Options Startup File Extension, 537, 751
Options Startup Menu Tree, 537, 751, 806
Options Startup Quit, 751
Options Startup Startup Macro, 536, 578, 580, 751
Options Startup Use Dialogs, 358, 537, 752
Options Update, 193, 415, 514, 537, 579, 752, 806
Options Values, 752
Options WYSIWYG ZOOM %, 534, 752
Order of calculation, arithmetic formulas, 43
OVR, 19
  status indicator, 12

P

Page breaks
  adding, 156–157

elimination of, 156, 168
errors in, 149
printing defaults for, 146
spreadsheet, printing, 156–157, 168
Page length
    changing setting, 153–154
    printing defaults for, 146
    setting for, 153
    spreadsheet, printing, 153–154
Palette colors, settings for, 528–529
PANELOFF, 668–669
PANELON, 669–670
Paper, advancing and printer, 148, 520
Paradox, 437–440
    combined with Quattro Pro, 437–440
    exporting data to, 185, 187, 189
    on network, 437, 541
Parenthesis
    in arithmetic formulas, 45
    functions, 232
Parity, 518
Passwords
    removing password protection, 183
    and saving, 183
Path, 179
PATH command, 24
Pause between pages, printing, 520
@PAYMT, 291–293
PGUP and PGDN keys, 16, 17
@PI, 311–312
Pie graph, 342
    See also Graphs
PLAY, 670
Playback Block, 594, 595
Playback speed, Transcript, setting, 596
Plotter speed, setting, 518
@PMT, 290–291
POINT, mode indicator, 13
Pointing method
    arithmetic formulas, 45–48
    with mouse, 47
    steps in, 46
    formula links, 204–205
POINT mode
    formulas, entering, 45–48
    and hidden columns, 109
Point size, 123
Polygon icon, 380
Polyline icon, 380
Portrait orientation, graphs, 404, 405
PostScript, 122
@PPAYMT, 294
Preview
    of printed graph, 406
    of printed spreadsheet, 4, 161–163

Print Adjust Printer, 753, 806–807
Print Adjust Printer Align, 149
Print Adjust Printer Form Feed, 148
Print Adjust Printer Skip Line, 148
Print Block, 147, 148, 224, 753–754, 807
Print Copies, 152, 754
Print Destination, 484, 754–755, 807
Print Destination Graphics Printer, 406
Print Destination Screen Preview, 161–162
Printer
    adjustment of
        advancing paper, 148
        resetting top of page indicator, 149
    changing printers, 172–174
    customization of, 516–520
        advance of paper, 520
        default printer, setting, 518
        fonts, 519
        pause between pages, 520
        plotter speed, 518
        scaling, 519–520
        selection of printer, 517–518
Print Format, 755
Print Go, 808
Print Graph Go, 402
Print Graph Print Destination, 755–756
Print Graph Print Destination Graph Printer, 406
Print Graph Print Go, 756
Print Graph Print Layout, 404–406, 756–757
Print Graph Print Layout Reset, 406
Print Graph Print Layout Update, 406
Print Graph Print Name, 393, 402, 757
Print Graph Write Graph File, 757
Print Headings, 758
Printing
    error messages, 149
    in File Manager, 224
    graphs, 400–406
        fonts, 341, 354–355
        graph layout, 404, 406
        named graph, 402
        preview of graph, 406
        printer requirements, 401
        resetting options, 406
        rotation of graph, 404
        sending graph to file, 402–403
        sending graph to second printer, 402
    international characters, by overstriking, 533
    interrupting printing, 149–150
    macro for, 585–586
    printer driver, 3, 516
    Print Manager, 170–171
    spreadsheet, 144–174

Index 869

adjusting printer, 148–149
background printing, 170–172
changing printers, 172–174
default settings, 144–146, 170
expanding/compressing spreadsheet, 164–165
headers and footers, 155–156
headings, 154–155
Hewlett-Packard LaserJet Printer, 169
hiding columns in, 157–158
layout options, 150–151
margins, 152–153, 168–169
number of copies, 152
output options, 151–152
page breaks, 156–157, 168
page length, 153–154
preview of printed spreadsheet, 161–163
printing cell contents, 158–160
print problems, types of, 149–150
resetting print block, 147–148
resetting settings, 158
rotation of spreadsheet, 163–164
selection of print block, 146–147
setup strings, use of, 165–166, 169
sideways printing, 163–164
text files, special issues, 167–169
wider column widths, 168
view before printing, 4
See also Fonts
Print job, 171
Print Layout, 150, 168, 537
Print Layout Break Pages, 156, 758
Print Layout Dimensions, 758
Print Layout Footer, 759
Print Layout Header, 759
Print Layout Margins, 760
Print Layout Orientation, 761
Print Layout Orientation Banner, 164
Print Layout Orientation Landscape, 163
Print Layout Orientation Portrait, 163
Print Layout Percent, 164
Print Layout Percent Scaling, 761
Print Layout Quit, 761
Print Layout Reset, 406, 762
Print Layout Reset All, 170
Print Layout Reset Headings, 154, 155
Print Layout Reset Layout, 170
Print Layout Reset Print Block, 147
Print Layout Setup String, 165, 166, 762
Print Layout Update, 158, 406, 762–763
Print Layout Values, 150, 763
Print Manager, 170–171
Print Page Layout, 808–809
Print Print Manager, 171, 763–764
Print Print-To-Fit, 164, 764

Print Quit, 764, 809
Print Reset, 809
Print spooler, and Print Manager, 170–171
Print Spreadsheet Print, 149, 164, 764
Product costing, macro for, 587–588
Pro forma spreadsheets, 74, 76
@PROPER, 251, 253
Property sheet, Graph Annotator, 378
Protection
  defaults, 551
  spreadsheet, 90–93
    activation of, 92
    changing protection status, 92–93
    for formulas, 93, 551
PRTSC key, 19, 20
PRV button, 192
Punctuation, international, changing style, 531–532
PUT, 615–617
@PV, 301–302
@PVAL, 302–303

Q

QARGS, and use of resource files, 513–514
QUATTRO.LOG, 596–597
Quattro Pro
  basic concepts, 1–3
    data management, 2–3
    graphics, 2
    spreadsheet, 1–2
  customization of. *See* Customizing Quattro Pro
  defaults, 20
  display, 5–11
  equipment requirements
    hard drive, 3
    memory options, 4
    mouse, 4–5
    printing devices, 3–4
    storage capacity, 4
  with expanded memory, 687
  with extended memory, 686
  help, 23–24
  installation of, 3, 683–686
  keyboard, 11–20
  menu selection, 20–23
  start-up, 24–25
Query
  database
    assigning names to fields, 421–422
    defining block for search, 420–421
    deleting matching records, 435
    steps in query, 419

? command, 634–636
Queue Background, 171
Queue Network, 171
QUIT, 630

R

@RADIANS, 314
@RAND, 312
@RATE, 297–298
READ, 660–662
READLN, 662–663
READY mode
   indicator, 13
   and status line, 10
REC, mode indicator, 13
RECALC, 617–618
RECALCCOL, 618–620
Recalculation
   defaults
      changing number of iterations, 550–551
      changing order of spreadsheet calculation, 548–549
      choosing manual or automatic calculation, 548
   of formulas, 48–49
   with link references, 210
RECORD mode, steps in use of, 573–574
Records, database, 410
Rectangle icon, 380
Redrawing the screen, setting for, 540
Reference types, 48, 49
   absolute references, 48, 49
   in copied formulas, 72–76
   mixed references, 48, 49
   in moved formulas, 83
   relative references, 48, 49
Regression analysis, 471–474
   steps in, 472–473
   use of results of, 473–474
Relative address, 48, 49
   and copied formulas, 72–73
Renaming files, File Manager, 226
@REPEAT, 259
@REPLACE, 261–263
Reset Row Height, 115
Resolution, screen, 515
Resource files
   and defaults, 513–514
   use of, 513–514
RESTART, 631
Restore To Here, 594
Retrieving files, 189–194
   automatic retrieval, 192–193
   buttons to select file, 191–192
   in different format, 193–194
   file name extensions for, 186
RETURN, 631–634
@RIGHT, 255–256
Rotated bar graph, 344
Rotation
   of graph, 404
   of spreadsheet, 163–164
@ROUND, 306–308
Rounded rectangle icon, 380
Row commands
   Edit Delete Row Block, 109
   Edit Delete Rows, 107
   Edit Insert Row Block, 107
   Edit Insert Rows, 106
   Reset Row Height, 115
   Set Row Height, 115
@ROWS, 332–333
Rows
   height, setting height, 115
   hiding borders of, 121–122
   search of, 99
   spreadsheet
      blocks of rows, 107, 109
      deleting, 107
      height, 115
      insertion of, 106

S

@S, 263
Sales projection, creation of, 138–142
Saving
   file name extensions and, 186
   graphs
      graphic image, 394
      and naming graph, 392–393
      in other format, 403
      spreadsheet, 393–394
   number of steps performed before save, setting, 597
   part of file, 486–487
   spreadsheet, 181–189
      and passwords, 183
      saving in different format, 185, 187, 189
      saving to different directory, 184
      in SQZ! format, 184–185
      steps in, 181–182
Scaling
   graphs, 341, 370–373
   settings for, 519–520
Scientific notation, 39
Scientific numeric format, 543

Index 871

SCR, status indicator, 12
Screen, customization of, 514–516
SCROLL LOCK keys, 19, 20
Search and replace
   options in, 98–99
   spreadsheet, 96–99
   steps in, 96–97
@SECOND, 273–274
Select key, selecting block with, 65
Selector, spreadsheet, 6
Select Reset Width, 111
; command, 673
Series, graphs, 341, 346–348, 359, 365
SETPOS, 664
Set Row Height, 115
Setup strings
   printing
      defaults for, 146
      entering strings through menu, 165–166
      and Hewlett Packard LaserJet Printer, 166
      use of, 165–166, 169
      and use of another program, 169
Shading, 525
   Hewlett-Packard LaserJet Printer, 169
   setting for, 519
   spreadsheets, 129–130
Shadow, 523
SHIFT key, 19
@SIN, 315
Slide show, 394–399
   with graph buttons, 397–399
   with spreadsheet table, 394–395
   transition effects, 396–397, 399
@SLN, 287
Sort, 224, 809–810
Sorting
   database
      changing order of, 415
      data integrity during, 417–419
      sort keys, 413–415
      specifying records for, 412–413
   File Manager files, 223–224
   international characters, changing sort order, 532
SPDINST, and fonts, 126
Special keys
   advanced features, 19
   listing of, 20
Special values, formulas, 49–50
SpeedBar, 7
   customization of, 538
Spreadsheet, 1–2
   adding spreadsheets, 491–486
   auditing, 483–486

automatic loading of file, 536
blocks, 62–65
   copying, 77–82
   erasing, 85
   formatting, 66–69
   generate series of values, 101–104
   moving, 82–85
   naming, 85–90
   reformatting text blocks, 99–101
   specifying block, 63–65
bullet characters, 127
calculation
   changing order of, 548–549
   iterations, changing number of, 550–551
   manual or automatic, 548
columns
   blocks of columns, 107, 109
   deleting, 106
   hiding, 109
   insertion of, 104, 106
   width, 110–115
copying
   blocks, 77–82
   one cell to another, 70, 72
   one cell to several cells, 76–77
   one spreadsheet to another, 488–491
   reference styles in copied formulas, 72–76
date, 54–56
   date calculations, 55–56
   documentation for, 57
   formats for, 54
display area for, 5–7
documentation for, 158
entries, 27–32
   correcting mistakes, 30–32
   finalizing entries, 30, 31
   label entries, 28–29
   making entries, 29–30
   and memory, 27–28
   and mode indicator, 28, 29
   organization of, 27
   value entries, 29
erasing data, 85
errors, circular references, 485
fonts, 122–127
formulas, 41–54
   arithmetic formulas, 42, 43–48
   conversion to result of formula, 93–94
   display of, 43–44
   documentation for, 57
   logical formulas, 42, 50–52
   and operators, 43
   protection for, 93
   recalculation of, 48–49

reference types, 48, 49
special values, 49–50
string formulas, 42, 52
testing formulas, 53–54
graphs
  adding to, 399–400
  copying graph to another spreadsheet, 393
invoice form, creation of, 57–60
labels, 32–37
  alignment, 34–35
  long labels, 33–34
  with numeric characters, 37
  purposes of, 32
  repeating labels, 35
  rules for, 32
lines and boxes, 127, 129
linking files, 203–216
  advantages of, 203
  primary spreadsheet, 203
  supporting spreadsheets, 203
map view, 120–121
mouse, use of, 18
named styles, use of, 130–134
numeric format, changing, 66–69
printing, 144–174
protection, 90–93
  activation of, 92
  changing protection status, 92–93
  for formulas, 93
recalculation, defaults, 546–551
rows
  blocks of rows, 107, 109
  deleting, 107
  height, 115
  insertion of, 106
sales projection, creation of, 138–142
saving, 181–189
search and replace, 96–99
selector, 6
shading, 129–130
subtracting spreadsheets, 496–497
time, 56
  formats for, 56
  time calculations, 56
titles, 116–117
transposing entries, 94–95
Undo, corrections with, 134, 137–138
values, 38–41
  alignment, 41
  correcting mistakes, 40
  default display, 39–40
  entering values, 39–40
  formulas, 38
  length of values, 39
  numeric constants, 38
  rules for, 38
windows, 117–122
  colors, changing, 524–525
  hiding column/row borders, 121–122
  hiding/displaying grid lines, 121
  map view, 120–121
  panes, creating, 118
  removing window, 119
  synchronizing windows, 119
Spreadsheet commands
  Database Data Entry, 689–690
  Database Paradox Access, 690
  Database Query, 690–692
  Database Restrict Input, 692
  Database Sort, 692–693
  Edit Copy, 693–694
  Edit Copy Special, 694
  Edit Delete Column Block, 694–695
  Edit Delete Columns, 695
  Edit Delete Row Block, 695
  Edit Delete Rows, 695
  Edit Erase Block, 695–696
  Edit Fill, 696
  Edit Insert Column Block, 696
  Edit Insert Columns, 679
  Edit Insert Row Block, 679
  Edit Insert Rows, 679
  Edit Move, 679–698
  Edit Names Create, 698–699
  Edit Names Delete, 699
  Edit Names Labels, 699
  Edit Names Make Table, 699
  Edit Names Reset, 700
  Edit Search & Replace, 700–701
  Edit Transpose, 701
  Edit Undo, 701–702
  Edit Values, 702
  File Close, 702
  File Close All, 703
  File Directory, 703
  File Erase, 703
  File Exit, 703–704
  File New, 704
  File Open, 704–705
  File Retrieve, 705
  File Save, 705–706
  File Save All, 706
  File Save As, 706–707
  File Utilities DOS Shell, 707
  File Utilities File Manager, 707
  File Utilities SQZ!, 707–708
  File Workspace Restore, 708
  File Workspace Save, 708
  Graph Annotate, 708–709

Graph Customize Series Bar Width, 709
Graph Customize Series Bubbles, 709–710
Graph Customize Series Colors, 710
Graph Customize Series Fill Patterns, 710–711
Graph Customize Series Interior Labels, 711–712
Graph Customize Series Markers & Lines Formats, 712
Graph Customize Series Markers & Lines Line Styles, 712
Graph Customize Series Markers & Lines Markers, 713
Graph Customize Series Markers & Lines Quit, 713
Graph Customize Series Override Type, 713–714
Graph Customize Series Pies Colors, 714
Graph Customize Series Pies Explode, 714–715
Graph Customize Series Pies Label Format, 715
Graph Customize Series Pies Patterns, 715
Graph Customize Series Pies Quit, 716
Graph Customize Series Pies Tick Marks, 716
Graph Customize Series Quit, 716
Graph Customize Series Reset, 716–717
Graph Customize Series Update, 717
Graph Customize Series Y-Axis, 717
Graph Fast Graph, 717–718
Graph Graph Type, 718–719
Graph Hide, 719–720
Graph Insert, 720
Graph Name Autosave Edits, 720
Graph Name Create, 721
Graph Name Display, 721
Graph Name Erase, 721
Graph Name Graph Copy, 721–722
Graph Name Reset, 722
Graph Name Slide, 722
Graph Overall Background Color, 722
Graph Overall Color/B & W, 723
Graph Overall Drop Shadow Color, 723
Graph Overall Grid, 723–724
Graph Overall Outlines, 724
Graph Overall Three-D, 724
Graph Quit, 725
Graph Series, 725–726
Graph Text 1st Line, 729
Graph Text 2nd Line, 729
Graph Text Font, 726–727
Graph Text Legends, 727–728
Graph Text Quit, 728
Graph Text Secondary Y-Axis, 728
Graph Text X-Title, 728
Graph Text Y-Title, 729
Graph View, 729–730
Graph X-Axis, 730–731
Graph Y-Axis, 731–732
Options Colors Conditional, 732
Options Colors Desktop, 733
Options Colors File Manager, 733
Options Colors Help, 734
Options Colors Menu, 734
Options Colors Palettes, 734–735
Options Colors Quit, 735
Options Colors Spreadsheet, 735–736
Options Display Mode, 736
Options Formats Align Labels, 736–737
Options Formats Global Width, 737
Options Formats Hide Zeros, 737
Options Formats Numeric Format, 737–738
Options Formats Quit, 738
Options Graphics Quality, 738
Options Hardware Coprocessor, 739
Options Hardware EMS memory, 739
Options Hardware Mouse Button, 739
Options Hardware Normal Memory, 739
Options Hardware Printers 1st Printer, 742
Options Hardware Printers 2nd Printer, 742
Options Hardware Printers Auto LF, 739
Options Hardware Printers Background, 740
Options Hardware Printers Default Printer, 740
Options Hardware Printers Fonts, 740–741
Options Hardware Printers Plotter Speed, 741
Options Hardware Printers Quit, 741
Options Hardware Printers Single Sheet, 741–742
Options Hardware Screen, 743
Options International, 743–745
Options Network, 745–746
Options Other Clock, 746
Options Other Expanded Memory, 746
Options Other Macro, 746–747
Options Other Paradox, 747
Options Other Undo, 747
Options Protection, 747–748
Options Quit, 748
Options Recalculation, 748–749
Options Speedbar, 749
Options Startup Autoload File, 750
Options Startup Beep, 750
Options Startup Directory, 750
Options Startup Edit Menus, 750
Options Startup File Extension, 751

Options Startup Menu Tree, 751
Options Startup Quit, 751
Options Startup Startup Macro, 751
Options Startup Use Dialogs, 752
Options Update, 752
Options Values, 752
Options WYSIWYG ZOOM %, 752
Print Adjust Printer, 753
Print Block, 753–754
Print Copies, 754
Print Destination, 754–755
Print Format, 755
Print Graph Print Destination, 755–756
Print Graph Print Go, 756
Print Graph Print Layout, 756–757
Print Graph Print Name, 757
Print Graph Write Graph File, 757
Print Headings, 758
Print Layout Break Pages, 758
Print Layout Dimensions, 758
Print Layout Footer, 759
Print Layout Header, 759
Print Layout Margins, 760
Print Layout Orientation, 761
Print Layout Percent Scaling, 761
Print Layout Quit, 761
Print Layout Reset, 762
Print Layout Setup String, 762
Print Layout Update, 762–763
Print Layout Values, 763
Print Print Manager, 763–764
Print Print-To-Fit, 764
Print Quit, 764
Print Spreadsheet Print, 764
Style Alignment, 765
Style Block Size, 765–766
Style Column Width, 766
Style Define Style Create, 766–767
Style Define Style Erase, 767
Style Define Style File, 767–768
Style Define Style Quit, 768
Style Define Style Remove, 768
Style Font, 768–769
Style FontTable, 769–770
Style Hide Column, 770–771
Style Insert Bread, 771
Style Line Drawing, 771–772
Style Numeric Format, 772–773
Style Protection Protect, 773
Style Protection Unprotect, 773
Style Reset Width, 773
Style Shading, 774
Style Use Style, 774
Tool Macro Execute, 782
Tools Advanced Math Invert, 774

Tools Advanced Math Multiply, 775
Tools Advanced Math Regression, 775
Tools Audit, 776–777
Tools Combine Add, 777
Tools Combine Copy, 778
Tools Combine Subtract, 778–779
Tools Frequency, 779
Tools Import, 779–780
Tools Library, 780
Tools Macro Clear Breakpoints, 780
Tools Macro Debugger, 781–782
Tools Macro Instant Replay, 782
Tools Macro Key Reader, 782–783
Tools Macro Library, 783
Tools Macro Macro Recording, 783
Tools Macro Name, 784
Tools Macro Paste, 784–785
Tools Macro Record, 785
Tools Macro Transcript, 785–786
Tools Optimizer, 786–789
Tools Parse, 789
Tools Reformat, 789–790
Tools Solve For, 790
Tools Update Links, 790–791
Tools What-If, 791–792
Tools Xtract, 793
Window Move/Size, 793
Window Options Clear, 794
Window Options Grid Lines, 794
Window Options Horizontal, 794
Window Options Locked Titles, 794–795
Window Options Map View, 795
Window Options Print Block, 795
Window Options Row & Col Borders, 796
Window Options Sync, 796
Window Options Vertical, 796
Window Pick, 797
Window Stack, 797
Window Tile, 797
Window Zoom, 797–798
@SQRT, 310–311
SQZ! format, saving in, 184–185
Stacked bar graph, 342
Start-up, Quattro Pro, 24–25
Statistical functions, 238–249
   @AVG, 243–244
   @COUNT, 240–241
   @MAX, 239
   @MIN, 240
   @STD, 246–247
   @STDS, 247–248
   @SUM, 241, 243
   @SUMPRODUCT, 249
   @VAR, 244–245
   @VARS, 245–246

Index 875

See also Database, statistical functions
Statistics of series, graphing, 349–350
Status indicators
    listing of, 12
    status line, 11
Status line
    and EDIT mode, 10
    file name, 10
    mode indicators, 11
    nature of, 8–11
    and READY mode, 10
    status indicators, 11
    window number, 10
@STD, 246–247
@STDS, 247–248
Step mode, debugger, 604
STEPOFF, 651–653
STEPON, 653–654
Stop bits, 518
@STRING, 258
String, nature of, 232, 237, 249, 264
String formulas, 42, 52
    string constants in, 52
    uses of, 42, 52
String functions, 249–265
    @CHAR, 264
    @CLEAN, 253
    @CODE, 263–264
    @EXACT, 259–260
    @FIND, 260–261
    @HEXTONUM, 264
    @LEFT, 253, 255
    @LENGTH, 249–250
    @LOWER, 250
    @MID, 256–257
    @N, 263
    @NUMTOHEX, 265
    @PROPER, 251, 253
    @REPEAT, 259
    @REPLACE, 261–263
    @RIGHT, 255–256
    @S, 263
    @STRING, 258
    @TRIM, 253
    @UPPER, 251
    @VALUE, 257–258
Style Alignment, 765
Style Block Size, 111, 765–766
Style Block Size Auto Width, 112, 502, 546
Style Block Size Height, 115
Style Block Size Set Width, 111–112, 546
Style Block Widths, 115
Style Block Widths Auto Width, 159, 168
Style Block Widths Set Width, 168
Style Column Width, 110–111, 114, 115, 546, 766

Style Define Style Create, 131, 132, 134, 766–767
Style Define Style Erase, 132, 767
Style Define Style File, 767–768
Style Define Style File Retrieve, 133
Style Define Style File Save, 133
Style Define Style Quit, 768
Style Define Style Remove, 132, 768
Style Font, 123, 125, 133, 355, 768–769
Style FontTable, 123, 126, 769–770
Style FontTable Edit Fonts, 125, 355
Style FontTable Reset, 126
Style FontTable Update, 126
Style Hide Column, 770–771
Style Hide Column Expose, 109, 158
Style Hide Column Hide, 109, 157
Style Insert Bread, 771
Style Insert Break, 157, 164
Style Line Drawing, 525, 771–772
Style Numeric Format, 62, 66–69, 130, 159, 456, 543, 544, 584, 772–773
Style Numeric Format Date, 265, 531
Style Numeric Format Date Time, 275, 532
Style Numeric Format Reset, 68, 69
Style Protect, 93
Style Protection Protect, 93, 551, 773
Style Protection Unprotect, 92, 93, 440, 551, 773
Style Reset Width, 111, 773
Style Shading, 129–130, 525, 774
Style Shading Grey, 169
Style Shading None, 130
Style Use Named Style, 132
Style Use Style, 132, 134, 774
Subdirectories
    and File Manager, 226–227
    nature of, 178–179
Subtracting spreadsheets, 496–497
@SUM, 204, 205, 206, 207, 241, 243
@SUMPRODUCT, 249
Swiss fonts, 122
@SYD, 288–289
System customization options, 511, 513
System functions, 333–335
    @CURVALUE, 334
    @MEMAVAIL, 334–335
    @MEMEMSAVAIL, 335
    @VERSION, 335

T

Table functions, 327–333
    @CHOOSE, 329–331
    @COLS, 333

@HLOOKUP, 328–329
@INDEX, 331–332
@ROWS, 332–333
@VLOOKUP, 327–328
@TAN, 315–316
@TERM, 294–296
Text
   in graphs, legend, 353–354
   printing, special issues, 167–169
   text blocks, reformatting, 99–101
Text format, 68–69
Text graph, 344
Text icon, 379
Text mode display, 5
Three-dimensional graph, 344, 376
Tick marks, graphs, 341, 370–372
@TIME, 271
Time
   formats for, spreadsheet, 56
   international, changing format, 532
   setting clock display, 540–541
   spreadsheet, 56
   time calculations, 56
Time functions. *See* Date and Time functions
@TIMEVALUE, 275
Titles
   in graphs, 352–353
   spreadsheet, 116–117
      clearing titles, 117
      creation of, 116–117
@TODAY, 266
Toolbox, Graph Annotator, 377
Tool Macro Execute, 782
Tools Advanced Math Invert, 468, 588, 774
Tools Advanced Math Multiply, 469, 587, 775
Tools Advanced Math Regression, 351, 472, 775
Tools Audit, 484, 565, 776–777
Tools Audit Circular, 485, 551
Tools Audit Dependency, 484, 485
Tools Combine, 488
Tools Combine Add, 491, 494, 777
Tools Combine Copy, 488, 489, 778
Tools Combine Subtract, 496, 778–779
Tools Frequency, 463, 464, 779
Tools Import, 498, 779–780
Tools Library, 780
Tools Library Load, 238
Tools Macro, 573, 575
Tools Macro Clear Breakpoints, 608, 780
Tools Macro Debugger, 604, 609, 781–782
Tools Macro Execute, 579, 583
Tools Macro Instant Replay, 574, 782
Tools Macro Key Reader, 579, 782–783
Tools Macro Library, 581, 783

Tools Macro Macro, 592
Tools Macro Macro Recording, 783
Tools Macro Name, 577, 784
Tools Macro Name Create, 578
Tools Macro Name Delete, 580
Tools Macro Paste, 574, 576, 784–785
Tools Macro Record, 574, 576, 785
Tools Macro Recording Keystroke, 576
Tools Macro Transcript, 592, 595, 785–786
Tools Optimizer, 469, 477, 478, 552, 566, 786–789
Tools Optimizer Model Load, 482
Tools Optimizer Model Save, 481
Tools Optimizer Reset Options, 483
Tools Parse, 264, 501, 503–507, 661, 789
Tools Reformat, 100, 789–790
Tools Solve For, 475, 476, 790
Tools Solve For Parameters Max Iterations, 475
Tools Update Links, 790–791
Tools Update Links Change, 208
Tools Update Links Delete, 208
Tools Update Links Open, 209, 210
Tools Update Links Refresh, 209, 210
Tools What-If, , 457, 460, 461, 791–792
Tools What-If 1 Variable, 455–457
Tools What-If Reset, 457
Tools What-If 2 Variable, 458–460, 461
Tools Xtract, 488, 793
Trace cells, debugger, 607–608
Transcript, 592–597
   activation of, 592
   exiting, 597
   limitations of, 596
   log file size, setting limit for, 596–597
   number of steps performed before save, setting, 597
   playback speed, setting, 596
   replaying entries, 593–596
      block of commands, 594–595
      copying block to spreadsheet, 595–596
      restoring actions to point, 593–594
      undoing last command, 593
Transcript Add-in, 158
Transposing entries, spreadsheet, 94–95
Tree, 810
Tree Open, 222
Tree Resize, 222
Trends, graphing, 350–351
Trigonometric functions
   @ACOS, 316–317
   @ASIN, 316
   @ATAN2, 317–318
   @ATAN, 317
   @COS, 315

@DEGREES, 314
@RADIANS, 314
@SIN, 315
@TAN, 315-316
@TRIM, 253
@TRUE, 284

U

Undo
    corrections with, 134, 137-138
    effect on spreadsheet changes, 539
    setting, 539
Undo Last Command, 593
@UPPER, 251

V

@VALUE, 257-258
VALUE, mode indicator, 13
Values
    generation in blocks, 101-104
    solving for, 474-476
    spreadsheet, 29, 38-41
        alignment, 41
        correcting mistakes, 40
        default display, 39-40
        entering values, 39-40
        format code symbols for, 135-137
        formulas, 38
        numeric constants, 38
        rules for, 38
@VAR, 244-245
@VARS, 245-246
@VERSION, 335
Vertical line icon, 380
Virtual Real Time Object-Oriented Memory Manager (VROOMM), 4
@VLOOKUP, 327-328

W

WAIT, 654
    mode indicator, 13
What-If analysis, 454-462
    and database statistical functions, 460-462
    macro for, 588-592
    multiple spreadsheets in, 462
    with one variable, 454-458
    with two variables, 458-460
Width of columns. See Columns, width
Window Move/Size, 199, 793, 810

Window number, status line, 10
Window Options Clear, 119, 794
Window Options Grid Lines, 525, 794
Window Options Grid Lines Display, 121
Window Options Grid Lines Hide, 121
Window Options Horizontal, 794
Window Options Locked Titles, 525, 794-795
Window Options Map View, 121, 484, 485, 551, 795
Window Options Print Block, 795
Window Options Row & Col Borders, 796
Window Options Row & Col Borders Hide, 122
Window Options Sync, 119, 796
Window Options Unsync, 119
Window Options Vertical, 796
Window Pick, 197, 219, 797, 810-811
Windows
    closing a window, 197
    moving between windows, 197
    multiple windows, 201-202
        display options, 197-201
        other spreadsheets in formulas, 202
        other spreadsheets in Quattro's command, 201-202
    spreadsheet, 117-122
        colors, changing, 524-525
        hiding column/row borders, 121-122
        hiding/displaying grid lines, 121
        map view, 120-121
        opening with new spreadsheet, 196
        panes, 118
        removing window, 119
        synchronizing windows, 119
    and WYSIWYG mode, 198-199
WINDOWSOFF, 671
WINDOWSON, 672
Windows Options Map View, 485
Window Stack, 198, 797, 811
Window Tile, 198, 199, 797, 811
Window Zoom, 198, 797-798, 811
Workspaces, creating, 227
WRITE, 664-666
WRITELN, 666
WYSIWYG mode, 5, 33, 538
    and fonts, 123, 126
    operation of, 533-534
    setting colors for, 525
    and windows, 198-199

X

X commands, 674-679
    XC command, 674

XG command, 675
XI command, 676
XL command, 676
XM command, 677
XN command, 678
XQ command, 678–679
XR command, 679
XY graph, 342, 361, 363

Y

@YEAR, 268

Z

Zero values, hiding, 545
Zoom, to view graph, 355–356